Oxford Dictionary of Proverbs

オックスフォード
英語ことわざ・名言
辞典

ジェニファー・スピーク［編］

澤田治美［監訳］　赤羽美鳥・杉山正二［訳］

柊風舎

オックスフォード
英語ことわざ・名言辞典

Oxford Dictionary of Proverbs

ジェニファー・スピーク［編］

澤田治美［監訳］　赤羽美鳥・杉山正二［訳］

柊風舎

'Oxford' is the trade mark of Oxford University Press

©Oxford University Press 1982, 1992, 1998, 2003, 2008, 2015

Oxford Dictionary of Proverbs, Sixth Edition was originally published in English 2015. This translation is published by arrangement with Oxford University Press. SHUFUSHA CO. LTD. is solely responsible for this translation from the original work and Oxford University Press shall have no liability for any errors, omissions of inaccuracies or ambiguities in such translation or for any losses caused by reliance thereon.

Oxford Dictionary of Proverbs（第 6 版）（邦訳書名『オックスフォード英語ことわざ・名言辞典』）は元々 2015 年に英語で出版されたものである。この翻訳はオックスフォード大学出版局との契約によって出版されたものである。原著からのこの翻訳については柊風舎の側のみに責任があり、オックスフォード大学出版局の側には、この翻訳に関する誤り、省略、不正確、曖昧さ、あるいはこうした不備による損失については責任はない。

は じ め に

　本書『オックスフォード英語ことわざ・名言辞典 (*Oxford Dictionary of Proverbs*)』の第 6 版は、オックスフォード大学出版局の長期に及ぶことわざ編纂の最も新しい集大成である。また、1982 年に公刊された *Concise Oxford Dictionary of Proverbs* (以下 *CODP*) 以降の、英語における著しい変化も反映している。*CODP* は、1935 年に初版が世に出、その後 1970 年に F. P. ウィルソンによって大幅に修正された記念碑的辞典 *Oxford Dictionary of English Proverbs* (以下 *ODEP*) の縮約版である。膨大な歴史的研究に基づく *ODEP* は、公刊・未公刊の文献のコーパスに広く網を仕掛けて、古い英語から現代の英語にいたるまで数多くの豊富な比喩表現、慣用句、ことわざを収録した。しかし、*CODP* には当初から *ODEP* とは異なる目的があった。つまり、*ODEP* の歴史的観点を踏襲するものの、*CODP* は現代の用法と 20 世紀後半の英語話者がことわざとみなすものに焦点を当てているのである。ことわざの定義は、*CODP* の初代の編者ジョン・シンプソンが本書の「序文」で述べている通りである。*CODP* の方針は本書の根底にも流れている。なぜなら、本書自体が *CODP* から生まれたものにほかならないからである。

　本書を編集するにあたり、英米におけることわざは常に生命力にあふれ、変化してきたことを再認識することができた。*CODP* から本書に進化するまでには 30 年以上の時が経過したが、本書の完成には、他の追随を許さないほど便利で広範囲にわたる調査手段としてのインターネットが大きく貢献している。オンラインで閲覧可能なアーカイブスにより、多くの場合、現在使用されていることわざの初例を時には数十年前に遡らせることができた (例えば、There is no such thing as bad weather, only the wrong clothes.「悪い天候などというものはない。服装がおかしいだけだ」と Better to light one candle than to curse the darkness.「暗闇を呪うくらいならロウソクに火を灯せ」)。さらに、ある表現が特定の著名人に由来するという民間伝承が多くの場合、誤りであったという事実も確認することができた。なぜなら、当のことわざは特定の個人によって広められる以前にすでに一般に普及していたことがわかったからである。

　世界中から集められるオンライン上の情報は、かなり多数の古いことわざが継続して使用されてきたことを示す貴重な証拠となる。それらは活字化されていなかったため、20 世紀末には廃れていたように思われていたのである。また、古いことわざは、ことわざの形式は地域によって異なる可能性があることも示している。例えば、First up, best dressed.「最初の子供が最も良い身なりをしている」はオーストラリア生まれであるが、当初は First in, best dressed. という形であった。インターネットで検索すれば、英語圏内でことわざがいかに愛着を持って使われているかがわかる。例えば、書籍のタイトル、新聞の見出し、歌詞、商品の宣伝用コピー、店名、T シャツのロゴ、漫画や探偵の台詞などにことわざが実

によく登場するのである。

第 6 版である本書には新しいことわざも多数登場する。そのうちのいくつかは、多くの古いことわざと同様に、特定可能な個人による素晴らしい創作によるものであるが、ほとんどのことわざの明確な起源は不明である。しかし、たとえ起源が不明なものであっても本書に収録した理由は、それが広く世間に流通していること、異形を生み出す創造力を持っていること、すでに英語の語彙の一部となり、今後もその資格を保持しつづけることが予想されることである。このことを示す一端が、What happens in/on ... stays in/on ... という米国の最近の表現に見られる。例えば、What happens on the road stays on the road.「旅先で起きることは旅先だけの話」、What goes on tour stays on tour.「旅先で起こることは旅先だけの話」、What happens in Vegas stays in Vegas.「ラス・ベガスで起こることはラス・ベガスだけの話」が良い例である。電子メディアのおかげで、世界中の作家と話者は、どこで生まれたものであれ、新しいことわざを即座に入手し、さらに読者がすでにその表現に馴染んでいると想定することができる。例えば、英国の週刊誌『スペクテータ』の読者が What happens in Vegas ... and why I'm happy it doesn't happen here.「ベガスで起こることは…ここでは起こらないので安心」（2014 年 11 月 15 日、p.35）という見出しを目にしたとき、読者は What happens in Vegas stays in Vegas の意味を理解していることが前提とされる。しかし他方で、普及するには言葉の選択が独特すぎることわざもある。例えば、When you're up to your ass in alligators, it's too late to start figuring out how to drain the swamp.「ワニにめりこんでいる時には、沼地を干拓するしかたを理解しようとしても、すでに遅すぎる」（イェール著 *Dictionary of Modern Proverbs* より）ということわざは今のところ大西洋しか越えていない。それも draining the swamp「沼地を干拓する」という比喩表現の形式に限られる。この表現は英国のキャメロン元首相によって次のように使用されている。'We will "drain the swamp" which allows Muslim extremists to flourish'.「イスラム教徒の過激派がはびこる『沼地を干拓する』」（2014 年 6 月 3 日『デイリー・テレグラフ』の見出し）。

ことわざとそれを取り巻く世界は発展しつづけるが、1982 年刊行の *CODP* に収録されたことわざのうち、その後使用頻度が減ったせいで今回の改訂版から削除されたものは驚くほど少ない。1900 年以降に削除するだけの説得的な証拠がないことが一番の要因であるが、削除の候補となったことわざは、現在では主に骨董品的な興味の対象でしかないか、あるいは 21 世紀の感性からすると違和感を覚えるものである。前者の例として、Better a good cow than a cow of a good kind.「良い品種の牝牛よりも良い牝牛のほうがましだ」が挙げられる。これは、女性と家畜を同じ単語で評価するような小規模の廃れた農村地域の考え方を反映している。一方、意味不明な No moon, no man「月がないと、人もいない」は、新月のあいだに生まれた子供は病弱になるという古代の迷信に基づいている。次に、違和感を覚える例としては以下のものが挙げらる。A good Jack makes a good Jill.「男の方が良ければ女も良くなる」、A woman, a dog, and a walnut tree, the more you beat them the better they be.「女、犬、クルミの木は、叩けば叩くほど良くなる」である。これらのことわざが伝える真意を誰の怒りを買うこともなく発話できるような現代の場面を想定すること自体が困難である。

　さて、かつて英語圏ではきわめて馴染み深いことわざであったが、現代人が当初使われていた文脈を一般に意識しない、あるいは単に知らないという意味で、多少なりとも廃れてしまったものがある。その多くは聖書あるいはキリスト教教会に由来する。また別のタイプのことわざは天気と暦に関する実用的な情報を伝えている。それらは読み書きが満足にできない農耕社会に多く、実際たくさんの人々の役に立ったわけだが、今では魅力的な内容と風変わりな面白さから、限られた地域でのみ生き残っている。本書は、そのようなことわざの意味と用法に関する情報も提供する。そして、一般に、個々のことわざに関する注は、万人の興味をひくようにかなり広範囲に付けている。

　個々のことわざの歴史と使用を示す用例に関しては、当のことわざの発達過程を理解するのにほとんど寄与しない事例は、たとえ興味深いものであっても本書では割愛した。しかし、初例と認定される事例に関してはそのまま載せている。重要な異形と、月日とともに生じた意味変化を示す事例も同様に載せている。時を経ずして標準形が定着したことわざもあれば、異形に対してより寛容的なものもある。後者の場合、異形を辿ることによって、そのことわざの発達過程をうかがい知ることができる。リズムや類音反復の影響を受けて、語順が「固定化」される場合がある。その結果、より覚えやすく、簡潔な表現となっている。例えば、チョーサーの Wikkid haste is no profit.「あせりは無益」は、Haste makes waste.「せいては事をし損じる」と比べると心に響かない。このことわざは、ヘイウッドが *Dialogue of Proverbs* の中で紹介した1546年までにはすでに使われていたと想定される。一方、There's many a slip between cup and lip.「茶碗と唇のあいだには多くの邪魔が入るものだ」は古代ギリシア・ローマ時代に起源があり、ラテン語からの難解な翻訳借用の事例である。『エラスムスの格言集』のタヴァーナーの翻訳本 (1539年出版) に初例が見られるが、1783年まで many a slip の形式は英語の「古いことわざ」とされていた。

　一般的な苦境 (When all you have is a hammer, everything looks like a nail.「ハンマーしか持っていないと、すべてのものが釘に見えてしまう」) や真実 (Justice delayed is justice denied.「遅れた正義は正義の否定である」) を表わす洒落た表現は、様々な文脈で流通し、生き残り、そして進化していくということわざの力を示している。漫画家・ユーモア作家は、The opera isn't over till the fat lady sings.「そのオペラは例の太った女性が歌うまで終わらない」や Two heads are better than one.「2つの頭は1つの頭にまさる (三人寄れば文殊の知恵)」のようなことわざも読者には容易に理解されると想定することができる。作家は、すべてを言わずにことわざをほのめかすだけの場合がある。例えば、2015年1月24日の『スペクテータ』に次のような記述がある。「ボランティア団体に参加する人の多くは暇で他にすることがないのだ。(彼らの)空白を埋めるために悪魔が仕事を作る・・・」。この一節は、The Devil finds work for idle hands to do.「悪魔は何もしないで

怠けている手に仕事を見つけるものだ」に基づいているが、読者がこのことわざを知らなければ、上の文章はかなり奇異に響くであろう。ことわざは、言語学的には手抜きであり、クリシェ（決まり文句）とみなされるかもしれない。しかし、使用者の教養の高さを示すためにも同様に使われると思われる。なぜなら、思索を深め、言葉を楽しみ、あるいは言葉に少しばかりの彩りを添えるということわざの可能性を使用者が十分認識していることを示すからである。

　数年にわたり、多くの方々がこの仕事に興味を持ってくださり、いくつかのことわざを教示され、編者と議論までしてくださった。貴重な引用例を提供してくださった方もおられる。末筆ながらそれらすべての方々のご協力と励ましに感謝するものである。

ジェニファー・スピーク
オックスフォード
2015年 2 月

序　文

　本書 Concise Oxford Dictionary of Proverbs は過去200年にわたり英国において一般に使用されたことわざの歴史を概観するものである。ことわざの中には、長い間、英語圏で使用されているものもあれば、19〜20世紀になって地方（特にスコットランド）から一般に普及したものもある。米国と、英国以外の国々に起源をもつことわざ（例えば、If you don't like the heat, get out of the kitchen「熱さがいやなら、台所から出て行け」や、The apple never falls far from the tree「リンゴの実は木から遠く離れたところには決して落ちない」）でも、現在、英国で一般的に用いられている場合には、あるいは当該地域において特に普及している場合には本書に収録されている。

　ことわざとは、短くて含蓄のある形式で書かれた、忠告もしくはモラルを提示する伝統的な言葉である。逆説的になるが、今日、ことわざと呼ばれるものの多くは定義上、ことわざではない。例えば、fly on the wall「人の行動をひそかに観察している人」や as dead as the dodo「もはや重要ではない」のような表現もあるが、どちらも本書でいうことわざではない。このような混乱は18世紀以前に遡る。当時、proverb という語は比喩表現、直喩、罵り言葉なども含み、今日よりも幅広く使われていたからである。現在では、ことわざは、通常、文の形式である。ことわざは 3 つの主要なタイプに分類することができる。第 1 のタイプは、一般的な真実を抽象的に述べたもので、例えば、Absence makes the heart grow fonder.「離れていると情がなおいっそう深まる」や Nature abhors a vacuum.「自然は真空を嫌う」などである。第 2 のタイプは、より色彩豊かで、一般性を表わすために日常経験の具体的な観察に基づいた表現が使われる。例えば、You can take a horse to water, but you can't make him drink.「馬を水飲み場まで連れて行くことはできても、（馬にその気がなければ）無理やり水を飲ませることはできない」や、Don't put all your eggs in one basket.「すべての卵を 1 つの籠に入れるな」などである。第 3 のタイプは、伝統的な知恵と民間伝承の表現から生まれたものである。例えば、After dinner rest a while, after supper walk a mile.「豪華な食事の後ではしばらく休め、軽い夕食の後では 1 マイル歩け」や、Feed a cold and starve a fever.「風邪には大食を、熱には絶食を」のような健康に関することわざが挙げられる。これらは古典的な格言であるが、話し言葉の中に取り入れられている。さらに、農業、季節、天候などに関する伝統的な、地方のことわざもある。例えば、Red sky at night, shepherd's delight; red sky in the morning, shepherd's warning.「赤い夕焼けは羊飼いの喜び。赤い朝焼けは羊飼いへの警告」、や When the wind is in the west, 'tis neither good nor man nor beast.「（大陸から吹いてくる冷たい）東風は人にも獣にもよくない」などである。

　一般性の高い慣用句のいくつかも、ことわざの形式で使用されている場合は本書に含ま

れている。例えば、to cut off your nose to spite your face「顔に腹を立てて鼻を切り落とす」と、to throw the baby out with the bathwater「風呂の残り湯と一緒に赤ん坊を捨てる」という句は通常ならことわざに含まれないが、Don't cut off your nose to spite your face.「顔に腹を立てて鼻を切り落とすな」、Don't throw the baby out with the bathwater.「風呂の残り湯と一緒に赤ん坊を捨ててはならない」のようにことわざ形式で用いられることが多いのでことわざとして認めることにした。他の慣用句 (to win one's spurs「手柄を立てる」、to throw in the towel「降参する」など)、直喩 (as red as a rose「バラのように赤い」、as dull as ditchwater「ものすごく退屈な」)、格言的な引用文 (Power grows out of the barrel of a gun.「権力は銃身から得られる」) は除外されている。ただし、引用句として英語に由来することわざの中でも、例えば、Hope springs eternal.「希望は (胸の中に) 絶えることなく湧き出る」や Fools rush in where angels fear to tread.「愚か者は天使が恐れて足を踏み入れない所へも飛び込む」のように、その起源がもはや一般に認知されていない場合は本書に含めることにした。

　ことわざは流行おくれになりつつあるとか、クリシェに格下げられた、などと時折言われることがある。そのような見解は、英文学におけることわざの役割が変化した一方で、一般的には常に変わらず使用されつづけているという事実を見逃している。中世時代、さらには17世紀後期でさえ、多くの場合、ことわざは普遍的な真実という資格を持っていたし、議論を強化するために、あるいは反論するために使用された。ことわざの詳細なリストが論争中の学者の助けとなるように編纂された。その結果、ラテン語、ギリシア語、他のヨーロッパ大陸の言語から多数の表現が英語に導入された。しかし、18世紀までにはことわざの人気は教養ある作家の作品においては下火となった。なぜなら、彼らは陳腐な慣習的な知恵の伝達手段としてことわざを見下しはじめたからである。英国の小説家サミュエル・リチャードソンは Clarissa Harlowe (1748) の中で、主人公の Robert Lovelace は差し迫った結婚を祝福され、今までの愚かな振る舞いを直すよう忠告を受ける。彼の叔父が手紙に「It is a long lane that had no turning『曲がり角のない道は長い道 (どんな道にも曲がり角はある)』」ということわざがあるじゃないか。でも、ことわざを引用したからといって私を軽蔑しないでくれたまえ」と書いている。また、英国の作家ジョナサン・スウィフトは Polite Conversation (1738) の序において「読者は、ことわざと、会話を飾る美しい丁寧な言葉とを正しく区別できなければならない。・・・ことわざについて言えば、私は巧妙な会話の中からそれらを完全に排除する」と述べている。ことわざがいかに不評であったかは容易にわかる。なぜなら、一見して相矛盾することわざを組み合わせることさえできるからである。例えば、Too many cooks spoil the broth「料理人が多すぎるとスープをだめにしてしまう」と Many hands make light work「人手が多いと仕事は楽になる」や、Absence make the heart grow fonder「離れていると情がなおいっそう深まる」と Out of sight, out of mind「目に見えないところにあるものは忘れ去られる」のような逆の意味の組み合わせである。したがって、ことわざの使用は学識の高いグループ内では物笑いの種

になり、洗練された名文家によって今でも時折眉をひそめられる。それにもかかわらず、ことわざは人生に対する素朴な論評として、そして今日でも役に立つ先人の知恵を想起させるものとして人気の高さを維持している。この変化は辞書項目に使用される引用句にも反映されている。つまり、初期の頃は大作家の作品から頻繁に引用されたが、最近では無名作家の作品や新聞雑誌からの引用が多くなっている。

　古いことわざが廃れ、新しいことわざが次から次へと生まれるのは、ことわざの生命力の強さを物語っている。驚くべきことに、A trouble shared is a trouble halved「分かち合えば苦労も半分となる」は20世紀以前には記録がなく、A changing is as good as a rest「変化をつけるのは休むのと同じほどの価値がある」は19世紀の最後の10年になって初めて登場する。広く普及している A watched pot never boils.「じっと見つめていると鍋はなかなか煮え立たない」は1848年にやっと姿を現わした。コンピューターの世界では、最近になって古典的なことわざ Garbage in, garbage out「がらくたを入れると、がらくたが出てくる」が復活し、経済学の分野では There's no such thing as a free lunch.「無料の昼食などない」が生み出された。ことわざは、初期の収集家が飽きもせず述べてきたように、日常会話という食事に味つけをするソースとしての役割を果たしつづけることになる。

　ことわざ辞典はその配列方法に特徴が出る。どの方法を選ぶかは編者しだいである。初期のことわざ辞典で好まれた方法はアルファベット順で、aから始まることわざを順次掲載することである。例えば、A bird in the hand is worth two in the bush.「手の中の1羽は藪の中の2羽に値する」、A stern chase is a long chase.「真後ろからの追跡は長い追跡」と続き、最後はzで始まることわざで終わる。この方法の難点は、a、every、one、theなどで始まることわざが多くなりすぎることである。そのような語で始まることわざは互いに繋がりがないので、読者はお目当てのことわざを探し当てるまでに一苦労を強いられる。別の方法はテーマ別分類である。例えば、猫、犬、悪魔、自尊心などに関することわざが同じグループに分類される。このやり方には多くの長所があるが、明確なテーマが定められない場合、1つのことわざが複数のテーマに分類されるため、検索する際に混乱が生じる恐れがある。

　本書の採った方法は、近年出版された主要なことわざ辞典、例えば、M. P. ティリーの *Dictionary of the Proverbs in England I the Sixteenth and Seventeenth Centuries* (1950) と、B. J. ホワイティングの *Early American Proverbs and Proverbial Phrases* (1977) で採用されたもので、要するに、アルファベット順の長所と、主要語によるテーマ別配列の長所を組み合わせている。例えば、All cats are grey in the dark.「暗闇ではどの猫も灰色だ」は cats の項に、You cannot put an old head on young shoulders.「若者の肩に老練の頭脳を据えることはできない」は old の項に、そして Every picture tells a story.「すべての絵には物語がある」は picture の項に挙げられるという具合である。さらに、検索が困難な際に読者の助けとなるよう、相互参照が可能になるように編纂されている。例え

ば、All cats are grey in the dark. は grey と dark の項に、You cannot put an old head on young shoulders. は head、young、shoulder の項に、そして Every picture tells a story. は every、tell、story の項に相互参照できるように見出し語を挙げている。なお、掲載する価値がある場合は、異形体のことわざも挙げることにした。

ODEP と同様に、実例を記載しているのも本書の特徴である。文献に登場した初例を最初の用例として挙げている。おそらく多くのことわざは文献に登場する以前に口語で広く使用されていたが、本書は文献上の記録を重要視する。あることわざが英語より前に他の言語に存在していた場合は、用例の前にその旨を述べておく。例えば、There's many a slip 'twixt cup and lip.「茶碗と唇とのあいだには多くの邪魔が入るものだ」の初出は1539年であるが、このことわざはギリシア語とラテン語に由来するので、その情報を16世紀の英語の用例の前に加えている。同様に、Nothing succeeds like success.「成功ほど成功を呼ぶものはない」は1867年が初例であるが、その数十年前にすでにフランス語で一般的になっていた。興味深いことに、英語の伝統的なことわざの多くが実は外国産である。英語における多くの語と同様に、医学や法律の学者を介して、あるいは古典作家の作品から、ことわざもギリシア語とラテン語を経由して頻繁に入ってきた。またはノルマンコンクエスト以後フランスから直接入ったものもある。現代のことわざのいくつか、例えば、The opera isn't over till the fat lady sings.「そのオペラは例の太った女性が歌うまで終わらない」と The family that prays together stays together.「共に祈る家族は団結する」は米国産である。なお、予想されるように、It never rains but it pours.「降れば必ず土砂降り」という古いことわざはイングランド起源である。

各項目には理解を助けるためにいくつかの実例が添えられている。その中で、当のことわざが今日に至るまでにどのような文脈で使用されてきたかが示される。標準的な形は発達過程において変貌を遂げていくが、記録上の原形はつねに記載されている。ことわざの意味や用法が、実例から分からないほど不明瞭な場合、あるいは文法的・統語的に言及しておくべき点がある場合は簡単な頭注を付けてある。例えば、Possession is nine points of the law.「所有は法律の九分の強み」と Every dog is allowed one bite.「どんな犬も一度は嚙みつくことを許される」には法律上の含意があること、Caesar's wife must be above suspicion.「カエサルの妻たる者は貞操を疑われるようなことがあってはならない」と One might as well be hanged for a sheep as a lamb.「子羊を盗んで絞首刑になるくらいなら、親羊を盗んで絞首刑になった方がましだ」は史実に由来することが述べられている。また、Handsome is a as handsome does.「物事を立派にこなす人こそが立派なのである」における handsome のような語の原義も必要とあれば論じている。

本書の編纂上の仕事の多くは用例の検証に関わるものであった。振り返ってみると、語源辞典における用例は代々検証されることなく受け継がれてきた。特に古い用例はそのまま採用されることが多い。本書では、すべてのことわざが再検証され、関連作品の初版から引用されている。もしそうでない場合は、用例もしくは参考文献において言及する。他の

ことわざ辞典における多数の用例は日付が誤っていることが判明した。その原因は主に、当のことわざ辞典の初版以降の版（しばしば不適切な箇所を削除されたヴィクトリア朝時代の版）から引用されたことにある。さらに、真の初版本には馴染みの薄いことわざが挙げられていたり、もしくはまったくことわざらしきものが掲載されていないこともたびたびあった。

　用例では自明の短い書名がたびたび使用されるが、本書では可能な限り、書名と著者名は省略しないことにした。書名は現代風にアレンジされている場合もあるが、引用例（聖書とシェイクスピアの例を除く）には変更を加えていない。引用例は出典の章を示している。ただし、元々そのような分類がなされていない場合は原書のスタイルを踏襲した。聖書、シェイクスピアをはじめとして数名の著名な作家の作品は全作品を参照した。劇作品は幕と場面（場面が特定できない際はページ）を記載している。聖書からの引用は、特に断らない限り、1611年版の欽定訳聖書を使用した。類似したことわざが、欽定訳聖書以前の翻訳書、説教集、教会の説教集に見受けられることがしばしばあるが、現在使われている形は大抵欽定訳聖書のものである。短縮形のことわざは中世の文献でよく見られるが、本書では特に断ることなく短縮される以前の形に戻している。

ジョン・シンプソン

オックスフォード

1982年3月

目　　次

はじめに　3

序文　7

『オックスフォード英語ことわざ・名言辞典』　15

監訳者のことば　499

参考文献　503

主題索引　506

省 略 記 号

a	ante (before)	以前
Apr.	April	4 月
Aug.	August	8 月
AV	Authorized Version (of the Bible) , 1611	1611 年出版「欽定訳聖書」
BCP	Book of Common Prayer	祈禱書
c	circa (about)	およそ
cent.	century	世紀
cf.	confer (compare)	参照せよ
COD	Concise Oxford Dictionary	コンサイス・オックスフォード辞典
Dec.	December	12月
Dict.	dictionary (of)	(…の) 辞典
Du.	Dutch	オランダ語
ed.	edition	版
EETS	Early English Text Society	初期英語テクスト協会
esp.	especially	特に
et al.	et alii (and others)	およびそのほかの者たち
Feb.	February	2 月
Fr.	French	フランス語
Ger.	German	ドイツ語
Gr.	Greek	ギリシア語
Hist.	history (of) , historical	歴史、歴史的
Ibid.	ibidem (in the same place)	同一箇所に
Ital.	Italian	イタリア語
Jan.	January	1 月
L.	Latin	ラテン語
Mag.	Magazine	雑誌
Mar.	March	3 月
mod.	Modern	現代の
MS (S)	manuscript (s)	原稿・草稿
Nov.	November	11月
NY	NewYork	ニューヨーク
Oct.	October	10月
ODEP	Oxford Dictionary of English Proverbs	オックスフォード英語ことわざ・名言辞典
OED	Oxford English Dictionary	オックスフォード英語辞典
Pt.	part	部分
quot.	quotation	引用
rev.	revised	改訂された
Sept.	September	9 月
Ser.	series	一連の作品
St.	Saint	聖
STS	Scottish Text Society	スコットランド英語テクスト協会
tr.	translation (of)	(…の) 翻訳
U.S.	United States (of America)	アメリカ合衆国
vol.	volume	巻
†		参照せよ

＊本文中の「訳注」は監訳者によるものです。

A ⇒ Who SAYS A must say B.

abhors ⇒ NATURE abhors a vacuum.

a-borrowing ⇒ He that GOES a-borrowing, goes a-sorrowing.

abroad ⇒ GO abroad and you'll hear news of home.

ABSENCE makes the heart grow fonder.
離れていると情がなおいっそう深まる。
(訳注：「遠ざかるほど想いが募る」。「逢わねばいや増す恋心」)

†プロペルティウス『エレギア』II. xxxiiib. 1. 43 *Semper in absentes felicior aestus amantes*.「好きな人と会えないと、よりいっそう恋心が募るものだ」

□ *c*1850 In T. H. Bayly *Isle of Beauty* (rev.ed.) iii. Absence makes the heart grow fonder. **1923** *Observer* 11 Feb.9 These saws are constantly cutting one another's throats. How can you reconcile the statement that 'Absence makes the heart grow fonder' with 'Out of sight, out of mind'? **1992** A. LAMBERT *Rather English Marriage* (1993) xi. 178 Absence may have made his heart grow fonder, but it hasn't done wonders for mine. **2002** *Spectator* 9 Feb.63 In this way you can keep her at bay indefinitely, or at least until such time as her absence has made your heart grow fonder. ■ **absence** 不在；**love** 愛・恋愛

He who is ABSENT is always in the wrong.
その場にいない者がいつも悪者になる。
(訳注：he/she who…は「…する者は誰でも」の意．複数形は those who〈…するような人たち〉。There are *those who* say so.〈そう言う人々もいる〉)

当人がその場にいないと、皆、その人に場合、罪をなすりつけられてしまうものだ。†フランス語 *Les absents ont toujours tort*.「いない者はいつも悪者。欠席裁判」。*c*1440J. レッジナイト『王子の没落』(EETS) III.1.3927 For princis ofte…Wil cachche a qu[a]rel…Ageyn folk absent.「王子はよく口論する…その場にいない民と」

□ **1640** G. HERBERT *Outlandish Proverbs* no. 318 The absent partie is still faultie. **1736** B. FRANKLIN *Poor Richard's Almanack* (July) The absent are never without fault, nor the present without excuse. **1912** 'SAKI' *Unbearable Bassington* iv. The absent maybe always wrong, but they are seldom In a position to be inconsiderate. **1981** A. PRICE *Soldier no More* 57 I will quote first that fine old French saying-which covers any claim Charlie may or may not have on that cake-

16　absolute

'he who is absent is always in the wrong.' ■ **absence** 不在；error 間違い・過ち

absolute ⇒ POWER corrupts.

abundance ⇒ Out of the FULLNESS of the heart the mouth speaks.

ACCIDENTS will happen (in the best-regulated families) .
（どんなにきちんとした家庭でも）事故は起こるもの。

（訳注：家庭のみならず、2002 年の用例にあるように、社会についても用いられる。失敗の言い訳などによ
く使われる。will ＝「…するものだ」〈習性・傾向〉。Boys *will* be boys.〈男の子はやっぱり男の子《いた
ずらは仕方ない》〉。happen は occur となることもある。なお、accident はかなり重大な事故を指す）

どれほど慎重に暮らそうとしても、うまく事が運ばないときがある。

□**1700** VANBRUGH *Pilgrim* IV Such Accidents will happen sometimes, take what care we can.
1819 'P. ATALL' *Hermit in America* i. Accidents will happen in the best regulated families. **1850**
DICKENS *David Copperfield* xxviii. 'Copperfield,'said Mr. Micawber, 'accidents will occur in the
best-regulated families; and in families not regulated by…the influence of Woman, in the lofty
character of Wife, they must be expected with confidence, and must be borne with philosophy.'
1939 W. S. MAUGHAM *Christmas Holiday* x. Accidents will happen in the best regulated families;
and…if you find you've got anything the matter with you,…go and see a doctor right away.
2002 *Country Life* 14 Feb. 51 No-one should underestimate the pain and suffering caused. However, the CPS [Crown Prosecution Service] has to recognize that, even in this determinedly
scapegoat society, accidents do happen. ■ **misfortune** 不運

There is no ACCOUNTING for tastes.
人の好みは説明できない。

（訳注：there is no … ing は「…することはできない」の意。「蓼食う虫も好き好き」。If war breaks out,
there is no knowing how many people will be killed.〈もし戦争になったらどれほどの人が死ぬことに
なるかわからない〉）

人それぞれに好みが異なること、特に、自分が苦手とするものを好む人がこの世にいる
ということは説明できない。現在では tastes の代わりに taste も使われる。ラテン語 *Tag
de gustibus non est disputandum.*「好みについて論争することはできない」の翻訳で
ある。† 1599 J. ミンシュ『スペイン語での対話』6 Against ones liking there is no
disputing.「人の好みに対して異議を唱えることはできない」

□**1794** A. RADCLIFFE *Mysteries of Udolpho* I. xi. I have often thought the people he disap-
proved were much more agreeable than those he admired;—but there is no accounting for tastes.
1889 GISSING *Nether World* II. viii. There is no accounting for tastes. Sidney…not
once…congratulated himself on his good fortune. **1985** R. REEVES *Doubting Thomas* iv. 'You're
usually in here with a little guy, wears a rug. Looks like he gets his suits from Sears. Paisley
ties….There's no accounting for taste.' **2014** *Spectator* 13 Dec. 75 I read of an ornament which
is 'a plywood cutout of a giant boiled egg', but there's no accounting for taste, even bad taste. ■
idiosyncrasy 特異性・性癖；taste 趣味・味

accumulate ⇒ If you don't SPECULATE, you can't accumulate.

accuse ⇒ He who EXCUSES, accuses himself.

ADDLED 17

accuser ⇒ A GUILTY conscience needs no accuser.

acorn ⇒ GREAT oaks from little acorns grow.

act ⇒（名詞）SOW an act, and you reap a habit. ;（動詞）THINK global, act local.

ACTIONS speak louder than words.
行為は言葉よりも雄弁である。

米国起源。Deeds speak louder than words. という形も使われる。

□1628 J. PYM *Speech* 4 Apr.in *Hansard Parliamentary Hist. England* (1807) II. 274 'A word spoken in season is like an Apple of Gold set in Pictures of Silver,' and actions are more precious than words. **1736** *Melancholy State of Province* in A. M. Davis Colonial Currency (1911) III. 137 Actions speak louder than Words, and are more to be regarded. **1856** A. LINCOLN *Works* (1953) II. 352 'Actions speak louder than words' is the maxim; and, if true, the South now distinctly says to the North, 'Give us the measures, and you take the men.' **1939** M. STUART *Dead Men sing no Songs* xii. Deeds speak louder than words. First she tells you the most damning things she can…, and then she begs you to believe he's innocent in spite of them? **2008** *Times* 21 July 13 If he flares up at you…lock yourself in the bathroom and have a nice bath with a good book. Sometimes actions speak louder than words. ■ **words and deeds** 言動

When ADAM delved and Eve span, who was then the gentleman?
アダムが耕し、イブが紡いだとき、誰が領主だったというのか。

昔、皆が畑仕事で暮らしていた頃は階級の差などなかった。このことわざの脚韻（span と gentleman）は、英国におけるワットタイラーの乱（1381年）の指導者で、地方巡回牧師であったジョン・ボールが用いた。彼は重い年貢に対して農民に反乱を呼びかけるためにこの脚韻を効果的に用いた（2013年の用例参照）。

□*c*1340 R. ROLLE in G. G. perry *Religious Pieces* (EETS) 88 When Adam dalfe[dug] and Bue spane…Whare was than the pride of man? **1381** in Brown & Robbins *Index Middle English Verse* (1943) 628 Whan adam delffid and eve span, Who was than a gentilman? **1562** J. PILKINGTON *Aggeus & Abdias* I. ii. When Adam dalve, and Eve span, Who was than a gentle man? Up start the carle, and gathered good, And thereof came the gentle blood. **1979** C. E. SCHORSKE *Fin-de-Siècle Vienna* vi. When Adam delved and Eve span Who was then the gentleman? The question had ironic relevance for the arrive. **2013** *New Statesman May* (online) An oral peasant culture, such as still survives in the Balkan countryside, is a fertile context for the transmission of history and ideas through ballad and song. This is not so different from 'When Adam Delved and Eve Span', which we've inherited from our 14th century Peasants' Revolt. ■ **equality** 平等 ; **gentry** 紳士階級

As good be an ADDLED egg as an idle bird.
怠け者の鳥でいるくらいなら、腐った卵であるほうがましだ。

（訳注：as good 〈… as 〜〉とは、「〜するくらいなら…するほうがましだ」の意）

怠惰な人、つまり働かない人は腐った卵と同じくらいの使い道しかない。

□1578 LYLY *Euphues* l. 325 If I had not bene gathered from the tree in the budde, I should beeing blowne haue proued a blast, and as good it is to bee an addle egge as an idle bird. **1732** T. FULLER *Gnomologia* no. 681 As good be an addled Egg as an idle Bird. **1974** D. CARTER. *Ghost Writer* iii. The chickens are feeling the heat, poor creatures. I'm afraid I gave them a bit of a tick-

18　ADVENTURES

ing off. As good be an addled egg, I told them, as an idle bird. ■ **action and inaction** 行為と非行為 ; **idleness** 怠惰

ADVENTURES are to the adventurous.
冒険は冒険を恐れない者だけにある。

（訳注：the adventurous ＝「冒険心のある人々」。the ＋形容詞・分詞は「…な人々」を表わす。*the* rich〈金持ち〉）

心躍るようなことは臆病でない人、もしくは危険を恐れない人にしか起こらない。

□**1844** DISRAELI *Coningsby* III. I. 244 'I fear that the age of adventures is past.' … 'Adventures are to the adventurous,'said the stranger. **1952** 'T. HINDE' *Mr Nicholas* iv. He told himself that adventure was to the adventurous….If he could not make the effort for the small he would miss the big adventure. ■ **boldness** 大胆さ ; **opportunity, taken** 得られた機会 ; **risk** 危険

ADVERSITY makes strange bedfellows.
逆境に置かれると気心の知れない者とも仲間になるものだ。

（訳注：1611 年の用例からわかるように、シェイクスピアの『テンペスト』に出てくる名文句）

不幸な出来事が起こると、通常なら付き合わないような人々が仲間にならざるをえなくなる。根底に流れる考え方は同じでも、文頭の語にはいくつかの形がある。POLITICS makes strange bedfellows.「政治によって気心の知れない者とも仲間になる」

□**1611** SHAKESPEARE *Tempest* II.ii. 37 My best way is to creep under his gaberdine; there is no other shelter hereabout: Misery acquaints a man with strange bedfellows. **1837** DICKENS *Pickwick Papers* xli. (*heading*) illustrative…of the old proverb, that adversity brings a man acquainted with strange bedfellows. **1927** *Times* 27 Aug.12 The…alliance of 1923-5 was an illustration of the adage that adversity makes strange bedfellows. **1982** *Times* 15 Mar. 9 (*heading*) Poverty makes strange bedfellows. ■ **adversity** 逆境・困難 ; **misfortune** 不運

afraid ⇒ He who RIDES a tiger is afraid to dismount.

Africa ⇒ There is always something NEW out of Africa.

AFTER a storm comes a calm.
嵐の後には凪が来る。

（訳注：After 〈black〉 clouds 〈comes〉 clear weather.〈黒雲の後には晴天がやってくる〉。「待てば海路の日和あり」）

起源は古く、*a*1250『尼僧の戒律』(1962) 191 Iblescet ibeo thu laverd the makest stille efter storm.「嗚呼、神よ。嵐の後には静けさをもたらしたまえ」に由来する。**1337** ラングランド『農夫ピアズ』B. XVIII. 409 After sharpe shoures…moste shene [bright] is the sonne.「豪雨の後には輝く太陽」

□**1576** C. HOLYBAND *FrenchLittleton* E1ᵛ After a storme commeth a calme. **1655** T. FULLER *Church Hist. Britain* IX. Viii. After a storm comes a calm. Wearied with a former blustering they began now to repose themselves in a sad silence. **1979** 'J. LE CARRÉ' *Smiley's People* i. For the next two weeks nothing happened….After the storm had come the calm. ■ **peace** 平和 ; **trouble** やっかい・苦労

ALL   19

AFTER dinner rest a while, after supper walk a mile.
豪華な食事の後ではしばらく休め、軽い夕食の後では 1 マイル歩け。

dinnerは正式な食事なので消化を促すために小休止が必要だが、supperは軽めの食事なので運動した方が健康によいという考えに基づく（1979年の用例参照）。このことわざは中世ラテン語時代に使用されていた。*Post prandium stabis, post coenam ambulabis.*「午餐会の後は静かに休み、軽食の後は歩け」。この教訓は他のヨーロッパ言語にも浸透し、例えばスペイン語では *Despues de comer dormer, y de cenar pasos mil.*「豪華な食事の後は昼寝せよ、軽食の後は1000歩歩け」となった（J. コリンズ『スペイン語ことわざ辞典』1834, p. 108）。

□1582 G. WHETSTONE *Heptameron of Civil Discourses* E3 After dynner, talke a while, After supper, walke a mile. 1584 T. COGAN *Haven of Health* cod. That olde English saying: After dinner sit a whyle, and after supper walke a myle. 1979 *Daily Telegraph* 24 Dec. 3 'The physiological reaction to a heavy indigestible meal…seems to be to sleep it off.' What it all seems to boil down to is the old adage: After dinner rest a while, after supper walk a mile. ■ **health** 健康

AFTER the feast comes the reckoning.
ご馳走の後には請求書が待ち受けている。

快楽と食道楽の後にはつけが待っている。主に北米で使用される。

□1620 F. QUARLES *Feast for Wormes* VI. vi. But Young-man, know, there is a Day of doome, The Feast is good, untill the reck'ning come. 1869 *New York Times* 20 Nov. (online) After the feast comes the reckoning, says the proverb, and…the Viceroy of Egypt is beginning…to estimate the actual cost of his ambition and enterprise. 1999 *Time* 29 July (online; *heading*) After the Monica feast comes the reckoning. ■ **action and consequence** 行為と結果

after ⇒ It is easy to be WISE after the event.

Agamemnon ⇒ BRAVE men lived before Agamemnon.

Age ⇒ The age of MIRACLES is past. ; If YOUTH knew, if age could.

Agree ⇒ BIRDS in their little nests agree. ; TWO of a trade never agree.

Alive ⇒ If you want to LIVE and thrive, let the spider run alive.

ALL good things must come to an end.
すべて良い物事には必ず終わりが来るものだ。

（訳注：must ＝「必ず…する」。All human beings *must* die.〈人間は皆死ぬ運命にある〉）

形容詞 good はかなり最近になってから付けられた。当初の（good のない）形式は EVERYTHING *has an end.*「万事終わりがある」と同じと考えてよい。

□*c*1440 *Partonope of Blois* (EETS) 1. 11144 Ye wote [know] wele of all thing moste be an ende. 1738 SWIFT *Polite Conversation* i. 85 All Things have an End, and a Pudden [a kind of sausage] has two. 1857 H. H. RILEY *Puddleford Papers* xxiii. All things must have an end, and the grand caravan, in time, came to its end. 1924 'D. VANE' *Scar* xxv. All good things come to an end. The feast was over. 2002 *Washington Times* 17 Mar. Cl2 For more than a decade, Roy Kramer reigned as the most powerful figure in college athletics...But all good things must come to an end, and that end is now. ■ **finality** 終局 ; **good things** 良いもの

It takes ALL sorts to make a world.
世の中にはいろいろな種類の人がおり、ものがある。

人格、個性、望みの多様性は認めなければならないという意見であるが、皮肉を込めて用いられることが多い。sorts の代わりに kinds もよく使われる。

□**1620** T. SHELTON tr. *Cervantes' Don Quixote*II. vi. In the world there must bee of all sorts. **1767** S. JOHNSON *Letter* 17 Nov. (1952) I. 194 Some Lady surely might be found...in whose fidelity you might repose. The World, says Locke, has people of all sorts. **1844** D. W. JERROLD *Story of Feather* xxviii. Click can't get off this time?...Well, it takes all sorts to make a world. **1975** J. I. M. STEWART *Young Pattullo* iii. 'My father's a banker during the week and a country gent at week-ends. Takes all sorts, you know.' 'Takes all sorts?' 'To make a world.' **1993** B. RICHARDSON *Bachelor Brothers' Bed & Breakfast* (1997) 74 There is no nightlife....I suppose that what we have here is the working out of the adage that it takes all kinds to make a world. ■ **idiosyncrasy** 特異性・性癖 ; **tolerance** 寛容・忍耐 ; **variety** 多様性

ALL things are possible with God.
神の下では如何なることも可能である。

『マタイによる福音書』19章26節（欽定訳聖書）...with God all things are possible.「神の下では如何なることも可能である」を想起させることわざ。†ホメロス『オデュッセイアー』x.306 θεοί δέ τε πάντα δύνανται.「神の下ではすべて可能である」。欽定訳聖書の形式もよく使われ、1959年にはオハイオ州のモットーとして採用された。

□**1694** P. A. MOTTBUX tr. *Rabelais' Pantagruel* V. xliii. Drink...and you shall find its taste and flavor to be exactly that on which you shall have pitched. Then never presume to say that anything is Impossible to God. **1712** C. MATHER *Letter* 22 Nov. (1971) 117 However, take it again; all things are possible with God. **1826** L. BEECHER *Letter* 11 June in Autobiography (1865) II. viii. Sometimes it seems as if persons had too much...intellect to be converted easily. But all things are possible with God. **1965** M. SPARK *Mandelbaum Gate* vi. It would be interesting, for a change, to prepare and be ready for possibilities of, I don't know what, since all things are possible with God and nothing is inevitable. **1971** 'S. CHANCE' *Septimus and Danedyke Mystery* (1973) iii. 31 'All things are possible-but some are not very likely. As the Apostle should have said, but didn't.' ■ **possibility and impossibility** 可能性と不可能性

ALL things come to those who wait.
辛抱強く待っている人のところにはすべてがやって来る。

（訳注：those =「〈関係節を伴って〉…する人々、…の者たち」〈they〉。People who live in the countryside stay healthier than *those* who live in urban areas.〈田舎に住んでいる人々は都市部に住んでいる人々よりも健康に過ごしている〉。「石の上にも三年」。「待てば海路の日和あり」）

†フランス語 *Tout vient a celui qui sait attendre*.「待ち方を知っている人にはすべてがやってくる」

□**1530** A. BARCLAY *Eclogues* (EETS) II. 843 Somewhat shall come who can his time abide. **1642** G. TORRIANO *Select Italian Proverbs* 26 He who can wait, hath what he desireth. **1847** DISRAELI *Tancred* II. IV. Viii. I have got it at last, everything comes if a man will only wait **1872** V. FANE *Tout vient a qui sait Attendre in From Dawn to Noon* n. 85 Ah! 'All things come to those who wait'...They come, but often come too late. **2002** *Times* 2 14 Feb.7 Until last week I considered the proverb 'All things come to those who wait' to be up there with 'Every cloud has a silver lin-

angry 21

ing'on the list of fatuous remarks to make when your best friend has failed a vital job interview...or been trapped for hours on the Tube. ■ **patience and impatience** 忍耐と性急

all ⇒ All's for the BEST in the best of all possible worlds ; All CATS are grey in the dark ; DEATH pays all debts ; Why should the DEVIL have all the best tunes? ; Don't put all your EGGS in one basket ; All's FAIR in love and war ; All is FISH that comes to the net ; All that GLITTERS is not gold ; All is GRIST that comes to the mill ; When all you have is a HAMMER, everything looks like a nail ; HEAR all, see all, say nowt ; To KNOW all is to forgive all ; There is MEASURE in all things ; MODERATION in all things ; ONE size does not fit all ; To the PURE all things are pure ; A RISING tide lifts all the boats ; All ROADS lead to Rome ; The THIRD time pays for all ; All's WELL that ends well ; You can't WIN them all ; All WORK and no play makes Jack a dull boy.

Alone ⇒ He TRAVELS fastest who travels alone.

Alter ⇒ CIRCUMSTANCES alter cases.

Always ⇒ He who is ABSENT is always in the wrong ; There is always a FIRST time ; ONCE a —, always a — ; There is always ROOM at the top ; The UNEXPECTED always happens.

Good AMERICANS when they die go to Paris.
善良なアメリカ人は死に臨んでパリへ行く。

かつて one of the wittiest man「最もウイットに富む男の 1 人」はトーマス・ゴールド・アップルトン（1812-84）であった（1858年の用例）。米国人は洒落た旅の目的地としてパリに執着していた。ただし、2002年の用例はパリが暗示する天国のイメージを覆している。

□1858 O. W. HOLMES *Autocrat of Breakfast-Table* vi. To these must certainly be added that other saying of one of the wittiest of men: 'Good Americans, when they die, go to Paris.' 1894 O. WILDE *Woman of no Importance* I.I.16 They say...that when good Americans die they go to Paris. 1932 T. SMITH *Topper takes Trip* xxi. We are those good Americans who come to Paris when they die. 2002 *Times Literary Supplement* 22 Mar. 23 'Like any other city...Big, noisy, crowded.' You don't have to believe that Paris is worth a Mass or the place where good Americans go to die to disagree. ■ **death** 死 ; **just deserts** 当然の報い

and ⇒ If IFS and ands were pots and pans, there'd be no work for tinkers' hands.

angel ⇒ FOOLS rush in where angels fear to tread.

anger ⇒ Never let the SUN go down on your anger.

angry ⇒ A HUNGRY man is an angry man.

22 ANOTHER

ANOTHER day, another dollar.
もう 1 日、もう 1 ドル。

1897年の用例は、More days, more dollars「日数が増えると、ドルも増える」という形式と日雇いの船乗りを結び付けている。航海が長引けば長引くほど、収入が増えるからである。後に、Another day, another dollar「もう 1 日、もう 1 ドル」が生み出されたが、これは、生活費を稼ぐために重労働を強いられることに対しての恨み言葉として使われた。このことわざは多数の形を生み出している（1993年と2002年の用例参照）。

□**1897** J. CONRAD *Nigger of 'Narcissus'* (1955) v.114. The common saying, 'More days, more dollars,' did not give the usual comfort because the stores were running short. **1957** D. ERSKINE & P. DENNIS *Pink Hotel* (1958) 8 ''Nother sleepless night,' Mr. Baldwin said. 'Heard the clock strike four again.' 'That's a shame, Mr. Baldwin,' Mary said..., knowing that her landlord was about to say Another Day, Another Dollar. **1992** J. E. DOMINGUEZ & V. ROBIN *Your Money or Your Life* v.157 For those opting for Financial Independence it reinforces the awareness that work is no longer about 'another day, another dollar.' **1993** *Time International* 18 Jan.4 Another day, another deadline. And another backdown by Saddam Hussein, for what seems like the zillionth time. **2002** *Times* 2 10 Jan.7 And I haven't even mentioned...Bobby Fischer, stripped of his title by Fide in 1975 (another decade, another squabble), but never defeated... ■ **action and consequence** 行為と結果；**work** 仕事

answer ⇒ ASK a silly question and you get a silly answer ; A CIVIL question deserves a civil answe ; A SOFT answer turneth away wrath.

anvil ⇒ The CHURCH is an anvil which has worn out many hammers.

ANY port in a storm.
嵐のときにはどんな港でもありがたい。

絶望的な状況では安全な場所ならどこでも大歓迎である。

□**1749** J. CLELAND *Memoirs of Woman of Pleasure* II. 133 It was going by the right door, and knocking desperately at the wrong one....I told him of it: 'Pooh,' says he 'my dear, any port in a storm.' **1821** SCOTT *Pirate* I. iv. As the Scotsman's howf [refuge] lies right under your lee, why, take any port in a storm. **1965** J. PORTER *Dover Three* ii. It was not quite the sort of company with which Dover would mix from choice but, as the jolly sailors say, any port in a storm. **1983** M. BOND *Monsieur Pamplemousse* iv. On the principle of any port in a storm he made a dive for the nearest cubicle. ■ **necessity** 必要性・必然性；**trouble** やっかい・苦労

If ANYTHING can go wrong, it will.
間違える可能性があれば、それはきっと間違える。

（訳注：go wrong の go は思わしくない状態になることを表わす。反対に、良い状態になる場合は come を用いる。will ＝「必ず…する」〈必然性〉）

「マーフィーの法則」として広く知られている。多くの異形があるが、元々の概念は工学・科学領域のものである。**1878**『都市整備土木工学学会プロシーディングズ』li. 8（1877年11月13日の会議）。It is found that anything that can go wrong at sea generally does go wrong sooner or later.「海上で間違える可能性があれば、それは遅かれ早かれ間違えることがわかった」。なお、「法則」として定式化されたのは1949年で、ジョージ・ニコルズの手になると言われている。彼は当時カルフォルニア州にあるノースロ

ップ社の企画室長であったが、ライト・フィールド空軍演習場に所属していた同僚のマーフィー大尉の言葉を広めたのである。当初の実例からこのことわざの起源がわかる。**1955**『航空力学紀要』5‐6月号マーフィーの法則第11：If an aircraft part can be installed incorrectly, someone will install it that way.「飛行機の部品が間違って組み立てられるようになっていると、誰かが必ず間違って組み立てることになる」

□**1951** A. ROE 'Child Behavior, Animal Behavior, and Comparative Psychology', *Genetic Psychology Monographs* xliii. 204 [H]e realized that this was the inexorable working of the second law of the thermodynamics which stated Murphy's law 'If anything can go wrong it will.' **1956** *Scientific American* Apr.166 Dr. Schaefer's observation confirms this department's sad experience that editors as well as laboratory workers are subject to Murphy's Laws, to wit: l. If something can go wrong it will, [etc.]. **1980** A. E. FISHER *Midnight* Men vii. Of course, the up train was delayed. There was some vast universal principle. If anything can go wrong it will. **2000** *Washington Post* 28 Dec. El Tune out the pundits....I subscribe to a corollary of Murphy's Law ('Anything that can go wrong, will'), which is Pundit's Law: Anything experts predict will happen, will not ■ **error 間違い・過ち**

An APE's an ape, a varlet's a varlet, though they be clad in silk or scarlet.
絹衣を着ようが緋の服をまとおうが、猿は猿、下郎は下郎である。

varletはかつて使用人である召使いを指したが、「悪党」あるいは「ごろつき」という悪い意味を帯びるようになった。緋色は判事を含む様々な高位の人が着る公式、または儀礼的服装の色であった。†ルキアノス『無学なる書籍蒐集家に』4 πίθηκος ὁπίθηκος...κἂν χρυσέα ἔχη σύμβο λα.「猿は猿である…たとえ金色の勲章をつけようとも」。エラスムス『格言集』I.vii. *Simia simia est, etiamsi aurea gestet insignia.*「猿は猿である…たとえ金色の勲章をつけようとも」

□**1539** R. TAVERNER tr. Erasmus' Adages 21 An ape is an ape although she weare badges of golde. **1659** J. HOWELL *Proverbs* (English) I An Ape's an Ape, A Varlett's a Varlett. Though they be cladd in silk, or scarlett. **1732** T. FULLER *Gnomologia* no. 6391 An Ape's an Ape: a Varlet's a Varlet, Tho' they be clad in Silk or Scarlet. **1967** D. MORRIS *Naked Ape* i. The naked ape is in danger of...forgetting that beneath the surface gloss he is still very much a primate.('An ape's an ape, a varlet's a varlet, though they be clad in silk or scarlet.')Even a space ape must urinate. ■
appearance, deceptive 偽りの外見；nature and nurture 生まれと育ち

ape ⇒ The HIGHER the monkey climbs the more he shows his tail.

appear ⇒ TALK of the Devil, and he is bound to appear.

APPEARANCES are deceptive.
見かけは人を欺く。

米国では Appearances are deceiving. の方が一般的である。

□**1666** G. TORRIANO *Italian Proverbs* 12 Appearance oft deceives. **1784** in *Collections of Massachusetts Hist. Society* (1877) III.186 The appearances in those mountainous regions are extremely deceptive. **1846** H. MELVILLE *Typee* xxiv. Appearances...aredeceptive. Little men are sometimes very potent, and rags sometimes cover very extensive pretensions. **1927** E. F. BENSON *Lucia in London* v. Mr. merriall...watched the three figures at Georgie's door. 'Appearances are deceptive,'he said.'But isn't that Olga Shuttleworth and Princess Isabel?' **2002** A. VANNEMAN *Sherlock Holmes and Giant Rat of Sumatra* xviii.128 'Why, Mr. Holmes, you are the most wide-

24 APPETITE

awake man here.''Appearances are deceiving,'returned Holmes. ■ **appearance, deceptive 偽りの外見 ; deception ごまかし**

APPETITE comes with eating.
食欲は食べるほどにますます増すものだ。
（訳注：appetite には「情欲」の意味もある）

願望や能力は活動や習慣が継続するにつれて増していく。† **1534** ラブレー『ガルガンチュア』I. v. *L'appetit vient en mangeant.*「食欲は食べるほどにますます出てくるものだ」。**1600-1** シェイクスピア『ハムレット』I. ii. 143 Why, she would hang on him As if increase of appetite had grown By what it fed on.「そう、母上もあのころは父上を一時も離さず、満たされてますますつのる貪欲な愛にひたっておいでだった」

☐**1653** URQUHART & MOTTEUX tr. *Rabelais' GargantuaI.* v. Appetite comes with eating. *a*1721 M. PRIOR *Dialogues of Dead* (1907) 227 But as wesay in France, the Appetite comes in Eating; so in Writing You stil found more to write. **1906** W. MAXWELL *From Yalu to Port Arthur* i. Appetite comes with eating. Having absorbed Port Arthur and begun on Manchuria, Russia saw no reason why she should not have Korea also. **1943** S. CLOETE *Congo Song* xxiv. The appetite came with eating. The more he had of her, the more he wanted. ■ **wanting and having 不足と所持**

appetite ⇒ HUNGER is the best sauce.

An APPLE a day keeps the doctor away.
1 日にりんご 1 個で医者いらず。

民間伝承の知恵に基づく。りんごが健康によいことは現代栄養学からも証明されている。

☐**1866** *Notes & Queries* 3rd Ser. IX.153 A Pembrokeshire Proverb.—'Eat an apple on going to bed, And you'll keep the doctor from earning his bread.' **1913** E. M. WRIGHT *Rustic Speech* xiv. Ait a happle avore gwain to bed, An' you'll make the doctor beg his bread (Dev.); or as the more popular version runs: An apple a day keeps the doctor away. **2001** *Times* 12 Dec. 2 Have you resolved to be a well person?...Do you eat an apple a day to keep the doctor away? ■ **doctors 医者 ; health 健康**

The APPLE never falls far from the tree.
リンゴの実は木から遠く離れたところには決して落ちない。

どうやら東洋起源で、世代を超えて家系の特徴が継続されていくことを述べている。1839 年の用例は、人は生まれた場所に帰るといういくぶん異なる意味で使われている。† 16 世紀のドイツ語のことわざ *Der Apfel fellt nicht gerne weit vom Baume.*「リンゴはたいてい木から離れたところには落ちない」

☐**1839** EMERSON *Letter* 22 Dec.(1939) II. 243 As men say the apple never falls far from the stem, I shall hope that another year will draw your eyes and steps to this old dear odious haunt of the race. **1939** H. W. THOMPSON *Body, Boots & Britches* xix. As a...farmer remarked, 'If you breed a pa'tridge, you'll git a pa'tridge.' Another way of setting that truth forth is,...'An apple never falls far from the tree.' **1981** *Women's Journal* Apr.179 He's a fool, Muffle, as his father was. The apple never falls far from the tree. **2001** *Washington Post* 28 June C10 The social worker had summed up the child's future: 'Don't expect to do miracles. An apple can't fall too far from the tree.' ■ **family 家族・家系 ; nature and nurture 生まれと育ち ; origins 起源・生まれ**

apple ⇒ The ROTTEN apple injures its neighbours ; SMALL choice in rotten apples ; STOLEN fruit is sweet.

An APPLE-PIE without some cheese is like a kiss without a squeeze.
チーズのないアップルパイは抱擁のない口づけのようなものだ。

アップルパイとチーズを一緒に食べる習慣はヨークシャーを連想させることが多いが、米国でも広く普及している（1882年の用例参照）。脚韻（cheese と squeeze）の起源についても議論が分かれる。1889年、フォートワース『デイリーガゼット』(18 Sept.4)によると、この言葉はパーク・ベンジャミン（1809-64）に由来する。彼の言葉は「チーズのないアップルパイは抱擁のない口づけのようなものだ」であった。パーク・ベンジャミンは多作な米国のジャーナリスト兼編集者であった。

☐ **1882** W. G. MARSHALL *Through America* 99 Our transatlantic cousins are very fond of apple-pie…and (in some parts of America)…you will eat it with a bit of cheese, Yorkshire fashion. As an American lady once graphically put it Apple-pie without cheese is like a kiss without a squeeze. **1929** C. BROOKS *Seven Hells* v. 63 Let me advise you to take a bit of cheese with it They have a good proverb, these folks:'Apple pie without the cheese, is like the kiss without a squeeze.'**1989** *Courier-Journal* (Louisville, KY) 2 July 4M There was an old English rhyme popular about 1750 that went: An apple-pie without some cheese Is like a kiss without a squeeze. **2002** *Spectator* 21 Sept 61 'Apple cake without cheese,'they used to say in Yorkshire,'is like a kiss without a squeeze.' ■ **food and drink** 飲食物

APRIL showers bring forth May flowers.
4 月の雨は 5 月の花をもたらす。

イングランドの天気にまつわるよく知られた言葉であるが、実証されているわけではない（1921年の用例参照）。

☐ *c***1560** in T. Wright *Songs & Ballads* (1860) 213 Aprell sylver showers so sweet Can make May flowers to sprynge. **1670** J. RAY *English Proverbs* 41 April showers bring forth May flowers. **1846** M. A. DENHAM *Proverbs relating to Seasons*, &c. 36 March winds and April showers bring forth May flowers. **1921** *Sphere* 14 May 152 If there was anybody left to believe in the saying that 'April showers bring forth May flowers' their simple faith must have been rudely shattered by May's behaviour this year. **2001** *Washington Post* 1 July Fl If April showers bring May flowers, what do June brides bring? ■ **weather lore** 天気にまつわる伝承

architect ⇒ EVERY man is the architect of his own fortune.

arm ⇒ KINGS have long arms ; YORKSHIRE born and Yorkshire bred, strong in the arm and weak in the head.

An ARMY marches on its stomach.
軍隊は胃袋で進軍する。
（訳注：「腹が減ってはいくさはできぬ」）

軍隊が正常に機能するのは食料が十分供給されている場合である。ナポレオンとフリードリヒ 2 世の 2 人に由来すると言われている。(on one's) stomach「お腹いっぱいで」という慣用句は英語ではあまり使われない。

26　around

□**1904** *Windsor Magazine* Jan. 268 'An army marches on its stomach.''*C'est lasoupequifait le soldat.*' These Napoleonic aphorisms...have been increasingly appreciated by our War Office. **1977** J. B. HILTON *Dead-Nettle* x.'They say an army marches on its stomach,'Gilbert Slack began to say. 'You mean that Frank was a cook?' **1992** W. DONALDSON *Root into Europe* ii.16 'Didn't see service as such. Supply and demand myself. Pay and personnel. Laundry and so forth. An army marches on its stomach.' **2002** *Washington Times* 30Jan. E4 (*Hazel comic strip*) 'An army marches on its stomach.''And retreats on its...' **2015** *Spectator* 17 Jan.57 We all know that an army marches on its stomach—but what about hardworking aid workers or disaster victims? ■ **food and drink 飲食物 ; soldiers 兵士**

around ⇒ What GOES around comes around.

arrive ⇒ It is BETTER to travel hopefully than to arrive.

ART is long and life is short.
技芸は長く、人生は短い。

古代ギリシアの医学者ヒポクラテス（『箴言』I. I. ὁ βίος βραχύς, ἡ δὲ τέχνη μααρή.「人生は短いが、医術は長い」）は医学を習得する際に直面する困難と人生の短さを較べている。ヒポクラテスの言葉は、ローマの哲学者セネカの対話集 *On the Brevity of life*『人生の短さについて』の中に登場する (*De brevitate vitae I: vitam brevem esse, longam artem*)。ここからラテン語の格言 *Ars longa,vita brevis.*「技芸は長く、人生は短い」が生まれた。ことわざの中の *art* は習得するのに多大な時間を要する技術一般を指しているが、同時に1958年の用例が示しているように、芸術作品は人間の寿命よりも長く存在しつづけるという意味も含まれている。

□*c*1380 CHAUCER *Paliament of Fowls* 1. 1 The lyf so short, the craft so long to lerne. **1558** W. BULLEIN *Government of Health* 5ᵛ And although oure life be shorte, yet the arte of phisicke is long. **1581** G. PETTIE tr. *S. Guazzo's Civil* Conversation I.16 An art is long and life is short. **1710** S. PALMER *Proverbs* 380 Art is Long, Life Short. Our Philosophical Meditations on Time are very Obscure and Confus'd. **1869** M. ARNOLD *Culture & Anarchy* vi. If...we take some other criterion of man's well-being than the cities he has built...our Liberal friends...take us up very sharply. 'Art is long', says the Times, 'and life is short.' **1958** L. DURRELL *Balthazar* IV. xiii. The shapely hand on his shoulder still wore the great ring taken from the tomb of a Byzantine youth. Life is short, art long. **1987** 'C.AIRD' *Dead Liberty* viii.'The art is long,' Sloan heard himself saying aloud....'And life is short. I know that.' Dr. bressingham completed the quotation brusquely. ■ **life 人生 ; mortality 死すべき運命**

ash ⇒ When the OAK is before the ash, then you will only get a splash ; Beware of an OAK it draws the stroke.

ASK a silly question and you get a silly answer.
愚かな質問をすれば愚かな答えしか返ってこない。

（訳注：英語のことわざには「命令文 and ... 」の構文〈～すれば…となる〉が多い）

『箴言』26章 5 節（欽定訳聖書）Answer a fool according to his folly, lest he be wise in his own conceit.「愚かな者にはその愚かさにしたがって答えよ。彼が自分の目に自らを知恵ある者と見ないためだ」を思わせる。

ATTACK 27

□ *c*1300 *South-English Legendary* (EETS) 494 Ffor-sothe thou axest as a fol, and swich ansuere me schul the yive. **1484** CAXTON *Aesop* (1967) V. xiii. 158 And thus they wente withoute ony sentence For to a folysshe demaunde behoueth a folysshe ansuere. **1551** R. ROBYNSON tr. *T. Mare's Utopia*, E4 For SALOMON the wise sayeth: Answer a foole according to his folishnes, like as I do now. *c*1600 *Tarlton's Jests* (1638) E2ᵛ The fellow seeing a foolish question had a foolish answere, laid his legges on his neck, and got him gone. **1721** J. KELLY *Scottish Proverbs* 35 A thraward [perverse] Question should a thraward Answer. **1934** C. RYLAND *Murder on Cliff* vi. If you ask me damned silly questions, I'm going to give you damned silly answers. **1969** 'A. GIL-BERT' *Missingfromher Home* v. No, don't bother to answer that Ask a silly question and you get a silly answer. **1985** M. WESLEY *Harnessing Peacocks* (1990) v. 46 'Are you happy at school?' Ask a silly question. 'It's all right' 'What sort of answer is that?' she cried in distress. ■ **action and consequence** 行為と結果；**stupidity** 愚かさ

ASK no questions and hear no lies.
質問をしなければ嘘をつかれなくてすむ。
(訳注：子供がしつこく質問してくる時に、親がよく使うとされる)

相手が答えることができない、あるいは答えたくない質問をして嘘を言わせてはならない。通常、1906年のキップリングの小説にあるような Them that asks no questions isn't told a lie. という形、もしくはそれに影響を受けた形で用いられる（1997年の用例も参照）。

□ **1773** GOLDSMITH *She stoops to Conquer* III. 51 Ask me no questions and I'll tell you no fibs. **1818** SCOTT *Heart of Midlothian* I.ix.If ye'll ask nae questions, I'll tell ye nae lees. **1900** H. LAW-SON *Over Sliprails* 135'Where did you buy the steer, father?'she asked.'Ask no questions and hear no lies.' **1906** R. KIPLING *Puck of Pook's Hill* 252 Them that asks no questions isn't told a lie—Watch the wall, my darling, while the Gentlemen go by! **1997** R. BOWEN *Evans Above* vi. 65 Charlie put his finger to his nose.'Them that asks no questions, don't get told no lies, that's what my old mother used to say,' he said. ■ **curiosity** 詮索好き・好奇心；**lying** 嘘をつくこと

ask ⇒ If you WANT something done, ask a busy person.

a-sorrowing ⇒ He that GOES a-borrowing, goes a-sorrowing.

ATTACK is the best form of defence.
攻撃こそ最善の防御。

攻撃こそが最善の防御であるという考えは米国起源である。† **1775** W. H. ドレイトンの言葉。R. W. ギッブス『米国独立戦争ドキュメンタリー史』(1855) I. 174 It is a maxim, that it is better to attack than to receive one.「攻撃を受けるより攻撃する方がよいというのは名言である」。**1799** ジョージ・ワシントン『著作集』(1940) XXXVII. 250 Make them believe, that offensive operations, often times, is the surest, if not the only…means of defence.「彼らに信じさせよ、唯一の手段とは言わないが、しばしば攻撃するのが最も確実な防御であることを」。最近の用例は英米の差が顕著で、米国では The best DEFENCE is a good offense.「最上の攻撃こそよい防御」の方が一般的である。

□ **1930** C. F. GREGG *Murder on Bus* xxxvii. Inspector Higgins fired his revolver at the sound, deeming attack the better part of defence, whilst someone from the other side of the room had a similar notion. **1965** N. S. GRAY *Apple-Stone* xi. 'Attack', she said, 'is the best means of defence.' She sounded so smug that I told her the thought was not original. **1980** F. OLBRICH *Desouza in*

28　away

Stardustiv. Attack is the best form of defence, they say, and when politicians Jose their principles they play a dirty game. **2002** *Times* 19 June 24 Clearly,the big banks have stuck to their policy of attack being the best form of defence on this issue [of price controls]. ■ **boldness** 大胆さ ; **war-fare** 戦争

away ⇒ When the CAT'S away, the mice will play.

B

B ⇒ Who SAYS A must say B.

babe ⇒ Out of the MOUTHS of babes—.

baby ⇒ Don't THROW the baby out with the bathwater.

back ⇒ GOD makes the back to the burden ; What is GOT over the Devil's back is spent under his belly ; The LAST straw breaks the camel's back ; You SCRATCH my back, I'll scratch yours.

A BAD excuse is better than none.
まずい言い訳でもしないよりはまし。

逆の言い方もある。A bad excuse is worse than none.「まずい言い訳ならしないほうがましだ」は1864年7月に行なわれた、イギリスの著名なバプテスト派の牧師・伝道者・説教者スポルジョンの説教の演題である。『ルカによる福音書』14章18節（欽定訳聖書）に And they all with one consent began to make excuse.「すると、彼らはみな口実をもうけて、次々と断った」という一節がある。

□ **1551** T. Wilson *Rule of Reason* 56 This is as thei Saie in English, better a badde excuse, then none at all. **1579** S. GOSSON *School of Abuse* 24 A bad excuse is better, they say, then none at all. **1821** W. WIRT *Letter* 29 Aug. in J. P. Kennedy *Memoirs* (1849) II. vii.The old fellow's look had a glimpse of passing cunning as much as to say, 'A bad excuse is better than none.' **1981** P. VAN GREENAWAY *'Cassandra'Bill* xiii. What excuse is better than none? ■ **excuses** 言い訳

BAD money drives out good.
悪貨は良貨を駆逐する。
(訳注：goodの後にmoneyが省略された表現)

王立取引所の創始者トーマス・グレシャム（1519頃-79）にちなんで名づけられたグレシャムの法則として広く知られる。彼自身がこの表現を用いたという証拠はないが、貨幣の純潔度を保証する経済的必要性をよく理解していた。1902年の用例から、グレシャムがエリザベス1世へ宛てた手紙の中でこの原則が（ことわざとしてではなく）言及していることがわかる。**1858** H. D. マクラウド『政治経済学の要素』477 He [Gresham] was the first to perceive that a bad and debased currency is the cause of the disappearance of the good money.「グレシャムこそ、質の悪い貨幣が出回ると良貨が駆逐されてしまう原因となることに最初に気づいた人物であった」

□**1902** *New English Dictionary* VI. 116 *Gresham's law*, the principle, involved in Sir Thomas Gresham's letter to Q. Elizabeth in 1558, that 'bad money drives out good'. **1933** A. HUXLEY *Letter* 18 Nov. (1969) 438 Gresham's Law holds good in every field...and bad politics tends to drive out good politics just as bad money drives out good money. **1982** R. NISBET *Prejudices* 178 Genuine scholars receive grants too, but this misses the crucial point, which is that bad money drives out good, and that only a few years of such handouts to putterers will be enough to convince the American people that Everyman is a humanist. **2002** *Times 2* 12 June 5 In potatoes as in currency, Gresham's law applies: bad drives out good. The new new, in potatoes, is old. ■ **money** 金・金銭

BAD news travels fast.
悪い知らせはあっという間に伝わる。

（訳注：「悪事千里を走る」）

良い知らせよりも悪い知らせの方が速く伝わるものだ。† **1539** タヴァーナー訳『エラスムス格言集』II. A 4 Sad and heuy tydynges be easly blowen abroade be they never so vaine and false and they be also sone beleued.「悲しく辛い知らせはすぐに外に伝わる。たとえその根拠はなくとも、信じる者はいるのである」。1592 年と 1694 年の用例における動詞 flie、fly が示すように、当時は news は複数名詞と考えられていた。

□**1592** KYD *Spanish Tragedy* I. B2v Euill newes flie faster still than good. **1694** Terence's *Comedies made English* 46 Bad News always fly faster than good. **1792** T. HOLCROFT *Road to Ruin* II. i. All these bills...brought...this morning. Ill news travels fast. **1935** W. IRWIN *Julius Caesar Murder Case* xxv.'Where'd you get it [a knife]?''On the Plains of Philippi''Bad news travels fast,' said Hercules. **1991** L. SANDERS *McNally's Secret*(1992)iv.38 'I've already had a dozen phony sympathy calls—including one from a cousin in Sarasota. Bad news certainly travels fast.' **2012** *Christian Science Monitor* 30 Dec. (online) There's much more good news than bad news. But bad news travels fast and commands attention. ■ **misfortune** 不運 ; **news** 知らせ

A BAD penny always turns up.
偽金はいつも舞い戻って来るものだ。

（訳注：penny の代わりに shilling が用いられることもある。turn up like *a bad penny* という慣用句は「いやな奴がいやな時に現われる」の意味で用いられる）

比喩的に使われることもある（1766 年の用例参照）。評判の悪い厄介な人物は、しばらくいなくなった後、また戻ってくるものである。そうした望ましくない人物が戻ってくることは大体予測がつく。

□**1766** A. ADAMS in L H. Butterfield et al. *Adams Family Correspondence* (1963) I. 55 Like a bad penny it returnd, to me again. **1824** SCOTT *Redgauntlet* II. ii. Bring back Darsie? little doubt of that—the bad shilling is sure enough to come back again. **1884** R. H. THORPE *Fenton Family* iii. Just like as not he'll be coming back one of these days, when he's least wanted. A bad penny is sure to return. **1922** JOYCE *Ulysses* 149 Who's dead, when and what did he die of? Turn up like a bad penny. **1941** A. UPDEGRAFF *Hills look Down* vi. 'I miss Bart.' 'Oh, a bad penny always turns up again.' **1979** G. MITCHELL *Mudflats of Dead* iii. 'Stop worrying. The bad pennies always turn up.' 'Oh, Adrian, I don't think she's a bad penny, not really.' ■ **wrong-doers** 悪事をなす者

BAD things come in threes.
悪いことは三度起こる。
（訳注：「二度あることは三度」。「弱り目に祟り目」）

良いことでも悪いことでも三度連続で起こるという民間の迷信は欧米で今でも生き残っている。一度目の不運のあとにもう二度生じることは避けられないという考えは相当根強く、不運を避けるために何らかの行為がなされる場合もある。**1891**『ノーツ・アンド・クェリーズ』7 th Ser. XII. 489 One of my servants having accidentally broken a glass shade, asked for two other articles of little value, a wine bottle and jam crock, that she might break them, and so prevent the two other accidents.... which would otherwise follow. 「ガラスのランプ笠をうっかり割ってしまった使用人の 1 人が、割ってもかまわないような安い品物を 2 つ要求した。それらはワインボトルとジャムの瓶であった。彼女はその 2 つを割っておけば、後から起こるかもしれない 2 つの重大事故を避けられると思ったのである」。なお、bad things は accidents、deaths あるいは他の不運な出来事として具体的に述べられることもある。† MISFORTUNES never come singly. 「不幸は 1 度だけでは終わらない」

☐ **1997** O. HANSEN *Sole Survivor* xvi. 82 He was a superstitious man and believed that bad joss always struck in threes. **2002** *Times* 20 Mar. 22 They say bad things come in threes. I don't know who the they are that say this, mind, or how they found out that that was how bad things came, ...but...last weekend, they were spot on. **2014** *www.independent.ie* 29 Jan. It is said that bad things come in threes, but that certainly isn't the case with this secondary school. ■ **misfortune** 不運 ; **superstition** 迷信

There is no such thing as BAD weather. Only the wrong clothes.
悪い天候などというものはない。服装がおかしいだけだ。

スウェーデン、あるいはノルウェー起源と伝えられる。両言語では脚韻を踏む。スウェーデン語 *Det jinns inget ddligt viider, bara ddliga kliider.* 「悪い天候などというものはない。服装がおかしいだけだ」。2012 年の用例が示すように、山野散策家アルフレッド・ウエインライト (1907-91) の言葉と考えられている。しかし、彼の言葉であるという説と他の著名な散策家や探検家の言葉であるという説は、悪天候と服装の関連性の指摘よりも後の話である。† **1883**ラスキン『イングランドの歴史』218 [T]here was no such thing as bad weather, but only different kinds of pleasant weather. 「悪天候などというものはない。快適な天候といっても人によって違うだけだ」

☐ **1911** *New Outlook* xcvii. 975 I responded glibly, 'Some one has said there is no such thing as bad weather, there is only good clothes.' **1960** DUCHESS OF WINDSOR *San Diego Union* 13 Oct BS/1 After a long wet holiday..., an acquaintance of mine came up with the observation that there is no such thing as bad weather, only bad clothes. **1992** *Daily Telegraph* 23 Sept 13 As someone once said, there is no such thing as bad weather, only the wrong clothes. **2005** B. CONNOLLY in *Scotsman.com* 6 Oct I hate all those weathermen who tell you that rain is bad weather. There's no such thing as bad weather, just the wrong clothing. **2012** *www.theguardian.com* 4 June (*heading*) There's no such thing as bad weather, only unsuitable clothing. ■ **circumstances** 状況 ; **dress** 衣服 ; **weather lore** 天気にまつわる伝承

32 BAD

A BAD workman blames his tools.
下手な職人ほど道具に難癖をつける。

（訳注：bad の代わりに ill も用いられ〈An ill ...〉、workman の代わりに labourer も用いられる。未熟者に限って、自分が使っている道具に難癖をつけるものである。テニスが下手なのをラケットのせいにしてしまうといった類いである）

能力のない者は自分の失敗を自分以外のものになすりつけようとするもの。† 13 世紀末のフランス語 *Mauves ovriers ne trovera Ja bon hostill.*「腕の悪い職人は良い道具を見つけられない」

☐**1611** R. COTGRAVE *Dict. French & English* s.v. Outil, A bungler cannot find (or fit himselfe with) good tooles. **1640** G. HERBERT *Outlandish Proverbs* no. 67 Never had ill workeman good tooles. **1859** S. SMILES *Self-Help* iv. It Is proverbial that the bad workman never yet had a good tool. **1979** A. FOX *Threat Signal Red* xv. Damn! Dropped the screwdriver....Bad workmen blame their tools. **2001** *Washington Times* 19 Aug. B8 'Virtuous War' starts off with a bad idea, proceeds to a pair of disasters, then gets worse. As for the fundamental reason for its failure—for now let's just say, it's a poor workman who blames his lousy tools. ■ **efficiency and inefficiency** 能率と非能率；**work** 仕事

bad ⇒ Give a DOG a bad name and hang him；FIRE is a good servant but a bad master；A GOOD horse cannot be of a bad colour；HARD cases make bad law；HOPE is a good breakfast but a bad supper；NOTHING so bad but it might have been worse；THREE removals are as bad as a fire.

bag ⇒ EMPTY sacks will never stand upright；There's many a GOOD cock come out of a tattered bag.

bairn ⇒ FOOLS and bairns should never see half-done work；The SHOEMAKER's son always goes barefoot.

As you BAKE, so shall you brew.
パンを焼く具合に応じて、醸造するであろう。

人は自分の行為の結果に責任を負わなくてはならないものだ。順序を逆にしたものとして As you BREW, so shall you bake.「醸造する具合に応じて、パンを焼くであろう」がある。

☐*c*1577 *Misogonus* III. I. As thou bakst, so shat brewe. **1775** O. GABRICK *May-Day* ii.To keep...My bones whole and tight, To speak, nor look, would I dare; As they bake they shall brew. **1909** W. DE MORGAN *It never can happen Again* I. v. Each one [i.e. young person]...was...the centre of an Incubation of memories that were to last a lifetime. 'As they bake, so they will brew,'philosophized Mr. Challis to himself. ■ **action and consequence** 行為と結果

bake ⇒ As you BREW, so shall you bake.

bandit ⇒ The more LAWS, the more thieves and bandits.

bare ⇒ There goes more to MARRIAGE than four bare legs in a bed.

barefoot ⇒ The SHOEMAKER'S son always goes barefoot.

bargain ⇒ It takes TWO to make a bargain.

bark ⇒ DOGS bark, but the caravan goes on ; Why KEEP a dog and bark yourself?

A BARKING dog never bites.
吠えたてる犬は咬みつかぬ。

† Q. クルティウス『アレクサンドロス大王の謎の偉業』VII. iv. 13 *Canem timidum vehementius latrere quam mordere.*「臆病な野良犬は咬みつくよりも激しく吠えたてる」(バクトリア王国のことわざと伝えられる)。13世紀のフランス語 *Chascuns chiens qui abaie ne mort pas.*「吠えたてる犬は咬みつかぬ」

☐ c1550 *Thersytes* El Great barking dogges, do not most byte And oft It Is sene that the best men In the hoost Be not suche, that vse to bragge moste. **1595** *Locrine* (1908) IV. i. Soft words good sir....A barking dog doth sildome strangers bite. **1629** *Book of Merry Riddles* 22 A barking dog seldome bites. **1837** F. CHAMJER *Arethusa* III. x. Our dogs which bark, Abdallah, seldom bite. **1980** *Daily Telegraph* 1 May 18 A canvassing candidate came to a house where there was an Alsatian who barked ferociously. His agent said: 'Just go In. don't you know the proverb "A barking dog never bites"?' 'Yes,' said the candidate, 'I know the proverb, you know the proverb, but does the dog know the proverb?' ■ words and deeds 言動

BARNABY bright, Barnaby bright, the longest day and the shortest night.
明るいバルナバは 1 年中で昼間が一番長く、夜が一番短い。

(訳注：Barnabyはキリストの使徒でパウロの友人。英国の地方には子供たちがてんとう虫のことをBarnaby Bright と呼んで、てんとう虫に向かって、このように言うとされる)

旧暦 6 月11日の聖バルナバの日は一番日が長いと考えられていた (1978年の用例参照)。
† **1595** スペンサー『祝婚歌』1. 266 This day the sunne is in his chiefest hight, With Barnaby the bright.「この日太陽はバルナバの光とともに最も高くなる」

☐ **1659** J. HOWELL. *Proverbs* (English) 20 Barnaby bright, the longest day and shortest night. **1858** *Notes & Queries* 2nd Ser. VI. 522 In some parts of the country the children call the ladybird Barnaby Bright, and address it thus:—'Barnaby Bright, Barnaby Bright, The longest day and the shortest night' **1906** E. HOLDEN *Country Diary of Edwardian Lady* (1977) 72 Barnaby bright All day and no night. **1978** R. WHITLOCK *Calendar of Country Customs* vii. Barnaby bright, Barnaby bright, The longest day and the shortest night, Is a reminder that, before the change In the calendar In 1752, 11 June was the longest day of the year. ■ calendar lore 暦にまつわる伝承

basket ⇒ Don't put all your EGGS in one basket.

bathwater ⇒ Don't THROW the baby out with the bathwater.

battalion ⇒ PROVIDENCE is always on the side of the big battalions.

battle ⇒ The RACE is not to the swift, nor the battle to the strong.

34 BE

BE what you would seem to be.
他人からそう見られているなら、実際にそのような人間になれ。

偽善に対する警告として使われる。† アイスキュロス『テーバイ攻めの七将』l. 592 οὐ γὰρ δοκεῖν ἄριστος ἀ λλ εἶναι θέλει「彼は見かけでなく実際に最高でありたいと願っている」。サッルスティルス『カティリナ戦記』liv. *Esse, quam videri, bonus malebat.*「彼（カトー）は良く見えるというのではなく、実際に良くありたいと望んだ」

☐c1377 LANGLAND *Piers Plowman* B. x. 253 Suche as thow semest In syghte, be In assay [trial] y-founde. **1640** G. HERBERT *Outlandish Proverbs* no.724 Be what thou wouldst seeme to be. **1721** J. KELLY *Scottish Proverbs* 68 Be what you seem, and seem what you are. The best way! for Hypocrisy Is soon discovered. **1865** 'L. CARROLL' *Alice's Adventures in Wonderland*ix. It's a vegetable. It doesn't look like one, but it is....the moral of that is—'Be what you would seem to be.' **1980** G. SIMS in H. Watson *Winter Crimes12* 158 The Benningworth family motto *Esse quam videri*, 'To be rather than to seem to be'. ■ **appearance** 外見

bean ⇒ CANDLEMAS day, put beans in the clay, put candles and candlesticks away.

BEAR and forbear.
（苦痛を）我慢せよ、そして（快楽を）差し控えよ。
（訳注：古代ギリシアのストア派の哲学者エピクテトスの黄金律）

辛抱と自制を勧める訓戒。† エピクテトス『断章』x. *Avtxov real cbrt, tou.*「我慢せよ、そして耐えよ」。エラスムス『格言集』II, vii. 13 *Sustine et abstine.*「耐えよ、そして断念せよ」

☐**1573** T. TUSSER *Husbandry* (rev.ed.) II. 12ᵛ Both beare and forbeare, now and then as ye niay, then wench God a mercy [reward you], thy husband will say. **1688** BUNYAN *Discourse of Building, & C. House of God* 53 To bear and forbear here, will tend to rest. **1871** S. SMILES *Character* xi. The golden rule of married life Is, 'Bear and forbear'. **1940** H. W. THOMPSON *Body, Boots & Britches* xix. You must take two bears two live with you—Bear and Forbear. ■ **patience and impatience** 忍耐と性急；**tolerance** 寛容・忍耐

bear（名詞）⇒ Don't SELL the skin till you have caught the bear.

beard ⇒ It is MERRY in hall when beards wag all.

beast ⇒ When the WIND is in the east, 'tis neither good for man nor beast.

If you can't BEAT them, join them.
負かせない相手とは仲間になれ。
（訳注：「長いものには巻かれろ」）

米国では beat よりも lick「打ち負かす」の方が一般的である（訳注：以下の用例で 'em は話し言葉で them と同じ。古英語 hem に由来）。

☐**1941** Q. REYNOLDS *Wounded don't Cry*i. There is an old political adage which says 'If you can't lick'em, jine 'em'. **1953** P. GALLICO *Foolish Immortals* xvii. It was vital to him to get the reins back into his own hands again. He remembered an old adage: 'If you can't lick 'em, join ' em.' **1979** D. LESSING *Shikasta* 2661 said, Running things, what's the point? He said, If you can't beat them, Join them! **1996** *Washington Times* 2 July B8 Having taken it on the chin so convinc-

BEAUTY 35

ingly, brokers have decided that, if you can't beat 'em, join 'em. **2002** Washington *Times* 26 Feb. A20 In fact, he began an attempt to win over the Catholic party to his side; the Teutonic version of 'can't lick 'em, join 'em.' ■ **enemies** 敵 ; **self-preservation** 自己防衛

beat ⇒ One ENGLISHMAN can beat three Frenchmen ; It is easy to find a STICK to beat a dog.

beautiful ⇒ SMALL is beautiful.

BEAUTY draws with a single hair.
美貌は髪の毛 1 本で引く。

美貌には単なる物理的な力では測れないような魅力がある。1591 年の用例における Helen とはトロイのヘレネ（トロイ戦争の原因となった美女）を指している。

□**1591** J. FLORIO *Second Fruits* 183 Ten teemes of oxen draw much lesse, Than doth one haire of Helens tresse. **1640** G. HERBERT *Outlandish Proverbs* no.685 Beauty drawes more then oxen. **1666** G. TORRIANO *Piazza Universale* 199 One hair ofa woman draws more than a hundred yoke ofoxen. **1712** POPE *Rape of Lock* II. 28 And beauty draws us with a single hair. **1941** 'M. COLES' *They tell no Tales* xxii. Beauty draws me with a single hair if it's blonde enough. **1945** R. L. HINE *Confessions* (ed. 2) 91 The old adage…that 'beauty draws more than oxen.' ■ **beauty** 美・美貌

BEAUTY is in the eye of the beholder.
美貌は見る人しだいである。
（訳注：「あばたもえくぼ」）

美といっても、それは客観的に判断されるのではなく、見る人の主観に左右される。† テオクリトス『牧歌』vi.18 ἡ γὰρ ἔρωτι πολλάκις…τὰ μὴ καλὰ καλὰ πέφατναι.「愛する者の目には美しくないものも美しく見えることがある」。† **1742** ヒューム『道徳・政治・文学論集』II. 151 Beauty, properly speaking, lyes…in the Sentiment or Taste of the Reader.「美しさとは、正しくは、読者の心情や嗜好しだいである」

□**1769** F. BROOKE *Hist. Emily Montague* IV. 205 You should remember, my dear, that beautyis in the lover's eye. **1788** R. CUMBERLAND in *Observer* IV. cxviii. Beauty, gentlemen, is in the eye, I aver it to be in the eye of the beholder and not in the object itself. **1878** M. W. HUNGERPORD *Molly Bawn* I. xii. 'I have heard she is beautiful—is she?' 'Beauty is in the eye of the beholder.' quotes Marcia. **2001** *Spectator* 8 Dec. 58 This at once confirmed the conclusion that I had just reached after studying the photographs of the child Wladyslaw…: beauty is not merely in the eye but also in the imagination of the beholder. ■ **beauty** 美・美貌 ; **love** 愛・恋愛 ; **taste** 趣味・味

BEAUTY is only skin-deep.
美貌も皮一重。

美人だからと言って、その人が性格が良いとか、徳が高いとは言えない。† *a*1613 T. オーヴァーベリー『妻よ』(1614) B 8ᵛ All the carnall beautie of my wife, Is but skinne-deep.「私の妻の身体の美しさは皮一重にすぎない」

□**1616** J. DAVIES *Select Second Husband* B3 Beauty's but skin-deepe. **1829** COBBETT *Advice to Young Men* III.cxxix. The less favoured part of the sex say, that 'beauty is but skin deep'…but it is very agreeable though, for all that. **1882** B. M. JNGRAHAM *Bond & Free* xiii. Mother used to say that beauty was only skin deep, but I never before realized that bones could be so fearfully

36　bed

repulsive. **1978** A. PRICE *'44 Vintage* xix. Beauty is only skin-deep, but it's only the skin you see. ■ **beauty** 美・美貌

bed ⇒ EARLY to bed and early to rise, makes a man healthy, wealthy, and wise ; As you MAKE your bed, so you must lie upon it ; There goes more to MARRIAGE than four bare legs in a bed.

bedfellow ⇒ ADVERSITY makes strange bedfellows ; POLITICS makes strange bedfellows.

beer ⇒ He that DRINKS beer, thinks beer ; LIFE isn't all beer and skittles ; TURKEY, heresy, hops, and beer came into England all in one year.

Where BEES are, there is honey.
ミツバチのいる所、蜜あり。
（訳注：「火のない所に煙は立たぬ」）

原義は1670年の用例で説明されているが、1931年の用例は No SMOKE without fire.「火のない所に煙は立たぬ」に意味が近いことを示している。† *Ubi mel, ibi apes.*「蜜ある所ミツバチあり」

☐**1616** T. DRAXE *Adages* 77 Where Bees are, there is honie. **1670** J. RAY *English Proverbs* 60 Where Bees are, there is honey. Where there are industrious persons, there is wealth, for the hand of the diligent maketh rich. **1748** M. FREEMAN *Word in Season* 6 Take away the Bees, and...you shall have no Honey in the Hive,...but there always will be Honey where there are Bees. **1931** P. A. TAYLOR *Cape Cod Mystery* ix. It'd look...like they was something afoot, bein' as how there's bees where's honey. **2012** *www.esif.eu* 15 May (*article title*) Where bees are, there will be honey (even prehistoric). ■ **associates** 仲間 ; **diligence** 勤勉

beforehand ⇒ PAY beforehand was never well served.

beget ⇒ LOVE begets love.

Set a BEGGAR on horseback, and he'll ride to the Devil.
乞食を馬に乗せれば悪魔の所まで駆けていく。

多くの形があるが、簡略化されて使われることが多い。権力や贅沢に不慣れな者はいったんそれを手にすると乱用してしまうか、もしくはそれによって破滅するものだ。

☐**1576** G. PETTIE *Petit Palace* 76 Set a Beggar on horsebacke, and he wyl neuer alight. **1669** W. WINSTANLEY *New Help to Discourse* 151 Set a Beggar on Horse-back, and he will ride to the Devil. **1855** GASKELL *North & South* 1: x. You know the proverb...'Set a beggar on horseback, and he'll ride to the devil,' —well, some of these early manufacturers did ride to the devil in a magnificent style. **1923** C. WELLS *Affair at Flower Acres* II. I should think your early days of forced economy would have taught you not to be quite so extravagant But there's an old proverb —'Set a beggar on horse-back—' and so forth, that jolly well fits you. **1961** W. H. LEWIS *Scandalous Regent* x. He had a good deal of the vulgarity and insolence of the beggar onhorseback. ■ **good fortune** 幸運 ; **pride** 誇り・うぬぼれ

beggar ⇒ SUE a beggar and catch a louse ; If WISHES were horses, beggars would ride.

believing　37

BEGGARS can't be choosers.
乞食は選り好みはできぬ。

（訳注：Beggars should〈must〉be no choosers.とも言う）

貧乏であったり、困難な状況に置かれている場合には、選り好みなどする余地などない。助動詞 can't の代わりに must not を使うのは最近の傾向である。†15世紀半ばのフランス語では、*Qui empruncte ne peult choisir.*「借金のある者は選べないである」

□**1546** J. HEYWOOD *Dialogue of Proverbs* I. x. Dl Folke say alwaie, beggers shulde be no choosers. **1728** VANBRUGH *Journey to London* m. L My Lords, says I, Beggars must not be Chusers; but some Place about a thousand a Year...might do pretty weel. **1888** N. J. CLODFELTER *Snatched from Poor House* iv. Crawl out o' that bed! I'spose you do feel a little bad, but ',beggars can't be choosers!' **1939** J. SHEARING *Blanche Fury* 72 'I suppose...you would marry any man with a good character and a fine estate.'...'Beggars can't be choosers, you mean!' **2000** J. ALTMAN *Gathering of Spies* ix. 150 It would ruin the dress, no doubt about that But beggars couldn't be choosers. She drew a breath and then jumped, tucking and rolling as she came out of the train. ■ necessity 必要性・必然性；poverty 貧困

begin ⇒ CHARITY begins at home；A journey of a thousand miles begins with a single step；Life begins at forty；When THINGS are at the worst they begin to mend；⇒ BEGUN.

beginning ⇒ A GOOD beginning makes a good ending.

begun ⇒ The SOONER begun, the sooner done；WELL begun is half done.

beholder ⇒ BEAUTY is in the eye of the beholder.

BELIEVE nothing of what you hear, and only half of what you see.
耳で聞くことは何も信じるな、目で見ることは半分だけ信じよ。

† *a*1300『アルフレッド大王の格言集』(1907) 35 Gin thu neuere leuen alle monnis spechen,Ne alle the thinge that thu herest singen.「汝が耳にしたことのすべてを本当であると信じるな。それらがすべて本当だとは限らない」。**1770**『メリーランド歴史集』における 9 月 4 日付けのキャロル『書簡集』(1918) XIII. 58 You must not take Everything to be true that is told to you.「語られたことすべてが正しいと思ってはならない」

□**1845** E. A. POE in *Graham's Mag.* Nov. 194 You are young yet...but the time will arrive when you will learn to judge for yourself...Believe nothing you hear, and only one half that you see. **1933** 'R. ESSEX' *Slade of Yard* xlx. It's a good plan to believe half you see and nothing you hear. **1979** D. KYLE *Green River High* ii. I listened with the old magician's warning lively in my mind; believe nothing of what you hear—and only half of what you see! **2002** *Washington* Times 16 Aug. A19 The Democratic candidates are lined up, and they are making hot and heavy pitches for our votes. But, as the old saying goes, believe half of what you see and none of what you hear. ■ rumour 噂；trust and scepticism 信用と懐疑

believing ⇒ SEEING is believing.

38 BELLOWING

A BELLOWING cow soon forgets her calf.
鳴いている雌牛でも子牛のことはそのうち忘れる。
(訳注：「喉元過ぎれば熱さを忘れる」)

(特に死別の) ひどい悲しみもほどなく消えていくものだ。† **1553** ウィルソン『修辞学の技法』42 The Cowe lackyng her Caulfe, leaueth Loweyng within three or foure daies at the farthest.「子牛を失った雌牛もせいぜい 3 日か 4 日以内にその悲しみは忘れる」

☐ **1895** S. O. ADDY *Household Tales* 142 In the East Riding they say, 'A bletherin' coo soon forgets her calf,' meaning that excessive grief does not last long. **1928** *London Mercury* Feb. 439 Common proverb in the West Country Is 'A belving cow soon forgetsher calf.' **1945** F. THOMPSON *Lark Rise* xxxiv. When a woman, newly widowed, had tried to throw herself into her husband's grave at his funeral...some one...said drily...'Ah, you wait. The bellowing cow's always the first to forget Its calf.' ■ **forgetfulness** 物忘れ；**words and deeds** 言動

belly ⇒ What is GOT over the Devil's back is spent under his belly.

bent ⇒ As the TWIG is bent, so is the tree inclined.

All's for the BEST in the best of all possible worlds.
この世のすべてのものはあらゆる世界の中で最善になるようにできている。

フランスの啓蒙思想家・文学者ヴォルテールの言葉 *Tout est pour le mieux dans le meilleur des mondes possibles.* を翻訳したものである。楽観主義的哲学者のパングロスが『カンディード (あるいは楽天主義説)』(1759) の中で述べている意見であるが、物語の中で登場人物たちを襲う悲劇はこのことわざとは正反対のことを示している。

☐ **1911** G. B. SHAW *Shewing-up of Blanco Posnet* 299 The administrative departments were consuming miles of red tape in the correctest forms of activity, and everything was for the best in the best of all possible worlds. **1943** A. CHRISTIE *Moving Finger* xv. I agreed with happy Miss Emily that everything was for the best in the best of possible worlds. **1961** WODEHOUSE *Ice in Bedroom* II. Fate had handed him the most stupendous bit of goose [luck] and...all was for the best in this best of all possible worlds. ■ **content and discontent** 満足と不満足；**optimism** 楽観主義

The BEST is the enemy of the good.
最善は善の敵。
(訳注：often が挿入されることもある。the best, the good の定冠詞 the は形容詞に付けて、名詞に変える働きを持つ。「…であること」の意。the impossible〈不可能なこと〉。ほどほどにしておけばいいものを、最高のものにしようとして失敗してしまうことがある)

The GOOD is the enemy of the best.「善は最善の敵」のように主語と述語が倒置されることもたまにある。† **1770** ヴォルテール『百科事典に関する疑問』II. 250 *C'est bien ici qu'on peut dire n meglio e l'inimico del bene.* **1772** − *La Béguele in CEuvres Complètes* (1877) X. 50 *Le mieux est l'ennemi du bien.*「最善は善の敵」

☐ **1861** R. C. TRENCH *Commentary on Epistles to Seven Churches in Asia* p. v. 'The best is oftentimes the enemy of the good'; and...many a good book has remained unwritten...because there floated before the mind's eye...the ideal of a better or a best. **1925** *Times* 1 Dec. 16 This is not the first time In the history of the world when the best has been the enemy of the good;...one single step on...solid ground may be more profitable than a more ambitious flight.

1960 D. JONES *Letter* 1 June In R. Hague *Dai Greatcoat* (1980) III. 182 Tom told me a very good Spanish proverb: 'The best is the enemy of the good.' **2014** *Spectator* 3 May 14 Next time you hear somebody say that they worry about the potential risks of e-cigarettes, remind them of Voltaire's dictum—don't let the best be the enemy of the good. ■ **good things** よいもの

The BEST-laid schemes of mice and men gang aft agley.
ネズミと人間の完全犯罪は失敗に終わることが多い。

1911年の用例からわかるように、簡略化された形で暗示的に使われることが多い。*gang aft agley* とは often go awry「しばしば失敗する」の意。

□ **1786** BURNS *Poems* 140 The best laid schemes o' Mice an' Men, Gang aft agley. **1911** D. H. LAWRENCE *Letter* 21 Sept (1979) I. 305 I am sorry the bookbinding has gone pop. But there 'The best laid schemes' etc. etc. **1996** H. P. JEFFERS *Reader's Guide to Murder* xxvii. 179 But, like the man said, 'The best laid plans of mice and men often go awry.' ■ **intentions** 意図; **wanting and having** 不足と所持

The BEST of friends must part.
親友といえども別れざるを得ないものだ。

（訳注：must＝「必ず…する、…することは避けられない」。All human beings *must* die.〈人間は皆死ぬ運命にある〉。「会うは別れの始め」）

† *c*1385 チョーサー『トロイラスとクリセイデ』v. 343 Alwey frendes may nat ben yfeere [may not be together].「友人といえども別れざるを得ないものだ」

□ **1611** G. CHAPMAN *May-Day* IV, 70 Friends must part, we came not all together, and we must not goe all together. **1685** J. DUNTON In *Publications of Prince Society* (1867) 10 But the dearest friends must part. **1784** J. F. D. SMYTH *Tour in USA* I. xxxvii. Sooner or later, all, even the dearest of friends, must part. **1821** SCOTT *Kenilworth* I. xi. 'You are going to leave me, then?'…'The best of friends must part, Flibbertigibbet.' **1979** W. GOLDING *Darkness Visible* ii. 'Aren't there going to be any more lessons?'…'The best of friends must part.' ■ **absence** 不在; **friends** 友

The BEST of men are but men at best.
至高の人間といえども所詮は人間にすぎない。

（訳注：but＝「ただ、ほんの」。He is *but* a child.〈ほんの子供だ〉）

1680年の用例で言及されているランバート将軍は、議会派指導者ジョン・ランバート (1619-83) を指す。彼はイギリス市民戦争において王党派に対するクロムウェル軍の勝利を導く上で重要な役割を果たした。

□ **1680** J. AUBREY *Letter* 15 June In *Brief Lives* (1898) I. 12 I remember one sayeing of generall Lambert's, that 'the best of men are but men at best'. **1885** T. HARLEY *Moon Lore* 191 We can but repeat to ourselves the saying. 'The best of men are but men at best'. **2006** *Africa News* 16 April (online) The suave and customer friendly postal officers exercised the required social graces, ensuring that their customer understood…these seemingly able and efficient Kenyans, toiling under an imperfect International postal system. After all, 'the best of men are men at best.' ■ **human nature** 人間性; **pragmatism** 実用主義; **virtue** 長所・徳

The BEST things come in small packages.
最高のものは包みが小さい。

（訳注：The best wine comes out of an old vessel.〈最高の酒は古い壺から注がれる〉）

parcels（英）が packages（米）の代わりに使われることもある。† 13世紀のフランス語

Menue[s] parceles ensemble sunt beles.「小さい包みは美しく見える」。**1659** J.ハウエル『ことわざ集』(フランス語) 10 The best ointments are put in little boxes.「最高の軟膏は小さな箱の中に入っている」

☐**1877** B. FARJEON *Letter* 22 Jan. In E. Farjeon Nursery in Nineties (1935) v. As the best things are (said to be) wrapped In small parcels (proverb), I select the smallest sheet of paper I can find…to make you acquainted with the…state of affairs. **1979** R. Thomas *Eighth Dwarf* xviii. 'The little gentleman.'…'The best things sometimes come in small packages,' Jackson said, wincing at his own banality. **2002** *Country Life* 15 Aug. 61 Back at the lodge, the scalestum at 18 pounds, four ounces—my personal best, and an *über*-trout by any standards. . . . Sometimes good things come in big packages. ■ **great and small** 大小

The BEST things in life are free.
この世の最高のものは無料である。

☐**1927** B. G. DE SILVA et al. *Best Things In Life are Free (song)* 3 The moon belongs to ev'ryone, The best things in life are free, The stars belong to ev'ryone, They gleam there for you and me. **1955** W. GADDIS *Recognitions* II. ii. Someone once told them the best things in life are free, and so they've got in the habit of not paying. **2002** *Washington Post* 12 Jan. Cl2 The best things in life are free—friendships and sunshine still cost nothing—but some of the worst things are also free. ■ **good things** よいもの; **money** 金・金銭

It is BEST to be on the safe side.
安全な側にいるのが最上である。
(訳注：「君子危きに近寄らず」)

危険を冒すよりも、用心したり、用意周到である方が安全である。

☐**1668** DRYDEN & NEWCASTLE *Sir Martin Mar-all* v. I. I'm resolv'd to be on the sureside. **1811** J. AUSTEN *Sense & Sensibility* III. Iv. Determining to be on the safe side, he made his apology in form as soon as he could say any thing. **1847** MARRYAT *Children of New Forest* I. xi. Be on the safe side, and do not trust him too far. **1935** L. I. WILDER *Little House on Prairie* iii. Best to be on the safe side, it saves trouble in the end. **1981** *Economist* 28 Nov. 100 The Rowland-Molina hypothesis about the damaging effects of CFCs has not been disproved, so it is best to be on the safe side. ■ **prudence** 思慮・分別; **security** 安全

best ⇒ ACCIDENTS will happen (in the best-regulated families); ATTACK is the best form of defence; The best DEFENSE is a good offense; Why should the DEVIL have all the best tunes?; The best DOCTORS are Dr Diet, Dr Quiet, and Dr Merryman; EAST, west, home's best; EXPERIENCE is the best teacher; FIRST thoughts are best; FIRST up, best dressed; The GOOD is the enemy of the best; HONESTY is the best policy; HOPE for the best and prepare for the worst; HUNGER is the best sauce; He LAUGHS best who laughs last; LAUGHTER is the best medicine; If you have to LIVE in the river, it is best to be friends with the crocodile; It is best to be OFF with the old love before you are on with the new; An old POACHER makes the best gamekeeper; SECOND thoughts are best; SILENCE is a woman's best garment.

BETTER a century of tyranny than one day of chaos.
1日の混沌状態より100年の圧政の方がましだ。

イブン・タイミーヤは14世紀のダマスカスの学者であった。このことわざは1311頃-15

BETTER 41

年に書かれた *Kitāb al-Siyasa al-Shar'iya* (神によって定められた政治の書) に由来する
と考えられている (1966 年の用例参照)。ことわざの中で述べられている時間の長さは、
60 日、40 年など、そのつど変わる。

□ **1966** P. RAHMAN *Islam* 239 Ibn Tamiya Immediately follows up the...alleged Hadith with the
quotation, 'sixty days of an unjust ruler are much better than one night of lawlessness'. **1994** H.
MUTALIB *Islam In Malaysia* 64 Ibn Taymlyyah maintained that It is better to suffer a corrupt
leadership for sixty days rather than face one day of chaos and anarchy. **2004** 'Taking Hostages'
on *www.pbs.org* 30 Sept You know there's a very famous Arab saying that says...something like
40 years of tyranny, not one day of chaos. And this chaos...that has engulfed Iraq...is just devastating for the prospects of any future American backed government in Iraq. **2007** posting in
Arizona Republic on *www.azcentraLcom* 22 Jan. I wonder If, before waging war against Iraq,
President Bush had ever heard the famous Arab saying: 'Better a century oftyranny than one day
of chaos.' ■ **rulers and ruled** 支配者と被支配者

BETTER a dinner of herbs than a stalled ox where hate is.
牛舎で太らされた牛を食べて憎み合うよりも、野菜だけの食事の方がましだ。

参加者が互いに憎しみ合っている場所でごちそうを食べるより、仲良く乏しい配給食を
食べる方が良い。ここで herbs は食用として葉が使われる植物全般を指す古い意味で使
われている。stalled ox は食肉用に牛舎で太らされた牛である。『箴言』xv. 17 (ジュネー
ヴ聖書〈1560〉の翻訳は欽定訳聖書の直前に書かれている) を連想させる。Better is a
dinner of green herbs where love is, than a stalled ox and hatred therewith.「野
菜を食べて互いに愛するのは、肥えた牛を食べて互いに憎むのにまさる」

□ **1817** S. SMITH *Letter* 13 Mar. in S. Holland Memoir (1855) II. 138 When you think of that am-
orous and herbivorous parish of Covent Garden, and compare It with my agricultural benefice,
you will say, 'Better is the dinner of herbs where love is, than the stalled ox.' etc. etc. **1914** 'SAKI'
Beasts & Super-Beasts 227 The ox had finished the vase-flowers...and appeared to be thinking of
leaving its rather restricted quarters....I forget how the proverb runs....Something about 'better
a dinner of herbs than a stalled ox where hate is'. **1979** J. DRUMMOND *I saw Him Die* viii. Lunch
was a silent affair....I said, '"Better a dinner of herbs than a stalled ox where hate is."' ■ **content
and discontent** 満足と不満足 ; **food and drink** 飲食物 ; **malice** 悪意・恨み

BETTER are small fish than an empty dish.
空の皿より小魚でも載っているほうが良い。

たとえわずかでも与えられたものに感謝せよ。

□ **1678** J. RAY *English Proverbs* 204 Better are small fish then an empty dish. **1862** A. HISLOP
Proverbs of Scotland 171 Sma' fish are better than nane. **1874** painted on cornice at Ascott
House, Wing, Bucks., UK. Better are small fish than an empty dish. **1971** J. GLUSKI *Proverbs* 133
Better are small fish than an empty dish. **2000** *Pravda* 17 Oct. (English version online) Why
should the great ones of this world settle such particular questions? However, the answer is sim-
ple: better a small fish than an empty dish. ■ **content and discontent** 満足と不満足

BETTER be an old man's darling, than a young man's slave.
若者の奴隷になるより老人のお気に入りである方がまし。

年配の男性は妻を大事にするが、若い男性は妻をないがしろにする傾向がある (それな
ら、老人と結婚した方が良い)。

□ **1546** J. HEYWOOD *Dialogue of Proverbs* II. vii. 13ᵛ Many yeres sens, my mother seyd to me,

Hyr elders wold saie, it ys better to be An olde mans derlyng, then a yong mans werlyng [object of scorn]. **1721** J. KELLY *Scottish Proverbs* 74 Better an old Man's Darling, than a young Man's Wonderling, say the Scots, Warling, say the English. **1859** J. R. PLANCHÉ *Love & Fortune* 8 Let defeated rivals snarling, Talk of one foot in the grave. Better be an old man's darling, Than become a young man's slave. **1980** J. MARCUS *Marsh Blood* ix. Find yourself an older man. Much better to be an old man's darling, than a young man's slave. **1992** 'C. AIRD' 'Man Who Rowed for Shore' in *Injury Time* (1995) 14 [S]he had been brought up by her mother on the well-attested aphorism that it was better to be an old man's darling than a young's [sic]man's slave...

■ love 愛・恋愛 ; wives and husbands 夫婦

BETTER be envied than pitied.
同情されるよりねたまれる方がまし。

† ピンダー『デルフォイ頌歌』1.163 χρέσσων γὰρ οἰκτιρμοῦ φθόνος 「羨望は同情よりも強い」。ヘロドトス『歴史書』iii.52 φθονέεσθαι κρέσσον ἐστὶ ἢ οἰκτείρεσθαι. 「同情されるよりねたまれるほうがまし」。15世紀中頃のフランス語 *Trop plus vaut estre envie que plaint.* 「同情されるよりねたまれるほうが断然まし」。エラスムス『格言集』IV. iv. 87 *Praestat invidiosum esse quam miserabilem.* 「同情されるよりもねたまれる方がましである」

☐ **1546** J. HEYWOOD *Dialogue of Proverbs* 1: xi. D2v Sonne, better be envied then pitied, folke sey. *a* **1631** DONNE *Poems* (1633) 94 Men say, and truly, that they better be Which be envyed then pittied. **1902** G. W. B. RUSSELL *Onlooker's Note-Book* xxxiii. Her friend responded sympathetically, 'My dear, I'd much rather be envied than pitied.' **2014** *www.freepresshouston.com* 'American Girl in France' 24 Oct There's a French adage that goes 'It's better to be envied than pitied.' But, when you go to the bank to ask for money, it's better to be pitied than envied. ■

malice 悪意・恨み ; pity 哀れみ・同情

BETTER out than in.
内に閉じ込めるより吐き出した方がいい。

思っていることは栓をするより口に出した方がよい。好ましくない事実を語ることを正当化する際によく使われる（1880年の用例）。1912年の用例が示すように、文字通りの意味で使用されることもある。† **1740** フレーベル『全集』ii.559 But O how fain would we have this or that Affliction scrued out of the Frame of Providence, conceiving it would be far better out than in? 「しかし、内に閉じ込めるより吐き出した方がいいと考えて私たちは喜んであれやこれやの苦しみを配慮の枠から喜んで解放したことであろう」

☐ **1856** C. SPURGEON *Sermons* II. no. 59 Not 'pour out your fine words,'...but 'pour out your hearts.' 'I dare not,' says one, 'there Is black stuff in my heart.' Out with it then: it is better out than in. **1880** *Sunday at Home* xxvii 3 She said quietly: 'Cousin Felix, it's better out than in: you're a changed man of late—and, to be plain, the change Is no way for the better!' **1912** *Motor World* XXXIV. 39 The dust itself will do little harm provided the machine is not flooded with oil, though obviously it is better out than in. **1984** *Harvard Business Review : Managing to Save Time* 107 [D]etachment...Is usually the symptom of some feeling of affront. If you probe it, you will usually find that there is something bursting to come out, and that it is better out than in. **2014** *Times* 6 Nov. 31 Maybe it is bigotry but let's hear it. Possibly it is, as they say, better out than in.

■ speech and silence 発言と沈黙

BETTER 43

BETTER be out of the world than out of the fashion.
流行遅れになるくらいならこの世から消えた方がまし。

流行遅れになるより死んだ方がましなのである。

☐ **1639** J. CLARKE *Parremiologia Anglo-Latina* 171 As good out of th' world as out o' th' fashion. **1738** SWIFT *Polite Conversation* II. 117 'Why, Tom, you are high in the Mode.'...'It is better to be out of the World, than out of the Fashion.' **1903** E. F. MAITLAND *From Window in Chelsea* IV. Women seem seldom hindered by lack of money when it is a case of follow-my-leader. 'Better be out of the world than out of the fashion.' **1935** J. MAXTON *If I were Dictator* i.Dictatorships are fashionable just now. There was an old-time song which said 'If you are out of the fashion you had better leave the world.' ■ **novelty** 目新しさ

BETTER be safe than sorry.
後で後悔するより安全である方が良い。

(訳注：「後悔先に立たず」また、safe は sure ＝安全なになることもある）

用心深くすることの勧め。現在では（be を省略した）better safe than sorry の方がよく使われる。

☐ **1837** S. LOVER *Rory O'More* II. xxi. 'Jist countin' them,—is there any harm in that?' said the tinker: 'it's bebther be sure than sorry'. **1933** *Radio Times* 14 Apr. 125 Cheap distempers very soon crack or fade. Better be safe than sorry. Ask for Hall's. **1972** J. WILSON *Hide & Seek* vii. It's not that I want to shut you in...but—well, it's better to be safe than sorry. **2002** *Washington Post* 12 Jan. C10 (*Garfield comic strip*) 'You're breaking up with me? But we've never dated. You don't want to take any chances?' 'Better safe than sorry.' ■ **prudence** 思慮・分別 ; **security** 安全

BETTER late than never.
遅くても何もしないよりまし。

(訳注：例えば、2002 年の用例にあるように、3 日も遅れてバレンタインの花束を渡した際に「遅くても何も渡さないよりはましでしょう」と述べている。遅れたことをユーモラスに弁解する時に使われるとされる)

†ハウカルナサスのディオニシオス『古代ローマの遺物』9, κρεῖττον γάρ ἐστιν ὀψὲ ἄρξασθαι τὰ δέοντα πράττειν ἤμηδέποτε. 「全くしないより遅くなってもしなければならないことをしはじめるほうがよい」。リウィウス『歴史書』IV. ii. *Potius sero quam nunquam.* 「何もしないよりもむしろ遅い方がましである」

☐ *c***1330** in C. KELLER *Die Mittelenglische Gregoriuslegende* (1941) 146 A Better is lat than neuer blinne [cease].Our soules to maken fre. *c***1450** LYDGATE *Assembly of Gods* (EETS) I. 1204 Vyce to forsake ys bettyr late then neuer. **1546** J. HEYWOOD *Dialogueof Proverbs* I. x. C4 Things done, can not be vndoone,...But better late then neuer to repent this. **1708** S. OCKLEY *Conquest of Syria* I. 276 Whilst he was murdering the unhappy Aleppians, Caled (better late than never) came to their Relief. **1954** A. HUXLEY *Letter* 16 Sept (1969) 711 I am sorry your holiday will have to be postponed so long; but better late than never. **2002** *Washington Post* 17 Feb. SC4 (*Sally Forth comic strip*) 'Consider these a "late Valentine's Day" bouquet' 'It was three days ago.' 'I know, but better late than never, I always say.' 'Better never late, I always say.' ■ **lateness** 遅れ

BETTER one house spoiled than two.
2 軒の家より 1 軒の家がごたつく方がまし。

(訳注：性悪のひねくれた男女が結婚したときに用いられる。two〈houses〉＝「悪夫と善女との結婚によって生じる家庭と善男と悪女との結婚によって生じる家庭という 2 つの家庭」)

2 人の性悪の男女が結婚して不幸に陥っている家庭についてのコメント。spoiled (あるいは spilled「崩壊する」) は filled と対比的に使われることがある (1670年と1805年の用例参照)。

□**1586** T. B. tr. *de la Primaudaye's French Academy* xlvi. The wicked and reprobate, of whom that common proverbe is spoken, that it is better one house be ttoubled with them than twaine. **1587** R. GREENE *Penelope's Web* V. 162 The old prouerb is fulfild, better one house troubled than two. **1670** J. RAY *English Proverbs* 51 Better one house fill'd then two spill'd. This we use when we hear of a bad Jack who hath married as bad a Jyll. **1805** W. BENTLEY *Diary* 28 May (1911) III. 161 One of the company discovering a disposition to speak much of his own wife...the Gen. observed...One house filled was better than two spoiled. **1924** *Folk-Lore* XXXV. 358 Better one house spoilt than two (said when a witless a man marries a foolish woman). ■ **marriage 結婚**

The BETTER the day, the better the deed.
(これをしたのが) 良い日であればあれば、もっと良いことをしたことになる。
(訳注：1721年の用例からわかるように、日曜日に何か悪いことをした時の言い訳として使われる)

日曜や祝祭日に働いたことを正当化する際によく使われる。† 14世紀初頭のフランス語 *A bon jour bone euvre*.「良い日には良い行ないを」

□**1607** MIDDLETON *Michaelmas Term* III.i. Why, do you work a' Sundays, tailor? The better day the better deed, we think. **1721** J. KELLY *Scottish Proverbs* 328 The better Day, the better Deed. I never heard this used but when People say that they did such an ill thing on Sunday. **1896** J. C. HUTCHESON *Crown & Anchor* xiii. The better the day, the better the deed...It was only the Pharisees who objected to any necessary work being done on the Sabbath. **1995** D. WILLIAMS *Death of Prodigal*' And he was coming back here with us after, for Sunday lunch. I've just cleaned the car in his honour, too. The better the day, the better the deed, like.' ■ **action and inaction 行為と非行為**

BETTER the devil you know than the devil you don't know.
知らない悪魔より知っている悪魔の方がまし。
(訳注：「知らぬ仏よりなじみの鬼」に近い。Better the harm I know than that I know not. とも言う)

† **1539**R. タヴァーナー訳『エラスムス格言集』48 *Nota res mala, optima*. An euyl thynge knowen is best. It is good kepyng of a shrew [a scolding or ill-tempered woman] that a man knoweth「知っている悪事が最善である。男にとって知っている口やかましい (性悪な) 女と付き合うのは良いことである」。**1576** G. ペティー『小さな宮殿』84 You had rather keepe those whom you know, though with some faultes, then take those whom you knowe not, perchaunce with moe faultes.「たとえ多少欠点があろうとも、知っている人とつきあう方が知らない人とつきあうより良い。なぜなら後者はもっと欠点があるかもしれないから」。**1586**ローランド訳『ラサリーリョ・デ・トルメス』H 6ᵛ The olde prouerbe: Better is the euill knowne, than the good which is yet to knowe.「古いことわざ：未知の善よりも既知の悪の方が良い」

□**1857** TROLLOPE *Barchester Towers* II. vii. 'Better the d—you know than the d—you don't know,' is an old saying...but the bishop had not yet realised the truth of it. **1937** W. H. SAUMAREZ SMITH *Letter* 16 May in *Young Man's Country* (1977) ii. Habit has practically made me resigned to Madaripur—'Better the devil you know than the devil you don't.' **1987** S. STEWART *Lifting the Latch* 1661 knowed he'd never change, it 'ud always be 'Don't-be-so-daft' and no appreciation; but better the Black 'un thee knows than the devil thee don't. **2007** *Times* 14 Sept. 28

BETTER 45

More than half (54 per cent) think that it is time for a change, while about two fifths (43 per cent) say that it is 'better to stick with the devil you know'. ■ **familiarity** 慣れ親しみ

It is BETTER to be born lucky than rich.
金持ちに生まれるより幸運の星の下に生まれる方がいい。

この根拠が1926年の用例に説明されている。

□ **1639** J. CLARKE *Paræmiologia Anglo-Latina* 49 Better to have good fortune then be a rich mans child. **1784** *New Foundling Hospital for Wit* (new ed.) W. 128 Estate and honours!—mere caprich! Better be fortunate than rich: Since oft me find...ls verify'd what proverbs prate. **1846** M. A. DENHAM *Denham Tracts* (1892) I. 224 Better to be born lucky than rich. **1926** D. H. LAW-RENCE in *Harper's Bazaar* July 97 'Then what is luck, mother?' 'It's what causes you to have money. If you are lucky you have money. That's why it's better to be born lucky than rich. If you're rich you may lose your money. But if you're lucky, you will always get more money.' **1980** T. MORGAN *Somerset Maugham* xv. This was Mangham at his most lighthearted, exposing the fallacy of the moralist position. 'I'm glad to be able to tell you that it has a moral,' he said, 'and that is: it's better to be born lucky than to be born rich.' ■ **luck** 幸運・運 ; **riches** 富

BETTER to die on your feet than live on your knees.
ひざまずいて生きるより自分の足で立って死ぬ方がいい。

メキシコの革命指導者エミリアーノ・サパタ (1879-1919) の言葉 *Prefiero morir de pie que vivir de rodillas*「ひざまずいて生きるより自分の足で立って死ぬ方がいい」に由来する。実際は彼の言葉ではないが、彼を連想させる出来事として、サパタが彼の暗殺当時、貧民層によって彫られたスローガンの逸話の中に登場することが挙げられる。彼の言葉の英訳が次の作品に出ている。**1924** ハーバーマン「盗賊植民地」*Survey* LII.iii.148 Rebels of the South, it is more honourable to die on your feet than to live on your knees.「南部の反乱者よ、ひざまずいて生きるより自分の足で立って死ぬ方が名誉なのだ」。† **1936** ドロレス・イバルリ (1895-1989) の 9 月 3 日の言葉. *Il vaut mieux mourir debout que de vivre a genoux!*「ひざまずいて生きるより自分の足で立って死ぬ方がいい」を参照。ドロレスはスペイン共産党の指導者であった。

□ **1941** *Charleston Gflzette* 25 June 6/2 The president puts it in another way at Cambridge when he says: 'We would rather die on our feet that live on our knees'. **1955** *Evening Standard* (Uniontown, Pennsylvania) 18 Aug. 4/1 We face the fact that it [atomic war] demoralizes concepts that have perennially ruled the minds of free men. 'It is better to die on one's feet that live on one's knees' is no longer bravely proclaimed. **1993** *Washington Post* 7 Mar. (online) Better to die on your feet than live on your knees. Yeah. But what about sitting around in a Designated Smoking Area? Is that living? **2007** *Times Magazine* l Sept. 90 Few sights induce such ambivalence in me as a bird in a cage. [They] may live up to 15 years in captivity, as opposed to three or four in the wild, a classic quality versus quantity dilemma...Better to die on your feet, surely, or, er, talons, or wings, I suppose, than live on your knees...If owls have knees. ■ **courage** 勇気

It is BETTER to give than to receive.
与えるは受けるにまさる。

(訳注 : receive は take とも言う)

『使徒言行録』20章35節 (欽定訳聖書) It is more blessed to give, than to receive.「貰うより与える方が幸福である」の形式も使われる (2001年の用例参照)。

46 BETTER

□*c*1390 GOWER *Confessio Amantis* v. 7725 Betre is to yive than to take. *c*1527 T. BERTHELET tr. *Erasmus' Sayings of Wise Men* B2 It is better to gyue than to take, for he that takethe a gyfte of another is bonde to quyte [repay] It, so that his lyberte is gone. **1710** S. PALMER *Proverbs* 351 'Tis better to Give than to Receive, but yet 'tis Madness to give so much Charity to Others, as to become the Subject of it our Selves. **1980** *Times* (Christmas Supplement) 15 Nov. p. i. There is no harm in reminding your relatives and friends that it is better to give than to receive. **2001** *Washington Times* 2 July B9 (*Herb & Jamaal comic strip*) 'Herb, you know the old saying: "It is more blessed to give than to receive."' 'What, presents?' 'No, advice.' ■ **giving and receiving** 授受

BETTER to have loved and lost,than never to have loved at all.
全く愛したことがないよりも愛して失った方がいい。

□**1700** CONGREVE *Way of World* II. i. Say what you will, 'tis better to be left, than never to have lov'd. **1812** G. CRABBE *Tales* xiv. Better to love amiss than nothing to have lov'd. **1850** TENNYSON *In Memoriam* xxvii. 44 'Tis better to have loved and lost Than never to have loved at all. **1953** B. PYM *Jane & Prudence* i. One wondered if it was really better to have loved and lost than never to have loved at all, when poor Prudence seemed to have lost so many times. **2002** *Times* 2 15 Oct. 9 That cliché, It is better to have loved and lost than never to have loved at all, applies to me. ■ **love, blighted** くじかれた愛

BETTER to light one candle than to curse the darkness.
暗闇を呪うくらいならロウソクに火を灯せ。
（訳注：「暗いと不平を言うよりも進んで明かりをつけよう」）

米国クリストファー協会（1945年設立）のモットーで、協会によると、古代中国のことわざに由来する。

□**1970** W. L. WATKINSON *Supreme Conquest* 2l8 [D]enunciatory rhetoric…proves a popular temptation. Yet It is far better to light the candle than to curse thedarkness. **1962** ADLAI STEVENSON in *New York Times* 8 Nov. 34 She [Eleanor Roosevelt] would rather light a candle than curse the darkness, and her glow has warmed the world. **2000** *Straits Times* 26 Aug. (online) He is certainly one who believes it is better to light a candle than to curse the darkness. **2010** *Times* 30 Dec. 24 OK, so you might not be changing the world—but you will be changing your bit of it. Better to light one candle than blame the darkness. ■ **action and inaction** 行為と非行為

BETTER to live one day as a tiger than a thousand years as a sheep.
羊として1000年生きるより虎として１日生きる方がいい。

インドのマイソール王であるティプー・サーヒブ(1750頃–99)の思想とされている。1800年の用例参照。

□**1800** A. BEATSON *View of Origin and Conduct of War with Tippoo Sultaun* x. 153 'In this world I would rather live two days like a tiger, than two hundred years like a sheep.' **1997** *Daily Telegraph* 8 Mar. (online) The title of Anne Haverty's novel [*One Day as a Tiger*] derives from an old Tibetan proverb: 'It is better to have lived one day as a tiger than a thousand years as a sheep.' ■ **action and inaction** 行為と非行為 ; **boldness** 大胆さ

BETTER to marry than to burn.
情欲に身を焦がすくらいなら結婚した方がいい。

聖パウロの結婚を勧める言葉で、『コリント人への手紙一』7章 8‐9節（欽定訳聖書）が想起される。I say therefore to the unmarried and widows, It is good for them if they abide even as I. But if they cannot contain, let them marry: for it is better to marry than to burn.「独身の人や夫を亡くした婦人に言います。わたしのように今のままでいる方が良いのです。しかし、もし自分を制することができなければ結婚しなさい。結婚する方が、情欲に身を焦がすよりは良いからです」。聖パウロが言いたいことは、独身者が独り身でいることは望ましいことではあるが、それが叶わぬ場合、情欲で心身ともに消耗するくらいなら結婚した方がいいという教え。

□**1911** G. B. SHAW *Getting Married* 116 St Paul's reluctant sanction of marriage;...his contemptuous 'better to marry than to burn' is only out of date in respect of his belief that the end of the world was at hand and that there was therefore no longer any population question. **1973** J. PORTER *Murder with* Dover 58 'You didn't approve?' Miss Marsh pursed her lips. 'We are told it is better to marry than to burn,' she said. 'And he could have done worse, I suppose.' **2000** *Washington Times* 15 Nov. B12 (*Herb &Jamaal comic strip*) [T]hey say,...'It is better to marry than to burn'...But I'll tell ya, among the things they say, what I'm most curious about is...who are '*they*'? ■ **marriage 結婚**

It is BETTER to travel hopefully than to arrive.
目的地に着くことよりも着くことを夢みている時の方が楽しい。
（訳注：「待つうちが花」）

楽しい目的を達成する期待感は達成した目的そのものより価値がある場合が多い。

□**1881** R. L. STEVENSON *Virglnibus Puerisque* IV. 190 To travel hopefully is a better thing than to arrive, and the true success is to labour. **1918** D. H. LAWRENCE in *English Review* Jan. 29 Love is strictly a travelling. 'It is better to travel than to arrive,' somebody has said. **1959** 'J. DUNCAN' *My Friend Muriel* II. 83 Remember,...it is better to travel hopefully than to arrive. The satisfaction lies mainly in the travelling. **2002** *Rough News* Spring 2 (*comic strip*) 'They say it's better to travel than to arrive.' '"They" have obviously never been on this bus!' ■ **expectation 予期・期待；optimism 楽観主義；travel 旅行**

BETTER to wear out than to rust out.
錆び果てるより擦り切れる方がまし。

怠惰なまま生きるより活動的でありつづける方が望ましい。特に年配の人について使われる。現在の形は司教リチャード・カンバーランド (1718年没) に由来するとされることが多いものの、1820年の用例では、メソジストの預言者ジョージ・ホワイトフィールド (1714-70) の言葉となっている。† **1557** R. エッジワース『説教集』A1ᵛ Better it is to shine with laboure, then to rouste for idleness.「怠けて錆びるより働いて輝く方がいい」。**1598** シェイクスピア『ヘンリー四世』Pt. 2 I. ii. 206 I were better to be eaten to death with a rust than to be scoured to nothing with perpetual motion.「このからだは永久運動の機械じゃないんだ。のべつまくなく働かされてすり減っちまうよりは錆びついて朽ち果てる方がましだ」

□**1820** in Southey *Life of Wesley* II. xxv. I had rather wear out than rust out. **1834** M. EDGEWORTHHelen II. xiii. *Helen*...trembled for her health...but she repeated her favourite maxim-'Better to wear out, than to rust out' **1947** S. BELLOW *Victim* xvii. It was better to wear out than to rust out, as was often quoted. He was a hard worker himself. **1972** *Times* 24 May 16 'A man will rust out sooner'n he'll wear out' is one of his oft-repeated maxims. ■ **action and inaction 行為と非行為；old age 老年**

48　BETTER

BETTER wed over the mixen than over the moor.
嫁は遠方より近場からもらう方がいい。

（訳注：wed は「結婚する」を、mixen は「堆肥」を、moor は「泥炭地」を意味する）

遠くの素性の知れない者よりもなじみの近隣の者と結婚する方がいい。古風なスコットランドの方言形 *mixen* に関しては *a*1661 年の用例参照。

☐*a*1628 in M. L. ANDERSON *Proverbs in Scots* (1957) no. 320 Better to wow [woo] over middin, nor [than] over mure. *a*1661 T. FULLER *Worthies* (Cheshire) 174 Better Wed over the Mixon [midden] then over the Moor...that is, hard by or at home, Mixon being that heap of Compost which lyeth in the yards of good husbands. 1818 SCOTT *Heart of Midlothian* III. vi. He might hae dune waur [worse] than married me....Better wed over the mixen as over the moor, as they say in Yorkshire. 1874 T. Hardy *Far from Madding Crowd* I.xxii. 'That means matrimony.'...'Well, better wed over the mixen than over the moor,' said Laban Tall. 1920 *Garden: Illustrated Weekly Journal* lxxxiv. 539 [T]hey have never gone far afield for mates, but have followed the old local saying, 'Better wed over the mixen than over the moor'. 2013 A. R. DOBLE *Just Slightly Ahead* (online) [B]ack then [1850], people tended to marry within their own ethnic groups-remember 'Better wed over the mixen than over the moor'? ■ familiarity 慣れ親しみ；marriage 結婚

better ⇒ DISCRETION is the better part of valour ; The GREY mare is the better horse ; A LIVE dog is better than a dead lion.

BETWEEN two stools one falls to the ground.
2 つの腰掛の間で尻もちをつく。

（訳注：「虻蜂取らず」。「二兎を追う者一兎をも得ず」）

2 つ存在する見方や行動のどちらか一方を選べない場合、窮地に立たされる。現在では to fall between two stools「虻蜂取らずになる」の方が慣用句として一般的に使われている。†中世ラテン語 *Labitur enitens sellis herere duabus*.「2 つの椅子に座ろうとして尻もちをつく」。16世紀初頭のドイツ語でも使われた（†トマス・ムルナー『いたずら仲間』〈1516〉に登場する木こりの話）。

☐*c*1390 GOWER *Confessio Amantis* IV. 626 Thou farst [farest] as he betwen tuo stoles That wolde sitte and goth to grounde. *c*1530 R. HILL *Commonplace Book* (EETS) 129 Betwen two stolis, the ars goth to grwnd. 1841 DICKENS *Old Curiosity Shop* I. xxxlli. She was...still in daily occupation of her old stool opposite to that of her brother Sampson. And equally certain it is, by the way, that between these two stools a great many people had come to the ground. 1991 S. RUSHDIE *Imaginary Homelands* 15 Sometimes we feel we straddle two. cultures; at other times, that we fall between two stools. ■ decision and indecision 決断と優柔不断

beware ⇒ Let-the BUYER beware ; Beware of an OAK it draws the stroke.

bicycle ⇒ A WOMAN without a man is like a fish without a bicycle.

Never BID the Devil good morrow until you meet him.
会うまでは悪魔に朝の挨拶をしてはならない。

必要もないのに外出をして（何かを始めて）困難に遭遇してはならない。

☐1873 J. MORRIS *Wanderinss of Vagabond* II. 19 The firm of Giles & Morris never looked ahead to meet trouble, but were firm believers in an old Irish adage, which affirms that, 'It's time

big 49

enough to bid the devil good morning when you meet him.' **1905** A. CARNEGIE *James Watt* iv. 77 Roebuck, on the contrary, continued hopeful and energetic, and often rallied his pessimistic partner on his propensity to look upon the dark side. He was one of those who adhered to the axiom, 'Never bid the devil good-morning till you meet him.' **1923** *Seanad Eireann* 14 June (electronic ed.) Mr. Linehan: Have you any indication as to whether the National Health Insurance BUI will be certified as a Money Bill?...An Cathaoirleach: It may be, but never bid the devil good morrow until you meet him. **1929** P. D. GRIERSON *Green Diamond Mystery* vi. 66 By the time they reached Calais Kit had wisely resolved, in the classic phrase, not to bid the Devil good-morrow till he met him; in other words,to wait until he saw June, and then be guided by her reception of him. **1998** *Beloit Daily News* 19 Mar. (electronic ed.) Over the weekend, Ryan responded to hypothetical questions about having Fitzgerald on the ticket by saying 'We should never bid the devil good morning until we meet him.' ■ **good and evil** 正邪

BIG fish eat little fish.
大きな魚が小さな魚を食べる。
（訳注：「弱肉強食」）

裕福な権力者が貧しい弱者を滅ぼす。

☐ *a*1200 *Old English Homilies* (EETS) 2nd Ser. 179 The more [bigger] fishes in the se eten the lasse [smaller]. *c*1300 in J. Small *English Metrical Homilies* (1862) 136 Al this werld es bot a se,...And gret fisches etes the smale. For riche men of this werd [world] etes, That pouer [the poor] wit thair travail getes. **1608** SHAKESPEARE *Pericles* II.i.27 Master, I marvel how the fishes live in the sea.—Why, as men do a-land—the great ones eat up the little ones. **1979** *New Society* 6 Dec. 557 The state today...seems like nothing so much [as] a huge aquarium....Big fish eat little fish, and the great fish eat the big. ■ **great and small** 大小

BIG fleas have little fleas upon their backs to bite them, and little fleas have lesser fleas, and so *ad infinitum*.
大きなノミは自分を嚙む小さなノミを背中に乗せ、その小さなノミはさらに小さなノミを背中に乗せる、かくして無限に続いていく。

誰もが誰かの餌食になる。そして次にその誰かは別の誰かの餌食になる。

☐ **1733** SWIFT *Poems* II. 651 The Vermin only teaze and pinch Their Foes superior by an Inch. So Nat'ralists observe, a Flea Hath smaller Fleas that on him prey, And these have smaller Fleas to bite 'em, And so proceed ad infinitum. **1872** A. DE MORGAN *Budgetof Paradoxes* 377 Great fleas have little fleas upon their backs to bite 'em, And little fleas have lesser fleas, and so ad infinitum. And the great fleas themselves, in turn, have greater fleas to go on; While these again have greater still, and greater still, and so on. **1979** R. BARNARD *Posthumous Papers* ii. There will be a long article in the Sunday Chronicle...and I'm afraid the Sunday Grub has got onto the story as well. Big fleas and little fleas, you know—. **2001** *Times* 22 Dec.19 They [CERN scientists] would identify another lacuna in our knowledge which would require even bigger and better facilities to decide whether it could or could not be explained. 'Great fleas have little fleas upon their backs to bite 'em, and little fleas have lesser fleas and so ad infinitum.' ■ **associates** 仲間；**great and small** 大小

big ⇒ PROVIDENCE is always onthe side of the big battalions；SPEAK softly and carry a big stick.

50 BIGGER

The BIGGER they are, the harder they fall.
大きければ大きいほど倒れ方もひどい。

（訳注：「the 比較級，the 比較級」〈…すればするほどますます…だ〉の形式が使われている。*The* more, *the* merrier.【ことわざ】〈人多ければ楽しみ多し〉）

一般にはボクサーのボブ・フィッツモンズが1900年頃の試合前に語った言葉と考えられている（1902年の用例参照。1971年の用例が示すように are の代わりに come が使われることもある）。ただし、類似の形はそれ以前のことわざにも散見される。**1493**パーカー『金持ちと乞食』R 7 v It is more synne in the man For the higher degre [position] the harder is the fal「人間にはもっと罪深いものが潜んでいる。なぜなら位が高くなればなるほど没落も激しくなるからだ」。**1670**レイ『英語ことわざ集』102 The higher standing the lower fall.「高いところに立っていればいるほどより低いところに落ちる」。この考えは少なくとも 4 世紀のラテン語詩人クラウディアヌスにまで遡ることができる（*In Rujinum* I. 22 *Tolluntur in altum Ut lapsu grauiore ruant.*「人はより激しく落ちるために高い地位に引き上げられる」）

□ **1902** *National Police Gautte* 27 Sept. 6 'If I can get close enough,' he (Fitzsimmons] once said, 'I'll guarantee to stop almost anybody. The bigger the man, the heavier the fall.' **1905** H. R. DURANT 'Quitter' in *Everybody's Magazine* xii (Jan-June) 230 When the manager returned to the champion's dressing-room he said: '…A big gazabo, ain't he?' 'The bigger they are the harder they fall.' **1927** 'C. BOYER' *Mosaic Earring* i. 'I haven't seen…even an imitation of the blossom I would have to find before I surrender my sweet freedom.' 'The bigger they are, the harder they fall.' **1971** J. CLIFF (*song-title*) The bigger they come the harder they fall. **1981** H. & B. BRETT *Promises to Keep* ix. 'I thought a big, beautiful place llke this would be an exception to the general decline.' 'Sometimes,' Mrs. Benjamin said sagely, 'the bigger they are, the harder they fall.' **2002** *New Scientist* 30 Mar. 14 (*headline*) The bigger you are, the harder you fall. ■ **great and small** 大小 ; **misfortune** 不運

bill ⇒ DEATH pays all debts.

billet ⇒ Every BULLET has its billet.

bind ⇒ SAFE bind, safe find.

binding ⇒ You can't tell a BOOK by its cover.

A BIRD in the hand is worth two in the bush.
手の中の 1 羽は藪の中の 2 羽に値する。

（訳注：「明日の百より今日の五十」）

さらに手に入れようと欲張ってすべてを失う危険を冒すよりも、今持っているものを大事にして、それで満足する方が良い。† 13世紀のラテン語 *Plus valet in manibus avis unica quam dupla siluis.*「手の中の 1 羽は藪の中の 2 羽よりも価値がある」。1934年公開の映画『罪じゃないわよ』に出演した米国の女優メイ・ウエスト (1892-1980) によるパロディが有名である。A man in the house is worth two in the street.「家にいる 1 人の男性は通りにいる 2 人に値する」

□ *c*1450 J. CAPGRAVE *Life of St.Katharine* (EETS) II. iii. It is more sekyr [certain] a byrd in your

BIRDS   51

fest, Than to haue three in the sky a-boue. *c*1470 *Harley MS* 3362 f.4 Betyr ys a byrd in the hond than tweye in the wode. **1581** N. WOODES *Conflict of Conscience* JV.i. You haue spoken reasonably, but yet as they say, One Birde in the hande, is worth two in the bush. **1678** BUNYAN *Pilgrim's Progress* I. 42 That Proverb, A Bird in the hand is worth two in the Bush, is of more Authority with them, then are all…testimonies of the good of the world to come. **1973** G. GREENE *Honorary Consul* II. iii. We have an expression in English—A bird in the hand is worth two in the bush. I don't know anything about that 'afterwards'. I only know I would like to live another ten years. **2002** *Oxford Times* 18 Jan. 15 The firm could realise a very good price now.…The situation may not be as good as this in three or four years. A bird in the hand is worth two in the bush. ■ **prudence** 思慮・分別；**risk** 危険

A BIRD never flew on one wing.
鳥が片方の翼だけで飛んだためしはない。

主にスコットランドとアイルランドで使われている。現在では贈り物の追加、特に酒のおかわりを正当化する際に使われる。ただし、1721年の用例は、広範囲の政治活動の場から後援者を獲得するのが望ましいことを述べている。

□**1721** J. KELLY *Scottish Proverbs* 308 The Bird must flighter [flutter] that flies with one Wing. Spoken by them who have Interest only in one side of the House. **1824** S. FERRIER *Inheritance* III. xxxii. 'The bird maun flichter that flees wi' ae wing'—but ye's haud up your head yet In spite o' them a'. **1914** K. F. PURDON *Folk of Furry Farm* ii. He held out a shilling to Hughie. 'A bird never yet flew upon the one wing. Mr. Heffernan!' said Hughie, that was looking to get another shilling. **1925** S. O'CASEY *Juno & Paycock*III. 89 Fourpence, given to make up the price of a pint, on th' principle that no bird ever flew on wan wing. **1980** J. O'FAOLAIN *No Country for Young Men* iii. I'll just have another quick one. A bird never flew on wan wing. ■ **food and drink** 飲食物

bird ⇒ As good be an ADDLED egg as an idle bird ; You cannot CATCH old birds with chaff ; The EARLY bird catches the worm ; FINE feathers make fine birds ; It's an ILL bird that fouls its own nest ; In vain the NET is spread in the sight of the bird.

There are no BIRDS in last year's nest.
去年の巣の中に今年の鳥はもういない。
（訳注：「歳月人を待たず」）

時の流れは周りの状況を変えてしまう。

□**1620** T. SHELTON tr. *Ceruantes' Don Quixote* II. lxxiv. I pray you go not on so fast, since that in the nests of the last yeere, there are no birds of this yeere. Whilom [formerly] I was a foole, but now I am wise. **1732** T. FULLER *Gnomologia* no. 41163 There are no Birds this Year, in last year's Nest. **1845** LONGFELLOW *Poems* 62 All things are new…even the nest beneath the eaves; —There are no birds in last year's nest. **1946** H. CELROY *Unkindly Cup* I. ii. 23 'I am not as bad, or as unfeeling as I sound. It was my memory that was groaning—not the other part of my anatomy.' '"There are no birds in last year's nests",' Bland quoted sententiously. ■ **change** 変化；**circumstances** 状況

BIRDS in their little nests agree.
小さな巣の中の鳥は仲良くする。
（訳注：1715年の用例にあるように、英国の神学者・論理学者アイザック・ワッツ作の子供向けの讃美歌に由来する）

子育てに使われることわざで、小さな子供たちに口論しないように諭すのに使われる。

52 BIRDS

□ **1715** I. WATTS *Divine Songs* 25 Birds in their little Nests agree; And 'tis a shameful Sight, When Children of one Family Fall out, and chide, and fight. **1868** L. M. ALCOTT *Little Women* i. 'Birds in their little nests agree,' sang Beth, the peacemaker. **1961** J. STEINBECK Winter of our DiscontentI.i. 'Birds in their little nests agree,' he said. 'So why can't we?...You kids can't get along even on a pretty morning.' **1980** A. T. BLLIS *Birds of Air* (1983) 52 Her mother used to say to her and Mary: 'Birds in their little nests agree.' ■ **harmony and disharmony** 調和と不調和

BIRDS of a feather flock together.
同じ種類の鳥は群をなす（類は友を呼ぶ）。

（訳注：of a/an = the same〈同じ〉。なお、feather =「種類」。fur and *feather*〈鳥獣〉）

同じ（通常、無節制な）性格を持つ人々は、同じ種類の鳥が群れるように徒党を組むものである。†「聖書外典」（欽定訳聖書）『シラの書』27章9節 The birds will resort unto their like, so will truth return unto them that practise in her.「鳥はその仲間のもとに、誠実さはそれを行なう人のもとに帰る」

□ **1545** W. TURNER *Rescuing of Romlsh Fox* B8 Byrdes of on kynde and color flok and flye all-wayes together. **1599** J. MINSHEU *Spanish Grammar* 83 Birdes of a feather will flocke together. **1660** W. SECKER *Nonsuch Professor* 81 Our English Proverb...That birds of a feather will flock together. To be too intimate with sinners, Is to intimate that you are sinners. **1828** BULWER-LYITON *Pelham* III. xv. It is literally true in the systematised roguery of London, that 'birds of a feather flock together.' **2001** *Washington Times* 15 July D7 Birds of a feather flock together, so the second thing you should do is find another friend who's less troubled than the first. ■ **associates** 仲間；**human nature** 人間性；**similarity and dissimilarity** 類似性と相違性

Little BIRDS that can sing and won't sing must be made to sing.
歌えるのに歌おうとしない小鳥は歌うように仕向けるべきだ。

才能や技能は、それを持っている人によって行使されなければならない。

□ **1678** J. RAY *English Proverbs* (ed. 2) 343 The bird that can sing and will not sing must be made to sing. **1846** DICIKENS *Cricket on Hearth* ii. 'The bird that can sing and won't sing, must be made to sing, they say,' grumbled Tackleton. 'What about the owl that can't sing, and oughtn't to sing, and will sing?' **1888** A. QUILLER-COUCH *Troy Town* i. 'A little music might perhaps leave a pleasant taste.'...'Come, Sophy! Remember the proverb about little birds that can sing and won't sing?' **1904** G. K. CHESTERTON *Napoleon of Notting Hill* II. I. When the disdainful oligarchs declined to join in the songs of the men of the Broadway..., the great Republican leader, with his rough humour, said the words which are written in gold upon his monument, 'Little birds that can sing and won't sing, must be made to sing.' **1952** J. KNOX *Little Benders* 18 Heaven wasn't so far away when you could do your own singing about it Mama believed that and many a time she said, 'A body who can sing and won't sing ought to be made to sing.' ■ **obstinacy** 頑固さ；**speech and silence** 発言と沈黙

bite ⇒ （名詞）A BLEATING sheep loses a bite；Every DOG is allowed one bite；（動詞）A BARKING dog never bites；BIG fleas have little fleas upon their backs to bite them；DEAD men don't bite.

The man who has once been BITTEN by the snake fears every piece of rope.
蛇に咬まれたことのある人は紐を見ても怖がる。

（訳注：「あつものに懲りてなますを吹く」）

中国のことわざで、日本にもある。

□**1937** H. H. HART 700 *Chinese Proverbs* (1960) no. 527 One year bitten by a snake, for three years afraid of a grass rope. **1981** DALAI LAMA quoted in *Observer* 5 Apr. (online) Frankly speaking, It Is difficult to trust the Chinese. Once bitten by a snake you feel suspicious even when you see a piece of rope. **1995** E. C. SYMMES *Netsuke* 94 The snake appears in many Japanese proverbs—the man who has once been bitten by the snakefears every piece of rope, or 'once bitten, twice shy.' **2004** *New York Times* 25 June 9 (online) China's chief trade negotiator, Vice Premier Wu YI, cited a Chinese proverb, 'Once bitten by a snake, one is terrified of the mere sight of a piece of rope.' ■ experience 経験

bitten ⇒ ONCE bitten, twice shy.

black ⇒ It doesn't matter if a CAT is black or white...; The DEVIL is not so black as he is painted ; FEBRUARY fill dyke, be it black or be it white ; TWO blacks don't make a white.

blame ⇒ A BAD workman blames his tools ; COMMON fame is seldom to blame.

The BLEATING of the kid excites the tiger.
子供がめそめそ泣くと虎が暴れ出す。

犠牲者の苦痛の叫びは略奪者をかき立てる。キップリングはフランシス・ガルトン『旅の技法』(1855)からヒントを得て、いじめっ子たちに少しばかりの仕返しをする児童の話の中にこの考えを取り入れた。

□**1899** KIPLING 'Moral Reformers' in *Stalky & Co* Ruffle his hair, Turkey. Now you get down, too. 'The bleatin' of the kid excites the tiger.' **1921** F. HAMILTON *Here, There and Everywhere* 13 I have a strong suspicion that the unhappy goats played a part...and that they were tethered in different parts of the jungle, for, as we all know, 'the bleating of the kid excites the tiger.' **2006** *Jewish Russian Telegraph* 21 Feb. (online) Serial apologies too numerous to count, $50 million thrown to his tormentors in an attempt to make the issue go away...— none of this worked. It never works. On the contrary, once again the bleat of the lamb excited the tiger. ■ misfortune 不運

A BLEATING sheep loses a bite.
啼く羊は餌を食べ損なう。
（訳注：「口が動けば手がやむ」）

おしゃべりが過ぎると貴重な機会を失う。

□**1599** J. MINSHEU *Dialogues in Spanish* 20 That sheepe that bleateth looseth a bit [mouthful]. **1659** G. TORRIANO *English & Italian Dict.* 37 A bleating sheep loseth her pasture. **1861** T. HUGHES *Tom Brown at Oxford* II. vii. He said something about a bleating sheep losing a bite; but I should think this young man is not much of a talker. **1978** R. V. JONES *Most Secret War* xiv. I thought of reminding him [Churchill] of an adage that I had learnt from my grandfather: 'Every time a sheep bleats it loses a nibble.' ■ opportunity, missed 逃した機会 ; speech and silence 発言と沈黙

BLESSED is he who expects nothing, for he shall never be disappointed.
何も期待しない者は幸いである。なぜなら失望することがないからだ。
（訳注：1727年の用例にあるように、英国の詩人・作家 A. ポープは手紙の中で、『マタイによる福音書』の

54　blessed

8つの山上の垂訓に加えて、9つ目のものだと述べている）

教皇が聖書の一節「…する者は幸いである」(Blessed are...）をパロディ化したもの（1727年の用例参照）。元の言葉はキリストによる山上の垂訓の出だしであり、「真福八端」として知られている（『マタイによる福音書』5章2-11節）。

□**1727** POPE *Letter* 6 Oct (1956) II. 453 I have...repeated to you, a ninth Beatitude...'Blessed is he who expect nothing, for he shall never be disappointed.' **1739** B. PRANKLIN *Poor Richard's Almanack* (May) Blessed is he that expects nothing, for he shall never be disappointed. **1931** A. R. & R. K. WEEKES *Emerald Necklace* xix. 'When I get back...I shall expect to find all our luggage in the hall.' 'Blessed is he that expecteth nothing,' said Louis, 'for he shall not be disappointed.' **1997** *Washington Times* 28 Feb. C16 My dear grandmother...gave me a plaque many years ago that contains a motto to live by: 'Blessed are those who expect nothing, for they will not be disappointed.' ■ **blessings** 恵み・（神の）恩恵；**disappointment** 失望

blessed ⇒ It is BETTER to give than to receive ; Blessed are the DEAD that the rain rains on.

BLESSINGS brighten as they take their flight.
天恵は飛び去る時にこそ輝く。

† **1732** T. フラー『グノモロジア』no. 989 Blessings are not valued, till they are gone.「天恵は去りゆくまで価値がわからない」

□**1742** YOUNG *Night Thoughts* II.37 How blessings brighten as they take their flight. **1873** 'S. COOLIDGE' *What Katy Did* xi. Blessings brighten as they take their flight. Katy began to appreciate for the first time how much she had learned to rely on her aunt **1929** G. M. WHITE *Square Mark* i. It has been said that one never knows one's blessings until one has lost them. ■ **blessings** 恵み・（神の）恩恵；**gains and losses** 利益と損失

There's none so BLIND as those who will not see.
見ようとしない者ほど目の見えない者はいない。

（訳注：those who... ＝「…する人々」。There are *those who* say so.〈そう言う人々もいる〉）

見えているのにもかかわらずわざと見ようとしない者は目の見えない者と同じである。1546年の用例に挙げられているように、There's none so DEAF as those who will not hear.（「聞こうとしない者ほど耳の聞こえない者はいない」）と並行している。2つのことわざにおいて will notは「…する意志がない」もしくは「拒絶する」という強い意志を表わしている。

□**1546** J. HEYWOOD *Dialogue of Proverbs* II. ix. K4 Who is so deafe, or so blynde, as is hee, That wilfully will nother here nor see. **1551** CRANMER *Answer to Gardiner* 58 There is no manne so...blynd as he that will not see, nor so dull as he that wyll not vnderstande. **1659** P. HEYLYN *Examen Historicum* 145 Which makes me wonder...that having access to those Records...he should declare himself unable to decide the doubt...But none so blind as he that will not see. **1738** SWIFT *Polite Conversation* III.191 You know, there's none so blind as they that won't see. **1852** E. FITZGERALD *Polonius* 58 'None so blind as those that won't see.'...A single effort of the will was sufficient to exclude from his view whatever he judged hostile to his immediate purpose. **2000** P. LOVESEY *Reaper xv*. 185 Owen shook his head and picked up his drink. 'There's none so blind as those that will not see.' ■ **ignorance** 無知・無学；**obstinacy** 頑固さ

BLOOD 55

When the BLIND lead the blind, both shall fall into the ditch.
盲人が盲人を導くと 2 人とも穴に落ちることになる。

無知な者が無知な者に導かれると悲惨な結末に終わる。現在では the blind leading the blind「盲人を導く盲人」という慣用句でよく使われる。『マタイによる福音書』15 章 14 節（欽定訳聖書）Let them alone: they be blind leaders of the blind. And if the blind lead the blind, both shall fall into the ditch.「そのままにしておきなさい。彼らは盲人を導く盲人である。盲人が盲人を導けば、2 人とも穴に落ちてしまう」

□*c*897 ALFRED *Gregory's Pastoral Care* (EETS) i. Gif se blinda thone blindan læt, he feallath begen [both] on amne pytt. *c*1300 *Body & Soul* (1889) 49 Ac hwanne the blindelat the blinde, In dike he fallen bothe two. 1583 B. MELBANCKE *Philotimus* 165 In the ditch falls the blind that is led by the blind; 1836 CARLYLE *Sartor Resartus* II. iii. It is written, When the blind lead the blind, both shall fall into the ditch....May It not sometimes be safer, if both leader and led simply—sit still? 1908 H. M. SYLVESTER *Olde Pemaquid* 12 If the blind lead the blind, the ditch is but a little way on. 1947 L. P. HARTLEY *Eustace & Hilda* xvi. To get Hilda out of the house was a step forward, even in a Bath chair...even if they could see nothing beyond their noses, the blind leading the blind. ■ ignorance 無知・無学 ; rulers and ruled 支配者と被支配者

A BLIND man's wife needs no paint.
盲人の妻は夫に心で接する。

文字通りには、盲人の妻は外見以外の手段で夫を魅了しなければならないという意味であるが、もしその妻が化粧をするとしたら、それは夫以外の男の関心を引くためであるという女性差別的な意味合いも含まれている。ここで paint は make-up「化粧」を意味する。

□1659 J. HOWELL *Proverbs* (Spanish) 4 The blind mans wife needs no painting. 1736 B. FRANKLIN *Poor Richard's Almanack* (June) God helps them that help themselves. Why does the blind man's wife paint her self? 1892 C. M. YONGE *Old Woman's Outlook in Hampshire Village* 166 His [the schoolmaster's] copies too were remarkable. One was 'A blind man's wife needs no paint' 'Proverbs, sir, Proverbs,' he answered, when asked where it came from. 1998 L. KIRSCHEN *American Proverbs about Women* 47 The blind man's wife needs no makeup. ■ appearance 外見 ; wives and husbands 夫婦

blind ⇒ In the COUNTRY of the blind, the one-eyed man is king ; A DEAF husband and a blind wife are always a happy couple ; LOVE is blind ; A NOD's as good as a wink to a blind horse ; NOTHING so bold as a blind mare.

bliss ⇒ Where IGNORANCE is bliss, 'tis folly to be wise.

You cannot get BLOOD from a stone.
石から血は出ない。

一文無しの者から金銭をだまし取ろうとしても無駄であることから、無駄な努力という意味でよく使われる。stone「石」の代わりに、堅い、または動きそうにない物が使われることもある。北米では turnip「かぶ」もよく登場する（2002 年の用例参照）。

□*c*1435 J. LYDGATE *Minor Poems* (EETS) 666 Harde to likke bony out of a marbilstoon, For ther is nouthirlicour nor moisture. 1666 G. TORRIANO *Italian Proverbs* 161 There's no getting of

56 BLOOD

bloud out of that wall. **1836** MARRYAT *Japhet iv*. There's no getting blood out of a turnip. **1850** DICKENS *David Copperfield* xi. Blood cannot be obtained from a stone, neither can anything on account be obtained…from Mr. Micawber. **1925** J. S. FLETCHER False Scent ix. 'You'll never get it…' 'He'll have to pay me when he loses!' 'You can't get blood out of a stone.' **2001** K. HALL PAGE *Body in Moonlight* vii. 120 '"You can't get blood from a stone," Nick was saying. They were both really ripping. You could tell.' **2002** *London Review of Books* 3 Jan. 5 In Dr Eckener's time you couldn't get blood from a turnip, and you couldn't get helium from any place but the United States of America. ■ **meanness** けち・意地悪 ; **possibility and impossibility** 可能性と不可能性

BLOOD is thicker than water.
血は水よりも濃い。

(訳注：blood ＝「血液、血統、血縁」)

親族の絆が他のどの関係よりも重要であることを表わしている。†12世紀のドイツ語 *Ouch hoer ich sagen, daz sippebluot von wassere niht verdirbet*.「近親者の血は水によって汚されたりはしないという話を聞いたことがある」。**1412** リドゲイト『トロイの書』(EETS) III. 2071 For naturely blod will ay of kynde Draw vn-to blod, wher he may it fynde.

□**1813** J. RAY *English Proverbs* (ed. 5) 281 Blood's thicker than water. **1815** SCOTT *Guy Mannering* II. xvii. Weel—blood's thicker than water—she's welcome to the cheeses. **1914** WODEHOUSE *Man upstairs & Other Stories* 115 But though blood, as he was wont to remark while negotiating his periodical loans, is thicker than water, a brother-in-law's affection has 31 blow its limits. **2011** R. LARSON *Gabriel's Insurrection* 30 I like Jack a lot, but blood is still thicker than water and even, I suppose, whiskey: ■ **family** 家族・家系

The BLOOD of the martyrs is the seed of the Church.
殉教者の血こそが教会の種である。

キリスト教会は迫害を受けながら今日まで栄えてきた。†テルトゥリアヌス『護教論』I. *Semen estsanguis Christianorum*.「キリスト教徒の血こそが種である」

□**1560** J. PILKINGTON *Aggeus the Prophet* U4V Ciprlane wrytes that the bloud of Martirs is the seede of the Church. **1655** T. FULLER *Church Hist. Britain* I. iv. Of all Shires in England, Staffordshire was…the largest sown with the Seed of the Church, I mean, the bloud of primitive Martyrs. **1889** J. LUBBOCK *Pleasures of Life* II. xi. The Inquisition has even from its own point of view proved generally a failure. The blood of the martyrs is the seed of the Church. **1979** *Church Times* 15 June 10 It is not merely that 'the blood of the martyrs is the seed of the Church'; it is that a little persecution is good for you. **2014** *Spectator* 3 May 11 H…[Britain] ceases to be [a Christian country], this will not harm the Christian faith. Christianity was born in persecution and in the grim phrase 'The blood of the martyrs is the seed of the Church.' The harm will be to the country. ■ **adversity** 逆境・苦難 ; **Christianity** キリスト教

BLOOD will have blood.
血は血を生む。

(訳注：この場合の will は「傾向・習性」を表わす。次項の Blood will tell. も同じ用法である)

暴力は暴力を生む。†『創世記』9 章 6 節 (欽定訳聖書) Who so sheddeth man's blood, by man shall his blood be shed.「人の血を流すものは、人に血を流される」

□*a*1449 J. LYDGATE *Minor Poems* (EETS) 512 Blood will have wreche [vengeance], that wrongfully is spent. **1559** *Mirror for Magistrates* (1938) 99 Blood wyll haue blood, eyther first or last.

1605-6 SHAKESPEARE *Macbeth* III. iv. 122 It will have blood; they say blood will have blood. **1805** SOUTHEY *Madoc* I. vii. Blood will have blood, revenge beget revenge. **1974** A. FOREST *Cricket Term* i. 'Blood will have blood,' quoted Lawrie smugly. **2014** Guardian 4 Dec. (online; heading) Slaughter in Jerusalem: Blood will have blood. ■ **revenge** 復讐 ; **violence** 暴力

BLOOD will tell.
血は語る。
(訳注：will =「…するものだ」〈傾向・習性〉。Students *won't* study if it's not interesting.〈学生は面白くなければ勉強しないものだ〉)

家系の特徴や遺伝的な特徴を隠すことはできない。Blood will out.「血は隠せない」とも言う。

□ **1850** G. H. BOKER *World a Mask* IV. in S. BRADLEY *Glaucus* (1940) 38 He looked like the tiger in the Zoological, when I punch him with my stick....Game to the backbone—blood will tell. **1914** WODEHOUSE *Man upstairs & Other Stories* 253 Blood will tell. Once a Pittsburgh millionaire, always a Pittsburgh millionaire. **2002** *Oldie* June 63 By the end, she herself has turned out to be the cousin of 'darling Clare', and the daughter of long-lost Sir David Beaumont,...which is a bit of a cheat really because blood will out, won't It, and it's not surprising that Daisy is such a marvel. ■ **family** 家族・家系

bloom ⇒ When the FURZE is in bloom, my love's in tune ; When the GORSE is out of bloom, kissing's out of fashion.

blow ⇒ It's an ILL wind that blows nobody any good ; NORTH wind doth blow, we shall have snow ; SEPTEMBER blow soft, till the fruit's in the loft ; STRAWS tell which way the wind blows.

BLUE are the hills that are far away.
遥か遠くの丘は青い。
(訳注：「夜目遠目笠の内」。「遠きは花の香」)

遠景を見た時の視覚効果に関する観察で、A. E. ハウスマン『シロップシャーの若者』(1896) の一節 What are those blue remembered hills.「あの青い見覚えのある丘は何だ」にこの考えが見られる。ことわざとしては DISTANCE lends enchantment to the view.「人は遠くにあるものに魅了されるもの」に匹敵する。blue の代わりに green が使われることもある。† The GRASS is always greener on the other side of the fence.「隣の芝はいつも青い」

□ **1887** T. H. HALL CAINE *Deemster* I. v. 'What's it sayin', 'they would mutter, 'a green hill when far away from me; bare, bare, when it is near.' **1902** J. BUCHAN *Watcher by Threshold* iv. 236 'Blue are the hills that are far away' is an overcome [common expression] in the countryside. **1914** *Spectator* 6 June 955 It is the habit of the Celt to create fanciful golden ages in the past- 'Blue are the faraway hills,' runs the Gaelic proverb. **1949** J. L. MORRISSEY *Necktie for Norman* iii. 21 It was so much like the attitude of the habitual stay-at-home. They say that 'distant hills are always the greenest.' ■ **absence** 不在 ; **content and discontent** 満足と不満足

blush ⇒ TRUTH makes the Devil blush.

boat ⇒ A RISING tide lifts all the boats.

body ⇒ CORPORATIONS have neither bodies to be punished nor souls to be damned ; If you SIT by the river for long enough, you will ⇒ The body of your enemy float by.

boil ⇒ A WATCHED pot never boils.

bold ⇒ NOTHING so bold as a blind mare.

bolted ⇒ It is too late to shut the STABLE-door after the horse has bolted.

bond ⇒ An ENGLISHMAN's word is his bond.

bone ⇒ What's BRED in the bone will come out in the flesh ; You BUY land, you buy stones ; A DOG that will fetch a bone will carry a bone ; HARD words break no bones ; the NEARER the bone, the sweeter the meat ; STICKS and stones may break my bones, but words will never hurt me ; While TWO dogs are fighting for a bone, a third runs away with it.

You can't tell a BOOK by its cover.
本の善し悪しは表紙だけではわからない。

（訳注：tell ＝「〈…から〉識別する」。tell them apart 〈それらを区別する〉）

隠された内面は外観からはわからない。

□ **1929** *American Speech* IV. 465 You can't judge a book by its binding. **1946** ROLFE & FULLER *Glass Room* i. 'Forgive me, sir,' he said. 'I had you all wrong. You can never tell a book by its cover.' **1954** R. HAYDN *Journal of Edwin Carp* 131 This is a nice respectable street, wouldn't you say, sir?...Unfortunately, sir, you can't tell a book by its cover. **1984** D. CANNELL *Thin Woman* xii. Appreciate your allowing me to participate, but you should be less trusting, Ellie—can't always judge a book by its cover. **2001** *Bookseller* 9 Nov. 28 Don't judge a book by its cover, read it for yourself at BookBrowse.com. ■ **appearance, deceptive** 偽りの外見

book ⇒ A GREAT book is a great evil.

If you're BORN to be hanged then you'll never be drowned.
縛り首になる運命の者は決して溺死することはない。

他人の上辺だけの幸運をけなす際によく使われる。† 14世紀中頃のフランス語 *Noyer ne peut, cil qui doit pendre.*「絞首刑を受けなければならない者は溺死することはあり得ない」。c1503 A. バークレイ訳『グランゴールの労働の館』(1506) A 8 He that is drowned may no man hange.「溺死する者はおそらく縛り首にされる者ではない」

□ **1593** J. ELIOT *Ortho-Epia Gallica* 127 He thats borne to be hangd shall neuer be drownde. **1723** DEFOE *Colonel Jack* (ed. 2) 126 He had a Proverb in his Favour, and he got out of the Water...not being born to be drown'd, as I shall observe afterwards in its place. **1956** H. LEWIS *Witch & Priest* v. There is another picture, and underneath it says...if you're born to be hanged, then you'll never be drowned. **1986** M. SLUNG *More Momilies* 16 If you're born to hang, you won't drown. ■ **fate and fatalism** 運命と運命論；**luck** 幸運・運

born ⇒ It is BETTER to be born lucky than rich ; Because a MAN is born in a stable that does not make him a horse ; YORKSHIRE born and Yorkshire bred ; Strong in the arm and weak in the head

borrow ⇒ The EARLY man never borrows from the late man.

Neither a BORROWER nor a lender be.
借り手にも貸し手にもなるな。
　□1601 SHAKESPEARE *Hamlet* I. iii. 73 Neither a borrower nor a lender be; For loan oft loses both itself and friend. **1985** R. CURTIS & B. BLTON *Blackadder II* in R. Curtis et al. *Black-Adder* (1998) 192 Take heed the moral of this tale, Be not a borrower or lender, And if your finances do fail, Make sure your banker's not a bender. **2002** *Times* 2 11 Mar. 7 The moral architecture of my childhood was supported by a series of massive, neo-Victorian precepts, among which 'neither a borrower nor a lender be' occupied a particularly imposing position. ■ **borrowing and lending** 貸し借り

borrowing ⇒ He that GOES a-borrowing, goes a-sorrowing.

bottle ⇒ You can't put NEW wine in old bottles.

bottom ⇒ TRUTH lies at the bottom of a well ; Every TUB must stand on its own bottom.

bought ⇒ GOLD may be bought too dear.

bowls ⇒ Those who PLAY at bowls must look out for rubbers.

You can take the BOY out of the country but you can't take the country out of the boy.
田舎から少年を連れ出すことはできるが、少年の心の中から田舎を取り除くことはできない。
（訳注：「三つ子の魂百まで」）

居住地や環境が変わっても人の本質まで変わることはない。北米生まれのことわざであるが、ユーモア溢れる形がたくさんある。

　□1938 'B. BAER' in Baer & Major *Hollywood (caption to caricature of James Stewart)* You can take a boy out of the country but you can't take the country out of a boy. **1950** F. BUNCE *So Young a Body* vii. 'You can take the girl out of the country, but you can't take the country out of the girl,' Remington interjected casually. 'Ginnie's from a crossroads in Vermont, and she's still a small-town kid at heart.' **1978** W. B. MURPHY *Leonardo's Law* x. 'He was just something I picked up off the counter.' She smiled. I guess you can take the girl out of the chorus line but you can't take the chorus line out of the girl. **1997** *Times* 19 Sept 33 And, while you can take Björk out of Iceland, it seems you cannot take Iceland out of Björk's music. **2001** *National Review* 20 Aug. 56 My own visceral responses to the case are distinctly Southern...You can take the girl out of the South but you can't take the South out of the girl, e.g., 'Why doesn't her father kill him?' ■ **nature and nurture** 生まれと育ち ; **origins** 起源・生まれ

60 BOY

Never send a BOY to do a man's job.
大人の仕事をさせるのに少年を遣るな。

☐ **1874** *Daily Graphic* [NY] 12 Oct 736/4 Never send a boy to do a man's work. **1931** G. FOWLER *Great Mouthpiece* xii. Mr. Alfred J. Talley...took command of the...prosecution. He was an able man.... 'It's about time they gave me a run for the money,' Fallon said. 'The People shouldn't send boys on men's errands.' **1941** 'T. CHANSLOR' *Our Second Murder* xxviii. Never send a boy to do a man's work. **1967** E. MCGIRR *Hearse with Horses* vi. He blushed. Piron thought that he shouldn't have sent a boy to do a man's job. **2006** H. C. MANSFIELD *Manliness* 92 Somehow the passage from boy to man in his [Roosevelt's] case was not quite complete...If we consult the maxim 'never send a boy to do a man's job,' the difference may be considerable. ■ **efficiency and inefficiency 能率と非能率 ; work 仕事**

Two BOYS are half a boy, and three boys are no boy at all.
少年 2 人は少年 1 人の半人分の仕事しかせず、少年が 3 人集まると全く役に立たない。

仕事に関わる男の子の数が増えると、その分仕事をしなくなる。

☐ *c***1930** F. THOMPSON *Country Calendar* 114 Their parents do not encourage the joining of forces....We have a proverb here: 'Two boys are half a boy, and three boys are no boy at all.' **1971** *New York Times* 31 Jan. IV. 12 Rural New England of the mid-nineteenth century, not commonly sophisticated in mathematics but witty enough about man's condition, used to [say]...'One boy helping, a pretty good boy; two boys, half a boy; three boys, no boy.' **2002** *Times: Weekend* 6 Apr. 9 I...have been warned by my neighbours not to let him have any friends round. Because the more boys there are, the less work will get done. Apparently there is a country proverb that goes: 'One boy is a boy. Two boys are half a boy. And three boys are no boys at all.' ■ **assistance 援助 ; efficiency and inefficiency 能率と非能率 ; work 仕事**

BOYS will be boys.
男の子は男の子だ。

(訳注：男の子のいたずらは仕方がない。will＝「…するものだ」〈傾向・習性〉。Oil *will* float on water. 〈油は水に浮くものだ〉)

Girls will be girls. 「女の子は女の子だ」も使われることがある。

☐ **1601** A. DENT *Plain Man's Pathway* 64 Youth will be youthfull, when you haueside all that you can. **1826** T. H. LISTER *Granby* II. Vii. Girls will be girls. They like admiration. **1848** THACKBRAY *Vanity Fair* xiii. As for the pink bonnets...why boys will be boys. **1964** WODEHOUSE *Frozen Assets* iii. I tried to tell him that boys will be boys and you're only young once. **2000** W. NORTHCUTT *Darwin Awards* iv. 108 Firecrackers are illegal in Indonesia. However, they can be purchased on the black market during celebrations such as Eid AlFitr...And boys will be boys, the world over. ■ **human nature 人間性**

brae (slope, hill-side) ⇒ Put a STOUT heart to a stey brae.

BRAG is a good dog, but Holdfast is better.
ブラッグ（ほら吹き）は良い犬だが、ホールドファスト（黙々と働く人）はもっと良い。

粘り強さと慎重さは自慢や見栄張りよりも望ましい。 † **1580** A. マンディ *Zelauto* 146 Brag is a good Dogge, whyle he will holde out: but at last he may chaunce to

BRAVE 61

meete with his matche.「ブラッグは良い犬で、そのうえよく我慢する。しかし、やっと彼も恋の相手に出会えるかもしれない」。**1599** シェイクスピア『ヘンリー 5 世』2 幕 3 場 52 And Holdfast is the only dog, my duck.「食らいついたら離さない。これが一番いい犬さ」

☐ **1709** O. DYKES *English Proverbs* 123 Brag is a good Dog, but Hold-fast is a Better...Nothing edifies less in an Ingenuous Conversation, than Boasting and Rattle. **1752** S. JOHNSON *Rambler* 4 Feb. VIII. 92 When I envied the finery of any of my neighbours, [my mother] told me, that 'brag was a good dog, but holdfast was a better'. **1889** *Pictorial Proverbs for Little People* 11 Brag's a good dog, but Holdfast is better. **1937** A. W. WINSTON *It's Far Cry* xxi. In golf, as in life...the exceptional has no staying qualities. To quote a Southern [US] saying, 'Brag is a good dog, but Holdfast is better'. **1952** J. F. DOVIE *Some Part of Myself* vii. I remember my mother's repeating once after he left an old proverb: 'Brag's a good dog, but Hold Fast is a better.' ■
boasting 自慢 ; **words and deeds** 言動

brain ⇒ An IDLE brain is the Devil's workshop.

brass ⇒ Where there's MUCK there's brass.

None but the BRAVE deserve the fair.
美人にふさわしい者は勇者以外にいない。

(訳注：but =「…を除いて」。Everyone was there *but* him.〈彼以外は皆出席していた〉)

ドライデンの詩（『アレクサンドロス大王の祝宴』）に登場する 2 人は、アレクサンドロス大王とアテネの高級娼婦タイスである。

☐ **1697** DRYDEN *Poems* (1958) III. 148 Happy, happy, happy Pair!...None but the Brave deserves the Fair. **1829** P. EGAN *Boxiana* 2nd Ser. II. 354 The tender sex...feeling the good old notion that 'none but the brave deserve the fair', were sadly out of temper. **1873** TROLLOPE *Phineas Redux* II. xiii. All the proverbs were on his side. 'None but the brave deserve the fair,' said his cousin. **1978** F. WELDON *Praxis* xii. She frequented the cafe where the Rugger set hung out, and on a Saturday, after closing hours, could be seen making for the downs, laughing heartily and noisily in the company of one or other of the brave, who clearly deserved the fair, ■
courage 勇気 ; **just deserts** 当然の報い

BRAVE men lived before Agamemnon.
アガメムノーン以前にも勇者はいた。

トロイ戦争におけるミュケナイの王、アガメムノーン（ギリシア軍の総大将）の功績がホメロスと古代ギリシアの悲劇詩人らによって称えられた。このことわざはホラティウスのものであるが、言わんとするところは英雄の名前が広く知られ、後世にまで語り継がれるようになるためには、その英雄を称賛する作家が必要だということである。ホラティウス『頌歌』IV. ix. 25 *Vixere fortes ante Agamemnona multi.*「アガメムノーン以前にも勇者は大勢いたのだ」

☐ **1616** JONSON *Forest* VIII. 114 There were braue men, before Aiax or Idomen, or all the store That Homer brought to Troy. **1819** BYRON *Don Juan* I. v. Brave men were living before Agamemnon And since, exceeding valorous and sage. **1980** *Times* 23 June 16 Brave men lived before Agamemnon, lots of them. But on all of them...eternal night lies heavy, because they have left no records behind them. ■ **courage** 勇気 ; **fame and obscurity** 有名と無名

brave ⇒（名詞としても使われる形容詞）FORTUNE favours the brave;（動詞）ROBIN Hood could brave all weathers but a thaw wind.

The BREAD never falls but on its buttered side.
パンは落ちると必ずバターを塗った側が下になるものだ。
（訳注：「弱り目に祟り目」。「降れば土砂降り」）

マーフィーの法則 (if ANYTHING can go wrong, it will.「間違う可能性がある場合、必ず間違いが起きてしまう」）を想起させる。2013年の用例がこの現象の理由を述べている。

□ **1867** A. O. RICHARDSON *Beyond Mississippi* iii. His bread never fell on the buttered side. **1891** J. L. KIPLING *Beast & Man* x. We express the completeness of ill-luck by saying, 'The bread never falls but on its buttered side.' **1980** *Guardian* 3 Dec. 12 Murphy's (or Sod's) Law....Murphy's many relatives always quote it as 'Buttered bread falls buttered side down—and if it's a sandwich it falls open.' **2013** *Daily Mail* 3 Sept (online) [R]esearchers claim to have found the definitive answer as to why a piece of toast always seems to fall buttered side down. Apparently, it's all to do with the height of the table...after it topples off the edge, the toast only has time to perform a half-somersault before it lands. ■ luck 幸運・運; misfortune 不運

bread ⇒ HALF a loaf is better than no bread; MAN cannot live by bread alone.

break ⇒（名詞）Never give a SUCKER an even break;（動詞）HARD words break no bones; If it were not for HOPE, The heart would break; The LAST straw breaks the camel's back; OBEY orders, if you break owners; STICKS and stones may break my bones, but words will never hurt me; ⇒ BREAKING, BROKEN.

Breakfast ⇒ HOPE is a good breakfast but a bad supper; SING before breakfast, cry before night.

breaking ⇒ You cannot make an OMELETTE without breaking eggs.

What's BRED in the bone will come out in the flesh.
骨の中で育てられたものが肉体の中から染み出てくる。
（訳注：このことわざは元々は否定辞 not/never があった）

長年の習慣や受け継がれてきた特性はたとえ隠しても隠しきれるものではない（†BLOOD will tell.「血は語る」）。このことわざの形式と強調点は否定辞 not を省略することによって近年変化してきた。†中世ラテン語 *Osseradicatumraro de came recedit.*「骨の中に根付いているものはめったに肉体から顔を出さない」

□ **c1470** MALORY *Morte d'Arthur* (1947) I. 550 Sir Launcelot smyled and seyde, Harde hit ysto take oute off the fleysshe that ys bredde in the bone. **1546** J. HEYWOOD *Dialogue of Proverbs* II.viii.K2 This prouerbe prophecied many yeres agone, It will not out of the fleshe, thats bred in the bone. **1603** J. FLORIO tr. *Montaigne's Essays* III. xiii. They are effects of custome and vse: and what is bred in the bone will never out of the flesh. **1832** J. P. KENNEDY *Swallow Barn* III. v. What is bred in the bone—you know the proverb. *a***1957** L. I. WILDER *First Four Years* (1971) iv. We'll always be farmers, for what is bred in the bone will come out in the flesh. **1981** B. HEALEY *Last Ferry* iv. There's bad blood there....What's bred in the bone comes out in the flesh. ■ family 家族・家系; habit 習慣; human nature 人間性

bred ⇒ YORKSHIRE born and Yorkshire bred, strong in the arm and weak in the head.

breed ⇒ FAMILIARITY breeds contempt ; LIKE breeds like.

BREVITY is the soul of wit.
簡潔は分別の魂である。
(訳注：最初の用例にあるように、シェイクスピアの『ハムレット』の中でポローニアスは「簡潔は分別の精髄と申しますので、…手短に申し上げます」と述べる)

1600-1 年の用例における soul of wit は essence of wisdom「知恵の本質」と解釈できる。現在の wit は「機知」、つまり、「思いもかけない咄嗟の、そしてユーモア溢れるアイデアや表現の組み合わせによって知的な喜びを与える能力」(COD による定義) と一般に理解されている。

□ **1600-1** SHAKESPEARE *Hamlet* II. ii. 90 Since brevity is the soul of wit…I will be brief. **1833** M. SCOTT *Tom Cringle's Log* II. v. Brevity is the soul of wit, —ahem. **1996** *Washington Post* 8 Sept. CS Clinton is Southern and given to garrulousness while brevity, as they say, is the soul of wit. **2012** *Wall Street Journal* 22 May (online) If brevity is the soul of wit, then the Web by Awards might be the wittiest show of all time…[T]he show is curtailed by the Webby's policy of limiting acceptance speeches to just five words. ■ **brevity and long-windedness** 簡潔と冗漫

As you BREW, so shall you bake.
醸造する具合に応じて、パンを焼くであろう。
(訳注：人は自分の行為の結果に責任を負わなければならない。「因果応報」)

† As you BAKE, so shall you brew.「パンを焼く具合に応じて、醸造するであろう」という順序を逆にした言い方もある。中世の用例では、醸造とパン焼きよりも醸造と飲酒の繋がりの方が強かった。例えば、**1264** C. ブラウン『13世紀英詩歌集』(1932) 131 Let him habbe ase he brew, bale [misery] to dryng [drink]. *a***1325**『世界を走る者』(EETS) I. 2848 Nathing of that land [is not submerged], Suilk [such] als thai brued now ha thai dronken. *c***1450**『タウンリー第二羊飼い劇』(EETS) I. 501 Bot we must drynk as we brew And that is bot reson.「醸造する具合に応じて酒を飲まねばならない。そしてこれにも十分な理由がある」

□ *c***1570** T. INGELEND *Disobedient Child* D8^V As he had brewed, that so shulde bake. **1766** COLMAN & GARRICK *Clandestine Marriage* I. 3 As you sow, you must reap—as you brew, so you must bake. **1922** S. J. WEYMAN *Ovington's Bank* xxiii. No, you may go, my lad. As you ha' brewed you may bake. ■ **action and consequence** 行為と結果

brew ⇒ As you BAKE, so shall you brew.

You cannot make BRICKS without straw.
藁なしで煉瓦を作ることはできぬ。

必要な資材なしには何も作れない。to make bricks without straw「不可能なことを試みる」という慣用句としてよく使われる。『出エジプト記』5 章 7 節（欽定訳聖書）Ye shall no more give the people straw to make brick, as heretofore: let them go and gather straw for themselves.「これからは、今までのように、彼らにれんがを作る

64 BRIDE

ためのわらを与えるな。わらは自分たちで集めさせよ」に由来すると（間違って）考えられている。†**1624**バートン『憂鬱の解剖学』(第 2 版) I. ii. (Hard taske-masters as they [patrons] are) they take away their straw & compell them to make their number of bricke.「(彼らは無理難題を押し付ける者たち〈客〉なので) 藁を奪って煉瓦を作らせようとする」

□**1658** T. HYDE *Letter in Verney Memoirs* (1904) II. xxxviii. I have made the enclosed. It is an hard task to make bricks without straw, but I have raked together some rubbish. **1737** in *Publications of Prince Society* (1911) III. 170 Let Men be never so willing and industrious, they can't make Brick without Straw. **1909** A. BENNETT *Literary Taste* iv. You can only acquire really useful general ideas by first acquiring particular ideas.... You cannot make bricks without straw. **1995** A. G. TAYLOR *Simeon's Bride* xxxi. 208 'What would you have us do, sir?' Jack asked. 'We can't make bricks without straw.' ■ **possibility and impossibility 可能性と不可能性 ; work 仕事**

Happy is the BRIDE that the sun shines on.
太陽が降り注ぐ花嫁は幸せである。

(訳注：心掛けの良い者は結婚式に青天となる。ことわざの文体は『マタイによる福音書』の山上の垂訓を想起させる)

同様の迷信として Blessed are the DEAD that the rain rains on.「雨が降り注ぐ死者は幸せである」がある。

□**1648** HERRICK *Hesperides* 129 Blest is the Bride, on whom the Sun doth shine. And thousands gladly wish You multiply, as doth a fish. **1787** F. GROSE *Prouincial Glossary* (Superstitions) 61 It is reckoned a good omen, or a sign of future happiness, if the sun shines on a couple coming out of the church after having been married.... Happy is the bride that the sun shines on. **1926** 'P. WENTWORTH' *Black Cabinet* xxxvi. 'Happy's the bride that the sun shines on,' is how the proverb goes. But where there's real true love...there's always sunshine in a manner of speaking. **1984** C. A. O'MARIE *Novena for Murder* 181 And the weather is cooperating! 'Blessed the bride that the sun shines on!' ■ **blessings 恵み・(神の) 恩恵 ; weddings 結婚式**

Always a BRIDESMAID, never a bride.
つねに花嫁の付添人では花嫁になれない。

常に 2 番手になるように運命づけられた人を指すのに使われる。(1951 年の用例が示すように) always ではなく often を使用した形が1920 年代以降、マウスウォッシュ商品の宣伝シリーズで一般的になった。その宣伝では、縁遠い花嫁付添人が抱える問題は口臭であることをほのめかしていた。

□**1882** E. M. INGRAHAM *Bond & Free* i. Always a maiden [bridal attendant], never a wife. **1903** V. S. LEAN *Collectanea* II. 81 Three times bridesmaid, never a bride. **1917** LEIGH, COWNS, & MORRIS *'Why am I always the Bridesmaid?' (song)* Why am I always the bridesmaid, Never the blushing bride? **1951** WODEHOUSE *Old Reliable* xi. Then they'd leave me...and go off and buy candy and orchids for the other girls.... Often a bridesmaid but never a bride. **1995** G. MAGUIRE *Wicked Witch of West* V. xiv. 478 Always the bridesmaid, never the bride. Always the godfather, never the god. ■ **weddings 結婚式**

It is good to make a BRIDGE of gold to a flying enemy.
逃げる敵には金の橋を造ってやるのがよい。

(訳者：gold は silver になることもある)

このことわざが言わんとしていることは、「追い詰められた敵は絶望的になっているかも

しれない…それなら何としてでも自由に逃してやる方が良い」である。(T. フィールディング『世界のことわざ集』〈1824〉14)。この発想はギリシア総督のアリスティデス(紀元前480年)に由来する。彼はテミストクレスに、ペルシアの統治者クセルクセスがギリシアに侵攻するためにヘレスポント海狭に架けた橋を破壊せずに、ペルシア側が退却できるように手つかずのまま残しておくように警告した(プルタルコス『テミストクレス』xvi)。† 2005年の用例参照。† エラスムス *Apophthegms* viii. *Hostibus fugientibus pontem argenteum exstruendum esse.*「逃げる敵には銀の橋が造られるべきである」

☐**1576** W. LAMBARDE *Perambulation of Kent* 323 It was well sayde of one…If thine enemie will flye, make him a bridge of Golde. **1642** T. FULLER *Holy State* IV. xvii. He [the good general] makes his flying enemy a bridge of gold, and disarms them of their best weapon, which is necessity to fight whether they will or no. **1889** R. L. STEVENSON *Master of Ballantrae* iv. You may have heard a military proverb: that it is a good thing to make a bridge of gold to a flying enemy. I trust you will take my meaning. **2005** *Mideast Mirror* 22 July (online) Bar-Lev, a former commander of the IDF's elite Duvdevan unit preferred to cite Mao Tse Tung, who spoke about laying down a bridge of gold for the enemy's retreat. ■ enemies 敵; warfare 戦争

bridge ⇒ Don't CROSS the bridge till you come to it ; Everyone SPEAKS well of the bridge which carries him over.

brighten ⇒ BLESSINGS brighten as they take their flight.

bring ⇒ NIGHT brings counsel ; The WORTH of a thing is what it will bring.

If it ain't BROKE, don't fix it.
壊れていないのなら直すな。

(訳注：ain't = isn't、broke = broken。いずれも非標準。「触らぬ神に祟りなし」。「寝た子は起こすな」)

米国の軍事力に関する技術的な文脈において1960年初頭に生まれた。この言葉は、バート・ランスが1976年に最初に用いたとされることが多いが、実はそれ以前に誕生したことになる(1977年の用例参照)。これに相当する英国の表現は Let well alone.「そのままにしておけ」である。

☐**1964** *Approach: Naval Aviation Safety Review* IX. x. 42 But be sure it's real leakage that you're measuring. As someone recently said, 'if it ain't broke don't fix it.' **1977** *Nation's Business* 27 May Bert Lance [President Carter's Director of the Office of Management and Budget] believes he can save Uncle Sam billions if he can get the government to adopt a single motto: 'If it ain't broke, don't fix it.' **1984** R. Wilder *You All Spoken Here* 25 If it ain't broke, don't fix it: Don't mess with a clock that runs on time. **1988** *Washington Post* 5 Dec. Cl 1 The sleep pattern you have worked out is normal for you, and since you have been fairly successful in planning your life around it, why change? 'If it ain't broke, don't fix it.' **2001** *Times Literary Supplement* 30 Nov. 14 A healthy libertarianism rubs shoulders with the 'if it ain't broke, don't fix it' style of conservatism. ■ busybodies おせっかい屋; content and discontent 満足と不満足

broken ⇒ PROMISES, like pie-crust, are made to be broken ; RULES are made to be broken.

broom ⇒ NEW brooms sweep clean ; SWEEP the house with broom in May, you sweep the head of the house away.

broth ⇒ TOO many cooks spoil the broth.

build ⇒ FOOLS build houses and wise men live in them ; Where GOD builds a church, the Devil will build a chapel ; It is easier to PULL down than to build up.

built ⇒ ROME was not built in a day.

Every BULLET has its billet.
銃弾には皆着弾点がある。

(訳注：弾丸に当たるも当たらぬも運しだいである。its billet の代わりに a lighting place も使われる)

誰が殺されるかは運命しだいである。1922 年の用例では、より一般的に運命が人間のすべての営みにおいて役割を果たすと述べられている。

□ **1575** G. GASCOIGNE *Fruits of War* i. 155 Suffiseth this to proove my theame withall, That every bullet hath a lighting place. **1765** WESLEY *Journal* 6 June (1912) V. 130 He never received one wound. So true is the odd saying of King William [III], that 'every bullet has its billet'. **1922** JOYCE *Ulysses* 366 The ball rolled down to her as if it understood. Every bullet has its billet. **1932** R. C. WOODTHORPE *Public School Murder* XI. iv. 237 It is said that every bullet finds its billet I am afraid this is yet another instance of a shaft at random sent finding a mark the archer never meant. **1986** *Canadian Medical Association Journal* CXXXV. vii. 790 (*article title*) Every bullet has its billet. ■ **death** 死 ; **fate and fatalism** 運命と運命論

A BULLY is always a coward.
弱い者いじめをする者は皆臆病者である。

□ **1817** M. EDGEWORTH *Ormond in Harrington & Ormond* III. xxiv. Mrs. M'Crule, who like all other bullies was a coward, lowered her voice. **1826** LAMB *Elia* in *New Monthly Magazine* XVI. 25 A Bully is always a coward....Confront one of the silent heroes with the swaggerer of real life, and his confidence in the theory quickly vanishes. **1853** T. C. HALIBURTON *Wise Saws* iv. I never saw a man furnished with so much pleasure in my life. A brave man is sometimes a desperado. A bully is always a coward. **1981** *Times* 9 May 2 The old adage holds good: all bullies are cowards, and most cowards are bullies. ■ **cowardice** 臆病

bung-hole ⇒ SPARE at the spigot, and let out at the bung-hole.

burden ⇒ GOD makes the back to the burden.

bum（動詞）⇒ BETTER to marry than to burn.

burned ⇒ ONCE bitten, twice shy.

A BURNT child dreads the fire.
やけどをした子は火を怖がる。

(訳注：あつものに懲りてなますを吹く」)

人は経験によって避けるべきものを覚える。† ONCE bitten, twice shy.「1 度咬まれ

ると 2 度目は臆病になるものだ」

□*c*1250 *Proverbs of Hending in Anglia* (1881) IV. 199 Brend child fuir fordredeth [is in dread of]. c 1400 *Romaunt* of Rose I. 1820 'For evermore gladly,' as I rede, 'Brent child offierbath mychdrede.' 1580 LYLY *Euphues & his England* II. 92 A burnt childe dreadeth the fire....Thou maysthappely forsweare thy selfe, but thou shalt neuer delude me. 1889 *Pictorial Proverbs for Little People* 5 She will not touch a match or a lighted candle...which proves that the proverb is true which says: a burnt child dreads the fire. 1948 WODEHOUSE *Uncle Dynamite* II. vii. The burnt child fears the fire, and bitter experience had taught Pongo Twistleton to view with concern the presence in his midst of Ickenham's fifth earl. 1984 *Newsweek* 5 Nov. 98 The burned child fears the fire and when dawn breaks next Tuesday voters may pull the covers over their ringing heads and refuse to get out of bed. ■ **experience** 経験

burnt ⇒ If you PLAY with fire you get burnt.

bury ⇒ Let the DEAD bury the dead.

bush ⇒ A BIRD in the hand is worth two in the bush ; GOOD wine needs no bush ; Do not grieve that ROSE-TREES have thorns,...

The BUSIEST men have the most leisure.
一番忙しい人が一番暇がある。

IDLE people have the least leisure.「なまけ者には全く暇がない」と逆である。さらに If you WANT something done, ask a busy person.「何かをやってもらいたい時は忙しい人に頼め」を逆から見た際の道理でもある。† 1866 S. スマイルズ『自己援助』(新版) i. Those who have most to do...will find the most time.「やるべきことが最も多い人が…最も時間を見つける」。異なった言い方に、The busiest men find the most time.「最も忙しい人が最も多くの時間を見つける」がある。

□1884 J. PAYN *Canon's Ward* II. xxxiv. It is my experience that the men who are really busiest have the most leisure for everything. 1911 *Times Literary Supplement* 6 Oct. 365 The busiest men have always the most leisure; and while discharging the multifarious duties of a parish priest and a guardian he found time for travelling. 2012 *Sydney Morning Herald* 23 Sept. (online; *heading*) The busiest do not find the most time.

BUSINESS before pleasure.
楽しむ前にまず仕事。

business と pleasure という 2 つの語はことわざ以外の表現においてもたびたび対比される。† *c*1640 *Grobiana's Nuptials* (*MS Bodley 30*) 15 Well to the businesse. − On; businesse is senior to complement.「仕事に取りかかれ。仕事は遊びに優先する」。1767 T. ハッチンソン『日記と書簡集』(1883) I. v. Pleasure should always give way to business.「快楽よりもつねに仕事を優先すべきだ」

□1837 C. G. F. GORE *Stokeshill Place* III. vi. 'Business before pleasure' is a golden rule which most of us regard as iron. 1943 S. STERLING *Douin among Dead Men* v. This is business, Sarge. You know what business comes before. 1986 J. HESS *Strangled Prose* vi. Douglas drifted past with the department chairman, engrossed in conversation. He gave me a quick nod, but steered his captive toward a sofa. Business before pleasure. 1997 R. BOWEN *Evans Above* xxii. 232 'I think I

68 BUSINESS

should buy you a drink first.'...'Business before pleasure, major,' Evan said. ■ **business** ビジネ
ス・商売；**work** 仕事

BUSINESS is war.
ビジネスは戦争である。

これが日本のモットーであるという不確かな主張は1992クライトン『ライジングサン』
の中で繰り返し使われたことによる。

□1905 *New York Times* 9 Apr. (online) That business is war is truer of nothing in modern com-
merce than the railway business. **1984** *New York Times* 14 Nov. (online) Declaring that 'business
is war', Mr Tramiel also said his company was reducing prices. **2000** *Linux Journal* Aug. (online)
Their conceptual metaphors are 'business is war' and 'markets are battlefields'. ■ **business** ビジ
ネス・商売

business ⇒ EVERYBODYS business is nobody's business ; PUNCTUALITY is the soul of
business.

busy ⇒ If you WANT something done, ask a busy person.

butter ⇒（名詞）The same FIRE that melts the butter hardens the egg ; There are more
WAYS of killing a dog than choking it with butter ;（動詞）FINE words butter no parsnips.

buttered ⇒ The BREAD never falls but on its buttered side.

You BUY land, you buy stones. ; You buy meat, you buy bones.
土地を買ったら石も買うことになる；肉を買ったら骨も買うことになる。

（訳注：土地や肉を買えば余分なものにまで金を払わねばならないが、ビールの場合にはビール以外のもの
に金を払う必要がない）

† **1595** *Pedler's Prophesy* B4ᵛ You shall be sure to haue good Ale, for that haue
no bones.「あなたは必ずおいしいビールが飲めるだろう。なぜならビールには骨がない
（ビール以外のものに金を払う必要がない）から」

□1670 J. RAY *English Proverbs* 211 He that buys land buys many stones; He that buys flesh
buys many bones; He that buys eggs buys many shells, But he that buys good ale buys nothing
else. **1721** J. KELLY *Scottish Proverbs* 172 He that buys Land, buys Stones; He that buys Beef,
buys Bones; He that buys Nuts, buys shells; He that buys good Ale, buys noughtelse. **1970** *Countryman* Autumn 172 Welsh butcher to customer complaining of bony meat: 'Well, missus, you
buy land, you buy stones; buy meat, you buy bones.' ■ **buying and selling** 売買；**property** 財産

buy ⇒ Why buy a cow when milk is so cheap? ; MONEY can't buy happiness ; One WHITE
foot, buy him.

Let the BUYER beware.
買い手は用心すべし。

買い手は取引をする前に商品の性質と価値を吟味しなければならないという警告。ラテ
ン語のことわざ*Caveat emptor*「買手は用心すべし」もそのまま使われる。*Caveat emp-*

tor, quiaignorare non debuit quod jus alienum emit.「買手は用心すべし。なぜなら他人から買おうとしている物の特徴を知らないで済むはずはないから」

☐**1523** J. FITZHERBERT *Husbandry* 36 And (if) he [a horse] be tame and haue hen rydden vpon than caveat emptor be ware thou byer. **1592** NASHE *Pierce Penniless* I. 155 Sed caueat emptor, Let the interpreter beware. **1607** E. SHARPHAM *Fleire* II. C4 They are no prouerb breakers: beware the buyer say they. **1927** *Times* 29 Sept. 10 We dislike very much, whether it is put in Latin or in English, the phrase 'Let the buyer beware!' **1974** D. FRANCIS *Knock Down* xi. 'Caveat emptor,' I said. 'What does that mean?' 'Buyer beware.' 'I know one buyer who'll beware for the rest of his life.' **2001** *Washington Times* 24 Sept. All It's caveat emptor as charities and others appeal for relief donations in the wake of the Sept. 11 terrorist attacks. Only this time 'let the buyer beware' should probably read 'let the donor beware.' ■ **buying and selling 売買**；**caution 用心**

The BUYER has need of a hundred eyes, the seller of but one.
買い手は100の目が必要だが、売り手は1つの目だけでよい。

（訳注：but ＝「たった、ほんの」。This took him *but* a few minutes.〈これをするのにものの数分もあればよかった〉）

† イタリア語 *Chi compra ha bisogna di cent' occhi; chi vende n 'ha assai di uno.*
「買う側は百の目が必要であるが、売る側は1つの目だけでよい」

☐**1640** G. HERBERT *Outlandish Proverbs* no. 390 The buyer needes a hundred eyes, the seller not one. **1745** B. FRANKLIN *Poor Richard's Almanack* (July) He who buys had need have 100 Eyes, but one's enough for him that sells the Stuff. **1800** M. EDGEWORTH *Parent's Assistant* (ed. 3) III. 86 He taught him…to get…from customers by taking advantage of their ignorance.…He often repeated…'The buyer has need of a hundred eyes, the seller of but one.' **1928** *Illustrated Sporting & Dramatic News* 7 Jan. 27 (caption) The buyer has need of a hundred eyes. The seller of but one. ■ **buying and selling 売買**；**caution 注意**

Let BYGONES be bygones.
済んだことは済んだことにしよう。

過去の怒りや悲しみは忘れて未来に目を向けるべきだ。類似のものに Forgive and forget.「許し、そして忘れよ」がある。済んだこととは過ぎ去った出来事のことで、この意味での名詞用法は明らかにスコットランド起源である。† **1568** Mary of Scots *Commission* (in H. キャンベル『スコットランドのメアリー女王のラブレター』補遺29) For good amitie, as well for bygonnes as to come, betwixt them…「2人の良き親交のため、将来のことも過ぎ去ったことと同様に…」

☐**1636** S. RUTHERFORD *Letters lxii* (1862) I. 166 Pray…that byegones betwixt me and my Lord may be byegoiles. **1648** F. NETHERSOLE *Parables* 5 Let bygans be bygans. **1856** A. LINCOLN *Speech* 10 Dec. Thus let bygones be bygones. Let past differences, as nothing be. **2000** D. TUTU in J. Hopkins *Art of Peace* 99 A third option is do nothing. You say, 'Let bygones be bygones, let's forget the past.' **2011** Z. M. CHOUDHURY *Fight for Bangladesh* 84 The population of every country transitioning out of war…comprises, roughly speaking, two camps—those who want justice, and those who want to let bygones be bygones. ■ **forgiveness 許し・寛容**；**past 過去・過ぎ去った**

C

CAESAR's wife must be above suspicion.
カエサルの妻たる者は貞操を疑われるようなことがあってはならない。

古代ギリシアの作家・道徳論者プルタルコスによると、ローマ帝国の提督ユリウス・カエサル（紀元前100-44）は、妻のポンペイアと離婚した理由を尋ねられてこのように答えたと言われる。彼は、神聖冒瀆が争点のプブリウス・クロディウスの裁判にまつわるスキャンダルに妻が間接的に関与していたので、自分の地位と名誉が傷つけられたと考えたのである。† **1580** リリー『ユーフュイーズとイングランド』II. 101 Al women shal be as Caesar would haue his wife, not onelye free from sinne, but from suspition. 「カエサルが妻として迎える女は罪がないだけではなく、疑われるようなこともあってもならない」

☐**1779** A. ADAMS *Letter* 4 Jan. in L. H. Butterfield et al. *Adams Family Correspondence* (1973) III. 148 It is a very great misfortune that persons imployed in the. most important Departments should...have seperate interests from the publick whom they profess to serve. Caesars wife ought not to be suspected. **1847** J. C. & A. W. HARE *Guesses at Truth* (ed. 3) 1st Ser. 263 Caesar's wife ought to be above suspicion....Caesar himself ought to be so too. **1990** *Washington Times* 9 July D2 He [i.e. Governor D. Wilder] ought to bear in mind the maxim of one of Caligula's more lucid predecessors: Caesar's wife must be above suspicion. And so should Caesar. ■ **associates** 仲間 ; **conduct** 行ない・品行

cake ⇒ You cannot HAVE your cake and eat it.

calf ⇒ A BELLOWING cow soon forgets her calf.

call ⇒ Call no man HAPPY till he dies ; He who PAYS the piper calls the tune.

called ⇒ MANY are called but few are chosen.

calm ⇒ AFTER a storm comes a calm.

camel ⇒ The LAST straw breaks the camel's back ; TRUST in God but tie your camel.

CANDLEMAS　71

He who CAN, does; he who cannot, teaches.
能力のある者は自分で行ない、能力のないものは人に教える。

　（訳注：he =「〈関係節を伴って〉…する者は誰でも〈性別は問わない〉」。*He who* has all the gold makes all the rules.〈金をすべて持つ者が法をすべて支配する〉）

このことわざには（しばしば滑稽な）多くの異なった言い方がある。

□ **1903** G. B. SHAW *Maxims for Revolutionists in Man & Superman* 230 He who can, does. He who cannot, teaches. **1979** *Daily Telegraph* 6 Aug. 8 A version of an old adage came to me those who can, do, those who can't, attend conferences. **1981** P. SOMERVILLE-LARGE *Living Dog* i. He who can, does sang the train wheels, he who cannot, teaches. **2002** *Washington Times* 11 July D8 (*Herb & Jamaal comic strip*) 'Rev. Croom, as a man of the cloth, do you consider yourself an example of perfection?' 'No....I may wear this collar, but I struggle with being a human as much as the next guy. I guess that's what's meant when they say...'He who can, does; he who cannot, preaches.' ■ **efficiency and inefficiency 能率と非能率 ; work 仕事**

candle ⇒ BETTER to light one candle...; CANDLEMAS day, put beans in the clay, put candles and candlesticks away.

candlelight ⇒ Never CHOOSE your women or your linen by candlelight.

If CANDLEMAS day be sunny and bright, winter will have another flight. ; If Candlemas day be cloudy with rain, winter is gone, and won't come again.
聖燭祭日が明るく晴れているなら、冬は再びやって来る。；聖燭祭日が曇りで雨なら、冬は過ぎ去り、再び戻ってくることはない。

キリスト教の暦では聖母マリアの純潔と寺院内のキリストの存在を称える祝祭は 2 月 2 日に該当する。その日は祝祭日の礼拝の際に蠟燭が浄められることから聖燭祭日と呼ばれる。北米では、2 月 2 日は "Groundhog Day" と呼ばれる。この日にウッドチャックが冬眠から覚めて穴を出て、明るい太陽の下で自分の影に驚くとさらに 6 週間の冬眠に逆戻りし、春の到来が遅れるという言い伝えがある。この迷信は少なくとも 16 世紀初頭から知られていた。† **1523** スケルトン『作品集』I. 418 Men were wonte for to discerne By candlemas day what wedder shulde holde.「人々は聖燭祭の日の天気によって、その後どのような天気になるかを予測した」。1584 年の用例の脚韻 (daie と raie) は 1678 年の用例におけるラテン語の脚韻 (purificante と ante) と似ている。

□ **1584** R. SCOT *Discovery of Witchcraft* XI. xv. If Maries purifieng daie, Be cleare and bright with sunnie raie, The frost and cold shalbe much more, After the feast than was before. **1678** J. RAY *English Proverbs* (ed. 2) 51 If Candlemas day be fair and bright Winter will have another flight If on Candlemas day it be showre and rain, Winter is gone and will not come again. This is a translation...of that old Latin Distich; *Si Sol splendescat Maria purificante, Major eritglacies post festum quam fuit ante.* **1980** *Times* 2 Feb. 11 Today is Candlemas Day. So let us see if the old legend holds good again as it did last year. 'If Candlemas day be sunny and bright, winter will have another flight; if Candlemas day be cloudy with rain; winter is gone and won't come again.'
■ **weather lore 天気にまつわる伝承**

72　CANDLEMAS

CANDLEMAS day, put beans in the clay, ; put candles and candlesticks away.
聖燭祭日には豆を土に入れ、ロウソクと燭台は片付けよ。

聖燭祭日（2月2日）に関しては1つ前のことわざを参照。このことわざの前半と後半は明らかに比較的最近になって合体したものである。種蒔きの指示が聖バレンタインデー（2月14日）からずれているのは暦が旧暦から新暦に移行したことによる。†脚韻（day, clay）の部分は、このことわざが *c*1640 On Saint Valentine's Day cast beans in clay But on Saint Chad（2 Mar.）sow good or bad.「聖バレンタインデーには豆を土に入れよ。しかし、聖チャドの日（3月2日）には良し悪しを問わず種を蒔け」（ジョン・スミス『バークレイ草稿』33. no. 89）に由来することの証しである。

□**1678** J. RAY *English Proverbs* (ed. 2) 344 On Candlemas day throw candle and candlestick away. **1876** T. F. THISELTON-DYER *British Popular Customs* 55 From Candlemas the use of tapers at vespers and litanies, which had continued through the whole year, ceased until the ensuing All Hallow Mass...On Candlemas Day, throw candle and candlestick away. **1948** F. THOMPSON *Still glides Stream* ii. Broad beans were planted...on Candlemas Day. Candlemas Day, stick beans in the clay, Throw candle and candlestick right away, they would quote. **1974** K. BRIGGS *Folklore of Cotswolds* ii. Candlemas Day was the time...when lights were extinguished....An old rhyme said: Candlemas Day, put beans in the clay: Put candles and candlesticks away. ■ **calendar lore** 暦にまつわる伝承；**garden lore** 庭にまつわる伝承

If the CAP fits, wear it.
帽子が合うなら、その帽子を被れ。
（訳注：その批評が当たっていると思うなら、その批評を生かせということ）

名前や行動によって示されるその人物の適性を示す際に使われる。† If the SHOE fits, wear it.「靴が合うなら、その靴を履け」。次例が示すように、ここでの capは、元々は「馬鹿帽子」（覚えの悪い生徒に罰としてかぶらせた円錐型の紙帽子）であった。**1600** N. ブルトン『パスキルの馬鹿帽子』A 3 Where you finde a head fit for this Cappe, either bestowe it vpon him in charity, or send him where he may haue them for his money.「この帽子に合う頭を見つけたら、ただで彼に授けよ。あるいは自分の金で買える所に彼を連れて行け」

□**1732** T. FULLER *Gnomologia* no. 2670 If any Fool finds the Cap fit him, let him wear it. **1750** RICHARDSON *Clarissa* (ed. 3) VII. ii. If indeed thou find est...that the cap fits thy own head, why then...clap it on. **1854** DICKENS *Hard Times* II. vii. 'Mercenary....Who is not mercenary?' ...'You know whether the cap fits you....If it does, you can wear it' **1985** 'J. GASH' *Pearlhanger* xi. Little crooks get chased. Big crooks...get knighted and freedom. I don't mean bankers and insurance syndicates, incidentally, though if the cap fits... ■ **conduct** 行ない・品行；**reputation** 評判

capacity ⇒ GENIUS is an infinite capacity for taking pains.

caravan ⇒ DOGS bark, but the caravan goes on.

Where the CARCASE is, there shall the eagles be gathered together.
死体があるところハゲワシが集まる。

『マタイによる福音書』24章28節（欽定訳聖書）Wheresoever the carcase is, there will the Eagles be gathered together. 「死体があるところには禿鷲が集まる」を想起させる。現代の聖書訳では eagles「ハゲワシ」の代わりに vultures「ハゲワシ、コンドル」が使われる。

□*c*1566 W. P. tr. *Curio's Pasquin in Trance* 33 Where the caraine [carrion] is, thither do the Eagles resort. **1734** B. FRANKLIN *Poor Richard's Almanack* (Jan.) Where carcasses are, eagles will gather, And where good laws are, much people flock thither. **1929** C. BUSH *Perfect Murder Case* x. On the way he explained his appearance at the inquest on the twin lines of busman's holiday and that where the carcass is there will the vultures be gathered together. **1979** 'S. WOODS' *Proceed to Judgement* 190 [He] was surprised to find Sir Nicholas and Vera, as well as Roger and Meg, having tea with Jenny. 'Where the carcase is, there shall the eagles be gathered together,' he commented, not very politely. ■ **associates** 仲間

card ⇒ LUCKY at cards, unlucky in love.

CARE killed the cat.
心配は猫も殺した。

(訳注：猫は9つの命を持っているとされる。その猫でさえも「心配」は殺してしまうのである)

† CURIOSITY killed the cat.「詮索好きは猫も殺した」の方がよく使われる。care には「心配ごと、悲しみ」と「注意深さ、用心深さ」の2つの意味がある。1962年の用例では、「悩み」というよりも「過度の手入れ」という意味で使われている。

□**1598-9** SHAKESPEARE *Much Ado about Nothing* V. i. 133 Though care kill'd a cat, thou hast mettle enough in thee to kill care. **1726** SWIFT *Poems* II. 761 Then, who says care will kill a cat? Rebecca shews they're out in that. **1890** 'R. BOLDREWOOD' *Miner's Right* II. xxiii. He was always ready to enjoy himself....'Care killed a cat'. **1949** S. SMITH *Holiday* xii. We must be careful of that. Care killed the cat, said Caz. **1962** A. CHRISTIE *Mirror Crack'd* xxii. Care killed the cat, they say....You don't want kindness rubbed into your skin,...do you? **1979** F. SELWYN *Sergeant Verity & Blood Royal* xx. 'Pretty sure, Mr. Crowe? I was bloody near ten feet short of it, that's all!' ...'Come on now, Verity. Care might kill a cat! Look to the future!' ■ **stress** ストレス

Don't CARE was made to care.
「かまうもんか」と言う人がかまわれた。

伝統的な児童詩の一節で、I don't care!「かまうもんか！」と言う人、特に子供に対するしっぺ返しとして用いられる。1959年の用例はロンドンのハックニーにおいて収集された実例である。

□**1927** R. GRAVES (ed.) *Less Familiar Nursery Rhymes* 18 Don't Care didn't care. Don't Care was wild: Don't Care stole plum and pear Like any beggar's child. Don't Care was made to care, Don't Care was hung: Don't Care was put in a pot And boiled till he was done. **1959** I & P. OPIE *Lore and Language of Schoolchildren* iii. 50 To 'don't-cares' the traditional saying is: Don't care was made to care...**1992** D. LESSING *African Laughter* 223 Look at the maize. How do we know what bugs the Portuguese brought in with maize? We don't know! We don't care! Well, don't care was made to care. **2001** *Spectator* 19 May 13 And as the crime spawned by permissiveness reaches even into the most secluded cul-de-sac, they will find that an egalitarian government is neutral between victim and offender, so that while they cannot defend themselves, there is nobody out there to protect them. Don't care will be made to care then. ■ **trouble** やっかい・苦労

care ⇒ CHILDREN are certain cares, but uncertain comforts ; Take care of the PENCE and the pounds will take care of themselves.

74 CAREFUL

Be CAREFUL what you pray for, you might get it.
願い事には気をつけろ。逆のものが手に入るかもしれないから。

高望みし過ぎると当初の望みとは逆のものだったということになりかねないという警告。
Be careful what you wish for.「望むものには注意せよ」という言い方もある。

☐ **1933** *Oakland Tribune* 24 Feb B7 At 11 a.m., the Rev. Tob Watt, pastor, will preach on 'Be Careful What You Pray For—You Might Get It.' **1995** *CNN*, 2 Mar. Public opinion polls show well over 70 percent of Americans are in favor. But it reminds me of a little prayer you hear—or adage you hear from time to time—'Be careful what you pray for, you just might get it.' Is it your sense that the majority of Americans who do want a balanced budget really know what they're in for? **2002** *Times* 4 Mar. 4 Howard had been thoroughly upbeat about the future. 'These last few weeks I've had to say: Be careful what you pray for, because it might happen!' **2014** J. ARCHER *Be Careful What You Wish For* (*book title*). ■ **caution** 用心 ; **hope** 望み

careful ⇒ If you can't be GOOD, be careful.

The CARIBOU feeds the wolf, but it is the wolf who keeps the caribou strong.
トナカイは狼の餌となるが、トナカイを強くしているのはほかならぬ狼である。

イヌイットのことわざで、獲物を取る側と獲物になる側との相互関係を述べている。

☐ **1963** F. MOWAT *Never Cry Wolf* (1979) 90 This is why the caribou and the wolf are one: for the caribou feeds the wolf but it is the wolf who keeps the caribou strong. **2006** World Wild Life Fund website 31 Oct 'Arctic Wolf' In most Native American mythologies, the wolf is revered as a powerful spirit and its place in the web of life is seen as vital. An old Inuit saying from the Kivalliq Region in northern Canada, says: 'The caribou feeds the wolf, but it is the wolf who keeps the caribou strong.' **2007** 'Without a Park to Range' weblog 30 Jan. If you don't believe biologists, heed an Inuit proverb based on thousands of years of observation: 'The caribou feeds the wolf, but it is the wolf who keeps the caribou strong.' ■ **strength and weakness** 強弱

A CARPENTER is known by his chips.
大工の技量は木端でわかる。

人の仕事にはその人の仕事ぶり、つまり力量 (技) が残っている。

☐ **a1533** LD. BERNERS *Hist. Arthur* (1582) 162[b] I know well my lorde Arthur hath been here.... He is a good carpenter, for he hath made here a faire sight of chips. **1546** J. HEYWOOD *Dialogue of Proverbs* I. vii. 14 Muste she not (quoth he) be welcome to vs all, Amonge vs all, lettyngsuche a farewell fall? But such carpenters, such chips. Quoth she folke tell. **1738** SWIFT *Polite Conversation* II.153 'You have eaten nothing.'...'See all the Bones on my Plate: They say, a carpenter's known by his Chips.' **1962** *Washington Daily News* 24 July 14 In the idiom of the Middle West, you can tell a wood chopper by his chips. President Kennedy's economic report...was based on the scientific estimates of his Council of Economic Advisers. ■ **appearance** 外見 ; **human nature** 人間性

carry ⇒ A DOG that will fetch a bone will carry a bone ; SPEAK softly and carry a big stick ; Everyone SPEAKS well of the bridge which carries him over.

cart ⇒ Don't PUT the cart before the horse.

case ⇒ CIRCUMSTANCES alter cases ; HARD cases make bad law ; No one should be

JUDGE in his own cause.

Ne'er CAST a clout till May be out.
5月が過ぎるまで冬服を脱いではならない。

（訳注：be は仮定法現在形の形で古い言い方。現代英語では is となる。*Be* it even so humble, there's no place like home.〈いかに粗末であろうともわが家にまさる所はない〉）

5月末までは今まで着ていた冬服を脱いではならないという警告。5月の花が咲くまでという意味ではないことに注意。

□ **1706** J. STEVENS *Spanish & English Dict*. s.v. Mayo, Hasta passado Mayo note quites el sayo, Do not leave off your Coat till May be past. **1732** T. FULLER *Gnomologia* no. 6193 Leave not off a Clout [item of clothing], Till May be out **1832** A. HENDERSON *Scottish Proverbs* 154 Cast ne'er a clout till May be out. **1948** R. GRAVES *White Goddess* x. In ancient Greece, as in Britain, this [May] was the month in which people went about in old clothes—a custom referred to in the proverb 'Ne'er cast a clout ere May be out,' meaning 'do not put on new clothes until the urtlucky month is over.' **1970** N. STREATFEILD *Thursday's Child* xxv. I still wear four petticoats...Ne'er cast a clout till May be out. **1996** C. DUNN *Murder on Flying Scotsman* i. 7 Brought up on 'Ne'er cast a clout till May be out' (May month or may blossom? she had always wondered), Daisy was wearing her green tweed winter coat. ■ **calendar lore** 暦にまつわる伝承；**dress** 衣服

cast ⇒ COMING events cast their shadows before ; OLD sins cast long shadows ; Do not throw PEARLS to swine.

castle ⇒ An ENGLISHMAN'S house is his castle.

casualty ⇒ TRUTH is the first casualty of war.

It doesn't matter if a CAT is black or white, as long as it catches mice.
鼠を捕まえてくれさえすれば、黒猫だろうが白猫だろうがかまわない。

中国のことわざで、実用主義を支持する際に使われる。鄧小平（とうしょうへい）(1904-97) の言葉とされる。1997年の用例参照。

□ **1968** *China Reconstructs* XVII. viii. 18 [A] handful of class enemies...openly declared, 'So long as a cat catches mice it is a good cat, whether it is black or white.' **1997** *Daily Telegraph* 20 Feb. (obituary of Deng Xiaoping. quoting from early 1960s) It doesn't matter if a cat is black or white, as long as it catches mice. **2006** *South China Morning Post* 9 May (online) Director of Broadcasting Chu Pui-hing...said RTHK...also had to abide by the rules. 'There is a saying: "It doesn't matter whether it's a black cat or white cat. It's a good cat as long as it catches mice."...[W]e are well aware that catching mice alone doesn't make us a good cat. We need to be a cat that catches mice according to the rules.' ■ **efficiency and inefficiency** 能率と非能率；**pragmatism** 実用主義

A CAT in gloves catches no mice.
手袋をした猫は鼠を捕れない。

抑制と用心（あるいは引っ込み思案）も度を超すと何も達成できない。† 14世紀のフランス語 *Chat engaunte ne surrizera ja bien*.「手袋をした猫は鼠を上手に捕まえない」

76　CAT

□**1573** J. SANFORDE *Garden of Pleasure* 105 A gloued catte can catche no myse. **1592** G. DELA-MOTHE *French Alphabet* n. 1 A mufled Cat is no good mouse hunter. **1758** B. FRANKLIN *Poor Richard's Almanack* (Preface) Handle your Tools without Mittens; remember that the Cat in Gloves catches no Mice. **1857** DICKENS *Little Dorrit* II. xiv. Mrs. General, if I may reverse the common proverb...is a cat in gloves who will catch mice. That woman...will be our mother-in-law. **1979** *Country Life* 21 June 2047 There is hardly one [cat] but flings back the lie in the face of the old saying that a cat in gloves catches no mice. Why dirty your paws when your servants will do It for you? ■ **efficiency and inefficiency　能率と非能率**

A CAT may look at a king.
猫でさえ王様を見てもいい。
（訳注：may＝「…してよい、…して差し支えない」〈許可〉）

たとえ卑しい身分の者でも身分の高い人の前で平身低頭する必要はない。

□**1546** J. HEYWOOD *Dialogue of Proverbs* II. v. H3 What, a cat maie looke on a king, ye know. **1590** R. GREENE *Never too Late* VIII. 181 A Cat may look at a King, and a swaynes eye hath as high a reach as a Lords looke. **1721** N. BAILEY *English Dictionary* s.v. Cat, A Cat may look upon a King. This is a saucy Proverb, generally made use of by pragmatical Persons. **1935** I. COMP-TION-BURNETI *House & its Head* xi. There is no harm in that, dear. A cat may look at a king; and it is only in that spirit that my poor brother looks at Alison. **2001** *Times* 23 Nov. 20 Our trivia quiz shows are intended to show that taxi drivers are as clever as philosophers and poets. A cat may look at a king. ■ **equality　平等；society　社会**

When the CAT's away, the mice will play.
猫がいないとネズミがはしゃぐものだ。
（訳注：will＝「…するものだ」〈傾向・習性〉。Truth will out.〈真実は明るみに出るものだ〉。「鬼の居ぬ間に洗濯」）

上の者に告げ口する人、あるいは、尊敬できない人物が不在だと人々は反乱を起こす。†14世紀のフランス語 *Ou chat na rat regne*.「猫がいないとネズミが王様になる」。*c*1470 *Harley MS 3362* in *Retrospective Review* (1854) May 309 The mows lordchy-pythe [rules] ther a cat ys nawt.「猫がいないとネズミが支配する」。**1599** シェイクスピア『ヘンリー5世』I. ii. 172 To her unguarded nest the weasel Scot Comes sneaking, and so sucks her princely eggs, Playing the mouse in absence of the cat.「スコットランドというイタチが親鳥のいない巣へこっそりと忍び寄り、王者の卵を吸いつくすからです。猫の居ぬ間のハッカネズミ同様…」

□**1607** T. HEYWOOD *Woman killed with Kindness* II. 135 Mum; there's an old prouerbe, when the cats away, the mouse may play. **1670** J. RAY *English Proverbs* 68 When the cat is away, the mice play. **1876** I. BANKS *Manchester Man* III. xiv. Mrs. Ashton, saying 'that when the cat's away the mice will play', had decided on remaining at home. **1925** S. O'CASEY *Juno & Paycock* i. 13 It's a good job she has to be so often away, for when the cat's away, the mice can play! **2001** R. HILL *Dialogues of Dead* xxx. 258 'When I'm having the time of my life, you'd not deprive me of the pleasure of thinking about all those poor sods back here working their fingers to the bone.' 'You don't really believe that, do you? When the cat's away...' ■ **discipline　規律；opportunity, taken　得られた機会**

The CAT, the rat, and Lovell the dog, rule all England under the hog.
猫と鼠と犬のラベルが猪の下でイギリス全土を治めている。
（訳注：Richard IIIの下でCatisby、Ratclyffl、Lovelrの3人がイングランドを支配していた。）

CATCH 77

この風刺の意味は1516年の用例で説明されている。

□**1516** R. FABYAN New *Chronicles of England & France* vm. 219ᵛ The Cane the Ratte And Louell our dogge Rulyth all Englande under a hogge. The whiche was ment that Catisby Ratclyffe And the Lord Louell Ruled the lande under the kynge. **1586** R. HOLINSHED *Chronicles* III. 746 [Richard III executed] a poore gentleman called Collingborne [in 1484], for making a small rime of three of his...councellors,...lord Louell, sir Richard Ratcliffe...and sir William Catesbie....The Cat, the Rat, and Louell our dog, Rule all England vnder an hog. Meaning by the hog, the...wild boare, which was the Kings cognisance [coat of arms]. **1816** SCOTT *Antiquary* ii.'His name...was Lovel' 'What! The cat, the rat, and Lovel our dog? Was he descended from King Richard's favourite?' **1973** A. CHRISTIE *Postern* of Fate I. ii. The cat, the rat and Lovell the dog, Rule all England under the hog....The hog was Richard the Third. ■ **rulers and ruled** 支配者 と被支配者

The CAT would eat fish, but would not wet her feet.
猫は魚を食べたいが、足を濡らすのはまっぴら御免だ。
（訳注：「河豚は食いたし命は惜しし」）

ある特定の行為を嫌う人は、望みを達成できないかもしれない。†中世ラテン語 *Catus amat piscem, sed non vult tingere plantas*.「猫は魚が好きだが、足を濡らすのは御免だ」

□*c*1225 in Englische Studien (1902) XXXI. 7 Cat lufat visch, ache nele his fethwete. *c*1380 CHAUCER *House of Fame* III. 1783 For ye be lyke the sweynte (tired) cat That wolde have fissh; but wostow [do you know] what? He wolde nothing wete his clowes. *c*1549 J. HEYWOOD *Dialogue of Proverbs* I. xi. B8v But you lust not to do, that longeth therto. The cat would eate fyshe, and wold not wet her feete. **1605-6** SHAKESPEARE *Macbeth* vii. 44 Letting 'I dare not' wait upon 'I would', Like the poor cat i' th' adage. **1732** T. FULLER *Gnomologia* no. 6130 Fain would the Cat Fish eat, but she's loth her Feet to wet. **1928** *Sphere* 7 Jan. 36 'The cat would fain eat fish, but would not wet his feet'...In modem days one might paraphrase it into 'bad sailors would fain enjoy the sun, but would not cross the channel'. ■ **decision and indecision** 決断と優柔不断；**wanting and having** 不足と所持

cat ⇒ CARE killed the cat ; CURIOSITY killed the cat ; Feed a DOG for three days and he will remember your kindness for three years...; DOGS look up to you, cats look down on you, pigs is equal ; KEEP no more cats than will catch mice ; WANTON kittens make sober cats ; There is more than one WAY to skin a cat ; There are more WAYS of killing a cat than choking it with cream ; ⇒ CATS.

You cannot CATCH old birds with chaff.
年を取った鳥は籾殻などでは捕まらない。

経験豊かで賢い者は、たとえ魅力ありそうでも価値のないものには容易に騙されない。1481年の用例は、籾殻（トウモロコシの皮）と good corn「良いトウモロコシ」の区別を明確に説明している。

□**1481** CAXTON *Reynard the Fox* (1880) xl. Wenest [do you think] thou thus to deceyue....I am no byrde to be locked ne take by chaf. I know wel ynowh good corn. *c*1590 *Timon* (1842) IV. ii. Tis well.—An olde birde is not caught with chaffe. **1670** J. RAY *English Proverbs* 126 You can't catch old birds With chaff. **1853** THACKERAY *Newcomes* II. Xv. They ogled him as they sang...with which chaff our noble bird was by no means to be caught. **1961**'L. BRUCE' *Die All,*

78 catch

Die Merrily (1986) xx. 188 'But why, headmaster? On what do you base that?' 'Aha,' said Mr. Gorringer, 'old birds are not to be caught with chaff. I sensed it as soon as you failed to name him among your "possible."' ■ experience 経験 ; wisdom 賢明・知恵

catch ⇒ It doesn't matter if a CAT is black or white, as long as it catches mice ; A CAT in gloves catches no mice ; A DROWNING man will clutch at a straw ; EAGLES don't catch flies ; The EARLY bird catches the worm ; FIRST catch your hare ; HONEY catches more flies than vinegar ; KEEP no more cats than will catch mice ; If you RUN after two hares you will catch neither ; A SHUT mouth catches no flies ; If the SKY falls we shall catch larks ; SUB a beggar and catch a louse ; Set a THIEF to catch a thief ; ⇒ caught

CATCHING's before hanging.
絞首刑にする前にまず逮捕せよ。

犯人を逮捕してはじめて罰することができる。

□1818 A. N. ROYALL *Letters from Alabama* (1830) xxxvi. Yes, says Marchant, but catching's before hanging—the villain's cleared out. **1876** W. G. NASH *New England Life* vii. Catchin' before spankin' is the rule. **1961** B. SEEMAN *In Anns of Mountain* 60 Ketchin' comes before hangin', I always say. ■ action and consequence 行為と結果

All CATS are grey in the dark.
暗闇ではどの猫も灰色だ。

夜になると、生物が持つ顕著な特徴がわからなくなる。しばしば女性に対して軽蔑的に使われる。

□*c*1549 J. HEYWOOD *Dialogue of Proverbs* I. V. A6v When all candels be out, all cats be grey. All thyngs are then of one colour. **1596** T. LODGE *Margarite of America* H2ᵛ All cattes are grey in the darke…and therefore (good madam) you doe well to referred the eie. **1745** B. FRANKLIN *Letter* 25 June in Papers (1961) III. 31 And as in the dark all Cats are grey, the Pleasure of corporal Enjoyment with an old Woman is at least equal, and frequently superior. **1886** H. JAMES *Princess Casamassima* I. xiv. 'If she isn't, what becomes of your explanation?'…'Oh, It doesn't matter; at night all cats are grey.' **1990** R. RICHARDSON *Dying of Light* xi. 130 He braked as a cat scuttled in front of him…'Was that black?' 'All cats are grey in the dark,' Tess quoted. 'But it could have been. That's lucky.' **2007** New Scientist 30 June 45 There is a French expression which in English becomes 'at night all cats are grey', but the Hungarian version of this translates as 'at night all cows are black'. ■ similarity and dissimilarity 類似性と相違性

cattle ⇒ HURRY no man's cattle.

Caught ⇒ Don't SELL the skin till you have caught the bear.

Cause ⇒ No one should be JUDGE in his own cause.

Cease ⇒ WONDERS will never cease.

Century ⇒ BETTER a century of tyranny than one day of chaos.

CHANGE 79

Certain ⇒ CIIIDREN are certain cares, but uncertain comforts ; NOTHING is certain but death and taxes ; NOTHING is certain but the unforeseen.

Chaff ⇒ You cannot CATCH old birds with chaff ; A KING'S chaff is worth more than other men's corn.

A CHAIN is no stronger than its weakest link.
鎖の強度とは一番弱い輪の強度に他ならない。

□**1856** C. KINGSLEY *Letter* 1 Dec. (1877) II. 499 The devil is very busy, and no one knows better than he, that 'nothing is stronger than its weakest part'. **1868** L. STEPHEN in *Cornhill Mag.* XVII. 295 A chain is no stronger than its weakest link; but if you show how admirably the last few are united...half the world will forget to test the security of the...parts which are kept out of sight. **1986** L. J. PETER *Peter Pyramid* ii. A chain is only as strong as its weakest link; and the longer the chain, the more weak links. **2015** *Spectator* 17 Jan. 28 [B]ecause—as fighting men have appreciated through most of history...—you're only as strong as your weakest link. If one of you caves, you all die... ■ strength and weakness 強弱

Don't CHANGE horses in mid-stream.
川の真ん中で馬を取り替えるな。

いったんある作戦や行為に決めてしまったら、途中で制度や指導者を変えずに最後までやり遂げるのが肝要である。to change horses in mid-stream「途中で別の馬に鞍替えする（中途で方針を変える）」という慣用句でも使われる。

□**1864** A. UNCOLN *Collected Works* (1953) VII. 384 I am reminded...of a story of an old Dutch farmer, who remarked to a companion once that 'it was best not to swap horses when crossing streams'. **1929** R. GRAVES *Good-bye* to All That xxiii. 'If ours is the true religion why do you not become a Catholic?'...'Reverend father, we have a proverb in England never to swap horses while crossing a stream'. **1967** RIDOUT & WITTING *English Proverbs Explained* 41 Don't change horses in mid-stream....If we think it necessary to make changes, we must choose the right moment to make them. **1979** D. MAY *Revenger's Comedy* ix. Changing horses, love? I should look before you leap. ■ decision and indecision 決断と優柔不断

A CHANGE is as good as a rest.
変化をつけるのは休むのと同じほどの価値がある。

20世紀中に、当初の A change of work is as good as a rest. に取って代わったと考えられる。A change is as good as a holiday. という言い方もなされる。

□*c***1882** F. COBLEY *On Foot Through Wharfedale* vi 42 The old saying, 'a change is as good as a rest,' is as true as ever; and if the visitor to this or to any other part is at all anxious that his tour may do him good, he must take care not to carry the 'shop' about with him. **1890** A. CONAN DOYLE in *Lippincott's Monthly Mag.* Feb. x. 198 Well, I gave my mind a thorough rest by plunging into a chemical analysis. One of our greatest statesmen has said that a change of work is the best rest. So it is. **1895** J. THOMAS *Randigal Rhymes* 59 Change of work is as good as touchpipe [a short interval of rest]. **1903** V. S. LEAN *Collectanea* III. 439 Change of work is rest. (Manx.) **1967** O. MILLS *Death enters Lists* viii. There would be no fish-bits for Whiskers...but she could buy him some fish-pieces; and a change was as good as a rest, she remembered. **1984** D. CANNELL *Thin Woman* xiii. Me old grandpa used to say 'a change is as good as a rest', and at my time of life variety don't often come aknocking. **2012** *Daily Mail* 28 Nov. (online; heading) A change is as good as a rest? No thanks! Unadventurous Brits have had the same haircut their

80 CHANGE

entire lives. ■ change 変化；recreation 気晴らし

CHANGE the name and not the letter, change for the worse and not the better.
（結婚予定の女性が）文字ではなく名前を変えると、良い方にではなく、悪い方に変えることになる。

ウィリアム・ヘンダーソン『イングランドの北部郡と境界線上の民間伝承に関する覚書』
(1866) 26で次のように説明されている。It is unlucky for a woman to marry a man
whose surname begins with the same letter as her own.「女性が自分と同じ文字で
始まる苗字の男性と結婚するのは不幸になる」

□ 1853 *Notes & Queries* 1st ser. VIII. 150 Is the following distich known in any part of England?
'To change the name but not the letter, Is to marry for worse, and not for better.' I met with it in
an American book, but it was probably an importation. **1936** T. C. H. JACOBS *Appointment with
Hangman* ii. 18 'Change the name and not the letter, change for the worse and not the better.
She ought to be warned about that.' **1950** woman from Forfar, Angus, quoted in I. OPIE & M. TA-
TEM *Oxford Dictionary of Superstitions* (1996) 238 A change of name and not of letter Is a
change for the worse and not the better. ■ marriage 結婚；superstition 迷信

change ⇒（動詞）If you are not the LEAD dog, the view never changes；The LEOPARD
does not change his spots；TIMES change and we with time.

chaos ⇒ BETTER a century of tyranny than one day of chaos.

Chapel ⇒ Where GOD builds a church, the Devil will build a chapel.

CHARITY begins at home.
慈善は我が家から始まる。

（訳注：charity は本来は「思いやり、人間愛」の意味である。out of *charity*.〈思いやりの心から〉）

現在は自分および自分の家族の利益を優先することを正当化したり、慈善団体に寄付を
しないことを正当化することを暗示している。しかし、元来は他人に対する一般的な愛
や関心を指していた。そのような愛は家庭から始まり、そこから社会へと広がって行っ
たのである。

□ *c*1383 in Wyclif *English Works* (EETS) 78 Charite schuld bigyne at hem-self. *a*1625 BEAUMONT
& FLETCHER *Wit without Money* V. ii. Charity and beating begins at home. **1659** T. FULLER *Appeal of Injured Innocence* I. 25 Charity begins, but doth not end, at home....My Church-
History...began with our own Domestick affairs....I intended...to have proceeded to forrain
Churches. **1748** SMOLETT *Roderick Random* I. vi. The world would do nothing for her if she
should come to want—charity begins at home. **1910** 'SAKI' Reginald in Russia 2 With her, as with
a great many of her sex. charity began athomeliness and did not generally progress much farther.
1985 C. MACLEOD *Plain Old Man* xiv. 'You know Aunt Emma never gives anybody a compli-
mentary ticket. If she did,...there'd be no money raised for charity.' 'I thought charity began at
home.' **1996** *Washington Post* 30 July Cl6 True, charity begins at home, but it shouldn't end
there. ■ charity 慈善；home 家庭・母国

CHARITY covers a multitude of sins.
慈善は多くの罪を覆う。

『ペトロの手紙一』(欽定訳聖書) 4 章 8 節 [H]ave fervent charity among yourselves; for charity shall cover the multitude of sins. 「何よりもまず互いに心を尽くして愛し合いなさい。愛は多くの罪を覆うからです」を想起させる。この聖書の文脈は人間に対する愛を持つと罪を免れることができるという教えであるが、慈善は不道徳を隠すために偽善的に実践されることもあるという皮肉とも取れる。†エラスムス *Responsio ad Albertum Pium* (1529) 35ᵛ *quid est charitas? Est pallium monachi. Qui sic? Quia operit multitudinem peccatorum.* 「慈善とは何か。修道僧の服である。なぜか。それは多くの罪を隠すからである」

□*a*1633 G. HERBERT *Priest to Temple* (1652) xii. Many and wonderfull things aie spoken of thee....To Charity is given the covering of sins. **1794** J. Q. ADAMS *Letter* 26 May in Writings (1913) I. 191 Faction covers at least as great a multitude of sins as charity. **1836** E. HOWARD *Rattlin the Reefer* I. xxx. The blue coat, like charity, covereth a multitude of sins. **1908** 'O. HENRY' *Gentle Grafter* 47 According to the old proverb, 'Charity covers a multitude of skins'. **1982** G. HAMMOND *Game* xvi. Charity, after all, can cover up a multitude of sins. ■ **charity** 慈善；**forgiveness** 許し・寛容

chase ⇒ A STERN chase is a long chase.

It is as CHEAP sitting as standing.
立っていても座っていても値段は同じだ。
(訳注：どうせただなのだから立っていないで座っていたほうがましだ)

文字どおりの意味で一般に使われる。

□**1666** G. TORRIANO *Italian Proverbs* 277 The English say, It is as cheap sitting as standing, my Masters. **1858** SURTEES *Ask Mamma* xlix. Let's get chairs, and be snug; it's as cheap sitting as standing. **1932** 'J. J. CONNINGTON' *Sweepstake Murders* ix. He returned to Tommie Redhill's car. 'Jump in, Inspector,' Tommie suggested, opening the door at his side. 'It's as cheap sitting as standing.' **1946** 'R. T. CAMPBELL' *Bodies in Bookshop* xix. The old man...grunted angrily and lowered himself into a chair. I had already taken a seat. It was as cheap to sit as to stand. ■ **idleness** 怠惰

cheap ⇒ Why buy a cow when milk is so cheap ; TALK is cheap.

CHEATS never prosper.
ごまかしが栄えることはない。

特に米国では cheaters も使われる。† *a*1612 J.ハリントン『警句集』(1618) IV. 5 Treason doth neuer prosper, what's the reason? For if it prosper, none dare call it Treason. 「裏切りは決してうまくいかない。なぜか。それはもしそれが成功すると、誰もそれを裏切りとは呼ばないからである」

□**1805** R. PARKINSON *Tour in America* II. Xxix. It is a common saying in England, that 'Cheating never thrives': but, in America, with honest trading you cannot succeed. **1903** V. S. LEAN *Collectanea* II. 38 'Cheating never prospers.' A proverb frequently thrown at each other by young people when playing caids. **1935** R. CROMPTON *William—the Detective* vi. They avenged themselves upon the newcomer...by shouting the time-honoured taunt 'Cheats never prosper.'

82　cheek

1971 R. L. FISH *Green Hell Treasure* ii. 'So you figured…that someone in the classroom had been helping him with his homework, and that was cheating. Which you frown on.' 'With reason,' Da Silva said virtuously. 'Cheaters never prosper.' **2001** *Washington* Times 30 Aug. B8 Cheaters never prosper. They only receive the keys to the city from Mayor Rudolph Giuliani. ■ **wrong-doers** 悪事をなす者

cheek ⇒ There is always one who KISSES, and one who turns the cheek.

Cheeping ⇒ MAY chickens come cheeping.

Cheese ⇒ An APPLE-PIE without some cheese is like a kiss without a squeeze.

A CHERRY year, a merry year; a plum year, a dumb year.
さくらんぼのなり年は陽気な年、プラムのなり年は陰気な年。

　□**1678** J. RAY *English Proverbs* (ed. 2) 52 A cherry year a merry year: A plum year a dumb year. This is a puerile and senceless rythme…as far as I can see. **1869** R. INWARDS *Weather Lore* 14 The progress of the seasons may be watched by observing the punctuality of the vegetable world. …A cherry year, a merry year. A plum year, a dumb year. **1979** V. CANNING *Satan Sampler* ix. Warboys was studying an arrangement of cherry blossom.…The blossom was good this year. A cherry year, a merry year. ■ **garden lore** 庭にまつわる伝承

chicken ⇒ Don't COUNT your chickens before they are hatched ; CURSES, like chickens, come home to roost ; MAY chickens come cheeping.

Monday's CHILD is fair of face.
月曜日に生まれた子供は器量がよい。

　この詩は長詩の一部であり、各行が独立して使われることがある（1838 年の用例参照）。1 週間の各曜日に関する伝承を下に挙げる。1838 年の用例が示す Christmas「クリスマス」はあまり使われず、Sabbath「安息日」の方がはるかに一般的である。

　□**1838** A. E. BRAY *Traditions of Devon* IT. 287 Monday's child is fair of face; Tuesday's child is full of grace, Wednesday's child is full of woe, Thursday's child has far to go, Friday's child is loving and giving, Saturday's child works hard for its living, And a child that's born on the Christmas day Is fair and wise and good and gay. **1915** J. BUCHAN *Salute to Adventurers* i. I was a Thursday's bairn, and so, according to the old rhyme, 'had far to go'. **1935** D. JONES *Journal* 12 Nov. in R. Hague *Dai Greatcoat* (1980) II. 81 Which day's child is 'loving and giving' in the rhyme?…Is it Wednesday's? **1957** V. BRITTAIN *Testament of Experience* I. Ii. From the outset Shirley sustained the nursery adage which commends 'Sunday's child', for she put on weight steadily and was the easiest of infants to rear. **1980** A. WILSON *Setting World on Fire* II. iii. She showed her contrition by stroking his hair. 'Saturday's child works hard for his living,' she murmured. **1997** *Washington Post* 18 Dec. C27 Monday's child is fair of face. | Tuesday's child is full of grace. | Wednesday's child is full of woe. | Thursday's child has far to go. | Friday's child is loving and giving. | Saturday's child works hard for a living. | And the child born on the Sabbath day | Is bonny and blithe, and good and gay. ■ **children** 子供

The CHILD is the father of the man.
子供は大人の父である。

　（訳注：1807 年の用例にあるように、ロマン派を代表する英国の桂冠詩人 W. ワーズワースの「虹を見る時

CHILDREN　83

我が心はおどる」という有名な短詩の第7行にこの句がある。「三つ子の魂百まで」）

成人になってからの性格、興味、能力は子供の頃にすでにその兆しを見せている。†1671
ミルトン『復楽園』IV 220 The childhood shews the man, asmorning shews the day.
「朝がその日を表わしているように、子供時代は大人を表わしている」

□**1807** WORDSWORTH *Poems* (1952) I. 226 My heart leaps up when I behold A rainbow in the
sky: So was it when my life began...The Child is father of the Man. **1871** S. SMILES *Character* ii.
Tire influences which contribute to form the character of the child...endure through life....'The
child is father of the man.' **1907** E. GOSSE *Father & Son* xii. We are the victims of hallowed proverbs, and one of the most classic of these tells us that 'the child is the father of the man'. **2002**
Washington Post 31 May C7 'The child is father of the man' is an idea that's been around for a
while, but Gail Tsukiyama takes this notion and tweaks it, ever so gently. ■ **children　子供；human
nature　人間性**

child ⇒ A BURNT child dreads the fire ; An OLD man is twice a child ; PRAISE the child,
and you make love to the mother ; SPARE the rod and spoil the child ; It takes a whole VIL-
LAGE to bring up a child ; It is a WISE child that knows its own father.

CHILDREN and fools tell the truth.
子供と愚か者は本当のことを言う。

子供と愚か者は単純なので嘘をつくことができず、つい本当のことを言ってしまう。†14
世紀後半のフランス語 *Pour savoir vrai de chose toute, yvre, runke, sot et femme
escoute.*「すべてのことについて真実を知るためには、酔っぱらい、子供、愚か者そして
女性の話を聞け」。*c*1425『アングリア』(1885) VIII. 154に Atte laste treuthe was tryed
oute of a childe and drunken man.「ついに真実が子供と酔っ払いの口から出た」とい
う記述が見られる。

□**1537** in *Letters & Papers of Reign of Henry VIII*(1929) Addenda I. 1. 437 It is 'an old saying that
a child, a fool and a drunken man will ever show...the truth'. **1591** LYLY *Endymion* IV. ii. Children must not see Endimion, because children and fooles speake true. **1652** J. TATHAM *Scots
Figgaries* III. 23 I am a fool 'tis confest, but children and fooles tell truth sometimes; you know.
1805 SCOTT *Letter* Jan. (1932) I. 233 It is a proverb, that children and fools talk truth and I am
mistaken if even the same valuable quality may not sometimes be extracted out of the tales made
to entertain both. **1921** *Evening Standard* 21 Oct 9 Solicitor...'Are you telling the truth in this
case?'Witness.—Only children and fools tell the truth. **1972** 'O. SHANNON' *Murder with Love* ii.
All he said was that children and fools speak the truth. ■ **children　子供；fools　愚か者；truth　真実・
真理**

CHILDREN are certain cares, but uncertain comforts.
子供が苦労の種になるのは確かであるが、慰めを与えてくれるかどうかは確かでは
ない。

1915年の用例では、喜びを与えてくれるのは確かであるが、苦労の種でもあると述べて
いる。

□**1639** J. CLARKE *Parremiologia Anglo-Latina* 240 Children are uncertaine comforts, but cer-
taine cares. **1641** R. BRATHWAIT *English Gentleman* (ed. 3) 27 Children reflect constant cares,
but uncertaine comforts. **1732** T. FULLER *Gnomologia* no. 1095 Children are certain Cares, but
uncertain comforts. **1885** B. J. HARDY *How to be Happy though Married* xvi. Children are not

84 CHILDREN

'certain sorrows and uncertain pleasures' when properly managed. **1915** J. WEBSTER *Dear Enemy* 203 My new little family has driven everything out of my mind. Bairns are certain joy, but nae sma' care. ■ children and parents 親子

CHILDREN should be seen and not heard.
子供は見られるだけにしておき、話すのを聞かれるべきではない。
(訳注：子供は行儀よくしていなくてはならない。その場にいてもいいが、目下の人の前ではむやみにしゃべってはならないというしつけ)

(下の古い用例からわかるように) 元々は特に (若い) 女性に対して用いられた。

□*c*1400 J. MIRK *Festial* (EETS) I. 230 Hytys an old Englysch sawe [saying]: 'A mayde schuld be seen, but not herd.' **1560** T. BECON *Works* i. Bbb2 This also must honest maids provide, that they be not full of tongue....A maid should be seen, and not heard. **1773** R. GRAVES *Spiritual Quixote* I. III. xviii. It is a vulgar maxim, 'that a pretty woman should rather be seen than heard'. **1820** J. Q, ADAMS *Memoirs* (1875) V. xii. My dear mother's constant lesson in childhood, that children in company should be seen and not heard. **1959** M. BRADBURY *Eating People is Wrong* ii. 'You think that children should be seen and not heard then?' asked the novelist. **2002** *Times* 22 May 8 But although mothers may not want to draw attention to themselves,...there is never any guarantee that their baby...has yet learnt the old maxim that children should be seen and not heard. ■ children 子供 ; manners しつけ

children ⇒ The DEVIL'S children have the Devil's luck ; FOOLS and bairns should never see half-done work ; HEAVEN protects children, sailors, and drunken men.

Chip ⇒ A CARPENTER is known by his chips.

Choice ⇒ You PAYS your money and you takes your choice ; SMALL choice in rotten apples.

Choke ⇒ It is idle to SWALLOW the cow and choke on the tail.

choking ⇒ There are more WAYS of killing a cat than choking it with cream ; There are more WAYS of killing a dog than choking it with butter.

Never CHOOSE your women or your linen by candlelight.
女とリンネルはロウソクの灯りの下で選ぶな。
(訳注：暗い所では欠点も見落としてしまう)

このアドバイスの理論的根拠が1980年の用例の中で述べられている。

□**1573** J. SANFORDE *Garden of Pleasure* 51 Choose not a woman, nor linnen clothe by the candle. **1678** J. RAY *English Proverbs* (ed. 2) 64 Neither women nor linnen by candle-light. **1737** B. FRANKLIN *Poor Richard's Almanack* (May) Fine linnen, girls and gold so bright. Chuse not to take by candlelight. **1980** *Woman's Journal* Dec. 105 'Never choose your women or your linen by candlelight,' they used to say: a testimony to the soft, flattering glow that candles always give. ■ appearance, deceptive 偽りの外見 ; women 女性

choose ⇒ Of two EVILS choose the less.

cite 85

chooser ⇒ BEGGARS can't be choosers.

chosen ⇒ MANY are called but few are chosen.

Christmas ⇒ The DEVIL makes his Christmas pies of lawyers' tongues and clerks' fingers ; A DOG is for life, not just for Christmas ; A GREEN Yule makes a fat churchyard.

The CHURCH is an anvil which has worn out many hammers.
教会は多くのハンマーをすり減らした鉄床(かなとこ)である。

教会はこれまでいかなる迫害にも屈しなかった。今後も存続していくであろう。このことわざはカルヴァン派の神学者であるテオドール・ド・ベーズ(1519-1605)が1562年3月、ヴァシーにおけるユグノーの虐殺の後ナヴァール王へ送った返信に由来する。王はプロテスタントがギーズ公とその従者たちを投石によって怒らせたという理由で大虐殺を許そうとしていた。

☐1853 G. DE FELICE *Hist. Protestants of Prance* I. II. v. 156 (tr. Beza to King of Navarre, 1562) It is the peculiarity of the Church of God...to endure blows, not to give them; but yet you will be pleased to remember, that it is an anvil on which many a hammer has been broken. **1908** A. MA-CLAREN *Acts of Apostles* I. 136 The Church is an anvil which has worn out many hammers and the story of the first collision is, in essentials, the story of all. **1920** J. BUCHAN *Path of King* vii. 'From this day I am an exile from France so long as it pleases God to make His Church an anvil for the blows of His enemies.'...'God's church is now an anvil, but remember...It is an anvil which has worn out many hammers.' ■ **Christianity** キリスト教

church ⇒ The BLOOD of the martyrs is the seed of the Church ; Where GOD builds a church, the Devil will build a chapel ; The NEARER the church, the farther from God.

churchyard ⇒ A GREEN Yule makes a fat churchyard.

CIRCUMSTANCES alter cases.
事情によって事態も違ってくるものだ。

（訳注：cases ＝「事態、実情、真相」。That's the *case*.〈それは事実だ〉）

☐1678 T. RYMER *Tragedies of Lost Age* 177 There may be circumstances that alter the case, as when there is a sufficient ground of partiality. **1776** W. HEATH *Memoirs* (1798) 92 Our General reflected for a moment, that as circumstances alter cases, Gen. Washington...might possibly wish for some aid. **1895** J. PAYN *In Market Overt* xxxix. Circumstances alter cases even with the best of us, as was shown in a day or two in the conduct of the Lord Bishop. **1938** A. CHRISTIE *Appointment with Death* xiii. It is undoubtedly true that circumstances alter cases. I do feel...that in the present circumstances decisions may have to be reconsidered. **1998** 'C. AJRD' *Stiff News* (2000) v. 56 'I didn't say anything before,' the Matron murmured awkwardly, 'because I couldn't imagine that it could be important.' 'Circumstances alter cases,' said Crosby prosaical-ly. ■ **circumstances** 状況

circus ⇒ If you can't RIDE two horses at once, you shouldn't be in the circus.

cite ⇒ The DEVIL can quote Scripture for his own ends.

86 CITY

The CITY for wealth, the country for health.
裕福になりたければ都会で、健康になりたければ田舎で暮らせ。

> バランスのとれた生活のためには、都会と田舎の両方が必要である。都会でお金を稼ぎ、田舎でのんびり暮らせばよい。

□ **1838** T. E. HOOK *Gurney Married* i. 158 'He has written to me…to tell me he has been obliged to go to London.' 'Ah, poor man, I pity him,' said the lady; 'the city for wealth, the country for health.' **1874** painted on cornice at Ascott House, Wing, Bucks., U. K. The city for wealth, the country for health. **1970** M. E. MARTY *Righteous Empire* 157 [T]heir readers as the century wore on were coming to be young urbanites. God had given the good, or rural, environment; man was spoiling it with a man-made, or urban, milieu. 'The city for wealth, the country for health'; so taught a textbook. ■ health 健康 ; riches 富

city ⇒ If every man would SWEEP his own doorstep the city would soon be clean.

A CIVIL question deserves a civil answer.
丁寧に質問すれば、丁寧な答が返ってくる。

□ **1853** T. C. HALIBURTON *Sam Slick's Wise Saws* II. ii. Give a civil answer to a civil question. **1858** S. A. HAMMETT *Piney Woods Tavern* xxvii. The Squire there asked me a civil question, and that desarves a civil answer, —at least that's manners where I come from. **1935** E. GREENWOOD *Pins & Needles* xi. 'Thank you for those few words,' Aunt said effusively. 'I've got what I wanted—a civil answer to a civil question.'

CIVILITY costs nothing.
礼節には費用はかからない。

> 類似したことわざに NOTHING is lost by civility.「礼節によって失うものは何もない」がある。現在では politeness がしばしば civility の代わりに使われる。† 15 世紀後半のフランス語 *De bouche honnestete. petit couste et vault plente.*「礼儀正しい言葉使いは…ほとんどお金がかからない。しかし、その価値は高い」

□ **1706** J. STEVENS *Spanish & English Dict.* s. v. Cortesia, Mouth civility is worth much and costs little. **1765** LADY M. W. MONTAGU *Letter* 30 May (196 7) III. 107 Remember Civility costs nothing, and buys every thing. **1765** H. TIMBERLAKE *Memoirs* 73 Politeness…costs but little. **1873** W. ALLINGHAM *Rambles* xiv. Civility costs nothing, it is said—Nothing, that is, to him that shows it; but it often costs the world very dear. **1980** E. HARRIS *Medium for Murder* x. 'It made me hopping mad to hear you kow-towing to him.'…'Politeness costs nothing,' said Brooker. **1992** C. GRAHAM *Death in Disguise* v. 95 There was no call, Jill's boss had agreed whilst comforting his employee with an iced Malibu, to take that tone. Politeness cost nothing. ■ manners 礼儀・作法 ; politeness 礼儀正しさ

civility ⇒ There is NOTHING is lost by civility.

claws ⇒ A CLEVER hawk hides its claws.

clay ⇒ CANDLEMAS day, put beans in the clay, put candles and candlesticks away.

clean ⇒ A clean CONSCIENCE is a good pillow ; NEW brooms sweep clean ; If every man would SWEEP his own doorstep the city would soon be clean.

CLIMBERS　87

CLEANLINESS is next to godliness.
清潔は敬虔に近い。

(訳注：next ＝「…の次に、隣に」。古英語で nēah「近い」の最上級 nēhsta「最も近い」から来ている)

ここでの next は順番上「直後に続く」を意味する。† 1605 ベーコン『学問の進歩』II. 44 Cleannesse of bodie was euer esteemed to proceed from a due reuerence to God. 「体の清潔さは神への畏敬の念から生じると考えられた」

□*a*1791 WESLEY *Works* (1872) VII.16 Slovenliness is no part of religion. . . . 'Cleanliness is indeed next to godliness.' 1876 F. G. BURNABY *Ride to Khiva* x. 'Cleanliness is next to Godliness.' The latter quality, as displayed in a Russian devotee, is more allied with dirt than anything else. 1979 C. EGLETON *Backfire* i. The hospital staff had a thing about personal cleanliness, next to godliness, you might say. 2002 *Washington* Post 14 Aug. C2 But a $6,000 shower curtain? Even if cleanliness is next to godliness, isn't that kinda steep? ■ **cleanliness** 清潔さ

CLERGYMEN's sons always turn out badly.
牧師の息子はろくでなしになるのが常だ。

(訳注：牧師はしばしば、息子に厳しく接するだけで、真の宗教を教えない場合がある。「賢が子賢ならず」)

この一般化に対する根拠が1885年の用例で示されている。

□1885 E. J. HARDY *How to be Happy though Married* xix. The Proverb says that 'Clergymen's sons always turn out badly'. . . because the children are surfeited with severe religion, not with the true religion of Christ. 1922 W. R. INGE *Outspoken Essays* 2nd Ser. vii. An Eton boy. . . when asked why the sons of Eli turned out badly, replied 'The sons of clergymen always turn out badly'. 1982 B. PYM *Unsuitable Attachment* iii. Yes, sons of the clergy often go to the bad, and daughters, too. ■ **children and parents** 親子

clerk ⇒ The DEVIL makes his Christmas pies of lawyers' tongues and clerks' fingers.

A CLEVER hawk hides its claws.
能ある鷹は爪を隠す。

日本のことわざ。

□1994 S. NISON *Beyond Candlesticks* i. There is a Japanese saying, 'A clever hawk hides its claws.' For over a century, the claws of Japanese technical analysis, that is candlestick charts, were a secret hidden from the western world. 2007 J. HUIZENGA 'Ten Tips for Teaching English as a Foreign Language' on *www.transltionsabroad.com* In classrooms outside the U.S., however, showing solidarity with classmates. . . is often more important than looking good for the teacher. . . This holds true in Japan and China. . . where proverbs express the cultural idea in a nutshell:. . . 'The clever hawk hides its claws'. ■ **guile** 狡猾・策略

client ⇒ A man who is his own LAWYER has a fool for his client.

Climb ⇒ He that would EAT the fruit must climb the tree ; The HIGHER the monkey climbs the more he shows his tail.

Hasty CLIMBERS have sudden falls.
急いで登る者は急に落下する。

(訳注：「急いては事をし損じる」)

88 CLOGS

野心家は頂上を目指して急ぎ過ぎて、足を滑らせることが多い。

☐*a*1439 J. LYDGATE *Fall of Princes* (EETS) ill. 953 The wheel of Fortune tourneth as a ball; Sodeyn clymbyng axeth a sodeyn fall. *c*1511 S. HAWES *Comfort of Lovers* (1975) A4 Clymbe not to fast, lest sodenlye ye slyde. **1592** R. GREENE *Repentance in Works* XII. 158 For a yong man led on by selfe will....Hee forseath not that such as clime hastely fall sodainely. **1605** Capt. Thomas *Stukeley* DI But there are many daungers by the way, and hastie climers quicklie catch a fall. **1616** N. BRETON *Crossing of Proverbs* II. A4 Hasty climbers haue sodaine falles....Not if they sit fast. **1869** C. H. SPURGEON *John Ploughman's Talk* xix. Hints as to thriving....Hasty climbers have sudden falls. **1987** *Daily Telegraph* 27 Apr. 12 The ambition to send spaceships to the red planet reminds me of the old saying: 'Hasty climbers quickly catch a fall.' ■ **ambition** 野心・野望

From CLOGS to clogs is only three generations.
木靴から木靴まではわずか 3 世代である。

成り上がりの家は没落するのも早いというランカシャー地方の言い伝えに由来する。類似のことわざに From SHIRTSLEEVES to shirtsleeves in three generations.「シャツからシャツまではわずか 3 世代である」がある。木靴は厚い木製の靴底がついており、イングランド北部においてかつて工場や他の手工業の職人が履いていた。† **1700** ドライデン『寓話の中のバースの女房、今昔』493 Seldom three descents continue good.「3 世代が続けて繁栄することはめったにない」。**1721** ケリー『スコットランドことわざ集』312 The Father buys, the Son biggs [builds], The Grandchild sells, and his Son thiggs [begs].「父親が買い、子供が建て、孫が売る。最後にその子供 (ひ孫) が物乞いになる」

☐**1871** *Notes & Queries* 4th Ser. VII. 472 'From clogs to clogs is only three generations.' A Lancashire proverb, implying that, however rich a poor man may eventually become, his great-grandson will certainly fall back to poverty and 'clogs'. **1938** R. G. COLLINGWOOD *Principles of Art* V. But the poor, who are always the last guardians of a tradition, knew that the curse of God rested on idleness, and spoke of three generations from clogs to clogs. **1993** 'C. AIRD' *Going Concern* (1994) vii. 51 Claude Miller, Chairman and Managing Director of Chernwoods' Dyestuffs, was a living exemplification of the old saw about it being 'only three generations from clogs to clogs.' His father hadn't been the man his father was and, worse still, Oaude Miller wasn't even the man his father had been. ■ **family** 家族・家系 ; **poverty** 貧困

close ⇒ When ONE door shuts, another opens.

cloth ⇒ CUT your coat according to your cloth.

CLOTHES make the man.
衣装が人を作る。

(訳注 : the man =「立派な人」。「馬子にも衣装」)

† ギリシア語 εἵματα ἀνήρ.「人は服である。」エラスムス『格言集』*'Divitiae' vestis virum facit.*「衣装が人を作る」。**1626** ジョンソン『ニュースの源』I. ii. 3 Taylor makes the man.「仕立屋が人を作る」

☐*a*1400 *Prov. Wisdom* I. 59 in *Archiv* (1893) XC. 245 Euer maner and clothyngmakyth man. *c*1445 *Peter Idley's Instructions to his Son* (1935) 1. 82 Ffor clothyng oft maketh man. **1591** J. FLORIO *Second Fruits* 115 Though manners makes, yet apparel shapes. **1836** CARLYLE *Sartor* I.

COBBLER 89

V. Qothes gave us individuality, distinctions, social polity. Clothes have made men of us. 1933 J. HILTON *Lost Horizon* 3 Still, it did happen—and it goes some way to show that clothes make the man, doesn't it? 2001 *Washington Post* 17 Dec. Cl2 Gem of the day (credit Mark Twain): Clothes make the man. Naked people have little or no influence on society. ■ appearance, significant 重要な外見 ; dress 衣服

clothes ⇒ There is no such thing as BAD weather, only the wrong clothes.

Every CLOUD has a silver lining.
どんな雲にも銀の裏地がついている。

最も憂鬱に見える物の中にも希望の光、または慰めの面が含まれているという詩的感情を表す。† 1634 ミルトン『仮面劇コーマス』I. 93 Was I deceiv'd, or did a sable cloud Turn forth her silver lining on the night? 「私は騙されたのか、それとも黒雲が夜に裏地をめくって見せたのか」

☐ 1863 D. R. LOCKE *Struggles of P. V. Nasby* (1872) xxiii. Tuer is a silver linin to evry cloud. 1869 P. T. BARNUM *Struggles & Triumphs* 406 'Every cloud', says the proverb, 'has a silver lining.' 1991 T. MO *Redundancy of Courage* xxii. 283 This misfortune of hers had done wonders for our up and down relationship—all clouds have a silver lining, don't they say. 2002 *Spectator* 13 Apr. 74 Still, every cloud has a silver lining, and he was quiet for the rest of the meal, which is something of a delightful first. ■ optimism 楽観主義

clout ⇒ Ne'er CAST a clout till May be out.

clutch ⇒ A DROWNING man will clutch at a straw.

coat ⇒ CUT your coat according to your cloth.

Let the COBBLER stick to his last.
靴屋には己れの靴型に専念させよ。
(訳注：人は皆、自分の専門の仕事とかけ離れたことについて軽々しく判断を下すべきではない)

ギリシアの画家アペレス（紀元前 4 世紀）の言葉とされる。1721 年の用例参照。shoemaker「靴屋」を使った形式が英国のことわざでは伝統的であるが、今では主に北米で使われる。last「靴型」とは、靴屋が靴やブーツを作る際に用いる木製、または金属製の靴型のことである。† プリニウス『博物誌』xxxv. 85 *Ne supra crepidam sutor iudicaret.* 「靴屋は靴型を超えて判断すべきではない」。エラスムス『格言集』I. vi. 16 *Ne sutor ultra crepidam.* 「靴匠は靴型を超えてはならない」

☐ 1539 R. TAVERNER tr. *Erasmus' Adages* 17 Let not the shoemaker go beyond hys shoe. 1616 J. WITHALS *Dict.* (rev. ed.) 567 Cobler keepe your last. 1639 J. CLARKE *Parremiologia Anglo-Latina* 21 Cobler keepe to your last. 1721 J. KELLY *Scottish Proverbs* 242 Let not the Cobler go beyond his last....Taken from the famous Story of Apelles, who could not bear that the Cobler should correct any part of his Picture beyond the Slipper. 1868 W. CLIFT *Tim Bunker Papers* Iix. I understood the use of a plow...better than the use of a pen...remembering the old saw 'Let the cobbler stick to his last.' 1930 C. F. GREGG *Murder on Bus* xxx. Yet even then, Mapell had been mixed up with a gang of blackmailers. The shoemaker sticks to his last! 1984 A. MACLEAN *San Andreas* viii. Point taken, Mr. McKinnon. You see before you a rueful cobbler who will stick to

90 COBBLER

his last from now on. ■ **work 仕事**

The COBBLER to his last and the gunner to his linstock.
靴屋は靴型を、兵士は導火棹を守れ。

（訳注：人は各自の持ち場を守るべきで、他人の領域を侵してはならない）

１つ上のことわざに脚色を加えた言い方。「導火棹」は火のついたマッチを保つために熊手状の頭の形状をしている。

□**1748** SMOLLETT *Roderick Random* II. xiii. I meddle with no body's affairs but my own; The gunner to his linstock, and the steersman to the helm, as the saying is. **1893** H. MAXWELL *Life of W. H. Smith* II. v. He…never showed any disposition to trespass on the province of science or literature….There is sound sense in the adage, 'The cobbler to his last and the gunner to his linstock.' ■ **work 仕事**

cobbler ⇒ The SHOEMAKER'S son always goes barefoot.

Every COCK will crow upon his own dunghill.
どの雄鶏も自分の糞の山の上に立てば威勢よく時を告げる。

（訳注：「お山の大将」）

誰しも自分の本拠地にいるときは自信を持つものだ。†セネカ *Apocolocyntosis vii. gallus in suo sterquilinio plurimum posse.*「雄鶏は自分の糞の山の上にいるときが最も威勢がいい」。セネカの言葉には、ローマ皇帝クラウディウスの死後、彼を神として崇拝することに対する皮肉が込められている。ここで*gallus*には雄鶏と古代ガリア人という２つの意味があることから、セネカはクラウディウスが田舎出身であることと彼の権益とを駄洒落にしていることがうかがえる。

□*a*1250 *Ancrene Wisse* (1952) 62 Coe is kene [bold] on his owune mixerne [midden]. **1387** J. TREVISA tr. *Higden's Polychronicon* (1879) VIII. 5 As Seneca seith, a cok is most myghty on his dongehille. **1546** J. HEYWOOD *Dialogue of Proverbs* I. xi. D2 He was at home there, he myght speake his will. Euery cocke is proude on his owne dunghill. **1771** SMOLLETT *Humphry Clinker* II. 178 Insolence…akin to the arrogance of the village cock, who never crows but upon his own dunghill. **1935** D. L. SAYERS *Gaudy Night* xix. 'I believe you're showing off.'…'Every cock will crow upon his own dunghill.' **1980** M. GILBERT *Death of Favourite Girl* vii. Mariner seemed to be easy enough. A cock on his own dunghill. ■ **home 家庭・母国**

cock ⇒ There's many a GOOD cock come out of a tattered bag ; The ROBIN and the wren are God's cock and hen.

COLD hands, warm heart
手の冷たい人は心が暖かい。

科学的根拠のない一般的な民間伝承である（2008年の用例参照）。人の愛情や感情の暖かさは手の冷え具合から測定することはできないし、逆に温かい手が冷淡さを示すわけでもない。

□**1903** V. S. LEAN *Collectanea* III. 380 A cold hand and a warm heart. **1910** W. G. COLLINGWOOD *Dutch Agnes* 206 I did take her hand…Cold hand, warm heart! **1962** B. LININGTON *Knave of Hearts* xv. A hot, humid night, but her hands cold. Cold hands, warm heart. **1985** D. & S. ROSEN *Death & Blintzes* xxvi. 'Belle, your hands are cold,' he said. 'Cold hands, that's fun-

COMMON 91

ny?' 'You know the old saying, "cold hands, warm heart".' **2008** *Telegraph* 28 Oct. (online; heading) Cold hands, warm heart is a myth, scientists reveal. ■ **love 愛・恋愛**

cold ⇒ (名詞) As the DAY lengthens, so the cold strengthens ; FEED a cold and starve a fever ; (形容詞) REVENGE is a dish that can be eaten cold.

colour ⇒ A GOOD horse cannot be of a bad colour.

come ⇒ ALL things come to those who wait ; The BIGGER they are, the harder they fall ; Don't CROSS the bridge till you come to it ; EASY come, easy go ; Never do EVIL that good may come of it ; FIRST come, first served ; What GOES around comes around ; All is GRIST that comes to the mill ; LIGHT come, light go ; Come LIVE with me and you'll know me ; MARCH comes in like a lion, and goes out like a lamb ; If the MOUNTAIN will not come to Mahomet, Mahomet must go to the mountain ; When POVERTY comes in at the door, love flies out of the window ; QUICKLY come, quickly go ; When THIEVES fall out, honest men come by their own ; TOMORROW never comes.

comfort ⇒ CHILDREN are certain cares, but uncertain comforts.

COMING events cast their shadows before.
出来事の前には前兆がある。

将来起こる出来事には、その徴候が前もって感じ取れることがある。

□**1803** T. CAMPBELL *Poetical Works* (1907) 159 'Tis the sunset of life gives me mystical love, And coming events cast their shadows before. **1857** TROLLOPE *Barchester Towers* II. V. The coming event of Mr. Quiverful's transference to Barchester produced a delicious shadow in the shape of a new outfit for Mrs. Quiverful. **1979** N. LESSING *Shikasta* 231 'Coming events cast their shadows before.' This Shikastan [Earthly] observation was of particular appropriateness during an epoch when the tempo of events was so speeded up. ■ **future 未来**

command ⇒ He that cannot OBEY cannot command.

COMMON fame is seldom to blame.
世間の評判の方が間違っていることはめったにない。

（訳注：fame =【スコットランド英語】「評判」）

世間の一般的な評判といえども完全に間違っているわけではない。† **1597**ロック『さまざまなキリスト教徒の受難』149 Though prouerbe truely say, by fames affect, Gods iudgement lightly doth a truth detect.「ことわざが正しく言っているように、世間の評判に基づいて、神は真実を直ちに明らかにする」

□**1639** J. CLARKE *Parremiologia Anglo-Latina* 227 Common fame's seldome to blame. **1721** J. KELLY *Scottish Proverbs* 80 Common Fame sindle [seldom] to blame. A man will seldom be under an universal ill Report, unless he has given some occasion for it. **1853** R. C. TRENCH *Lessons in Proverbs* 13 Common fame is seldom to blame. **1936** R. A. J. WALLING *Corpse in Crimson Slippers* i. But though, as the proverb says, common fame is seldom to blame, don't believe everything you hear about me. ■ **public opinion 世論**

communication ⇒ EVIL communications corrupt good manners.

A man is known by the COMPANY he keeps.
人はつきあっている仲間で分かる。

元来は結婚相手を探す段階での道徳的格言あるいは訓戒であった。

□**1541** M. COVERDALE tr. *H. Bullinger's Christian State of Matrimony* F6 So maye much be spyed also, by the company and pastyme that a body vseth. For a man is for the moost parte condicioned euen tyke vnto them that he kepeth company wythe all. **1591** H. SMITH *Preparative to Marriage* 42 If a man can be known by nothing els, then he maye bee known by his companions. **1672** W. WYCHERLEY *Love in Wood* I. i. There is a Proverb, Mrs. Joyner, You may know him by his Company. **1912** 'SAKI' *Chronicles of Clovis* 286 (heading) A man is known by the company he keeps. **1976** L. ALTHER *Kinflicks* ii. People knew a man by the company he kept, but they generally knew a woman by the man who kept her. **2002** *Washington Times* 5 Feb. A19 Planned Parenthood denies that [Margaret] Sanger was a racist or an eugenicist, but there's truth to the adage that we are known by the company we keep. ■ **associates** 仲間

The COMPANY makes the feast.
仲間こそがご馳走である。

（訳注：「鯛も一人はうまからず」。「朋あり遠方より来る。亦楽しからずや」）

□**1653** I. WALTON *Compleat Angler* iii. Take this for a rule, you may pick out such times and such companies, that you may make yourselves merrier, ... for 'tis the company and not the charge [expense] that makes the feast. **1911** F. W. HACKWOOD *Good Cheer* xxxii. 'Epicurus maintained that you should rather have regard to the company with whom you eat ... than to what you eat. ... This has been crystallised into the terse English proverb, 'The company makes the feast.' **1981** 'J. STURROCK' *Suicide most Foul* vi. It is the company which makes the occasion, not the surroundings. ■ **friends** 友 ; **hospitality** もてなし

company ⇒ MISERY loves company ; TWO is company, but three is none.

COMPARISONS are odious.
比較されるのは嫌なもの。

比較をすることはたいていどちらか一方に（あるいは時に両方に）不利益をもたらす。†
14世紀初頭のフランス語 *Comparaisons sont hayneuses*.「比較は不愉快である」

□*c***1440** J. LYDGATE *Minor Poems* (EETS) 561 Odious of old been all comparisouns. **1456** Gilbert of Hay's Prose MS (STS) 282 I will nocht here mak questiounn ... quhy [why] that always comparisoun is odious. *c***1573** G. HARVEY *Letter-Book* (1884) 7 But thal wil sai, Comparisons ar odius: in deed, as it fals out, thal ar too odious. **1724** SWIFT *Drapier's Letters* X. 82 A Judge ... checked the Prisoner ... taxing him with 'reflecting on the court by such a Comparison, because Comparisons were odious'. **1939** G. MITCHELL *Printer's Error* ii. 'I will study the psychology of pigs instead of that of ... refugees.' 'Comparisons are odious.' Observed Carey. **2001** P. J. O'ROURKE *CEO of Sofa* v. 82 And poets? Comparisons being odious, only a comparison will do to illustrate the odium of modern poesy. ■ **similarity and dissimilarity** 類似性と相違性

He that COMPLIES against his will is of his own opinion still.
意志に反して従う者はまだ自分の意見を秘めたままである。

（訳注：he that/who ... ＝「〈…するところの〉者は〈誰でも〉」。He who laughs last laughs best.〈最後に笑う者がいちばんよく笑う〉）

CONSCIENCE 93

誰かに強制的に何かをさせることはできても、その人の考え方まで変えることはできない。

□ **1678** S. BUTLER *Hudibras* III. iii. He that complies against bis Will, Is of his own Opinion still; Which he may adhere to, yet disown, For Reasons to himself best known. **1965** M. SPARK *Mandelbaum Gate* v. No one should submit their mind to another mind: He that complies against his will Is of his own opinion still—that's my motto. I won't be brainwashed. **1985** G. V. HIGGINS *Penance for Jerry Kennedy* xiii. But Ed Maguire did what he did against his own convictions. And what they say is true…'A man convinced against his will is of the same opinion still.' ■ **free will and compulsion** 自由意志と強制

CONFESS and be hanged.
自白すると絞首刑にされてしまう。

(訳注：confess の形は命令形。「命令文＋and…」の構文で「…すれば…」の意味となる)

過ちや罪を白状することは、取り返しのつかないことになりかねない。

□ **1589** 'MISOPHONUS' *De Gaede Gallorum Regis* A2ᵛ Confesse and be hangede man In English some sale. **1604** SHAKESPEARE *Othello* IV. i. 37 Handkerchief—confessions—handkerchief! To confess, and be hanged for bis labour. **1672** MARVELL *Rehearsal Transprosed* 74 After so ample a Confession as he bath made, must he now be hang'd too to make good the Proverb? **1821** SCOTT *Pirate* III. xii. At the gallows!…Confess and be hanged is a most reverend proverb. **1951** M. C. BARNES *With all my Heart* vii. 'People who commit high treason get hanged.'…'Very well, confess and be hanged!' ■ **confession** 告白・懺悔

confessed ⇒ A FAULT confessed is half redressed.

CONFESSION is good for the soul.
懺悔(ざんげ)は心の安らぎである。

聖職者に自分の罪を正式に告白することはローマカトリックと他のキリスト教の伝統において要求されることであるが、このことわざはほとんどいつも皮肉を込めて使われる(1721年の用例参照)。

□ c**1641** in B. BEVERIDGE *D. Fergusson's Scottish Proverbs* (1924) no. 159 Ane open confessione is good for the soul. **1721** J. KELLY *Scottish Proverbs* 270 Open Confession is good for the Soul. Spoken ironically, to them that boast of their ill Deeds. **1881** J. PAYN *Grape from Thorn* III. xxxix. Confession may be good for the soul; but it is doubtful whether the avowal of incapacity to the parties desirous of securing our services is quite judicious. **1942** R. A. J. WALLING *Corpse with Eerie Eye* v. That's open confession, but I don't know that it does my soul any good. **1983** R. HILL *Deadheads* IV. iv. Confession may be good for the soul but it's pretty lousy for marriages. **2002** *Washington Times* 1 Sept D7 Confession may be good for the soul but not if it's being broadcast. ■ **confession** 告白・懺悔

A clean CONSCIENCE is a good pillow.
清らかな良心は安眠のための枕である。

清らかな良心の持ち主は、たとえ嵐の中でもぐっすり眠ることができるという考えは数多くの伝統的な表現によって表わされている。c**1605** シェイクスピア『マクベス』IV. i. 85 I may tell pale-hearted fear it lies, And sleep in spite of thunder. 「そうすれば蒼ざめた恐怖心など叱り飛ばし、雷鳴のなかでも安眠できよう」。†ドイツ語 *Gut Gewissen ist ein sanftes Ruhekissen.* 「清らかな良心は安眠のための枕である」。フランス語

Une conscience pure est un bon oreiller.「清らかな良心は安眠のための枕である」

□ **1721** J. KELLY *Scottish Proverbs* 14 A safe Conscience makes a sound Sleep. **1747** B. FRANK-LIN *Poor Richard's Almanack* (July) A quiet conscience sleeps in thunder. **1902** P. E. HULUME *Proverb Lore* 216 A good conscience makes an easy couch. **1929** 'P. OLDFELD' *Alchemy Murder* ii. 18 [The bed] was hard and cold, and he found poor comfort in a copybook maxim which came back vaguely to him-something about a good conscience providing the softest pillow for a weary head. **1992** MIEDER *Dict. American Proverbs* 112 A clean conscience is a good pillow. ■ **conscience 良心**

CONSCIENCE makes cowards of us all.
良心は誰をも臆病にする。

（訳注：make A of B ＝「B〈人・物〉を A〈状態・種類〉にする、変える」。*make* a friend *of* an enemy.〈敵を味方にする〉）

自責の念があると、正しい行ないをするときでさえ躊躇してしまう。cowards を cowboys に変えている 1912 年の用例はこのことわざの滑稽な誤用である。† **1594** シェイクスピア『リチャード 3 世』I. iv. 133 Where's thy conscience now? —I'll not meddle with it—it makes a man a coward.「良心はどこへ行った。あいつと関わりを持つのは危険だ。あいつは人を臆病にする」

□ **1600-1** SHAKESPEARE *Hamlet* III. i. 83 Conscience does make cowards of us all. **1697** VAN-BRUGH *Provoked Wife* v. 75 It mayn't be amiss to deferr the Marriage till you are sure they [mortgages] are paid off....Guilty Consciences make Men Cowards. **1912** 'SAKI' *Chronicles of Clouts* 134 The English have a proverb, 'Conscience makes cowboys of us all.' **1941** H. G. WELLS *You can't be too Careful* viii. 'Why doesn't he face it out?'...'Conscience makes cowards of us all, Whittaker.' **1976** J. S. SCOOT *Poor Old Lady's Dead* iv. There was something funny here. Bloody funny. So the Inspector, who lived, like any other policeman, with the sure knowledge that conscience doth make cowards of us all, began to lean. ■ **conscience 良心；cowardice 臆病**

conscience ⇒ A GUILTY conscience needs no accuser.

Consent ⇒ SILENCE means consent

CONSTANT dropping wears away a stone.
絶えず滴り落ちる水は石さえ穿つ。

（訳注：「継続こそ力なり」。「雨だれ石を穿つ」）

元来、辛抱強さは、困難な目的をも達成するという意味であった（ただし 1912 年の用例参照）。米国では continual「断続的な」が constant の代わりによく使われる。† サモスのコイリロス『断章』(Kinkel) πέτρην κοιλαίνει ρανίς ὕδατος ἐνδελεχείη.「水滴が何年も続くと石に穴をあける」。ティブルス『哀歌』I. iv.18 *Longa dies molli saxa peredit aqua.*「長い時間の間に、柔らかい水でも石に穴を開ける」

□ *a***1250** *Ancrene Wisse* (1962) 114 Lutle dropen thurleth (pierce) the flint the (that) ofte falleth theron. *c***1477** CAXTON *Jason* (EETS) 26 The stone is myned and holowed by contynuell drop-pyng of water. **1591** SHAKESPEARE *Henry VI*, Pt 3 III. ii. 50 He plies her hard; and much rain wears the marble. **1793** T. COKE *Extracts from Journals* III.ii.50 The Negroes of Barbadoes...are much less prepared for the reception of genuine religion. But constant dropping. 'tis said, will wear out a stone. **1841** DICKENS *Old Curiosity Shop* I. vii. As to Nell, constant dropping will wear away a stone, you know you may trust me as far as she is concerned. **1912** D. H. LAWLENCE *Let-*

COUNCILS 95

ter 19 Dec. (1962) I. 169 She says a woman can only have one husband....Constant dropping will wear away a stone, as my mother used to say. **1963** E. S. GARDNER *Case of Mischievous Doll* vii. The constant dripping water...can wear away the toughest stone. ■ **persistence** ねばり強さ

contempt ⇒ FAMILIARITY breeds contempt.

continual ⇒ CONSTANT dropping wears away a stone.

contrary ⇒ DREAMS go by contraries.

cook ⇒ GOD sends meat, but the Devil sends cooks ; TOO many cooks spoil the broth.

corn ⇒ A KING'S chaff is worth more than other men's corn.

CORPORATIONS have neither bodies to be punished nor souls to be damned.
法人には処罰される体もなければ、非難される魂もない。

大きな組織は民間人と違って、責任を問われる心配がないので、不正に振る舞ったり、高圧的に振る舞うことがある。

□**1658** E. BULSTRODE *Reports* II. 233 The opinion of Manwood, chief Baron [*c*1580], was this, as touching Corporations, that they were invisible, immortall, and that they had no soule; and therefore no Subpœma lieth against them, because they have no Conscience nor soule. *c*1820 J. POYNDER *Literary Extracts* (1844) I. 268 Lord Chancellor Thurlow said [*c*1775] that the corporations have neither bodies to be punished nor souls to be damned. *a*1845 S. SMITH in S. Holland *Memoir* (1855) I. xi. Why, you never expected justice from a company, did you? They have neither a soul to lose, nor a body to kick. **1932** ERNST & LINDEY *Hold your Tongue* xii. A corporation is just like any natural person, except that it has no pants to kick or soul to damn, and, by God, it ought to have both. ■ **business** ビジネス・商売; **conscience** 良心

corrupt ⇒ EVIL communications corrupt good manners ; POWER corrupts.

cost ⇒ CIVILITY costs nothing.

cough ⇒ LOVE and a cough cannot be hid.

COUNCILS of war never fight.
軍事会議は戦わない。

集団で議論している人々は慎重になり、個人ならやりかねないような類いの行動をする決定など下さないものだ。

□**1863** H. W. HALLECK *Telegram* 13 July (1877) III. 148 Act upon your own judgment and make your Generals execute your orders. Call no counsel [sic] of war. It is proverbial that counsels of war never fight. **1891** A. FORBES *Barracks, Bivouacs & Battles* 191 Solomon's adage that in the multitude of counselors there is wisdom does not apply to war. 'Councils of war never fight' has passed into a proverb. **1998** *Washington Times* 28 Sept. A21 A council of war never fights, and in a crisis the duty of a leader is to lead and not to take refuge behind the generally timid wisdom of a multitude of councilors. ■ **action and inaction** 行為と非行為; **decision and indecision** 決断と優

96　counsel

柔不断；warfare　戦争

counsel ⇒ A FOOL may give a wise man counsel ; NIGHT brings counsel.

Don't COUNT your chickens before they are hatched.
卵からかえる前にひよこを勘定するな。

(訳注：「取らぬ狸の皮算用」)

間違っているかもしれないような（都合がいい、あるいは楽観的な）仮定を立てたり、その仮定のもとで行動してはならない。†1532 ラブレー『パンタグリュエル』III. Xiii. *Ad praesens ova,eras pullis sunt meliora.*「今日の卵の方が明日の鶏よりよい」（法律家によって使われる一連のラテン語の決まり文句の１つである）。to count one's chickens は「都合の良い結果を前提にする」という意味の慣用句。

□ c1570 T. HOWELL *New Sonnets* C2 Counte not thy Chickens that vnhatched be. **1579** S. GOS-SON *Ephemerides of Phialo* 19 I woulde not haue him to counte his Chickens so soone before they be hatcht, nor tryumphe so long before the vlctorie. **1664** S. BUTLER Hudibras II. iii. To swallow Gudgeons ere th'are catch'd, And count their Chickens th'are hatch'd. **1829** SCOTT *Journal* 20 May (1946) 69 I see a fund…capable of extinguishing the debt…in ten years or earlier.…But we must not reckon our chickens before they are hatchd. **1964** RIDOUT & WIT-TING *English Proverbs Explained* 42 Mr. Smith hoped to be made manager before the end of the year.…'Don't count your chickens before they are hatched,' warned his wife. **2002** *New Scientist* 5 Jan. 17 Ultimately it's a question of how much oil is down there, and how quickly it can be extracted. No one really knows, but the geological evidence suggests that the US might be counting its chickens before they're hatched. ■ optimism 楽観主義

In the COUNTRY of the blind, the one-eyed man is king.
盲人の国では片目の男でも王になれる。

(訳注：the blind ＝「盲目の人々」。king の前に不定冠詞が付いていないのは、king を人でなく、役職と捉えているため。elect a person chairman〈人を議長に選ぶ〉の chairman の場合と同じである)

「愚かな人々の間では、少しでも知力があれば、その人は天才になれる」(T. フィールディング『世界ことわざ集』〈1824〉23)。知性に加えて、能力にも使われる。†エラスムス『格言集』III. iv. *In regione caecorum rex est luscus.*「盲人の王国では片目の男が王である」。

□ 1522 J. SKELTON Works (1843) II. 43 An one eyed man is Well syghted when He Is amonge blynde men. **1640** G. HERBERT *Outlandish Prouerbsno.* 469 In the kingdome of blind men the one ey'd is king. **1830** J. L. BURCKHARDT *Arabic Proverbs* 34 The one-eyed person is a beauty In the country of the blind. **1904** H. G. WELLS In *Strand* Apr. 405 Through his thoughts ran this old proverb…'In the Country of the Blind, the One-Eyed Man Is king.' **1937** W. H. SAUMAREZ SMITH *Letter* 7 Mar. In *Young Man's* Country (1977) ii. You exaggerate the alleged compliment paid to me by the Bengal Govt. In wanting to retain my services. 'In the country of the blind the one-eyed man is king.' **2002** B. MONAHAN *Sceptred Isle Club* i. 9 His success with crime-solving suggested an extraordinary Intelligence, but he could never know from his limited vantage point In provincial Brunswick whether he was merely the one-eyed man in the land of the blind and the Jekyl Island Club solution a fluke. ■ ignorance 無知・無学；rulers and ruled 支配者と被支配者

COW 97

Happy is the COUNTRY which has no history.
歴史を持たない国は幸せである。

スコットランドの批評家・歴史家 T. カーライルによると、フランスの政治哲学者モンテスキュー（1689-1755）に由来する（1864年の用例参照）。† **1740** B. フランクリン『哀れなリチャード年鑑』（2 月）Happy that Nation,—fortunate that age, whose history is not diverting.「歴史が変わらない国は幸せで、歴史が変わらない時代は幸運である」

☐**1807** T. JEFFERSON *Letter* 29 Mar. In Writings (1904) XL 182 Blest is that nation whose silent course of happiness furnishes nothing for history to say. **1860** G. BUOT Mill on Floss VI. iii The happiest women, like the happiest nations, have no history. **1864** CARLYLE *Frederick the Great* IV. XVI. i. Happy the people whose annals are blank in history. **1957** V. BRITTAIN *Testament of Experience* I. iv. Quoting the familiar dictum: 'Happy is the country which has no history,' I remarked that I belonged, like Edward VIII, to a generation which was still on the early side of middle age but had already seen almost more history than any generation could bear. **1981** *Nature* 23 Apr. 698 An old proverb...tells us that 'happy is the nation that has no history.' ...DNA...is the unhappiest of molecules, for it is the subject of innumerable biographies. ∎
blessings 恵み・（神の）恩恵 ; history 歴史

country ⇒ You can take the BOY out of the country but you can't take the country out of the boy ; The CITY for wealth, the country for health ; GOD made the country, and man made the town ; A NATION without a language is a nation without a heart ; OTHER times, other manners ; A PROPHET is not without honour save in his own country.

couple ⇒ A DEAF husband and a blind wife are always a happy couple.

The COURSE of true love never did run smooth.
真の愛の流れが平らに流れたためしはない。

（訳注：1595年の用例では、シェイクスピアの『真夏の夜の夢』の中で、ライサンダーが「本を読んだり…した限りでは、まことの恋が平穏無事に進んだためしはない」と述べている）

☐**1595** SHAKESPEARE *Midsummer Night's Dream* I. i. 134 For aught that I could ever read...The course of true love never did run smooth. **1836** M. SCOTT *Cruise of Midge* I. xi. 'The course of true love never did run smooth.' And the loves of Saunders Skelp and Jessy Miller were no exception to the rule. **1980** *Tablet* 26 Jan. 89 The course of true love could never run smooth with Sybylla's temperament. ∎ **love, blighted くじかれた**

course ⇒ HORSES for courses.

court ⇒ HOME is home, as the Devil said when he found himself in the Court of Session.

cover ⇒ （名詞）You can't tell a BOOK by its cover ; （動詞）CHARITY covers a multitude of sins.

Why buy a COW when milk is so cheap?
ミルクは安いのになぜわざわざ雌牛を買うのか。

（訳注：when =「…であるのに、…であるのにもかかわらず」〈対照・譲歩〉。How can he get high grades *when* he cuts classes so often?〈サボってばかりいるのにいい成績なんて取れるはずもない〉）

最も問題の少ない選択肢を選べという主張として、特に男が結婚するのに反対する際によく用いられる。修辞疑問文の形式をとる数少ないことわざの1つである。† Why KEEP a dog and bark yourself?「犬を飼っていながら、なぜわざわざ飼い主のあなたが吠えたりするのか」

☐1659 J. HOWELL *Proverbs* p. ii. It is better to buy a quart of Milk by the penny then keep a Cow. 1680 BUNYAN *Mr. Badman* 293 Who would keep a Cow of their own, that can have a quart of milk for a penny? Meaning, Who would be at the charge to have a Wife, that can have a Whore when he listeth [wishes]? 1942 S. ACRE *Yellow Overcoat* v. 'He ain't marryin'...any more!...'Why buy a cow when milk is so cheap, eh?' 1984 W. TEVIS *Color of Money* vi. 'I don't have a wife.' 'That's the best way. Why buy a cow when you can get milk free?' 2000 B. GUNN *Five Card Stud* iii.36 She said she thought people who wanted to live together 'ought to get married and be done with it' 'I don't want to be done with it.' Trudy said.'I want it to go on and on.' 'Fat chance of that. Men don't buy the cow if they can get the milk for—' ■ **marriage 結婚**

cow ⇒ A BELLOWING cow soon forgets her calf ; It is idle to SWALLOW the cow and choke on the tail ; THREE things are not to be trusted.

coward ⇒ A BULLY is always a coward ; CONSCIENCE makes cowards of us all

COWARDS die many times before their death.
臆病者は死ぬ前に何度も死ぬ。

(訳注：deathがdeathsと複数形になっていないのは『ジュリアス・シーザー』からの誤った引用である。そこでは、their deathsとなっている)

一般的に知られているこの形はシェイクスピアの誤った引用である（1599年の用例参照）。† 1596 ドレートン『モーテマー物語』SI Every houre he dyes, which ever feares.「彼は死ぬ度ごとに恐れる」。1927年の用例は劇作家の姓（Coward）とCowards「臆病者」の駄洒落。

☐1599 SHAKESPEARE *Julius Caesar* II. ii. 32 Cowards die many times before their deaths: The valiant never taste of death but once. 1800 M. EDGEWORTH *Castle Rackrent* p. xliv. In Ireland, not only cowards, but the brave 'die many times before their death.' 1927 *Sphere* 3 Dec. 414 It is true that cowards die many times before their death, and Noel Coward will come back again and again, and...win his niche among the great dramatists. ■ **cowardice 臆病**

The COWL does not make the monk.
僧帽を被っただけで修道士になれるわけではない。

(訳注：cowlの代わりにhabit、hoodなども使われる)

外見はその人物の本質を知るうえで信頼できる指針とはならない。† 中世ラテン語 *Cucullus non facit monachum*「僧帽が修道士を作るわけではない」。a1250『尼僧の戒律』(1962) 10 Her in is religiun, nawt i the wide hod ne i the blake cape.

☐1387 T. USK *Testament of Love in Chaucer Complete Works* (1897) II. xi. For habit maketh no monk; ne weringe of gilte spurres maketh no knight. 1613 SHAKESPEARE *Henry VIII* III.i. 23 They should be good men, their affairs as righteous; But all hoods make not monks. 1617 R. GREENE *Aleida* B3 The Hood makes not the Monke, nor the apparrell the man. 1820 SCOTT *Abbot* II. xi. 'Call me not doctor...since I have laid aside my furred gown and bonnet.'...'O, sir...the cowl makes not the monk.' 1891 G. B. SHAW *Music in London* (1932) I. 217 Such impostures are sure of support from the sort of people...who think that it is the cowl that makes

CRIME 99

the monk. **1940** 'S. ASHE' *I Am Saxon Ashe* 58'Darling — there is a Latin tag that runs: A cowl does not necessarily hide a monk. Let me vary it for you: the clown is not necessarily a fool.' ∎ **appearance, deceptive 偽りの外見**

cradle ⇒ The HAND that rocks the cradle rules the world.

A CREAKING door hangs longest.
きしる扉は長くちょうつがいに付いているものだ。
(訳注：「柳に雪折れなし」)

体の弱い人について、あるいは体の弱い人が、さらには体の弱い人に対して使われる場合が多い。ただし、欠陥のある物は長く迷惑でありつづけることを含意する場合もある。door「扉」の代わりに gate「門」が用いられることもある。

☐ **1776** T. COGAN *John Buncle, Junior* I. vi. They say a creaking gate goes the longest upon its hinges; that's my comfort. **1888** F. HUME *Madame Midas* II. ii. It is said that 'creaking doors hang the longest'. Mrs. Pulchop...was an excellent illustration of the truth of this saying. **1944** A. CHRISTIE *Towards Zero* 62 But it seems I am one of these creaking gates—these perpetual invalids who never die. **1970** L. DIDGHTON *Bomber* vi. The Flight Engineer said, 'A creaking door hangs longest' Digby christened her [anaeroplane] 'Creaking Door'. **1985** J. MORTIMER *Paradise Postponed* viii. I'll probably last like this another thirty years. I'll be a creaking gate...and they goes on swinging forever. ∎ **mortality 死すべき運命；old age 老年**

cream ⇒ There are more WAYS of killing a cat than choking it with cream.

Give CREDIT where credit is due.
栄誉を受けてしかるべき者には栄誉を与えよ。

古い言い方では、creditではなく honour（主に「尊敬、敬意」の意味）が使われていた。今では稀。†『ローマの信徒への手紙』xiii. 7（ランス）Render therefore to all men their due:...to whom honour, honour.「それゆえ、すべての人に報酬を与えよ。名誉ある人には名誉を与えよ」。

☐ **1777** S. ADAMS *Letter* 29 Oct in *Collections of Massachusetts Hist. Society* (1917) LXXII. 375 May Honor be given to whom Honor may be due. **1834** M. FLOY *Diary* 17 Jan. (1941) 50 Loudon must be a man of taste...and disposed to give all credit where any credit is due. **1894** *Girl's Own Paper* 6 Jan. 228 The justice and magnanimity which would show 'honour to whom honour is due'...is not always found equal to the occasion when it involves the granting of a degree. **1968** M. WOODHOUSE *Rock Baby* xxii. You aren't half as daft as I thought....Credit where credit's due. **1976** T. SHARPE *Wilt* viii. 'Some maniac....' 'Come now, give credit where credit is due,' interrupted Dr. Board. **2002** *Washington Post* 1 Jan. Cl4 Express your gratitude. Give credit when it's due—and even when it isn't. ∎ **fair dealing 公正な取引；just deserts 当然の報い**

CRIME doesn't pay.
犯罪は割りに合わない。

米国の犯罪撲滅運動のスローガンで、ラジオドラマの犯罪シリーズ *The Shadow* の最後の場面で毎回主人公によって語られる決め台詞でもある（1937年の用例参照）。また、漫画の探偵ディック・トレーシーの決まり文句でもあった（1954年の用例参照）。かなり最近になって、and neither does farming「そして農業も割に合わない」が付け加えられた。

100　crime

□**1892** *Catholic World* Dec. 364 Until our laws are so made and executed as to prove that crime doesn't pay…then only will religion and common-sense…work out the great plan of creation. **1905** *Harper's Weekly* 18 Feb. 231/2 If only Christopher had stuck to Sherlock Holmes it would have been impressed upon him that crime doesn't pay, and that the cleverest criminal gets caught. **1937** E. H. BIERSTADT *Shadow: Death House Rescue* 26 Sept. (script of radio broadcast) 18 The weed of crime bears bitter fruit.…Crime does not pay.…The Shadow knows.…(Laugh). **1954** S. BECKER *Comic Art in America* 5 Dick Tracy is the daddy of all cops-and-robbers strips, and Chester Gould…has been announcing to the world since 1931 that crime does not pay. **1959** *Times Literary Supplement* 12 June 356 War, like crime, may not pay, but that does not make the problem of preventing it any easier. **2001** *Country Life* 20/27 Dec 85 We hear of…David Steele's meanness (he was known as 'Crime' because he never bought a drink—'Crime doesn't pay'). ■ **action and consequence** 行為と結果

crime ⇒ POVERTY is not a crime.

crocodile ⇒ If you have to LIVE in the river, it is best to be friends with the crocodile ; No matter how long a LOG stays in the water….

crop ⇒ Good SEED makes a good crop.

Don't CROSS the bridge till you come to it.
橋を渡るのは橋のたもとに着いてからでいい。
（訳注：「来年のことを言うと鬼が笑う」）

将来起こるかもしれない問題は、その時がくるまで悩む必要はないという忠告。†Never TROUBLE trouble till trouble troubles you.「悩み事が汝を悩ませるまでは悩み事で悩むな」。現在では to cross one's bridges when one comes to them「その時になったら考える」という慣用句としても使われる。

□**1850** LONGFELLOW *Journal* 29 Apr. in *Life* (1886) II. 165 Remember the proverb, 'Do not cross the bridge till you come to it.' **1895** S. O. ADDY *Household Tales* xiv. One who anticipates difficulty is told not to cross the bridge till he gets to it. **1927** 'J. TAINE' *Quayle's Invention* xv. Why cross our bridges before we come to them? **1967** T. STOPPARD *Rosencrantz & Guildenstern are Dead* II. 43 We cross our bridges when we come to them and burn our bridges behind us, with nothing to show for our progress except a memory of the smell of smoke, and a presumption that once our eyes watered. ■ **trouble** やっかい・苦労

cross （名詞） ⇒ NO cross, no crown.

CROSSES are ladders that lead to heaven.
十字架は天国へ通じる梯子である。
（訳注：「艱難汝を玉にす」）

ここでの cross には 2 つの意味がある。1 つは「十字架」、もう 1 つは「苦難」である（訳注：No cross, no crown. 〈苦難なくして栄冠なし〉の場合では後者の意味で使われている）。

□**1616** T. DRAXE *Adages* 36 The Crosse Is the ladder of heauen. **1670** J. RAY *English Proverbs* 6 Crosses are ladders that do lead to heaven. **1859** S. SMILES *Self-Help* xi. If there be real worth in the character…it will give forth its finest fragrance when pressed. 'Crosses' says the old proverb, cup 101

'are ladders that lead to heaven.' 1975 J. O'FAOLAIN *Women in Wall* iv. The cross, they say, is the ladder to heaven and so I have sent your lordship…two. ■ misfortune 不運

crow ⇒（名詞）On the FIRST of March, the crows begin to search ; HAWKS will not pick out hawks' eyes ; ONE for the mouse, one for the crow ;（動詞）Every COCK will crow upon his own dunghill ; ⇒ CROWING.

crowd ⇒ You can't SHOUT 'Fire' in a crowded theatre ; TWO is company, but three is none.

crowing ⇒ A WHISTLING woman and a crowing hen are neither fit for God nor men.

crown ⇒（動詞）The END crowns the work ;（名詞）NO cross, no crown.

Don't CRY before you're hurt.
まだ怪我もしていないのに泣き叫ぶな。

怪我を負ってもいないのに大騒ぎをしてはならない。†14世紀初頭のフランス語 Follie *fait plorer deuant que on soit batu.*

□1548 *Reliquim Antique* (1843) II. 16 Ye may the better understand that I cry notbefore I am pricked. 1678 J. RAY *English Proverbs* (ed. 2) 237 You cry before you're hurt. 1721 J. KELLY *Scottish Proverbs* 204 It Is time enough to cry, Oh, when you are hurt. Spoken to dissuade People from groundless Fears. 1930 N. B. MAVITY *Other Bullet* xxviii. Don't cry out before you're hurt. 1981 J. WRIGHT *Devil's Parole* xvi. You mean…that one shouldn't cry before one is hurt. ■ cowardice 臆病 ; expectation 予期・期待

cry ⇒ MUCH cry and little wool ; SING before breakfast, cry before night.

It is no use CRYING over spilt milk.
こぼれたミルクを嘆いても仕方がない。

（訳注：「覆水盆に返らず」。なお、There is no use in… の言い方もある〈1884年の用例参照〉）

不備を改善しようにも手遅れになった場合は、後悔したり、嘆いても意味がない。

□1659 J. HOWELL *Proverbs* (British) 40 No weeping for shed milk. 1738 SWIFT *Polite Conversation* I. 27 'I would cry my Byes out'…"Tis a Folly to cry for spilt Milk.' 1884 J. PAYN *Canon's Ward* I. xv. There would be a row…but he would say, like a wise man, 'There's no use in crying over spilt milk.' 1936 M. DE LA ROCHE *Whiteoak Harvest* xxv. It's no use crying over spilt milk. The money's gone…and that's that. 2015 C. PRICE *Emotion* 54 In these cases [of grief, regret, etc.]…it is hard to see what use our emotional response could have, since it is now too late to affect the situation. After all, there is no use in crying over spilt milk. ■ misfortune 不運 ; past 過去・過ぎ去った

cup ⇒ FULL cup, steady hand ; The LAST drop makes the cup run over ; There's MANY a slip between cup and lip.

He that will to CUPAR maun to Cupar.
どうしてもクーパーに行こうとする者はクーパーに行かなければ気がすまない。

（訳注：he that/who... ＝「…するところの」者は〈だれでも〉。maun ＝【スコットランド英語】must。will と maun の後に動詞 go を補う）

クーパーはスコットランドのファイフにある町を指す。このことわざは忠告を無視して我を張ろうとする強情者に対する警告。中世におけるクーパーはファイフにおける司法の中心地であった。ゆえに、クーパーは愚かで向こう見ずな者、あるいは犯罪者が最後に行きつく場所であるという含意がある。

☐ **1721** J. KELLY *Scottish Proverbs* 141 He that will to Cowper [Cupar], will to Cowper. A Reflection upon obstinate Persons, that will not be reclaim'd. **1817** SCOTT *Rob Roy* III. i. The Hecate…ejaculated, 'A wilfu' man will hae his way—them that will to Cupar maun n[must] to Cupar!' **1893** R. L. STEVENSON *Catriona* xiii. He stood part of a second…, hesitating. 'He that will to Cupar, maun to Cupar,' said he, and…was hauled into the slclff. **1958** J. CANNAN *And be Villain* v. 'I shall take the first plane to Paris.'…'Well, he who will to Cupar maun to Cupar, but I think it's very silly of you.' ■ **obstinacy** 頑固さ

cure ⇒ NO cure, no pay ; PRBVBNTION is better than cure.

What can't be CURED must be endured.
治せないものなら耐えなければならない。

何かが修復できないときは辛抱せよという教え。† **1377** ラングランド『農夫ピアズ』B. x. 439 When must comes forward, there is nothing for it but to suffer.「義務が先行すれば、苦しむ以外に仕方がない」。c**1408** リドゲート『理性と官能性』(EETS) I. 4757 For thyng that may nat be eschiwed But of force mot be sywed [followed].「避けることのできないものについては、なんとしても従わなければならない」

☐ c**1579** SPENSER *Shepherd's Calendar* (Sept.) 88 And cleanly couer, that cannot be cured. Such ii, as is forced, mought nedes be endured. **1763** C. CHURCHILL *Prophecy of Famine* 18 Patience is sorrow's salve; what can't be cur'd, so Donald right areeds [counsels], must be endur'd. **1870** C. KINGSLEY *Madam How* i. That stupid resignation which some folks preach…is merely saying —what can't be cured, must be endured. **1936** W. HOLTBY *South Riding* VI. i. We all have our bad turns. What can't be cured must be endured, you know. **1997** *Washington Post* 18 Dec. Cl 'What cannot be cured must be endured,' the chained man says, trying to smile. But it comes out as a grimace. ■ **patience and impatience** 忍耐と性急

CURIOSITY killed the cat.
詮索好きは猫も殺した。

自分に関係のないことを詮索してはならないという警告。

☐ **1921** E. O'NEILL *Different* II. 252 'What'd you ask 'em, for instance?'…'Curiosity killed a cat! Ask me no questions and I'll tell you no lies.' **1973** A. CHRISTIE *Pastern of Fate* I. iv. 'A curiosity death,' said Tommy. 'Curiosity killed the cat' **1984** J. R. RIGGS *Last Laugh* Iii. 'I'm curious, that's all.' 'Curiosity killed old tom.' **2002** *Times 2* 17 May 9 'Well, you've probably heard the saying, "curiosity killed the cat". Well that's what I'm doing here.' For one horrible minute, I thought that he was about to…reveal that he was Ben Vol-au-Vent from Curiosity Killed the Cat, killing a cat. ■ **curiosity** 詮索好き・好奇心

CUT 103

curried (combed) ⇒ A SHORT horse is soon curried.

curse (動詞) ⇒ BETTER to light one candle than to curse the darkness.

CURSES, like chickens, come home to roost.
呪いは雛鳥のようにねぐらに戻るものだ。

呪いはしばしば呪った人の元に戻る。2001年の用例が示すように、呪いに関して特に言及しない場合もある。

□*c*1390 CHAUCER *Parson's Tale* l. 620 And ofte tyme swich cursynge wrongfully retometh agayn to hym that curseth, as a bryd that retometh agayn to his owene nest. **1810** SOUTHEY *Kehama (title-page)* Curses are like young chicken; they always come home to roost. **1880** S. SMILES *Duty* iv. Their injustice will return upon them. Curses, like chickens, come home to roost. **1932** S. GIBBONS *Cold Comfort Farm* vii. Curses, like rookses, flies home to nest in bosomses and baroses. **1986** *Washington Post* 10 July A23 The proverb teaches us that 'curses, like chickens, come home to roost.' The Supreme Court taught that lesson one more time last week in an opinion that combined bad law with rough justice. **2001** *Spectator* 8 Dec. 71 The Brits used diplomatic language which is as useless as the Draft Dodger's oath in a court of law. As they say down on the farm, the chickens have come home to roost. ■ **malice** 悪意・恨み ; **retribution** 当然の報い

The CUSTOMER is always right.
客こそがつねに正義である。

サービス産業に従事する従業員向けのスローガン。1905年と1980年の用例は、このことわざが米国の小売業界における二大巨大企業に由来することを示している。1917年の用例におけるフランス語版 (The customer is never wrong.「客は決して間違っていない」) は、スイスのホテル経営者セザール・リッツ (1850-1918) の言葉に由来する。彼はパリとロンドンにあるリッツホテルの創設者である。

□**1905** *Boston Daily Globe* 24 Sept. Mr Field adheres to the theory that 'the customer is always right.' **1914** Mill Supplies IV. ix. 45 (heading) Successful Salesmanship: Is the Customer Always Right? **1917** B. PAIN *Confessions of Alphonse* iii. The great success of a restaurant is built up on this principle—*le patron n'a jamais tort*—the customer is always in the right! **1941** D. LODGE *Death & Taxes* ii. 'I'm drunk.'…'You shouldn't do it, George.' 'Business,' he said solemnly. 'The customer is always right.' **1980** *Times* 30 Sept. 9 That the customer is always right is a theory attributed to John Wanamaker, the American retail prince who founded the stores which bear his name. **2001** *Washington Times* 3 Sept. Al2 The old man wasn't much on theory, but he understood value received, good will, repeat business, that the customer is always right and above all the importance of a trusted brand. ■ **buying and selling** 売買

Don't CUT off your nose to spite your face.
顔に腹を立てて鼻を切り落とすな。
（訳注：「短気は損気」）

自分を傷つけたり、自分の損になるような行為をしてはならない。慣用句 to cut off one's nose to spite one's face「腹立ちまぎれに自分に損になることをする」もよく使われる。†中世ラテン語 *Male ulciscitur dedecus sibi illatum, qui amputat nasum suum.*「自分の鼻を切り落とす者は被った恥のために哀れな復讐をする者である」。14世紀中頃のフランス語 *Qui cope son nes, saface est despechie.*「自分の鼻を切り落とす

ような男は自分の顔を嫌っている男である」

□*c*1560 *Deceit of Women* II He that byteth hys nose of, shameth hys face. **1788** F. GROSE *Dict. Vulgar Tongue* (ed. 2) U3ᵛ He cut off his nose to be revenged of his face, said of one who, to be revenged of his neighbour, has materially injured himself. **1889** R. L. STEVENSON *Master of Ballantrae* x. He was in that humour when a man—in the words of the old adage will cut off his nose to spite his face. **1964** RIDOUT & WITTING *English Proverbs Explained* 43 Don't cut off your nose to spite your face. **1980** A. CRAIG *Pint of Murder* vi. So the next thing anybody knew she'd run off an' married that no-good Bob Bascom an' if that ain't cuttin' off your nose to spite your face, I'd like to know what is. ■ malice 悪意・恨み ; revenge 復讐

CUT your coat according to your cloth.
衣服は布に応じて裁て。

（訳注：cut は「〈衣服を〉裁断する」の意。The jacket was cut too long.〈その上着の仕立ては長過ぎた〉）

振る舞いは自分の生活状態や資力にふさわしくなければならない。慣用句 to cut one's coat according to one's cloth「収入に合った暮らしをする」もよく使われる。

□**1546** J. HEYWOOD *Dialogue of Proverbs* I. viii. Cl I shall Cut my cote after my cloth. **1580** LYLY *Euphues & his England* II. 188 Be neither prodigall to spende all, nor couetous to keepe all, cut thy coat according to thy cloth. **1778** G. WASHINGTON *Writings* (1936) XIII. 79 General Mclntoch...must...yield to necessity; that is, to use a vulgar phraze, 'shape his Coat according to his Cloth'. **1951** 'P. WENTWORTH' *Miss Silver comes to Stay* xxxvii. 'You must cut your coat according to your cloth.'...'My trouble is that I do like the most expensive cloth.' **2014** *Australian* 7 June (online) [T]here are very few ways of raising serious additional revenue that do not involve significant economic costs. Cutting your coat according to your cloth is a message we can all understand. ■ circumstances 状況 ; poverty 貧困 ; thrift 質素倹約

cut ⇒（過去分詞の形容詞的用法）A SLICE off a cut loaf isn't missed ;（動詞）DIAMOND cuts diamond ; MEASURE seven times, cut once ; MEASURE twice, cut once ; THINK twice, cut once.

D

daisy ⇒ It is not SPRING until you can plant your foot upon twelve daisies.

damned ⇒ CORPORATIONS have neither bodies to be punished nor souls to be damned.

They that DANCE must pay the fiddler.
踊る者こそがバイオリン弾きの報酬を払わなければならない。

（訳注：they that…は「…する人々」の意。*They that* live longest must die at last.〈生者必滅〉）

娯楽やサービスには報酬を支払う必要がある。†米国では He who PAYS the piper calls the tune.「笛吹きに演奏代を払う者が曲を決める」のように強調語句が逆転する場合もある。

□**1638** J. TAYLOR *Taylor's Feast In Works* (1876) 94 One of the Fidlers said, Gentlemen, I pray you to remember the Musicke [musicians], you have given us nothing yet...Alwayes those that dance must pay the Musicke. **1837** A. LINCOLN *Speech* 11 Jan. In Works (1953) I. 64 I am decidedly opposed to the people's money being used to pay the fiddler. It is an old maxim and a very sound one, that he that dances should always pay the fiddler. *a***1957** L. I. WILDER *First Four Years* (1971) i. Laura was going to have a baby....She remembered a saying of her mother's: 'They that dance must pay the fiddler.' ■ **action and consequence 行為と結果**

dance ⇒ He that LIVES in hope dances to an ill tune ; If you can WALK you can dance....

danger ⇒ The post of HONOUR is the post of danger ; OUT of debt, out of danger.

dangerous ⇒ DELAYS are dangerous ; A LITTLE knowledge is a dangerous thing.

dark ⇒ All CATS are grey in the dark.

The DARKEST hour is just before the dawn.
夜明けの直前こそが最も暗い時間帯である。

最も危険で絶望的な時といえども、それは物事が良い方向に向かう直前である。†When THINGS are at the worst they begin to mend.「物事は最悪のときに好転しはじめる」

□**1650** T. FULIER *Pisgah Sight* II. xi. It is always darkest just before the Day dawneth. **1760** In J. Wesley *Journal* (1913) IV. 498 It is usually darkest before day break. You shall shortly find pardon. **1897** J. MCCARTHY *Hist. our Own Times* V. iii. Ayoob Khan now laid siege to

106 darkness

Candahar....As so often happens In the story of England's struggles In India, the darkest hour proved to be that just before the dawn. **2002** *Washington Times* 4 Feb. B5 It is always darkest before the dawn, the old saying. goes, and often a declarer reaches a dark point during the early play that precedes his ultimate step toward victory. ■ **hope and despair 希望と絶望**

darkness ⇒ BETTER to light one candle than to curse the darkness.

darling ⇒ BETTER be an old man's darling. than a young man's slave.

daughter ⇒ Like FATHER, like son ; Like MOTHER, like daughter ; My SON is my son till he gets him a wife, but my daughter's my daughter all the days of her life.

dawn ⇒ The DARKEST hour is just before the dawn.

As the DAY lengthens, so the cold strengthens.
日が長くなるにつれて寒さも強まる。

冬至を過ぎると日は長くなるが、気温は下がっていく。

□**1631** E. PELLHAM *God's Power* 27 The New Year now begun, as the Days began to lengthen, so the Cold began to strengthen. **1639** J. CLARKE *Paræmiologia Anglo-Latina* 18 As the day lengthens so the cold strengthens. **1899** A. WEST *Recollections* II. xxi. The weather at this time was bearing out the old adage and the cold strengthened as the days lengthened. **1978** R. WHIT-LOCK *Calendar of Country Customs* iii. As the day lengthens, So the cold strengthens, is still a well-known country proverb, applicable to January and early February. **2015** *Times* 15 Jan. 60 Long after the shortest day, the coldest day of the year usually comes In January or February-as an old saying goes, 'The cold grows stronger as the days grow longer'. This lag between the shortest day and the coldest day is the result of the seas around Britain. ■ **weather lore 天気にまつわる伝承**

Be the DAY weary or be the day long, at last it ringeth to evensong.
一日がどんなに辛かろうが長かろうが、ついには夕べの祈りの鐘が鳴る。

(訳注：ringeth = rings)

一日がどんなに疲れ果てたものであっても、最後には終わりがくる。機械時計が出現する前は、教会や修道院の夕べの祈り（evensong）を告げる鐘の音が労働時間の終わりを示していた。

□**1509** S. HAWES *Pastime of Pleasure* xlii. R8ᵛ For thoughe the day, be neuer so longe, At last the belles ryngeth to euensonge. **1612** T. ADAMS *Gallant's Burden* 20 If you could indent with the Sunne to stand still...yet it shall sette: Be the day never so long, at length comes evensong. **1732** T. FULLER *Gnomologia* no. 6132 Be the day never so long, At length cometh Even-song. **1935** 'J. J. CONNINGTON' *In whose Dim Shadow* xv. '"Be the day weary or be the day long, At last it rin-geth to evensong",' quoted the Chief Constable. **1969** N. HALE *Life in Studio* 120 Be the day short or be the day long, At length it cometh to evensong. ■ **perseverance 我慢強さ**

One DAY honey, one day onion.
蜂蜜を食べる日もあれば、玉葱を食べる日もある。

人生には浮き沈みがあるというアラビアの教え。

1979 A. DUNCAN *Money Rush* 129 You get all sorts of figures in this country...one day honey, another onion. **2000** D. CARMI *Samir and Yonatan* 90 It's like the saying, 'One day honey, one day onion.' **2003** A. HARTLEY *Zanzibar Chest* 136 He lived long enough to be philosophical about the ups and downs and said, 'One day honey, one day an onion.' **2006** M. K. NYDELL *Understanding Arabs* 102 The world is changeable, one day honey and the next day onions. (This rhymes in Arabic.) ■ fate and fatalism 運命と運命論

day ⇒ ANOTHER day, another dollar ; An APPLE a day keeps the doctor away ; BARNABY bright, Barnaby bright, the longest day and the shortest night ; BETTER a century of tyranny than one day of chaos ; The BETTER the day, the better the deed ; BETTER to live one day as a tiger...; Every DOG has his day ; Feed a DOG for three days and he will remember your kindness for three years...; FAIR and softly goes far in a day ; FISH and guests smell after three days ; OTHER times, other manners ; ROME was not built in a day ; My SON is my son till he gets him a wife, but my daughter's my daughter all the days of her life ; SUFFICIENT unto the day is the evil thereof ; TOMORROW is another day.

Let the DEAD bury the dead.
死者に死者を葬らせよ。
(訳注：the dead ＝「死者」。*the sick*「病人」)

手の施しようのない人たちは同じ状態にある他の人たちの手にゆだねるべきである。『マタイによる福音書』8 章22節（欽定訳聖書）Jesus said unto him, Follow me; and let the dead bury their dead.「イエスは仰せになった。わたしに従いなさい。死者は死者に葬らせなさい」。これは、父親の埋葬に出席しなければならなかったため、イエスにすぐに従えなかったという言い訳をした、イエスの弟子になり得る者に対する言葉である。

a1815 L. DOW *Hist. Cosmopolite* (1859) 340 A religious bigot made a motion to mob me; but none would second it A worldling replied to him, 'Let the dead bury their dead.' **1931** J. S. HUXLEY *What dare I Think?* vi. Let, then, the dead bury the dead. The task for us is to rejuvenate ourselves and our subject. **1997** *Spectator* 8 Nov. 28 There is something repellent, as well as profoundly unhistorical, about judging the past by the standards or prejudices of another age. Let the dead bury the dead. ■ death 死

DEAD men don't bite.
死者はかみつかない。

自分の身を守る最も確かな方法は危険人物を抹殺することである。† DEAD men tell no tales.「死人に口なし」。この言葉はプルタルコスがテオドトスに語らせたものであった。テオドトスは修辞学の教師で、エジプト人にローマ帝国の将軍ポンペイを殺害するように忠告した。ポンペイは紀元前48年のファルサリアの戦いで敗北した後、エジプトに避難場所を探しに来たのである。プルタルコス『ポンペイ』lxxvii. νεκρὸς οὐ δάκνει.「死者はかみつかない」。†エラスムス『格言集』III. vi. *Mortui non mordent.*「死者はかみつかない」

a1547 E. HALL *Chronicle* (1548) Hen. VI 92ᵛ A prouerbe...saith, a dead man doth no harme: Sir John Mortimer...was attainted [convicted] of treason and put to execucion. **1655** T. FULLER *Church Hist Britain* IX. iv. The dead did not bite; and, being dispatch'd out of the way, are forgotten. **1883** R. L. STEVENSON *Treasure Island* xi. 'What are we to do with 'em anyway?...Cut 'em down like that much pork?'...'Dead men don't bite,' says he. **1902** A. LANG *Hist Scotland* II. xii. The story that Gray 'whispered in Elizabeth's ear, The dead don't bite', is found in Camden. **1957** L. REVELL *See Rome & Die* xvi. A dead man cannot bite, as it says somewhere in Plutarch. Pompey's murderers, I think. Anyhow, that was the way their minds worked then. ■ **revenge** 復讐

DEAD men tell no tales.
死人に口なし。

死者は秘密を漏らさない（死んでくれればもう安全である）。類似した意図のものに DEAD men don't bite.「死者はかみつかない」がある。† **1560** ベーコン『作品集』II.97 He that hath his body loden with meat and drinke is no more mete to prai vnto god then a dead man is to tel a tale.「体が肉と酒でいっぱいの者は、死人が語ることができないのと同じく、神への祈りにふさわしくない」

□ **1664** J. WILSON *Andronicus Comnenius* I. iv. 'Twere best To knock 'um i' th' head....The dead can tell no tales. **1702** G. FARQUHAR *Inconstant* v. 76 Ay, ay, Dead Men tell no Tales. **1850** C. KINGSLEY *Alton Locke* I. iv. Where are the stories of those who have...ended in desperation?...Dead men tell no tales. **2001** S. KENDRICK *Night Watch* iv. 159 Dead men tell no tales. But their bodies sometimes do. ■ **revenge** 復讐；**speech and silence** 発言と沈黙

Blessed are the DEAD that the rain rains on.
雨に降られる死者は幸いである。

（訳注：日頃の心掛けの良い者は葬式の時に雨が降る。このことわざの文体は『マタイによる福音書』の山上の垂訓を想起させる）

類似の民間伝承には Happy is the BRIDE that the sun shines on.「太陽が降り注ぐ花嫁は幸いである」がある。

□ **1607** *Puritan* I. i. If, Blessed bee the coarse [corpse] the raine raynes vpon, he had it, powring downe. **1787** P. GROSE *Provincial Glossary* (Superstitions) 61 It is...esteemed a good sign if it rains whilst a corpse is burying:...Happy is the corpse that the rain rains on. **1925** F. S. FITZGERALD *Great Gatsby* 210 I could only remember, without resentment, that Daisy hadn't sent a message or a flower. Dimly I heard someone murmur, 'Blessed are the dead that the rain falls on.' ■ **blessings** 恵み・(神の)恩恵；**death** 死

dead ⇒ The only GOOD Indian is a dead Indian；It's ILL waiting for dead men's shoes；A LIVE dog is better than a dead lion；Never SPEAK ill of the dead；STONE-dead hath no fellow；THREE may keep a secret, if two of them are dead.

deadly ⇒ The FEMALE of the species is more deadly than the male.

There's none so DEAF as those who will not hear.
聞こうとしない者ほど耳の聞こえない者はいない。

（訳注：those＝「〈関係節を伴って〉…する人々、…の者たち」〈they〉。People who live in the countryside stay healthier than *those who* live in urban areas.〈田舎に住んでいる人々は都市部に住んでいる人々よりも健康に過ごしている〉。「心ここにあらざれば聞けども聞こえず」）

言われたことを意図的に無視する人は完全に耳の聞こえない人のようなものだ。類似のものに There's none so BLIND as those who will not see.「見ようとしない者ほどに

DEATH 109

目の見えない者はいない」がある。†14世紀中頃のフランス語 *Il n'est si mavais sours que cliuis ch'oër ne voeilt*.「聞きたがらない人ほど耳の聞こえない人はいない」

□**1546** J. HEYWOOD *Dialogue of Proverbs* 11. ix. K4 Who is so deafe, or so blynde, as is hee, That wilfully will nother here nor see? *c***1570** T. INGELEND *Disobedient Child* C2ᵛ I perceyve by thys geare, That none is so deaf, as who wyll not heare. **1766** in B. FRANKLIN *Papers* (1969) XIII. 18 I have not interfered in this Trial one word, only in my Applications to you and Mr. Foxcraft, both of which turn a deaf Ear: for none so deaf as those who will not hear. **1993** F. SECOMBE 'Hello, Vicar!' in *Chronicles of a Vicar* (1999) i. 8 'Don't worry, Vicar. Of course you've got to be up at the parish church more than here. He ought to know that but there you are, there's none so deaf as him who won't listen.' ■ **obstinacy** 頑固さ

A DEAF husband and a blind wife are always a happy couple.
耳の聞こえない夫と目の見えない妻はすべて幸せな夫婦である。

妻の小言が聞こえず、夫の欠点が見えない夫婦は互いに心満たされるであろう。

□**1578** J. FLORIO *First Fruits* 26 There neuer shal be chiding in that house, where the man is blynd, and the wife deafe. **1637** T. HEYWOOD *Pleasant Dialogues* VI. 334 Then marriage may be said to be past in all quietnesse, When the wife is blind, and the husband deafe. **1940** H. W. THOMPSON *Body, Boots & Britches* xix. When the wooing is o'er and the maid wed...the neighbours will observe...'A deaf husband and a blind wife are always a happy couple.' **1988** *Washington Times* 8 July B2 Nothing brings out advice mongers like a summer wedding....'A deaf husband and a blind wife are always a happy couple.' ■ **harmony and disharmony** 調和と不調和；**marriage** 結婚

dear ⇒ EXPERIENCE keeps a dear school ; GOLD may be bought too dear.

DEATH is the great leveler.
死は万人を平等にする。

（訳注：leveller＝「平等にする者」）

地位や富などのあらゆる差も死とともに消え去る。†クラウディウス『ペルセポネの略奪』II. 302 *Omnia mors aequat*.「死はすべてを平等にする」

□**1732** T. FULLER *Gnomologia* no. 1250 Death is the grand leveller. **1755** E. YOUNG *Centaur* ii. Is diversion grown a leveller, like death? **1961** M. DICKENS *Heart of London* I. 101 'All this is going to be a great leveller.'...'It is death which is the great leveller.' **1973** 'C. AIRD' *His Burial Too* vi. Dr. Dabbe took a last look....'A classic case, you might say, Sloan, of Death, the Great Leveller.' ■ **death** 死

DEATH pays all debts.
死はすべての借金を支払う。

借金と義務は死によってすべて帳消しにされる。†1597-8 シェイクスピア『ヘンリー4世』Pt. 1 III. ii. 157 The end of life cancels all bands [bonds].「死をもって償います。この誓約を一言半句でも破るくらいなら」

□**1611** SHAKESPEARE *Tempest* III. ii. 126 He that dies pays all debts. **1827** SCOTT *Two Drovers* in *Chronicles of Canongate* I. xiv. 'It must be sorely answered.'...'Never you mind that Death pays all debts; it will pay that too.' **1979** K. BONFIGLION *After You* xvi. I have no particular objection to death as such; it pays all bills. **1991** G. KEILLOR *WLT: Radio Romance* xii. I am not responsible anymore. Death pays all debts. Fix the damn furnace yourself. ■ **death** 死

110 death

death ⇒ COWARDS die many times before their death ; NOTHING is certain but death and taxes ; There is a REMEDY for everything except death.

debt ⇒ DEATH pays all debts ; OUT of debt, out of danger ; SPEAK not of my debts unless you mean to pay them.

deceive ⇒ FOOL me once, shame on you…

deceptive ⇒ APPEARANCES are deceptive.

deed ⇒ The BETTER the day, the better the deed ; No GOOD deed goes unpunished.

deep ⇒ STILL waters run deep.

defence ⇒ ATTACK is the best form of defence.

The best DEFENSE is a good offense.
最善の防御は効果的な攻撃となる。

通常の米国版は ATTACK is the best form of defence.「攻撃こそ最善の防御」である。また A good offense is the best defense.「効果的な攻撃は最善の防御である」と逆さにすることもある。

☐1989 *Washington Times* 13 Sept C9 The reigning corporate strategy these days is that the best defense is a good offense. **1992** MIEDER *Dict. Of American Proverbs* 436 A good offense is the best defense. **2002** *Washington Times* 6 Apr. B2 There is a saying. 'The best defense is a good offense. 'Your sister-in-law's behavior was an example of that. ■ **boldness 大胆さ ; warfare 戦争**

deferred ⇒ HOPE deferred makes the heart sick.

defiled ⇒ He that TOUCHES pitch shall be defiled.

delayed ⇒ JUSTICE delayed is justice denied.

DELAYS are dangerous.
遅れは危険である。

† *c*1300 ハヴェロック (1915) I. 1352 Dwelling haueth ofte scathe [harm] wrouht.「遅れはしばしば危険をもたらす」

☐**1578** LYLY *Euphues* I. 212 Delayes breed daungers, nothing so perillous as procrastination. **1655** J. SHIRLEY *Gentlemen of Venice* v. 62 Shall we go presently [immediately], delaies are dangerous. **1824** J. FAIRFIELD *Letters* (1922) p. xxxi. I have always found on all subjects that 'delays are dangerous'….It Is expedient that we marry young. **1930** B. FLYNN *Murder en Route* xxxiii. What a pity Master Hector left It too late….Delays are proverbially dangerous. ■ **action and inaction 行為と非行為 ; procrastination 先延ばし**

DEVIL 111

delved ⇒ When ADAM delved and Eve span, who was then the gentleman?

denied ⇒ JUSTICE delayed is justice denied.

Derbyshire ⇒ YORKSHIRE born and Yorkshire bred, strong in the arm and weak in the head.

deserve ⇒ None but the BRAVE deserve the fair ; A CIVIL question deserves a civil answer ; One GOOD turn deserves another.

DESPERATE diseases must have desperate remedies.
絶望的な病には荒療治を施さなければならない。

> 極限状態を解決するためには極端な手段が必要となる。多くの形がある。†ラテン語 *Extremis malis extrema remedia*.「重病には荒療治が必要である」

□**1539** R. TAVERNER tr. *Erasmus' Adages* 4 A strange disease requyreth a strange medicine. **1601** SHAKESPEARE *Hamlet* IV. Ill. 9 Diseases desperate grown By desperate appliance are rel-lev'd, Or not at all. **1659** J. RUSHWORTH *Hist. Collections* I. 120 According to the usual Proverb; A desperate disease must have a desperate remedy. **1748** RICHARDSON *Clarissa* VI. 292 I must...have an interview with the charmer of my Soul: For desperate diseases must have desperate remedies. **1935** 'A. WYNNE' *Toll House Murder* ix. These circumstances are wholly exceptional. Desperate diseases, they say, call for desperate remedies. **1961** 'A. GILBERT' *She shall Die* xl. She'd have sold the roof over her head sooner than have you know. Desperate situations require desperate remedies. **2001** W. NORTHCUTT *Darwin Awards* 112 Desperate times call for desperate measures, which are often sensible when you consider the bleak alternative. ■ **necessity** 必要性

destiny ⇒ HANGING and wiving go by destiny.

destroy ⇒ Whom the GODS would destroy, they first make mad.

details ⇒ The DEVIL is in the details.

The DEVIL can quote Scripture for his own ends.
悪魔も自分の都合で聖句を引くこともある。

> 悪賢くて偽善的な人は自分の政策に対する支持を訴えるために聖書を引用することすらある。このことわざは悪魔によるキリストの誘惑を想起させる（『マタイによる福音書』4章6節）。『マタイによる福音書』は『詩篇』91篇からこの一節を引用している。

□**1596** SHAEKSPEARE *Merchant of Venice* I. iii. 93 The devil can cite Scripture for his purpose. An evil soul producing holy witness Is like a villain with a smiling cheek. **1761** C. CHURCHILL *Apology* 15 Thus Candour's maxims flow from Rancour's throat, As devils, to serve their purpose, Scripture quote. **1843** DICKENS *Martin Chuzzlewlt* xi. Is any one surprised at Mr. Jonas making such a reference to such a book for such a purpose? Does any one doubt the old saw that the Devil (being a layman) quotes Scripture for his own ends. **1937** 'C. DICKSON' *Ten Teacups* xiii. The versatile personage in our popular proverbs, who...quotes Scripture for his own ends. **1997** *Washington Times* 25 July A4 The devil can quote Scripture, as we all know, so why not a politician? ■ **good and evil** 正邪；**hypocrisy** 偽善

The DEVIL finds work for idle hands to do.
悪魔は何もしないで怠けている手に仕事を見つけるものだ。

（訳注：「小人閑居して不善をなす」）

聖ヒエロニムス『手紙』cxxv. xi. *Jae et aliquid operis,ut semper te diabolus inveniat occupatum.*「悪魔にいつもあなたが忙しいと思せるように何かをしておけ」の中で、怠惰と悪が結び付けられている。*c*1386 チョーサー『メリベ物語』I. 1594 Therefor seith Seint Jerome:'Doothe somme goode dedes that the devel, which is oure enemy. Ne fynde yow nat unoccupied.'

☐**1715** I. WATTS *Divine Songs* 29 In Works of Labour or of Skill I would be busy too: For Satan finds some mischief still for idle Hands to do. **1721** J. KELLY *Scottish Proverbs* 221 If the Devil find a Man idle, he'll set him on Work. **1792** M. WOLLSTONECRAPT *Vindication of Rights of Woman* ix. There is a homely proverb, which speaks a shrewd truth, that whoever the devil finds idle he will employ. **1941** A. UPDEGRAFF *Hills lookDown* iv. Better keep busy, and the devil won't find so much for your idle hands to do. **2002** *Washington Times* 14 Mar. D6 (*Crock comic strip*) 'J've slaved in your salt mines for twenty years without a day off.' 'You can have thirty minutes off.' 'Why didn't you give the poor soul more time off?' 'Idle hands work for the devil, Poulet' **2015** *Spectator* 24 Jan. 29 Many who join voluntary organisations have time on their hands and nothing else to do. The Devil then makes work to fill the lacunae… ■ **idleness** 怠惰

Why should the DEVIL have all the best tunes?
なぜ悪魔は最高の調べを持っているのか。

（訳注：should は驚きを表わしている。Why *should* he say that to you? 〈どうしてあなたにそんなことを言ったりするのか〉）

多くの賛美歌が世俗的なはやりのメロディにのせて歌われる。これは特にメソジスト教会によって好まれた習慣であった。このことわざは、イギリス人の福音伝道者ローランド・ヒル (1744-1833) の言葉であると一般に考えられている。

☐**1859** W. CHAPPELL *Popular Music* n. 748 The Primitive Methodists…acting upon the principle of 'Why should the devil have all the pretty tunes?' collect the airs which are sung at pot and public houses, and write their hymns to them. **1879** J. E. HOPKINS *Work amongst Working Men* vi. If Wesley could not see why the devil should have all the good tunes, still less should we be able to see why he should have all the good amusements. **1933** G. B. SHAW *Letter* 29 June in *In Great Tradition* III. 261 Why should the devil have all the fun as well as all the good tunes? **2015** *Country Life* 7 Jan. 19 [J]ust as the Devil was said to have all the best tunes, so Scottish nationalism has the best politicians. ■ **good and evil** 正邪

The DEVIL is in the details.
悪魔は細部に宿る。

一見したところ重要でない些細な箇所も計画や企画全体の実現可能性にとっては重大な問題になるかもしれない。1978年の用例はこのことわざがドイツに起源があるということを示しているが、確証はない。ただし、God is in the details.「神は細部に宿る」という逆の記述は、美術歴史家アビ・ヴァールブルク (1866-1929) と建築家ミース・ファン・デル・ローエ (1886-1969) の言葉とされる。2人ともドイツ生まれであるが、だからと言って、必ずしもどちらか一方に由来するというわけではない。単数形 detail もよく使

DEVIL 113

われる。

□**1963** R. MAYNE *Community of Europe* 92 [O]n the principle that 'the devil is in the details', what should have been a merely formal occasion developed into a debate about the Community's official languages and the site of its headquarters. **1978** *Washington Post* 8 July C7 There is an old German saying...that the devil is in the details. **1990** *Automotive News* 5 Mar. l Many issues remain unresolved. As one...official put it, 'the devil is in the details, and we don't know what those details are yet.' **2007** *Times* 24 Sept 6 I can't decide if the hall is modelled on Hell or a bordello...Red floor, red walls, red everything. The devil may be in the detail but this year he's also done the decor. ■ **great and small** 大小

The DEVIL is not so black as he is painted.
悪魔は絵に描かれているほどには黒くない。

どんなに評判の悪い人や物でも、世評ほどには悪くはないかもしれない。†15世紀後半のフランス語 *Toutesfois n'est il pas sy deable qu'il est noir.*「人は必ずしも黒いほどには悪魔ではない」

□**1534** MORE *Dialogue of Comfort* (1553) III. xxii. Some saye in sporte, and thlnke in earnest: The devill is not so blacke as he is painted. **1642** J. HOWELL. *Instructions for Foreign Travel* xiv. The Devill is not so black as he is painted, no more are these Noble Nations and Townes as they are tainted. **1834** MARRYAT *Peter Simple* II. x. Fear kills more people than the yellow fever.....The devil's not half so black as he's painted. **1953** A. CHRISTIE *Pocket full of Rye* xxiii. Lance patted her on the arm. 'You didn't believe the devil was as black as he was painted? Well, perhaps he wasn't.' ■ **good and evil** 正邪 **; reputation** 評判

The DEVIL looks after his own.
悪魔は自分の仲間の面倒をよく見る。

邪悪な人が繁栄するのを保証するのは悪魔である。† **1606** J. デイ『カモメの島』D4ᵛ You were worse then the devil els, for they say hee helps his Servants.「あなたは悪魔よりもひどかった。悪魔だって自分の召使いは助けると言うではないか」

□**1721** J. KELLY *Scottish Proverbs* 310 The Dee'ls ay good to his own....Spoken when they whom we affect not, thrive and prosper in the World; as if they had their Prosperity from the Devil. **1837** F. CHAMIER *Arethusa* II. i. Weazel was the only midshipman saved besides myself: the devil always takes care of his own. **1940** R. A. J. WALLING *Why did Trethewy Die?* vii. 'The devil looks after his own,' said Pierce. 'Yes, doesn't he? But even he's not so clever, either.' **1985** B. KNOX *Wavecrest* vii.140 He saw Andy Grey's worried face and winked at him. 'Cheer up. The devil looks after his own.' ■ **associates** 仲間 **; good fortune** 幸運

The DEVIL makes his Christmas pies of lawyers' tongues and clerks' fingers.
悪魔は弁護士の舌と書記の指でクリスマスのパイを作る。
（訳注：clerk =「書記」）

元々は悪徳弁護士に対するネガティブなことわざであったが、他の職業にも応用可能である（1980年の用例参照）。

□**1591** J. FLORIO *Second Fruits* 179 Of three things the Deuill makes his messe, Of Lawyers tongues, of Scriveners fingers, you the third may gesse [i.e. women]. **1629** T. ADAMS *Workes* 1059 Corrupt and consciencelesse lawyers you will confesse to be sharp and wounding brambles....The Italians haue a shrewd prouerbe against them. The Deuill makes his Christmas-pyes of lawyers tongues, and clerkes fingers. *a***1697** J. AUBREY *Brief Lives* (1898) I. 422 Sir Rob-

114 DEVIL

ert Pye, attorney of the court of wardes,…happened to dye on Christmas day: the newes being brought to the serjeant, said he 'The devill haz a Christmas pye.' **1952** 'E. QUEEN' *Calendar of Crime* 248 Well, well, it couldn't have happened at a more appropriate season; there's an old English proverb that says the Devil makes his Christmas pies of lawyers' tongues. **1980** *Times* 24 Dec. 8 The Devil makes his Christmas-pies of television personalities' tongues and journalists' typing fingers: old English proverb, adapted. ■ **honesty and dishonesty 正直さと不正直；law and lawyers 法と法律家**

The DEVIL's children have the Devil's luck.
悪魔の子には悪魔の運がついている。
（訳注：「憎まれ子世に憚（はばか）る」）

悪人には不当に幸運がついてまわっている。† The DEVIL looks after his own.「悪魔は自分の仲間の面倒をよく見る」

□**1678** J. RAY *English Proverbs* (ed. 2) 126 The Devils child the Devils luck. **1721** J. KELLY *Scottish Proverbs* 333 The Dee'ls Bairns have Dee'ls luck. Spoken enviously when ill People prosper. **1798** LD. NELSON *Letter* 20 July (1845) III. 42 It is an old saying, 'the Devil's children have the Devil's luck.' I cannot find…where the French Fleet are gone to. **1938** R. A. J. WALLING *Corpse with Grimy Glove* vii. They must have had her hidden up somewhere…and waited till after sundown to get away. The devil's own luck—but the devil looks after his children. **1980** G. RICHARDS *Red Kill* viii. The Devil's son has the Devil's luck. We're going to need that kind of luck. ■ **luck 幸運・運**

DEVIL take the hindmost.
仕事が一番遅い者は悪魔に捕まってしまえ。
（訳注：take は仮定法現在形で、祈願を表わしている。God *save* the Queen!〈女王陛下万歳〉。「遅れた者は鬼に食われろ」）

EVERY man for himself, and devil take the hindmost.「皆自分の仕事に精を出せ。仕事が一番遅い者は悪魔に捕まってしまえ」の短縮版である。ラテン語版はホラティウス『詩論』417 *Occupet extremum scabies.*「仕事が一番遅い者は疥癬（かいせん）に捕まってしまえ」である。

□**1620** BEAUMONT & PLETCHER *Philaster* v. i. What if…they run all away, and cry the Devil take the hindmost. **1725** DEFOE *Everybody's Business* 29 In a few years the navigation…will be entirely obstructed.…Every one of these gentlemen-watermen hopes it will last his time, and so they all cry, the Devil take the hindmost. **1824** *Tales of American Landlord* I. ix. The troops…hurried away…with a precipitation which seemed to say 'De'il tak the hindmost.' **1953** P. GALLICO *Foolish Immortals* vii. Hannah grew up in…a land of unlimited resources and opportunity for acquiring them and let the devil take the hindmost. **2002** *Times* 22 Feb. 24 And Devil take the hindmost. In a better world than the infernal Circle Line, women and children first is still a noble sentiment. ■ **self-preservation 自己防衛**

The DEVIL was sick, the Devil a saint would be；the Devil was well, the devil a saint was he!
悪魔が病気になった、悪魔は修道士になろうと思った。悪魔は元気になった、悪魔は悪魔のままであった。
（訳注：the devil a saint = no saint at all. the devil はこの場合否定を強めている）

逆境の時になされたけなげな約束も順境の時には反古（はご）にされるものだ。† 中世ラテン語

Aegrotavit daemon, monachus tune esse volebat; daemon convaluit, daemon ut ante fuit.「悪魔が病気の時は修道士になろうと思った。悪魔が元気になると、やはり前と同様悪魔であった」。**1586** J. WITHALS『ラテン語辞典』(改訂版)K 8 The diuell was sicke and crasie; Good woulde the monke bee that was lasie.「悪魔は具合が悪く、気も狂っていた。回復したら修道士になろうとしたが、そうしなかった」

☐ **1629** T. ADAMS *Works* 634 God had need to take what deuotion he can get at our hands in our misery; for when prosperity returns, wee forget our vowes....The Deuill was sicke, the deuill a Monke would be, The Deuill was well, the deuill of [sic] Monke was he [i.e. no sort of monk at all]. **1881** D. C. MURRAY *Joseph's Coat* II. xvii. A prisoner's penitence is a thing the quality of which it is very difficult to judge until you see it...tried outside. 'The devil was sick.' **1913** H. JAMES *Small Boy* xxviii. The old, the irrepressible adage...was to live again between them: 'When the devil was sick the devil a saint would be; when the devil was well the devil a saint was he!' **1959** E. CADELL *Alice, where art Thou?* xii. 185 Laurie...offers to do penance for his past, to make amends in the future....My father's comment is that the devil a monk was he.
■ adversity 逆境・困難 ; hypocrisy 偽善

Devil ⇒ Set a BEGGAR on horseback, and he'll ride to the Devil ; BETTER the devil you know than the devil you don't know ; Never BID the Devil good morrow until you meet him ; EVERY man for himself, and devil take the hindmost ; GIVE a thing, and take a thing, to wear the Devil's gold ring ; GIVE the Devil his due ; Where GOD builds a church, the Devil will build a chapel ; GOD sends meat, but the Devil sends cooks ; What is GOT over the Devil's back is spent under his belly ; HASTE is from the Devil ; HOME is home, as the Devil said when he found himself in the Court of Session ; An IDLE brain is the Devil's workshop ; NEEDS must when the Devil drives ; PARSLEY seed goes nine times to the Devil ; It is easier to RAISE the Devil than to lay him ; He who SUPS with the Devil should have a long spoon ; TALK of the Devil, and he is bound to appear ; TELL the truth and shame the Devil ; TRUTH makes the Devil blush ; YOUNG saint, old devil.

DIAMOND cuts diamond.
ダイヤモンドだけがダイヤモンドを切れる。
（訳注：毒を以て毒を制す」）

狡猾さの裏をかく狡猾さといったように抜きつ抜かれつの競走をしている人たちのことを指すのに使われる。また、diamond cut diamond.「しのぎを削る」という慣用句でもよく使われる。† **1593** ナッシュ『キリストの涙』II. 9 An easie matter is it for anie man to cutte me (like a Diamond) with mine own dust.「私の亡骸で（ダイヤモンドのように）私を切ることは誰にとっても簡単だ」

☐ **1604** MARSTON *Malcontent* IV. i. None cuttes a diamond but a diamond. **1629** J, FORD *Lover's Melancholy* 1. 18. We're caught in our own toyles. Diamonds cut Diamonds. **1863** C. READE *Hard Cash* II. xi. You might say I robbed you....It is diamond cut diamond. **1958** M. STEWART *Nine Coaches Waiting* xi. I'll always have prospects. Diamond cuts diamond. **1979** *Guardian* 19 Apr. 26 When the boat comes in: Diamond cut diamond. James Bolam as the rough one turned smoothie. ■ similarity and dissimilarity 類似性と相違性

116 DIE

You can only DIE once.
人は一度しか死なない。

危険な企て、あるいは性に合わない企てを引き受けるのを渋っている人を励ます際に使われる。

□*c*1435 *Torrent of Portugal* (EETS) I. 993 A man schall But onnys Dyee. 1597-8 SHAKESPEARE *Henry IV*, Pt. 2 III. ii. 228 A man can die but once. *a*1721 M. PRIOR in *Literary Works* (1971) I. 533 With great Submission I pronounce That People dye no more than once. 1818 F. HALL *Travels In Canada & United States* xxxvii. He replied…that he was too ill to come out, and should die if she forced him; 'You can die but once,' said the beldame. 1840 MARRYAT *Olla Podrida* I. xii. 'A man cannot die more than once,'…but…a man can die…once professionally or legally, and once naturally. 1980 M. GILBERT *Death of Favourite Girl* ii. 'Why not,' said Sally. 'You can only die once.' ■ death 死; fate and fatalism 運命と運命論

die ⇒ Good AMERICANS when they die go to Paris; BETTER to die on your feet than live on your knees; COWARDS die many times before their death; We must BAT a peck of dirt before we die; BAT, drink, and be merry, for tomorrow we die; Whom the GODS love die young; The GOOD die young; Call no man HAPPY till he dies; He who LIVES by the sword dies by the sword; OLD habits die hard; OLD soldiers never die; YOUNG men may die, but old men must die; ⇒ DYING.

diet ⇒ The best DOCTORS are Dr Diet, Dr Quiet, and Dr Merryman.

differ ⇒ TASTES differ.

DIFFERENT strokes for different folks.
人にはそれぞれのやり方がある。

（訳注：「十人十色」）

米国起源。ここで strokes は承諾または祝福を表わす励ましのジェスチャーを意味する。急速に広まり様々なパロデイ版が登場している。例えば、1974年のフォルクスワーゲン社の CM コピーは Different Volks for different folks.「人それぞれのフォルクスワーゲン」であった。

□1973 *Houston* (Texas) *Chronicle Magazine* 14 Oct 4 The popular saying around P[almer] D[rug] A[buse] P[rogram] is 'different strokes for different folks', and that's the basis of the program. 1990 A. STODDARD *Gift of Letter* iii. Peter sends and receives letters. He dictates everything he writes. I send and receive handwritten letters. I write out everything. Different strokes for different folks. 2002 *Washington Post* 25 Feb. C2 There are many people who box for the sheer joy of it, there are even more who love to watch them do so; it's not my own. cuppa—though for many years it was—but what it says here is different strokes for different folks, so let the games begin. ■ tact 機転; ways and means 方法と手段

The DIFFICULT is done at once; the impossible takes a little longer.
難しいことはすぐ片付き、不可能なことは少しだけよけい時間がかかる。

（訳注：the difficult＝「困難〈なこと〉」、the impossible＝「不可能〈なこと〉」。こうした場合、抽象概念を指し、単数扱いとなる。an eye for the beautiful〈美に対する鑑識眼〉)

米国軍隊のスローガン The difficult we do immediately; the impossible takes a little longer.「困難なことは直ちに行なう。不可能なことは少し時間がかかっても行なう」として有名である。1873年の用例で、このことわざの由来とされているのが「フランスの大臣」ことシャルル・アレクサンドル・ド・カロンヌ (1734-1802) である。彼は1783年ルイ14世によって財政大臣に任命された。*Si c'est possible, c'est fait; impossible? cela se fera.*「可能であるなら、なされると考えよ。不可能なら、どうするか。いずれできると考えよ」(J. ミシュレ『フランス革命史』〈1847〉I. ii. 8 からの引用)

□**1873** TROLLOPE *Phineas Redwc* II. xxix. What was it the French Minister said. If It Is simply difficult it is done. If it is impossible, it shall be done. **1967** H. HARRISON *Technicolor Time Machine* iv. The impossible may take a while, but we do it, you know the routine. **1981** P. MC-CUTCHAN *Shard calls Tune* iv. A well-worn precept of the British Navy was that the difficult was done at once; the impossible took a little longer. **1997** *National Review* 29 Sept 66 That's good, utilitarian, achievement-oriented American lingo. We do the difficult immediately, the impossible takes a little longer. ■ **possibility and impossibility** 可能性と不可能性

difficult ⇒ It is the FIRST step that is difficult.

difficulty ⇒ ENGLAND's difficulty is Ireland's opportunity.

digging ⇒ When you are in a HOLE, stop digging.

DILIGENCE is the mother of good luck.
勤勉は好運の母。

着実で慎重な仕事をしていると好運がもたらされる。

□**1591** W. STEPNEY *Spanish Schoolmaster* L2ᵛ Diligence is the mother of good fortune. *La diligencia es madre de Tabuena ventura.* **1736** B. FRANKLIN *Poor Richard's Almanack* (Feb.) Diligence is the mother of good Luck. **1875** S. SMILES *Thrift* ix. Diligence is the mother of good luck....A man's success in life will be proportionate to his efforts. **1972** B. EMECHETA *In Ditch* vi. Where do people get a system that allows a Dian to be better off when out of work?...People...used to say that diligence was the mother of fortune. ■ **diligence** 勤勉; **luck** 幸運・運

Dinner ⇒ AFTER dinner rest a while, after supper walk a mile ; BETTER a dinner of herbs than a stalled ox where hate is.

Throw DIRT enough, and some will stick.
泥でもたくさん投げればくっつくものもある。

執拗に誹謗中傷をしていると最後には真実として通ることになる。†ラテン語 *Calumniare fortiter, et aliquid adhaerebit.*「ひどく中傷せよ。本当のことになるものもある」

□**1656** *Trepan* 34 She will say before company, Have you never had the French Pox? speak as in the sight of God: let them Reply what they will, some dirt will stick. **1678** B. R. *Letter to Popish Friends* 7 'Tis a blessed Line in Matchiavel—If durt enough be thrown, some will stick. **1705** B. WARD *Hudibras Redivivus* II. 11 Scurrility's a useful Trick, Approv'd by the most Politic; Fling Dirt enough, And some will stick. **1857** T. HUGHES *Tom Brown's Schooldays* I. viii. Whatever harm a...venomous tongue could do them, he took care should be done. Only throw dirt enough

118 dirt

and some of it is sure to stick. **2000** P. LOVESEY *Reaper* xvi. 201 'We both know Owen is full of wind and piss.' 'The trouble is not everyone knows that Throw enough mud, and some will stick.' ■ malice 悪意・恨み；slander 誹謗中傷

dirt ⇒ We must EAT a peck of dirt before we die.

DIRTY water will quench fire.
泥水でも火を消すものだ。

（訳注：will ＝「…するものだ」〈傾向・習性〉。Accidents *will* happen.〈事故は起きるものだ〉）

どんな女性でも、たとえ醜い売春婦であろうとも男性の性欲を満たすことができるという意味で主に使われる。

☐**1546** J. HEYWOOD *Dialogue of Proverbs* I. v. B2 As this prouerbe saieth, for quenchyng hot desire, Foul water as soone as fayre, wyl quenche hot fire. **1796** COBBETT *Political Censor* Sept 62 That I have inade use...of the British Corporal for a good purpose, I have little doubt—Dirty water will quench fire. **1945** O. ONIONS *Ragged Robin* vi. It's flocks and straw for us....Well, dirty water's good enough to quench a fire with. **1995** A. G. Taylor *Simeon's Bride* xxvi. 173 She had the thick ugly feet of a streetwalker;...How could anyone go with her?' Dew! shrugged. 'They do say dirty water puts out fire just as well.' ■ necessity 必要性・必然性；ways and means 方法と手段

dirty ⇒ It's an ILL bird that fouls its own nest；Don't THROW out your dirty water until you get in fresh；One does not WASH one's dirty linen in public.

disappointed ⇒ BLESSED is he who expects nothing, for he shall never be disappointed.

DISCRETION is the better part of valour.
思慮深さが勇気の大半を占めている。

確かに勇気は美徳であるが、危険な試みを実行する際には思慮深さもまた大切である。†エウリピデス『救いを求める女たち』I. 510 καὶ τοῦτ᾽ ἐμοί τἀνδρεῖον ἡ προμηθία,「勇気は予見から成る」。*c***1477** キャクストン『イアソン』(EETS) 23 Than as wyse and discrete he withdrewe him sayng that more is worth a good retrayte than a folisshe abydinge.

☐**1597-8** SHAKESPEARE *Henry IV. Pt. 1* v. iv. 121 The better part of valouris discretion; in the which better part, I have saved my life. **1885** C. LOWE *Prince Bismarck* I. v. Napoleon...had vowed that he would free Italy 'from the Alps to the Adriatic', but...he acted on the maxim that discretion is the better part of valour. **2002** *Washington Times* 12 Jan. F10 (*Fox Trot comic strip*) 'Who knew you weren't supposed to club him or kick him or lob fireballs, just because he's huge and fierce and can squash you at will!' 'You've heard the saying, "Discretion is the better part of valor"? Think of this as a valuable life lesson.' ■ discretion 思慮分別；prudence 思慮・分別

disease ⇒ DESPERATE diseases must have desperate remedies.

disgrace ⇒ POVERTY is no disgrace, but it is a great inconvenience.

dish ⇒ BETTER are small fish than an empty dish；REVENGE is a dish that can be eaten

Divided 119

cold.

dismount ⇒ He who RIDES a tiger is afraid to dismount.

dispose ⇒ MAN proposes, God disposes.

DISTANCE lends enchantment to the view.
距離は景色に魅力を添える。

(訳注：1799年の用例にある "'Tis distance lends…" は "It is distance that lends…"「…に魅力を添えるのは距離である」の意。「夜目遠目傘の内」)

遠くから見ると、近くから見たときよりも美しく見えるもの。

☐ **1799** T. CAMPBELL *Pleasure of Hope* 1. 3 Why do those cliffs of shadowy tint appear More sweet than all the landscape smiling near? —'Tis distance lends enchantment to the view, And robes the mountain in its azure hue. **1827** T. HOOD *Poems* (1906) 78 What black Mont Blancs arose, Crested with soot and not with snows....I fear the distance did not 'lend enchantment to the view'. **1901** C. FITCH *Captain Jinks* II. 118 'I wish you'd taike me hout of the second row and put me in the front.'...'You forget the old adage,... "Distance lends enchantment"' **1974** T. SHARPE *Porterhouse Blue* xviii. As ever with Lady Mary's affections, distance lent enchantment to the view, and...she was herself the intimate patroness of this idol of the media. ■ **absence** 不在

ditch ⇒ When the BLIND lead the blind, both shall fall into the ditch.

DIVIDE and rule.
分裂させて統治せよ。

派閥が互いに競り合い、一致団結して統治者に反旗を翻さないなら、政府は容易に維持される。一般的な格言 (ラテン語 *divide et impera*、ドイツ語 *entzwei und gebiete*) であるので、(1732年の用例には反するが) イタリアの政治哲学者ニッコロ・マキャヴェッリ (1469-1527) の言葉であると考えるべきではない。実は、彼はこの原則を非難していたからである。† **1588** tr. *M. Hurault's Discourse upon Present State of France* 44 It hath been alwaies her [Catherine de Medici's] custome, to set in France, one against an other, that in the meane while shee might rule in these diuisions.「キャサリンがこの地域を統治している間はフランス国内を互いに反目し合う状態にしておくことが彼女のいつもの習慣であった」

☐ **1605** J. HALL *Meditations* 1. 109 For a Prince...is a sure axiome, Diuide and rule. **1732** SWIFT *Poems* III. 805 As Machiavel taught 'em, divide and ye govern. **1907** *Spectator* 20 Apr. 605 The cynical maxim of 'Divide and rule' has never clouded our relations with the daughter-States. **1979** D. WILLIAMS *Genesis & Exodus* ii. Matters concerning the estate were put in the hands of a secretary and a steward who were responsible not to Benson but to the Governors. But 'divide and rule' was not in his nature. **2014** *Guardian* 30 Apr. (online; *heading*) Benefits crackdown leads to divide and rule within poor communities. ■ **power** 権力 ; **rulers and ruled** 支配者と被支配者 :

Divided ⇒ A HOUSE divided cannot Stand ; UNITED we stand, divided we fall.

120　divine

divine ⇒ To ERR is human (to forgive divine) ; On SAINT Thomas the Divine kill all turkeys, geese, and swine.

DO as I say, not as I do.
私のするとおりにではなく、私の言うとおりにせよ。

私の行ないでなく私の命令、指示に従いなさい。†『マタイによる福音書』23章3節 Do not ye after their works: for they say, and do not.「彼らの行ないを見習ってはいけない。彼らは口先だけで、実行しないからである」

□*a*1100 in N. R. KER *Anglo-Saxons* (1959) 277 Ac theah ic wyrs do thonne ic the lære ne do thu na swa swa ic do, ac do swa ic the lære gyf ic the wel lære [Although I do worse than I teach you, do not do as I do, but do as I teach you if I teach you well]. **1546** J. HEYWOOD *Dialogue of Proverbs* II. v. H4v It Is as folke dooe, and not as folke say. **1689** J. SELDON *Table-Talk* 45 Preachers say, Do as I say, not as I do. **1911** *Spectator* 24 June 957 It has always been considered allowable to say…to children, 'Do as I say, rather than as I do.' **1979** D. CLARK *Heberden's Seat* v. I saw you spooning sugar into coffee…Do as I say, not as I do. **2001** *Spectator* 4 Aug. 28 Do as I say, not as I do. The government's White Paper on competition is a bad example in itself, for why should there only be one of it? ■ **hypocrisy　偽善**；**words and deeds　言動**

DO as you would be done by.
自分が人にしてもらいたいように人にしてあげよ。

（訳注：would＝「〈できれば〉…したいと思う」〈願望〉。Nutritionists *would* have us all eat whole grains.〈栄養士たちは皆に精白していない穀物を食べてもらいたいと思っている〉）

聖書の DO unto others as you would they should do unto you.「自分が人にしてもらいたいように人にもしてあげなさい」の簡略版である。1991年の用例が示すように、元の版と簡略版とが混ざり合うこともある。

□*c*1596 A. MUNDAY et al. *Sir Thomas More* 9 A [he] saies trewe: letts do as we may be doon by. **1747** CHESTERFIELD *Letter* 16 Oct. (1932) III. 1035 'Do as you would be done by,' Is the surest method that I know of pleasing. **1863** C. KINGSLEY *Water Babies* v. I shall grow as handsome as my sister…the loveliest fairy in the world;…her name is Mrs. Doasyouwouldbedoneby. **1928** 'J. J. CONNINGTON' *Mystery at Lynden Sands* viii. 'Do unto others as you'd be done by' is my motto. **1965** M. PRAYN *Tin Men* i. 'Always treat a man as you would wish to be treated yourself.…' 'Do as you would be done by.' 'It's good human relations.…' Mr. Vulgurian paused and stroked his hair, doing to It as he would be done by. **1991** T. MO *Redundancy of Courage* xxix. 394 'Do unto others as you would be done by' was a more positive social prescription of societies like Toronto. ■ **reciprocity　相互扶助**；**society　社会**

DO right and fear no man.
正しいことをし、誰も恐れるな。

良心的にふるまうならば、誰の非難も恐れる必要はない。

□*c*1450 *Proverbs of Good Counsel in Book of Precedence* (EETS) 68 The beste wysdom that I Can [know], Ys to doe well, and drede no man. **1721** J. KELLY *Scottish Proverbs* 89 Do well and doubt [fear] no Man. But rest satisfied in the Testimony of a good Conscience. **1979** *Guardian* 31 Mar. 10 It used to be, 'Do right and fear no man. Don't write and fear no women.' ■ **action and consequence　行為と結果**；**conscience　良心**

DOG 121

DO unto others as you would they should do unto you.
自分が人にしてもらいたいように人にもしてあげなさい。

(訳注：would については、2つ前のことわざの訳注参照)

2つ前の Do as you would be done by. を見よ。『ルカによる福音書』6章31節（欽定訳聖書）As ye would that men should do to you, do ye also to them likewise.「あなた方は人からしてほしいことを人にもしなさい」

□*a*901 *Laws of Alfred* in F. Llebermann *Gesetze Angelsachsen* (1903) I. 44 Tluet ge willen, tluet othre men eow ne don, ne doth ge thmt othrum monnum [What you do not wish others to do to you, do not to other men].　1477 A. WYDEVILLE *Dicts of Philosophers* 62 Do to other as thou woldest they should do to the, and do to noon other but as thou woldest be doon to. **1790** W. HAZLITT *Letter* 9 July (1979) 48 He wished to have him out, merely because 'he would do to others as he would be done to'. **1903** G. B. SHAW *Man & Superman* 227 Do not do unto others as you would that they should do unto you. Their tastes may not be the same. **2000** *Washington Post* 27 Nov. A21 Maybe all I'm doing is overcomplicating a lesson first taught two millennia ago: Do unto others as you would have others do unto you. ■ reciprocity 相互扶助；society 社会

do ⇒ Never do EVIL that good may come of it；The KING can do no wrong；Whatever MAN has done, man may do；MONKEY see, monkey do；When in ROME, do as the Romans do；If you WANT a thing done well, do it yourself；⇒ DOES, DOING, DONE.

doctor ⇒ An APPLE a day keeps the doctor away.

The best DOCTORS are Dr Diet, Dr Quiet, and Dr Merryman.
最高の医者はドクター食事、ドクター安静、ドクター快活である。

これら3人の「医者」は患者の回復にとっての重要な看護ケアの要素である。† 1449 リドゲート『小詩集』(EETS) 704 Tore lechees [doctors] consaruea mannys myht, First a glad hert…Temperat diet…And best of all, for no thyng take no thouht.「第1は喜びに満ちた心、第2は適切な食事、そして最も大切なのは心配しないことである」。† LAUGHTER is the best medicine.「笑いは最高の薬である」

□**1558** W. BULLEIN *Government of Health* 50ᵛ I should not staye my selfe vpon the opinion of any one phisicion, but rather vpon three.…The first was called doctor diet, the seconde doctor quiet, the thirde doctor mery man. **1738** SWIFT *Polite Conversation* II. 154 The best Doctors in the World, are Doctor Dyet, Doctor Quiet, and Doctor Merryman. **1909** *Spectator* 30 Jan. 175 A proverb prescribes for sickness Dr. Diet, Dr. Quiet, and Dr. Merryman. The merry heart goes all the way in all but the worst sicknesses. ■ doctors 医者；health 健康

does ⇒ He who CAN, does；It's DOGGED as does it；EASY does it；HANDSOME is as handsome does；PRETTY is as pretty does.

Feed a DOG for three days and he will remember your kindness for three years.；feed a cat for three years and she will forget your kindness in three days.
犬に3日餌をやれば、3年間その恩義を忘れない。猫に3年餌をやっても3日も過ぎればその恩義を忘れる。

日本のことわざ。Keep a dog... も使われる。

□**1892** L. HEARN 'In a Japanese Garden' in *Atlantic Monthly* July 26 Cats are ungrateful. 'Feed a dog for three days,' says a Japanese proverb, 'and he will remember your kindness for three years; feed a cat for three years, and she will forget your kindness in three days.' **1921** C. VAN VECHTEN *Tiger in the House* 137 A Japanese proverb has it that A dog will remember a three days' kindness three years while a cat will forget a three years' kindness in three days. This may be regarded as a compliment to the intelligence of the cat. **2007** 'Sagara Likes Kaname?' posting on *www. forums. animesukl.com* 31 Jan. Maybe familiarity breeds attraction, in this case. What is the Japanese saying? Feed a dog for three days and it becomes attached to you? (shrug). ◼
animals 動物；**gratitude and ingratitude** 感謝と忘恩

Give a DOG a bad name and hang him.
犬に悪評が立てばその犬は縛り首になってしまう。

（訳注：このことわざでは、「犬に悪評を立てよ」と「その犬を縛り首にせよ」という 2 つの命令文が並列されている。しかし、実際にそうせよと命令しているのではない。犬に悪評を立てたければ勝手にそうするがいい。しかし、そうすると、その犬は縛り首になってしまうぞと警告しているのである。命令文を並列して、どちらもやってはいけないと警告していることわざに、Spare the rod and spoil the child.〈鞭を惜しむと子供をだめにする〉、Marry in haste and repent at leisure.〈慌てて結婚、ゆっくり後悔〉などがある）

ひとたび悪い評判が立つともはや挽回不可能な窮地に立たされてしまうものである。2002 年の用例の解釈は、どこか劣るものという犬の俗語的な意味によるところが大きい。

□**1706** J. STEVENS *Spanish & English Dict.* s. v. Perro, We say, Give a Dog an ill name and his work is done. **1721** J. KELLY *Scottish Proverbs* 124 Give a Dog an ill Name, and he'll soon be hanged. Spoken of those who raise an ill Name on a Man on purpose to prevent his Advancement. **1803** *Norfolk* [VA] *Herald* 14 Apr. 3 It is an old saying, 'give a dog a bad name and hang him.' **2002** *Times: Weekend* 20 July 4 Give a dog a bad name seems to have become a workaday motto for the wine trade. And the sillier the name on the bottle, the less chance there is of anything drinkable inside. **2005** *Telegraph* 15 Jan. (online) 'Give a dog a bad name...' runs the pessimistic old saw, 'and hang him.' If that were so, you would have to regard with gloom the chances of...successfully 'rehoming' the 53 Staffordshire bull terriers...currently abiding in Battersea Dogs Home. ◼ **reputation** 評判；**slander** 誹謗中傷

DOG does not eat dog.
犬は犬を食ったりはしない。
（訳注：「同類相食まず」)」

同じ種類あるいは同じ職業の人は互いに傷つけ合うべきではない。†ウァロ『ラテン語論』VII. 32 *Canis caninam non est*.「犬は犬の肉を食べぬ」。

□**1543** W. Turner *Hunting of Romish Fox* A2ᵛ The prouerb...on dog will not eat of an other dogges fleshe. **1790** 'P. PINDAR' *Epistle to Bruce* 31 Dog should not prey on dog, the proverb says: Allow then brother-trav'lers crumbs of praise. **1866** C. KINGSLEY *Hereward the Wake* II. xi. Dog does not eat dog and it is hard to be robbed by an Englishman, after being robbed a dozen times by the French. **1933** F. D. GRIERSON *Empty House* viii. Dog doesn't eat dog, my dear fellow. To put it more politely, the physician attends his brother practitioner without charge. **1993** 'C. AIRD' *Going Concern* (1994) viii. 67 'Apparently Harris and Marsh've been trying for a takeover of Chemwoods' for quite a while now.' 'I always thought that dog doesn't eat dog.' objected Leeyes. 'But I suppose I'm old-fashioned.' ◼ **reciprocity** 相互扶助

DOG 123

Every DOG has his day.
どんな犬でも良い時がある。

たとえ地位が低く無視される人でも、成功あるいは栄光の機会に恵まれるときもある。

☐ **1545** R. TAVERNER tr. *Erasmus' Adages* (ed. 2) 63 A dogge hath a day. **1600-1** SHAKESPEARE *Hamlet* v. i. 286 Let Hercules himself do what he may, The cat will mew, and dog will have his day. **1611** R. COTGRAVE *Dict. French & English* s.v. Fevrier, Euerie dog hath his day. **1726** POPE *Odyssey* V. xxii. Dogs, ye have had your day; ye fear'd no more lilysses vengeful from the Trojan shore. **1837** CARLYLE *French Revolution* III. I. i. How changed for Marat, lifted from his dark cellar!...All dogs have their day; even rabid dogs. **1863** C. KINGSLEY *Water Babies* ii. Young blood must have its course, lad, And every dog his day. **1978** 'M. CRAIG' *Were He Stranger* x. 'She could be his sister.' 'No way—not with a face like that.' 'Well, every dog deserves his day.' **2003** *Spectator* 17 May 22 Nevertheless, every dog has his day, and David Blunkett is no exception. ■ opportunity, taken 得られた機会 ; success 成功

Every DOG is allowed one bite.
どんな犬も一度は噛みつくことを許される。

古いイングランドの法律に基づく（少なくとも17世紀に遡る）。この規則によって、家畜の所有者は、もし自分がその家畜の横暴な性質を知らなかった場合には、その家畜がもたらした被害については法的責任を問われなくてすむ。1913年の用例はこの考え方の理由を説明している。

☐ **1902** V. S. LEAN *Collectanea* I. 439 Every dog is allowed his first bite i.e. is not punished. **1913** *Spectator* 15 Mar. 440 Every dog is allowed by the law one free bite. After the dog has once bitten a person it is presumed that its owner knows it to be 'savage'. **1968** P. FOOT *Politics of Harold Wilson* x. In March 1967...Wilson rounded on the Left at a Parliamentary Party meeting, warning them that 'a dog is only allowed one bite' and threatening them with a General Election unless they came to heel. **1980** 'A. BLAISDELL' *Consequence of Crime* (1981) ii. She got arrested....They say every dog [is] allowed one bite....But it was a vice thing....I told her to get out. ■ reputation 評判

A DOG is for life, not just for Christmas.
犬は一生かけて世話をするもの。たんにクリスマスの時だけにあらず。

英国の National Canine Defence League のスローガンである。クリスマスプレゼントとして子犬は適切でないという意図で1978年に導入された。元の形式で広く使われるが、多くのユーモアに富む形が生み出されている。

☐ **1998** R. RAY *Certain Age* 344 A tree is for life, not just for decorating with small shiny objects. **1999** *Jewish Chronicle* 30 July 42 And remember, a pet is for life, not just for Rosh Hashanah. **2014** *Country Life* 31 Dec. 27 [Alt least we can say that a moth orchid is for life, not just for Christmas. ■ constancy and inconstancy 安定と不安定

The DOG returns to its vomit.
犬は自分の吐いたものを食べに戻ってくる。

人はしばしばかつての悪い習慣や悪い仲間に戻るものである。この表現はしばしば比喩的・暗示的な形を取って使われている。例えば、以下の用例に見られるように to return like a dog to his vomit「愚か者は愚かな行為を繰り返す」が挙げられる。1534年以前は、聖書の初期の形や註釈の形を取ってだいたい同じ表現となっている。この考え方は中世

124 DOG

に広く一般的に受け入れられていた。当該の聖書の一節とは、『箴言』26章11節（欽定訳聖書）As a dog returneth to his vomit: so a fool returneth to his folly.「犬が自分の吐いたものを食べに戻ってくるように、愚か者は自分の愚かな習慣を繰り返す」。『ペテロの手紙一』2章22節（1534年の用例参照）にも言及がある。

□ *c***1390** CHAUCER *Parson's Tale* 1. 137 Ye trespassen so ofte tyme as dooth the hound that retoumeth to eten his spewyng. **1534** W. TYNDALE tr. *Bible* 2 Peter ii. 22 It is happened vnto them according to the true proverbe: The dogge is turned to his vomet agayne. **1832** S. WARREN *Diary of Late Physician* II. vi. His infatuated wife betook herself—'like a dog to his vomit'...—to her former...extravagance and dissipation. **1981** P. MCCUTCHAN *Shard calls Tune* xvi. The old saying that the dog returns to his vomit, the criminal to the scene of his crime. **1993** G. LANDRUM *Rotary Club Murder Mystery* 44 'You know what the Bible says,' Harriet replied. '"The dog shall return to his vomit and the old hog to his wallowing in the mire."' ■ **habit** 習慣 ; **human nature** 人間性

A DOG that will fetch a bone will carry a bone.
骨を取ってくる犬はそれを別の場所へ持って行くものだ。

（訳注：will＝「…するものだ」〈傾向・習性〉）

ゴシップは他人のスキャンダルをあなたに伝えてくれるが、逆に彼らの元にあなたの話も伝える。

□ **1830** R. FORBY *Vocabulary of East Anglia* 429 'The dog that fetches will carry.'—i.e. a talebearer will tell tales *of* you, as well as *to* you. **1941** L. I. WILDER *Little Town on Prairie* xv. So Nellie twisted what you said and told it to Miss Wilder....'A dog that will fetch a bone, will carry a bone.' **1959** E. SCHIDDEL *Devil in Bucks County* II. iii. All this gossip reminded Shirley...of the saw *The dog who brings a bone also will carry one away.* ■ **slander** 誹謗中傷

dog ⇒ A BARKING dog never bites ; BRAG is a good dog, but Holdfast is better ; The CAT, the rat, and Lovell the dog, rule all England under the hog ; Why KEEP a dog and bark yourself? ; If you are not the LEAD dog, the view never changes ; If you LIE down with dogs, you will get up with fleas ; A LIVE dog is better than a dead lion ; LOVE me, love my dog ; It is a POOR dog that's not worth whistling for, let SLEEPING dogs lie ; It is easy to find a STICK to beat a dog ; You can't TEACH an old dog new tricks ; THREE things are not to be trusted ; While TWO dogs are fighting for a bone, a third runs away with it ; There are more WAYS of killing a dog than choking it with butter, there are more WAYS of killing a dog than hanging it ; Do not call a WOLF to help you against the dogs.

It's DOGGED as does it.
事を成し遂げるには根気が必要である。

（訳注：強調構文の形を取っている。dogged＝persistent。方言で as＝that。「継続は力なり」）

粘り強く続けると、最後には結果が付いてくる。類似表現に EASY does it.「慌てずゆっくりやれば事は成し遂げられる」がある。

□ **1864** M. B. CHESNUT *Diary* 6 Aug. (1949) 429 'It's dogged as does it,' says Isabella. **1867** TROLLOPE *Last Chronicle of Barset*lxi. There ain't nowt a man can't bear if he'll only be dogged....It's dogged as does it. It's not thinking about it. **1916** J. BUCHAN *Greenmantle* i. We've got the measure of the old Boche now, and it's dogged as does it. **1965** K. GILES *Some Beasts no More* v. It was Colonel Rodgers. 'Any progress?'...'Very little, it's dogged as does it, sir.' **2006**

Scientific American 22 Jan. (online ; *heading*) It's Dogged as Does It Retracing Darwin's footsteps…reveals how revolutions in science actually evolve. ■ **perseverance** 我慢強さ

DOGS bark, but the caravan goes on.
犬は吠えても、キャラバン隊は意に介せず進んでいく。
（訳注：反対意見があっても事は方針通りに進行する）

1956年の用例はこのことわざを面白おかしくひっくりかえしたものである。大半の例では caravan は「砂漠を共に旅する一行」という原義で使われている。しかし、1956年の用例では mobile home「動く家（トレーラーハウス）」を意味する。

☐ **1891** J. L. KIPLING *Beast & Man in India* ix. 252 'The dog barks but the elephant moves on' is sometimes said to Indicate the superiority of the great to popular clamour, but the best form of the phrase Is, 'Though the dog may bark the caravan (*kafila*) moves on.' **1924** C. K. SCOTIT MONCRIEFF tr. *Proust's Within Budding Grove* I. 45 In the words of a fine Arab proverb, 'The dogs may bark; the caravan goes on!'…Its effect was great, the proverb being familiar to us already. It had taken the place, that year, among people who 'really counted', of 'He who sows the wind shall reap the whirlwind.' **1930** *Time* 4 July 17 I was struggling to explain the situation to an old Moor….After thinking it over he murmured: 'Dogs bark but the caravan goes on.' **1956** D. SMITH *Hundred & One Dalmatians* xiv. The shut-in Romany dogs heard them [the Dalmatians] and shook the caravans in their efforts to get out…'The caravans bark but the dogs move on,' remarked Pongo, when he felt they were out of danger. **2002** *Spectator* 6 July 28 The dogs bark, but the caravan moves on. ICC, Kyoto, Arafat, Iraq…early chapters in a long story. If you want to be part of it, join America. If you want to impede it, join a terrorist group. ■ **great and small** 大小 ; **malice** 悪意・恨み

DOGS look up to you, cats look down on you, pigs is equal.
犬は人を尊敬し、猫は人を見下し、豚は我々と対等である。

英国の政治家・著述家・首相 W. チャーチル (1874-1965) の言葉とされる。I am fond of pigs. Dogs look up to us. Cats look down on us. Pigs treat us as equals.「私は豚が好きだ。犬は人を見上げる。猫は人を見下す。豚は人を同等に見てくれる」（M. ギルバート『決して諦めるな』〈1988〉304 からの引用）

☐ **1937** W. R. INGE *Rustic Moralist* 319 'You see cats look down upon you, dogs look up to you, but pigs is equals.' He was right about cats and dogs. **1980** *Christian Science Monitor* (Boston, MA) 10 Jan 20 Geraldine, a Wessex Saddleback sow, of intermediate age, established herself in the order of things from the first moment of her arrival on our farm…I've heard it said that, while a dog looks up to you, and a cat looks down on you, a pig looks you straight in the eye. When she fixed you with her gaze you knew it was a privilege to be considered an equal by Geraldine. **2002** *Times* 24 Sept. 21 Back in the 1960s our transplantation team had every good reason to credit the old country adage, 'dogs look up to you, cats look down on you, pigs is equal'. ■ **animals** 動物 ; **equality** 平等

doing ⇒ If a THING's worth doing, it's worth doing well.

dollar ⇒ ANOTHER day, another dollar.

What's DONE cannot be undone.
いったんなされてしまったことは元に戻せない。

より簡潔で略式の表現 What's done is done. も使われる（1605-6 年の用例参照）。†ソフォクレス『アジャックス』1. 378 οὐ γὰρ γένοιτ᾽ ἂν ταῦθ᾽ ὅπως οὐχ ὧδ᾽ ἔχειν.「物事はもはやなかったことにはできない」。14世紀初頭のフランス語 *Mez quant ja est la chose fecte, ne puet pas bien estre desfecte.*「いったんなされたことは、元には戻せない」

☐*c*1450 *King Ponthus* in *Publications of Modern Language Association of America* (1897) XII. 107 The thynges that be doone may not be undoone. **1546** J. HEYWOOD *Dialogue of Proverbs* I. x. C4 Things done, can not be undoone. **1605-6** SHAKESPEARE *Macbeth* III. ii. 12 Things without all remedy Should be without regard. What's done is done. Ibid. v. I. 65 What's done cannot be undone. **1818** S. FERRIER *Marriage* III. xxi. I hope you will think twice about it Second thoughts are best What's done cannot be undone. **1967** H. HARRISON *Technicolor Time Machine* vii. What's done is done...I'll see you don't suffer for it. **1998** K. NEVILLE *Magic Circle* 92 'And although I am very, very sorry I involved you in this, Ariel, what has been done cannot be undone.' ■ past 過去・過ぎ去った

done ⇒ DO as you would be done by ; Whatever MAN has done, man may do ; NOTHING should be done in haste but gripping a flea ; The SOONER begun, the sooner done ; If you WANT something done, ask a busy person ; WELL begun is half done.

A DOOR must either be shut or open.
扉は閉まっているか開いているか、どちらかでなければならない。
（訳注：両方を同時に満たすことはできない）

2 つの相互に排他的な選択肢について使われる。†フランス語 *Il faut qu'une porte soit ouverte ou fermée.*「扉は開いているか閉まっているか、どちらかでなければならない」

☐**1762** GOLDSMITH *Citizen of World* I. xlix. There are but the two ways; the door must either be shut, or it must be open. **1896** G. SAINTSBURY *Hist Nineteenth-Century Literature* vii. Fiction...pleads in vain for detailed treatment. For all doors must be shut or open; and this door must now be shut. **1953** S. BEDFORD *Sudden View* I. ix. We...returned to France, the land of good sense...where a door has got to be either open or shut. ■ choices 選択

door ⇒ A CREAKING door hangs longest ; A GOLDEN key can open any door ; When ONE door shuts, another opens ; OPPORTUNITY never knocks twice at any man's door ; A POSTERN door makes a thief ; When POVERTY comes in at the door, love flies out of the window ; It is too late to shut the STABLE-door after the horse has bolted.

doorstep ⇒ If every man would SWEEP his own doorstep the city would soon be clean.

When in DOUBT, do nowt.
疑わしいときは何もするな。

nowt は nought (= nothing) の方言形で doubt と脚韻を踏むために使われている。

☐**1874** G. J. WHYTE-MELVILLE *Uncle John* xx. I should wait. When in doubt what to do, he is a wise man who does nothing. **1884** G. WEATHERLY *'Little Folks' Proverb Painting Book* 64 Err ever ort the side that's safe, And when in doubt, abstain. **1917** J. C. BRIDGE *Cheshire Proverbs*

155 When in doubt, do nowt. This shows the cautious Cheshlreman at his best. **1952** H. CECIL *Ways & Means* ii. I don't know. I think it's one of those occasions where it's best to follow the maxim: When in doubt, don't. **1972** E. GRIERSON *Confessions of Country Magistrate* vii. 'When in doubt say nowt' is a precept enshrined over most magistrates' courts. **1981** E. AGRY *Assault Force* i. What to do?... 'When in doubt, do nowt,' had always been my grandfather's advice. ■ action and inaction 行為と非行為 ; decision and indecision 決断と優柔不断

down ⇒ Up like a ROCKET, down like a stick ; What goes UP must come down.

drag ⇒ With a SWEET tongue and kindness, you can drag an elephant by a hair.

Whosoever DRAWS his sword against the prince must throw the scabbard away.
主君にさからって刀を抜く者は誰であれ、その鞘を投げ捨てなければならない。

主君の暗殺・退位を企てる者は、その後常に自分の身を守る準備をしておかなければならない。抜いた剣は決して元の鞘に戻ることはないのである。

□**1604** R. DALLINGTON *View of France* F3ᵛ His King, against whom when yee drawe the sword, ye must throw the scabberd into the riuer. **1659** J. HOWELL *Proverbs* (English) 17 Who draweth his sword against his Prince, must throw away the scabbard. **1962** S. E. FINER *Man on Horseback* viii. [The Military] must still fear the results of a fall from power.... 'Whosoever draws his sword against the prince must throw the scabbard away'...pithily express[es] the logic of the situation. ■ hope and despair 希望と絶望 ; rulers and ruled 支配者と被支配者

draws ⇒ BEAUTY draws with a single hair.

dread ⇒ A BURNT child dreads the fire.

DREAM of a funeral and you hear of a marriage.
葬式の夢を見ると、結婚の噂を聞く。
（訳注：命令文 and ... の構文で、「～すれば…する」の意）

DREAMS go by contraries.「夢は逆夢になる」の原則を表わしている。このことわざは逆の形式（Dream of a marriage and you hear of a funeral.）で使われることもある。

□**1639** J. CLARKS *Paræmiologia Anglo-Latina* 236 After a dreame of weddings comes a corse [corpse]. **1766** GOLDSMITH *Vicar of Wakefield* x. My wife had the most lucky dreams in the world.... It was one night a coffin and cross-bones, the signs of an approaching wedding. **1883** C. S. BURNE *Shropshire Folklore* xx. We have the sayings...'Dream of a funeral, hear of a wedding' ...and vice versa. **1909** *British Weekly* 8 July 331 'Dream of a funeral and you hear of a marriage'...has probably been verified many times in the experience of ordinary people. ■ dreams 夢

dream ⇒ MORNING dreams come true.

DREAMS go by contraries.
夢は逆夢になる。

□*c***1400** *Beryn* (EETS) I. 108 Comynly of these swevenys [dreams] the contrary man shul fynde.

128　dressed

1584 LYLY *Sappho & Phao* IV. iii. I dreamed last night, but I hope dreams are contrary, that...all my hair blazed on a bright flame. **1673** W. WYCHERLEY *Gentleman Dancing-Master* IV.64 Ne're fear It, dreams go by the contraries. **1731** FIELDING *Grub-Street Opera* 1. xi. Oh! the perjury of men! I find dreams do not always go by contraries. **1860** T. C. HALIBURTON *SeasonTicket* 30 The events of life, like dreams, appear in the words of the old proverb, 'to go by contraries'. **1932** J. H. WALLIS *Capital City Murder* iv. There was no sign...of Lester Armande. 'Dreams go by contraries,' said Lily. **1973** 'P. SIMPLE' *Stretchford Chronicles* (1980) 198 They say dreams go by opposites....Perhaps you'll dream about that AA man again. ■ **dreams 夢**

dressed ⇒ FIRST up, best dressed.

drink ⇒ EAT, drink, and be merry... ; You can take a HORSE to the water, but you can't make him drink.

He that DRINKS beer, thinks beer.
ビールを飲む人はビールのことしか頭にない。

(訳注：he＝「〈関係節を伴って〉…する者は誰でも〈性別は問わない〉」。*He that* is not with me is against me.〈私に味方しない者は私に敵対する〉〈『マタイによる福音書』12章30節〉)

ビールは飲む人の思考を鈍らせる。これはビールが下層階級の人たちの主要な酒であった時代に遡る汚名の1つである。

□ **1820** W. IRVING *Sketch Book of Geoffrey Crayon* vii. 70 (*footnote*) They who drink beer will think beer. **1867** A. O. RICHARDSON *Beyond Mississippi* i. 'They who drink beer think beer,' but Catawba and Muscatel neither muddle the brain nor fire the passions. **1912** R. A. FREEMAN *Mystery of 31, New Inn* v. 'You despise the good old British John Barleycorn.' 'He that drinks beer thinks beer,' retorted Thorndyke. **1958** D. G. BROWNE *Death in Seven Volumes* xii. 'He who drinks beer, thinks beer,' was one of his favourite aphorisms. ■ **action and consequence 行為と結果 ; drunkenness 酩酊 ; food and drink 飲食物**

A DRIPPING June sets all in tune.
6月に雨が降ると万事うまく運ぶ。

雨の多い6月は多くの花を咲かせ、その結果、豊かな実りをもたらすという考えから。

□ **1742** *Agreeable Companion* 35 A dripping June Brings all Things in Tune. **1883** W. ROPER *Weather Sayings* 22 A dry May and a dripping June brings all things in tune. **1912** *pectator* 28 Dec. 1094 'A dripping June sets all in tune,' and on sandy soils not only farm crops but garden flowers do best in a wet summer. ■ **weather lore 天気にまつわる伝承**

You can DRIVE out Nature with a pitchfork, but she keeps on coming back.
人の本性は熊手で追い払うことはできても、必ず戻ってくる。

(訳注：この場合の you は総称的な用法で、話し手や聞き手を含めた一般の人々を指している。one よりくだけた使い方。*You* never can tell what's going to happen.〈何が起きるかは誰にもわからない〉)

ホラティウス『書簡集』1. x. 24 *Naturam expelles furca, tamen usque recurret.*「熊手で本性を追い出すことはできるが、つねに戻ってくる」に由来する。

□ **1539** R. TAVERNER tr. *Erasmus' Adages* 44 Thurst out nature wyth a croche [staff], yet woll she styli runne backe agayne. **1831** T. L. PEACOCK *Crotchet Castle* i. Mr. Crotchet...seemed...to settle down...into an English country gentleman....But as, though you expel nature with a pitchfork, she will always come back. **1980** C. GAVIN *How sleep Brave* xiv. There was feminine logic for you!...'You can drive out Nature with a pitchfork,...but she keeps on coming back.' **2002** *Times* 31 May 41 'Pitchfork nature out of doors and it will come back through a window' was a comment on many would-be papal reforms. ■ **Nature** 自然・造物主; **persistence** ねばり強さ

drive ⇒ BAD money drives out good; HUNGER drives the wolf out ofthe wood; NEEDS must when the Devil drives; ONE nail drives out another.

drop ⇒ The LAST drop makes the cup run over.

dropping ⇒ CONSTANT dropping wears away a stone.

drowned ⇒ If you're BORN to be hanged then you'll never be drowned.

A DROWNING man will clutch at a straw.
溺れる者は藁をもつかもうとする。
　（訳注：will ＝「…するものだ」〈傾向・習性〉。at にも注意。clutch at... 「…をつかもうとして何度も手を出す」）

人はすべての希望がなくなっていくと、どんなにわずかなチャンスにも手を伸ばそうとする。clutch は比較的最近の形で、初期の catch よりさらに絶望の意味を強調している。to clutch at a straw (or straws)「藁にも縋ろうとする」は慣用句としてよく使われる。

□ **1534** MORE *Dialogue of Comfort* (1553) iii. Lyke a man that in peril of drowning catcheth whatsoeuer cometh next to hand...be it neuer so simple a sticke. **1583** J. PRIME *Fruitful &Brief Discourse* 1. 30 We do not as men redie to be drowned, catch at euery straw. **1748** RICHARD-SON *Clarissa* VII. i. A drowning man will catch at a straw, the Proverb well says. **1877** W. COL-LINS *My Lady's Money* xv. His gratitude caught at those words, as the drowning man is said to catch at the proverbial straw. **1915** CONRAD *Victory* IV. viii. Wang seemed to think my insistence...very stupid and tactless. But a drowning man clutches at straws. **1967** RIDOUT & WITTING *English Proverbs Explained* 49 A drowning man will clutch at a straw. **1967** T. STOP-PARD *Rosencrantz & Guildenstern are Dead* III. 80 We drift down time, clutching at straws. But what goad's a brick to a drowning man? ■ **hope and despair** 希望と絶望

drunken ⇒ CHILDREN and fools tell the truth; HEAVEN protects children, sailors, and drunken men.

druv (drove, driven): ⇒ SUSSEX won't be druv.

dry ⇒ You never MISS the water till the well runs dry; Sow dry and set wet; Put your TRUST in God, and keep your powder dry.

due ⇒ Give CREDIT where credit is due; GIVE the Devil his due.

dumb ⇒ A CHERRY year, a merry year.

dunghill ⇒ Every COCK will crow upon his own dunghill.

130   dust

dust ⇒ A PECK of March dust is worth a king's ransom.

duty ⇒ The FIRST duty of a soldier is obedience.

dying ⇒ You cannot SHIFT an old tree without it dying.

dyke ⇒ FEBRUARY fill dyke, be it black or be it white.

E

eagle ⇒ Where the CARCASE is, there shall the eagles be gathered together.

EAGLES don't catch flies.
鷲はハエなど捕まえない。

大物は些細な事柄や取るに足りない人々に関わらない。†エラスムス『格言集』III. ii. *Aquila non captat muscas.*「鷲はハエなぞ捕まえぬ」

☐ **1563** *Mirror for Magistrates* (1938) 405 The iolly Egles catche not little flees. **1581** G. PETTIE tr. *S. Guazzo's Civil Conversation* II. 48v That is the right act of a Prince, and therefore it is well saide, That the Egle catcheth not flies. **1786** H. L. PIOZZI *Anecdotes of Johnson* 185 With regard to slight insults ... 'They sting one (says he) but as a fly stings a horse; and the eagle will not catch flies.' **1942** H. C. BAILEY *Nobody's Vineyard* i. 'Eagles don't catch flies.' 'What do you mean?' 'Inspectors of Police don't trail urchins.' **1980** A. T. ELLIS *Birds of Air* (1983) 92 'Aquila non captat muscas,' she told him in a reassuring whisper. 'Eagles don't catch flies.' ■ **great and small 大と小**

ear ⇒ FIELDS have eyes, and woods have ears; LITTLE pitchers have large ears; You can't make a SILK purse out of a sow's ear; WALLS have ears.

The EARLY bird catches the worm.
早起き鳥が虫を捕まえる。
（訳注：「早起きは三文の得」）

2001 年の用例にある it's the second mouse that gets the cheese.「チーズを取るのは結局のところ 2 番目のネズミである」という帰結を述べたのは米国のコメディアン、スティーブン・ライト（1955-）である。特に企業開発あるいは技術革新の分野で使われる。その分野では 1 番（つまり 1 番のネズミ）である優勢者が追随者や模倣者（2 番目のネズミ）に先を越されることがある。それは、2 番手が直面するリスクの方が 1 番手よりも低いからである。

☐ **1636** W. CAMDEN *Remains concerning Britain* (ed. 5) 307 The early bird catcheth the worme. **1859** H. KINGSLEY *Geoffrey Hamlyn* II. xiv. Having worked ... all the week ... a man comes Into your room at half-past seven ... and Informs you that the 'early bird gets the worm'. **1892** ZANG-WILL *Big Bow Mystery* i. Grodman was not an early bird, now that he had no worms to catch. He could afford to despise proverbs now. **1996** R. POE *Return to House of Usher* ix. 167 'I got home at midnight last night and I'm here at seven. Where are they? ... Well, it's the early bird that catches the worm, and no mistake.' **2001** *Washington Post* 4 Sept. C13 The early bird may

132 EARLY

catch the worm, but it's the second mouse that gets the cheese. Don't be in a hurry to take a winner. ■ **diligence** 勤勉；**efficiency and inefficiency** 能率と非能率

The EARLY man never borrows from the late man.
早く種を蒔く者が遅く種を蒔く者から（穀物を）を借りることは決してない。

（訳注：1659年と1732年の用例にある borrow of の of は「…から」の意）

早く種を蒔く農家は遅く種を蒔く農家より収穫も早い。

☐ **1659** J. HOWELL *Proverbs* (English) 17 The rath [early] sower never borroweth of the late. **1732** T. FULLER *Gnomologia* no. 4492 The early Sower never borrows of the Late. **1978** R. WHIT-LOCK *Calendar of Country Custom* iii. Oats, too, benefit from early sowing.... Another agricultural proverb ... declares that, 'the early man never borrows from the late man'. ■ **borrowing and lending** 貸し借り

EARLY to bed and early to rise, makes a man healthy, wealthy, and wise.
早寝早起きは人を健康に、金持ちに、そして賢くする。

（訳注：makes と make に 3 単現の -s が付いているのは、early to bed and early to rise〈早寝早起き〉が 1 つの概念として捉えられているため）

たとえ健康、富、知恵が目に見えて増えなくても、早寝がもたらす恩恵は科学的にも裏打ちされている（2002年の用例参照）。

☐ **1496** *Treatise of Fishing with Angle* Hl As the olde englysshe prouerbe sayth in this wyse. Who soo woll ryse erly shall be holy helthy and zely [fortunate]. **1523** J. FITZHERBERT *Husbandry* (1530) 52ᵛ At gramer scole I lerned a verse, ... erly rysynge maketh a man hole in body, holer in soule, and rycher in goodes. **1639** J. CLARKE *Parremiologia Anglo-Latina* 91 Earley to bed and early to rise, makes a man healthy, wealthy, and wise. **1853** SURTEES *Sponge's Sporting Tour* ix. Early to bed and earlyto rise being among Mr. Sponge's maxims, he was enjoying the view ... shortly after daylight. **2002** *New Scientist* 29 June 57 A lot of sleep doesn't make us happier.... It's going to bed earlier that counts. There really is much to be said for 'early to bed early to rise, makes one healthy, wealthy and wise.' ■ **diligence** 勤勉；**health** 健康；**riches** 富

earned ⇒ A PENNY saved is a penny earned.

easier ⇒ It is easier to PULL down than to build up; It is easier to RAISE the Devil than to lay him; ⇒ EASY.

EAST is east. and west is west.
東は東、西は西である。

東洋と西洋にはどうしても埋められない文化の差があることを述べている。

☐ **1892** R. KIPLING *Barrack-room Ballads* 75 Oh, East is East, and West is West, and never the twain shall meet. **1909** M. BARING *Orpheus in Mayfair* 271 Sledge said 'Goodnight' again, but when he was on the stairs he called back: 'In any case remember one thing, that East is East and West is West. Don't mix your deities.' **1994** *English Today* Oct. 19/2 East is east and west is west, and it will be a long time before fishermen from the bookends of Canada agree on delicate matters of taste over a plate of oysters. ■ **familiarity** 慣れ親しみ；**harmony and disharmony** 調和と不調和；**opposites** 逆

EAT 133

EAST, west, home's best
東に行こうが、西に行こうが、我が家こそが一番である。

どれだけ遠方に旅をしても、結局、我が家にまさる所はない。

□1859 W. K. KELLY *Proverbs of all Nations* 36 'East and west, at home the best' (German)....
Ost und West; daheim das Best. 1869 C. H. SPURGEON *John Ploughman's Talk* xiii. East and
west, Home is best. 1920 E. V. LUCAS *Verena in Midst* cxiii. None the less I don't envy the travel-
ler. 'East, west, home's best.' 1994 'C. AIRD' 'Fair Cop' in *Injury Time* (1995) 27 As the police
professional in Calleshire most involved with murder, Detective Inspector Sloan would have been
the last man in the world to subscribe to the view that 'East or West, Home's Best' since home
was where most victims of murder met their end. ■ **home 家庭・母国**

east ⇒ When the WIND is in the east, 'tis neither good for man nor beast.

EASY come, easy go
簡単に入ってくる物は簡単に出ていく。
（訳注：「悪銭身につかず」）

簡単に手に入ったもの（特に金銭）は、たちまち消えてしまうもの。LIGHT come, light
go. と QUICKLY come, quickly go. の2つも同じ考え方を述べているが、それほど一般
的ではない。†15世紀初頭のフランス語 *Tost acquis tost se despens.*「早く手に入る
と、早くなくなる」

□1650 A. BRADSTREET *Tenth Muse* 126 That which easily comes, as freely goes. 1832 S. WAR-
REN *Diary of Late Physician* II. xi. 'Easy come, easy go' is . . . characteristic of rapidly acquired
commercial fortunes. 1960 I. JEFFERIES *Dignity & Purity* ii. She's your only daughter, isn't
she.... Well, easy come, easy go. 2002 *National Review* 11 Mar. 28 After all, if tattoos can be removed at public expense, why bother to think very carefully about having them done in the first
place? Easy come, easy go. ■ **getting and spending 取得と消費**

EASY does it
慌てずゆっくりやれば事は成し遂げられる。

落ち着いてやると良い結果が生まれる。同様な意味で Gently does it. も使われる。類似
した形式としては It's DOGGED as does it.「事を成し遂げるには根気が必要である」が
挙げられる。

□1863 T. Taylor *Ticket-of-Leave Man* IV. i. Easy does it, Bob. Hands off, and let's take things
pleasantly. 1928 J. P. MCEVOY *Showgirl* 21 No high pressure stuff, sis. Easy does it with Dick.
1972 A. PRICE *Colonel Butler's Wolf* iii. Easy does it—the nails are big, but they are old and brit-
tle. 1981 S. RUSHDIE *Midnight's Children* I. 103 Important to build bridges ... between the
faiths. Gently does it. ■ **tact 機転 ; ways and means 方法と手段**

easy ⇒ It is easy to find a STICK to beat a dog; It is easy to be WISE after the event; ⇒
EASIER.

You are what you EAT.
人は食べているものからできている。

ドイツ語 *Mann ist was Mann isst.*「人は食べているものからできている」。†ヤコブ・

モレスホット『食物学』の中の哲学者ルートヴィヒ・フォイエルバッハ (1804-72) の言葉。また、『市民のために』(1850) の「広告コピー」*Der Mensch ist, was er isst.*「人は食べているものからできている」としても使われた。このことわざはフランスの食通家アンテルム・ブリア＝サヴァランに由来すると言われることもある。彼は『味覚の生理学 (美味礼讃)』(1825) の中で次のように述べているからである。*Dis-moi ce que tu manges, je te dirai ce que tu es.*「いつも食べているものを言ってごらん。君がどのような人物か当ててみせよう」

□ **1930** J. GOLLOMB *Subtle Trail* ii. 55 There flashed through her mind the German saying, 'One is what one eats.' **1940** V. H. LINDLAHR (*title*) You are what you eat. **1980** FARE&ARMELAGOS *Consuming Passions* 3 Food faddists in recent decades have declared, 'You are what you eat'. **2014** *Times* 29 May 24 It is certainly time ... for consumers to take far more seriously the old adage that you are what you eat. ■ **food and drink** 飲食物

We must EAT a peck of dirt before we die.
人は一生のうちに、1 ペックの泥を食べなければならない。

文字通り慰めの意味でよく使われる (1979 年の用例参照)。さらに、少しくらいの泥なら食べても心配ないよと安心させる場合にも使われる (1738 年の用例参照)。なお、peck とは 2 ガロン (約 9 リットル) を示す乾量単位である。† **1603** H. CHETTLE et al. *Patient Grisel* A3ᵛ I thinke I shall not eate a pecke of salt: I shall not liue long sure. 「1 ペックもの塩を食べようとは思わない。そんなに長生きしないだろうから」

□ **1738** SWIFT *Polite Conversation* I. 48 'Why then, here's some Dirt m my Tea-cup.' ... 'Pohl you must eat a Peck of Dirt before you die.' **1819** KEATS *Letter* 19 Mar. (1952) 314 This is the second black eye I have had since leaving school ... we must eat a peck before we die. **1979** M. BABSON *Twelve Deaths of Christmas* xxix. She tried to rinse off the ice cubes. 'Never mind.... They say, we all have to eat a peck of dirt before we die!' **2010** *Tufts Nutrition* XI. ii (online) 'We will all eat a peck of dirt before we die,' or so the adage goes. I'll bet our ancestors never imagined that antibiotic-resistant bacteria and modern-day pesticides would one day be included in the dished-up dirt. ■ **health** 健康 ; **mortality** 死すべき運命

EAT, drink, and be merry, for tomorrow we die.
食べて飲んで楽しめ。どうせ明日は死ぬのだから。

聖書の中の 2 つのことわざが融合したもの。1 つは『コヘレトの言葉』8 章 15 節 (欽定訳聖書) Then I commended mirth, because a man hath no better thing under the sun, than to eat, and to drink, and to be merry ...「そこで私は歓楽をたたえる。それは日の下では、人にとって、食い、飲み、楽しむよりほかに良いことはないからである …」。もう 1 つは『イザヤ書』22 章 13 節 (欽定訳聖書) Let us eat and drink; for to morrow we shall die.「われわれは食い、かつ飲もう。明日は死ぬのだから」。多くの滑稽な言い方がある (2001 年の用例参照)。

□ **1870** D. G. ROSSETTI 'The Choice' in House of Life, Sonnet bod. Eat thou and drink; tomorrow thou shalt die. **1884** E. LYALL *We Two* xii. 240 But far from prompting him to repeat the maxim 'Let us eat and drink, for tomorrow we die!' it spurred him rather to a sort of fiery energy, never satisfied with. what it had accomplished. **1960** O. MANNING *Great Fortune* (1988) 42 Inchcape ... complained: 'I've never before seen. this place in such a hubbub.' 'It's the war.' said Clarence. 'Eat, drink and be merry, for tomorrow we may be starving to death.' **1975** N. GUILD *Lost and Found Man* 87 No point in getting morbid.... What the hell. Eat, drink, and be merry,

eating　135

and all that crap. Lukas signaled the waiter and ordered another two croissants. **2001** *New Scientist* 22/29 Dec. 45 Eat, drink and be merry, for tomorrow we die. ■ **life** 人生；**opportunity** 機会・好機

He that would EAT the fruit must climb the tree.
果物が食べたい者は木に登らなければならない。

(訳注：he =「〈関係節を伴って〉…する者は誰でも〈性別は問わない〉」。*He that* is not with me is against me.〈私に味方しない者は私に敵対する〉〈『マタイによる福音書』12章30節〉。「虎穴に入らずんば虎児を得ず」)

何かを楽しみたいなら、まずそれを手に入れなければならない。† **1577** J. グランジェ *Golden Aphroditis* Ml Who will the fruyte that haruest yeeldes, must take the payne.「熟れた果物が欲しい者は危険を冒さなければならない」。1970年の用例は明らかに性的な意味合いを帯びている。

□**1721** J. KELLY *Scottish Proverbs* 141 He that would eat the Fruit must climb the Tree. **1843** 'R. CARLTON' *New Purchase* I. xxiv. It is a proverb, 'He that would eat the fruit must first climb the tree and get it': but when that fruit is honey, he that wants it must first cut it down. **1970** V. CANNING *Great Affair* xiv. 'Son, are you one of those who like to eat the fruit and then walk away from the tree?' 'I want to marry her.' ■ **wanting and having** 不足と所持

EAT to live, not live to eat.
生きるために食え、食うために生きるな。

アテネの哲学者ソクラテスの言葉とされる（ディオゲネス・ラエルティオス『ソクラテス』II. xxxiv 参照）。ἐλεγέ τε τοὺς μὲν ἄλλους ἀνθρώπους ζῆν ἵν᾽ ἐσθίοιεν; αὐτὸς δὲ ἐσθίειν ἵνα ζώη.「食べるために生きる人もいるが、私は生きるために食べるのだと彼は言った。」† キケロ *Rhetoricorum* IV. vii. *Edere oportet ut vivas, non vivas ut edas.*「人は生きるために食べなければいけない、食べるために生きてはならない」。フランス語 **1668** モリエール『守銭奴』III. v. Suivant le dire d'un ancien, 'il faut manger pour vivre, et non pas vivre pour manger'.

□**1387** J. TREVISA tr. *Higden's Polychronicon* (1871) III. 281 Socrates seide that many men wll leve forto ete and drynke, and that they wolde ete and drynke ... forto lyve. *c* **1410** in *Secreta Secretorum* (1898) 67 I will ete so that y leue, and noghtlyfthaty ete. **1672** T. SHADWELL *Miser* 46 Bat to live, not live to eat; as the Proverb says. **1912** A. W. PINERO *Preserving Mr. Panmure* II.85 I shall eat sufficient ... But I eat to live; I don't live to eat. **2001** *Country Life* 20/27 Dec. 80 If I had to give a yes or a no to the old question 'Do you live to eat or eat to live?' I should say yes to the first part. ■ **food and drink** 飲食物

eat ⇒ The CAT would eat fish, but would not wet her feet; DOG does not eat dog; You cannot HAVE your cake and eat it; When the LAST tree is cut down, ... you will realize that you cannot eat money; If you won't WORK you shan't eat.

eaten ⇒ REVENGE is a dish that can be eaten cold.

eating ⇒ APPETITE comes with eating; The PROOF of the pudding is in the eating.

136 eavesdroppers

eavesdroppers ⇒ LISTENERS never hear any good of themselves.

egg ⇒ As good be an ADDLED egg as an idle bird; The same FIRE that melts the butter hardens the egg; You cannot make an OMELETTE without breaking eggs; There is REASON in the roasting of eggs; Don't TEACH your grandmother to suck eggs.

Don't put all your EGGS in one basket.
すべての卵を 1 つの籠に入れるな。

　1 つの投機的事業にすべてを賭けるのではなく、危険を分散させよ。*to put all one's eggs in one basket*「全資産を 1 つの事業に投じる」は慣用句として一般的に使われている。

　□**1662** G. TORRIANO *Italian Proverbial Phrases* 125 To put all ones Eggs in a Paniard, viz. to hazard all in one bottom [ship]. **1710** S. PALMER *Proverbs* 344 Don't venture all your Eggs in One Basket. **1894** 'M. TWAIN' *Pudd'nhead Wilson in Century Mag.* XLVII. VI. 817 Behold, the fool saith, 'Put not all thine eggs in the one basket' —which is but a manner of saying, 'Scatter your money and your attention'; but the wise man saith, 'Put all your eggs in the one basket and— watch that basket.' **1967** RIDOUT & WITTING *English Proverbs Explained* 46 Don't put all your eggs in one basket. **2002** *Washington Post* 23 May E3 What part of 'don't put all your eggs in one basket' isn't clear? Putting all or most of your money into one stock is gambling, not investing. ■ **prudence** 思慮・分別

eight ⇒ FALL down seven times, get up eight; SIX hours' sleep for a man, seven for a woman, and eight for a fool.

elephant ⇒ With a SWEET tongue and kindness, you can drag an elephant by a hair.

When ELEPHANTS fight, it is the grass that suffers.
象どうしが戦ったら、被害を被るのは草地である。

　アフリカのことわざで、強者同士の争いの中では弱者が傷つく。

　□**1936** *New York Times* 26 Mar. (online) As citizens of a country whose fate depends on the policies and changing moods of powerful neighbours, Belgians quote frequently these days a proverb learned in the Congo: 'When elephants fight it is the grass that suffers.' **1986** *New York Times* 23 Nov. (online) 'Angolans say "When two elephants fight, it is the grass that suffers,"' an aide worker here commented. **2003** *Journal of Literacy Research* Spring (online) 'When elephants fight, only the grass gets trampled.' This African proverb is used regularly to describe ... officials and leaders whose disputes and divisions end up hurting innocent ... people. ■ **strength and weakness** 強弱; **violence** 暴力

eleven ⇒ POSSESSION is nine points of the law; RAIN before seven, fine before eleven.

Every ELM has its man.
どのヤシの木の下にも人がいる。

　ヤシの木は前触れもなしに枝を落とすとされる。**1906** キップリング『プークヶ丘の妖精パック』32 Ellum she hateth mankind, and waiteth Till every gust be laid To drop a limb on the head of him That any way trusts her shade. 「ヤシの木の下に人がいる。ヤシの木は突風が吹いて、木陰を求めてやって来た人の頭に大枝が落ちるのを待っている」

□ **1928** *Times* 29 Nov. 10 Owing to the frequency with which this tree sheds its branches, or is uprooted in a storm, it has earned for itself a sinister reputation. 'Every elm has its man' is an old country saying. **2007** N. P. MONEY *Triumph of Fungi* 30 The proverb stating that 'Every elm has its man' is utterly opaque. ■ **death** 死 ; **fate and fatalism** 運命と運命論

emperor ⇒ The MOUNTAINS are high, and the emperor is far away.

EMPTY sacks will never stand upright.
空の袋はたてには立てぬ。

（訳注：will ＝「…するものだ」〈傾向・習性〉。Oil *will* float on water. 〈油は水に浮くものだ〉）

極度の貧困は生存を不可能にする。何かを飲んだり食べたりしなくてはならないという論拠としても使われる（1978年の用例参照）。

□ **1642** G. TORRIANO *Select Italian Proverbs* 90 Sacco vuoto non puo star in piedi. An emptie sack cannot stand upright: nota, Applied to such as either pinch themselves, or are pincht by hard fortune. **1758** B. FRANKLIN *Poor Richard's Almanack* (Introduction) Poverty often deprives a Man of all Spirit and Virtue; 'Tis hard for an empty Bag to stand up-right. **1860** G. ELIOT *Mill on Floss* I. I. viii. There's folks as things 'ull allays go awk'ard with: empty sacks 'ull never stand upright. **1958** B. BEHAN *Borstal Boy* III. 310 We've a long night before us and an empty sack won't stand. **1978** J. MCGAHERN *Getting Through* 99 'Give this man something.' ... 'A cup of tea will do fine,' he had protested.... 'Nonsense.... Empty bags can't stand.' ■ **hunger** 飢え・空腹 ; **poverty** 貧困

EMPTY vessels make the most sound.
空の入れ物が一番大きな音を立てる。

言うべき内容を持たない浅はかな者ほどおしゃべりで、騒々しい。ここで vessel は drinking-vessel「水差し」のような容器を指す。

□ **a1430** J. LYDGATE *Pilgrimage of Man* (EETS) L 15933 A voyde vessel ... maketh outward a gret soun, Mor than ... what yt was ful. **1547** W. BALDWIN *Treatise of Moral Philosophy* IV. Q4 As emptye vesselles make the lowdest sounde: so they that haue least wyt, are the greatest babblers. **1599** SHAKESPEARE *Henry V* IV. iv. 64 I did never know so full a voice issue from so empty a heart but the saying is true—The empty vessel makes the greatest sound. **1707** SWIFT *Essay on Faculties of Mind* I. 249 Empty Vessels sound loudest. **1967** RIDOUT &WITTING *English Proverbs Explained* 51 Empty vessels make the most sound. **1982** J. BINGHAM *Brock &Defector* xiii. 'All talk and no action.... ' 'Empty vessels make the most noise,' Brock agreed. **2002** *Times* : *Register* 21 Oct 10 The adage 'empty vessels make most noise' has certainly come to mind as I have listened to many other politicians. ■ **boasting** 自慢 ; **words and deeds** 言動

empty ⇒ BETTER are small fish than an empty dish; Don't THROW the baby out with the bathwater.

enchantment ⇒ DISTANCE lends enchantment to the view.

The END crowns the work.
仕上げが仕事の最後を飾る。

仕事の善し悪しはうまく仕上がった時に初めて決まる。†ラテン語 *Finis coronat opus.*「仕上げが作品に栄誉を与える」。15世紀のフランス語 *La fin loe l'œuvre.*「仕上げが作品を称賛する」

□**1509** H. WATSON *Ship of Fools* Ddl For the ende crowneth. **1592** G. DELAMOTHE *French Alphabet* I. 29 The end doth crowne the worke.... La fin couronne l'amvre. **1602** SHAKESPEARE *Troilus & Cressida* IV. v. 223 The end crowns all; And that old common arbitrator, Time, Will one day end it. **1820** SCOTT *Abbot* I. xiii. As the end crowns the work, it also forms the rule by which it must be ultimately judged. **1870** DICKENS *Edwin Drood* xviii. Proof, sir, proof, must be built up stone by stone.... As I say, the end crowns the work. **1961** J. WEBB *One for my Dame* iii. That the end should crown the work, that I had given no more lies than I had been told made no difference. You either played it straight or you didn't. ■ **finality** 結末・終局

The END justifies the means.
目的は手段を正当化する。
(訳注：「嘘も方便」)

ある重要な目的を達成するためには、よこしまで違法な手段に訴えることも許されるという考え方。†オウィディウス『名婦の書簡』ii. 85 *Exitus acta probat.*「結果が行動を正当化する」。こうした考え方は多くの場合、道徳的に問題があるので否定形もしばしば使われる（2001年と2014年の用例参照）。

□**1583** G. BABINGTON *Exposition of Commandments* 260 The ende good, doeth not by and by make the meanes good. **1718** M. PRIOR *Literary Works* (1971) I. 186 The End must justify the Means: He only Sins who ill intends. **1941** 'H. BAILEY' *Smiling Corpse* 238 'The police don't like to have their bodies moved.' ... 'In this case the end justifies the means.' **2001** *Washington Times* 2 Aug. Al6 The conservatives' war on drugs is an example of good intentions that have had unfortunate consequences. As often happens with noble causes, the end justifies the means, and the means of the drug war are inconsistent with the U.S. Constitution and our civil liberties. **2014** *Tirnes* 17 Dec. 31 The end does not justify the means, and it is never right to commit an evil in the hope of eradicating another evil. ■ **action and consequence** 行為と結果

end ⇒（名詞）ALL good things must come to an end; The DEVIL can quote Scripture for his own ends; EVERYTHING has an end; He who WILLS the end, wills the means;（動詞）All's WELL that ends well.

ending ⇒ A GOOD beginning makes a good ending.

endured ⇒ What can't be CURED must be endured.

The ENEMY of my enemy is my friend.
敵の敵は味方。

古代アラビアのことわざ（2001年の用例参照）と伝えられるが、確証はない。

□**1985** M. KORDA *Queenie* III. xiii. 347 In California, I'm an outsider. So is Wolff, so we're natural allies. "The enemy of my enemy is my friend," as I believe the Arabs say. **1992** MIEDER Dict. *American Proverbs* 181 The enemies of my enemies are my friends. **2000** *New Yorker* 25 Sept

56/1 The enemy-of-my-enemy-is-my-friend logic ... dominates central-African politics. **2001** *Spectator* 24 Nov. 36 The hack right-wing answer ... is to quote what the quoters claim to be 'the old Arab proverb': 'The enemy of my enemy is my friend.' **2008** K. M. HILL *Tax Revolt* 5 The old axiom of 'the enemy of my enemy is my friend', which built alliances, was reversed to 'the friend of my enemy is my enemy', which built coalitions of enemies. ■ enemies 敵 ; friends 友

enemy ⇒ The BEST is the enemy of the good; It is good to make a BRIDGE of gold to a flying enemy; The GOOD is the enemy of the best; There is no LITTLE enemy; SAVE us from our friends; If you SIT by the river for long enough, you will ⇒ The body of your enemy float by.

ENGLAND is the paradise of women, the hell of horses, and the purgatory of servants.
イングランドは女にとっては天国、馬にとっては地獄、召使いにとっては煉獄である。

多くの異なった言い方のある古いことわざ。† **1558** ボナヴェンチュール・デ・ペリエ『笑話集』N1ᵛ *Paris ... c' est le paradis des femmes, l'enfer des mules, et le purgatorie des soliciteurs.* 「パリは女性にとっては天国、雌ラバにとっては地獄、弁護士にとっては煉獄である」。**1583** R. D. *Mirrour of Mirth* K1ᵛ *Paris* is a paradise for women, a hel for mens horse, and a Purgatory for those that followe suits of Law. 「パリは女性にとって天国、雄馬にとって地獄、訴訟に従うものにとっては煉獄である」

□**1591** J. FLORIO *Second Fruits* 205 She takes her ease, and followes her busines at home.... England is the paradise of women, the purgatory of men, and the hell of horses. **1617** F. MORYSON *Itinerary* III. I. iii. England ... is said to be the Hell of Horses, the Purgatory of Seruants, and the Paradice of Weomen. **1787** F. GROSE *Provincial Glossary* S. V. England, England is the paradise of women, hell of horses, and purgatory of servants. **1962** E. S. TURNER *What Butler Saw* i. An ancient proverb said that England was 'the hell of horses, the purgatory of servants and the paradise of women'. When the eighteenth century came in, England was still the hell of horses, but there were loud complaints that it had become the paradise of servants and the purgatory of women. ■ national characteristics 国民性

ENGLAND's difficulty is Ireland's opportunity.
イングランドのピンチはアイルランドのチャンス。

アイルランドとイングランドの何世紀にも渡る敵対関係を表わしている。1856 年の用例におけるオコンネルとはダニエル・オコンネル (1775-1847) を指す。彼は the Liberator (解放者) として知られるアイルランド・ローマカトリック国粋主義者のリーダーである。The difficulty-opportunity「ピンチ—チャンス」の型は他の文脈でもよく使われる (2015 年の用例参照)。

□**1856** *Tribune* 19 Jan. 188 Some few years ago, we followed O'Connell, and when he declared that 'England's difficulty is Ireland's opportunity', we threw our hats in the air. **1916** G. B. SHAW in *New York Times* (Mag.) 9 Apr. 2 The cry that 'England's Difficulty Is Ireland's Opportunity' is raised in the old senseless, spiteful way as a recommendation to stab England in the back when she is fighting some one else. **1969** T. PAKENHAM *Year of Liberty* i. Successive plantations—of Scottish Presbyterians in illster ... did not secure Ireland. The Catholics' watchword remained: 'England's difficulty is Ireland's opportunity.' **2015** *Spectator* 31 Jan. 12 The triumph of the Syriza

140　England

party in Greece presents [David Cameron] with a glorious opportunity to solve the European question ... Europe's difficulty is Cameron's opportunity. ■ **opportunity** 機会 ; **politics** 政治

England ⇒The CAT, the rat, and Lovell the dog, rule all England under the hog; What MAN-CHESTER says today, the rest of England says tomorrow; TURKEY, heresy, hops, and beer came into England all in one year.

The ENGLISH are a nation of shopkeepers.
英国人とは商人である。

〈訳注：nation =「〈集合的に単数・複数扱い〉国民〈people〉」。the French nation〈フランス国民〉）

B. E. オメーラの『流刑中のナポレオン』(1822) I. 103で述べられたナポレオンの言葉 *L'Angleterre est une nation de boutiquiers.*「英国は商人の国である」に由来するが、英国が商人の国というイメージはそれ以前からある。**1766** J. タッカー『商人からの手紙』46 Shop-keeper will never get the more Custom by beating his Customers; and what is true of a Shop-keeper, is true of a Shop-keeping Nation.「商人は客を殴ることで、得意先を増やすことはできない。商人に当てはまることは商人の国にも当てはまる」。**1776** アダム・スミス『国富論』II. IV. vii. To found a great empire for the sole purpose of raising up a people of customers, may at first sight appear a project fit only for a nation of shopkeepers.「商売相手を増やすという目的だけで帝国を作ることは、一見すると、商人の国だけに適合する事業計画に思えるかもしれない」

□**1831** DISRAELI *Young Duke* I. xi. Hast thou brought this, too, about that ladies' hearts should be won ... over a counter.... We are indeed a nation of shopkeepers. **1911** *Times Weekly* 17 Feb. 132 Napoleon ... described the English as a nation of shopkeepers. Uttered in a sneering spirit, it embodied ... the profound truth that our prosperity is based upon our trade. **1981** R. RENDELL *Put on by Cunning* xiv. Americans ... are a nation of salesmen just as the English are a nation of small shopkeepers. **2002** *Times* 5 Jan. 25 England is indeed a nation of shopkeepers, but it has always preferred to draw these shopkeepers from among the newly Anglicised. ■ **national characteristics** 国民性

One ENGLISHMAN can beat three Frenchmen.
1 人の英国人で 3 人のフランス人を倒せる。

現在は他の国に対しても、そして異なる人数の割合でも使われている。

□**1599** SHAKESPEARE *Henry V* III. vi. 144 When they were in health.... I thought upon one pair of English legs Did march three Frenchmen. **1745** H. WALPOLE *Letter* 13 July (1941) IX. 17 We, who formerly ... could any one of us beat three Frenchmen, are now so degenerated that three Frenchmen can evidently beat one Englishman. **1834** MARRYAT *Peter Simple* III. viii. My men ... there are three privateers.... It's just a fair match for you—one Englishman can always beat three Frenchmen. **1851** G. BORROW *Lavengro* I. xxvi. In the days of pugilism it was no vain boast to say, that one Englishman was a match for two of t'other race [the French]. **1913** A. LUNN *Harrovians* i. Peter knew that an Englishman can tackle three foreigners, and forgot that the inventor of this theory took care to oppose three Englishmen to one foreigner as often as possible. **1981** *London Review of Books* 16 July-5 Aug. 5 Spain's conquest of Mexico 'gave Europeans a new and potent myth', the conviction of one European as equal to twenty others. ■ **boasting** 自慢 ; **national characteristics** 国民性

ENOUGH   141

An ENGLISHMAN's house is his castle.
英国人にとって家庭は城である。

(訳注：英国人は他人が家庭のプライバシーを犯すのを許さない。それは法律でしっかりと守られている)

□ **1581** R. MULCASTER *Positions* xl. He is the appointer of his owne circumstance, and his house is his castle. **1642** T. FULLER *Fast Sermon* 28 It was wont to be said A mans house is his Castle but if this Castle of late hath proved unable to secure any, let them make their conscience their castle. **1791** BOSWELL *Life of Johnson* II. 284 In London ... a man's own house is truly his castle, in which he can be in perfect safety from intrusion. **1837** DICKENS *Pickwick Papers* xxiv. Some people maintains that an Englishman's house is his castle. That's gammon [nonsense]. **1998** *Garden* (*RoyalHorticultural Society*) May 313 An Englishman's house may be his castle, but does it follow that his garden is his forest? **2002** *Washington Times* 1 Aug. Al4 An Englishman's home is no longer his castle. Thanks to gun control zealots, England has become the land of choice for criminals. ■ **home** 家庭・母国 ; **national characteristics** 国民性

An ENGLISHMAN's word is his bond.
英国人の言葉は証文である。

口頭での約束を守ることは名誉ある人の証であると考えられている。一度約束がなされると、法的文書の資格を有しているかのように尊重されるべきである。しかしながら、下に挙げられているこの自己満悦的なことわざの用例からわかるように当初の言い方では英国人にはついても一言も触れられてはいない。

□ *c***1500** *Lancelot of Lake* (STS) I. 1671 O kingis word shuld be o kingis bonde. *a* **1606** *Nobody & Somebody* C2ᵛ Nobodies worde is as good as his bond. **1642** T. FULLER *HolyState* V. XIII. He hath this property of an honest man, that his word is as good as his band. **1754** RICHARDSON *Grandison* I. Letter ix. I am no flincher.... The word of Sir Rowland Meredith is as good as his bond. **1841** DICKENS *Old Curiosity Shop* Iviii. 'Marchioness,' said Mr. Swiveller, rising, 'the word of a gentleman is as good as his bond—sometimes better, as in the present case.' **1916** F. VANE *Letter* 14 Sept. in M. Gibbon *Inglorious Soldier* iii. [List of fictions underlying national conceit:] 3. That English justice is something much more superfine than any other sort of justice (owing to Public School training!) and that an Englishman's word is his bond. **1981** A. GRAHAM-YOOLL *Forgotten Colony* xvi. If a verbal promise is made the native, to seal the contract, usually says palabra de ingles, ... meaning that he will act as an Englishman, whose word is his bond. ■ **honour** 尊敬・名誉 ; **national characteristics** 国民性

ENOUGH is as good as a feast.
十分はごちそうも同然。

(訳注：何事も過度はいけない。ほどほどで一番である。足るを知らなければならない)

飲食に関して、文字通りの意味で使われる場合（1375年の用例）と、過度の期待に対する警告として比喩的に用いられる場合とがある（2000年の用例）。

□ *c***1375** J. BARBOUR *Bruce* (EETS) XIV. 363 He maid thame na gud fest, perfay [truly], And nocht-for-thi [nevertheless] yneuch had thai. *c* **1470** MALORY *Morte d'Arthur* (1967) I. 246 Inowghe is as good as a feste. **1546** J. HEYWOOD *Dialogue of Proverbs* II. xi. Ml Here is enough, I am satisfied (sayde he) ... For folke say, enough Is as good as a feast. **1833** LAME *Elia's Last Essays* vi. That enough is as good as a feast. Not a man, woman, or child in ten miles round Guildhall, who really believes this saying. **1928** D. H. LAWRENCE *Woman who rode Away* 165 I'll live with another woman but I'll never marry another. Enough is as good as a feast. **2000** T. & R. MAGUOZZI *In Our Humble Opinion* 208 And now we know from our Happiness equation that the problem is high Expectations. Enough is as good as a feast. ■ **content and discontent** 満足と不満足 ; **food and drink** 飲食物

142 ENOUGH

ENOUGH is enough.
十分で十分。

満足の表現（† ENOUGH is as good as a feast.「十分はごちそうも同然」）としての古い用法を経て、今では不適切な行動や行き過ぎた行動をやめさせるための言葉となっている。

☐1546 J. HEYWOOD *Dialogue of Proverbs* 11. xi. M1 Sens enough is enough (sayd I) here maie we With that one word take end good. **1832** W. IRVING *Alhambra* II. 40 'I will descend for no more,' said the Moor, doggedly; 'enough is enough for a reasonable man—more is superfluous.' **1915** T. DREISER *Titan* (ed. 3) xlvii. 404 I realize all its merits just as well as you do. But enough is enough. **2007** *New Scientist* 20 Oct 59 Also then I'd get talking about people that I still see, and I didn't think much would be gained by it ... Enough is enough. ■ **content and discontent** 満足と不満足；**moderation** 節度・中庸

enough ⇒ Throw DIRT enough, and some will stick; Give a man ROPE enough and he will hang himself; A WORD to the wise is enough.

envied ⇒ BETTER be envied than pitied.

equal ⇒ DOGS look up to you, cats look down on you, Pigs is equal.

To ERR is human (to forgive divine)
過ちは人の常（許すは神の業）。

ラテン語の原文（*Humanum est errare.*「過ちをするのが人間である」）と、より古い時代の英語の形もあるが、一般にはイギリスの詩人ポープの言葉として引用されることが多い（1711年の用例参照）。† **1386** チョーサー『メリベ物語』I. 1264 The proverbe seith that 'for to do synne is mannyssh, but certes for to persevere longe in synne is werk of the devel.'「ことわざに曰く、罪を犯すのは人間だが、罪を長引かせるのは悪魔の仕業である」。**1539** モリソン訳『J. L. ビーベスの学問入門』D 7 It is naturally gyuen to al men, to erre, but to no man to perseuer ... therein.「すべての人間は生まれながらに罪を犯すように作られているが、その罪を背負って耐えていく力は与えられていない」。

☐1578 H. WOTTON tr. *J. Yver's Courtly Controversy* E3 To offend is humaine, to repent diuine, and to perseuere diuelish. **1659** J. HOWELL *Proverbs* (French) 12 To erre is humane, to repent is divine, to persevere is Diabolicall. **1711** POPE *Essay on Criticism* I. 525 Good-Nature and Good-Sense must ever join; To Err is Humane; to Forgive, Divine. **1908** *Times Literary Supplement* 27 Mar. I The modern moralist pardons everything, because he is not certain of anything, except that to err is human. **2000** T. DALRYMPLE *Life at Bottom* (2001) 222 To err is human, to forgive divine: and the police have now taken up the role of divinities, making allowances for wrongdoers instead of apprehending them. ■ **forgiveness** 許し・寛容；**wrong-doers** 悪事をなす者

escape ⇒ LITTLE thieves are hanged, but great ones escape.

eternal ⇒ HOPE springs eternal.

EVERY 143

Eve ⇒ When ADAM delved and Eve span, who was then the gentleman?

even ⇒ (形容詞) Don't get MAD, get even; Never give a SUCKER an even break; (副詞) Even a WORM will turn.

evensong ⇒ Be the DAY weary or be the day long, at last it ringeth to evensong.

event ⇒ COMING events cast their shadows before; It is easy to be WISE after the event.

ever ⇒ NOTHING is for ever.

EVERY little helps.
どんなに小さいものでも役に立つ。

(訳注:「塵も積もれば山となる」)

† **1590** G. モーリア *Deviz Familiers* A 6 *Peu ayde, disçoit le formy, pissant en mer en plein midy*.「どんなに小さな助けでも、正午に海に小便をするくらいは役に立つと蟻が言った」

☐**1602** P. GAWDY *Letters* (1906) 118 The wrenn sayde all helpte when she—in the sea. **1623** W. CAMDEN *Remains concerning Britain* (ed. 3) 268 Euery thing helpes, quoth the Wrenwhen she pist i' the sea. **1787** E. HAZARD in *Collections of Massachusetts Hist. Society* (1877) 5th Ser. II. 477 A guinea is a guinea, and every little helps. **1840** MARRYAT *Poor Jack* xiii. It's a very old saying, that every little helps.... Almost all the men were on the larboard side. **1988** J. MORTIMER *Rumpole and Age of Miracles* (1989) 48 'I'll get him to make a few inquiries relative to the bird in question. Every little helps.' **2014** *New Scientist* 11 Oct. 41 It is slow progress, and we are still looking for the killer material ... But in the uphill battle against thermodynamics, every little helps. ■ **assistance** 援助 ; **great and small** 大小

EVERY man for himself.
各自皆自分のことをやれ。

後になって拡張された形式 Every man for himself, and devil take the hindmost.「皆、自分の仕事に精を出せ。仕事が一番遅い者は悪魔に捕まってしまえ」と Everyman for himself, and God for us all.「人は皆自分自身のために、神は万人のために」も参照。

☐**c1386** CHAUCER *Knight's Tale* I. 1182 At the kynges court, my brother, Ech man for hymself, ther is noon oother. **1478** J. WHETLEY *Letter* 20 May in Paston Letters (1976) II. 427 Your moder ... hath made herwyll, the wyche ye shall understond more when I corn, for ther is every man for hym selff. **1678** J. RAY *English Proverbs* (ed. 2) (Scottish) 366 Every man for himself (quoth the Merteine). **1795** D. YANCEY *Letter* 6 June in *Virginia Magazine of Hist. &Biography* (1922) XXX. 224 The old adage might well be applied in many cases. Every man for himself. **1974** A. PRICE *Other Paths to Glory* II. vi. It was pretty much every man for himself. But I was hit quite early on. ■ **self-preservation** 自己防衛

EVERY man for himself, and devil take the hindmost.
皆、自分の仕事に精を出せ。仕事が一番遅い者は悪魔に捕まってしまえ。

(訳注 : DEVIL take the hindmost. に関する訳注を参照)

144 EVERY

誰もが自分の利益のためだけに動き、失敗した人やついてこれない人に何が起ころうと誰も心配しないような状況について使われる。以下の 2 つの最も初期の用例は、次に登場することわざと形がよく似ている。DEVIL take the hindmost. だけが独立して使われることもある。

☐ **1530** A. BARCLAY *Eclogues* (EETS) I. 1009 Eche man for him selfe, and the fiende for all. **1573** J. SANFORDE 108ᵛ Euery man for him selfe; and the Deuill for all. **1858** D. M. MULOCK *Women's Thoughts about Women* ii. The world is hard enough, for two-thirds of it are struggling for the dear life— 'each for himself, and de'il talc the hindmost' **1939** L. I. WIWER *By Shores of Silver Lake* xxv. There wasn't any standing in line.... It was each fellow for himself and devil take the hindmost. **2001** *Spectator* 24 Nov. 29 One senses that ... Tories are hostile to that extra refinement of civilisation: it's every man for himself, and devil take the hindmost Remember what Mrs Thatcher said about not helping 'lame ducks' ... ? ■ **self-preservation** 自己防衛

EVERY man for himself, and God for us all.
人は皆は自分自身のために、神は万人のために。

誰もが自分自身の利益を追求するが、その結果がどうなるかを決めるのは神である。

☐ **1546** J. HEYWOOD *Dialogue of Proverbs* II. ix. 12 Praie and shifte eche one for hym selfe, as he can. Every man for hym selfe, and god for us all. **1615** T. ADAMS *White Devil* (ed. 2) 83 That by-word, Euery man for himselfe, and God for vs all, is vncharitable, vngodly. **1830** MARRYAT *King's Own* III. xiii. The captain ... ordered the sailor to leave the boat 'Every man for himself, and God for us all!' was the cool answer of the refractory sea-man. **1979** *Times* 29 Dec. 12 Each for himself, and God for us all, as the elephant said when he danced among the chickens. ■ **self-preservation** 自己防衛

EVERY man has his price.
どんな人でも、その人を買える値段がある（買収できない人はいない）。

多額の金銭や報奨を差し出せば、どんな人をも買収できる。

☐ **1734** W. WYNDHAM in *Bee* III. 97 'It is an old Maxim, that every Man has his Price,' if you can but come up to it. **1845** G. P. R. JAMES *Smuggler* I. x. 'You can do nothing with Mowle. He never took a penny in his life.' 'Oh, every man has his price.' **1949** N. MAILER *Naked & Dead* II. xi. It was the sort of deal his father might have pulled. 'Every man has his price.' **2015** *Spectator* 10 Jan. 36 'You can't buy Dave,' Mark tells him ... Still, and as it turns out, everyone does have their price. ■ **bribery and corruption** 賄賂と腐敗

EVERY man is the architect of his own fortune.
人はみな自分の運命を作ることができる。

ローマの監察官アピウス・クラウディウス・カエクス（紀元前 4 – 3 世紀）の言葉。Pseudo-Sallust *Ad CaesaremSenem* i. *Sed res docuit id uerum esse, quod in carminibus Appius ait, fabrum esse suae quemque fortunae.*「様々な経緯からアピウスが詩の中で言ったことが正しいことがわかった。つまり人は自らの運命を作ることができるのである」。フランシス・ベーコン（1561-1626）が「運命について」というエッセイの中で、*Faber quisquefortunae suae* というラテン語をそのまま引用している（1991 年の用例参照）。

☐ **1533** N. UDALL *Flowers for Latin Speaking* (1560) 24 A prouerbiall spekyng.... Eueryman ... is causer of his own fortune. **1649** MILTON *Eikonoklastes* III. 542 They in whomsoeuer these ver-

EVERY 145

tues dwell ... are the architects of thir own happiness. **1707** J. DUNTON *Athenian Sport* 454 We are ... architects of our own fortune. **1818** S. FERRIER *Marriage* III. vi. As every man is said to be the artificer of his own fortune, so every one ... had best be the artificer of their own friendship. **1873** *Notes & Queries* 4th Ser. XII. 514 We have not a commoner saying among us than 'Every man is the architect of his own fortune,' and we have very few much older. **1991** *Times* 5 June 18 Educationists complain of the limitations on their resources; but quantifying this in league tables proves the long-term truth of Bacon's dictum *quisquefaber suae fortunae*, each the maker of his own fate. ■ self-help 自助

EVERY man to his taste.
人それぞれに好みがある。
(訳注：「十人十色」。「蓼食う虫も好き好き」)

誰にでも好き嫌いがある。†スタティウス『シルウァエ』II. ii. 73 *Sua cuique uoluptas.* 「誰にでも自分だけの楽しみがある」。フランス語*Chacun a son goftt.*「1人ひとり好みがある」

□ **1580** LYLY *Euphues & his England* II. 161 Betweene them it was not determined, but euery one as he lyketh. *a* **1640** MIDDLETON et al. *Old Law* II. ii. Every one to their liking. But I say An honest man's worth all. **1760** STERNE *Tristram Shandy* I. vii. I own I never could envy Didius in these kinds of fancies of his:—But every man to hisown taste. **1849** BULWER-LYTION *Caxtons* III. XVII. i. 'Sheep are dull things to look at after a bull-hunt.' ... 'Every man to his taste in the Bush.' **1929** E. UNKLATBR *Poet's Pub* xxvi. 'I like fairy tales,' said the professor.... 'Every man to his taste,' agreed the landlord. **1986** J. SMITH *Tourist Trap* xviii. Tried to get me to try one, and our son and daughter-in-law too. But we wouldn't do it I said, '"Everybody to their own taste," said the old lady as she kissed the cow.' ■ idiosyncrasy 特異性・性癖 ; taste 趣味・味

EVERY man to his trade
人それぞれに自らの職業がある。
(訳注：trade＝「〈熟練を要する〉職業」。He followed the *trade* of his father.〈彼は父親の仕事を継いだ〉。「餅は餅屋」)

人は自分の職業を極めることに専念すべきである。『コリントの信徒への手紙一』7章20節（欽定訳聖書）を想起させる。Every man abide in the same calling wherein he was called.「信仰者として召された人は、各々召された時の境遇に留まりなさい」。† **1539** タヴァーナー訳『エラスムス格言集』El Let euerye man exercise hym selfe in the facultie that he knoweth.「皆に自分自身の能力を発揮せしめよ」**1590-1.** シェイクスピア『ヘンリー六世』第二部IV. ii. 15 And yet it is said 'Labour in thy vocation'; which is as much to say as 'Let the magistrates be labouring men'; and therefore should we be magistrates.「それなのに、『職業に励み、よく働くべし』って言うだろ、ってことはつまり、『お役人は働きものたるべし』ってことだ。ってことはつまり、おれたち働きものがお役人たるべしってことさ」

□ **1597-8** SHAKESPEARE *Henry IV,Pt. 1* II. ii. 75 Every man to his business. **1605** MARSTON *Dutch Courtesan* I. i. Every man must follow his trade, and every woman her occupation. *a* **1721** M. PRIOR *Dialogues of Dead* (1907) 221 Every man to his trade, Charles, you should have challenged me at long pike or broad sword. **1930** C. BUSH *Murder at Fenwold* viii. 'I dabble in Mathematics but ... I'd rather have your Latinity.' 'Every man to his trade.' **1990** 'C. AIRD' *Body Politic* (1991) x. 110 'Too early at the crem [crematorium], of course,' said Tod, surprised. 'That's always bad.' 'Yes, I can see that,' agreed Sloan. Every man to his own trade. ■ business ビジネ

146 every

ス・商売；trades and skills 職業と技術；work 仕事

every ⇒ Every CLOUD has a silver lining; Every COCK will crow upon his own dunghill; Every DOG has his day; Every DOG is allowed one bite; Every ELM has its man; There is an EXCEPTION to every rule; every HERRING must hang by its own gill; Every JACK has his Jill; Every LAND has its own law; Every PICTURE tells a story; If every man would SWEEP his own doorstep the city would soon be clean; Every TUB must stand on its own bottom; There are TWO sides to every question.

EVERYBODY loves a lord.
人は皆、貴族を好む。

人は自分よりも高い地位の人物との付き合いを好む。

□1869 F. J. FURNIVALL in *Queen Elizabeth's Academy* (EETS) p. xii. The second tract … is printed, not mainly because 'John Bull loves a Lord' … but because the question of Precedence was so important a one in old social arrangements. 1908 *Spectator* 3 July 9 It is always said that an Englishman loves a lord. It would be more exact to say that he is in love with lordliness. 1980 M. NICHOLLS *Importance of being Oscar* (1981) 58 If pressed, he would probably have admitted that he was no exception to the adage that 'Everybody Loves a Lord'. ■ society 社会

What EVERYBODY says must be true.
誰もが言っていることは本当にちがいない。

現在では、一般に、多くの人が言ったり、信じているから本当だと主張することに対する皮肉として使われる。

□*a*1400 *Legends of Saints* (STS) III. 105 For I fynd suthfastnes [truth], that almen sais, is nocht les [lies]. *c* 1475 in *Modern Philology* (1940) XXXVIII. 118 Hitys cominly truye that all men sayth. *c* 1518 A. BARCLAY tr. *Mancinus' Mirror of Good Manners* FI^v It nedes muste be trewe which euery man doth say. 1748 RICHARDSON *Clarissa* IV. 74 The most accomplished of women, as every one says; and what every one says must be true. 1905 A. MACLAREN *Gospel according to St. Matthew* II. 246 'What everybody says must be true' is a cowardly proverb…. What most people say is usually false. ■ public opinion 世論；truth 真実・真理

EVERYBODY's business is nobody's business.
皆の仕事は誰の仕事でもない（誰もやろうとしない）。

（訳注：business＝「〈課せられた〉仕事、用事」。take care of *business*〈仕事を片づける〉）

もしあることが集団全体に関わっているにもかかわらず、その担当責任者がいない場合、そのことは棚上げにされることが多い。†アリストテレス『政治学』II. i. ἥκιστα γὰρ ἐπιμελείας τυγχάνει τὸ πλείστων κοινόν「大半の人に共通する問題は最も関心が薄くなる」。

□1611 R. COTGRAVE *Dict. French & English* s.v. Ouvrage, Euerie bodies worke is no bodies worke. 1655 I. WALTON *Compleat Angler* (ed. 2) 1. ii. A wise friend of mine did usually say, That which is every bodies businesse, is no bodies businesse. 1725 DEFOE (*title*) Every-Body's Business, is No-Body's Business; … exemplified in the pride of our Woman-Servants. 1914 G. B. SHAW *Misalliance* 10 'The danger of public business is that it never ends' … 'What I say is that everybody's business is nobody's business.' 1981 D. CLARK *Longest Pleasure* v. It's unfair to try to make points by misquoting. What you should have said is 'everybody's business is nobody's

EVIL　147

business', and that doesn't fit our present case at all. ■ **busybodies** おせっかい屋

everyone ⇒ You can't PLEASE everyone; Everyone SPEAKS well of the bridge which carries him over.

EVERYTHING has an end.
あらゆるものには終わりがある。

† 14世紀中頃のフランス語 *Mais il n'est chose qui ne fine, ne qui ne viengne à son termine.*「終わりのないもの、結論に到達しないものはない」

□*c*1385 CHAUCER *Troilus & Criseyde* III. 615 At the laste, as every thyng hath ende, She took hire leve. **1616** N. BRETON *Crossing of Proverbs* A6 'Euery thing hath an end' ... 'Not so, a Ring hath none.' **1841** DICKENS *Barnaby Rudge* xx. Everything has an end. Even young ladies in love cannot read their letters for ever. **1980** D. FRANCIS *Reflex* viii. Can't go on for ever, more's the pity. Everything ends, doesn't it. ■ **finality** 結末・終局

everything ⇒ ALL things come to those who wait; When all you have is a HAMMER, everything looks like a nail; MONEY isn't everything; A PLACE for everything, and everything in its place; There is a REMEDY for everything except death; There is a TIME and place for everything; There is a TIME for everything.

evidence ⇒ What the SOLDIER said isn't evidence.

EVIL communications corrupt good manners.
悪い付き合いは良い習慣を害する。
（訳注：「朱に交われば赤くなる」。「悪貨は良貨を駆逐する」）

悪い手本は、それが言葉であれ行ないであれ、ふるまいに悪い影響を及ぼす。『コリントの信徒への手紙一』15章33節（欽定訳聖書）Be not deceived: evil communications corrupt good manners.「悪い付き合いは善い習慣を損なう」を想起させる。

□*c*1425 J. ARDERNE *Treatises of Fistula* (EETS) 5 Shrewed speche corrumpith gode maners. **1533** MORE *Debellation* [subjugation] *of Salem* xiv. (As saynt Poule speketh ofsuch heresyes) euyl communication corrupteth good maners. **1749** FIELDING *Tom Jones* IV. XII. iii. I heartily wish you would ... not think of going among them.—Evil Communication corrupts good Manners. **1874** TROLLOPE *PhineasRedux* I. xvi. [The horse] would have taken the fence ... but Dandolo had baulked ... and evil communications will corrupt good manners. **1939** W. S. MAUGHAM *Christmas Holiday* ii. A disposition of such sweetness that no evil communication could corrupt his good manners. **1973** 'M. INNES' *Appleby's Answer* ii. One can't be too careful in choosing a well-bred cat's company.... Evil communications corrupt good manners. ■ **conduct** 行ない・品行；**example, good and bad** 好例と悪例

EVIL to him who evil thinks.
邪念を抱く者に災いあれ。

中世のフランス語 *Honi soit qui mal y pense*「邪念を抱く者に災いあれ」はガーター勲章のモットーである。それはイングランド王、エドワード 3 世によって 1348 年、あるいは 1349 年に始められた。現在の様々な言い方に加えてフランス語の形式でもよく使われ

148 EVIL

る。1589 年と1650年の用例はこのことわざがフランス語の翻訳であることを示している。

□*c*1460 SIR R. ROS *La Belle Dame in Skeat* (ed.) Chaucer VIII. 397 Who thinketh il, no good may him befal. **1546** J. HEYWOOD *Dialogue of Proverbs* I. ix. C2 And shame take him that shame thinkth. **1589** G. PUTTENHAM *Arte of English Poesie* (Arber) 116 Commonly thus Englished, Ill be to him that thinks ill, but in mine opinion better thus, Dishonoured is he that meanes dishonorably. **1650** R. COTGRAVE *Dict. French & English* (Rowell's Epistle Dedicatory) We English it, Ill be to him who thinks ill; though the true sense be, let him be beray'd who thinks any ill, being a metaphor taken from a child that hath berayed [fouled] his clouts [clothes], and in Francether's not one in a hundred who understands this word nowadayes. **1668** DENHAM in Dryden *Miscellany* v. 76 Who evil thinks, may evil him confound. **1954** B. FLYNN *Doll's Done Dancing* xvii. 158 'The ... er ... hoi polloi ... can always be found ready to point the finger or shrug the shoulder or ... er ... nod the head. Whereas the understanding ... erudite person ... with the right instincts, makes no comment. Evil to him who evil thinks.' ■ **good and evil 正邪**

Never do EVIL that good may come of it.
善が生じるようにと悪を行なったりしてはならない。

（訳注：that＝「…であるように」〈目的・意図〉。He works hard *that* his family may live in comfort.〈家族が安楽に暮せるように懸命に働いている〉）

『ローマの信徒への手紙』3 章 8 節（欽定訳聖書）And not ... Let us do evil, that good may come.「『善が生じるように悪を行なおう』というのではいけない」を想起させる。

□**1583** P. STUBBES *Anatomie of Abuses* KS We must not doo euil, that good may come of it: yet the lawes In permitting certain reasonable gain to be received for the Ioane of money lent ... haue not doone much amisse. **1689** G. BULKELEY *Letter* in *Coll Connecticut Hist. Society* (1860) I. 59 IfI knew any thing whereby to justify the present proceeding. I should not conceal it; but we must not do evil that good may come of it. **1882** C. M. YONGE *Unknown to History* II. ix. Walsingham's agents ... did evil that good might come, thinking Mary's death alone would ensuie them from Pope and Spaniard. **1950** J. CANNAN *Murder Included* 127 What ... were the ethics? A promise made to a silly child, was it binding? You mustn't do evil that good may come of it ... but the boy was only fourteen and practically half-witted, and Lisa was an absurd little Quixote. ■ **good and evil 正邪**；**ways and means 方法と手段**

evil ⇒ A GREAT book is a great evil; IDLENESS is the root of all evil; MONEY is the root of all evil; ⇒ No evil, hear no evil, speak no evil; SUFFICIENT unto the day is the evil thereof.

Of two EVILS choose the less.
2 つの悪の中からどちらかを選ばなければならないとしたら少しでもましな方を選べ。

† アリストテレス『ニコマコス倫理学』II. ix. 1109a κατὰ τὸν δεύτερον, φασί, πλοῦν τὰ ἐλάχιστα ληπτέον τῶν κακῶν.「2 番目に最善の道として、悪の中でも最も悪でないものを選べと言われている」。キケロ『義務について』III. xxix. *Minima de malis*.「悪の中なら、最もましな方を選べ」

□*c*1385 CHAUCER *Troilus & Criseyde* II. 470 Of harmes two, the lesse is for to chese. *c* **1440** *Gesta Romanorum* (EETS) 10 Of too Evelis the lasse Evill is to be chosyn. **1546** J. HEYWOOD *Dialogue of Proverbs*. v. B2 Of two yls, chose the least while choyse lyth in lot. **1785** J. BOSWELL *Journal of Tour to Hebrides* 464 'O ho! Sir, (said I), you are flying to me for refuge!' ... 'It is of two evils choosing the least.' **1891** A. FORBES *Barracks, Bivouacs & Battles* 187 Either the Turks

would make a prisoner of me ... or I must ... take my chance of the Russian fire ... : 'Of two evils choose the less,' says the wise proverb. **2013** *Yorkshire Evening Post* 16 Jan. (online) Campaigners against the proposed £250m Leeds trolleybus are urging council bosses to choose the lesser of two evils if they must-and not sacrifice one of the city's green space gems to the project.
■ **choices** 選択

EXAMPLE is better than precept.
実例は教訓に勝る。

†セネカ『書簡集』vi. 5 *Longum iter est per precepta, breve et efficax per exempla.*「教訓に従うと道は長くなり、実例に従うと道は短く効果的となる」

□**1400** J. MIRK *Festial* (EETS) 216 Then saythe Seynt Austeyn [Augustine] that an ensampull yn doyng ys mor commendabull then ys tecbyng other [or] precbyng. *a* **1568** R. ASCHAM *Schoolmaster* (1570) 1. 20 One example, is more valiable ... than xx. preceptes written in bookes. **1708** M. PRIOR *Literary Works* (1971) I. 535 Example draws where Precept fails, And Sermons are less read than Tales. **1828** D. M. MOIR *Mansie Wauch* xix. Example is better than precept, as James Batter observes. **1981** P. O'DONNELL *Xanadu Talisman* ii. Example is always better than precept, remember. ■ **example, good and bad** 好例と悪例；**words and deeds** 言動

The EXCEPTION proves the rule.
例外は規則が存在する証しである。

ブルーワー曰く、The very fact of an exception proves there must be a rule.「例外が存在するという事実こそ規則が存在することの証である」。現在では誤解され、矛盾を正当化するために使われることが多い。†ラテン語 *Exceptio probat regulam in casibus non exceptis.*「例外は例外でないものの規則を確証する」

□**1640** G. WATTS *Bacon's Advancement of Learning* VIII.iii. Exception strengthens the force of a Law in Cases not excepted. **1664** J. WILSON *Cheats* A2ᵛ I think I have sufficiently justif'd the Brave man, even by this Reason, That the Exception proves the Rule. **1765** S. JOHNSON *Shakespeare Preface* C2ᵛ There are a few passages which may pass for imitations, but so few that the exception only confirms the rule. **1863** W. S. GILBERT in *Cornhill Mag.* Dec. VIII. 727 As for the dictum about Temple Bar, why, the case of Poddle and Shaddery might be one of those very exceptions whose existence is necessary to the proof of every general rule. **1907** H. W. FOWLER *Si Mihi* 80 It is one of those cryptic sayings, like 'The exception proves the rule', which always puzzle me. **1994** 'C. AIRD' 'Fair Cop' In *Injury Time* (1995) 27 [H]ome was where most victims of murder met their end. This instance, he was prepared to concede, might just be the exception that proved the rule. ■ **rules** 規則

There is an EXCEPTION to every rule.
いかなる規則にも例外はある。

The EXCEPTION proves the rule.「例外は規則が存在する証しである」と RULES are made to be broken.「規則は破られるためにある」も参照。

□**1579** T. F. *News from North* D1ᵛ There is no rule so generall, that it admitteth not exception, albeit i dout not ... that honors chaunge maners. **1608** T. HEYWOOD *Rape of Lucrece* V. 169 A general concourse of wise men.... Tarquln, if the general rule have no exceptions, thou wilt have an empty consistory [council chamber]. **1773** R. GRAVES *Spiritual Quixote* III. IX. xviii. The rules of Grammar cannot, in any language, be reduced to a strict analogy; but all general rules have some exceptions. **1836** MARRYAT *Midshipman Easy* I. xii. I have little reason to speak in its favour ... but there must be exceptions in every' rule. **1981** *Listener* 21 May 683 'There is still

150 EXCHANGE

something awe-inspiring about a duke,' we are informed. Only those who share such values will want to read Heirs and Graces. Even they should remember that there is an exception to every rule.

■ **rules** 規則

A fair EXCHANGE is no robbery.
正当な交換は盗みではない。

何かがそれと同程度の価値のものと交換される場合には、それは正当な取引である。しかし、このことわざは、人から何かを奪い、それよりも価値の劣るものと交換することを正当化するための口実として使われることが多い。

☐ **1546** J. HEYWOOD *Dialogue of Proverbs* II. iv. G4 Chaunge be no robbry for the changed case. *c* **1590** *John of Bordeaux* (1936) I. 213 Exchaung is no roberie. *a* **1628** in M. L. ANDERSON *Proverbs in Scots* (1957) no. 540 Fair shifts [exchange] na robberie. **1721** J. KBLLY *Scottish Proverbs* 105 Fair Exchange is no Rob'ry. Spoken when we take up one Thing, and lay down another. **1748** SMOLLETT *Roderick Random* II. xii Casting an eye at my hat and wig ... he took them off, and clapping his own on my head, declared, that a fair exchange was no robbery. **1960** N. MITFORD *Don't tell Alfred* xx. 'So it was you who took away the Harar frescoes?' 'Took away? We exchanged them.... A good exchange is no robbery, I believe?' **1999** J. CUTLER *Dying to Score* i. 5 'Superintendent Groom, sir, I have to report that I was just considering my spring-cleaning,' I said. 'And, since fair exchange is no robbery, what about your thoughts?' ■ **fair dealing** 公正な取引

excites ⇒ The BLEATING of the kid excites the tiger.

excuse ⇒ A BAD excuse is better than none; IGNORANCE of the law is no excuse for breaking it.

He who EXCUSES accuses himself.
言い訳をする者は自らを責めているのだ。

(訳注：he =「〈関係節を伴って〉…する者は誰でも〈性別は問わない〉」。*He who* hesitates is lost. 〈しり込みする者は負けだ〉。*He who* carries nothing loses nothing. 【ことわざ】〈持たざれば失うことなし〉)

言い訳をするという行為自体、その人が罪の意識を持っていることを示している。†ラテン語 *Dum excusare credis, accusas.*「言い訳をしようとするのは、自らを責めることだ」。フランス語 *Qui s'excuse, s'accuse.*「言い訳をする者は自らを責めているのだ」

☐ **1611** R. COTGRAVE *Dict. French & English* s. v. Excuser, Some when they mean to excuse, accuse, themselues. **1884** J. PAYN *Canon's Ward* II. xxxi. It is very difficult for a person in my position to excuse without accusing himself, but I should like you to feel that Miss Gilbert's fortune has formed no part of her attraction for me. **1936** J. STAGGE *Murder gone to Earth* vi. She spoke with such venom that I remembered the good old French proverb of 'he who excuses, accuses himself.' **1968** G. WAGNER *Elegy for Corsica* xi. The tests would be underground, every precaution taken, impossible to contaminate anything. One had heard these pleas before ... Who excuses himself accuses himself. ■ **conscience** 良心; **excuses** 言い訳

expand ⇒ WORK expands so as to fill the time available.

EXPERIENCE   151

What can you EXPECT from a pig but a grunt?
ブーブー鳴く以外、ブタなどに何を期待できようか。

(訳注：but=「…を除いて」。All *but* him were present.〈彼以外は皆、出席していた〉)

下品でがさつな振る舞いを指す修辞的用法である。

□ **1731** *Poor Robin's Almanack* C6 If we petition a Hog, what can we expect but a grunt. **1827** SCOTT *Journal* 10 Apr. (1941) 41 They refuse a draught of £20, because, in mistake, it was £8 overdrawn. But what can be expected of a sow but a grumph? **1910** P. W. JOYCE *English as We speak it In Ireland* x. Of a coarse, ill-mannered man, who uses unmannerly language: 'What could you expect from a pig but a grunt' **1997** *Spectator* 22 Nov. 37/2 References in Mr Cole's letter to the 'bottle' were, to say the least, distasteful. But then, as they say, 'What can you expect from a pig but a grunt?' ■ conduct 行ない・品行 ; human nature 人間性

expect ⇒ BLESSED is he who expects nothing, for he shall never be disappointed.

EXPERIENCE is the best teacher.
経験こそが最良の師。

ラテン語の決まり文句 *Experientia docet*.「経験が教えてくれる」は多くのことわざを生み出した。標準的な形式はなく、以下に挙げたことわざは One learns (also, Fools learn) by experience.「人は経験によって学ぶ (愚か者も同じである)」と Experience is a hard teacher.「経験は厳しい教師である」という主題を表わしている。EXPERIENCE keeps a dear school.「経験は授業料の高い学校を経営している」も参照。

□ *a***1568** R. ASCHAM *Schoolmaster* (1570) I. 19 Erasmus ... saide wiselie that experience is the common scholehouse of foles. **1618** N. BRETON *Court & Country* B4 Let ignorance be an enemy to wit, and experience be the Mistris of fools. **1670** J. RAY *English Proverbs* 86 Experience is the mistress of fools. Experientia stultorum magistra. Wise men learn by others harms, fools by their own. **1732** T. FULLER *Gnomologia* no.1484 Experience teacheth Fools; and he is a great one, that will not learn by it. **1856** F. M. WHITCHER *Widow Bedott Papers* xxix. I ... didnt know how to do anything as well as I do now.... Experience is the best teacher, after all. **1874** G. J. WHYTE-MELVILLE *Uncle John* I. x. Experience does not make fools wise.... Most proverbs are fallacious. None greater than that which says it does. **1962** *Infantry* Nov.-Dec. 26 Experience is a hard teacher, and we cannot afford to learn on the battlefield what should be taught during normal training. **2002** *Washington Post* 11 Jan. C1O Whoever said 'experience is the best teacher' got it right—as you can certainly testify. ■ experience 経験

EXPERIENCE is the father of wisdom.
経験は知恵の父。

(訳注：この後に、and memory the mother「記憶は知恵の母」と続く)

† アルクマン『断章』cxxv. (Page) πῆρά τοι μαθήσιος ἀρχά.「経験は知識の第一歩である」。

□ **1539** R. TAVERNER *Garden of Wisdom* II. 24ᵛ This be commonly true, for experience is mother of prudence, yet suche prudence & wysedom cost the comon weale moch. *a* **1547** E. HALL *Chronicle* (1548) Rich. III 31 He by the longe and often alternate proof ... had gotten by greate experience the very mother and mastres of wisedome. **1581** G. PETTIE tr. *S. Guazzo's Civil Conversation* I.11 Experience is the father of wisedom, and memorie the mother. **1788** *American Museum* III. 183 If it be true, that experience is the mother of wisdom, history must be an improving teacher. **1981** P. O'DONNELL *Xanadu Talisman* ii. Experience is the father of wisdom, remember. ■ experience 経験 ; wisdom 賢明・知恵

152 EXPERIENCE

EXPERIENCE keeps a dear school.
経験は授業料の高い学校を経営している。

□**1743** B. FRANKLIN *Poor Richard's Almanack* (Dec.) Experience keeps a dear school, but Fools will learn in no other. **1897** C. C. KING *Story of British Army* vii. But the British leaders were to learn the fact, they might have foreseen, in the 'only school fools learn in, that of experience'. **1938** E. O. LORIMER tr. *W. Frischauer's Twilight in Vienna* vii. The various Governments had ... to learn their lesson in blood and tears, for 'experience keeps a dear school'. **2000** *Washington Post* 17 July C2 You are never going to be any of these people—for which it says here you should be eternally grateful—but that isn't going to stop you from trying, is it? In the immortal words of (talk about success gurus) Benny Franklin: 'Experience keeps a dear school, but fools will learn in no other.' ■ **experience** 経験

EXTREMES meet.
両極端は一致する。

例えば、教義（1822年の用例参照）と政治的な立場（1978年の用例参照）の中で対極に位置するものには共通点が多い。† *a* **1662** パスカル『パンセ』（1835年の新版）I. iv. 109 *Les extremes se touchent*.「両極端は一致する」

□**1762** J. WATTS in *Collections of New York Hist Society* (1928) LXII. 48 But as extremes meet we may possibly the sooner have a peace for it. **1822** SCOTT *Nigel* III. iii. This Olifaunt is a Puritan?—not the less like to be a Papist ... for extremities meet. **1836** E. HOWARD *Rattlin the Reefer* I. xiv. Let us place at least one 'barring out' [i.e. action of schoolboys barricading themselves in a room] upon record, in order to let the radicals see, and seeing hope, when they find how nearly extremes meet, what a slight step there is from absolute despotism to absolute disorganization. **1905** J. B. CABELL *Line of Love* vi. It is a venerable saying that extremes meet. **1978** *Economist* 16 Dec. 22 Groups of the extreme left and extreme right are each other's total opposites and avowed enemies. But in some respects these extremes meet. ■ **human nature** 人間性 ; **opposites** 両極

extremity ⇒ MAN'S extremity is God's opportunity.

What the EYE doesn't see, the heart doesn't grieve over.
目に見えないものに心は痛まない。

† 聖ベルナルド『説教集』v. *All Saints, vulgo dicitur: Quod non videt oculus cor non dolet*.「目に見えないものを心は悲しまないと言われる」。14世紀初頭のフランス語 *Car on dit que ce que on ne voit au cueur ne deult*.「人は見えないものに心を痛めることはないと言われる」

□**1545** R. TAVERNER tr. *Erasmus' Adages* (ed. 2) 13 That the eye seeth not, the hart rueth not. **1576** G. PETTIE *Petit Palace* 145 As the sence of seeinge is most sharp, so is that paine most pinching, to see the thing one seeketh, and can not possesse it... : And as the common saying is, that which the eye seeth, the hart greeueth. **1721** J. KELLY *Scottish Proverbs* 341 What the Eye sees not, the Heart rues not. Men may have Losses, but if they be unknown to them they give them no Trouble. **1830** J. L. BURCKHARDT *Arabic Proverbs* 109 When the eye does not see, the heart does not grieve. **1883** C. S. BURNE *Shropshire Folklore* xxxvi. These ... seem to be popular legal maxims.... What the eye doesn't see, the heart doesn't grieve. **1939** G. HEYER *No Wind of Blame* iii. Anyone knows what men are, and what the eye doesn't see the heart won't grieve over. **1986** 'J. GREENWOOD' *Mists Over Mosley* (1987) xix. 122 'But they have a saying in these parts. "What the eye don't see, the heart don't grieve," and I've always said to myself, that's not

EYES 153

a bad motto for a man.' ■ **ignorance** 無知・無学 ; **trouble** やっかい・苦労

The EYE of a master does more work than both his hands.
主人の目玉１つの方が両手よりも多くの事を成す。

よく監視していると労働者はよく働く。

□**1744** B. FRANKLIN *Poor Richard's Almanack* (Oct.) The eye of a Master, will do more Work than his Hand. **1876** I. BANKS *Manchester Man* I. xiv. She was wont to say, 'The eye of a master does more work than both his hands,' accordingly in house or warehouse her active supervision kept other hands from idling. **1907** *Washington Post* 9 Jan. 8/4 (advertisement) The Eye of a Master Does Better Work Than Both His Hands. **1995** A. ZUGARRAMURDI et al. *Economic Engineering* 242 [T]he owner is usually the plant manager, and therefore prevention of mistakes and waste is considered a basic task of management ('The eye of a master does more work than both his hands'). ■ **employers and employees** 雇用者と被雇用者

eye ⇒ BEAUTY is in the eye of the beholder; The BUYER has need of a hundred eyes, the seller of but one; FIELDS have eyes, and woods have ears; FOUR eyes ⇒ More than two; HAWKS will not pick out hawks' eyes.

The EYES are the window of the soul.
目は心の窓である。

（訳注：「目は口ほどに物を言う」。「目は心の鏡」）

目（あるいは表情）はその人物の性格を知る鍵である。多くの別の言い方があるが、The face is the index of the mind.「表情は心を表わす。」はその１つである。†キケロ『弁論家について』lx. *Ut imago est animi voltus sic indices oculi.*「顔は心を映し出す絵であり、目はそれを解読する鍵である」。ラテン語 *Vultus est index animi* （または *oculus animi index*）.「顔は（目は）心を表わす」

□**1545** T. PHAER *Regiment of Life* 14 The eyes … are the wyndowes of the mynde, for both ioye & anger … are seene … through them. *a* **1575** J. PILKINGTON *Nehemiah* (1585) i. The affections of the minde declare them selues openlie in the face. **1601** JONSON *Cynthia's Revels* D3ᵛ I can refell [refute] that Paradox … of those, which hold the face to be the Index of the minde. **1781** A. ADAMS in L. H. Butterfield et al. *Adams Family Correspondence* (1973) IV. 215 I did not study the Eye that best Index to the mind. **1940** G. SEAVER *Scott of Antarctic* II. 48 The eye, which is the reflector of the external world, Is also the mirror of the soul within. **1979** J. GERSON *Omega Factor* iii. If the old saying, the eyes are the window of the soul, were true then this young girl had misplaced her soul. **2000** J. W. HALL *Rough Draft* (2001) i. 23 He'd never believed in reading things into people's eyes. All that windows-of-the-soul bullshit. ■ **appearance, significant** 重要な外見

F

face ⇒ Don't CUT off your nose to spite your face; The EYES are the window of the soul.

FACT is stranger than fiction.
事実は小説よりも奇なり。

(訳注：strange は「予想を超えた」を意味する)

TRUTH is stranger than fiction. の頭韻 (fact と fiction) を踏んだバージョンである。

☐**1853** T. C. HALIBURTON *Sam Slick's Wise Saws* 5 Facts are stranger than fiction, for things happen sometimes that never entered into the mind of man to imagine or invent. **1881** A. JES-SOPP *Arcady for Better or Worse* iii. I have no desire to convince the world that ... in this ... case fact is stranger than fiction. But the following instance of Mr. Chowne's 'cunning' may be verified. **1929** E. J. MILLWARD *Copper Bottle* 64 Facts may be stranger than fiction, ... but fiction is generally truer than facts. **1980** *Christian Science Monitor* 30. May B3 Some of the research seems almost eerie to the outsider, covering some genuine fact-is-stranger-than-fiction ground. ■ **reality and illusion 現実と幻想**

FACTS are stubborn things.
事実は頑なである。

事実は動かしようがない。この後に but statistics are more pliable「しかし統計値は操作できる」(2013年の用例) を付け加えたのは米国のユーモア作家マーク・トゥエインであると言われているが、根拠はない。なぜなら facts と statistics を並置した初例 (www. barrypopik.com) が、**1927**『レジスター新聞』(イリノイ州ロックフォード) 16/ 8 FACTS are stubborn, but statistics are more pliable.「事実は動かしようがないが、統計値は柔軟である」において既に見られるからである。

☐**1732** E. BUDGELL *Liberty & Progress* ii. Plain matters of fact are terrible stubborn things. **1749** J. ELIOT *Continuation of Essay on Field Husbandry* 20 Facts are stubborn things. **1866** BLACK-MORE *Cradock Nowell* III. vi. Facts, however, are stubborn things, and will not even make a bow to the sweetest of young ladies. **1942** L. THAYER *Murder is Out* xxvii. You're ... too intelligent to think that suggestion would have any weight with a jury.... Facts are stubborn things. **2013** B. WEISS *When Doctor Says, Alzheimer's* 22 AB Mark Twain has famously said, 'Facts are stubborn things, but statistics are more pliable.' ■ **reality and illusion 現実と幻想**

fail ⇒ When all FRUIT fails, welcome haws.

failure ⇒ SUCCESS has many fathers, while failure is an orphan.

FAIR 155

FAINT heart never won fair lady.
気弱な男が美女を射止めたためしはない。

† *c*1390 ガウワー『恋する男の告解』v. 6573 Bot as men sein, wher herte is failed, Ther schal no castell ben assailed. 「勇気がなければどんな城も攻め落とせないと人は言います」

☐1545 R. TAVERNER tr. *Erasmus' Adages* (ed. 2) 10 A coward verely neuer obteyned the loue of a faire lady. 1580 LYLY *Euphues & his England* II. 131 Faint hart Philautus neither winneth Castell nor Lady: therfore endure all thinges that shall happen with patience. 1614 W. CAMDEN *Remains concerning Britain* (ed. 2) 306 Faint heart neuer wonne faire Lady. 1754 RICHARDSON *Grandison* I. xvi. Then, madam, we will not take your denial.... Have I not heard it said, that faint heart never won fair lady. 1899 G. GISSING *Crown of Life* xiii. Could he leave England, this time, without confessing himself to her? Faint heart—he mused over the proverb. 2002 *New Scientist* 11 May 37 Those who risk all might die in the attempt, but this is no worse genetically speaking than sitting around and dying childless; they might, by risking all, do very well indeed. Faint heart never won fair lady. ■ **boldness** 大胆さ ; **love** 愛・恋愛

FAIR and softly goes far in a day
あわてずゆっくりと進めば、1日で遠くまで進める。

(訳注：go でなく goes となっているのは fair and softly を 1 つの概念として捉えているため)

このことわざの合理的な理由が1670年の用例で示されている。類似したものにラテン語 *Festina lente.*「ゆっくり急げ」がある。

☐*c*1350 *Douce MS52* no. 50 Fayre and softe me [one] ferre gose. 1670 J. RAY *English Proverbs* 87 Fair and softly goes far in a day.... He that spurs on too fast at first setting out, tires before he comes to his journeys end. 1818 SCOTT *Heart of Midlothian* IV. viii. Reuben Butler isna the man I take him to be, if he disna learn the Captain to fuff [puff] his pipe some other gate [place] than in God's house, or [before] the quarter be ower. 'Fair and softly gangs far,' said Meiklehose. 1914 K. F. PURDON *Folk of Furry Farm* ii. Maybe I'm like the singed cat, better than I look! I'm slow, but fair and easy goes far in a day. ■ **gentleness** 優しさ ; **tact** 機転

All's FAIR in love and war.
恋と戦争においてはすべてが正当化される。

† 1578 リリー『ユーフュイーズ』I. 236 Anye impietie may lawfully be committed in loue, which is lawlesse. 「どんな卑劣な手段も恋では許される。恋は無法地帯なのだから」

☐1620 T. SHELTON tr. *Cervantes' Don Quixote* II. xxi. Love and warre are all one.... It is lawfull to use sleights and stratagems to ... attaine the wished end. 1845 G. P. R. JAMES *Smuggler* II. iv. In love and war, every stratagem is fair, they say. 1986 S. BRETT *Nice Class of Corpse* xl. Then Eulalie's eyes narrowed and she looked hard at her companion. 'Do you believe that all is fair in love and war?' 2002 *Spectator* 15 June 63 All is fair in love and war, and it is important that you sustain your marriage. You must therefore take the following, deceitful steps. ■ **fair dealing** 公正な取引 ; **love** 愛・恋愛 ; **warfare** 戦争

FAIR play's a jewel.
フェアプレイは宝石である。

不正に対する禁止として使われる。

156　fair

☐1809 W. IRVING *Hist. New York* II. VI. vii. The furious Risingh, in despight of that noble max-im … that 'fair play is a jewel', hastened to take advantage of the hero's fall. 1823 J. F. COOPER *Pioneers* II. v. Well, fair play's a jewel. But I've got the lead of you, old fellow. 1935 B. F. BEN-SON *Lucia's Progress* viii. There's been a lil'mistake…. I want my lil' rubber of Bridge. Fair play's a jewel. 1948 L. A. G. STRONG *Trevannion* iv. 'It ain't good to win crooked.' 'Good for you, Stan. I agree. Fair play's a jewel' ■ **fair dealing** 公正な取引

fair ⇒ None but the BRAVE deserve the fair; A fair EXCHANGE is no robbery; FAINT heart never won fair lady; GIVE and take is fair play; If SAINT Paul's day be fair and clear, it will betide a happy year; SAINT Swithun's day, if thou be fair, for forty days it will remain; TURN about is fair play.

FAITH will move mountains.
信念は山をも動かす。

『マタイによる福音書』17章20節 (欽定訳聖書) If ye have faith as a grain of mustard seed, ye shall say unto this mountain; Remove hence to yonder place; and it shall remove.「もし、あなた方に一粒のからし種ほどの信仰があれば、この山に向かってここからあそこへ移れと言えば、山は移る」を想起させる。†『コリントの信徒への手紙一』13章2節 (欽定訳聖書) though I have all faith; so that I could remove moun-tains; and have not charity, I am nothing.「たとえ山を移すほどの完全な信仰があっても、愛がなければ、私は何ものでもない」

☐1897 'S. GRAND' *Beth Book* xvi. If mountains can be moved by faith, you can surely move your own legs! 1933 J. BETJEMAN *Ghastly Good Taste* iii. As faith can move mountains, so noth-ing was impossible to Holy Church. 1948 B. STEVENSON *Home Book of Proverbs* (rev. ed.) 745 Faith will move mountains. 1980 C. PREMLIN *With no Crying* xix. Faith moves mountains, they say: and Hope lights up our darkness. ■ **faith** 信念

FALL down seven times, get up eight.
七転び八起き。

日本のことわざである。

☐1997 *New York Times* 24 Aug. (online) 'I always told him, "Fall down seven times, get up eight,"' said John Kim, the bridegroom's father. 'That's a martial arts motto.' 2006 R. PAGE on *www.russpage.net* 10 Apr. I saw a Dwayne Wade commercial this morning that showed him fall-ing down on the basketball court numerous times. Seven times to be exact. Toward the end of the commercial, it shows him lying face down on the court as he lifts up his head and smiles be-fore standing up. The final line says something like 'Fall down seven times. Get up eight,' It seems very motivational. ■ **perseverance** 我慢強さ

fall ⇒ (名詞) Hasty CLIMBERS have sudden falls; PRIDE goes before A fall; A STUMBLE may prevent a fall; (動詞) The APPLE never falls far from the tree; BETWEEN two stools one falls to the ground; The BIGGER they are, the harder they fall; When the BLIND lead the blind, both shall fall into the ditch; The BREAD never falls but on its buttered side; A REED before the wind lives on, while mighty oaks do fall; If the SKY falls we shall catch larks; When THIEVES fall out, honest men come by their own; As a TREE falls, so shall it lie; UNITED we

far 157

stand, divided we fall.

fame ⇒ COMMON fame is seldom to blame.

FAMILIARITY breeds contempt.
慣れ親しむとあなどりが生まれる。
　（訳注：「親しき仲にも礼儀あり」）

過度の親しみ深さを見せると、相手の心の中に軽蔑心が生まれる（1539年の用例参照）。現在では、物、人、日課に慣れ親しみすぎることによって生まれる不注意や嫌悪感まで含むように拡大されている。✝聖アウグスティヌス『楽園の梯子』8（ミーニュ40, col. 1001）*Vulgare proverbium est, quod nimia familiaritas parit contemptum.*「よく知られたことわざに、慣れすぎると軽蔑の念が生じるというのがある」

☐*c*1386 CHAUCER *Tale of Melibee* I. 1685 Men seyn that 'over-greet hoomiesse [familiriarity] engendreth dispreisynge'. **1539** R. TAVERNER *Garden of Wisdom* II. 4 Hys specyall frendes counsailled him to beware, least his ouermuche familiaritie myght breade him comptempte. **1654** T. PULLER *Comment on Ruth* 176 With base and sordid natures familiarity breeds comptempt. **1869** TROLLOPE *He knew He was Right* II. lvi. Perhaps, if I heard Tennyson talking every day, I shouldn't read Tennyson. Familiarity does breed contempt. **1928** D. H. LAWRENCE *Phoenix* II (1968) 598 We say ... Familiarity breeds contempt ... That is only partly true. It has taken some races of men thousands of years to become contemptuous of the moon. **2015** *Times* 27 Jan. 28 Yet familiarity, while it might not always breed contempt, can more easily breed a numbed triviality. ■ **familiarity** 慣れ親しみ

The FAMILY that prays together stays together.
共に祈る家族は団結する。

コピーライターのアル・スカルポーネによって作られ、パトリック・ペイトン神父が設立した「ロザリオの十字軍」（P. ペイトン『すべては彼女のために』〈1967〉のスローガンとして使用された。この十字軍は1942年に始まり、スローガンはラジオ番組『ファミリーシアター』の中で1947年3月6日に初放送された。英国における十字軍は1952年に始まり、それ以来、この表現には多くの（しばしば滑稽な）言い方が生まれている。

☐**1948** *St. Joseph Mag.* (Oregon) Apr. 3 'More things are wrought by prayer than this world dreams of', and 'The family that prays together stays together.' Such religious themes are hardly what one would expect to hear propounded over the air waves of our modem radio. **1954** *Parents'Magazine* Feb.119 The family that plays together stays together. **1980** R. HILL *Spy's Wife* xxi. The family that spies together, sties together. Old Cockney Russian proverb. **1996** *Washington Post* 15 Mar. B3 First, Mother Teresa opined on the divorce of Princess Di and Prince Charles.... 'The family that prays together stays together; and if you stay together, you will Jove one another with the same Jove with which God loves each one of us.' **2001** *Times* 22 Dec.19 Those who cook together stay together. Maybe because they cannot decide who should get the blender. ■ **family** 家族・家系

family ⇒ ACCIDENTS will happen (in the best-regulated families).

far ⇒ BLUE are the hills that are far away; FAIR and softly goes far in a day; GOD is high above, and the tsar is far away; The MOUNTAINS are high, and the emperor is far away.

fare ⇒ GO further and fare worse.

fashion ⇒ BETTER be out of the world than out of the fashion; When the GORSE is out of bloom, kissing's out of fashion.

fast ⇒ BAD news travels fast; A MONEYLESS man goes fast through the market.

fastest ⇒ He TRAVELS fastest who travels alone.

fasting ⇒ It's ill speaking between a FULL man and a fasting.

The FAT man knoweth not what the lean thinketh.
太っている人には痩せている人の気持ちは分からない。
（訳注：knoweth、thinketh はそれぞれ knows、thinks の古い形）

裕福な人はそうでない人の気持ちが分からない。

☐**1640** G. HERBERT *Outlandish Proverbs* no. 605 The fatt man knoweth not, what the leane thinketh. **1952** C. R. SHORT *Devil's Power* 111 Tony Gowar grunted. He was thinking of an old proverb he had read in a seventeenth-century book of proverbs in his father's library: 'The fat man knoweth not what the lean thinketh!' ■ **ignorance** 無知・無学

fat ⇒ A GREEN Yule makes a fat churchyard; The OPERA isn't over till the fat lady sings.

You do not FATTEN a pig by weighing it.
いくら豚を量っても太らせることはできない。

児童の学習成果を測定するのに試験を乱用する人たちがいる。そのような人へ反対意見を述べる際に教育者によって好んで使われる。

☐**1997** J. W. FRASER *Reading, Writing, Justice* 24 Offer the tests to see if the students meet them [but] ... As the old Highland Scots saying goes, 'You don't fatten a sheep by weighing it.' **2004** *Times* 7 June 19 The chairman, a wise farmer ... studied the figures for a time and then put them aside saying: 'You do not fatten a pig by weighing it!' **2009** B. OBAMA *Speech* 11 June There's a saying In Illinois I learned when I was down in a lot of rural communities ... 'Just weighing a pig doesn't fatten it.' ■ **reality and illusion** 現実と幻想

Like FATHER, like son.
この父親にしてこの息子あり。
（訳注：「蛙の子は蛙」）

Like father, like daughter も使われる。Like MOTHER, like daughter「この母親にしてこの娘あり」はこれとは独立して生まれた。しかし、Like FATHER, like son. と Like MOTHER, like daughter. の両方とも 17 世紀にこの形式で固定した。†ラテン語 *Qualis pater talis filius*.「父がそうであるように息子もそうである」

☐*c***1340** R. ROLL *Psalter* (1884) 342 Ill sunnys folous ill fadirs. **1509** A. BARCLAY *Ship of Fools* 98 An oldeprouerbe bath longe agone be sayde That oft the sone in maners lyke wyll be Vnto the Father. **1616** T. DRAXE *Adages* 149 Like father like sonne. **1709** O. DYKES *English Proverbs* 30 Like Father, like Son.... How many Sons inherit their Fathers Failings, as well as Estates? **1936**

W. HOLTBY *South Riding* v.i. Perhaps Lydia might do it once too often.... Like father, like daughter. **1983** 'M. INNES' *Appleby & Honeybath* xii. And like son, like father, If one may so vary the old expression. Neither of them reading men. **2012** G. HARDING *Painter of Silence* 71 Like father, like son. When Paraschiva saw the talent her son had inherited it made her uneasy. ■ **children and parents** 親子；**similarity and dissimilarity** 類似性と相違性

father ⇒ The CHILD is the father of the man; EXPERIENCE is the father of wisdom; SUCCESS has many fathers, while failure is an orphan; It is a WISE child that knows its own father; The WISH is father to the thought.

A FAULT confessed is half redressed.
自ら認めた過ちは半ば償われている。
（訳注：confess＝「〈罪などを〉認める」。*confess* one's crime〈犯罪を認める〉）

過ちを認めることによって、事態は円満な解決へと進んでいく。

□**1558** *Interlude of Wealth & Health* D2ᵛ Yf thou haue doone amisse, and be sory therfore, Then helfe a mendes is made. **1592** *Arden of Feuersham* Hlᵛ A fault confessed is more than half amends, but men of such ill spirite as your selfe Worke crosses [arguments] and debates twixt man and wife. **1732** T. PULLER *Gnomologia* no. 1140 Confession of a Fault makes half amends. **1822** SCOTT *Nigel* III. v. Come, my Lord, remember your promise to confess; and indeed, to confess is, in this case, in some slight sort to redress. **1855** H. G. BOHN *Handbook of Proverbs* 285 A fault confessed is half redressed. **1981** P. O'DONNELL *Xanadu Talisman* x. A fault confessed is half redressed, so I hope he will forgive us. ■ **confession** 告白・懺悔；**error** 間違い・誤ち

favour ⇒（名詞）KISSING goes by favour;（動詞）FORTUNE favours fools; FORTUNE favours the brave.

FEAR the Greeks bearing gifts.
贈り物をしてくるギリシア人には用心せよ。
（訳注：たとえ和解しても、かつて敵であった者に心を許してはならない）

暗示的に使われることが多い。元のラテン語版もそのまま引用される。ウェルギリウス『アエネーイス』II. 49 *Timeo Danaos, et dona ferentes.*「たとえ贈り物を持ってきたとしても、私はギリシア人を恐れる」（トロイ人に対して、トロイの城壁の中に木馬を入れないように警告したラオコオーンの言葉）。**1777** S. ジョンソン『書簡集』3 May (1952) II. 515 Tell Mrs. Boswell that I shall taste her marmalade cautiously at first. *Timeo Danaos et dona ferentes.* Beware, says the Italian proverb, of a reconciled enemy.「ボスエル夫人にマーマレイドは最初、用心していただきますと伝えてください。イタリアのことわざ *Timeo Danaos et dona ferentes.* がいみじくも述べているように、和睦した敵には気をつけなければなりませんから」

□**1873** TROLLOPE *Phineas Redux* I. xxxiii. The right honourable gentleman had prided himself on his generosity as a Greek. He would remind the right honourable gentleman that presents from Greeks had ever been considered dangerous. **1929** *Times* 26 Oct 13 Mr. Moses ... must now be reflecting on the wisdom of the advice to 'fear the Greeks even when they bring gifts'. **1943** B. S. GARDNER *Case of Drowsy Mosquito* vi. 'It wasn't a trap, I tell you.' Nell Sims said ... 'Fear the Greeks when they bear olivebranches.' **1980** J. GERSON *Assassination Run* iv. Fear the Greeks bearing gifts was the maxim to be drummed into every novice in the department. ■ de-

160　fear

ception ごまかし；giving and receiving 授受

fear ⇒ The man who has once been BITTEN by the snake fears every piece of rope; No right and fear no man; FOOLS rush in where angels fear to tread; Man fears TIME, but time fears the pyramids.

feast ⇒ AFTER the feast comes the reckoning; The COMPANY makes the feast; ENOUGH is as good as a feast.

feather ⇒ BIRDS of a feather flock together; FINE feathers make fine birds.

FEBRUARY fill dyke, be it black or be it white.
2月というのは黒であれ、白であれ、溝が溢れる月である。

(訳注："be it ..."の中のbeは仮定法現在で、「譲歩」を示している。whether ... or ...〈…であろうと…であろうと〉の形に相当する)

イングランドでは、2月は伝統的に大雨（黒）か雪（白）の月である。1978年の用例を参照。† In FEBRUARY there be no rain, 'tis neither good for hay nor grain.「2月に雨が降らなければ、干し草にも穀粒にも良くない」

□ 1557 T. TUSSER *Husbandry* DI Feuerell fill dyke, doth good with his snowe. **1670** J. RAY *English Proverbs* 40 February fill dike Be it black or be it white.; But if it be white, It's the better to like. **1906** B. HOLDEN *Country Diary of Edwardian Lady* (1977) 13 February fill dyke Be it black or be it white. **1978** R. WIUTLOCK *Calendar of Country Customs* iii. Though February is notoriously associated with floods, as in the appellation 'February fill-dyke', it is statistically one of the driest months of the year. ■ calendar lore 暦にまつわる伝承

If in FEBRUARY there be no rain, 'tis neither good for hay nor grain.
2月に雨が降らなければ、干し草にも穀物にも良くない。

(訳注：このことわざにおける if there be no rainのbeも仮定法現在できわめて古風な表現)

晩冬に雨が少ないと、年末の作物に悪影響をもたらす。この考えを表わした先例は**1670** J. レイ『英語ことわざ集』40 All the moneths in the year curse a fair Februeer.「1年は晴れた2月を呪う」である。2月の天候が残りの1年の繁栄を示すという考えはヨーロッパ諸国において多く見られるが、時に相反することわざもある。**1869** R. INWARDS『天気に関する伝承』「天気の知恵」21 If February give much snow, A fine summer it doth foreshow.「もし2月に多く雪が降れば、快適な夏が予想される」。フランス語に由来する。† If CANDLEMAS day be sunny and bright ...「もし聖燭祭が上天気であれば…」

□ *a*1706 J. STEVENS *Spanish & English Dict.* s.v. Febrero, When it does not rain in February, there's neither good Grass nor good Rye. **1906** E. HOLDEN *Country Diary of Edwardian Lady* (1977) 13 If February bring no rain 'tis neither good for grass nor grain. **1978** R. WHITLOCK *Calendar of Country Customs* iii. One farming adage asserts that 'If in February there be no rain Tis neither good for hay nor grain.' ■ weather lore 天気にまつわる伝承

fence 161

FEED a cold and starve a fever.
風邪には大食を、熱には絶食を。

おそらく 2 つの独立した忠告として意図されたものであるが、2 つが組み合わさった表現の背後にある合理的な理由が2002 年の用例に説明されている。初期の医学的な忠告として **1574** J. Withals『食事』66 Fasting is a great remedie in feuers.「断食は高熱を下げるのに適した治療法である」がある。

☐**1852** E. FITZGERALD *Polonius* p. ix. 'Stuff a cold and starve a fever' has been grievously misconstrued, so as to bring on the fever it was meant to prevent **1867** 'M. TWAIN' *Celebrated Jumping Frog* 69 It was policy to 'feed a cold and starve a fever'. **1939** C. MORLEY *Kitty Foyle* xxxi. I said I better go downstairs and eat a square meal, 'feed a cold and starve a fever.' ... 'You misunderstand that,' he says. 'It means if you feed a cold you'll have to starve a fever later.' **1997** *Washington Times* 19 Nov. A8 'Forget about feeding a cold and starving a fever,' Dr. Edelman said, adding there is no medical reason for diet changes. **2002** *New Scientist* 9 Feb. 51 The saying should be: 'If you feed a cold you will have to starve a fever.' The theory goes that if you carry on eating when you have a cold, your body will have to use up vital energy digesting the food rather than ... fighting the cold. You are therefore more likely to allow the cold to develop and become a fever. Your body will then have no option but to shut down your desire to eat in order to direct all its energy into fighting the fever. ■ **health** 健康

feed ⇒ The CARIBOU feeds the wolf, but it is the wolf who keeps the caribou strong; Feed a DOG for three days and he will remember your kindness for three years....

feel ⇒ A MAN is as old as he feels, and a woman as old as she looks; PRIDE feels no pain.

feet ⇒ BETTER to die on your feet than live on your knees; The CAT would eat fish, but would not wet her feet; ⇒ FOOT.

fell ⇒ LITTLE strokes fell great oaks.

fellow ⇒ STONE-DEAD hath no fellow.

The FEMALE of the species is more deadly than the male.
すべての種において、雌は雄より凶暴である。

慣用句 the female of the species「種の中の雌の方（生命力の強い方）」はこのことわざを想起させる表現としてよく使われる。

☐**1911** R. KIPLING in *Morning Post* 20 Oct 7 The she-bear thus accosted rends the peasant tooth and nail, For the female of the species is more deadly than the male. **1922** *WODEHOUSE Clicking of Cuthbert* ix. The Bingley-Perkins combination, owing to some inspired work by the female of the species, managed to keep their lead. **1979** *Guardian* 28 Apr. 12 We know phrases about the female of the species being more deadly than the male, but the suffragettes ... seemed to have gone into ... abeyance. ■ **women** 女性

fence ⇒ GOOD fences make good neighbours; The GRASS is always greener on the other side of the fence.

fetch ⇒ A DOG that will fetch a bone will carry a bone.

fever ⇒ FEED a cold and starve a fever.

few ⇒ MANY are called but few are chosen; You WIN a few, you lose a few.

fiction ⇒ FACT is stranger than fiction; TRUTH is stranger than fiction.

fiddle ⇒ There's many a GOOD tune played on an old fiddle.

fiddler ⇒ They that DANCE must pay the fiddler.

FIELDS have eyes, and woods have ears.
野に目あり、森に耳あり。
（訳注：「壁に耳あり、障子に目あり」）

思いもよらない場所で目撃されたり、話しを聞かれたりすることがある。都会でならば WALLS have ears.「壁に耳あり」となる。

□*c*1225 in *Englische Studien* (1902) XXXI. 8 Veld haued hege [eye], and wude haued heare- Campus habet lumen et habet nemus auris acumen. *c* 1386 CHAUCER *Knight's Tale* 1. 1522 But sooth is seyd, go sithen manyyeres, That 'feeld hath eyen and the wode hath eres'. 1640 J. HOW- ELL *Dodona's Grove* A4ᵛ Hedges have eares, tlie rurall Proverb sayes. 1738 SWIFT *Polite Conver- sation* III. 199 'O, Miss; 'tis nothing what we say among ourselves.' ... 'Ay Madam; but they say Hedges have Eyes, and Walls have Ears.' 1905 S. J. WEYMAN *Starvecrow Farm* xxviii. Heedful of the old saying, that fields have eyes and woods have ears, she looked carefully round her before she laid her hand on the gate. ■ **eavesdroppers** 盗み聞きする人

FIGHT fire with fire.
火をもって火と戦え。
（訳注：「毒をもって毒を制す」）

敵と同じものを使用して対抗せよという警告。† 14世紀初頭のフランス語*Lungfeu doit estaindre lautre*.「火を使って別の火を消さなければならない」。1608 シェイクスピア『コリオレーナス』IV. vii. 54 One fire drives out one fire; one nail, one nail.「こうして火は火に消され、釘は釘に追い出される」。これとは逆の主張がされることもある。You cannot fight fire with fire.「火で火と闘うことはできない」

□1846 J. F. COOPER *Redskins* III. i. If 'Fire will fight fire', 'Indian' ought to be a match for 'In- jin'any day. 1869 P. T. BARNUM *Struggles & Triumphs* xl. I write to ask what your intentions are.... Do you intend to fight fire with fire? 1980 C. SMITH *Cut-out* ix. 'You think the other Pales- tinians have hired some heavies as well?' 'Why not? Fight fire with fire.' 2015 *Irish Examiner* 16 Jan. (online) 'We will make sure we fight fire with fire and be physically ready to match Munster and take them beyond that,' said the [Saracens'] full-back. ■ **similarity and dissimilarity** 類似性と相違性 ; **ways and means** 方法と手段

fight ⇒ COUNCILS of war never fight; When ELEPHANTS fight, it is the grass that suffers; While TWO dogs are fighting for a bone, a third runs away with it.

FINDINGS 163

He who FIGHTS and runs away, may live to fight another day.
戦って生き延びた者は、次にまた戦う機会がある。

(訳注：he ＝「〈関係節を伴って〉…する者は誰でも〈性別は問わない〉」。*He who* hesitates is lost.〈しり込みする者は負けだ〉。「三十六計逃げるにしかず」)

戦いから逃げることが生命と後日新たに戦う力の再生を保証してくれるなら、それは分別ある行動となるであろう。to live to fight another day「別の日に戦う機会を得る」という慣用句も暗示的に使われる。†メナンドロス *Sent.* 56 (Jaekel) ἀνὴρ ὁ φεύγων καὶ πάλιν μαχήσεται.「逃げる者は再び戦う」。現在の形は、次のような簡潔な中英語の形に取って代わったものである。*a* 1250『梟と小夜鳴鳥』(1960) 1.176 'Wel fight that wel flight,' seth the wise.「賢者曰く、『上手く逃げる者は上手く戦う』」

□ **1542** N. UDALL *Erasmus' Apophthegms* II. 335[V] That same manne, that renneth awaye, Maye again fight, an other daye. **1678** S. BUTLER *Hudibras* III. iii. For, those that fly, may fight againe, Which he can never do that's slain. **1747** J. RAY *Complete Hist. Rebellion* 61 The Dragoons ... thought proper ... a sudden Retreat; as knowing that, He that fights and runs away, May turn and fight another Day; But he that is in Battle slain, Will never rise to fight again. **1876** J. A. AULLS *Sparks & Cinders* 5 For be it known he kept in view That ancient adage, trite but true, That 'He who fights and runs away, May live to fight another day.' **1981** *Daily Telegraph* 10 June 2 (*caption*) He who fights and runs away ... lives to fight another day! ■ discretion 思慮分別 ; ways and means 方法と手段

fill ⇒ FEBRUARY fill dyke, be it black or be it white; WORK expands so as to fill the time available.

find ⇒ The DEVIL finds work for idle hands to do; Those who HIDE can find; LOVE will find a way; SAFE bind, safe find; SCRATCH a Russian and you find a Tartar; SEEK and ye shall find; SPEAK as you find; It is easy to find a STICK to beat a dog.

FINDERS keepers (losers weepers).
見つけた人が持ち主となる（無くした人は泣くしかない）。

下の例からわかるように、口語にはいろいろな言い方がある。

□ **1825** J. T. BROCKETT *Glossary of North Country Words* 89 No halfers—findee keepee, lossee seekee. **1856** C. READE *Never too Late* III. xiii. We have a proverb—'Losers seekers finders keepers.' **1874** E. EGGLESTON *Circuit Rider* xv. If I could find the right owner of this money, I'd give it to him; but I take it he's burled.... 'Finders, keepers,' you know. **1969** *Daily Express* 17 Mar. 9 Where I come from it's finders keepers, losers weepers. **2002** *Washington Times* 23 Jan. E4 (*Crankshaft comic strip*) 'Mr. Crankshaft ... I think I left my pencil box on your bus! Can I look in your lost and found box?' 'Forget it ... I don't have one! Haven't you ever heard of the legal concept "Finders keepers, losers weepers"?' ■ gains and losses 利益と損失

FINDINGS keepings
拾いものは自分のもの。

(訳注：Findings の後に are が省略されている)

上のことわざも参照。†プラウトゥス『三文銭』I. 63 *Habeas ut nanctu's.*「見つけた者は持ち主となる」。この原則は現在の形になる以前に既にイングランドで成立していた。

164 FINE

1595 A. クック *Country Errors in Harley MS 5247* 108^v That a man finds is his own, and he may keep it. 「見つけたものは自分のものである。だから持っていてもよい」

☐**1863** J. H. SPEKE *Discovery of Source of Nile* v. The scoundrels said, 'Findings are keepings, by the laws of our country; and as we found your cows, so we will keep them.' **1904** *Daily Chronicle* 27 Sept.1 Harsh sentences of imprisonment for 'findings-keepings' offences. **1963** G. GREENE *Sense of Reality* 38 'I found them in the passage.' ... 'Finding's [i.e. the action or fact of finding, rather than the objects found, as in earlier examples] not keeping here,' he said, 'whatever it may be up there.' **1996** H. HODGKINSON Findings Keepings (*poem title*). ■ **gains and losses** 利益と損失

FINE feathers make fine birds.
美しい羽が美しい鳥を作る
（訳注：「馬子にも衣装」）

立派に装えば立派に見え、実際以上の人物だと見られる。†16世紀初頭のフランス語 *Les belles plumes font les beaux oiseaux.*「美しい羽が美しい鳥を作る」**1583** J. スポンダヌスの書いた『オデッセイ』VI.81の解説からバスク語のことわざと見なされる。*Apud meos Vascones ... hac parcemia ... : speciosae plumae avem speciosam constituent.*「これは私の愛するバスク語のことわざである。美しい羽が美しい鳥を作る」

☐**1592** G. DELAMOTHE *French Alphabet* II. 29 The faire feathers, makes a faire foule. **1658** E. PHILLIPS *Mysteries of Love & Eloquence* 162 Fine feathers make fine birds. As you may see in Hide Park. **1858** SURTEES *Ask Mamma* x. Mrs. Joe ... essayed to pick her to pieces, intimating that she was much indebted to her dress—that fine feathers made fine birds. **1968** I. PETITE *Life on Tiger Mountain* xiv. I feel, ... if, indeed, 'fine feathers make a fine bird,' then I would just as soon not be that peculiar kind of fine bird. ■ **appearance, significant** 重要な外見；**dress** 衣服

FINE words butter no parsnips.
美辞麗句を並べたところで、パースニップにバターも塗れない。
（訳注：parsnip=「パースニップ、アメリカホウフウ」〈セリ科の草〉。クリーム色をした野菜でその根が食用となる。通称サトウニンジン）

口先だけでは何にもならない。

☐**1639** J. CLARKE *Parremiologia Anglo-Latina* 169 Faire words butter no parsnips. **1692** R. L'ESTRANGE *Fables of Aesop* cccxl. Relations, Friendships, are but Empty Names of Things, and Words Butter No Parsnips. **1763** A. MURPHY *Citizen* I. ii. What becomes of his Greek and Latin now? Fine words butter no parsnips. **1848** THACKERAY *Vanity Fair* xix. Who ... said that 'fine words butter no parsnips'? Half the parsnips of society are served and rendered palatable with no other sauce. **1997** C. M. SCHULZ *Washington Post* 27 Jan. Cl2 (*Peanuts comic strip*) [Charlie Brown:] 'Yes, ma'am, he's a very smart dog. Thank you for saying so.'[Snoopy:] 'Fine words butter no parsnips.' **2001** *Spectator* 1 Dec. 66 While it may be a truth universally acknowledged that fine words butter no parsnips, I have to say that in my experience parsnips are seldom cooked in butter. ■ **hypocrisy** 偽善；**words and deeds** 言動

fine ⇒ RAIN before seven, fine before eleven.

fire 165

FINGERS were made before forks.
指はフォークができる前からあった。
（訳注：フォークのない頃は手を使って食事をしたものである。よって食事は形式ばる必要はない）

食卓で両手を使って食べることに対する丁寧な言い訳として使われる。

□ **1567** *Loseley MSS* (1836) 212 As God made hands before knives, So God send a good lot to the cutler's wives. **1738** SWIFT *Polite Conversation* II. 136 (Colonel talces them [some fritters] out with his Hand.) Col. Here, Miss, they say, Fingers were made before Forks, and Hands before Knives. **1857** TROLLOPE *Barchester Towers* II. iii. Miss Thorne ... was always glad to revert to anything and ... would doubtless In time have reflected that fingers were made before forks, and have reverted accordingly. **1983** J. WAINWRIGIIT *Heroes no More* 37 'This is ridiculous. However, fingers were made before forks.' She lifted one of the king prawns from its resting place and began to nibble at it ■ **excuses** 言い訳 ; **manners** 礼儀・作法

fingers ⇒ The DEVIL makes his Christmas pies of lawyers' tongues and clerks' fingers.

FIRE is a good servant but a bad master.
火は従順な召使いにも、暴君にもなる。

首尾よく支配されれば有益で役に立つものでも、支配する側になれば危険である。

□ **1615** T. ADAMS *Englands Sickness* 20 The world, like fire, may be a good seruant, will bee an ill Master. **1738** SWIFT *Polite Conversation* II. 183 Why, Fire and Water are good Servants, but they are very bad Masters. **1808** J. ADAMS *Works* (1850-6) VI. 533 Like fire, they [i.e. the aristocracy] are good servants, but all-consuming masters. **1948** H. BESTON *Northern Farm* xxxvi. 'Fire is a good servant but a bad master.' So runs the proverb. **1973** J. CAIRD *Murder Remote* xx. Is not whisky the wonderful thing? But like fire, like fire—a good servant but a bad master. ■ **ways and means** 方法と手段

The same FIRE that melts the butter hardens the egg.
同じ火でもバターを溶かすこともすれば、卵を固くすることもする。

人々は同じ経験に対して異なる反応を示す。当初は他の言い方もあった。† **1623** ベー コン『生と死の歴史』(online) In one and the same fire, clay grows hard and wax melts.「同じ火でも粘土が固くもなれば蠟が溶けもする」

□ **1952** J. F. BENDER *Make Your Business Letters Make Friends* 220 An approach that works In one Instance may kill a sale In another. Remember the fire that hardens the egg softens the butter. **1995** D. T. LYKKEN *Antisocial Personalities* 81 The first day In school or a first rollercoaster ride will be a pleasurable excitement for some children ... but a terrifying and destructive experience for other children; ... the same fire that melts the butter hardens the egg. **2000** D. DE ARMAS WILSON *Ceruantes, Novel, and New World* 131 The same fire that melts the butter hardens the egg. The same books that craze Don Quixote lead Dorotea ... out of a wilderness of seductions and betrayal. ■ **experience** 経験

fire ⇒ A BURNT child dreads the fire; DIRTY water will quench fire; FIGHT fire with fire; You should KNOW a man seven years before you stir his fire; If you PLAY with fire you get burnt; You can't SHOUT 'Fire' in a crowded theatre; No SMOKE without fire; THREE removals are as bad as a fire.

FIRST catch your hare.
まずは、兎を捕らえよ。

（訳注：「捕らぬ狸の皮算用」）

一般にグラス夫人の『料理の技』(1747)、またはビートン夫人の『家政読本』(1851)で紹介された兎スープのレシピに由来すると考えられているが、実はそのような記述は見当たらない（1896年の用例参照）。意味が似てるものとして CATCHING's before hanging.「縛り首にする前にまずは捕えよ」がある。† *c* 1300 ブラクトン『イングランドの法と慣習法』IV. xxi. *Vulgariter dicitur, quod primo opportet cervum capere, & postea cum captus fuerit ilium excoriare.*「よく言われるように、まずは鹿を捕えよ。皮を剥ぐのはその後だ」

☐ **1801** *Spirit of Farmers' Museum* 55 How to dress a dolphin, first catch a dolphin. **1855** THACKERAY *Rose & Ring* xiv. 'To seize wherever I should light upon him—' 'First catch your hare!' ... exclaimed his Royal Highness. **1896** *Daily News* 20 July 8 The familiar words, 'First catch your hare,' were never to be found in Mrs. Glasse's famous volume. What she really said was, 'Take your hare when it is cased [skinned].' **1984** 'C. AIRD' *Harm's Way* iii. Sloan took his reply straight from the pages of an early cookery book. ... 'First, catch your hare.' ■ **ways and means　方法と手段**

FIRST come, first served.
最初に来た者が最初にもてなしを受けることができる。

（訳注：「早い者勝ち」。come は過去形でなく、過去分詞）

一番早く到着する者がまずもてなしを受ける。形と意味が類似したものとして FIRST up, best dressed.「最初の子供が最も良い身なりをしている」がある。† 13世紀後半のフランス語 *Qui ainçois vient au molin ainçois doit molder.*「水車場に最初に来る者が最初に粉を挽くことができる」

☐ *c***1390** CHAUCER *Wife of Bath's Prologue* I. 389 Whoso that first to mille comth, first grynt. **1548** H. BRINKBLOW *Complaint of Roderick Mors* xvii. Ye haue a parciall lawe in making of tachmentes [attachments, i.e. judicial seizure of one's person or goods (obsolete)], first come first serued. **1608** R. ARMIN *Nest of Ninnies* DI He found Sexton ... making nine graues ... and who so dyes next, first comes, first served. **1819** SCOTT *Montrose in Tales of my Landlord* 3rd Ser. IV. Xii. All must ... take their place as soldiers should, upon the principle of, first come, first served. **2002** *Rough Guide: Hong Kong & Macau* 170 You can't reserve seats on the ferries: it's first come, first served, so get there early at busy times. ■ **orderliness　整然としていること**

The FIRST duty of a soldier is obedience.
軍人の大義とは忠節である。

1915年の用例はこの古くからの有名な軍事教訓の異形の１つである。第２次世界大戦後に開かれたニュルンベルクの戦争犯罪裁判以降、この考え方には疑問を抱く傾向がある（2006年の用例参照）。

☐**1831** 'ANTI-RADICAL' in *United Service Journal* II. 540 I have at this moment some instructions lately issued from the Horse-guards, and the maxim under the head of 'Articles of War' is, Obedience is the first duty of a soldier. **1847** J. GRANT *Romance of War* IV. xv. 'What do the wiseacres at head-quarters mean, in sending a detachment there?''I suppose they scarcely know themselves. But obedience—We all know the adage.' **1867** MCCALL V. MCDOWELL *California Circuit Court* 25 Apr. 10 The first duty of a soldier is obedience, and without this there can be neither discipline nor efficiency in an army. **1872** G. J. WHYTE-MELVILLE *Satanella* II. xxiv. 'The first duty of a soldier is obedience,' he answered in great glee. **1915** F. M. HUEFFER *Good Soldier* m. iii. She had been taught all her life that the first duty of a woman is to obey. **2006** *Journal of Moral Education* XXXV. ii. 141 Finding all 24 of the defendants guilty of war crimes, that tribunal wrote an opinion acknowledging that a military soldier's first duty is to obey, but nonetheless rejected the defence of superior orders and called for independent thinking by the soldier. ■ **obedience** 従順・服従；**soldiers** 兵士

FIRST impressions are the most lasting.
第一印象が最も長く続く。

（訳注：the most〈＝最も〉は most でも可。動詞の後の形容詞・副詞を修飾する場合は the を付けないことがある。She is〈the〉most beautiful.〈彼女が一番美しい〉。）

人や物に対する第一印象はその後もずっと変わらずに残る。

□**1700** CONGREVE *Way of World* IV. i. How shall I receive him? ... There is a great deal in the first Impression. **1791** H. JACKSON in *Publications of Colonial Society of Massachusetts* (1954) XXXVI. 112 I am afraid it is too late ... and you know that first impressions are the most lasting. **1844** DICKENS *Martin Chuzzlewit* v. I didn't like to run the chance of being found drinking it ... for first impressions, you know, often go a long way, and last a long time. **1926** R. M. OGDEN *Psychology & Education* xii. Primacy is popularly expressed by the statement that 'first impressions are lasting'. **1946** J. B. PRIESTLEY *Bright Day* ii. He ought to look neat and tidy.... It's half the battle ... making a good first impression. ■ **appearance, significant** 重要な外見

On the FIRST of March, the crows begin to search.
3 月 1 日、カラスがつがいを探し始める。

カラスの繁殖期は 3 月から始まる。

□**1846** M. A. DENHAM *Proverbs relating to Seasons, &c.* 39 On the first of March, the crows begin to search. Crows are supposed to begin pairing on this day. **1847** R. CHAMBERS *Popular Rhymes of Scotland* (ed. 2) 165 On the first of March, The craws begin to search; By the first o'April, They are sitting still. **1906** E. HOLDEN *Country Diary of Edwardian Lady* (1977) 132 By the 1st of March the crows begin to search, By the 1st of April they are sitting still, By the Ist of May they are flown away, Creeping greedy back again With October wind and rain. ■ **calendar lore** 暦にまつわる伝承

It is the FIRST step that is difficult.
難しいのは最初の一歩である。

このことわざにはいくつか他の言い方がある。殉教したパリの司教、聖ドニの話はフランスのことわざを想起させるもので、1979 年の用例に挙げられている。†フランス語 *Ce n'est que le premjer pas qui coute.*「労力を要するのは最初の一歩だけである」

□*c*1596 A. MUNDAY et al. *Sir Thomas More* 11 Would I were so far on my Journey. The first stretch is the worst methinks. **1616** J. WITHALS *Dict.* (rev. ed.) 576 The first step is as good as halfe ouer. **1876** A. B. MEACHAM *Wi-Ne-Ma & her People* iv. He had fortified himself against the charms of the Indian maiden, as he thought, but consented to visit her. Ah! my man, have you not learned that when the first step is taken the next follows easily. **1979** J. BARNETT *Backfire is Hostile* xi. St Denis was executed.... Afterwards he picked up his head and walked for six miles. ... The wise man said, 'The distance ... is not Important. It was the first step that was difficult.' **1991** 'P. RUELL' *Only Game* vii. 193 What is It they said about that Frenchman who walked three miles after his head had been chopped oil? It's the first step that counts. ■ **beginnings and endings** 最初と最後

168 FIRST

FIRST things first.
大事なことから先にやれ。

優先順位は正しく設定されなければならない。

☐**1894** G. JACKSON (*title*) *First things first*; addresses to young men. **1920** W. RILEY *Yorkshire Suburb* 136 The dear lady was … incapable … of putting first things first. **1979** 'L BLACK' *Penny Murders* Iv. They dropped the talking; first things first, as Kate always felt about a pleasant meal. **2002** *Spectator* 10 Aug. 20 'I think the principle of "first things first" does apply,' says Al Gore, 'and has to be followed if we are to have any chance of success.' ■ **orderliness 整然としていること**

FIRST thoughts are best.
最初の考えが最善である。

(訳注：Second thoughts are best.「2番目の考えが最善である」ということわざもある)

最初の自然に生まれた考え方こそ正しいということがよくある。

☐**1922** J. JOYCE *Ulysses* 354 First kiss does the trick. The propitious moment. Something inside them goes pop. Mushy like, tell by their eye, on the sly. First thoughts are best. Remember that till their dying day. **1929** 'P. OLDFELD' *Alchemy Murder* viii. 95 'I have thought it over. First thoughts are best' **1943** M. LOWRY *Letter* 7 Sept in S. E. Grace *Sursum Corda!* (1995) I. 427 Don't shrink the Branches too much—first thoughts often best. **2001** *New York Times* 8 Apr. (online) 'First thought, best thought' was his [i.e. Ginsburg's] governing principle: no heed to the high-modernist idea of poem as patiently constructed artifact … ■ **decision and indecision 決断と優柔不断**

There is always a FIRST time.
何事にも初めがある。

以前に起こっていない、あるいは、なされていないからと言って、これ以後も起こらない、あるいはなされないという保証はどこにもない。There's a first time for everything. という形でも使われる。

☐**1792** A. HAMILTON *Papers* (1961-) XII. 504 But there is always 'a first time'. **1929** W. R. BUR-NETT *Little Caesar* III. vii. 'I ain't got nothing to spill.… Did I ever do any spiling?' 'There's a first time for everything.' **1987** 'M. HEBDEN' *Pel among Pueblos* xvi. 'He has no record.' 'Doesn't mean a thing. There's always a first time.' **2001** R. JOHANSEN *Beyond Belief* iii. 48 'You don't think I can do it?' 'I think you can try.' 'I've never failed yet' She shrugged. 'There's a first time for everything.' ■ **beginnings and endings 最初と最後**

FIRST up, best dressed.
最初の子供が最も良い身なりをしている。

イングランド北部のことわざで、貧乏な大家族では下の子供は上の子供のおさがりをもらうことになる（1969年の用例参照）。First in, best dressed. は特にオーストラリアで使われる (2014年の用例参照)。† FIRST come, first served.「最初に来た者が最初にもてなしを受けることができる」

☐**1919** B. CLASSEN *Outlines of History of English Language* 263 The same dislike of assertive-ness is responsible for … the frequency of such short pregnant phrases as … 'first up, best dressed' … **1969** *Times* 23 Sept 9 'It's like first up, best dressed in this family' Mr. F told me. A crane slinger, he was injured at work in February 1969 … Since then he and his wife and eight children have been living on approximately £25 a week. **2007** *Times Educational Supplement* 8

FISH 169

June 32 The inability of many parents to send their children to school in clothes that have seen the inside of a washing machine in the past six months (teachers in more challenging schools will be familiar with the concept of 'first up, best dressed') can lead to dilemmas. **2014** *Sydney Morning Herald* 30 Dec. (online; *heading*) Sydney New Year's Eve: First in, best dressed for fireworks display. ■ **punctuality** 時間厳守

first ⇒ Every DOG is allowed one bite; Whom the GODS would destroy, they first make mad; LAST in, first out; SELF-PRESERVATION is the first law of nature; If at first you don't SUCCEED, try, try, try again; THINK first and speak afterwards; He that will THRIVE must first ask his wife; TRUTH is the first casualty of war.

The FISH always stinks from the head downwards.
魚はいつも頭から腐る。

死んだ魚の鮮度は魚の頭の状態から判断できる。したがって、社会、国、企業などの上層部が腐敗していると、残りもすぐに腐っていく。ἰχθὺς ἐκ τῆς κεφαλῆς ὄζειν ἄρχεται.「魚は頭から腐る」

□**1581** G. PETIIE tr. *S. Guozzo's Civil Conversation* III. 51 If the prouerbe be true, ... that a fishe beginneth first to smell at the head, ... the faultes of our seruantes will be layed vppon vs. **1611** R. COTGRAVE *Dict. French & English* s. v. Teste, Fish euer begins to taint at the head; the first thing that's deprau'd in man's his wit. **1915** W. S. CHURCHILL *Letter* 3 Dec. in M. Gilbert Winston S. Churchill (1972) III. Compan. II. 1309 The guilt of criminality attaches to those responsible. 'Well,' said the Aga Khan, 'fish goes rotten by the head.' **1981** *Sunday Telegraph* 3 May 16 'The fish', as the saying goes, 'always stinks from the head downwards.' Last Sunday we deplored Mr. Michael Foot's liking for the street politics of marches and 'demos'. Since then, a hundred Labour MPs ... have followed their leader's example. **2012** *Times* 2 July 20 The fish rots from the head. The appetite of employees for dishonesty is largely governed by the signals from the top floor. ■ **rulers and ruled** 支配者と被支配者

FISH and guests smell after three days.
魚と客は 3 日経つと臭くなる。

† プラウトゥス『ほら吹き兵士』I. 7 41 *Nam hospes nullus tarn in amici hospitium devorti potest, quin, ubi triduom continuom fuerit, iam odiosus siet.*「訪問してきた友人を 3 日後も飽きないでいるほど心優しい主人はいない」

□**1580** LYLY *Euphues & his England* II. 81 As we say in Athens, fishe and gestes in three dayes are stale. **1648** HERRICK *Hesperides* 169 Two dayes y'ave larded here; a third yee know, Makes guests and fish smell strong; pray go. **1736** B. FRANKLIN *Poor Richard's Almanack* (Jan.) Fish and visitors smell in three days. **1869** *Notes & Queries* 4th Ser. N. 272 'See that you wear not out your welcome.' This is an elegant rendering of the vulgar saying that 'Fish and company stink in three days'. **1985** J. S. BORTHWICK *Down East Murders* iv. How long should she stay? She remembered the universal truth that fish and guests smell after three days. **2001** *Washington Times* 21 Nov. BI Fish and visitors smell after three days, the old adage goes. Yet the experience of hosting a crowd for ah extended time over the holidays need not leave a bad taste—or odor—for someone prepared to cope. ■ **hospitality** もてなし

170 FISH

There are as good FISH in the sea as ever came out of it.
海にはこれまでに捕られたことのないほどの良い魚がいる。

（訳注：好機は1度しかないというものではない。チャンスはまだある）

現在では失恋した人に対する慰めの言葉となっている。There are plenty more fish in the sea.「海にはもっとたくさんの魚がいる」

□*c*1573 G. HARVEY *Letter-Book* (1884) 126 In the mayne sea theres good stoare of fishe, And in delicate gardens ... Theres always great varietye of desirable flowers. **1816** T. L. PEACOCK *Headlong Hall* xiv. There never was a fish taken out of the sea, but left another as good behind. **1822** *SCOTT Nigel* III. x. Ye need not sigh sae deeply.... There are as gude fish in the sea as ever came out ofit. **1944** W. S. MAUGHAM *Razor's Edge* iii. I'm a philosopher and I know there are as good fish in the sea as ever came out. I don't blame her. You're young. I've been young too. **2000** *Washington Post* 30 Nov. C11 (*Garfield comic strip*) 'Yesiree, Garfield, there are lot of women out there. Yesiree.... Plenty of fish in the sea. I'll just cast out the old line.' 'Your bait's dead.' ■ **love, blighted** くじかれた愛

All is FISH that comes to the net.
網にかかるものはすべて魚である。

自分のところに来る物はすべて利益であり、みな利用する。しばしば性的な文脈で使われる（1636年の用例参照）。これと意味がよく似たものに All is GRIST that comes to the mill.「水車小屋に来るものはすべて自分の穀物である」がある。

□*c*1520 in *Ballads from MSS* (1868-72) I. 95 Alleys ffysshe that commyth to the nett. **1564** W. BULLEIN *Dialogue against Fever* 70 Takyng vp commoditie [opportunity], refusyng nothyng: all is fishe that commeth to the nette. **1631** F. LENTON *Characterismi* C4 [A]ll's fish that comes to net with her [a bawd]. **1680** BUNYAN *Mr. Badman* 19 What was his fathers could not escape his fingers, all was fish that came to his net. **1848** DICKENS *Dombey & Son* ix. 'All's fish that comes to your net, I suppose?' 'Certainly,' said Mr. Brogley. 'But sprats an't whales, you know.' **1936** A. CHRISTIE *Murder in Mesopotamia* xix. I don't know that she cares for one more than the other. ... All's fish that comes to her net at present. ■ **gains and losses** 利益と損失；**opportunity** 機会・好機

fish ⇒ BETTER are small fish than an empty dish; BIG fish eat little fish; The CAT would eat fish, but would not wet her feet; When the LAST tree is cut down, the last fish eaten, ... you will realize that you cannot eat money; LITTLE fish are sweet; A WOMAN without a man is like a fish without a bicycle.

fish-guts ⇒ KEEP your own fish-guts for your own sea-maws.

fit ⇒ If the CAP fits, wear it; ONE size does not fit all; If the SHOE fits, wear it.

fix ⇒ If it ain't BROKE, don't fix it.

flag ⇒ TRADE follows the flag.

flattery ⇒ IMITATION is the sincerest form of flattery.

flea ⇒ BIG fleas have little fleas upon their backs to bite them; If you LIE down with dogs, you will get up with fleas; NOTHING should be done in haste but gripping a flea.

flesh ⇒ What's BRED in the bone will come out in the flesh.

flew ⇒ A BIRD never flew on one wing.

flight ⇒ BLESSINGS brighten as they take their flight.

float ⇒ If you SIT by the river for long enough, you will ⇒ the body of your enemy float by.

flock ⇒ BIRDS of a feather flock together.

flower ⇒ APRIL showers bring forth May flowers.

fly ⇒（名詞）EAGLES don't catch flies; HONEY catches more flies than vinegar; A SHUT mouth catches no flies;（動詞）TIME flies; ⇒ FLEW.

flying ⇒ It is good to make a BRIDGE of gold to a flying enemy.

folk ⇒ DIFFERENT strokes for different folks; There's NOWT so queer as folk; YOUNG folks think old folks to be fools, but old folks know young folks to be fools.

follow ⇒ TRADE follows the flag.

He that FOLLOWS freits, freits will follow him.
前兆を追い求める者は、前兆に追いかけられる。

スコットランドのことわざ。前兆を探し求める者は、振り返ってみると前兆通りのことが起こっていることに気が付く。ここで freits は「前兆、予感、虫の知らせ」を意味する。

□c1700 in J. PINKERTON *Scottish Tragic Ballads* (1781) I. 47 Wha luik to freits, my master deir, Freits will ay follow them. **1721** J. KELLY *Scottish Proverbs* 128 He that follows Freets, Freets will follow him. He that notices superstitious Observations (such as spilling of Salt) ... it will fall to him accordingly. **1804** M. PARK in Lockhart *Life of Scott* (1837) II. i. He answered, smiling, 'Freits (omens) follow those who look to them.' ... Scott never sahim again. **1914** *Times Literary Supplement* 9 Apr. 178 The Kings of Scots have always been beset by omens, and ... to him who follows freits, freits follow. ■ future 未来 ; omens 前兆

folly ⇒ Where IGNORANCE is bliss, 'tis folly to be wise.

fonder ⇒ ABSENCE makes the heart grow fonder.

172 FOOL

A FOOL and his money are soon parted.
馬鹿者はすぐに金を使ってしまう。

愚かで何でもすぐに真に受ける者は、簡単に騙されて金を奪われてしまう。

☐ **1573** T. TUSSER *Husbandry* (rev. ed.) ix. A foole and his money be soone at debate: which after with sorow repents him too late. **1587** J. BRIDGES *Defence of Government in Church of England* xv. 1294A foole and his money is soone parted. **1616** T. DRAXE *Adages* 166 A foole, and his money are soone parted. **1771** SMOLLETT *Humphry Clinker* I. 17 4 She tossed her nose in distain, saying, she supposed her brother had taken him into favour … : that a fool and his money were soon parted. **1981** C. BERMANT Patriarch xx. I can see now I was a fool, perhaps even a greedy fool, and a fool and his money are soon parted. **2002** *Washington Times* 1 Jan. D4 (*Herb & Jamaal comic strip*) 'Herb, you ought to know better than to get mixed up in a get-rich scheme! It's like the old saying: "A fool and his money are soon parted."' 'Yeah, you are right! So, how much did you lose?' ■ **money** 金・金銭 ; **stupidity** 愚かさ

A FOOL at forty is a fool indeed.
40歳になってもまだ馬鹿な奴は全くの馬鹿である。

知恵は経験によって身に付けなければならない。ゆえに、40歳に到達した人は若い時代の愚かさから卒業してしかるべきである。† **1557** R. エッジワース『説教集』301 When he [Rehoboarn] begonne hys raigne he was one and fortye yeares of age.... And he that hath not learned some experience or practice and trade of the world by that age will neuer be wise. 「彼（レホボアン）の治世が始まったとき、彼は40歳であった。その歳までに、ある程度の経験や世界の慣習と貿易状況について知らなかったのだから、今から賢くなることはなかろう」

☐ **1725** E. YOUNG *Universal Passion* II. 16 Be wise with speed; A fool at forty is a fool indeed. **1751** N. COTTON *Visions in Verses* 13 He who at fifty is a fool, Is far too stubborn grown for school. **1908** L. MITCHELL *New York Idea*III. 112 I shall come or not [to your wedding] as I see fit. And let me add, my dear brother, that a fool at forty is a fool indeed. **1982** B. EMECHETA *Destination Biafra* i. 'What is it they say about a fool at forty?' 'I don't think you'll be a fool forever, sir.' ■ **middle age** 中年 ; **stupidity** 愚かさ

There's no FOOL like an old fool.
年寄りの馬鹿ほどの馬鹿はいない。

老齢になっても愚かなことを続けるのは真の愚か者の証である。

☐ **1546** J. HEYWOOD *Dialogue of Proverbs* II. ii. F4ᵛ But there is no foole to the olde foole, folke saie. **1721** J. KELLY *Scottish Proverbs* 256 No fool to an old Fool. Spoken when Men of advanc'd Age behave themselves, or talk youthfully, or wantonly. **1732** T. FULLER *Gnomologia* no. 3570 No Fool like the old Fool. **1814** SCOTT *Waverley* III. xv. And troth he might hae ta'en warning, but there's nae fule like an ould fule. **1910** R. KIPLING *Rewards & Fairies* 257 'There are those who have years without knowledge.' 'Right,' said Puck. 'No fool like an old fool.' **2001** *Washington Post* 8 July B5 But these fantasies are more proper to ayoung person; beyond the age of, say, 50, they become the fantasy of that fool like whom we are told there is no other, the old fool. ■ **old age** 老年 ; **stupidity** 愚かさ

A FOOL may give a wise man counsel.
愚か者でも賢者に知恵を貸すこともある。

（訳注：may ＝「…でも〈時々〉… することがある」。この意味では can もよく用いられる。Even cautious

FOOLS 173

people *may* sometimes be off their guard.〈用心深い人も時に油断することがある〉。Lightning *can* be dangerous.〈稲妻も危険なことがある〉)

愚か者でさえ時には自分より賢い人に役立つ忠告をすることもある。

□*a*1350 *Ywain & Gawain* (EETS) I. 1477 Bot yit a fole that litel kan [knows], May wele cownsail another man. **1641** D. FERGUSSON *Scottish Proverbs* (STS) no. 84 A Fool may give a wyse man a counsell. **1721** J. KELLY *Scottish Proverbs* 25 A Fool may give a wise Man counsel by a time. An Apology of those who offer their Advice to them, who may be supposed to excel them in Parts and Sense. **1818** SCOTT *Heart of Midlothian* IV . viii. If a fule may gie a wise man a counsel, I wad hae him think twice or [before] he mells [meddles] wi' Knockdunder. **1942** E. P. OPPENHEIM *Man who changed Plea* xvii. Aren't we all fools ... in one or two things? ... Even a fool, though, can sometimes give good advice. ■ advice 忠告・助言 ; fools 愚か者

FOOL me once, shame on you; fool me twice, shame on me.
1 度私を騙したのなら、あなたの恥。 2 度私を騙したのなら、私の恥。

誰しも 1 度は騙される。その場合、騙した人の方が悪い。しかし、もし同じことが再び起これば、今度は騙された人の方が悪い。なぜなら、経験から何も学ばず、用心を怠ったからである。fool の代わりに動詞 deceive「騙す」が使われることがある。

□**1611** *Tarlton's Jests* (1844) 11 For Who deceives me once, God forgive him; if twice, God forgive him; but if thrice, God forgive him, but not me, because I could not beware. **1650** A. WELLDON *Secret History of King James I* (1690) 88 The Italians having a Proverb, He that deceives me Once, it's his Fault; but Twice it is my fault. **1659** N. R. *Proverbs English, French, Dutch, Italian & Spanish* 54 He that deceives me once, it is his faul[t]; if twice, it is mine. **1980** *Forbes* 17 Mar. 69 The important thing in dealing with the Japanese is not to believe everything you hear. Or, as the saying goes: Fool me once, shame on you. Fool me twice, shame on me. **2001** *Washington Times* 3 Oct. Al7 You know the old saying, 'Fool me once, shame on you; fool me twice, shame on me.' How does that apply in the aftermath of the Sept. 11 act of war against our country? **2002** P. LOVESEY *Diamond Dust*xxx. 297 'Did you give him any?' 'No. I wouldn't be so daft. You know that old saying? He that deceives me once, shame fall him; if he deceives me twice, shame fall me.' ■ deception ごまかし

fool ⇒ CHILDREN and fools tell the truth; FORTUNE favours fools; A man who is his own LAWYER has a fool for his client; MORE people know Tom Fool than Tom Fool knows; SIX hours' sleep for a man, seven for a woman, and eight for a fool; YOUNG folks think old folks to be fools, but old folks know young folks to be fools; also FOOLS.

foolish ⇒ PENNY wise and pound foolish.

FOOLS and bairns should never see half-done work.
愚か者と子供は未完成の作品を見てはならない。

(訳注：bairn=〈スコットランド・北イングランドで〉「子供」)

標題の 2 人は、製作途中の見かけの悪さから完成品の質を間違って非難することがある。

□**1721** J. KELLY *Scottish Proverbs* 108 Fools should not see half done Work. Many fine Pieces of Work will look ... aukward when it is a doing. **1818** SCOTT *Letter* Dec. (1933) V. 265 'Bairns and fools' ... according to our old canny proverb should never see half done work. **1913** A. & J. LANG *Highways & Byways in Border* ix. To the lay eye improvement is yet barely perceptible: 'Fools and bairns', however, they tell us, 'should never see half-done work.' **1934**V. MACCLURE

174 FOOLS

Death on Set ii. He has never really liked anybody seeing the roughs except the technical staff. Said it gave the players ideas they were better without. 'Fools and children, and unfinished work,' you know. ■ **fools 愚か者；work 仕事**

FOOLS ask questions that wise men cannot answer.
愚か者は賢者が答えられない質問をするものだ。

愚か者は馬鹿げた質問（1738年の用例）をするという意味か、または愚か者は一見単純だが、実は鋭い、あるいは一筋縄ではいかない質問（1973年の用例）をするという意味で使われる。どちらの場合にせよ、賢者は答えを出すのが難しい。

☐ **1666** G. TORRIANO *Italian Proverbs* 249 One fool may ask more than seven wise men can answer. **1738** SWIFT *Polite Conversation* II. 156 'Miss, can you tell which is the white Goose?' ... 'They say, a Fool will ask more Questions than the wisest body can answer.' **1871** J. S. JONES *Life of J. S. Batkins* liv. Bean appeared always to be fond of Amanda.... I asked him one day.... He looked at me, and said, 'Batkins, fools ask questions that wise men cannot answer.' **1973** *Amarillo Globe-Times* 27 Mar. 20/1 We are well acquainted with the old adage that fools can ask questions which wise men cannot answer. Yet we would pose the question simply—'Why?' Why do young Americans use heroin? **1997** M. WALTERS *Echo* iv. 60 '[H]e was a right nutter most of the time, but ... I reckon I learnt a thing or two off of him.' 'Like what?' Terry grinned. 'Like, fools ask questions that wise men cannot answer.' ■ **fools 愚か者；wisdom 賢明・知恵**

FOOLS build houses and wise men live in them.
愚か者が家を建て、賢者がそこに住む。

より簡潔な形式 Fools build and wise men buy.「愚か者が建て、賢者が買う」は家以外の財産にも使うことができる（1997年の用例参照）。

☐ **1670** J. RAY *English Proverbs* 91 Fools build houses, and wise men buy them. **1721** J. KELLY *Scottish Proverbs* 110 Fools Big [build] Houses and wise Men buy them. I knew a Gentleman buy 2000 1. worth of Land, build a House upon it, and sell both House and Land to pay the Expences of his building. **1875** A. B. CHIIALES *Proverbial Folk-Lore* 43 Fools build houses, and wise men live in them is another proverb on this subject; it is partly true. **1934** J. ALEXANDER *Murder at Eclipse* III. ii. 86 On his retirement, the first baron did not build himself a palace such as he could well have afforded. Perhaps he remembered the old adage that 'fools build and wise men buy.' **1997** *Country Life* 14 Aug. 28 Arthur Ransome, self-mocking, said of boating folk: 'Fools build and wise men buy.' There is a similar put-down of people who breed their own horses. ■ **fools 愚か者；home 家庭・母国**

FOOLS for luck.
幸運の例なら、愚か者を見よ。

この形式は明らかに1834年の用例から来ている。Fools for Luckは W. C. フィールズとチェスター・コンクリンが出演した1928年の映画のタイトルとなった。FORTUNE favours fools.「運命の女神は愚か者を贔屓する」も同じ考え方を表わしている。1981年の用例はこのことわざを一部だけ切り取ったものである。† **1631**ジョンソン『バーソロミューの市』II. ii. Bring him a sixe penny bottle of Ale; they say, a fooles handsell [gift] is lucky.「彼に6ペンスの酒瓶を1本やってくれ。愚か者への贈り物は幸運であると言うではないか」

☐ **1834** *Narrative of Life of David Crockett* xiii. The old saying—'A fool for luck. and a poor man for children.' **1854** J. B. JONES *Life of Country Merchant* xix. They attribute your good fortune to the old hackneyed adage, 'A fool for luck'. **1907** D. H. LAWRENCE *Phoenix II* (l968) 6 'You'll make our fortunes.' 'What!' he exclaimed, 'by making a fool of myself? They say fools for luck. What fools wise folks must be.' **1981** T. HARLING *Bikini Red North* xi. All fools are lucky; isn't that the adage? ■ **fools** 愚か者 ; **luck** 幸運・運

FOOLS rush in where angels fear to tread.
愚か者は天使が恐れて足を踏み入れない所へも飛び込む。

（訳注：fools と angels が対比されている。「愚か者の怖いもの知らず」。1711 年の用例にあるように、英国の詩人・作家ポープの有名な一行である）

愚か者は慎重な取扱いが必要とされる状況に、無防備にあるいは下手に介在する。しばしば Fools rush in. と短縮される。これは1997年の映画のタイトルとなった。

☐ **1711** POPE *Essay on Criticism* I. 625 No Place so Sacred from such Fops is barr'd, Nor is Paul's Church more safe than Paul's Church-yard: Nay, fly to Altars; there they'll talk you dead; For Fools rush in where Angels fear to tread. **1858** G. J. MCREE *Iredell's Life & Correspondence* II. 277 Rash presumption illustrates the line, 'Fools rush in where angels fear to tread'. **1922** JOYCE *Ulysses* 649 Prying into his private affairs on the fools step in where angels principle. **1943** H. MCCLOY *Do not Disturb* ii. The folly of the officious is proverbial: don't rush in where angels fear to tread. **1975** 'C. AIRD' *Slight Mourning* xv. 'The deceased was of—er—a forceful personality. Not over-sensitive, either, from all accounts.' 'Ah, I see. Fools rush in where angels fear to tread.' ■ **fools** 愚か者 ; **ignorance** 無知・無学

foot ⇒ It is not SPRING until you can plant your foot upon twelve daisies; One WHITE foot, buy him; ⇒ FEET.

forbear ⇒ BEAR and forbear.

foretold ⇒ LONG foretold, long last.

FOREWARNED is forearmed.
前もっての警戒は前もっての武装。

（訳注：「転ばぬ先の杖」）

† ラテン語 *Praemonitus, praemunitus*. 「あらかじめ警戒し、あらかじめ武装せよ」

☐ *c*1425 J. ARDERNE *Treatises of Fistula* (EETS) 22 He that is wained afore is noght bygiled. c **1530** J. REDFORD *Wit & Science* I. 1093 Once warnd, half armd folk say. **1587** R. GREENE *Card of Fancy* IV. 23 I giue thee this Ring of golde, wherin is written … Praemonitus, Premunitus … inferring this sense, that hee which is forewarned by friendlie counsoule of imminent daungers, is fore-armed against all future mishappe. *a* **1661** T. FULLER *Worthies* (Devon) 272 Let all ships passing thereby be fore-armed because forewarned thereof. **1885** 'LE JEMLYS' *Shadowed to Europe* xxv. 'Forewarned is forearmed,' he thought, as he complimented himself upon his success in baffling the attempt to ensnare him. **2014** *Spectator* 13 Dec 105 A couple of competitors dropping dead of fugu poisoning might be just the ticket. Forewarned is forearmed. ■ **foresight and hindsight** 先見の明と後知恵 ; **prudence** 思慮・分別

forget ⇒ A BELLOWING cow soon forgets her calf; Feed a DOG for three days and he will remember your kindness for three years …

forgive ⇒ To ERR is human (to forgive divine); To know all is to forgive all.

fork ⇒ FINGERS were made before forks.

FORTUNE favours fools.
運命の女神は愚か者を贔屓する。

愚か者、あるいは愚かな行動が幸運に変わることもある。†ラテン語 *Jortuna javet fatuis*.「運命の女神は愚か者を贔屓する」

□**1546** J. HEYWOOD *Dialogue of Proverbs* II. vi. II^v They saie as ofte, god sendeth fortune to fooles. **1563** B. GOOGE *Eclogues* ES But Fortune fauours Fooles as old men saye And lets them lyue And take the wyse away. **1738** GAY *Fables* 2nd Ser. II. xii. 'Tis a gross error, held in schools, That Fortune always favours fools. **1922** E. PHILLPOTTS *Red Redmaynes* xviii. Thus he became exceedingly useful as time passed; yet fortune favours fools and his very stupidity selved him well at the end. **1960** O. MANNING *Great Fortune* I. vi. Fortune favours fools.... We were forced to tarry while he slumbered. ■ **fools** 愚か者 ; **luck** 幸運・運

FORTUNE favours the brave.
運命の女神は勇者に味方する。
(訳注：the brave=「勇者」。the=「…な人々」。the elderly〈お年寄り〉)

†エンニウス『年代記』257 (Vahlen) *Fortibus est Jortuna viris data*.「幸運は勇敢な者に与えられる」。ウェルギリウス『アエネーイス』x. 284 *Audentes Jortuna iuvat*.「幸運は勇敢な者に手を貸す」

□*c*1385 CHAUCER *Troilus & Criseyde* IV. 600 Thenk ek Fortune, as wel thiselves woost, Helpeth hardy man to his enprise. *c* **1390** GOWER *Confessio Amantis* VII. 4902 And seith, 'Fortuneunto the bolde Is favorable forto helpe'. *a* **1625** BEAUMONT & FLETCHER *Prophetess* IV.vi. He is the scorn of Fortune: but you'll say, That she forsook him for his want of courage, But never leaves the bold. **1752** in W. JOHNSON *Papers* (1939) IX. 86 Make no doubt but Fortune will favour the brave. **1885** TROLLOPE *Dr. Thorne* II. vii. Fortune, who ever favours the brave, specially favoured Frank Gresham. **2001** *Spectator* 17 Nov. 25 The luck element has aroused doubts in some quarters, but Lord Guthrie has a standard retort: 'Fortune favours the brave.' He has been proved right, so far. ■ **courage** 勇気 ; **luck** 幸運・運

fortune ⇒ EVERY man is the architect of his own fortune; OPPORTUNITY never knocks twice at any man's door.

forty ⇒ A FOOL at forty is a fool indeed; LIFE begins at forty; SAINT Swithun's day, if thou be fair, for forty days it will remain.

foul ⇒ It's an ILL bird that fouls its own nest; NO harm, no foul.

FOUR eyes see more than two.
4 つの目は 2 つの目より多くのものを見る。
(訳注：「3 人寄れば文殊の知恵」)

1 人でチェックするよりダブルチェックのほうが望ましい。TWO heads are better

than one.「2 つの頭は 1 つよりよい」も同じ発想である。ビジネス界と財界では Four-Eyes Principle「4 つ目の原則」(2014 年の用例) に進化した。この原則はすべての重要な書類は腐敗や見落としを前もって防ぐために、少なくとも 2 人の重役によって目を通さなければならないというものである。ラテン語 *Plus vident oculi, quam oculus.*「複数の目は 1 つの目より良く見える」

☐ **1591** A. COLYNET *True Hist. Civil Wars France* 31 Two eyes doo see more then one. **1592** G. DELAMOTHE *French Alphabet* II. 45 Foure eyes can see more then two. **1642** T. PULLER *Holy State* IV. v. Matters of inferiour consequence he will communicate to a fast friend, and crave his advice; for two eyes see more than one. **1898** F. M. MULLER *Auld Lang Syne* 80 But who has ever examined any translation from any language, without finding signs of ... carelessness or ignorance? Four eyes see more than two. **1962** H. REILLY *Day She Died* vii. What he wanted was a look at the cars the variegated crowd of people had arrived in. Four eyes were better than two. **2014** *L'Osservatore Romano* Aug. (online) Thus the 'four eyes principle' is being applied 'so that any significant piece of business cannot be conducted only by one person'. ■ **assistance** 援助 ; **observation** 観察

four ⇒ There goes more to MARRIAGE than four bare legs in a bed.

There's no such thing as a FREE lunch.
無料の昼食などない。
(訳注 :「ただより高いものはない」)

ただでは何も手に入らない。元々は米国経済における口語的な格言であったが、今では一般的に使われている。

☐ **1967** R. A. HEINLEIN *Moon is Harsh Mistress* xi. 'Oh, "tanstaafl." Means "There ain't no such thing as a free lunch." And isn't,' I added, pointing to a FREE LUNCH sign across the room, 'or these drinks would cost half as much.' **1969** *Newsweek* 29 Dec. 52 I was taught ... the first and only law of economics: 'There is no such thing as a free lunch.' **1971** *New Yorker* 25 Sept 76 There is no such thing as a free lunch.... The idea has proved so illuminating for environmental problems that I am borrowing it from its original source, economics. **1979** L. ST. CLAIR *Obsessions* xi. There's no such thing as a free lunch. So, In return for your help, what do you ask? **2001** *Spectator* 29 Dec. 26 I believe that the old saying 'There is no such thing as a free lunch' applies here. Pornography and permissiveness will have a price. ■ **bribery and corruption** 賄賂と腐敗 ; **reciprocity** 相互扶助

free ⇒ The BEST things in life are free; PREEDOM is not free; THOUGHT is free.

FREEDOM is not free.
自由はただではない。

自由を維持する代価を想起させる。Freedom costs.「自由は金がかかる」というスローガンとしても使われる。米国起源で、ワシントン D.C. の朝鮮戦争退役軍人記念碑に刻まれている。歌のタイトルや T シャツなどを通じて大衆文化の中に広く行き渡っている。1943 年の用例におけるように拡大された形でもよく使われる。

☐ **1943** *American Forests* XLIX. 195 (*advertisement*) Freedom is not free—It's Priceless. **1991** G. BUSH speech 4 July in *Public Papers of Presidents of United States*: *George Bush, 1991* 827 (quoting letter from Michigan teacher Martha Williams) I try to teach my young people that freedom isn't free, its price is dedication to an ideal ... **2015** *Spectator* 17 Jan. 28 This troubles me.

Not the bit about people not wanting to die—that's normal—but this apparent failure to accept that freedom isn't free. ■ **freedom** 自由

freit (omen)：⇒ He that FOLLOWS freits, freits will follow him.

Frenchman ⇒ One ENGLISHMAN can beat three Frenchmen.

fresh ⇒ Don't THROW out your dirty water until you get in fresh.

Friday ⇒ Monday's CHILD is fair of face.

A FRIEND in need is a friend indeed.
まさかの時の友こそ真の友。
　　(訳注：in need と indeed が韻を踏んでいる)

　friend in need とは窮地の際に助けてくれる友人を指す。†エウリピデス『ヘカベ』l. 1226 ἐν τοῖς κακοῖς γὰρ ἀγαθοὶ σαφέστατοι φίλοι.「苦境のとき、よい友人が最も傍にいる」。エンニウス *Scaenica* 210 (Vahlen) *Amicus certus in re incerta cemitur.*「本当の友かどうかは不安定な時代のときにわかる」。これをパロディ化したものに1960年代のスローガン A friend with weed [marijuana] is a friend indeed.「マリファナを持っている友こそ真の友」がある。

　□*c*1035 *Durham Proverbs* (1956) 10 lilt thearfe man sceal freonda cunnian [friend shall be known in time of need]. *a* 1400 *Titus & Vespasian* (1905) 98 I shal the save When tyme cometh thou art in nede; Than ogh men frenshep to shewe in dede. *a* 1449 LYDGATE *Minor Poems* (EETS) II. 755 Ful weele is him that fyndethe a freonde at neede. **1678** J. RAY *English Proverbs* (ed. 2) 142 A friend in need is a friend indeed. **1773** R. GRAVES *Spiritual Quixote* II. VIII. xx. (*heading*) A Friend in Need is a Friend Indeed. **1866** C. READE *Griffith Gaunt* III. xv. You came to my side when I was in trouble.... A friend in need is a friend indeed. **1985** D. WILLIAMS *Wedding Treasure* viii. He never felt quite right about calling up scripture—at least not in private. 'Friend in need is a friend Indeed,' he added. That was better. ■ **adversity** 逆境・苦難；**friends** 友

friend ⇒ The BEST of friends must part; The ENEMY of my enemy is my friend; LEND your money and lose your friend; If you have to LIVE in the river, it is best to be friends with the crocodile; SAVE us from our friends; SHORT reckonings make long friends.

The FROG in the well knows nothing of the sea.
井の中の蛙大海を知らず。

　日本のことわざで、自分の経験は狭すぎて外の世界を知らなくてはならないということを教えている。†中国語 The frog in the well cannot talk of Heaven.「井戸の中の蛙は天国の話はできない」

　□**1918** E. J. BANFIELD *Tropic Days* 189. Among coastal blacks—all of whom may be said to be fishermen—some are ardent devotees to the sea. Others of the same camp restrict themselves to unsensational creeks and lagoons. The frog in the well knows nothing of the salt sea, and its aboriginal prototype contents himself with milder and generally less remunerative kind of sport than that in which his bolder cousins revel. **1976** R. STORRY 'Soldiers of the Showa Empire' in

Pacific Affairs vol. 49 (spring) 105 Japanese officers could be forgiven for supposing that they were the wave of the future. In reality they were prisoners of the past and (in the apt if trite Japanese phrase) 'frogs in a well'. [footnote] *I no naka no kawazu taikai wo shirazu* (the frog in the well knows nothing of the great ocean). **2006** 'Oregon Caves' on *www.nps.gov* 11 Sept Amphibians ... 'The frog in the well knows nothing of the great ocean.' **2007** D. KENNEDY 'Faust—The Seven Games ofthe Soul' on *www.justadventure.com* 14 Feb. The paper reads 'Thefrog in the well knows nothing about the high seas.' Recall that there is a well outside the house. ■ **experience 経験 ; ignorance 無知・無学**

frost ⇒ So many MISTS in March, so many frosts in May.

When all FRUIT fails, welcome haws.
あらゆる果物が手に入らなければ、たとえサンザシの実でもありがたい。

年配の女性、あるいは若くても好ましくない愛人をやむを得ず妻にめとる人に対してよく使われる。haws とはサンザシの木の実で、食べられるが、あまり美味しくなく手触りも好ましくない。

□ **1721** J. KELLY *Scottish Proverbs* 350 When all Fruit fa's welcome ha's.... Spoken when we take up with what's coarse, when the good is spent. **1914** K. F. PURDON *Folk of Furry Farm* vii. 'Lame of a leg, and grey In the head! ... That's a fancy man for a girl to take!' 'Marg was none too young herself ... and when all fruit fails, welcome haws! She wanted someone.' **1958** B. BEHAN *Borstal Boy* III. 266 So even the excommunicated will do; when It's not easy to getanyone else. When all fruit falls, welcome haws. ■ **necessity 必要性・必然性 ; old age 老年**

fruit ⇒ He that would EAT the fruit must climb the tree; SEPTEMBER blow soft, till the fruit's in the loft; STOLEN fruit is sweetest; The TREE is known by its fruit.

FULL cup, steady hand.
コップが満杯の時こそしっかり持て。
(訳注：「おごる平家は久しからず」)

快適な、または羨ましい状況 (満杯など) を不注意な行動によって台無しにしないよう注意しなければならない。

□ *c* **1025** *Durham Proverbs* (1956) 15 Swa fulre fiet swa hit mann sceal liegror beran [the more full the cup, the more carefully must one carry it]. *c* **1325** *Proverbs of Hending in Anglia* (1881) IV. 293 When the coppe is fullest, thenne her hire feyrest. **1721** J. KELLY *Scottish Proverbs* 346 When the Cup's full carry it even. When you have arrived at Power and Wealth, take a care of Insolence, Pride, and Oppression. **1889** C. M. YONGE in *Monthly Packet Christmas* 46 Poor things! They were so happy—so open-hearted. I did long to caution them. 'Full cup, steady hand.' **1903** G. H. KNIGHT *Master's Questions* xxi I would listen ... to this question ... whenever ... I am eagerly reaching out my hands to grasp what may satisfy an unlikely ambition. All hands are not steady enough to carry a full cup. **2012** *www.scoop.co.nz* 1 Aug. (*heading*) New Zealand sheepmeat—'full cup, steady hand'. ■ **good fortune 幸運 ; prudence 思慮・分別**

It's ill speaking between a FULL man and a fasting.
満腹な人と空腹の人は折り合いが悪い。
(訳注：a fasting の後に man を補う)

空腹な人と満腹な人が仲良くなることはまずない。1824年の用例では、食事を促す表現として使われている。

180 FULLNESS

□*a*1641 D. FERGUSSON *Scottish Proverbs* (STS) no. 1349 Thair is nothing betuix a bursten body and a hungered. **1824** SCOTT *Redgauntlet* I. xi. Ye maun eat and drink, Steenie ... for we do little else here, and it's ill speaking between a fou man and a fasting. **1934** J. BUCHAN *Free Fishers* ii. It's ill speaking between a full man and a fasting, but two fasting men are worse at a crack. ■ hunger 飢え・空腹 ; quarrelsomeness 口論になりやすさ

Out of the FULLNESS of the heart the mouth speaks.
口は心から溢れ出ることを語るものである。

感情が高ぶっている人は思いついたことを心おきなく語るものである。『マタイによる福音書』12章34節 (欽定訳聖書) Out of the abundance of the heart the mouth speaketh.「口は心から溢れ出ることを語るものである」

□*c*1390 CHAUCER *Parson's Tale* I. 626 After the habundance of the herte speketh the mouth ful ofte. **1699** T. CHALKLEY *Fruits of Divine Meditation in Works* (1751) II. 26 Out of the Abundance of the Heart the Mouth speaketh. **1861** TROLLOPE *Framley Parsonage* II. x. As out of the full head the mouth speaks, so is the full heart more prone to speak at such periods of confidence as these. **1932** 'S. POWLER' *Hand-Print Mystery* ii. The murder ... had been in the background of her mind all the time. 'Out of the fullness of the heart the mouth speaketh.' ■ speech and silence 発言と沈黙

One FUNERAL makes many.
葬式は 1 度あると何度も続けてある。

One WEDDING brings another.「婚礼は婚礼を生む」と同じ発想である。この理由が下の用例において示されている。例えば、悪天候の中、屋外にいると、参列者、特に年配者は体調を崩し、その結果命取りになるからである。

□**1894** BLACKMORE *Perlycross* I. vii. It has been said, and is true too often ... that one funeral makes many. A strong east wind ... whistled through the crowd of mourners. **1935** R. C. WOODTHORPE *Shadow on Downs* V.iv. 137 The funeral went off very well.... I am glad we had such a fine day for it Standing about bareheaded in driving rain ... always makes such an occasion rather trying. and there is a good deal of truth in the saying that one funeral brings others. **1951** M. DURHAM *Forked Lightning* xx. 132 Poured catsand dogs for my poor father's funeral, it did.... My poor mother took a fever and it carried her off in a fortnight. They say one funeral makes another. ■ death 死

funeral ⇒ DREAM of a funeral and you hear of a marriage.

further ⇒ GO further and fare worse.

fury ⇒ HELL hath no fury like a woman scorned.

When the FURZE is in bloom, my love's in tune.
ハリエニシダが咲いている時は私の恋は好調である。

同じ主題を表わす When the GORSE is out of bloom, kissing's out of fashion.「ハリエニシダが咲いていない時は口づけをする人は誰もいない」を逆から言ったもの。
†*c*1225『英語研究』(1902) XXXI. 5 Whanne bloweth [flowers] the brom, thanne wogeth [woos] the grom; Whanne bloweth the furs, thanne wogeth he wurs.「花が

咲いている時、若者は求愛する。ハリエニシダが咲いている時、彼は求愛する」

□**1752** *Poor Robin's Almanack* Aug. B3ᵛ Dog-days are in he'll say's the reason Why kissing now is out of season: but Joan says furze [gorse] in bloom still, and she'll be kiss' d if she's her will. **1908** *Spectator* 9 May 740 At almost any season of the year gorse can be found in ... flower.... When the furze is in bloom, my love's in tune. ■ **love, prosperous** 順調な（恋）

G

gain ⇒ (名詞) One man's LOSS is another man's gain; There's no great LOSS without some gain; NO pain, no gain; (動詞) What you LOSE on the swings you gain on the roundabouts; NOTHING venture, nothing gain.

gallows ⇒ The SEA refuses no river.

game ⇒ LOOKERS-on ⇒ most of the game.

gamekeeper ⇒ An old POACHER makes the best gamekeeper.

gander ⇒ What's SAUCE for the goose is sauce for the gander.

GARBAGE in, garbage out.
がらくたを入れると、がらくたが出てくる。

> 米国起源である。データ処理の分野において、garbage は「不正確なインプット」を意味する。そのようなインプットは当然ながら誤ったアウトプットを産出する。頭文字語として GIGO も使われる。
>
> □**1957** B. B. BLANCHE 'Applying New Electronic Computers to Traffic and Highway Problems' *Traffic Quarterly* xl. 411 When the basic data to be used by a computer are of questionable accuracy or validity, our personnel have an unusual expression—GIGO—to characterize such information and the answers the computer produces. It simply means 'garbage in—garbage out.' **1964** *CIS Glossary of Automated Typesetting & Related Computer Terms* (Composition Information Services, LA.) 15 The relationship between input and output is sometimes—when Input is incorrect—tersely noted by the expression 'garbage in, garbage out'. **1987** *Washington Times* 10 Sept. F4 The computer rule, 'garbage in, garbage out' applies to the human mind just as much as it does to the computer. **1996** *Washington Times* 26 Feb. Al9 This brings into play the old computer-Industry dictum: Garbage In, Garbage Out. ■ **action and consequence** 行為と結果 ; **error** 間違い・誤ち

garment ⇒ SILENCE is a woman's best garment.

gate ⇒ A CREAKING door hangs longest; One man may STEAL a horse, while another may not look over a hedge.

GENIUS 183

gather ⇒ He who PLANTS thorns should not expect to gather roses; A ROLLING stone gathers no moss.

gathered ⇒ Where the CARCASE is, there shall the eagles be gathered together.

geese ⇒ On SAINT Thomas the Divine kill all turkeys, geese, and swine.

generation ⇒ From CLOGS to clogs is only three generations; From SHIRTSLEEVES to shirtsleeves in three generations.

It takes three GENERATIONS to make a gentleman.
紳士 1 人を作るのに 3 世代かかる。

1823 年の用例以前にはこの形式での表現がないものの、3 世代という概念そのものはルネサンス期に既にあった。例えば、**1598** J. KEPERS 訳『ロメイの延臣アカデミー』187 He may bee called absolutely noble, who shall have lost the memory of his ignobilitie ... during the reuolution of three generations「彼は完全に高貴だと称されるようになるかもしれない。というのは、彼は 3 世代かかって自分の下品さを消してしまっているであろうから」。**1625** F. マーカム『名誉の 50 年』ii. Three perfit descents, do euer so conclude a perfit Gentleman of Blood.「完璧な紳士 1 人が生まれるには完璧な 3 世代が必要である」

☐**1823** J. F. COOPER *Pioneers* I. xviII. You will find it no easy matter to make a gentleman of him. The old proverb says, that 'it takes three generations to make a gentleman'. **1915** W. S. MAUGHAM *Of Human Bondage* xxvii. He remembered his uncle's saying that it took three generations to make a gentleman: it was a companion proverb to the silk purse and the, sow's ear. **1940** 'M. INNES' *Comedy of Terrors* i. It has always been possible to make a gentleman in three generations; nowadays ... the thing is done in two. ■ **family** 家族・家系 ; **gentry** 紳士階級

generous ⇒ Be JUST before you're generous.

GENIUS is an infinite capacity for taking pains.
天才とは努力することをいとわない無限の能力のことである。

(訳注：pains=「〈複数形で〉」骨折り、苦労、努力。He took great pains with the job.〈彼はその仕事にひじょうに苦労した〉)

† **1858** カーライル『フリードリヒ 2 世』I. IV. iii. 'Genius' ... means transcendent capacity of taking trouble, first of all.「『天才とは』…まず第一に、苦労を受け入れる優れた能力を意味する」

☐**1870** J. B. HOPKINS *Work amongst Working Men* iv. Gift, like genius, I often think, only means an infinite capacity for taking pains. **1959** M. BRADBURY *Eating People is Wrong* iv. Genius is an infinite capacity for taking pains. But we should still foster it, however much of an embarrassment it may be to us. **1974** T. SHARPE *Porterhouse Blue* xiv. The modem fashion [of research] comes, I suppose, from a literal acceptance of the ridiculous dictum that genius is an infinite capacity for taking pains. ■ **diligence** 勤勉

184 gentleman

gentleman ⇒ When ADAM delved and Eve span, who was then the gentleman?; An ENG-LISHMAN'S word is his bond; It takes three GENERATIONS to make a gentleman.

gently ⇒ EASY does it; if you gently touch a NETTLE it'll sting you for your pains.

get ⇒ You cannot get BLOOD from a stone; Be CAREFUL what you pray for, you might get it; If you don't like the HEAT, get out of the kitchen; If you LIE down with dogs, you will get up with fleas; Don't get MAD, get even; The MORE you get, the more you want; What a NEIGHBOUR gets is not lost; You cannot get a QUART into a pint pot; What you SEE is what you get; You don't get SOMETHING for nothing; also GOT.

Never look a GIFT horse in the mouth.
贈り物の馬の口を覗いてはならない。

幸運な機会や贈り物の質や便利さを疑ったり、不平を言ってはならない。馬の年齢は一般に歯の状態で測定する。† *a* 420 聖ヒエロニムス *Commentary on Epistle to Ephesians*「序文」*noli ...ut vulgare proverbium est, equi dentes inspicere donati.*「ことわざが言うように、贈り物の馬の歯を見てはならない」

☐*a*1510 J. STANBRIDGE *Vulgaria* (EETS) 27 A gyuen hors may not [be] Joked in the tethe. **1546** J. HEYWOOD *Dialogue of Proverbs* I. v. B2ᵛ Where gyfts be gyuen freely, est west north or south, No man ought to Joke a geuen hors in the mouth. **1659** N. R. *Proverbs* 80 No man ought to look a guift Horse in the mouth. **1710** S. PALMER *Proverbs* 40 Never look a Gift Horse in the Mouth. **1892** G. & W. GROSSMITH *Diary of a Nobody* xviii. I told him it was a present from a dear friend, and one mustn't look a gift-horse in the mouth. **2002** *Oldie* Mar. 34 Gather ye rosebuds while ye may, let not the grass grow under thy feet, and never look a gift horse in the mouth. ■ **giving and receiving** 授受 ; **gratitude and ingratitude** 感謝と忘恩

gift ⇒ FEAR the Greeks bearing gifts.

gill ⇒ Every HERRING must hang by its own gill.

girl ⇒ BOYS will be boys.

GIVE and take is fair play.
双方の譲歩こそがフェアプレイである。

（訳注：日本語の「ギブアンドテイク」は物などを「あげたらもらう」という相互交換の意味だが、英語の意味とは異なる）

たとえ競合していても公正な取引を薦める際に使われる。

☐*c*1778 F. BUBNEY *Evelina* I. xxv. This here may be a French fashion ... but Give and Take Is fair in all nations. **1832** MARRYAT *Newton Forster* III. x. Give and take is fair play. All I say Is, let it be a fair stand-up fight **1873** 'TWAIN' & WARNER *Gilded Age* xxxiii. She thought that 'give and take was fair play', and to pany an offensive thrust with a sarcasm was a neat and legitimate thing to do. **2005** T. BARKER *Leadership for Results* 122 In combating the primary barrier of internal competitiveness, the crucial behavior is that of cooperation, in particular the implementation of the principle that 'give and take is fair play.' ■ **fair dealing** 公正な取引 ; **tolerance** 寛容・忍耐

GIVES   185

GIVE a thing, and take a thing, to wear the Devil's gold ring.
一度くれた物を取り返すなんて、悪魔の金の指輪をしている。
（訳注：子供に与えた物を子供から取り戻してはならない。）

子供が用いる脚韻表現 (thing, ring) で、何かを与えた後でそれを返すように求められる際に使われる。この概念自体はとても古くから見られる。†プラトン『ピレボス』19E καθάπερ οἱ παῖδες, ὅτι τῶν ὀρθῶς δοθέντων ἀφαίρεσις οὐκ ἔστι. 「子供の場合にあてはまることだが、正当に与えた物は取り返すことはできない」

□ 1571 J. BRIDGES *Sermon at Paul's Cross* 29 Shal We make God to say the worde, and eate his worde? to giue a thing, and take a thing, little children say, This Is the diuels goldring, not Gods gift. 1611 R. COTGRAVE *Dict. French & English* s. v. Retirer, To glue a thing and take a thing; to weare the diuels gold-ring. 1721 J. KELLY *Scottish Proverbs* 120 Give a Thing, and take a Thing, Is the ill Man's Goud Ring. A Cant among Children, when they demand a Thing again, which they had bestowed. 1894 *Notes & Queries* 8th Ser. VI. 155 Another saying among boys is—Give a thing and take a thing, To wear the devil's gold ring. 1959 I. & P. OPIE *Lore & Language of Schoolchildren* viii. It is a cardinal rule amongst the young that a thing which has been given must not be asked for again.... [Somerset] Give a thing, take a thing, Dirty man's plaything.... [Cheshire] Give a thing, take a thing, Never go to God again. ■ **giving and receiving** 授受

GIVE the Devil his due.
悪魔にも当然与えるべきものは与えよ。
（訳注：「盗人にも三分の理あり」）

悪人、あるいはあなたが嫌っている人に対してさえも、その人にすぐれたところがあるなら、それを認めてやらなければならない。慣用句 to give the devil his due「悪人をも公平に評する」としても使われる。

□ 1589 LYLY *Pap with Hatche* III. 407 Giue them their due though they were diuels ... and excuse them for taking anie money at interest. 1596 NASHE *Saffron Walden* III. 36 Giue the diuell his due. 1642 *Prince Rupert's Declaration* 2 The Cavaliers (to give the Divell his due) fought very valiantly. 1751 SMOLLETT *Peregrine Pickle* I. xviL You always used me in an officer-like manner, that I must own, to give the devil his due. 1936 H. AUSTIN *Murder of Matriarch* xxiii. To give the devil his due ... I don't think that Irvin planned to incriminate anyone else. 1978 R. L. HILL *Evil that Men Do* vi. Giving the devil his due will always jostle the angels. 2011 *Independent* 31 July (online; *heading*) Give the devil his due: 'Lucifer' [a variety of crocosmia] has never looked more appealing. ■ **fair dealing** 公平な取引

give ⇒ It is BETTER to give than to receive; Give CREDIT where credit is due; Give a DOG a bad name and hang him; Give a man ROPE enough and he will hang himself; Never give a SUCKER an even break.

He GIVES twice who gives quickly.
早く与える者は 2 度与えるに等しい。

†プブリリウス・シュルス『格言集』ccxxxv. *Inopi beneficium bis dat, qui dat celeriter.*「困っている人にすぐに援助する人は 2 倍助けてくれる人である」。14世紀中頃のフランス語 *Qui tost donne, deus fois donne.* また、*c* 1385 チョーサー『善女伝説　序』l. 451 For whoso yeveth a yifte, or dooth a grace. Do it by tyme [in good time], his thanks ys wel the more. 「贈り物をする人、あるいは親切な行為をする人へ。良いタイ

186 GLASS

ミングでしてあげなさい。相手の感謝はより大きくなるから」もある。ラテン語 *bis dat qui cito dat* はおそらくプブリリウス・シュルスの形式よりも一般的である。1617 年 5 月 17 日、英国の随筆家・政治家・哲学者 F. ベーコン が国璽尚書に就任する際に行なった演説の中でこのラテン語が引用されている。

□ *c*1553 T. WILSON *Art of Rhetoric* 65ᵛ He geueth twise, that geueth sone and chearefully. **1612** T. SHELTON tr. *Ceruantes' Don Qutxote* I. iv. It is an old proverbe, that bee that gives quickly, gives twice. **1775** J. BOSWELL *Life of Johnson* I. 443 I did really ask the favour twice; but you have been even with me by granting it so speedily. *Bis dat qui dto dat*. **1980** *Times* 17 Oct. 13 'He gives twice who gives quickly.' ... We have everything to gain by generous action at once. ■ **charity** 慈善；**giving and receiving** 授受

Those who live in GLASS houses shouldn't throw stones.
ガラスの家に住む者は石を投げてはならない。

（訳注：「人を呪わば穴 2 つ」。Whose house 〈or head〉 is of glass must not throw stones at another. という言い方もある）

自分の状況やふるまいが同様の批判に晒されている相手を批判してはならない。† *c*1385 チョーサー『トロイラスとクリセダ』II. 867 Who that bath an bed ofverre [glass], Fro cast of stones war hym in the werre!

□ **1640** G. HERBERT *Outlandish Proverbs* no. 196 Whose house is of glasse, must not throw stones at another. **1754** J. SHEBBEARE *Marriage* Act II. lv. Thee shouldst not throw Stones, who hast a Head of Glass thyself.... Thee canst have no Title to Honesty who lendest the writings to deceive Neighbour Barter. **1778** T. PAINE in *Pennsylvania Packet* 22 Oct. i. He who lives in a glass house, says a Spanish proverb, should never begin throwing stones. **1861** TROLLOPE *Framley Parsonage* I. vi. Those who live in glass houses shouldn't throw stones.... Mr. Robarts's sermon will be too near akin to your lecture to allow of his laughing. **2001** W. NORTHCUTT *Darwin AwardsII* i. 16 Judea and Samaria district police jointly determined that the accidental crash was caused by the stone-throwing young men. People who live in glass houses shouldn't throw stones. ■ **hypocrisy** 偽善；**self-preservation** 自己防衛；**slander** 誹謗中傷

All that GLITTERS is not gold.
輝くものすべてが金とは限らない。

（訳注：1596 年の用例にあるシェイクスピアの『ヴェニスの商人』第 2 幕 7 場の文句「輝くもの必ずしも金ならず」は良く知られた言葉である。この場合、all ... not は「すべてが…だとは限らない」という部分否定となっていることに注意）

シェイクスピアに glisters という権威ある動詞があるが、今では glitters の方が普通である。1987 年の用例に示されている All is not gold that glitters. も一般的である。ラテン語 *Non omne quod nitet aurum est*.「輝くものすべてが金というわけではない」に由来する。

□ *c*1220 *Hall Meidenhad* (EETS) ii. Nls hit nower neh gold al that ter [there] schineth. *c* **1390** CHAUCER *Canon's Yeoman's Tale* I. 962 But al thyng which that shlneth as the gold Nls nat gold, as that I have herd it told. **1596** SHAKESPEARE *Merchant of Venice* II. vii. 65 All that glisters is not gold, Often have you heard that told. *c* **1628** W. DRUMMOND *Works* (1711) 222 All is not Gold which glittereth. **1847** C. BRONTë *Jane Eyre* II. ix. I wished to put you on your guard. It Is an old saying that 'all is not gold that glitters'. **1880** *Dict. English Proverbs* (Asprey Reference Library) 39 All that glitters is not gold. **1933** E. B. BLACK *Ravenelle Riddle* iv. All that glitters is not gold ... Every bird who calls himself an American doesn't happen to be one. **1987** D. FISKE *Murder Bound* (1989) ii.II The old saw 'all is not gold that glitters' still holds true despite its standing as a platitude. **1998** *Country Life* 22 Jan. 50 (*caption*) In the volatile world of jewellery investment, all that glisters is not gold. ■ **appearance, deceptive 偽りの外見**

global ⇒ THINK global, act local.

glorify ⇒ Until the LIONS produce their own historian, ...

glove ⇒ A CAT in gloves catches no mice.

GO abroad and you'll hear news of home.
外国へ行ってはじめて母国のことがわかるものだ。
(訳注：「灯台もと暗し」)

ニュースと噂は遠くまで伝わる。

☐ **1678** J. RAY *English Proverbs* (ed 2) 345 You must goe into the countrey to hear what news at London. **1887** T. HARDY *Woodlanders* I. iv. Well, what was the latest news at Shottsford.... As the saying is, 'Go abroad and you'll hear news of home.' **1937** J. P. MARQUAND *Late George Apley* x. It seems one must leave home to learn the news of home. ■ **home 家庭・母国；news 知らせ；travel 旅行**

GO further and fare worse.
遠くへ行けば行くほど事態は悪化する。
(訳注：fare =「事が運ぶ」He *fared* well in his profession. 〈彼は仕事が順調にいった〉)

遠く離れた場所を探して最終的に事態を悪化させるよりも身近なところで満足せよ。

☐ **1546** J. HEYWOOD *Dialogue of Proverbs* II. iv. G3ᵛ You rose on your right syde here ryght And might haue gon further, and haue faren wurs. **1738** SWIFT *Polite Conversation* II. 58 Come, Sir John, you may go further, and fare worse. **1848** THACKERAY *Vanity Fair* iv. She's just as rich as most of the girls who came out of India. I might go farther and fare worse. **1988** G. GREENE in *Spectator* 12 Aug. 271 He would have said, perhaps, with his plainness and simplicity and the smirk of satisfaction you see on his portrait, that one can fare further and fare worse. ■ **content and discontent 満足と不満足**

go ⇒ EASY come, easy go; LIGHT come, light go; QUICKLY come, quickly go; He that would go to SEA for pleasure, would go to hell for a pastime; SELL in May and go away; Never let the SUN go down on your anger; Don't go near the WATER until you learn how to swim; The WEAKEST go to the wall; Many go out for WOOL and come homeshorn; ⇒ GOES.

You cannot serve GOD and Mammon.
神とマモン（宝の神）の両者に仕えることはできない。

2 つの相反する原理、つまり神と物質主義を同時に支持することはできない。『マタイによる福音書』6 章 24 節（欽定訳聖書）No man can serve two masters ... Ye cannot serve God and mammon.「誰も 2 人の主人に兼ね仕えることはできない。…あなた方は神と富に仕えることはできない」。*Mammon*「マモン」とはアラム語で「富」を意味する。強欲な神を表わす固有名詞として中世の作家によって使われたが、現在では災いを

もたらす財産を意味する語として使われている。

☐ **1531** W. BONDE *Pilgrimage of Perfection* (rev. ed.) III. vii. No person may serue god eternall and also the Mammonde of Iniquite: whiche Is golde and syluer and other richesse. **1860** TROLLOPE *Framley Parsonage* II. i. Lady Lofton … would say of Miss Dunstable that It was impossible to serve both God and Mammon. **1982** P. MCGINLEY *Goosefoot* v. The city and the country repel each other like oil and water. And like God and Mammon, they can't be served at the same time by the same person. ■ **money** 金・金銭

Where GOD builds a church, the Devil will build a chapel.
神が教会を建てている場所に悪魔も礼拝堂を建ててくる。

悪は崇高な事業や計画でさえも腐敗させ、その中に潜り込んでくる。1942年の用例は英国の詩人・聖職者 G. ハーバート の『奇妙なことわざ集』(1640) no. 674. の形式を使用している。

☐ **1560** T. BECON *Works* I. 516ᵛ For commonly, where so ever God buildeth a church, the Deuyll wyl builde a Chappell iuste by. **1701** DEFOE *True-born Englishman* 4 Wherever God erects a House of Prayer, The Devil always builds a Chapel there: And 'twill be found upon Examination, The latter has the largest Congregation. **1903** G. H. KNIGHT *Master's Questions* xiii. Nowhere does the devil build his little chapels more cunningly than close under theshadow of the great temple of Christian liberty. A thing in itself completely right and good, may be, in its effects on others, completely evil. **1942** M. MABLETT *Devil Builds a Chapel* (*epigraph*) No sooner Is a temple built to God, but the Devil builds a chapel hard by. **2001** S. KENDRICK *Night Watch* iv. 134 'I'm beginning to think there's great truth in the old saying "Wherever God builds a church, the devil builds a chapel next door."' ■ **good and evil** 正邪

GOD helps them that help themselves.
神は自ら助くる者を助く。

自助努力を勧める説教として使われる。†アイスキュロス『断章』395 φιλεῖ δὲ τῷ κάμνοντισυσπεύδειν θεός.「神は骨を折って働く者を好んで助ける」。15世紀初頭のフランス語 *Aidez uous,Dieu uos aidera*.「自らを助けよ、そうすれば神があなたを助けてくれる」

☐ **1545** R. TAVERNER tr. *Erasmus' Adages* (ed. 2) 57 Diifacientes adiuuant. The goddes do helpe the doers. **1551** T. WILSON *Rule of Reason* SIᵛ Shipmen cal to God for helpe, and God will helpe them, but so not withstandying, if they helpe them selfes. **1668** R. B. *Adagia Scotica* 21 Help thy self, and God will help thee. **1736** B. FRANKLIN *Poor Richard's Almanack* (June)God helps them that help themselves. **1990** C. FREMLIN *Listening in Dusk* xxvii. A widow of eighty-nine … had hit an intruder over the head with the family Bible and sent him flying. 'The Lord helps those who help themselves!' she'd declared, cackling with triumph in front of the cameras. **2002** *Spectator* 19 Jan. 33 And what does the future hold? He quotes his grandmother: 'The Lord helps those who help themselves'. ■ **providence**（神の）摂理 ; **self-help** 自助

GOD is high above, and the tsar is far away.
神ははるか上空に、ツァー（ロシアの皇帝）ははるか遠くにいる。

ロシアのことわざで、中央権力は地方の利害・関心事には我関せずの状態であるから遠く離れたところに位置するという意味である。相当する中国のことわざは、The MOUNTAINS are high, and the emperor is far away.「山は高く、皇帝ははるか遠い」である。

☐ **1891** G. KENNAN *Siberia and Exile System* preface The lot of the 'unfortunates' to whom 'God is high above and the Tsar is far away.' **1915** A. C. LAUT *Pioneers of Pacific Coast* 34 'God is high

GOD 189

in the heavens, and the Czar is far away,' they said. The object was quick profit, and plundering was the easiest way to attain it **1970** M. LIEBMAN *Russian Revolution* 24 A vast and miserable mass of peasants for whom, as an old Russian saw had it, God was too high and the Tsar too far away. **1995** B. GRANT *In Soviet House of Culture* 5 Russian peasants across Siberia knew their relative independence in the maxim, 'God is high in the sky and the tsar is far away.' ■ **independence** 独立・自立 ; **power** 力・権力 ; **rulers and ruled** 支配者と被支配者

GOD made the country, and man made the town.
神が田園を、人間が都市を作った。

† ウァロ『農業論』III. i. *Divina natura dedit agros, ars humana aedijicavtt urbes.*
「神聖なる自然がわれらに野を与え、人間の技術が町を作った」

☐ **1667** A. COWLEY in J. Wells *Poems* 2 My father said ... God the first Garden made, & the first City, cain. **1785** COWPER *Task* 40 God made the country, and man made the town. **1870** H. TENNYSON *Memoir* 25 Jan. (1897) II. 96 There is a saying that if God made the country, and man the town, the devil made the little country town. **1941** H. MACINNES *Above Suspicion* x. God made the country, man made the town. Pity men couldn't learn better. **1977** G. TINDALL *Field & Beneath* i. It has been said that 'God made the country and man made the town', but ... the town is simply disguised countryside. ■ **Nature** 自然・造物主

GOD makes the back to the burden.
神は重荷を背負うために背中をお作りになった。
(訳注：神は力に余る試練を与えない。to the burden は「重荷に合わせて」の意)

状況がどんなに耐えきれないものであろうと、または困ったものであろうと、神はそれに耐えるだけの力は与えてくださっている。

☐ **a1822** COBBETT *Weekly Register* 12 Jan. 94As 'God has made the back to the burthen,' so the clay and coppice people make the dress to the stubs and bushes. **1839** DICKENS *Nicholas Nickleby* xviii. Heaven suits the back to the burden. **1939** E. F. BENSON *Trouble for Lucia* ii. 'Spare yourself a bitty' I've said, and always she's replied 'Heaven fits the back to the burden.' **1979** E. ANTHONY *Graue of Truth* viii. So many questions and nobody to answer them; it was a true penance for her.... God made the back for the burden.... An Irish nun ... had taught them that saying from her native land. ■ **providence** （神の）摂理 ; **trouble** やっかい・苦労

GOD never sends mouths but He sends meat.
神様が子供をお授けになったからにはきっと食物もお授けになる。
(訳注：子供の養育に無頓着な親に対しての言葉。1905 年の用例にも見られるが、He の H が大文字となっているのは〈キリスト教の〉神を意味しているためである。but ＝「…なしで」。meat ＝「食物」)

神はすべての人に与えて下さる。

☐ **1377** LANGLAND *Piers Plowman* B. XIV. 39 For lente neuere was lyf but lyflode [livelihood] were shapen. **1546** J. HEYWOOD *Dialogue of Proverbs* I.iv. Bl God neuer sendeth mouthe, but he sendeth meat. **1832** J. P. KENNEDY *Swallow Barn* I. xxvlii. God never sends mouths ... but he sends meat, and any man who has sense enough to be honest, will never want wit to know how to live. **1905** A. MACLAREN *Gospel accordingto St. Matthew* I. 103 We are meant to be righteous, and shall not in vain desire to be so. God never sends mouths but He sends meat to fill them. ■ **hunger** 飢え・空腹 ; **providence** （神の）摂理

GOD sends meat, but the Devil sends cooks.
神は食物を与えてくださるのに、悪魔が料理人をよこす。

下手な料理人は神の恵みの食べ物を台無しにしてしまう。

☐1542 A. BORDE *Dietary of Health* xi. It is a common prouerbe, God may sende a man good meate, but the deuyll may sende an euyll coke to dystrue it. *c* 1607 T. DELONEY *Thomas of Reading* B3 God sends meat, and the diuel sends cookes. 1738 SWIFT *Polite Conversation*II. 155 This Goose is quite raw: Well, God sends Meat, but the Devil sends Cooks. 1822 SCOOT *Nigel* III. iii. That homely proverb that men taunt my calling wlth,—'God sends good meat, but the devil sends cooks.' 1979 *Country Life* 13 Sept 807 Another old saying ... that God sends good meat but the devil sends the cooks. ■ **food and drink 飲食物**

GOD's in his heaven; all's right with the world.
神は天国にまします。この世はすべて安泰である。

標準的な形式は満足した心の状態を表わしている (1841 年の用例参照)。当初は God is where he was.「神は至る所にいる」という慰めの表現であったが (1530年、1612年、1678年の用例参照)、今ではこの言い方の方が良く使われている。

☐1530 J. PALSGRAVE *L'eclaircissement de la Langue Française* 213 Neuer dlspayre man, god is there as he was. 1612 T. SHELTON tr. *Cervantes' Don Qutxote* I. IV. iii. God is in heaven. 1678 J. RAY *English Proverbs* (ed. 2) 147 God is where he was. Spoken to encourage People in any distress. 1841 R. BROWNING *Works* (1970) 327 The snail's on the thorn: God's in his heaven— All's right with the world. 1906 R. KIPLING *Puck of Pook's Hill* 240 Cheer up, lad.... God's where He was. 1928 B. WAUGH *Decline & Fall* I. v. When you've been in the soup as often as I have, it gives you a sort of feeling that everything's for the best, really. You know, God's in His heaven; all's right with the world. 1988 P. MORTIMER *Handyman* xv. When she heard his car draw up, on the dot of seven, it was as though she had been injected with a great feeling of calm, a reassurance that God was in his heaven and all [was] right with her world. ■ **content and discontent 満足と不満足**

GOD tempers the wind to the shorn lamb.
弱い者には吹く風も柔らか。

神は、不幸な出来事が弱者や救われない者をこれ以上苦しめないように、慈悲深く手を差し伸べてくださる。to temper the wind (to the shorn lamb)「弱い者には風を弱める」という慣用句もよく使われている。† 1594 H. エティエンヌ『プレミス』47 *Ces termes, Dieu mesure le froid a la brebis tondue, sont les propres termes du prouerbe.*「神は毛を刈り取られた羊に対してその寒さを手加減するという表現が、このことわざの正しい表現である」

☐1640 G. HERBERT *Outlandish Proverbs* no. 867 To a close shorn sheep, God gives wind by measure. 1768 L. STERNE *Sentimental Journey*II. 175 How she had home it ... she could not tell —but God tempers the wind, said Marla, to the shorn lamb. 1933 V. BRITTAIN *Testament of Youth* I. ii. There is an unduly optimistic proverb which declares that God tempers the wind to the shorn lamb. My subsequent history was hardly to justify such naive faith in the Deity. 1996 *American Spectator* Mar. 56 But as Laurence Sterne was wont to remind us, the Lord tempers the wind for the shorn lamb. There were bars. ■ **providence（神の）摂理；trouble やっかい・苦労**

GODS 191

God ⇒ ALL things are possible with God; EVERY man for himself; And God for us all; MAN proposes, God disposes; MAN'S extremity is God's opportunity; The MILLS of God grind slowly, yet they grind exceeding small; The NEARER the church, the farther from God; PROVIDENCE is always on the side of the big battalions; The ROBIN and the wren are God's cock and hen; TAKE the goods the gods provide; TRUST in God but tie your camel; Put your TRUST in God, and keep your powder dry; The VOICE of the people is the voice of God; A WHISTLING woman and a crowing hen are neither fit for God nor men; ⇒ GODS, HEAVEN.

godliness ⇒ CLEANLINESS is next to godliness.

Whom the GODS love die young.
神々に愛された者は若くして死ぬ。

（訳注：「佳人薄命」）

† メナンドロス『2 度だまし』「断章」4 (Sandbach) ὃν οἱ θεοὶ φιλοῦσιν ἀποθνῄσκει νέος.「神が愛する者は早く死ぬ」。プラウトゥス『バッキデス』I. 817 *Quem di diligunt, Adolescens moritur.*「神々が愛する人は若くして死ぬ」

☐ **1546** W. HUGHE *Troubled Man's Medicine* B8ᵛ Most happy be they and best belouid of god, that dye whan they be young. **1553** T. WILSON *Art of Rhetoric* 40 Whom god loueth best, those he talceth sonest. **1651** G. HERBERT *Jacula Prudentum* no. 1094 Those that God loves, do not live long. **1821** BYRON *Don Juan* IV. xii. 'Whom the gods love die young,' was said of yore, And many deaths do they escape by this. **1972** A. PRICE *Colonel Butler's Wolf* xx. 'Whom the gods love die young,' the war taught us that. **2014** *Telegraph* 27 Nov. (online) [Phillip] Hughes was in the prime of life. That euphemism about 'those whom the gods love die young' offers us little by way of consolation. ■ **death** 死；**youth** 若さ・若者

The GODS send nuts to those who have no teeth.
神は歯のない者に胡桃を授ける。

絶好の機会や快楽は享受するには時すでに遅しということがよくある。それが人生なのだ。† フランス語 *Le pain vient a qui les dents faillent.*「歯のない者にパンが与えられる」

☐ **1929** *American Speech* IV. 463 God gives us nuts to crack when we no longer have teeth. **1967** RIDOUT &WITTING *English Proverbs Explained* 68 The gods send nuts to those who have no teeth. In this life we either have too little of what we do want, or too much of what we don't want or can't use. **2000** 'C. AIRD' *Little Knell* (2001) xiv. 161 'It's seeing the gardens I—we—would have been going for,' Insisted Sloan, 'Not the luxury.' 'Quite right,' said Leeyes, adding obscurely, 'The nuts come when the teeth have gone.' ■ **old age** 老年；**opportunity, missed** 逃した機会

Whom the GODS would destroy, they first make mad.
神は破滅させたい者がいれば、まず気を狂わせる。

（訳注：would ＝「〈できれば〉…したいと思う」〈願望〉。Do as you *would* be done by.〈自分がしてもらいたいように他人にもせよ〉）

† *Trag. Graec. Fragm. Adesp.* 296 (ナウク) ὅταν γὰρ ὀργὴ δαιμόνων βλάπτῃ τινά, τοῦτ᾽ αὐτὸ πρῶτον, ἐξαφαιρεῖται φρενῶν τὸν νοῦν τὸν ἐσθλόν.「神の怒りがある者を滅ぼすとき、

192　GOES

まずその人の優れた感性を奪う」。ラテン語 *Quos Deus vult perdere, prius dementat.* 「神は自分が滅ぼそうと欲する人をまず狂わせる」

□**1611** JONSON *Catiline* V. 481 A madnesse, Wherewith heauen blinds 'hem, when it would confound 'hem. **1640** G. HERBERT *Outlandish Proverbs* no. 688 When God will purtish, hee will first take away the understanding. **1817** BYRON *Letter* 2 Apr. (1976) V. 204 God maddens him whom 'tis his will to lose, And gives the choice of death or phrenzy—Choose! **1875** M. THOMPSON *Hoosier Mosaics* 180 Whom the gods would destroy they first make mad. **1981** *Daily Telegraph* 24 July 4 Already Commonwealth Finance Ministers have elected not to meet on New Zealand's defiled soil. If greater penalties follow, the Commonwealth will confirm that those whom the gods would destroy they first make mad. ■ **fate and fatalism 運命と運命論 ; fools 愚か者**

He that GOES a-borrowing, goes a-sorrowing.
借金をする者は悲しい思いをする。

借金は貸付金を返済しなければならない時、悩みの種となる。

□*c***1470** In WRIGHT & HALLIWELL *Reliquite Antiquæ* (1841) I. 316 He that fast spendyth must nede borowe; But whan he schal paye ayen, then ys al the sorowe. **1545** R. TAVERNER tr. *Erasmus' Adages* (ed. 2) 46ᵛ He that goeth a borowynge goeth a sorowynge. **1836** MARRYAT *Midshipman Easy* I. viii. You had made your request for the loan ... fully anticipating a refusal, (from the feeling that he who goes a borrowing goes a sorrowing). **1925** S. O'CASEY *Juno & Paycock* III. 84 Ah, him that goes a borrowin' goes a sorrowin'! ... An' there Isn't hardly a neighbour In the whole street that hasn't lent him money on the strength of what he was going to get. **1995** *American Spectator* Feb. 82 Who goes a-borrowing goes a-sorrowing. Yes, the balanced-budget amendment Is sort of a dumb idea, because It can so easily be evaded by cunning congressional accounting. ■ **borrowing and lending 貸し借り**

What GOES around comes around.
出て行ったものは再び報いとして戻って来るものだ。

米国起源の現代のことわざで、2011 年の用例が示すように、As you SOW, so you reap. 「自分で蒔いた種は自分で刈り取らねばならない」と同じ意味を表わしている。

□**1961** *Proceedings of Fourteenth Biennial Convention of International Longshoremen's and Warehousemmen's Union* 242 I don't think you can deny him this right And if you do, you are taking away the rights belonging to you, because the old saying goes, 'What goes around comes around.' **1974** E. STONE *Donald writes no More* xv. No one can say why Donald Goines and Shirley Sailor were murdered. The ghetto philosophy, 'what goes around comes around', Is the only answer most people can give. **1982** H. STEIN *Ethics* 108 At this juncture another, more recent, adage springs to mind: What goes around comes around. It is, all in all, a terrific statement, and I know a lot of people who would turn handsprings if only they could be assured it was true. **1989** *Washington Times* 19 Apr. Fl No sooner had the royal accusers sent Louis XVI and his queen to the guillotine, than they themselves were being hoist onto the tumbrels by men whose own heads would later drop into the basket. What goes around comes around. **2011** *www.huffingtonpost.com* 11 Nov. 'What goes around comes around' or 'as you sow, so shall you reap' is the basic understanding of how karma, the law of cause and effect, works. ■ **fate and fatalism 運命と運命論 ; retribution 天罰・報復**

goes ⇒ There goes more to MARRIAGE than four bare legs in a bed; PRIDE goes before a fall; What goes on TOUR stays on tour; What goes UP must come down.

GOLDEN 193

When the GOING gets tough, the tough get going.
状況が困難になれば本当に強いやつらの出番となる。

（訳注：going ＝「進行のしかた、その状況」。hard *going*〈事がはかどらない状況〉）

米国の政治家、実業家，そしてジョン・Ｆ・ケネディ大統領の父親であるジョセフ・Ｐ・ケネディ (1888-1969) のお気に入りの家訓だと言われている。アメリカンフットボールのコーチ、フランク・レフィー (1908-73) のスローガンに由来すると考えられている（1954年の用例参照）。1956年にドワイト・Ｄ・アイゼンハウワーが米国大統領に立候補した際、レフィーがこの言葉を使って応援演説を行なったことで広く普及し、政治の世界で使われるようになった。

□ **1954** Charleston [WV] *Daily Mail* 4 May Frank Leahy ... is back coaching football in front of a camera ... He also inserted his own personal football motto into the dialogue: 'When the going gets tough, the tough get going.' **1962** J. H. CUTLER *'Honey Fitz'* xx. Joe [Kennedy] made his children stay on their toes.... He would bear down on them and tell them, 'When the going gets tough, the tough get going.' **1970** *New Yorker* 3 Oct. 33 Baron Marcel Bich, the millionaire French pen magnate probably spoke for them all last month when he said, 'When the going gets tough, the tough get going!' ('Quand le chemin devient dur, Jes durs se cheminent!') **1979** J. CRUMLEY *Last Good Kiss* xvi. 'When the going gets tough, the tough get going?' she asked slyly. 'Make fun if you want to, but that's what character is all about.' **2007** T. French *In the Woods* 199 O'Kelly kept giving us rousing, arm-waving speeches about how ... when the going gets tough the tough get going. ■ **opportunity, taken** 得られた機会；**politics** 政治；**stress** ストレス

GOLD may be bought too dear.
たとえ金でも高すぎる値で買われることがある。

（訳注：may ＝「…のこともある」。今では can の方が一般的。This illness can be fatal.〈こんな病気でも命取りになることもある〉）

高い価値があるものでも、法外な高値が要求されることがある。

□ **1546** J. HEYWOOD *Dialogue of Proverbs* II. vii. 14 Well (quoth she) a man maie bie golde to dere. **1642** T. FULLER *Holy State* II. xxi. Fearing to find the Proverb true, That Gold may be bought too dear, they returned to their ships. **1889** J. LUBBOCK *Pleasures of Life* (ed. 2) II. ii. It is well worth having ... but it does not requite too great a sacrifice. A wise proverb tells us that gold may be bought too dear. **1908** *Times* 28 Nov.11 Gold may be bought too dear; and little improvements in the regulation of the drink traffic are too heavily loaded when they carry with them confiscatory legislation, local option, ruinous harshness to individuals ... ■ **money** 金・金銭；**value** 価値

gold ⇒ It is good to make a BRIDGE of gold to a flying enemy; GIVE a thing, and take a thing, to wear the Devil's gold ring; All that GLITTERS is not gold.

A GOLDEN key can open any door.
黄金の鍵はどんな扉でも開けることができる。

（訳注：a golden key ＝「金銭」。「地獄の沙汰も金次第」。A silver key can open an iron lock.〈銀の鍵は鉄の錠をも開けることができる〉ということわざもある）

金さえあれば、いかなる障害をも克服できる。

□ **1580** LYLY *Euphues & his England* II. 71 Who is so ignorant that knoweth not, gold be a key for euery locke, chieflye with his Ladye. **1660** W. SECKER *Nonsuch Professor* 11. ix. The gates of the new Jerusalem ... are not got open by golden keys. **1842** TENNYSON *Poems* (1969) 694 Ev-

194 golden

ery door is barr'd with gold, and opens but to golden keys. **1945** F. THOMPSON *Lark Rise* xix.
Their better-educated neighbours ... did not call on the newly rich family. That was before the
days when a golden key could open any door. ■ **bribery and corruption** 賄賂と腐敗 ; **money** 金・金
銭

golden ⇒ SILENCE is golden; SPEECH is silver, but silence is golden.

If you can't be GOOD, be careful.
大人しくできないなら、気をつけてやれ。

性交渉の文脈で与えられる忠告である。元のことわざに次のようなユーモラスな追加が
なされる。and if you can't be careful, buy a pram.「そしてもし気をつけてできない
なら、乳母車を買え」。†11世紀中頃のラテン語 *Si non caste tamen caute*「大人しくで
きないなら、気をつけてやれ」。**1303** R. BRUNNE『罪の処理』(EETS) 1. 8316 The
apostle seyth thys autoryte [dictum], 'Gyf thou be nat chaste, be thou pryue [se-
cret].'「その使徒が言うには、『もし貞節を守れないなら、秘密にやりなさい』」。**1528** W.
ティンダル『キリスト教徒の服従』73 As oure lawears saye, *si non caste tamen
caute*, this is, ifye live not chaste, se ye cary clene [act properly], and playe the
knave secretly.「『おとなしくできないなら、気をつけてやれ』と言われているが、その
意味とは、『もし貞節を守れないなら、うまくやりなさい。うまくやれないなら、秘密に
やりなさい』である」

☐**1902** G. ADE *Forty Modem Fables* 185 Just one Word in Parting. Always count your Change,
and if you can't be Good, be Careful. **1903** A. M. EINSTEAD *Pitcher in Paradise* viii. [A]lways
bear in mind what the country mother said to her daughter who was coming up to town to be ap-
prenticed to the Bond Street millinery, 'For heaven's sake be good; but if you can't be good, be
careful.' **1982** S. GRANT DUFF *Parting of Ways* xvii. Tommy ... gave me a stem warning....
'Never meet a German in Prague ... Be good, and if you can't, be very careful.' ■ **caution** 用心

If you can't be GOOD, be lucky.
うまくできないなら、幸運にすがれ。

If you can't be GOOD, be careful.「大人しくできないなら、気をつけてやれ」をモデル
としたことわざ。スポーツ界に起源があるので、スポーツの場面でよく使われる。

☐**1935** *Los Angeles Times* 3 Apr. The Angels should have won the game ... but the Cubs,
weighted down by horseshoes and rabbits' feet, staved off a deserved defeat ... The moral, if
any, seems to be: If you can't be good; be lucky. **1994** B. A. LOOMIS *Time, Politics, and Policies* If
you can't be good, be lucky, the saying goes. The children's advocates had been good, but they
were also lucky. Their good fortune came at Senator Bogina's expense. **2011** *www.bathchronicle.
co.uk* 7 Feb. There's an old saying: 'If you can't be good, be lucky'. On this evidence Brighton
appears to be both, which probably helps to explain why they look set to be plying their trade in
the Championship next year. ■ **luck** 幸運・運 ; **success** 成功

A GOOD beginning makes a good ending.
始め良ければ終わり良し。

何事もスタートが良ければ結果も良くなるものだ。

☐*c*1300 *South-English Legendary* (EETS) I. 216 This was atte uerste me thingth [it seems to me] a
god bygynnynge. Ther after was the betere hope to come to god endynge. *c* 1350 *Douce MS 52*

GOOD 195

no. 122 Of a gode begynnyng comyth a gode endyng. **1710** S. PALMER *Proverbs* 1 A good Beginning makes a good End.... 'Tis a great point of Wisdom ... to begin at the right end. **1850** 'M.
TENSAS' *Odd Leaves from Life of Louisiana 'SwampDoctor'* 109 I hope my future lot will be verification of the old adage, that a 'bad beginning makes a good ending', for mine is bad enough.
1934 G. WESTON *His First Million Women* xvi. I was brought up to believe that 'Of a good beginning cometh a good ending.' ... 'You can't do a good plastering job if your laths aren't right to
begin with.' ■ **beginnings and endings 最初と最後**

There's many a GOOD cock come out of a tattered bag.
ぼろぼろの袋から上等な鶏がたくさん出てくる。

（訳注：many a [an] ＋単数名詞＝「多くの、いくつもの」。*Many* a man lost his way in the woods.
〈たくさんの人が森の中で道に迷った〉）

見かけや第一印象から人の性格や実力を判断することはできない。このことわざは闘鶏
に起源がある。意味が類似したものに、**1721**J. ケリー『スコットランドことわざ集』7
An ill Cow may have a good Calf. Bad People may have good Children.「病気の雌
牛からでも丈夫な子牛が生まれ、悪人からでも良い子が生まれることがある」がある。

□**1883** C. S. BURNE *Shropshire Folklore* xxxvi. There'll come a good cock out of a ragged
bag.... A cockfighting simile, lately used by a farmer, whose buildings were out of repair, but his
stock in good condition. **1953** R. SUTCLIFF *Simon* xiv. 'There's many a good cock come out of a
tattered bag,' said the dark shape, slowly. There was an instant of ... silence, and then Simon
said, 'And a good tune played on an old fiddle.' ■ **appearance, deceptive 偽りの外見**

No GOOD deed goes unpunished.
処罰されない善行はない。

アイルランド出身の劇作家・詩人・小説家 O. ワイルドに由来するとされることもあるが、
彼の作品中にこの言葉は見当たらない。1938年の用例におけるパヴィアは、音楽家のイ
シドーレ・レオ・パヴィア (1875-1945) である。

□**1938** J. AGATE *Ego* 3 25 Jan. 275 Pavia was in great form to-day: 'Every good deed brings its
own punishment.' **1967** J. ORTON *Diaries* (1986) 13 June 209 Very good line George came out
with at dinner: 'No good deed ever goes unpunished.' **2002** *Washington Post* 11 Jan. C3 Finally,
the wages of purity, naivete and an excessive love of mankind catch up with her. As they say, no
good deed goes unpunished, no unloved and unimportant humans can expect not to be
squashed. **2011** *Spectator* 10 Sept. 17 But no good deed goes unpunished, so it didn't take long
for doubts to creep in. ■ **just deserts 当然の報い**

The GOOD die young.
善人は早死にする。

（訳注：the good ＝「善人」。「the ＋形容詞・分詞」で「…な人々」を意味する。*the* able 〈有能な人たち〉。
「佳人薄命」）

類似したものに Whom the GODS love die young.「神々に愛された者は若くして死
ぬ」がある。

□**1697** DEFOE *Character of Dr. Annesley* 3 The best of Men cannot suspend their Fate; The
Good die early, and the Bad die late. **1814** WORDSWORTH *Excursion* I. 27 The good die first,
And they whose hearts are dry as summer dust Bum to the socket. **1852** A. CARY *Clovernook* 39
Sarah ... was dead ... aged nineteen years.... The old truth was again reasserted ... in the often
repeated verse which followed, that the good die young. 1987 L. BARNES *Trouble of Fools* v.

196 GOOD

'Live hard, die young,' I said.... 'You got it wrong, Carlotta,' Mooney said. 'I learned it in school. It's "Only the good die young." Before they get a chance to fool around.' **2002** *Washington Post* 18 Jan. C1 It [Black Hawk Down] teaches stuff they don't know, only thesmallest and most bitter of lessons: that ammunition is more important than water, that cover is more important than concealment, and that the good die young. ■ **death** 死 ; **youth** 若さ・若者

GOOD fences make good neighbours.
良い垣根は良い隣人を作る。

頑丈で正確に分けられた境界は、隣同士の調和のとれた関係を強固にする。

□**1640** E. ROGERS *Letter in Winthrop Papers* (1944) N. 282 A good fence helpeth to keepe peace between neighbours; but let vs take heed that we make not a high stone wall, to keepe vs from meeting. **1815** H. H. BRACKENRIDGE *Modern Chivalry* (rev. ed.) IV. II. xiii. I was always with him [Jefferson] in his apprehensions of John Bull.... Good fences restrain fencebreaking beasts, and ... preserve good neighbourhoods. **1914** R. FROST *North of Boston* 12 My apple trees will never get across And eat the cones under his pines, I tell him. He only says, 'Good fences make good neighbours.' **2001** *Washington Times* 7 Sept. A4 Mr. Fox insists that the United States overhaul immigration by the end of this year.... He said he doesn't believe the American folk wisdom that good fences make good neighbors. ■ **harmony and disharmony** 調和と不調和 ; **neighbours** 隣人

A GOOD horse cannot be of a bad colour.
駿馬の毛色が悪かろうはずがない。

優れた馬なら、毛色などどうでもいい。馬は優れているということだけで評価される。

□*a***1628** J. CARMICHAELL *Proverbs in Scots* no. 1621 There is gude horse of all hewis. **1653** I. WALTON *Compleat Angler* iv. It is observed by some, that there is no good horse of a bad colour. **1732** T. FULLER *Gnomologia* no. 1713 Good Horses can't be of a bad Colour. **1891** J. L. KIPLING *Beast & Man* viii. 'A good horse is never of a bad colour' ... is wildly irreverent from the Oriental point of view. **1912** *Spectator* 28 Dec. 1094 Virgil ... did not hold that 'a good horse cannot be of a bad colour'; he liked bays and grays. ■ **appearance, significant** 重要な外見 ; **horse lore** 馬にまつわる伝承

It's a GOOD horse that never stumbles and a good wife that never grumbles.
決して躓かないのが名馬、決して文句を言わないのが良妻。

1943年の用例は、たとえどんなに立派な人でも時には過ちを犯す（あるいは不平を漏らす）ことを示している。前半部分の It's a GOOD horse that never stumbles. だけで使われることも多い（1867年と1961年の用例参照）。

□**1732** T. FULLER *Gnomologia* no. 6440 It's a good Horse that never stumbles; And a good Wife that never grumbles. **1867** C. M. TIDY *Coal and its Products* 13 'It's a good horse that never stumbles;' so it must be indeed a good result that has no ills attending it. **1870** C. H. SPURGEON *John Ploughman's Talks* x (online) It is a good horse that never stumbles, And a good wife that never grumbles. But surely such horses and wives are only found in the fool's paradise, where dumplings grow on trees. **1943** *Farmer's Digest* vii. 64 It's a good horse that never stumbles. The horseman's way of saying we all err at times. **1961** H. WELLS *Cherry Ames, Rural Nurse* iv. 42 'It's a good horse that never stumbles, Ma.' 'You've been stumbling much of your life,' his mother said sadly. ■ **error** 間違い・過ち ; **words and deeds** 言動

GOOD 197

The only GOOD Indian is a dead Indian.
良いインディアンと呼べるのは死んだインディアンだけである。

元来は北米の原住民（ネイティブアメリカン）を指して使われた。現在では他の国籍や集団の構成員について中傷的に使われる。

☐ **1868** J. M. CAVANAUGH in *Congressional Globe* (US) 28 May 2638 I have never in my life seen a good Indian (and I have seen thousands) except when I have seen a dead Indian. **1886** A. GURNEY *Ramble through United States* 29 The Government ... is at length earnestly endeavouring to do tardy justice to the conquered race; but it was distressing to hear again and again from American lips the remark that 'A good Indian is a dead Indian.' **1895** E. S. ELLIS *People's Standard History U.S. N.* lxxxiv. In January, 1869, ... Old Toch-a-way ... , a chief of the Comanches, ... [said]: 'Me, Tock-a-way; me good Injun.' ... General [Sheridan] ... set those standing by in a roar by saying: 'The only good Indians I ever saw were dead.' **1934** G. B. SHAW *On Rocks* (Preface) 146 'The only good nigger is a dead nigger' say the Americans of the Ku-Klux temperament. **1935** L. I. WILDER *Little House on Prairie* xvii. She did not know why the government made treaties with Indians. The only good Indian was a dead Indian. **1980** R. BUTLER *Blood-Red Sun at Noon* II. vi. The only good Jap is a dead Jap. **1994** *Washington Times* 18 Jan. Al5 Unfortunately, some liberals sound as if they believe that the only good gun owner is a dead gun owner. **1998** K. NEVILLE *Magic Circle* 457 Sam had escorted me, and as we'd passed some other boys in the hallway, one had whispered just loud enough for Sam to hear: 'The only good Indian is a dead Indian.' ■ **national characteristics** 国民性；**reputation** 評判

The GOOD is the enemy of the best.
善は最善の敵。

（訳注：the good ＝「善」。the は抽象概念を指している。It approaches *the* impossible. 〈それは不可能に近い〉）

The BEST is the enemy of the good.「最善は善の敵である」のように最初と最後の語を逆にした言い方になることもある。

☐ **1912** J. KELMAN *Thoughts on Things Eternal* 108 Every respectable Pharisee proves the truth of the saying that 'the good is the enemy of the best.' ... Christ insists that we shall not be content with a second-best, though it be good. **1939** R. A. HABAS *Morals for Moderns* vii. 'The good', runs the old aphorism, 'is the enemy of the best.' Nowhere is this ... better exemplified than in connection with ... self-deceit. ■ **good things** よいもの

GOOD men are scarce.
善人は少ない。

まさしく文字通りの意味で解釈される場合と、だからこそ善人を大事にすべきであると解釈される場合とがある。

☐ **1609** D. TUVILL *Essays Moral & Theological* 92 Good men are scarce, no age so many brings As Thebes hath gates. **1721** J. KELLY *Scottish Proverbs* 124 Good Folks are scarce, you'll take care of one. Spoken to those who carefully provide against ill Weather, or cowardly shun Dangers. **1836** DICKENS *Sketches by Boz* I. 285 One of the women has agreed to stand a glass round, jocularly observing that 'as good people's were scarce, what I says is, make the most on 'em.' **1979** 'J. LE CARRé' *Smiley's People* xii. Time you had some shut-eye, isn't it? Good men are scarce, I always say. ■ **good and evil** 正邪

There's many a GOOD tune played on an old fiddle.
古いヴァイオリンでも良い曲がたくさん弾ける。

（訳注：「many a/an ＋単数名詞」＝「数々の、多くの」。Many a man comes and goes.〈多くの人が往来する〉。さらに、この場合の there 構文〈＝存在文〉は「…が〜されている」という状態を表わしている）

老齢だからと言って人生を楽しむことに何の支障もない。

□*a*1902 S. BUTLER *Way of All Flesh* (1903) lxi. Beyond a haricot vein in one ofmy legs I'm as young as ever I was. Old indeed! There's many a good tune played on an old fiddle. **1979** N. FREELING *Widow* xxx. He looked at her casually.... 'Not all that bad at that. Many a good tune played on an old fiddle.' **2002** G. PHINN *Head over Heels in Dales* 9 Dun't really matter what it looks like, though, does it? It's what inside that counts, my grandad says. Same wi' people, he says. 'Many a good tune played on an old fiddle.' ■ **appearance, deceptive 偽りの外見**; **old age 老年**

One GOOD turn deserves another.
親切は親切に値する。

（訳注：turn ＝「〈good, bad, kind などを伴って〉行為」。よい行ないにはよい行ないで報いるべきである。「情けは人のためならず」）

† 14世紀初頭のフランス語 *Lune bonte requiert lautre*.「善行は善行に値する」

□*c*1400 in *Bulletin of John Rylands Library* (1930) XN. 92 O [one] good turne asketanother. **1620** J. HALL *Contemplations* V. XIV. 28 One good turne requires another.... Justly should they haue been set at the vpper end of the table. **1638** T. RANDOLPH *Amyntas* V. vi. One good turne deserves another. **1929** S. T. WARNER *True Heart* 11. 151 You've given me the best laugh I've had for months, and one good turn deserves another. **1979** T. SHARPE *Wilt Alternative* xiv. Noblesse oblige? You know, one good turn deserves another and whatnot. ■ **reciprocity 相互扶助**

GOOD wine needs no bush.
良酒には看板などいらない。

優れた商品は宣伝など不要である。蔦の一房（bush）はかつて酒屋の外看板に吊るされた目印であった。

□*a*1430 J. LYDGATE *Pilgrimage of Man* (EETS) I. 20415 And at tavemys (withoute wene [doubt]) Thys tooknys [signs] nor thys bowys grene ... The wyn they mende nat. **1545** R. TAVERNER tr. *Erasmus' Adages* (ed. 2) 42 Wyne that is saleable and good nedeth no bushe or garland of yuye [ivy] to be hanged before. The english prouerbe is thus Good wyne neadeth no signe. **1599** SHAKESPEARE *As You like It* (Epilogue) 3 If it be true that good wine needs no bush, 'tis true that a good play needs no epilogue. **1711** ADDISON *Spectator* 13 Nov. I was never better pleased than with a plain man's compliment, who upon his friend's telling him that he would like the Spectator much better if he understood the motto, replied, that good wine needs no bush. **1983** D. CLARK *Monday Theory* vi. 'Doesn't advertise much, does she, Chief?' said Reed. 'Relies on the principle that good wine needs no bush, perhaps,' replied Masters. ■ **public relations 広報・宣伝活動**; **reputation 評判**

good ⇒ As good be an ADDLED egg as an idle bird; ALL good things must come to an end; Good AMERICANS when they die go to Pans; BAD money drives out good; The BEST is the enemy of the good; Never BID the Devil good morrow until you meet him; BRAG is a good dog, but Holdfast is better; It is good to make a BRIDGE of gold to a flying enemy; A CHANGE is as good as a rest; CONFESSION is good for the soul; A clean CONSCIENCE is a good pillow; The best DEFENSE is a good offense; Why should the DEVIL have all the best tunes?; DILIGENCE is the mother of good luck; ENOUGH is as good as a feast; EVIL communications corrupt good manners; Never do EVIL that good may come of it; FIRE is a good servant but a bad master; There are as good FISH in the sea as ever came out of it; HOPE is a good breakfast but a bad supper; It's an ILL wind that blows nobody any good; JACK is as good as his master; A LIAR ought to have a good memory; LISTENERS never hear any good of themselves; A MISS is as good as a mile; MONEY, like manure, does no good till it is spread; NO news is good news; A NOD's as good as a wink to a blind horse; There is NOTHING so good for the inside of a man as the outside of a horse; See a PIN and pick it up, all the day you'll have good luck; Any PUBLICITY is good publicity; The ROAD to hell is paved with good intentions; Good SEED makes a good crop; If it SOUNDS too good to be true, it probably is; One STORY is good till another is told; You can have TOO much of a good thing; When the WIND is in the east, 'tis neither good for man nor beast.

goods ⇒ ILL gotten goods never thrive; TAKE the goods the gods provide.

goose ⇒ What's SAUCE for the goose is sauce for the gander; ⇒ GEESE.

When the GORSE is out of bloom, kissing's out of fashion.
ハリエニシダの花が咲いていない時は、口づけする人は誰もいない。
> (訳注：1846 年の用例に、"Whins are never out of bloom."〈ハリエニシダの花が咲いていないことは決してない〉とあるが、そうであるならば、恋人たちの愛は一年中廃れることはないことになる)

1846 年、1860 年、そして 2015 年の用例が、このことわざと類似のことわざ When the FURZE is in bloom, my love's in tune.「ハリエニシダの花が咲いている時は私の愛もうまくいく」の背後にある理由を説明している。ブリテン島の様々な地域で低木の ulex europaeus「ハリエニシダ」は gorse、furze、whin などと呼ばれている。

☐ **1846** M. A. DENHAM *Proverbs relating to Seasons*, &c. 12 When whins are out of bloom, Kissing's out offashion.... Whins are *never* out of bloom. **1860** G. J. WHYTE-MELVILLE *Holmby House* I. iii. 'When the gorse is out of bloom, young ladies,' quoth Sir Giles,'then is kissing out of fashion!' ... There is no day in the year when the blossom is off the gorse. **1974** A. DWYER-JOYCE *Brass Islands* 175 'What's that old jingle about the gorse?' ... 'When the gorse is out of bloom, kissing is out of fashion.' **2015** *Times* 13 Jan. 29 [I]n Pembrokeshire gorse flowers all year round—hence the old rhyme [*sic*], 'When the gorse is out of bloom, kissing is out of season'. ■
love, prosperous 順調な (恋) 愛

What is GOT over the Devil's back is spent under his belly.
悪魔の背中で得られたものは、悪魔の腹の下で費やされる。

不当な手段で手に入ったものはくだらない快楽や放蕩に費やされる。

☐ **1582** S. GOSSON *Plays Confuted* G7ᵛ That which is gotten ouer, the deuils backe, is spent vnder his belly. **1607** MIDDLETON *Michaelmas Term* IV. i. What's got over the devil's back (that's by knavery), must be spent under his belly (that's by lechery). **1670** J. RAY *English Proverbs* 80 What is gotten over the Devils back, is spent under his belly.... What is got by oppression or extortion is many times spent in riot and luxury. **1821** SCOTT *Pirate* III. iv. You shall not prevail on me to go farther in the devil's road with you; for ... what is got over his back is spent—you wot

200　got

how. **1952** N. TYRE *Mouse in Eternity* 93 What I say is what goes over the devil's back is sure to come under his belly. ■ **getting and spending 取得と消費**

got ⇒ A PENNY saved is a penny earned.

grain ⇒ If in FEBRUARY there be no rain, 'tis neither good for hay nor grain.

grandmother ⇒ Don't TEACH your grandmother to suck eggs.

While the GRASS grows, the steed starves.
草が伸びるのを待っているあいだに馬が餓死する。

夢や期待が叶うのは時間がかかりすぎることがある。†中世ラテン語 *Dum gramen crescit, equus in moriendo quiescit.*「草が育つあいだに馬が死んでいく」

□*c*1350 *Douce MS 52* no. 20 While the grasse growes, the goode hors sterues. *a* **1500** in WRIGHT & HALLIWELL *Reliquæ Antiquæ* (1841) I. 208 While the grasse growes the steede starues. **1600-1** SHAKESPEARE *Hamlet* III. ii. 333 You have the voice of the King himself for your succession. —Ay, sir, but 'While the grass grows' —the proverb is something musty. **1821** J. GALT *Ayrshire Legatees* x. Until ye get a kirk there can be no marriage. But the auld horse may die waiting for the new grass. **1911** G. B. SHAW *Doctor's Dilemma* III. 56 I shall sell them next year fast enough, after my one-man-show; but while the grass grows the steed starves. **1973** 'M. INNES' *Appleby's Answer* ii. 'The working capital?' 'Well ... while the grass grows the steed mustn't starve. Say five hundred down.' ■ **expectation 予期・期待**

The GRASS is always greener on the other side of the fence.
垣根の向こう側では芝生はいつも青々している。
(訳注：「隣の芝生は青い」)

†オウィディウス『アルス・アマトリア』I. 349 *Fertilior seges est alienis semper in agris.*「収穫高はいつも他人の畑のほうが多い」

□**1959** H. & M. WILLIAMS in J. C. Trewin *Plays of Year* XIX. 13 (*title*) The grass is greener. **1965** *Which?* Mar. 91 'The grass always looks greener on the other side of the fence,' said another informant, explaining that while stores who do practise the system are uneasy about it ... those outside constantly wonder whether results might not justify it. **2001** *Spectator* 15/22 Dec. 26 They push their heads through fences and get stuck (the grass on the other side really is greener: sheep invented the axiom). ■ **content and discontent 満足と不満足**

grass ⇒ When ELEPHANTS fight, it is the grass that suffers.

grease ⇒ The SQUEAKY wheel gets the grease.

A GREAT book is a great evil.
偉大なる書物は大いなる災いである。
(訳注：evil は misfortune とも言う。War brings many *evils*. 〈戦争は多くの害悪をもたらす〉)

†カリマコス『断章』465 (ファイファー) τὸ μέγα βιβλίον ἴσον ... εἶναι τῷ μεγάλῳ κακῷ.「偉大な書物は大いなる災いである」

great 201

□**1628** BURTON *Anatomy of Melancholy* (ed. 3) 7 Oftentimes it falls out ... a great Booke is a great mischiefe. **1711** ADDISON *Spectator* 23 July We do not expect to meet with any thing in a bulky Volume.... A great Book is a great Evil. **1933** *Oxford English Dictionary* (Preface) p. vii. If there is any truth in the old Greek maxim that a large book is a great evil, English dictionaries have been steadily growing worse ever since their inception more than three centuries ago.
■ **brevity and long-windedness** 簡潔と冗漫

GREAT minds think alike.
偉人の考え方は似通っている。

同時に、自画自賛に対して皮肉を込めて使われることが多い。最近では、推論を働かせて and fools seldom differ「同時に、愚か者の考えが異なることもめったにない」が付け足されることもある。ここで使われている minds という名詞も think という動詞も、初期の頃から今に至るまで様々な形が登場してきた。1898年の用例が現在の形の初例である。1618年、1716年、1889年にある「全く同意見である」、または「一致する」という意味の jump は今日では廃れている。

□**1618** D. BELCHIER *Hans Beer-Pot* Dl Though he made that verse, Those words were made before.... Good wits doe iumpe. **1761** STERNE *Tristram Shandy* III. IX. Great wits jump: for the moment Dr. Slop cast his eyes upon his bag ... the very same thought occurred. **1889** A. JAMES *Journal* 1 Dec. (1964) 61 As great minds jump this proves ... that my Mind is Great! **1898** C. G. ROBERTSON *Voces Academicae* 24 Curious how great minds think alike. My pupil wrote me the same explanation about his non-appearance.... **1922** *Punch* 27 Dec. 601 Lord Riddell considers that Mr. H. G. Wells is one of the world's greatest minds. Great minds, as the saying is, think alike. **2002** *Washington Times* 28 May C9 (*Bottomliners cartoon*) 'Great minds think alike—that's why we're never in agreement.' **2014** *Deccan Chronicle* 25 Oct. (online) What are the qualities you admire in each other ... ? Manish: You may call it 'great minds think alike' or 'fools seldom differ'—that's the best answer I can give. ■ **coincidence** 偶然の一致 ; **harmony and disharmony** 調和と不調和

GREAT oaks from little acorns grow.
樫の大木も小さなどんぐりから。

たとえ始まりは小さくても、その後偉大な結果をもたらすことがある。

□**c1385** CHAUCER *Troilus & Criseyde* II. 1335 As an ook comth of a litel spir [shoot], So thorugh this letter ... Encressen gan desir. **1579** S. GOSSON *School of Abuse* 20ᵛ But Tall Cedars from little graynes shoote high: great Oakes, from slender rootes spread wide. **1584** J. WITHALS *Dict.* (rev. ed.) D4 Of a nut springes an hasill, and of an Alcorn an hie or tall oke. **1732** T. FULLER *Gnomologia* no. 4576 The greatest Oaks have been little Acorns. **1777** D. EVERETT in *Columbian Orator* (1797) 58 Large streams from little fountains flow, Tall oaks from little acorns grow. **1923** *Times* 13 Oct. 7 Here in England, as nowhere else in the world, 'great oaks from little acorns grow'. The oak, as the emblem of British strength, has been symbolic in many ways. **2002** *Times* 28 Mar. 27 One shouldn't sneer. From little acorns do mighty oak trees grow. ■ **beginnings and endings** 最初と最後 ; **great and small** 大小

great ⇒ BIG fleas have little fleas upon their backs to bite them; DEATH is the great leveller; LITTLE strokes fell great oaks; LITTLE thieves are hanged, but great ones escape; There's no great LOSS without some gain; POVERTY is no disgrace, but it is a great inconvenience; THRIFT is a great revenue; TIME is a great healer.

The GREATER the sinner, the greater the saint.
罪が深ければ深いほど、偉大な聖人になる。

(訳注：「the ＋比較級 …，the ＋比較級 …」＝「…すればするほどますます…」。The more she practiced, the better she played.〈練習すればするほどますます上手になった〉。次のことわざも同じ構文)

過去に大罪を犯した者は、その後悔い改め、以前悪事に費やしたのと同じくらいの熱意を持って良いことに従事するよう自分を変えることができる。1773年の用例におけるホワイトフィールドとは、メソジスト派の牧師ジョージ・ホワイトフィールド（1714-70）のことである。

□**1773** R. GRAVES *Spiritual Quixote* II. VII. xi. It was a maxim with Mr. Whitfield, 'The greater the Sinner, the greater the Saint.' **1856** B. HINCHCLIFFE *Barthomley* vi. How well is the old proverb illustrated in this foul seducer.... 'The greater the sinner, the greater the Saint.' **1964** M. LAVIN *Stories* i. 293 Ah, well, I always heard it's the biggest divils that make the best saints, and now I can believe it! ■ **good and evil** 正邪 ; **wrong-doers** 悪事をなす者

The GREATER the truth, the greater the libel
誹毀された内容が真実であればあるほど、その誹毀も大きくなる。

批判的・攻撃的だが本当のことが記事になった場合、見当違いで誇張された攻撃を受けた場合よりも、当該人物にとってより不愉快なものになる。1787年と1882年の用例におけるマンスフィールドとはウィリアム・マレーのことである。彼は初代マンスフィールド伯爵（1705-93）で、政治家・判事であった。

□*c***1787** BURNS *Poems* (1968) I. 349 Dost not know that old Mansfield, who writes like the Bible, Says the more 'tis a truth, sir, the more 'tis a libel? **1828** BULWER-LYTTON *Pelham* i. xxiv. 'You won't catch an old lawyer in such impudence.' 'The greater the truth the greater the libel,' said Warburton, with a sneer. **1882** S. A. BENT *Short Sayings of Great Men* 371 The greater the truth, the greater the libel. A maxim of the law in vogue ... while Mansfield presided over the King's Bench.... The maxim is said to have originated in the Star Chamber. **2002** *Spectator* 23 Nov. 50 On the contrary: there is an old adage, 'The greater the truth, the greater the libel', for rioting is bound to be more serious if the incitement is known to be based on fact rather than on gross exaggeration. ■ **slander** 誹謗中傷 ; **truth** 真実・真理

When GREEK meets Greek, then comes the tug of war.
ギリシア人がギリシア人に出会うと、綱引きが始まる。

評判の良くない人同士が出会うと、互いに競い合い、あげくの果てに共倒れする。16世紀以降、Greekは英語の俗語で狡猾な騙し合いを意味する。それゆえ、英国の作家 G. グリーンは1954年の詐欺師の物語のタイトルとして *When Greek Meets Greek* を使っている。

□**1677** N. LEE *Rival Queens* IV. 48 When Greeks joyn'd Greeks, then was the tug of War. **1804** W. IRVING *Journals & Notebooks* (1969) I. 69 Two upright Postilions ... were disputing who was the greatest rogue.... 'When Greek meets Greek then comes the tug of war.' **1926** A. HUXLEY *Two or Three Graces* 175 When Greek meets Greek then comes, in this case, an exchange of anecdotes about the deposed sovereigns of eastern Europe—in a word, the tug of bores. **1979** M. A. SCREECH *Rabelais* iii. One is reminded of an adage Erasmus used ... Magus cum mago: 'magician meets magician' —Greek, as we say, meets Greek. ■ **enemies** 敵 ; **similarity and dissimilarity** 類似性と相違性

Greek ⇒ FEAR the Greeks bearing gifts.

A GREEN Yule makes a fat churchyard.
冬が温暖だと墓地が肥える。

(訳注：Yule＝「【古】クリスマス〈の季節〉。」異常気象のため、冬に雪が降らないと病気になる人が多くなるから)

クリスマスまでに雪が降らない暖冬の異常気象を主題にしたもので、色々な言い方がある。

☐ **1635** J. SWAN *Speculum Mundi* v. They also say, that a hot Christmas makes a fat Churchyard. **1670** J. RAY *English Proverbs* 42 A green winter makes a fat Church-yard. This Proverb was sufficiently confuted Anno 1667, in which the winter was very mild; and yet no mortality ... ensued the Summer or Autumn following. **1721** J. KELLY *Scottish Proverbs* 30 A green yule makes a fat Church-yard. This, and a great many proverbial Observations, upon the Seasons of the Year, are groundless. **1858** G. ELIOT *Amos Barton in Scenes of Clerical Life* I. vi. I shouldn't wonder if it takes the old lady off. They say a green Yule makes a fat Churchyard; but so does a white Yule too. **1945** M. SARSFIELD (*book-title*) Green December Fills the Graveyard. **1950** B. PYM *Some Tame Gazelle* xviii. They say a green Christmas means a full churchyard.... I dare say some old people will be taken. **1997** *Times: Weekend* 27 Dec. 16 So a green Christmas maketh a fat churchyard, as we say in SEIO. ■ **death** 死 ; **weather lore** 天気にまつわる伝承

greener ⇒ The GRASS is always greener on the other side of the fence.

The GREY mare is the better horse.
灰色の雌馬のほうが優れた馬である。

かかあ天下、つまり、妻の方が夫より有能であることを述べている。† **1529** モア『イメージについての対話』III. v. Here were we fallen in a grete questyon of the law, whyther the gray mare be the better horse ... or whither he haue a wyse face or not that loketh as lyke a foole as an ewe loketh lyke a shepe.「ここで私たちは法則の大問題にぶつかったのである。それは、灰色の雌馬の方が優れた馬なのか、それとも、牡馬は賢い顔つきをしているのか、それとも、雌馬が羊のように見えるように、愚か者のような顔つきをしているのかという問題である」

☐ **1546** J. HEYWOOD *Dialogue of Proverbs* II. iv. G4 The grey mare is the better hors. **1664** S. BUTLER *Hudibras* II. ii. 117 A Riding [charivari], us'd of Course, When the Grey Mare's the better Horse. When o're the Breeches greedy Women Fight, to extend their vast Dominion. **1906** J. GALSWORTHY *Man of Property* I. vi. D'you think he knows his own mind? He seems to me a poor thing. I should say the gray mare was the better horse! **1981** V. POWELL *Flora Annie. Steel* vii. She did not wish it to seem, to quote an old fashioned expression, that the grey mare was the better horse.... She strove to avoid prejudicing her husband's position. ■ **wives and husbands** 夫婦

grey ⇒ All CATS are grey in the dark.

grieve ⇒ What the EYE doesn't see, the heart doesn't grieve over; Do not grieve that ROSE-TREES have thorns....

grind ⇒ The MILL cannot grind with the water that is past; The MILLS of God grind slowly, yet they grind exceeding small.

gripping ⇒ NOTHING should be done in haste but gripping a flea.

All is GRIST that comes to the mill.
水車小屋へ来るものはすべて自分の穀物である。

受け取ったり、獲得したものはすべて利用すること。grist は挽かれる穀物を指す。the mill の定冠詞 the が所有代名詞や代名詞句によって置き換わる場合が多い。類似したことわざとして、より古い形の All is FISH that comes to the net.「網にかかるものはすべて魚である」がある。慣用句 grist to one's mill「人にとっての利益の種」としても使われる。

☐ **1655** T. FULLER *Church Hist. Britain* III. iii. Forein Casuists bring in a bundle of mortal sins, all grist for their own Mill. **1770** S. FOOTE *Lame Lover* L 28 Well, let them go on, it brings grist to our mill: for whilst both the sexes stick firm to their honour, we shall never want business. **1896** A. WHYTE *Bible Characters* I. xii. Your stumble, your fall, your misfortune ... all is grist to the mill of the mean-minded man. **1943** A. CHRISTIE *Moving Finger* ix. You're failing to allow for the mentality of a Poison Pen—all is grist that comes to their mill. **1979** G. MITCHELL *Mudflats of Dead* iii. All was grist which came to a novelist's mill, and he was still hoping that something, somewhere, would bring him what he still thought of as inspiration. **2000** 'G. WILLIAMS' *Dr. Mortimer and Aldgate Mystery* (2001) xviii. 94 'I should very much like to know,' she said, 'what picture was there that Agar felt was so eminently worth stealing. In my pursuit of him, all is grist to my mill.' ■ gains and losses 利益と損失; opportunity 機会・好機

ground ⇒ BETWEEN two stools one falls to the ground.

grow ⇒ While the GRASS grows, the steed starves; GREAT oaks from little acorns grow; ONE for the mouse, one for the crow.

grumble ⇒ It's a GOOD horse that never stumbles and a good wife that never grumbles.

grunt ⇒ What can you EXPECT from a pig but a grunt?

guest ⇒ FISH and guests smell after three days.

A GUILTY conscience needs no accuser.
やましい心は自らを責める。

† 『カトの二行格言詩集』I. *xvii. Conscius ipse sibi de se putat omnia dici.*「良心の呵責がある者はいつも自分が噂の的になっていると思ってしまう」

☐ *c***1390** CHAUCER *Canon's Yeoman's Prologue* l. 688 For Catoun [Dionysius Cato] seith that he that gilty is Demeth alle thyng be spoke of him. **1721** J. KELLY *Scottish Proverbs* 9 A guilty Conscience self accuses. A Man that has done ill ... shews his Guilt. 17 44 *Life & Adventures Matthew Bishop* viii. It is an old saying, a guilty conscience needs no accuser. **1881** D. C. MURRAY *Joseph's Coat* I. viii. 'Where are you off to?' asked George with a great effort.... A guilty con-

science needs no accuser. **1952** *Ellery Queen's Mystery Mag.* Apr. 25 'Why should I think that?' I said, groping for his identity. 'Because you were thinking about me.' Then I knew he was speaking of Hinckman's murder and must be the murderer—'a guilty conscience needs no accuser.' ■
conscience 良心 ; **wrong-doers** 悪事をなす者

gunner ⇒ The COBBLER to his last and the gunner to his linstock.

H

habit ⇒ OLD habits die hard; SOW an act, and you reap a habit.

What you've never HAD you never miss.
手に入れたことのないものに対しては、それがなくて困るという気持ちにはならない。

> 人生のすばらしいものを享受する機会が今までなかった場合には、そうしたものを奪われた気持ちにもならない。

□1912 'J. WEBSTER' *Daddy-Long-Legs* (1913) 232 You mustn't get me used to too many luxuries. One doesn't miss what one has never had. **1939** T. BURKE *Living in Bloomsbury* ii. It has been said that what you've never had you never miss, and from all one can gather, those people were not aware of suffering from lack of holiday. **1987** S. STEWART *Liftingthe Latch* 189 I ent never fled in an aeroplane. Don't want to. Too far to drop. What you've never had you never miss. ■ content and discontent 満足と不満足 ; gains and losses 利益と損失

hair ⇒ BEAUTY draws with a single hair; With a SWEET tongue and kindness, you can drag an elephant by a hair.

HALF a loaf is better than no bread.
たとえ半塊のパンでも全くないよりはまし。
> (訳注：Any port in a storm.〈嵐の時はどんな港でもありがたい〉。「枯れ木も山の賑わい」)

> 類似した意味のものに SOMETHING is better than nothing.「何もないより何かあった方が良い」がある。

□1546 J. HEYWOOD *Dialogue of Proverbs* I. xi. D4^V Throwe no gyft agayne at the giuers head, For better is halfe a lofe then no bread. **1636** W. CAMDEN *Remains concerning Britain* (ed. 5) 297 Halfe a loafe is better than no bread at all. **1841** DICKENS *Old Curiosity Shop* I. xxxiii. 'Mr. Swiveller,' said Quilp, 'being pretty well accustomed to the agricultural pursuits of sowing wild oats, Miss Sally, prudently considers that half a loaf is better thanno bread.' **1979** *Guardian* 6 Aug. 10 Half a loaf is better than no bread at all. The ending of half a war is immensely better than no truce at all. **2002** A. MCNEILLIE 'Half a Loaf' in *Times Literary Supplement* 12 Apr. 4 Half a loaf's better than no bread. A crumb of wisdom finds a world, in a grain of wheat. ■ content and discontent 満足と不満足

The HALF is better than the whole.
半分は全部に勝る。

節約・節度を勧めることわざ。†ヘシオドス『仕事と日々』40：πλέον ἥμισυπαντός.「半分は全部に勝る」

□**1550** H. LATIMER *Sermon before King's Majesty* G3 Tuer is a proverb ... Dimidium plus toto: The halfe somtymes more then the hole. The meane lyfe is the best Jyfe and the most quyet lyfe of al. **1828** I. DISRAELI *Curiosities of Literature* 2nd Ser. I. 419 The half is better than the whole. **1906** A. C. BENSON *From College Window* v. It is true of conversation as of many other things, that the half is better than the whole. People who are fond of talking ought to beware of being lengthy. ■ **moderation** 節度・中庸

One HALF of the world does not know how the other half lives.
この世の半分の人はもう半分の人の人生を知ってはいない。

他人の生活を取り巻く環境について人は無知であることを述べている。†**1532** ラブレー『パンタグリュエル物語』II. xxxii. *La moytie du monde ne sçait comment l'autre Vit.*「世界の半分はもう半分の人生を知ってはいない」

□**1607** J. HALL *Holy Observations* xvii. One half of the world knowes not how the other liues: and therefore the better sort pitty not the distressed ... because they knowe it not. **1640** G. HERBERT *Outlandish Proverbs* no. 907 Halfe the world knowes nothow the other halfe lives. **1755** B. FRANKLIN *Poor Richard's Almanack* (Preface) It is a common saying, that One Half of the World does not know how the other Half lives. **1830** MARRYAT *King's Own* I. x. It is an old proverb that 'one half the world do not know how the other half live'. Add to it, nor where they live. **1945** C. S. LEWIS *That Hideous Strength* i. 'I didn't even know this was Bracton property.' 'There you are! ... One half of the world doesn't know how the other half lives.' **1979** A. MORICE *Murderin Outline* vi. It just proved how true that saying is about one half knowing so little of the other, even when both halves are living under the same roof. ■ **ignorance** 無知・無学；**society** 社会

HALF the truth is often a whole lie.
真実の半分しか語らないのは大嘘をつくのと等しい場合が多い。

(訳注：例えば、明日と明後日の両方の日に試験があるのを知っていながら、友人に「明日は試験があるよ」と伝えたような場合、真実を半分しか語っていないとみなしてよい。しかし、その友人がそのため明後日の試験を受けずに落第したとしたら、故意に嘘をついたと言われても仕方ない)

間違った印象を与えるために真実を半分しか伝えないのは、まっかな嘘をついているようなものである。

□**1758** B. FRANKLIN *Poor Richard's Almanack* (July) Half the Truth is often a great Lie. **1859** TENNYSON *Poems* (1969) 1107 That a lie which is half a truth is ever the blackest of lies, That a lie which is all a lie may be met and fought with outright, But a lie which is part a truth is a harder matter to fight. **1875** A. B. CHEALES *Proverbial Folklore* 166 Half the truth is often a whole lie ... is a proverb which Tennyson has most admirably versified. **1979** H. HOWARD *Sealed Envelope* xiii. 'You've been lying.' ... 'Half the truth can be worse than a straight lie.' ■ **lying** 嘘をつくこと

half ⇒ BELIEVE nothing of what you hear, and only half of what you see; Two BOYS are half a boy, and three boys are no boy at all; A FAULT confessed is half redressed; WELL begun is half done.

half-done ⇒ FOOLS and bairns should never see Half-done work.

halfway ⇒ A LIE is halfway round the world; Do not MEET troubles halfway.

hall ⇒ It is MERRY in hall when beards wag all.

Don't HALLOO till you are out of the wood.
森を抜けるまでは安堵の叫びをあげるな。

危険や困難が過ぎ去るまでは早まって有頂天になってはならない。ここでの halloo は「叫ぶ」の意。

□**1770** B. FRANKLIN *Papers* (1973) XVIII. 356 This is Hollowing before you are out of the Wood. **1800** A. ADAMS *Letter* 13 Nov. (1848) 381 It is an old and a just proverb, 'Never halloo until you are out of the woods.' **1866** C. KINGSLEY *Hereward the Wake* I. iii. Don't holla till you are out of the wood. This is a night for praying rather than boasting. **1936** 'B. C. R. LORAC' *Crime Counter Crime* i. Don't halloo till you're out of the wood. I'll bet my head to a china orange we shall have trouble before to-morrow night. **1947** M. LONG *Dull Thud* x. 99 'Don't whistle till you're out of the woods,' I advised her. 'The investigation hasn't even begun.' ■ peril 危険；trouble やっかい・苦労

halved ⇒ A TROUBLE shared is a trouble halved.

When all you have is a HAMMER, everything looks like a nail.
ハンマーしか持っていないと、すべてのものが釘に見えてしまう。

主に北米で使われる。

□**1966** A. MASLOW *Psychology of Science* (foreword) x If the only tool you have is a hammer, it is tempting to treat everything as if it were a nail. **1981** *New York Times* 11 Nov. Dl3 'There is frequently a lack of understanding of what power is—I've got power, therefore I'm right,' he said. 'When you've got a hammer, everything looks like a nail.' **1989** *PC Magazine* 14 Mar. 78 That kind of crude misapplication of PCs and PC software—the computer world's equivalent of the old saw that 'when all you have is a hammer, everything starts to look like a nail' —means death for productivity. **2014** *Times* 29 May 27 US military action cannot be the only ... component in every instance. Just because we have the best hammer does not mean that every problem is a nail. ■ necessity 必要性・必然性；ways and means 方法と手段

hammer ⇒ The CHURCH is an anvil which has worn out many hammers；(動詞) The NAIL that sticks up gets hammered down.

One HAND for yourself and one for the ship.
片方の手は自分のため、もう片方は船のために使え。

船舶に関することわざで、他にも様々な言い方がある。1902 年の用例の説明参照。

□**1799** *Port Folio* (Philadelphia, 1812) VII. 130 Did I not tell you never to fill both hands at once. Always keep one hand for the owners, and one for yourself. **1822** J. F. COOPER *Pilot* I. vii. The maxim, which says, 'one hand for the owner, and t'other for yourself,' ... has saved many a hearty fellow from a fall that would have balanced the purser's books. **1902** E. LUBBOCK *Round Horn* 58 The old rule on a yard is, 'one hand for yourself and one for the ship,' which means, hold on with one hand and work with the other. **1968** L. MORTON *Long Wake* i. I did not know then the old adage 'one hand for oneself and one hand for the company.' **1993** B. CALLISON *Crocodile Trapp* (1994) x. 169 'Now you allus remember the seaman's golden rule from now on, Mister Despytoff,' Spew chastised gently. 'One hand f'r the ship—or in your case, f'r the *aeroplane*, eh? heh, heh … an' one hand f'r yerself.' ■ **prudence** 思慮・分別；**security** 安全

The HAND that rocks the cradle rules the world.
揺り籠を揺らす手が世界を支配する。

子供に対する影響力が大きいゆえに、女性（母親）は重要な役割を果たしている。

□**1865** W. R. WALLACE in J. K. Hoyt *Cyclopedia of Practical Quotations* (1896) 402 A mightier power and stronger Man from his throne has hurled, For the hand that rocks the cradle Is the hand that rules the world. *a* **1916** 'SAKI' *Toys of Peace* (1919) 158 You can't prevent it; it's the nature of the sex. The hand that rocks the cradle rocks the world, in a volcanic sense. **1996** *Washington Times* 10 May A2 The habits of the home in one generation become the morals of society in the next. As the old adage says: 'The hand that rocks the cradle rules the world.' ■ **women** 女性

One HAND washes the other.
一方の手がもう片方の手を洗う。

親切な行為は互いのためであり、またそうでなければならない。†エピカルモス『格言集』273（カイベル）ά δὲ χεὶρ τὰν χεῖρα νίζει. 「片方の手がもう片方の手を洗う」。セネカ『アポコロキュントシス』ix. *Manus manum lavat.* 「手が手を洗う」

□**1573** J. SANFORDE *Garden of Pleasure* 110ᵛ One hand washeth an other, and both wash the face. **1611** R. COTGRAVE *Dict. French & English* s.v. Main, One hand washes the other; applyable to such as giue vpon assurance, or hope, to be giuen vnto; or vnto such as any way serue one anothers turne. **1836** P. HONE *Diary* 12 Mar. (1927) I. 203 Persons in business … make, as the saying is, 'one hand wash the other'. **1983** H. RESNICOW *Gold Solution* ix. And three years ago, Erik was on a design jury that picked the dean's firm's entry as a winner. One hand washes the other. **2001** P. J. O'ROURKE *CEO of Sofa* xii 250 One hand washes the other: for I the lord thy God am a jealous God, visiting the iniquity of the fathers upon the children unto the third and fourth generation of them that hate me—unless they seek counseling, of course. ■ **reciprocity** 相互扶助

hand ⇒ A BIRD in the hand is worth two in the bush; COLD hands, warm heart; The DEVIL finds work for idle hands to do; The EYE of a master does more work than both his hands; FULL cup, steady hand; If IFS and ands were pots and pans, there'd be no work for tinkers' hands; MANY hands make light work.

HANDSOME is as handsome does.
物事を立派になす人こそが立派なのである。
（訳注：「見目より心」。as は関係代名詞で、先行詞 one が省略されている。Handsome is one who does handsomely. の意）

形容詞 handsome は一般には外見の良さを指すが、ここでは礼儀正しさや上品さを指す。2 番目に登場する handsome は厳密には副詞である。一般的な米語のことわざに関しては PRETTY is as pretty does. 「物事をみごとになす人こそがみごとである」を参照。

□*c*1580 A. MUNDAY *View of Sundry Examples* in J. P. Collier John A Kent (1851) 78 As the ancient adage is, goodly is he that goodly dooth. **1659** N. R. *Proverbs* 49 He is handsome that handsome doth. **1766** GOLDSMITH *Vicar of Wakefield* i. They are as heaven made them, handsome enough if they be good enough; for handsome is that handsome does. **1845** *Spirit of Times* 23 Aug. 297 Handsome is as handsome does. **1873** M. YONGE *Pillarsof House* II. xvii. 'Don't you think her much better looking than Alda?' 'If handsome is that handsome does.' **1979** A. WILLIAMSON *Funeral March for Siegfried* xxiv. 'But he's such a handsome, chivalrous, man.' Handsome is as handsome does, thought York grimly. ■ **appearance 外見 ; conduct 行ない・品行**

HANG a thief when he's young, and he'll no' steal when he's old.
泥棒は若いうちに縛り首にしてしまえ。そうすれば年を取ってから盗みを働くことはすまい。

〈訳注：no' は not に等しい〈1832年の用例参照〉〉

□**1832** A. HENDERSON *Scottish Proverbs* 115 Hang a thief when he's young, and he'll no [not] steal when he's auld. **1896** A. CHEVIOT *Proverbs of Scotland* 126 Hang a thief when he's young and he'll no steal when he's auld. This was a favourite saying of Lord Justice Clerk Braxfield [Robert MacQueen, Lord Braxfield (1722–99), Scottish judge], who invariably acted upon its teaching. **1979** J. LEASOR *Love & Land Beyond* x. So much killing.... It reminds me of the Scots proverb, 'Hang a thief when he's young, and he'll no' steal when he's old.' ■ **wrong-doers 悪事をなす者**

hang ⇒ A CREAKING door hangs longest; Give a DOG a bad name and hang him; Every HERRING must hang by its own gill; Give a man ROPE enough and he will hang himself.

One might as well be HANGED for a sheep as a lamb.
子羊を盗んで絞首刑になるくらいなら、親羊を盗んで絞首刑になった方がましだ。

〈訳注：might 〈may〉〈just〉as well A 〈as B〉〈A, B は動詞句〉＝「〈B するくらいなら〉A した方が〈まだ〉ましだ」。このことわざでは、as a lamb=as be hanged for a lamb である。話し手は A することにあまり気乗りがしないが、ほかに選択肢はない。This movie is not interesting. I *might just as well* be back home.〈この映画は面白くない。家に帰ったほうがましだ〉。「毒を食らわば皿まで」〉

かつて羊盗みが受けた処罰を示している。ここでの発想は次の用例の中で描かれている。**1662** N. ロジャーズ『富める愚か者』253 As some desperate Wretches, Who dispairing of life still act the more villainy, giving this desperate Reason of it, As good be hanged for a great deal, as for a little. 「自暴自棄になった悪漢どもは、人生を絶望しつつも次のようなやけくその理由を挙げて、さらなる狼藉を働いた。すなわち、『ちょっとのことで絞首刑になるくらいなら、大きなことで絞首刑になったほうがましだ』と」

□**1678** J. RAY *English Proverbs* (ed. 2) 350 As good be hang'd for an old sheep as a young lamb. Somerset. **1732** T. FULLER *Gnomologia* no. 683 As good be hang'd for a Sheep as a Lamb. **1836** MARRYAT *Midshipman Easy* n. ii We may as well be hanged for a sheep as a lamb.... I vote that we do not go on board. **1841** DICKENS *Barnaby Rudge* liii. Others ... comforted themselves with the homely proverb, that, being hung at all, they might as well be hung for a sheep as a lamb. **1915** D. H. LAWRENCE *Rainbow* vi. One might as well be hung for a sheep as for a lamb. If he had lost this day of his life, he had lost it. **1977** B. PYM *Quartet in Autumn* xv. Letty ... decided that she might as well be hung for a sheep as a lamb and make the most of her meal. ■ **conduct 行ない・品行 ; risk 危険**

HAPPY 211

hanged ⇒ If you're BORN to be hanged then you'll never be drowned; CONFESS and be hanged; LITTLE thieves are hanged, but great ones escape; Never mention ROPE in the house of a man who has been hanged.

HANGING and wiving go by destiny.
絞首刑と妻を娶（めと）ることは運命次第である。

絞首刑になるか、良い結婚をするかといった事態は運命による。1951年の用例では（中世イングランド、ウェセックス地方の王であった）アルフレッド大王（在位871-99）の言葉とされるが、初期中英語の『アルフレッド大王ことわざ集』には記載がない。こうした誤解が生じたのは、賢者でかつ教育者としての彼の名声から多くのことわざが彼に由来すると考えられたからである。

☐ **1546** J. HEYWOOD *Dialogue of Proverbs* I. iii. Weddyng is desteny, And hangyng lykewise. **1596** SHAKESPEARE *Merchant of Venice* II. ix. 82 The ancient saying is no heresy: Hanging and wiving goes by destiny. **1678** S. BUTLER *Hudibras* II. i. 270 If Matrimony and Hanging go By Dest'ny, why not Whipping too? **1738** SWIFT *Polite Conversation* 1. 78 'Twas her Fate; they say, Marriage and Hanging go by destiny. **1951** E. MARSHALL *Viking* iii. King Alfred said that wiving and hanging go by destiny. **2006** V. P. ZICKAFOOSB 'Vrrtuous Crown' 366 (doctoral thesis) If 'hanging and wiving go by destiny' nowhere ... was Orzechowski more subject to his own fate.
■ fate and fatalism 運命と運命論 ; marriage 結婚

hanging ⇒ CATCHING's before hanging; there are more WAYS of killing a dog than hanging it.

ha'porth ⇒ Do not spoil the SHIP for a ha'porth of tar.

happen ⇒ ACCIDENTS will happen (in the best-regulated families); What happens on the ROAD stays on the road; The UNEXPECTED always happens; What happens in VEGAS stays in Vegas.

happiness ⇒ MONEY can't buy happiness.

If you would be HAPPY for a week take a wife; if you would be happy for a month kill a pig; but if you would be happy all your life plant a garden.
1週間幸せになりたければ妻をめとれ。1か月幸せになりたければ豚をつぶせ。しかし一生幸せになりたければ庭に木を植えよ。

（訳注：would =「〈できれば〉…したいと思う」〈願望〉。Do as you *would* be done by.〈自分がしてもらいたいように他人にもせよ〉）

このテーマに関しては、ほとんど無限の言い方が生まれる可能性がある。ただし、結婚は短期間の満足しかもたらさないものの中に含まれていることが多い。

☐ **a 1661** T. FULLER *Worthies Wales* 6 I say the Italian-humor, who have a merry Proverb, Let him that would be happy for a Day, go to the Barber; for a Week, marry a Wife; for a Month, buy him a New-horse; for a Year, build him a New-house; for all his Life-time, be an Honest man. **1809** S. PEGGE *Anonymiana* II. xix. If you would live well for a week, kill a hog; if you would live well for a month, marry; if you would live well all your life, turn priest.... Turning priest ... al-

212 HAPPY

ludes to the celibacy of the Romish Clergy, and has a pungent sense, as much as to say, do not marry at all. **1973** *New Earth Catalog* 55 If you would be happy for a week take a wife; If you would be happy for a month kill a pig; But if you would be happy all your life plant a garden. **1996** *National Review* 25 Nov. 6 For those of a philosophical turn of mind, I pass on something that the distinguished economist Peter Bauer said last week: 'If you want to be happy for a day, get drunk; for a month, get married; for a lifetime, take up gardening.' ■ happiness 幸福

Call no man HAPPY till he dies.
人が幸福であったかどうかは死んでからしかわからない。
（訳注：人間の幸・不幸は生前には断定できないものである）

1545年の用例で言及されている物語は古代ギリシアの歴史家ヘロドトスの『歴史』I. xxxiiで語られている。When the great Athenian lawgiver Solon visited Croesus, the fabulously wealthy king of Lydia, the latter asked Solon who was the happiest man he had ever seen—expecting the answer to be himself.「偉大なるアテネの法律家ソロンが、リディアのきわめて裕福な王クレオスを訪れた時、王はソロンに自分であると期待しながら問うてみた。今まで会った中で誰が一番幸せな男であるかと」。†ソフォクレス『オイディプス王』I. 1529 μηδέν’ὀλβίζειν, πρὶν ἂν τέρμα τοῦ βίου περάον μηδὲν ἀλγεινὸν πάθων.「悲惨な思いをせずに人生の最後を過ごすことができるまでは、幸せな人生を送ったと考えるな」。オウィディウス『変身物語』iii. 135 *Dicique beatus Ante obitum nemo ... debet.*「その人が死ぬまでは幸せであったと言うべきではない」

□**1545** R. TAVERNER tr. *Erasmus' Adages* (ed. 2) 53ᵛ Salon aunsered kynge Cresus, that no man could be named happy, tyl he had happely and prorouslye passed the course of his lyfe. **1565** T. NORTON &S. SACKVILLE *Gorboduc* III. i. Oh no man happie, till his ende be seene. **1603** J. FLORIO tr. *Montaigne's Essays* I. xviii. We must exspect of man the latest day, Nor e'er he die, he's happie, can we say. **1891** *Times* 5 Dec. 9 Call no man happy till he dies is the motto ... suggested by the career of Dom Pedro [emperor of Brazil]. **1967** C. S. FORESTER *Hornblower & Crisis* 163 'Call no man happy until he is dead.' ... He was seventy-two, and yet there was still time for this dream ... to change to a nightmare. ■ good fortune 幸運 ; happiness 幸福

happy ⇒ Happy is the BRIDE that the sun shines on; Happy is the COUNTRY which has no history; A DEAF husband and a blind wife are always a happy couple; Happy's the WOOING that is not long a-doing.

HARD cases make bad law.
厄介な事件が悪法を作る。

困難な事件が起こると、例外やゆがんだ解釈によって法律の明確さが失われてしまう。

□**1854** G. HAYES in W. S. *Holdsworth Hist. English Law* (1926) IX. 423 A hard case. But hard cases make bad law. **1945** W. S. CHURCHIIL in *Hansard* (Commons) 12 June 1478 Well, of course, hard cases do not make good laws. **1991** *Times* 17 Sept. 29 Hard cases not only make bad law. They also create bad feeling between judges. **2001** *Spectator* 21 July 18 Hard cases make bad law, no doubt, and maybe bad policy, but this case is far from unique. ■ law and lawyers 法と法律家 ; rules 規則

HARD words break no bones.
きつい言葉を言われてもそれで骨折することはない。

HASTE 213

STICKS and stones may break my bones, but words will never hurt me.「棒や石なら私の骨は折れるかもしれないが、言葉などで私は傷ついてたまるものか」の内容を簡潔に述べたもの。† c 1450『タウンリーのノアの箱舟劇』(EETS) I. 380 Thise grete wordis shall not flay me.「このようにひどい言葉でも私を鞭で打つことはない」

☐ **1697** G. MERITON *Yorkshire Ale* (ed. 3) 84 Foul words break neay Banes. **1806** H. H. BRACK-ENRIDGE *Gazette Publications* 250 Hard words, and language break nae bane. **1814** G. MORRIS *Letter* 18 Oct. (1889) II. xlix. These ... are mere words—hard words, if you please, but they break no bones. **1882** BLACKMORE *Christowell* III. xvi. 'Scoundrel, after all that I have done—.' 'Hard words break no bones, my friend.' **1980** G. NELSON *Charity's Child* i. Soft words! They butter no parsnips.... Would you prefer hard ones? ... Hard words break no bones. ■ malice 悪意・恨み

hard ⇒ OLD habits die hard.

hardens ⇒ The same FIRE that melts the butter hardens the egg.

harder ⇒ The BIGGER they are, the harder they fall.

hare ⇒ FIRST catch your hare; If you RUN after two hares you will catch neither; You cannot RUN with the hare and hunt with the hounds.

harm ⇒ NO harm, no foul.

HASTE is from the Devil.
焦りは悪魔から生まれる。
(訳注：of=「〈be, come などの動詞の後で〉…から」。she comes *of* a good family.〈彼女は名門の出だ〉)

早まって行動したり、焦って行動することは良くない。1835 年と1929 年の用例が示すように、このことわざと東洋との繋がりが主張されるのは、ハディース（預言者ムハンマドの言葉と行動）の記録などにこの言葉が登場するからである。*Calmness and patient deliberation is from Allah and haste is from Satan.*「沈着冷静な判断はアラーの神から、焦りは悪魔から生まれる」

☐ **1633** J. HOWELL *Familiar Letters* 5 Sept. (1903) II. 140 As it is a principle in chemistry that Omnis festinatio est a Diabolo, All haste comes from Hell, so in ... any business of State, all rashness and precipitation comes from an ill spirit. **1835** SOUTHEY *Doctor* III. lxxxiii. If any of my readers should ... think that I ought to have proceeded to the marriage without delay ... I must admonish them in the words of a Turkish saying, that 'hurry comes from the Devil, and slow advancing from Allah.' **1929** *Times* 12 Sept. 14 Listening patiently to the views ... [f]or he understood the East; he knew that for an Intelligence officer 'haste is from the devil.' ■ haste 性急; patience and impatience 忍耐と性急

More HASTE, less speed.
急がば回れ。
(訳注：speed の語源は「幸運、隆盛、素早さ」である。「せいては事をし損ずる」)

ここでの speed の意味は「行動や操作における迅速さ」である。

□c1350 *Douce MS 52* no. 86 The more hast, the worse spede. 1546 J. HEYWOOD *Dialogue of Proverbs* I. ii. A3ᵛ Moste tymes he seeth, the more haste the lesse speede. 1595 *Locrine* (1908) I. ii. My penne is naught; gentlemen, lend me a knife. I thinke the more haste the worst speed. 1705 E. WARD *Hudibras Redivivus* I. i. A mod'rate pace is best indeed. The greater hurry, the worse speed. 1887 BLACKMORE *Springhaven* III. xi. Some days had been spent by the leisurely Dutchman in providing fresh supplies, and the stout bark's favourite maxim seemed to be—'the more haste the less speed.' 1919 S. J. WEYMAN *Great House* xxvii. Tell me the story from the beginning. And take time. More haste, less speed, you know. 1993 'C. AIRD' *Going Concern* (1994) iv. 31 'Working against the clock doesn't make for considered thought.' 'More haste, less speed,' said Detective Constable Crosby helpfully. ■ haste 性急; patience and impatience 忍耐と性急

HASTE makes waste.
あわてると損をする。

（訳注：「せいては事をし損じる」）

waste は物を無駄にすることであるが、ここでは厳密に言うと、時間や金などの浪費を指す。

□c1386 CHAUCER *Tale of Melibee* I. 1053 The proverbe seith ... in wikked haste is no profit. 1546 J. HEYWOOD *Dialogue of Proverbs* 1. ii. A3 Som thyngs ... show after weddyng, that haste maketh waste. 1663 S. BUTLER *Hiulibras* I. iii. Festina lente, not too fast; For haste (the Proverb says) makes waste. 1853 R. C. TRENCH *On Lessons in Proverbs* i. Many Proverbs, such as Haste makes waste ... have nothing figurative about them. 1997 *Washington Post: Washington Business* 29 Dec. 15 But I've let myself be an impulsive Internet shopper, too, and I usually regret it. In '98, my motto is 'haste makes waste.' ■ haste 性急; patience and impatience 忍耐と性急; waste 浪費

Make HASTE slowly.
ゆっくり急げ。

（訳注：ローマ皇帝アウグストゥスはこの格言を座右の銘として、会話の中でしばしば使ったり、手紙の中で引用したりしたとされる〈エラスムス『格言集』〉）

†ラテン語 *Festina lente.*「ゆっくり急げ」。スエトニウス『アウグストゥス』XXV. 4. *Nihil autem minus perfecto duci quam festinationem temeritatemque convenire arbitratur. crebro itaque ilia iactabat: σπεῦδε βραδέως.*「彼（アウグストゥス）は、せっかちな振る舞いはすぐれたリーダーにふさわしくないと考え、常々『ゆっくり急げ』ということわざを口ずさみながら出かけた」。c 1385 チョーサー『トロイラスとクリセダ』I. 956 He hasteth wel that wisly kan [knows how to] abyde.「とどまり方をよく知っている者は上手に急ぐ」

□1683 DRYDEN *Poems* (1958) I. 336 Gently make haste.... A hundred times consider what you've said. 1744 B. FRANKLIN *Poor Richard's Almanack* (Apr.) Make haste slowly. 1989 C. G. HART *Little Class on Murder* xii. 'Festina lente,' Miss Dora suggested slyly. 'Not bad advice,' Max said cheerfully. At Annie's glare, he added quickly, 'Make haste slowly.' ■ haste 性急; patience and impatience 忍耐と性急

haste ⇒ MARRY in haste and repent at leisure; NOTHING should be done in haste but gripping a flea.

柊風舎 出版案内

東京都新宿区上落合1-29-7 ムサシヤビル5F
TEL 03(5337)3299 FAX 03(5337)3290
http://www.shufusha.co.jp/ 〈呈内容見本〉

The Worldwide History of Dress

世界の民族衣装文化図鑑
【合本普及版】

日々の暮らしや特別な儀礼の中で身に着けてきた衣服や装飾品の数々を、各地域の自然環境や歴史的背景についても解説しながら、多数の図版とともに紹介。

本書の特色

1. 服飾・衣服の歴史を約1000点の写真・図版とともに概観。

2. 男女の基本的服装、履き物、外衣、髪型、被り物、衣料小物、宝飾類、武具、特別な衣装、服の飾り、顔と体の装飾、変わりゆく服装などを地域ごとに紹介。

3. 各地域の生活相や文化変容、交易、時代的背景、社会構造についても丹念に考察。

4. 巻末に、本文注、参考文献、総索引を付記。

5. 関連語彙集約330項目を所収。

パトリシア・リーフ・アナワルト=著
蔵持不三也=監訳

A4変型判／上製／608ページ／フルカラー
定価：本体28,000円＋税
ISBN978-4-86498-046-3

Fragile Languages

滅びゆく世界の言語小百科

消滅の危機に瀕している言語30。その地域社会、歴史、多様な問題を、印象的なカラー写真とともに考察する。

本書で取り上げる言語30
◆カルク語／ハイダ語／セリ語／ガリフナ語／ミクマク語◆アイマラ語／ワラオ語／マプドゥング語／ケチュア語（サンティアゴ・デル・エステロ州）／ティクナ語◆ロマンシュ語／北部サーミ語／コーンウォール語／ルシン語／ツァコニア語◆スパ語／ハヅァ語／スィウィ語／オンゴタ語／バデ語◆アイヌ語／アカ語／トゥヴァ語／メフリ語／テムアン語◆チャモロ語／グンバインギル語／マオリ語／ロトゥマ語／ティウィ語

ジニー・ナイシュ＝著
伊藤眞＝監訳

A4変型判／上製／289ページ／フルカラー
定価：本体15,000円＋税
ISBN978-4-86498-035-7

Living, Endangered, and Lost: ONE THOUSAND LANGUAGES

【ビジュアル版】世界言語百科
現用・危機・絶滅言語1000

人類の知的基盤としての民族言語の特徴を、多様な観点から描き出す"ことばの博物館"。

本書の特色
1. 話者が数億人から数人までの1000の言語を収録。
2. 主要な約300の言語については、起源・歴史、使用地域、話者数、文字、特徴、基本語彙数等を解説。
3. 言語分布を示した地図、言語の実例や10までの数え方などがわかるコラムも充実。索引、用語解説も完備。

ピーター・K・オースティン＝編
澤田治美＝日本語版監修

A4変型判／上製／288ページ／フルカラー
定価：本体13,000円＋税
ISBN978-4-903530-28-4

Textiles & Vêtements DU MONDE

少数民族の染織文化図鑑
伝統的な手仕事・模様・衣装

伝統的な織物に魅了された著者が各地を訪ね、衣服や装飾品の多様性や、人々の生活に密着した染織技術を記録。模様や色、形に込められた意味や民間伝承も紹介する。約700枚のカラー写真を掲載。

カトリーヌ・ルグラン 著
福井正子 訳

B4変型判／上製／240ページ／フルカラー
定価：本体13,000円＋税
ISBN978-4-903530-58-1

目次より
[ベトナム、ラオス、タイ] ステッチのことば／…[オリッサ、ラジャスターン、グジャラート] インドのプリント布／星、ストライプ、ミラー [メキシコとグアテマラ] アイデンティティの糸／どの人もみな優美 [パナマ] 色の迷宮／モラ、織物の旅 [ルーマニア] 生きている伝統／…[ベナン] 藍の空、藍の海／西アフリカの色

The Chronology of Pattern

【ビジュアル版】
世界の文様歴史文化図鑑
青銅器時代から現代までの3000年

紀元前1100年から現代まで。衣類、宝飾品、織物、壁紙、家具、陶磁器、絵画、彫刻、建築物などの文様に込められた意味と文化的・歴史的・社会的背景を探る。様式と発達を通観する。

本書の特色
1. 東西交易による交流や文化の伝播によって、変形・再生・合体を繰り返しながら生み出されてきた文様の様式と発達を通観する。
2. 「基本のページ」、「文様の細部に注目するページ」、「文様の刷新を推進した人物のページ」から成る構成で多角的に考察。
3. 巻末に、年表・用語解説・引用／参考文献・索引を掲載。

ダイアナ・ニューオール／
クリスティナ・アンウィン＝著
蔵持不三也＝日本語版監修
松平俊久＝監訳

A4変型判／上製／288ページ
定価：本体13,000円＋税
ISBN978-4-903530-93-2

RHS Companion to Scented Plants

英国王立園芸協会
香り植物図鑑
花・葉・樹皮の香りを愉しむ

1000種を超える香り植物を、多くのカラー写真やコラムを交えて紹介した"香りの指南書"。ガーデニングや街づくりにどう活かせばよいかを丁寧に解説する。

本書の特徴
1. 概説ではガーデニングや街づくりのヒントになる植栽方法や香りの愉しみ方を、「植物解説」では個々の植物の香りの性質、花や葉の色、形、質感、生育環境などを紹介。
2. 巻末に「香りのカレンダー」、「生育環境別にみる香りの植物」、「学名（約1800項目）・英名（約500項目）・和名等（約1200項目）索引」を掲載。

スティーブン・レイシー＝著
アンドリュー・ローソン＝写真
小泉祐貴子＝訳

A4変型判／上製／320ページ／フルカラー
定価：本体15,000円＋税
ISBN978-4-86498-038-8

Remarkable Plants That Shape Our World

【ビジュアル版】
世界有用植物誌
人類の暮らしを変えた驚異の植物

人類の歴史に密接に関わってきた80種以上の植物を8つのテーマに分け、それぞれの植物のルーツや利用法を紹介する。植物と人類の壮大な歴史ドラマ！

本書の特徴
1. 植物が文明の発展や日常生活（食べ物、住居、衣服、乗り物、薬剤など）に与えてきた影響を探る。
2. キュー植物園所蔵の植物画を中心に約200枚の写真を掲載。
3. 学名280項目、植物名300項目、事項600項目の索引を完備。

ヘレン＆ウィリアム・バイナム＝著
栗山節子＝訳

A4変型判／上製／240ページ／フルカラー
定価：本体12,000円＋税
ISBN978-4-86498-032-6

柊風舎 出版案内
しゅう ふう しゃ

東京都新宿区上落合1-29-7 ムサシヤビル5F
TEL 03(5337)3299　FAX 03(5337)3290
http://www.shufusha.co.jp/ 〈呈内容見本〉

Encyclopedia of Historic Places

世界歴史地名大事典
【全3巻】

それはどこにあるのか？　いつ頃から存在するのか？　そこで何が起きたのか？　世界のあらゆる地域の歴史地名15000を五十音順に掲載。歴史的背景に重点をおいた、地名事典の新機軸！　欧文・漢字索引を付記。歴史的背景を重点的に解説した、新しい地名事典

本書の特色

1. 現在の都市に加え、今では存在しない古代の地名も収録。

2. その土地の地理的な情報のほか、その場所で起きた出来事・文化・建築・政治・経済・人物など歴史的背景を重点的に解説。

3. 関連する地名には＊を付してあり、相互参照しやすい。

4. 旧地名や別称などは、本見出しを参照できるよう見出し語として立項。

5. 第3巻の巻末に欧文索引、漢字索引を付記。

〈分売可〉
第1巻　ア〜サ《発売中》
ISBN978-4-86498-049-4
第2巻　シ〜ヒ《発売中》
ISBN978-4-86498-050-0
第3巻　フ〜ン（2018年1月刊行）
ISBN978-4-86498-051-7

**コートランド・キャンビー／
デイビッド・S・レンバーグ＝著
植松靖夫＝日本語版監修**

菊判／上製／函入り／各巻約770ページ
各巻定価：本体19,000円＋税

History Year by Year

【ビジュアル版】
人類の歴史大年表

古今東西の事象を年表形式で語り、印象的なエピソード、ドラマチックなイラスト、地図、グラフをフルカラーで掲載。人類が歩んできた歴史をあらゆる角度から眺めるのに最適な一冊。

本書の特色
1. その年の出来事にアクセスしやすい年表。
2. ヨーロッパや北アメリカでの事件や発見や業績を、中東、極東、インド、アフリカ、南アメリカ、環太平洋での動きと対比できる。
3. 農業の起源から天体物理学上の最新の発見にいたる主要なトピックを、精細なイラストと明解な説明で描く特集ページも収録。
4. 約200項目の用語集と、約6000項目の索引を完備。

ドーリング・キンダースリー＝編著
樺山紘一＝日本語版監修
藤井留美＝訳

B4変型判／上製／512ページ／フルカラー
定価：本体19,000円＋税
ISBN978-4-86498-007-4

Science Year by Year

【ビジュアル版】
世界科学史大年表

石器・火・鉄の使用、ペニシリンの発見、宇宙探査の始まり、インターネットの登場……世界を変えた発明・発見を年表とビジュアルで辿る壮大な旅！

本書の特色
1. 科学の歴史を年ごとに追い、大発見や大発明にいたる思想的な道筋や人物の相関関係を描き出す。
2. 詳細なイラスト、グラフをフルカラーで掲載。
3. 道具・機器のコレクションから、車輪やロボット工学などの発達史を紹介する特集ページも収録。
4. 約6000項目の索引を完備。

ロバート・ウィンストン＝編
荒俣宏＝日本語版監修
藤井留美＝訳

B4変型判／上製／400ページ／フルカラー
定価：本体19,000円＋税
ISBN978-4-86498-025-8

A Dictionary of London Place Names

ロンドン歴史地名辞典

世界に大きな影響を与え続ける都市、ロンドン。そんなロンドンやその付近の歴史に刻まれた地名の成り立ちがわかる画期的な辞典。オックスフォード大学出版局刊行本！

本書の特色
1. 文学作品や映画でもお馴染みのストリートや公園など、1700の地名の起源・由来を解説。
2. 約100ページに及ぶ序論で、地名の成り立ちや他言語との関わり、地名形成に至る各種類のタイプと構造を概説。
3. 地名に現われる構成要素の用語（約700項目）をアルファベット順に分類。
4. 参考文献と和名索引を完備。

A. D. ミルズ=編
中林正身／今野史昭=訳

A5判／上製／500ページ
定価：本体15,000円＋税
ISBN978-4-86498-047-0

The Great Trade Routes

世界の交易ルート大図鑑
陸・海路を渡った人・物・文化の歴史

文明の興隆にも影響を与えながらどのような交易品がどう世界を巡ったのか。輸送手段はどう変化したのか。陸・海路・内陸水路に沿った都市や港は、どのように繁栄したのか。交易でたどる、ヒト・モノ・カネのもう一つの世界史

本書の特色
1. 先史時代から現代までの交易ルートの歴史を、多数の写真や地図を交えてわかりやすく解説。
2. 歴史上重要な100におよぶ交易ネットワークを網羅。
3. 当時の交易の状況を示す証言を、書物や手紙、旅行記などから引用し、100以上のコラムで紹介。
4. 巻末に索引（約2000項目）と参考文献を完備。

フィリップ・パーカー=編著
蔵持不三也／嶋内博愛=訳

B4変型判／上製／320ページ／フルカラー
定価：本体18,000円＋税
ISBN978-4-86498-024-1

Encyclopaedia of the Viking Age

【図説】ヴァイキング時代百科事典

8世紀末に始まったヴァイキングによる襲撃。広範囲にわたるその活動は、ヨーロッパの歴史において、重要な、時に決定的な役割を果たした。彼らの社会・生活、法、習慣、産業、芸術、文学、神話、宗教、民間信仰などから、その本当の姿に迫る。

本書の特色
1. ヴァイキングの実像に多角的に迫る。
2. ヴァイキングおよびその敵対者の主要人物も紹介。
3. ヴァイキング時代を概観する地図と、レファレンスに役立つ「年表」「ヴァイキングの君主・統治者」。
4. 項目数500、写真・図版300点。

ジョン・ヘイウッド=著
伊藤盡=監訳
村田綾子=訳

A5判／上製／448ページ
定価：本体15,000円＋税
ISBN978-4-86498-042-5

Dictionary of Ancient Egypt

【図説】古代エジプト文明辞典

ナイル河谷に誕生した古代文明の最も総合的な辞典

王と王朝、神と女神、ヒエログリフやミイラ製作、寺院と墓、考古遺跡、美術・宗教・言語・医学など。古代エジプト文明の魅力的な"宝物"を集め、様々な角度からの探求を可能にした辞典。

本書の特色
1. 紀元前3000年における国家の統一から、紀元前332年のアレクサンドロス大王の征服の間に即位した全ての王に対し項目を設ける。
2. エジプトの地図およびギザ、サッカラ、王家の谷、ルクソール神殿、カルナク神殿の遺跡平面図を収録。
3. 項目数1100、収録図版300点余。
4. 充実のレファレンス機能。

トビー・ウィルキンソン=著
大城道則=監訳

A5判／上製／400ページ
定価：本体15,000円＋税
ISBN978-4-86498-036-4

hasty ⇒ Hasty CLIMBERS have sudden falls.

hatched ⇒ Don't COUNT your chickens before they are hatched.

hate ⇒ BETTER a dinner of herbs than a stalled ox where hate is.

What you HAVE, hold.
まずは今持っているものを手放すな。

現在持っているものを手放さないことが肝要である。

□ *c*1450 *Towneley Play of Killing of Abel* (EETS) I. 142 It is better hold that I haue then go from doore to doore and craue. **1546** J. HEYWOOD *Dialogue of Proverbs* 1. x. D1 Hold fast whan ye haue it (quoth she) by my lyfe. **1876** L. BANKS *Manchester Man* I. x. Then ... rang, clear and distinct, Humphrey Chetham's motto—'Quod tuum, tene!' (What you have, hold!) **1979** *Times* 23 Nov. 5 There had been a simple 'what we have we hold' approach by the established parties. ■ **property** 財産

You cannot HAVE your cake and eat it.
ケーキを食べて、なおかつそれを持っているというわけにはいかない。

（訳注：世の中は2ついいことはない。この文では、"have your cake and eat it"〈ケーキを食べて、なおかつそれを持っている〉ということが1つのまとまった概念となっており、それが"cannot"〈できない〉となっている）

何かを消費したり、使い果たすことと、それを保持しつづけることとは両立しない。つまり、ケーキを食べれば、なくなってしまうのである。You cannot eat your cake and have it.「ケーキを食べて、なおかつそれを持っていることはできない」のように、have と eat の順番を逆にした言い方もある。

□ **1546** J. HEYWOOD *Dialogue of Proverbs* II. ix. L2 I trowe ye raue, Welde ye bothe eate your cake, and haue your cake? **1611** J. DAVIES *Scourge of Folly* no. 271 A man cannot eat his cake and haue it stil. **1812** in R. C. KNOPF *Document Transcriptions of War* of 1812 (1959) VI. 204 We cannot have our cake and eat it too. **1938** P. MCGUIRE *Funeral in Eden* ii. Not that the savages were especially savage. They have always been a sensitive people, and when they ate a man they probably felt genuinely sorry that they could not have their cake and eat it, so to speak. **2002** R. J. BERNSTEIN *Radical Evil* 32 Why does Kant allow himself to get entangled in such difficulties and paradoxes? It looks as if he wants to have his cake and eat it too!

have ⇒ The MORE you get, the more you want; NOTHING venture, nothing have; you can have TOO much of a good thing.

haw ⇒ When all FRUIT fails, welcome haws.

hawk ⇒ A CLEVER hawk hides its claws.

HAWKS will not pick out hawks' eyes.
鷹は別の鷹の目をくり抜くようなことはしない。

（訳注：will ＝傾向・習性〈…するものだ〉。Accidents *will* happen.〈事故はどうしても起こるもの〉）

捕食動物（略奪者）や悪漢の間でさえ仲間意識はある。

☐ **1573** J. SANFORDE *Garden of Pleasure* 104 One crowe neuer pulleth out an others eyes. **1817** SCOTT *Rob Roy* III. iii. I wadna ... rest my main dependence on the Hielandmen—hawks winna pike out hawks' een.—They quarrel amang themsells ... but they are sure to join ... against a' civilized folk. **1883** J. PAYN *Thicker than Water* III. xii. Members of his profession ... while warning others of the dangers of the table, seem to pluck from them the flower Safety. (Is it that, since hawks do not peck out hawks' een, they know they can be cured for nothing?) **1915** J. BUCHAN *Salute to Adventurers* vi. I have heard that hawks should not pick out hawks' eyes. What do you propose to gain? **1975** J. O'FAOLAIN *Women in Wall* xiv. The crow doesn't pluck out the crow's eye but poor folk bear the brunt. ■ reciprocity 相互扶助

hay ⇒ If in FEBRUARY there be no rain, 'tis neither good for hay nor grain; MAKE hay while the sun shines; A SWARM in May is worth a load of hay.

head ⇒ The FISH always stinks from the head downwards; Where MACGREGOR sits is the head of the table; You cannot put an OLD head on young shoulders; A STILL tongue makes a wise head; SWEEP the house with broom in May, you sweep the head of the house away; TWO heads are better than one; YORKSHIRE born and Yorkshire bred, strong in the arm and weak in the head.

heal ⇒ PHYSICIAN, heal thyself.

healer ⇒ TIME is a great healer.

health ⇒ The CITY for wealth, the country for health.

healthy ⇒ EARLY to bed and early to rise, makes a man healthy, wealthy, and wise.

HEAR all, see All, say nowt, tak' all, keep all, gie nowt, and if tha ever does owt for nowt do it for thysen.
すべてを聞いて、すべてを見て、何も言わず。すべてを取って、すべてを自分のものとし、何も与えず。ただで何かをするようなことがあったとしても、それは自分のためだけ。

今では伝統的にヨークシャー生まれのことわざとされており、色々な言い方がある。ここではヨークシャー出身の人が中傷ばかりする人として風刺的に描かれている。つまり、抜け目がなく、気難しく（say nowt「何も言わない」）、貪欲で（gie nowt「何も与えず」）、利己的（if tha ever does owt for nowt do it for theysen「ただで何かをすることがあったとしても、それは自分のためだけ」）という人物像である。

☐ *a* **1400** *Proverbs of Wisdom* in Archiv (1893) XC. 246 Hyre and se, and saynowght. Be ware and wyse, and lye nought ... and haue thy will. **1623** J. WODROEPHE *Spared Hours of Soldier* 276 Heare all, see all, and hold thee still If peace desirest with thy will. **1913** D. H. LAWRENCE *Letter* 1 Feb. (1962) I. 183 It seems queer, that you do it and get no profit. I should think you've forgotten the Yorkshire proverb, 'An' if tha does owt for nowt, do it for thysen.' **1925** *Notes & Queries* 412 The famous Yorkshire motto ... is invariably recited with an air of superior bravado, and will be found upon mugs, post cards, etc. The authentic version, (believe, is, 'Hear all, see all, say now't, tak' all, keep all, gie now't, and if tha ever does ow't for now't do it for thysen.' **1984** G. SMITH *English Companion* 265 'Hear all, see all, say nowt; sup all, eat all, pay nowt', is said by detractors to be the Yorkshlreman's motto. ■ **self-preservation** 自己防衛；**speech and silence** 発言と沈黙

hear ⇒ ASK no questions and hear no lies; BELIEVE nothing of what you hear, and only hall of what you see; There's none so DEAF as those who will not hear; DREAM of a funeral and you hear of a marriage; GO abroad and you'll hear news of home; LISTENERS never hear any good of themselves; SEE No evil, hear no evil, speak no evil.

heard ⇒ CHILDREN should be seen and not heard.

heart ⇒ ABSENCE makes the heart grow fonder; COLD hands, warm heart; What the BYE doesn't see, the heart doesn't grieve over; FAINT heart never won fair lady; Out of the FULLNESS of the heart the mouth speaks; HOME is where the heart is; HOPE deferred makes the heart sick; If it were not for HOPE, the heart would break; A NATION without a language is a nation without a heart; It is a POOR heart that never rejoices; Put a STOUT heart to a stey brae; The WAY to a man's heart is through his stomach.

If you don't like the HEAT, get out of the kitchen.
熱さがいやなら、台所から出て行け。

苦境に耐えられないなら、それから抜け出すべきである。If you can't stand the heat, get out of the kitchen.「熱さに耐えることができないなら、台所から出て行け」という言い方もある。米国第33代大統領トルーマンがこのことわざを世に広めたとされるが（1952年の用例）、実際はパーセル判事という人物の言葉であると考えられる。なぜなら、もっと早い1931年の用例に彼の言葉が記されているからである。

□ **1931** *Independence Examiner* [Missouri] 1 Jan. [I]f a man can't stand the heat, he ought to stay out of the kitchen. **1952** *Time* 28 Apr. 19 President [Truman] gave a ... down-to-earth reason for his retirement, quoting a favorite expression of his military jester, Major General Harry Vaughan: 'If you don't like the heat, get out of the kitchen.' **1970** *Financial Times* 13 Apr. 25 Property people argue that hoteliers are not facing the facts of economic life, and that if they cannot stand the heat they should get out of the kitchen. **2002** *Times* 29 Aug. 22 (*heading*) If you can't stand the Heat, then you need to get out of Hello!'s kitchen. ■ **politics** 政治；**stress** ストレス

HEAVEN protects children, sailors, and drunken men.
天は子供、水夫、飲んだくれを守ってくださる。

様々な言い方がある。近年、米国においては the United States「米国」がしばしば付け加えられる（1997年、2001年の用例参照）。このことわざで言及されている人たちは、贔屓されたり、特別な保護が必要とされる人たちである。

□ **1861** T. HUGHES *Tom Brown at Oxford* I. xii. Heaven, they say, protects children, sailors, and drunken men; and whatever answers to Heaven In the academical system protects freshmen. **1865** G. MACDONALD *Alec Forbes* III. xi. I canna think hoo he cam' to fa' sae sair; for they say there's a special Providence watches over drunk menand bairns. **1980** S. KING *Firestarter* 57 She

218　heaven

didn't even have a bruise—God watches over drunks and small children. **1997** *Washington Times* 18 Nov. A15 As we become once more the fool, we can only pray the old epigram is still true: 'God protects fools, drunkards and the United States.' **2001** *Washington Times* 15 Nov. A16 We've all likely heard at some time or other the stale, snide European-ism: 'The Lord looks after fools, drunks, and the United States.' Sometimes you have to wonder: Does He really?　■ **provi-dence（神の）摂理**

heaven ⇒ CROSSES are ladders that lead to heaven; GOD'S in his heaven, all's right with the world; MARRIAGES are made in heaven; ⇒ GOD.

hedge ⇒ One man may STEAL a horse, while another may not look over a hedge.

heir ⇒ WALNUTS and pears you plant for your heirs.

HELL hath no fury like a woman scorned.
恐ろしい地獄といえども、軽蔑された女に匹敵するほどの復讐の女神はいない。

（訳注：ここで用いられている fury には、ギリシア・ローマ神話に登場する「復讐の女神」と「激怒」という2つの意味が込められていると考えられる。この女神は、エリニュス〈複数形はエリニュエス〉と称され、尊属殺人者に特にきびしく報復し、罪人を追いつめて苦しめる。頭髪は蛇で、翼があり、手に鞭とたいまつを持っている。通常、アレクト、メガイラ、ティシフォネの3姉妹がエリニュエスとされる〈ローマ神話では、フリアイ、もしくはディライと呼ばれる〉。彼女たちは英語では the Furies と称される）

ギリシア・ローマ神話では、冥界の底タルタロスには恐ろしい復讐の3女神が住んでおり、自然の法を犯した罪や重い罪に対して復讐した。現代の fury には、「激怒」という意味も込められているかもしれない。†エウリピデス『メディア』I. 263 γυνὴ γὰρ τἄλλα μὲν φόβου πλέα κακέ τ ἐς ἀλκὴν καὶ σίδηρον εἰσορᾶν : ὅταν δ' ἐς εὐνὴν ἠδικημένη κυρῇ, οὐκ ἔστιν ἄλλη φρὴν μιαιφονωτέρα.「他の場合なら女性は恐怖心で身動きがとれず、力あるものや冷酷なものに対峙することを避ける。しかし、女性ということで軽蔑されると、今までにないほどの残酷な感情が芽生えるのである」。この考え方はルネサンス時代には一般的であった。例えば、*a* **1625** ボーモント＆フレッチャー『マルタの騎士』l. i. *The wages of scorn'd Love is baneful hate.*「蔑まれた恋人（女性）の報いは命を奪うほどの憎しみとなる」参照。

□**1696** C. CIBBER *Love's Last Shift* IV. 71 No Fiend in Hell can match the fury of a disappointed Woman!—Scorned! slighted; dismissed without a parting Pang! **1697** CONGREVE Mourning Bride m. 39 Heav'n has no Rage, like Love to Hatred turn'd, Nor Hell a Fury, like a Woman scorn'd. **1886** M. HOLMES *Chamber over Gate* xxvi. You know 'Hell hath no fury,' etc. If your wife should ever wake up to the true state of the case ... I'm afraid she'd be an ugly customer. **2002** *Washington Post* 15 Jan. B4 'Hell hath no fury like a woman scorned,' ... Calvert deputy state's attorney ... told jurors yesterday ... 'The defendant, Adele Freeman, felt like a woman scorned.' **2007** T. FRENCH *In the Woods* 495 But nothing I had done to her ... warranted this ... Hell hath no fury.　■ **love, blighted くじかれた愛；malice 悪意・恨み；women 女性**

hell ⇒ ENGLAND is the paradise of women; The ROAD to hell is paved with good intentions; He that would go to SEA for pleasure, would go to hell for a pastime.

help ⇒ EVERY little helps; GOD helps them that help themselves; A MOUSE may help a lion; Help you to SALT, help you to sorrow; Do not call a WOLF to help you against the dogs.

hen ⇒ The ROBIN and the wren are God's cock and hen; A WHISTLING woman and a crowing hen are neither fit for God nor men.

herb ⇒ BETTER a dinner of herbs than a stalled ox where hate is.

heresy ⇒ TURKEY, heresy, hops, and beer came into England all in one year.

hero ⇒ NO man is a hero to his valet.

Every HERRING must hang by its own gill.
どのニシンも自分のえらでぶら下がらなければならない。

> 我々はみな自分の足で立たなければならない。このことわざはハリソン編『雑録』(1869) の中でマン島のことわざとして紹介されている。そこでは次のように説明される。ニシンは網の目にえらが引っかかって捕まる。そして頭がすべて同じ方向に向く(p.17)。しかし、1998年の用例でtailsが使われているところを見ると、魚が燻製されるときは頭ではなく、尻尾で吊るされることがわかる。

> □**1609** S. HARWARD *MS* (Trinity College, Cambridge) 85 Lett every herring hang by his owne tayle. **1639** J. CLARKE *Parremiologia Anglo-Latina* 20 Every herring must hang by th'owne gill. **1670** J. RAY *English Proverbs* 102 Every herring must hang by its own gill.... Every man must. **1865** SURTEES *Facey Romford's Hounds* xxi. One man is no more a criterion for another man than one horse is a criterion for another.... Every herring must hang by its own head. **1890** T. H. HALL *CAINE Bondman* II. ii. Adam, thinking as little of pride, said No, that every herring should hang by its own gills. **1998** *Times* 16 June 22 You believe, like Bill Tilman who sailed leaky pilot cutters up Greenland fjords until he was 80, that 'every herring should hang by its own tail.' ■ **independence** 独立・自立

He who HESITATES is lost.
ためらう者は破滅する。

> 当初の用例では、「ためらう者」とは女性のことであった。

> □**1713** ADDISON *Cato* IV. i. When love once pleads admission to our hearts ... The woman that deliberates is lost. **1865** TROLLOPE *Can You forgive Her?* II. x. It has often been said of woman that she who doubts is lost ... never thinking whether or no there be any truth in the proverb. **1878** J. H. BEADLE *Western Wilds* xxi. In Utah it is emphatically true, that he who hesitates is lost—to Mormonism. **1887** BLACKMORE *Springhaven* xiii. Dolly hesitated, and with the proverbial result. **2001** *Washington Times* 8 Nov. D6 (Herb & Jamaal comic strip) 'Sometimes he who hesitates is lost ... and ends up several miles from the next freeway exit.' ■ **decision and indecision** 決断と優柔不断

hid ⇒ LOVE and a cough cannot be hid.

Those who HIDE can find.
何かを隠す者は他人が隠したものを見つけることもできる。

（訳注：「蛇の道は蛇」。those who ... =「…する人々」。God helps those who help themselves.〈天は自ら助けるものを助ける〉）

ここでの hide は「意図的に何かを隠す」という意味で、自動詞として使われている。

□ *c*1400 *Seven Sages of Rome* (1815) 68 He may wel fynde that hyde him selven. **1639** J. CLARKE *Parremiologia Anglo-Latina* lll They that hide can find. **1842** MARRYAT *Percival Keene* I. ill. 'I could have told you where it was.' 'Yes, yes, those who hide can find.' **1922** JOYCE *Ulysses* 542 (She ... unrolls the potato from the top of her stocking.) Those that hides knows where to find. **1979** 'E. PETERS' *One Corpse too Many* ix. Only those who had hidden here were likely ever to find. The full leafage covered all. ■ concealment 隠すこと・隠蔽

hides ⇒ A CLEVER hawk hides its claws.

high ⇒ GOD is high above, and the tsar is far away; The MOUNTAINS are high, and the emperor is far away.

The HIGHER the monkey climbs the more he shows his tail.
猿は、高く登れば登るほど自分の尻も見せる羽目になる。

適任者でない人物が高い地位に昇れば昇るほど、その人物の無能力さがより一層目立つことになる。下の用例からわかるように、丁寧な言い方もあればそうでない言い方もある。

□ *c*1395 WYCLIF *Bible* (1850) Proverbs iii. 35 (*gloss*) The filthe of her foll aperith more, as the filthe of the hynd partis of an ape aperith more, whanne he stieth [climbs] on high. *c* **1594** BACON *Promus* 102 He doth like the ape that the higher he clymbes the more he shews his ars. **1670** J. RAY *English Proverbs* S7 The higher the Ape goes, the more he shews his tail.... The higher beggars or base bred persons are advanced, the more they discover the lowness and baseness of their spirits and tempers. **1743** POPE *Dunciad* IV. 157 (note) The higher you climb, the more you shew your A—. **1873** TROLLOPE *Phineas Redux* I. xxxiv. He's to be pitchforked up to the Exchequer.... The higher a monkey climbs—; you know the proverb. **1985** *Washington Post* 3 Nov. C3 Let me tell you something Cookie and try to remember it the rest of your life, will you? The higher a monkey climbs the more he shows his ass. **2000** *Washington Post* 12 Dec. D6 The great expectations cost Norv Turner his job. And the attending soap opera quality made Dan Snyder a villainous stick figure across the nation. The lesson is obvious: The higher you attempt to climb, the more your behind shows. ■ ambition 野心・野望 ; human nature 人間性

hill ⇒ BLUE are the hills that are far away.

hindmost ⇒ DEVIL take the hindmost; EVERY man for himself, and devil take the hindmost.

HINDSIGHT is always twenty/twenty.
後知恵はいつも視力が20/20である。

（訳注：20/20は正常視力1.0を表わす。慣用句 twenty-twenty hindsight〈過去を振り返る際の鋭い洞察力〉参照）

事が起こった後でのみ、完全な全体像を把握することができる。最終的にうまくいかな

HISTORY 221

かった決定を下した人を慰めたり、強く非難する際に用いられることが多い。スネレン視力表は視力測定の尺度として使われている（2012年の用例）。米国起源のことわざで、1949年の用例は、アメリカの詩人・作家 R. アーマー（1906-89）の言葉に由来することを示している。しかし、J. R. コロンボの『映画製作者のウイットと知恵』（1979）vii においては、アメリカの映画監督・脚本家 B. ワイルダー（1906-2002）の言葉として紹介されている。

□ *a* 1949 Van Nuys [CA] *News* 17 Feb. Most people's hindsight is 20-20. **1984** *West Coast Review of Books* x. 32 Sure, it's not objective, and all the facts aren't in yet, but let the historians shake their heads-hindsight is always twenty-twenty. **1998** B. KINGSOLVER *Poisonwood Bible* (2000) 522 Like they always say, the rearview mirror is twenty-twenty. **2001** A. LANDERS *Washington Post* 18 Oct (online) Please stop blaming yourself. You did what you thought was best for your children. Hindsight is always 20/20. **2012** A. L. PROVOST *Gathering of Thieves* 8 As any optometrist worth his Snellen eye chart will tell you, hindsight is always twenty-twenty. So James Curry should not be faulted for not … taking the extremely difficult CPA examination. ■ **foresight and hindsight** 先見の明と後知恵; **wisdom** 賢明・知恵

hire ⇒ The LABOURER is worthy of his hire.

historian ⇒ Until the LIONS produce their own historian, …

HISTORY repeats itself.
歴史は繰り返される。

ここで述べられている循環的な歴史観はしばしば懐疑論と合致する（1957年の用例参照）。ドイツの経済学者・哲学者 K. マルクスの言葉とされることがあるが、彼はドイツの哲学者 G. W. F. ヘーゲル（1770-1831）の言葉を引用しているにすぎない。Hegel says somewhere that all great events and pesonalities in world history reappear in one fashion or another. He forgot to add: the first time as tragedy, the second as farce. 「ヘーゲルがどこかで述べているように、世界史に残る偉大な業績と人物は形を変えて再び現われるものである。ただし、ヘーゲルは最初は悲劇であったものが、次は茶番劇に変わるということを言い忘れている」（『ルイ・ボナパルトのブリュメール18日』〈1852〉I）。† 1989年の用例参照。

□ **1858** G. ELIOT *Janet's Repentance in Scenes of Clerical Life* II. x. History, we know, is apt to repeat itself. **1865** H. SEDLEY *Marian Rooke* III. v. i. History, it is said, repeats itself.… Few but are reminded almost every day … of something that has gone before. **1957** V. BRITTAIN *Testament of Experience* 11 History tends to defy the familiar aphorism; whether national or personal, it seldom repeats itself. **1971** A. PRICE *Alamut Ambush* xiii. Maybe history repeats itself—but I have to have facts. **1989** J. BARNES *History of World in 9½ Chapters* Does history repeat itself, the first time as tragedy, the second time as farce? ■ **history** 歴史

HISTORY is written by the victors.
歴史は勝者によって書かれる。

英国の政治家・著述家 W. チャーチルの言葉とされることが多いが、1919年の用例参照。† ドイツ語 *Der Sieger schreibt die Geschichte*. 「勝者が歴史を書く」

□ **1903** C. A. EVANS 'Introduction' in H. W. Thomas *History of the Doles-Cook Brigade* ix It is an

222 history

old saying, that the victor writes the history of a struggle. **1919** A. VON TIRPITZ *My Memoirs* I. 254 (tr.) [I]t could be taken as proof of the saying that history is written by the victors. **2001** B. HALPERN *David's Secret Demons* 108 'History is written by the victors' is another way of saying that history is written by the historians whose work survives. ■ **history 歴史**

history ⇒ Happy is the COUNTRY which has no history.

hog ⇒ The CAT, the rat, and Lovell the dog, rule all England under the hog.

hold ⇒ What you HAVE, hold.

Holdfast ⇒ BRAG is a good dog, but Holdfast is better.

When you are in a HOLE, stop digging.
穴の中にいるときは掘るのをやめろ。

困難な状況に陥っていることに気づいたら、そうした状況の原因となった行為を続けてはならない。状況を悪化させるだけである。

□**1977** *Wall Street Journal* 16 Sept. A senior official ... suggests the administration needs to learn 'the rule of holes': When you're in a hole, you don't keep digging. **1988** D. HEALEY *Observer* in J. Care (ed.) *Sayings of the Eighties* It is a good thing to follow the first law of holes; if you are in one, stop digging. **1989** *U.S. News & World Report* 23 Jan. CVI. iii. 46 (*headline*) When you're in a hole, stop digging. **1997** *Times* 15 Sept.1 WILLIAM HAGUE seems to have forgotten the first rule of politics: when you are in a hole, stop digging. **2001** *Spectator* 1 Dec. 32 Parliament would be unwise to hand to somebody in Tehran, Lambeth Palace or Salt Lake City the power, by pronouncing something hateful, to create an offence under English law. You're in a hole, Home Secretary. Stop digging. ■ **prudence 思慮・分別; trouble やっかい・苦労**

HOME is home, as the Devil said when he found himself in the Court of Session.
我が家にまさる所はない。このことは、高等裁判所で裁かれた時、悪魔が言った通りだ。

民事高等裁判所はスコットランドの最高国家裁判所で、1532年に設立された。

□**1832** W. MOTHERWELL in A. Henderson *Scottish Proverbs* lxix. Nothing more bitter was ever uttered ... against our Supreme Court of Judicature, than the saying ... Hame is hamely, quo' the Dell, when he fund himself in the Court of Session. **1915** J. BUCHAN *Salute to Adventurers* iv. I saw nothing now to draw me to ... law.... 'Hame's hame,'runs the proverb, 'as the devil said when he found himself in the Court of Session,' and I had lost any desire for that sinister company. ■ **law and lawyers 法と法律家**

HOME is home though it's never so homely.
どんなにみすぼらしくあろうとも我が家にまさる所はない。
（訳注：埴生の宿も我が宿である。「住めば都」）

たとえ豪邸でなくても、家庭には家庭としての価値がある。never soは古い表現で、ever so「この上なく」と同義で、形容詞homelyを強めている。ここでのhomelyは「醜い」（米国ではこの意味が多い）ではなく、「質素な、つつましい」の意。

honest 223

□**1546** J. HEYWOOD *Dialogue of Proverbs* 1. iv. Bl Home is homely, though it be poore in syght. **1569-70** *Stationers' Register* (1875) I. 192 A ballett intituled home ys homelye be yt neuer so ill. **1670** J. RAY *English Proverbs* 103 Home is home though it be never so homely. **1857** DICKENS *Little Dorrit* II. ix. 'Just as Home is Home though it's never so Homely, why you see,' said Mr. Meagles, adding a new version to the proverb, 'Rome is Rome though it's never so Romely.' **1915** J. WEBSTER *Dear Enemy* 46 Hame is hame, be't ever sae hamely. Don't you marvel at the Scotch? ■ content and discontent 満足と不満足; home 家庭・母国

HOME is where the heart is.
家庭とは心の通う場所である。

(訳注:houseが建物としての「家」であるのに対し、homeは「家庭」であり、人が住むことに焦点が置かれている〈homeの語源は「住む所」である〉)

家は必ずしも実際に住んでいる場所ではなく、愛情のある場所である。

□**1870** J. J. MCCLOSKEY in Goldberg & Heffner *Davy Crockett & Other Plays* (1940) 79 'As I am to become an inmate of your home, give me a sort of a panoramic view.' ... 'Well, home, they say, is where the heart is.' **1950** H. M. GAY *Pacific Spectator* IV. 91 'Home is where the heart is,' she said, 'if you'll excuse the bromide (trite remark).' **1979** K. BONFIGLIONI *After You with Pistol* xxi. 'Where is "home", please,' I asked.... 'Home's where the heart is,' he said. ■ content and discontent 満足と不満足; home 家庭・母国

home ⇒ CHARITY begins at home; CURSES, like chickens, come home to roost; EAST, west, home's best; An ENGLISHMAN's house is his castle; GO abroad and you'll hear news of home; The LONGEST way round is the shortest way home; There's no PLACE like home; A WOMAN's place is in the home; Many go out for WOOL and come home shorn.

HOMER sometimes nods.
ホメロスも時にはうっかり間違いをする。

(訳注:「弘法も筆の誤り」。「猿も木から落ちる」)

誰も始終最高の状態や明晰な状態を保つことはできない。紀元前10世紀のギリシアの叙事詩人ホメロスのような偉大な詩人でも同様である。ここでnodは「居眠りする」を意味する。したがって、「一時的な集中力の欠如のため失敗する」という意味になる。ホラティウスの『詩論』359 *Indignor quandoque bonus dormitat Homerus.* 「偉大なホメロスが居眠りすると、腹が立つ」に由来する。

□**1387** J. TREVISA tr. *Higden's Polychronicon* (1874) V. 57 He may take hede that the grete Homerus slepeth somtyme, for in a Jong work it is Jaweful to slepe som time. **1677** DRYDEN in *State of Innocence* BI^v Horace acknowledges that honest Homer nods sometimes: he is not equally awake in every line. **1887** T. H. HUXLEY in *Nineteenth Century* Feb.196 Scientific reason, like Homer, sometimes nods. **1979** D. CLARK *Heberden's Seat* vi. 'We're half asleep, not to have asked where they are before this.' 'Homer nods.... You can't ask every question.' **2002** *National Review* 6 May 16 Thanks for the studious illumination. But isn't it easier to go the even-Homer-nods routeon this, than to question the rule that plural subjects require a plural form of the verb? ■ error 間違い・過ち

honest ⇒ When THIEVES fall out, honest men come by their own.

224 HONESTY

HONESTY is the best policy.
正直こそ最善の策である。

正直さは、生来の徳ではなく、単なる実用的な生き方の指針にすぎないとしても、推奨されるべきものである。1854年の用例はこのことわざが孕む矛盾を突いている。

☐ **1605** E. SANDYS *Europre Speculum* K3 This over-politick ... order may reach a note higher than our grosse conceipts, who think honestie the best policie. *a* **1763** J. BYROM *Poems* (1773) I. 75 I'll filch no filching;—and I'll tell no lye; Honesty's the best policy,—say I. **1854** R. WHATELY *Detached Thoughts* 11. xviii. 'Honesty is the best policy'; but he who acts on that principle is not an honest man. **1928** J. GALSWORTHY *Swan Song* vi. It had been in his systems just as the proverb 'Honesty is the best policy' was in that of the private banking which then obtained. **2001** *Washington Times* 17 July A18 It is not a phrase I'm particularly fond of, for it endorses a virtue not for itself but for practical reasons, yet it bears repeating: Honesty is still the best policy. ■ **conduct** 行ない・品行; **honesty and dishonesty** 正直と不正直

HONEY catches more flies than vinegar.
酢よりも蜂蜜の方がハエをたくさん捕まえる。

柔らかくて巧みな言葉の方が厳しい言葉よりも有効である。†聖フランシスコ・サレジオ (1567-1622) in L. de la Rivière『聖フランシスコ・サレジオの生涯』(1624) 584: *Souvenez-vous que l'on prends plus de mouches avec une cuillerée de miel qu'avec cent barils de vinaigre.*「100バレルの酢よりスプーン1杯の蜂蜜の方がハエをよけいに捕獲できることを忘れてはならない」

☐ **1666** G. TORRIANO *Italian Proverbs* 149 Honey gets more flyes to it, than doth viniger. **1744** B. FRANKLIN *Poor Richard's Almanack* (Mar.) Tart Words make no Friends: spoonful of honey will catch more flies than Gallon of Vinegar. **1955** W. C. MACDONALD *Destination Danger* x. I ... know the old saying relative to honey catching more flies than vinegar.... If this is an act, you might as well save your breath. **1996** *Washington Post* 25 Oct. B4 Ask his advice frequently, and thank him profusely for his wisdom and guidance. Remember that old adage 'You can catch more flies with honey than with vinegar.' ■ **tact** 機転

honey ⇒ Where BEES are, there is honey; One DAY honey, one day onion.

There is HONOUR among thieves.
盗人の間にも義理はある。

この考え方は次の引用例に見受けられる。*c* **1622-3** *Soddered Citizen* (1936) l. 305 Theeues haue betweene themselues, a truth, And faith, which they keepe finne, by which They doe subsist.「盗人たちの間にも信義・忠義がある。彼らはそれを順守し、それに従って生きている」。**1703** P. A. モントゥー『ドン・キホーテ』II. lx. The old proverb still holds good, Thieves are never rogues among themselves.「この古いことわざは今でも有効である。盗人は盗人の間では悪漢ではない」

☐ **1802** J. BENTHAM *Works* (1843) N. 225 A sort of honour may be found (according to a proverbial saying) even among thieves. **1823** J. BEE *Dict. Turf* 96 'There is honour among thieves, but none among gamblers,' is very well antithetically spoken, but not true in fact. **1984** J. REEVES *Murder before Matins* vi. Honour among thieves was an empty phrase to all three of them: every professional criminal they'd known would sell his sidekick unhesitatingly if the price were right. **2002** R. J. BERNSTEIN *Radical Evil* 25 And a moral scoundrel may occasionally do

HOPE 225

what duty requires (honor among thieves). ■ honour 尊敬・名誉; wrong-doers 悪事をなす者

The post of HONOUR is the post of danger.
名誉ある地位は危険な地位でもある。

（訳注：of honour、of danger の of は「…のある、…という特徴をもつ」〈性質・特徴〉の意。「of ＋名詞」が形容詞に相当し、前の名詞の修飾語や補語になる。A man of courage〈勇気のある男〉、The disease is of two types.〈その病気には 2 種類ある〉）

名誉を得ると、自らを危険にさらすことになる。

□*a*1533 LD. BERNERS *Huon* (EETS) xx. Where as lyeth grete parelles there lieth grete honour. **1613** T. HEYWOOD *Brazen Age* III. 211 The greater dangers threaten The greater is his honour that breaks through. *a* **1625** J. FLETCHER *Rule Wife* (1640) IV. i. I remembered your old Roman axiom, The more the danger, still the more the honour. **1711** *Spectator* 1 Dec.1 We consider Human Life as a State of Probation, and Adversity as the Post of Honour in it. **1832** A. HENDERSON *Scottish Proverbs* 33 The post of honour is the post of danger. **1905** *British Weekly* 14 Dec. 1 The Chancellorship of the Exchequer ... is preeminently the post of danger, and therefore the post of honour in the new Government. ■ honour 尊敬・名誉; peril 危険

honour ⇒ Give CREDIT where credit is due; A PROPHET is not without honour save in his own country.

hoof ⇒ NO foot, no horse.

hop ⇒ TURKEY, heresy, hops, and beer came into England all in one year.

HOPE deferred makes the heart sick.
望みがなかなかかなわないと心が折れる。

『箴言』13章12節（欽定訳聖書）Hope deferred maketh the heart sick.「望みがなかなか叶わないと心を悩ます」に由来する。† *c* **1395** ウィクリフ聖書 (1850)『箴言』13章13節 Hope that is deferrid, torrnenteth the soule.「かなわぬ望みは心をくじく」。*c* **1527** J. ラステル『カリストとメリベーア』A5ᵛ For long hope to the hart mych troble wyll do.「望みがなかなか叶わないと、心が折れる」

□**1557** R. EDGEWORTH *Sermons* 130 v The hope that is deferred, prolonged, and put of, vexeth the minde. **1733** J. TALCOIT in *Collections of Connecticut Hist. Society* (1892) IV. 285 As hope deferred makes the heart sick: so I am in long expectation of your answers. **1889** GISSING *Nether World* II. vii. There was a heaviness at his heart. Perhaps it came only of hope deferred. **1981** *Observer* 26 Apr. 14 If hope deferred makes the heart sick, despair is a poor counsellor also. ■ hope and despair 希望と絶望

HOPE for the best and prepare for the worst.
最善を望み、最悪に備えよ。

楽観的であれ。しかし、まさかの時に備えて用心も怠るな。

□**1565** T. NORTON & T. SACKVILLE *Gorboduc* I. ii. Good is I graunt of all to hope the best, But not to liue still dreadles of the worst. **1581** W. AVERELL *Charles & Julia* D7 To hope the best, and feare the worst, (Joe, such is Loouers gaines). **1706** E. WARD *Third Volume* 337 This Maxim ought to be carest, Provide against the worst, and hope the best. **1813** J. JAY *Correspondence*

226　HOPE

(1893) IV. 367 To hope for the best and prepare for the worst, is a trite but a good maxim. **1836** E. HOWARD *Rattlin the Reefer* II. xxix. The youngest of us cannot always escape—hoping, trusting, relying on the best, we should be prepared for the worst. **1999** 'H. CRANE' *Miss Seeton's Finest Hour* i. 7 'We must all hope for the best,' Mrs. Seeton chided him gently. 'As my nanny used to say: "Hope for the best, expect the worst—and take what comes."' ■ **foresight and hindsight　先見の明と後知恵**

HOPE is a good breakfast but a bad supper.
希望は朝食にはよいが、夕食にはよくない。

（訳注：「一日の計は朝にあり」）

現実的な望みを抱くことは精神衛生上好ましいが、その望みがなかなかかなわないと、失望や絶望の原因となる。† HOPE deferred maketh the heart sick.「望みがなかなかかなわないと心が折れる」

☐**1661** W. RAWLEY *Resuscitatio* (ed. 2) 298 But, said the fisher men, we had hope then to make a better gain of it. Saith Mr. [Francis] Bacon well my Maisters, then lie tell you; hope is a good Breakfast but it is a Bad supper. **1817** H. L. PIOZZI *Autobiography* (1861) II. 188 He was a wise man who said Hope is a good breakfast but a bad dinner. It shall be my supper ... when all's said and done. **1986** C. M. SCHULZ *Washington Post* 27 Aug. D15 (*Peanuts comic strip*) 'I hope I get better grades this year. I hope I'll be the prettiest and smartest girl in the whole class ... ' '"Hope is a good breakfast, but it is a bad supper."' ■ **disappointment　失望**; **hope and despair　希望と絶望**

HOPE springs eternal.
希望は（胸の中に）絶えることなく湧き出る。

（訳注：1732年の用例にあるように、英国の詩人・作家 A. ポープの思想詩『人間論』からの引用。While there is life there is hope.〈生きている限り、希望はある〉ということわざも参照）

希望を抱くことはいつの世も変わらぬ人間の本性である。

☐**1732** POPE *Essay on Man* I. 95 Hope springs eternal in the human breast. Man never Is, but always To be blest. **1865** DICKENS *Our Mutual Friend* II. III. x. Night after night his disappointment is acute, but hope springs eternal in the scholastic breast. **1935** H. SPRING *Rachel Rosing* viii. 'It was understood, wasn't it, that we could not dine together?' 'Oh yes—but you know how it is. Hope springs eternal and so forth.' **2014** *Spectator* 22 Nov. 87 I have never actually won anything on the Lottery since the then prime minister, John Major, introduced it in 1994, but hope springs eternal. ■ **hope and despair　希望と絶望**

If it were not for HOPE, the heart would break.
希望がなかったら、心が折れてしまう。

（訳注：if it were not for ... ＝「仮に…がなかったら」。仮定法過去形を用いた反実仮想で、主節の would と呼応する。but for と同義。現実には人は皆心の中に希望を抱いて生きているので、「希望がなかったら」は非現実のこととして述べられている）

希望は困難と悲しみに立ち向かう原動力となる。

☐*a* **1250** *Ancrene Wisse* (1962) 43 Ase me seith, yefhope nere heorte to breke [as one says, if there were not hope, the heart would break]. *c* **1440** *Gesta Romanorum* (EETS) 228 Yf hope wer not, hert schulde breke. **1616** J. WITHALS *Dict.* (rev. ed.) 582 If it were not for hope, the heart would breake. **1748** RICHARDSON *Clarissa* VI. xxix. No harm in hoping, Jack! My uncle says, Were it not for hope, the heart would break. **1911** J. LUBBOCK *Use of Life* (rev. ed.) xv. There is an old proverb that if it were not for Hope the heart would break. Everything may be retrieved except despair. ■ **hope and despair　希望と絶望**

HORSES 227

hope ⇒ While there's LIFE there's hope; He that LIVES in hope dances to an ill tune.

hopefully ⇒ It is BETTER to travel hopefully than to arrive.

You can take a HORSE to the water, but you can't make him drink.
馬を水飲み場まで連れて行くことはできても、（馬にその気がなければ）無理やり水を飲ませることはできない。

人に機会を与えることはできるが、強制的にそれをさせることはできない。the waterの定冠詞 the はよく省略される。また、take の代わりに lead が使われることもある。

□c1175 *Old English Homilies* (EETS) 1st Ser. 9 Hwa is thet mei thet hors wettrien the him self-nule drinken [who can give water to the horse that will not drink of its own accord]? **1546** J. HEYWOOD *Dialogue of Proverbs* 1. xi. D3 A man may well bryng a horse to the water, But he can not make hym drynke without he will. **1658** E. PHILLIPS *Mysteries of Love & Eloquence* 160 A man may lead his Horse to water, but he cannot make him drink unless he list. **1857** TROLLOPE *Barchester Towers* III. i. 'Well,' said she ... 'one man can take a horse to water but a thousand can't make him drink.' **1970** J. MITFORD in *Atlantic* (1979) July 50 The dropout rate [for the course] must be close to 90 percent. I guess you can take a horse to the water, but you can't make him drink. **1997** M. LAZARUS *Washington Post* 7 Dec. (*Momma comic strip*) We could send you out to a firm and convince them to hire you, but we're not sure you'd be willing to learn the job. In other words, you can lead a horse to water, but you can't make it drink. ■ **free will and compulsion** 自由意志と強制

horse ⇒ Don't CHANGE horses in mid-stream; ENGLAND is the paradise of women; Never look a GIFT horse in the mouth; A GOOD horse cannot be of a bad colour; It's a GOOD horse that never stumbles and a good wife that never grumbles; While the GRASS grows, the steed starves; The GREY mare is the better horse; Because a MAN is born in a stable that does not make him a horse; NO foot, no horse; A NOD's as good as a wink to a blind horse; There is NOTHING so good for the inside of a man as the outside of a horse; Don't PUT the cart before the horse; If you can't RIDE two horses at once, you shouldn't be in the circus; A SHORT horse is soon curried; It is too late to shut the STABLE-door after the horse has bolted; One man may STEAL a horse, while another may not look over a hedge; THREE things are not to be trusted; If TWO ride on a horse, one must ride behind; For WANT of a nail the shoe was lost; If WISHES were horses, beggars would ride.

horseback ⇒ Set a BEGGAR on horseback, and he'll ride to the Devil.

HORSES for courses.
競走路に応じて馬がいる。

（訳注：「餅は餅屋」）

元来は競馬用語で、各競走路にふさわしい競走馬がそれぞれ揃っているという意味であった。現在では競馬以外の文脈でも使用される。

□**1891** A. E. T. WATSON *Turf* vii. A familiar phrase on the turf is 'horses for courses'.... The Brighton Course is very like Epsom; and horses that win at one meeting often win at the other. **1929** *Daily Express* 7 Nov. 18 Followers of the 'horses for courses' theory will be interested in the acceptance of Saracen, Norwest and Sir Joshua. **1985** 'J. GASH' *Pearlhanger* xxiii. It seemed to me I'd need a massacre, and immediately thought of Big John Sheehan. Horses for courses. **2001** *Times* 7 Nov. 16 Likewise it is horses for courses in Parliament. Mr Blair has a huge majority. There is no point in 'nursing a constituency' which offers no threat. ■ **efficiency and inefficiency** 能率と非能率

hot ⇒ A LITTLE pot is soon hot; STRIKE while the iron is hot.

hound ⇒ You cannot RUN with the hare and hunt with the hounds.

One HOUR's sleep before midnight is worth two after.
夜の12時前に 1 時間寝ると、それ以降の 2 時間の睡眠に値する。

（訳注：midnight ＝「夜の12時」）

2002年の用例は EARLY to bed and early to rise, makes a man healthy, wealthy, and wise.「早寝早起きは、人を健康に、裕福にそして賢明にする」をパロディ化して、「早寝早起きは、人を無愛想にし、目を充血させる」と述べている。

□**1640** G. HERBERT *Outlandish Proverbs* no. 882 One houres sleepe before midnight is worth three after. **1670** J. RAY *English Proverbs* 37 One hours sleep before midnight's worth two hours after. **1829** COBBETT *Advice to Young Men* I. xxxviii. It is said by the country-people that one hour's sleep before midnight is worth more than two are worth after midnight; and this I believe to be a fact. **1937** A. THIRKELL *Summer Half* iii. Now, Mr. Winter, remember my boys when you come up! Every hour's sleep before twelve is worth two afterwards, you know. **2002** *Times* 16 Feb. 26 Some maintain that 'An hour before midnight is worth two after it', which is utter nonsense because, as everyone knows: *Early to bed, early to rise, Makes a man surly, and gives him red eyes.* ■ **health** 健康

hour ⇒ The DARKEST hour is just before the dawn; Six hours' sleep for a man, seven for a woman, and eight for a fool.

A HOUSE divided cannot stand.
内輪もめの家は立ちゆかない。

内部分裂は家族、地域、国家を崩壊させる。『マタイによる福音書』12章25 節（欽定訳聖書）Every city or house divided against itself shall not stand.「どんな町や家も内輪で争えば成り立っていかない」

□*a* **1050** DEFENSOR *Liber Scintillarum* (EETS) 133 Drihten segth … relc ceaster oththe hus todreled ongean hit sylf, hit na stynt. *c* **1704** in T. CHALKLEY *Journal in Works* (1751) 42 My Mother would often say, A House divided could not stand. **1858** A. LINCOLN *Speech* 16 June in *Works* (1953) II. 461 'A house divided against itself cannot stand.' I believe this government cannot endure, permanently half slave and half free. **2001** *Times* 12 Dec.17 A house divided against itself cannot stand. And if Britain is to provide a secure home for all its peoples, there must be a shared sense of what values the nation holds in common. ■ **quarrelsomeness** 口論になりやすさ； **unity and division** 統一と分断

My HOUSE, my rules.
私の家には私のやり方。

（訳注：日本語でも、「私は私」、「我が家は我が家」と言う場合、自分、我が家には自分なりの、我が家なりのやり方・流儀があることを主張している）

定型句 My/Your —, my/your rules で始まる多くのことわざの1つであり、ある特定の場所や状況の下で、ある特定の人物が独断で規則を設定するという場面で使われる。以下の用例にあるように、"my game, my rules"、"my house, my party"、"my money, my rules"など色々な言い方がなされる。

□ **1983** *Pittsburgh Courier* 27 Aug. At home he lives by his father's motto 'It's my house, my rules.' **1984** J. PASLÉ-GREEN and J. HAYNES *Hello, I Love You!* 93 I felt a requirement each time I was with a girl that it be my game, my rules, so to speak … **1991** *Daily Pennsylvanian* 3 Dec. Remember, this is my house, my party. I'm inviting you. **2008** L. L. TROUPE *If I Only Knew* 32 You have to obey my rules when I'm paying the bills. Tuition bills, car payment, rent for that apartment. My money, My rules. **2012** *www.huffingtonpost.com* 15 Nov. [W]e treat them [i.e. our grown-up children] like responsible adults, capable of making their own decisions, right up to the moment when they cross our thresholds and then—my house, my rules? ■ **circumstances** 状況；**rules** 規則

house
⇒ BETTER one house spoiled than two; An ENGLISHMAN's house is his castle; FOOLS build houses and wise men live in them; Those who live in GLASS houses shouldn't throw stones; LEARNING is better than house and land; Never mention ROPE in the house of a man who has been hanged; SWEEP the house with broom in May, you sweep the head of the house away.

human
⇒ To ERR is human (to forgive divine).

hundred
⇒ The BUYER has need of a hundred eyes, the seller of but one.

HUNGER drives the wolf out of the wood.
空腹に耐えかねて狼も森から出てくる。

必要に迫られると人は不慣れな行動でもやってしまう。† 14世紀のフランス語 *La Jains enchace le louf dou bois.*「空腹に耐えかねて狼も森から出てくる」

□ **1483** CAXTON *Cato* B6ᵛ As hunger chaceth the wolfe out of the wode thus sobrete [sobriety] chaseth the deuyl fro the man. **1591** J. FLORIO *Second Fruits* 125 Hunger driues the wolfe out of the wood, if I had not great neede of monie, you should neuer haue them so dog cheape. **1748** SMOLLETT *Gil Blas* (1749) IV. XII. vii. This one … I own is the child of necessity. Hunger, thou knowest, brings the wolf out of the wood. **1872** R. BROWNING *Works* (1897) III. 323 Hunger, proverbs say, allures the wolf from the wood. **1905** J. B. CABELL *Line of Love* iv. Hunger … causes the wolf to sally from the wood. **2008** G. UCHITEL *Don't Judge Book by Cover* 90 Hunger drives the wolf out of the woods. ■ **hunger** 飢え・空腹；**necessity** 必要性・必然性

HUNGER is the best sauce.
空腹こそが最上のソースである。
（訳注：ひもじい時にまずい物なし）

† キケロ『善と悪の究極について』II. xxviii. *Cibi condimentum esse jamem.*「空腹は食べ物のスパイスである」。15世紀のフランス語 *N'est saucequi vaillefain.*「空腹に匹敵するソースはない」

□ **1530** A. BARCLAY *Eclogues* (EETS) 11. 743 Make hunger thy sause be thou neuer so nice, For there shalt thou finde none other kind of spice. **1539** R. TAVERNER *Garden of Wisdom* I. Bl He

230 HUNGRY

[Socrates] sayd, the beste sawce is hungre. **1555** R. EDEN tr. *P. Martyr's Decades of New World* II.iii.(*margin*) Hunger is the best sauce. **1850** C. KINGSLEY *Alton Locke* I. ix. If hunger is, as they say, a better sauce than any Ude invents, you should spend ... months shut out from every glimpse of Nature, if you would taste her beauties. **1929** F. M. MCNEILL *Scots Kitchen* iii. Mere hunger, which is the best sauce, will not produce cookery, which is the art of sauces. **1939** L. I. WILDER *By Shores of Silver Lake* xxi. 'The gravy is extra good too.' 'Hunger is the best sauce,' Ma replied modestly. **2013** *New Scientist* 27 July 65 That hunger is the best sauce is proverbial in various languages. But remember that many of our ancestors were intimately familiar with famine. ■ **food and drink** 飲食物；**hunger** 飢え・空腹

A HUNGRY man is an angry man.
空腹の人は怒りっぽくなる。

空腹でイライラしていると、どうしても乱暴なふるまいをしがちである。

□*c***1641** O. FERGUSSON *Scottish Proverbs* (STS) no. 553 Hungry men ar angry. **1659** J. HOWELL *Proverbs* (English) 13 A hungry man, an angry man. **1738** SWIFT *Polite Conversation* 11. 119 'I'm hungry.' ... 'And I'm angry, so let us both go fight.' **1909** *Spectator* 22 May 824 The Acharnians [in a play of that name by Aristophanes] ... made fun of the Athenians.... 'A hungry man is an angry man' ... and the Athenians were certainly hungry. **1922** J. JOYCE *Ulysses* 161 Hungry man is an angry man. **1981** B. MARLEY in *Times* 17 Oct. 7 A hungry mob is an angry mob, a pot a cook but the food not enough. **2011** *sacsis.org.za* 11 Aug. Our [i.e. South Africa's] staggering levels of unemployment and inequality provide the ingredients for social unrest. As the dub poet Linton Kwesi Johnson said, 'A hungry man is an angry man.' ■ **hunger** 飢え・空腹

hunt ⇒ Until the LIONS produce their own historian, ... ; You cannot RUN with the hare and hunt with the hounds.

hunter ⇒ Until the LIONS produce their own historian, ...

HURRY no man's cattle.
他人の牛（もしくは、馬）を急がせるな。

（訳注：1811年、1907年の用例にあるように、後ろに「自分自身はロバを持つ身になるかもしれないぞ」という意味の表現〈you may come to have a donkey of your own〉が続くことが多い）

「早く、早く！」とせかす短気な子供に対する警告。cattle は現在は「牛」を意味するが、かつては horses「馬」の俗語であった。

□**1811** *Spirit of Public Journals for 1811*(1812) XV. 326 'I want my dinner sadly, and am in a hurry.'—'Hurry,' says I, 'that's good Indeed! Hurry no man's cattle; you may have a jack-ass of your own some of these days, and perhaps have got one when you're at home.' **1822** SCOTT *Pirate* I. ix. 'A' in gude time,' replied the jagger [pedlar]; 'hurry no man's cattle.' **1907** W. C. HAZLITT *English Proverbs & Proverbial Phrases* 236 Hurry no man's cattle; you may come to have a donkey of your own. Sometimes said to an impatient child. **1932** J. S. PLETCHER *Murder of Ninth Baronet* xxi. I knew that in due time he would tell me the result of these mental exercises; in the meantime I stood by the old adage—hurry no man's cattle. ■ **patience and impatience** 忍耐と性急

hurt ⇒ Don't CRY before you're hurt; What you don't KNOW can't hurt you; STICKS and stones may break my bones, but words will never hurt me.

The HUSBAND is always the last to know.
最後に知るのはいつも夫である。
（訳注：「知らぬは亭主ばかりなり」）

たとえ不倫が世間話や噂話の話題になっても、欺かれた夫は自分の妻の不倫に最後まで気づかない。1936年、2002年の用例からわかるように、The wife is always the last to know.「いつも最後に知るのは妻である」は20世紀に生まれた言い方である。

☐ **1604** MARSTON *What you Will* I. i. A cuckold ... a thing that's hoodwinked with kindness.... He must be the last must know it. **1659** N. R. *Proverbs* 95 The good man is the last that knows whats amisse at home. **1756** STENE *Tristram Shandy* VIII. iv. 'It is with love as with cuckoldom' —the suffering party is at least the third, but generally the last who knows anything about the matter. **1893** R. KIPLING *Many Inventions* 250 The most disconnected witness knew ... the causes of offence; and the prisoner (i.e. the cuckolded husband), who naturally was the last of all to know, groaned in the dock while he listened. **1936** M. MITCHELL *Gone with Wind* liv. I thought surely the whole town knew by now. Perhaps they all do, except you. You know the old adage: 'The wife is always the last one to find out.' **1979** C. MACLEOD *Family Vault* iii. 'Do you mean he hasn't heard?' Leila whooped. 'They say the husband's always the last to know,' Harry chimed in. **2002** B. MONAHAN *SceptredIsle Club* vii. 138 John knew that, just as in affairs of the heart the wife is the last to know, with affairs of business, professional associates seldom had warnings when their seemingly secure friend went bankrupt. ■ **deception** ごまかし；**wives and husbands** 夫婦

husband ⇒ A DEAF husband and a blind wife are always a happy couple.

232 Ice

I

Ice ⇒ The RICH man has his ice in the summer and the poor man gets his in the winter.

An IDLE brain is the Devil's workshop.
暇人の頭は悪魔の仕事場である。

（訳注：ラテン語のことわざ Otium est pulvinar diaboli.〈閑散は悪魔の座席である〉に由来するとされる。「小人閑居して不善をなす」）

怠惰によって良からぬ考えが生じることに対する警告。† IDLENESS is the root of all evil.「怠惰は諸悪の根源」。最近の米語用法は、明らかにこのことわざと the DEVIL finds work for idle hands to do.「悪魔は何もしないで怠けている手に仕事を見つけるものだ」との合成である（2001 年の用例参照）。

□*a* **1602** W. PERKINS *Works* (1603) 906 The idle bodie and the idle braine is the shoppe [workshop] of the deuill. **1732** T. FULLER *Gnomologia* no. 3053 Idle Brains are the Devil's Workhouses. **1855** H. G. BOHN *Hand-Book of Proverbs* 311 An idle brain is the devil's workshop. **1859** S. SMILES *Self-Help* viii. Steady employment ... keeps one out of mischief, for truly an idle brain is the devil's workshop. **1930** E. D. BIGGERS *Charlie Chan Carries On* xxii. Tell him to be [a] good boy and study hard. An idle brain is the devil's workshop. **1988** C. G. HART *Design for Murder* ix. 'Idle minds are the devil's workshop.' She lifted the watch ... and stared at it accusingly. 'Five minutes after eight Is no one else here?' **2001** *Washington Times* 3 Sept. A12 Young people need to learn to work. Their parents must not let them be idle all summer for, as they say, idle hands are the devil's workshop. ■ **idleness 怠惰；wrong-doers 悪事をなす者**

IDLE people have the least leisure.
無精者には一番暇がない。

The BUSIEST men have the most leisure.「一番忙しい人が一番暇がある」からの推論。

□**1678** J. RAY *English Proverbs* (ed. 2) 161 Idle folks have the most labour. **1853** SURTEES *Sponge's Sporting Tour!* vii. 'Got a great deal to do', retorted Jog, who, like all thoroughly idle men, was always dreadfully busy. **1855** H. G. BOHN *Hand-Book of Proverbs* 414 Idle folks have the least leisure. **1908** *Spectator* 10 Oct. 535 The difference between leisureliness and laziness runs parallel with that between quickness and haste. 'Idle people', says the proverb, 'have the least leisure.' ■ **efficiency and inefficiency 能率と非能率；idleness 怠惰**

idle ⇒ As good be an ADDLED egg as an idle bird; The DEVIL finds work for idle hands to do; It is idle to SWALLOW the cow and choke on the tail.

IGNORANCE 233

IDLENESS is the root of all evil.
怠惰は諸悪の根源。
（訳注：「小人閑居して不善をなす」）

この考えはクレルヴォーの聖ベルナルド（1090頃-1153）の言葉に由来する。† 14世紀初頭のフランス語 *Oiseusete atrait viches*.「怠惰は悪を引き寄せる」。*c* **1390** チョーサー『カンタベリー物語』「第二の尼僧の物語の序」l. 1 The ministre and the norice [nurse] unto vices, which that men clepe [call] in Englissh ydlenesse.「悪の召使いにして悪の養い手、人が英語で安逸と称するもの」

□**1422** J. YONGE in *Secreta Secretorum* (1898) 158 Idylnysse is the ... rote of vicis. **1538** T. BECON *Governance of Virtue* B8ᵛ Idleness ... is the well-spring and root of all vice. **1707** G. FARQUHAR *Beaux' Stratagem* 1. i. Idleness is the Root of all Evil; the World's wide enough, let 'em bustle. **1850** DICKENS *David Copperfield* x. 'The boy will be idle there,' said Miss Murdstone, looking into a pickle-jar, 'and idleness is the root of all evil.' **1966** *Gleaner* (Kingston, Jamaica) 2 Aug. 22/7 We too can help by our behaviour and our industry and by working harder and spending less time in idleness. There is a well-known adage that idleness is the root of all evil. **2000** N. N. ERIKSEN *Kierkegaard's Category of Repetition* 27 Plebeians think that idleness is the root of all evil; but this would be true only if work were the destiny of human life. ■ **good and evil** 正邪; **idleness** 怠惰

If IFS and ands were pots and pans, there'd be no work for tinkers.
「もしも」が鍋や釜になるのなら、鋳掛職人の仕事はなくなってしまう。
（訳注：ifs = ands であり、想像していることが現実のものになったら、鋳掛職人、すなわち貧乏人だって金持ちになれるのになあと述べている。If Wishes Were Horses という童謡から来ているとされる。どう考えても鋳掛職人の仕事がなくなるなどということはあり得ない。人生は思い通りには行かないものなのである。) if ifs and ands were pots and pans =「想像していることがすべて現実になるのなら」)

とうてい信じられないような楽観的希望に対して、ユーモアを込めて応酬する際に使われる。条件節の事柄があり得ない以上、主節の事柄もあり得ない。ands は等位接続詞 and の廃れた意味の「もしも」（その場合、弱形の an となる）という意味を表わしているが、ここでは、臨時に「反実仮想」を表わす名詞として使われている。

□**1850** C. KINGSLEY *Alton Locke* I. x. 'If a poor man's prayer can bring God's curse down.' ... 'If ifs and ans were pots and pans.' **1886** *Notes & Queries* 7th Ser. I. 71 There is also the old doggerel-If ifs and ands Were pots and pans Where would be the work for Tinkers' hands? **1981** J. ASHFORD *Loss of Culion* xvi. As my old aunt used to say, 'If ifs and ands were pots and pans, there'd be no work for tinkers' hands.' **2002** *Washington Times* 14 Aug. B5 A reader signed 'Desperate in Ohio' reported that a verse her aunt told her many years ago was rattling around in her head, but she couldn't remember the last line. It went, 'If "ifs" and "ans" were pots and pans ... ' My column yesterday was filled with letters from readers eager to provide the missing line, ' ... there'd be no work for tinkers.' ■ **wanting and having** 不足と所持

Where IGNORANCE is bliss, 'tis folly to be wise.
知らないことが幸福な場合、知ることは愚かである。
（訳注：「知らぬが仏」）

現在では Ignorance is bliss.「知らないことは幸せ」と短縮されることが多い。

□**1742** GRAY *Poems* (1966) 10 Thought would destroy their paradise. No more; where ignorance is bliss, 'Tis folly to be wise. **1865** SURTEES *Facey Romford's Hounds*lxxi. Of course Facey knew nothing about Lucy, and, upon the principle that where ignorance is bliss 'twere folly to be wise,

234 IGNORANCE

Soapey was not extra-inquisitive about her. **1925** S. O'CASEY *Juno & Paycock* II. 49 'You ought to be ashamed o' yourself ... not to know the History o' your country.' ... 'Where ignorance's bliss 'tis folly to be wise.' **1983** 'J. GASH' *Sleepers of Erin* I. Antique dealers haven't a clue. Pathetic. God knows. why, but dealers always want to prove that ignorance really is bliss. **2001** *Times* 23 Nov. 20 And the moral of our present situation is:If ignorance is bliss, why aren't more people happy? ■ **ignorance** 無知・無学

IGNORANCE of the law is no excuse.
法律を知らなかったことは何の言い訳にもならない。

†古代ラテン語の法律に関する格言 *Ignorantia iuris neminem excusat*.「法律を知らなかったからといって誰も容赦されない」

□*c***1412** T. HOCCLEVE *Degimene Principum* (EETS) 92 Excuse schal hym naght his ignorance. **1530** C. ST. GERMAN *Dialogues in English* II. xlvi. Ignorance of the law though it be inuincible doth not excuse. **1616** T. DRAXE *Adages* 100 The ignorance of the law excuseth no man. *a* **1654** J. SELDIIN *Table-Talk* (1689) 30 Ignorance of the Law excuses no man; not that all Men know the Law, but because 'tis an excuse every man will plead, and no man can tell how to confute him. **1830** N. AMES *Mariner's Sketches* xxviii. Ignorance of the law excuses nobody.... The gates of mercy are forever shut against them. **1979** *Private Eye* 17 Aug. 6 [He] was fined £5 at Marylebone Court when he learned that ignorance of the law is no excuse for breaking it. ■ **excuses** 言い訳 ; **law and lawyers** 法と法律家

It's an ILL bird that fouls its own nest.
自分の巣を汚すのは悪い鳥。

自分の家族、国などを誹謗中傷する人を戒める表現として使われる。†中世ラテン語 *Nidos commaculans inmundus habebitur ales*.「自分の巣を汚す鳥は不潔である」

□*a* **1250** *Owl & Nightingale* (1960) 1. 99 Dahet habbe [a curse on] that ilke best that fuleth his owe nest. *c* **1400** N. BOZON *Moral Tales* (1889) 205 Hyt ys a fowle brydde that fylyth hys owne neste. **1591** H. SMITH *Preparative to Mamage* 82 It becommeth not any woman to set light by her husband, nor to publish his infirmities for they say, it is an euill bird that defileth his owne nest. **1670** J. RAY *English Proverbs* 62 It's an ill bird that beraies its own nest. **1817** SCOTT *Rob Roy* II. xiii. Where's the use o' vilifying ane's country.... It's an ill bird that files its ain nest. **1926** *Times* 7 Sept. 17 Nothing ... can excuse the bad taste of Samuel Butler's virulent attack upon his defenceless family.... It's an ill bird that fouls its own nest. **2000** C. GOFF *Rant of Ravens* i. 2 Miriam cleared her throat. 'It's an ill bird that fouls its own nest, dear. If you ask me, it's about time you dumped him.' ■ **malice** 悪意・恨み

ILL gotten goods never thrive.
不正に入手したものはすぐに浪費されてしまう。

†キケロ『フィリッピカ』II. xxvii. 65 *Male parta, male dilabuntur*.「不正に入手したものは浪費されてしまう」。同じ内容でもう少し控えめな表現に What is GOT over the Devil's back is spent under his belly.「悪魔の背中で得られたものは、悪魔の腹の下で費やされる」がある。

□**1519** W. HORMAN *Vulgaria* 77 Euyll gotten ryches wyll neuer proue longe. *c* **1577** J. NORTHBROOKE *Treatise* ... Dicing 95 Euill gotten goods shall neuer prosper. **1609** JONSON *Case is Altered* v. xii. Ill gotten goods ne'er thriue, I plaid the thiefe, and now am robd my selfe. **1670** J. RAY *English Proverbs* 96 Ill gotten goods, seldom prosper. **1826** C. LAMB *Elia's Last Essays* (1833) ii. That ill-gotten gain never prospers ... is the trite consolation administered to the easy dupe, when he has been tricked out of his money or estate. **1937** D. L. SAYERS *Busman's Honeymoon* x. Ill gotten goods never thrive.... Because he hath oppressed and forsaken the poor. ■ **action and consequence** 行為と結果；**retribution** 天罰・報復

It's ILL waiting for dead men's shoes.
死者の靴を待ち望むのはよくない。

遺産相続を期待して誰かの死を待つようなことはすべきでない。*c* 1549 年と 1721 年の用例に挙げられている当初の言い方は現在使われていない。以下の用例では慣用句 to wait for dead men's shoes「人の遺産をねらう」の意味でも使われていることに注意。

□**1530** J. PALSGRAVE *L'eclaircissement de la Langue Franlyllise* 306ᵛ Thou lokest after deed mens shoes. *c* **1549** J. HEYWOOD *Dialogue of Proverbs* I. xi. C5 Who waitth for dead men shoen, shal go long barfote. **1721** J. KELLY *Scottish Proverbs* 148 He goes long bare Foot that wears dead Mens Shoon. Spoken to them who expect to be some Man's Heir, to get his Place, oife, if he should dye. **1758** A. MURPHY *Upholsterer* I. ii. You have very good pretensions; but then its waiting for dead Men's Shoes. **1815** SCOTT Guy *Mannering* II. xvi. That's but sma' gear, puir thing; she had a sair time o't with the auld Leddy. But it's ill waiting for dead folk's shoon. **1912** E. V. LUCAS *London Lavender* iv. I pointed out that I was executor to no fewer than three persons ... 'It's ill waiting for dead men's shoes,' Naomi quoted. **1963** C. BUSH *Case of Heavenly Twin* xvi. Perhaps I was right when I suggested he told Staffer he was waiting for a dead man's shoes. ■ **expectation** 予期・期待

ILL weeds grow apace.
雑草はすぐに伸びる。

（訳注：apace ＝「すぐに、早く」〈文語〉。Ill news runs *apace*.〈悪事千里を走る〉。「憎まれっ子世に憚る」）

†14 世紀のフランス語 *Male herbe croist*.「悪い草は蔓延る」

□*c***1470** in *Anglia* (1918) XLII. 200 Wyi[d] weed ys sone y-growe. Creuerat herba satis, que nil habet utilitatis. **1546** J. HEYWOOD *Dialogue of Proverbs* I. x. C4 v Ill weede growth fasles [Alice], wherby the come is Jome [lost]. **1578** J. FLORIO *First Fruits* 31ᵛ An yl weede groweth apace. **1594** SHAKESPEARE *Richard III* II. iv. 13 'Ay,' quoth my uncle Gloucester, 'Small herbs have grace: great weeds do grow apace.' ... I would not grow so fast, Because sweet flow'rs are slow and weeds make haste. **1738** SWIFT *Polite Conversation* I. 23 'Don't you think Miss is grown?' ... 'Ay; ill Weeds grow a-pace.' **1905** A. MACLAREN *Gospel according to St. Matthew* II. 208 The roots of the old lay hid, and, in due time, showed again above ground. 'Ill weeds grow apace.' **1986** M. SLUNG *More Momilies* 67 It's always the weeds that grow the best. ■ **good and evil** 正邪；**wrong-doers** 悪事をなす者

It's an ILL wind that blows nobody any good.
誰にも利益を吹き与えてくれない風は悪い風。

（訳注：この場合、blow は間接目的語〈＝ nobody〉と直接目的語〈＝ any good〉の 2 つを取る授与動詞となっている。すなわち、blow には give〈与える〉の意味が含まれている。I bought her a new car.〈彼女に新車を買い与えた〉の buy の場合と並行している。「甲の損は乙の得」。「泣く者あれば笑う者あり」）

航海における比喩表現で、どんなに悪い物事でも誰かには利益になっていることを述べている。

□**1546** J. HEYWOOD *Dialogue of Proverbs* II. ix. LI An yll wynde that blowth no man to good, men saie. **1591** SHAKESPEARE *Henry VL* Pt. 3 11. v. 55 Ill blows the wind that profits nobody. **1655** T. FULLER *Church Hist. Britain* II. ii. It is an ill wind which bloweth no man Profit. He is cast on the Shoar of Freezland ... where the Inhabitants ... were by his Preaching converted to Christianity. **1832** S. WARREN *Diary of Late Physician* I. i. My good fortune (truly it is an ill wind that blows nobody any good) was almost too much for me. **1979** J. SCOTT *Angels in your Beer* xxviii. It is an ill wind that blows nobody any good, but then John Quinlan ... was about as close to being a nobody as anyone could get. **2002** *Washington Times* 11 Jan. A4 It's an ill wind that blows nobody any good, as the wise man said, and certain Democrats and pundits think the wiod that blew Enron away was a warm breeze from Eden. ■ **misfortune** 不運

ill ⇒ BAD news travels fast; EVIL to him who evil thinks; It's ill speaking between a FULL man and a fasting; He that LIVES in hope dances to an ill tune; It is ill SITTING at Rome and striving with the Pope; A sow may whistle, though it has an ill mouth for it; Never. SPEAK ill of the dead; ⇒ BAD.

IMITATION is the sincerest form of flattery.
真似ることこそは最も誠実な追従である。
（訳注：たんなる追従ならば誠実とは言えないが、その人のやり方・生き方を真似て、お手本にすることは、心からの「追従」と言える）

2世紀のローマ皇帝マルクス・アウレリウスが『瞑想録』(X viii iv) の中で同様の考えを述べている。You should consider that Imitation is the most acceptable part of Worship, and that the Gods had much rather Mankind should Resemble, than Flatter them.「模倣は申し分のない形の崇拝であり、神々には人間がへつらうよりもむしろ自らを似せるべきものをたくさん有していたと考えるべきである (J. Collier 訳『皇帝マルクス・アウレリウスの自省録』〈1701〉186 より)」。1714年の用例における artless は「心からの」の意。

☐**1714** *Spectator* 11 Oct. (1776) 207 [Y]ou maybe sure a woman loves a man, when she uses his expressions, tells his stories, or imitates his manner ... for imitation is a kind of artless flattery. **1820** C. C. COLTON *Lacon* I. 113 Imitation is the sincerest of flattery. **1843** SURTEES *Handley Cross* I. xv. Imitation is the sincerest of flattery. **1940** E. PAYNE *Malice Domestic* 13 Penny's [clothes] all seemed to be homemade copies of the expensive models her sister wore.... Imitation may be the sincerest form of flattery but ... I wondered whether there might not be more to it. **2001** *Washington Post* 8 Sept. C11 It has been said that 'imitation is the sincerest form of flattery,' but being stalked and copied can indeed be frightening. ■ **imitation** 模倣

impossible ⇒ The DIFFICULT is done at once.

impression ⇒ FIRST impressions are the most lasting.

IN for a penny, in for a pound.
1ペニーを稼ぐ仕事を始めた以上は1ポンドを稼ぐ仕事をなし遂げるまでやり抜かねばならない。
（訳注：〈be〉in fo ... , in for ... ＝「…に手を出した以上は…もやらなければならない〈もうあとへは引けない〉。」1ペニーは100分の1ポンド。penny には「小銭」の意味もある）

いったん何かを始めたなら、とことんやり抜かねばならない。

☐**1695** E. RAVENSCROFT *Canterbury Guests* v.i. It concerns you to ... prove what you speak.... In for a Penny, in for a Pound. **1815** SCOTT *Guy Mannering* III. vii. Sampson ... thought to him-

iron 237

self, in for a penny in for a pound, and he fairly drank the witch's health in a cupfull of brandy. **1841** DICKENS *Old Curiosity Shop* II. lxvi. Now, gentlemen, I am not a man who does things by halves. Being in for a penny, I am ready as the saying is to be in for a pound. **1979** P. NIESE-WAND *Member of Club* viii. 'Do you want to go and have a look, sir?' ... 'Why not? ... In for a penny, in for a pound.' **2001** *Oldie* Nov. 66 Have you ever suggested that you take the children away for a few days or even a week—in for a penny, in for a pound—after Christmas or near their birthdays? ■ **action and consequence** 行為と結果 ; **perseverance** ねばり強さ ; **risk** 危険

inclined ⇒ As the TWIG is bent, so is the tree inclined.

inconvenience ⇒ POVERTY is no disgrace, but it is a great inconvenience.

index ⇒ The EYES are the window of the soul.

Indian ⇒ The only GOOD Indian is a dead Indian.

infinite ⇒ GENIUS is an infinite capacity for taking pains.

inside ⇒ There is NOTHING so good for the inside of a man as the outside of a horse.

intention ⇒ The ROAD to hell is paved with good intentions.

invention ⇒ NECESSITY is the mother of invention.

Ireland ⇒ ENGLAND's difficulty is Ireland's opportunity.

iron ⇒ STRIKE while the iron is hot.

J

Every JACK has his Jill.
どのジャックにもお似合いのジルがいる。

（訳注：Jack and Jill とは「〈若い〉男女、恋人同士」を指す。「割れ鍋に閉じ蓋」）

どの男性にも、お似合いの女性がいるもの。固有名詞の Jack と Jill（または Gill）は任意の男性と女性を指している。

□ **1611** R. COTGRAVE *Dict. French & English* s.v. Demander, Like will to like; a Iacke lookes for a Gill. **1619** in C. W. BARDSLEY *Curiosities of Puritan Nomenclature* (1880) i. The proverb is, each Jacke shall have his Gill. **1855** G. J. WHYTE-MELVILLE *General Bounce* ii. 'Every Jack has his Gill,' if he and she can only find each other out at the propitious moment. **1940** H. W. THOMPSON *Body, Boots & Britches* xix. Every Jack has his Jill; If one won't, another will. **1986** M. SLUNG *More Momilies* 47 For every Jack, there is a Jill. ■ **men and women 男女**

JACK is as good as his master.
ジャックといえど主人と同じ人間である。

（訳注：この場合の Jack とは「下男・使用人」の意）

Jack は船乗り、一般男性、召使い、日雇い労働者の名前としてさまざまな場面で使われる。

□ **1706** J. STEVENS *Spanish & English Dict.* s.v. Pedro, Peter is as good as his Master. Like Master, like Man. **1868** READE & BOUCICAULT *Foul Play* II. xx. Is it the general opinion of seamen before the mast? Come, tell us. Jack's as good as his master in these matters. **1936** W. HOLTBY *South Riding* I. iv. She was far from thinking Jack as good as his master and explained failure in plebeian upstarts by saying with suave contempt: 'Well, what can you expect? Wasn't bred to power.' **1987** R. HILL *Child's Play* viii. 1945 might have seen Britain ready at last for the political assertion that Jack was as good as his master, but it was still light years away from any meaningful acknowledgment that Black Jack was as good as White Jack. ■ **employers and employees 雇用者と被雇用者；equality 平等**

JACK of all trades and master of none.
ジャックは色々な仕事に手を出すが、どの仕事も極めることができない。

（訳注：trade ＝「職業、生業」。the carpenter's *trade* 〈大工の職〉。Two of a *trade* never agree.〈同業者は仲が悪いもの〉の trade も同じ意味で使われている。「多芸は無芸」）

ここでの Jack は未熟な労働者の意味で使われており、徒弟期間を修了した熟練者である master と対比されている。

□ **1732** T. FULLER *Gnomologia* no. 3051 Jack of all Trades is of no Trade. **1804** M. EDGEWORTH 'The Will' in *Popular Tales* ii. 152 'How comes it that I am so unlucky?' 'Jack of all trades, and master of none!' said Goodenough, with a sneer. **1878** S. WALPOLE *History of England* I. 311 It would be unfair to say of Lord Brougham that he was 'Jack of all trades and master of none'. **1987** O. S. CARD *Seventh Son* (1988) vi. 47 To have every possible skill ... and to have it in exactly even proportions. Far from being average, the child was extraordinary ... Jack of all trades and master of none? Or master of all? **2002** *Oxford Times Weekend* 9 He is quick to point out that the reverse side of the renaissance man is jack of all trades, who, as we all know, is often considered a master of none. ■ **trades and skills** 職業と技術

Jack ⇒ All WORK and no play makes Jack a dull boy.

JAM tomorrow and jam yesterday, but never jam today.
明日と昨日がジャムの日で、今日はジャムの日ではない。

(訳注：1871 年の用例からわかるように、英国の童話作家・数学者 L. キャロルの『鏡の国のアリス』に登場する女王さまのセリフである。女王さまは、週に 2 ペンスと 1 日おきのジャムという条件でアリスを侍女として雇おうと言うが、実は、規則では、明日と昨日がジャムの日で、今日はジャムの日ではないと決まっているので、今日はアリスにジャムを与えることはできない。それに対して、アリスが「今日はジャムの日」という日だってあるでしょうと言うと、女王はそれはないという。「1 日おきのジャム」なので、1 日おけば、今日は明日になってしまうというのである。よって、「ジャムの日」は永遠に来ないことになる。成句で jam tomorrow は「明日の楽しみ」という意味で用いられる。He is concerned only with jam tomorrow. 〈彼女は明日の楽しみしか頭にない〉。

手に入れようのないものを愚弄するのに用いられる。

□ **1871** 'L. CARROLL' *Through Looking-Glass* v. 'The rule is, jam to-morrow and jam yesterday— but never jam to-day.' 'It must come sometimes to "jam to-day",' Alice objected. 'No, it can't,' said the Queen. **1951** 'J. WYNDHAM' *Day of Triffids* xii. Just put the Americans into the jam-to-morrow-pie-in-the-sky department awhile. **1979** *Guardian* 9 June 10 The manageress of the launderette calls me darling.... 'Jam yesterday, jam tomorrow, but never jam today.' **2012** *www.ipe. com* Nov. To paraphrase Lewis Carroll's Alice, when the going gets tough, Jam today always trumps jam tomorrow. ■ **disappointment** 失望

jaw (rush of water) : ⇒ JOUK and let the jaw go by.

jest ⇒ Many a TRUE word is spoken in jest.

jewel ⇒ FAIR play's a jewel.

Jill ⇒ Every JACK has his Jill.

job ⇒ Never send a BOY to do a man's job; If a THING's worth doing, it's worth doing well.

join ⇒ If you can't BBAT them, join them.

JOUK and let the jaw go by.
身を屈めて奔流をやりすごせ。

(訳注：スコットランド英語で jouk は「身を屈める」を jaw は「奔流」を表わす。)

スコットランドのことわざで、危険に晒されたときの対処のしかたを説いている。to

240 JOURNEY

jouk and let the jaw go by という成句にもなっている。

□ **1721** J. KELLY *Scottish Proverbs* 189 Juck [stoop], and let the jaw [rush of water] go o'er you. That is, prudently yield to a present Torrent. **1817** SCOTT *Rob Roy* II. xii. Gang your ways hame, like a gude bairn—jouk and let the jaw gae by. **1927** J. BUCHAN *Witch Wood* xv. A man must either joule and Jet the jaw go bye, as the owercome [commonexpression] says, or he must ride the whirlwind. ■ **prudence** 思慮・分別；**self-preservation** 自己防衛

A JOURNEY of a thousand miles begins with a single step.
1000マイルの旅も一歩から。

（訳注：このことわざは、老子の「千里之行、始於足下」〈千里の行も足下より始まる〉の英訳である。人間行動の合理的基盤を説いていると考えられる。「千里の道も一歩から」）

道教の始祖・老子（紀元前604頃-531頃）の言葉とされる。

□ **1904** *Sayings of Lao Tzu* tr. L Giles 51 A journey of a thousand miles began with a single step. **1947** L. LEE *Twisted Mirror* x. 87 Willie looked at him with all the solemnity of an old Chinese priest 'Even a journey of a thousand miles, my honored superior,' he intoned, 'begins with but a single step.' **1983** *National Review* 29 Apr. 485 Of the 15,000 people treated there ... , nearly all smoked marijuana. Which proves nothing. Except that the longest journey begins with a single step. **2001** *Washingt on Times* 28 July F9 (*Herb & Jamaal comic strip*) 'They say life is a journey.... And there's an old saying: "A Journey of a thousand miles begins with one step." My first step was into an abandoned shaft.' **2012** *Times* 10 Mar. 2 A Chinese proverb, crystallising the spirit of endeavour, says: 'A journey of a thousand miles must begin with a single step.' Today we'd add: 'But who says it's you who need do the walking?' ■ **beginnings and endings** 最初と最後

JOVE but laughs at lovers' perjury.
ジュピターは恋人たちの偽誓を笑ってすます。

（訳注：ジョーブとはジュピターであり、ローマ神話の最高神ユピテルの英語読みである。ギリシア神話ではゼウスに相当する。この神は天空を支配する全能神であるが、好色な神であり、結婚と離婚を繰り返し、また、浮気も繰り返していた。標題のことわざはこのことに関係がある。ジョーブの神からは多くの子供が生まれたが、このことは強力な神々や半神半人を生み出し、全宇宙や人間界の基盤を整えることとなった）

ジュピターは古代の神々の王で、好色で知られていた。†ヘシオドス『断章』124 (M-W)，ἐκ τοῦ δ'ὅρκον ἔθηκον ἀποίνιμον ἀνθρώποισι δ'νοσφιδίων ἔργων περὶ κύπριδος.「その時以来、彼（ゼウス）はアフロディーテの秘密の行為の中で立てられた誓いに対して男たちには罰を科すことはしなくなった」。ティブルス『エレジー』III. vi. 49 *Periuria ridet amantum Iuppiter*.「ジュピターは恋人たちの偽証を笑う」。a **1500** W. W. スキート『チョーサー及び他の作品集』(1897) 311 Your [lovers'] othes laste No lenger than the wordes ben ago! And god, and eke his sayntes, laughe also.「恋人たちの誓いは言った端から破られる。神や聖人たちも笑う」

□ *c***1550** tr. A. S. *Piccolomini's Lady Lucres* E4ᵛ Pacorus ... confesseth the faut asketh forgeuenes and ... ryghte well knewe he that Jupyter rather laughethe, then taketh angerlye the periuringe of louers. c **1595** SHAKESPEARE *Romeo & Juliet* II. ii. 92 At lovers' perjuries, They say Jove laughs. **1700** DRYDEN *Poems* (1958) IV. 1487 Love endures no Tie, And Jove but laughs at Lovers Perjury! **1922** *Evening Standard* 17 Oct 5 Perjury in the Divorce Court has been openly permitted to the upper classes for many years, following the maxim ... that 'Jove but laughs at lovers' perjury.' **1973** I. MURDOCH *Black Prince* III. 299 Zeus, they say, mocks lovers' oaths. ■ **love** 愛・恋愛

JUST 241

No one should be JUDGE in his own cause.
誰も自分の訴訟事件の判事になるべきではない。

†ラテン語で書かれた法律に関する格言。*Nemo debet esse iudex in propria causa.*
「誰も己の訴訟で判事になるべきではない」。1604 シェイクスピア『尺には尺を』V. i. 166
In this I'll be impartial; be you judge Of your own cause.「この裁判に私はかかわる
まい、自分への訴えを自分でさばくがいい」

□*c*1449 R. PECOCK *Repressor of Blaming of Clergy* (1860) II. 381 Noman oughte beiuge in his
owne cause which he hath anentis [against] his neighbour. **1775** WESLEY *Letter* 3 Nov. (1931) VI.
186 No man is a good judge in his own cause. I believe I am tolerably impartial. **1928** *Times* 22
Aug. 9. The principle that no judge could be a judge in his own case was generally accepted. The
chairman of a meeting was in a quasi-judicial capacity. **1981** *Daily Telegraph* 16 May 18 The
maxim that no one should be judge in his own cause. ■ **law and lawyers 法と法律家**

JUDGE not, that ye be not judged.
人を裁いてはならない、自分が裁かれないためである。

（訳注：that ye be not judged は現代英語に直すと、so that you may not be judged となり、「目的・意
図」を表す副詞節である。古い英語では本動詞は仮定法現在形が用いられ、be となっている。また、この場
合、ye〈汝ら〉は thou〈汝〉の複数形二人称主格である。*Ye are the salt of the earth.*〈汝らは地の塩な
り〉)

自分勝手な判断で他人をすぐに裁く人は逆に人から裁かれる。『マタイによる福音書』7
章1節（欽定訳聖書）Judge not, that ye be not judged.「裁いてはならない。裁かれな
いためである」を想起させる。

□**1481** CAXTON *Reynard* (1880) xxix. Deme[judge] ye noman, and ye shal not be demed. **1509**
H. WATSON *Ship of Fools* Hl Judge not but yf that ye wyl be judged. **1925** A. CLUTTONBROCK
Essays on Life x. The saying, 'Judge not, that ye be not judged,' is ... a statement of fact. Nothing
makes us dislike a man so much as the knowledge that he is always judging us and all men. **2001**
Washington Times 27 Nov. Al2 The purpose is neither to gloat, nor to deride nor to humiliate our
enemies and adversaries. Indeed, much wisdom and prudence is captured in the biblical injunction, 'Judge not, thatye be not judged.' ■ **reciprocity 相互扶助; tolerance 寛容・忍耐**

judge（動詞）⇒ You can't tell a BOOK by its cover.

June ⇒ A DRIPPING June sets all in tune.

Be JUST before you're generous.
気前よくおごる前に真っ当であれ。

借金を返済し、家族を養うことが先決であり、他人に気前よくおごるのはそれからであ
る。

□**1745** E. HAYWOOD *Female Spectator* II. VII. 35 There is, I think, an old saying, that we 'ought
to be just before we are generous'. **1780** SHERIDAN *School for Scandal* IV. i. Be just before you
are generous. **1834** MARRYAT *Peter Simple* I. xi. I owe every farthing of my money.... There's an
old proverb—be just before you're generous. **1908** *Spectator* 4 Apr. 529 A likeable man is tempted
to be generous before he is just. **1922** JOYCE *Ulysses* 521 Bloom—You had better hand over that
cash to me to take care of. Why pay more? Stephen—Be just before you are generous. ■ **fair
dealing 公正な取引**

242 JUSTICE

JUSTICE delayed is justice denied.
遅れた正義は正義の否定である。

現在では、警察が容疑者に不利な証拠があるか否かを調査しているあいだ、有罪として再勾留するか、もしくは無罪として保釈するかにかかわらず、容疑者を長期間とどめて置くことを非難する際によく使われる。遅延と正義の否定とを結びつける考えは古くからある（† 1215『マグナカルタ』To no man will we sell, or deny, or delay right or justice.「誰に対しても、権利や正義を売ったり、否定したり、遅らせることはできない」）。ウイリアム・ユワート・グラッドストン（1809-98）の言葉に由来すると考えられているが、この言い方は明らかに現代的なもので、主に米国で使用されている（1924年と1963年の用例参照）。

□**1924** Case of GOHMAN V. CITY OF ST. BERNARD 111 Ohio Street. 726, 737 This case should be classed as a leading case in support of the maxim that justice delayed is justice denied. **1963** M. L. KING '*Letter from Birmingham Jail*' 5 We must come to see with the distinguished jurist of yesterday that 'justice too long delayed is justice denied.' **1999** *Daily Nation* (*Nairobi*) 9 Dec. 6/1 As they say, justice delayed is justice denied, an expression that obtains especially in situations where a person may languish in remand prison for three years only to be found innocent of any charge. **2001** *Washington Times* 13 Dec. B1 The inscription on the front of the Alexandria Courthouse, next to the depiction of the tortoise and the hare, reads simply. 'Justice Delayed is Justice Denied.' That's the motto at the 'rocket docket,' the federal court known for speed, spies and a winning record for government prosecutors. **2014** *Spectator* 6 Dec. 11 [S]ome ... have been on bail for three years, their lives and careers on hold. As the old saying goes: justice delayed is justice denied. ■ **justice and injustice** 正義と不正

justify ⇒ The END justifies the means.

K

Why KEEP a dog and bark yourself?
犬を飼っていながら、なぜ飼い主のあなたが吠えたりするのか。

その仕事をさせるために他人を雇っておきながら自らがその仕事を行なうのは馬鹿げている。

☐ **1583** B. MELBANCKE *Philotimus* 119 It is smal reason you should kepe a dog, and barke your selfe. **1670** J. RAY *English Proverbs* 81 What? keep a dog and bark my self. That is, must I keep servants, and do my work my self. **1738** SWIFT *Polite Conversation* I. 17 'Good Miss, stir the Fire.' … 'Indeed your Ladyship could have stirr'd it much better.' … 'I won't keep a Dog and bark myself.' **1933** A. CHRISTIE *Thirteen at Dinner* xviii. Why keep a dog and bark yourself? **1999** S. PAWSON *Some by Fire* vii. 153 'I think you want me to start all over again at Edinburgh University and the Sorbonne, but you want me to volunteer because you daren't ask me yourself.' 'That's about it,' I admitted. 'Man with dog never has to bark.' ■ **employers and employees** 雇用者と被雇用者 ; **work** 仕事

KEEP a thing seven years and you'll always find a use for it.
物は 7 年とっておけ。そうすると必ず使い道が見つかる。

物を捨てないことのたんなる口実である。

☐ **1623** W. PAINTER *Palace of Pleasure* C5 Things of small value the old proverb say, Wise men seuen yeares will carefully vp lay. **1663** T. KILLIGREW *Parson's Wedding in Comedies & Tragedies* (1664) 100 According to the Proverb; Keep a thing seven years, and then if thou hast no use on't throw't away. **1816** SCOTT *Antiquary* II. vi. They say, keep a thing seven year, an' ye'll aye find a use for't. **1945** F. THOMPSON *Lark Rise* xx. 'I don't know that I've any use for it.' 'Use! Use! … Keep a thing seven years and you'll always find a use for it!' ■ **thrift** 質素倹約

KEEP no more cats than will catch mice.
ネズミを捕る猫以上の数の猫を飼うな。

どのような組織であっても、役に立つ人のみを雇用した方が賢明である。

☐ **1673** J. DARE *Counsellor Manners* ! xii. If thou hast a regard to Thrift, keep nomore Cats than will kill Mice. **1678** J. RAY *English Proverbs* (ed. 2) 350 I will keep no more cats then will catch mice (*i.e.* no more in family then will earn their living). *Somerset.* **1710** S. PALMER *Proverbs* 358 Keep no more Cats than will Catch Mice. Ecquipage and Attendance … must be agreeable to Character, Dignity and Fortune. **1910** R. KIPLING *Rewards & Fairies* 73 The King keeps no cats that don't catch mice. She must sail the seas, Master Dawe. ■ **efficiency and inefficiency** 能率と非能率 ; **work** 仕事

244 KEEP

KEEP your own fish-guts for your own sea-maws.
自分のカモメに与えるだけの塩辛はちゃんと確保しておけ。

類似のことわざに CHARITY begins at home.「慈善はまず家庭から」がある。

☐ **1721** J. KELLY *Scottish Proverbs* 118 Give your own Sea Maws [gulls] your own Fish Guts. If you have any Superfluities give them to your poor Relations, Friends, or Countrymen, rather than to others. **1816** SCOTT *Antiquary* I. xv. Ye ken my gudeman likes to ride the expresses himsel— we maun gie our ain fish-guts to our ain sea-maws. **1952** 'P. PIPER' *Death in Canongate* (1954) viii. 'Oh! it makes me a bit sick when you can be so liberal with anyone—' 'And not with you. That's what you are trying to say, isn't it?' 'I suppose so,' he said, and quoted lugubriously, '"Keep your ain fish guts for your ain sea maws."' ■ **charity** 慈善；**family** 家族・家系

KEEP your shop and your shop will keep you.
店をしっかり経営せよ。そうすれば店の方があなたを守ってくれる。

（訳注：「商い三年」）

米国の女優メイ・ウエスト（1892-1980）が1937年公開の映画『毎日が日曜日』の中でパロディ化している。I always say, keep a diary and some day it'll keep you.「いつも言っているの。日記をつけなさい、そうすればいつか日記を見ればあなた自身のことがつけてあるのがわかる」

☐ **1605** G. CHAPMAN et al. *Eastward Ho* A2ᵛ I ... garnished my shop ... with good wholsome thriftie sentences; As, 'Touchstone, keepe thy shopp, and thy shoppe will keepe thee.' **1712** ADDISON *Spectator* 14 Oct. Sir William Turner ... would say, Keep your Shop and your Shop will keep you. **1905** H. G. WELLS *Kipps* III. iii. A little bell jangled. 'Shop!' said Kipps. 'That's right Keep a shop and the shop'll keep you.' **1943** S. V. BENEÉT *Western Star* 1. 20 I keep my shop but my shop doth not keep me. Shall I give such chances [of making a fortune] the go-by and walk the roads? **1976** H. KEMELMAN *Wednesday Rabbi got Wet* vii. 'When I was home, Dad cared a lot more about the store than he did about me,' he said bitterly. She nodded.... 'That's because a store, if you take care of it, it takes care of you. Your father lives from that store, and your grandfather before him.' ■ **efficiency and inefficiency** 能率と非能率；**money** 金・金銭

keep ⇒ A man is known by the COMPANY he keeps; EXPERIENCE keeps a dear school; THREE may keep a secret, if two of them are dead; Put your TRUST in God, and keep your powder dry.

keeper ⇒ FINDERS keepers (losers weepers).

keeping ⇒ FINDINGS keepings.

key ⇒ A GOLDEN key can open any door.

kick ⇒ CORPORATIONS have neither bodies to be punished nor souls to be damned.

kid ⇒ The BLEATING of the kid excites the tiger,

kindness 245

What doesn't KILL you makes you stronger.
どんなに苦しくても死なない限り、人は強くなる。

† **1889** F. ニーチェ『偶像の黄昏』*Götzen-Dämmerung* Sprüche unde Pfeile 8 *Was mich nicht umbringt, macht mich starker.*「私を殺さないものは私をさらに強くする」

☐ **1997** *Journal of African Travel-Writing* ii-v. 56 A friend said to me once, when I was complaining about a difficult situation, 'What doesn't kill you, makes you stronger.' **2010** *London Review of Books* 25 Mar 10 Truly, in this game [politics], what doesn't kill you makes you stronger. **2015** *Times* 2 12 Jan. 3 Whereas once a bit of dirt was seen as good for stimulating the immune system ... modem, Western living conditions are too clean and provide too few opportunities to build resistance. The old adage 'what doesn't kill you makes you stronger' no longer seems in vogue. ■ **adversity** 逆境・苦難 ; **strength and weakness** 強弱

kill ⇒ It is the PACE that kills; It is not WORK that kills, but worry.

killed ⇒ CARE killed the cat; CURIOSITY killed the cat.

KILLING no murder.
命を奪うことは殺人には当たらない。

(訳注：言葉の意味だけから言えば、確かに、killとmurderは同じではない。killは最も一般的な語で、意図的、非意図的いずれの場合も可能である。人・病気・事故が主語となり、目的語は人・動植物いずれも可能である。それに対して、murderの場合、主語と目的語は人に限られ、計画的・意図的に殺害することを表わす。例えば、His father was killed in a traffic accident.〈彼の父親は交通事故で亡くなった〉のような文では、killedの代わりにmurderedを用いることはできない)

1657年の用例は、イングランド共和国の時代の護国卿であるO.クロムウエルを暗殺することが合法的で称賛に値することを主張し、暗殺を呼びかけるパンフレットのタイトル。

☐ **1657** SEXBY & TITUS (*title*) Killing noe murder. **1800** M. EDGEWORTH *Castle Rackrentp*. xliv. In Ireland, not only cowards, but the brave 'die many times before their death'. There killing is no murder. **1908** *Times Literary Supplement* 4 June 179 The exception is the share which he took in the conspiracy of Orsini against Napoleon III.... It was probably a case to which Holyoake would have applied the doctrine of 'killing no murder'. **1961** C. COCKBURN *View from West* vi. The British ... made, in England, propaganda out of the phrase—attributed to the Irish—'killing no murder', they were not foolish enough to take their own propaganda seriously. ■ **violence** 暴力

killing ⇒ There are more WAYS of killing a cat than choking it with cream; There are more WAYS of killing a dog than choking it with butter; There are more WAYS of killing a dog than hanging it.

kindness ⇒ Feed a DOG for three days and he will remember your kindness for three years ... ; With a SWEET tongue and kindness, you can drag an elephant by a hair.

246 KING

The KING can do no wrong.
国王は不正行為をなすことはできない。

時と場合により、king「王」が queen「女王」に変わる。†法律に関する格言 *Rex non potest peccare.*「王は間違ったことはできない」。*c* 1538 T. スターキー『ヘンリー 8 世統治下のイングランド』(EETS) 1. iv. Wyl you make a kyng to have no more powar then one of hys lordys? Hyt ys commynly sayd ... a kyng ys aboue hys lawys.「王が領主より権力を持たないようにするのがお望みか。よく言われるように、王は法律を超越しているのだぞ」

□*a* 1654 J. SELDEN *Table-Talk* (1689) 27 The King can do no wrong, that is no Process [action at law] can be granted against him. **1765** W. BLACKSTONE *Commentaries on Laws of England* 1. vii. The King can do no wrong.... The prerogative of the crown extends not to do any injury: it is created for the benefit of the people, and therefore cannot be exerted to their prejudice. **1888** C. M. YONGE *Beechcroft at Rockstone* II. xxii. 'So, Aunt Jane is your Pope.' 'No; she's the King that can do no wrong,' said Gillian, laughing. **1952** 'M. COST' *Hour Awaits* 191 It was very different with Augustus.... We had always expected that.... In his case, was it not rather a matter of the king can do no wrong. **1981** *Times* 28 July 14 The Queen [of Holland] has no power but some influence.... 'The Queen can do no wrong. The ministers are responsible.' ■ **rulers and ruled 支配者と被支配者**

A KING's chaff is worth more than other men's corn.
国王の籾殻は民の穀物以上の価値がある。

(訳注：chaffには「籾殻」以外にも「くず、がらくた」の意味もある。また、cornはその地域の主要作物を指している。アメリカ・カナダではトウモロコシ、イングランドでは大麦、スコットランドではカラスムギである)

この意味が1738年の用例で説明されている。類似のものには、**1612** T. シェルトン訳『セルバンデスのドン・キホーテ』I. IV. xii. A Kings crumme is more worth then a Lords loafe.「王様のパンくずは領主のパン 1 個以上の価値がある」がある。chaff「籾殻」を使った言い方はスコットランド生まれであると考えられる。

□*a*1628 J. CARMICHAELL *Proverbs in Scots* (1957) 101 The kings calf [chaff] is worth other mennis come. **1668** R. B. *Adagia Scotica* 33 Kings calf is worth otlier mens corn. **1738** *Gentleman's Mag.* VIII. 474 The King's chaff is worth more than other men's corn. This ... signifies that even the little perquisites, which attend the King's service, are more considerable than standing wages of private persons. **1788** BURNS 4tter 16 Aug. (1931) I. 245 The old Scots Proverb says well—'King's calf is better than ither folks' corn.' **1817** SCOTT *Rob Roy* III. vii. They say ... kings' chaff is better than otherfolk's corn, but I think that canna be said o' kings' soldiers, if they let themselves be beaten wi' a wheen [few] auld caries. **1957** *Times Literary Supplement* 13 Sept 552 A king's chaff is proverbially better than other men's corn. ■ **employers and employees 雇用者と被雇用者 ; value 価値**

king ⇒ A CAT may look at a king; In the COUNTRY of the blind, the one-eyed man isking; A PECK of March dust is worth a king's ransom.

kingdom ⇒ In the COUNTRY of the blind, the one-eyed man is king.

KISSING 247

KINGS have long arms.
王の腕は長い。

権力を持った支配者はその権力と影響力をはるか遠くの地にまで及ぼすことができる。†ギリシア語μακραὶτυράννων χεῖρες.「統治者の手は遠くまで届く」。オウィディウス『名婦の書簡』xvii. *An nescis longas regibus esse manus?*「王の手ははるか遠くまで届くことを知らないのか」

☐ 1539 R. TAVERNER tr. *Erasmus' Adages* A4ᵛ Kynges haue longe handes. They can brynge in men, they can pluck in thinges, though they be a great weye of. 1578 LYLY *Euphues* I. 221 Knowest thou not Euphues that kinges haue long armes, and rulers large reches? 1752 B. FRANKLIN *Poor Richard's Almanack* (Jan.) Kings haue long Arms, but misfortune longer. 1927 P. B. NOYES *Pallid Giant* iii. 'How will you insure Markham's safety if he takes refuge here?' ... 'Governments, proverbially, have long arms.' 1975 O. DUNNETT *Checkmate* V. x. 536 'I would ask you to be very careful ... in your doings when you return to Scotland. I have a long arm.' 'Monseigneur: you have no arm at all,' Lymond said, 'unless England allows you a sleeve for it'
■ justice and injustice 正義と不正 ; power 力・権力

kirtle ⇒ NEAR is my kirtle, but nearer is my smock.

kiss ⇒ An APPLE-PIE without some cheese is like a kiss without a squeeze.

There is always one who KISSES, and one who turns the cheek.
(積極的に) キスをしようとする人と (受身的に) 頬を差し出す人の両方のタイプがつねにいる。

男女の関係においては、常にどちらか一方がもう片方よりも積極的で情熱的である。†フランス語 *Il y a toujours l'un qui baise, et l'autre qui tourne la joue.*「キスをする人と頬を差し出す人がつねにいる」(英訳が世に出回る前に明らかにフランス語の原文が米国で知られていた。このことは、『ハーパーズ・マンスリー』(1870) に掲載された E. B. コブ「ダリントン嬢は何を見たのか」の中ですでにこのことわざが引用されていることからも明らかである。

☐ 1903 G. B. SHAW *Man and Superman* 40 Oh, I know you dont care very much about Tavy. But there is always one who kisses and one who only allows the kiss. Tavy will kiss; and you will only turn the cheek. And you will throw him over if anybody better turns up. 1933 J. GALSWORTHY *Over the River* 267 'In your experience, sir, are the feelings of lovers towards each other ever the same? ... You know the French proverb as to there being always one who kisses and the other who offers the cheek to the kiss?' 1951 N. MONSARRAT *Cruel Sea* 274 With calm despair, he stirred himself to sum up what was in his mind, what Was In his life ... Presently he muttered, aloud: *'Il y en a toujours l'un qui baise, et l'un qui tourne la joue.'* 2002 M. BYWATER in *Independent* on Sunday 3 Nov. (online) The French have it that there is always one who kisses,one who turns the cheek; but things change where the heart is concerned, and there's no guarantee that because you began as cheek-turner you may not end up as the victim of an adamant devotion. ■ love, blighted くじかれた愛

KISSING goes by favour.
キスをするのは好意からである。

誰に恩恵を授けるべきかを決定する際には、受取人の利益よりも当事者の個人的な感情

248　kissing

が影響を与える (1721 年の用例参照)。しかし、実際にキスをする場合には、favourが「好意」と「容貌」とに両義的になるように言葉遊び (駄洒落) が意図されている可能性もある。

□ **1616** T. DRAXE *Adages* 62 Kissing commeth by fauour. **1621** BURTON *Anatomy of Melancholy* II. iii. Offices are not alwaies given … for worth. *[note]* Kissing goes by Favour. **1721** J. KELLY *Scottish Proverbs* 225 Kissing goes by Favour. Men shew Regard, or do Service, to People as they affect. **1880** BLACKMORE *Mary Anerley* II. iii. 'I should like … to give you one kiss, Insie.' … Before he could give reason in favour of a privilege which goes proverbially by favour, the young maid was gone. **1929** 'L. THAYER' *Dead Man's Shoes* i. Kissing goes by favour all along the line. **1976** K. BONFIGLIOLI *Something Nasty in Woodshed* xii. Tell you what, Jock; you forget to mention hot buttered crumpets to Mrs Mortdecai and I'll forget to mention about you pinching her caviare. Kissing goes by favour, you know. ■ **bribery and corruption** 賄賂と腐敗

kissing ⇒ When the GORSE is out of bloom, kissing's out of fashion.

kitchen ⇒ If you don't like the HEAT, get out of the kitchen.

kitten ⇒ WANTON kittens make sober cats.

knees ⇒ BETTER to die on your feet than live on your knees.

knew ⇒ If YOUTH knew, if age could.

knock ⇒ OPPORTUNITY never knocks twice at any man's door.

To KNOW all is to forgive all.
すべてを知ることはすべてを許すことである。

† **1807** アンヌ・ルイーズ・ジェルメーヌ・ド・スタール『コリンヌ』III. xviii. v. *Tout comprendre rend très-indulgent.*「すべてを理解するととても寛大になる」。**1908** E. テリー『我が人生の物語』116 I had taken a course for which all blamed me, perhaps because they did not know enough to pardon enough—*savoir tout c'est tout pardonner.*「私はその時点ではすでにある処置を講じてしまっていたが、それに対して皆非難轟々であった。しかし、それは、彼らがその処置について十分に知らなかったために許せなかったからに他ならない。フランスのことわざに「すべてを知ることはすべてを許すことである」とある」

□ **1864** R. H. HORNE *Prometheus the Fire-Bringer* 48 To know all, is to forgive. **1952** K. FULLER *Silken Cord* xv. After all, to know all is to forgive all, as my poor dear father used to say. **1974** 'H. CARMICHAEL' Most Deadly Hate xviii. 'They say to know all is to forgive all,' Piper said. 'Except the killing of Arthur Harlow.' ■ **forgiveness** 許し・寛容; **tolerance** 寛容・忍耐

You should KNOW a man seven years before you stir his fire.
知り合ってから 7 年は経たないとその人の家の炉床の火をかき回すことはできない。

このことわざの合理的な理由は、よそ様の家の炉床の火をかき回すようななれなれしい

行為はその家でくつろいでいるからこそできるというものである。相手のことをよく知らないうちにそのようなことをしたりすることは失礼にあたる。

□ **1803** C. DIBDIN *Professional Life* I. p. xi. It is a well-meant saying, that you should know a man seven years before you stir his fire; or, in other words, before you venture at too much familiarity. **1904** V. S. LEAN *Collectanea* IV. 204 You may poke a man's fire after you've known him seven years, but not before. **1942** A. THIRKELL *Marling Hall* iii. 'Let me get you another drink,' said David, taking the glass. 'I know one ought to know people seven years to poke their fires, but I believe it's less for cocktails.' **1945** M. SARSFIELD *Green December Fills Graveyard* iv. 35 'I haven't known you ten years, or whatever the period is, but I'm going to poke your fire.' ■ **familiarity** 慣れ親しみ

What you don't KNOW can't hurt you.
知らないでおれば傷つかないですむ。

やっかいな質問をさせないようにするときによく使われる。「知らないでおれば傷つく」と述べている 2001 年の用例はこれとは逆の考えを示している。類似の発想のことわざとして、Where IGNORANCE is bliss, 'tis folly to be wise.「知らないことが幸福な場合、知ることは愚かである」が挙げられる。

□ **1576** G. PETTIE *Petit Palace* 168 Why should I seeke to take him in it? ... So long as I know it not, it hurteth mee not. **1908** E. WALTER *Easiest Way* III. 66 What a fellow doesn't know doesn't hurt him, and he'll love you just the same. **1979** 'S. WOODS' *This Fatal Writ* 54 'No, this is interesting.... I didn't know—' 'What you don't know can't hurt you,' said Maitland. **1992** A. LAMBERT *Rather English Marriage* (1993) vi. 115 Everyone's entitled to their privacy and what you don't know can't hurt you. **2001** *Times* 23 Nov. 20 A little ignorance can go a long way. But what you don't know will always hurt you. Cleverness is the saving grace of our humanity. ■ **ignorance** 無知・無学

KNOW thyself.
汝自身を知れ。

†ギリシア語 γνῶθι σαυτόν (or σεαυτόν) は、紀元前 6 世紀にデルフォイのアポロ神殿に刻まれたモットーで、古代の作家たちに引用されている（ソロンの言葉として紹介している作家もいる）。特にパウサニアス『ギリシア案内記』10. 24. 1 ならびにユウェナリス『風刺詩集』xi 参照。ラテン語 *Nosce te ipsum*.「汝自身を知れ」

□ **1387** J. TREVISA tr. *Higden's Polychronicon*(1665) I. 241 While the cherle smoot the victor, he schulde ofte seie to hym in this manere: ... Knowe thyself. **1545** R. ASCHAM *Toxophilus* II. 36 Knowe thy selfe: that is to saye, leame to knowe what thou arte able, fitte and apt vnto, and folowe that. **1732** POPE *Essay on Man* II. 1 Know then thyself, presume not God to scan; The proper study of Mankind is Man. **1849** BULWER-LYTION *Caxtons* III. XVI. x. 'Know thyself,' said the old philosophy. 'Improve thyself,' saith the new. **2002** *Washington Times* 7 Feb. A21 The self-esteem movement is based on simple-minded shibboleths such as 'Love thyself,' rather than 'Know thyself.' ■ **human nature** 人間性 ; **wisdom** 賢明・知恵

You never KNOW what you can do till you try.
やってみるまで自分に何ができるのかということは分からない。

人は、自分はこんなことまでできるのかと我ながら驚くこともある。とにかく試しにやってみなさいという勧めの言葉。

□ **1818** COBBETT *Year's Residence in USA* II. vi. A man knows not what he can do 'till he tries.

250 know

1890 M. WILLIAMS *Leaves of Life* i. xiii. On hearing the verdict he ... shouted out 'I told you so! You never know what you can do till you try'. **1968** D. FRANCIS *Forfeit* xiv. 'Ty, you aren't fit to drive.' 'Never know what you can do till you try.' ■ **boldness 大胆さ**

know ⇒ BETTER the devil you know than the devil you don't know; The FROG in the well knows nothing of the sea; One HALF of the world does not know how the other half lives; The HUSBAND is always the last to know; Come LIVE with me and you'll know me; MORE people know Tom Fool than Tom Fool knows; NECESSITY knows no law; It TAKES one to know one; It's not WHAT you know, it's who you know; It is a WISE child that knows its own father; ⇒ KNEW; KNOWN.

knoweth ⇒ The FAT man knoweth not what the lean thinketh.

KNOWLEDGE is power.
知識は力である。

形式上は MONEY is power.「金は力である」と類似しており、意味上は『箴言』24章5節（欽定訳聖書）A man of knowledge increaseth strength.「知識ある者は力が増す」と類似している。†**1597** F. ベーコン『異端の論について』x. *Nam et ipsa scientia potestas est.*「知識はそれ自体が力である」

□**1598** in *Bacon Essays* 27ᵛ Knowledge it selfe is a power whereby he [God] knoweth. **1806** B. RUSH *Letter* 25 Nov. (i951) II. 935 The well-known aphorism that 'knowledge is power.' **1853** BULWER-LYTTON *My Novel* I. 11. iii. He ... said half aloud, —'Well, knowledge is power!' **2014** *New Scientist* 25 Oct. 35 By establishing a formal concept of time you know when to expect seasonal events, such as the return of salmon to the local rivers. And knowledge is power. ■ **power 力・権力 ; wisdom 賢明・知恵**

knowledge ⇒ A LITTLE knowledge is a dangerous thing.

known ⇒ A CARPENTER is known by his chips; A man is known by the COMPANY he keeps; The TREE is known by its fruit.

Who KNOWS most, speaks least.
最も多く知る者は最も語らない。

□**1666** G. TORRIANO *Italian Proverbs* 189 Who knows most, speaks least. **1996** P. LOVESEY *Bloodhounds* xxi. 182 'Crafty old sod,' said Mr. Musgrave.... 'What's the old saying? "Who knows most, speaks least."' ■ **speech and silence 発言と沈黙**

The KUMARA does not speak of its own sweetness.
クマラはおのれの甘さを語らない。

マオリ族のことわざで、自画自賛に対する警告として使われる。クマラは（ニュージーランドの）さつまいものことである。

□**2001** *He Hinatore Ki Te Ao Maori A Glimpse into Maori World* on *www.justice.govt.nz* Self-praising is an undesirable trait in traditional Maori society. It is synonymous with the expression 'kaore te kumara e korero mo tona mangaroa—a kumara does not talkabout its own sweetness'

ie, self-praise is no recommendation. **2003** speech in New Zealand Parliament 5 Mar. on *www.hansard.parliament.govt.nz* I tell Mr Cunliffe that there is an old saying in Maoridom: 'The kumara never tells you how sweet it is.' ... [I]f one is really so good, one does not need to tell the nation, the nation will tell one. But the nation is not saying that **2004** weblog on *www.publicaddress.net* 24 Dec. Now, Arihia would kick me if she knew I was writing this. Kaore te kumara e korero mo tona ake reka—it is not for the kumara to peak of its own sweetness, after all. So I thought I'd give you a few tasting notes. She's a stellar person, a scholar and mentor without match. **2006** 'What is Maori Patient-Centred Medicine for Pakeha GPs?' on *www.bpac.org.nz* Oct. GPs that use their expertise for the good of others, show a sense of humility and are not arrogant about their position, gain particular respect. 'The kumara does not speak of its own sweetness.'
■ **boasting** 自慢

L

The LABOURER is worthy of his hire.
働く者が報酬を受けるのは当然である。

人はその仕事ぶりに応じて公正な報酬を得るべきである。『ルカによる福音書』10章7節（欽定訳聖書）The labourer is worthy of his hire.「働く者が報酬を受けるのは当然である」

□*c*1390 CHAUCER *Summoner's Tale* I. 1973 The hye God, that al this world hath wroght, eith that the orkman worthy is his hyre. **1580** J. BARET *Alveary* D697 Digna canis pabulo.... A Prouerbe declaring that the laborer is worthie of his hire: it is taken as well of the labour of the mind, as of the bodie. **1824** SCOTT *St Ronan's Well* I. x. Your service will not be altogether gratuitous, my old friend—the labourer is worthy of his hire. **1980** *Times* 4 Mar. 7 Forget haggling.... The labourer is worthy of his hire. **2001** R. HILL *Dialogues of Dead* ii. 11 Penn had no difficulty squaring his assertion that the labourer was worthy his hire with using Dee as his unpaid research assistant, but the librarian never complained. ■ **employers and employees** 雇用者と被雇用者; **money** 金・金銭; **work** 仕事

ladder ⇒ CROSSES are ladders that lead to heaven.

lady ⇒ FAINT heart never won fair lady; The OPERA isn't over till the fat lady sings.

lamb ⇒ The BLEATING of the kid excites the tiger; GOD tempers the wind to the shorn lamb; One might as well be HANGED for a sheep as a lamb; MARCH comes in like a lion, and goes out like a lamb.

Lancashire ⇒ What MANCHESTER says today, the rest of England says tomorrow.

Every LAND has its own law.
どの国にもその国独自の法律がある。

□*a*1628 J. CARMICHAELL *Proverbs in Scots* no. 469 Everie land hes the laich. **1721** J. KELLY *Scottish Proverbs* 92 Everyland hath its own Laugh, and every Com its own Caff [chaff]. Every Country hath its own Laws, Customs, and Usages. **1916** *British Weekly* 2 Nov. 84 'Every land', says the old Scottish proverb, 'has its ain lauch.' And every class has its own mode of thought and expression. ■ **idiosyncrasy** 特異性・性癖; **national characteristics** 国民性

land ⇒ You BUY land, you buy stones; LEARNING is better than house and land.

lane ⇒ It is a LONG lane that has no turning.

language ⇒ A NATION without a language is a nation without a heart.

large ⇒ A GREAT book is a great evil; LITTLE pitchers have large ears.

lark ⇒ If the SKY falls we shall catch larks.

The LAST drop makes the cup run over.
最後の一滴でコップから水がこぼれる。
（訳注：いかに些少のものでも限度を過すと破滅をもたらす。2つ下にある The last straw breaks the camel's back.「最後のわら1本でらくだの背骨が折れる」のことわざに等しい）

1655年の用例におけることわざと意味が似ている。

□**1655** T. FULLER *Church Hist. Britain* XI. ii. When the Cup is brim full before, the last (though least) superadded drop is charged alone to be the cause of all the running over. **1855** H. G. BOHN *Hand-Book of Proverbs* 509 The last drop makes the cup run over. **1876** J. PAYN *Halves* I. x. An application of her brother-in-law for a five-pound note ... was the last drop that caused Mrs. Raeburn's cup of bitterness to overflow. **2002** R. MARGGRAF- TURLEY *Writing Essays* 77 Be careful not to go overboard, though ... Use your discretion. Remember, the last drop makes the cup run over! ■ **excess** 過剰・過度

LAST in, first out.
最初に入った者が最初に出る。

時折、頭文字語の *LIFO*（ライフォ）として使われる。この原則が実施される分野としては、棚卸し、コンピューターメモリー、経理、銀行業務、職員の雇用・解雇などがある。最後の事例では、最後に雇われた者が最初に解雇される（2012年の用例参照）。選別基準は Last hired, first fired.「最後に雇われた者が最初に解雇される」である。

□**1914** *Popular Mechanics* Jan. 173 (*advertisement*) Last in, first out ... Whether you are packing up for a week or a weekend, the big red tin of SMOOTHEST TOBACCO is a mighty good companion to take along. **1987** *Chicago Tribune* 4 Oct (online) As the last hired and first fired, women miners have seen their number fall to about 2,000. **2012** *www.hrmagazine.co.uk* 30 Aug. (*heading*) 'Last in, first out' job fear can dissuade people from moving job. ■ **employers and employees** 雇用者と被雇用者

The LAST straw breaks the camel's back.
最後のわら1本でらくだの背骨が折れる。
（訳注：the last ［final］straw だけでも「我慢の限界を超えるできごと」という慣用句がある）

たとえ小さな荷物、問題でも度を超すと大きな被害を引き起こすことになる。特に the last straw という名詞句においては何かを暗示するような比喩となっている。

□**1655** J. BRAMHALL *Defence of True Liberty of Human Actions* 54 It is the last feather may be said to break an Horses back. **1793** in *Publications of Colonial Society of Massachusetts* (1954) XXXVI. 298 It is certainly true that the last feather will sinkthe camel. **1848** DICKENS *Dombey & Son* ii. As the last straw breaks the laden camel's back, this piece of underground information crushed the sinking spirits of Mr. Dombey. **1876** I. BANKS *Manchester Man* III. xv. The last straw breaks the camel's back. **1983** R. BARNARD *Case of Missing Bronte* iii. 'This is the picture, as far

254 LAST

as we have it,' he said, ... a sigh in his voice that suggested that the visit of the Prime Minister was the final straw that might break the camel's back of his professional equilibrium. ■ **excess** 過剰・過度

When the LAST tree is cut down, the last fish eaten, and the last stream poisoned, you will realize that you cannot eat money.
最後の木が切り倒され、最後の魚が食べられ、そして最後の川が汚染された時に人ははじめて金は食べられないことに気づく。

アメリカ先住民のことわざ。

☐ **1983** H. WASSERMAN *America Born and Reborn* 277 'When you have polluted the last river,' goes an Osage saying, 'when you have caught the very last fish, and when you have cut down the very last tree, it is too bad that then, and only then, will you realize that you can not eat all your money in the bank. **1995** *New York Times* 17 Aug. (online) 'A Modest Step to Save the Fish' ... brings to mind a prophecy of the Cree Indians: 'When the last tree is cut down, the last fish eaten and the last stream poisoned, you will realize that you cannot eat money.' **2006** L. S. JOUBERT *Scorched: South Africa's Changing Climate* 203 Once the last tree is cut and the last river poisoned, you will find that you cannot eat your money. **2007** *Sun2Surf* 5 Feb. (online) But that may be wishful thinking in the light of the Cree Indian prophecy that 'only after the last tree has been cut down, the last river poisoned, the last fish caught, will man find that money cannot be eaten'. ■ **environment** 環境 ; **money** 金・金銭

last（名詞）⇒ Let the COBBLER stick to his last; The COBBLER to his last and the gunner to his linstock.

last ⇒（形容詞）There are no BIRDS in last year's nest; The HUSBAND is always the last to know; The THIRD time pays for all;（副詞）He LAUGHS best who laughs last; He who LAUGHS last, laughs longest.

lasting ⇒ FIRST impressions are the most lasting.

late ⇒（形容詞）The BARLY man never borrows from the late man; It is NEVER too late to learn; It is NEVER too late to mend; It is too late to shut the STABLE-door after the horse has bolted;（副詞）BETTER late than never.

LAUGH and the world laughs with you; weep and you weep alone.
笑えば周りの人も一緒に笑い、泣けば 1 人で泣くことになる。

ホラティウス『詩について』101 *Ut ridentibus arrident, itajlentibus adsunt humani voltus.*「人は笑っている人を見ると笑い、泣いている人を見るとつられて泣いてしまう」の中で表現されている感情を一部変更したもの。†『ローマの信徒への手紙』12章15節（欽定訳聖書）Rejoice with them that do rejoice, and weep with them that weep.「喜んでいる者と共に喜べ、そして嘆いている者と共に悲しめ」

☐ **1883** E. W. WILCOX in *Sun* (New York) 25 Feb. 3 Laugh, and the world laughs with you; Weep, and you weep alone. For the sad old earth must borrow its mirth, But has trouble enough of its own. **1907** 'O. HENRY' *Trimmed Lamp* 211 Laugh, and the world laughs with you; weep, and

LAUGHTER   255

they give you the laugh. **1912** 'SAKI' *Chronicle of Clovis* 127 The proverb 'Weep and you weep alone,' broke down as badly on application as most of its kind. **1997** *Oldie* Aug. 27 Laugh, said the little clown, and the world laughs with you. Cry but don't Jet anyone catch you at it! **2001** R. HILL *Dialogues of Dead* xviii. 153 'Right joker, this Wordman, ain't he? What's it they say? Laugh and the world laughs with you.' ■ **merriment** 談笑・陽気な賑わい

laugh ⇒ JOVE but laughs at lovers' perjury; LOVE laughs at locksmiths.

He LAUGHS best who laughs last.
最後に笑う者が最もよく笑う。

(訳注：he ＝「〈関係節を伴って〉…する者は誰でも〈性別は問わない〉」。*He who* has all the gold makes all the rules.〈金をすべて持つ者が法をすべて支配する〉。勝つまでは、まだ勝負は終わってはいない。早まって喜んではならない)

どのような状況であれ、最後に勝った者こそが真の勝者である。1822年の用例における「フランス語のことわざ」とは *Rira bien qui rira le dernier.*「最後に笑う者が最もよく笑う」である。

□*c1607* *Christmas Prince* (1923) 109 Hee laugheth best that laugheth to the end. **1715** VANBRUGH *Country House* II. V. Does she play her jests upon me too! —but mum, he laughs best that laughs last. **1822** SCOTT *Peveril* IV. Iii. Your Grace knows the French proverb,'He laughs best who laughs last.' **1980** J. LINSSEN *Yellow Pages* iii. The mark of greatness is survival. He laughs best who laughs last. **1996** *Washington Post* 15 Jan. C2 This purchase ... was wildly out of character and the source of endless amusement to those who know me best ... Well, in the immortal words of Sir John Vanbrugh (1664-1726) : He laughs best who laughs last. ■ **revenge** 復讐 ; **winners and losers** 勝者と敗者

He who LAUGHS last, laughs longest.
最後に笑う者が一番長く笑う。

上のことわざの現代版である。

□**1912** J. MASEFIELD *Widow in Bye Street* IV. 66 In this life he laughs longest who laughs last. **1943** J. LODWICK *Running to Paradise* xxx. He who laughs last laughs longest, and in another four days I was able to look at my mug in the mirror without wincing. **1951** M. DE LA ROCHE *Renny's Daughter* ix. 'We'll see. He who laughs last, laughs ... 'So worked up was Eugene Clapperton that he could not recall the last word of the proverb. ■ **revenge** 復讐 ; **winners and losers** 勝者と敗者

LAUGHTER is the best medicine.
笑いは最良の薬。

笑いが健康に良いという考えは古くからある。『箴言』17章22節 (欽定訳聖書) A merry heart doeth good like a medicine: but a broken spirit drieth the bones.「心の楽しみは良い薬である。魂の憂いは骨を枯らす」。もっと古い英語の表現としては laugh and be fat「笑って太れ」(1596年から使われている) と laugh and be well「笑って健康になれ」(1737年)がある。Laughter, the Best Medicine「笑いこそ最良の薬」は『リーダーズダイジェスト』に掲載されている長期の連載ジョーク集のタイトルになっている。 † The best DOCTORS are Dr Diet, Dr Quiet, and Dr Merryman.「最高の医者は、ドクター食事、ドクター安静、ドクター快活である」

256　LAW

□**1992** MIEDER *Dict. American Proverbs* 362 Laughter is the best medicine. **2002** *Washington Post* 21 Jan. C10 Who could argue with the sage advice that an ounce of prevention is worth a pound of cure, ... or laughter is the best medicine? **2014** *Times of India* 11 Nov. (online) Laughter is the best medicine, is an age-old saying, and about 10,000 laughter clubs in India are a testimony to the fact that the therapy works. ■ **doctors 医者 ; health 健康 ; merriment 談笑・陽気な賑わい**

One LAW for the rich and another for the poor.
金持ち用の法律と貧乏人用と別々の法律がある。

(訳注：the rich や the poor の the は「…な人々」の意。そのような人々を包括的に表現する。*The strong must help the* weak.〈強者は弱者を助けなければならない〉)

賄賂を贈ったり、有能な弁護士を雇う余裕のない者は厳しい罰を受け、一方、裕福な者は罰を逃れることができる。こうした不正が生じる状況を述べたもの。

□**1830** MARRYAT *King's Own* I. xi. Is there nothing smuggled besides gin? Now, if the husbands and fathers of these ladies,—those who have themselves enacted the laws,—wink at their infringement, why should not others do so? ... There cannot be one law for the rich and another for the poor. **1944** A. THIRKELL *Headmistress* iv. 'You want one law for the people you think are rich and another law for the people you think are poor,' I said. 'Let me advise you to find out which are which before you make a fool of yourself.' **2001** *Spectator* 29 Dec. 48 If he gets community service and a suspended sentence the hustlers will be out in force screaming the old 'one law for the rich, another for the poor' chestnut. ■ **justice and injustice 正義と不正 ; law and lawyers 法と法律家**

law ⇒ HARD cases make bad law; IGNORANCE of the law is no excuse for breaking it; Every LAND has its own law; NECESSITY knows no law; NEW lords, new laws; POSSESSION is nine points of the law; SELF-preservation is the first law of nature.

The more LAWS, the more thieves and bandits.
法律が増えれば増えるほど、泥棒と盗賊が増える。

(訳注：「the 比較級，the 比較級」＝「…すればするほどますます…だ」。*The more* she thought about it, *the more* depressed she became.〈彼女はそのことを考えれば考えるほど、ますます落ち込んだ〉)

道教の始祖・老子（紀元前604頃-531頃）の言葉とされる。The more laws and orders are made prominent, The more thieves and bandits there will be.「法律と命令が際立てば際立つほど、より多くの泥棒と盗賊が生まれる」(*Tao-te Ching* lvii. in Wmg-Tsit Chan (ed.)『中国哲学原典』(1963) 166。†アルケシラオス（紀元前3世紀）：*Οπου νόμοι πλεῖοτοι, ἐκεῖ καὶ ἀδικίαν εἶναι μεγίδτην (ἔλεγε)* (ストバイオス『精華集』xliii. 91)；タキトゥス『年代記』iii. 27 *Corrupdssima republica plurimae leges*.「国が腐敗すればするほど、多くの法律が必要となる」

□**1573** J. SANFORDE *Garden of Pleasure* 4 Where there are many lawes, there be also or else haue ben many vices. *c* **1620** MIDDLETON & ROWLEY *World Tost at Tennis* (Works ed. Bullen VII. 176) The more laws you make The more knaves thrive by't. **1667** MILTON *Paradise Lost* xii. 283 So many Laws argue so many sins Among them. **1732** T. FULLER *Gnomologia* no. 4663 The more Laws the more offenders. **1766** O. GOLDSMITH *Vicar of Wakefield* xxvii. The multitude of laws produce new vices, and new vices call for fresh restraints. **2002** *Times* 19 Mar. 30 Citing the ancient Chinese Lao-tse's dictum, the more laws, the more thieves and bandits, Norberg insists that 'the commonest way of corrupting a nation through and through is by stipulating permits

LEAD 257

and controls for production, for imports, for exports and investments'. ■ **honesty and dishonesty** 正直と不正直; **law and lawyers** 法と法律家

A man who is his own LAWYER has a fool for his client.
自分が自分の弁護士である人は、依頼人が愚か者である。

自分自身で訴訟を行なう(すなわち、本人訴訟をする)ことへの警告。

☐**1809** *Port Folio* (Philadelphia) Aug; 132 He who is always his own counseller will often have a fool for his client. **1850** I. HUNT *Autobiography* II. xi. The proprietor of the Morning Chronicle pleaded his own cause, an occasion in which a man is said to have 'a fool for his client'. **1911** *British Weekly* 21 Dec. 386 There is a popular impression, for which there is a good deal to be said, that a man who is his own lawyer has a fool for his client. **1975** D. BAGLEY *Snow Tiger* xiii. You must have heard the saying that the man who argues his own case has a fool for a lawyer. **2002** *Spectator* 30 Mar. 35 The man who is his own lawyer has a fool for a client, and that goes double for retired law lecturers from Newcastle Polytechnic. ■ **law and lawyers** 法と法律家

lawyer ⇒ The DEVIL makes his Christmas pies of lawyers' tongues and clerks' fingers.

lay ⇒ It is easier to RAISE the Devil than to lay him.

LAY-OVERS for meddlers.
お前には関係ないことだ。いちいち詮索しないでよろしい。

生意気な、あるいは詮索好きな子供などに対する叱り。主にイングランド北部と米国の表現である。lay-oversはしつこい奴へのしっぺ返しのことで、layersまたはlayorsと短縮される(ただし1854年の用例も参照)。† **1699** B. E. *New Dict. Canting Crew* s.v. *Lare-Over*, said when the true name of the thing must (in decency) be concealed. 「事物の本質を(体面上)隠さねばならない場合に用いられる」

☐**1785** F. GROSE *Classical Dict. Vulgar Tongue* s.v. *Lareovers, Lareovers for medlers, an answer frequently given to children* ... as a rebuke for their impertinent curiosity. **1854** A. B. BAKER *Glossary of Northamptonshire Words & Phrases* I. 389 *Lay-o'ers-for-meddlers*, ... a contraction of lay-overs, i.e. things laid over, covered up, or protected from meddlers. **1882** NODAL & MILNER *Glossary of Lancashire Dialect* 179 'What have yo' getten i' that bag?' 'Layers-for-meddlers-does ta want to know?' **1936** M. MITCHELL *Gone with Wind* xxxii. When they asked who was going to lend the money she said: 'Layovers catch meddlers,' so archly they all laughed. **1945** B. MILLHAUSER *Whatever goes Up* xv. 'Know his address?' 'I certainly do. Ninety-seven Gramercy Park North, New York.' She closed the door firmly. 'Layovers for meddlers,' she muttered. ■ **busybodies** おせっかい屋; **curiosity** 詮索好き・好奇心

lazy ⇒ LONG and lazy, little and loud.

If you are not the LEAD dog, the view never changes.
犬ぞりのリーダー犬にならない限り、目の前の景色は変わらない。

犬ぞりについてのカナダのことわざ。リーダーでないなら、目の前しか見ることができない。

☐**1980** P. DICKSON *Official Explanations* 202 The scenery only changes for the lead dog. **1990** *Reauthorization of the Export Administration Act*: Hearings before the Subcommittee on Interna-

258 lead

tional Finance and Monetary Policy (United States Congress) (online) None of us should relish the hardly comic prospect of the US crying from the back of the cocom pack, 'Follow me.' As any dog-sledder will tell you, if you're not the lead dog, the scene never changes. **1999** *Discount Store News* 22 Feb. (online) He makes his point perfectly clear with a distinctly Canadian metaphor. 'If you're not the lead dog of a sled, the view never changes.' 2007 *New York Times* 11 Feb. (online) But Mr. Rau said action in Suffolk to stem scrap thefts could be a national model. 'If you are not the lead dog, the view is always the same,' he said. 'Let's take the problem on.' ■ **ambition** 野心・野望

lead ⇒ When the BLIND lead the blind, both shall fall into the ditch; CROSSES are ladders that lead to heaven; All ROADS lead to Rome.

leak ⇒ LITTLE leaks sink the ship.

lean ⇒ The FAT man knoweth not what the lean thinketh.

leap ⇒ LOOK before you leap.

learn ⇒ LIVE and learn; It is NEVER too late to learn; NEVER too old to learn; We must learn to WALK before we can run; Don't go near the WATER until you learn how to swim.

LEARNING is better than house and land.
学問は家や土地に勝る。

> 十分な教育は不動産を所有するよりも私たちを貧困から救ってくれる。

□**1773** O. GARRICK in Goldsmith *She stoops to Conquer* A3ᵛ When ign'rance enters, folly is at hand; Learning is better far than house and land. **1800** M. EDGEWORTH *Castle Rackrent* 19 I ... thanked my stars I was not born a gentleman to so much toil and trouble—but Sir Murtagh took me up short with his old proverb, 'learning is better than house or land.' **1859** J. R. PLANCHÉ *Love & Fortune* 8 'Learning is better than house and land.' A fact that I never could understand. **1939** *Daily Mall* (Hagerstown, Maryland) 16 Mar. 19 (advertisement) Learning is better than house and land. And learning about the offers among the Classified Ads will show you where to save money in buying house and land. ■ **learning** 学問・学び ; **property** 財産

learning ⇒ A LITTLE knowledge is a dangerous thing; There is no ROYAL road to learning.

LEAST said, soonest mended.
口数が最も少なければ、最も早く訂正できる。

> 侮辱されたり損傷を受けたりした際はできるだけ何も言わないのが一番良い。なぜなら非難と言い訳は状況を悪化させるだけだからである。

□*c***1460** in W. C. HAZLllT *Remains of Early Popular Poetry* (1864) III. 169 Who sayth lytell he is wyse ... And fewe wordes are soone amend. **1555** J. HEYWOOD *Two Hundred Epigrams* no. 169 Lyttle sayde, soone amended. *a* **1641** D. FERGUSSON *Scottish Proverbs* (STS) no. 946 Littl said is soon mended. **1776** T. COGAN *John Buncle, Junior* I. vi. Mum's the word; least said ls soonest mended. **1818** SCOTT *Heart of Midlothian* I. vi. A fine preaching has he been at the night ... but maybe least said is sunest mended. **1960** MISS READ *Fresh from Country* xii. A quiet word ...

should ... stop any further tale-bearing, and I really think it's a case of 'least said, soonest mended.' **1992** A. LAMBERT *Rather English Marriage* (1993) xvii. 289 He was tempted to go down and confront her, ... but he knew he was in the wrong. Least said, soonest mended: no good creating a fuss now. ■ discretion 思慮分別 ; speech and silence 発言と沈黙 ; tact 機転

least ⇒ IDLE people have the least leisure; Who KNOWS most, speaks least

There is nothing like LEATHER.
革に勝るものはない。

(訳注：市の防備は革に限ると革屋が言ったというイソップ物語に由来する。「手前味噌」)

1692年の用例で言及されているイソップ物語は、適切かどうかとは関係なく、人は限られた個人的経験に照らして問題の解決を導こうとすることを示している。市の防備のためにはどの材質が最も良いのかという議論になった時、職人たちは各々自分の馴染みの材質を推薦する。例えば、石工は石の壁を、船大工は木製の砦を提案するといった具合である。（イソップ物語と無関係に）文字通りの意味で使われることもある。

□ **1692** R. L'ESTRANGE *Fables of Aesop* cccxlviii. There was a council of mechanics called to advise about the fortifying of a city.... Up starts a currier [a person who dressed and coloured leather]; Gentlemen, says he, when y'ave said all that can be said, there's nothing in the world like leather. **1837** F. PALGRAVE *Merchant & Friar* iv. King Log [the birch] was ... forgotten.... 'Depend upon it, Sir, there is nothing like leather.' **1892** I. ZANGWILL *Big Bow Mystery* vi. Besides, meat might have reminded him too much of his work. There is nothing like leather, but Bow beefsteaks occasionally come very near it. **1909** *Votes for Women* 22 Oct 63 Nothing like leather for Suffragettes' wear. —Miss M. Roberta Mills makes Ties, Bags, Belts, [etc.]. **1937** C. ST. JOHN SPRIGG *Six Queer Things* v. 115 Morgan had a leathery mind There was no subtlety or sharpness about it, but it was tough.... No amount of discouragement or error wore it out There is nothing like leather. ■ strength and weakness 強弱

leave ⇒ LET well alone.

leg ⇒ There goes more to MARRIAGE than four bare legs in a bed.

leisure ⇒ The BUSIEST men have the most leisure; IDLE people have the least leisure; There is LUCK in leisure; MARRY in haste and repent at leisure.

lemon ⇒ If LIFE hands you lemons, make lemonade.

LEND your money and lose your friend.
金を貸すと友を失う。

(訳注：このことわざでは、「〈友人に〉金を貸せ」と「友人を失え」という 2 つの命令文が並列されている。しかし、実際にそうせよと命令しているのではない。友人に金を貸したければ勝手にそうするがいい。しかし、そうすると、友人を失うはめになるぞと警告しているのである。命令文を並列して、どちらもやってはいけないと警告していることわざに、Spare the rod and spoil the child. 〈鞭を惜しむと子供をだめにする〉、Marry in haste and repent at leisure. 〈慌てて結婚、ゆっくり後悔〉などがある)

友人間の借金は、返済を巡って問題が生じた場合、友情が壊れる危険性がある。1721 年の用例がこの点を明らかにしている。

260   lend

☐**1474** CAXTON *Game of Chess* (1883) III. iv. 112 And herof speketh Domas the philosopher and sayth that my frende borrowed money of me And I haue lost my frende and my money attones [simultaneously]. **1600-1** Shakespeare *Hamlet* I. iii. 75 Neither a borrower nor a lender be; For loan oft loses both itself and friend. **1721** J. KELLY *Scottish Proverbs* Lendyour Money, and lose your Friend. It is not the lending of our Money that loses our Friend; but the demanding it again. **1960** H. SLESAR *Enter Murderers* xiii. You know what they say about lending money, It's a sure way to lose friends. ■ **borrowing and lending 貸し借り; friends 友**

lend ⇒ DISTANCE lends enchantment to the view.

lender ⇒ Neither a BORROWER nor a lender be.

lengthen ⇒ As the DAY lengthens, so the cold strengthens.

The LEOPARD does not change his spots.
ヒョウは自分の斑点を変えられない。
（訳注：「三つ子の魂百まで」）

『エレミヤ書』13章23節（欽定訳聖書）Can the Ethiopian change his skin, or the leopard his spots?「エチオピア人は肌の色を変えることができるだろうか、あるいはヒョウは斑点を変えることができるだろうか」を想起させる。このことわざに対応するラテン語は *Lupus pilum mutat, non mentem.*「狼は毛の色は変えられるが、性格は変わらない」である。

☐**1546** J. BALE *irst Examination of Anne Askewe* 38 Their olde condycyons wyll they change, whan the blackemoreame change hys skyruie, and the cane of the mountayne [leopard] her spottes. **1596** SHAKESPEARE *Richard II* I. i. 174 Rage must be withstood.... Lions make leopards tame. —Yea, but not change his spots. **1869** A. HENDERSON *Latin Proverbs* 317 *Pardus maculas non deponit*, a leopard does not change his spots. **1979** J. SCOTT *Clutch of Vipers* iv. He always was a dirty old man ... and the leopard doesn't change his spots. **1997** *Washington Times* 24 July C16 Although he swears he has changed, leopards don't usually change their spots, especially those who don't cooperate in counseling. ■ **change 変化; human nature 人間性**

LESS is more.
より少ない方がより多い。

特に芸術の分野では、抑制された控え目な表現の方が派手な表現よりも深い印象を与える。

☐**1855** R. BROWNING *Andrea del Sarto* I. 78 in Poems (1981) I. 645 Well, less is more, Lucrezia: I am judged. **1947** P. JOHNSON *Mies uan der Rohe* 49 As in architecture, [Mies] has always been guided by his personal motto, 'less is more.' **1984** O. BANKS *Garavaggio Obsession* III. iii. Anyway, he spent years furnishing it with precious, ornamental works of art. This was in the twenties and thirlies, when 'less is more' was the golden rule. **1989** *Time* 20 Feb. 108 What Chiat and his associates seem to be betting on is that there is a mass market of low-income, style-conscious people who have grasped the hip message that less is more. **2001** *Washington Times* 3 Aug. A17 It was as if the pink flamingos had been taken off a Florida lawn, the sequins off Dolly Parton's cowgirl costume, the fins off a '50s Cadillac ... There are times when less is blessedly more. ■ **moderation 節度・中庸**

less ⇒ Of two EVILS choose the less; More HASTE, less speed.

LET well alone.
よいものは (手を出さずに) そのままにしておけ。

ここで、well は副詞ではなく名詞 (「良いもの」) として用いられている。このことわざは Leave well alone. という形でもよく使われる。2002 年の用例は、If it ain't BROKE, don't fix it.「壊れていなければわざわざ修理するな」と同じであることを示している。

□c1570 *Scoggin's Jests* (1626) 76 The shoemaker thought to make his house greater.... They pulled downe foure or flue pastes of the house.... Why said Scoggin, when it was well you could not let it alone. **1740** G. CHEYNE *Essay on Regimen* p. xxxvi. When a Person is tolerably well, and is subject to no painful or dangerous Distemper, I think it. his Duty ... to *let* Well *alone.* **1822** M. EDGEWORTH *Letter* 12 Jan. (1971) 317 Joanna quoted to me the other day an excellent proverb applied to health: 'Let well alone.' **1829** T. L. PEACOCK *Misfortunes of Elphin* ii. This Immortal work ... will stand for centuries.... It is well: it works well: let well alone. **1985** R. R. IRVINE *Ratings are Murder* xx. I don't think it's ever a good idea to tamper with tradition. Leave well enough alone, I say. **2002** *Washington Post* 17 May B6 From what I can tell, most people are members of the 'Let's Leave Well Enough Alone' and 'If It Ain't Broke, Don't Fix It' clubs. ■ **busybodies** おせっかい屋; **content and discontent** 満足と不満足

let ⇒ Let the COBBLER stick to his last; Let the DEAD bury the dead; LIVE and let live; Let SLEEPING dogs lie; SPARE at the spigot, and let out at the bung-hole; Never let the SUN go down on your anger.

leveler ⇒ DEATH is the great traveler.

A LIAR ought to have a good memory.
嘘つきは記憶力が良くなければならない。

† クインティリアヌス『雄弁家教育論』iv. ii. *Mendacem memorern esse oportet.*「嘘つきは物覚えが良くなければならない」

□*a* **1542** T. WYATI in *Poetical Works* (1858) p. xxxvii. They say, 'He that will lie well must have a good remembrance, that he agree in all points with himself, lest he be spied.' *c* **1690** R. SOUTH *Twelve Sermons* (1722) IV. 167 Indeed, a very rational Saying. That a lyar ought to have a good Memory. **1721** J. KELLY *Scottish Proverbs* 50 A Lyar should have a good Memory. Lest he tell the same Lye different ways. **1945** F. THOMPSON *Lark Rise* xiii. 'A liar ought to have a good memory,' they would say. **1999** C. HITCHENS *No One Left To Lie To* (2000) I. 19 Just as the necessary qualification for a good liar is a good memory, so the essential equipment of a would-be lie detector is a good timeline, and a decent archive. ■ **lying** 嘘をつくこと

libel ⇒ The GREATER the truth, the greater the libel.

lick ⇒ If you can't BEAT them, join them.

A LIE is halfway round the world before the truth has got its boots on.
真実が靴を履き終える前に、嘘は世界の半分を回っている。

（訳注：シェイクスピアの『ヘンリー四世』第二部の「序」では冒頭に「噂」〈Rumour〉が登場し、以下のよ

うに述べる。「日の昇る東のかたより日の沈む西の涯まで、風を早馬に仕立てて乗りまわし、この地上に起こるあらゆる出来事を伝えひろめるのがおれの役目だ」)

嘘がいかに早く伝わるかは、昔からよく知られたことである。ウェルギリウス『アエネーイス』iv. 174 *Fama, malum qua non aliud velocius alium*.「噂は他のどんな悪いことより早く伝わる」。この全文がシェイクスピア『ヘンリー四世』第二部 (1597-9) の序に取り入れられている。

☐ **1859** C. H. SPURGEON *Gems from Spurgeon* 74 It Is well said in the old proverb, 'a lie will go round the world while truth Is pulling its boots on'. **1996** *National Review* 6 May 6 'A lie Is halfway round the world before the truth has got Its boots on.' But, eventually, truth gets booted and spurred, and the lie gets a good licking. **2002** *Times* 21 Feb. 3 It is often said that a lie can get round the world quicker than the truth can get its shoes on. For Stephen McPherson, it was quicker than he could get his clothes on. ■ **rumour** 噂; **truth** 真実・真理

If you LIE down with dogs. you will get up with fleas.
犬と一緒に寝れば、蚤と一緒に起きることになる。
（訳注：「朱に交われば赤くなる」）

悪徳は悪い仲間とつきあうとすぐに身に付く。†ラテン語 *Qui cum canibus concumbunt cum pulicibus surgent*.「犬と寝る者は蚤と起きる」

☐ **1573** J. SANFORDE *Garden of Pleasure* 103ᵛ Chi va dormir con i cani, si leua con i pulici. He that goeth to bedde wyth Dogges, aryseth with fleas. **1640** G. HERBERT *Outlandish Proverbs* no. 343 Hee that lies with the dogs, rlseth with fleas. **1721** J. KELLY *Scottish Proverbs* 129 He that sleeps with Dogs, must rise with Fleas. If you keep Company with base and unworthy Fellows, you will get some m by them. **1791** 'P. PINDAR' *Rights of Kings* 32 To this great truth, a Universe agrees, 'He who lies down with dogs, will rise with fleas'. **1842** C. J. LEVER *Jack Hinton* xxii. If you lie down with dogs, you'll get up with fleas, and that's the fruits of travelling with a fool. **1996** *Washington Post* 26 Feb. B2 [W]e do well to bear in mind three axioms so hoary that their essential truth may no longer be adequately grasped. The first is 'He who lies down with dogs rises with fleas.' ■ **associates** 仲間

lie ⇒（名詞）ASK no questions and hear no lies; HALF the truth is often a whole lie;（動詞）As you MAKE your bed, so you must lie upon it; As a TREE falls, so shall it lie; TRUTH lies at the bottom of a well.

LIFE begins at forty.
人生は40歳から。
（訳注：1932年の用例からわかるように、アメリカの哲学者 W. B. ピトキンの著書『人生は40歳から始まる』〈*Life Begins at Forty*〉から広まった名言。ピトキンは、「今日の時点ではまだ完全な真理ではないが、明日には公理となる」と述べている。平均寿命が飛躍的に伸びた現在では、「人生は60歳から」あるいは「人生は70歳から」と考えてもいい）

年配の人に対する励ましの言葉。40歳になると新しい人生が待っている。

☐ **1932** W. B. PITKIN *Life Begins at Forty* i. Life begins at forty. This is the revolutionary outcome of our New Era.... Today it is half a truth. Tomorrow it will be an axiom. **1945** *Zionist Review* 14 Dec: 6 Among Palestine pioneers, life does not 'begin at forty'. **1952** 'M. COST' *Hour Awaits* 142 Life begins at forty.... I know you're only in your thirties, but it leaves a nice margin. **1990** J. R. MCCAHERY *Grave Undertaking* v. Life begins at forty, she reminded herself—give or take a couple of years. ■ **life** 人生; **middle age** 中年

LIFE 263

If LIFE hands you lemons, make lemonade.
人生でレモンを手渡されたら、レモネードを作れ。

（訳注：lemon には、俗語用法として「役立たず物、ポンコツ車」〈アメリカ英語〉、「愚か者」〈イギリス英語〉
といった否定的な意味がある）

たとえ将来性がないように思えても、訪れた機会を最大限に利用せよ。このことわざは
lemon の何か望ましくないものという俗語的な意味を利用している。

□**1910** W. G. HAUPT *Art of Business College Soliciting* 89 Don't be a pessimist, but be optimistic. If anyone 'hands you a lemon' take it home and make lemonade of it. **1996** F. POPCORN
Clicking iii. 408 And a little stand by-the-side-of-the-road is a good spot to learn from a wise saying: If life hands you lemons, make lemonade. But, we'd like to add, then market it, franchise It,
and sell It to a major international conglomerate as a fresh fruit drink. **2002** *Washington Post* 5
April CIO You are the perfect example of the adage 'When life hands you a lemon, make lemonade.' Not only have you strengthened your marriage, you have discovered new interests. ■ **adversity 逆境・苦難**

LIFE isn't all beer and skittles.
人生はビールと九柱戯づくめにあらず。

（訳注：skittle ＝「【英】9 柱戯、スキットル〈9 人一組で木でできたピンをボールを転がしてできるだけ
多く倒すことを競う《ボーリングに似た》ゲーム〉」。このことわざでは、all beer and skittles 全体が比喩
的に「楽しいことづくめ」という意味を表わしている。「楽あれば苦あり」）

人生は自己道楽と気休めづくめなどではない。

□**1855** T. C. HALIBURTON *Nature & Human Nature* I. ii. 'This life ain't all beer and skittles.'
Many a time ... when I am disappointed sadly I say that saw over. **1857** T. HUGHES *Tom Brown'
s Schooldays* 1. ii. Life isn't all beer and skittles. **1931** A. CHRISTIE *Sittaford Mystery* xxvi. 'It's an
experience, isn't it?' 'Teach him life can't be all beer and skittles,' said Robert Gardner mali-
ciously. **1985** B. J. MORISON *Beer & Skittles* iii. '"Life," as the saying goes,' he solemnly informed Persis, '"is not all beer and skittles."' ■ **life 人生**

While there's LIFE there's hope.
生きている限り希望がある。

†テオクリトス『牧歌』iv. 42 ἐλπίδες ἐν ζωοῖσιν.「人生の中に希望がある」。キケロ『アッ
ティクス宛書簡集』IX. X. *Dum anima est, spes esse dicitur.*「ことわざに言うように、
命ある限り希望がある」『コレヘトの言葉』9 章 4 節（A LIVE dog is better than a dead
lion.「生ける犬は、死せる獅子に勝る」参照）。より簡潔なラテン語版 *Dum spiro, spero.*
「私が息をしている間は、私は望みを持つ」はサウスカロライナ州のモットーの一部にな
っている。

□**1539** R. TAVERNER tr. *Erasmus' Adages* 36ᵛ The sycke person whyle he bath lyfe, bath hope.
1670 J. RAY *English Proverbs* 113 While there's life, there's hope, he cry'd; Then why such
haste? So groan'd and dy'd. **1868** READE & BOUCICAULT *Foul Play* I. xi. They lost, for a few moments, all idea of escaping. But ... 'while there's life there's hope.' **1939** C. H. B. KITCHIN *Death
of his Uncle* v. But so far it's only the poor gentleman's clothes that have been found, isn't it? I
mean, while there's life there's hope. **1996** *Washington Times* 29 Jan. Cl4 I will be pleasantly surprised If corporate America acts on your 'wake-up call'—but where there's life there's hope.
■ **life 人生 ; optimism 楽観主義**

264　life

life ⇒ ART is long and life is short; The BEST things in life are free; A DOG is for life ... ; If you would be HAPPY for a week take a wife; My SON is my son till he gets him a wife, but my daughter's my daughter all the days of her life; VARIBTY is the spice of life.

lift ⇒ A RISING tide lifts all the boats.

LIGHT come, light go.
簡単に入ってくるものは簡単に出ていく。

　（訳注：light ＝「容易に」。lightly の方が普通。「悪銭身につかず」）

　EASY come, easy go. の方がよく用いられる。†14世紀後半のフランス語 [*argent*] *legierement vous sont venu et legierement sont perdu*. 「簡単に手に入った金は簡単に出ていく」

　□*c*1390 CHAUCER *Pardoner's Tale* L 781 And lightly as it comth, so wol we spende. *a*1475 J. FORTESCUE *Works* (1869) I. 489 For thyng that lightly cometh, lightly goeth. **1546** J. HEYWOOD *Dialogue of Proverbs* II. ix. 11 Lyght come lyght go. **1712** J. ARBUTHNOT *John Bull still in his Senses* iv. A thriftless Wretch, spending the Goods and Gear that his Fore Fathers won with the Sweet of their Brows; light come, light go. **1861** C. READE *Cloister & Hearth* II. x. Our honest customers are the thieves.... With them and with their purses 'tis lightly come, and lightly go. **1937** G. HEYER *They found Him Dead* iv. He was a bad husband to her. Light come light go. ■ **getting and spending** 取得と消費

light ⇒ （形容詞）MANY hands make light work; （動詞）BETTER to light one candle ...

LIGHTNING never strikes the same place twice.
雷は同じところに二度は落ちない。

　悪いことは重ならないという楽観的な主張。

　□**1857** P. H. MYERS *Prisoner of Border* xii. They did not hit me at all.... Lightning never strikes twice in the same place, nor cannon balls either, I presume. **1942** P. WILDE *Tinsley's Bones* x. The Witness: They say that lightning never strikes twice in the same place. Mr Blodgett It don't because the second time the place ain't there. **1979** M. YORK *Death in Account* x. His bank had been raided the moment his back had been turned. 'Well, lighting never strikes the same place twice.... I expect We'll be safe enough now.' **2001** M. DAHL *Viking Claw* viii. 59 'You gave us our disaster for the climb,' he said. 'Most climbs have only one disaster, so now we are good for the rest of the trip.' 'Like lightning never strikes twice, eh?' said Roobick. ■ **misfortune** 不運

LIKE breeds like.
同類は同類を生む。

　（訳注：like は「〈…に〉似た人［物］」の意。compare *like* with *like* 〈似たものどうしを比較する〉）

　人の性格の特徴は似た人と付き合うことで強化される。『詩篇』18章25- 6 節 (BCP) With the holy thou shalt be holy: and with a perfect man thou shalt be perfect. With the clean thou shalt be clean: and with the froward thou shalt learn frowardness. 「あなたはいつくしみある者には、いつくしみある者となり、欠けたところのない者には、欠けたところのない者となり、清い者には、清い者となり、ひがんだ者には、ひがんだ者となられます」

□1557 A. EDGEWORTH *Sermons* 178ᵛ Wyth a frowarde [evilly disposed] synner, a man shall be naughtye [wicked] ... for tyke maketh like. *c*1577 *Misogonus* 2ᵛ The like bredes the like (eche man sayd). **1842** TENNYSON *Poems* (1969) 703 Like men, like manners: Like breeds like, they say. **1931** 'N. FROME' *Strange Death of Martin Green* xiv. Murder is an awfully bad thing for anybody to get away with, even once. Like breeds like. **1969** A. P. HANNUM *Look back with Love* xxv. The Richard saga seemed ... summed up in her grandfather's words ... 'Like begets like in spite of the Devil.' ■ similarity and dissimilarity 類似性と相違性

LIKE will to like.
似たもの同士は集まるものだ。

(訳注：will＝「…するものだ」〈傾向・習性〉。Students *won't* study if it's not interesting.〈学生は面白くなければ勉強しないものだ〉。willの後ろにdraw＝「集まる」、もしくはcome to＝「やって来る」を補う）

† ホメロス『オデュッセイア』xvii. 218 ὡς αἰεὶ τόν ὁμοῖον ἄγει θεός ὡς τόν ὁμοῖον.「神は常に似たもの同士を集める」。キケロ『老年について』III. vii. *Pares autem vetere proverbio cum paribus facillime congregantur*.「古いことわざによると、同類の者が最も混ざりやすい」。14世紀初頭のフランス語 *Lung semblable quiert lautre*.「似たものは似たものを探す」。† BIRDS of a feather flock together.「類は友を呼ぶ」

□a1400 *Legends of Saints* (STS) I. 226 In proverbe I haf hard say That lyk to lyk drawis ay. *c*1450 *Proverbs of Good Counsel in Book of Precedence* (EETS) 70 This proverbe dothe specify, 'Lyke wyll to lyke in eche company'. **1648** HERRICK *Hesperides* 378 Like will to like, each Creature loves his kinde. **1822** SCOTT *Peveril* II. ii. How could I help it? like will to like— the boy would come—the girl would see him. **1855** T. C. HALIBURTON *Nature & Human Nature* I. xi. Jessie had a repugnance to the union.... 'Jessie ... nature, instead of forbiddin' it approves of it; for like takes to like.' **1922** S. J. WEYMAN *Ovington's Bank* xxxi. He's learned this at your d—d counter, sir! That's where it is. It's like to like. **1981** R. BARNARD *Mother's Boys* xiv. Mrs. Hodsden's connection with his house will be quite plain to you when you meet my husband. Like clings to like, they say.... And those two certainly cling. ■ similarity and dissimilarity 類似性と相違性

like ⇒（形容詞）Like FATHER, like son; Like MASTER, like man; Like MOTHER, like daughter; Like PEOPLE, like priest;（動詞）If you don't like the HEAT, get out of the kitchen.

linen ⇒ Never CHOOSE your women or your linen by candlelight; One does not WASH one's dirty linen in public.

lining ⇒ Every CLOUD has a silver lining.

link ⇒ A CHAIN is no stronger than its weakest link.

linstock (a forked staff to hold a lighted match)：⇒ The COBBLER to his last and the gunner to his linstock.

lion ⇒ A LIVE dog is better than a dead lion; MARCH comes in like a lion, and goes out like a lamb; A MOUSE may help a lion; When SPIDER webs unite, they can tie up a lion.

266 LIONS

Until the LIONS produce their own historian, the story of the hunt will glorify only the hunter.
ライオンが自分たちのための歴史家を生み出すまでは、狩りの物語は狩人だけに栄誉を与える。

物語の勝者側が語られる側となり、敗者は忘れられるものである。米国人の作家・社会学者の W. E. B. デュボイス (1868-1963) の言葉という説があるが、その証拠はない (1971年の用例参照)。† HISTORY is written by the victors. 「歴史は勝者によって書かれる」

☐ **1971** W. R. JOHNSON in *Africa Today* xviii. i. 23 Until the lions have their own historians, stated W. B. B. DuBois, the tales will continue to glorify the hunters. **2000** C. ACHEBE *Home and Exile* 73 'Until the lions produce their own historian, the story of the hunt will glorify only the hunter.' **2004** *Road to Democracy in South Africa* I. vii Thus it was said 'The hunters will always be the victors until the lions have their own historian.' **2006** on *www.womenscenter.ut.edu* I would like to give special thanks to the Women's Center. Their work reminds me of a Benin, Ghana, and Togo proverb: *Gnatola ma no kpon sia, eyenabe adelan to kpo mi sena.* (Ewe-mina) *Until the lion has his or her own storyteller, the hunter will always have the best part of the story.* Thank you all for being the storytellers of unequal powers. ■ **fame and obscurity** 有名と無名；**history** 歴史

lip ⇒ There's MANY a slip between cup and lip.

LISTENERS never hear any good of themselves.
立ち聞きする者の耳には自分の悪口しか聞こえてこない。

（訳注：listeners は listen に接尾辞 -er が付いた形。listen は聞こうとして耳を傾けることを意味する。I *listened* to people moving around upstairs.〈人々が 2 階で動き回っているのに聞き耳を立てた〉。一方、hear は聞く意志の有無にかかわらず音・声が聞こえることを意味する。I *listened*, but could not *hear* anything.〈聞き耳を立てたが、何も聞こえなかった〉）

現在では listeners より eavesdroppers「盗み聞きする人」の方がはるかに一般的である。

☐ **1647** *Mercurius Elencticus* 26 Jan.-2 Feb. 76 The old Proverb is, Hearkners never heare good of them selves. **1678** J. RAY *English Proverbs* (ed. 2) 75 Listners ne'er hear good of themselves. **1839** Dickens *Nicholas Nickleby* xiii. 'If It is fated that listeners are never to hear any good of themselves,' said Mrs. Browdie, 'I can't help it, and I am very sorry for it.' **1881** J. C. HARRIS *Uncle Remus* x. Brer Fox wuz stannin' at de back do' wid one. year at de cat-hole lissenin'. Bavedrappers don't hear no good er deyse'f, en de way Brer Fox was 'bused dat day wuz a caution. **1907** B. NESBIT *Enchanted Castle* v. He ... opened the door suddenly, and there ... was Eliza.... 'You know what listeners never hear,' said Jimmy severely. **1977** *A Newman Evil Streak* IV. 178 They say listeners never hear any good of themselves but there is no excuse for ... ingratitude. **1992** A. LAMBERT *Rather English Marriage* (1993) xvii. 289 'Eavesdroppers never hear good of themselves,' Grace would have said, and she'd have been right. ■ **eavesdroppers** 盗み聞きする人

There is no LITTLE enemy.
小敵などいない。

（訳注：「油断大敵」）

たとえ取るに足らない敵でも、侮ったり、軽蔑することは危険である。† *c***1386** チョーサー『カンタベリー物語』「メリベ物語」I. 1322 Ne be nat necligent to kepe thy persone, nat oonly fro thy gretteste enemys, but fro thy leeste enemy. Senek seith: 'A man that is well avysed, he dredeth his leste enemy.'

□1659 J. HOWELL *Proverbs* 8 There's no enemy little, viz. we must not undervalue any foe. **1733** B. FRANKLIN *Poor Richard's Almanack* (Sept) There is no little enemy. **1887** J. LUBBOCK *Pleasures of Life* I. V. To be friendly with every one Is another matter; we must remember that there is no little enemy. **2006** *Florida Times-Union* 22 Apr. M-18 Students also sent her their favorite quotes … Student Saye Kotee chose the quote 'there Is no little enemy.' ■ **enemies** 敵；**malice** 悪意・恨み

LITTLE fish are sweet.
小魚もおいしい。

（訳注：「気は心」）

たとえ些細なものでも、その利益や喜びはありがたい。

□**1830** R. FORBY *Vocabulary of East Anglia* 434 'little fish are sweet'—It means small gifts are always acceptable. **1914** K. F. PURDON *Folk of Furry Farm* vii. 'They'll sell at a loss,' he went on, with a sigh, 'but sure, little fish is sweet! And the rent has to be made up.'**1981** J. BINGHAM *Brock* 92 Wealthy proprietor of the Melford Echo and three or four small newspapers in the country. ('Little fish are sweet, old boy.') **2011** *Spectator* 10 Sept 57 The moments to relish so far? 'Any day you have a winner. Little fish are sweet.' ■ **great and small** 大小

A LITTLE knowledge is a dangerous thing.
生半可な学問ほど危険なものはない。

（訳注：英国の詩人・作家 A. ポープの『批評論』の中の有名な言葉〈1711年の用例参照〉。ポープは、"To err is human, to forgive divine."〈過ちは人の常、許すは神の業〉など、多くの名言を残している。「生兵法は大怪我のもと」）

生半可な知識は自分に学識があると思い込ませるという点で危険である。1711年のポープによる用例における The *Pierian spring*「ピエリアの泉」は、モーセがギリシア北部のピエリア地域で生まれたという言い伝えを指している。knowledge の代わりに本来のlearning も使われることがある。

□**1711** POPE *Essay on Criticism* I. 215 A little Learning is a dang'rous Thing; Drink deep, or taste not the Plerian Spring. **1829** P. EGAN *Boxiana* 2nd Ser. II. 4 The sensible idea, that 'A little learning is a dangerous thing!' **1881** T. H. HUXLEY *Science & Culture* iv. If a little knowledge Is dangerous, where is the man who has so much as to be out of danger? **1974** T. SHARPE *Porterhouse Blue* xviii. His had been an intellectual decision founded on his conviction that if a little knowledge was a dangerous thing, a lot was lethal. **2002** *Washington Post* 14 Jan. D9 If a little knowledge is a dangerous thing, then extensive-but-incomplete knowledge is a constant torment. ■ **ignorance** 無知・無学；**learning** 学問・学び

LITTLE leaks sink the ship.
小さな水漏れでも船を沈める。

（訳注："Little strokes fell great fell great oaks."〈小さな打撃でも樫の巨木を切り倒す〉参照。ship は大型の大洋航行用の船を指す。a naval *ship*〈軍艦〉、a fleet of *ships*〈艦隊〉。「点滴岩をもうがつ」）

□**1616** T. ADAMS *Taming of Tongue* 28 in Sacrifice of Thankefulnesse It is a little leake that drowneth a shippe. **1642** T. FULLER *Holy State* 1. viii. If servants presume to dispose small things without their masters allowance (besides that many little leaks may sink a ship) this will widen tjleir consciences to give away greater. **1745** B. FRANKLIN *Poor Richard's Almanack* (Jan.) Beware of little Expences; a small leak will sink a great ship. **1809** L. DOW *Chain of Lorenzo* 60 Methinks none will make that reply, but those who love and plead for a little sin; one leak will sink a ship. **1927** M. P. SHIEL *How Old Woman got Home* II. xlll. 'Don't mind spending a few pounds for me: you won't miss it' ... 'Won't miss it ... I don't know so much about that it's the little leaks sink the ship.' **2014** M. CARBONELL *Grail Messenger* xi. 'We won't make it,' the navigator warned. 'I'm not afraid of two small leaks.' 'little leaks sink the ship.' ■ **great and small 大小**

LITTLE pitchers have large ears.
小さな水差しに大きな耳がついている。

（訳注：ear は、茶碗、ドア・窓などの、耳の形をした取っ手を指す。この場合は水差しの取っ手。下の用例からわかるように、large は、wide, long, big などにもなる。）

子供は自分以外のことにも聞き耳を立てている。水差しの ears「耳」は取っ手を指す。

☐**1546** J. HEYWOOD *Dialogue of Proverbs* II. V. G4ᵛ Auoyd your children, small pitchers haue wide eares. **1594** SHAKESPEARE *Richard HI* II. iv. 37 Good madam, be not angry with the child. —Pitchers have ears. **1699** B. E. *New Dict. Canting Crew* s.v. Pitcher-bawd, Little Pitchers have large ears. **1840** R. H. BARHAM *Ingoldsby Legends* 1st Ser. 226 A truth Insisted on much in my earlier years, To wit, 'Little pitchers have very long ears!' **1972** A, PRICE. *Colonel Butler's Wolf* i. He watched her shoo her sisters safely away.... He had been lamentably careless in forgetting that little pitchers had large ears. **2002** *Washington Times* 10 Feb. D2 Are you familiar with the old saying, 'Little pitchers have big ears'? Conversations ... within your son's hearing about your problems or about the problems you're having with him will affect his behavior negatively. ■ **eavesdroppers 盗み聞きする人**

A LITTLE pot is soon hot.
小鍋はすぐに熱くなる。

小人は怒りや感情におぼれやすい。

☐**1546** J. HEYWOOD *Dialogue of Proverbs* r. xi. D2 It is wood [mad] at a woorde, little pot soone whot. **1593** Shakespeare *Taming of Shrew* IV. i. 6 Now were not I a little pot and soon hot, my very lips might freeze to my teeth. **1670** J. RAY *English Proverbs* 115 A little pot's soon hot ... Little persons are commonly. Cholerick. **1884** C. READE *Perilous Secret* II. Xv. Cheeky little beggar, But ... 'a little pot is soon hot.' **1930** R. K. WEEKES *Mignonette* xxiii. 'Oh well,' she quite obviously swallowed down her grievance, still simmering, 'I suppose you'll say little pots are soon hot.' ■ **anger 怒り ; great and small 大小**

LITTLE strokes fell great oaks.
小さな打撃でも樫の巨木を切り倒す。

（訳注：stroke＝「斧などの一撃」。fell＝「〈木を〉切り倒す」。「塵も積もれば山となる」。「点摘岩をもうがつ」）

斧で何回も打つと最も大きな木でさえ倒れる。†エラスムス『格言集』I. viii. *Multis ictibus deiicitur quercus*.「樫の木も何度も打つと倒れる」。LITTLE leaks sink the ship.「小さな水漏れでも船を沈める」と意味が類似している。一方、1981 年の用例は little strokes「小さな打撃」でなくては木を切り倒せないことを示している。

☐*c*1400 *Romaunt of Rose* I. 3688 For no man at the firste strok Ne may nat felle down an ok. **1539** R. TAVERNER tr. *Erasmus' Adages* 26ᵛ Wyth many strokes is an oke ouerthrowen. Nothing is so strange but that lyttell and lyttell maye be brought downe. **1591** SHAKESPEARE *Henry VI*, Pt. 3 II. i. 54 And many strokes, though with a little axe, Hews down and fells the hardest-timber'd oak. By many hands your father was subdu'd. **1757** B. FRANKLJN *Poor Richard Improved* : **1758** (Mar.) Stick to it steadily and you will see great Effects; for ... Little Strokes fell great Oaks.

1869 C. H. SPURGEON *John Ploughman's Talk* xxii. 'By little strokes Men fell great oaks.' By a spadeful at a time the navvies digged ... the embankment. **1981** *Family Circle* Feb. 57 From the cradle to the grave we are reminded that ... great oaks are only felled by a repetition of little strokes. ■ **great and small 大小**

LITTLE thieves are hanged, but great ones escape.
こそ泥が処刑され、大泥棒が逃げ失せる。

† 14世紀後半のフランス語 *Les petits larrons sont penduez, non pas les grands.*「こそ泥は処刑されるが、大物は処刑されない」

□ **1639** J. CLARKE *Parremiologia Anglo-Latina* 172 Little theeves are hang'd, but great ones escape. **1979** *Daily Telegraph* 22 Nov. 18 1n view of the Blunt affair, I am reminded of the proverb, 'Little thieves are hanged but great ones escape.' ■ **great and small 大小 ; justice and injustice 正義と不正 ; wrong-doers 悪事をなす者**

LITTLE things please little minds.
小人は小事で喜ぶ。

些細なことで笑ったり楽しんだりした者を見下す言葉としてよく使われる。Small things amuse small minds. とも言う。† オウィディウス『アルス・アマトリア』I. 159 *Parva leves capiunt animos.*「小人は些細なことで夢中になる」

□ **1576** G. PEITIE *Petit Palace* 139 A litle thyng pleaseth a foole. **1584** LYLY *Sappho & Phao* II. iv. Litle things catch light mindes. **1845** DISRAELI *Sybil* II. ii. Little things affect little minds. Lord Marney ... was kept at the station which aggravated his spleen. **1880** C. H. SPURGEON *John Ploughman's Pictures* 81 Precious little is enough to make a man famous in certain companies ... for ... little things please little minds. **1963** O. LESSING *Man & Two Women* 74 Small things amuse small minds. **1973** *Galt Toy Catalogue* 35 As the saying goes-little things please little minds. **1998** J. JONKER *Try Little Tenderness* (online) She pushed her chair back and glared. 'I'll leave you to the [Christmas] tree, then. They say small things amuse small minds.' ■ **great and small 大小**

little ⇒ （形容詞）BIG fish eat little fish; BIG fleas have little fleas upon their backs to bite them; BIRDS in their little nests agree; Little BIRDS that can sing and won't sing must be made to sing; EVERY little helps; GREAT oaks from little acorns grow; LONG and lazy, little and loud; MANY a little makes a mickle; MUCH cry and little wool; （副詞）LOVE me little, love me long.

LIVE and learn.
長生きすればいろいろなことがわかってくる。

（訳注：このことわざでは、「生きろ」と「学べ」を並列しているが、実際には、「長生きすれば、いろいろなことがわかってくる」と述べている。日常生活で、失敗を経験した時などに、「やれやれ、何事も経験してみないとわからないものだ」といった気持ちで使われるとされる。learn はたんに「勉強して学ぶ、教わる」といった狭い意味ではなく、「経験や失敗から学び取る、悟る」といった広い意味を表している。learn by experience〈経験から学ぶ〉。）

経験こそが物事を知る確かな方法である。

□ **c1620** in *Roxburghe Ballads* (1871) I. 60 A man may liue and learne. **1771** SMOLLETT *Humphry Clinker* III. 168 'Tis a true saying, live and learn—O woman, what chuckling and

270 LIVE

changing have I seen! **1894** J. LUBBOCK *Use of Life* vi. No doubt we go on learning as long as we live: 'Live and learn,' says the old proverb. **1984** J. MINAHAN *Great Diamond Robbery* xi. 'Y' want steins, gov, go to Germany; 'ere we only got pints.' Live and learn. **2002** *Washington Times* 17 May Cl2 Live and learn. That has become something of a mantra for mutual fund investors.
■ **experience** 経験

LIVE and let live.
自分も生き、他人も生かせ。

（訳注：このことわざでは、「生きろ」と「他人を生かせ」を並列しているが、その心は、「互いにじゃませずにやっていく」ということである。Our idea is to *live and let live*.〈我々の考えは、互いにじゃませずにやっていくことである〉）

忍耐の勧め。

□**1622** G. DE MALYNES *Ancient Law-Merchant* 1. xiv. According to the Dutche prouerbe ... Leuen ende laeten leuen, To liue and to let others liue. **1641** D. FERGUSSON *Scottish Proverbs* (STS) no. 582 Live and let live. **1762** SMOLLETT *Sir Launcelot Greaves* II. xvi. He deals very little in physic stuff, ... whereby he can't expect the pothecary to be his friend. You knows, master, one must live and let live, as the saying is. **1843** SURTEES *Handley Cross* II. vii. Live and let live, as the criminal said to the hangman. **1979** C. BRAND *Rose in Darkness* iv. Not that Sari cared two hoots how other people conducted their private lives. Live and let live. **2007** *Times* 21 Sept 19 Too late to start quoting live and let live ... and all the various little mantras and sermons of tolerance that stop the human race from tearing itself apart like weasels in a sack. ■ **tolerance** 寛容・忍耐

If you have to LIVE in the river, it is best to be friends with the crocodile.
川の中で生きざるを得ないのなら、ワニと仲良くするのが一番だ。

（訳注：if 節の中で、「川の中で生きざるを得ない」を意味するのに、must でなく、have to が使われていることに注意。一般に、must は話し手が課す義務や主語の決意を表わすのに対し、have to は周囲の事情からやむなくそうせざるを得ない状況にあることを表わす。You *must* be back by ten.〈10時までに戻ってきなさい〉。You *have to* be back by ten.〈あなたは10時までに戻らざるを得ない《門限》〉。I *must* stop smoking.〈禁煙するぞ《＝決意》〉、I *have to* stop smoking.〈私は禁煙せざるを得ない《＝医者の命令》〉）

インドのことわざ。近くの権力者と良い関係を保つに越したことはない。

□**1882** W. L. WILKINSON 'Shells from Strange Shores' in Wray(ed.) *Golden Hours* CLIX. 180/2 (Mar.) To be on bad terms with those und. er whose authority we are placed is 'To live in the river and be at enmity with the crocodile.' **1990** H. SABAHI *British Policy in Persia* 1918-1925 242 He repeatedly impressed upon the senior khans that they had little choice but to cooperate with Reza Khan. To hammer home his message, he quoted them an Indian proverb: 'If you have to live in the river, it is best to be friends with the crocodile.' **2002** J. VAN DER UNDEN in M. Pacione (ed.) *City* 608 However bad the patrons' image, the clients often have no other option than to consider their patrons an unavoidable evil ... : 'If you live in the river, it is better to stay friends with the crocodile.' ■ **pragmatism** 実用主義

If you want to LIVE and thrive, let the spider run alive.
金持ちになりたいなら、蜘蛛は生かしておけ。

蜘蛛を殺すなといういましめ。古来、蜘蛛は幸運をもたらすものと考えられてきた。蜘蛛に関する古い迷信の中でも、このことわざは衣服に付いた蜘蛛がお金を呼ぶ蜘蛛であったら、その蜘蛛が付いた人はまもなくお金を得ることになるという民間伝承と結びつ

いている。

□**1867** *Notes & Queries* 3rd Ser. XI. 32 The proverb so often used in Kent: 'He who would wish to thrive Must let spiders run alive.' **1903** V. S. LEAN *Collectanea* II. 204 He that would thrive Must let spiders live. **1957** H. P. BECK *Folklore of Maine* iv. If you want to live and thrive let the spider run alive. ■ **superstition** 迷信

A LIVE dog is better than a dead lion.
生ける犬は、死せる獅子に勝る。

『コヘレトの言葉』9 章 4 節（欽定訳聖書）を想起させる。To him that is joined to all the living, there is hope: for a living dog is better than a dead lion. 「すべて生ける者には望みがある。生ける犬は、死せる獅子に勝るからである」

□**c1390** in *Minor Poems of Vernon MS* (BETS) 534 Better is a quick [living] and an hol hounde Then a ded lyon … And better is pouert with godnes Then richesse with wikkedness. **1566** J. BARTHLET *Pedigree of Heretics* 2ᵛ A lyuing Dogge, is better than a dead Lion. **1798** 'P. PINDAR' *Tales of Hoy* 41 It was a devil of a trick … but, 'A living Dog is better than a dead Lion,' as the saying is. **1864** TROLLOPE *Can You forgive Her?* II. vii. He had so often told the widow that care killed the cat, and that a live dog was better than a dead lion. **1953** 'G. CULLINGFORD' *Post Mortem* iv. I take my walks without following a ball about like a dog. Which reminds me of the old proverb that a live dog is better than a dead lion. ■ **great and small** 大小 ; **life** 人生

They that LIVE longest, see most.
最も長生きする者が最も多くの事を見る。

（訳注：they＝「〈関係節を伴って〉…する人々、…の者たち」〈those〉。*They that* live longest must die at last. 【ことわざ】〈生者必衰〉）

†14世紀初頭のフランス語 *Qui vit trop voit*. 「長く生きる者がたくさん見る」。**1605-6** シェイクスピア『リア王』v. iii. 325 We that are young Shall never see so much nor live so long. 「若いわれわれにはこれほどの苦しみ、たえてあるまい」

□**1620** T. SHELTON tr. *Cervantes' Don Quixote* II. Iii. My Mother was vsed to say, That 'twas needful to live long, to see much. **1837** T. HOOK *Jack Brag* III. ii. Them as lives longest sees the most. **1961** N. LOFTS *House at Old Vine* VI. Vi. Them that live longest see most. You remember that, young man, if ever you're down on your luck. **1971** 'M. ERSKINE' *Brood of Folly* v. Mrs Parslowe gave her a glance that was both sly and knowing. 'Those that live longest will see most,' she answered cryptically. ■ **experience** 経験 ; **old age** 老年

Come LIVE with me and you'll know me.
私と一緒に暮らせば、私のことが分かる。

（訳注：この場合の "come and … " は命令文で用いられ、「…しに来る」の意。Please come and dine with us next Saturday.〈今度の土曜日に食事にいらしてください〉）

単なる顔見知りでは人の性格を十分理解するには不十分である。

□**1925** S. O'CASEY *Juno & Paycock* II. 49 I only seen him twiced; if you want to knowme, come an' live with me. **1960** C. S. LEWIS *Four Loves* iii. You must really give no kind of preference to yourself; at a party it is enough to conceal the preference. Hence the old proverb 'come live with me and you'll know me'. ■ **familiarity** 慣れ親しみ

live ⇒ BETTER to die on your feet than live on your knees; BETTER to live one day as a tiger … ; EAT to live, not live to eat; He who FIGHTS and runs away, may live to fight another day; Those who live in GLASS houses shouldn't throw stones; One HALF of the world does not know how the other half lives; MAN cannot live by bread alone; A REED before the wind lives on; While mighty oaks do fall; THREATENED men live long.

lived ⇒ BRAVE men lived before Agamemnon.

He who LIVES by the sword dies by the sword.
剣で生きるものは剣で死ぬ。

（訳注：he ＝「〈関係節 who ... や that ... を伴って〉…する者は誰でも〈性別は問わない〉」。下の 2 つのことわざにおける he の場合も同様である。He who hesitates is lost.〈しり込みする者は負けだ〉。He who carries nothing loses nothing.〈【ことわざ】持たざれば失うことなし〉）

暴力は暴力で報復される。暴力を使う者は暴力的な結末に遭う。1997 年の用例が示すように、the sword「剣」でなく銃といった武器が使われることもある。『マタイによる福音書』26 章 52 節（欽定訳聖書）「剣を取るものすべて剣で滅びるだろう」を想起させる。

†**1601** A. マンデー他『ハンティンドン伯爵ロバートの死』L l Alas for woe: but this is iust heauens doome On those that liue by bloode: in bloode they die.「なんと痛ましいことだ。しかし、これは血で生きる者の天命だ。彼らは血で死ぬ」

□**1652** R. WILLIAMS *Complete Writings* (1963) N. 352 All that take the Sword ... shall perish by it. **1804** G. MORRIS *Diary & Letters* (1889) II. xiv. To quote the text, 'Those who live by the sword shall perish by the sword.' **1916** J. BUCHAN *Greenmantle* vi. I did not seek the war.... It was forced on me.... He that takes the sword will perish by the sword. **1978** 'M, CRAIG' *Were He Stranger* xiii. Mark me, Sydney, he who lives by the sword dies by the sword. **1997** *Washington Post* 12 Mar. Bl Wallace's friends, with whom he had sold dope out of a garbage can ... , had pretty much summed up the situation in a sentence: 'When you live by the gun.' **2007** *Editing Matters* Jan/Feb 10 And he [David Crystal] says ... 'It seems to be one of the consequences of becoming a usage critic that your own usage will be pilloried sooner or later.' Er, yes—those who live by the sword die by the sword. ■ **retribution 天罰・報復**

He that LIVES in hope dances to an ill tune.
希望を抱いて生きる者は下手な音楽にでも合わせて踊れる。

† HOPE deferred makes the heart sick.「望みを失うと心も折れる」

□**1591** J. FLORIO *Second Fruits* 149 'This argument of yours is lame and halting, but doo not you knowe that He that dooth liue in hope, dooth dance in narrowe scope. **1640** G. HERBERT *Outlandish Proverbs* no. 1006 Hee that lives in hope danceth without musick. **1732** T. FULLER *Gnomologia* no. 2224 He that liveth in Hope, danceth without a Fiddle. **1977** J. AIKEN *Five Minute Marriage* ii. 'He that lives in hope danceth to an ill tune,' remarked Mrs. Andrews, who was full of proverbs. ■ **disappointment 失望 ; hope and despair 希望と絶望**

He LIVES long who lives well.
良く生きる者こそが長く生きるというものだ。

節度ある人生を送るなら、その方がたんに長生きするよりも重要である。

□**1553** T. WILSON *Art of Rhetoric* 45ᵛ They lyued long enough, that have liued well enough. **1642** T. FULLER *Holy State* I. vi. If he chance to die young, yet he lives long that lives well. **1861** H. BONAR in *Hymns of Faith & Hope* 2nd Ser. 129 He liveth long who liveth well! All other life is short and vain. **2007** *India Today* 12 Feb. 18 There's a proverb which says: 'He lives long who lives well'. That was way before the days when caloric intake, low fat, high fibre, stress management and working out became lifestyle mantras. ■ **life** 人生

load ⇒ A SWARM in May is worth a load of hay.

loaf ⇒ HALF a loaf is better than no bread; A SLICE off a cut loaf isn't missed.

local ⇒ THINK global, act local.

lock ⇒ It is too late to shut the STABLE-door after the horse has bolted.

locksmith ⇒ LOVE laughs at locksmiths.

loft ⇒ SEPTEMBER blow soft, till the fruit's in the loft.

No matter how long a LOG stays in the water, it doesn't become a crocodile.
丸太はどんなに長く水の中につかっていても、ワニにはならない。

マリのバンバラ族のことわざ。人の本性は外の環境によって変化することはない。西アフリカと中央アフリカのいくつかの言語において異なった言い方が観察されている。

□**1976** K. M. AITHNARD *Some Aspects of Cultural Policy in Togo* 36 As two Togolese proverbs say, 'If you do not know where you are going try at least to know where you have come from', for 'it is not because the log has floated for a long time in the water that it will become a crocodile.' **1987** P. STOLLER & C. OAKES *In Sorcery's Shadow* 21 Although the people of Mehanna professed their eternal friendship, I was a stranger ... I knew that I would never cross the invisible threshold to become an insider ... A floating log does not become a crocodile. **2001** *www.afri-prov.org* 'African Proverb of the Month' June No matter how long a log stays in the water, it doesn't become a crocodile. **2007** M. K. ASANTE *An Afrocentric Manifesto* 36 'We were Africans who retained much of Africa even through the slavery institution and we also were deeply affected by Europe in America, but we remained Africans.' Wolof wisdom says, 'Wood may remain in water for ten years but it will never become a crocodile.' ■ **appearance, deceptive** 偽りの外見; **circumstances** 状況

London ⇒ What MANCHESTER says today, the rest of England says tomorrow.

LONG and lazy, little and loud; fat and fulsome, pretty and proud.
のっぽの女は怠け者、小さい女は高調子、太っちょ女は好色で、きれいな女はうぬぼれ屋。

□*c***1576** T. WHITEHORNE *Autobiography* (1961) 23 Hy women be layzy and low be lowd, fair be sluttish, and ret be proud. **1648** HERRICK *Hesperides* 166 *Long and lazie.* That was the Proverb. Let my mistress be Lasie to others, but be long to me—*Ibid.* 248 *Little and loud.* Little you are; for Womans sake be proud; For my sake next, (though little) be not loud. **1659** J. HOWELL *Proverbs* (English) 10 Long and lazy, little and loud, fatt and fulsome, pretty and proud; in point of women. **1872** BLACKMORE *Maid of Sker* I. xiii. You are long enough, and lazy enough; put your hand to the bridle. **2007** H. VALBORG *Symbols of Eternal Doctrine* 281 [S]he placed guards to protect the dwarfs from the giants, only to find that the latter were mercilessly preyed upon by the former ... The guards' instructions were altered but the incident gave credence to the old

274　LONG

folk saying, 'Long and lazy, little and loud.' ■ **women 女性**

LONG foretold, long last; short notice, soon past.
前触れが早いのは長く続き、前触れが遅いのはすぐに終わる。

† 1863 R. フィッツロイ *Weather Book* 15 The longer the time between the signs and the change foretold by them, the longer such altered weather will last; and, on the contrary, the less the time between a warning and a change, the shorter will be the continuance of such predicted weather. 「その天気の兆候と出現までの時間が長ければ長いほど、その天気は長く続く。一方、その天気の警告と出現の間の時間が短ければ短いほどその天気は早く終わる」

☐1866 A. STEINMBTZ *Manual of Weathercasts* xiv. Old saws [sayings] about the barometer. Long foretold, long last; short notice, soon past. **1889** J. K. JEROME *Three Men in Boat* v. The barometer is ... misleading.... Boots ... read out a poem which was printed over the top of the oracle, about 'Long foretold, long last; Short notice, soon past.' The fine weather never came that summer. **2002** *Times* 6 Apr. (online) 'Long foretold, long last; short notice, soon past' the old saying says, meaning that a long rise in atmospheric pressure brings a long spell of high pressure, which there was. ■ **future 未来**；**weather lore 天気にまつわる伝承**

It is a LONG lane that has no turning.
曲がり角のない道は長い道（どんな道にも曲がり角はある）。

（訳注：この場合の a long lane とは、「長い道」というよりも、「あり得ない道」を指している。下の用例からわかるように、lane の代わりに、run や road も用いられる。lane ＝「〈垣根・家などの間の〉小道、通路、路地」。一般に、狭い車道を指す。人が通る小道は path, footpath。A blind lane〈袋小路〉。「待てば海路の日和あり」）

望ましくない状況も最終的には好転する。

☐1633 *Stationers' Register* (1877) N. 273 (*ballad*) Long runns that neere tumes. **1670** J. RAY English Proverbs 117 It's a long run that never turns. **1732** T. FULLER *Gnomologia* no. 2863 It is a long Lane that never turns. **1748** RICHARDSON *Clarissa* IV. xxxii. It is a long lane that has no turning —Do not despise me for my proverbs. **1945** F. P. KEYES *River Road* VIII. xxxvii. 'You're through in politics, Gervais. You might just as well face it.' ... 'It's a long lane that has no turning.' **2002** *Country Life* 11 Apr. 117 'It's a long road that doesn't have to turn some time,' says Mr Plant, who intends to continue sheep farming, like his father and grandfather before him. ■ **circumstances 状況**；**perseverance 我慢強さ**

long ⇒（形容詞） ART is long and life is short; Be the DAY weary or be the day long, at last it ringeth to evensong; KINGS have long arms; NEVER is a long time; OLD sins cast long shadows; SHORT reckonings make long friends; A STERN chase is a long chase; He who SUPS with the Devil should have a long spoon;（副詞）He LIVES long who lives well; No matter how long a LOG stays in the water ... ; LOVE me little, love me long; If you SIT by the river for long enough ... ; THREATENED men live long; Happy's the WOOING that is not long a-doing.

The LONGEST way round is the shortest way home.
一番遠い回り道が一番近い帰り道。

（訳注：「急がば回れ」）

回り道を行った方が直線ルートよりも結果として早く着くこともある。この考えは古くからある。**1580** Lyly *Euphues & his England* II. 96 Thou goest about (but yet the neerest way) to hang me vp for holy-dayes.「あなたは回り道をして（しかし、その方が結局近道だけれど）私を休日に備えて帽子掛けにつるす」(実は、この場合、go aboutは「回り道をする」と「…しようと努める」という 2 つの意味に取れる。「私」とは帽子掛けにつるす帽子のことで、擬人的に使われている)。

□**1635** F. QUARLES *Emblems* iv. ii. The road to resolution lies by doubt: The next way home's the farthest way about. **1776** G. COLMAN *Spleen* II. 24 The longest way about is the shortest way home. **1846** J. K, PAULDING *Letter* 9 May (1962) vii The Potatoes arrived … via New York … in pursuance of the Old Proverb, that 'the longest way round is the shortest way home.' **1942** K. ABBEY *And let Coffin Pass* xviii. 'The longest way round is the shortest way home.' … 'We'll make the best time by skirting the pines.' **1990** F. LYALL *Croaking of Raven* vi. 2. 64' … when I was training my old boss used to say: "If in doubt take the long road round. It'll prove to be the shortest in the end."' ■ **patience and impatience** 忍耐と性急 ; **ways and means** 方法と手段

longest ⇒（形容詞）BARNABY bright, Barnaby bright, the longest day and the shortest night;（副詞）A CREAKING door hangs longest; He who LAUGHS last, laughs longest; They that LIVE longest, ⇒ Most.

LOOK before you leap.
跳ぶ前によく見よ。
（訳注：「転ばぬ先の杖」。「念には念を入れよ」）

軽率で無分別な行為を戒める警告。

□*c*1350 *Douce MS 52* no. 150 First Joke and aftirward lepe. **1528** W. TYNDALE *Obedience of Christian Man* 130 We say … Loke yer thou lepe, whose literall sence is, doo nothinge sodenly or without avisement. **1567** W. PAINTER *Palace of Pleasure* II. xxiv. He that looketh not before he leapeth, may chaunte to stumble before he sleapeth. **1621** BURTON *Anatomy of Melancholy* II. iii. Looke before you leape. **1836** MARRYAT *Midshipman Easy* I. vi. Look before you leap is an old proverb…. Jack … had pitched into a small apiary, and had upset two hives of bees. **1941** C. MACKENZIE *Red Tapeworm* i. Do you remember the rousing slogan which the Prime Minister gave the voters … on the eve of the last General Election? … Look Before You Leap. **1979** D. MAY *Revenger's Comedy* ix. Changing horses, love? I should look before you leap. ■ **caution** 用心

look ⇒ A CAT may look at a king; The DEVIL looks after his own; DOGS look up to you, cats look down on you, Pigs is equal; Never look a GIFT horse in the mouth; When all you have is a HAMMER, everything looks like a nail; A MAN is as old as he feels, and a woman as old as she looks; Take care of the PENCE and the pounds will take care of themselves; Those who PLAY at bowls must look out for rubbers; One man may STEAL a horse, while another may not look over a hedge.

LOOKERS-ON see most of the game.
傍観者にはゲームが一番よく見える。
（訳注：試合をしている人よりもそれを見ている人の方が試合がつかめるものだ。「岡目八目」）

局外者の方が当事者よりも事態がよく理解できる。最近では lookers-on の代わりに

onlooker(s) もよく使われる。

☐1529 J. PALSGRAVE in *Acolastus* (EETS) p. xxxviii. It fareth between thee and me as it doth between a player at the chess and a looker on, for he that looketh on seeth many draughts that the player considereth nothing at all. **1597** BACON *Essays* 'Of Followers' 7ᵛ To take aduise of friends is euer honorable: For lookers on many times see more then gamesters. **1666** G. TORRIANO *Italian Proverbs* III As the English say, The stander by sees more than he who plays. **1850** F. E. SMEDLEY *Frank Fairlegh* vii. Remembering the old adage, that 'lookers-on see most of the game,' I determined ... to accompany him. **1998** 'C. AIRD' *Stiff News* (2000) iii. 29 So it fell out that Mrs Maisie Carruthers, still too frail to attend the funeral, but not too immobile to get to the window of her room at the Manor, became the onlooker who saw most of the game. **1999** 'H. CRANE' *Miss Seeton's Finest Hound* x. 164 Mrs. Morris, it was clear, did not suspect that her warm regard for the works manager was no secret from her assistant—an assistant who by training was an acute observer. Was not another adage that the looker-on saw most of the game? ■ **observation 観察**

lord ⇒ EVERYBODY loves a lord; NEW lords, new laws.

What you LOSE on the swings you gain on the roundabouts.
ブランコで損をした分は回転木馬で取り戻す。

(訳注：この場合の you は総称的な用法で、話し手や聞き手を含めた一般の人々を指している。*You* never can tell what's going to happen.〈何が起きるかは誰にもわからない〉。次のことわざの you も同様。「海の疲れは山で直す」)

ある領域での損失は他の領域での利益によって取り戻す。よって、最終的にプラスマイナスゼロとなる。催し場に関する比喩で、様々な言い方がある。

☐**1912** P. CHALMERS *Green Days & Blue Days* 19 What's lost upon the roundabouts we pulls up on the swings. **1927** *Times* 24 Mar. 15 By screwing more money out of taxpayers he diminishes their savings, and the market for trustee securities loses on the swings what it gains on the roundabouts. **1978** G. MOORE *Farewell Recital* 129 There are compensations: what you lose on the swings you gain on the roundabouts. And let's face it, a cup of tea or a cup of coffee are all very well but they are not so much fun as polygamy. ■ **winners and losers 勝者と敗者**

You cannot LOSE what you never had.
持っていないものはなくせない。

このことわざの趣旨はいろいろな言い方で表現される。例えば、1974年の用例に挙げられている "Only them as has them can lose them." (それらを持っている者だけがそれらを失うことができる) はイングランド北部のヨークシャー地方の言い方である。よく似たものに What you've never HAD you never miss. 「手に入れたことのないものには、それがなくて困るという気持ちにはならない」が挙げられる。

☐*a*1593 MARLOWE *Hero & Leander* I. 276 Of that which hath no being do not boast, Things that are not at all are never lost. **1676** I. WALTON *Compleat Angler* (ed. 5) 1. v. 'He has broke all; there's half a line and a good hook lost' 'I [Aye] and a good Trout too.' 'Nay, the Trout is not lost, for ... no man can lose what he never had.' **1788** WESLEY *Works* (1872) VII. 41 He only seemeth to have this.... No man can Jose what he never had. **1935** *Oxford Dict. English Proverbs* 601 You cannot Jose what you never had. **1974** 'J. HERRIOT' *Vet in Harness* viii. 'Only them as has them can lose them,' she said firmly, her head tilted as always. I had heard that said many times and they were brave Yorkshire words. ■ **winners and losers 勝者と敗者**

louse 277

lose ⇒ A BLEATING sheep loses a bite; LEND your money and lose your friend; The SUN loses nothing by shining into a puddle; A TALE never loses in the telling; USE it or lose it; You WIN a few, you lose a few.

loser ⇒ FINDERS keepers (losers weepers).

One man's LOSS is another man's gain.
甲の損は乙の得。
（訳注：「甲の薬は乙の毒」）

誰かが負けるということは他の誰かが勝つということである。

□*c*1527 T. BERTHELET tr. *Erasmus' Sayings of Wise Men* D1ᵛ Lyghtly whan one wynneth, an other loseth. **1733** J. BARBER in *Correspondence of Swift* (1965) IV. 189 Your loss will be our gain, as the proverb says. **1821** SCOTT *Pirate* I. vi. Doubtless one man's Joss is another man's gain. **1918** D. H. LAWRENCE *Letter* 21 Feb. (1962) I. 544 I am glad to have the money from your hand. But ... one man's gain is another man's loss. **1979** R. LITTELL *Debriefing* vi. Well, their loss is my gain! ■ **gains and losses** 利益と損失

There's no great LOSS without some gain.
どんな大損でもいくらは利益があるものだ。
（訳注：否定語 without〈…なしに〉の後ろに any でなく some があることに注意。必ず利益があることを強調している）

不測の事態、不利な状況でもプラスの面を探すことを促す慰めの言葉。

□*a*1641 D. FERGUSSON *Scottish Proverbs* (STS) no. 1408 Thair was never a grit loss without som small vantag. **1868** W. CLIFT *Tim Bunker Papers* 134 However, 'there is no great loss but what there is some small gain,' and Jake Frink claims that he has got his money's worth in experience. **1937** L. WILDER *On Banks of Plum Creek* xxv. The hens ... were eating grasshoppers.... 'Well, we won't have to buy feed for the hens.... There's no great loss without some gain.' **1957** M. P. HOOD *In Dark Night* viii. I didn't think there'd be enough business on the wharf for him to need me this afternoon.... No loss without some small gain. ■ **gains and losses** 利益と損失

lost ⇒ BETTER to have loved and lost, than never to have loved at all; he who HESITATES is lost; What a NEIGHBOUR gets is not lost; There is NOTHING lost by civility; For WANT of a nail the shoe was lost.

lottery ⇒ MARRIAGE is a lottery.

loud ⇒ LONG and lazy, little and loud.

louder ⇒ ACTIONS speak louder than words.

louse ⇒ SUE a beggar and catch a louse.

278 LOVE

LOVE and a cough cannot be hid.
恋と咳は隠せない。

咳の発作を止めることができないように、恋をしている人はうっかり秘密を漏らしてしまう。†ラテン語 *Amor tussisque non celantur*.「恋と咳は隠せない」

□*a*1325 *Cursor Mundi* (EETS) I. 4276 Luken Juue at the end wil kith [concealed love will show itself in the end]. **1573** J. SANFORDE *Garden of Pleasure* 98ᵛ Foure things cannot be kept close, Loue, the cough, fyre, and sorrowe. **1611** R. COTGRAVB *Dict. French & English* s.v. Amour, We say, Loue, and the Cough cannot be hidden. **1640** G. HERBERT *Outlandish Proverbs* no. 49 Love and a Cough cannot be hid. **1863** G. EUOT *Romola* I. vi. If there are two things not to be hidden —love and a cough—I say there is a third, and that is ignorance. **1994** R. DAVIES *Cunning Man* 458 Love and a cough cannot be hid. **2002** *Washington Times* 14 Feb. A21 Three things are hard to hide, says the Yiddish proverb: a cough, poverty and love. ■ **love** 愛・恋愛；**secrecy** 秘密

One cannot LOVE and be wise.
恋と分別とは両立し得ない。

(訳注：恋は盲目である。この場合、love and be wise〈恋をしていながら賢明であること〉がひとかたまりになって、cannot に続いている)

†プブリリウス・シルス『金言集』xxii. *Amare et sapere vix deo conceditur*.「恋をして、同時に賢明であることを神様が許してくれることはめったにない」

□*c*1527 T. BERTHELET tr. *Erasmus' Sayings of Wise Men* Blᵛ To have a sadde [serious] mynde and loue is nat in one person. **1539** R. TAVERNER tr. *Erasmus' Adages* II. A5 To be in loue and to be wyse is scase graunted to god. **1612** BACON *Essays* 'Of Love' xii. It is impossible to loue and bee wise. **1631** R. BRATHWAIT *English Gentlewoman* 32 The Louer is euer blinded ... with affection ... whence came that vsuall saying One cannot loue and be wise. **1872** G. ELIOT *Middlemarch* II. III. xxvii. If a man could not love and be wise, surely he could flirt and be wise at the same time? **2012** M. MARNU *Sky's the Limit* 49 One cannot love and be wise at the same time. It is said that affection blinds reason and lovers are always mad ... ■ **love** 愛・恋愛；**wisdom** 賢明・知恵

LOVE begets love.
愛は愛を生む。

Love breeds love. という言い方もある。†ラテン語 *Amor gignit amorem*.「愛は愛を生む」

□**1648** HERRICK *Hesperides* 297 Love love begets, then never be Unsoft to him who's smooth to thee. **1812** E. NARES *I'll consider of It* iii. 'Love' says the proverb, 'produces love.' **1909** A. MACLAREN *Epistle to Ephesians* 275 Love begets love, and ... if a man loves God, then that glowing beam will glow whether it is turned to earth or turned to heaven. **1958** R. FENISONG *Death of Party* vi. The cliche that 'love breeds love' was a blatant lie. **2013** C. G. VICKERY *Om* (online) The great thinkers whose words I have included ... knew this simple fact—that happiness begets happiness, love breeds love ... ■ **love** 愛・恋愛；**reciprocity** 相互依存

LOVE is blind.
恋は盲目。

(訳注：「あばたもえくぼ」)

恋には理性が働かないことを観察したもの。弓矢を持った裸の美少年クピド（キューピッド）が目隠しをされている場面がよく描かれている。†テオクリトス『牧歌』x. 19

LOVE 279

τυφλὸς...ὁ...Ἔρως.「恋は盲目である」。プラウトゥス『ほら吹き兵士』l. 1259 *Caeca amore est.*「彼女は恋で周囲が見えなくなっている」

□*c*1390 CHAUCER *Merchant's Tale* l. 1598 For love is blynd alday, and may nat see. **1591** SHAKESPEARE *Two Gentlemen of Verona* II. i. 61 If you love her you cannot see her.—Why?—Because Love is blind. **1978** A. MALING *Lucky Devil* xii. 'How did you ever come to marry an idiot like Irving?' ... 'Love is blind.' **2002** *Spectator* 25 May 70 And, if love is blind, how come lingerie is so popular? ■ **love** 愛・恋愛

LOVE laughs at locksmiths.
恋は錠前屋などものともしない。

(訳注：恋する男は鍵を壊してでも女の許へ行く。laugh at ＝「…をものともしない、一笑に付す」。Love *laughs at* distance.〈惚れて通えば千里も一里〉)

同じ心情をさらに生き生きと表現したものに LOVE will find a way.「恋に不可能はない」がある。† **1592-3** シェイクスピア『ヴィーナスとアドーニス』l. 576 Were beauty under twenty locks kept fast, Yet love breaks through and picks them all at last.「たとえ20個の錠前で美人を固く守っても、恋はそれらを破って入る」

□**1803** G. COLMAN (*title*) Love laughs at locksmiths: an operatic farce. **1901** F. R. STURGIS *Sexual Debility in Man* ix. Love is said to laugh at locksmiths, and incidentally at parental authority, and this young man was no exception. **1922** 'N. YATES' *Jonah & Co* iv. And now push off and lock the vehicle. I know Love laughs at locksmiths, but the average motor-thief's sense of humour is less susceptible. **2015** *Times* 24 Jan. 28 Love laughs at locksmiths, and casual romance has always enjoyed a good snigger at the expense of authoritarian regimes. ■ **love** 愛・恋愛

LOVE makes the world go round.
愛がこの世を回らせている。

† フランス語 *C'est l'amour, l'amour, l'amour, Quifait le monde A la ronde* (Dumerson & Segur *Chansons Nationales & Populaires de France*, 1851, 11. 180)「地球を回転させているのは愛、愛、愛である」

□**1865** 'L. CARROLL' *Alice's Adventures in Wonderland* ix. '"Oh, 'tis love, 'tis love that makes the world go round!"' 'Somebody said,' Alice whispered, 'that it's done by everybody minding their own business.' **1902** 'O. HENRY' in *Brandur Mag.* 27 Sept 4 It's said that love makes the world go round. The announcement lacks verification. It's the wind from the dinner horn that does it. **2002** *Washington Times* 14 Feb. A21 It is a well-known factoid that love makes the world go 'round; less well-known is love's ability to stop the planet dead flat in midspin when it ends, replacing Paris in the spring with Chicago in January. ■ **love** 愛・恋愛

LOVE me little, love me long.
少し愛して、長く愛して。

安定した控えめな愛情の方が突然の情熱的な愛より長続きがする。

□*a*1500 in *Archiv* (1900) CVI. 274 Love me lytyll and longe. **1546** J. HEYWOOD *Dialogue of Proverbs* II. ii. Gl Olde wise folke saie, loue me lyttle loue me long. **1629** T. ADAMS *Works* 813 Men cannot brooke poore friends. This inconstant Charitie is hateful as our Engllsh phrase premonisheth; Loue me little, and Loue me Long. **1721** J. KELLY *Scottish Proverbs* 229 Love me little, love me long. A Dissuasive from shewing too much, and too sudden Kindness. **1907** *Times Literary Supplement* 8 Mar. 77 Mrs. Bellew is a lady who cannot love either little or long. She ... tires very quickly of the men who are irresistibly drawn to her. **1991** *Washington Times* 14 Feb.

280 LOVE

G3 'Love me a little less but longer' is an old folk phrase. ■ **constancy and inconstancy** 安定と不安定；love 愛・恋愛

LOVE me, love my dog.
私を愛するなら、私の犬も愛して。

(訳注：「坊主憎けりゃ袈裟まで憎い」を逆にしたものと言われる。私を本当に愛しているのなら、私のペットも愛してほしいと訴えている。「愛は屋烏に及ぶ」ということわざに近い。このことわざは、誰かを深く愛すると、その人の家の屋根にとまっているカラスまでも好きになるものだと述べている)

†聖ベルナルド *Sermon：In Festa Sancti Michaelis* iii. *Qui me amat, amat et canem meum.*「私を愛する人は私の犬も愛して」。14世紀初頭のフランス語 *Et ce dit le sage qui mayme il ayme man chien.*「賢人も言っているように、私を愛する人には私の犬も愛してほしい」

□*a*1500 in *Archiv* (1893) XC. 81 He that lovyeth me lovyeth my hound. **1546** J. HEYWOOD *Dialogue of Proverbs* II. ix. K4ᵛ Ye haue bene so veraie [veritable] a hog, To my frends. What man, loue me, loue my dog. **1692** R. L'ESTRANGE *Fables of Aesop* cvi. Love Me, Love my Dog.... For there are certain Decencies of Respect due to the Servant for the Master's sake. **1826** LAMB *Elia's Last Essays* (1833) 262 That you must love me, and love my dog.... We could never yet form a friendship ... without the intervention of some third anomaly ... the understood dog in the proverb. **2001** *Spectator* 1 Dec. 28 Sir Michael had agreed to take his new job only on the condition that Mr Bolland remained at his right hand. 'It's a case of love me, love my dog,' a courtier told me. ■ **associates** 仲間；love 愛・恋愛

LOVE will find a way.
恋に不可能はない。

恋には抗し難い力がある。

□*a*1607 T. DELONEY *Gentle Craft* (1648) I. Xv. Thus love you see can finde a way, To make both Men and Maids obey. **1661** 'T. B.' (*title*) Love will finde out the way. **1765** in T. PERCY *Reliques* iii. III. 236 Over the mountains, And over the waves; ... Love will find out the way. **1962** 'S. NASH' *Killed by Scandal* ix. But he's so fond of June that I'm sure it's going to be all right. Love will find a way. **1975** *Listener* 16 Oct. 504 The red-plush curtain fell on a reprise of 'Love will find a way'. ■ love 愛・恋愛

love ⇒ (名詞) The COURSE of true love never did run smooth; All's FAIR in love and war; When the FURZE is in bloom, my love's in tune; LUCKY at cards, unlucky in love; MONEY is the root of all evil; It is best to be OFF with the old love before you are on with the new; PITY is akin to love; When POVERTY comes in at the door, love flies out of the window; PRAISE the child, and you make love to the mother; The QUARREL of lovers is the renewal of love; (動詞) EVERYBODY loves a lord; Whom the GODS love die young.

loved ⇒ BETTER to have loved and lost, than never to have loved at all.

Lovell ⇒ The CAT, the rat, and Lovell the dog, rule all England under the hog.

lover ⇒ LOVE but laughs at lovers' perjury; The QUARREL of lovers is the renewal of love.

There is LUCK in leisure.
運は暇の中にある。
（訳注：「果報は寝て待て」）

行動を起こす前に待つ方がいい場合が多い。

□**1683** G. MERITON *Yorkshire Dialogue* 9 There's luck in Leizur. **1859** 'SKITT' *Fisher's River* vii. Thinks I, 'There's luck in leisure,' as I've hearn folks say.... So I jist waited a spell. **1936** J. ESTE-VEN *While Murder Waits* xxii. 'You ... won't decide now?' ... 'There's luck in leisure, Victoria.'
■ **patience and impatience** 忍耐と性急；**procrastination** 先延ばし

There is LUCK in odd numbers.
奇数は縁起がよい。
（訳注：奇数とは 2 で割り切れない整数をいうが、洋の東西を問わず、縁起がよい、重要な、根本的なといった意味が含まれているようである。「世界の七不思議」〈the Seven Wonders of the World〉、子供の成長・健康を祝う「七五三」などからもわかるように、特に 3 、7 などは重要な数とされている。3 に関しては、キリスト教の「三位一体」〈父なる神、子なるキリスト、精霊〉、仏教の「三世」〈前世、現世、来世〉、「三宝」〈仏、仏の教えである法、その教えを奉じる僧〉、日本のことわざに「三人寄れば文殊の知恵」などがある。7 に関しては、ギリシアの「七賢人」日本の「七福神」などが想起されよう。1598 年のシェイクスピアの『ウィンザーの陽気な女房たち』からの用例では、「これが 3 度目だ。奇数には幸運が宿っておればいい」と述べられている）

THIRD *time lucky*「3 度目の幸運」とよく似た迷信である。†ウェルギリウス『牧歌』viii. 75 *Numero deus impare gaudet.*「神は奇数を好む」

□**1598** SHAKESPEARE *Merry Wives of Windsor* V. i. 3 This is the third time; I hope good luck lies in odd numbers. **1837** S. LOVER *Rory O'More* I. (*title-page*) 'There's luck in odd numbers,' says Rory O'More. **1883** J. PAYN *Thicker than Water* I. i. She was ... by no means averse to a third experiment in matrimony.... 'There was luck in odd numbers.' **1963** N. FITZGERALD *Day of Adder* i. You can make that five then.... There's luck in odd numbers. ■ **luck** 幸運・運；**super-stition** 迷信

luck ⇒ The DEVIL'S children have the Devil's luck; DILIGENCE is the mother of good luck; FOOLS for luck; See a PIN and pick it up, all the day you'll have good luck.

LUCKY at cards, unlucky in love.
トランプでつくと、恋でつまずく。

この発想は 18 世紀にすでにはやっていた。スウィフト『上品な会話』(1738)III. 213 Well, Miss, you'll have a sad Husband, you have such good Luck at Cards.「お嬢さん、あなたはご主人には恵まれせんな。こんなにトランプで運を使い果たしたんですから」

□**1866** T. W. ROBERTSON *Society* II. ii. 'I'm always lucky at cards!' ... 'Yes, I know an old prov-erb about that.... Lucky at play, unlucky in—.' *a***1871**—?—*Play* (1889) III. ii. Unlucky in love, lucky at cards. **1941** P. CHEYNEY *Trap for Bellamy* iv. 'Lucky at cards, unlucky in love.' ... I'm going to find out if the proverb's true.... What are they playing tonight? **1981** *Oxford Mail* 29 Aug. 5 Arthur and Hilda Cover have defied the old proverb by being lucky at cards and lucky in love. **2003** *Times* 1 Jan. 30 You had never believed the phrase 'lucky in cards, unlucky in love' until that night when you were the victim of a drive-by shooting from a jealous ex-girlfriend shortly after being dealt a full house. ■ **love** 愛・恋愛；**luck** 幸運・運

282　lucky

lucky ⇒ It is BETTER to be born lucky than rich; If you can't be GOOD, be lucky; THIRD time lucky.

lunch ⇒ There's no such thing as a FREE lunch.

M

Where MACGREGOR sits is the head of the table.
マグレガーが座ると、そこが上座となる。

ハイランドの略奪者であるキャンベルのロバート・マグレガー（通称ロブ・ロイ：1671-1734）の言葉とされることがある。the MacGregor（1903年の用例）とはマグレガー一族の長を意味する。マグレガー以外の名前が使われることもある。このことわざの発想は次の2つの用例で説明される。1つは**1580**リリー『ユーフュイーズと彼のイングランド』II. 39 When ... Agesilaus sonne was set at the lower end of the table, and one cast it in his teeth as a shame, he answered: this is the vpper end where I sit「アゲシラオスの息子がテーブルの下座に座らされたので、そのようなところに座るなんてとんでもないと言ったところ、彼は答えた。私が座ったところこそが上座である」。もう1つは**1732** T. フューラー（英国の医師）の格言集『グノモロジア』no. 4362 That is the upper End, where the chief Person sits.「ここ、つまり、中心人物が座る場所こそが上座である」

☐**1837** EMERSON *American Scholar* 19 Wherever Macdonald [the head of the Macdonald clan] sits, there is the head of the table. Linnaeus makes botany the most alluring of studies and wins it from the farmer and the herb-woman. **1903** K. D. WIGGIN *Rebecca of Sunnybrook Farm* viii. If wherever the MacGregor sat was the head of the table, so ... wherever Rebecca stood was the centre of the stage. **1918** A. G. GARDINER *Leaves in Wind* 197 There are ... people who carry the centre of the stage with them.... 'Where O'Flaherty sits is the head of the table.' **1940** J. W. BELLAH *Bones of Napoleon* 69 Like Macdonald—where Lord Innes sat was the head of the table. **1980** *Times* 12 May 15 (letter from His Honour Judge MacGregor) Sir, Where MacGregor sits is the head of the table. ■ **honour** 尊敬・名誉；**pride** 誇り・うぬぼれ

Don't get MAD, get even.
怒るな、やり返すのだ。

☐**1975** J. F. KENNEDY in B. Bradlee *Conversations with Kennedy* 25 Some of the reasons have their roots in that wonderful law of the Boston Irish political jungle: 'Don't get mad; get even.' **1990** *Evening Standard* 28 Feb. 13 Nancy Reagan made more than $2 million from her 'don't get mad, get even' ... memories. **2001** *Washington Times* 25 May A22 The episode was especially moving inasmuch as forgiveness is not in the Kennedy tradition. JFK was the author of the famous dictum, 'Don't get mad, get even.' **2014** *Guardian* 24 Apr. (online; heading) The FCC [Federal Communications Commission] is about to axe-murder net neutrality. Don't get mad—get even. ■ **revenge** 復讐

mad ⇒ Whom the GODS would destroy, they first make mad.

made ⇒ GOD made the country, and man made the town; PROMISES, like pie-crust, are made to be broken; RULES are made to be broken; ⇒ MAKE.

Mahomet ⇒ If the MOUNTAIN will not come to Mahomet, Mahomet must go to the mountain.

MAKE hay while the sun shines.
日の照るうちに草を干せ。
（訳注：「好機逸すべからず」）

チャンスを逃してはならない。

☐ **1546** J. HEYWOOD *Dialogue of Proverbs* I. iii. A4 When the sunne shynth make hey. **1583** B. MELBANCKE *Philotimus* 24 Yt is well therefore to make hay while the sunne shines. **1835** J. CARLYLE *Letters & Memorials* (1883) I. 21 'It is good to make hay while the sun shines,' which means, in. the present case ... to catch hold of a friend while she is in the humour. **1924** E. BAGNOLD *Serena Blandish* vi. The countess's enthusiasm was cooling. Martin ... said warningly, 'You must make hay, my child, while the sun shines.' **1999** 'H. CRANE' *Miss Seeton's Finest Hour* xii. 100 'Our local garage must have made a fortune out of me since this blackout nonsense began.... Mind you,' the doctor added in a noncommittal voice, 'I imagine they think of it more along the lines of making hay while the sun shines ... ' ■ **opportunity, taken 得られた機会**

As you MAKE your bed, so you must lie upon it.
自分で寝床を作るのだから自分がそこに寝なければならない。
（訳注：いくらいやでも、自分がしたことの始末は自分でつけねばならない。「自業自得」）

どんなに不愉快であろうと、自分の行ないの結果は受け止めなければならない。† 15世紀後半のフランス語 *Comme onfaictson lict, on le treuve.*「自分で寝床を作るのだから、そこを寝場所とせよ」

☐ *c*1590 G. HARVEY *Marginalia* (1913) 88 Lett them ... go to there bed, as themselues shall make it. **1640** G. HERBERT *Outlandish Proverbs* no. 340 He that makes his bed ill, lies there. **1721** J. KELLY *Scottish Proverbs* 16 As you make your bed, so you lye down. According to your Conditions you have your Bargain. **1832** S. WARREN *Diary of Late Physician* II. vi. As soon as his relatives ... heard ... they told him ... that as he had made his bed, so he must lie upon it. **1921** A. P. HERBERT *House by River* V. There's no doubt she was out with one of them ... and went further than she meant, ... but if you make your bed you must lie on it. **1997** *Spectator* 29 Nov 14 Your mother says serves you right, you've made your bed and now you lie on it, I never liked him. ■ **action and consequence 行為と結果**

make ⇒ You cannot make BRICKS without straw; CLOTHES make the man; Make HASTE slowly; If you don't make MISTAKES you don't make anything; You cannot make an OMELETIE without breaking eggs; You can't make a SILK purse out of a sow's ear.

male ⇒ The FEMALE of the species is more deadly than the male.

Mammon ⇒ You cannot serve GOD and Mammon.

MAN   285

MAN cannot live by bread alone.
人はパンだけでは生きられない。

このことわざは、『申命記』8 章 3 節 (欽定訳聖書) Man doth not live by bread only, but by every word that proceedeth out of the mouth of the Lord doth man live. 「人はパンだけでは生きられず、神の口から出たあらゆる言葉に従って生きる」と、『マタイによる福音書』4 章 4 節 (欽定訳聖書) Man shall not live by bread alone. 「人はパンだけでは生きられない」から来ていることは明らかである。

□ **1875** EMERSON in *North American Review* May-June 418 Man does not live by bread alone, but by faith, by admiration, by sympathy. **1927** J. BUCHAN *Witch Wood* iii. Man canna live by bread alone, but he assuredly canna live without it. **1973** *Galt Toy Catalogue* 35 As the saying goes—Man cannot live by bread alone. **2012** *Yorkshire Life* 8 Oct. (online) Of course, man cannot live on bread alone. But in Yorkshire, faced with an astounding array of top bakery talent, it might be fun to try. ■ **food and drink 飲食物 ; life 人生**

Whatever MAN has done, man may do.
人は、人のしたことならどんなことでもやれる。

(訳注 : may =「…できる」〈能力〉。may の語源は「できる」である。I'll help you as best I *may*.〈できるだけ援助しましょう〉。Cather roses while you *may*.【ことわざ】〈摘めるうちにバラを摘め。若いときは二度と来ない〉。「彼も人なり、我も人なり」)

これとよく似た考えが **1723** G. S. キンボール『ロードアイランド植民地総督通信録』(1902) I. 9 における S. クランストンの言葉 But as the Proverb is what hath been may be againe. 「ことわざにあるように、今までなされたことは再びなされうる」の背後に見られる。

□ **1840** *New Jerusalem Mag.* Dec. XIV. 144. [S]hall not a father's good sense and paternal compassion rescue his own children from the miseries attaching to this worship of the gods of Greece and Rome? This ill-considered usage [compulsory classical education] props itself a good deal, upon the vulgar adage, that—What man has done, man may do. **1863** C. READE *Hard Cash* TI. xiv. 'Dark Deeds are written in an unknown tongue called "Lawyerish" ... ; pick it out if you can.' 'Whatever man has done man may do,' said Dr. Sampson stoutly. **1910** 'SAKI' *Reginald in Russia* 14 I fell in love ... with the local doctor's wife.... On looking back at past events it seems to me that she must have been distinctly ordinary, but I suppose the doctor had fallen in love with her once, and what man has done man can do. **2010** M. WALTERS *Echo* 78 I'm not the first to do it, and I sure as hell won't be the last ... Whatever man has done, man can do. ■ **possibility and impossibility 可能性と不可能性**

A MAN is as old as he feels and a woman as old as she looks.
男の年は気持ち相応、女の年は顔つき相応。

(訳注 : このことわざでは、"x as ... as y" の構文が用いられている。この構文は、「x の程度は少なくとも y ほどはある」と解釈される。すなわち、x の程度が y のそれを多少上まわることはあっても、下まわることはない。Mary is as tall as Jane is. 〈メアリーの背の高さは少なくともジェーンほどはある〉)

このことわざの前半と後半はそれぞれ単独で使われることもある。(1891 年と 1990 年の用例参照)。

□ **1871** V. LUSH *Thames Journal* 27 Aug. (1975) 114 She is always making me out so much older than I am and that's not fair, for a man is only as old as he feels and a woman is only as old as she looks. **1891** W. MORRIS *News from Nowhere* iii. 'How old am I, do you think?' 'Well,' quoth I, 'I have always been told that a woman is as old as she looks.' **1907** *Illustrated London News* 25

286　MAN

May 794 The adage that a man is as old as he feels, and a woman as old as she looks, may be said to contain much inherent truth. **1900** 'C. AIRD' *Body Politic* (1991) xi. 123 'He might still marry.' Sloan was bracing. 'A man is only as old as he feels.' ■ **men and women　男女**；**old age　老年**

MAN is the measure of all things.
人間は万物の尺度である。

世界の中心が人間であるという考え方を正当化する際に使われる。†プラトン『クラテュロス』vi.におけるプロタゴラスの言葉 πάντων χρημάτων μέτρον εἶναι ἄνθρωπον.「人間は万物の尺度である」。プロタゴラス（紀元前 5 世紀）はソフィストで修辞学教師であった。

☐**1547** W. BALDWIN *Morall Phylosophie* III. xvi. O6ᵛ Man is the measure of all thynges. **1631** G. CHAPMAN *Warres of Pompey & Caesar* II. E2 As of all things, man is said the measure, So your full merits measure forth a man. **1948** 'H. BESTON' *Northern Farm* xii. 'Man the measure of all things.' A good adage. **1980** *Times Greece Supplement* 15 Dec. p. iv. The belief that man was the measure of all things ... led the Greeks into ... new disciplines. ■ **human nature　人間性**

MAN proposes, God disposes.
計画は人に、決裁は神にあり。

（訳注：propose ＝「…を企てる、計画する」、dispose ＝「…を整理する、処理する」。この違いは、語源の違いにも反映されている。pro- は「前に」であり、dis- は「離れて」である）

人間の努力の結果は神のみぞ知る。†14世紀初頭のフランス語 *Car se li homme mal propose, Diex … le dispose.*「たとえ人間が悪事を企もうとも、神がそれを決済する」。*c*1420 トマス・ア・ケンピス『キリストにならいて』I. xix. *Homo proponit, sed Deus disponit*「計画は人に、決裁は神にあり」（1450年の用例参照）。

☐*c*1440 J. LYDGATE *Fall of Princes* (EETS) 1. 3291 A man off malice may a thyng purpose ... But God a-boue can graciousli dispose [determine] Ageyn such malice to make resistence. *c*1450 tr. T. a Kempis' De lmitatione Christi (EETS) 1. xix. For man purposith and god disposith. **1640** G. HERBERT *Outlandish Proverbs* no. 1 Man Proposeth, God disposeth. **1853** R. C. TRENCH *On Lessons in Proverbs* (ed. 2) iii. A proverb ... Man proposes, God disposes ... that every nation in Europe possesses. **1958** L. DURRELL *Mountolive* IV. 88 In diplomacy one can only propose, never dispose. That is up to God, don't you think? **1997** *Times* 9 Aug. 8 God's will is not something to be commanded; recall the saying 'Man proposes, God disposes'. ■ **fate and fatalism　運命と運命論**；**providence　（神の）摂理**

MAN's extremity is God's opportunity.
人間の窮地は神の出番である。

（訳注：extremity「窮地、難局」。複数形になることもある。drive a person to the ⟨utmost⟩ *extremity/extremities* ⟨人を窮地に追い込む⟩）

逆境や被害に直面すると人は神に祈りたくなる。

☐**1629** T. ADAMS *Works* 619 Heere is now a deliuery fit for God, a cure for the Almightie hand to vndertake. Mans extremity is Gods opportunitie. **1706** LD. BELHAVEN in *Defoe Hist. Union* (1709) v. 34 Man's Extremity is God's opportunity.... Some unforeseen Providence will fall out, that may cast the Ballance. **1916** E. A. BURROUGHS *Valley of Decision* viii. In the first winter of the war ... we were all much encouraged by tales of a new thirst for religion among the majority of the men.... 'Man's extremity, God's opportunity.' **1949** N. SMITH *I capture Castle* xiii. 'You should look in on the church if ever you're mentally run down.' ... ' You mean "Man's extremity is God's opportunity"?' **1980** *Times* 4 Dec. 17 Those extremities which have, until now, been of-

MANCHESTER 287

ten God's opportunity. ■ **necessity** 必要性・必然性；**opportunity** 機会

Because a MAN is born in a stable that does not make him a horse.
人は馬小屋で生まれたからといって馬になるわけではない。

ウェリントン伯爵（1769-1852）の言葉とされることがある。1969年の用例参照。

□**1833** M. SCOTT *Tom Cringle's Log* I. iv. 'I am an Englishman and no traitor, nor will I die the death of one.' ... 'Truly ... a man does sometimes become a horse by being born in a stable.' **1906** *Times Literary Supplement* 27 Apr. 147 Except on the principle that the man who is born in a stable is a horse, [he] was not an Irishman at all. **1969** E. LONGFORD *Wellington: Years of Sword* viii. If Wellington was ever chaffed for being an Irishman and replied with a notorious quip, it was probably during this period (1807): Because a man is born in a stable that does not make him a horse. **1980** J. O'FAOLAIN *No Country for Young Men* ii. Father Casey ... has a theory that the Irish back in Ireland have less claim to Irishness than men like himself. Something to do with ... being born in a stable not necessarily making you a horse. ■ **human nature** 人間性；**origins** 起源・生まれ

man ⇒ BETTER be an old man's darling, than a young man's slave; A BLIND man's wife needs no paint; Never send a BOY to do a man's job; The CHILD is the father of the man; CLOTHES make the man; In the COUNTRY of the blind, the one eyed man is king; DO right and fear no man; A DROWNING man will clutch at a straw; The EARLY man never borrows from the late man; EVERY elm has its man; EVERY man for himself; EVERY man for himself, and devil take the hindmost; EVERY man for himself, and God for us all; EVERY man has his price; EVERY man is the architect of his own fortune; EVERY man to his taste; EVERY man to his trade; It's ill speaking between a FULL man and a fasting; A HUNGRY man is an angry man; You should KNOW a man seven years before you stir his fire; A man who is his own LAWYER has a fool for his client; One man's LOSS is another man's gain; MANNERS maketh man; Like MASTER, like man; One man's MEAT is another man's poison; MONEY makes a man; A MONEYLESS man goes fast through the market; NEEDLES and pins, ... when a man marries, his trouble begins; NINE tailors make a man; NO man can serve two masters; NO man is a hero to his valet; There is NOTHING so good for the inside of a man as the outside of a horse; An OLD man is twice a child; The RICH man has his ice in the summer and the poor man gets his in the winter; Give a man ROPE enough and he will hang himself; Six hours' sleep for a man, seven for a woman, and eight for a fool; One man may STEAL a horse, while another may not look over a hedge; The STYLE is the man; TIME and tide wait for no man; Man fears TIME, but time fears the pyramids; For WANT of a nail the shoe was lost; The WAY to a man's heart is through his stomach; A WILFUL man must have his way; When the WIND is in the east, 'tis neither good for man nor beast; A WOMAN without a man is like a fish without a bicycle; A YOUNG man married is a young man marred; ⇒ MEN.

What MANCHESTER says today, the rest of England says tomorrow.
マンチェスターが今日語ることが明日イングランドすべての意見になる。

このことわざは様々なバリエーションがある。1902年の用例は歴史的な文脈で使われて

288 Manchester

いる。1846 年に廃止された穀物法は外国産の穀物の輸入を制限したものであるが、マンチェスター（当時はイングランド北部のランカシャーの一部であった）は自由貿易の本拠地とみなされており、輸入制限法に反対するリーダー的存在であった。

□**1898** R. KIPLING *Day's Work* 51 What the horses o' Kansas think to-day, the horses of America will think to-morrow; an' I tell you that when the horses of America rise in their might, the day o' the Oppressor is ended. **1902** V. S. LEAN *Collectanea* I. 116 What Lancashire thinks to-day all England will think to-morrow. This was in the days of the Anti-Com-Law League. Since then the initiative in political movements proceeds from Birmingham. **1944** C. MILBURN *Journal* 24 Aug. in *Diaries* (1979) xiii. Manchester rang its bells yesterday—a day before St. Paul's ... thus justifying its words, so often used: 'What Manchester says today, the rest of England says tomorrow!' **1980** *Listener* 6 Mar. 300 What Manchester does today— ... is the old boast that 'What Manchester does today London thinks tomorrow.' ■ imitation 模倣; opinions 意見; public opinion 世論

Manchester ⇒ YORKSHIRE born and Yorkshire bred, strong in the arm and weak in the head.

MANNERS maketh man.
礼儀作法が人を作る。

（訳注：man ＝「立派な人」。manners ＝「礼儀作法、行儀」。That child has good *manners*.〈あの子は行儀が良い〉。Where're your *manners*?〈お行儀良くしなさい〉。manners には、「〈国民・民族などの〉風習、慣習」という意味もある。Manners are stronger than law.【ことわざ】〈慣習は法律よりも強し〉。「金が人を作る」〈Money makes a man.〉参照）

教養人としての地位を作るのは我々の礼儀作法である。このことわざを座右の銘にしていたウィカムのウィリアム（1324-1404）は、ウィンチェスターの司教、イングランドの高官、ウィンチェスター大学とオックスフォード大学ニューカレッジの創立者であった（1661 年の用例参照）。

□*c*1350 *Douce MS* 52 no. 77 Maner makys man. *c*1450 in *Archiv* (1931) CLIX. 88 Maners and clothyng makes man. **1509** A. BARCLAY *Ship of Fools* 118 An old prouerbe ... Sayth that good lyfe and maners makyth man. *a*1661 T. FULLER *Worthies* (Hants.) 3 Manners makes a man, Quoth William Wickham. This generally was his Motto, inscribed frequently on the places of his Founding. **1721** J. KELLY *Scottish Proverbs* 246 Meat feeds, Cloth deeds, but Manners makes the Man.... Good Meat, and fine Cloaths, without good Breeding, are but poor Recommendations. **1824** BYRON *Don Juan* xv. xviii. The difference is, that in days of old Men made the manners; manners now make men. **1983** R. BARNARD *Case of Missing Bronte* vi. Gracious little twit The idea that manners makyth man clearly went out of the educational system before he went into it.
■ manners 礼儀・作法

manners ⇒ EVIL communications corrupt good manners; OTHER times, other manners.

manure ⇒ MONEY, like manure, does no good till it is spread.

MANY a little makes a mickle.
小さなものでもたくさん集まれば大きなものになる。

（訳注：many a/an ＝「たくさんの」〈単数扱い〉。「塵も積もれば山となる」。下の 2 つのことわざの many a も同様である *Many a* member has supported the plan.〈多くの会員がその計画を支持している〉）

次に挙げることわざの正式な形である。1905年の用例で使われている pickle は「少量」を表わすスコットランド語。mickle「大量」もスコットランドでしか使われない。

☐ *a*1250 *Ancrene Wisse* (1962) 32 Thys ofte as me seith, of lutel muchel waxeth. *c*1390 CHAUCER *Parson's Tale* l. 361 The proverbe seith that 'manye smale maken a greet.' **1545** R. TAVERNER tr. *Erasmus' Adages* (ed. 2) G5 We commonly say in englyshe: Many a lyttle maketh a great. **1614** W. CAMDEN *Remains concerning Britain* (ed. 2) 310 Many a little makes a mickle. **1822** CARLYLE in *J. A. Froude Life* (1884) I. xii. 'Many a little makes a mickle.' It will be a long ... and weary job, but I must plod along. **1905** *Westminster Gazette* 29 Apr. 3 'There is the Tithe Relief.... But that is a small item.' 'Yes, but many a pickle makes a muckle.' **1979** C. COLVIN *Maria Edgeworth* in France & Switzerland 196 Many a pickle (or little) makes a mickle. ■ **great and small** 大小

MANY a mickle makes a muckle.
小さなものでもたくさん集まれば大きなものになる。

（訳注：「塵も積もれば山となる」）

上のことわざの崩れた形で、よく使われる。muckle はスコットランド方言 *mickle*「大量」に等しい。

☐ **1793** G. WASHINGTON *Writings* (1939) XXXII. 423 A Scotch addage, than which nothing in nature is more true ... 'many mickles make a muckle.' **1940** *Huntly Express* 19 Jan. 3 He said at the close of his address 'As the Scots say, and they should know, mony a mickle male's a muckle.' ... As the Scots know, he had quoted the proverb wrongly. **1993** 'C. Aird' *Going Concern* (1994) i. 5 Amelia's mind had gone off at a complete tangent, trying to work out however many Puckles there must be in the firm. The old saw about thrift came into her mind: 'Many a mickle makes a muckle....' Could it be a case of many a client making a Puckle? ■ **great and small** 大小

There's MANY a slip between cup and lip.
茶碗と唇のあいだには多くの邪魔が入るものだ。

（訳注：slip ＝「しくじり、間違い」。いよいよそれを飲もうとする寸前に思わぬ邪魔が入って、それを飲めなくなることがあるものだ。「油断大敵」、「百里を行く者は九十九里をもって半ばとす」）

† アウルス・ゲッリウス『アッティカの夜』XIII. xviii. 1 における大カトーの言葉 (*saepe audivi*) *inter os atque offam multa intervenire posse*.「口と食べ物のあいだに多くのこと（＝邪魔）が入ることがある」、『パラティン詞華集』x. 32 におけるパラダスの言葉 32 πολλὰ μεταξὺ πέλει κύλικος καὶ χείλεος ἄκρου.「杯と唇のあいだに多くの多くのこと（＝邪魔）が入る」

☐ **1539** R. TAVERNER tr. *Erasmus' Adages* 15 Many thynges fall betwene the cuppe and the mouth.... Betwene the cuppe and the lyppes maye come many casualties. **1783** in *Collections of Massachusetts Hist. Society* (1877) 5th Ser. II. 216 Have a care, and remember the old proverb of 'many a slip,' &c. **1840** R. H. BARHAM *Ingoldsby Legends* 1st Ser. 280 Doubtless the adage, 'There's many a slip 'Twixt the cup and the lip,' hath reference to medicine. **1979** E. KYLE *Summer Scandal* xiii. 'I thought you were here for life.' ... 'There's many a slip between cup and lip.' **2014** *Spectator* 8 Nov. 78 In Soho we lost two of our party between quitting the taxi and entering the first club. One of these was last seen on the very doorstep. There's many a slip 'twixt the cup and the lip, we supposed. ■ **disappointment** 失望；**error** 間違い・過ち

290 MANY

MANY are called but few are chosen.
多くの者が招かれるが、選ばれる者はほとんんどいない。

『マタイによる福音書』22章14節（『欽定訳聖書』）For many are called, but few are chosen.「多くの者が招かれるが、選ばれる者はほとんどいない」を想起させる。

□**1871** J. S. JONES *Life J. S. Batkins* xxviii. The saying that 'many shall be called, but few chosen.' **1980** P. VAN GREENAWAY *Dissident* iii. 'Many are called ... but few are chosen.' He's right. Those of us conscious of our destinies may fairly be termed 'elitistes'. ■ **choice 選択; fate and fatalism 運命と運命論**

MANY hands make light work.
人手が多いと仕事は楽になる。

†ヘシオドス『仕事と日々』380 πλείων μὲν πλεόνων μελέτη. 手が増えるとは労働力が増すことを意味する。エラスムス『格言集』II. iii. 95. *Multae manus onus levius reddunt*.「人手が多いと仕事が楽になる」

□*c***1330** *Sir Beves* (EETS) I. 3352 Ascopard be strong and sterk [physically powerful], Mani hondes maketh light werk! **1678** S. BUTLER *Hudibras* III . ii. Most Hands dispatch apace, And make light work, (the proverb says). **1721** J. KELLY *Scottish Proverbs* 244 Many Hands make light Work. Because it is but little to every one. **1923** *Observer* 11 Feb. 9 What is the use of saying that 'Many hands make light work' when the same copy-book tells you that 'Too many cooks spoil the broth'? **2002** B. D'AMATO *White Male Infant* i. 16 Tony immediately began to prepare the bone marrow ... His assistant ... simultaneously ran up smears with less usual stains ... Many hands make light work. ■ **assistance 援助; work 仕事**

many ⇒ There's many a GOOD tune played on an old fiddle; Many a TRUE word is spoken in jest; Many go out for WOOL and come home shorn.

MARCH comes in like a lion, and goes out like a lamb.
3 月はライオンのようにやって来て子羊のように去って行く

イングランドの天気は伝統的に 3 月初旬は荒れるが、下旬になると穏やかになる。

□*a***1625** J. FLETCHER *Wife for Month* (1717) II. i. 'I would chuse March, for I would come in like a Lion.' ... 'But you'd go out like a Lamb when you went to hanging.' **1670** J. RAY *English Proverbs* 41 March hack ham [hackande = annoying] comes in like a lion, goes out like a lamb. **1849** C. BRONTë *Shirley* II. iv. Charming and fascinating he resolved to be. Like March, having come in like a lion, he purposed to go out like a lamb. **1906** E. HOWEN *Country Diary of Edwardian Lady* (1977) 25 March has come in like a lamb with a warm wind ... from the South-west. **2002** *Times* 2 Mar. 26 'When March comes in like a lion, it goes out like a lamb' goes the old folklore saying ... The reverse, however, is also true, and the saying continues: 'When March comes in like a lamb, it goes out like a lion,' which does not bode well for us this year. ■ **weather lore 天気にまつわる伝承**

March ⇒ APRIL showers bring forth May flowers; On the FIRST of March, the crows begin to search; So many MISTS in March, so many frosts in May; A PECK of March dust is worth a king's ransom.

march ⇒ An ARMY marches on its stomach.

MARRY 291

mare ⇒ The GREY mare is the better horse; MONEY makes the mare to go; NOTHING so bold as a blind mare.

market ⇒ A MONEYLESS man goes fast through the market.

MARRIAGE is a lottery.
結婚は運である。

□ **1642** T. FULLER *Holy State* III. xxii. Marriage shall prove no lottery to thee, when the hand of providence chuseth for thee, who, if drawing a blank, can turn into a prize by sanctifying a bad wife unto thee. **1875** S. SMILES *Thrift* xii. 'Marriage is a lottery.' It may be so, if we abjure the teachings of prudence. **1939** F. SULLIVAN *Sullivan at Bay* 14 What is marriage? ... Marriage is a lottery. ■ **luck** 幸運・運; **marriage** 結婚

There goes more to MARRIAGE than four bare legs in a bed.
結婚にはベッドの中の四本の素足より大切なものがある。

セックスや性的な魅力では幸せな結婚生活を維持することはできない。

□ **c1549** J. HEYWOOD *Dialogue of Proverbs* I. viii. Bl In house to kepe household, whan folks wyll wed, Mo thyngs belong, than foure bare legs in a bed. **1623** W. CAMDEN *Remains concerning Britain* (ed. 3) 273 Longs more to marriage then foure bare legges in a bed. **1738** SWIFT *Polite Conversation* I. 84 Consider, Mr. Neverout, Four bare Legs in a Bed; and you are a younger Brother. **1958** in M. L. Wolf *Dict. Painting* p. vii. As the old proverb has it, 'there goes more to marriage than four bare legs in a bed.' ■ **marriage** 結婚

marriage ⇒ DREAM of a funeral and you hear of a marriage; HANGING and wiving go by destiny.

MARRIAGES are made in heaven.
結婚は天の定めである。

以下の用例では、結婚が天の定めであるという考えはほとんど支持されてはいない。

□ **1567** W. PAINTER *Palace of Pleasure* xxiii. True it is, that marriages be don in Heaven and performed in earth. **1580** LYLY *Euphues & his England* II. 223 Mariages are made in heauen, though consumated in yearth. **1738** SWIFT *Polite Conversation* I. 78 They say, Marriages are made in Heaven; but I doubt, when she was married, she had no Friend there. **1932** S. GIBBONS *Cold Comfort Farm* I. I prefer the idea of arrangement to that other statement, that marriages are made in Heaven. **1980** 'S. Woods' *Weep for Her* 187 She's a sentimental sort who believes marriages are made in heaven. ■ **marriage** 結婚

married ⇒ A YOUNG man married is a young man marred.

Never MARRY for money, but marry where money is.
金のために結婚してはならないが、どうせなら金がある人と結婚せよ。

結婚相手を選ぶ際に、純粋に金目当ての結婚であってはならない。とはいえ、愛と幸せな結婚生活に必要なものが備わっているなら、自分よりも裕福な人と結婚する方がいい。

□ **1870** TENNYSON *Northern Farmer, New Style in The Holy Grail* 163 Doänt thou marry for munny, but goä wheer munny is! **1968** 'W. Haggard' *Cool Day for Killing* ii. He'd have heard the

ancient saw. Never marry for money, but marry where money is. **1991** *Bookseller* 16 Aug. 403
'Never marry money but go where money is.' For the book as an entity to make news consistently, it must go where news is consistently made—as with the royal family. ■ **marriage 結婚；mon-
ey 金・金銭**

MARRY in haste and repent at leisure.
慌てて結婚、ゆっくり後悔。

（訳注：at leisure ＝「ゆっくりと、時間をかけて」。このことわざでは、「慌てて結婚せよ」と「ゆっくり後
悔せよ」という 2 つの命令文が並列されているが、しかし、実際にそうせよと命令しているのではない。あ
わてて結婚すると後々後悔することになると警告しているのである。命令文を並列して、どちらもやって
はいけないと警告していることわざに、Spare the rod and spoil the child.〈鞭を惜しむと子供をだめに
する〉などがある。I will debate this matter *at leisure*.〈この問題はゆっくりと時間をかけて論じます〉）

このことわざは早急な結婚だけでなく、それ以外の早急な行動にも広く適用される。
1998 *Spectator* 10 Jan. 6 All modern governments legislate in haste and repent
at leisure.「すべての近代政府は慌てて法律を作り、後からじっくり後悔する」。最近の
言い方として、Act in haste, repent at leisure.がある。**1998** *Times* 26 Jan. 21 'Act in
haste, repent at leisure' would be a poor epitaph for the UK's presidency [of the
EU].「慌てて行動、ゆっくり後悔」という言葉は英国が EU の議長国になったりしたら哀
れな墓碑銘になるであろう。

□**1568** E. TILNEY *Duties in Marriage* B4 Some haue loued in post hast, that afterwards haue repented them at leysure. **1615** J. DAY *Festivals* x. Marrying in hast, and Repenting by leasure. **1734**
B. FRANKLIN *Poor Richard's Almanack* (May) Grief often treads upon the heels of pleasure,
Marry'd in haste, we oft repent at leisure. **1872** W. STIRLING-MAXWELL *Works* (1891) VI. xvii.
'Marry in haste and repent at leisure' is a proverb that may be borne in mind with advantage in
the choice of a party as well as of a wife. **2002** *National Review* 11 Mar. 28 One might with justice adapt the old proverb about marriage to the adorning of the skin in this savage fashion: Tat-
too in haste, repent at leisure. ■ **haste 性急；marriage 結婚；regrets 後悔**

MARRY in May, rue for aye.
5 月に結婚すると、後々後悔する。

（訳注：このことわざでも、「5 月に結婚せよ」と「後々後悔する」という 2 つの命令文が並列されている
が、しかし、その意味は、5 月に結婚すると後々後悔することになると警告している。for〈ever and〉
ay〈e〉＝「【方言・詩】永久に」。Their love will last *for aye*.〈彼らの愛は永久に続く〉）

これより初期の関連することわざが以下の用例に示されている。5 月が結婚に悪影響を
及ぼすという古い迷信は多い。例えば、MAY chickens come cheeping.「5 月のひよこ
はピヨピヨ鳴きながらやって来る」。SWEEP the house with broom in May, you
sweep the head of the house away.「5 月に箒で家を掃くと家の主人も掃き出してし
まう」などである。†オウィディウス『祭暦』489 *Si te proverbia tangunt, mense malum
Maio nubere volgus ait*.「もしことわざを信じるなら、巷の人は 5 月の結婚は不幸を招
くと言っている」

□**1675** *Poor Robin's Almanack* May, The Proverb saies … Of all the Moneths 'tis worst to Wed
in May. **1821** J. GALT *Annals of Parish* vl. We were married on the 29th day of April … on account of the dread that we had of being married in May, for it is said, 'Of the marriages in May,
The bairns die of a decay.' **1879** W. HENDERSON *Notes on Folk-Lore of Northern Counties* (rev.
ed.) i. The ancient proverb still lives on the lips of the people of Scotland and the Borders—Marry in May, Rue for aye. **1913** E. M. WRIGHT *Rustic Speech* xiii. May … is an evil month for mar-

MAY 293

riage.... Marry in May, you'll rue it for aye, is a Devonshire saying. **1981** *Observer Magazine* 28 June 27 On weddings and engagements we are told that May is an unlucky month for getting married; 'Marry in May, rue for aye.' ■ calendar lore 暦にまつわる伝承；marriage 結婚；regrets 後悔

marry ⇒ BETTER to marry than to burn.

Martin ⇒ The ROBIN and the wren are God's cock and hen.

Martyr ⇒ The BLOOD of the martyrs is the seed of the Church.

Like MASTER, like man.
この主人にしてこの召使いあり。

ここでの man は「召使い」の意味で使われている。女性の場合、like mistress や like maid となる。†ペトロニウス『サテュリコン』I viii. *Qualis dominus, talis et servus.*「主人のように召使いもなる」。14世紀初頭のフランス語 *Lon dit a tel seigneur tel varlet.*「よく言われることだが、こんな主人にはこんな召使いが仕えるものだ」

□**1530** J. PALSGRAVE *L'eclatrcissement de la Langue Française* 120ᵛ Suche maystre suche man. **1538** T. ELYOT *Dict.* S. V. Similes, A lewde [foolish] servaunt with an yll master.... Lyke master lyke man. **1620** T. SHELTON tr. *Cervantes' Don Quixote* II. X. The Prouerbe be true that ays, 'like master, like man', and I may add, 'like lady, like maid'. Lady Hercules was fine, but her maid was still finer. **1979** M. G. EBERHART *Bayou Road* iv. 'Like master, like man,' Marcy' s father had said bitterly ... of the disappearance of an entire set of Dresden plates. **1990** 'C. AIRD' *Body Politic* (1991) xii. 131 'I'm sorry,' said Miss Finch, 'but she just doesn't like men.' Like mistress, like maid, was what Sloan's grandmother would have said to that, but Sloan himself, wise in his own generation, kept silent. ■ employers and employees 雇用者と被雇用者

master ⇒ The EYE of a master does more work than both his hands; FIRE is a good servant but a bad master; JACK is as good as his master; JACK of all trades and master of none; NO man can serve two masters.

What MATTERS is what works.
大事なことはうまくいくことである。

あらゆる状況で最も大切な考慮すべきことは、どのような行為にせよ、それが効果的になるように見守ることである。

□**1998** Department of Transport, Environment, and the Regions *Modernising Local Government: Improving Local Services through Best Value* ii. 9 There is no reason why services should. be delivered directly if other more efficient means are available. What matters is what works. **2001** *Spectator* 3 Nov. 22 Given that the unions had all bought into 'what matters is what works', it struck me as confrontational. ■ efficiency and inefficiency 能率と非能率

MAY chickens come cheeping.
5月のひよこはピヨピヨ鳴きながらやって来る。

文字通りの意味は、5月生まれのひよこは常にか細い声で鳴いていることから、明らか

294　May

に虚弱だということである。病気がちな子供についても使われる。

□1868 A. HISLOP *Proverbs of Scotland* 223 May birds are aye cheeping. This refers to the popular superstition against marrying in … May, the children of which marriages are said to 'die of decay'. **1895** S. O. ADDY *Household Tales* II. viii. Children born in the month of May require great care in bringing up, for 'May chickens come cheeping.' **2002** N. ASTLEY *End of My Tether* 216 May-farrowing sows will eat their own litters … And May chickens come cheeping. ■ **calendar lore** 暦にまつわる伝承 ; **misfortune** 不運

May ⇒ APRIL showers bring forth May flowers; Ne'er CAST a clout till May be out; MARRY in May, rue for aye; So many MISTS in March, so many frosts in May; SELL in May and go away; A SWARM in May is worth a load of hay; SWEEP the house with broom in May, you sweep the head of the house away.

may ⇒ He that WILL not when he may, when he will he shall have nay.

means ⇒ The END justifies the means; he who WILLS the end, wills the means.

MEASURE seven times, cut once.
7 度寸法を測り、1 度で裁断せよ。

ロシアのことわざで、元来は大工仕事と針仕事を指していた。意味は準備段階での細心の注意が過ちを未然に防いでくれるというものである。† MEASURE twice, cut once.「2 度寸法を測り、1 度で裁断せよ」。THINK twice, cut once.「2 度考え、1 度で裁断せよ」

□**1853** W. FELGATE trans. Tapparelli d'Azeglio, Marchese Massimo *Maid of Florence* 213 'However, measure seven times before you cut once' 'The more I think of it, the more do I repent not having done it.' **1990** *New York Times* 1 June (online) Boris Yeltsin has been accusing the present regime of half-measures when drastic action is needed, while 'Measure seven times, cut once' is the go-slow Gorbachev adage. **2004** posting on *www.eng.yabloko.ru* 13 Aug. Putin, they said, is not interested in thrashing around aimlessly. Before launching radical reforms, he will measure seven times and cut seven times. Now, sadly, it must be noted that the 'warming-up period' was wasted after all. ■ **caution** 用心

MEASURE twice, cut once.
2 度寸法を測り、1 度で裁断せよ。

大工仕事と一般に関係がある。類似のものに THINK twice, cut once.「2 度考え、1 度で裁断せよ」がある。

□a**1901** *Manitoba Morning Free Press* 15 Nov. 7 (*advertisement*) 'Measure twice, cut but once.' Experiment till you find the uniformly good make of shoe—the shape, size and width you need. Then stick to it—don't speculate. **1964** *Cedar Rapids Gazette*, 29 Mar. 20E Accurate measurements are the backbone of good construction. There's an old saying among carpenters that if you measure twice, you will have to cut only once. **1992** *Independent* 22 Oct.14 Ross Perot said the key to reducing the deficit will be to measure twice and cut once. Boy, too bad his barber didn't follow that advice. **2000** *Houston Chronicle* 10 Aug. 29 'My dad always taught me: "Measure twice, cut once,".... 'Someone forgot to measure twice here.' **2005** posting on *www.pipeline.corante.com* 16 Mar. This law of mine comes down to the old advice of 'Measure Twice, Cut Once.' It's a hard rule to remember, when you've got a box of saws and the wood is just sitting there, daring you to have at it. ■ caution 用心

There is MEASURE in all things.
何事にも限度がある。

(訳注：measure ＝「節度、限度、限界、妥当な範囲」。above *measure*〈法外に〉、know no *measure*〈限度を知らない〉）

度を越して失敗しないようにという警告として使われる。類似のものに MODERATION in all things.「何事にも限度がある」がある。ホラティウス『風刺詩』I. i. 106 *Est modus in rebus.*「物事には限度がある」

□ *c*1385 CHAUCER *Troilus & Criseyde* II. 715 In every thyng, I woot, there lith mesure [moderation]. **1598-9** SHAKESPEARE *Much Ado about Nothing* II. i. 59 If the prince be too important, tell him there is measure in every thing. **1616** T. DRAXE *Adages* 131 There is a measure in all things. **1910** R. KIPLING *Rewards & Fairies* 84 There's no clean hands in the trade. But steal in measure.... There is measure in all things made. **1942** A. THIRKELL *Marling Hall* iii. 'Good God, mamma dear,' said Oliver. 'You cannot throw old governesses together like that There is measure in everything.' **1958** M. RENAULT *King must Die* II. i. One expects some fooling when they bring the bridegroom, but there is measure in everything. ■ moderation 節度・中庸

measure ⇒ MAN is the measure of all things.

One man's MEAT is another man's poison.
ある人の食物が別の人には毒となる。

(訳注：meat ＝「【古】食物」。*meat* and drink〈飲食物〉、green *meat*〈青物〉。「甲の薬は乙の毒」)

† ルクレティウス『事物の本性について』IV. 637 *Quod ali cibus est aliis fuat acre venenum.*「ある人にとっての食物が別の人にとっては苦い毒となる」。† EVERY *man to his taste.*「めいめいお気に召すまま」

□ *c*1576 T. WHYTHORNB *Autobiography* (1961) 203 On bodies meat iz an otherz poizon. **1604** *Plato's Cap* B4 That ould moth-eaten Prouerbe ... One mans meate, is another mans poyson. *a* **1721** M. PRIOR *Dialogues of Dead* (1907) 246 May I not nauseate the food which you Covet; and is it not even a Proverb, that what is meat to one Man Is Payson to another. **1883** TROLLOPE *Autobiography* x. It is more true of novels than perhaps of anything else, that one man's food is another man's poison. **1986** J. S. SCOTT *Knife between Ribs* xvi. 'I don't see what he sees in her.' 'One man's meat is another man's poison.' **2000** *Washington Post* 9 Mar. C2 If one man's meat is another man's poison, then by the same token one man's joke is another man's snooze. ■ idiosyncrasy 特異性・性癖；taste 趣味・味

meat ⇒ You BUY land, you buy stones; GOD never sends mouths but he sends meat; GOD sends meat, but the Devil sends cooks; The NEARER the bone, the sweeter the meat.

medicine ⇒ LAUGHTER is the best medicine.

meddler ⇒ LAY-OVERS for meddlers.

296 MEET

Do not MEET troubles halfway.
苦労を途中までわざわざ出迎えに行くな。

(訳注：meet /borrow trouble halfway ＝【成句】「取り越し苦労をする」。You are just *meeting trouble halfway*.〈君は取り越し苦労をしているにすぎない〉)

いくつか同じ線に沿ったことわざがある。Never TROUBLE trouble till trouble troubles you.「困り事が君を困らせるまでは困り事を困らせるな」。†セネカ『書簡集』XIII. x. *Quid iuvat dolori suo occurrere?*「困難に出会うためになぜわざわざ出かけるのか」。1598-9 シェイクスピア『から騒ぎ』I. i. 82 Are you come to meet your trouble? The fashion of the world is to avoid cost, and you encounter it.「わざわざ厄介者をお出迎えか？ ものいりは避けるのが世の習い。それを喜んで引き受けようとなさるのだな」

□ **1896** J. C. HUTCHESON *Crown & Anchor* xvi. I can't see the use of anticipating the worst and trying to meet troubles halfway. **1940** M. SAOLEIR *Fanny by Gaslight* III. ii. What happens when she goes? ... Do not meet troubles halfway.... When need arises we will see what can be done. **1980** G. THOMPSON *Murder Mystery* xx. Don't go meeting trouble half-way. There might just be something we can do. ■ misfortune 不運

meet ⇒ Never BID the Devil good morrow until you meet him; EXTREMES meet; When GREEK meets Greek, then comes the tug of war.

melts ⇒ The same FIRE that melts the butter hardens the egg.

memory ⇒ A LIAR ought to have a good memory.

So many MEN, so many opinions.
人の数だけ意見がある。

(訳注：紀元前 2 世紀、共和政ローマ時代の劇作家テレンティウスの名言。彼は「私は人間である。およそ人間に関わることで私に無縁なことは 1 つもない」、「恋人どうしの喧嘩は恋の更新である」など幾多の名言を残している。so many ... so many ＝「同数の、それだけの数の」。*So many* men, *so many* minds.【ことわざ】〈十人十色〉)

人の意見が異なるのは当然である。ラテン語がそのまま使われることもある。†テレンティウス『フォルミオ』n. iv. *Quothomines tot sententiae.*「人の数だけ意見がある」。14世紀中頃のフランス語 *Que tant de testes, tant de sens.*「人の数だけ意見がある」

□ **c1390** CHAUCER *Squire's Tale* I. 203 As many heddes, as manye wittes ther been. **1483** Vulgaria abs Terencio Q3ᵛ Many men many opinyons. Euery man has his guyse. **1692** R. L'ESTRANGE *Fables of Aesop* ccclviii. So many Men, so many Minds; and this Diversity of Thought must necessarily be attended with Folly, Vanity, and Error. **1754** RICHARDSON *Grandison* VI. xx. Doctors differ. So many persons, so many minds. **1924** 'A. CARP' *Augustus Carp, Esq.* xii. They were all those things, and they would remember the old saying, so many men, so many opinions. ■ idiosyncrasy 特異性・性癖; opinions 意見

men ⇒ The BEST-laid schemes of mice and men gang aft agley; The BEST of men are but men at best; BRAVE men lived before Agamemnon; The BUSIEST men have the most leisure; DEAD men don't bite; DEAD men tell no tales; GOOD men are scarce; When THIEVES fall out, honest men come by their own; THREATENED men live long; One VOLUNTEER is worth two pressed men; YOUNG men may die, but old men must die.

mend ⇒ It is NEVER too late to mend; When THINGS are at the worst they begin to mend.

mended ⇒ LEAST said, soonest mended.

mending ⇒ A WOMAN and a ship ever want mending.

mention ⇒ Never mention ROPE in the house of a man who has been hanged.

merrier ⇒ The MORE the merrier.

It is MERRY in hall when beards wag all.
皆の顎髭が揺れると、大広間は陽気になる。

（訳注：1598年のシェイクスピアの『ヘンリー四世』第二部の第三場で地方判事のサイレンスが酔っ払って歌う歌には「男どうしで愉快に飲もう」と、このことわざが取り入れられている。beards wag＝「〈食べる時口を動かすと〉あごひげも同時に揺れる」。「鯛も一人はうまからず」）

御馳走、飲酒、会話の楽しさを描いたこの古い脚韻（hallとall）は、今では主にシェイクスピアの『ヘンリー四世』第二部の登場人物、地方判事のサイレンスの酔っぱらいの歌として知られている（1598年の用例）。

□*c*1300 *King Alisaunder* (EETS) I. 1164 Swithe [so] mury hit is in halle, When the burdes wawen alle! **1546** J. HEYWOOD *Dialogue of Proverbs* 11. vii. 13v It is mery in halle, When herds wag all. **1598** SHAKESPEARE *Henry IV, Pt. 2* v. iii. 35 Be merry, be merry, my wife has all.... 'Tis merry in hall when beards wag all. **1738** SWIFT *Polite Conversation* 11. 170 Come; they say, 'Tis merry in Hall, when Beards wag all. **1857** TROLLOPE *Barchester Towers* III. iv. "Twas merry in the hall when the beards wagged all;' and the clerical beards wagged merrily ... that day. **1976** 'J. Davey' *Treasury Alarm* i. Presumably this is how the Treasury greybeards get their fun. Are they in fact greybearded. One rather assumes a great wagging of beards: *'Tis merry in hall when beards wag all.* ■ hospitality もてなし；merriment 談笑・陽気な賑わい

merry ⇒ A CHERRY year, a merry year; EAT, drink, and be merry ...

Merryman ⇒ The best DOCTORS are Dr Diet, Dr Quiet, and Dr Merryman.

mice ⇒ The BEST-laid schemes of mice and men gang aft agley; It doesn't matter if a CAT is black or white, as long as it catches mice; A CAT in gloves catches no mice; When the CAT's away, the mice will play; KEEP no more cats than will catch mice.

mickle ⇒ MANY a little makes a mickle; MANY a mickle makes a muckle.

midge ⇒ The MOTHER of mischief is no bigger than a midge's wing.

midnight ⇒ One HOUR's sleep before midnight is worth two after.

mid-stream ⇒ Don't CHANGE horses in mid-stream.

MIGHT is right.
力は正義である。

（訳注：might ＝【名詞】「〈巨大な〉力、権力」。形容詞 mighty は「強力な、強大な」の意。助動詞 may の語源は「できる、力がある」であるが、これと同語源。mighty を用いたことわざとして、The pen is *mightier* than the sword.〈ペンは剣よりも強し〉がよく知られている）

強者は力によって自分の見解、願望、権威などを押し付けてくる。†プラトン『国家』I. 338c φημὶ γὰρ ἐγὼ εἶναι τὸ δίκαιον οὐκ ἄλλο τι ἢ τὸ τοῦ κρείττονος ξυμφέρον. 「正義とは、より強い立場の者の利益以外の何物でもないと私（トラシュマコス）は言っているのだ」。ルカヌス『ファルサリア（内乱）』I. 175 *Mensuraque iuris vis erat.* 「力が正義の基準であった」

□ *a*1327 in T. Wright *Political Songs* (1839) 254 For miht is right, the lond is laweless. **1546** J. HEYWOOD *Dialogue of Proverbs* II. v. H2ᵛ We se many tymes myght ouercomth ryght **1790** J. TRUSLER *Proverbs Exemplified* 78 The law is so expensive.... Might too often overcomes right. **1892** J. NICHOL *Carlyle* iv. [In] Chartism ... he clearly enunciates 'Might is right'—one of the few strings on which ... he played through life. **1979** *Guardian* 17 May 24 By adult examples, pupils are being taught such evil doctrines as 'Might is right'. **2001** *Times* 7 Nov. 16 All this means is that in politics, as in war, might is right ■ justice and injustice 正義と不正 ; power 力・権力

mightier ⇒ The PEN is mightier than the sword.

mighty ⇒ A REED before the wind lives on, while mighty oaks do fall.

mile ⇒ A JOURNEY of a thousand miles begins with a single step; A MISS is as good as a mile.

milk ⇒ Why buy a cow when milk is so cheap? ; It is no use CRYING over spilt milk.

The MILL cannot grind with the water that is past.
ひき臼は流れ去った水で粉をひくことはできない。

（訳注：mill ＝「水車小屋、ひき臼」。このことわざは 2 つの意味に解釈できよう。1 つは「好機を逸するな」であり、もう 1 つは「逸した好機をいたずらに嘆くな」である。「好機逸すべからず」）

一度逃した機会は永遠に戻ってこない。

□ **1616** T. DRAXE *Adages* 151 The water that is past, cannot make the mill goe. **1640** G. HERBERT *Outlandish Proverbs* no. 153 The mill cannot grind with the water that's past. **1856** R. C. TRENCH *Poems* 197 Oh seize the instant [present] time; you never will With waters once passed by impel the mill. **1980** G. RICHARDS *Red Kill* xiv. It did no good to think back. The mill cannot grind with the water that is past, as the old people in the mountains used to say. ■ opportunity, missed 逃した機会 ; past 過去・過ぎ去った

mill ⇒ All is GRIST that comes to the mill.

The MILLS of God grind slowly, yet they grind exceeding small.
神のひき臼はゆっくりとだが、きわめて細かくひく。

(訳注：天罰は後になってから下されるが、しかし必ず下される。何人もその天罰から逃れることはできない。「天網恢々疎にして漏らさず」)

水車の車輪が穀物を粉に砕くイメージを描いたもの。古代ギリシアの医者・哲学者セクスタス・エンピリカス『教授に対して』1. 287 ὀψὲ θεῶν ἀλέουσι μύλοι, ἀλέουσι δὲ λεπτά. 「神のひき臼は粉をひくのは遅いが、細かくひく」に引用されている。

☐ **1640** G. HERBERT *Outlandish Proverbs* no. 747 Gods Mill grinds slow, but sure. **1870** LONG-FELLOW *Poems* (1960) 331 Though the mills of God grind slowly, yet they grind exceeding small; Though with patience he stands waiting, with exactness grinds he all. **1942** 'F. BEEDING' *Twelve Disguises* i. That's my business.... The mills of God grind slowly, but they grind exceeding small. **1989** R. HART *Remains to be Seen* vii. Military record keepers were like the mills of God. They ground slow, and exceeding small, but only at their own pace. ■ **justice and injustice 正義と不正；retribution 天罰・報復**

mind ⇒ The EYES are the window of the soul; GREAT minds think alike; LITTLE things please little minds; OUT of sight, out of mind; TRAVEL broadens the mind.

The age of MIRACLES is past.
奇跡の時代は終わった。

主流を占めるプロテスタント教会によると、奇跡の時代とは聖書によって書かれている時代を指す。そこでは奇跡がしばしば描かれている。

☐ **1599** SHAKESPEARE *Henry V* I. i. 67 It must be so; for miracles are ceas'd; And therefore we must needs admit the means How things are perfected. **1602** —*All's Well that Ends Well* II. iii. 1 They say miracles are past; and we have our philosophical persons to make modern and familiar things supernatural and causeless. **1840** CARLYLE *On Heroes & Hero Worship* iv. The Age of Miracles past? The Age of Miracles is for ever here! **1988** J. MORTIMER *Rumpole and Age of Miracles* (1989) 108 'A total victory,' I agreed. 'The Age of Miracles is not past.' ■ **marvels 不思議**

mischief ⇒ The MOTHER of mischief is no bigger than a midge's wing.

MISERY loves company.
不幸な者は仲間を愛する。

(訳注：このことわざにおける misery は「不幸、悲惨」という抽象的な意味というよりも、「不幸な状況にある人々」〈=people in misery〉という具体的な意味に解釈できる。company ＝「仲間」。Two is company, 〈but〉 three is a crowd.【ことわざ】〈2 人では気が合うが、3 人では仲間割れ〉。「同病相憐む」)

† 14世紀初頭のラテン語 *Gaudium est miseris socios habuisse penarum.*「悲惨な目にあった人は災難の中でも仲間ができると慰められる」。*a*1349 C. ホーストマン『ヨークシャーの作家たち』(1895) I. 101 に収められた R. ロル『キリスト受難の瞑想録』の中に次の言葉がある。It is solace to haue companie in peyne.「悲しみの中でも仲間がいると慰められる」

☐ **1578** LYLY *Euphues* i. 238 In miserie Euphues it is a great comfort to haue a companion. **1620** T. SHELTON tr. *Cervantes' Don Quixote* u. xiii. If that which is commonly spoken be true, that to haue companions in misery is a lightner of it, you may comfort me. **1775** T. GILBERT *Letter* 4 May in W. B. Clark et al. Naval Documents of American Revolution (1964) I. 279 All my Letters are inter septed by those Rebels who want Every one to be kept in Dark like themselves. (Misery Loves Company). **1851** H. D. THOREAU *Journal* 1 Sept. (1949) II. 440 If misery loves company, misery has company enough. **2005** J. VAN DE RUIT *Spud* (2006) 315 Fatty reckons that Geoff Lawson is suicidal because of Amanda and Emberton. I laughed loudly—misery loves company. **2014** *Spectator* 15 Nov. 52 Misery loves company. Anyone who doubts this old adage should pop into their local bookshop, because ... what keep the tills ringing are misery memoirs. ■ **malice** 悪意・恨み；**misfortune** 不運

MISFORTUNES never come singly.
不幸は単独ではやって来ない。

（訳注：以下のことわざ参照。It never rains but it pours.【ことわざ】〈降るときは必ずどしゃ降り〉〈＝不幸は必ず重なるものだ〉。「泣き面に蜂」。「弱り目に祟り目」）

†14世紀初頭のフランス語 *Ung meschief ne vient point seul.*「不幸は単独ではやって来ない」。迷信に BAD *things come in threes*.「不幸は3回は続く」がある。

□*c*1300 *King Alisaunder* (EETS) I. 1276 Men telleth in olde mone [lament] The qued [harm] comuth nowher alone. **1509** A. BARCLAY *Ship of Fools* 236 Wyse men sayth, and oft it fallyth so ... That one myshap fortuneth neuer alone. **1622** J. MABBE tr. *Aleman's Guzman d'Alfarache* I. iii. Misfortunes seldome come alone. **1711** J. ADDISON *Spectator* 8 Mar. The Lady ... said to her Husband with a Sigh, My Dear, Misfortunes never come single. **1791** T. BURR *Letter* 27 July in M. L. Davis *Memoirs of Aaron Burr* (1836) I. 301 We certainly see the old proverb very often verified. 'That misfortunes never come singly,' that poor little woman is a proof. **1931** 'L. CHARTERIS' *Wanted for Murder* v. Blessings, like misfortunes, never come singly. There was even a packet of Havana cigarettes ... behind the bath salts. **1981** G. MITCHELL *Death-Cap Dancers* v. 'The car ... skidded and hit a tree.' 'Misfortunes never come singly.' ■ **misfortune** 不運

A MISS is as good as a mile.
小さな失敗でも、1マイルもの大失敗に等しい。

（訳注：good ＝「相当の、かなりの」。ほんのわずかな失敗でも、失敗は失敗だ）

たとえわずかの差で目的を達成できなくても、結果は大幅に失敗した場合と同じである。このことわざは an inch in a miss を a miss と短縮したことによって統語法が歪んでいる。元の形は1614年の用例から明らかである。

□**1614** W. CAMDEN *Remains concerning Britain* (ed. 2) 303 An ynche in a misse is as good as an ell [a former measure of length equal to about 1.1 m]. **1655** T. FULLER *Hist. Cambridge* 37 An hairs breadth fixed by a divine-finger, shall prove as effectuall a separation from danger as a miles distance. **1788** *American Museum* Apr. 382 A miss is as good as a mile. **1825** SCOTT *Journal* 3 Dec. (1939) 28 He was very near being a poet—but a miss is as good as a mile, and he always fell short of the mark. **1978** T. SHARPE *Throwback* vii. If you aimed at a grouse it was hit or miss and a miss was as good as a mile. **2014** *Scotsman* I Dec. (online; *heading*) Miss is as good as a mile ... The 150-ft wide lump of rock may be 17,200 miles away but this in asteroid terms is a close shave. ■ **error** 間違い・過ち

You never MISS the water till the well runs dry.
井戸が干上がるまで水のありがたさはわからない。

（訳注：you ＝「人、誰でも」〈総称用法〉。*You* never can tell.〈先の事など誰もわからない〉。次のことわざにおける you も同じく総称用法）

MODERATION　301

あたりまえだと思っているものはそれを失ってはじめてありがたさがわかるものだ。

□ *a*1628 J. CARMICHAELL *Proverbs in Scots* no. 1140 Manie wats [know] not quhairof [whereof] the wel sauris [tastes] quhill [until] it fall drie. **1659** J. HOWELL *Proverbs* (British) 24 Of the Well we see no want, till either dry, or Water skant. **1721** J. KELLY *Scottish Proverbs* 351 We'll never know the worth of Water 'till the well go dry. **1874** H. UNN *You never miss Water* 5 Do not let your chances, like sunbeams pass you by; For you never miss the water till the well runs dry. **1996** *Washington Times* 18 July A6 'There is an old adage,' Sen. Robert Byrd ... recalled this week, 'that "you never miss the water until the well runs dry."' ■ **blessings** 恵み・(神の)恩恵；**gratitude and ingratitude** 感謝と忘恩

miss ⇒ What you've never HAD you never miss; A SLICE off a cut loaf isn't missed.

If you don't make MISTAKES you don't make anything.
失敗しなければ得るものもない。

失敗する恐怖が勝ると何も達成できない。

□ **1896** CONRAD *Outcast of Islands* III. ii It's only those who do nothing that make no mistakes, I suppose. **1925** *Times* 9 Nov. 17 The comforting assurance that 'a man who never makes mistakes never makes anything.' **1980** M. DRABBLE *Middle Ground* 86 If you don't make mistakes you don't make anything, she said, a motto which Hugo seemed to remember having seen pinned over the desk. ■ **error** 間違い・過ち；**risk** 危険

mistress ⇒ Like MASTER, like man.

So many MISTS in March, so many frosts in May.
3 月の降霧の回数だけ 5 月に降霜がある。

(訳注：so many ... so many ＝「同数の、それだけの数の」。*So many* men, *so many* opinions.【ことわざ】〈人の数だけ意見がある〉)

英国の気候に関する経験上の観察で、3 月の霧は 5 月に季節外れの霜をもたらす傾向がある。

□ **1612** A. HOPTON *Concordancy of Years* xxx. Some say, so many mistes in March, so many hoare frosts after Easter. **1678** J. RAY *English Proverbs* (ed. 2) 344 So many frosts in March so many in May. **1978** R. WHITLOCK *Calendar of Country Customs* iii. Many old country beliefs are not content with generalities but strive to be more precise. A well-known proverb is: So many mists in March, So many frosts in May. ■ **weather lore** 天気にまつわる伝承

mixen ⇒ BETTER wed over the mixen than over the moor.

MODERATION in all things
何事も中庸こそ肝要。

この発想を表わした最近のことわざに There is MEASURE in all things.「何事にも限度がある」がある。ラテン語の *modus* は moderation または measure と訳されるが、前者の方が後者よりも広く使われている。おそらく measure が多義であるため、誤解を招くからであろう。ヘシオドス『仕事と日』I. 694 μέτρα φυλάσσεσθαι καιρὸς δ'ἐπὶ πᾶσιν ἄριστος.「しかるべき節度を守れ」。プラウトゥス『カルタゴ人』I. 238 *Modus omnibus rebus ... optimus est habitu.*「すべてのことにおいて中庸が最善である」

□**1849** H. MELVILLE *Mardi* II. lxxvii. I am for being temperate in these things.... All things in moderation are good; whence, wine in moderation is good. **1879** W. H. G. KINGSTON tr. *Swiss Family Robinson* ii. 'Oh, father, sugar canes.... Do let us take a lot home to mother.' ... 'Gently there.... Moderation in all things.' **1980** S. T. HAYMON *Death & Pregnant Virgin* ii. Norfolk ... [is] on the same scale I am. No Niagaras, no hills higher than hills ... ought to be. Moderation in all things. **2002** *Times Crème* 3 July 5 It can hardly be described as good for you ... but all things in moderation, as they say. ■ **moderation** 節度・中庸

Monday ⇒ Monday's CHILD is fair of face.

MONEY can't buy happiness.
幸せは金では買えない。

物質主義への非難という昔から繰り返される主題であるが、このことわざは明らかに比較的最近のものである。

□**1856** G. C. BALDWIN *Representative Women* 215 Gold cannot buy happiness, and parents who compel their daughters to marry for money, or station, commit a grievous sin against humanity and God. **1873** E. KELLOGG *Arthur Brown* vii. 118 'I had rather have friends who love me for my own sake ... than all the money in the world.' 'Money won't buy happiness, Walter.' **1984** ANON. in R. Byrne *Other* 637 Best Things Anybody Ever Said (1985) I. no. 220 Whoever said money can't buy happiness didn't know where to shop. **2002** *Washington Post* 19 June Cl5 (*Blondie comic strip*) 'Bumstead, your problem is that you worry too much about money. Money can't buy happiness, you know.' 'Has it bought you happiness, boss?' 'Yeah, but that's just me!' ■ **happiness** 幸福；**money** 金・金銭

MONEY has no smell.
金はにおわない。

そのお金をどこからどのようにして得たのかは、そのお金の価値とは無関係である。ラテン語 *Non olet.*「(金は) におわない」。ローマの歴史家・伝記作者スエトニウスは、ローマ皇帝ウェスパシアヌスの息子ティトゥスが公衆便所に課税したことを批判したいきさつを語っている。ウェスパシアヌスは最初に支払われたお金からコインを1枚取り出し、息子の鼻に押し当て、臭いかどうか尋ねた。ティトゥスは「いいえ」と答えた。ウェスパシアヌスはこう応じた。「しかしその金は小便から得られたものだぞ」(スエトニウス『ウェスパシアヌス』xxiii)。

□**1914** 'E. Bramah' *Max Carrados* 45 The Romans, Parkinson, had a saying to the effect that gold carries no smell. That is a pity sometimes. What jewellery did Miss Hutchins wear? **1922** A. BENNETI *Mr. Prohack* iii. The associations of the wealth scarcely affected him. He understood in the flesh the deep wisdom of that old proverb ... that money has no smell. **1940** R. CHANDLER *Farewell, my Lovely* xxxiv. He punched the cash-register and dropped the bill into the drawer. They say money don't stink. I sometimes wonder. **2002** *Times* 20 Feb. 3 Mr Justice Jacob ... asked rhetorically: 'Should procurers, pimps, panders ... pay VAT? That is the question on this appeal ... In this case, as the Latin poet [sic] said, pecunia non olet money doesn't smell. I allow the appeal.' ■ **money** 金・金銭

MONEY isn't everything.
金がすべてではない。

物事を考慮する際に、お金を第一に考えてはならない。とりわけ、お金を稼ぐ方法がいや

MONEY 303

なので、その仕事に気が向かないような時に用いられる（2007 年の用例参照）。

☐**1922** *Vanity Fair* Sept 39 (*heading*) Money Isn't Everything. **1927** E. O'NEILL *Marco Millions* iii. Money isn't everything, not always. *a***1947** F. THOMPSON *Still glides Stream* (1948) ii. He said quite angrily that money was not everything, there was the satisfaction of knowing you'd turned out a good job. **1975** J. 1. M. STEWART *Young Pattullo* xv. If one owns property one can always have a little money follow one around. But we all know that money isn't everything. **2007** *Times* 25 July 7 Ah yes, he said glumly, but the hours are relentless, the people dismal and the work very dull. Besides … money isn't everything. ■ **money 金・金銭**

MONEY is power.
金は力である。

KNOWLEDGE is power. 「知識は力である」の方がより一般的である。

☐**1741** N. AMES *Almanack* 4 Laws bear Name, but Money has the Power. **1789** F. AMES *Letter* 16 May in Works (1854) I. 39 Money is power, a permanent revenue is permanent power, and the credit which it would give was a safeguard to the government. **1818** M. EDGEWORTH *Letter* 13 Oct. (1971) 115 Now he had money 'and money is power'. **1930** MEANS & Thacker *Strange Death of President Harding* iv. One can do nothing—be nothing, without money, not even in the White House. Money is power. **1980** J. O'FAOLAIN *No Country for Young Men* i. The lads would have to have … money if they were to get guns…. Money was power. ■ **money 金・金銭 ; power 力・権力**

MONEY is the root of all evil.
金は諸悪の根源である。

†『テモテへの手紙一』6 章 10 節（欽定訳聖書）The love of money is the root of all evil.「金を愛することは諸悪の根源である」。聖書にある the love of money is … と money is … という短縮版とが両方使われている。

☐*c***1000** AELFRIC *Homilies* (1843) I. 256 Seo gytsung is ealra yfelra thinga wyrtruma [covetousness is the root of all evil things]. *c***1449** R. PECOCK *Repressor of Blaming of Clergy* (1860) II. 555 Loue to money … is worthi to be forbom … as Poul seith, it is 'the roote of al yuel'. **1616** J. WITHALS *Dict.* (rev. ed.) 546 Riches are the root of all euill. **1777** in L H. Butterfield et al. *Adams Family Correspondence* (1963) II. 345 Many have been loth to believe … That Money is the Root of all Evil. **1858** TROLLOPE *Dr. Thorne* I. xii. 'But, doctor, you'll take the money.' … 'Quite impossible … ' said the doctor, … valiantly rejecting the root of all evil. **2001** R. HILL *Dialogues of Dead* xliii. 355 'Anyway there we have it, a dollar sign and a Roman coin. I suppose it could be some kind of statement about money being the root of all evil?' ■ **good and evil 正邪 ; money 金・金銭**

MONEY, like manure, does no good till it is spread.
金は肥やしのようなもので、ばら撒かなければ役に立たない。

（訳注：英国の哲学者・政治家 F. ベーコンが『随想集』15 章「反乱と騒動について」の中で述べた言葉。この書には、「読書は充実した人間を作り、会話は気がきく人間を、書くことは正確な人間を作る」といった名言もある〈50 章「学問について」〉。ベーコンは、ほかにも「希望は朝食にはよいが、夕食にはよくない」〈Hope is a good breakfast, but it is a bad supper.〉、「知識は力なり」〈Knowledge is power.〉などの名言を残している）

金は 1 人の人間によってためこまれる必要はなく、社会で流通しなければ意味がない。ベーコンによる、あまり上品とは言えない表現は今なお使われている（1625 年の用例参照）。

304 MONEY

□ **1625** F. BACON 'Of Seditions and Troubles' in *Essays* 65 Money is like muck; not good except it be spread. **1816** W. MAVOR *English Spelling-Book* (ed. 198) 103 Money, like manure, does no good till it is spread. **2001** *Las Vegas Review-Journal* 7 Oct (electronic ed.) 'Jack always says,' Wagner recalled, 'money's like manure. You've got to spread it around in your company to make things grow.' ■ **money** 金・金銭

MONEY makes a man.
金が人を作る。

（訳注：man＝「立派な人」。内容はまったく異なるが、形がよく似ていることわざとして「礼儀作法が人を作る」〈Manners maketh man.〉参照）

財産によって人の地位が決まる。†ラテン語 *Divitiae virum faciunt.*「財産が人を作る」

□ *a***1500** in R. L. Greene *Early English Carols* (1935) 263 Ytys allwayes sene nowadayes That money makythe the man. *a***1661** T. FULLER *Worthies* (Hants.) 3 We commonly say ... In the Change [Exchange], Money makes a man, which puts him in a solvable condition. **1828** BULWER-LYTTON *Pelham* i. xxxiv. The continent only does for us English people to see.... Here, you know, 'money makes the man.' **1920** D. H. LAWRENCE *Letter* 7 May (1962) I. 629 Money maketh a man; even if he was a monkey to start with. **1950** C. E. VULLIAMY *Henry Plumdew* 203 I doubt whether he understands the place of money in vulgar estimation.... Money maketh man. ■ **money** 金・金銭

MONEY makes money.
金が金を生む。

金を持っている人は金儲けにたけている。

□ **1572** T. WILSON *Discourse upon Usury* 54ᵛ Mony getteth money. *a***1654** J. SELDEN *Table Talk* (1689) 57 'Tis a vain thing to say, Money begets not Money; for that no doubt it does. **1776** A. SMITH *Wealth of Nations* I. 1. ix. Money, says the proverb, makes money. When you have got a little, it is often easy to get more. **1865** DICKENS *Our Mutual Friend* III. v. We have got to recollect that money makes money, as well as makes everything else. **1935** A. CHRISTIE *Miss Marple's Final Cases* (1979) 60 Everything she did turned out well. Money made money. **1988** C. H. SAWYER *J. Alfred Prufrock Murders* v. Well ... maybe she made some clever investments? But no, she would have had to have money to begin with—it takes money to make money, my husband always said. ■ **money** 金・金銭

MONEY makes the mare to go.
金は雌馬をも進ませる。

（訳注：使役動詞 make が to 不定詞を従えているのは調子を整えるため。「地獄の沙汰も金次第」）

金さえあればたいていのことは達成できる。

□ *a***1500** in R. L. Greene *Early English Carols* (1935) 262 In the heyweyes [highways] ther joly [spirited] palfreys Yt [money] makyght to ... praunce. **1573** J. SANFORDE *Garden of Pleasure* 105ᵛ Money makes the horsse to goe. **1670** J. RAY *English Proverbs* 122 It's money makes the mare to go. **1748** RICHARDSON *Clarissa* IV. 187 A leading man in the House of Commons, is a very important character; because that house has the giving of money: And Money makes the mare to go. **1930** L. MEYNELL *Mystery at Newton Ferry* xiii. 'Tis money makes the mare go.... They're all after it, every one of them. **1978** *Countryman Spring* 193 Weardale farmer's advice to daughter about to reject a proposal of marriage from a wealthy tradesman: 'Never cock your snoop at money, my lass, 'cos it's money that makes the mare to go'. ■ **money** 金・金銭

MONKEY 305

MONEY talks.
金がものをいう。

金の影響力は大きい。

□ **1666** G. TORRIANO *Italian Proverbs* 179 Man prates, but gold speaks. **1681** A. BEHN *Rover II*. III. i. Money speaks in a Language all Nations understand. **1903** *Saturday Evening Post* 5 Sept. 12 When money talks it often merely remarks 'Good-by'. **1915** WODEHOUSE *Something Fresh* iii. The whole story took on a different complexion for Joan. Money talks. **1984** A. BROOKNER *Hotel du Lac* (1985) xi. 'At least I assume they are millionaires?' 'That is what they would like you to assume, certainly. And if money talks, … they are certainly making the right amount of noise.' **2002** *Washington Post* 15 Jan. E3 Why did all these people look the other way for so long? Money talks. Or, with Enron, shouts. ■ money 金・金銭; power 力・権力

money ⇒ BAD money drives out good; A FOOL and his money are soon parted; When the LAST tree is cut down, the last fish eaten, … you will realize that you cannot eat money; LEND your money and lose your friend; Never MARRY for money, but marry where money is; Where there's MUCK there's brass; You PAYS your money and you takes your choice; PUT your money where your mouth is; TIME is money.

A MONEYLESS man goes fast through the market.
金のない人は市場を急ぎ足で通り抜ける。

1721年の用例では、because以下でこのことわざの理由（すなわち、お金がないと買うことも値切ることもできない）が述べられている。最後の1977年の用例はこのことわざを少し変えたもので、その趣旨は、人は自分に不足しているものが見つかりそうなところであればどこへでも駆けつけるものだということである。† 14世紀後半のフランス語 *Cilz qui n'a point d'argent n'a que faire au marchié.*「金のない者は市場に行くだけしかできない（つまり、何も買うことはできない）」

□ **1721** J. KELLY *Scottish Proverbs* 10 A silverless Man goes fast through the Market. Because he does not stay to cheapen [bargain] or buy. **1732** T. FULLER *Gnomologia* no. 330 A Moneyless Man goes fast thro' the Market. **1977** J. AIKEN *Five-Minute Marriage* iv. Found your way here at last, then, miss, have you? A moneyless mare trots fast to the market. ■ buying and selling 売買; poverty 貧困

monk ⇒ The COWL does not make the monk.

MONKEY see, monkey do.
猿は見て真似をする。

人はたとえその内容は理解できなくても、観察し模倣することで覚えるものである。米国生まれのことわざで、人真似をするという猿のよく知られた習性をほのめかしている（1908年の用例参照）。また、1891年の用例が示すように、軽蔑的な意味合いを持つ場合がある。この例では、広告主が競争相手を猿真似していると、けなしている。現在の形は単数名詞に動詞の複数形が呼応するという非標準的なものであるが、初期のMonkey sees, monkey does. に取って代わった。現在の形の起源は不詳で、西アフリカの民話から中国人のピジン英語に至るまで多くの説がある。

306　monkey

□**1891** *Cedar Rapids Evening Gazette* 17 Mar. 4/1 (advertisement) It's the old saying what 'Monkey sees Monkey Does' and it turned out true. Notice how some of the other dry goods merchants are imitating and copying Denecke & Yetter's ways of advertising. **1908** F. F. SEC *Classroom Conversation Book* 117 Monkeys are great imitators, hence the saying, 'Monkey see, monkey do.' **2011** *Science Daily.com* 2 Aug. We are all familiar with the phrase 'monkey see, monkey do'—but have we actually thought about what it means? Over the last two decades, neuroscience research has been investigating whether this popular saying has a real basis in human behavior. **2013** *Seattle Times* 25 Apr. (online) You don't have to be a teenager to want to fit in at the school lunchroom. Some wild animals seem to follow similar monkey see, monkey-do behavior to follow the crowd and find the best eats … ■ **imitation　模倣**

monkey ⇒ The HIGHER the monkey climbs the more he shows his tail; If you PAY peanuts, you get monkeys; SOFTLY, softly, catchee monkey.

moor ⇒ BETTER wed over the mixen than over the moor.

MORE people know Tom Fool than Tom Fool knows.
頓馬のトムが知っている以上の人が頓馬のトムを知っている。

顔見知りでもなく、名前すら知らない相手によって知られているという状況を表わしている。Tom Fool とは、愚か者、または演劇や仮装舞踏会で愚か者の役を演じている役者に与えられてきている名前。

□**1656** S. HOLLAND *Wit & Fancy* II. i. In all Comedies more know the Qown, then the Clown knows. **1723** DEFOE *Colonel Jack* (ed. 2) 347 It was no satisfaction to me that i knew not their faces, for they might know mine … according to the old English proverb, 'that more knows Tom Fool, than Tom Fool knows'. **1865** SURTEES *Facey Romford's Hounds* xxxii. 'Good mornin', Mr. Swig,' said the man; for the aphorism that 'more people know Tom Fool than Tom Fool knows,' holds particularly good as regards huntsmen and field servants. **1980** L. MEYNELL *Hooley & Prancing Horse* iv. Hooky asked … 'How's the great pulsating world of journalism?' Mac was … surprised; but he consoled himself with the thought that more people know Tom Fool than Tom Fool knows. **2000** 'C. AIRD' *Little Knell* (2001) xv. 170 'I reckon that just at this minute, sir, there's more that we don't know about this girl's murder than what we do … ' 'More people always know Tom Fool, Crosby.' ■ **associates　仲間；fame and obscurity　有名と無名**

The MORE the merrier
多ければ多いほど楽しい。

(訳注：「the ＋比較級 … the ＋比較級」(＝「…であればあるほどますます…だ」の構文が用いられている。*The* sooner, *the* better.〈早ければ早いほどよい〉。下のことわざも同じである。「枯れ木も山の賑わい」)

余分に加えられた人や物でも喜ばしい。

□*c***1380** *Pearl* (1953) 1. 850 The mo [more] the myryer, so God me blesse. **1546** J. HEYWOOD *Dialogue of Proverbs* II. vii. 13 The mo the merier, we all daie here [hear] and se. Ye but the fewer the better fare (saied he). **1614** T. ADAMS *Devil's Banquet* IV. 196 The company is … all the Patriarchs, Prophets, Saints…. The more the mirrier, yea, and the better cheare to. **1855** C. KINGSLEY *Westward Ho!* III. iv. the old proverb comes true—'the more the merrier: but the fewer the better fare.' **1976** L. ALTHER *Kinflicks* xiii. 'Take my word for it. Have another baby.' … 'The more, the merrier!' **2001** M. DAHL *Viking Claw* vii. 56 A third rope was tossed through the hole. 'Clip that on, too!' yelled out Uncle Stoppard. Why not? The more the merrier. ■ **hospitality　もてなし；merriment　談笑・陽気な賑わい**

The MORE you get the more you want.
持てば持つほど欲しくなる。
(訳注：「欲に頂きなし」)

さらに簡潔な形であるMUCH would have more.「たくさんあるともっとたくさん欲しくなる」と同様に、人の貪欲さを述べている。現在ではセックスや金銭以外の物に対する執着心を指すこともある（2011年の用例参照）。†ホラティウス『使徒書簡』II. ii.147 *Quanto plura parasti, tanto plura cupis.*「人は既に持っているものと同じだけのものをまた欲しがる」

□*c*1340 R. ROLLE *Psalter* (1884) 97 The mare that a man has the brennandere [more ardently] he askis. *a*1450 *Castle of Perseverance* I. 3268 in Macro Plays (EETS) The more he hadde, the more he cravyd, Why! the lyf lefte hym with-Inne. 1578 J. FLORIO *First Fruits* 32 The more a man bath, the more he desireth. 1798 W. MANNING *Key of Liberty* (1922) 9 In short he is never easy, but the more he has the more he wants. 1940 G. H. COXE *Glass Triangle* x. I was averaging eighty to a hundred [dollars] a week. Well, you know how it is. The more you get the more you want. 2011 *www.psychology today.com* 22 Mar. How about 'The more you get—the more you want?' Have you noticed that the word 'insatiable' goes so well with the word 'desire'? ■ greed 貪欲 ; riches 富

more ⇒ More HASTE, less speed; The more LAWS, the more thieves and bandits; LESS is more; MUCH would have more; The more you STIR it the worse it stinks; There are more WAYS of killing a cat than choking it with cream; there are more WAYS of killing a dog than choking it with butter; There are more WAYS of killing a dog than hanging it

MORNING dreams come true.
朝の夢は正夢。

古代の迷信で、インドでも信じられている。†モスコス『エウローペー』2 νυκτὸς ὅτε τρίτατον λάχος ἵσταται, ἐγγύθι δ᾽ ἠώς, ... εὖτε καὶ ἀτ ρεκέων ποιμαίνεται ἔθνος ὀνείρων.「夜の第三更、夜明けが近づくと、…正夢の群れがかすめて通る」。ホラティウス『風刺詩』I. x. 33 *Post mediam noctem visus, cum somnia vera.*「夜の12時を過ぎて夢がかなう時、彼は私の前に姿を現わした」

□1540 J. PALSGRAVE *Acolastus* II. i. After mydnyght men saye, that dreames be true. 1616 JONSON *Love Restored* VIII. 385 All the morning dreames are true. 1813 W. B. RHODES *Bombastes Furioso* III. 7 This morn ... I dreamt (and morning dreams come true, they say). 1909 A. MACLAREN *Romans* 87 Our highest anticipations and desires are not unsubstantial visions, but morning dreams, which are proverbially sure to be fulfilled. ■ dreams 夢

morning ⇒ Never BID the Devil good morrow until you meet him; RED sky at night, shepherd's delight.

moss ⇒ A ROLLING stone gathers no moss.

most ⇒ Who KNOWS most, speaks least.

Like MOTHER, like daughter
この母にしてこの娘あり。

Like FATHER, like son.「この父にしてこの息子あり」の女性版。『エゼキエル書』16章44節（欽定訳聖書）Every one … shall use this proverb against thee, saying, As is the mother, so is her daughter.「すべてことわざを用いる者は、あなたについて、『この母にして、この娘あり』ということわざを用いる」

□ a1325 *Cursor Mundi* (EETS) I. 18857 0 suilk [such] a moder, wel slik [such] a child. **1474** CAXTON *Game of Chess* II. ii. For suche moder suche daughter comunely. **1644** R. WILLIAMS *Bloody Tenent of Persecution* xcix. Is not this as the Prophet speaks, Like mother, like daughter? **1861** C. READE *Cloister & Hearth* II. xvii. 'Mother, you were so hot against her.' … 'Ay…. Like mother like daughter: cowardice it is our bane.' **1992** A. LAMBERT *Rather English Marriage* (1993) xi. 188 'Darling, you are hopeless! Why are you always so broke?' (Like mother, like daughter, she thought to herself.) ■ children and parents 親子; similarity and dissimilarity 類似性と相違性

The MOTHER of mischief is no bigger than a midge's wing.
災害の元はブヨの羽ほどの大きさもない。

小さくて一見すると何の害もないように見えるものでも厄難をもたらすことがある。

□ a1628 J. CARMICHAELL *Proverbs in Scots* no. 1468 The mother of mischief, is na mair nor [than] a midgewing. **1796** M. EDGEWORTH *Parent's Assistant* (ed. 2) 149 'The mother of mischief', says an old proverb, 'is no bigger than a midge's wing.' **1858** D. M. MULOCK *Woman's Thoughts about Women* viii. Fatal and vile as her [Gossip's] 'progeny may be, 'the mother of mischief, says the proverb, 'is no bigger than a midge's wing.' **2005** *Times Magazine* 5 Nov. 13 (*heading*) 'The mother of mischief is no bigger than a midge's wing'. ■ beginnings and endings 最初と最後; great and small 大小; trouble やっかい・苦労

mother ⇒ DILIGENCE is the mother of good luck; NECESSITY is the mother of invention; PRAISE the child, and you make love to the mother.

If the MOUNTAIN will not come to Mahomet, Mahomet must go to the mountain.
山がムハマンド（マホメット）の所に来ないのなら、ムハマンドの方が山の所へ行かねばならない。

（訳注：英語のことわざとしては、英国の哲学者・政治家 F. ベーコン『随想集』12章「大胆について」の中で述べられた言葉〈1625年の用例参照〉。この言葉は、以下のような故事に基づくとされる。ある時、ムハマンドが丘に対して自分のところに来るようにと呼びかけた。しかし、丘はじっとしたままであった。奇跡を起こそうとしたが、失敗したのである。その時、ムハマンドは少しも悪びれず、「ムハマンドの方から丘に行こう」と言ったという。思い通りにことが運ばない場合には、方針転換をしなければならないのである）

一方の側が妥協しないなら、他方が歩み寄らねばならない。1625年の用例にこのことわざの背後にある逸話が挙げられている。

□ **1625** BACON *Essays* 'Of Boldness' xii. Mahomet cald the Hill to come to him … And when the Hill stood still, he was neuer a whit abashed, but said; If the Hill will not come to Mahomet, Mahomet wil go to the hil. **1732** T. FULLER *Gnomologia* no. 2707 If the Mountain will not come to Mahomet, Mahomet must go to the Mountain. **1975** O. BAGLEY *Snow Tiger* xvii. You couldn't go to see him, so the mountain had to go to Mahomet It was … important to him. **2001** *Washington*

mouth   309

Times 27 Jan. F23 (*Herb & Jamaal comic strip*) 'I've waited too long for Jamaal to ask me out It's time for me to take action! As they say, "If the mountain won't come to Mohammed, then Mohammed will go to the mountain".' ■ **necessity** 必要性・必然性；**obstinacy** 頑固さ

mountain ⇒ FAITH will move mountains.

The MOUNTAINS are high, and the emperor is far away.
山は高くそびえ、皇帝ははるか遠くにいる。
（訳注：中央権力は地方の民の利害・関心事には我関せずの状態であるという嘆き）

中国のことわざで、ロシアのことわざ GOD is high above, and the tsar is far away.「神ははるか上空に、ツァーははるか遠くにいる」に相当する。

□ **1910** P. W. SERGEANT *Great Empress Dowager of China* 153 'The mountains are high,' say the Chinese, 'the Emperor is far away.' A brief lull in the persecution was followed in 1895 by an extremely violent outburst. **1974** P. J. SEYBOLT *Through Chinese Eyes* 73 This is wild hillcountry: As they used to say in the old days, 'the mountains are high and the emperor is far away.' **1995** *New York Times* 4 Dec. (online) A foreigner who spends two weeks in the region quickly learns that autonomy has its limits. Granted … many Uighur traditions are tolerated. Married couples are legally permitted two rather than one child per family, the limit elsewhere in China. and those leading a nomadic life have no limits. This is illustrative of an oft-heard saying. 'The mountains are high and the emperor is far away.' **2003** R. PISKE *Political Corruption* 81 Often in the provinces during the classical communist period it had been said with a shrug that 'shan gao huangdi yuan', or 'the mountains are high and the Emperor is far away.' ■ **independence** 独立・自立；**power** 力・権力；**rulers and ruled** 支配者と被支配者

A MOUSE may help a lion.
ネズミでもライオンを助けることがある。
（訳注：may＝「…でも〈時々〉…することがある」。この意味では can も用いられる。Even cautious people *may* sometimes be off their guard.〈用心深い人も時に油断することがある〉、Lightning *can* be dangerous.〈稲妻も危険なことがある〉）

キャクストンの『寓話』(1484) 40 に登場するライオンとネズミのイソップ物語を想起させる。ライオンが捕まえたネズミの命を助けたところ、その取るに足らない小さなネズミがいつか恩返しをすると誓い、ライオンを笑わせた。ところが間もなく、そのライオンは罠の網にかかり、万事休すとなったとき、かつてのネズミがロープを噛み切るために助けにやって来たという話である。

□ *a***1563** *Mirror for Magistrates* (1938) 274 The mouse may sometyme help the Lyon in nede…. O prynces seke no foes. **1732** T. FULLER *Gnomologia* no. 264 A Lyon may come to be beholding to a Mouse. **1842** MARRYAT *Percival Keene* i. xvil. A mouse may help a lion, as the fable says. **1935** J. BUCHAN *House of Four Winds* xi. I only offer to show my gratitude by doing what I can…. A mouse may help a lion. ■ **assistance** 援助；**great and small** 大小

mouse ⇒ ONE for the mouse, one for the crow; ⇒ MICE.

mouth ⇒ Out of the FULLNESS of the heart the mouth speaks; Never look a GIFT horse in the mouth; GOD never sends mouths but He sends meat; PUT your money where your mouth is; A SHUT mouth catches no flies; A sow may whistle, though it has an ill mouth for it.

Out of the MOUTHS of babes—
幼子の口から…が出てくる。

幼子と言えども、時に驚くほど賢く、また的を射たことを口にすることがある。このことわざは省略形と暗示形で使われる場合が多く、原形が使われることはあまりない。『詩編』8 章 2 節 (欽定訳聖書) Out of the mouth of babes and sucklings hath thou ordained strength.「幼子と乳飲み子との口によって、褒めたたえられています」。『マタイによる福音書』21 章 16 節 (欽定訳聖書) Jesus saith unto them [the Pharisees], Yea; have ye never read, Out of the mouth of babes and sucklings thou hast perfected praise.「イエスは彼らに言われた、『そうだ、あなたがたは " 幼子、乳飲み子たちの口に賛美を備えられた " とあるのを読んだことがないのか」」

□ *a*1899 R. KIPLING *Stalley & Co.* II In the present state of education I shouldn't have thought any three boys would be well enough grounded.... But out of the mouths—. **1979** 'C. AIRD' *Some die Eloquent* xviii. It was something Crosby said.... 'About the source of the money.' 'Out of the mouths,' conceded Leeyes. **2003** S. A. MONACO *Suicide Squeeze* 342 'I know that God told you to write to me and that you would be my real daddy someday.' Nick ... sighed. Out of the mouths of babes. He'd forgotten that he'd written those words. ■ **children** 子供; **wisdom** 賢明・知恵

move ⇒ FAITH will move mountains.

MUCH cry and little wool
悲鳴のわりに毛はほとんど刈れない。

(訳注:「大山鳴動してネズミ一匹」)

1711 年の用例が示すように、商品に実質的な中身が何もないという事実を覆い隠すために、自己宣伝と大きなはったりの声が意図的に使われることがある。この例における cry は、かつて通りで商品名と性能を叫びながら宣伝する行商の習慣を指している。豚の毛を刈ること (*a*1475 年と1659 年の用例) は完全に徒労に終わる作業であり、豚の悲鳴が上がるだけでそれほど毛が刈り取れるわけではない。16 世紀のブラバンド公国 (現在のオランダ) の画家ピーテル・ブリューゲル (父) の絵画『ネーデルラントのことわざ』(1559) の下の部分で、1 人の農夫がまさにこの行ないをやっている場面が描かれている。

□ *a*1475 J. FORTESCUE *On Governance of England* (1885) x. His hyghnes shall haue theroff, but as hadd the man that sherid is [sheared his] hogge, much crye and litil woll. **1659** J. HOWELL *Proverbs* (English) 13 A Great cry and little wooll, quoth the Devil when he sheard the hogg. **1711** J. ADDISON *Spectator* 18 Dec. Those ... make the most noise, who have least to sell ... to whom I cannot but apply that old Proverb of Much cry, but little wool. **1922** *Punch* 29 Nov. 520 Ministers have taken good care that the adage, 'Much cry and little wool,' shall not apply to them. **1958** M. RENAULT *King must Die* I. v. They keep it [the codpiece] on under their kilts ... ; much cry and little wool as the saying goes. ■ **boasting** 自慢; **words and deeds** 言動

MUCH would have more.
あればあるほど欲しくなる。

† The MORE you get, the more you want.「持てば持つほど欲しくなる」

□ *c*1350 *Douce* MS 52 no. 65 Mykull [much] wulle more. *a*1400 *Wars of Alexander* (EETS) I. 4397 Mekill wald have mare as many man spellis [tells]. **1597** T. MORLEY *Plain Introduction to Music* murder 311

II, 70 The Common Prouerb is in me verified, that much would have more. **1732** T. FULLER *Gno-mologia* no. 3487 Much would have more; but often meets with less. **1897** J. MCCARTHY *Hist. Own Times* V. 131 Expedition after expedition has been sent out to extend the Egyptian frontier.... 'Much will have more,' the old proverb says; but in this case ... much is compelled for the sake of ... security to try to have more. **1928** J. S. FLETCHER *Ransom for London* v. iv. Why should ten millions satisfy these people? ... There is an old adage to the effect that much wants more. ■ greed 貪欲 ; riches 富

much ⇒ You can have TOO much of a good thing.

Where there's MUCK there's brass.
こやしのあるところに金がある。

(訳注：muck ＝「こやし、泥、ふん、ごみ」。農民だけでなく、ごみにまみれる仕事をする職人などにも当てはまるとされる。1678年の用例に挙がっている Muck and money go together. 〈金とこやしは道連れ〉もよく知られたことわざ)

畑仕事はこやしと泥にまみれているものの、それが財を生み出す源であることを意味していた。ここで使われている brass は money「金」を意味する俗語で、方言。

□**1678** J. RAY *English Proverbs* (ed. 2) 179 Muck and money go together. **1855** H. G. BOHN *Hand-Book of Proverbs* 564 Where there is muck there is money. **1943** J. W. DAY *Farming Adventure* xii. 'Where there's muck there's money' is as true now as then. But farms today lack the mud. **1967** *Punch* 13 Sept. 396 'Where there's muck there's brass' synopsised for many a North-country businessman the value of dirt in the profit-making process. **2001** *Spectator* 15/22 Dec. 28 Where there's muck, there's brass, and it was the job of the stercorarius to empty the cesspits and sell on the contents to farmers on city outskirts. ■ money 金・金銭

muckle ⇒ MANY a mickle makes a muckle.

mud ⇒ Throw DIRT enough, and some will stick.

multitude ⇒ CHARITY covers a multitude of sins.

MURDER will out.
殺人は明らかになるものだ。

(訳注：will ＝「性質・習性」。glass *will* break. 〈ガラスは割れるものだ〉。「天網恢恢疎にして漏らさず」)

隠そうとしているものはなんであれ、いずれ明るみに出る。類似した形式にTRUTH will out.「真実は明らかになるものだ」がある。

□*c***1325** *Cursor Mundi* (EETS) I. 1084 For-thl [therefore] men sais into this tyde [time], Is no man that murthir may hide. *c***1390** CHAUCER *Nun's Priest's Tale* I. 4242 Mordre wol out that se we day by day. **1596** SHAKESPEARE *Merchant of Venice* II. ii. 73 Truth will come to light; murder cannot be hid long. **1860** W. COLLINS *Woman in White* II. 64 Crimes cause their own detection, do they? And murder will out (another moral epigram), will it? **1978** F. NEUMANN *Seclusion Room* ix. 'Murder will out,' Berman announced, smiling fatuously. ■ concealment 隠すこと・隠蔽 ; violence 暴力

murder ⇒ KILLING no murder.

312 MUST

What MUST be, must be.
そうなると決まっていることは、きっとそうなる。

(訳注：must＝「〈必然を表わして〉必ず…になる」。All human beings *must* die.〈人間は皆死ぬ運命にある〉。「運は天にあり」)

物事に対する運命的な見方を表わしており、イタリア語 (che sara sara) とスペイン語 (Que sera, sera) のことわざに似た言い方でも知られている。これらのことわざはイタリア語でもスペイン語でも非文法的であり、またあまりなじみがないため、それらが英語に入ったのではなく、英語のことわざ What will be, will be.「なるようにしかならない」がイタリア語やスペイン語に入ったかのように見える。とはいえ、これらのことわざは英国に入り、16世紀には英国の合言葉にまでなった。そして、1956年には Que sera, sera「ケセラセラ」という歌が国際的なヒット曲となった。† **1604** マーロー『フォースタス博士』73 We must sinne, and so consequently die ... What doctrine call you this, Che sera, sera, what wil be, shall be? Diuinitie, adieu. (マーロー版はスペイン語とイタリア語の融合した形である)。

□*c***1386** CHAUCER *Knight's Tale* I. 1466 Whan a thyng is shapen, it shal be. **1519** W. HORMAN *Vulgaria* 20ᵛ That the whiche muste be wyll be. **1546** J. HEYWOOD *Dialogue of Proverbs* II. i. F3 That shalbe, shalbe. **1616** BEAUMONT & FLETCHER *Scornful Lady* III. i. I must kiss you.... What must be, must be. **1841** S. WARREN *Ten Thousand a Year* I. i. It's really very inconvenient ... for any of my young men to be absent ... but—I suppose—what must be must be. **1850** DICKENS *David Copperfield* lvii. 'My love,' observed Mr. Micawber, ' ... I am always willing to defer to your good sense. What will be—will be.' **1981** J. BINGHAM *Brock* 70 Oh well, what must be, must be. ■ **fate and fatalism** 運命と運命論

N

The NAIL that sticks up gets hammered down.
飛び出た釘はハンマーで打ちつけられる。
（訳注：「出る杭は打たれる」）

日本のことわざで、個人の才能・手腕よりも周囲との調和の方が重んじられるという考え方を表わしている。

☐ **1972** J. HOHENBERG *New Era in Pacific* 145 It will be a long time before the Japanese give up faith in the group creed: 'The nail that sticks up must be hammered down.' **1982** K. OHMAE *Mind of Strategist* 228 Whenever I wanted to do my own thing. I was constantly reminded that the nail that sticks up gets hammered down. **2007** J. HUIZENGA 'Ten Tips for Teaching English as a Foreign Language' on *www.trailsitionsabroad.com* In classrooms outside the U.S., however, showing solidarity with classmates ... is often more important than looking good for the teacher ... This holds true in Japan and China, ... where proverbs express the cultural idea In a nutshell: ... 'The nail that stands up must be pounded down.' ■ **action and consequence** 行為と結果；**pride** 誇り・うぬぼれ

nail ⇒ When all you have is a HAMMER, everything looks like a nail; ONE nail drives out another; For WANT of a nail the shoe was lost.

name ⇒ Give a DOG a bad name and hang him; NO names, no pack-drill.

A NATION without a language is a nation without a heart.
国語を持たない国は心を持たない国である。

ウェールズのことわざ。アイルランド版は2007年の用例参照。†アイルランド人の国粋主義者トーマス・デーヴィス（1814-45）の言葉。A people without a language of its own is only half a nation (Our National Language).「国語を持たない国民は半人前の国にすぎない」

☐ **1917** *Zionist Review* 110 It is recognized that a nation without a language is like a body without a soul. **1972** *Proceedings of the Institute on Narcotic Addition among Mexican Americans in the South West* As one great citizen of this world said, 'A country without a language is like a country without a heart.' **1993** B. THOMAS *Industrial Revolution and Atlantic Economy* 229 The striking leveling-off in the rate of decline between 1971 and 1981 is a great tribute to the whole-hearted labours of thousands of Welsh patriots who have made the language the centre-piece of the national effort Cenedl heb iaith, cenedl heb gallon. A nation without a language is a nation without a heart. **2007** posting 11 Feb. on *anthropology.net* In Ireland we have a saying '*Tu gan* *teanga, tir gan anam*' a country without a language is a country without a soul. The same applies to a people. ■ **national characteristics** 国民性

nation ⇒ Happy is the COUNTRY which has no history; The ENGLISH are a nation of shop-keepers.

NATURE abhors a vacuum.
自然は真空を嫌う。

古代の自然科学の原理で、**1534** ラブレー『ガルガンチュア』I. v において *Natura abhorret vacuum*.「自然は真空を嫌う」として引用されている。

□ *c***1551** CRANMER *Answer to Gardiner* 299 Naturall reason abhorreth vacuum. **1642** T. FULLER *Holy State* v. ii. Queen Joan ... (hating widowhood as much as Nature doth vacuum) marled James King of Majorca. **1686** R. BOYLE *Free Inquiry* VII. 292 The Axiom of the Schools, that Nature abhors a Vacuum. **1771** S. JOHNSON *Letter* 20 June (1952) I. 249 Whatever philosophy may determine of material nature, it is certainly true of intellectual nature, that it abhors a vacuum: our minds cannot be empty. **2001** *Washington Times* 30 Oct. A4 The White House should have expected this, of course, since the media, like nature, abhors a vacuum. ■ **Nature** 自然・造物主; **opportunity, taken** 得られた機会

nature ⇒ You can DRIVE out Nature with a pitchfork, but she keeps on coming back; SELF-preservation is the first law of nature.

nay ⇒ He that WILL not when he may, when he will he shall have nay.

NEAR is my kirtle, but nearer is my smock.
ガウンは私の肌に近いが、下着の方がもっと近い。

最近では下のことわざ NEAR is my shirt, but nearer is my skin.「シャツは私の肌に近いが、肌はもっと近い」の方がよく使われる。ここで kirtle は女性用のスカートやガウンを指し、smock は婦人用の肌着を指す。† プラウトゥス『三文銭』l. 1154 *Tunica propior palliost*.「私のブラウスはコートよりももっと近い」。よく似たことわざが19世紀初頭のフランス語 (*Ma chemise m'est plus proche que ma robe.*)、イタリア語、スペイン語にも見られる。

□ **1461** *Paston Letters* (1976) II. 228 Nere is my kyrtyl but nerre is my smok. **1545** R. TAVERNER tr. *Erasmus' Adages* (ed. 2) B7v The Englysshe prouerbe sayethe thus: nere is my cote, but nerer is my shyrt. **1622** J. HOWELL *Familiar Letters* 1 May (1903) I. 126 That king ... having too many irons in the fire at his own home ... answered them that his shirt was nearer to him than his doublet. **1861** C. READE *Cloister & Hearth* IV. xxlx. You must not think all of him and none of yourself. Near is your kirtle, but nearer is your smock. **2007** J. JENKINS & O. BERTRAND in Renevey & Whitehead *Medieval Translator* 17 Dickson would have preferred him to substitute the English equivalent 'Near is my kirtle, but nearer is my smock'. In other words, he would have preferred an ethnocentric translation. ■ **self-preservation** 自己防衛

NEAR is my shirt, but nearer is my skin.
シャツは私の肌に近いが、肌の方がもっと近い。

NEAR is my kirtle, but nearer is my smock.「ガウンは私の肌に近いが、下着はもっ

と近い」と意味が似ている。†14世紀初頭のフランス語*Plus pres m'est char que n'est chemise.*「私の肌はシャツより私に近い」

☐*c*1570 in J. P. COLLIER *Old Ballads* (1840) 99 Neerer is my skin then shirte. **1631** J. HENSHAW *Spare Hours of Meditations* 63 His charitie beginnes at home, and there it ends; neere is his coat, but neerer is his skinne. **1712** J. ARBUTHNOT *Lewis Baboon* V. My Shirt (quoth he) is near me, but my Skin is nearer: Whilst t take care of the Welfare of other Folks, no body can blame me, to apply a little Balsam to my own Sores. **1890** T. H. HALL CAINE *Bondman* II. x. 'We can't trust you.' ... 'Not your own brother?' said Jacob. '"Near is my shirt, but nearer is my skin," as the saying is.' **2009** P. PECINA *Roots of Evil* 39 It is the nature of human beings ... to be interested in one's own affairs first, and in everything else after ... 'Near is my shirt, but nearer is my skin,' as the saying goes. ■ **self-preservation** 自己防衛

The NEARER the bone, the sweeter the meat.
骨に近い肉ほど味がいい

（訳注：次のことわざ同様、「the 比較級 , the 比較級」〈…すればするほどますます…だ〉の形式が使われている。*The* more, *the* merrier.【ことわざ】〈人多ければ楽しみ多し〉。ここでの sweet は「おいしい」を意味するが、sweet の語源的意味は「おいしい」である）

このことわざは 2 通りに解釈できる。 1 つの意味は、昔から骨に近い肉が味がいいということであり（*a*1398 年の用例参照）、もう 1 つの意味は、骨に近い肉は残っている最後の肉であるだけによけい味わいがあるということである（1945 年の用例参照）。

☐*a*1398 J. TREVISA tr. *Bartholomew's On Properties of Things* (1975) xix. 1 The nerer the boon the swetter is the flesshe. *a*1661 T. PULLER *Worthies* (Wales) 2 As the sweetest flesh is said to be nearest the bones, so most delicious vallies are interposed betwixt these Mountains. **1778** in B. FRANKLIN *Writings* (1906) VIII. 258 We all agree the nearer the bone the sweeter the meat. **1945** F. THOMPSON *Lark Rise* i. 'The nearer the bone the sweeter the meat,' they used to say, and they were getting very near the bone.... Their children ... would have to depend wholly upon whatever was carved for them from the communal joint. **1979** 'TREVANIAN' *Shiborni* I. 38 A little skinny ... for my taste, but, like my ol' daddy used to say: the closer the bone, the sweeter the meat. **1996** *Washington Post* 27 Nov. B7 He inserts the rib in his mouth. 'The closer to the bone, the sweeter the meat,' he notes. ■ **value** 価値

The NEARER the church, the farther from God.
教会に近づけば近づくほど、神からは遠ざかる。

1879 年の用例では物理的な意味で使われているものの、一般にはこのことわざは宗教の見せかけだけの姿・形は真の信仰や徳とは関係がないという考えを表わしている。†Where GOD builds a church, the Devil will build a chapel.「神が教会を建てる場所に悪魔も礼拝堂を建てようとする」

☐**1303** R. BRUNNE *Handlyng Synne* (EETS) I. 9242 Tharfor men seys, an weyl ys trowed [believed], 'the nere the cherche, the fyrther fro God.' **1620** T. SHELTON tr. *Ceruantes' Don Quixote* II. xlvii. Eat nothing of all this meat ... for this dinner was presented by Nunnes, and it is an olde saying, The neerer the Church, the farther from God. **1879** J. B. HOPKINS *Work amongst Working Men* i. I fear it was a practical comment on the truth of the uncomfortable proverb, 'The nearer the church, the farther from God,' that so bad a district should adjoin one of the great head-quarters of the church. **1957** A. GRAVES *They hanged my Saintly Billy* ii. 'The nearer the church, the farther from God,' is a proverb of doubtful truth. But true it is that William Palmer, as a child, had two churches frowning down on him. ■ **Christianity** キリスト教

NECESSITY is the mother of invention.
必要は発明の母である。

逆境や欠乏こそが独創的な解決策を生みだす原動力となる。†ペルシウス『風刺詩』序10 *Magister artis ingenique largitor venter.*「空腹が芸術の師であり、発明の才の源である」。こうした考え方は **1519** W. ホーマン *Vulgaria* 52 Nede taught hym wytte. *Necessitasingenium dedit.*「必要が人に発明の才を教えた」においてより簡潔に述べられている。

□**1545** R. ASCHAM *Toxophilus* II. 18ᵛ Necessitie, the inuentor of all goodnesse (as all authours in a maner, doo saye) ... inuented a shaft heed. **1608** G. CHAPMAN *Tragedy of Byron* IV. i. The great Mother, Of all productions (graue Necessity). **1658** R. FRANCK *Northern Memoirs* (1694) 44 Art imitates Nature, and Necessity is the Mother of invention. **1726** J. SWIFT *Gulliver's Travels* IV. x. I soaled my Shoes with wood, which I cut from a Tree.... No man could more verify the Truth ... That, Necessity is the Mother of invention. **1861** C. READE *Cloister & Hearth* II. vi. 'But, dame, I found language too poor to paint him. I was fain to invent You know Necessity is the mother of—'. 'Ay! ay, that is old enough, o'conscience'. **2001** *Washington Post* 18 Nov. B7 If necessity is the mother of invention, calamity is not uncommonly the source of legislation. ■ **necessity** 必要性・必然性

NECESSITY knows no law.
必要の前に法律なし。
（訳注：「背に腹は代えられぬ」）

緊急の必要性は法律に従う義務に勝る。†ラテン語 *Necessitas non habet Legem.*「必要の前に法律なし」

□**1377** LANGLAND *Piers Plowman* B. xx. 10 Nede ne hath no lawe, ne neure shal falle in dette. *c*1530 W. TYNDALE *Answer to More* B1 Two things are without law, God and necessity. *a*1555 N. RIDLEY *Lamentation of Miserable Estate of Church* (1556) D4 The latter reason ... includeth a necessitie which after the common sayinge bathe no law. **1680** DRYDEN *Kind Keeper* III. ii. Necessity has no Law; I must be patient. **1776** F. RHINELANDER *Letter* 23 Feb. in H. C. VAN SCHAACK *Life of Peter Van Schaack* (1842) 54 Troops ... quarter themselves in any houses they find shut up. Necessity knows no law. **1864** MRS H. WOOD *Trevlyn Hold* II. xiv. Necessity has no law, and he was obliged to rise. **1939** 'D. YATES' *Gale Warning* vi. '"Don't speak to the man at the wheel" is a very good rule.' 'So', said I, 'is "Necessity knows no law,"' **1977** S. T. WARNER *Kingdoms of Elfin* 107 Necessity knows no law. I must admit it. From time to time, I flew. ■ **necessity** 必要性・必然性

need ⇒ (名詞) A FRIEND in need is a friend indeed; (動詞) GOOD wine needs no bush; A GUILTY conscience needs no accuser.

NEEDLES and pins, needles and pins, when a man marries, his trouble begins.
針とピンを買ってやらなきゃ、針とピンを買ってやらなきゃ、結婚すると男の悩みが始まる。

かつて男は結婚すると妻に針やピンなどの必需品を買い与えなければならなかったが、機械による大量生産がなされる前は、これらの品は高価であった。

□**1843** J. O. HALLIWELL *Nursery Rhymes of England* 122 Needles and pins, needles and pins, When a man marries his trouble begins. **1876** R. N. BLACKMORE *Cripps* III. 214 Cripps was come to a turn of the track—for it scarcely could be called a road—and was sadly singing to Dobbin and himself that exquisite elegiac— 'Needles and pins, needles and pins, When a man marries, his trouble begins!' 1952 'J. CANNAN' (1983) *Body in Beck* vii. 165 Thank God I steered clear of females. Needles and pins, needles and pins, when a man marries his trouble begins. Good God, where did I get that from? 2000 *Washington Times* 15 Nov. El2 (*Herb & Jamaal comic strip*) They say, 'Needles and pins, needles and pins, when a man marries, his troubles begin,' ... But I'll tell ya, among the things they say, what I'm most curious about is ... who are '*they*'? ■ **marriage** 結婚

NEEDS must when the Devil drives.
悪魔に追い立てられれば、ぜがひでも行かなければならぬ。

(訳注：needs＝「必ず、どうしても」〔通例 must の前後で〕。You *needs* must do your duty.〈ぜがひでも義務を果たさなければならない〉。「泣く子と地頭には勝てぬ」)

必要性に迫られて、たとえやりたくなくてもやらなければならない時がある。needs must は one needs must go「ぜひとも行かなければいけない」の省略形。

□*c*1450 J. LYDGATE *Assembly of Gods* (EETS) 1. 21 Hit ys oftseyde by hem that yetlyues He must nedys go that the deuell dryues. **1602** SHAKESPEARE *All's Well that ends Well* I. iii 29 He must needs go that the devil drives. **1835** SOUTHEY *Doctor* III. lxxxiii. Needs must go when the Devil drives. **1843** SURTEES *Handley Cross* III. xi. Needs must when the devil drives! ... But I'd rather do any thing than injure that poor blue-eyed beauty. **1978** T. SHARPE *Throwback* iii. I don't want to marry the damned woman either, but needs must when the devil drives. **2002** *Times* 22 Feb. 24 Applied conscientiously in the rush hour it [the rule 'women and children first'] would ensure that no male adult would ever reach his office on time, if at all. Needs must when the Devil drives is a more realistic motto for the Underground. ■ **necessity** 必要性・必然性

What a NEIGHBOUR gets is not lost.
隣人が手に入れたものはあなたが失くしたものではない。

親しい人が何かを手に入れたとしても、あなたが何かを失ったわけではない。それゆえその人の幸運を祝福すべきである。neighbour の代わりに friend もよく使われる。

□**1567** L. WAGER *Mary Magdalene* D4ᵛ There is nothyng lost that is done for such a friende. **1721** J. KELLY *Scottish Proverbs* 198 It is no tint [not lost], a Friend gets. **1891** J. L. KIPLING *Beast & Man* viii. The public at large have reaped much of the crop sown by Government for its own army, but, as the Scottish saying has it, 'What a neighbour gets is not lost' **1933** N. GORDON *Shakespeare Murders* xv. 237 'Every one is naturally interested in the whereabouts of a million pounds, even if it does not belong to oneself. It isn't lost, what a friend gets.' ■ **neighbours** 隣人；**winners and losers** 勝者と敗者

neighbour ⇒ GOOD fences make good neighbours.

nest ⇒ There are no BIRDS in last year's nest; BIRDS in their little nests agree; It's an ILL bird that fouls its own nest.

In vain the NET is spread in the sight of the bird.
鳥の目の前で網を張るのは無駄である。

罠は狙った獲物がそれを知っている場合、何の役にも立たない。似た意味を持つものに FOREWARNED is forearmed「前もっての警戒は前もっての武装」がある。『箴言』1 章

318 net

17節（欽定訳聖書）Vain the net is spread in the sight of any bird.「鳥の目の前で網を張るのは無駄である」を想起させる。† *c*1395 ウィクリフ聖書（1850）『箴言』1 章17節 A net is leid in veyn before the ighen [eyes] ofbriddis.「鳥の目の前に網を仕掛けても無駄に終わる」

☐**1581** G. PETTIE tr. *S. Guazzo's Civil Conversation* I. 20ᵛ In vaine (as the Prouerb sayth) The net is pitcht in the sight of the birdes. **1888** J. E. T. ROGERS *Economic Interpretation of Hist.* xxi. The landowners in Pitt's time foresaw this.... They would certainly be caught, and the net was spread in vain in sight of the bird. **1941** 'M. COLES' They tell No Tales x. 'Keep a good look out' ... 'In vain is the net spread in the sight of the bird, anyway.' **1961** L. S. DE CAMP *Dragon of Ishtar Gate* viii. 'If they come, we shall be ready,' said Bessas. 'In vain the net is spread in the sight of the bird.' ■ **deception** ごまかし；**futility** 無益

net ⇒ All is FISH that comes to the net.

If you gently touch a NETTLE it'll sting you for your pains; grasp it like a lad of mettle, an' as soft as silk remains.

イラクサには優しく触っても棘は刺さる。ならば、男らしくそれを摑め。摑んでしまえば絹のように柔らかい。

このことわざの真意（すなわち、面倒な連中には断固として立ち向かうべきだ）が1830年の用例の中で説明されている。慣用句 to grasp the nettle「困難に恐れずに立ち向かう」はよく使われる。

☐**1578** LYLY *Euphues* I. 212 True it is Philautus that he which toucheth ye nettle tenderly, is soonest stoung. **1660** W. SECKER *Nonsuch Professor* I. 156 Sin is like the nettle, that stings when it is gently touched, but doth hurt not when it is ruggedly handled. **1753** A. HILL *Works* IV. 120 Tender-handed stroke a nettle, And it stings you, for your pains: Grasp it like a man of mettle, And it soft as silk remains. **1830** R. FORBY *Vocabulary of East Anglia* 430 'Nip a nettle hard, and it will not sting you' —i.e. Strong and decided measures prevail best with troublesome people. **1925** S. O'CASEY *Juno & Paycock* I. 35 Be firm, Captain.... If you gently touch a nettle it'll sting you for your pains; grasp it like a lad of mettle, an' as soft as silk remains. ■ **boldness** 大胆さ

NEVER is a long time.

「決して」は長い時間にわたる言葉である。

（訳注：文字通りには、「『決して』は長い時間にわたる言葉である」である。never とは not〈…ない〉＋ ever〈永久に、いつまでも〉から成っている。それゆえ、このことわざの趣旨は、たとえ今はできなくても、永久にできないわけではないので、すぐにあきらめてはならないということである）

意味がよく似たものとして、最近のことわざ NEVER say never.「『決して』という言葉は決して使うな」が挙げられる。

☐*c*1390 CHAUCER *Canon's Yeoman's Tale* I. 1411 Nevere to thryve were to long a date. **1721** J. KELLY *Scottish Proverbs* 260 Never is a long Term.... Spoken to them that say they will never get such a Thing effected. **1887** BLACKMORE *Springhaven* I. xvii. She never could pay her rent. But 'never is a long time' ... and ... she stood clear of all debt now. **1979** H. HOWARD *Sealed Envelope* iii. 'I never reveal my sources.' ... 'Never is a long time.' ■ **future** 未来

NEVER say never.
「決して」という言葉は決して言うな。

おそらく上のことわざを簡潔に言い換えたものである。当然のことながら、20世紀中頃から Never say always.「『いつも』という言葉は決して使うな」も用いられることがある。

□**1977** *Economist* 9 Apr. 6 Mr Colley ... is politician enough never to say never. **1978** *Washington Post* 2 Mar. Al Marshall did not rule out a resumption of talks, saying 'you can never say "never" in this business'. **1984** *Washington Post* 27 Apr. A23 A president should 'never say never.' **2014** *www.telegraph.co.Uk* 14 Sept And I guess I'm here to say to other women in their fifties, 'Never say never. It isn't over yet' ■ **future** 未来

It is NEVER too late to learn.
学ぶのに遅すぎることはない。

† NEVER too old to learn.「年を取り過ぎて学べないということはない」

□**1678** R. L'ESTRANGE *Seneca's Morals* II. xx. It is never too late to learn what it is always necessary to know. **1721** J. KELLY *Scottish Proverbs* 266 Never too late to learn. **1856** W. COLLINS *Lady of Glenwith Grange in After Dark* II. 3 'It is never too late to learn,' cried he. 'I will make a fisherman of you in no time, if you will only attend to my directions.' **1927** B. F. BENSON *Lucia In London* ii. We want to know what the cosmopolitan mind is thinking about. Of course we're old, but it is never too late to learn. **2002** *Washington Times* 17 Feb. B3 To his credit. Norman Mailer later said that he felt 'a very large responsibility' for Mr. Adan's murder, and admitted that he 'never thought Abbott was close to killing ... I was not sensitive to the fact' It's never too late to learn. ■ **lateness** 遅れ; **learning** 学問・学び

It is NEVER too late to mend.
改めるのに遅すぎるということはない。

（訳注：mend =「〈態度・欠点などを〉改める、直す」。*mend* one's manners〈態度を改める〉、Least said, sooner *mended*.【ことわざ】〈口数少なければ言い直しもたやすい、口は災いのもと〉）

何かのために修正したり、改善したりするのに遅すぎるということは決してない。

□**1590** R. GREENE (*title*) Never too late. **1594** WOGE & GREENE *Looking-Glass for London* 13ᵛ Amends may neuer come too late. *c*1645 J. HOWELL *Familiar Letters* 9 Nov. (1903) III. 139 We have both of us our failings that way ... but it is never too late to mend. **1856** C. READE (*title*) It is never too late to mend. **1934** H. SPRING *Shabby Tiger* iv. Adolf shrugged a shoulder which suggested that it's never too late to mend. **1961** I. JEFFERIES *It wasn't Me!* i. How kind. ... Never too late to mend. ■ **improvement** 改善; **lateness** 遅れ

NEVER too old to learn
年を取り過ぎて学べないということはない。

（訳注：「六十の手習い」）

† セネカ『使徒書簡』LXXVI. iii. *Tamdiu discendum est, quamdiu nescias: si proverbio credimus, quamdiu vivas.*「我々は知らないものがある限り、あるいはことわざを信じるなら、生きている限り学び続けなければならない」。† It is NEVER too late to learn.「学ぶのに遅すぎることはない」

□**1530** A. BARCLAY *Eclogues* (EETS) II. 538 Corid. on thou art not to olde for to lere. **1555** *Institution of Gentleman* B7ᵛ No man can be to olde to learne. **1670** J. RAY *English Proverbs* 112

Never too old to learn. **1712** J. ARBUTHNOT *Law is Bottomles Pit* I. vii. A Lawyer I was born, and a Lawyer I will be; one is never too Old to learn. **1858** TROLLOPE *Dr. Thorne* I. x. One should never be too old to learn—there's always something new worth picking up. **1990** 'C. AIRD' 'Lord Peter's Touch' in *Injury Time* (1995) 45 'All right then, tell me. I suppose I'm never too old to learn.' ■ **learning** 学問・学び ; **old age** 老年

never ⇒ BETTER late than never; never send a BOY to do a man's job; Never do EVIL that good may come of it; What you've never HAD you never miss; PAY beforehand was never well served; Never let the SUN go down on your anger.

NEW brooms sweep clean.
新しい箒はきれいに掃ける。

（訳注：とかく新任者ははりきって仕事をする。また、改革にも熱心である。a new broom =「改革に熱心な新任の指導者」。What is needed right now is *a new broom*. 〈今こそ新しいリーダーが必要だ〉。sweep =「掃ける」。These scissors *cut* well. 〈このハサミはよく切れる〉の cut と同じ用法）

慣用句 new broom「人事や仕事の手順」はこのことわざから生まれた。

□**1546** J. HEYWOOD *Dialogue of Proverbs* II. i. F3v Som therto said, the grene new brome sweplth cleene. **1578** LYLY *Euphues* I. 232 Ah well I wotte [know] that a newe broome sweepeth cleene. **1616** J. WITHALS *Dict.* (rev. ed.) 569 New bromes sweepe cleane, yet old friendship still retaine. **1776** G. COLMAN *New Brooms!* 15 I am glad he is gone—Glad!—To be sure. New Brooms, you know. **1877** J. A. FROUDE *Short Studies* 3rd Ser. 55 New brooms sweep clean. Abbot Thomas, like most of his predecessors, began with attempts at reformation. **1979** F. OLBRICH *Sweet & Deadly* iv. He was all right at first It was a case of a new broom sweeping clean. ■ **improvement** 改善 ; **innovation** 革新

What is NEW cannot be true.
新しいからといって正しいとは言えない

新しいものはその正しさがまだ証明されてないので信用できない。

□**1639** J. CLARKE *Parœmiologia Anglo-Latina* 228 The newest things, not always truest. **1791** J. BOSWELL *Life of Johnson* II. 283 I found that generally what was new was false. **1880** J. NICHOL *Byron* ix. We are told ... that he knew little of art or music.... It is true but not new. But when Hunt proceeds to say that Byron had no sentiment ... it is new enough, but is manifestly not true. **1928** *Times* 4 Feb. 8 Sir Arthur Evans has fallen a victim ... to the old slogan 'What is new cannot be true.' ■ **innovation** 革新

NEW lords, new laws
領主が変わると法も変わる。

新しい統治者は新しい法を導入する。† **1450** 聖エディッタ（1883）96 Willyham Conquerour was made here kyng, And made newe lordus and eke new lawe.「ウィリアム征服王はここで王になり、新しい領主となり、そして新しい法を制定した」

□*a***1547** E. HALL *Chronicle* (1548) Hen. VI 169 Tholde spoken prouerbe, here toke place: New Lordes, new lawes. **1824** SCOTT *St. Ronan's Well* II. i. But new lords new laws—naething but fine and imprisonment, and the game no a feather the plentler. **1874** T. HARDY *Far from Madding Crowd* I. viii. 'I was lately married to a woman, and she's my vocation now.' ... 'New lords new laws, as the saying is.' **2004** *News Bulletin* (dateline: Sochi) 28 Mar. (Interfax) The EU presidency rotates every six months. 'As a Russian proverb says: new lords, new laws. The EU has new pri-

new　321

orities with every new president It is difficult to work in these conditions.' ■ change 変化 ; circumstances 状況

You can't put NEW wine in old bottles.
新しい酒を古い革袋に入れてはならない。

（訳注：この場合の you は総称的な用法で、話し手や聞き手を含めた一般の人々々を指している。one よりくだけた使い方。Unless *you* cultivate *your* land, *you* won't have good crops.〈土地を耕さなければ、よい作物はできない〉）

新約聖書でこの理由が説明されている。『マタイによる福音書』9 章17節（欽定訳聖書）Neither do men put new wine into old bottles: else the bottles break, and the wine runneth out, and the bottles perish.「新しい酒を古い革袋に入れてはいけない。さもなくば、袋が破れ、酒がこぼれ、袋が腐ることになる」。この考え方は慣用句 new wine in old bottles「旧来の形式では扱えない新説」として比喩的に表わされている。

□**1912** L. STRACHEY *Landmarks in French Literature* vi. The new spirits had animated the prose of Chateaubriand and the poetry of Lamartine; but ... the form of both these writers retained most of the important characteristics of the old tradition. It was new wine in old bottles. **1948** A. J. TOYNBEE *Civilization on Trial* vi. The new wines of industrialism and democracy have been poured into old bottles and they have burst the old bottles beyond repair. **1960** I. JEFFERIES *Dignity & Purity* viii. 'I don't thinkyou can put new wine in old bottles.' I looked doubtful. ... 'A lot of this could be rationalized.' **1974** T. SHARPE *Porterhouse Blue* x. 'Motives? ... Good old-fashioned lust' 'That hardly explains the explosive nature of his end.' ... 'You can't put new wine in old bottles.' ■ innovation 革新

There is always something NEW out of Africa.
新しいものはいつもアフリカからやってくる。

ラテン語 *ex Africa semper aliquid novi* は、アフリカに生息する動物の異種交配を描いた大プリニウスの『博物誌』(viii. 16) における一節を言い変えたものである。その一節とは、*unde etiam vulgare Graeciae dictum semper aliquid novi African afferre.*「アフリカはいつも新しいものを生み出し続けるというギリシアのよく知られたことわざ」である。アリストテレス『動物誌』viii. 28, 7 には、Ἀεὶ Λιβύη φέρει τι καινόν.「リビアはいつも新しいものを見せてくれる」とある。ラテン語のことわざに由来するこのことわざは、少なくともエラスムスの『格言集』(1500) 以来、イングランドではずっと使われ続けている。

□**1559** W. BAVARDE tr. *A Woorke of Ioannes Ferrarius* 81 It is saied that Affricque bringeth foorthe alwaies some newe thing. **1642** J. HOWELL *Instructions for Forreine Travel* (Arber ed.) III. 22 France, which as Africk produceth always something New, for I never knew week passe in Paris but It brought forth some new kinds of Authors. **1976** D. ARDEN (*title*) *Out of Africa something new?* **1988** R. KELLY 'Stone Wall in Providence' in *Under Words* 112 Always something new/out of Africa. Rubadubdub of the new desires squeezing/into the convenient old places of the sleepstonewall. **2000** CBS NEWS (web site) 11 June It is a thing of rare beauty nonetheless: Humans and dangerous animals at peace and in harmony with each other-proving once again that there is always something new out of Africa. ■ novelty 目新しさ

new ⇒ There is NOTHING new under the sun; It is best to be OFF with the old love before you are on with the new; You can't TEACH an old dog new tricks.

news ⇒ BAD news travels fast; GO abroad and you'll hear news of home; NO news is good news.

nibble ⇒ A BLEATING sheep loses a bite.

NIGHT brings counsel.
夜になると助言が訪れる。

ある問題や決断を考えながら眠りにつくと、しばしば頭が冴え、進むべき進路が明確になるという考え（1928年の用例参照）。† メナンドロス『名言集』no. 222 Ἐν νυκτὶ βουλὴ τοῖς σοφοῖσι γίγνεται.「夜になると、賢者のところに助言が降りてくる」。ラテン語 In nocte consilium.「夜に降りてくるのは助言である」。フランス語 La nuit porte conseil.「夜になると助言が訪れる」

□ **1590** SPENSER *Faerie Queene* I. i. 291 Vntroubled night ... giues counsell best. **1640** G. HERBERT *Outlandish Proverbs* no. 746 Night is the mother of Councels. **1660** DRYDEN *Astrrea Redux* I. 93 Well might the Ancient Poets then confer On Night the honout'd name of Counsels. **1928** L. THAYER *Darkest Spot* xviii. The saying that night brings counsel is often true.... Peter ... woke next morning with a plan of campaign fully developed. **1967** N. FREELING *Strike out where not Applicable* 184 'Home you go, boy. Night brings counsel.' Night did bring counsel. Or rather Verbiest, the young inspector, brought it ■ **advice** 忠告・助言

night ⇒ BARNABY bright, Barnaby bright, the longest day and the shortest night; All CATS are grey in the dark; Red sky at night, shepherd's delight; SING before breakfast, cry before night.

NINE tailors make a man.
仕立て屋 9 人で男一人前。

（訳注：このことわざには諸説ある。仕立て屋は職業柄体力がなく、9 人で一人前の力であるといった俗説に由来するという説、紳士たるもの服を仕立てる際にはたくさんの仕立て屋から選ぶべきであるという忠告であるという説、さらには、tailors は tellers 〈葬儀の際の弔いの鐘の回数〉を意味しており、大人の葬式では鐘は 3 × 3 ＝ 9 回鳴らされるという説もある）

文字通りの意味は、紳士たる者は服を様々な店から厳選しなければならないというものであるが、現在は、特に（教会での）鐘の鳴らし方に関連して使われることが多い（1908年と1934年の用例参照）。

□ **1613** *Tarlton's Jests* C1 Two Taylors goes to a man. **1647** N. WARD *Simple Cobbler* 26 It is a more common then convenient saying, that nine Taylers make a man; it were well if nineteene could make a woman to her minde. **1776** *Poor Robin's Almanack* II. C6v Do ye know how many Taylors make a Man? Why Nine—Nine Taylors make a Man. **1819** SCOTT *Letter* 26 July (1933) V. 427 They say it take nine tailors to make a man—apparently, one is sufficient to ruin him. **1908** H. B. WALTERS *Church Bells* v. When the Knell is rung, it is a frequent practice to indicate the ... sex of the deceased.... The old saying 'nine tailors make a man' is really 'nine tellers' [strokes], or three times three. **1912** A. BRAZU. *New Girl at St. Chad's* i. There's a saying that it takes nine tailors to make a man, so if your name is Taylor you can only be the ninth part of a lady! **1934** D. L. SAYERS *Nine Tailors* IV. iii. The voice of the bells of Fenchurch St Paul.... Nine Tailors Make a Man. ■ **dress** 衣服

NO 323

nine ⇒ PARSLEY seed goes nine times to the Devil; POSSESSION is nine points of the law; It is not SPRING until you can plant your foot upon twelve daisies; A STITCH in time saves nine.

NO cross, no crown
十字架（苦難）なくして栄冠なし。

ここでは cross が二重の意味で使われている。1 つは「キリストの十字架」であり、もう 1 つは「苦難」である。したがって、もし十字架を背負わなければ、つまり苦難を経験しなければ、究極の天の報酬（crown「栄冠」）は得られないという意味になる。†CROSS-ES are ladders that lead to heaven.「十字架は天国へ通ずる梯子である」

□ **1609** T. BRETNOR *Almanac March* Good days A crosse before a Crowne. **1621** F. QUARLES *History of Queene Ester: Meditations* ix. The way to Blisse lyes not on beds of Downe, And he that had no Crosse, deserues no Crowne. **1669** W. PENN (*title*) No Cross no Crown. **1944** 'A. GIL-BERT' *Death at Door* (1945) xiii. 135 They were always at loggerheads, those two. No Cross, No Crown, that's their motto. **1996** L. ANDREWS *Sinister Side* vii. 123 He sighed piteously. 'I suppose I'll have to hang on for it' 'No cross, no crown, Julian.' He realised he had overplayed the martyr. ■ misfortune 不運

NO cure, no pay
治らなければ、支払いなし。

ロイズ救助契約標準書式でよく用いられている。

□ **1800** J. COBB *Ramah Droog* I iv You'll never have reason to complain of my want of confidence. Besides, the worst come to the worst ... 'No cure, no pay.' **1836** W. C. RISLEY *Early Victorian Squarson* 13 (16 Dec.) ... a travelling doctor of smoaking chimneys ... made his appearance here. I agreed to buy his skill ... on the principle of No Cure, No Pay. **1907** A. R. KENNEDY *Treatise ... Law of Civil Salvage* (ed. 2) 270 (*heading*) Salvage agreement on basis of Lloyd's standard form of 'no cure—no pay' agreement. **1933** *Reports of Tax Cases* (*Inland Revenue*) XVII. 352 The charges of those accountants ... were made on the 'No cure, no pay' principle. **1982** *Listener* 6 May 10 The divers ... will earn their money.... If they find nothing, they will receive nothing.... No cure, no pay. ■ just deserts 当然の報い

NO foot, no horse
蹄（ひづめ）なくして馬はなし。

（訳注：このことわざは北米で18世紀の半ばから使われている〈1751 年の用例参照〉。蹄は馬の命である。蹄の世話をしなければ馬に危害が及ぶ）

北米では No hoof, no horse. という形式で使われる。

□ **1751** J. BRIDGES (*title*) *No Foot, No Horse*. An essay on the anatomy of the foot of ... a horse. **1893** A. T. FISHER *The Farrier* or '*No Foot, No Horse*' 2 'No foot, no horse' exactly expresses that which I desire to impress on the reader in the following pages. Without the full and perfect use of its feet, the horse is useless. **2001** R. FREEMAN *www.horseshoes.com* (web site) It was while hanging around the barns with a friend who trained horses that I quickly gained an appreciation for the old adage, 'no hoof, no horse'. **2007** *Times* 2 27 Apr. The great fascination of extreme old age will ... be ... how do you behave when you reach your destination? ... in the manner of old-fashioned trench warfare, with a mixture of chiropody and raw courage. No foot, no horse, says the old stables maxim, and it goes for humans too. ■ horse lore 馬にまつわる伝承

NO harm, no foul
害がなければ、反則もなし。

損害が発生していない場合には、罰は与えられない。バスケットボールの世界で生まれた米国のことわざ。たとえ選手のプレーが反則行為であっても対戦相手側に害を及ぼさないなら、審判は罰を与えるべきではない（1956年の用例参照）。現在では、法律の分野でもよく使われる（2014年の用例参照）。

☐ **1956** *Hartford Courant* 2 Dec. 1D 1 (online) The conference coaches also agreed that Big Ten officials this winter should emphasize a principle of 'no harm, no foul'. **1975** B. MEGGS *Matter of Paradise* (1976) V. 31 So they quietly divorced: no harm, no foul. Mainly, no children. **2014** *www. dailyherald.com* 11 Dec.(*heading*) Target customers face no harm-no foul argument in suit. ■ **action and consequence 行為と結果**

NO man can serve two masters.
誰も 2 人の主人に仕えることはできない。

『マタイによる福音書』6 章24節 (欽定訳聖書)No man can serve two masters ... Ye cannot serve God and mammon.「誰も 2 人の主人に仕えることはできない…神と強欲の 2 人に仕えることはできない」を想起させる。

☐ *c***1330** in T. Wright *Political Songs* (1839) 325 No man may wel serve tweie lordes to queme [please]. *c***1477** CAXTON *Jason* (EETS) 57 No man may wel serve two maistres, for that one corurnpeth that other. **1642** D. ROGERS *Naaman* vi. You cannot have your will ... and Christ too; no man can serve two masters. **1853** R. C. TRENCH *On Lessons in Proverbs* V. Our lord ... has said: 'No man can serve two masters.' ... So the Spanish proverb: He who has to serve two masters, has to lie to one. **1979** 'C. AIRD' *Some die Eloquent* V. The Coroner's Officer existed in a sort of leaderless no-man's-land. Hostilities had broken out over this more than once ... No man can serve two masters. ■ **employers and employees 雇用者と被雇用者**

NO man is a hero to his valet.
誰も従者にとっては英雄たり得ない。

(訳注：下の解説で引用されている、16世紀ルネサンス期フランスを代表する哲学者モンテーニュは、『エセー』第 3 巻第 2 章「後悔について」で、「何人も、自分の家においてばかりでなく、自分の故郷においても、預言者でなかった」と述べている。これは、「預言者郷里に容れられず」ということであり、たとえすぐれた人物であっても、身近な人には理解されにくいのである)

身辺周りの世話をする従者にとっては主人もただの人にすぎない。このことわざはルイ14世の愛人であった著名なフランスの貴婦人コルニュエル夫人 (1605-94) の言葉 *Il n'y a pas de héros pour son valet-de-chambre*.「従者にとっても英雄であるような人はいない」に由来する。しかし、この考え方自体は、古代マケドニアのアレクサンドロス大王に仕えた将軍アンティゴノス (紀元前 4 世紀) にまで遡る。プルタルコス『格言集』Hermodotus in his poems called him Son of the Sun. He that attends my close-stool, said he [Antigonus], sings me no such song.「ヘルモドトスはアンティゴノスのことを太陽の息子と呼んだが、アンティゴノスによると、室内用便器の世話をする自分の従者は自分のことをそのように賛美してくれないという」。† **1603** M.E.de モンテーニュ『エセー』(J. フロリオ訳) III. ii. Few men haue beene admired of their familiers.... In my climate of Gascoigne they deeme it as iest to see mee in print.「自分の家族によって賛美されているような人はいない。…わがガスコーニュの土地では、

皆が私の著作が公にされたのを見ておかしがっている」

☐ **1764** S. FOOTE *Patron* II. 31 It has been said ... that no man is a hero to his valet de chambre; now I am afraid when you and I grow a little more intimate ... you will be horribly disappointed in your high expectations. **1910** *Times* 20 Jan. (Literary Supplement) 17 Many men have been heroes to their valets, and most (except Pope and Poe) to their biographers. **1940** A. CHRISTIE *One, Two, buckle my Shoe* i. It has been said that no man is a hero to his valet. To that may be added that few men are heroes to themselves at the moment of visiting their dentist. **2002** *Washington Times* 9 May C2 All of which is a mere footnote to the longest presidency in American history, and one of the greatest. But it is a useful reminder that just as no man is a hero to his valet so, it seems, not even a president is immune to the ministrations of a Chef From Hell.

■ **employers and employees** 雇用者と被雇用者；**familiarity** 慣れ親しみ

NO names, no pack-drill
無名であれば、懲罰軍装行進の罰を受けることもない。

何かの責任を負わされるほど有名でなければ、責められたり、罰を受けることもない。ま
た、微妙な話題に関しては寡黙であるにこしたことはない。pack-drillとは軍の刑罰の 1
つで、違反者は隊列を崩さずに何度も行進を強要される。一般には第 1 次世界大戦時に
生まれたと考えられているが、実際はそれよりはるか以前に遡る（1874年の用例参照）。

☐ **1874** Winnipeg *Daily Free Press*, 28 July NO NAMES—NO PACK DRILL-*old saw* [saying]. **1903** *Bucks Herald* 11 Apr. He saw Burke in the custody of Rolfe, and charged him with the theft of the clock. Witness asked him who the other man was, and he said, 'No names, no pack drill.' **1925** S. O'CASEY *Juno & Paycock* II. 61 I know some as are as sweet as the blossoms that bloom in the May—oh; no names, no pack drill. **2000** P. LOVESEY *Reaper* iv. 47 'Do you know, I've heard of churches—no names, no pack-drill—who wait until the end of the year before stomping up.' ■ **speech and silence** 発言と沈黙

NO news is good news.
便りのないのは良い便り。

連絡がないということは、何も悪いことが起こっていないということである。BAD news
travels fast.「悪事千里を走る」はこの楽観的な考え方の理由を示している。

☐ **1616** JAMES I in *Loseley MSS* (1836) 403 No newis is bettir then evill newis. **1640** J. HOWELL *Famlliar Letters* 3 June (1903) 11. 144 I am of the Italians mind that said, 'Nulla nuova, buona nuova', (no news, good news). **1850** F. E. SMEDLEY *Frank Fairlegh* x. Arguing ... (on the 'no news being good news' system) that I should have heard again if anything had gone wrong, I dismissed the subject from my mind. **1974** T. SHARPE *Porterhouse Blue* xxi. 'He can't reply,' the Senior Tutor pointed out 'I find that most consoling. After all no news is good news.' **2002** *Washington Post* 12 Feb. Cl3 (*Mother Goose & Grimm comic strip*) 'Sigh ... No news is good news.' 'I'll say ... It means no rolled-up newspaper.' ■ **news** 知らせ

NO pain, no gain
苦労なくして、得るものなし。
（訳注：「苦は楽の種」）

努力なしには何も達成できない。

☐ **1577** N. BRETON *Works of Young Wit* 33ᵛ They must take pain that look for any gayn. **1648** HERRICK *Hesperides* 298 No Paines, no Gaines. If little labour, little are our gaines: Mans fortunes are according to his paines. **1853** R. C. TRENCH *On Lessons in Proverbs* iv. For the most part they courageously accept the law of labour, *No pains, no gains,—No sweat no sweet*, as the

326 NO

appointed law and condition of man's life. **1985** *Washington Post* 22 May (Health Supplement) 14 Forget the coach's rule of 'no pain, no gain'. Today, exercise researchers are replacing it with the 'talk rule'. **2000** M. BERMAN *Twilight of American Culture* i. 58 [T]here is very little tolerance on the part of students for any real work; 'no pain, no gain' is not part of their emotional vocabulary. ■ **wanting and having** 不足と所持

NO penny, no paternoster
一文無しではお祈りを頼むこともできない。
（訳注：かつて宗教改革以前の時代にはお金を払わなければお祈りの儀式をしてもらえなかった）

お金を払わないと何もできない。ここでの文脈は、祈禱料を払って自分のために司祭に祈りをあげてもらうというものである。paternoster（Our Father「我らの父」）とは主の祈りを意味する。

□ **1528** W. TYNDALE *Obedience of Christian Man* fo. lxxxiiv After the commune sayenge, no peny no Pater noster. **1648** HERRICK *Hesperides* 302 Who … Can't send for a gift A Pig to the Priest for a Roster [roast], Shall heare his Clarke say, … No pennie, no Pater Noster. **1721** J. KELLY *Scottish Proverbs* 259 No Penny, no Pater Noster. **1925** J. I. C. CLARKE *My Life* ix. If the churchly motto 'No penny, no Paternoster' was true, how could a church … stay downtown when its congregation was moving north. **1940** D. TBILHET *Broken Face Murders* ii. No penny, no paternoster. I neither pay the piper nor do I dance. ■ **just deserts** 当然の報い

no ⇒ HALF a loaf is better than no bread; There's no great LOSS without some . gain; There's no PLACE like home; If there were no RECEIVERS, there would be no thieves; There is no ROYAL road to learning; ⇒ No evil, hear no evil, speak no evil; SHROUDS have no pockets; No SMOKE without fire; TIME and tide wait for no man; No TIME like the present.

nobody ⇒ EVERYBODY's business is nobody's business; It's an ILL wind that blows nobody any good.

A NOD's as good as a wink to a blind horse.
盲馬にとっては来だけでも目配せに劣らぬほどの効力がある。

相手に自分の気持ちを伝えるにはただほのめかすだけで十分であり、言葉に出す必要はないということを動物を用いて述べたもの。1822年の用例が示すように簡略形で用いられることが多い。

□ **1794** W. GODWIN *Caleb Williams* I. viii. Say the word; a nod is as good as a wink to a blind horse. **1822** B. MALKIN *Gil Blas* (rev. ed.) I. II. ix. I shall say no more at present; a nod is as good as a wink. **1925** S. O'CASEY *Shadow of Gunman in Two Plays* 1. 142 You needn't say no more—a nod's as good as a wink to a blind horse. **1979** L. MEYNELL *Hooky & Villainous Chauffeur* vi. The way he behaves … Other men's wives. Still, I expect you know as much about that as I do…. They say a nod's as good as a wink to a blind horse. **1992** W. DONALDSON *Root into Europe* ii. 34 Got a good PR machine working for you, I expect. Say no more…. Nod's as good as a wink. ■ **hints** ヒント・暗示 ; **tact** 機転

nod ⇒ （動詞） HOMER sometimes nods.

noise ⇒ EMPTY vessels make the most sound.

none ⇒ A BAD excuse is better than none; There's none so BLIND as those who will not see; None but the BRAVE deserve the fair; There's none so DEAF as those who will not hear; JACK of all trades and master of none; TWO is company, but three is none.

no one ⇒ No one should be JUDGE in his own cause.

NORTH wind doth blow, we shall have snow.
北風が吹けば、雪になる。
　（訳注：doth = does）

ブリテン島では北風は北極地方から寒気がやってくる兆しである。

□**1805** *Songs for Nursery* 3 The north wind doth blow, And we shall have snow, And what will poor Robin do then? Poor thing! **1980** A. T. ELLIS *Birds of Air* (1983) 113 Mary was thinking. 'The north wind doth blow and we shall have snow and what will the robin do then ...' ■ **weather lore** 天気にまつわる伝承

nose ⇒ Don't CUT off your nose to spite your face.

NOTHING comes of nothing.
無からは何も生じない。
　（訳注：of =「〈由来・起源・出所を表わし，be, come などの後で〉…から」。See what comes *of* being in such a hurry.〈それごらん、そんなに慌てるからこんなになるんだ〉。「蒔かぬ種は生えぬ」）

†アルカイオス『断章』cccxx. (Lobel-Page) οὐδὲν ἐκ δενός γένοιτο.「無から何も生じない」。ラテン語 *Ex nihilo nihil fit.*「無からは何も生じない」

□*c***1380** CHAUCER *Boethius* v. pr. i. For this sentence is verray and soth, that 'no thing hath his beynge of naught'. **1551** CRANMER *Answer to Gardiner* 369 *Sicut ex nlhilo nihil fit, Ita nihil in nihilum redigitur*, As nothyng can be made of nought, so nothynge can be tourned into nought **1605-6** SHAKESPEARE *King Lear* I. i. 89 Nothing will come of nothing. Speak again. **1818** SCOTT *Heart of Midlothian* I. i. You are to give me all your business.... If you have none, the learned gentleman here knows nothing can come of nothing. **1946** E. R. CURTIS *Lady Sarah Lennox* iv. 'What did you think of it?' 'Nothing. Sir.' 'Nothing comes of nothing!' the King exclaimed impatiently. **1998** T. DALRYMPLE *Life at Bottom* (2001) 233 Well, as King Lear said, nothing comes of nothing: and the journalist's hatred of the police was unlikely to have sprung completely at random and fully informed from his consciousness. ■ **reciprocity** 相互扶助

NOTHING for nothing.
金がないと何も買えない。

何も提供しなければ、何ももらえない。

□*a***1704** T. BROWN *Works* (1707) I. 131 Thou know'st the proverb, nothing due for nought. **1800** M. EDGEWORTH *Castle Rackrent* 167 Nothing for nothing, or I'm under a mistake with you, Jason. **1858** G. J. WHYTE-MELVILLE *Interpreter* xxv. Sir Harry ... recollected the old established principle of himself and his clique, 'Nothing for nothing, and very little for a halfpenny.' **1908** A. MACLAREN *Ezekiel* 172 The last touch in the picture is meanness, which turned everything into money.... Is not 'nothing for nothing' an approved maxim to-day? **1981** N. FREELING *One Damn*

Thing after Another iv. Their heart's not in it. Nothing for nothing and not much for sixpence. ■ **reciprocity** 相互扶助

NOTHING is certain but death and taxes.
死と税金以外、確実なものはない。

（訳注：but＝「…を除いて」。次のことわざにおける but も同様。She could do nothing *but* weep.〈彼女は泣く以外になすすべがなかった〉）

死と税金の追っ手から逃れることができる人はいない。

□ **1726** DEFOE *Hist. Devil* II. vi. Not the Man in the Moon, ... not the Inspiration of Mother Shipton, or the Miracles of Dr. Faustus, Things as certain as Death and Truces, can be more firmly believ'd. **1789** B. FRANKLIN *Letter* 13 Nov. in *Writings* (1907) X. 69 In this world nothing can be said to be certain, except death and taxes. **1939** L. I. WILDER *By Shores of Silver Lake* xxv. Everything's more or less a gamble.... Nothing is certain but death and taxes. **2001** *Washington Times* 20 Dec. C10 In **1789**, Benjamin Franklin said, 'In this world, nothing is certain but death and taxes.' Well, there is one way to avoid capital-gains truces on investments—hold them until you die. ■ **certainty and uncertainty** 確かさと不確かさ

NOTHING is certain but the unforeseen.
予想外の事を除いて、（人生において）確実なものは何もない。

（訳注：the unforeseen の the は「〈形容詞・過去分詞につけて〉…な物・事柄」の意。抽象的概念を表わし、単数扱いとなる。Have an eye for *the* beautiful〈審美眼がある〉、With him, you should always expect *the* unexpected.〈彼の場合には何が起こるかわからないことを知っておいたほうがいい〉）

類似のものに The UNEXPECTED always happens.「予想外の事はつねに起こるものだ」がある。

□ **1886** J. A. FROUDE *Oceana* vii. There is a proverb that 'nothing is certain but the unforeseen,' and in fact few things turn out as we expect them. **1905** A. MACLAREN *Gospel according to St. Matthew* I. 322 There is nothing certain to happen, says the proverb, but the unforeseen. Tomorrow will have its cares. ■ **certainty and uncertainty** 確かさと不確かさ；**foresight and hindsight** 先見の明と後知恵

NOTHING is for ever.
永遠に続くものはない。

Nothing lasts forever. という形式でも使われる。† NEVER is a long time.「『決して』長い時間にわたる言葉である」

□ **1984** *Defense Electronics* 144/2 Nothing is forever, and political-military alliances are less forever than most. **1992** MIEDER *Dict. American Proverbs* 433 Nothing can last for ever. **2001** *Times* 7 Nov. 16 Mr Blair may treat Parliament's support as unconditional, but nothing is for ever. **2005** D. S. MARTIN 'Nothing Lasts Forever' in *Poetry for Rest of Us* 3 Nothing is forever except the earth and sky. ■ **change** 変化

There is NOTHING lost by civility.
礼節によって失われるものは何もない。

† よく似たものとして CIVILITY costs nothing.「礼節には費用はかからない」がある。

□ **1892** G. & W. GROSSMITII *Diary of Nobody* xviii. 225 I made myself useful, and assisted several ladies to ices, remembering an old saying that 'There is nothing lost by civility.' **1903** *Association Boys* ii. 162 There is nothing lost by civility, and we should accord to the boy the same courtesy which we demand from him. **2009** D. JEFFERSON *Phantom of Fonthill Abbey* (2010) 273 'As they say, there is nothing lost by civility. I should be thanking you for opening my eyes to what is really happening in my life all around me.' ■ **politeness 礼儀正しさ**

There is NOTHING new under the sun.
太陽の下に新しき物なし。

『コヘレトの言葉』1 章 9 節（欽定訳聖書）There is no new thing under the sun. 「太陽の下に新しいものはない」を想起させる。

□**1592** G. DELAMOTHE *French Alphabet* II. 7 Under the large Cope of heauen, we see not a new thing. **1664** A. BRADSTREET *Works* (1867) 53 There is no new thing under the sun. **1801** T. JEFFERSON *Writings* (1904) X. 229 We can no longer say there is nothing new under the sun. **1850** C. KINGSLEY *Alton Locke* I. xviii. There is nothing new under the sun; all that, is stale and trite to a septuagenarian, who has seen where it all ends. **2014** *New Scientist* 25 Oct. 30 Apparently the Incas also encountered some of the problems ... such as multiple interpretations of one knot. As they say, there's nothing new under the sun. ■ **familiarity 慣れ親しみ；novelty 目新しさ**

NOTHING should be done in haste but gripping a flea.
ノミを捕まえること以外に，急いですべきことは何もない。

（訳注：but＝「…を除いて」。Everyone was there *but* him. 〈彼以外は皆出席していた〉）

焦って何かをしようとすることに対する警告。

□**a1655** N. L'ESTRANGE in *Anecdotes & Traditions* (1839) I. 55 A grave gentleman in this Kingdome us'd this phrase often: 'Do nothing rashly, but catching of fleas.' **1678** J. RAY *English Proverbs* (ed. 2) 151 Nothing most be done hastily but killing of fleas. **1721** J. KELLY *Scottish Proverbs* 261 *Nothing to be done in haste, but gripping of Fleas....* Spoken when we are unreasonably urged to make haste. **1927** J. BUCHAN *Witch Wood* xii. What's the need o' hurry when the body's leg is still to set. As my auld mither used to say, naething suld be done in haste but grippin' a flea. **1969** B. LEHANE *Compleat Flea* i. 'Do nothing hastily but catching of fleas,' warns a wary proverb.

NOTHING so bad but it might have been worse.
災難はすべて、それよりもっとひどかった可能性もある。

（訳注：文頭に There is を補うと、There is nothing so bad but it might have been worse. となる。文字通りには、「もっと悪かったかもしれないということがあり得ないような悪い事というのはない」の意。so は、否定を含意する but 節の内容を指している。but 節の内容である it might have been worse. 〈もっと悪かったかもしれない〉という文は仮定法過去完了構文の帰結節だけが表わされたものであり、「運が悪ければ」、「下手をすると」といった内容の条件節を補うことができる。どんな災難であれ、下手をするとこれよりもっとひどかった可能性もあるのである。このように考えると、これでよしとしなくてはならないという救われた気持ちになる）

これに対応する肯定的な言い方は **1817** スコット『ロブ・ロイ』II. xiii. There's naething sae gude on this side o' time but it might hae been better. 「今この時点で、どんなに良いことが起こったとしても、もしかしたらもっと良かった可能性だってある」

□**1876** I. BANKS *Manchester Man* III. xiii. However, there is nothing so bad but it might be worse. **1885** E. J. HARDY *How to be Happy though Married* xxi. Let us resolve to look at the bright side of things.... 'Nothing so bad but it might have been worse.' **1908** *Times* 5 Oct. 3 Farmers ... will regard the ... meteorological changes as illustrating the ancient axiom to the effect that circumstances are never so bad that they cannot be worse. ■ **good and evil 正邪；optimism 楽観主義**

NOTHING so bold as a blind mare.
目隠しをされた雌馬ほど、向こう見ずなものはいない。

何かについてすべての事実を知らない人は、目隠しをされた馬と同じ状況に置かれている。こうした人は、通常の状態なら恐れていたものが見えないのである。スコットランドのことわざ。

☐ *a*1628 J. CARMICHAELL *Proverbs in Scots* no. 1435 The blind horse is hardiest. **1721** J. KELLY *Scottish Proverbs* 266 Nothing so bold as a blind Mare. **1922** J. BUCHAN *Huntingtower* x. He spoke of the still unconquered enemy with ... disrespect, so that Mrs Morran was moved to observe that there was 'naething sae bauld as a blind mear'. ■ **boldness** 大胆さ；**ignorance** 無知・無学

There is NOTHING so good for the inside of a man as the outside of a horse.
馬の外側ほど人間の内側に効くものはない。

乗馬ほど健康にいいものはない。パーマストン子爵（1906年の用例）が使った聖書外典に由来する説に加えて、W. チャーチルと D. レーガンの言葉とされることもある。

☐ **1906** G. W. E. RUSSELL *Social Silhouettes* xxxii. The Squire will wind up ... with an apocryphal saying which he attributes to Lord Palmerston —'There's nothing so good for the inside of a man as the outside of a horse.' **1946** M. C. SELF *Horseman's Encyclopredia* 338 'There is something about the outside of a horse which is good for the inside of a man.' This adage is wiser than might first appear. But one should not consider just the hours spent in the saddle as beneficial. **1987** *Time* 28 Dec. 52 There is nothing better for the inside of a man than the outside of a horse. Ronald Reagan President. ■ **health** 健康

NOTHING succeeds like success.
成功ほど成功を呼ぶものはない。

（訳注：「一事なれば万事なる」）

いったん成功すると、それがきっかけになってさらに成功を呼ぶ。†フランス語*Rien ne reussit comme le success*.「成功ほど成功を呼ぶものはない」

☐ **1867** A. D. RICHARDSON *Beyond Mississippi* xxxiv. 'Nothing succeeds like success.' There was much Southern sympathy on the island; now all are our dear friends. **1872** W. BESANT *Ready-Money Mortiboy* I. ix. In Mr. Mortiboy's judgment no proverb could be better than ... 'Nothing succeeds like success.' Success dazzled him. **1980** H. TREVOR-ROPER *History & Imagination* 9 Nothing succeeds like success, and if Hitler had founded his empire ... we can well imagine how later historians would have treated him. ■ **success** 成功

NOTHING venture, nothing gain
何の危険も冒さなければ何も得ることはできない。

（訳注：解説に用例が挙がっている著者 W. キャクストンは英国の印刷業者・翻訳家。1476年ウェストミンスターに英国最初の印刷機を据えた。また、最初に印刷した本はチョーサーの『カンタベリー物語』であるとされている。キャクストンは出版を通して英語の標準化〈方言の均質化〉に大きく貢献した。「虎穴に入らずんば虎児を得ず」）

次項のことわざ NOTHING venture, nothing have.「何の危険も冒さなければ何も得ることはできない」の別の言い方である。†14世紀後半のフランス語 *Qui onques rien n'enprist riens n'achieva*.「何も実行しない者は何も達成しなかった」。**1481**W. キャクストン『キツネのレイナルド』(1880) xii. He that will wynne he muste Iaboure and auenture. 「勝利する者は努力と命を賭けなければならない」

□ **1624** T. HEYWOOD *Captives* IV. i. I see hee that nought venters, nothinge gaynes. **1668** C. SEDLEY *Mulberry Garden* III. ii. Who ever caught any thing With a naked hook? nothing venture, nothing Win. **1876** BLACKMORE *Cripps* III. iv. We must all have been in France ... if—well, never mind. Nothing venture, nothing win. **1967** N. MORRIS *Naked Ape* iv. For him [the withdrawn individual] the old saying: 'Nothing ventured, nothing gained' has been rewritten: 'Nothing ventured, nothing lost'. **1979** A. PRICE *Tomorrow's Ghost* vii. That was decidedly interesting-'And Pearson Cole?' Nothing venture, nothing gain. **2001** *Washington Times* 15 Dec. B2 Though there are no guarantees, it does seem sad that a chance at true love was stillborn because one of the parties had low self-esteem. Nothing ventured, nothing gained. ■ **boldness** 大胆さ; **wanting and having** 不足と所持; **risk** 危険

NOTHING venture, nothing have.
何の危険も冒さなければ何も得ることはできない。

上のことわざ NOTHING venture, nothing gain. と類似しており、今ではこれに取って代わられたようである。

□ *c***1385** CHAUCER *Troilus & Criseyde* II. 807 He which that nothing undertaketh, Nothing n'acheveth, be hym looth or deere [be it hateful or pleasing to him]. **1546** J. HEYWOOD *Dialogue of Proverbs* I. xi. El Noght venter noght haue. **1559** T. COOPER *Bibliotheca* (ed. 3) s. v. Fortis, Fortune foretherethe [furthers] bolde aduenturers, nothyng venture, nothyng haue. **1791** J. BOSWELL *Life of Johnson* II. 166 I am, however, generally for trying 'Nothing venture, nothing have'. **1841** DICKENS *Old Curiosity Shop* I. xxix. I'm sorry the gentleman's daunted—nothing venture, nothing have—but the gentleman knows best. **1957** R. DOWNING *All Change Here* v. 36 'Jonah, aren't you taking a hell of a risk?' 'Of course. We all are. But then "nothing venture nothing have."' ■ **boldness** 大胆さ; **wanting and having** 不足と所持; **risk** 危険

nothing ⇒ BELIEVE nothing of what you hear, and only half of what you see; BLESSED is he who expects nothing, for he shall never be disappointed; CIVILITY costs nothing; The FROG in the well knows nothing of the sea; There is nothing like LEATHER; You don't get SOMETHING for nothing; SOMETHING is better than nothing; The SUN loses nothing by shining into a puddle.

notice ⇒ LONG foretold, long last.

There's NOWT so queer as folk.
人ほど奇妙なものはない。

人間の奇行を観察したもので、特にイングランド北部の人々について用いられている。nowt は nought で、nothing の方言形である。

□ **1905** *English Dialect Dict.* IV. 304 There's nowt sae queer as folk, *Old saying.* **1939** J. WOOD *Letter* 30 May in J. Chambers *Letters* (1979) 186 I trust you ... find plenty of interest in people & their doings. Really 'there is nowt so funny as folk'. **1955** R. E. MEGARRY *Miscellany-at-Law* I. 72 There is the infinite charm and variety of human nature itself: 'there's nowt so queer as folk.' **1993** B. D'AMATO *Hard Women* xxi. 243 'You never really know anything about people. As LJ sometimes says, "There's nowt so strange as folk." It's not like you can work people out on a chessboard.' **2002** *Oldie* Apr. 57 ... and his creed that everyone is good copy. Or, as they would put it up North, that there's nowt so queer as folk. ■ **idiosyncrasy** 特異性・性癖

332   nowt

nowt ⇒ When in DOUBT, do nowt; HEAR all, ⇒ All, say nowt.

number ⇒ There is LUCK in odd numbers; There is SAFETY in numbers.

nut ⇒ The GODS send nuts to those who have no teeth.

O

When the OAK is before the ash, then you will only get a splash; when the ash is before the oak, then you may expect a soak.
樫の木がトネリコより先に芽吹くと小雨ですむが、トネリコが樫より先に芽吹くと大雨になるかもしれない。

> 昔からの言い伝えによるとイングランドの夏が雨になるか晴れになるかは、春に樫とトネリコのどちらが先に芽吹くかによってわかる。

☐**1852** *Notes & Queries* 1st Ser. V. 581 When the oak comes out before the ash, there will be fine weather in harvest. I ... find it generally correct. **1911** *Times Literary Supplement* 4 Aug. 285 One of the commonest weather rhymes in most parts of England deals with the budding of the oak and the ash: —When the oak's before the ash Then you'll only get a splash, When the ash is before the oak Then you may expect a soak. But in North Germany the signs are exactly inverted, and also in Cornwall. **2014** *Times* 5 May 27 [A]nother el Niño is expected, and ... this might imply a wet summer. Here in Somerset the oak is almost in full leaf, and the ash lies dormant. This is unusual, and the saying goes 'if the oak before the ash then there will only be a splash'. I wonder if country Jore will beat scientific meteorology. ■ **weather lore** 天気にまつわる伝承

Beware of an OAK, it draws the stroke; avoid an ash, it counts the flash; creep under the thorn, it can save you from harm.
樫に用心せよ。雷をおびき寄せるぞ。トネリコを避けよ。稲妻がよく落ちるぞ。トゲの下に潜れ。難から逃れられるぞ。

> 嵐の間、稲光を避けるにはどこが安全かを教えている。

☐**1878** *Folk-Lore Record* i. 43 Mothers teach their children to say—Beware of an oak, It draws the stroke; Avoid an ash; It counts the flash; Creep under the thorn, It can save you from harm. **1945** F. THOMPSON *Lark Rise* xvii. Some one would ... warn him to keep away from trees during a thunderstorm.... Others would quote: Under oak there comes a stroke, Under elm there comes a calm, And under ash there comes a crash. ■ **necessity** 必要性・必然性 ; **security** 安全

oak ⇒ GREAT oaks from little acorns grow; LITTLE strokes fell great oaks; A REED before the wind lives on, while mighty oaks do fall.

obedience ⇒ The FIRST duty of a soldier is obedience.

334 OBEY

He that cannot OBEY cannot command.

服従できない者は命令することもできない。

〈訳注：he＝「〈関係節を伴って〉…する者は誰でも〈性別は問わない〉」。*He that* is not with me is against me.〈私に味方しない者は私に敵対する〉『『マタイによる福音書』12章30節〉〉

統制は命令に従う側と命令を出す側の両方にとって重要である。†セネカ『怒りについて』II. xiv. *Nemo regere potest nisi qui et regi.*「自分が規則に従えない者は他人を規則に従わせることもできない」

□*a*1500 tr. *T. à Kempis' De Imitatione Christi* (1893) xxiv. No man surely comaunclith but he that hath lerned to obeye. **1581** G. PETTIE tr. *S. Guazzo's Civil Conversation* III. 48ᵛ Those onely knowe well how to commaund, which know well howe to obaye. **1734** B. FRANKLIN *Poor Richard's Almanack* (Aug.) He that cannot obey, cannot command. **1850** H. MELVILLE *White Jacket* vi. As the only way to learn to command, is to learn to obey, the usage of a ship of war is such that midshipmen are constantly being ordered about by the Lieutenants. **1972** S. CLOETE *Victorian Son* ix. I did not mind the army because I knew I must learn to obey before I could command. ■ **obedience** 従順・服従；**rulers and ruled** 支配者と被支配者

OBEY orders, if you break owners.

たとえ船主の言うことが間違っていてもその命令には従え。

船舶関係のことわざで、たとえ間違っているとわかっていても言われた通りにせよと述べている（1924年の用例参照）。

□**1782** W. GORDON *Letter* 30 Nov. in *Proceedings of Massachusetts Hist. Society* (1930) LXIII. 476 You will be safe, though you break orders that would break your owners. **1823** J. F. COOPER *Pilot* vii. The old rule runs, 'Obey orders, if you break owners.' **1924** R. CLEMENTS *Gipsy of Horn* iii. What could be sounder than 'Obey orders, if you break owners' —meaning, do as you're told, even if you know it's wrong. **1976** J. R. L. ANDERSON *Death on North Sea* iv. I was brought up on the old sea maxim, 'Obey orders if you break owners.' ■ **obedience** 従順・服従

odd ⇒ There is LUCK in odd numbers.

odious ⇒ COMPARISONS are odious.

It is best to be OFF with the old love before you are on with the new.

新しい恋を始める前に古い恋に終止符を打っておくのが最上の策である。

このことわざを引用している歌が18世紀後半に流行し、1835年に出版された『イングランドとスコットランドの歌』(II. 73) に収められている。

□**1801** M. EDGEWORTH *Belinda* I. x. I can give you my advice gratis, in the formula of an old Scotch song.... ''Tis good to be off with the old love, Before you be on with the new.' **1819** SCOTT *Bride of Lammermoor* III. ii. It is best to be off wi' the old love Before you be on wi' the new. **1891** A. LANG *Essays in Little* 6 Dumas … met the great man at Marseilles, where … Alexandre chanced to be 'on with the new love' before being completely 'off with the old'. **1923** B. V. LUCAS *Advisory Ben* XXXIX. That proverb about being off with the old love is a very sound one. **1980** I. ST. JAMES *Money Stones* III. vi. Off with the old and on with the new. Why not just come out with it? Tell her it's all finished. ■ **constancy and inconstancy** 安定と不安定；**love** 愛・恋愛

OLD 335

OFFENDERS never pardon.
相手を害する者は決してその相手を許すようなことはない。

他人を傷つけたことのある人は、罪の意識を持たず、相手をとことんまで恨みつづける。

□**1640** G. HERBERT *Outlandish Proverbs* no. 561 The offender never pardons. **1672** DRYDEN *Conquest of Granada* II. I. ii. Forgiveness to the Injur'd does belong; But they ne'r pardon who have done the wrong. **1876** I. BANKS *Manchester Man* III. xiii. He was of Mrs. Ashton's mind, that, 'as offenders never pardon', Augusta needed a friend. **1984** B. H. HONG *Forgiveness* 95 There are some people from whom I cannot receive forgiveness. 'Offenders never pardon,' says an old proverb. ■ **forgiveness 許し・寛容 ; wrong-doers 悪事をなす者**

offense ⇒ ATTACK is the best form of defence; The best DEFENSE is a good offense.

OLD habits die hard.
長年の習慣は簡単には断てない。

長年の習慣を断つのはきわめて難しい。

□**1758** B. FRANKLIN in *London Chronicle* 26–28 Dec. 632 I hear the reader say, Habits are hard to break, and those ... accustomed to idleness or extravagance do not easily change their manners. **1792** J. BELKNAP *Foresters* ix. Old habits are not easily broken, and ... they endeavoured ... to transfer the blame from him to his wife. **1944** 'H. TALBOT' *Rim of Pit* xv. 'Miss Daventry ... started to run. Naturally I ran after her.' Rogan smiled. 'Old habits Die hard.' **2007** *Times* 13 Sept. 18 Things may have changed, but old habits die hard and Portugal's historic habits more than justify suspicions about its police force's methods, motives and obsessional secrecy. ■ **habit 習慣**

You cannot put an OLD head on young shoulders.
若者の肩に老練な頭脳を据えることはできない。

(訳注 : この場合の you は総称的な用法で、話し手や聞き手を含めた一般の人々を指している。one よりくだけた使い方。*You* can't be happy if you are negative.〈悲観的だと幸福にはなれない〉)

若者に年配者のような分別ある行動を期待するのは無理である。

□**1591** H. SMITH *Preparative to Marriage* 14 It is not good grafting of an olde head vppon young shoulders, for they will neuer beare it willingly but grudgingly. **1794** B. DRINKER *Journal* 31 Dec. (1889) 256 Tis not the way I could wish my children to conclude the year—in parties—but we can't put old heads on young shoulders. **1951** *Sport* 30 Mar.–5 Apr. 11 I no longer believe in the old proverb that you cannot put an old head on young shoulders. **1975** J. PORTER *Package included Murder* xvi. The Hon. Con generously forgave her. Well, you can't expect old heads on young shoulders, can you? ■ **wisdom 賢明・知恵 ; youth 若さ・若者**

An OLD man is twice a child.
老人は子供に帰る。

(訳注 : 人は、老いると童子、赤子に戻るという発想はギリシア時代からあるとされる。日本でも、東北地方には「二度童子 (にどわらし)」という言葉がある)

年を取ってくると人は幼児に帰る。そこで 'Once a man, twice a child'「年を取ると子供に帰る」は高齢者の認知症を指すようになった。

□**1601** SHAKESPEARE II. ii. 381 Happily he [Polonius] is a second time come to them [i.e. infant's swaddling clothes]; for they say an old man is twice a child. **1821** W. HAZLITT *Table Talk* 284 An old man is twice a child: the dying man becomes the property of his family. **1841** *Tract*

Mag. and Christian Miscellany viii. 62 The old word is, that an old man is twice a child; but I say, happy is he that is thus a child always. It is a great imperfection to want [i.e. lack] knowledge; but of the two, it is better to be a child in understanding than a man in maliciousness. **1980** B. MARLEY 'Real Situation' (*song*) Once a man and twice a child. ■ **old age 老年**

OLD sins cast long shadows.
過去の罪は長い影を落とす。

† **1638** サックリン『アグラウラ』v. in *Plays* (1971) 110 Our sins, like to our shadowes, When our day is in its glorie scarce appear: Towards our evening how great and monstrous they are!「我らの罪は、影のように我らが全盛期にあるうちはほとんど姿を現わさないが、夕べになるとなんと大きく恐ろしいものになることよ」

☐ **1924** D. VANE *Scar* xxiii. 'You don't look well.... No fresh worry, I hope.' 'No,' wearily. 'Only old sins have long shadows.' **1957** V. BRIITAIN *Testament of Experience* I. iii. If he hadn't been killed, they would probably never have become what they were.... Bygone battles, like old sins, cast long shadows. **1987** C. GRAHAM *Killings at Badger's Drift* viii. 'The father was no good. Drove his poor wife into her grave.' 'So I understood.' 'Old sins cast long shadows.' ■ **past 過去・過ぎ去った ; wrong-doers 悪事をなす者**

OLD soldiers never die.
老兵は死なず。

(訳注：D. マッカーサー元帥は、1951 年 4 月に、米上下両院の合同会議で52 年間の軍役の退任演説をした。軍歌の一節であるこの言葉は、この演説で引用されたことによって一躍有名になった。「老兵は死なず」という言葉は、「ただ消え去るのみ」(they just fade away) という言葉とセットで使われている。彼は、この言葉を用いて自らの去り際を誇り高く公言したのである)

広く愛唱され、パロディ化されることの多い英国の軍歌。マッカーサー陸軍元帥が引退演説 (1951) で引用したことで米国でも馴染みとなった。Old soldiers never die,—Young ones wish they would「老兵は死なず。だが若い兵士はそれを願っている」という一節を含む形式もある。

☐ *a***1920** J. FOLEY (*song-title*) *Old soldiers never die.* **1930** BROPHY & PARTRIDGE *Songs & Slang of British Soldier* 1914-1811. 67 Old soldiers never die —They simply fade away. **1933** F. RICHARDS. *Old Soldiers never Die* xxviii. We generally wound up our evenings with the old song, set to the tune of a well-known hymn, 'Old soldiers never die, they simply fade away'. **1940** *Times* 6 Apr. 4 There is an old saying that 'Old soldiers never die' —but they may starve ... when other State pensioners are receiving increased benefits. **2000** *Washington Times* 7 Apr. A18 Meanwhile, regardless of the case's outcome, Gen. Kennedy plans to retire this summer, proving, once again, that old soldiers never die. These days, they just file harassment charges. ■ **old age 老年 ; soldiers 兵士**

old ⇒ BETTER be an old man's darling, than a young man's slave; you cannot CATCH old birds with chaff; There's no FOOL like an old fool; There's many a GOOD tune played on an old fiddle; HANG a thief when he's young, and he'll no' steal when he's old; A MAN is as old as he feels, and a woman as old as she looks; NEVER too old to learn; You can't put NEW wine in old bottles; It is best to be OFF with the old love before you are on with the new; An old POACHER makes the best gamekeeper; You cannot SHIFT an old tree without it dying; You can't TEACH an old dog new tricks; YOUNG folks think old folks to be fools, but old folks know young folks to be fools; YOUNG men may die, but old men must die; YOUNG saint, old devil.

You cannot make an OMELETTE without breaking eggs.
卵を割らないでオムレツを作ることなどできはしない。

（訳注：この場合の you は総称的な用法で、話し手や聞き手を含めた一般の人々を指している。one よりくだけた使い方。*You* never can tell what's going to happen.〈何が起きるかは誰にもわからない〉）

価値のある事業にはそれなりの代償はつきものである。†フランス語 *On ne fait pas d'omelette sans casser des œufs.*「卵を割らずにオムレツは作れない」

□ **1859** T. P. THOMPSON *Audi Alteram Partem* II. xc. We are walking upon eggs and ... the omelet will not be made without the breaking of some. **1897** R. L. STEVENSON *St Ives* viii. You cannot make an omelette without breaking eggs, ... and it is no bagatelle to escape from Edinburgh Castle. One of us, I think, was even killed. **1974** J. MANN *Sticking Place* iv. 'In your philosophy, it seems that some men have no right to live at all.' ... 'You can't make an omelette without breaking eggs, Mother.' **2000** *National Review* 20 Mar. 22 Nor should anyone be satisfied with the argument that eggs must be broken to make an omelet—the idea, in other words, that effective law enforcement requires the occasional slaying of an innocent citizen. ■ **pragmatism** 実用主義；**ways and means** 手段と方法

ONCE a—, always a—.
いったん…になると、ずっと…のまま。

この定型句は多くのことわざを生み出している。その多くはなかなか悪習・悪癖から抜け出せないことを述べたものであるが（1622年の用例）、べつに悪いわけではないものもある（1655年の用例）。長期に渡る存続期間を述べたもの（例えば ONCE a priest, always a priest.「いったん牧師になると、ずっと牧師のまま」や ONCE a whore, always a whore.「いったん売春婦になると、ずっと売春婦のまま」）もあれば、1回ぽっきりのものもある。この型を持つことわざを以下に挙げる。

□ **1622** J. MABBE tr. *Aleman's Guzman* I. I. i. Once a knaue, and euer a knaue: ... For he that hath once beene naught, is presumed to bee so still ... not considering ... whether ... hee had reformed his manners or no. **1655** T. FULLER *Church Hist. Britain* VII. xxviii. Latimer by the courtesie of England (once a bishop, and ever a bishop) was in civility saluted Lord. **1706** J. STEVENS *Spanish & English Dict.* s. v. Hurtar, Once a Thief, always a Thief. **1820** M. EDGEWORTH *Letter* 15 Nov. in *Maria Edgeworth in France & Switzerland* (1979) 277 She loses her rank ... by marrying one of inferior rank.... French and Russians are with reason surprised with the superior gallantry of our customs which say once a Lady and always a lady. **1953** R. CHANDLER *Long Good-bye* xliv. I went out of the door and got out of the building fast. Once a patsy [dupe], always a patsy. **2002** *Times* 2 21 May 6 Yet although lapsed Catholics may rebel on the surface, they cannot escape the Once a Catholic, Always a Catholic dictum. **2010** *www.telegraph.co.uk* 15 Oct (*heading*) Once a pit bull, always a pit bull—Brian Moore keeps dishing out the pain. ■ **constancy and inconstancy** 安定と不安定；**human nature** 人間性

ONCE a priest, always a priest.
いったん牧師になると、ずっと牧師のまま。

1870年8月9日にイングランド国教会の聖職者が辞職することを可能にする法律（the Clerical Disabilities Act）が制定された。

338 ONCE

□*a*1859 G. A, SALA *Twice round Clock* 290 The great case of Home Tooke versus the House of Commons —'Once a priest forever a priest'. **1865** L. STEPHEN *Life & Letters* (1906) ix. As in this ... country we stick to the maxim, 'once a parson, always a parson,' I could not ... go in for law. **1916** JOYCE *Portrait of Artist* (1967) iv. You must be quite sure, Stephen, that you have a vocation because it would be terrible if you found afterwards that you had none. Once a priest always a priest, remember. **2002** *Washington Times* 14 June AI 'Once a priest, always a priest' is a fundamental belief among Catholics. But that tenet may be tested as bishops consider firing hundreds of priests. ■ constancy and inconstancy 安定と不安定

ONCE a whore, always a whore.
いったん売春婦になると、ずっと売春婦のまま。

□**1613** H. PARROT *Laquei Ridiculosi* II. cxxi. Well you may change your name, But once a Whore, you shall be still the same. **1659** N. R. *Proverbs* 82 Once a whore and alwaies a whore. **1754** *World* 31 Jan. 344 Supposing him to have acquired so much wealth, the proverb of 'Once a whore, and always a whore', is less significant. **1824** H. MARSHALL *Hist. Kentucky* II. v. 'Once a prostitute, and always a prostitute,' is a fair mode of argument—at least, among politicians. **1981** N. LOFTS *Old Priory* v. iii. There is a saying, 'Once a whore, always a whore.' ■ constancy and incontancy 安定と不安定；wrong-doers 悪事をなす者

ONCE bitten, twice shy.
一度嚙まれると二度目は臆病になる。
(訳注：「あつものに懲りてなますを吹く」)

異形の Once burned, twice shy.「一度やけどをすると二度目は臆病になる」は特に米国で一般的である。米国版はおそらく A BURNT child dreads the fire.「やけどをした子は火を怖がる」の影響を受けている。

□**1853** SURTEES *Sponge's Sporting Tour* xxxvii. Jawleyford had been bit once, and he was not going to give Mr. Sponge a second chance. **1894** G. F. NORTHALL *Folk-Phrases* 20 Once bitten, twice shy. **1920** CONRAD *Rescue* III. ix. Once bit twice shy. He had no mind to be kidnapped. **1949** 'S. STERLING' *Dead Sure* xv. She was especially on her guard ... because she'd been victimized in a stupid swindle herself, recently. Once burned, twice shy, you know. **1981** H. ENGEL *Ransom Game* xvi. I can't imagine why this man would be harassing my wife again, Mr. Cooperman. You'd think 'Once burned, twice shy' wouldn't you. **1998** *Times* 7 Jan. 27/6 Once bitten, twice shy when thinking of certain shops. ■ experience 経験

once ⇒ You can only DIE once; FOOL me once, shame on you ... ; MEASURE seven times, cut once; MEASURE twice, cut once; THINK twice, cut once.

When ONE door shuts, another opens.
1つのドアが閉まっても、もう1つのドアが開く。
(訳注：「捨てる神あれば拾う神あり」)

たとえある1つの好機が失われても、すぐに別の好機が訪れるものである。

□**1586** D. ROWLAND tr. *Lazarillo* D3ᵛ This proverbe was fulfild, when one doore is shut the other openeth. **1620** T. SHELTON tr. *Cervantes' Don Quixote* III. vii. Where one door is shut another is opened. **1710** S. PALMER *Proverbs* 49 When one Door Shuts another Opens.... How often does the Divine Bounty smprize us with unthought of Felicity! **1821** J. GALT *Annals of Parish* xxvi. Here was an example ... of the truth of the old proverb that as one door shuts another opens; ... A full equivalent for her [the light-headed Lady Macadam] was given in this hot and fiery Mr.

Cayenne. **1925** S. O'CASEY *Juno & Paycock* I. 16 'The job couldn't come at a betther time.' ... 'Ah, God never shut wan door but he opened another.' **1987** S. STEWART *Lifting the Latch* 105 They say one door in life doesn't close without another opening. **2002** *Washington Post* 30 Jan. C15 (*Rhymes with Orange comic strip*) 'I always say, "When one door closes, another will open." In this case, when my office door closes behind you, Security will escort you to the exit and open that door for you.' ■ opportunity 機会・好機

ONE for sorrow, two for mirth; three for a wedding, four for a birth.
1 羽なら悲しみ、2 羽なら喜び、3 羽なら結婚、4 羽なら出産。

ある場所でカササギを見た時、その数で将来がわかるという迷信である。イングランドの田舎に残る昔からの言い伝えで、様々な言い方がある。

□*a***1846** B. HAYDON *Autobiography* (1853) I. v. During the journey four magpies rose ... and flew away.... I repeated ... the old saw, 'one for sorrow, two for mirth, three for a wedding, and four for death.' **1846** M. A. DENHAM *Proverbs relating to Seasons*, &c. 35 One for sorrow: two for mirth: three for a wedding: four for a birth: five for silver: six for gold: seven for a secret, not to be told: eight for heaven: nine for hell: and ten for the devil's own sel [self]. **1913** A. C. BENSON *Along Road* 162 I never see magpies myself without relating the old rhyme: 'One for sorrow, Two for mirth, Three for a death, Four for a birth; Five, you will shortly be In a great company.' **1999** A. I. BARKER *Haunt* (2000) 53 A magpie flew up from the road, almost under his wheels. 'One for sorrow,' said the girl 'But there's another in the hedge—two for joy.' ■ bird lore 鳥にまつわる逸話 ; omens 前兆

ONE for the mouse, one for the crow, one to rot, one to grow.
1 つはネズミのもの、1 つはカラスのもの、1 つは腐るもので、後の 1 つが生えるもの。

4 粒の種のうち 1 つだけが育つもので、残り 3 つは害獣や湿気でやられてしまう。crow/grow の脚韻部分は共通するが、この昔からのことわざには以下のようないろいろな言い方がある。2002 年の用例はニューイングランドのもの。

□**1850** *Notes & Queries* 1st Ser. II. 515 How to sow Beans. 'One for the mouse, One for the crow, One to rot, One to grow.' **1941** L. I. WILDER *Little Town on Prairie* ii. 'Kernels,' said Pa. 'Four kernels.... One for the blackbird, One for the crow, And that will leave Just two to grow.' **1961** N. LOFTS *House at Old Vine* I. 34 Careful farmers ... sow their seed broadcast, saying: One for wind and one for crow One to die and one to grow. **2002** E. CUTTING in *Voices: Journal of New York Folklore* XXVIII (online) I was trying to remember the verse about planting corn. One for the cutworm, one for the crow ... **2013** www.saga.co.uk You will need to sow plenty of seeds. 'One for the mouse, one for the crow, one to rot and one to grow' as the saying goes. ■ garden lore 庭にまつわる伝承

ONE nail drives out another.
1 本の釘がもう 1 本の釘を追い出す。

古い恋、悲しみ、病気などが新しいものに取って代わられる状況を述べている。†アリストテレス『政治学』1314 a ἧλῳ γὰρ ὁ ἧλος, ὥσπερ ἡ παροιμία.「ことわざによれば、1 本の釘がもう 1 本を追い出す」。同じ表現がフランス語 *Un clou chasse l'autre.*「1 本の釘がもう 1 本の釘を追い出す」とスペイン語 *Un clavo saca otro clavo.*「1 本の釘がもう 1 本の釘を追い出す」にも見られる。

□*a***1250** *Ancrene Wisse* (1962) 206 An neil driueth ut then other. **1555** J. HEYWOOD *Two Hun-*

340　ONE

dred Epigrams no. 112 One nayle dryueth out an other. **1591** SHAKESPEARE *Two Gentlemen of Verona* II. iv. 189 As one nail by strength drives out another, So the remembrance of my former love Is by a newer object quite forgotten. *c***1645** J. HOWELL *Familiar Letters* 17 Sept (1903) III. 87 Languages and words … may be said to stick in the memory like nails or pegs in a wainscot door, which used to thrust out one another oftentimes. **1852** E. FITZGERALD *Polonius* cxvii. One nail drives out another. **1979** V. CANNING *Satan Sampler* ix. He needed a home with a woman in it. One nail drove out another. ■ **change** 変化

ONE size does not fit all.
１つのサイズですべてが間に合うわけではない。

当初の形式は、異なる足には異なる大きさの靴が必要であるという比喩に基づいていた。† **1587** J. ブリッジス『英国国教会の統治の擁護』86 Diverse feete have diverse last-es. The shooe that will serve one, may wring another.「それぞれの足には大きさに合った靴型がある。１人の人に合う靴でも別の人には窮屈かもしれない」

□**1616** B. RICH *My Ladle's Looking Glasse* 21 As every shooe Is not flt for everyfoote, nor every medicine to be applyed to every maladie, so every fashion, doth not befit every person, not every colour agree with every complexion. **1712** J. KELLY *Scottish Proverbs* 96 Every shoe fits not every foot. Every condition of life, every behaviour, every speech and gesture becomes not every body; that will be decent in one, which will be ridiculous in another. **1874** Ascott House, Buckinghamshire, UK (*painted on cornice*) Every shoe fits not every foot. **2002** *Times* 20 Mar. 26 Yesterday Sir Howard Davies … gave warning that there was a danger that Europe's approach to financial markets was in danger of trying to strap the different European markets into rigid rules that risked damaging their international competitiveness. One size does not fit all, he said. **2013** *Guardian* 28 Oct (online; *heading*) There is no 'one size fits all' solution to health and social care integration. ■ **ways and means** 方法と手段

ONE year's seeding makes seven years' weeding.
１年雑草の種が地に落ちるのを放っておくと、その後７年の草刈りが待ち受けている。

雑草を放置しておくと取り返しのつかないことになるという警告。比喩的にも使われる。

□**1866** *Rural American* 1 Dec. 354 It has been truly remarked that 'one year's seeding may cost ten years' weeding'. **1873** HARLAND & WILKINSON *Lancashire Legends* 190 One year's seeding makes seven years' weeding. **1889** T. F. THISTELTON-DYER *Folklore of Plants* xi. A weed that runs to seed Is a seven years' weed … implies that disagreeable actions … only too frequently cling to man in after years. **1980** *Daily Telegraph* 19 Jan. 20 My advice to weedpersons is: do not let your weeds grow to maturity and seed—'one year's seeding means seven years' weeding'. ■ **action and consequence** 行為と結果 ; **garden lore** 庭にまつわる伝承

one ⇒ BETTER one house spoiled than two; BETTER to live one day as a tiger … ; A BIRD never flew on one wing; Two BOYS are half a boy, and three boys are no boy at all; The BUYER has need of a hundred eyes, the seller of but one; Every DOG is allowed one bite; Don't put all your EGGS in one basket; One ENGUSHMAN can beat three Frenchmen; One FUNERAL makes many; One GOOD turn deserves another; One HALF of the world does not know how the other half lives; One HAND for yourself and one for the ship; One HAND washes the other; One HOUR's sleep before midnight is worth two after; One man's LOSS is another man's gain; One man's MEAT is another man's poison; One PICTURE is worth ten

OPPORTUNITY 341

thousand words; One man may STEAL a horse, while another may not look over a hedge; One STEP at a time; From the SUBLIME to the ridiculous is only a step; One SWALLOW does not make a summer; It TAKES one to know one; TWO heads are better than one; If TWO ride on a horse, one must ride behind; One VOLUNTEER is worth two pressed men; One WEDDING brings another.

one-eyed ⇒ In the COUNTRY of the blind, the one-eyed man is king.

onion ⇒ One DAY honey, one day onion.

open ⇒（形容詞）A DOOR must either be shut or open;（動詞）A GOLDEN key can open any door; When ONE door shuts, another opens.

The OPERA isn't over till the fat lady sings.
そのオペラは例の太った女性が歌うまで終わらない。

該当する歌姫は誰なのかを明らかにしようとする試みが今に至るまでずっと続いている。しかし、1978年の用例はこのことわざがスポーツ（ロデオ）の世界に起源があり、女性はおそらく想像上の人物に過ぎなかったことを示している。2002年の用例では sings「歌う」と singes「焦げる」の駄洒落が用いられている。

□1978 *Washington Post* 13 June Bl The opera isn't over till the fat lady sings.... One day three years ago, Ralph Carpenter, who was then Texas Tech's sports information director, declared to the press box contingent in Austin, 'The rodeo ain't over till the bull riders ride.' Stirred to top that deep insight, San Antonio sports editor Dan Cook countered with, 'The opera ain't over till the fat lady sings.' 1988 D. L. GILBERT *Black Star Murders* viii. As soon as the big blond Brünnhilde finished, it was over. All I could think about was the classic line about the opera never being over until the fat lady sings. 1992 *Independent* 11 Aug. 7 'You know, they say that the show's never over until the fat lady sings,' Mr Bolger said. 'Well, I think it was her we heard warming up in the wings this week.' 2002 *Times* 2 July 19 [T]he Royal Opera House's leading lady whose dress was set on fire by an on-stage candle is a classic case of it ain't over till the fat lady singes. ■ finality 結末・終局

opinion ⇒ He that COMPLIES against his will is of his own opinion still; so many MEN, So many opinions.

OPPORTUNITY makes a thief.
盗人は機会があるからこそ生まれる。

盗む機会がすぐ目の前にあれば、誰でも盗みの誘惑に負けてしまう。

□*c*1220 *Hali Meidenhad* (EETS) 23 Man seith that eise maketh theof. 1387 J. TREVISA tr. *Higden's Polychronicon* (1879) VII. 379 At the laste the bischop seide to hym, 'Me thenke that opportunitie makethe a thefe'. 1623 W. CAMDEN *Remains concerning Britain* (ed. 3) 275 Opportunity makes the thief. 1670 J. RAY *English Proverbs* 129 Opportunity makes the thief.... Therefore, masters ... ought to secure their moneys and goods under lock and key, that they do not give ... a temptation to steal. 1835 SOUTHEY *Doctor* III. cv. Opportunity, which makes thieves, makes lovers also. 1979 *Daedalus* Summer 107 A child steals from the sleeping woman's pocket, acting out the proverb 'Opportunity makes a thief.' **2008** *Wall Street Journal* 15 Feb. (online; *heading*) Opportunity Makes a Thief. ■ **honesty and dishonesty** 正直と不正直；**opportunity, taken** 得られた機会

OPPORTUNITY never knocks twice at any man's door.
好機は 2 度は訪れない。

（訳注：「鉄は熱いうちに打て」）

当初は opportunity の代わりに fortune が使われていた。以下に挙げた用例のいくつか
は元のことわざに基づいてはいるものの、やや異なる考えを表わしている。1809 年の用
例では、機会は 1 度以上ノックすることになっているが、他の例では 1 度だけである。
† 15 世紀初頭のフランス語 *Il n'est chance qui ne retourne*.「2 度訪れる好機などな
い」

☐ *a*1567 G. FENTON *Bandello* 216 Fortune once in the course of our life, dothe put into our
handes the offer of a good tome. **1809** *Port Folio* (Philadelphia) Nov. 431 Fortune knocks once, at
least, at every man's door. **1889** W. F. BUTLER *C. G. Gordon* iii. Fate, it is said, knocks once at
every man's door.... Gordon had just passed his thirtieth year when Fortune ... knocked at ...
the door which was to lead him to fame. **1891** J. J. INGALLS *Opportunity in Truth* (NY) 19 Feb.
17 I [Opportunity] knock unbidden once at every gate! If sleeping, wake: if feasting rise before I
turn away ... [for] I return no more! **1941** 'P. WENTWORTH' *Unlawful Occasions* xxiv. It was an
opportunity with a capital O, and if she threw it away it would never come back again. Opportunity never knocks twice at any man's door. **2001** *Washington Post* 18 Nov. F2 Experts are unique-
ly vulnerable to one weakness: Opportunity may knock only once, but the temptation to try to
make a contract the hard way—and make the newspapers—is always pounding at the expert's
door. ■ **opportunity** 機会・好機

opportunity ⇒ ENGLAND'S difficulty is Ireland's opportunity; MAN'S extremity is God's opportunity.

opposite ⇒ DREAMS go by contraries.

orders ⇒ OBEY orders, if you break owners.

orphan ⇒ SUCCESS has many fathers, while failure is an orphan.

OTHER times, other manners.
時代が違えば風習も違う。

（訳注：times ＝「〈歴史上の〉時代、時期」〈複数形〉。Roman *times*〈ローマ時代〉、keep up with *times*
〈時流に遅れないようにする〉。「移れば変わる世の習い」）

様々な形式と言語において観察されることわざである。†ピンダロス『断章』ccxxv.
(Bowra), ἄλλοτ᾿ ἀλλοῖα φρόνει.「異なる時代には異なる考え方をせよ」。フランス語 *Autres temps, autres mreurs*.「時代が違えば、風習も違う」

☐ **1576** G. PETTIE *Petit Palace* 34 Other times, other wayes. **1902** A. DOBSON *Samuel Richardson* iv. Notwithstanding the favourite explanation of 'other times, other manners', contemporary
critics of Clarissa found very much the same fault with her history as people do to-day. **1945** F.
THOMPSON *Lark Rise* viii. Other days, other ways.... The old country midwives did at lea. st

succeed in bringing into the world many generations of our forefathers. **1978** G. GREENE *Human Factor* IV. ii. 'We used to have better funerals in Africa.' ... 'Oh well—other countries, other manners.' ■ change 変化; circumstances 状況; past 過去・過ぎ去った

other ⇒ DO unto others as you would they should do unto you; The GRASS is always greener on the other side of the fence; One HALF of the world does not know how the other half lives; One HAND washes the other.

An OUNCE of practice is worth a pound of precept.
１オンスの実行は１ポンドの訓戒に値する。
（訳注：１オンスは、重さの単位としては１/16ポンド、金属・薬量の単位としては１/12ポンド）

形式が類似していることわざを以下に挙げている。比喩的に「少量」の意味を表わす an ounce が、**1567** C. リード『秘書セシル』(1955) xxi. に収められている W. セシル『手紙』で使われている。Marry [to be sure], an ounce of advice is more worth to be executed aforehand than in the sight of perils.「結婚となると、（間違いなく）１オンスの助言でも、いざという時にあわてふためく前に、事前に従っておくにこしたことはありません」。また 2002 年の用例は、このことわざと PREVENTION is better than cure.「予防は治療に勝る」とが互いによく似ていることを示している。

☐*c*1576 T. WHYTHORNE *Autobiography* (1961) 142 I ment not to be on of thoz who waith [esteems] A chip of chauns [luck] mor then A pownds wurth of witt. **1592** G. DELAMOTHE *French Alphabet* II. 55 An ounce of discretion, is better worth, then a pound of hardinesse [audacity]. **1616** T. ADAMS *Sacrifice of Thankfulness* 19 The prouerbe is true; an Ounce of Discretion, is worth a pound of Learning. **1748** J. ELIOT *Essays upon Field Husbandry* 12 It used to be the Saying of an old Man, That an Ounce of Experience is better than a Pound of Science. **1866** BLACKMORE *Cradock Nowell* II. ix. Remember that rigid probity, and the strictest punctuality ... are the very soul of business, and that an ounce of practice is worth a pound of precept. **1925** J. GALSWORTHY *Caravan* 667 'Define it [Beauty], Mr. Vaness.' 'An ounce of fact is worth a ton of theory. —It stands before me.' **1981** P. O'DONNELL *Xanadu Talisman* ix. She said rather primly, 'An ounce of wisdom is worth a pound of wit.' **2002** *Washington Times* 5 Apr. A20 Yet, if the IRS is attempting to reduce the incidence of obesity, ... shouldn't it permit deduction for activities and products that prevent one from becoming obese in the first place? After all, an ounce of prevention could be worth a literal pound of cure. ■ example, good and bad 好例と悪例; words and deeds 言動

OUT of debt, out of danger.
借金なければ危険もなし。

借金から解放されると、借金の取り立ての圧力からも解放される。

☐*a*1639 J. CLARKE *Paræmiologia Anglo-Latina* 82 Out of debt and deadly danger. **1667** H. PEACHAM *Worth of Penny* (ed. 2) 8 How bold, confident, merry, lively, and ever in humour are moneyed men (for being out of debt, they are out of danger). **1710** S. PALMER *Proverbs* 132 Out of Debt out of Danger.... A Man in Debt is a Slave, and can't act with Liberty. **1908** E. M. SNEYD-KYNNERSLEY *H.M.I.* xxi. Call it 'distributing capital expenditure over a term of years', and even a rural dean succumbs. 'Out of debt, out of danger,' but 'out of debt, out of progress.' **1977** 'C. AIRD' *Parting Breath* vii. 'Well, they're important, aren't they?' said Leeyes largely. 'Out of debt, out of danger.' ■ security 安全; thrift 質素倹約

344 OUT

OUT of sight, out of mind.
目に見えない所にあるものは忘れ去られる。
（訳注：「去る者日々に疎し」）

目の前に存在しない人や物は忘れ去られてしまう。†ラテン語*Absens haeres non erit.*
「近くにいない者は相続人にはなれぬ」

□*c*1250 *Proverbs of Alfred* (1907) 46 He that is ute bi-loken [shut out] He is inne sone foryeten [forgotten]. *c*1450 tr. *T. à Kempis' De Imitatione Christi* (EETS) r. xxxiii. Whan Man is oute of sight, son be he passith oute ofmynde. 1545 R. TAVERNER tr. *Erasmus' Adages* (ed. 2) D6ᵛ Whereunto also agreethe oure Englyshe proverbe which sayethe: Oute of syght, oute of mynde. 1797 A. RADCUFFE *Italian* III. ix. Old women now-a-days are not much thought of; out of sight out of mind with them. 1863 C. KINGSLEY *Water Babies* i. Sir John and the rest saw no more of her; and out of sight was out of mind. 1979 'S. WOODS' *This Fatal Writ* 45 The brief ... was promptly concealed.... He was working on the principle 'out of sight, out of mind'. 2002 *Spectator* 13 Apr. 38 'Once word gets out, people will come,' they say. 'Out of sight, out of mind.' ■
absence 不在 ; **forgetfulness** 物忘れ

out ⇒ BETTER out than in; BETTER be out of the world than out of the fashion; There are as good FISH in the sea as ever came out of it; When the GORSE is out of bloom, kissing' s out of fashion; Don't HALLOO till you are out of the wood; LAST in, first out; Out of the MOUTHS of babes―; MURDER will out; never tell TALES out of school; TRUTH will out.

outside ⇒ There is NOTHING so good for the inside of a man as the outside of a horse.

over ⇒ The OPERA isn't over till the fat lady sings; The SHARPER the storm, the sooner it's over.

own ⇒ The DEVIL looks after his own; When THIEVES fall out, honest men come by their own.

owner ⇒ OBEY orders, if you break owners.

owt ⇒ HEAR all, see all, say nowt; You don't get SOMETHING for nothing.

ox ⇒ BETTER a dinner of herbs than a stalled ox where hate is.

P

It is the PACE that kills.
速度が命取りになる。

乗馬による狩猟から生まれたことわざ。全速力で駆けている馬が転倒すると、馬も騎手
も大怪我をする。

□**1855** S. A. HAMMETT *Wonderful Adventures of Captain Priest* xv. The well-known sporting
maxim, that 'It is the pace that kills'. **1901** S. LANE-POOLE *Sir H. Parkes in China* xx. There is an
old proverb about the pace that kills, and ... Sir Harry was killing himself by work at high pressure. **1936** N. MARSH *Death in Ecstasy* II. xvii. Don't overdo it.... This is the pace that kills.
■ haste 性急 ; stress ストレス

package ⇒ The BEST things come in small packages.

pack-drill ⇒ NO names, no pack-drill.

padlock ⇒ WEDLOCK is a padlock.

pain ⇒ GENIUS is an infinite capacity for taking pains; NO pain, no gain; PRIDE feels no
pain.

paint ⇒ A BIIND man's wife needs no paint

painted ⇒ The DEVIL is not so black as he is painted.

pan ⇒ If IFS and ands were pots and pans, there'd be no work for tinkers' hands.

paradise ⇒ ENGLAND is the paradise of women.

parcel ⇒ The BEST things come in small packages.

pardon ⇒ OFFENDERS never pardon.

Paris ⇒ Good AMERICANS when they die go to Paris.

346 PARSLEY

PARSLEY seed goes nine times to the Devil.
パセリの種は 9 回悪魔に食べられる。

(訳注：パセリの種は 9 回悪魔に食べられるので、10回も蒔かねばならない。)

1908年の用例から、他の野菜の種に比べてパセリは発芽までの期間が長いため、このことわざが生まれたことがわかる。

☐ **1658** in Mennis & Smith *Wit Restored* 35 There is a saying in the North Riding of Yorkshire that The weed [parsley] before it's borne Nine times the devill sees. **1885** *Notes & Queries* 6th Ser. XI. 467 Parsley seed (when it has been sown) goes nine times to the devil. **1908** D. H. LAWRENCE *Letter* 4 May (1962) I. 7 People say parsley seed goes seven times (some are moderate, discarding the holy number as unfit, and say five) to the Old Lad, it is so long a-germinating. **1981** in A. Hewins *Dillen* xiv. It's a queer plant, parsley: 'sow on Good Friday, seven times down to Hell afore it chits [sprouts].' ■ **garden lore** 庭にまつわる伝承 ; **superstition** 迷信

parsnip ⇒ FINE words butter no parsnips.

part ⇒ （名詞）DISCRETION is the better part of valour; If you're not part of the SOLUTION, you're part of the problem; （動詞）The BEST of friends must part.

parted ⇒ A FOOL and his money are soon parted.

Things PAST cannot be recalled.
過ぎ去ったことは取り戻せない。

(訳注：past ＝「〈時が〉過ぎ去った」。pass の過去分詞 passed は形容詞として用いることはできない。よって past が用いられる。The incident is now three weeks *past*. 〈その出来事はもう 3 週間前のことになる〉。「後悔先に立たず」)

† 14世紀後半のフランス語 *Ce qui est passe ne poet on recouver.*「過ぎ去ったことは取り戻せない」。ここで recalled は recovered「取り戻す」という意味で使われている。

☐ *a*1500 H. MEDWALL *Nature* H3ᵛ A thyng don can not be called agayn. *a*1535 MORE *Edward V* in J. Hardyng *Chronicle* (1543) II. 36 Sith [since] thynges passed cannot be gaine called, muche more ought wee to bee ware. **1616** T DRAXE *Adages* 151 That that is past, cannot be recalled or helped. **1804** M. EDGEWORTH *Popular Tales* II. 130 Since a thing past can't be recalled … we may be content. **1979** *Country Life* 24 May 1683 Visually, another period's realities are palpably inaccessible. Things past cannot be—perfectly—recalled. ■ **past** 過去・過ぎ去った ; **regrets** 後悔

pastime ⇒ He that would go to SEA for pleasure, would go to hell for a pastime.

paternoster ⇒ NO penny, no paternoster.

PATIENCE is a virtue.
忍耐は美徳である。

† 『カトの二行格言集』I. xxxviii. *Maxima enim … patientia virtus.*「忍耐は最大の美徳である」。14世紀中頃のフランス語 *Patience est une grant vertu.*「忍耐は偉大なる美徳である」。18世紀の童謡、Patience is a virtue,/Virtue is a grace/Both put together/Make a very pretty face.「忍耐は美徳、美徳は優雅、2 つが 1 つになると、とても美し

PAY 347

い顔になる」は現在、Patience is a virtue/Virtue is a grace,/Grace is a little girl/
Who wouldn't wash her face.「忍耐は美徳、美徳は優雅である。美徳（グレース、ここ
では女性の名前）は女の子、その子が顔を洗おうとしないなんて」とパロディ化され、広
く使われている。

□**1377** LANGLAND *Piers Plowman* B. XJ. 370 Suffrance [forbearance] is a souereygne vertue.
*c***1386** CHAUCER *Tale of Melibee* I. 1517 Pacience is a greet vertu of perfeccioun. **1594** LYLY
Mother Bombie v. iii. Patience is a vertue, but pinching is worse than any vice! **1754** RICHARD-
SON *Grandison* II. xvii. Aunt Prue in Yorkshire ... will be able to instruct you, that patience is a
virtue; and that you ought not to be in haste to take a first offer, for fear you should not have a
second. **1858** TROLLOPE *Dr. Thorne* I. xiv. That was only three days ago. Why don't you ... fer-
ret her out? ... Patience is and always was a virtue. **1979** A. FOX *Threat Warning Red* iv. 'I ...
can't wait for you.' ... 'Patience is said to be a virtue?' **2014** *Wall Street Journal* 4 Aug. (online;
heading) Patience Is a Virtue on Vulcan's Rocky Road. ■ **patience and impatience** 忍耐と性急

Paul ⇒ If SAINT Paul's day be fair and clear, it will betide a happy year.

paved ⇒ The ROAD to hell is paved with good intentions.

PAY beforehand was never well served.
（職人に）前払いをすると満足のいく仕事をしてもらえない。

仕事が仕上がる前に職人に賃金を支払ってしまうと、職人が働く動機づけがなくなるた
め、依頼した仕事が満足に仕上がっていないことに気づくことになる。

□**1591** J. FLORIO *Second Fruits* 39 He that paieth afore hand, hath neuer his worke well done.
1721 J. KELLY *Scottish Proverbs* 278 Pay beforehand was never well serv'd. It is common to see
... Labourers, to go about a piece of Work with great Uneasiness, which is to pay a just Debt.
1786 G. WASHINGTON *Letter* 7 Jan. in *Writings* (1938) XXVIII. 370 I have had some reason to
remember an old adage, that one of the bad paymasters is him that pays before hand. **1819**
SCOTT *Bride of Lammermoor* iii. 'Your honour is the bad pay-master,' he said, 'who pays before
it is done.' **1928** A. C. BROWN *Dr. Glazebrook's Revenge* xi. The old Scots adage that 'fore-hand
payments mak' hint-hand wark'. ■ **employers and employees** 雇用者と被雇用者 ; **work** 仕事

He that cannot PAY, let him pray.
支払えない者は祈るがよい。

（訳注：he ＝「〈関係節を伴って〉…する者は誰でも〈性別は問わない〉」。*He that* is not with me is against
me.〈私に味方しない者は私に敵対する〉《『マタイによる福音書』12章30節》）

貧乏な人はお祈りに頼らなければならない。

□*a***1611** R. COTGRAVE *Dict. French & English* s. v. Argent, He that cannot pay let him pray.
1732 T. FULLER *Gnomologia* no. 6362 He that cannot pay, Let him pray. **1954** R. STOUT *Three
Men Out* v. They're quotations from things. One of them says, 'He that cannot pay, let him pray.'
■ **money** 金・金銭 ; **poverty** 貧困

If you PAY peanuts, you get monkeys.
ピーナッツを賃金にすれば、猿しか手に入らない。

（訳注：この場合の you は総称的な用法。*You* never can tell what's going to happen.〈何が起きるかは
誰にもわからない〉）

ここで peanuts は少額のお金（特に不十分な支払い、賃金）を意味する。この比喩は米国

348 PAYING

で20世紀中頃に生まれた俗語である。

□**1966** L. COULTHARD in *Director* Aug. 228 Shareholders want the best available businessmen to lead the companies and recognise that you get what you pay for. If you pay in peanuts, you must expect to get monkeys. **1979** P. ALEXANDER *Show me Hero* iii. 'That's forty thousand we're giving away. Seems an awful lot' 'If you pay peanuts,' said Ashman, 'you get monkeys.' **1979** *Guardian* 11 Sept. 30 The companies' chief negotiator … was greeted with shouts of 'if you pay peanuts, you get monkeys'. **1994** S. REUBEN *Origin and Cause* xvii. 107 'How much is … this photo-enhancement going to cost my client?' 'A bundle.… But in my experience, if you pay peanuts, you get monkeys.' ■ **employers and employees** 雇用者と被雇用者；**money** 金・金銭

If you're not PAYING, you're the product.
金を払っていないといっても、あなた自身が商品となっている。

インターネットユーザーとして無料サービスを受けていると思っているかもしれないが、あなたの個人情報は市場調査などを行なう会社に売られている。この発想は2010年の用例において説明されている。

□**2010** A. LEWIS [aka MetaFilter user blue_beetle] 'if you're not paying for something, you're not the customer; you're the product being sold' … as you scour the internet and stores for holiday deals, keep in mind that when you're not paying with cash you're paying with your personal information. **2013** *Spectator* 7 Dec 13 The majority of Brits now use Facebook, Twitter, Instagram or another social media account—none of which charge [sic] us a penny. As the saying goes: if you're not paying, you're the product ■ **business** ビジネス・商売

pay ⇒（名詞）NO cure, no pay；（動詞）CRIME doesn't pay; They that DANCE must pay the fiddler; DEATH pays all debts; SPEAK not of my debts unless you mean to pay them; The THIRD time pays for all.

He who PAYS the piper calls the tune.
笛吹きにお金を払う者こそが曲を名指す権利がある。

（訳注：he＝「〈関係節を伴って〉…する者は誰でも〈性別は問わない〉」。*He who* hesitates is lost.〈しり込みする者は負けだ〉）

催し物の費用を支払う者こそがその内容・手順について指図する権利を持つ。このことわざは They that DANCE must pay the fiddler.「踊る者こそがバイオリン弾きの報酬を払わなければならない」の意味を逆にしたもの。

□**1895** *Daily News* 18 Dec. 9 Londoners had paid the piper, and should choose the tune. **1910** *Spectator* 22 Oct. 643 Until British electors know that the dollars have been returned they will be wise in placing little trust in Nationalist 'loyalty'. He who pays the piper calls the tune. **2002** *Times* 2 Jan. 14 In no profession is the saying 'He who pays the piper, calls the tune' more apt than government ■ **action and consequence** 行為と結果；**money** 金・金銭

You PAYS your money and you takes your choice.
自分が払うのだから自分の好きな方を選べ。

商品や行為の手順などにおいて、どちらが望ましいかがよく分からない時に使われる。単数形動詞の pays と takes は両方とも非標準的な口語体である。

□**1846** *Punch* X. 16 'Which is the Prime Minister?' … 'Which ever you please, my little dear. You pays your money, and you takes your choice.' **1904** V. S. LEAN *Collectanea* IV. 205 You pays your money and you takes your choice. You pays your money and what you sees is A cow or a donkey just as you pleases. 2014 *Times* 22 Dec. 6 You pays your money and takes your choice, but I wouldn't bother with either echinacea or vitamin C. ■ **choices** 選択；**money** 金・金銭

If you want PEACE, you must prepare for war.
平和を望むなら戦の準備をしなければならぬ。
（訳注：備えあれば憂いなし）

4世紀のローマの軍事作家フラウィウス・ウェゲティウス『軍事論』III.（序論）*Qui desiderat pacem, praeparet bellum.*「平和を望むものは戦の準備をしなければならない」に基づいている。英語版は、簡潔なラテン語の言い換え *Si vis pacem, para bellum.* を翻訳したものである。2001年の用例は、誤ってスキピオ・アフリカヌスの言葉としている。彼は、ハンニバルに向って、ザマの戦い（紀元前202年）の前に *Bellum parate, quoniam pacem pati non potuistis*「今までがまんをして平和を保つことができなかったのだから、今や戦に備えよ（リウィウス『ローマ建国史』（紀元前17年）XXX. Xxxの中に記載されている）」と伝えている。

☐*a*1547 B. HALL *Chronicle* (1548) Edw. IV 209 He forgat the olde adage, saynge in tyme of peace prouyde for warre. **1593** M. SUTCLIFFE *Practice of Arms* A2ᵛ He that desireth peace, he must prepare for warres. **1624** BURTON *Anatomy of Melancholy* (ed. 2) II. iii. The Commonwealth of Veriice in their Armory haue this inscription, Happy is that Citty which in time of peace thinkes of warre, a fit Motto for euery mans priuate house. **1885** C. LOWE *Prince Bismarck* II. x. Lord Beaconsfield had acted on the maxim that 'if you want peace, you must prepare for war'. **1929** *Listener* 28 Aug. 278 'If you want peace, prepare for peace.' This is the reverse of the old motto, 'If you want peace, prepare for war'. **2001** *Washington Times* 13 July Al 7 Do you want peace? Scipio Africanus, the Roman who defeated Hannibal, put it this way: 'If you want peace, prepare for war.' ■ **peace** 平和；**prudence** 思慮・分別

peanut ⇒ If you PAY peanuts, you get monkeys.

pear ⇒ WALNUTS and pears you plant for your heirs.

Do not throw PEARLS to swine.
豚に真珠を投げ与えるな。
（訳注：「猫に小判」）

価値が分からない者に高価なものを与えてはならない。『マタイによる福音書』7章6節（欽定訳聖書）Give not that which is holy the dogs, neither cast ye your pearls before swine.「聖なるものを犬にやるな。また真珠を豚に投げてやるな」を想起させる。慣用句 to cast pearls before swine「豚に真珠を投げ与える」もよく使われる。

☐**1340** *Ayenbite of Inwit* (EETS) 152 Thet we ne thrauwe naght oure precious stones touore the zuyn. **1362** LANGLAND *Piers Plowman* A. XI. Noli mittere Margeri, perles Among hogges. **1526** *Pilgrimage of Perfection* II. iii. The holy fathers thought it nat expedient to disclose the secrete misteryes to euer; worldly person.... Cast not your perles before hogges. **1550** R. CROWLEY *Epigrams* A3 Before suche swyne no pearles maye be caste. **1816** S. SMITH *Letter* in S. Holland *Memoir* (1855) II. 134 Elgin has done a very useful thing in taking them [the Elgin Marbles] away from the Turks. Do not throw pearls to swine. **1925** WODEHOUSE *Sam the Sudden* xi. 'Young women do not interest me.' The proverb about casting pearls before swine occurred to Sam. **2001**

Spectator 3 Nov. 8 I am always inclined to toss such people a copy of *The Way of All Flesh* to show them what great late-Victorian fiction-writing was really about, but that would be pearls before swine. ■ **gratitude and ingratitude** 感謝と忘恩 ; **waste** 浪費

A PECK of March dust is worth a king's ransom.
3 月のほこり 1 ペックは王の身代金の価値がある。

（訳注：1 ペック＝約 9 リットル。イングランドの 3 月は晴天の日が少ない。人々は 3 月の乾いた晴天の日を重宝した。下の解説にあるトーマス・フラー〈Thomas Fuller〉は英国の聖職者・歴史家。「自分のいないところで自分を褒めてくれる者こそが友である」〈He's my friend that speaks well of me behind my back.) など、多くの名言で有名である〉）

イングランドの 3 月は伝統的に湿気が多く風も強い。かつて 1 ペックは 2 ガロンに相当する乾量単位であった。トーマス・フラーは『英国名士列伝』(1662, p. 87) の中でこのことわざに触れ、king's ransom「王の身代金」とは、リチャード 1 世解放に支払うために 1193-4 年に工面された 10 万ポンドであるとしている。リチャード 1 世は聖地 (パレスチナ) への十字軍遠征から帰国途中、ドイツで拉致された。

☐ **1533** J. HEYWOOD *Play of Weather* DI And now to mynde there is one olde prouerbe come: 'One bushell of march dust is worth a kynges raunsome.' **1685** R. BOYLE *Discourse of Causes of Insalubrity of Air* 55 It is proverbially said in England, that a Peck of March Dust is worth a King's Ransom: So infrequent is dry Weather, during that Month. **1936** H. C. BAILEY *Clue for Mr. Fortune* 36 The flower borders ... were planted with bush roses ... stunted by the rigours of that grim March.... 'Bushel of March dust worth a king's ransom,' Reggie murmured. **1978** R. WHITLOCK *Calendar of Country Customs* iii. [The farmer] values dry, cold weather, such as often occurs in late February and March. 'A peck of dust in March is worth a king's ransom,' is still an oft-quoted proverb. ■ **weather lore** 天気にまつわる伝承

peck ⇒ We must BAT a peck of dirt before we die.

The PEN is mightier than the sword.
ペンは剣よりも強し。

意見や出来事に及ぼす作家の影響力は腕力より効果がある。†キケロ『義務について』I. xxii. *Cedant arma togae.*「武力は説得に屈する」

☐ **1582** G. WHETSTONE *Heptameron of Civil Discourses* iii. The dashe of a Pen, is more greeuous then the counter use of a Launce. *a***1712** W. KING *Eagle & Robin in Poetical Works* (1781) III. 49 Poor Bob ... A goosequill on for weapon ty'd, Knowing by use that now and then A sword less hurt does than a pen. **1839** BULWER-LYTTON *Richelieu* II. ii. Beneath the rule of men entirely great, The pen is mightier than the sword. **2002** *Washington Post* 6 Mar. Cl In the long run, casualties and causality may be equally important—or maybe Laura Bush and her conference on education had the edge, yesterday, the pen being mightier than the sword and all. **2015** *Times* 9 Jan. 29 The lesson of [the Charlie Hebdo attack in] Paris is not the simple one that the sword is mightier than the pen, or even vice versa. It is that cartoonists armed with a pen have no defence against ... idiots bearing both a Kalashnikov and a stupid idea. ■ **persuasion** 説得 ; **words and deeds** 言動

Take care of the PENCE and the pounds will take care of themselves.
ペニーを大事にせよ。そうすれば自然にポンドがたまる。

（訳注：1 ペニー＝100 分の 1 ポンド。「塵も積もれば山となる」）

penny 351

小銭（ペニー）でも貯めると最後には相当な額になるというのが文字通りの意味であるが、お金以外にも、個人の習慣などについても比喩的に用いられる（1912年と1999年の用例参照）。1750年の用例に挙げられている、このことわざの生みの親 Mr. Lowndes とは、ウィリアム・ロンダー（1652-1724）を指している。

□**1750** CHESTERFIELD *Letter* 5 Feb. (1932) IV. **1500** Old Mr. Lowndes, the famous Secretary of the Treasury, ... used to say ... Take care of the pence, and the pounds will take care of themselves. **1912** G. B. SHAW *Pygmalion* II. 132 Take care of the pence and the pounds will take care of themselves is as true of personal habits as of money. **1979** R. CASSILIS *Arrow of God* IV. xvii. Little things, Master Mally. Look after the pennies, Master Mally, and the pounds will look after themselves. **1999** 'H. CRANE' *Miss Seeton's Finest Hour* xi. 92. 'Yes, it sounds on the melodramatic side,' he said cheerfully, 'but in wartime you can't be too careful about the smallest detail. Think of it as along the lines of taking care of the pennies, and the pounds will take care of themselves.' ■ **money** 金・金銭 ; **thrift** 質素倹約

A PENNY saved is a penny earned.
１ペニーの貯蓄は１ペニーの儲け。

ある額の金を貯蓄することは、同じ額の金を稼ぐのと等しい。なぜなら、両方ともその金は自分の思い通りになるからである。

□**1640** G. HERBERT *Outlandish Proverbs* no. 506 A penny spar'd is twice got. *a***1661** T. FULLER *Worthies* (Hunts.) 51 By the same proportion that a penny saved is a penny gained, the preserver of books is a Mate for the Compiler of them. **1695** B. RAVENSCROFT *Canterbury Guests* II. iv. This I did to prevent expences, for ... a penny sav'd, is a penny got. **1853** DICKENS *Bleak House* ix. I saved five pounds out of the brickmaker's affair.... It's a very good thing to save one, let me tell you: a penny saved, is a penny got! **1923** WODEHOUSE *Inimitable Jeeves* xi. I can save money this way; and believe me, laddie, nowadays ... a penny saved is a penny earned. **2001** *Washington Post* 6 Dec. C11 (*Family Circus comic strip*) 'A penny saved is a penny earned, but what can I buy with it?' ■ **thrift** 質素倹約

PENNY wise and pound foolish.
ペニー（小銭）に賢く、ポンド（大金）に愚か。

少額の支出、例えば何かの修理代や保険金（1864年の用例参照）を渋ると、後で多額の支出を払わなければならない羽目になる。

□**1607** E. TOPSELL *Four-footed Beasts* 609 If by couetousnesse or negligence, one withdraw from them their ordinary foode; he shall be penny wise, and pourid foolish. **1712** J. ADDISON *Spectator* 7 Feb. I think a Woman who will give up herself to a Man in Marriage, where there is the least room for such an Apprehension ... may very properly be accused ... of being Penny wise and Pound foolish. **1864** MRS H. WOOD *Trevlyn Hold* II. xxi. He never would insure his ricks.... Miss Diana has often told him he deserved to have his ricks take fire for being penny wise and pound foolish. **2001** *Washington Post* 17 June Hl I didn't stop because I was too focused on saving that 2 cents a gallon. l was, without a doubt, being penny-wise and pound-foolish. ■ **meanness** けち・意地悪 ; **stupidity** 愚かさ

penny ⇒ A BAD penny always turns up; IN for a penny, in for pound; NO penny, no paternoster.

352 PEOPLE

Like PEOPLE, like priest.
教区民は牧師に似る。

（訳注：people ＝「一定の団体などに属する人々」。この場合は parish〈教区〉の人々を指す）

1670年の用例からわかるように、軽蔑的な意味が含まれている。つまり、民と指導者は共に劣っており、愚かであるということである。『ホセア書』4 章 9 節（欽定訳聖書）Like people, like priest.「祭司も民と同じようになる」を想起させる。

□*c*1589 *Pasquil's Return* C3 Like people, like Priest begins now to be verified. 1670 J. RAY *English Proverbs* 114 Like priest, like people.... Always taken In the worse sense. 1893 R. HEATH *English Peasant* IV. iii. He had so deep a reverence for the clergy, that It never entered into his mind that perhaps, after all, it was 'like people, like priest'. 1963 *Delaware County Daily Times* 17 May 7/2 The President sets the moral standards for the nation. 'Like people, like priest' Surely our nation is at a low ebb morally. ■ similarity and dissimilarity 類似性と相違性

people ⇒ IDLE people have the least leisure; MORE people know Tom Fool than Tom Fool knows; The VOICE of the people is the voice of God.

perfect ⇒ PRACTICE makes perfect.

perish ⇒ He who LIES by the sword dies by the sword.

perjury ⇒ JOVE but laughs at lovers' perjury.

PHYSICIAN, heal thyself.
医者よ、まず汝自らを治せ。

（訳注：「医者の不養生」）

（医師・教育者など）専門家や道を説く権威者に対して、自らの教えを自らが守ってみよと述べている。『ルカによる福音書』4 章 23 節（欽定訳聖書）Ye will surely say unto me this proverb, Physician, heal thyself.「あなた方はきっと『医者よ、自分自身を癒せ』ということわざをわざわざ引く」(VULGATE *medice cura teipsum.*「医者よ、まず君らを治せ」）を想起させる。

□*c*1400 tr. *Honorius of Autun's Elucidarium* (1909) 29 Blynde leches [doctors], heeleth first youre silf! 1519 J. COLET *Sermon to Convocation* B5ᵛ If you wyll ponder and Joke vpon oure mottis [motes] fyrst take awaye the blockes out of your eies. Hit is an olde Prouerbe: Phisition heale thy selfe. 1780 T. FRANCKLIN tr. *Lucian's Works* I. 320 According to the old adage, 'physician, cure thyself'. 1875 S. SMILES *Thrift* ii. How can a man ... teach sobriety or cleanliness, if he be himself drunken or foul? 'Physician, heal thyself,' is the answer of his neighbours. 1979 G. SWARTHOUT *Skeletons* 150 Tell me the truth. Don't dig yourself in any deeper. Physician, heal thyself. 2002 *National Review* 11 Feb. 26 As for those who get bent out of shape when they're 'Dr.' -less, all we can say is, 'Ph.D., heal thyself.' ■ doctors 医者

pick ⇒ HAWKS will not pick out hawks' eyes; ⇒ A PIN and pick it up, all the day you'll have good luck.

pickle（少量）： ⇒ MANY a little makes a mickle.

PIN   353

One PICTURE is worth ten thousand words.
1 枚の絵は 1 万語に匹敵する。
（訳注：「百聞は一見に如かず」）

1925 年と 1927 年の用例では中国のことわざとしているが、根拠はない。

□c1921 *Printers' Ink* 8 Dec. 96 One look is worth a thousand words. **1925** *Washington Post* 26 July (Amusements section) 2/2 'The picture is worth ten thousand words.' So says an old Chinese proverb. **1927** *Printers' Ink* 10 Mar. 114 Chinese proverb, One picture is worth ten thousand words. **1954** R. HAYDN *Journal of Edwin Carp* 90 'One picture speaks louder than ten thousand words.' Mr. Bovey repeated the adage this morning when ... he handed me my finished portrait. **2001** *New Scientist* 17 Nov. 59 [In a photograph] the mask is being worn with the bottom strap cut off or dangling. A picture is worth a thousand words, but here are eight to redress the balance: 'If there's only one strap, it's probably crap.' ■ example, good and bad 好例と悪例 ; illustration 例示

Every PICTURE tells a story.
すべての絵には物語がある。

1847 年の用例 C. ブロンテ『ジェーン・エア』から、このことわざがある企業の宣伝用キャッチコピーとして使用される以前から存在していたことがわかる。

□a1847 C. BRONTë *Jane Eyre* I. i. The letter-press ... I cared little for.... Each picture told a story. **1904** *Daily Mail* 26 Feb. 8 A London woman and Doan's Backache Kidney Pills.... 'Every picture tells a story.' **1967** E. WILLIAMS *Beyond Belief* IV. xxiii. Every Picture Tells a Story.... Sergeant Carr stood with his ... back to the fireplace, the lady next to the budgie, the dog next to her. **2001** *Times Literary Supplement* 2 Nov. 8 'We extend that which is limited by a frame to before and after, and through the craft of telling stories ... we lend the immutable picture an infinite and inexhaustible life.' This is not merely a gloss on 'every picture tells a story', but an unfashionably specific and an unfashionably true observation. ■ example, good and bad 好例と悪例 ; illustration 例示

pie ⇒ The DEVIL makes his Christmas pies of lawyers' tongues and clerks' fingers.

pie-crust ⇒ PROMISES, like pie-crust, are made to be broken.

pig ⇒ DOGS look up to you, cats look down on you, pigs is equal; What can you EXPECT from a pig but a grunt? ; You do not FATTEN a pig by weighing it.

pillow ⇒ A clean CONSCIENCE is a good pillow.

See a PIN and pick it up, all the day you'll have good luck; ⇒ A pin and let it lie, bad luck you'll have all the day.
ピンを見たらすぐ拾え。そうするとその日はずっと好運に恵まれる。しかし、ピンを見てそのまま放置すると、その日はずっと不幸になる。
（訳注：「一文銭も小判の端」）

倹約する徳を奨励している。類似のものとして次のものが挙げられる。**1668** S. ピープス『日記』2 Jan. (1976) IX. 7 The King answered to it with great indifference. Sir W. Coventry answered: I see your Majesty doth not remember the old English

354 pin

proverb, 'He that will not stoop for a pin will never be worth a pound'.「国王は全く無関心に答えた。するとコベントリー卿は次のように答えた。『国王陛下が「ピンのためにかがまない者は１ポンドの財も所有することはない』という古いことわざをご存じないことがわかりました」

☐*a*1843 J. O. HALLIWELL *Nursery Rhymes* 120 See a pin and let it lay, Bad luck you'll have all the day! **1883** C. S. BURNE *Shropshire Folklore* xxi. Pins are held … unlucky … in the North of England … but side by side with this we have the thrifty maxim—See a pin and let it lie, You'll want a pin another day; See a pin and pick it up, All the day you'll have good luck. **1935** A. CHRISTIE *Tape-Measure Murder in Miss Marple's Final Cases* (1979) 'There's a pin in your tunic.' … He said, 'They do say, "See a pin and pick it up, all the day you'll have good luck."' **1966** D. FRANCIS *Flying Finish* ix. In the little hall hung more time-worn poker work 'See a pin and pick it up, all the day you'll have good luck See a pin and let it lie, you will want before you die.'
■ luck 幸運・運；thrift 質素倹約

pin ⇒ NEEDLES and pins, … when a man marries, his trouble begins; It's a SIN to steal a pin.

pint ⇒ You cannot get a QUART into a pint pot.

piper ⇒ He who PAYS the piper calls the tune.

pitch ⇒ He that TOUCHES pitch shall be defiled.

The PITCHER will go to the well once too often.
水差しは調子に乗ってしょっちゅう井戸に運ばれると、しまいには壊れてしまう。

（訳注：once too often ＝「〈余計な１回のために悪い結果に至ったことを示して〉またもや、図に乗って」。The clerk lied *once too often* and was fired.〈その店員は《懲りずに》またもや嘘をついて、ついにくびになった〉。「おごる平家は久しからず」）

調子に乗ってやりすぎると失敗してしまうことに対する警告。†14世紀のフランス語 *Tant va pot a eve qu'il brise.*「水差しは井戸で使われすぎると壊れてしまう」

☐*a*1340 *Ayenbite of Inwit* (EETS) 206 Zuo longe geth thet pot to the wetere: thet hit comth tobroke horn. **1584** J. WITHALS *Dict.* (rev. ed.) B1 So oft goeth the pitcher to the well, that at last it commeth broken home. **1777** N. SHAW *Collections of New London County Hist. Society* (1933) I. 223 I shall send down what I have, but dont you think the Pitcher will go to the well once too often? **1880** *Church Times* 30 Apr. 275 Some of Mr. Gladstone's feats in the way of sweeping obstacles out of his path have been wonderful; but the proverb tells us that the pitcher which goes oft to the well will be broken at last. **1996** 'C. AIRD' *After Effects* xvi. 187 Superintendent Leeyes would have to be disturbed on a Saturday all over again. And it was odds on that he wouldn't like it. That quotation about the pitcher going to the well once too often had more than a ring of truth to it as far as the superintendent was concerned. ■ misfortune 不運；persistence ねばり強さ

pitcher ⇒ LITTLE pitchers have large ears.

pitchfork ⇒ You can DRIVE out Nature with a pitchfork, but she keeps on coming back.

pitied ⇒ BETTER be envied than pitied.

PITY is akin to love.
哀れみは恋に近い。

（訳注：よく知られているように、漱石の『三四郎』の中で、広田先生はこのことわざを「可哀想だた惚れたってことよ」と訳した）

同情に含まれる感情は恋愛から遠いものではない。

□*a*1601 SHAKESPEARE *Twelfth Night* III. i. 119 I pity you. —That's a degree to love. **1696** T. SOUTHERNE *Oroonoko* II. i. Do, pity me: Pity's a-kin to Love. *a*1895 F. LOCKER-LAMPSON *My Confidences* (1896) 95 They say that Pity is akin to Love, though only a Poor Relation; but Amy did not even pity me. **1942** 'C. KINGSTON' *Murder Tunes In* (1943) iii. 44 'It may not be love—it may be only pity.' 'You're wrong,' said Mrs. Armitage with the cheerfulness of one discussing something exceedingly pleasurable. 'It's not the pity that is akin to love—it's love itself.' ■ **love** 愛・恋愛 ; **pity** 哀れみ・同情

A PLACE for everything, and everything in its place.
物にはそれぞれふさわしい置き場所がある。その場所に置くべきだ。

整理整頓を奨励する際に使われる。

□**1640** G. HERBERT *Outlandish Proverbs* no. 379 All things have their place, knew wee how to place them. **1842** MARRYAT *Masterman Ready* II. i. In a well-conducted man-of-war … every thing in its place, and there is a place for every thing. **1855** T. C. HALIBURTON *Nature & Human Nature* I. vi. There was a place for everything, and everything was in its place. **1928** D. L. SAYERS *Lord Peter views Body* x. 'I thought you were rather partial to anatomical specimens.' 'So I am, but not on the breakfast-table. "A place for everything and everything in its place," as my grandmother used to say.' **2002** A. VANNEMAN *Sherlock Holmes and Giant Rat of Sumatra* ix. 80 The sailor's apothegm—'a place for everything, and everything in its place' —guided us, until at length everything was stowed away … ■ **orderliness** 整然としていること

There's no PLACE like home.
我が家に勝る所はない。

†ヘシオドス『仕事と日』I. 365 οἴκοι βέλτερον εἶναι. 「我が家ほどの場所はない」

□**1571** T. TOSSER *Husbandry* (rev. ed.) H1ᵛ Though home be but homely, yet huswife is taught, That home hath no fellow to such as haue aught. **1823** J. H. PAYNE *Clari* I. i. 'Mid pleasures and palaces though we may roam, Be it ever so humble, there's no place like home.' **1939** E. F. BENSON *Trouble for Lucia* xi. 'What a joy to have it back at Mallards again!' … 'No place like home is there, dear?' **2015** *Times* 26 Jan. 10 Yet his real message remains that of The Wizard of Oz: there's no place like home. ■ **content and discontent** 満足と不満足 ; **home** 家庭・母国

place ⇒ LIGHTNING never strikes the same place twice; There is a TIME and place for everything; A WOMAN's place is in the home.

plant ⇒ It is not SPRING until you can plant your foot upon twelve daisies; WALNUTS and pears you plant for your heirs.

356 PLANTS

He who PLANTS thorns should not expect to gather roses.
サンザシの木を植える者はバラを摘み取れるなどと期待すべきではない。
（訳注：thorn＝「とげのある植物〈イバラ、サンザシなど〉」）

中近東のことわざで、英語の as you SOW, so you reap.「自分が蒔いた種は自分で刈り取らねばならない」に相当する。

☐ **1883** J. PLATT *Platt's Essays* 49 He has got it into his head, with Pope, that 'Man never is, but always to be, blest.' This view of life must be reversed. Men must realize that 'he that plants thorns will not gather roses.' **1971** O. FLAKSER *Marxism, Ideology and Myths* 205 The means to the end tend to block the full realization of the end. 'He who plants thorns should not expect to gather roses.' **1999** P. TREMAYNE *Monk who Vanished* xx 'That is a young man with fire in his head,' he observed. 'He will plant thorns and expect to gather roses unless he is dissuaded,' agreed Fidelma. ■ **action and consequence** 行為と結果

Those who PLAY at bowls must look out for rubbers.
（芝生で行なう）ボウリングをする者は障害物を見つけ出さなければならない。
（訳注：この場合のボウリングは芝生で行なわれる競技。木球をジャックという目標のボールのできるだけ近くに転がす）

ある行為をする場合、途中で起こりうる困難なことに注意を払う必要がある。ここで rubber は明らかに rub（ボウリング競技の際の障害物やでこぼこ）の異形である（1907年の用例参照）。† **1595** シェイクスピア『リチャード2世』III. iv. 4 Madam, we'll play at bowls. —'Twill make me think the world is full of rubs.「お妃様、球転がしはいかがでしょう？」「それでは球をそらす障害がこの世に多いことを思い出すわ」

☐ **1762** SMOLLETT *Sir Launcelot Greaves* I. x. (*heading*) Which sheweth that he who plays at bowls, will sometimes meet with rubbers. **1874** L. STEPHEN *Hours in Library* I. 384 De Quincey … admits … that the fanaticism of the rub was 'much more reasonable' than the fanaticism of Priestly; and that those who play at bowls must look out for rubbers. **1907** F. W. HACKWOOD *Old English Sports* xi. Another term used in common speech and derived from this game [bowls] is 'rub'; as when we say … 'he who plays at bowls must look out for rubs' —that is, he must consider the inequalities of the ground, and … make due allowance for them. **1991** J. P. FOKKEL-MAN *Narrative Art in Genesis* 41 Those who play at bowls must look out for rubs, those who ride on clouds must reckon with cloud-bursts; God stands no nonsense. ■ **caution** 用心；**foresight and hindsight** 先見の明と後知恵；**trouble** やっかい・苦労

If you PLAY with fire you get burnt.
火遊びすると火傷する。
（訳注：get＝「〈受身を表わして〉…される」。被害・影響などを強く意識した場合に使われることが多い。He *got* hit by a car last week.〈彼は先週車にはねられた〉、*get* bitten by a dog.〈犬にかまれる〉）

慣用句 to play with fire「重大問題を軽々しく扱う」もよく知られている。† **1655** H. ヴォーン『火花散る石英ガラス』II. 15 I played with fire, did counsell spurn, … But never thought that fire would burn, Or that a soul could ake.「私は火遊びをし、忠告を無視した。…しかし、発火するとは思わず、心が痛むとも思わなかった」

☐ **1884** R. H. THORPE *Fenton Family* xiv. If people will play with fire, they must expect to be burned by it some time. If I had not learned the game, and thought myself a good player, I'd never have lost Mother's money. **1980** P. KINSLEY *Vatchman Switch* xxiv. If you play with fire you get burnt. Shouldn't mess around in Crown Colonies. **2014** www.kspr.com 14 Nov. Play with fire, you'll get burned. That's the message the Springfield Fire Department wants young people to hear. ■ action and consequence 行動と結果 ; peril 危険

play ⇒（名詞）FAIR play's a jewel; GIVE and take is fair play; TURN about is fair play; All WORK and no play makes Jack a dull boy;（動詞）When the CAT's away, the mice will play.

You can't PLEASE everyone.
全員を満足させることはできない。

（訳注：この場合の you は総称的な用法。*You never* can tell what's going to happen.〈何が起きるかは誰にもわからない〉。not every で部分否定となっている。「あちら立てればこちらが立たぬ」）

相反する利害関係を有する人たちの集まりで、すべての側を満足させるようなことはできないという警告。

□1472 E. PASTON *Letter* 16 May in *Paston Letters* (1971) I. 635 I am in serteyn the contrary is true—yt is nomore but that he can not plese all partys. **1616** T. DRAXE *Adages* 45 One can hardly please all men. **1844** RUSKIN *Journal* 30 Apr. In *Diaries* 1835-47 (1956) 274 At Ward's about window-nothing done. Gastineau came up and don't like mine: can't please everybody. **1981** *Dally Telegraph* 16 May 18 The old adage, 'you can't please everyone', holds good. ■ **conduct** 行ない・品行 ; public relations 広報・宣伝活動

please ⇒ LITTLE things please little minds.

pleasure ⇒ BUSINESS before pleasure; He that would go to SBA for pleasure, would go to hell for a pastime.

plum ⇒ A CHERRY year, a merry year.

An old POACHER makes the best gamekeeper.
老練な密猟者こそが最もすぐれた猟場人になる。

（訳注：make =「…になる」。She *made* a good wife.〈彼女はよい奥さんになった〉。「蛇の道はヘビ」）

類似したものに Set a THIEF to catch a thief.「泥棒を捕えるには泥棒を使え」がある。かつて密猟者だった者は、密猟者の思考法に対して専門的な知識と洞察力を持っているため、効果的な監視人になることができる。

□*c*1390 CHAUCER *Physician's Tale* I. 83 A theef of venysoun, that hath forlaft His likerousnesse [depravity] and al his olde craft, Kan kepe a forest best of any man. **1695** T. FULLER *Church Hist. Britain* IX. iii. Always set a—to catch a—; and the greatest dear-stealers, make the best Parke-keepers. **1878** R. JEFFERIES *Gamekeeper at Home* ix. There is a saying that an old poacher makes the best gamekeeper, on the principle of setting a thief to catch a thief. **1970** V. CANNING *Great Affair* iii. What the Church needed, possibly, was a good leavening of sinners in its ministry, on the principle that poachers make the best gamekeepers. **1978** T. SHARPE *Throwback* i. 5 'You'll have heard the saying that a poacher makes the best gamekeeper? ... Well, Dodd's the reverse. He's a gamekeeper who would have made the best poacher.' ■ **guile** 狡猾・策略 ; wrongdoers 悪事をなす者

pocket ⇒ SHROUDS have no pockets.

point ⇒ POSSESSION is nine points of the law.

358   poison

poison ⇒ One man's MEAT is another man's poison.

poke ⇒ You should KNOW a man seven years before you stir his fire.

policy ⇒ HONESTY is the best policy.

politeness ⇒ CMLITY costs nothing; PUNCTUALITY is the politeness of princes.

POLITICS makes strange bedfellows.
政治は見知らぬ者たちをも仲間にする。

　「政治」という意味でのpoliticsは、従来複数名詞と見なされてきたが、最近は単数名詞としての用法も認められつつある。表題のものは、ADVERSITY makes strange bedfellows.「不幸は見知らぬ者たちをも仲間にする」のよく知られた異形である。

☐**1839** P. HONE *Diary* 9 July (1927) I. 404 Party politics, like poverty, bring men 'acquainted with strange bedfellows'. **1870** C. D. WARNER *My Summer in Garden* (1871) 187 The Doolittle raspberries have sprawled all over the strawberry-beds: so true is It that politics makes strange bed-fellows. **1936** M. MITCHELL *Gone with Wind* viii. Ashley Wilkes and I are mainly responsible. Platitudinously but truly, politics make strange bedfellows. **1980** P. VAN GREENAWAY *Dissident* vii. Even enemies have something in common. Statecraft produces strange bedfellows. **1995** *Washington Times* 31 Mar. A4 Politics makes strange bedfellows, if Mr. Hyde will forgive the unforgivable but irresistible metaphor. ■ **associates** 仲間 ; **politics** 政治

It is a POOR dog that's not worth whistling for.
口笛で呼んでもらう価値のないのは哀れな犬である。

（訳注：どんな犬でも口笛で呼んでもらう価値はある。形式と意味の点から、前に挙がっている It is a long lane that has no turning.〈曲がり角のない道は長い道だ《どんな道にも曲がり角はある》〉ということわざと類似している。下のことわざにも同じことが言える）

たとえ取るに足らないものでも、保存したり、取り戻したりするだけの価値はあるものだ。

☐**1546** J. HEYWOOD *Dialogue of Proverbs* I. xi. It is, as I haue learned in lystnyng, A poore dogge, that is not worth the whlstlyng. **1614** W. CAMDEN *Remains concerning Britain* (ed. 2) 303 A poore dog that is not worth the whystllng. **1738** SWIFT *Polite Conversation* I. 41 Because, Miss, you never ask'd me; and 'tis an ill Dog that's not worth whistling for. **1952** W. S. HOOLE *Alias Simon Suggs* i. It was a poor dog indeed that wasn't worth whistling for. ■ **value** 価値

It is a POOR heart that never rejoices.
決して喜ばないのは貧しい心である。

たとえ最も不運な人でも時には楽しいことがあるものだ。

☐*c***1834** MARRYAT *Peter Simple* I. v. 'Well,' continued he, 'It's a poor heart that never rejoiceth.' He then poured out half a tumbler of rum. **1841** DICKENS *Barnaby Rudge* iv. What happened when I reached home you may guess.... Ah! Well, it's a poor heart that never rejoices. **1935** E. P. BENSON *Lucia's Progress* viii. They were all men together, he said, and it was a sad heart that never rejoiced. **1979** J. SCOTT *Clutch of Vipers* iv. 'It's a poor heart', Frankie told him, 'that never rejoices.' ■ **happiness** 幸福

POSTERN 359

poor ⇒ One LAW for the rich and another for the poor; The RICH man has his ice in the summer and the poor man gets his in the winter.

Pope ⇒ It is ill SITTING at Rome and striving with the Pope.

port ⇒ ANY port in a storm.

POSSESSION is nine points of the law.
所有は法律の九分の強み。
（訳注：「預かりものは半分の主」）

この概念は広く容認されているが、これを支持する特定の法律はない。当初の用法では、十分な資格や所有権を証明するためにはいくつかの点、例えば、10 点（時に 12 点）を満たすことが一般に主張された。ここでは所有権が 9 点（時に 11 点）で示されているので、10 点に最も近いことになる。† 1595『エドワード 3 世』E 3 Tis you are in possession of the Crowne, And thats the surest poynt of all the Law.「王冠を所有しているのはあなたである。それはすべての法律の中で最も確実なことである」

☐ 1616 T. DRAXE *Adages* 163 Possession is nine points in the Law. **1659** J. IRETON *Oration* 5 This Rascally-devill ... denys to pay a farthing of rent. Tis true, possession is nine points of the Law, Yet give Gentlemen, right's right. **1709** O. DYKES *English Proverbs* 213 Possession is a mighty Matter indeed; and we commonly say, 'tis eleven Points of the Law. It goes a great Way to the giving of Security, but not any Right **1920** J. GALSWORTHY *In Chancery* II. xiv. We're the backbone of the country. They [Leftists] won't upset us easily. Possession's nine points of the Law. **2002** *Washington Times* 17 Feb. B2 Mrs. Clinton told the New York Post, 'You know, we followed every single law.' And they did So what if it was the law of the jungle (possession is nine-tenths of the law) ... ? ■ property 財産

possible ⇒ ALL things are possible with God; All's for the BEST in the best of all possible worlds.

post ⇒ The post of HONOUR is the post of danger.

A POSTERN door makes a thief.
盗人は裏口があるからこそ生まれる。
（訳注：裏口を作ると、召使いが家の食料品などをそこから持ち出してしまう）

類似したものに OPPORTUNITY makes a thief.「盗人は機会があるからこそ生まれる」がある。a postern door とは正面ドアから離れたところに配置されている裏口、または側面の入り口を指す。

☐ *c*1450 *Proverbs of Good Counsel in Book of Precedence* (EETS) 69 A nyse wyfe, and a back dore, Makyth of ten tymus A ryche man pore. **1573** J. SANFORDE *Garden of Pleasure* 107 The posterne dore destroyeth the house. **1611** J. DAVIES *Scourge of Folly* 146 The Posterne doore makes theefe and whore. But, were that dam'd with Stone, or Clay, Whoores and Theeues would find a way. **1732** T. FULLER *Gnomologia* no. 6176 The Postern Door Makes Thief and Whore. **1977** J. AIKEN *Five-Minute Marriage* xi. 'I shall never be able to sleep securely in this room, if thieves are to be always breaking in and waking me up!' 'A postern door do always make a thief.'

360 pot

■ honesty and dishonesty 正直と不正直 ; opportunity, taken 得られた機会

pot ⇒ If IFS and ands were pots and pans, there'd be no work for tinkers' hands; A LITTLE pot is soon hot; You cannot get a QUART into a pint pot; A WATCHED pot never boils.

pound ⇒ IN for a penny, in for a pound; An OUNCE of practice is worth a pound of precept; Take care of the PENCE and the pounds will take care of themselves; PENNY wise and pound foolish.

pour ⇒ It never RAINS but it pours.

When POVERTY comes in at the door, love flies out of the window.
貧困がドアから入ってくると愛は窓から飛び出していく。

(訳注 : 解説に挙がっている W. キャクストンは英国の印刷業者・翻訳家。1476年ウェストミンスターに英国最初の印刷機を据えたことで有名)

家計が苦しいと結婚は破綻する。意味が類似したものに、**1474** キャクストン *Game of Chess* III. iii. Herof men saye a comyn prouerbe in englond that loue lastest as longe as the money endurith.「これについては、英国のよく知られたことわざに『愛はお金がある間に限って続く』がある」がある。

□**1631** R. BRATHWAIT *English Gentlewoman* vi. It bath been an old Maxime; that as pouerty goes in at one doore, loue goes out at the other. **1639** J. CLAEKE *Parremiologia Anglo-Latina* 25 When povertie comes in at doores, love leapes out at windowes. **1790** *Universal Asylum* Aug. 84 I hope, ladies, none of you may ever experience, that 'when poverty comes in at the door, love flies out at the windows'. **1894** J. LUBBOCK *Use of Life* iii. It is a mean proverb that, 'When poverty comes in at the door, love flies out of the window'. **1968** J. N. LOCH *Fringe of Blue* 6 Edith's family all believed that love flew out of the window when poverty came in at the door. ■ **love, blighted** くじかれた愛 ; **poverty** 貧困

POVERTY is no disgrace, but it is a great inconvenience.
貧困は不名誉ではないが、たいそう不自由なものである。

貧困だからといって道徳的に恥じ入る必要はないが、貧困ゆえにやりたいことができなくなる。

□**1591** J. FLORIO *Second Fruits* 105 Neuer be ashamed of thy calling. for Pouertie is no vice, though it be an inconvenience. **1721** J. KELLY *Scottish Proverbs* 278 Poortha [poverty] is a Pain, but no Disgrace. Unless it be the Effects of Laziness, and Luxury. **1945** F. THOMPSON *Lark Rise* i. 'Poverty's no disgrace, but 'tis a great inconvenience' was a common saying among the Lark Rise people; but ... their poverty was no less than a hampering drag upon them. ■ **poverty** 貧困

POVERTY is not a crime.
貧困は犯罪にあらず。

(訳注 : crime =「〈法律上の〉罪」、sin =「道徳・宗教上の罪」。Poverty is no sin.〈貧乏は罪にあらず〉とも言う。1640年、1973年の用例参照。)

意味が類似したものに POVERTY is no disgrace.「貧困は不名誉ではない」がある。

□**1591** J. FLORIO *Second Fruits* 105 Pouertie is no vice. **1640** G. HERBERT *Outlandish Proverbs* no. 844 Poverty is no sinne. **1785** C. MACKLIN *Man of World* IV. 56 Her Poverty is not her crime,

PRACTISE 361

Sir, but her misfortune. **1839** DICKENS *Nicholas Nickleby* lv. 'Remember how poor we are.' Mrs. Nickleby ... said through her tears that poverty was not a crime. **1945** F. THOMPSON *Lark Rise* ii. There's nothing the matter with Lark Rise folks but poverty, and that's no crime. If it was, we should likely be hung ourselves. **1973** G. MIKES *Spy who died of Boredom* 50 The English say: poverty is not a sin but something much worse. ■ **poverty 貧困**

poverty ⇒ ADVERSITY makes strange bedfellows.

powder ⇒ Put your TRUST in God, and keep your powder dry.

POWER corrupts.
権力は腐敗する。

このことわざは現在、権力者の悪について述べている1887年の用例を暗に指して広く使われている。

□**1876** TROLLOPE *Prime Minister* IV. viii. We know that power does corrupt, and that we cannot trust kings to have loving hearts. **1887** W. ACTON *Letter in Life & Letters of Mandel Creighton* (1904) I. xiii. Power tends to corrupt, and absolute power corrupts absolutely. Great men are almost always bad men, even when they exercise influence and not authority. **1957** V. BRITTAIN *Testament of Experience* II. ix. The processes by which 'power corrupts' are perhaps inevitable. **1979** MCCARRY *Better Angels* IV. xii. He doesn't know that power corrupts; there's nothing dark in him. **2001** *Washington Times* 1 Sept. A10 To paraphrase Lord Acton: Power corrupts. Extended service in Congress corrupts absolutely. ■ **power 力・権力**

power ⇒ KNOWLEDGE is power; MONEY is power.

PRACTICE makes perfect.
練習することによってこそ完璧になる。
（訳注：「習うより慣れよ」）

練習を積み重ねるとどんなこともできるようになる。

□**1553** T. WILSON *Art of Rhetoric* 3 Eloquence was vsed, and through practice made parfect. **1599** H. PORTER *Two Angry Women of Abington* I. 913 Forsooth as vse makes perfectnes, so seldome seene is soone forgotten. **1761** J. ADAMS *Diary* (1961) I. 192 Practice makes perfect. **1863** C. READE *Hard Cash* III. iv. He lighted seven fires, skillfully on the whole, for practice makes perfect. **1979** D. LESSING *Shikasta* 185 It is like playing the piano or riding a bicycle. Practice makes perfect. **2002** *Country Life* 14 Feb.49 The quality of the [blackbird's] song improves as the season progresses.... This, presumably, is a matter of practice makes perfect. ■ **diligence 勤勉**

practice ⇒ An OUNCE of practice is worth a pound of precept.

PRACTISE what you preach.
人に説くことを自分でも実行せよ。
（訳注：このことわざは、前に挙がっている Physician, heal thyself.〈医者よ、まず汝自らを治せ〉を想起させる）

人に作法を説くのなら、自分でもそれを実行しなければならない。

362 PRAISE

□**1377** LANGLAND *Piers Plowman* B. XIII.79 This goddes gloton … Hath no pyte on vs pore. He perforneth yuel [does evil], That he precheth he preueth [demonstrates] nought. **1639** T. FULLER *Holy War* I. xxiii. The Levites … had 48 cities … being better provided for then many English ministers, who may preach of hospitalltie to their people, but cannot go to the cost to practice their own doctrine. **1678** R. L'ESTRANGE *Seneca's Morals* II. ii. We must practise what we preach. **1725** B. YOUNG *Universal Passion* III. 48 Ye doctors sage, who thro' Pamassus teach, Or quit the tub, or practise what you preach. **1945** F. THOMPSON *Lark Rise* iv. Songs of a high moral tone, such as: … practise what you preach. **1970** D. CLARK *Deadly Pattern* iv. He was more than scornful of drink know-alls who practised what they preached even against their own palates. ■ **words and deeds** 言動

PRAISE the child, and you make love to the mother.
子供を褒めよ。そうすれば母親に気に入られる。

make loveの意味は当初は「…に気に入られる」であった。この表現の意味変化については2013年の用例参照。

□**1829** COBBETT *Advice to Young Men* IV. clxxxi. It is an old saying, 'Praise the child, and you make love to the mother'; and it is surprising how far this will go. **1885** B. J. HARDY *How to be Happy though Married* xix. 'Praise the child, and you make love to the mother,' and It is a thing that no husband ought to overlook. **2013** D. T. SIEBERT *Mortality's Muse* II Even the phrase 'making love' once meant something as innocent as 'ingratiating oneself' … The old saying 'Praise the child, and you make love to the mother' would be misunderstood today. ■ **children and parents** 親子

praise ⇒（名詞）SELF-praise is no recommendation.

pray ⇒ Be CAREFUL what you pray for, you might get it; The FAMILY that prays together stays together; He that cannot PAY, let him pray.

precept ⇒ EXAMPLE is better than precept; An OUNCE of practice is worth a pound of precept.

prepare ⇒ HOPE for the best and prepare for the worst; If you want PEACE, you must prepare for war.

present ⇒ No TIME like the present.

preservation ⇒ SELF-preservation is the first law of nature.

pressed ⇒ One VOLUNTEER is worth two pressed men.

PRETIY is as pretty does.
物事をみごとにこなす人こそがみごとである

（訳注：as pretty doesのprettyは「美しく」の意）

米国の版は HANDSOME is as handsome does.「物事を立派にこなす人こそが立派で

PRIDE 363

ある」である。

□**1853** T. C. HALIBURTON *Sam Slick's Wise Saws* i. 136 A very smart little boy; and Old Hundreth ... tells me you are a very good boy, and that's better, for pretty is as pretty does. *a***1871** A. CARY 'Pretty is that Pretty Does' in M. C. Ames *Memorial of Alice and Phoebe Cary* (1874) 238 My child, who reads this simple lay With eyes down-dropt and tender, Remember the old proverb says That pretty is, which pretty does And that worth does not go nor stay For poverty nor splendor. **1991** H. P. MCADOO in *Journal of Negro Education* lx. 362 On special occasions a big (and I do mean big) bow was placed on top of my head. As my mother wrestled with my hair she often tossed out little proverbs such as 'Pretty is as pretty does.' **2002** *Washington Times* 23 July B5 There is an old saying, 'Pretty is as pretty does.' It's a wise woman who learns that lesson early. ■ appearance 外見 ; conduct 行ない・品行

prevent ⇒ A STUMBLE may prevent a fall.

PREVENTION is better than cure.
予防は治療にまさる。

† *c***1240** ブラクトン『慣習法』v. x. *Melius & utilius [est] in tempore occurrere, quam post causam vulneratam quaerere remedium.*「損害が発生した後で解決案を探すより、前もって問題に対峙しておく方が賢明かつ有益である」

□**1618** T. ADAMS *Happiness of Church* 146 Preuention is so much better then healing, because it saues the labour of being sicke. **1732** T. FULLER *Gnomologia* no. 3962 Prevention is much preferable to Cure. **1826** J. PINTARD *Letter* 19 Apr. (1940) II. 257 Prevention is better than cure.... With perseverance we shall save numbers of little Devils from becoming big ones. **1954** R. HAYDN *Journal of Edwin Carp* 148 'Why do you wear those old galoshes when the sun's shining?' ... 'Prevention's better than Cure.' **2014** *Times* 2 16 Dec. 7 The modern mantra that prevention is better than cure has resulted in a shift away from focusing on the poorly individual to identifying whole populations who are ... at higher than average risk of trouble in the future. ■ foresight and hindsight 先見の明と後知恵 ; prudence 思慮・分別

price ⇒ EVERY man has his price.

PRIDE feels no pain.
おしゃれは苦痛知らず。
（訳注：「伊達者の薄着」）

どのような不快も意に関しないほどおしゃれに熱心な人を指すのに使われる。最近の米国版 Beauty knows no pain.「美しさは苦痛知らず」も同じ趣旨である。

□**1614** T. ADAMS *Devil's Banquet* II. 73 Pride is neuer without her own paine, though shee will not feele it: be her garments what they will, yet she will neuer be too hot, nor too colde. **1631** JONSON *New Inn* II. i. Thou must make shift with it Pride feeles no pain. Girt thee hard, Pru. **1721** J. KELLY *Scottish Proverbs* 277 Pride finds no cold. Spoken ... to Beaus [fops] with their open Breasts, and Ladles with their extravagant Hoops [hooped skirts]. **1865** SURTEES *Facey Romford's Hounds* xxxii. It was hard upon the old boy, who ... was not at all adapted for the sport; but pride feels no pain, and he went at it like a man. **1981** *Radio Times* 28 Feb.-6 Mar. 43 (*advertisement*) Pride feels no pain, the saying goes. Thankfully, with Clarks [shoes] it doesn't have to. ■ pride 誇り・うぬぼれ

364　PRIDE

PRIDE goes before a fall.
高ぶりは滅びに先立つ。
（訳注：「おごる平家は久しからず」）

プライドが高すぎると躓くことになる。『箴言』16章18節（欽定訳聖書）Pride goeth before destruction, and an haughty spirit before a fall.「高ぶりは滅びに先立ち、誇る心は倒れに先立つ」の簡略版である。

□ *c*1390 GOWER *Confessio Amantis* I. 3062 Pride ... schal doun falle. **1509** A. BARCLAY *Ship of Fools* 195ᵛ First or last foule pryde wyll haue a fall. **1784** S. JOHNSON *Letter* 2 Aug. (1952) III. 191 I am now reduced to think ... of the weather. Pride must have a fall. **1856** H. MELVILLE *Piazza Tales* 431 The bell's main weakness was where man's blood had flawed it And so pride went before the fall. **1930** W. S. MAUGHAM *Cakes & Ale* v. I suppose he thinks he'd be mayor himself.... Pride goeth before a fall. **1980** M. L. WEST in K. J. Dover Ancient Greek Literature iii. The spectacle of Xerxes' defeat tremendously reinforced the traditional conviction that pride goes before a fall. **2001** K. HALL PAGE *Body in Moonlight epilogue* 233 Millicent had disagreed. Vanity, pure and simple. Pride goeth before a fall. It was one of the maxims by which Millicent lived. ■ pride　誇り・うぬぼれ；retribution　天罰・報復

priest ⇒ ONCE a priest, always a priest; Like PEOPLE, like priest.

prince ⇒ Whosoever DRAWS his sword against the prince must throw the scabbard away; PUNCTUALITY is the politeness of princes.

problem ⇒ If you're not part of the SOLUTION, you're part of the problem; A TROUBLE shared is a trouble halved.

PROCRASTINATION is the thief of time.
先延ばしは時間泥棒。
（訳注：1742年の用例に示されているように、英国のよく知られた詩人エドワード・ヤングの詩集『夜想』〈*Night Thoughts*〉からの引用。「思い立ったが吉日」）

物事を先延ばしするのは時間の浪費である。

□**1742** E. YOUNG *Night Thoughts* I. 18 Procrastination is the Thief of Time; Year after year it steals, till all are fled. **1850** DICKENS *David Copperfield* xii. Never do to-morrow what you can do to-day. Procrastination is the thief of time. **1935** O. NASH *Primrose Path* 100 Far from being the thief of Time, procrastination is the king of it. **2000** D. UNDSAY *Cutting Edge of Barney Thomson* xxi. 219 'Ach, well, ye know how it is, ... an' so I procrastinated, I must admit I know what ye must be thinking. Laddie ... Procrastination is the thief of time, aye, isn't that the truth.' ■ procrastination　先延ばし

product ⇒ If you're not PAYING, you're the product.

PROMISES, like pie-crust, are made to be broken.
約束というものは、パイの皮と同じく、破られるためになされるものだ。

英国の叙情詩人クリスティーナ・ロセッティ（1830-94）の詩のタイトルに Promises like Pie-crust「パイの皮のような約束」がある。その冒頭部分は Promise me no promises,

So will I not promise you「私に約束しないと約束して。私もあなたに約束しないから」となっている。

□ **1681** *Heraclitus Ridens* 16 Aug. He makes no more of breaking Acts of Parliaments, than if they were like Promises and Pie-crust made to be broken. **1871** TROLLOPE *Ralph the Heir* II. iv. 'Promises like that are mere pie-crust,' said Ralph. **1981** *Family Circle* Feb. 66 Promises, like pie-crusts, they say, are made to be broken. Not at Sainsbury's. Every single pie they sell lives up to the promise of its famous name. **2002** *Oldie* Aug. 26 Unhappily for most of those zillionaire twenty-somethings—and for those who invested in the New Economy they thought they had invented-their promises turned out to be piecrust. ■ **deception** ごまかし

The PROOF of the pudding is in the eating.
プディングの味は食べてみないとわからない。
（訳注：「論より証拠」）

物事の本当の価値はそれを経験することによってのみ試すことができる。ここでのproofは通常の「証明する」ではなく、「試す」という意味で使われている。

□ **c1300** *King Alisaunder* (EETS) I. 4038 Jt is ywrite that euery thing Hymself sheweth in the tastyng. **1623** W. CAMDEN *Remains concerning Britain* (ed. 3) 266 All the proofe ofa pudding is in the eating. **1666** O. TORRIANO *Italian Proverbs* 100 (*note*) As they say at the winding up, or the proof of the pudding is in the eating. **1738** SWIFT *Polite Conversation* II. 132 The Proof of the Pudden is in the Eating. **1924** J. GAISWORTHY *White Monkey* III. xii. Let us ... look at the thing more widely. The proof of the pudding is in the eating. **1997** *New Scientist* 19 July 41 Lindzen for one argues that if the models get the detail wrong. they will get the big picture wrong, too. But modellers say the proof of the pudding is in the eating. ■ **appearance** 外見 ; **reality and illusion** 現実と幻想

A PROPHET is not without honour save in his own country.
預言者は自分の祖国以外でしか尊敬されない。
（訳注：save ＝「…を除いては」）

長年周りの人々となじみ深くなった人はやがて尊敬されなくなってしまう。『マタイによる福音書』13章57節（欽定訳聖書）A prophet is not without honour, save in his own country, and in his own house.「預言者は自分の郷里や自分の家以外では、どこでも敬われないことはない」を想起させる。

□ **a1485** CAXTON in Malory *Works* (1967) I. p. cxiv. The word of God ... sayth that no man is accept for a prophete in his owne contreye. **1603** J. FLORIO tr. *Montalgne's Essays* m. ii. No man bath beene a Prophet ... in his owne country, saith the experience of histories. **1771** SMOLLETT *Humphry Clinker* III. 92 The captain, like the prophets of old, is but little honoured in his own country. **1946** W. S. MAUGHAM *Then & Now* xxx. In Florence ... they had no great confidence in his judgment and never followed his advice. 'A prophet is not without honour save in his own country.' **2002** *Spectator* 2 Feb. 48 'I hope you don't mind, but my wife is in love with your Prime Minister.' 'Mind? Not I,' I coughed. 'A prophet is not without honour save in his own country,' another quoted. ■ **familiarity** 慣れ親しみ ; **honour** 尊敬・名誉

propose ⇒ MAN proposes, God disposes.

prosper ⇒ CHEATS never prosper.

366　protect

protect ⇒ HEAVEN protects children, sailors, and drunken men.

prove ⇒ The EXCEPTION proves the rule.

provide ⇒ TAKE the goods the gods provide.

PROVIDENCE is always on the side of the big battalions.
神は常に大軍に味方する。
　（訳注：「勝てば官軍」）

現在では Providence の代わりに God がよく使われる。† **1673** セヴィニエ夫人『書簡』22 Dec. *La fortune est toujours, comme disait le pauvre M. de Turenne, pour les gros bataillons.*「哀れなテュレンヌがかつて言っていたように、幸運はつねに大軍に味方する」。フランスの啓蒙思想家ヴォルテールは次のようなウイットに富む矛盾した言葉によって称賛されている。*Dieu n'est pas pour les gros bataillons, mats pour ceux qui tirent le mieux*「神は決して最強の軍隊に味方するのではない、…」(2011 年の用例参照)

☐**1822** A. GRAYDON *Memoirs* v. Heaven was ever found favourable to strong battalions. **1842** A. ALLISON *Hist. Europe* X. lxxviii. Providence was always on the side of dense battalions. **1904** 'SAKI' *Reginald* 63 Someone has observed that Providence is always on the side of the big dividends. **1943** R. A. J. WAILLING *Corpse by any Other Name* iii. Our statesmen ... ought to have learned years ago that Providence is always on the side of the big battalions. **1979** *Guardian* 9 July 9 Many thousands more voices now are raised in the name of sanity. But I dare say God is still on the side of the big battalions. **2011** *FT [Financial Times]* 10 Mar. (online) Turenne was killed on the battlefield by a stray cannon ball, a fate that prompted Voltaire to remark that 'God is on the side not of the great battalions, but of the best shots'. **2014** *London Evening Standard* 3 Dec. (online) The experience of the last European war — only 40 years earlier — had shown that God was on the side of the big battalions. ■ **great and small** 大小 ; **providence**（神の）摂理

public ⇒ One does not WASH one's dirty linen in public.

Any PUBLICITY is good publicity.
どのような宣伝もよい宣伝。

証拠はないが、米国の実業家で興行師のフィニアス・T・バーナム (1810-91) の言葉とされることが多い。

☐**1925** *Fresno* [CA] *Bee* 1 Aug. The prevailing psychology of Hollywood is that any publicity is good publicity. **1933** R. CHANDLER in *Black Mask* Dec. 26 Rhonda Farr said: 'Publicity, darling. Just publicity. Any kind is better than none at all.' **1974** P. CAVE *Dirtiest Picture Postcard* xiv. Haven't you ever heard the old adman's adage ... 'any publicity is good publicity'? **1986** 'C. AIRD' *Dead Liberty* xii. Bill wasn't too worried. Like the old trouper he is, he insisted that all publicity is good publicity. **2002** *Washington Times* 9 May C8 Mike Tyson may have disproved the adage that any publicity is good publicity. ■ **public relations** 広報・宣伝活動

pudding ⇒ The PROOF of the pudding is in the eating.

puddle ⇒ The SUN loses nothing by shining into a puddle.

PURE 367

It is easier to PULL down than to build up.
建てるより壊すほうがたやすい。

確立されている制度・評判などを破壊することに対する警告。

□**1577** R. STANYHURST *Hist. Ireland* In Hollnshed *Chronicles* 89 It is easie to raze, but hard to buylde. **1587** J. BRIDGES *Defence of Gouernment in Church of England* VI. 518 We may quicklier pull downe with one hande, than wee can easlle builde againe With both. **1644** J. HOWELL *Dodona's Grove* 134 In politicall affaires, as well as mechanicall, it is farre easier to pull downe, then build up. **1909** *Times* 29 Apr. 9 Turkey and her new rulers ... have astonished those who thought they knew the Turks best by ... the vigour ... With which the great change has been conducted.... But it is easier always and everywhere to pull down than to build up. **1932** C. BROGAN *Ghost Walks* 22 Some of the local boys tried it in the usual way. You know the kind of thing ' ... the fair fame of our city is impugned, the great achievements of our forefathers are being distorted by a morbid mind, it is easier to knock down than build up,' and so on. ■ **destruction 破壊**

PUNCTUALITY is the politeness of princes.
時間厳守は君主の礼節。

フランス語 *L'exactitude est la politesse des rois.*「時間厳守は君主の礼節」（ルイ 18 世〈1755-1824〉の言葉とされる）

□**1834** M. EDGEWORTH *Helen* II. ix. 'Punctuality is the virtue of princes.' ... Mr. Harley ... would have ridiculed so antiquated a notion. **1854** SURTEES *Handley Cross* (ed. 2) xli. Punctuality is the purlitness o' princes, and I doesn't like keepln' people waitin'. **1930** G. MITCHELL *Mystery of Butcher Shop* (1990) iii. 31 'Now do try to be down In time for breakfast to-morrow morning. Remember—"Punctuality is the politeness of princes." So charming of them, I always think.' **1981** P. MCCUTCHAN *Shard calls Tune* xv. One should never keep people waiting; punctuality was the politeness of princes. ■ **politeness 礼儀正しさ；punctuality 時間厳守**

PUNCTUALITY is the soul of business.
時間厳守はビジネスの精髄。

商売上の取引において時間厳守は最も大切である。

□**1853** T. C. HALIBURTON *Wise Saws* I. iii. 'Punctuality,' sais I, 'my lord, is the soul of business.' **1911** W. CROSSING *Folk Rhymes of Devon* 16 Punctuality is the soul of business, and In these days of cheap watches there can be no excuse for anybody failing to cultivate the habit. **1940** C. DICKSON *And so to Murder* 181 Punctuality ... has been called the politeness of kings. It's more than that it's plain good business. ■ **business ビジネス・商売；punctuality 時間厳守**

punished ⇒ CORPORATIONS have neither bodies to be punished nor souls to be damned.

To the PURE all things are pure.
清い人にはすべてが清らかである。

（訳注：the pure の the は「…な人々」の意。そのような人々を包括的に表現する。*The strong* must help the weak.〈強者は弱者を助けなければならない〉）

『テトスへの手紙』1 章 15 節（欽定訳聖書）Unto the pure all things are pure: but unto them that are defiled and unbelieving is nothing pure.「清い人々には、すべてのものが清いのです。しかし、汚れた、不信仰な人々には、何一つ清いものはありません」

368 purgatory

□**1854** S. M. HAYDEN *Early Engagements* II. Would that our earth were more frequently bright-ened and purified by such spirits.... 'To the pure all things are pure.' **1895** G. ALLEN *Woman who Did* vii. Herminia, for her part, never discovered she was talked about To the pure all things are pure. **1996** 'C. AIRD' *After Effects* xiv. 161 Sloan's mother, a great churchwoman in her day, always insisted that to the pure all things were pure. ■ **virtue** 長所・徳

purgatory ⇒ ENGLAND is the paradise of women.

purpose ⇒ The DEVIL can quote Scripture for his own ends.

purse ⇒ You can't make a SILK purse out of a sow's ear.

Don't PUT the cart before the horse.
馬の前に荷車を置いたりするな。
（訳注：「本末転倒」）

物事は適切な順序で取り扱わなければならない。慣用句の (*putting*) *the cart before the horse*「本末転倒する」として一般的に使われる。

□*c***1520** R. WHITINGTON *Vulgaria* (1527) 2 That techer setteth the carte before the horse that preferreth imitacyon before preceptes. **1589** G. PUTTENHAM *Arte of English Poesie* (Arber) 181 We call it In English prouerbe, the cart before the horse, the Greeks call it Histeron proteron. **1801** M. EDGEWORTH *Belinda* iii. Esteem ever followed affection, instead of affection following esteem. Woe be to all who In morals preposterously put the cart before the horse! **2013** (*www. weeklystandard.com*) 21 Mar. Speaking at a press conference today In Ramallah, President Obama said he doesn't 'want to put the cart before the horse' In terms of dealing with the so-called settlement issue before the security issue. ■ **patience and impatience** 忍耐と性急; **ways and means** 方法と手段

PUT your money where your mouth is.
口出しするところには金も出せ。

自分の発言は行動で、特に金銭で、支えなければならない。ただし、比喩的に他の文脈でも使われる（2015年の用例）。† PUT *up or shut up*.「拳を構えよ、さもなくば黙れ」

□**1913** *New-York Tribune* 24 Aug. (online) The Utah Senator explained that he did not have them [i.e. the figures] with him. 'Put your money where your mouth is,' retorted Senator Shep-pard. 'I am surprised that that remark should by made by any Senator, even from Texas,' replied Senator Smoot. **1928** H. W. ODUM *Rainbow round my Shoulder* 132 'Bet your money, go to hell.' 'Put your money where your mouth is.' 'It is down, turn them dam' cards ... ' **2014** *www.ft.com* 19 Sept. (*heading*) Put your money where your mouth is. Why director share buying is such an important indicator. **2015** *Spectator* 17 Jan. 28 [E]very now and then you've got to put your money where your mouth is ... and sacrifice your wellbeing for the greater cause. ■ **words and deeds** 言動

Never PUT off till tomorrow what you can do today.
今日やれることを明日に延ばすな。

延滞に対する警告として使われるが、ユーモアを込めてよく前後が逆転する（1869年と1980年の用例参照）。†14世紀中頃のフランス語 *Le bien que tu peus faire au matin,*

n'attens pas le soir ne l'endemain.「午前中にできる良いことをその日の晩や翌日が
くるのを待ってはならない」

☐ *c*1386 CHAUCER *Tale of Melibee* I. 1793 An olde proverbe ... seith that 'the goodnesse that thou mayst do this day, do it, and abide nat ne delaye it nat til to-morwe'. **1616** T. DRAXE *Adages* 42 Deferre not vntill to morrow, if thou canst do it to day. **1633** J. HOWELL *Familiar Letters* 5 Sept. (1903) II. 140 Secretary Cecil ... would ofttimes speak of himself, 'It shall never be said of me that I will defer till to-morrow what I can do to-day.' **1749** CHESTERFIELD *Letter* 26 Dec. (1932) IV. 1478 No procrastination; never put off til to-morrow what you can do today. **1869** C. H. SPURGEON John *Ploughman's Talk* vii. These slow coaches think that tomorrow is better than to-day, and take for their rule an old proverb turned topsy-turvy 'Never do to-day what you can put off till tomorrow.' **1980** J. LEES-MILNE *Harold Nicolson* xv. Lord Sackville was ... a lovable, easy-going but indolent peer whose philosophy is best summarized in one of his pet sayings: 'Never do what you can possibly put off until tomorrow.' **2002** *Washington Post* 16 Feb. Cl3 (*Born Loser comic strip*) 'Brutus, weren't you going to take down the Christmas lights this weekend?' 'No ... Next weekend, Gladys! Never put off till tomorrow what you can put off till next weekend!' ■ **efficiency and inefficiency** 能率と非能率；**procrastination** 先延ばし

PUT up or shut up.
拳を構えよ、さもなくば黙れ。

元々はボクシングの俗語で、話を止めて賞金の掛け金額をつり上げるか、それとも拳を構えて戦いに備えるか、どちらかにせよという挑発として使われる。PUT your money where your mouth is.「口出しするところに金も出せ」に述べられた考えをより素朴に表わしたものである。2014年の用例は、英国の財政取締官が、株式公開買い付け（TOB）を申し出る際に会社側に厳しい時間制限を課していることを指している。

☐ **1858** *Marysville* (Ohio) *Tribune* 21 July (online) Now, if he means business, let him put up, or shut up, for this is the last communication that will come from me in regard to this fellow. **1995** *www.independent.co.uk* 23 June John Major yesterday spectacularly put his five-year tenure of Downing Street on the line by ... inviting dissidents to 'put up or shut up' and giving them just a week to mount a challenge against him. **2014** *Wall Street Journal* 27 Nov. (online) Stryker ... is one of several companies that have had plans for large acquisitions thwarted by the rule known as 'Put Up or Shut Up'. ■ **words and deeds** 言動

put ⇒ Don't put all your EGGS in one basket; You can't put NEW wine in old bottles; You cannot put an OLD head on young shoulders; Put a STOUT heart to a stey brae; Put your TRUST in God, and keep your powder dry.

pyramids ⇒ Man fears TIME, but time fears the pyramids.

The QUARREL of lovers is the renewal of love.
恋人たちの口喧嘩は恋の更新である。

 † テレンティウス『アンドロス島の女』l. 555 *Amantium irae amoris integratiost*.「恋人たちの口喧嘩は恋の更新である」

 ☐*c*1520 *Terence in English* C1 The angers of louers renew love agayn. **1576** R. EDWARDES *Paradise of Dainty Devises* 42 Now haue I founde, the prouerbe true to proue, The fallyng out of faithfull frends, is the renuyng of love. **1754** RICHARDSON *Grandison* III. xviii. The falling out of Lovers ... is the renewal of love. Axe we not now better friends than if we had never differed? **1874** TROLLOPE *Phineas Redux* II. xxix. She knew that 'the quarrel of lovers is the renewal of love'. At any rate, the woman always desires that it may be so, and endeavours to reconcile the parted ones. **1905** *Graphic* (Christmas) 14 (*caption*) The quarrel of lovers is the renewal of love. **1980** M. GILBERT *Death of Pauourlie Girl* ii. Bear in mind, ladies, that a lovers' quarrel sometimes signifies the rebirth of love. ■ **love** 愛・恋愛

quarrel ⇒（名詞）**It takes TWO to make a quarrel;**（動詞）**A BAD workman blames his tools.**

You cannot get a QUART into a pint pot.
1 パイント入りの壺に 1 クォート入れることはできない。

 1 クォートは 2 パイントに相当する、液量の英国の標準的単位である。したがって、このことわざは、あるものを、その半分の大きさしかないもののために設計された空間や容器などに無理やり合わせることはできないことを表わしている。慣用句の to get (or put) a quart into a pint pot「無理なことをする」も使われる。

 ☐*c*1896 *Daily News* 23 July 4 They had been too ambitious. They had attempted what he might describe in homely phrase as putting a quart into a pint pot. **1934** C. F. GREGG *Execution of Diamond Deutsch* xi. He whistled thoughtfully. 'You can't get a quart into a pint pot—is that it?' asked the South African officer, quick to see the reason. **1974** W. FOLEY *Child in Forest* I. 101 A quart may not go into a pint pot, but my feet had to go into those boots. **2005** S. STICKLAND *Is It an Omen?* 284 And there we were trying to cram what were still masses of things into quite a small house! ... How do you get a quart into a pint pot? ■ **great and small** 大小 ; **possibility and impossibility** 可能性と不可能性

queer ⇒ **There's NOWT so queer as folk.**

quench ⇒ **DIRTY water will quench fire.**

quote 371

question ⇒ ASK a silly question and you get a silly answer; ASK no questions and hear no lies; A CIVIL question deserves a civil answer; FOOLS ask questions that wise men cannot answer; There are TWO sides to every question.

QUICKLY come, quickly go.
すぐに手に入るものはすぐに出て行く。

（訳注：「悪銭身につかず」）

類似したものに EASY come, easy go.「簡単に入ってくるものは簡単に出て行く」がある。

☐*c*1583 B. MELBANCKE *Philotimus* 151 Quickly spent, thats easely gotten. **1631** J. MABBE tr. *F. de Rojas' Celestina* I. 8 Quickly be wonne, and quickly be lost. **1869** W. C. HAZLITT *English Proverbs* 322 Quickly come, quickly go. **1947** C. MACKENZIE *Whisky Galore* iii. Quick come, quick go. The wind got up in a moment and it will drop just as suddenly. **1979** N. GOLLER *Tomorrow's Silence* iv. 'Was he alright when you came home?' … 'Yes, what comes quickly must go quickly, that's what I say.' ■ **getting and spending 入手と浪費**

quickly ⇒ He GIVES twice who gives quickly.

quiet ⇒ The best DOCTORS are Dr Diet, Dr Quiet, and Dr Merryman.

quote ⇒ The DEVIL can quote Scripture for his own ends.

R

The RACE is not to the swift, nor the battle to the strong.
競走は必ずしも足の速い者が勝つわけではなく、戦いは必ずしも強い者が勝つわけではない。

（訳注：the swift、the strongの the は「…な人々」の意。そのような人々を包括的に表現する。the old〈老人〉、the unemployed〈失業者〉。*The* poor are getting poorer.〈貧しい人々はさらに貧しくなりつつある。「勝敗は時の運」）

『コヘレトの言葉』9章11節（欽定訳聖書）The race is not to the swift, nor the battle to the strong.「必ずしも速い者が競争に勝つのではなく、強い者が戦いに勝つものでもない」を想起させる。

□ **1632** BURTON *Anatomy of Melancholy* (ed. 4) II. iii. It is not honesty, learning, worth, wisdome, that preferres men, The race is not to the swift, nor the battell to the stronger [1638 strong]. **1873** C. M. YONGE *Pillars of House* III. xxxii. Poor child! she lay ... trying to work out ... why the race is not to the swift, nor the battle to the strong. **1901** G. B. SHAW *Caesar & Cleopatra in Three Plays for Puritans* 96 The descendants of the gods did not stay to be butchered, cousin. The battle was not to the strong; but the race was to the swift. **2002** *Washington Times* 7 Mar. Al6 The race is not to the swift, nor the battle to the strong—but how come? One good reason: Ours is an imperfect world, full to the brim with imperfect people. ■ success 成功

race ⇒ SLOW and steady wins the race.

ragged ⇒ There's many a GOOD cock come out of a tattered bag.

RAIN before seven, fine before eleven.
7 時前に雨が降れば11時前には晴れる。

英国の気象に関する観察であるが、部分的にしか該当しない。

□ **1853** *Notes & Queries* 1st Ser. VIII. 218 Weather Proverbs.... Rain before seven, fine before eleven. **1909** *Spectator* 20 Mar. 452 'Rain before seven, shine before eleven,' is one of the most trustworthy of all country saws. **1940** B. DE VOTO (*title*) Rain before seven. **1961** THIRKELL & LEJUNE *Three Score & Ten* vii. The morning of the Agricultural dawned fair and bright. Naturally there were wisebeards who shook their heads over this and said Ar, that were a bad sign for certain sure, rain before seven, fine before eleven, and stands to reason the contrairy [*sic*] holds. ■ weather lore 天気にまつわる伝承

rain ⇒ Blessed are the DEAD that the rain rains on; If in FEBRUARY there be no rain, 'tis neither good for hay nor grain; SAINT Swithun's day, if thou be fair, for forty days it will remain.

It never RAINS but it pours.
降れば必ず土砂降り。

(訳注：never ... but ＝「…すれば必ず…する」。He *never* listened to the symphony *but* tears came to his eyes.〈彼はその交響曲を聞くと必ず目に涙を浮かべた〉。「泣き面に蜂」。「2 度あることは 3 度」)

一般的には、不運な出来事 (2014年の用例参照) は続けて起こることが多いことを述べている。連続して発生する不可避の状況を導く but は古風な用法である。

□**1726** J. ARBUTHNOT (*title*) It cannot rain but it pours. **1770** C. BURNEY *Music, Men and Manners in France and Italy* (1974) 22 July 54 The singers were the same as I had heard at the Burletta.... 'It never rains, but it pours!' **1857** TROLLOPE *Barchester Towers* III. xii. A wife with a large fortune too. It never rains but it pours, does it, Mr. Thorne? **1979** L. BARNEA *Reported Missing* vii. I listened to the radio. Ben Gurion had suffered a stroke.... It never rains but it pours. **2002** *Washington Post* 1 Mar. C5 When it rains, it pours, and Matt Sullivan is being flooded out by women who want to have sex with him. **2014** *Times* 29 May 3 First embroiled in a racism controversy, then petitioned for divorce by his wife—it never rains but it pours. ■ misfortune 不運

It is easier to RAISE the Devil than to lay him.
悪魔は寝かすより起こす方がたやすい。

(訳注：「寝た子を起こすな」)

厄介なことを引き起こしてはならないという警告。悪の魂を呼び出すことは、悪魔を送り返すよりもたやすい。同じく、危害を加えることは元通りにすることよりたやすい。

□**1655** T. FULLER *Church Hist Britain* x.iv. The Boy having gotten a habit of counterfeiting ... would not be undeviled by all their Exorcisms, so that the Priests raised up a Spirit which they could not allay. **1725** N. BAILEY tr. *Erasmus' Colloquies* 202 'Tis an old Saying and a true, 'Tis an easier Matter to raise the Devil, than 'tis to lay him. **1845** MACAULAY *Works* (1898) XII. 136 Did you think, when, to serve your turn, you called the Devil up, that it was as easy to lay him as to raise him? **2003** *National Post's Financial Post & FP Investing* (Canada) 5 May FP6 The latest revelation about Qwest wasn't the only reminder that, as Erasmus once said, it's easier to raise the devil than to lay him to rest. ■ good and evil 正邪 ; prudence 思慮・分別

ransom ⇒ A PECK of March dust is worth a king's ransom.

rat ⇒ The CAT, the rat, and Lovell the dog, rule all England under the hog.

reap ⇒ Sow an act, and you reap a habit; As you sow, so you reap; They that sow the wind shall reap the whirlwind.

There is REASON in the roasting of eggs.
卵を焼くなどという行動にもそれなりの理由がある。

(訳注：roast ＝「〈肉野菜などを〉オーブンまたは直火で焼く」。卵の場合には、普通はそのようなことはしない)

たとえどれほど奇妙に思えても、いかなる行動にもそれなりの理由がある。

□**1659** J. HOWELL *Proverbs* (English) 12 Ther's reason in rosting of Eggs. **1785** J. BOSWELL

Journal of Tour of Hebrides 24 (*note*) Every man whatever is more or less a cook, in seasoning what he himself eats. —Your definition is good, said Mr. Burke, and I now see the full force of the common proverb, 'There is reason in roasting of eggs'. **1867** TROLLOPE *Last Chronicle of Barset* II. lxxv. But there's reason in the roasting of eggs, and ... money is not so plentiful ... that your uncle can afford to throw it into the Barchester gutters. **1915** SOMERVILLE & ROSS *In Mr. Knox's Country* ix. I seemed to myself merely an imbecile, sitting in heavy rain, staring at a stone wall. Half an hour, or more, passed. 'I'm going out of this,' I said to myself defiantly; 'there's reason in the roasting of eggs.' ■ idiosyncrasy 特異性

recalled ⇒ Things PAST cannot be recalled.

receive ⇒ It is BETTER to give than to receive.

If there were no RECEIVERS, there would be no thieves.
そもそも盗品を買う者がいなかったら、盗人もいない。

（訳注：if ... would という仮定法過去形の構文を用いて、現実に反する仮想、すなわち、「反実仮想」を表わしている。それゆえ、現実には盗品を買う者がおり、盗人もいることが含意されている。このことわざが意味することは、The receiver is as bad as the thief.〈盗品を買う者も、盗人と同じ程度には悪人であるということである〉）

receivers は盗品を買ったり、横流しする輩を指す。彼らがいなければ、盗みは盗人にとって割に合わない行為である。

□ *c*1390 CHAUCER *Cook's Tale* 1. 4415 There is no theefwith-oute a lowke [accomplice], That helpeth hym to wasten and to sowke [cheat]. **1546** J. HEYWOOD *Dialogue of Proverbs* I. xii F1 This prouerbe preeues, Where be no receyuers, there be no theeues. **1614** T. ADAMS *Devil's Banquet* II. 67 The Calumniator is a wretched Thiefe, and robs man of the best thing he hath.... But if there were no receiuer, there would be no Thiefe. **1884** R. JEFFERIES *Red Deer* v. No one would buy a stolen deer, knowing the inevitable consequences, and as there are no receivers ... there are no thieves. **1926** *Times* 22 Nov. 11 It had often been said in those Courts that if there were no receivers there would be no thieves. ■ associates 仲間 ; wrong-doers 悪事をなす者

reckoning ⇒ AFTER the feast comes the reckoning; SHORT reckonings make long friends.

recommendation ⇒ SELF-praise is no recommendation.

RED sky at night, shepherd's delight; red sky in the morning, shepherd's warning.
赤い夕焼けは羊飼いの喜び。赤い朝焼けは羊飼いへの警告。

（訳注：「朝焼けは雨、夕焼けは晴」）

天候に関することわざの中でも最も古いものの 1 つで、羊飼いのみならず、船乗りによっても使われる（1893 年と 1995 年の用例参照）。『マタイによる福音書』16 章 2 - 3 節（欽定訳聖書）When it is evening, ye say, It will be fair weather: for the sky is red. And in the morning, It will be foul weather to day: for the sky is red and louring. 「あなたがたは夕方になると、空がまっかだから晴れだと言い、また明け方には空が曇ってまっかだから今日は荒れだと言う」を想起させる。*c*1395 ウィクリフ聖書『マタイによる福音書』16 章 2 - 3 節 The eeuenynge maad, ye seien, It shal be cleer, for the

heuene is lijk to reed; and the morwe, To day tempest, for heuen shyneth heuy,
or sorwful.「イエスは彼らに言われた。『あなた方は夕方になると、"空がまっかだから
晴れだ"と言い、また明け方には"空が曇ってまっかだから今日は荒れだ"と言う』」

□*c*1454 R. PECOCK *Follower to Donet* (EETS) 54 We trowen [believe] that this day schal be
a reyny day for that his morownyng was reed, or that to morow schal be a fayre day for that his
euentide is reed. 1893 R. INWARDS *Weather Lore* 53 Sky red in the morning Is a sailor's sure
warning; Sky red at night Is the sailor's delight. 1920 *Punch* 14 July 36 Red sky at night shepherd's delight ... Red sky in the morning shepherd's warning. 1979 P. ALEXANDER *Show me
Hero* xxv. 'Going to be a fine day,' he said at last 'Red sky in the morning, shepherd's warning,'
Ashman said. 1995 R. ORMEROD *And Hope to Die* ii. 15 The next morning it was raining steadily, this in spite of the flush of sunset the evening before.... Red sky at night, shepherds' delight
Well all right, perhaps so, if they'd been praying for rain. 2002 M. DAHL *Coral Coffin* ii. 16 Pink
clouds sailed high over the island. What was that saying I had heard from Uncle Stoppard? Red
skies at night: a sailor's delight Red skies at morning: a sailor takes warning. ■ **weather lore** 天気
にまつわる伝承

redressed ⇒ A FAULT confessed is half redressed.

A REED before the wind lives on, while mighty oaks do fall.
嵐に対して葦は生き延びるが、強い樫の木は倒れる。
　（訳注：on =〈ある動作を〉続けて、どんどん、ずっと」。walk *on*〈歩き続ける〉。「柳に雪折れなし」）

背が低く柔軟性のある葦は、背の高い樫の木を倒すような嵐の中でも生き残る。

□*c*1385 CHAUCER *Troilus & Criseyde* II. 1387 And reed that boweth down for every blast, Ful
lightly, cesse wynd, it wol aryse. 1621 BURTON *Anatomy of Melancholy* II. iii. Though I liue obscure, yet I liue cleane and honest, and when as the lofty oake is blowne downe, the silly [frail]
reed may stand. 1732 T. PULLER *Gnomologia* no. 3692 Oaks may fall, when Reeds stand the
Storm. 1954 R. HAYDN *Journal of Edwin Carp* 20 Remembering that 'a reed before the wind lives
on—while mighty oaks do fall,' I attempted to remove the pencil marks with my pocket eraser.
■ **great and small** 大小 ; **strength and weakness** 強弱

refuse ⇒ The SEA refuses no river.

regulated ⇒ ACCIDENTS will happen (in the best-regulated families).

rejoice ⇒ It is a POOR heart that never rejoices.

There is a REMEDY for everything except death.
死以外のあらゆるものには治療法がある。

より良いものを望み、そしてそのために働くことを推奨する際に使われる。 †中世ラテ
ン語 *Contra malum mortis, non est medicamen in hortis.*「死という悪魔に対しては
庭（この世）には治療薬はない」

□*c*1430 J. LYDGATE *Dance of Machabree* (EETS) I. 432 Agens deeth is worth [useful] no medicine. 1573 J. SANFORDE *Garden of Pleasure* 52 There is a remedie for all things, sauing for
death. 1620 T. SHELTON tr. *Cervantes' Don Quixote* II. lxiv. There is a remedy for everything but
death, said Don Quixote; for tis but hauing a Barke ready at the Sea side, and in spite of all the
world we may embarke our selues. *a*1895 F. LOCKER-LAMPSON *My Confidences* (1896) 95 There

is a remedy for everything except Death ... so the bitterness of this disappointment has long passed away. **1974** *Times* 30 Sept 25 I found the same readiness to wait reflected in a Spanish proverb which was quoted to me: *Para todo hay remedio menos para la muerte* (there is a cure for everything except death). It was a housewife speaking of Gibraltar's present difficulties, and she meant that sooner or later a way out would be found. ■ **death** 死 **; finality** 終末・終局

remedy ⇒ DESPERATE diseases must have desperate remedies.

remember ⇒ Feed a DOG for three days and he will remember your kindness for three years....

removal ⇒ THREE removals are as bad as a fire.

renewal ⇒ The QUARREL of lovers is the renewal of love.

repair ⇒ A WOMAN and a ship ever want mending.

repeat ⇒ HISTORY repeats itself.

repent ⇒ MARRY in haste and repent at leisure.

rest ⇒ (名詞) A CHANGE is as good as a rest; (動詞) AFTER dinner rest a while, after supper walk a mile.

return ⇒ A BAD penny always turns up; The DOG returns to its vomit; The TONGUE always returns to the sore tooth.

REVENGE is a dish that can be eaten cold.
復讐は冷えた状態でも食べられる料理である。

（訳注：この場合の cold は eat a dish cold〈食事を冷めた状態で食べる〉という意味的な関係になっている。eat fish raw〈魚を生で食べる〉の場合の raw と並行している）

復讐は急いで実行する必要はない。ただし逆の場合もある。† **1620** T. SHELTON tr. *Cervantes' Don Quixote* II. lxiii. Reuenge is not good in cold bloud. 「復讐は冷えた状態ではおいしくない」。Revenge is a dish best served cold. 「復讐は冷えた状態で出すのが最高の料理である」

☐**1885** C. LOWE *Prince Bismarck* I. iv. He had defended Olmütz, it is true, but ... with a secret resolution to 'eat the dish of his revenge cold instead of hot'. **1895** J. PAYN *In Market Overt* xvii. Invective can be used at any time; like vengeance, it is a dish that can be eaten cold. **1975** J. O'FAOLAIN *Women in Wall* iii. Revenge ... is a meal that's as tasty cold as hot Tastier cold sometimes. **1997** *Washington Post* 6 Nov. E6 Revenge is a dish best served cold. Let's see what happens one of these cold Octobers. **2015** *Times* 2 20 Jan.7 I had wondered ... which of my organs would be most vulnerable to the 'crab' [i.e. cancer]. Would it be the demon rum's revenge— his dish eaten 30 years cold? ■ **patience and impatience** 忍耐と性急 **; revenge** 復讐

RICH 377

REVENGE is sweet.
復讐は甘美である。

† ホロメス『イーリアス』XVIII. 109 χόλος...ὅς τε πολὺ γλυκίων μέλιτος καταλειβομένοιο ἀνδρῶν ἐν στήθεσσιν ἀέξεται ἠΰτε καπνός.「怒りは…したたる蜜よりはるかに甘く、男たちが吐き出すタバコの煙のように湧き出てくる」

☐ a1566 W. PAINTER *Palace of Pleasure* 300 Vengeance is sweete vnto him, which in place of killing his enemy, giueth life to a perfect frende. **1609** JONSON *Silent Woman* IV. v. O reuenge, how sweet art thou! **1658** *Whole Duty of Man* xvi. 346 'Tis, a devilish phrase in the mouth of men, that revenge is sweet.... Is it possible there can be any such sweetnesse in it? **1775** SHERIDAN *St. Patrick's Day* II. 22 'Revenge is sweet' ... and though disappointed of my designs upon your daughter, ... I'm revenged on her unnatural father. **1861** H. KINGSLEY *Ravenshoe* II. x. Revenge is sweet—to some. Not to him. **1980** J. PORTER *Dover beats Band* xv. He came to the conclusion that though revenge may be sweet, knowledge ... is better than money in the bank. ■ **revenge 復讐**

revenue ⇒ THRIFT is a great revenue.

REVOLUTIONS are not made with rose-water.
革命はバラの香水をふりかけることではなし得ない。

（訳注：解説で言及されているシャンフォール〈N. Chamfort〉はフランスの作家。機知に富んだ警句・箴言でよく知られている。標題の言葉のほかにも、「機会が二度扉を叩くなどと思うな」、「真の幸福は眼に映らない」、「信念は精神の良心である」など幾多の名言を残している）

1789 シャンフォールの言葉。マルモンテル『作品集』(1818) II. 294 *Voulez-vous qu'on vous fasse des revolutions a l'eau rose.*「革命はバラの香水をふりかけてなされるべきだと言うのですか」

☐ **1819** BYRON *Letter* 3 Oct. (1976) VI. 226 On either side harm must be done before good can accrue—revolutions are not to be made with rose water. **1894** J. LUBBOCK *Use of Life* xi. It is sometimes said that Revolutions are not made with rose-water. Greater changes, however, have been made in the constitution of the world by argument than by arms. *a***1931** T. M. HEALY letter in F. Callanan *T. M. Healy* (1996) The Sinns won in three years what we did not win in forty. You cannot make revolutions with rosewater, or omelettes without breaking eggs. ■ **politics 政治**；**rulers and ruled 支配者と非支配者**；**ways and means 方法と手段**

reward ⇒ VIRTUE is its own reward.

The RICH man has his ice in the summer and the poor man gets his in the winter.
夏でも氷が手に入るのが金持ち、冬にならないと氷が手に入らないのが貧乏人。

（訳注：his ＝「彼のもの」。The car is *his*.「その車は彼のものだ」）

☐ **1921** W. B. MASTERSON in *Morning Telegraph* (NY) 27 Oct. 7 There are those who argue that everything breaks even in this old dump of a world of ours.... These ginks who argue that way hold that because the rich man gets ice in the Summer and the poor man gets it in the winter things are breaking even for both. *a***1957** L. I. WILDER *First Four Years* (1971) ii. Everything evens up in the end.... The rich man has his ice in the summer and the poor man gets his in the winter. **1986** J. W. RIDER *Jersey Tomatoes* xi. The rich get ice in the summer and the poor get it in the winter, so some people figure everyone gets an even break. ■ **equality 平等**；**poverty 貧困**；

378 rich

riches 富

rich ⇒ It is BETTER to be born lucky than rich; One LAW for the rich and another for the poor.

If you can't RIDE two horses at once, you shouldn't be in the circus.
同時に 2 頭の馬を乗りこなすことができなければ、サーカス団にいるべきではない。

英国独立自由党の国会議員（在職期間1932-46）を務めたジェームス・マクストンの言葉とされる（1935年の用例参照）。デニス・ヒーリー（2002年の用例参照）も英国労働党の議員であり、おそらく意識的にマクストンの言葉を引用している。

□**1935** G. MCALLISTER *James Maxton* xiv. Maxton made a brief intervention in the debate to say ... that he did not believe it was necessary to pass a resolution for disaffiliation [of the ILP from the Labour Party]. He had been told that he could not ride two horses. 'My reply to that is', he said ... 'that if my friend cannot ride two horses—what's he doing in the bloody circus?' **1979** *Daily Telegraph* 15 Mar. 15 A producer who 'can't ride two horses at the same time shouldn't be in the circus.' ... Current affairs television should be both serious and entertaining. **2002** *National Review* 3 June 18 But politics is a practical activity, not an intellectual one. As Denis Healey once said, if you can't ride two horses at once, you shouldn't be in the bloody circus. ■ **efficiency and inefficiency** 能率と非能率 ; **stress** ストレス

ride ⇒ Set a BEGGAR on horseback, and he'll ride to the Devil; If TWO ride on a horse, one must ride behind; If WISHES were horses, beggars would ride.

He who RIDES a tiger is afraid to dismount.
虎の背中に乗っている者はこわくて降りることができない。

（訳注：降りると虎に襲われてしまう。he＝「〈関係節を伴って〉…する者は誰でも〈性別は問わない〉」。*He who* has all the gold makes all the rules.〈金をすべて持つ者が法をすべて支配する〉）

ひとたび危険で難儀な冒険的投資が開始されたら、最も安全なコースは最後までやり通すことである。

□**1875** W. SCARBOROUGH *Collection of Chinese Proverbs* no. 2082 He who rides a tiger is afraid to dismount.... Ch'i 'hu nan hsia pei. **1902** A. R. COLQUHOUN *Mastery of Pacific* xvi. These colonies are ... for her [France] the tiger which she has mounted (to use the Chinese phrase) and which she can neither manage nor get rid of. **1983** W. HARRISS *Bay Psalm Book Murder* x. 'But no doubt about it, I've got a tiger by the tail now.' 'And there's an Oriental saying that the man who rides the tiger is afraid to get off. Watch your step.' ■ **peril** 危険

ridiculous ⇒ From the SUBLIME to the ridiculous is only a step.

right ⇒ The CUSTOMER is always right; DO right and fear no man; GOD's in his heaven, all's right with the world; MIGHT is right; TWO wrongs don't make a right.

ring ⇒ GIVE a thing, and take a thing, to wear the Devil's gold ring.

ripe ⇒ SOON ripe, soon rotten.

ROAD 379

rise ⇒ EARLY to bed and early to rise, makes a man healthy, wealthy, and wise; A STREAM cannot rise above its source.

A RISING tide lifts all the boats.
上げ潮はあらゆる船を持ち上げる。

主に米国で使われる。ケネディ家によって世に広まったことわざの 1 つである。現在では一般に経済の分野で使用される。ここで tide は幸運の時流を意味するが、1915年の用例は社会的、精神的資本を指している。

☐**1915** Charlotte [NC] *Observer* 26 Sept 'The rising tide lifts all ships.' ... A sense of solidarity In fellowship and service increases the 'esprit de corps.' **1963** J. F. KENNEDY *Address* 25 June in Public Papers of Presidents of U.S. (1964) 519 As they say on my own Gape Cod, a rising tide lifts all the boats. And a partnership, by definition, serves both partners, without domination or unfair advantage. **1990** *Washington Times* 6 Mar. C2 The country was in a sharp economic expansion coming out of '82. This made everybody look smart—you know, the rising tide lifts all boats. **2011** *Times* 1 Jan. 41 A rising tide floats all boats, and the extraordinary wave of business optimism that ripples out from Asia will continue to lap beneficially at shores even as far away as Britain. ■ **good fortune 幸運**

river ⇒ If you have to LIVE in the river, it is best to be friends with the crocodile; The SEA refuses no river; If you SIT by the river for long enough....

The ROAD to hell is paved with good intentions.
地獄への道は善意で舗装されている。

当初の形では最初の 3 語 (The ROAD to) が省略されていた。†聖フランシスコ・サレジオ『書簡集』lxxiv. *Le proverbe tire de notre saint Bernard, 'L'enfer est plein de bonnes volontes ou desirs'.*「『地獄は善意や願望に満ちている』ということわざは我らの聖ベルナルドに由来する」

☐**1574** E. HELLOWES tr. *Guevara's Epistles* 205 Hell is full of good desires. **1654** R. WHITLOCK *Observations on Manners of English* 203 It is a saying among Divines, that Hell is full of good Intentions, and Meanings. **1736** WESLEY *Journal* 10 July(l910) I. I. 246 It is a true saying, 'Hell is paved with good intentions'. **1847** J. A. PROUDE *Shadows of Clouds* ix. I shall have nothing to hand in, except intentions, —what they say the road to the wrong place is paved with. **1855** H. G. BOHN *Hand-Book of Proverbs* 514 The road to hell is paved with good intentions. **2011** *Washington Times* 5 Dec. D8 (*Herb & Jamaal comic strip*) 'I'm sorry if I made things a mess with you and Yolanda. But I'll have you know that I had nothing but good intentions.' 'They say, "The road to ruin is paved with good intentions." ... and you keep making potholes.' ■ **action and inaction 行為と非行為 ; intentions 意図**

What happens on the ROAD stays on the road.
道中で起きることは道中だけの話。
（訳注：「旅の恥はかき捨て」）

† What goes on TOUR stays on tour.「旅先で起こることは旅先だけの話」。What happens in VEGAS stays in Vegas.「ラス・ベガスで起こることはラス・ベガスだけの話」(この街は賭博で有名)も同じ趣旨。

380 road

□**2001** M. LOVELACE in C. Lindahl *Perspectives on Jack Tales* 158 Nothing of this bet is revealed to the faithful sweetheart at home, of course … As contemporary athletes say about the sexual opportunities on road trips: 'What happens on the road, stays on the road.' **2011** B. BERRY *Chronicles of Idiot* 97 Vicki remembers that she saw a rock star who, when talking about affairs on the road said, 'What happens on the road, stays on the road.' She thinks it may be as simple as switching out 'road' for 'Vegas' and there is your slogan. ■ **discretion** 思慮分別 ; **speech and silence** 発言と沈黙

road ⇒ There is no ROYAL road to learning.

All ROADS lead to Rome.
すべての道はローマに通ず。

（訳注：同じ目的を達するにも方法・手段はいろいろある。解説で言及されているチョーサーの著作『アストロラーベに関する論文』の「アストロラーベ」*Astrolabe* とは、古代の天文学者や占星術者が用いた天体観測用の機器を指している）

実際のものであれ、比喩的なものであれ、すべてのルートは1つの中心地に集まる。この表現を生み出した歴史的な状況は、当時の人々がローマ帝国の最大都市ローマに魅了されていたということである（2002年の用例参照）。†中世ラテン語 *Mille vie ducunt hominem per secula Romam*.「千の道は人を常にローマに連れて行く」。*c*1391 チョーサー『アストロラーベに関する論文』序 I. 40 Right as diverse pathes Ieden diverse folk the righte way to Rome.「様々な道が様々な民を正しくローマに導くように正しい」

□**1806** R. THOMSON tr. *La Fontaine's Fables* IV. XII. xxiv. All roads alike conduct to Rome. **1872** W. BLACK *Strange Adventures of Phaeton* vi. You know all roads lead to Rome, and they say that Oxford is half-way to Rome. **1912** J. S. HUXLEY *Individual in Animal Kingdom* vi. All roads lead to Rome: and even animal individuality throws a ray on human problems. **2002** *Spectator* 16 Feb. 21 All roads, of course, led to Rome: an expression of Rome's control over the empire's landscape and populace. ■ **beginnings and endings** 最初と最後 ; **ways and means** 方法と手段

roasting ⇒ There is REASON in the roasting of eggs.

robbery ⇒ A fair EXCHANGE is no robbery.

The ROBIN and the wren are God's cock and hen; the martin and the swallow are God's mate and marrow.
コマドリとミソサザイは神が定めた雄鶏と雌鶏である。イワ燕と燕は神が定めたつがいの相手である。

小さくてか弱い鳥も特別な神の保護下にある（1787年の用例参照）。†『ルカによる福音書』12章6節（欽定訳聖書）Are not five sparrows sold for two farthings, and not one of them is forgotten before God?「5羽の雀は2アサリオンで売っているでしょう。そんな雀1羽でも、神の御前には忘れられてはいません」。marrow は廃語（方言は除く）で、「他のものと対をなすもの」を意味する。脚韻（wren と hen、swallow と marrow）は多くの異形でも使われる。*a*1508 J. スケルトン『詩集』(1969) 45 The pretty wren … is our Ladyes hen.「美しいミソサザイは…女王の雌鶏である」

ROLLING 381

□**1787** F. GROSE *Provincial Glossary* (Popular Superstitions) 64 There is a particular distich in favour of the robin and wren: A robin and wren Are God Almighty's cock and hen. Persons killing [them] ... or destroying their nests, will infallibly, within the course of a year, break a bone, or meet with some other dreadful misfortune. On the contrary, it is deemed lucky to have martins and swallows build their nests in the eaves of a house. **1826** R. WILBRAHAM *Cheshire Glossary* (ed. 2) 105 The following metrical adage is common in Cheshire: The Robin and the Wren Are God's cock and hen, The Martin and the Swallow are God's mate and marrow. **1945** F. THOMPSON *Lark Rise* ix. No boy would rob a robin's or a wren's nest ... for they believe that: The robin and the wrens Be God Almighty's friends. And the martin and the swallow Be God Almighty's birds to follow. ■ **bird lore 鳥にまつわる逸話**

ROBIN Hood could brave all weathers but a thaw wind.
ロビンフッドはいかなる天気にも耐えることができたが、霜解け風だけには耐えられなかった。

（訳注：but =「…を除いて」。All *but* him were present.〈彼以外はみな出席していた〉）

イングランド北部の特に厳しい天候を指す表現で、我慢強さの代名詞とも言える有名な無法者（つまりロビンフッド）でさえ耐えられない寒さを指す。thaw wind「霜解け風」とはイングランド南部や東南部から吹いてくる冷たい肌を刺すような風のことで、長期に及んだ霜を溶かすことで知られている（J. ブリッジ『チェシャーのことわざ集』）。

□**1855** W. NEVILLE *Life & Exploits of Robin Hood* ii. Every one, at least every Yorkshireman, is familiar with the observation that Robin Hood could brave all weathers but a thaw wind. **1931** J. BUCHAN *Blanket of Dark* xii. I dread the melting wind which makes seas of rivers and lakes of valleys. Robin Hood feared little above ground, but he feared the thaw-wind. ■ **weather lore 天気にまつわる伝承**

rock ⇒（名詞）who won't be RULED by the rudder must be ruled by the rock;（動詞）The HAND that rocks the cradle rules the world.

Up like a ROCKET, down like a stick.
ロケットのように上昇し、棒のように落下する。

フランス革命に関して行なわれた庶民院での論争において、エドマンド・バークの詭弁をトマス・ペインが愚弄した言葉に由来する（1792年の用例参照）。2014年の用例はこのことわざを財政の文脈に置き換えたもので、現在ではこちらの方が主流となっている。

□**1792** T. PAINE *Letter to Addressers on Late Proclamation* 4 As he rose like a rocket, he fell like the stick. **1922** JOYCE *Ulysses* 364 Up like a rocket, down like a stick. **1974** A. MENEN *Fonthill* (1975) 53 I believe he died loaded with debts. Well, up like a rocket and down like the stick, I always say. **2014** *www.fidelity.co.uk* 5 June Paine was not talking about share prices when he first coined the expression 'up like a rocket, down like a stick'. But ... it is a great description of the parabolic rise and rapid collapse that marks the fall from grace of a stock market darling. ■ **ambition 野心・野望；pride 誇り・うぬぼれ**

rod ⇒ SPARE the rod and spoil the child.

A ROLLING stone gathers no moss.
転石苔むさず。

（訳注：転職などを肯定的に捉えて、いい意味に解釈される場合もある）

いつも休むことなく旅をしたり、職を変えたり、交際する人を変えたりする人は決して成功したり、満足することはない。†エラスムス『格言集』III. iv. λίθος κυλινδόμενος τὸ φῦκος οὐ ποιεῖ.「転がる石には海藻はつかぬ」。*Musco lapis volutus haud obducitur.* 「転がる石は苔で覆われることはない」

☐ **1362** LANGLAND *Piers Plowman* A. x. 101 Selden Moseth [becomes mossy] the Marbelston that men ofte treden. **1546** J. HEYWOOD *Dialogue of Proverbs* I. xi. D2 The rollyng stone neuer gatherth mosse. **1579** S. GOSSON *Ephemerides of Phialo* 5ᵛ A rowling stone gathers no mosse, and a running hed wil neuer thriue. **1710** A. PHILIOPS *Pastorals* II. 8 A Rolling Stone is ever bare of Moss. **1841** DICKENS *Old Curiosity Shop* II. xlviii. Your popular rumour, unlike the rolling stone of the proverb, is one which gathers a deal of moss in its wanderings up and down. **1979** *Listener* 5 July 16 A roadside notice ... said in one long line: *Loose stones travel slowly*. Well, I dare say they do: rolling stones, we know, gather no moss. ■ constancy and inconstancy 安定と不安定 ; human nature 人間性

When in ROME, do as the Romans do.
ローマではローマ人のごとく振る舞え。
（訳注：「郷に入っては郷に従え」）

現在暮らしている土地の習慣に従うのが賢明である。†聖アンブロシウスの言葉で、聖アウグスティヌス『書簡集』xxxvi. 32 (Migne), *Quando hie sum, non ieiuno sabbato; quando Romae sum, ieiuno sabbato.*「ここ（つまりミラノ）にいるときは土曜日はゆっくり過ごす。しかし、ローマにいるときは土曜日でも忙しくしている」に引用されている。**1660** ジェレミー・テイラー *Ductor Dubitantium* (1851) I. i. 5. 5 *Cumfueris Romae, Romano vivito more, cum fueris alibi, vivito sicut ibi.*「ローマではローマ人のごとく暮らせ。よそにいるときは当地の人々のごとく暮らせ」では韻文の形式を取っている。

☐ *c***1475** in *Modern Philology* (1940) XXXVIII. 122 Whan tho herd hat Rome Do so of ther the dome [when you are at Rome do as they do there]. **1552** R. TAVERNER tr. *Erasmus' Adages* (ed. 3) 51ᵛ That which is commonly in euery mans mouth in England Whan you art at Rome, do as they do at Rome. **1836** B. HOWARD *Rattlin the Reefer* I. xxii. 'Do at Rome as the Romans do,' is the essence of all politeness. **1960** N. MITFORD *Don't tell Alfred* viii. 'I thought the English never bothered about protocol?' 'When in Rome, however, we do as the Romans do.' **2001** *Washington Post* 8 Dec. A25 One woman stationed there [Saudi Arabia] who purports to be comfortable with the rules said, 'When in Rome, do as the Romans do.' But how far does that go? To feeding the lions? ■ circumstances 状況 ; conduct 行ない・品行

ROME was not built in a day.
ローマは一日にして成らず。
（訳注：「大器晩成」）

大事業は短時間で達成するものではない。†中世フランス語 *Rome ne fut pas faite toute en un jour.*「ローマは一日にしてならず」

☐ **1545** R. TAVERNER tr. *Erasmus' Adages* (ed. 2) D1ᵛ Rome was not buylt in one daye. **1546** J. HEYWOOD *Dialogue of Proverbs* I. xi. D4 Rome was not bylt on a daie (quoth he) and yet stood Tyll it was fynysht **1646** in *Publications of Prince Society* (1865) I. 236 Rome was not built in a day.... Let them produce any colonie ... where more hath been done in 16 yeares. **1849** C. BRONTË *Shirley* I. vi. As Rome ... had not been built in a day, so neither had Mademoiselle Gerard Moore's education been completed in a week. **2001** *Times 2* 6 Nov. 15 Even then, £14 mil-

ROPE 383

lion must still be found from private sources. Not easy.... Still, Rome wasn't built in a day. ■
haste 性急；patience and impatience 忍耐と性急

Rome ⇒ All ROADS lead to Rome; It is ill SITTING at Rome and striving with the Pope.

There is always ROOM at the top.
最上の地位はいつも空いている。

米国の政治家ダニエル・ウェブスター（1782-1852）の言葉である（1866年の用例参照）。

□**1866** *Bangor* [ME] *Daily Whig & Courier* 27 Feb. 3/4 When Daniel Webster was a young man
... he was advised not to enter the legal profession, for it was already crowded. His reply was, —
'There is room enough at the top'. *a***1871** A. CARY 'A Sermon' in Poetical Works of Alice &
Phoebe Cary (1882) 274 Believe me there's truth in the saying: 'There always is room at the top'.
1900 W. JAMES *Letter* 2 Apr. (1920) II. 121 Verily there is room at the top. S—seems to be the
only Britisher worth thinking of. **1914** A. BENNEIT *Price of Love* vii. The Imperial had set out to
be the most gorgeous cinema in the Five Towns; and it simply was. Its advertisements read:
'There is always room at the top.' **1957** J. DRAINE *Room at Top* xxviii. You're the sort of young
man we want. There's always room at the top. **1980** M. DRABBLE *Middle Ground* 140 There's
room at the top, maybe, but only for the clever ones. ■ ambition 野心・野望

roost ⇒ CURSES, like chickens, come home to roost.

root ⇒ IDLENESS is the root of all evil; MONEY is the root of all evil.

Give a man ROPE enough and he will hang himself.
人に縄を存分に与えると、首を吊ってしまう。

ここでは、ropeは文字通りの意味「縄」と比喩的な意味「許可、自由」の両方の意味で使わ
れている。

□**1639** T. FULLER *Holy War* v. vii. they were suffered to have rope enough, till they had haltered
themselves. **1670** J. RAY *English Proverbs* 148 Give a thief rope enough, and he'll hang himself.
1698 in *William & Mary College Quarterly* (1950) VII. 106 The Kings prerogative ... will be hard
for his Successor to retrieve, though there's a saying give Men Rope enough, they will hang
themselves. **1876** TROLLOPE *Prime Minister* II. xvii. Give Sir Orlando rope enough and he'll hang
himself. **1941** G. BAGBY *Red is for Killing* x. 'I like to build a pretty complete case before making
an arrest.' ... 'If you give a man enough rope he hangs himself.' **2014** *Spectator* 22 Nov. 80 True,
there wasn't always an enormous difference between letting the interviewees speak for themselves and giving them enough rope. ■ ways and means 方法と手段；wrong-doers 悪事をなす者

Never mention ROPE in the house of a man who has been hanged.
縛り首になった人の家ではロープの話は禁物である。

話相手を悲しませるような話題を口にすることは無作法で礼儀に反する。1995年の用例
では、フランクリン・D・ルーズベルト（1882-1945）の言葉とされているが、起源はさら
に遡る。

□**1599** J. MINSHEU *Spanish Dialogues* I. A man ought not to make mention of a halter in the
house of a man that was hanged. **1620** T. SHELTON tr. *Don Quixote* III. xi. why doe I name an
Asse with my mouth, seeing one should not make mention of a rope in ones house that was
hanged? **1890** J. PAYN *Burnt Million* xxxii. Miss Grace, whom he pictured ... as sensitive upon

384 rope

the matter as though If her parent had been hung she would have been to an allusion to a rope. **1958** 'J. S. Strange' *Night of Reckoning* viii. Never mention rope in the house of a man who has been hanged. **1995** *Washington Times* 14 July A4 Whenever he hears the very word 'Vietnam' shame could compel Mr. Clinton to excuse himself.... He should remember FDR's famous admonition to avoid speaking of rope in the house of a man recently hanged. ■ **tact 機転**

rope ⇒ The man who has once been BITTEN by the snake fears every piece of rope.

No ROSE without a thorn.
とげのない薔薇はない。

（訳注：「楽あれば苦あり」）

望まれるものには常に負の側面がある。†クラウディウスの言葉。 *In Nuptias Honorii ... Fescennina* iv. 10 *Armat spina rosas, mella tegunt apes.*「とげで武装した薔薇、蜂が蜜を隠すようだ」に引用されている。

□**1430-40** LYDGATE *Bochas* Prol. ix There is no rose ... in garden, but there be sum thorne. **1579** LYLY *Euphues* i. 184 The sweetest Rose hath his prickel. **1603** J. FLORIO tr. *Montaigne's Essays* III. iii. 68 But no good without paines; no Roses without prickles. **1670** J. RAY *English Proverbs* 138 No rose without a thorn. **1922** JOYCE *Ulysses* Queer the number of pins they always have. No roses without thorns. **1965** H. ACTON *Old Lamps* 218 'But everything depends on the baby. What a bore.' 'No rose without a thorn, eh?' ■ **good and evil 正邪**

roses ⇒ He who PLANTS thorns should not expect to gather roses; Do not grieve that ROSE-TREES have thorns.

Do not grieve that ROSE-trees have thorns, rather rejoice that thorny bushes bear roses.
薔薇の木にとげがあることを嘆いてはならない。むしろとげのあるやぶに薔薇が咲くことを喜べ。

アラビアのことわざ。

□**1965** S. RADHAKRISHNAN 'Failure of the UN and nuclear weapons' (on *www.indian embassy. org*) We have to protect humanity against war. Peace is not the absence of war ... It is the disarmament of minds that is called for. The future is not all bleak. An old Arab proverb says, 'Do not grieve that rose trees have thorns, rather rejoice that thorny bushes bear roses'. **2005** C. VIDYA SAGAR 'Independence of judiciary under cloud' in *Daily Excelsior* 15 Mar. (*on www.southasianmedia.ne*) 'Do not grieve that rose trees have thorns, rather rejoice that thorny bushes have roses.' Mr Hans Raj Bhardwaj, right from the day he took over as Union Law Minister, has been, day in and day out, grieving that there is malfunctioning of judicial system in our country. ■ **content and discontent 満足と不満足**

rose-water ⇒ REVOLUTIONS are not made with rose-water.

rot ⇒ ONE for the mouse, one for the crow; WINTER never rots in the sky.

rule   385

The ROTTEN apple injures its neighbor.
腐ったりんごは周りのりんごも腐らせる。
（訳注：「朱に交われば赤くなる」）

性悪の人は接する人すべてを堕落させてしまうので注意せよという警告。以下に挙げるように多くの異なった言い方がある。†ラテン語*Pomum compunctum cito corrumpit sibi junctum.*「腐ったりんごは周りのりんごをすぐに腐らせる」

□**1340** *Ayenbite of Inwit* (EETS) 205 A roted eppel amang the holen [whole ones], maketh rotie the yzounde [sound]. **1577** J. NORTHBROOKE *Treatise against Dicing* 95 A peny naughtily [dishonestly] gotten, sayth Chrysostome, is like a rotten apple layd among sounde apples, which will rot all the rest. **1736** B. FRANKLIN *Poor Richard's Almanack* (July) The rotten apple spoils his companion. **1855** H. G. BOHN *Hand-Book of Proverbs* 514 The rotten apple injures its neighbour. **1979** D. MACKENZIE *Raven feathers his Nest* 19 The police ... have a deserved reputation for uprightness.... But one bad apple can spoil the whole barrel. ■ **associates 仲間 ; example, good and bad 好例と悪例**

rotten ⇒ SMALL choice in rotten apples; SOON ripe, soon rotten.

roundabout ⇒ What you LOSE on the swings you gain on the roundabouts.

There is no ROYAL road to learning.
学問に王道なし。

ギリシアの数学者エウクレイデス（ユークリッド）（紀元前300年頃活躍）が、エジプト王プトレマイオス１世に幾何学を習得する簡単な方法があるかどうか尋ねられたときの返答だとされる。†プロクロス『ユークリッド原論に関する管見』（フリードライン）68, μὴ εἶναι βασιλικὴν ἀτραπὸν ἐπὶ γεωμετρίαν.「幾何学には王の近道などない」。**1745** E. ストーン訳『ユークリッド原論』（第 2 版）II. A 2ᵛ There is no other Royal Way or Path to Geometry.「幾何学を習得するための王道はない」

□**1824** EMERSON *Journal* (1961) II. 268 There is no royal road to Learning. **1857** TROLLOPE *Barchester Towers* II. i. There is no royal road to learning; no short cutto the acquirement of any valuable art. **1941** H. G. WELLS *You can't be too Careful* II. vi. 'There's no Royal Road to Learning,' said Mr. Myame. 'No. "Thorough" has always been my motto.' **1995** *Nature* 26 Jan. 297/3 There are well-established criteria by which to distinguish homology from homoplasy but there is still no royal road to truth. ■ **diligence 勤勉 ; learning 学問・学び ; ways and means 方法と手段**

rubber ⇒ Those who PLAY at bowls must look out for rubbers.

rudder ⇒ Who won't be RULED by the rudder must be ruled by the rock

rue ⇒ MARRY in May, rue for aye.

rule ⇒ （名詞）The EXCEPTION proves the rule; There is an EXCEPTION to every rule; （動詞）DIVIDE and rule; The HAND that rocks the cradle rules the world.

Who won't be RULED by the rudder must be ruled by the rock.
舵によって支配されようとしない者は暗礁（あんしょう）によって支配されざるを得ない。

航海におけることわざで、案内されることを拒否する者は災難（岩礁）（がんしょう）に出くわすことを意味している。

□ **1666** G. TORRIANO *Italian Proverbs* 286 That ship which will have no *rudder*, must have a rock. **1823** I. DISRAELI *Curiosities of Literature* 2nd Ser. I. 459 There is a Cornish proverb, 'Those who will not be ruled by the rudder must be ruled by the rock' —the strands of Cornwall, so often covered with wrecks, could not fail to impress on the imaginations of its inhabitants the two objects from whence they drew this salutary proverb. **1911** B. WILBERFORCE *Secret of Quiet Mind* 79 Jesus ... is weeping because the spiritual blindness of the people made ... the destruction of Jerusalem ... inevitable. 'He who will not be ruled by the rudder must be ruled by the rock,' but ruled he must be. **1984** R. HENDERSON *Salty Words* 165 The nautical saying Who won't be ruled by the rudder must be ruled by the rock ... means 'those who won't listen to reason must bear the consequences'. ■ **action and consequence 行為と結果 ; discipline 規律**

RULES are made to be broken.
規則は破られるためにある。

規範を無視することを勧める言葉としてよく使われる。

□ **1858** F. NIGHTINGALE *Subsidiary Notes ... Female Nursing* 61 There is nothing so fatal to discipline as to require by regulations what it is known and admitted cannot be performed. Such rules are made to be broken. **1899** *Locomotive Firemen's Mag.* May 579/2 'Rules are made to be broken,' some one has said, and such would appear to be the case on railroads, where rules are constantly being made. **1938** F. VIVIAN *Black Alibi* xxiii. 212 'An old rule says Tell your lawyer everything, Mr. Moy.' ... 'An old saying asserts that rules were made to be broken. You must remember that also!' **2001** *Washington Post Book World* 28 Jan. 13 It's a rule of crime fiction that recurring main characters rarely get knocked off; but during Flavia's final confrontation with a sadistic murderer, Pears gives his uneasy readers cause to remember that rules are made to be broken. ■ **rules 規則**

rules ⇒ My HOUSE, my rules.

If you RUN after two hares you will catch neither.
二兎を追う者一兎も得ず。

2 つの目的を同時に達成しようとすると、どちらも達成できない。†エラスムス『格言集』III. ccxxxvii. *Duos insequens lepores, neutrum capit.*「2 羽のウサギを追う者はどちらも捕まえられない」

□ **1509** A. BARCLAY *Ship of Fools* H5 A fole is he ... Whiche with one haunde tendyth [intends] to take two harys in one instant. **1580** LYLY *Euphues & his England* II. 157 I am redie to take potions ... yet one thing maketh to feare, that in running after two Hares, I catch neither. **1732** T. FULLER *Gnomologia* no. 2782 If you run after two Hares, you will catch neither. **1880** C. H. SPURGEON *John Ploughman's Pictures* 24 If we please one we are sure to get another grumbling. We shall be like the man who hunted many hares at once and caught none. **1981** P. O'DONNELL *Xanadu Talisman* v. Let's take things a step at a time. You know what they say. If you run after two hares you will catch neither. ■ **decision and indecision 決断と優柔不断 ; wanting and having 不足と所持**

rust 387

You cannot RUN with the hare and hunt with the hounds.
野兎と一緒に逃げながら猟犬と一緒に狩りをすることはできない。

（訳注：run with the hares〈野兎と一緒に逃げる〉と hunt with the hounds〈猟犬と一緒に狩りをする〉という 2 つの事柄全体が cannot に続いている）

目的、関心などが真逆である 2 つの組織が関与する状況では、どちらの側に属するのかを決める必要がある。また、慣用句 to´run with the hare and hunt with the hounds「（議論などで）右についたり左についたりして意見を容易に変える」としても使われる。1546 年の用例における tytifils は、かつて悪魔の一般的な呼び名であった Titivil に由来する。

☐*a*1449 J. LYDGATE *Minor Poems* (EETS) 821 He ... holdeth bothe with hounde and hare. **1546** J. HEYWOOD *Dialogue of Proverbs* I. x. C3 There is no mo [more] suche tytifils [scoundrels] in Englands grounde, To holde with the hare, and run with the hounde. **1694** *Trimmer's Confession of Faith* I I can hold with the Hate, and run with the Hound: Which no Body can deny. **1896** M. A. S. HUME *Courtships of Queen Elizabeth* xii. Leicester, as usual, tried to run with the hare and hunt with the hounds, to retain French bribes and yet to stand in the way of French objects. **1975** J. O'FAOLAIN *Women in Wall* v. Clotair's henchmen say: 'You cannot run with the hare and hunt with the hounds.' The peasants have an even clearer way of putting this: 'You cannot', they say, 'side with the cow and the clover'. ■ **choices 選択**

run ⇒ He who FIGHTS and runs away, may live to fight another day; the LAST drop makes the cup run over; STILL waters run deep; While TWO dogs are fighting for a bone, a third runs away with it; We must learn to WALK before we can run.

rush ⇒ FOOLS rush in where angels fear to tread.

Russian ⇒ SCRATCH a Russian and you find a Tartar.

rust ⇒ BETTER to wear out than to rust out.

S

Sabbath ⇒ Monday's CHILD is fair of face.

sack ⇒ EMPTY sacks will never stand upright.

SAFE bind, safe find.
確実にしばっておけば確実に見つかる。

しっかり閉じ込められたものは、探しに行ったとき必ずその場所にある。Fast bind, fast find. という言い方もある。

□ **1546** J. HEYWOOD *Dialogue of Proverbs* I. iii. A4 Than catche and hold while I may, fast bind, fast fynde. **1573** T. TUSSER *Husbandry* (rev. ed.) II. 8 Drie sunne, drie winde, safe bind, safe find. **1655** T. FULLER *Church Hist. Britain* IV. iv Because sure binde, sure finde, he [Richard III] is said, and his Queen, to be Crowned again in York with great solemnity. **1890** D. C. MURRAY *John Vale's Guard* I. vi. 'Safe bind, safe find,' said Uncle Robert, locking the door and pocketing the key. **1937** D. L. SAYERS *Busman's Honeymoon* XX. As I says to Frank Crutchley, safe bind, safe find, I says. **1947** M. GILBERT *Close Quarters* viii. 'A careful man, the late head verger,' remarked Hazlerigg. 'Careful of his own and his master's property. Fast blind, fast find.' ■ **gains and losses** 利益と損失 ; **security** 安全

safe ⇒ It is BEST to be on the safe side; BETTER be safe than sorry.

There is SAFETY in numbers.
多数なら安全。

(訳注：numbers ＝「多数、多勢」。「寄らば大樹の陰」)

同じように考えたり、行動したりする人がたくさんいると安心する。現在では元の文脈よりも広い領域で使われる。『箴言』11章14節（欽定訳聖書）In the multitude of counsellors there is safety.「助言者の多いところには、救いがある」

□ **1680** BUNYAN *Mr. Badman* 133 I verily think, (since in the multitude of Counsellors there is safety) that if she had acquainted the Congregation with it, ... she had had more peace. **1816** J. AUSTEN *Emma* II. i. She determined to call upon them and seek safety in numbers. **1914** T. DREISER *Titan* xvii. He was beginning to run around with other women. There was safety in numbers. **2001** *Washington Post* 12 Sept. C15 (*Jeff MacNelly's Shoe comic strip*) 'Whoever said there's safety in numbers ... never took a math test.' ■ **associates** 仲間 ; **security** 安全

said ⇒ LEAST said, soonest mended; What the SOLDIER said isn't evidence.

SAINT 389

sailor ⇒ HEAVEN protects children, sailors, and drunken men.

If SAINT Paul's day be fair and clear, it will betide a happy year.
聖ポールの祭日が晴れたら、1年間幸福である。

（訳注：If Saint Paul's day be ... の be は仮定法現在形。if 節に仮定法現在形を使うのはきわめて形式的な表現。次のことわざの場合も同様である。If she *change* her will, she will tell her children about it.〈もし彼女が自分の決心を変えるとすれば、そのことについて子供たちに話す〉）

聖ポールの改宗は伝統的に1月25日に祝福される。このことわざは、主に農業社会において、いかに教会の暦のサイクルとその土地における季節行事が繋がっていたかを示している。† c1340 エイブバリーのロバート『歴史書』(1720) 266 *Clara dies Pauli bona tempora denotat anni.* 「聖ポールの祭日が晴れたら、1年間幸福である」

□ **1584** R. SCOT *Discovery of Witchcraft* XI. XV. If Paule th'apostles daie be cleare, it dooth foreshew a luckie yeare. **1687** J. AUBREY *Gentilism & Judaism* (1881) 94 The old verse so much observed by Countrey-people: 'If Paul's day be faire and cleare It will betyde a happy yeare' **1846** M. A. DENHAM *Proverbs relating to Seasons, &c.* 24 If St. Paul's day be fine and clear, It doth betide a happy year; But if by chance it then should rain, It will make dear all kinds of grain. **1975** M. KILLIP *Folklore of Isle of Man* xiii. In January the testing day was ... the 25th: St Paul's Day stormy and windy, Famine in the world and great death of mankind, Paul's day fair and clear, Plenty of corn and meal in the world. ■ **weather lore** 天気にまつわる伝承

SAINT Swithun's day, if thou be fair, for forty days it will remain; Saint Swithun's day, if thou bring rain, for forty days it will remain.
聖スウィジンよ、もし汝の祝日が晴れならその後40日は晴れとなる。聖スウィジンよ、もし汝の祝日が雨ならその後40日は雨となる。

イングランドの天候に関する予言として使われる。聖スウィジンはウィンチェスターの司祭であった。彼は862年に亡くなり、彼の祝祭日は7月15日にあたる。聖スウィジンと雨天続きとの組み合わせは少なくとも14世紀初頭の MS 27 in Emmanuel College, Cambridge (fo. 163; quoted in I. Opie and M. Tatem *Dictionary of Superstitions*): In the daye of seynte Svithone rane ginneth rinigge Forti dawes mid ywone 「聖スウィジンの祝日には、たいてい雨が降りはじめ、その後40日間は雨となる」にまで遡る。脚韻 (rain, remain) には多くの異形がある。

□ **1600** JONSON *Every Man out of Humour* I. iii. O, here, S. Swithin's the xv day, variable weather, for the most part raine.... Why, it should raine fortie daies after, now, more or lesse, it was a rule held afore I was able to hold a plough. **1697** *Poor Robin's Almanack* July B2ᵛ In this month is St. Swithin's day; On which, if that it rain, they say, Full forty days after it will, Or more or less some rain distill. **1846** M. A. DENHAM *Proverbs relating to Seasons*, &c. 52 St. Swithin's day, if thou dost rain, For forty days it will remain: St. Swithin's day, if thou be fair, For forty days 'twill rain na mair. **1892** C. M. YONGE *Old Woman's Outlook* 169 St. Swithin's promise is by no means infallible, whether for wet or fair weather. In ... Gloucestershire, they prefer a shower on his day, and call it christening the apples; but Hampshire ... hold[s] that—If Swithun's day be fair and clear, It betides a happy year; If Swithun's day be dark with rain, Then will be dear all sorts of grain. **1978** R. WHITLOCK *Calender of Country Customs* viii. Even today innumerable people take note of the weather on St Swithun's Day, 15 July.... St. Swithun's Day, if thou be fair, For forty days it will remain. St Swithun's Day, if thou bring rain, For forty days it will remain. ■ **weather lore** 天気にまつわる伝承

390 SAINT

On SAINT Thomas the Divine kill all turkeys, geese, and swine.
聖トーマスの日に神は七面鳥、ガチョウ、豚をすべて殺してしまう。

十二使徒の1人聖トーマス（トマス）の祝祭日は、伝統的に西洋では12月21日に当たる。1979年の引用例はクリスマスの準備としてのこの行事の重要性を説明している。

☐ **1742** *Agreeable Companion* 59 Thomas Divine, Brewing and Baking, and Killing of Swine. **1846** M. A. DENHAM *Proverbs relating to Seasons* &c. 64 The day of St. Thomas, the blessed divine, Is good for brewing, baking, and killing fat swine. **1979** C. MORSLEY *News from English Countryside* 164 This couplet reminded farmers of the day on which they should make their last slaughters for the Christmas table. On St Thomas the Divine Kill all turkeys, geese and swine. ■ **calendar lore** 暦にまつわる伝承

saint ⇒ The DEVIL was sick, the Devil a saint would be ... ; The GREATER the sinner, the greater the saint; YOUNG saint, old devil.

Help you to SALT, help you to sorrow.
塩を取るか、悲しむか、どちらか好きにしろ。

塩を巡って多くの迷信が作られている。それは、塩が何世紀ものあいだ、入手困難で貴重な必需品であったからである。その中で今なお行なわれている迷信の1つが、悪運を避けるために左肩の上に塩をふりかけるというものである。

☐ **1666** G. TORRIANO *Italian Proverbs* 245 At table, one ought not to present any one, either salt, or the head of any creature. **1872** J. GLYDE *Norfolk Garland* i. The spilling of salt is very ominous, and the proverb is well known: Help me to salt, Help me to sorrow. **1945** F. THOMPSON *Lark Rise* xxxvi. No one would at table spoon salt on to another person's plate, for 'Help you to salt, help you to sorrow'. **1969** 'S. MAYS' *Reuben's Corner* xiv. There was no end to the prohibitions we learned as youngsters.... Never help anyone to salt: Help you to salt, help you to sorrow. ■ **misfortune** 不幸 ; **superstition** 迷信

Saturday ⇒ Monday's CHILD is fair of face.

What's SAUCE for the goose is sauce for the gander.
雌ガチョウにとっておいしいものは雄ガチョウにとってもおいしい。

女性にとってふさわしいものは男性にとってもふさわしいものである。2002年の用例が示すように、女性や男性以外の文脈でも使われることがある。

☐ **1670** J. RAY *English Proverbs* 98 That that's good sawce for a goose, is good for a gander.... This is a woman's Proverb. **1692** R. L'ESTRANGE *Fables of Aesop* ccii. Sauce for a Goose is Sauce for a Gander. **1894** BLACKMORE *Perly-cross* III. v. A proverb of large equity ... declares ... that 'sauce for the goose is sauce for the gander'. This maxim is pleasant enough to the goose. **2002** *National Review* 28 Jan. 39 To buttress his case, the Russian leader pointed out that NATO itself had recently insisted that Macedonia implement this same principle in behalf of its Albanian ethnic minority. What was sauce for the Albanian goose was sauce for the Baltic gander. ■ **men and women** 男女

sauce ⇒ HUNGER is the best sauce.

SAVE us from our friends.
友人から私たちを救いたまえ。

（訳注：save ＝「〈悪・罪などから〉人を救う、救済する」）

前もって用心する明らかな敵よりも、信用している友達の方が危険かもしれないという考えは古くからある。†オウィディウス『アルス・アマトリア』I. 751 *Non est hostis metuendus amanti. Quos credis fidos effuge: tutus eris.*「敵は愛する人によって恐れられない。友人と信じている人とは距離を置きなさい。そうすれば安全である」。標題に挙げた簡略版とGodが主語となっている1604年の拡大版の両方が使われる。

□*a*1477 A. WYDEVILLE *Dicts. of Philosophers* 127 Ther was one that praied god to kepe him from the daunger of his frendis. **1585** Q. ELIZABETH in J. E. Neale *Elizabeth I & her Parliament* (1957) iv. There is an Italian proverb which saith, From my enemy let me defend myself; but from a pretensed friend, good Lord deliver me. **1604** J. MARSTON *Malcontent* IV. ii. Now, God deliver me from my friends ... for from mine enemies I'll deliver myself. **1884** *Railway Engineer* V. 265 The old proverb, 'Save us from our friends', may be well applied to the diligent gentlemen who ... toiled through labyrinths of reports since 1877, to dress up a few exaggerated cases against the ... brake. **1979** 'S. WOODS' *Proceed to Judgement* 140 Heaven save us from our friends! **2002** *Washington Times* 26 Mar. B5 'Defend me from my friends; I can defend myself from my enemies.' So cried a famous French general to Louis XIV long before bridge was invented. ■ friends 友

save ⇒ A STITCH in time saves nine.

saved ⇒ A PENNY saved is a penny earned.

say ⇒ Do as I say, not as I do; When in DOUBT, do nowt; What EVERYBODY says must be true; HEAR all, see all, say nowt; What MANCHESTER says today, the rest of England says tomorrow; NEVER say never; ⇒ SAID.

Who SAYS A must say B.
Aを言う者はBも同時に言わなければならない。

人は自分の言動が導く論理的帰結に従わなければならない。英語の中で唯一記録が残っているのは北米起源のものである。†オランダ語 *Wie a zegt, moet ook b zeggen.*「aを言う者はbも同時に言わなければならない」。

□**1838** J. C. NEAL *Charcoal Sketches* 190 Not so easy as you think.... If you say A, they'll make you say B. **1988** *Washington Times* 16 Sept. F3 But who says 'A' must say 'B', Mr. McCarthy. You can't talk about victims and caring and knowing cows individually while, at the same time, you treat carrots as nobodies! **2001** *National Review* 11 June 8 Either the state has the right to take life in cold blood, ... or it does not. If it does not, then McVeigh must be carefully supported, at public expense, even to the point of guarding him from other prisoners who might do him harm, for the rest of his natural days. Who says A, must say B. ■ action and consequence 行為と結果；necessity 必要性・必然性

scabbard ⇒ Whosoever DRAWS his sword against the prince must throw the scabbard away.

scarce ⇒ GOOD men are scarce.

scarlet ⇒ An APE's an ape, a varlet's a varlet, though they be clad in silk or scarlet.

scheme ⇒ The BEST-laid schemes of mice and men gang aft agley.

school ⇒ EXPERIENCE keeps a dear school; Never tell TALES out of school.

scorned ⇒ HELL hath no fury like a woman scorned.

You SCRATCH my back, I'll scratch yours.
私の背中を掻いてくれるなら、あなたの背中を掻いてあげよう。

（訳注：2つの文の間に and〈＝そうすれば〉を補って解釈する。「魚心あれば水心あり」）

意味が類似しているものに One HAND washes the other.「一方の手がもう片方の手を洗う」がある（1961年の用例参照）。

☐**1704** E. WARD *All Men Mad* 18 Scratch me, says one, and I'll scratch thee. **1858** 'A. WARD' *Letter* 27 Jan. in Maine: Guide 'Down East' (1937) ill. 363 You scratch my back and i will scratch your back. **1928** *Manchester Guardian Weekly* 10 Aug. 104/1 He goes on to spoil the effect by accusing Liberals of hypocrisy and being false to the principle of justice embodied in the phrase 'Scratch me and I'll scratch you'. **1961** J. HELLER *Catch-22* (1962) iv. 33 A little grease is what makes this world go round. One hand washes the other. Know what I mean? You scratch my back, I'll scratch yours. **2002** *Washington Times* 3 Mar. D1 Psychologist Lawrence Kohlberg outlined the stages of moral development in children: ... 2. Doing right for self-serving reasons: 'You scratch my back, and I'll scratch yours.' ■ **reciprocity 相互扶助**

SCRATCH a Russian and you find a Tartar.
ロシア人の皮をはがすと、タタール人が現われる。

ロシア人は文明人の仮面を被っているが、一皮むけば今でも略奪を繰り返す、ステップ地域に暮らす野蛮な遊牧民であるという主張である。特に他の国民を指す際に暗示的に使われることもある。†フランス語*Grattez le Russe et vous trouverez le Tartare*.「ロシア人の皮をはがすとタタール人が現われる」はナポレオンの言葉である。

☐**1823** J. GALLATIN *Diary* 2 Jan. (1914) 229 Very true the saying is, 'Scratch the Russian and find the Tartar.' c**1863** J. R. GREEN in *Notes & Queries* (1965) CCX. 348 They say, if you scratch a Russian you always find the Tartar beneath. **1899** F. A. OBER *Puerto Rico* xii. Scratch a Puerto Rican and you find a Spaniard underneath, so the language and home customs of Spain prevail here. **1911** *Spectator* 2 Dec. 964 Until a short time ago the aphorism, 'Scratch a Russian and you find a Tartar,' was the sum of British comprehension of the Russian character. **1947** J. FLANNER in *New Yorker* 31 May 6 Scratch a Pole and you find a Pole, even if he is a Communist. **1967** D. BLOODWORTH *Chinese Looking Glass* xxxiv. Mao ... discovered many years ago that you only had to scratch a Russian Communist to find a Tatar. ■ **human nature 人間性; national characteristics 国民性**

Scripture ⇒ The DEVIL can quote Scripture for his own ends.

He that would go to SEA for pleasure, would go to hell for a pastime.
娯楽で海へ行ったりしようものなら暇つぶしで地獄に落ちてしまう。

(訳注：he＝「〈関係節を伴って〉…する者は誰でも〈性別は問わない〉」。*He that* is not with me is against me.〈私に味方しない者は私に敵対する〉『『マタイによる福音書』12章30節)。he that would … の would は will〈＝意志〉の仮定法過去形、would go … の would は「仮想」の would)

船乗りと海の愛憎関係を示している。

□**1899** A. J. BOYD *Shellback* viii. Shentlemens vot goes to sea for pleasure vould go to hell for pastime. **1910** D. W. BONE *Brassbounder* xxvi. He gave a half-laugh and muttered the old formula about 'the man who would go to sea for pleasure, going to hell for a pastime!' **1924** R. CLEMENTS *Gipsy of Horn* iii. 'He who would go for sea for pleasure, would go to hell for a pastime' is an attempt at heavy satire. **1986** *Newsweek* 27 Jan. 62 Just before Steven Callahan set out to sail alone from Penzance to Martinique, a Comish seaman warned him that 'a fella who'd go to sea for pleasure'd sure go to hell for pastime.' ■ **idiosyncrasy** 特異性・性癖

The SEA refuses no river.
海はどんな川も拒まない。

(訳注：「河海は細流を選ばず」)

海が流れ込むすべての川を受け入れるように、死は万人を受け入れる。

□**1614** T. GENTLEMAN *England's Way to win Wealth* 45 (*marginal note*) The Sailors Prouerbe: The Sea and the Gallowes refuse none. **1699** E. WARD *Trip to New England* 4 It often puts me in mind of the old Proverb, The Sea and the Gallows refuses none. **1850** H. MELVILLE *White Jacket* II. xliii. 'The gallows and the sea refuse nothing,' is a very old sea saying. **1969** R. NYE *Tales I told my Mother* 124 The sea refuses no river. ■ **greed** 貪欲

sea ⇒ There are as good FISH in the sea as ever came out ofit; The FROG in the well knows nothing of the sea.

sea-maws ⇒ KEEP your own fish-guts for your own sea-maws.

search ⇒ On the FIRST of March, the crows begin to search.

SECOND thoughts are best.
2 番目の考えが最善である。

(訳注：「念には念を入れよ」)

第一印象で即決するよりも慎重に考慮する方が賢明である。†エウリピデス『ヒッポリュトス』I. 436 αἱ δεύτεραί πως φροντίδες σοφώτεραι.「2 番目の考えの方がつねにましである」

□**1577** HOLINSHED *Chronicles* 438 Oftentymes it chaunceth, that latter thoughts are better aduised than the first. **1581** G. PETTIE tr. *S. Guazzo's Civil Conversation* i. 23ᵛ I finde verified that Prouerbe, That the second thoughts are euer the best. **1681** DRYDEN *Spanish Friar* II. 22 Second thoughts, they say, are best: I'll consider of it once again. **1813** BYRON *Letter* 11 Dec. (1974) III. 196 In composition I do not think second thoughts are best, though second expressions may improve the first ideas. **1908** C. FITCH *Beau Brummel* I. i. Second thoughts seem to be always the best. **1981** P. O'DONNELL *Xanadu Talisman* v. That was my first thought.... But second thoughts are always best. ■ **prudence** 思慮・分別

394 secret

secret ⇒ THREE may keep a secret, if two of them are dead.

What you SEE is what you get.
あなたが目にしているものはあなたの手に入るもの。

米国起源。特にコンピューター用語で wysiwyg（ヴィジウィグ）と頭文字で使われることが多い。これは印刷する際のスクリーンフォーマットの再現可能なシステムを指している。

□ **1971** *New York Times* 14 Nov. 17 'What you see, is what you get' ... is one of those recurring gag lines from the Flip Wilson Show that has quickly drifted into the language, all but become a household expression. **1983** G. PETIEVICH *To die in Beverly Hills* vii. The teleprinter raced as it printed the names of arrestees nicknamed Bones. 'What you see is what you get,' she said, squinning to point her breasts. 'I mean the printout of course.' **1990** *Washington Post* 10 Sept. (Business Section) 59 The lenders who would lend to anyone who said 'real estate' aren't lending now. So we aren't going to build any more product. What you see is what you get. **2007** *Times 2* 13 Sept 3 She then proudly told us that she had read them all, as evidence of her upfront nature ('What you see is what you get!' she. boasted). ■ appearance, significant 重要な外見

SEE no evil, hear no evil, speak no evil.
悪を見ず、悪を聞かず、悪を言わず。
（訳注：「見ざる、聞かざる、言わざる」）

伝統的に 3 匹の猿の像や絵で表象される。その 3 匹の猿はそれぞれ両手で目、耳、口を塞いでいる。

□ **1926** *Army & Navy Stores Catalogue* 197 The three wise monkeys. 'Speak no evil, see no evil, hear no evil.' **1939** I. OELLRICHS *Man who didn't Answer* viii. 'Hear no evil, see no evil and speak no evil' was all right in its place, but Matt knew ... they gossiped as much there as in any other smallish town. **1978** T. L. SMITH *Money War* III. 233 It's the sort of thing they want done but do not want to know about. See no evil, hear no evil, speak no evil. **2014** *Spectator* 22 Nov. 23 [Y]ou can ... squeeze your eyes shut like a child in a storm, determined to see no evil, hear no evil, speak no evil—and still that evil storm may come at you with hands like knives one day. ■ good and evil 正邪

see ⇒ BELIEVE nothing of what you hear, and only half of what you see; There's none so BLIND as those who will not see; What the EYE doesn't see, the heart doesn't grieve over; HEAR all, see all, say nowt; They that LIVE longest, see most; LOOKERS-on see most of the game; MONKEY see, monkey do; See a PIN and pick it up, all the day you'll have good luck; ⇒ SEEING, SEEN.

Good SEED makes a good crop.
良い種こそが良い作物となる。
（訳注：「善因善果」）

1492 *Dialogue of Salomon & Martolphus* (1892) 5 He that sowyth chaf shall porely mowe.「もみ殻を蒔く者は刈り取りも少ない」において早い時期から使われている。

□ **1569** W. WAGER *Longer Thou Livest* A2 To be a good man it is also expedient Of good Parents to be begotten and borne.... Commonly of good Seed procedeth good Corne. **1700** T. TRYON

Letters i. If the Seed he Sowes be good ... his Crop is according; ... If he Sows Tares ... will he expect Wheat? **1940** L. I. WILDER *Long Winter* xvii. Seed-time's pretty sure to come around.... And good seed makes a good crop. ■ **beginnings and endings 最初と最後**

seed ⇒ The BLOOD of the martyrs is the seed of the Church; PARSLEY seed goes nine times to the Devil.

seeding ⇒ ONE year's seeding makes seven years' weeding.

SEEING is believing.
見ることは信じることである。
（訳注：「百聞は一見にしかず」）

自分自身の目で見た証拠があると、真実として受け入れるようになる。ただし、（見た目でだまされやすいという）1848年の用例にも注意。

□ **1609** S. HARWARD *MS* (Trinity College, Cambridge) 85 Seeing is leeving. **1639** J. CLARKE *Paremiologia Anglo-Latina* 90 Seeing is beleeving. **1712** J. ARBUTHNOT *Lewis Baboon* iv. There's nothing like Matter of Fact; Seeing is Believing. **1848** J. C. & A. W. HARE *Guesses at Truth* (ed. 2) 2nd Ser. 497 Seeing is believing, says the proverb.... Though, of all our senses, the eyes are the most easily deceived, we believe them in preference to any other evidence. **2001** *Washington Times* 14 Dec. A4 Seeing, as the old saw goes, is believing. and in the postliterate age the visual is more persuasive than it used to be. ■ **trust and scepticism 信用と懐疑**

SEEK and ye shall find.
求めよ、さらば見出さん。
（訳注：ye ＝「汝ら、あなたがた」。Ye are the salt of me earth.〈汝らは地の塩なり〉『マタイによる福音書』5章13節）

† ソフォクレス『オイディプス王』I. 110–11 τὸ δὲ ζητούμενον ἁλωτόν, ἐκφεύγειν δὲ τἀμελούμενον.「求めている物は見つかる。無視している物は逃げていく」。さらに直接の出所は『マタイによる福音書』7章7節（欽定訳聖書）Ask, and it shall be given you: seek, and ye shall find.「求めよ、そうすれば、与えられるであろう。捜せ、そうすれば、見出すであろう」

□ **1530** in J. PALSGRAVE *L'eclaircissement de la Langue Française* A5 He that wyll seke may fynde And in a brefe tyme attayne to his utterest desire. *c***1538** J. BALE *King Johan* (1931) I. 192 Serche and ye shall fynd, in every congregacyn that long [belongs] to the pope. **1783** J. JAY *Letter* 14 Nov. (1891) III. 95 'Seek and you shall find' does not, it seems, always extend to that [health] of the body. **1980** R. COLLINS *Case of Philosopher's Ring* xiii. There is danger in the saying. 'Seek and ye shall find'. ■ **diligence 勤勉**；**wanting and having 不足と所持**

seem ⇒ BE what you would seem to be.

seen ⇒ CHILDREN should be seen and not heard.

SELF-praise is no recommendation.
自賛は賞賛にならない。
（訳注：「一人自慢のほめ手なし」）

396　SELF

自慢する人に対する軽蔑（1967年の用例参照）。†ラテン語 *Laus in proprio ore sordescit.*「自分の口から出た自分の称賛は不愉快である」

□**1826** COBBETT *Weekly Register* 17 June 7 43 In general it is a good rule ... that self-praise is no commendation. **1853** DICKENS *Bleak House* Iv. Self-praise is no recommendation, but I may say for myself that I am not so bad a man of business. **1967** RIDOUT & WITTING *English Proverbs Explained* 137 'I admit I didn't score any of the goals, but it was largely due to me that we won the game.' 'Self-praise is no recommendation.' ■ **boasting　自慢**

SELF-preservation is the first law of nature.
自己保存は自然界の第一法則である。

†キケロ『最高善と最大悪について』IV. x. 25 *Primamque ex natura hanc habere appetitionem, ut conservemus nosmet ipsos.*「自然の摂理に従って、我らの最初の鼓動は我々自身を保存するためにある」

□*a***1631** *Donne Biathanatos* (1646) I. ii. It is onely upon this reason, that selfe-preservation is of Naturall Law. **1675** [MARVELL] *Complete Poems* (1872) I. 439 Self-preservation, Nature's first great Law. **1681** DRYDEN *Spanish Friar* IV. ii. Self-preservation is the first of Laws: ... When Subjects are oppress'd by Kings, They justifie Rebellion by that Law. **1821** SCOTT *Pirate* I. v. Triptolemus ... had a reasonable share of that wisdom which looks towards self-preservation as the first law of nature. **1952** 'A. A. FAIR' *Top of Heap* xvii. Loyalty is a fine thing ... but self-preservation is the first law of nature. **1975** P. D. JAMES *Black Tower* vii. What it amounted to was that he'd do a great deal for dear Maggie but that self-preservation was the first law of nature. ■ **self-preservation　自己防衛**

SELL in May and go away.
5 月に売って、姿をくらませ。

元来はロンドン株式取引所の活動周期に関することわざであった。かつて、5 月は会計年度が始まった直後で、多忙な時期であるが、その後は株の売り買いも停滞し、ロンドン子（株式仲買人も含む）は投資から離れて夏の休暇を満喫した。2002年の用例のような拡張版でも使われる。それは、9 月初旬に開催されるドンカスターの古典的なセントレジャー競馬——イングランドの夏の伝統的な行事の終わりを示すもの——を指している。

□**1979** *Daily Telegraph* 27 July 19 That hoary old adage sell in May and go away, has yet again been vindicated with the Financial Times 30 share index falling 97 points, from 559 on the 4 May post-election day to last night's 462 and with little immediate relief in sight. **1992** *Economist* 11 July 87/1 'Sell in May and go away,' says the old adage. This year it has been right on the button: a bad June for world stockmarkets is being followed by a worse July. **2001** *New York Times* The pattern [of stock market fluctuation] is the factual basis for the saying 'Sell in May and go away.' **2002** *Times* 15 May 34 In the City, you are about as likely to hear someone utter the old adage 'sell in May, go away, come back on St Leger's Day' as you are to spot gentlemen wearing bowler hats and carrying rolled umbrellas. ■ **business　ビジネス・商売**

Don't SELL the skin till you have caught the bear.
熊を捕ってもいないのにその皮を売るな。
（訳注：「捕らぬ狸の皮算用」）

まだ所有してもいないのにそれを売ることはできない。起源は1490年代に編纂された『イソップ物語』に15世紀イタリアの学者 L. アブステミウスが追加した寓話の中に見出

される。

□**1578** H. WOTTON tr. J. YVER *Courtly Controversie of Cupids Cantles* N4ᵛ His eyes, greedily fixed vpon his faire Mistresse, solde vnto him (as men say) the skin before the beast is taken. **1580** LYLY *Euphues & his England* ii. 53 I trusted so much, that I solde the skinne before the Beaste was taken. **1641** CHARLES I *Comment (on Remonstrance)* 1 Dec. in *Rushworth Historical Collections* (1692) III. v. 1, 436 We must not dispose of the Bears skin till the Bear be dead. **1692** R. L'ESTRANGE *Aesop* (ed. 3) 270 He bade me have a care for the future, to make sure of the bear before I sell his skin. **1721** KELLY *Scottish Proverbs* 376 You sell the Bear Skin on his Back. **1999** R. CARPENTER *Scarlet Pimpernel* (*BBC TV, episode 1*) [Chauvelin:] The trap is set, and he's about to walk into it. [Marguerite:] Don't sell the skin till you've caught the bear. ■ **optimism** 楽観主義

seller ⇒ The BUYER has need of a hundred eyes, the seller of but one.

send ⇒ Never send a BOY to do a man's job; GOD never sends mouths but He sends meat; GOD sends meat, but the Devil sends cooks.

SEPTEMBER blow soft, till the fruit's in the loft.
果物を小屋の 2 階にしまうまで 9 月が静かな風を吹かせてくれますように。

(訳注：blow は「祈願」を表わす仮定法現在形。God *save* the Queen!〈女王陛下万歳〉)

果物の収穫が終わるまで、秋の強風が吹かないで欲しいという願い。

□**1571** T. TUSSER *Husbandry* (rev. ed.) F2 September blowe soft, Till fruite be in loft. **1732** T. PULLER *Gnomologia* no. 6214 September, blow soft, Till the Fruit's in the Loft. **1906** B. HOWEN *Country Diary of Edwardian Lady* (1977) 121 September blow soft,—Till the fruit's. in the loft. **1928** *Daily Mail* 3 Sept 10 'September blow soft till the apple's in the loft' is what we desire of this traditionally beautiful month. ■ **weather lore** 天気にまつわる伝承

servant ⇒ ENGLAND is the paradise of women; FIRE is a good servant but a bad master.

serve ⇒ You cannot serve GOD and Mammon; NO man can serve two masters.

If you would be well SERVED, serve yourself.
十分に仕えてもらいたければ、自らが自らに仕えよ。

満足のいくまで仕事を遂行できる最良の人物とは実はあなた自身である。よく似たものに If you WANT a thing done well, do it yourself.「仕事を首尾よくやってもらいたければ、それを自分でやれ」がある。

□**1659** G. TORBIANO *English & Italian Dict.* 39 Who hath a mind to any thing let him go himself. **1706** J. STEVENS *Spanish & English Dict.* s.v. Querer, If you would be well serv'd, serve yourself. **1871** J. B. AUSTEN-LEIGH *Memoir of Jane Austen* (ed. 2) ii. 'If you would be well served, serve yourself.' Some gentlemen took pleasure in being their own gardeners. **1981** *Times* 28 Apr. 15 Absurd that the important things in one's life should be made by another person—'One is never so well served as by oneself.' ■ **efficiency and inefficiency** 能率と非能率; **self-help** 自助

served ⇒ FIRST come, first served; PAY beforehand was never well served; YOUTH must be served.

session ⇒ HOME is home, as the Devil said when he found himself in the Court of Session.

set ⇒ Set a BEGGAR on horseback, and he'll ride to the Devil; Sow dry and set wet; Set a THIEF to catch a thief.

seven ⇒ PALL down seven times, get up eight; KEEP a thing seven years and you'll always find a use for it; You should KNOW a man seven years before you stir his fire; MEASURE seven times, cut once; ONE year's seeding makes seven years' weeding; PARSLEY seed goes nine times to the Devil; RAIN before seven, fine before eleven; SIX hours' sleep for a man, seven for a woman, and eight for a fool.

shadow ⇒ COMING events cast their shadows before; OLD sins cast long shadows.

shame ⇒ (名詞) POOL me once, shame on you; (動詞) TELL the truth and shame die Devil.

shared ⇒ A TROUBLE shared is a trouble halved.

The SHARPER the storm, the sooner it's over.
嵐は激しければ激しいほど早く過ぎ去る。

　　（訳注：「the 比較級，the 比較級」〈…すればするほどますます…だ〉の形式が使われている。*The* sooner, *the* better.〈早ければ早いほどよい〉。「夕立は一日は降らず」）

樹しさゆえにすぐに終わってしまう猛攻撃を指す。†セネカ『自然研究』VII. ix. *Procellae, quanta plus habent virium, tantominus temporis.*「嵐は激しければ激しいほど長続きしない」

　　□**1872** P. KILVERT *Diary* 9 June (1977) II. 207 Mrs. Vaughan will have a good family soon. Her children come fast But the harder the storm the sooner 'tis over. **1913** *Folk-Lore* XXIV. 76 The sharper the storm, the sooner it's over. **2002** *Washington Post* 11 Feb. Cl3 (*One Big Happy comic strip*) ' … She'll be very, very angry!' 'I know, but the sharper the storm, the sooner it's over.' 'I'm about to be killed, and you're giving me weather reports?!' ■ **weather lore** 天気にまつわる伝承

sheep ⇒ BETTER to live one day as a tiger than a thousand years as a sheep; A BLEATING sheep loses a bite; One might as well be HANGED for a sheep as a lamb.

shepherd ⇒ RED sky at night, shepherd's delight.

You cannot SHIFT an old tree without it dying.
老木は植えかえると枯死する。

　　（訳注：この場合の you は総称的な用法。*You* can't judge a book by its cover.【ことわざ】〈人はうわべだけでは判断できない〉）

樹齢の高い木を移植することは枯れてしまう危険性が高い。1721 年の用例が示すように、長年住みなれた家を離れざるを得ない老人によって使われたり、そうせざるを得ない老

人について使われることが多い。

□*c*1518 A. BARCLAY tr. *Mancinus' Mirror of Good Manners* G4ᵛ An old tre transposed shall fynde smal auauntage. **1670** J. RAY *English Proverbs* 22 Remove an old tree, and it will wither to death. **1721** J. KELLY *Scottish Proverbs* 284 Remove an old Tree, and it will wither. Spoken by a Man who is loth to leave a Place in his advanc'd years, in which he has long lived. **1831** W. M. PRAED *Political & Occasional Poems* (1888) 166 I'm near three-score; you ought to know You can't transplant so old a tree. **1906** R. KIPLING *Puck of Pook's Hill* 259 'You've cleaved to your own parts pretty middlin' close, Ralph.' 'Can't shift an old tree 'thout it dyin'.' ■ **habit** 習慣 ; **old age** 老年

shine ⇒ Happy is the BRIDE that the sun shines on; MAKE hay while the sun shines.

shining ⇒ The SUN loses nothing by shining into a puddle.

Do not spoil the SHIP for a ha'porth of tar.
半ペンス分のタールを惜しんで船（または羊）を台無しにするな。

（訳注：ha'porth ＝ halfpenny-worth〈半ペンス分の〉。「一文惜しみの百失い」）

ここで ship「船」は sheep「羊」の方言発音で、このことわざの原義は「わずかばかりのタールを惜しんで羊を死なせてはならない」という意味であった。タール（黒い粘着性物質）はハエから羊の傷や痛みを保護するために使われる。（1623 年と 1670 年の用例参照）hog をレイは豚と理解したと思われるが（1670 年の用例の注参照）、実は初めて羊毛を刈られる前の若い羊を指す方言形として広く使われていた。現在の形式は 19 世紀中頃までにはすでに標準的になっていた。慣用句 to spoil the ship for a ha'porth of tar「半ペニーのタールを惜しんで船を失う」も使われる。

□**1623** W. CAMDEN *Remains concerning Britain* (ed. 3) 265 A man will not lose a hog, for a halfeperth [halfpennyworth] of tarre. **1631** J. SMITH *Advertisements for Planters* XIII. 30 Rather … lose ten sheepe, than be at the charge of halfe penny worth of Tarre. **1670** J. RAY *English Proverbs* 103 Ne're lose a hog for a half-penny-worth of tarre [(ed. 2) 154 Some have it, lose not a sheep, &c. Indeed tarr is more used about sheep than swine]. **1861** C. READE *Cloister & Hearth* I. i. Never tyne [lose] the ship for want of a bit of tar. **1869** W. C. HAZL1TI *English Proverbs* 432 To spoil the ship for a halfpennyworth of tar. In Cornwall, I heard a different version, which appeared to me to be more consistent with probability: 'Don't spoil the sheep for a ha'porth of tar.' **1992** 'C. AIRD' 'Man Who Rowed for Shore' in *Injury Time* (1995) 22 As Millicent, his late wife, would have said, it was just like Norman to spoil the ship for a ha'p'orth of tar. **2014** *Economist* 22 Sept. (online) It [i.e. America] has an interest in giving the new [Afghan] government a chance; "They won't spoil the ship for a ha'p'orth of tar," says one Western official. ■ **meanness** けち・意地悪

ship ⇒ One HAND for yourself and one for the ship; LITTLE leaks sink the ship; A WOMAN and a ship ever want mending.

shirt ⇒ NEAR is my shirt, but nearer is my skin.

From SHIRTSLEEVES to shirtsleeves in three generations.
腕まくりから腕まくりに戻るには三代しかかからない。

家族の財を築く一代目は、腕まくりをして働く肉体労働者である。二代目は一代目の家業を継承する。しかし、三代目で廃業となり、また肉体労働者に戻る。一般には、米国とスコットランドの製造業者で博愛主義者のアンドリュー・カーネギー（1835-1919）の言葉とされるが、確証はない。From CLOGS to clogs is only three generations.「木靴から木靴に戻るには三代しかかからない」も同じ考え。

□ **1874** *Appleton's Journal* 27 June 802/3 In America, where there are 'but three generations from shirt-sleeves to shirt-sleeves,' the whole of a son's fortune is well spent upon his training, though he must go out into life with the tastes of a gentleman, and no income to support them. **1907** N. M. BUTLER *True & False Democracy* ii. No artificial class distinctions can long prevail in a society like ours [in the US] of which it is truly said to be often but three generations 'from shirt-sleeves to shirt-sleeves'. **1957** J. S. BRUNER in *Psychological Review* I.XIV. 125 From shirt-sleeves to shirtsleeves in three generations: we are back with the founding and founded content of the pre-Gestalt Gestalters. **1980** J. KRANTZ *Princess Daisy* xvii. What's this? Shirtsleeves to shirtsleeves in three generations. ■ **family** 家族・家系；**poverty** 貧困

If the SHOE fits, wear it.
靴がぴったり合うなら、それを履け。

主として米国で使われる形式で、If the CAP fits, wear it.「帽子があうなら、それをかぶれ」と同じ意味である。

□ **1773** *New-York Gazette & Weekly Mercury* 17 May Why should Mr. Vanderbeek apply a general comparison to himself? Let those whom the shoe fits wear it. **1876** W. G. NASH *Century of Gossip* 125 If the shoe fits you, you can wear it a little wile [sic], Jack; but we won't quarrel about that. **1934** J. GREGORY *Emerald Murder Trap* 260 Some one, devilishly inspired, had made a noose in the end and the knot was what is so widely known as a Hangman's knot.... 'There's an old saying, you know; if the shoe fits, wear it. The words might be made to apply to knots, I suppose!' **2001** *Washington Post* 13 Dec. Cl 1 (*Baby Blues comic strip*) 'Zee, you're a know-it-all-crybaby-tattletale brat!' 'I'm telling Mommy that you said that!' ... 'What did Mommy say?' 'She said, "If the shoe fits, wear it!"' ■ **conduct** 行ない・品行；**reputation** 評判

shoe ⇒ It's ILL waiting for dead men's shoes; For WANT of a nail the shoe was lost.

The SHOEMAKER's son always goes barefoot.
靴屋の息子はいつも裸足で歩く。

熟練の技術を持つ職人などは、おうおうにして自分の家族にはその技術の恩恵を与えないものである。son の代わりに wife、children などいろいろな形で使われる。

□ **1546** J. HEYWOOD *Dialogue of Proverbs* I. xi. Elv But who is wurs shod, than the shoemakers wyfe, With shops full of newe shapen shoes all hir lyfe? **1773** R. GRAVES *Spiritual Quixote* I. III. ii. The Shoe-maker's wife often goes in ragged shoes.... Although there had been a [Methodist] Society begun here by Mr. Whitfield, yet ... the people of Gloucester are not much the better for having had so great a Prophet born amongst them. **1876** S. SMILES *Life of Scotch Naturalist* xvii. His large family ... were all ... well shod, notwithstanding the Scottish proverb to the contrary. 'The Smith's meer [mare] and the shoemaker's bairns are aye the worst shod.' **1981** 'E. PETERS' *Saint Peter's Fair* 30 Spruce in his dress, but down at heel, Cadfael noticed—proof of the old saying that the shoemaker's son is always the one who goes barefoot! **1987** S. STEWART *Lifting the*

shortest 401

Latch 58 They say the cobbler's children go the worst shod. Dad made sure we children went dry-shod by giving us a penny-a-week for the Boot-fund. **2001** *Spectator* 4 Aug. 28 The cobbler's children go barefoot, and Pearson, which publishes the Financial Times, has lost £233 million in six months. ■ **family** 家族・家系

shoemaker ⇒ Let the COBBLER stick to his last.

shop ⇒ KEEP your shop and your shop will keep you.

shopkeeper ⇒ The ENGLISH are a nation of shopkeepers.

shorn ⇒ GOD tempers the wind to the shorn lamb; Many go out for wool and come home shorn.

A SHORT horse is soon curried.
小さな馬はすぐに馬ぐしがかかる。

(訳注: 似たことわざに、A fair bride is soon busked and a short horse is soon whisked. 〈美人の花嫁はすぐに飾りつけができ上がり、小さい馬はすぐにブラシかけがすむ〉がある)

小さな仕事はすぐに終了することを意味する。curry は (馬に) 馬ぐしをかけることを表わす。

□*c*1350 *Douce MS* 52 no. 17 Short hors is son j-curryed. *a*1530 R. HILL *Commonplace Book* (EETS) 128 A shorte hors is son curried. **1732** T. FULLER *Gnomologia* no. 395 A short Horse is soon curried. **1820** SCOTT *Abbot* I. xi. A short tale is soon told—and a short horse soon curried. **1939** L. I. WILDER *By Shores of Silver Lake* xxx. A short horse is soon curried. This is our tightest squeeze yet, ... but it's only a beginning. **1965** Springfield Court of Appeals, Missouri, Travelers Indemnity Company v. Chumbley 394 S. W. 2d 418, 21 July The appeal as to *defendant Chumbley* is 'a short horse soon curried.' ■ **efficiency and inefficiency** 能率と非能率; **work** 仕事

SHORT reckonings make long friends.
短期の勘定は友情を長続きさせる。

short reckoning「短期の勘定」とは代金を早く払うことを意味する。†フランス語 *Les bons comptes font les bons amis.*「勘定のけじめは友情のかなめ」

□*a*1530 R. WHITFORDE *Work for Householders* A4 The commune prouerbe is that ofte rekenynge boldest longe felawship. **1641** D. FERGUSSON *Scottish Proverbs* (STS) no. 668 Oft compting makes good friends. **1673** J. DARE *Counsellor Manners* xciii. Short reckonings (we say) make long friends. **1842** S. LOVER *Handy Andy* viii. There must be no nonsense about the wedding.... Just marry her off, and take her home. Short reckonings make long friends. **1918** BARONESS OR-CZY *Man in Grey* 15 Short reckonings make long friends. I'll have a couple of hundred francs now. ■ **business** ビジネス・商売; **punctuality** 時間厳守

short ⇒ ART is long and life is short; LONG foretold, long last.

shortest ⇒ BARNABY bright, Barnaby bright, the longest day and the shortest night; The LONGEST way round is the shortest way home.

402　shoulder

shoulder ⇒ You cannot put an OLD head on young shoulders.

You can't SHOUT 'Fire' in a crowded theatre.
満席の劇場で「火事だ」などと叫ぶことは許されない。

〈訳注：you は総称的な用法。*You* never can tell what's going to happen.〈何が起きるかは誰にもわからない〉〉

言論の自由があるからといって、それを扇動的・無責任な形で乱用することに対する警告。

□1919 O. WENDELL HOLMES JR, opinion in *Schenck* v. *United States* 249 U.S. 47 The most stringent protection of free speech would not protect a man in falsely shouting fire in a theatre and causing a panic. **2015** *Spectator* 17 Jan. 28 The excuses offered [i.e. for the massacre at *Charlie Hebdo*] sound superficially plausible—'You can't shout fire in a crowded theatre.' ■
speech and silence　発言と沈黙

show ⇒ TIME will tell.

shower ⇒ APRIL showers bring forth May flowers.

SHROUDS have no pockets.
（死者を包む）経かたびらにポケットはない。

『テモテへの手紙一』6 章 7 節 For we brought nothing into this world, and it is certain we can carry nothing out.「私たちは何ひとつこの世に持って来なかったし、また何ひとつ持って出ることもできません」において述べられている内容を簡潔に表現している。

□1854 R. C. TRENCH *On Lessons in Proverbs* (ed. 2) v. With an image Dantesque in its vigour, that 'a man shall carry nothing away with him when he dieth', take this Italian, Our last robe, that is our winding sheet, is made without pockets. **1909** A. MACLAREN *Epistle to Ephesians* 41 There is nothing that is truly our wealth which remains outside of us, and can be separated from us. 'Shrouds have no pockets.' **1961** M. KELLY *Spoilt Kill* II. 20 'He had a win on the pools and it's burning him.' 'Shrouds don't need pockets, love,' he said with a grin. **2002** *Spectator* 13 Apr. 57 So we take into the afterlife only what we have given away. Shrouds have no pockets.
■ **death　死；money　金・金銭**

A SHUT mouth catches no flies.
閉じた口にハエは入ってこない。

〈訳注：「口は災いの門」〉

黙っておればトラブルに巻き込まれなくてすむ。

□1599 J. MINSHEU *Spanish Grammar* 83 In a closed vp mouth a flie cannot get in. **1640** G. HERBERT *Outlandish Proverbs* no. 219 Into a mouth shut flies flie not. **1659** T. FULLER *Appeal of Injured Innocence* 1. 12 The Spanish Proverb ... is necessary in dangerous ... Times, *Where the mouth is shut no Fly doth enter.* **1897** 'H. S. MERRIMAN' *In Kedar's Tents* xxiii. Concha, remembering ... that no flies enter a shut mouth, was silent. **1926** T. A. WILLARD *City of Sacred Well* xv. Tell each of them that a shut mouth catches no flies. We may find ... nothing ... and ... we do not want the other men laughing at us behind our backs. **1984** 'M. HEBDEN' *Pel and Pirates* (1987) v. 43 'People keep a tight lip. In bocca chiusa non entra mai mosca.... It's an old Italian

SILENCE 403

saying. The people on the Island use it.' 'What's it mean?' 'A fly never enters a closed mouth. They don't talk much.' ■ **discretion** 思慮分別 ; **speech and silence** 発言と沈黙

shut ⇒ A DOOR must either be shut or open; When ONE door shuts, another opens; PUT up or shut up; It is too late to shut the STABLE-door after the horse has bolted.

shy ⇒ ONCE bitten, twice shy.

sick ⇒ The DEVIL was sick, the Devil a saint would be ... ; HOPE deferred makes the heart sick.

side ⇒ It is BEST to be on the safe side; The BREAD never falls but on its buttered side; The GRASS is always greener on the other side of the fence; PROVIDENCE is always on the side of the big battalions; There are TWO sides to every question.

sight ⇒ In vain the NET is spread in the sight of the bird; OUT of sight, out of mind.

SILENCE is a woman's best garment.
沈黙こそが女性の最高の装飾品である。

†ソフォクレス『アイアース』I. 293 γυναιξὶ κόσμον ἡ σιγὴ φέρει.「沈黙こそが女性の装飾品である」。1539年の用例において聖パウロの言葉を思わせる一節が『コリントの信徒への手紙』14章34節（欽定訳聖書）Let your women keep silence in the churches, for it is not permitted unto them to speak.「女は会衆の中では黙っていなさい。話すことは許可されていないからです」にある。

□ **1539** R. TAVERNER tr. *Erasmus' Adages* 50 *Mulierem omat silentium*. Silence garnysheth a woman ... whych thynge also the Apostle Paule requyreth. **1659** J. HOWELL *Proverbs* (English) 11 Silence the best ornament of a woman. **1732** T. FULLER *Gnomologia* no. 4166 Silence is a fine Jewel for a Woman; but it's little worn. **1977** J. AIKEN *Five-Minute Marriage* iv. Quiet, miss! Silence is a woman's best garment. ■ **speech and silence** 発言と沈黙 ; **women** 女性

SILENCE is golden.
沈黙は金。

完全版の SPEECH is silver, but silence is golden.「雄弁は銀、沈黙は金」も使われる。

□ **1865** W. WHITE *Eastern England* II. ix. Silence is golden, says the proverb. We apprehend the full significance ... in some lone hamlet situate amid a 'thousand fields'. **1923** A. HUXLEY *Antic Hay* xx. Silence is golden, as her father used to say when she used to fly into tempers and wanted to say nasty things to everybody within range. **2002** *Washington Post* 4 Apr. C13 (*Mother Goose & Grimm comic strip*) 'What I don't understand is ... how can campaign money be free speech ... but silence is golden?' ■ **speech and silence** 発言と沈黙

SILENCE means consent.
沈黙は承諾を意味する。

（訳注：解説にあるトマス・モアは宗教改革時代の代表的な人文主義者で、『ユートピア』の作者。離婚問題などでヘンリー8世を批判したため、大逆罪で1535年に処刑された）

404 silence

近代イングランドの法で認められた原則ではない。しかし、トマス・モア卿（1478-1535）が、裁判において、教会に対する国王の優位性を承認するか否かを問われたときなぜ沈黙を貫いたのか尋ねられた際に、次のラテン語の格言を用いて言い返したと言われている。†ラテン語 *Qui tacet consentire videtur.*「黙っている者は同意したと受け取られる」

☐*c*1380 WYCLIF *Select English Works* (1871) III. 349 Oo [one] maner of consent is, whanne a man is stille and tellith not. **1591** LYLY *Endymion* v. iii. Silence, Madame, consents. *c*1616-30 *Partial Law* (1908) v. iv. 'I will nothing say.' ... 'Then silence gives consent.' **1847** A. HELPS *Friends in Council* ix. I have known a man ... bear patiently ... a serious charge which a few lines would have entirely answered.' ... 'Silence does not give consent in these cases.' **1914** L. WOOLF *Wise Virgins* v. He ... did not speak. 'I assume that silence means consent,' said Arthur. **1986** 'C. AIRD' *Dead Liberty* ii. 'Silence is consent,' said the superintendent. His knowledge of law had a magpie quality about it and he had picked up the phrase from somewhere. ■ **speech and silence 発言と沈黙**

silence ⇒ SPEECH is silver, but silence is golden.

You can't make a SILK purse out of a sow's ear.
豚の耳で絹の財布を作ることはできない。

質の劣る材料から貴重なものが作り出されることはない。物だけでなく人についても使われる（1672年の用例参照）。

☐**1518** A. BARCLAY *Eclogues* (EETS) v. 360 None can ... make goodly silke of a gotes flece. **1579** S. GOSSON *Ephemerides of Phialo* 62ᵛ Seekinge ... too make a silke purse of a Sowes eare, that when it shoulde close, will not come togeather. **1672** W. WALKER *English & Latin Proverbs* 44 You cannot make a ... silk purse of a sows ear; a scholar of a blockhead. **1834** MARRYAT *Peter Simple* I. xii. The master ... having been brought up in a collier, he could not be expected to be very refined ... 'It was impossible to make a silk purse out of a sow's ear.' **1915** D. H. LAWRENCE *Rainbow* i. You can't make a silk purse out of a sow's ear, as he told his mother very early, with regard to himself. **1985** M. SLUNG *Momilies* 83 You can't make a silk purse out of a sow's ear. ■ **possibility and impossibility 可能性と不可能性**

silk ⇒ An APE's an ape, a varlet's a varlet, though they be clad in silk or scarlet.

silly ⇒ ASK a silly question and you get a silly answer.

silver ⇒ Every CLOUD has a silver lining; SPEECH is silver, but silence is golden.

It's a SIN to steal a pin.
ピン１本でも盗むと罪になる。

（訳注：この場合の to steal ... には「…を盗むと」といった条件的意味がある。*To* see her is to love her.〈彼女に会えば一目でほれる〉）

どんなに些細なことでも不誠実は許されない。

☐**1875** A. B. CHEALES *Proverbial Folk-Lore* 129 It is a sin To steal a pin, as we, all of us, used to be informed in the nursery. **1945** F. THOMPSON *Lark Rise* xiii. Children were taught to 'know it's a sin to steal a pin' ... when they brought home some doubtful finding. **1956** O. M. DISNEY *Un-*

appointed *Rounds* xvii. I brought that boy up ... and I taught him to be honest.... I used to say to him. ''Tis a sin to steal a penny or a pin,' and he'd say it after me. ■ **honesty and dishonesty** 正直と不正直；**theft** 窃盗

sin ⇒ CHARITY covers a multitude of sins; OLD sins cast long shadows.

sincerest ⇒ IMITATION is the sincerest form of flattery.

SING before breakfast, cry before night.
朝食を食べる前に歌い、夜が来る前に泣く。
（訳注：喜びはしばしば苦しみの始まりである）

前後を逆にした形式でも使われる（1954年の用例参照）。

☐ **1530** J. PALSGRAVE *L'eclaircissernent de la Langue Française* 404 You waxe mery this morning god gyue grace you wepe nat or [before] nyght. **1611** R. COTGRAVE *Dict. French & English* s.v. Soir, Some laugh arnornings who ere night shed teares. **1721** J. KELLY *Scottish Proverbs* 332 They that laugh in the Morning may greet [weep] e'er Night. **1940** 'T. CHANSLOR' *Our First Murder* xii. 'You remember the saying. "Sing before breakfast—"' 'Oh dear— "cry before night."' **1954** A. SETON *Katherine* xxxi. Cry before breakfast, sing before supper. ■ **merriment** 談笑・陽気な賑わい

sing ⇒ Little BIRDS that can sing and won't sing must be made to sing; The OPERA isn't over till the fat lady sings; If you can WALK you can dance, if you can talk you can sing.

single ⇒ BEAUTY draws with a single hair; A journey of a thousand miles begins with a single step.

singly ⇒ MISFORTUNES never come singly.

sink ⇒ LITTLE leaks sink the ship.

sinner ⇒ The GREATER the sinner, the greater the saint.

If you SIT by the river for long enough, you will see the body of your enemy float by.
川辺にじっと座っていれば、敵の死体が流れていくのが見える。
（訳注：you は総称的な用法。*You* never can tell what's going to happen.〈何が起きるかは誰にもわからない〉。「石の上にも 3 年」。「待てば海路の日和あり」）

現代のことわざで、敵と相対するときは積極的に復讐するよりも我慢することを推奨する中国語（1995年と2000年の用例参照）、あるいは日本語（2004年の用例参照）のことわざに由来すると考えられている。

☐ **1995** S. FRENCH in *New Statesman* Aug. (online) My other favourite Confucius saying goes as follows: 'If you sit by the river for long enough, you will see the body of your enemy float by.' **2000** *New York Times* 10 May (online) A high-stakes gambler..., Mr. Edwards then acknowledged that his luck might finally have run dry. 'The Chinese have a saying that if you sit by the river

406　sit

long enough, the dead body of your enemy will come floating down the river,' he said … 'I suppose the feds sat by the river long enough, and here comes my body.' **2004** 'The long, slow painful death of Film Festivals' posting 28 Dec. on *www.filmthreat.com* Remember the old Japanese proverb 'If you sit by the river long enough, sooner or later the body of your enemy will go floating by.' ■ action and inaction 行為と結果；patience and impatience 忍耐と性急；revenge 復讐

sit ⇒ Where MACGREGOR sits is the head of the table.

It is ill SITTING at Rome and striving with the Pope.
ローマにいながら、法王と敵対するのはまずい。

権威者の支配下にある場所で反抗的な態度をとるのは賢明でない。

　　□*a*1628 J. CARMICHAELL *Proverbs in Scots* no. 1847 Ye may not sit in Rome and strive with the Pape. **1721** J. KELLY *Scottish Proverbs* 194 It is hard to sit in Rome, and strive against the Pope. It is foolish to strive with our Governours, Landlords, or those under whose Distress we are. **1908** A. MACLAREN *Ezekiel* 58 'It is ill sitting at Rome and striving with the Pope.' Nebuchadnezzar's palace was not precisely the place to dispute with Nebuchadnezzar. ■ conduct 行い・品行；prudence 思慮・分別

sitting ⇒ It is as CHEAP sitting as standing.

situation ⇒ DESPERATE diseases must have desperate remedies.

SIX hours' sleep for a man, seven for a woman, and eight for a fool.
男には 6 時間、女には 7 時間、愚か者には 8 時間の睡眠が必要である。

多くの異なった言い方があるが、ナポレオンが登場する以前から使われていたことは確かである（2013 年の用例参照）。

　　□1623 J. WODROEPHE *Spared Hours of Soldier* 310 The Student sleepes six Howres, the Traueller seuen; the Workeman eight, and all Laizie Bodies sleepe nine houres and more. **1864** J. H. FRISWELL *Gentle Life* 259 John Wesley … considered that five hours' sleep was enough for him or any man.… The old English proverb, so often in the mouth of George III, was 'six hours for a man, seven for a woman, and eight for a fool'. **1908** *Spectator* 19 Dec. 1047 Is there not a proverb that a man requires six hours' sleep, a woman seven, a child eight and only a fool more? If this be true, thousands of great men were, and are, fools. **2013** *www.bbc.co.uk/news/magazine* When Napoleon Bonaparte was asked how many hours sleep people need, he is said to have replied: 'Six for a man, seven for a woman, eight for a fool.' ■ health 健康

size ⇒ ONE size does not fit all.

skin ⇒（名詞）NEAR is my shirt, but nearer is my skin; Don't SELL the skin till you have caught the bear;（動詞）There is more than one WAY to skin a cat.

skin-deep ⇒ BEAUTY is only skin-deep.

skittle ⇒ LIFE isn't all beer and skittles.

SLICE 407

If the SKY falls we shall catch larks.
空が落ちてくればヒバリが捕れる。

「たとえ起こりそうにないことであっても、もしそれが起こったなら、多くのことができる」とほらを吹く人を嘲る際に使われる。フィールディング『世界ことわざ集』(1824) 22. 参照。

□*c*1445 *Peter Idley's Instructions to his Son* (1935) I. 178 We shall kacche many larkis whan heuene doith falle. **1546** J. HEYWOOD *Dialogue of Proverbs* I. iv. B1v When the sky faith we shal haue larks. **1670** J. RAY *English Proverbs* 143 If the sky falls we shall catch larks. **1721** J. KELLY *Scottish Proverbs* 343 What if the Lift [sky] fall, you may gather Laverocks [larks]. **1914** G. B. SHAW *Misalliance* p. xxx. I cannot be put off by the news that our system would be perfect if it were worked by angels ... Just as I do not admit that if the sky fell we should all catch larks. **1950** C. S. LEWIS in *Month* Oct. 234 If ... the total content of time were spread out before me ... I could do what the Historicist says he is doing.... Yes; and if the sky fell we should all catch larks. ■ possibility and impossibility 可能性と不可能性

sky ⇒ RED sky at night, shepherd's delight; WINTER never rots in the sky.

slave ⇒ BETTER be an old man's darling, than a young man's slave.

sleep ⇒ One HOUR's sleep before midnight is worth two after; SIX hours' sleep for a man, seven for a woman, and eight for a fool.

Let SLEEPING dogs lie.
寝ている犬を起こすな。

（訳注：「やぶをつついて蛇を出すな」。「寝た子は起こすな」）

わざわざトラブルを引き起こすのは賢明でない。† 14世紀初頭のフランス語 *N'esveillez pas lou chien qui dort.*「寝ている犬を起こすな」

□*c*1385 CHAUCER *Troilus & Criseyde* III. 764 It is nought good a slepyng hound to wake. **1546** J. HEYWOOD *Dialogue of Proverbs* I. x. D1v It is euill wakyng of a slepyng dog. **1681** S. COLVIL *Whigs' Supplication* II. 27 It's best To let a sleeping mastiff rest. **1824** SCOTT *Redgauntlet* I. xi. Take my advice, and speer [ask] as little about him as he does about you. Best to let sleeping dogs lie. **1976** T. SHARPE *Wilt* xx. He would be better off sticking to indifference and undisclosed affection. 'Let sleeping dogs lie,' he muttered. **1996** M. MACDONALD *Death's Autograph* ix. 98 'They don't have to prove it! He's dead. It can't do him any harm now.' She said distinctly, 'Let sleeping dogs lie, then.' ■ action and inaction 行為と非行為; busybodies おせっかい屋

A SLICE off a cut loaf isn't missed.
切ったパンを一切れ取っても気づかれない。

新しいパン1斤は切り取ればすぐにばれるが、パン一切れなら、すでに切られたものの中から一切れ取ってもなかなか気づかれない。性的な文脈で使われ、当該人物が処女ではないことを示唆する。

□**1592** SHAKESPEARE *Titus Andronicus* II. i. 87 More water glideth by the mill Than wots [knows] the miller of; and easy it is Of a cut loaf to steal a shlve [slice]. **1732** T. FULLER *Gnomologia* no. 3012 It is safe taking a slice off a Cut Loaf. **1901** F. E. TAYLOR *Wit & Wisdom of South Lancashire Dialect* 11 A shoive off a cut loaf's never miss't. (A satirical remark.) **1981** N. LOFTS

408　slip

Old Priory v. iii. I went into this with my eyes open and a slice off a cut loaf ain't missed. ■ **gains and losses** 利益と損失

slip ⇒ There's MANY a slip between cup and lip.

SLOW and steady wins the race.
遅くても着実な者が競争に勝つ。

（訳注：winsと単数形になっているのは、slow and steadyが 1 つのまとまった概念となっているため。「せいては事をし損じる」）

カメとウサギの競争を描いた『イソップ物語』から導き出される道徳観を要約したものである。つまり、自信過剰のウサギが途中で昼寝をした結果、遅いけれどもずっとついて来る競争相手に最後は負けてしまうという教訓である。† SLOW *but sure*.「遅くても確実にせよ」

□**1762** R. LLOYD *Poems* 38 You may deride my awkward pace, But slow and steady wins the race. **1894** G. F. NORTHALL *Folk-Phrases* 22 Slow and steady wins the race. **2002** *Washington Post Book World* 4 Apr. 4 In Gould's theory, slow and steady sometimes wins the race, but more often than not life is punctuated by catastrophic contingencies that fall in the realm of unique historical narratives rather than predictable natural laws. ■ **patience and impatience** 忍耐と性急 ; **ways and means** 方法と手段

SLOW but sure.
遅くても確実にせよ。

sureは正確に言うと「着実な、慎重な」という意味で、しばしばslowと対比して用いられる。例えば、**1562** G. Legh *Accidence of Armoury* 97 Although the Asse be slowe, yet is he sure.「ロバはとろいが、着実に進む」を参照。よく似たものに SLOW and steady wins the race.「遅くても着実な者が競走に勝つ」があり、この影響で表記のことわざでも wins the raceが後に続くことがある。1859 年の用例参照。

□**1692** R. L'ESTRANGE *Fables of Aesop* ccclxix. Slow and sure in these cases, is good counsel. **1859** S. SMILES *Self-Help* xi. Provided the dunce has persistency and application, he will inevitably head the cleverer fellow without these qualities. Slow but sure, wins the race. **1947** M. PENN *Manchester Fourteen Miles* xvii. No dressmaker ... ever learnt her trade in a hurry. 'Slow but sure' was the beginner's motto. **1985** D. & S. ROSEN *Death & Blintzes* xxi. But you know how we work, slow but sure. Getting the facts first and then narrowing things down. **2014** *Telegraph* 27 Dec. (online; *heading*) Design trends for 2015: slow but sure A reaction against the throwaway society has encouraged a renewed appreciation of craftmanship and thought ■ **patience and impatience** 忍耐と性急 ; **ways and means** 方法と手段

slowly ⇒ Make HASTE slowly; The MILLS of God grind slowly, yet they grind exceeding small.

SMALL choice in rotten apples
腐ったリンゴの中では選択の余地はほとんどない。

示された提案がすべてだめなものばかりである時に使われる。

□**1593** SHAKESPEARE *Taming of Shrew* I. i. 129 Faith, as you say, there's small choice in rotten apples. **1931** C. WELLS *Umbrella Murder* iv. 'I'm going upstairs, and you can come with me, or stay behind, as you choose.' 'Small choice in rotten apples.' **1958** 'S. DEAN' *Dishonor among Thieves* xxiii. It's a choice of rotten apples. ■ **choices** 選択 ; **necessity** 必要性・必然性

SMALL is beautiful.
小さなものは美しい。

シューマッハーの著名な本のタイトル（1973年の用例）で、製品の使用者に適した小規模な企画と技術を推奨する人々のスローガンとなっている。

□**1971** J. V. TAYLOR in *International Review of Mission* Ix. 328 (title)'Small is Beautiful'. **1973** E. F. SCHUMACHER (*title*) *Small is Beautiful. A Study of Economics As If People Mattered.* **1977** O. JAMES *Spy at Evening* xxiv. Small Is Beautiful—but big pays more. **1991** *Washington Post* 13 Jan. G8 In the 19th century, some classical composers forgot (if they had ever known) the principle that 'small is beautiful.' **2002** *Times* 2 May 23 Small isn't always beautiful and really small, like Nanoarchaeum equitans, which measures a whole 100 millionth of a millimetre less than the tiniest bacterium, may be a long way from even being visible to the naked eye. ■ **great and small** 大小

small ⇒ The BEST things come in small packages; BETTER are small fish than an empty dish; LITTLE things please little minds; There's no great LOSS without some gain; The MILLS of God grind slowly, yet they grind exceeding small.

smell ⇒ （名詞）MONEY has no smell; （動詞）FISH and guests smell after three days.

smock ⇒ NEAR is my kirtle, but nearer is my smock.

No SMOKE without fire
火のない所に煙は立たぬ。

煙の存在は火がどこかで燃えていることを示しているように、噂話もある程度の真実に基づいていることを示唆している。†プラウトゥス『クルクリオ』53 *Flamma fumo est proxima*.「炎は煙の真横にある」。13世紀後半のフランス語 *Nul feu est sens fumee ne fumee sens feu*.「煙が出ない火はなく、火のない所に煙も出ない」。c1375 J. バブアー『ブルース』(EETS) IV. 81 And thair may no man fire sa covir, [Bot] low or reyk [flame or smoke] sail it discovir.

□**c1422** T. HOCCLEVE *Works* (EETS) I. 134 Wher no fyr maad is may no smoke aryse. **1592** G. DELAMOTHE *French Alphabet* n. 39 No smoke without fire. **1655** T. FULLER *Church Hist. Britain* II. x. There was no Smoak but some Fire: either he was dishonest, or indiscreet. **1869** TROLLOPE *He knew He was Right* II. lii. He considered that ... Emily Trevelyan had behaved badly. He constantly repeated ... the old adage, that there was no smoke without fire. **1948** 'M. INNES' *Night of Errors* iv. 'Chimneys! ... Who the deuce cares whether there's smoke from every chimney in the house.' 'I do. No smoke without fire.' **2002** *Times* 8 July 8 'I've been found not guilty, but mud sticks. Some people will say: "There's no smoke without fire."' ■ **public opinion** 世論 ; **rumour** 噂

smooth ⇒ The COURSE of true love never did run smooth.

snake ⇒ The man who has once been BITTEN by the snake fears every piece of rope.

410 snow

snow ⇒ NORTH wind doth blow, we shall have snow.

so ⇒ So many MEN, so many opinions.

sober ⇒ WANTON kittens make sober cats.

A SOFT answer turneth away wrath.
柔らかい答えは怒りを鎮める。

（訳注：「笑顔に刃は向けられぬ」）

穏やかな、あるいは従順な対応は相手の怒りを鎮める。『箴言』15章1節（欽定訳聖書）A soft answer turneth away wrath.「柔らかい答えは怒りをそらす」を想起させる。†c1395ウィクリフ聖書 (1850)『箴言』15章1節 A soft answere brekith ire.「柔らかい答えは怒りをなだめる」

□c1445 *Peter Idley's Instructions to his Son* (1935) 1. 84 A softe worde swageth [assuages] Ire. **1693** C. MATHER *Wonders of Invisible World* 60 We would use to one another none but the Soft Answers, which Turn away Wrath. **1826** SOUTIIEY *Letter* 19 July (1912) 414 A soft answer turneth away wrath. There is no shield against wrongs so effectual as an unresisting temper. **1922** JOYCE *Ulysses* 597 A soft answer turns away wrath. **1979** J. SCOTT *Clutch of Vipersvi*. 'Yes, sir!' ... Soft answer, no wrath. ■ anger 怒り ; tact 機転

soft ⇒ SEPTEMBER blow soft, till the fruit's in the loft.

SOFTLY, softly, catchee monkey.
そっと、そっと、猿をつかめ。

望まれる結果は忍耐と策略を駆使することで首尾よく得られる。

□**1907** G. BENHAM *Cassell's Book of Quotations* 849 (Proverbs) 'Softly, softly.' caught the monkey—(Negro). **1939** H. C. BAILEY *Veron Mystery* xx. 'Softly talkee, catchee monkey,' Hopley summed up the method thus prescribed to him. **1941** F. VIVIAN *Death of Mr. Lomas* iv. 80 'Managed to dig out a suitable motive for Steadfall?' the Chief Constable asked slyly. 'I haven't done with him yet.' came the slow reply. 'Softly, softly, catchee monkee.... ' **1978** E. ST. JOHNSTON *One Policeman's Story* vii. They took with them the unique motto of the Lancashire Constabulary Training School, 'Softly, Softly, Catchee Monkey' which inspired the new programme's title, 'Softly, Softly'. ■ guile 狡猾・策略 ; patience and impatience 忍耐と性急 ; ways and means 方法と手段

softly ⇒ FAIR and softly goes far in a day; SPEAK softly and carry a big stick.

What the SOLDIER said isn't evidence.
兵士の話は証拠にならない。

噂話を証拠として報告してはならない。

□**1837** DICKENS *Pickwick Papers* III. xxxiii. 'You must not tell us what the soldier ... sail, sir.' interposed the judge; 'it's not evidence.' **1931** 'V. LODER' *Red Stain* xii. 'It was true!' ... 'True to you, ... but you have no means of proving it to us. What the soldier said is not evidence.' **1971** P. MOYES *Season of Snows & Sins* ix. 'There is an English *mot* about a *poilu*—no? ... What *le poilu* say cannot be in Court—is that it?' Henry grinned. 'What the soldier said isn't evidence.' ■ rumour 噂; soldiers 兵士; truth 真実・真理

soldier ⇒ The FIRST duty of a soldier is obedience; OLD soldiers never die.

If you're not part of the SOLUTION, you're part of the problem.
もしあなたが解決策の一部でなければ、あなたは問題の一部となっている。

クレヴァーの言葉 (1968年の用例参照) が現在でも使われているが、この発想自体はそれ以前からある。

□**1937** J. R. ALITUCKER in *California Journal of Secondary Education* xii. 158 Does the individual citizen so live, act, and react that he becomes a part of the problem or a part of its solution? **1968** E. CLEAVER *Speech in R. Scheer, Eldridge Cleaver* (1969) 32 What we're saying today is that you're either part of the solution or you're part of the problem. **1975** M. BRADBURY *History Man* v. 'If you're not the solution,' says Peter Madden, 'you're part of the problem.' 'It would be terribly arrogant of me to believe I was the solution to anything.' **1977** C. MCFADDEN *Serial* xxvi. Listen, don't you realize if you're not part of the solution you're part of the problem. **2001** *New Scientist* 24 Nov. 112 MTV used to broadcast environmental messages featuring the punchline 'if you're not part of the solution, you're part of the problem'. Indeed. ■ **assistance** 援助; **trouble** やっかい・苦労

some ⇒ You WIN a few, you lose a few.

You don't get SOMETHING for nothing.
ただで何かを手に入れることはできない。

イングランド北部には異なった言い方があり、それはYou don't get owt [anything] for nowt [nothing]. 「ただで何も手に入れることはできない」である。† **1845**ディズレーリ『シビル』I. I. v. To do nothing and get something formed a boy's ideal of a manly career. 「何もせずに何かを手に入れることが、男の成功に関する少年の理想となった」

□**1870** P. T. BARNUM *Struggles & Triumphs* viii. When people expect to get 'something for nothing' they are sure to be cheated. **1947** M. PENN *Manchester Fourteen Miles* xiii. No stranger, she declared emphatically, ever sent to another stranger 'summat for nowt' It would … be against nature. **1952** F. PRATT *Double Jeopardy* i. You don't get something for nothing, even in medicine. Perizone has a peculiar secondary effect. It releases all inhibitions. **1979** *Guardian* 18 June 10 Stravinsky and Auden … [are] saying 'You don't get something for nothing.' If you want the lovely things … you can't have them unless you're prepared to pay for them. **1979** *Church Times* 29 June 13 You don't get owt for nowt. **2014** *www.independent.ie* 22 Nov. It's often said that you don't get something for nothing but with taking hardwood cuttings this is simply not true. ■ **reciprocity** 相互扶助

SOMETHING is better than nothing.
何もないより何かあった方がよい。
(訳注：「枯れ木も山のにぎわい」)

心情的に類似したものに HALF a loaf is better than no bread. 「半塊のパンでも全くないよりはましだ」がある。† 15世紀初頭のフランス語*Mieubc vault aucun bien que neant.* 「無いよりあるほうがましだ」

□**1546** J. HEYWOOD *Dialogue of Proverbs* I. ix. DI And by this prouerbe appereth this o [one]

412　something

thyng, That alwaie somwhat is better than nothyng. **1612** T. SHELTON tr. *Ceruantes' Don Quixote*
III. vii. I will weare it as I may: for something is better then nothing. **1842** J. T. IRVING *Attorney*
xvii. Something is better than nothing—nothing is better than starving. **1980** *Country Life* 24 Apr.
1283 Mrs Smith worked out her own charitable rules: give what can be given in kind (for something is better than nothing) but never give money. ■ **content and discontent　満足と不満足**

something ⇒ If ANYTHING can go wrong, it will.

My SON is my son till he gets him a wife, but my daughter's my daughter all the days of her life.
私の息子は彼が妻を迎えるまでは私の息子であるが、私の娘は彼女が生きている限り私の娘である。

　　息子は結婚すると独立し、自分の家庭を持つが、娘はずっと実家の近くに住み、心理的に
　　もおそらく経済的にも親に依存するという考え方に基づく親子関係を述べている。1981
　　年の用例は「古臭い」ことわざだとしている。

　□**1670** J. RAY *English Proverbs* 53 My son's my son, till he hath got him a wife, But my daughter's my daughter all days of her life. **1863** C. READE *Hard Cash* I. v. 'Oh, mamma,' said Julia
wannly, 'and do you think all the marriage in the world … can make me lukewarm to my …
mother? … It's a son who is a son only till he gets him a wife: but your daughter's your daughter, all-the-days-of her life. **1943** A. THIRKELL *Growing Up* iii. She doesn't hear from him for
months at a time now of course and then it's only a wire as often as not, but your son's your son
till he gets him a wife, as the saying is. **1981** *Listener* 27 Aug. 206 There's a very old-fashioned
sort of saying we have in the North which goes, 'My son is my son till he finds him a wife, but
my daughter is my daughter the rest of her life.' ■ **children and parents　親子**

son ⇒ CLERGYMEN's sons always turn out badly; The DEVIL's children have the Devil's
luck; Like FATHER, like son; The SHOEMAKER's son always goes barefoot.

SOON ripe, soon rotten
早熟れの早腐り。

　　早熟の果物は早く腐りやすい。†ラテン語 *Cito maturum cito putridum*.「早く熟すと、
　　早く腐る」

　□**1393** LANGLAND *Piers Plowman* C. XIII. 233 And that that rathest [earliest] rypeth, roteth
most saunest. **1546** J. HEYWOOD *Dialogue of Proverbs* I. x. C4v In youth she was towarde
[promising] and without euill. But soone rype sone rotten. **1642** D. ROGERS *Naaman* x. Some indeed … are moved to … clisdaine by their inferiours forwardnesse, called them hastings, soone
ripe, soone rotten. **1887** S. SMILES *Life & Labour* vi. Very few prize boys and girls stand the test
of wear. Prodigies are almost always uncertain; they illustrate the proverb of 'soon ripe, soon rotten'. **1976** L. ROSTEN *O KAPLAN! My KAPLAN!* II. iii 'Parkhill,' Mr. Robinson steelily murmured,
'we may all profit from the ancient adage: "*Presto maturo, presto marcio?!*" Yes: "The sooner
ripe, the sooner rotten!" That applies to pupils no less than fruit!' ■ **youth　若さ・若者**

The SOONER begun, the sooner done.
(仕事は) 早く始めれば始めるほど早く終わる。
　　(訳注:「the 比較級, the 比較級」〈…すればするほどますます…だ〉の形式が使われている。*The* sooner,
　　the better.〈早ければ早いほどよい〉)

気の乗らない仕事を先延ばしにすることに対する警告。

□**1578** T. GARTER *Most Virtuous Susanna* (1937) I. 948 The sooner that we do begin, the sooner is it done. **1872** TROLLOPE *Golden Lion* xx. ' I suppose I might as well go to him alone,' said Michel, groaning. 'Well, yes.... Soonest begun, soonest over.' **1955** M. BOROWSKY *Queen's Knight* 46 Sooner task's begun, sooner task is done—so it's said. **1987** B. J. MORISON *Voyage of Chianti* vii. 'Would you like Viola and me to begin on her book tomorrow?' Amy asked him. 'The sooner begun, the sooner done.' ■ **beginnings and endings** 最初と最後; **efficiency and inefficiency** 能率と非能率

sore ⇒ The TONGUE always returns to the sore tooth.

sorrow ⇒ ONE for sorrow, two for mirth; Help you to SALT, help you to sorrow.

sorrowing ⇒ He that GOES a-borrowing, goes a-sorrowing.

sorry ⇒ BETTER be safe than sorry.

sort ⇒ It takes ALL sorts to make a world.

soul ⇒ BREVITY is the soul of wit; CONFESSION is good for the soul; CORPORATIONS have neither bodies to be punished nor souls to be damned; The EYES are the window of the soul; A NATION without a language is a nation without a heart; PUNCTUALITY is the soul of business.

sound ⇒ EMPTY vessels make the most sound.

If it SOUNDS too good to be true, it probably is.
その話はうますぎて本当と思えないなら、おそらくその勘は当たっている。

セールスマンや詐欺師が言ううまい話に乗せられてはならない。

□**1997** *Washington Times* 3 June B7 I'm sure you've heard the expression, 'If something sounds too good to be true, it probably is.' Well, in the investment world, I say, 'If something sounds too good to be true, it definitely is.' **2007** *New Scientist* 10 Nov. 76 In a few decades ... we'll be able to program robots to provide all the good stuff of relationships without the bad. If that sounds too good to be true, it probably is. **2014** *Times* 11 Oct. 63 Finally, the age-old adage still applies—if it sounds too good to be true, it probably is. Most scammers over the years ... have relied on victims not questioning their promises because they were so tempting. ■ **reality and illusion** 現実と幻想

source ⇒ A STREAM cannot rise above its source.

SOW dry and set wet.
乾いた土に種をまき、湿った土に苗を植えよ。

湿った土地にまかれた種は芽を出す前に腐ってしまうことから。† **1580** T. タッサー『農業経済』(rev. ed.) xxxv. 38ᵛ By sowing in wet, Is little to get. 「湿った土地に種をまく

と、ほとんど育たない」

☐**1660** S. RIDERS *Riders:1660 British Merlin* [observation on Apr.] In gardening never this rule forget To sowe dry, and set wet. **1846** M. A. DENHAM *Proverbs relating to Seasons*, &c. 11 This rule in gardening never forget—Sow dry and plant wet. **1985** *Observer* 3 Mar. 51 There is an adage for March which says 'This rule in gardening ne'er forget: Sow dry and set wet.' March is the month when most people's gardening year starts. ■ **garden lore** 庭にまつわる伝承

A SOW may whistle, though it has an ill mouth for it.
雌豚でも口笛を吹けるかもしれないが、その口は口笛には向いていない。

自分にふさわしくないことに必死で取り組んでいる人を指すのに使われる。1802 年の用例で言及されているグラナード侯はジョージ・フォーブス（1760-1837）のことで、グラナードの第 6 代伯爵で初代男爵でもあった。

☐**1802** M. EDGEWORTH *Letter* 19 Oct in *Maria Edgeworth in France & Switzerland* (1979) 10 He waddles on dragging his boots along in a way that would make a pig laugh. As Lord Granard says, a pig may whistle though he has a bad mouth for it. **1846** J. GRANT *Romance of War* I. xii. 'I dare say the Spanish sounds very singular to your ear.' 'Ay, sir; it puts me in mind o' an auld saying o' my faither the piper. "A soo may whussle, but its mouth is no made for't."' **1927** J. BUCHAN *Witch Wood* xvii. Ye say he has the speech o' aguid Christian? Weel-a-weel, a soo may whistle, though it has an ill mouth for it. ■ **possibility and impossibility** 可能性と不可能性

SOW an act, and you reap a habit.
行為という種を蒔け、そうすれば習慣という実が刈り取れる。

次のことわざ As you SOW, so you reap.「自分で蒔いた種は自分で刈り取らねばならない」をもっと詳しくしたもの。2 つの文が互いに独立しているとも取れるし、因果関係を持っているとも取れる。劇作家・小説家のチャールズ・リード（1814-84）の言葉とされることがあるが，1853 年と1881 年の用例では両方とも作者「不明」とされている。

☐**1853** W. LOVETT *Social and Political Morality* 6 Sow an act, and you reap a habit; sow a habit, and you reap a character; sow a character, and you reap a destiny. **1881** S. SMILES *Life and Labour* 1 Sow a thought, and you reap an act; Sow an act, and you reap a habit ... **1989** S. R. COVEY *7 Habits of Highly Effective People* I. 46 Our character, basically is a composite of our habits. 'Sow a thought, reap an action; sow an action, reap a habit; sow a habit, reap a character; sow a character, reap a destiny,' the maxim goes. **2011** R. LARSON *Gabriel's Insurrection* 3 Give him time and he'll outgrow it ... I don't know about that. Sow and [sic] act and reap a habit, as the saying goes. ■ **action and consequence** 行為と結果 ; **habit** 習慣

As you SOW, so you reap.
自分で蒔いた種は自分で刈り取らねばならない。
（訳注：「自業自得」）

『ガラテヤの信徒への手紙』6 章 7 節（欽定訳聖書）Whatsoever a man soweth, that shall he also reap.「人は自分の蒔いたものを、刈り取ることになる」

☐*a***900** Cynewulf *Christ in Anglo-Saxon Poetic Records* (1936) III. 5 Swa eal manna beam sorgurn sawath, swa eft ripath [just as each son of man sows in grief, so he also reaps]. *c***1470** *Mankind in Macro Plays* (1962) I. 180 Such as thei haue sowyn, such xall thei repe. **1664** S. BUTLER *Hudibras* II. ii. And look before you ere you leap; For as you sow, you are like to reap. **1871** J. A. FROUDE *Short Studies* 2nd Ser. 10 As men have sown they must still reap. The profligate ... may recover ... peace of mind ... but no miracle takes away his paralysis. **1978** F. WELDON *Praxis*

xxiv. 'You should never have left them,' said Irma 'As you sow, Praxis, so you reap.' 2000 'C. AIRD' *Little Knell* (2001) iii. 29 'But like it says in the Bible,' said Jennifer, 'as you sow, so shall you reap.' ■ action and consequence 行為と結果

They that SOW the wind shall reap the whirlwind.
風を蒔く者はつむじ風を刈り取るはめになる。

このことわざの後半部分は慣用句 to reap the whirlwind「愚かな振る舞い、悪意のある行為には必ず報いがある」としても使われる。『ホセア書』8 章 7 節 (欽定訳聖書) They have sown the wind, and they shall reap the whirlwind.「彼らは風を蒔いて、つむじ風を刈り取る」を想起させる。

□ **1583** J. PRIME *Fruitful & Brief Discourse* 11. 203 They who sowed a win de, shall reap a whirlewind, but they that sowed in iustice shall reape mercie. **1853** G. W. CURTIS in *Putnam's Magazine* Apr. 386 Ask the Rev. Cream Cheese to ... preach from this text: 'They that sow the wind shall reap the whirlwind.' **1923** O. DAVIS *Icebound* III. 98 Well—what's passed is passed. Folks that plant the wind reap the whirlwind! **1981** J. STUBBS *Ironmaster* xvii. I know that he who sows the wind shall reap the whirlwind. I dislodge a clod of earth, and start a landslide. ■ action and consequence 行為と結果

sow ⇒（名詞）You can't make a SILK purse out of a saw's ear.

span ⇒ When ADAM delved and Eve span, who was then the gentleman?

SPARE at the spigot, and let out at the bung-hole.
樽の止め釘を惜しんだばかりに、注ぎ口であふれ出させる。
(訳注：「一文惜しみの百知らず」)

1721 年の用例で意味が説明されている。ここで spigot は貯蔵樽の栓から流れ出る液体を調節するために使われる止め釘を指す。一方、bung-hole は (それよりはるかに大きい) 注ぎ口で、そこから樽を一杯にしたり、空にしたりする。なお、注ぎ口自体は止め釘によって閉められている。

□ **1642** G. TORRIANO *Select Italian Proverbs* 50 He holdeth in at the spicket, butletteth out at the bunghole. **1670** J. RAY *English Proverbs* 193 Spare at the spigget, and let it out at the bung-hole. **1721** J. KELLY *Scottish Proverbs* 299 Spare at the Spiggot, and let out at the Bung Hole. Spoken to them who are careful and penurious in some trifling Things, but neglective in the main Chance. **1885** E. J. HARDY *How to be Happy though Married* xiii. People are often saving at the wrong place.... They spare at the spigot, and let all run away at the bunghole. **1935** H. ZINSSER *Rats, Lice & History* xvi. It is all a part of the strange contradictions between idealism and savagery that characterize the most curious of all mammals. It leads to the extraordinary practice of what is spoken of as 'saving at the spigot and wasting at the bung'. **1966** L. BEERS *Wild Apples & North Wind* xxvii. That might fix it now, but next summer you'd be in as bad a squeeze.... If you save at the spigot you lose at the bung. ■ getting and spending 取得と消費；waste 浪費

SPARE the rod and spoil the child.
鞭を惜しむと子供をだめにする。

(訳注：このことわざでは、「鞭を惜しめ」と「子供をだめにせよ」という 2 つの命令文が並列されている。しかし、実際にそうせよと命令しているのではない。子供をだめにしたければ勝手にそうするがいい。しかし、そうすると、子供がだめになるぞと警告しているのである。命令文を並列して、どちらもやってはい

416 SPARE

けないと警告していることわざに、Marry in haste and repent at leisure.〈慌てて結婚、ゆっくり後悔〉などがある）

この and は帰結を導入する。『箴言』13章24節（欽定訳聖書）He that spareth his rod, hateth his son.「鞭を加えない者は、その子を憎んでいるのである」を想起させる。

□*c*1000 AELFRIC *Homilies* (1843) II. 324 Se the sparath his hild [stick], he hatath his cild. **1377** LANGLAND *Piers Plowman* B. v. 41 Salamon seide ... Qui parcit virge, odit filium. The Englich of this latyn is ... Who-so spareth the sprynge [switch], spilleth [ruins] his children. **1560** *Nice Wanton* Al^v He that spareth the rod, the chyld doth hate. **1639** J. CLARKE *Parremiologia Anglo-Latina* 161 Spare the rod and spoyle the child. **1876** I. BANKS *Manchester Man* II. Vii. 'Spare the rod and spoil the child' had not been abolished from the educational code fifty-five years back. **1907** E. GOSSE *Father & Son* ii. This action [caning] was justified, as everything he did was justified, by reference to Scripture— 'Spare the rod and spoil the child'. **2002** *Oldie* Aug. 64 It was good to hear ... how the Lord Chamberlain, the wonderfully named Sir Norman Bodkin, changed 'Spare the rod and spoil the child' to 'Spare the cane and spoil the child.' ■ **children 子供；discipline 規律**

SPARE well and have to spend.
十分に節約すれば、お金が必要になった時に安心である。

お金を節約する習慣が身についていると、お金を使う必要が生じた時に貯えがあって安心である。

□**1541** M. COVERDALE tr. *H. Bullinger's Christian State of Matrimony* xix. Spare as though thou never schuldest dye and yet as mortal spend measurably. To spare that thou mayest have to spend in honestye for goodes sake. **1635** J. GORE *Way to Well-doing* 25 A good sparer makes a good spender. **1721** J. KELLY *Scottish Proverbs* 297 Spare when you're young, and spend when you're old.... He that saveth his Dinner will have the more for his Supper. **1832** A. HENDERSON *Scottish Proverbs* 16 Spare weel and hae weel. **1977** J. AIKEN *Five-Minute Marriage* x. I've given them a polish and they've come up real tip-top! Spare well and have to spend, I allus say. ■ **thrift 質素倹約**

SPEAK as you find.
自分で見た通りに話せ。

他人の意見や報告に影響されるのではなく、自分の体験のみを語るべきである。

□**1594-8** SHAKESPEARE *Taming of Shrew* II. i. 66 Mistake me not; I speak but as I find. **1666** TORRIANO *Italian Proverbs* 294 no. 115 The English say, Let every one speak as he finds. **1937** A. QUILLER-COUCH 'Captain Knot' in *Q's Mystery Stories* 150 'There's a silly proverb tells ye to speak of a man as you find him. I found Kennedy well enough.' **1988** H. MANTEL *Eight Months on Ghazzah Street* 175 Look, I don't have any theories. I just go issue by issue. I just speak as I find. ■ **reputation 評判**

Never SPEAK ill of the dead.
死者の悪口を言ってはならない。

† τὸν τεθνηκότα μὴ κακολογεῖν.「死者の悪口を言ってはならない」（紀元前6世紀のスパルタのエフォロイ〈行政官〉を務めたチルトンの言葉に由来する）。またラテン語 *De mortuis nil nist bonum*「死者に関しては良いこと以外何も言ってはならない」も参照。

□**1540** R. TAVERNER tr. *Erasmus' Flores Sententiarum* A6 Rayle not vpon him that is deade. **1609** S. HARWARD *MS* ('Trinity College, Cambridge) 81^v Speake not evill of the dead. **1682** W.

PENN *No Cross, No Crown* (ed. 2) xix. Speake well of the dead. **1783** S. JOHNSON *Lives of Poets* (rev. ed.) IV. 381 He that has too much feeling to speak ill of the dead ... will not hesitate ... to destroy ... the reputation ... of the living. **1945** F. THOMPSON *Lark Rise* xiv. 'Never speak ill of the dead' was one of their maxims. **2002** K. HALL PAGE *Body in Bonfire* viii. 201 Faith remembered the conversation she'd overhead. No need to speak ill of the dead. But devastating as it might be, his wife's death had solved a major problem for the headmaster. ■ **reputation 評判；slander 誹謗中傷**

SPEAK not of my debts unless you mean to pay them.
私の借金を払ってくれる気がないのなら私の借金の話はするな。

他人の経済状態について口を出す人に対する叱責。

☐**1640** G. HERBERT *Outlandish Proverbs* no. 998 Speake not of my debts, unlesse you meane to pay them. **1875** A. B. CHEALES *Proverbial Folk-Lore* 88 Special proverbs supply us with some excellent admonitions.... Dont talk of my debts unless you mean to pay them. **1981** *Times* 2 Jan.10An old proverb recommends you not to speak of my debts unless you mean to pay them. ■ **money 金・金銭；tact 機転**

SPEAK softly and carry a big stick.
穏やかに話し、同時に大きな棒を持て。

物静かに話したり、外交を行なう際には武力に支えられている必要がある。米国大統領のセオドア・ルーズベルト（1858-1919）が多くの場面でこのことわざを用いている。彼はこのことわざが古くから使われているもの、あるいは（1900年の用例参照）西アフリカに起源があるものと主張しているが、そのような根拠はどこにもない。異形の walk softly ... も時折使われる。

☐**1900** T. ROOSEVELT letter 26 Jan. in *Letters* (ed. E. E. Morison, 1951-4) II. 1141 I have always been fond of the West African proverb: 'Speak softly and carry a big stick; you will go far.' **1982** *Christian Science Monitor* 21 July 9 Carry a big stick but speak softly—a lot more softly. That, in effect, is the wisdom being urged upon America's official information agency, the International Communications Agency (ICA), by its national oversight commission. **2007** *Times Mag.* 30 June 90 Strange game, diplomacy, I reflect ... Speak softly and carry a big stick, as someone once put it. I feel I let myself down on both counts. ■ **efficiency and inefficiency 能率と非能率；power 力・権力**

speak ⇒ ACTIONS speak louder than words; Out of the FULLNESS of the heart the mouth speaks; Who KNOWS most, speaks least; The KUMARA does not speak of its own sweetness; ⇒ No evil, hear no evil, speak no evil; TALK of the Devil, and he is bound to appear; THINK first and speak afterwards; ⇒ SPOKEN.

speaking ⇒ It's ill speaking a FULL man and a fasting.

Everyone SPEAKS well of the bridge which carries him over.
人は皆自分が渡る橋を褒め称えるべきものだ。

☐**1678** J. RAY *English Proverbs* (ed. 2) 106 Let every man praise the bridge he goes over. *i.e.* Speak not ill of him who hath done you a courtesie, or whom you have made use of to your benefit; or do commonly make use of. **1797** F. BAILY *Journal* 11 May (1856) 279 Let every one speak well of the bridge which carries him safe over. **1850** C. KINGSLEY *Alton Locke* I. x. Every one

418 species

speaks well of the bridge which carries him over. Every one fancies the laws which fill his pockets to be God's laws. **1886** G. DAWSON *Biographical Lectures* i. Our love of compromise ... has also been our great strength.... We speak well of the bridge that carries us over. **1996** C. STROHMER *Gospel and New Spirituality* (2004) xiv. 117 'Everyone speaks well of the bridge that carries him over,' says an ancient proverb. Non-Christian spiritual enthusiasts may speak favorably of the gospel when we have built communication bridges into their world. ■ **assistance** 援助; **public opinion** 世論

species ⇒ The FEAMALE of the species is more deadly than the male.

If you don't SPECULATE, you can't accumulate.
投機せずして財を得ず。

(訳注:「ノーリスク・ノーリターン」)

利益を得たいと思うなら、投資する危険も冒さなければならない。

☐**1925** WODEHOUSE 'Bit of Luck for Mabel' in *Eggs, Beans and Crumpets* (1963) 127 You can't accumulate if you don't speculate. So, though funds were running a bit low by this time, I invested a couple of bob in a cab. **1941** D. DODGE *Death & Taxes* xxiii. Krebs took out his billfold. 'Can you give me any assurance that you have useful information?' 'Nope.' ... 'You never accumulate if you don't specuate.' **1957** WODEHOUSE *Something Fishy* iv. Don't spoil the ship for a ha'porth of tar, or, putting it another way, if you don't speculate, you can't accumulate. **2009** B. ELTON *Meltdown* (2010) 29 'Can't accumulate if you don't speculate, babes. Gotta be in it to win it.' ■ **gains and losses** 利益と損失; **riches** 富; **risk** 危険

SPEECH is silver, but silence is golden.
雄弁は銀、されど沈黙は金なり。

短縮版の SILENCE is golden.「沈黙は金なり」も参照。

☐**1834** CARLYLE in *Fraser's Magazine* June 668 As the Swiss Inscription says: *Sprechen ist silbern, Schweigen ist golden* (Speech is silvern, Silence is golden). **1865** A. RICHARDSON *Secret Service* ii. A taciturn but edified listener, I pondered upon ... 'speech is silver, while silence is golden'. **1936** W. HOLTBY *South Riding* I. iv. She will give a pound note to the collection if I would cut my eloquence short, so in this case, though speech is silver, silence is certainly golden. **1961** M. SPARK *Prime of Miss Jean Brodie* i. Speech is silver but silence is golden. Mary, are you listening? ■ **speech and silence** 発言と沈黙

speed ⇒ More HASTE, less speed.

spend ⇒ SPARE well and have to spend.

spent ⇒ What is GOT over the DEVIL's back is spent under his belly.

sphere ⇒ A WOMAN's place is in the home.

spice ⇒ VARIETY is the spice of life.

SPRING 419

When SPIDER webs unite, they can tie up a lion.
蜘蛛の糸が結束すればライオン 1 頭でも縛ることができる。

アフリカのことわざで、一致団結することの大切さを述べている。

☐ **1987** J. SHREEVE *Nature* 66 'When spider webs unite,' says an Ethiopian proverb, 'they can halt a lion.' Large deer and antelope—the caribou, wildebeest, impalas, and the like—cannot. **2006** 'In the News' 18 Dec. on *www.redcross.org* There is an old African proverb that says: 'When spider webs unite, they can tie up a lion.' On Thursday, Dec. 14, the American Red Cross and our Malaria No More Partners will unite so that we can tie up the deadly lion of malaria.
■ **great and small** 大小 ; **strength and weakness** 強弱 ; **unity and division** 統一と分断

spider ⇒ If you want to LIVE and thrive, let the spider run alive.

spigot ⇒ SPARE at the spigot, and let out at the bung-hole.

spilt ⇒ It is no use CRYING over spilt milk.

spite ⇒ Don't CUT off your nose to spite your face.

splash ⇒ When the OAK is before the ash. Ten you will only get a splash.

spoil ⇒ Do not spoil the SHIP for a ha'porth of tar; SPARE the rod and spoil the child; TOO many cooks spoil the broth.

spoiled ⇒ BETTER one house spoiled than two.

spoken ⇒ Many a TRUE word is spoken in jest.

spoon ⇒ He who SUPS with the Devil should have a long spoon.

spot ⇒ The LEOPARD does not change his spots.

spread ⇒ MONEY, like manure, does no good till it is spread; in vain, the NET is spread in the sight of the bird.

It is not SPRING until you can plant your foot upon twelve daisies.
雛菊を12本踏みつけるまでは春が来たことにならない。

（訳注：plant＝「〈杭・足などを〉地面にしっかりと立てる、置く」）

雛菊は暖かくて快晴の時しか咲かないことに由来する。なお、踏まれる花の本数は様々である。

☐ **1863** R. CHAMBERS *Book of Days* I. 312 We can now plant our 'foot upon nine daisies' and not until that can be done do the old-fashioned country people believe that spring is really come. **1878** T. F. THISELTON-DYER *English Folk-Lore* i. 'It ain't spring until you can plant your foot upon twelve daisies,' is a proverb still very prevalent. **1910** *Spectator* 26 Mar. 499 Spring is here when you can tread on nine daisies at once on the village green; so goes one of the country

420 spring

proverbs. **1972** CASSON & GRENFELL *Nanny Says* 52 When you can step on six daisies at once, summer has come. ■ **calendar lore** 暦にまつわる伝承

spring（動詞）⇒ HOPE springs eternal.

The SQUEAKY wheel gets the grease.
きしむ車輪は油をさしてもらえる。

とかく、文句を言って大騒ぎする者やトラブルを引き起こす者に限って注意・関心が向けられがちである。

□**1903** C. STEWART *Uncle Josh Weathersby's Punkin Centre Stories* 6 I don't believe in kickin', It aint apt to bring one peace; But the wheel what squeaks the loudest Is the one that gets the grease. *a***1937** in J. BARTLETT *Familiar Quotations* 518 The wheel that squeaks the loudest Is the one that gets the grease. **1974** *Hansard* (Commons) 17 Oct. 502 It is the old story: the squeaky wheel gets the grease. **2001** *Washington Times* 29 June A20 We are all acquainted with the adage 'the squeaky wheel gets the grease.' For the past decade or so, liberals have been squeaking loudly and getting more than their fair share of the grease. ■ **trouble** やっかい・苦労

squeeze ⇒ An APPLE-PIE without some cheese is like a kiss without a squeeze.

stable ⇒ Because a MAN is born in a stable that does not make him a horse.

It is too late to shut the STABLE-door after the horse has bolted.
馬が逃げてから馬小屋の戸を閉めても遅すぎる。
（訳注：「火事の後の火の用心」）

当初は馬泥棒のことであった。当初は is stolen「盗まれる」であったが、今では has bolted「逃げてしまう」になった。†中世のフランス語 *A tartferme on l'estable, quant li chevaux est perduz.*「馬がいなくなった後で馬小屋の戸を閉めても遅すぎる」

□*c***1350** *Douce* MS 52 no. 22 When the hors is stole, steke [lock] the stabull-dore. *c***1490** in *Anglia* (1918) XLII. 204 Whan the stede ys stole, than shytte the stable-dore. **1578** LYLY *Euphues* I. 188 It is to late to shutte the stable doore when the steede is stolen: The Trojans repented to late when their towne was spoiled. **1886** R. L. STEVENSON *Kidnapped* xiv. A guinea-piece … fell … into the sea.... I now saw there must be a hole, and clapped my hand to the place.... But this was to lock the stable door after the steed was stolen. **1979-80** *Verbatim* Winter 2 It is too late … to shut the stable door after the horse has bolted. **1998** O. HARSTAD *Eleven Days* (1999) viii. 71 'Mike, maybe we should talk to Rothberg … ' 'Doesn't do much good to close the barn door after the horse is out' ■ **foresight and hindsight** 先見の明と後知恵；**futility** 無益；**lateness** 遅れ

stalled ⇒ BETTER a dinner of herbs than a stalled ox where hate is.

stand ⇒ EMPTY sacks will never stand upright; If you don't like the HEAT, get out of the kitchen; A HOUSE divided cannot stand; Every TUB must stand on its own bottom; UNITED we stand, divided we fall.

standing ⇒ It is as CHEAP sitting as standing.

step 421

starve ⇒ FEED a cold and starve a fever; While the GRASS grows, the steed starves.

stay ⇒ The FAMILY that prays together stays together; What happens on the ROAD stays on the road; What goes on TOUR stays on tour; What happens in VEGAS stays in Vegas.

steady ⇒ FULL cup, steady hand; SLOW and steady wins the race.

One man may STEAL a horse, while another may not look over a hedge.
馬を盗んでも許される人もおれば、生垣越しに中をうかがうことさえ許されない人もいる。

1670年の用例が説明しているように、我々は、えこひいきや偏見でもってその人の意図や行為を決めてしまいがちである。

☐ **1546** J. HEYWOOD *Dialogue of Proverbs* II. ix. K4 This prouerbe ... saith, that some man maie steale a hors better, Than some other maie stande and Joke vpone. **1591** LYLY *Endymion* III. iii. Some man may better steale a horse, then another looke ouer the hedge. **1670** J. RAY *English Proverbs* 128 One man may better steal a horse, then another look over the hedge. If we once conceive a good opinion of a man, we will not be perswaded he doth any thing amiss; but him whom we have a prejudice against, we are ready to suspect on the sleigh test occasion. **1894** J. LUBBOCK *Use of Life* ii. 'One man may steal a horse, while another may not look over a hedge' ... because the one does things pleasantly, the other disagreeably. **1921** A. BENNETT *Things that have interested Me* 315 Strange how one artist may steal a horse while another may not look over a hedge. **1957** R. WEST *Fountain Overflows* xi. Fancy him caring for her after all these years. Particularly when she treated him the way she did. But there, some people, can steal a horse, and others aren't allowed to look over the gate. ■ **reputation** 評判

steal ⇒ HANG a thief when he's young, and he'll no' steal when he's old; It's a SIN to steal a pin.

steed ⇒ While the GRASS grows, the steed starves.

One STEP at a time.
一度に一歩。

無理をして先を急ぐよりも用心して一歩一歩進む方が良い。

☐ **1853** C. M. YONGE *Heir of Redclyffe* II. i. One step at a time is all one wants. **1901** R. KIPLING *Kim* vi. It's beyond me. We can only walk one step at a time in this world. **1919** J. BUCHAN *Mr. Standfast* xvi. I did not allow myself to think of ultimate escape.... One step at a time was enough. **1986** M. SLUNG *More Momilies* 69 One step at a time is all it takes to get there. ■ **caution** 用心 ; patience and impatience 忍耐と性急

step ⇒ It is the FIRST step that is difficult; a journey of a thousand miles begins with a single step; From the SUBLIME to the ridiculous is only a step.

A STERN chase is a long chase.
真後ろからの追跡は長い追跡。

stern chase とは、追跡する船が追跡される船の船尾を追う追跡を指す。主に、風の影響を受ける帆船時代の話である。

□**1823** J. F. COOPER *Pilot* xv. 'If we can once get him in our wake I have no fears of dropping them all.' 'A stern chace is a long chase.' **1919** J. A. BRIDGES *Victorian Recollections* xiv. English poetry has had a start of some centuries, and a stern chase is proverbially a long one. **1929** G. B. VALE *Mystery of Papyrus* vii. 52 Followed again to-day by shabby native, but threw him off with complete success by getting rapidly into a taxi and driving round about. A stern chase is a long chase. **1994** L. NIVEN and J. POURNELLE *Griping Hand* 383 'Then their best bet is to take it easy,' Rawlins said. 'A stern chase is a long chase. Easy to use all your fuel in the chase and have none for the battle.' ■ **futility 無益 ; persistence ねばり強さ**

stey (steep)：⇒ Put a STOUT heart to a stey brae.

It is easy to find a STICK to beat a dog.
犬を叩こうと思えば叩くための棒はすぐに見つかる。

（訳注：この場合の to beat a dog には「犬を叩こうと思えば」といった条件的意味がある。*To see her is to love her.*〈彼女に会えば一目でほれる〉）

他人を苦しめようと思えば、酷い仕打ちや罵り言葉など、容易に見つかるものだ。

□**1564** T. BECON *Works* I. C5ᵛ Howe easye a thying it is to fynde a staffe if a man be mynded to beate a dogge. **1581** G. PETTIE tr. S. *Guazzo's Civil Conversation* III. 50 It is an easie matter to finde a staffe to beate a dog. **1782** F. HOPKINSON *Miscellaneous Essays* I. 266 A proverb ... naturally occurs on this occasion: It is easy to find a stick to beat a dog. **1875** S. SMILES *Thrift* xiv. Excuses were abundant.... It is easy to find a stick to beat a sick dog. **1908** *Times Literary Supplement* 6 Nov. 391 The reviewer seems ... predisposed to the view that any stick is good enough to beat a dog with. **1987** *Washington Times* 30 Apr. 11A When you want to beat a dog, any stick will do. ■ **excuses 言い訳**

stick ⇒（名詞）Up like a ROCKET, down like a stick; SPEAK softly and carry a big stick;（動詞）Let the COBBLER stick to his last; Throw DIRT enough, and some will stick; The NAIL that sticks up gets hammered down.

STICKS and stones may break my bones, but words will never hurt me.
棍棒や石なら私の骨は折れるかもしれないが、言葉などで傷ついてたまるものか。

元来は、悪口を言われた子供が相手に言い返した言葉であった。しかし、2001 年の用例はこれとは逆の主張をしている。なぜならマスコミによる言葉の暴力は度を越しているからである。類似したものに HARD words break no bones.「激しい言葉でも骨は折れない」がある。

□**1872** MRS. G. CUPPLES *Tappy's Chricks* 78 Sticks and stones may break my bones, But names will never hurt me. **1980** *Cosmopolitan* Dec. 137 'Sticks and stones may break my bones,' goes the children's rhyme, 'but words will never hurt me.' One wonders whether the people on the receiving end ... would agree. **2001** *Times* 28 Dec. 20 Sticks and stones may break some bones, but, as every journalist knows, words truly hurt. They rouse the fiends of fury, litigation and letters to the press. ■ **malice 悪意・恨み ; words and deeds 言動**

STIR 423

A STILL tongue makes a wise head.
物静かなら頭が賢くなる。

物静かな人は賢明である。A still tongue keeps a wise head. も使われる。

□ **1562** J. HEYWOOD *Works* Dd3ᵛ Hauyng a styll toung he had a besy head. **1776** T. COGAN *John Buncle, Junior* I. 238 Mum's the word.... A quiet tongue makes a wise head, says I. **1869** W. C. HAZLITT *English Proverbs* 35 A still tongue makes a wise head. **1892** A. QUILLER-COUCH *I saw Three Ships* vii. A still tongue makes a wise head. **1937** J. WORBY *Other Half* iv. 'I believe in the old saying "A still tongue keeps a wise head".' 'I guess you're right.... It's no business of mine.' **2005** R. BULLARD in H. Churchill *Prisoners on Kwai* 120 They were soldering some wires in a radio set. I never mentioned this; the old saying a still tongue keeps a wise head. ■ **speech and silence 発言と沈黙；wisdom 賢明・知恵**

STILL waters run deep.
静かな流れは水深し。
（訳注：「浅瀬(あだ)に徒浪(あだ)」）

一般に、穏やかな外見は情熱的または鋭敏な内面を隠すという意味で使われる。† Q. クルティウス『アレクサンドロス大王史』VII. iv. 13 *Altissima quaeque flumina minimo sono labi.* 「最も深い川が最も静かに流れる」（バクトリア地方のことわざだと言われている）

□ *c***1400** *Cato's Morals* in *Cursor Mundi* (EETS) 1672 There the flode is deppist the water standis stillist. *c***1410** J. LYDGATE *Minor Poems* (EETS) 476 Smothe waters ben ofte sithes [oftentimes] depe. **1616** T. DRAXE *Adages* 178 Where riuers runne most stilly, they are the deepest. **1721** J. KELLY *Scottish Proverbs* 287 Smooth Waters run deep. **1858** D. M. MULOCK *Woman's Thoughts about Women* xii. In maturer age ... the fullest, tenderest tide of which the loving heart is capable may be described by those 'still waters' which 'run deep'. **1979** M. UNDERWOOD *Victim of Circumstances* II. 86 As for her, still waters run deep, it seems. She always looked so solemn.... Fancy her shooting him! **2001** *National Review* 30 Apr. 60 Still waters run deep, so they say. The stillest and deepest belonged to Greta Garbo, who abruptly ended a dispute with Hollywood's moguls by saying, 'I tink I go home now.' She meant Sweden. ■ **appearance, deceptive 偽りの外見；speech and silence 発言と沈黙**

sting ⇒ If you gently touch a NETTLE it'll sting you for your pains.

stink ⇒ The FISH always stinks from the head downwards; FISH and guests smell after three days; The more you STIR it the worse it stinks.

The more you STIR it the worse it stinks.
掻き回せば回すほど臭う。
（訳注：「the 比較級, the 比較級」〈…すればするほどますます…だ〉の形式が使われている。*The* sooner, *the* better. 〈早ければ早いほどよい〉）

あやしい取引について詳しく調べれば調べるほど、いっそうあやしいとわかる。it は糞（1546 年と 1971 年の用例参照）。

□ **1546** J. HEYWOOD *Dialogue of Proverbs* II. vi. The more we stur a tourde [turd], the wours it will stynke. **1639** J. CLARKE *Parœmiologia Anglo-Latina* 200 The more you stirre it the worse it stinkes. **1706** P. A. MOTTEUX tr. *Cervantes' Don Quixote* II. xii. The more ye stir, the more 'twill stink. **1929** T. COBB *Crime without Clue* xx. The more we stir the worse it stinks, inspector. One would never imagine there were so many shady histories in this harmless-looking village. **1971** H. VAN DYKE *Dead Piano* iv. I could tell you.... But like my mama always used to say, 'The more you stir shit, the more it stinks.' ■ action and consequence 行為と結果; busybodies おせっかい屋

stir ⇒ You should know a man seven years before you stir his fire.

A STICH in time saves nine.
手遅れにならない一針は後で九針縫う手間を省く。

（訳注：「今日の一針、明日の十針」）

□**1732** T. FULLER *Gnomologia* no. 6291 A Stitch in Time May save nine. **1797** F. BAILY *Journal* 30 Apr. (1856) 268 After a little while we acquired a method of keeping her [a boat] in the middle of the stream, by watching the moment she began to vary, and thereby verifying the vulgar proverb, 'A stitch in time saves nine.' **1868** READE & BOUCICAULT *Foul Play* I. ix. Repairing the ship. Found a crack or two in her inner skin.... A stitch in time saves nine. **1979** *Homes & Gardens* June 105 Looking after oneself is like looking after a house: a stitch in time ... **2014** *www.daily-news.co.tz* 2 Dec. (*heading*) Medical checkup: A stitch in time saves nine.

STOLEN fruit is sweetest.
盗んだ果物が最も甘い（盗んだ快楽が最も楽しい）。

法で禁じられている快楽が最も楽しい。様々な異形を持つが、主にイヴの誘惑を想起させる（『創世記』3 章 6 節）。*c*1390 チョーサー『カンタベリー物語』「牧師の話」l. 332 The fleesh hadde delit in the beautee of the fruyt defended [forbidden].「肉体は禁じられた果実の美しさに心を奪われた」。類似した意味の STOLEN waters are sweet.「盗んだ水はおいしい」よりもよく使われる。

□**1614** T. ADAMS *Devil's Banquet* III. 98 But as the Proverbe bath it ... Apples are sweet, when they are plucked in the Gardiners absence. Eve liked no Apple in the Garden so well as the forbidden. **1668** F. KIRICMAN *English Rogue* 11. Bl^v So eager are these sort of people to buy any thing that is unlicensed, following the Proverb, that stolen meat is sweetest. **1855** GASKELL *North & South* II. vi. I can remember ... your being in some disgrace ... for stealing apples, ... Some one had told you that stolen fruit tasted sweetest. 1935 H. SPRING *Rachel Rosing* xxiv. He knew that he did not love her.... What else, then? ... He was not going to pretend that this stolen fruit was not sweet. 2001 J. MUDDIMAN and J. BARTON (eds) *Pauline Epistles* (2010) 74 Law is the parental command not to raid the biscuit tin, an injunction that ... makes all the more desirable the very thing it prohibits. As the old saying goes, Stolen fruit is sweetest. ■ theft 窃盗

STOLEN waters are sweet.
盗んだ水は甘い。

『箴言』9 章 17 節（欽定訳聖書）Stolen waters are sweet, and bread eaten in secret is pleasant.「盗んだ水は甘く、ひそかに食べるパンはうまい」を想起させる。† *c*1395 ウィクリフ聖書『箴言』9 章 17 節 Stoln watris ben swettere.「盗んだ水は甘い」。聖書の文脈では、通行人を誘惑する売春婦を指している。それゆえ、このことわざは違法な性交渉を指す際に使われる（1760 年の用例参照）。† STOLEN fruit is sweetest.「盗んだ果物が最も甘い（盗んだ快楽が最も楽しい）」の方がよく使われる。

□*c*1548 *Will of Devil* (1863) 9 This saying of the retcheles [reckless] woman in Salomon (Stollen waters ar sweete). **1614** T. ADAMS *Devil's Banquet* I. 3 Sinne shewes you a faire Picture—Stollen waters are sweet. **1721** J. KELLY *Scottish Proverbs* 298 Stoln Waters are sweet. People take great Delight in that which they can get privately. **1760** W. ANDREWS *Ephemeris for Year 1760* 'Touching the Spring Quarter' Stolen Waters are sweet and Stolen Wives may be sweeter, if no Bitterness follow after. **1976** A. J. RUSSELL *Pour Hemlock* ii. Lucarelli, fond of quoting scripture, ended the memo with 'Stolen waters are sweet'. ■ theft 窃盗

stomach ⇒ An ARMY marches on its stomach; The WAY to a man's heart is through his stomach.

stone ⇒ You cannot get BLOOD from a stone; You BUY land, you buy stones; CONSTANT dropping wears away a stone; Those who live in GLASS houses shouldn't throw stones; A ROLLING stone gathers no moss; STICKS and stones may break my bones, but words will never hurt me.

STONE-dead hath no fellow.
石のように硬くなった人（完全に死んだ人）には仲間はいない。

死刑推進派によってよく使われる（1926年の用例参照）。誤って、英国の将軍・護民官 O.クロムウェルの言葉とされることがあるが、実際はロバート・デヴァルーに由来する。彼はエセックスの第3代伯爵（1591-46）で、チャールズ王1世の相談役を務めたストラフォード伯爵（*a*1641年の用例参照）の処刑を迫るためにこの言葉を用いたとされる。ここで fellow は「仲間」を意味する。

☐*c*1633 *Soddered Citizen* (1936) l. 2618 'Is your ffather dead?' ... 'Laid with both Leggs Sir, in one lynnen bootehose That has noe fellowe, stone dead. *c*1641 CLARBNDON *Hist. Rebellion* (1702) I. Ⅲ. 191 The Earl of Essex ... answer'd, 'Stone Dead bath no Fellow.' **1828** MACAULAY *Essays* (1843) I. 144 Stonedead hath no fellow. **1926** *Times* 27 Aug. 11 The execution of the death sentence had been postponed for a week, an unusual period in a country where the adage' stone-dead bath no fellow' wins general support. ■ death 死; finality 結末・終局

stool ⇒ BETWEEN two stools one falls to the ground.

stop ⇒ When you are in a HOLE, stop digging.

storm ⇒ AFTER a storm comes a calm; ANY port in a storm; The SHARPER the storm, the sooner it's over.

One STORY is good till another is told.
1つの話が立派なのは次の話が語られるまでである。

人は最も新しく聞いた話の方を受け入れる傾向がある。

☐**1593** R. GREENE *Mamillia* II. 222 One tale is always good vntil another is heard. *a*1661 T. FULLER *Worthies* (Kent) 65 One story is good till another is heard. **1769** *Boston Gazette* 24 Apr. 2 The proverb, however homely it may be, will be allow'd by impartial men to be just, that 'one story is good, till another is told.' **1831** MACAULAY in *Edinburgh Review* Jan. 515 A theory is not proved ... because the evidence in its favour looks well at first sight.... 'One story is good till another is told!' **1922** JOYCE *Wysses* 121 One story good till you hear the next. ■ good things よいもの; novelty 目新しさ

story ⇒ Until the LIONS produce their own historian, ... ; Every PICTURE tells a story.

Put a STOUT heart to a stey brae.
険しい坂を登るには強い心を持て。

強い決意を持って難儀なことに臨めという意味で使われる。スコットランドのことわざ で、慣用句としても使われる。stey brae とは「険しい坂」を指す。

□*a*1585 A. MONTGOMERIE *Cherry & Sloe* (1821) xxxvi. So gets ay, that sets ay, Stout stomack is to the brae. **1721** J. KELLY *Scottish Proverbs* 287 Set a stout Heart to a stay Brea. Set about a difficult Business with Courage and Constancy. **1821** J. GALT *Annals of Parish* i. I began a round of visitations; but oh, it was a steep brae that I had to climb, and it needed a stout heart. For I found the doors ... barred against me. **1916** J. BUCHAN *Greenmantle* xii. He ... shouted to me ... to 'pit a stoot hert tae a stey brae'. **1937** S. SCOTT *Crazy Murder Show* v. Like the walls of Jericho, their resistance will eventually crumble if you peg away long enough. A stout heart to a stey brae, as my Inverness grandmother used to say. ■ **boldness** 大胆さ ; **perseverance** 我慢強さ

strange ⇒ ADVERSITY makes strange bedfellows; POLITICS makes strange bedfellows.

stranger ⇒ FACT is stranger than fiction; TRUTH is stranger than fiction.

straw ⇒ You cannot make BRICKS without straw; A DROWNING man will clutch at a straw; The LAST straw breaks the camel's back.

STRAWS tell which way the wind blows.
麦わらで風向きがわかる。

たとえ些細な兆候でも、将来の出来事や世間一般の感情・意見などを教えてくれる。慣 用句 a straw in the wind「風向き（世論）・予兆」としても使われる。

□*a*1654 J. SELDEN *Table-Talk* (1689) 31 Take a straw and throw it up into the Air, you shall see by that which way the Wind is.... More solid things do not shew the Complexion of the times so well, as Ballads and Libels. **1799** COBBETT *Porcupine's Works* (1801) X. 161 'Straws' (to make use of Callender's old hackneyed proverb)' ... 'served to show which way the wind blows.' **1927** A. ADAMS *Ranch on Beaver* vii. As straws tell which way the wind blows ... this day's work gives us a clean line on these company cattle. **1968** R. H. R. SMITHIES *Shoplifter* vii. You must remember that I was present at the contretemps which occurred at your house two days ago. Straws show which way the wind blows, Mrs. Pride! ■ **hints** ヒント・暗示 ; **omens** 前兆

A STREAM cannot rise above its source.
河の水位は水源地より高くはなれない。

何事もそれが生まれた源を超えることはできない。

□**1663** S. TUKE *Adventures of Five Hours* (Prologue) He would be ever w'you, but wants force; The Stream will rise no higher than the Source. **1732** T. FULLER *Gnomologia* no. 4771 The Stream can never rise above the Spring-head. **1905** H. A. VACHELL *Hill* 84 Clever chap.... But one is reminded that a stream can't rise higher than its source. **1921** T. R. GLOVER *Pilgrim* 125 It is held that a stream cannot rise above its source; but ... [a] river may have many tributaries, and one of them may change the character of what we call the main stream. **1952** R. A. KNOX *Hidden Stream* iv. Because after all the stream doesn't rise higher than its source, and God, however we conceive him, must be higher in the scale of being than anything he has created. ■ **be-**

stubborn　427

ginnings and endings 最初と最後

stream ⇒ Don't CHANGE horses in mid-stream; When the LAST tree is cut down, ... and the last stream poisoned, ... you will realize that you cannot eat money.

strength ⇒ UNION is strength.

strengthen ⇒ As the DAY lengthens, so the cold strengthens.

STRIKE while the iron is hot.
鉄は熱いうちに打て。

状況の機が熟したときであるならただちに行動せよという意味で使われる。鍛冶職人の言葉に由来する。†13世紀後半のフランス語 *Len doit batre le fer tandis cum ii est chauz.*「鉄は熱いうちに打たなければならない」

☐*c*1386 CHAUCER *Tale of Melibee* I. 1035 Whil that iren is hoot, men sholden smyte. **1546** J. HEYWOOD *Dialogue of Proverbs* I. iii. A4 And one good lesson to this purpose I pyke [pick] From the smiths forge, whan thyron is hote stryke. **1576** G. PETTIE *Petit Palace* 181 I think it wisdome to strike while the iron is hot. **1682** BUNYAN *Holy War* 18 Finding ... the affections of the people warmly inclining to him, he, as thinking 'twas best striking while the iron is hot, made this ... speech. **1771** SMOLLETT *Humphry Clinker* Ill. 242 If so be as how his regard be the same, why stand shilly shally? Why not strike while the iron is hot, and speak to the 'squire without loss of time? **1848** THACKERAY *Vanity Fair* xxi. Let George cut in directly and win her.... Strike while the iron's hot. **1974** T. SHARPE *Porterhouse Blue* xx. 'It seems an inopportune moment,' said the Senior Tutor doubtfully.... 'We must strike while the iron is hot,' said the Dean. **2000** 'G. WILLIAMS' *Dr. Mortimer and Aldgate Mystery* (2001) xxxii. 158 'Excellent!' I replied. 'Let us take up the invitation this very weekend: strike while the iron is hot.' ■ **opportunity 機会・好機**

strike ⇒ LIGHTNING never strikes the same place twice.

striving ⇒ It is ill SITTING at Rome and striving with the Pope.

stroke ⇒ DIFFERENT strokes for different folks; LITTLE strokes fell great oaks; Beware of an OAK, it draws the stroke.

strong ⇒ The CARIBOU feeds the wolf, but it is the wolf who keeps the caribou strong; GOOD fences make good neighbours; The RACE is not to the swift, nor the battle to the strong; YORKSHIRE born and Yorkshire bred, strong in the arm and weak in the head.

stronger ⇒ A CHAIN is no stronger than its weakest link; What doesn't KILL you makes you stronger.

stubborn ⇒ FACTS are stubborn things.

A STUMBLE may prevent a fall.
つまずいたおかげで転ばなくてもすむこともある。

小さな事故や障害が危険に気づかせてくれ、その結果、大きな事故や問題が回避されることもある。

□**1732** T. FULLER *Gnomologia* no. 424 A Stumble may prevent a Fall. **2010** *Chronicle Telegram* 3 Mar. (online) As the saying goes, 'a stumble may prevent a fall.' When it comes to balance a stumble may indeed be a wake-up call that all is not well. ■ **foresight and hindsight** 先見の明と後知恵 ; **prudence** 思慮・分別

stumble（動詞）⇒ It's a GOOD horse that never stumbles and a good wife that never grumbles.

The STYLE is the man.
文体は人なり。
（訳注：「文は人なり」）

書き方や話し方はその人の個性を示す。†ラテン語*Stylus virum arguit.*「文体は人を表わす」。ジョルジュ＝ルイ・ルクレール・ド・ビュフォン『博物誌』(1753) VII. p. xvii. *Le style est l'homme même.*「文体は人そのものである」

□**1901** A. WHYTE *Bible Characters* V. civ. If the style is the man in Holy Scripture also … we feel a very great liking for Luke. **1942** H. F. HEARD *Reply Paid* ix. Usually I don't like to have my style modified. 'The style is the man.' ■ **human nature** 人間性 ; **idiosyncrasy** 特異性・性癖

From the SUBLIME to the ridiculous is only a step.
崇高から滑稽まではほんの一歩にすぎない。
（訳注：「天才と気違いは紙一重」）

これは、駐ポーランド大使ド・プラド (D. G. ド・プラド『大使の歴史』…〈1815〉215)に贈られたナポレオンの言葉 *Du sublime au ridicule il n'y a qu'un pas.*「崇高から滑稽まではほんの一歩にすぎない」に由来する。ナポレオンの言葉は1812年のモスクワからの撤退の後で発せられたものであるが、実はこの考えはナポレオン独自のものではない。**1795** トマス・ペイン『理性の時代』II. 20 The sublime and the ridiculous are often so nearly related, that it is difficult to class them separately. One step above the sublime, makes the ridiculous; and one step above the ridiculous, makes the sublime again.「崇高と滑稽は紙一重なのではっきり区別し難い時もある。崇高から一歩はみ出すと滑稽になり、滑稽から一歩はみ出すと再び崇高に戻る」

□**1879** M. PATTISON *Milton* 116 The Hague tittle-tattle … ls set forth in the pomp of Milton's loftiest Latin.… The sublime and the ridiculous are here blended without the step between. **1909** *Times Literary Supplement* 17 Dec. 492 In the case of Louis XVIII, indeed, the ridiculous was, as it is commonly said to be, only a step removed from the sublime. **1940** W. & B. MUIR tr. *L. Feuchtwanger's Paris Gazette* II. xxx. viii. From the sublime to the ridiculous is only a step, but there's no road that leads back from the ridiculous to the sublime. **1983** 'M. INNES' *Appleby & Honeybath* iii. 'At least' he said, 'we can now go next door. Architecturally speaking, it's to move from the sublime to the ridiculous.' ■ **great and small** 大小

SUCKER 429

If at first you don't SUCCEED, try, try, try again.
たとえ最初はうまくいかなくても何度も何度もやってみよ。

特に米国において、短詩 Try (try) again は、19世紀児童文学において困難に直面した際に辛抱強く耐えることを勧める言葉としてよく引用された (1840年の用例参照)。一般には、W. E. ヒクソン (彼は『道徳的な歌』〈1857〉p.8の中で 3 つの try を使った上の表現を引用している) に由来すると考えられているが、パーマーの方が先である。この表現はすぐにことわざとして独自に使われるようになった。日曜大工の際に出くわすトラブルから生まれた現代のユーモラスな形式は、If at first you don't succeed, try reading the instructions. 「もし最初にうまくいかなければ、説明書をお読みください」である。

☐ **1840** T. H. PALMER *Teacher's Manual* 223 'Tis a lesson you should heed, Try, try again. If at first you do n't succeed, Try, try again. **1915** B. B. HOLT *Freudian Wish* iii. The child Is frustrated, but not instructed; and it is in the situation where, later on in life, we say to ourselves, 'If at first you don't succeed, Try, try, try again!' *a*1979 A. CHRISTIE *Miss Marple's Final Cases* 39 You mustn't give up, Mr. Rossiter, 'If at first you don't succeed, try, try, try again.' **2001** *Washington Times* 3 Aug. Al 7 John F. Hams reports, 'Bill Clinton this week will begin a second attempt at beginning his ex-presidency.' (If at first you don't succeed, try and try again.) ■ **perseverance** 我慢強さ; **success** 成功

succeed ⇒ NOTHING succeeds like success.

SUCCESS has many fathers, while failure is an orphan.
成功には多くの父親がいるが、失敗は孤児である。

人は、成功した業績で果たした自分の役割を自慢するが、失敗には口をつぐんでしまう。† **1942** G. チアノ『日記』9 Sept. (1946) II. 196 *La vittoria trova cento padre, e nessuno vuole riconoscere l'insuccesso.* 「勝利には百人の父親がいるが、失敗を自ら認める者は皆無である」

☐ **1961** J. F. KENNEDY *News Conference* 21 Apr. in Public Papers of Presidents of U.S. (1962) 312 There's an old saying that victory has 100 fathers and defeat is an orphan. **1991** *Washington Times* 29 Jan. Gl In the aftermath of the impeccably executed aerial attack that initiated the war with Iraq, the old saw that success has many fathers while failure is an orphan comes to mind. **2002** *Times* 11 June 19 In war, it has often been noted, victory has a hundred fathers, but defeat is an orphan. ■ **success** 成功

suck ⇒ Don't TEACH your grandmother to suck eggs.

Never give a SUCKER an even break.
乳飲み子には平等なチャンスなど無用である。

(訳注: break =「機会、チャンス」。Give him a *break*.〈彼にチャンスを与えてやれ〉)

愚か者、あるいは騙されやすい人は公正な機会を与える (または得る) に値しない。このことわざは E. F. アルビーと W. C. フィールズをはじめとする様々な人々の言葉に由来する。ミュージカルコメディ『ポピー』(1923) の中で、フィールズが台本には書かれていないこの言葉をアドリブで使ったことから一般に広まった。『ポピー』は1925年にサイレント映画化され、『曲馬団のサリー』というタイトルがつけられた。その後1936年にトー

キー（1936年の用例参照）としてリメイクされ、1941年に主演フィールズで *Never Give a Sucker an Even Break* として映画化された。

☐ **1925** *Collier's* 28 Nov. 26 'That line of mine that brings down the house always was true, wasn't it?' 'Which line?' I asked. 'Never give a sucker an even break' he [W. C. Fields] answered. **1936** *N. Y. Herald Tribune* 15 Mar. v. 1 Wasn't it 'Poppy' that provided him with his immortal motto, 'Never give a sucker an even break'? **1940** WODEHOUSE *Eggs, Beans & Crumpets* 158 Never give a sucker an even break.... But your sermon has made me see that there is something higher and nobler than a code of business ethics. **1979** *Daily Telegraph* 3 Nov. 24 The basic American business philosophy of 'never give a sucker an even break' runs rampant in those [money] markets. **2014** www.nzherald.co.nz 22 May 'It's all about never giving a sucker an even break ... I was never going to come off the field unless I was carried off and I never wanted. to give anyone else a chance.' ■ **fair dealing** 公正な取引；**fools** 愚か者

suckling ⇒ Out of the MOUTHS of babes—.

sudden ⇒ Hasty CLIMBERS have sudden falls.

SUE a beggar and catch a louse.
乞食を訴えてもしらみを得るのがおち。

（訳注：このことわざでは、「乞食を訴えよ」と「しらみを得よ」という2つの命令文が並列されているが、実際にそうせよと命令しているのではない。乞食を訴えても無駄だと警告しているのである）

財産を所有しない者に対して訴訟を起こしても無駄である。なぜなら、得られるものはなく、高額な裁判費用を支払うのが関の山であるからである。

☐ **1639** J. CLARKE *Parremiologia Anglo-Latina* 72 Sue a begger and get a louse. **1659** J. HOWELL *Proverbs* (English) 2 Goe to Law with a beggar, thou shalt et a lowse. **1732** T. FULLER *Gnomologia* no. 4285 Sue a Beggar, and catch a Louse. **1819** SCOTT *Bride of Lammermoor* iii. I guess it is some law phrase—but sue a beggar, and—your honour knows what follows. **1937** R. WINSTON *It's a Far Cry* xi. Such suit would have been useless as he was insolvent. The case indeed would have been the old one of suing a beggar and catching a louse! ■ **futility** 無益；**law and lawyers** 法と法律家

suffer ⇒ When ELEPHANTS fight, it is the grass that suffers.

SUFFICIENT unto the day is the evil thereof.
その日の苦労はその日1日だけで十分である。

先々の不安について心配する必要はない。それに向き合わなければならない日が来た時に心配すれば十分である。類似した意図を表わすものに Never TROUBLE trouble till trouble troubles you.「悩み事が汝を悩ませるまでは悩み事で悩むな」がある。『マタイによる福音書』6章34節（欽定訳聖書）Sufficient unto the day is the evil thereof.「その日の苦労は、その日1日だけで十分である」を想起させる。

☐ **1766** in L. H. BUTTERFIELD et al. *Adams Family Correspondence* (1963) I. 56 Sufficient to the Day is the Evil thereof. **1836** J. CARLYLE *Letter* 1 Apr. In *Letters & Memorials* (1893) I. 57 In the meanwhile there were no sense In worrying over schemes for a future, which we may not live to see. 'Sufficient for the day is the evil thereof.' **1979** M. BABSON *So soon done For* vii. 'I'll deal with these [bills] later.' ... 'Sufficient unto the day,' Kay agreed. ■ **good and evil** 正邪

supper 431

sufficient ⇒ A WORD to the wise is enough.

summer ⇒ The RICH man has his ice in the summer and the poor man gets his in the winter; One SWALLOW does not make a summer.

Never let the SUN go down on your anger.
憤ったままで、日が暮れるようであってはならない。

(訳注：on your angerの on は「いい状態で」の意。on fire〈燃えている〉)

恨みを抱いたままにせず、素早く対処せよ。『エフェソの信徒への手紙』4章26節（欽定訳聖書）Let not the sun go down upon your wrath. 「怒りに朝日を拝ませるな。」を想起させる。

□ 1642 T. FULLER *Holy State* III. viii. S. Paul saith, Let not the Sunne go down on your wrath; to carry news of the Antipodes In another world of thy revengefull nature. 1709 O. DYKES *English Proverbs* 189 We ought not to let the Sun go down upon our Wrath, or our Impenitence; neither ought we to let it conclude our Sluggishness. 1972 CASSON & GRENFELL *Nanny Says* 37 Never let the sun go down on your anger. 1981 M. MCMULLEN *Other Shoe* ii. Never let the sun go down on your anger, Clare's grandmother Herne used to say. ■ anger 怒り；forgiveness 許し・寛容；malice 悪意・恨み

The SUN loses nothing by shining into a puddle.
太陽は、たとえ泥水を照らしてもその価値は下がらない。

真に偉大で善良なるものは、たとえ無価値のものを扱っても汚れることはない。† ディオゲネス・ラエルティオス VI. Lxili. ὁ ἥλιος εἰς τοὺς ἀποπάτους, ἀλλ᾽ οὐ μιαίνεται. 「太陽は肥やしにも降り注ぐが、それで汚れることはない」。（ディオゲネスの言葉とされる）テルトゥリアヌス『見せ物について』xx. *Sol et in cloacam radios suos defert nee inquinatur.* 「太陽は下水道さえも照らすが、汚れることはない」

□ 1303 R. BRUNNE *Handlyng Synne* (EETS) I. 2299 The sunne, bys feymes neuer he tynes [loses], Thogh hyt on the mukhepe shynes. c1390 CHAUCER *Parson's Tale* l. 911 Though that hooly writ speke of horrible synne, certes hooly writ may nat been defouled, narnoore than the sonne that shyneth on the mixne [midden]. 1578 LYLY *Euphues* I. 193 The Sun shlneth vppon the dungehlll and is not corrupted. 1732 T. FULLER *Gnomologia* no. 4776 The Sun is never the worse for shining on a Dunghill. 1943 E. M. ALMEDINGEN *Frossia* iv. Dreadful words did fly about then, but the sun loses nothing by shining into a puddle. ■ associates 仲間；great and small 大小

sun ⇒ Happy is the BRIDE that the sun shines on; MAKE hay while the sun shines; There is NOTHING new under the sun.

sunny ⇒ If CANDLBMAS day be sunny and bright, winter will have another flight.

supper ⇒ AFTER dinner rest a while, after supper walk a mile; HOPE is a good breakfast but a bad supper.

He who SUPS with the Devil should have a long spoon.
悪魔と食事をしようとする者は長いスプーンを使うべきだ。

（訳注：he ＝「〈関係節を伴って〉…する者は誰でも〈性別は問わない〉」。*He who* has all the gold makes all the rules.〈金をすべて持つ者が法をすべて支配する〉）

危険な、あるいは悪意に満ちた人物とつき合う際の用心。

□ *c*1390 CHAUCER *Squire's Tale* I. 602 Therfore bihoueth hire a ful long spoon That shal ete with a feend. **1545** R. TAVERNER tr. *Erasmus' Adages* (ed. 2) 9ᵛ He had nede to haue a longe spone that shuld eate with the deuyl. **1590** SHAKESPEARE *Comedy of Errors* IV. iii. 59 He must have a long spoon that must eat with the devil. —What tell'st thou me of supping? **1721** J. KELLY *Scottish Proverbs* 147 He had need of a long Spoon that sups Kail with the Dee'! He that has to do with wicked ... Men, had need to be cautious. **1840** R. H. BARHAM *Ingoldsby Legends* 1st Ser. 270 Who suppes with the Deville sholde have a longe spoone! **1979** 'E. ANTHONY' *Grave of Truth* viii. Hindenburg and the army thought they could use [Hitler].... Who sups with the devil needs a long spoon. **2000** J. R. HAMPTON 'Clinical trial safety committees' on *europepmc.org* He who sups with the devil needs a long spoon. To cast the pharmaceutical industry in the role of the devil may seem a little unfair, but the British Biotech affair has shown ... that there are times when the industry must be kept at arm's length. ■ **associates** 仲間；**caution** 用心；**peril** 危険

sure ⇒ SLOW but sure.

suspicion ⇒ CAESAR's wife must be above suspicion.

SUSSEX won't be druve.
サセックスは操れない。

サセックスの人々は頑固で、自分の意志に反して何かを強制的にやらせることはできないことを主張する地域色豊かなことわざである。druv は drove の方言形である（標準的な英語では driven）。

□ **1910** in T. WALES *Sussex Garland* (1979) i. (*postcard*) Have got as fat as a Sussex [pig]—and 'wunt be druv' from Brighton. **1924** H. DE SELINCOURT *Cricket Match* vi. 'Well, we'd better be going, I suppose,' Gauvinier announced ... well aware that 'Sussex won't be druv'. **1939** 'D. FROME' *Pinkerton at Old Angel* vi. The sudden weariness in her frail face testified to years of patient leading. Mr. Pinkerton thought of the boast of the men of Sussex. They too couldn't be druv, they said. **1979** T. WALES *Sussex Garland* i. There ant no place like Sussex, Until ye goos above, For Sussex will be Sussex, And Sussex won't be druv! ■ **obstinacy** 頑固さ

One SWALLOW does not make a summer.
ツバメ 1 羽では夏が来たことにならない。

（訳注：「早合点は禁物」）

† ギリシア語 μία χελιδὼν ἔαρ οὐ ποιεῖ.「ツバメ一羽では夏が来たことにならない」。エラスムス『格言集』1. vii. *Una hirundo non facit ver.*

□ **1539** R. TAVERNER tr. *Erasmus' Adages* 25 It is not one swalowe that bryngeth in somer. It is not one good qualitie that maketh a man good. **1546** J. HEYWOOD *Dialogue of Proverbs* II. v. H3 One swalow maketh not sommer. **1659** J. HOWELL *Proverbs* (English) 11 One Swallow doth not make a Summer. **1844** DICKENS *Martin Chuzzlewit* xiii. One foul wind no more makes a winter, than one swallow makes a summer. **2000** 'G. WILLIAMS' *Dr. Mortimer and Aldgate Mystery* (2001) xiv. 78 One or two alfresco afternoons in the garden under the supervision of Ord and

Demmy did not spell liberation any more than one swallow made a summer ... 2014 *www.chron-iclelive.co.uk* 20 Oct One swallow doesn't make a summer. But a win is a win for Newcastle United. ■ **omens** 前兆

It is idle to SWALLOW the cow and choke on the tail.
牛1頭をまるまる飲み込んで尻尾をのどに詰まらせるのは愚の骨頂である。

1721年の用例からこの意味（＝出来もしないことをやり始めて途中で投げ出してしまう）がわかる。

□ **1659** J. HOWELL *Proverbs* (English) 13 To swallow an Ox, and be choaked with the tail. **1721** J. KELLY *Scottish Proverbs* 190 It is a Shame to eat the Cow, and worry [choke] on the Tail. It is a Shame to perform a great Task all but a little, and then give over. **1915** J. BUCHAN *Salute to Adventurers* xviii. We had gone too far to turn back, and as our proverb says, 'It is idle to swallow the cow and choke on the tail.' **1935** C. M. RUSSELL *Murder at Old Stone House* xvi. I'm not one to swallow a cow and choke on the tail. ■ **perseverance** 我慢強さ

swallow（名詞）⇒ The ROBIN and the wren are God's cock and hen.

swap ⇒ Don't CHANGE horses in mid-stream.

A SWARM in May is worth a load of hay; a swarm in June is worth a silver spoon; but a swarm in July is not worth a fly.
ミツバチの一群は5月なら干し草一荷分の値打ちがあるが、6月の一群は銀のスプーンの値打ちで、7月の一群は蝿一匹の値打ちもない。

（訳注：a swarm＝「ミツバチの一群」。worth…＝「…の値打ちがある」）

北半球におけるミツバチ飼育に関することわざである。ミツバチの群れによって巣が再生されるので、新しい巣を作り、春と夏の花々から蜜を収集する時間が多ければ多いほど望ましい結果となる（1879年の用例参照）。

□ **1655** S. HARTLIB *Reformed Commonwealth of Bees* 26 It being a Proverb, that a Swarm of Bees in May is worth a Cow and a Bottle [bundle] of Hay, whereas a Swarm in July is not worth a Fly. **1710** *Tusser Redivivus* 11 May The Proverb says, 'A Swarm in May is worth a Load of Hay'. **1879** R. JEFFERIES *Wild Life in Southern County* vii. 'A swarm in May is worth a load of hay; a swarm in June is worth a silver spoon; but a swarm in July is not worth a fly'— for it is then too late ... to store up ... honey before the flowers begin to fade. **1945** F. THOMPSON *Lark Rise* v. As she reminded the children: A swarm in May's worth a rick of hay; And a swarm in June's worth a silver spoon; while A swarm in July isn't worth a fly. **1985** N. FOSTER *Dog Rock* ii. A swarm of bees in May is worth a load of hay, A swarm of bees in June is worth a silver spoon, A swarm of bees in July is worth not a fly. On that basis, a swarm of bees now would be worth a milking cow, but I won't be joining it to one of my colonies. ■ **calendar lore** 暦にまつわる伝承

If every man would SWEEP his own doorstep the city would soon be clean.
皆が自宅の戸口を掃いてさえくれれば、町全体がすぐにきれいになるのだが。

共同体の利益に貢献することに対して全員が責任を持つ必要がある。個々の努力があれば、それがたとえどれだけ些細なものでも、全体の目標を達成するのに役立つ。

□ **1624** T. ADAMS *Temple* 65 When we would haue the street cleansed, let euery man sweep his owne doore, and it is quickly done. **1666** G. TORRIANO *Italian Proverbs* 41 If every one will sweep his own house, the City will be clean. **1930** *Times* 25 Mar. 10 It appears to be hard to draw a clear distinction between deciding a question of right and wrong for one's self and deciding it for others…. 'If every man would sweep his own doorstep the city would soon be clean.' **2002** *Washington Times* 14 Aug. B5 You're right—and if everyone swept his own doorstep, this world would be a cleaner place. ■ **cleanliness** 清潔さ ; **society** 社会

SWEEP the house with broom in May, you sweep the head of the house away.
5月に箒で家を掃けば、その家の主人を掃き出すことになる。

エニシダ（箒の材料）を魔女と魔法に結び付ける民間伝承は古くから浸透している。花が咲いているエニシダは不吉とされ、それが家に持ち込まれると死人が出ると考えられた。5月は不吉であるという考えはいくつかの古いことわざから見て取れる。例えば、MAR-RY in May, rue for aye.「5月に結婚するとのちのち後悔する」が挙げられる。

□**1873** *Folk-Lore Record* I. 52 The old gentleman … strictly forbade green brooms being used in his house during the month of May, and, as a reason for the prohibition, used to quote the adage — 'If you sweep the house with broom in May, You'll sweep the head of that house away'. **1943** H. C. BAILEY *Mr. Fortune Finds Pig* (1948) xvi. 64 'What hadn't you thought of? Rosen demanded sharply. '"Sweep the house with broom in May", 'Reggie murmured, "You sweep the head of the house away."' ■ **calendar lore** 暦にまつわる伝承 ; **superstition** 迷信

sweep ⇒ NEW brooms sweep clean.

With a SWEET tongue and kindness, you can drag an elephant by a hair.
甘い言葉と優しさがあれば、象を髪の毛1本で引っ張ることもできる。

イラン起源。… drag a snake …「…蛇を引っ張る…」という言い方もある。

□**2001** *Seattle Times* 31 Mar. All With a sweet tongue and kindness you can drag an elephant by a hair. —Persian proverb. **2006** *Times* 4 Sept 20 Another local maxim appears to capture the outside world's response to Iran's nuclear ambitions. It is akin to an ancient remark: 'A gentle hand may lead an elephant by a hair.' For that is clearly the approach that Kofi Annan, on behalf of the United Nations, and Javier Solana, for the European Union, are adopting. ■ **gentleness** 優しさ ; **tact** 機転

sweet ⇒ LITILE fish are sweet; REVENGE is sweet; STOLEN fruit is sweetest; STOLEN waters are sweet.

sweeter ⇒ The NEARER the bone, the sweeter the meat.

From the SWEETEST wine, the tartest vinegar.
最も甘いぶどう酒が最も酸っぱい酢になる。

（訳注：「可愛さ余って憎さ百倍」）

熱愛は憎悪に代わりやすいという文脈でよく使われる。

□**1578** LYLY *Euphues* I. 197 As the best wine doth make the sharpest vinaigar, so the deepest loue tourneth to the deadliest hate. **1637** J. HOWELL *Familiar Letters* 3 Feb. (1903) II. 140 He swears he had rather see a basilisk than her [his former love]. The sweetest wines may turn to the tartest vinegar. **1852** B. FITZGERALD *Polonius* 9 'It is … the sweetest wine that makes the sharpest vinegar,' says an old proverb. **1979** *Daedalus Summer* 121 The juxtaposition silently signals the cautionary maxim 'From the sweetest wine, the tartest vinegar'. ■ **opposites** 両極

sweetness ⇒ The KOMARA does not speak of its own sweetness.

swift ⇒ The RACE is not to the swift, nor the battle to the strong.

swim ⇒ Don't go near the WATER until you learn how to swim.

swine ⇒ Do not throw PEARLS to swine; On SAINT Thomas the Divine kill all turkeys, geese, and swine.

swing ⇒ What you LOSE on the swings you gain on the roundabouts.

Swithun ⇒ SAINT Swithun's day, if thou be fair, for forty days it will remain.

sword ⇒ Whosoever DRAWS his sword against the prince must throw the scabbard away; He who LIVES by the sword dies by the sword; The PEN is mightier than the sword.

T

table ⇒ Where MACGREGOR sits is the head of the table.

tail ⇒ Every HERRING must hang by its own gill; the HIGHER the monkey climbs the more he shows his tail; It is idle to SWALLOW the cow and choke on the tail.

tailor ⇒ NINE tailors make a man.

TAKE the goods the gods provide.
神が授けてくださるものは受け取りなさい。

† プラウトゥス『網曳き』I. 1229 *Habeas quod id ant boni.*「神が与えてくださったものは自分のものにしてよい」

☐ **1697** DRYDEN *Alexander's Feast* 5 Lovely Thais sits beside thee, Take the good the gods provide thee. **1880** TROLLOPE *Duke's Children* III. Xiv. 'It is only because I am the governor's son,' Silverbridge pleaded.... 'What of that? Take the goods the gods provide you.' **1980** M. MCMULLEN *Something of Night* viii. Take the goods the gods provide, and don't ... sulk when they are snatched away. ■ good fortune 幸運；opportunity 機会・好機

take ⇒ It takes ALL sorts to make a world; You can take the BOY out of the country but you can't take the country out of the boy; GIVE a thing, and take a thing, to wear the Devil's gold ring; GIVE and take is fair play; You can take a HORSE to the water, but you can't make him drink; You PAYS your money and you takes your choice; Take care of the PENCE and the pounds will take care of themselves; It takes TWO to make a bargain; It takes TWO to make a quarrel; It takes TWO to tango.

It TAKES one to know one.
君だって同類ではないか。

現在では、名指しで誰かを侮辱するような人を黙らせる言葉として使われることが多い（2009 年の用例参照）。

☐ **1977** *National Journal* 9 July 1090 In the it-takes-one-to-know-one category. Lester L. Kinsolving. among other jobs, is serving as national editor for the Panax Corp. newspapers. **1997** *Buffalo News* 27 Aug. 9D We hear that a local dude discourages his wife from buying antiques by saying. 'It takes one to know one.' **2001** R. HILL *Dialogues of Dead* xxiii. 200 'Sam just wasn't the suicidal type.' 'Takes a one to know a one, does it?' said Dalziel. **2007** *New Scientist* 23 June 37 (*heading*)

TALK 437

Birds that have never stolen do not re-hide their cache. It takes a thief to know a thief. **2009** C. SELL *Cup of Comfort* 255 I would swoop in with suggestions of snappy comeback lines for him to use in a pinch: 'Takes one to know one!' … And Andy's favorite, 'Get a life!' ■ **similarity and dissimilarity** 類似性と相違性

A TALE never loses in the telling.
話は繰り返されるたびに大げさになる。

1721 年の用例が示しているように、話というものは口から口へと伝わっていくうちにしばしば誇張されたり、脚色されたりする。また、慣用句 to lose (or grow) in the telling 「話が大きくなる」としても使われる。**1541**『女子校舎』A4ᵛ What soeuer commeth to memorye Shall not be loste, for the telling.「記憶される事柄というのは語り伝えられて、話が大きくなる」。**1581**『文房具店の記録簿』(1875) II. 388 A good tale Cannot to[o] often be Tolde.「いい話というものは繰り返し伝えられていくものではない (しだいに悪くなる)」

□**1609** S. HARWARD *MS* (Trinity College, Cambridge) 121 Tales lose nothing by the cariadge. **1721** J. KELLY *Scottish Proverbs* 44 A Tale never loses in the telling. Fame or Report … Commonly receives an Addition as it goes from hand to Hand. **1907** *Spectator* 16 Nov. 773 A story never loses in the telling in the mouth of an Egyptian. **1954** L. P. HARTLEY *White Wand* 15 No doubt Antonio was telling the story to his fellow-gondoliers and it would lose nothing in the telling. **1979** M. STEWART *Last Enchantment* 19 Like all strange tales, it will grow with the telling. ■ **rumour** 噂

tale ⇒ DEAD men tell no tales.

Never tell TALES out of school.
学校の外で内輪の話をするな (秘密を外に漏らすな)。

1721 年の用例が、仲間と同僚の間の秘密事項を守秘することが望ましいという一般的な意味について説明している。ただし、文字通り、学校内での人や物について不満を漏らす子供に対して使われることもある。また、慣用句 to tell tales out of school「秘密を外に漏らす」としても使われる。

□**1530** W. TYNDALE *Practice of Prelates* Blᵛ So that what cometh once in may never out for feare of elling tales out of scole. **1616** J. WITHALS *Dict.* (rev. ed.) 573 You must not tel tales out of the Taueme. **1721** J. KELLY *Scottish Proverbs* 303 Tell no School Tales. Do not blab abroad what is said in drink, or among Companions. **1876** I. BANS *Manchester Man* I. xv. All attempts to make known school troubles and grievances were met with 'Never tell tales out of school'. **1963** A. CHRISTIE *Clocks* xxiv. 'Well—.' … 'I understand. Mustn't tell tales out of school.' **2010** *www.telegraph.co.uk* 15 Oct. Does he worry about those he upsets? 'No … I don't tell tales out of school. I make it a rule that I won't write or say something that I won't say to their face.' ■ **malice** 悪意・恨み

TALK is cheap.
話すだけなら安い。
(訳注：「言うは易く行なうは難し」)

† *c*1600 A. マンデー他 *Sir T. More* (1911) 23 Woords are but wordes, and payes not what men owe.「言葉は言葉にすぎない。借金を支払ってはくれない」。**1639** チャ

438　TALK

ップマン & シャーリー *Ball* v. i. You may heare talke; but give me the man That has measur'd 'em: talkes but talke.「あなたはここでしゃべってもかまわない。しかし、それらを見積もった男を教えてくれ。話は話にすぎない」

　□**1668** R. B. Adagia *Scotica* 47 Seying goes good cheap. **1843** T. C. HALIBURTON *Attaché* I. ii. Talk is cheap, it don't cost nothin' but breath. **1929** K. C. STRAHAN *Footprints* i. Talk's cheap. You could never make me believe that. **2002** *Washington Times* 16 Mar. F15 (*Herb & Jamaal comic strip*) 'Talk is cheap ... because the supply always exceeds the demand.' ■ **boasting** 自慢 ; **words and deeds** 言動

TALK of the Devil, and he is bound to appear.
悪魔の噂をすると必ず悪魔が姿を現わす。
（訳注：「噂をすれば影がさす」）

Talk of the Devil!「噂をすればなんとやらか！」と省略される場合もある。ちょうど話題に上がっていた人物が偶然目の前に現われた時に使われる。(talkの代わりにspeakを用いて) Speak of the Devil.「悪魔の話をすると」という形でも使われる。

　□**1666** G. TORRIANO *Italian Proverbs* 134 The English say, Talk of the Devil, and he's presently at your elbow. **1721** J. KELLY *Scottish Proverbs* 299 Speak of the Dee'l, and he'll appear. Spoken when they, of whom we are speaking, come in by Chance. **1773** R. GRAVES *Spiritual Quixote* ll. VIII. V. 'How free he had made with the Devil's name.' ... 'Talk of the Devil, and he will appear.' **1830** MARRYAT *King's Own* II. V. The unexpected appearance of Mrs. Rainscourt made him involuntarily exclaim, 'Talk of the devil—"And she appears, Sir,' replied the lady. **1979** *Radio Times* 27 Oct.-2 Nov. 66 Talk of the Devil ... and he's bound to appear, they say, **2001** R. HILL *Dialogues of Dead* xiii. 107 'Talk of the devil, there he is. How do, Your Lordship! Who's looking after the maggots?' ■ **coincidence** 偶然の一致

talk ⇒ MONEY talks; If you can WALK you can dance, if you can talk you can sing.

tango ⇒ It takes TWO to tango.

tar ⇒ Do not spoil the SHIP for a ha'porth of tar.

Tartar ⇒ SCRATCH a Russian and you find a Tartar.

tartest ⇒ From the SWEETEST wine, the tartest vinegar.

taste ⇒ There is no ACCOUNTING for tastes; BVBRY man to his taste.

TASTES differ.
好みは人によって皆違う。
（訳注：「蓼食う虫も好き好き」）

意味が類似したものに EVERY *man to his taste*.「好みは人によって皆違う」がある。

　□**1803** J. DAVIS *Travels in USA* II. Tastes sometimes differ. **1868** W. COLLINS *Moonstone* I. xv. Tastes differ.... I never saw a marine landscape that I admired less. **1924** H. DE SEIJNCOURT *Cricket Match* iii. It's no use arguing about that.... Tastes differ. **1974** 'M. INNES' *Appleby's Other Story* xi. She seemed as alive as an electric eel, and no more comfortable for the purpose of mak-

teeth 439

ing passes at But tastes of course differ. **2014** *Spectator* 6 Dec. 29 The precise way he speaks seems to me a mirror of his clear thinking. Tastes differ. Two friends I subsequently asked said they couldn't stand [his] voice. ■ idiosyncrasy 特異性・性癖 ; taste 趣味・味

tattered ⇒ There's many a GOOD cock come out of a tattered bag.

tax ⇒ NOTHING is certain but death and taxes.

You can't TEACH an old dog new tricks.
老犬に新しい芸は仕込めない。

（訳注：you は総称的な用法。*You* never can tell what's going to happen.〈何が起きるかは誰にもわからない〉）

老人は自分のやり方を変えたがらない。

□**1530** J. FITZHERBERT *Husbandry* (ed. 2) G1ᵛ The dogge must leme it when he is a whelpe, or els It wyl not be; for it is harde to make an olde dogge to stoupe. **1636** W. CAMDEN *Remains concerning Britain* (ed. 5) 300 It is hard to teach an old dog trickes. **1672** W. WALKER *English & Latin Proverbs* 46 An old dog will learn no new tricks. **1806** J. RANDOLPH *Letter* 15 Feb. (1834) 14 There is an old proverb, 'You cannot teach an old dog new tricks.' **1987** J. HIGGINS *Little Death Music* v. He's listening to records with Vance. Downright rude, if you ask me, but you can't teach an old dog new tricks. **2002** *Times* 18 May 5 If ever there was a teacher who gave the lie to the proverb about old dogs and new tricks it is 89-year-old Donald Turner, whose classes on subjects as wide-ranging as line dancing and geography have left pupils asking for more. ■ habit 習慣 ; innovation 革新 ; old age 老年

Don't TEACH your grandmother to suck eggs.
祖母に卵の吸い方など教えるな。

（訳注：「釈迦に説法」。「孔子に論語」。「猿に木登り」。「河童に水練」）

自分よりも賢く経験豊かな人に助言などしてはならない。慣用句 to teach one's grandmother (to suck eggs)「釈迦に説法をする」としても使われる。

□**1707** J. STEVENS tr. *Queuedo's Comical Works* IV. 403 You would have me teach my Grandame to suck Eggs. **1738** SWIFT *Polite Conversation* I. 57 'I'll mend it, Miss.' ... 'You mend it! go, Teach your Grannam to suck Eggs.' **1882** BLACKMORE *Chrlstowell* II. iii. A ... twinkle, which might have been interpreted—'instruct your grandfather in the suction of gallinaceous products'. **1967** RIDOUT & WITTING *English Proverbs Explained* 48 Don't teach your grandmother to suck eggs. **2000** S. BOOTH *Black Dog* xxvii. 433 Hitchens was really warming up now. 'Teaching your grandmother to suck eggs' was an expression that sprang to the DCI's mind. ■ advice 忠告・助言

teach ⇒ He who CAN, does.

teacher ⇒ EXPERIENCE is the best teacher.

teeth ⇒ The GODS send nuts to those who have no teeth.

440 TELL

TELL the truth and shame the Devil.
真実を語れば悪魔も恥入る。

真実を語れば、悪魔を不愉快にさせる。なぜなら、悪魔は嘘と偽りを得意とするからである。† TRUTH makes the Devil blush.「真実は悪魔を恥じ入らせる」

□ **1548** W. PATTEN *Expedition into Scotland* A5 An Epigram ... the whiche I had, or rather (to saie truth and shame the deuel, for out it wool) I stale ... from a frende of myne. **1597-8** SHAKESPEARE *Henry IV*, Pt 1 III. i. 58 And I can teach thee, coz [cousin], to shame the devil By telling truth: tell truth, and shame the devil. **1639** J. CLARICE *Parǣmiologia Anglo-Latina* 316 Tell the truth, and shame the Devill. **1738** SWIFT *Polite Conversation* I. 93 Well; but who was your Author? Come, tell Truth and shame the Devil. **1945** F. THOMPSON *Lark Rise* xiv. A few homely precepts, such as ... 'Tell the truth and shame the devil.' **2007** *Times2* 8 June 7 Tell the truth and shame the devil, nanny used to say. But precepts such as that are perhaps too crude for the subtle minds who lead the modem C of E. ■ **truth** 真実・真理

tell ⇒ BLOOD will tell; You can't tell a BOOK by its cover; CHILDREN and fools tell the truth; DEAD men tell no tales; Every PICTURE tells a story; STRAWS tell which way the wind blows; Never tell TALES out of school; TIME will tell.

telling ⇒ A TALE never loses in the telling.

temper ⇒ GOD tempers the wind to the shorn lamb.

ten ⇒ One PICTURE is worth ten thousand words.

thaw ⇒ ROBIN Hood could brave all weathers but a thaw wind.

theatre ⇒ You can't SHOUT 'Fire' in a crowded theatre.

themselves ⇒ GOD helps them that help themselves; LISTENERS never hear any good of themselves.

thick ⇒ YORKSHIRE born and Yorkshire bred, strong in the arm and weak in the head.

thicker ⇒ BLOOD is thicker than water.

Set a THIEF to catch a thief.
泥棒を捕えるには泥棒を使え。
（訳注：「蛇の道は蛇」）

このことわざの背後にある発想は、泥棒の心理を知り尽くしており、それゆえ効果的に泥棒を捕え得る人物は泥棒にほかならないということである。It takes a thief to catch a thief.「泥棒を捕まえるには泥棒が必要である」という言い方もある。また1968年にはテレビドラマシリーズのタイトルとして It Takes a Thief. が使用された。同じ趣旨の表

現として、An old POACHER makes the best gamekeeper. 「老練な密猟者こそが最も すぐれた猟場人になる」がある。†カリマコス『エピグラム』xliii. φωρὸς δ᾽ ἴχνια φὼρ ἔμαθον. 「自分が泥棒なので、泥棒の足取りが認識できた」

□ **1654** B. GAYTON *Pleasant Notes upon Don Quixote* IV. ii. As they say, set a fool to catch a fool; a Proverb not of that gravity (as the Spaniards are), but very usefull and proper. **1665** R. HOWARD *Four New Plays* 74 According to the old saying, Set a Thief to catch a Thief. **1812** M. EDGEWORTH *Tales of Fashionable Life* VI. 446 'You have all your life been evading the laws.... Do you think this has qualified you peculiarly for being a guardian of the laws?' Sir Terence replied, 'Yes, sure, set a thief to catch a thief is no bad maxim.' **2002** *Washington Times* 13 Jan. A9 A pickpocket specialist with the Washington Metro Transit Police Department says it may take a thief to catch a thief, but cops who are trained to think like crooks can do. just as well. **2014** *Times* 15 Nov. 28 If you provide evidence that strips somebody else of their bonus, you get that bonus ... Set a thief to catch a thief. Maybe literally. ■ guile 狡猾・策略；wrong-doers 悪事をなす者

thief ⇒ HANG a thief when he's young, and he'll no' steal when he's old; There is HONOUR among thieves; The more LAWS, the more thieves and bandits; LITTLE thieves are hanged, but great ones escape; OPPORTUNITY makes a thief; A POSTBRN door makes a thief; PRO-CRASTINATION is the thief of time; If there were no RECEIVERS, there would be no thieves.

When THIEVES fall out, honest men come by their own.
泥棒たちが仲間割れすると、正直者が自分の物を失わずにすむ。

（訳注：come by their own ＝ keep what belongs to them〈自分の持ち物を保持する〉）

悪漢たちの仲間割れは正直者の利益になるように事が運ぶ。前半の When THIEVES fall out「泥棒たちが仲間割れすると」だけで表現されることもある。

□ **1546** J. HEYWOOD *Dialogue of Proverbs* II. Ix. L1 And olde folke vnderstood, Whan theues fall out, true men come to their good, Which is not alwaie true. *a***1640** *DAY & CHETILE Blind Beggar* (1659) IV. G2ᵛ Here's the old Proverb right, When false Theeves fall out, true men come to their own. **1681** S. COLVIL *Whigs' Supplication* II, 53 When thieves reckon, it's ofttimes known That honest people get their own. **1838** A. JACKSON *Letter* 26 Mar. in Correspondence (1931) V. 545 You must recollect the old adage, 'When rogues fall out, truth is revealed, and honest men get justice.' **2013** *www.guyanatimesgy.com* 21 Apr. But like the old people say, when thieves fall out, honest men come by their own ... meaning that they get what is rightfully theirs. ■ honesty and dishonesty 正直と不正直；wrong-doers 悪事をなす者

If a THING's worth doing, it's worth doing well.
いやしくもやる価値のあることなら、立派にやるだけの価値がある。

1910年の用例は表記のことわざと逆の主張をしているが、冗談にすぎない。また、thing 「物事」の代わりに job「仕事」が使われることもある。

□ **1746** CHESTERFIELD *Letter* 9 Oct (1932) ill. 783 Care and application are necessary.... In truth, whatever is worth doing at all is worth doing well. **1910** G. IC. CHESTERTON *What's Wrong with World* IV. xiv. The elegant female, drooping her ringlets over her water-colours, ... was maintaining the prime truth of woman, the universal mother: that if a thing is worth doing, it is worth doing badly. **1915** H. G. WELLS *Bealby* v. 'If a thing's worth doing at all,' said the professor ... 'it's worth doing well.' **1992** A. LAMBERT *Rather English Marriage* (1993) iii. 62 She'd never cared for dripdry, ... she'd rather see everything starched and crisply ironed. 'If a job's worth doing, it's worth doing well' was Gracie's motto. **2002** *Washington Times* 11 Mar. B5 Chil-

442 thing

dren should learn the value of completing tasks properly. The old saying, 'A job worth doing is worth doing well,' holds true. ■ **work 仕事**

thing ⇒ ALL good things must come to an end; ALL things are possible with God; ALL things come to those who wait; BAD things come in threes; The BEST things come in small packages; The BEST things in life are free; FACTS are stubborn things; FIRST things first; There's no such thing as a FREE lunch; GIVE a thing, and take a thing, To wear the Devil's gold ring; KEEP a thing seven years and you'll always find a use for it; LITTLE things please little minds; There is MEASURE in all things; MODERATION in all things; Things PAST cannot be recalled; To the PURE all things are pure; THREE things are not to be trusted; You can have TOO much of a good thing; If you WANT a thing done well, do it yourself; The WORTH of a thing is what it will bring.

When THINGS are at the worst they begin to mend.
物事は最悪になった時にこそ好転しはじめるものだ。
（訳注：「ピンチはチャンス」）

類似したものに The DARKEST hour is just before the dawn. 「夜明け前の道こそが最も暗い」がある。

☐**1582** G. WHETSTONE *Heptameron of Civil Discourses* vi. Thinges when they are at the worst, begin again to amend. The Feauer giueth place to health, when he hath brought the pacyent to deaths door. **1600** *Sir John Oldcastle* HIᵛ Patience good madame, things at worst will mend. **1623** J. WEBSTER *Duchess of Malfi* IV. i. Things being at the worst, begin to mend. **1748** RICHARDSON *Clarissa* III. liv. When things are at the worst they must mend. **1889** GISSING *Nether World* I. ii. When things are at the worst they begin to mend.... It can't be much longer before he gets work. **1928** M. SUMMERS *Vampire* v. If there be any truth in the old adage, that 'When things are at the worst they must amend,' the bettering of Spectral Melodrama is not distant.　■ **optimism 楽観主義**

THINK first and speak afterwards.
まず考えよ、話すのはそれからだ。
（訳注：「口は災いの元」）

然るべき考察をせずに話しはじめると後で後悔する。そのようなことが起こらないように注意せよという警告。

☐**1557** R. EDGEWORTH *Sermons* B6 Thinke well and thou shalt speak wel. **1623** W. PAINTER *Chaucer New Painted* BIᵛ Thinke twise, then speak, the old Prouerbe doth say. Yet Fooles their bolts will quickely shoot away. **1640** R. BRATHWAIT *Art asleep Husband?* vii. You thinke twice before you speake, and may be demanded twice before you answer. **1855** H. G. BOHN *Hand-Book of Proverbs* 528 Think to-day and speak to-morrow. **1902** E. HUBBARD in *Philistine* May 192 Think twice before you speak and then talk to yourself. **1943** L. I. WILDER *Happy Golden Years* i. You must do your thinking first and speak afterward. If you will ... do that, you will not have any trouble. **1981** P. O'DONNELL *Xanadu Talisman* iv. Please think before you speak. ■ **discretion 思慮分別；tact 機転**

THIRD 443

THINK global, act local.
考えは地球規模で、行動は地域で。

類似した表現 Think globally, act locally. は米国の環境保護活動家ヘイゼル・ヘンダーソンに由来する。このことわざはデーヴィッド・ブラウワー（1912-2000）が1969年に Friends of the Earth (FoE) を設立したときにスローガンとして採用したが、明らかにそれ以前から人口に膾炙していた（1947年と1981年の用例参照）。

□**1947** *Vidette-Messenger* 27 Mar.2 A letter was also read ... from Mrs. Jane Sense, worthy grand matron, Indiana grand chapter, OES, setting forth the objective and slogan of the right worthy grand matron of the general grand chapter: 'World Friendship' and 'think globally, act locally'. **1981** *Christian Science Monitor* (Boston, MA) 13 Oct. B3 'Think globally, act locally' is what we all have to do, she [Hazel Henderson] says. **1990** *Independent* 6 June 17 Bigness for its own sake in advertising has been largely discredited, and a more subdued charter—'Think global, act local'—is in vogue. **2007** S. O'REILLY in *Society of Antiquaries Salon* no. 165 [I]t is essential that the new processes do not lead to the creation of a 'democratic deficit', alienating people from the big decision-making processes that shape their lives and valued places. Think global, yes, but act local. ■ **environment** 状況 ; **great and small** 大小

THINK twice, cut once.
2 度考え、1 度で裁断せよ。

類似した MEASURE twice, cut once.「2 度寸法を測り、1 度で裁断せよ」ほどには使われていない。

□**1984** *New York Times* 9 Sept. (section 11 NJ) 8 'Think twice, cut once,' the amateur hobbyist is advised, and note that, beginning in 1871, it took 15 years to design and build the Statue of Liberty. **1994** *Independent* 18 Apr.18 Brushing up their skills at an Academy of Hair; Jeremy Ettinghausen visits a school where the first lesson is: 'Think twice, cut once'. **2011** *Country Life* 20 Apr. 269 Consider each operation before carrying it out, think twice and cut once. ■ **caution** 用心

think ⇒ EVIL to him who evil thinks; GREAT minds think alike; what MANCHESTER says today, the rest of England says tomorrow.

thinketh ⇒ The FAT man knoweth not what the lean thinketh.

THIRD time lucky
3 度目の幸運。
（訳注：「3 度目の正直」）

数字の 3 がラッキーナンバーであることはよく知られた迷信である。† The THIRD time pays for all.「3 度目がすべての埋め合わせをする」。2 度の失敗が続いたあとの 3 度目の試みは成功する確率が高いという呪<ruby>呪<rt>まじな</rt></ruby>いとして唱えられることが多い（1993年の用例参照）。

□c**1840** R. BROWNING *Letter* (1933) 5 'The luck of the third adventure' is proverbial. **1862** A. HISWP *Proverbs of Scotland* 194 The third time's lucky. **1882** R. L. STEVENSON *New Arabian Nights* II. 59 'The next time we come to blows—' 'Will make the third,' I interrupted.... 'Ay, true.... Well, the third time's lucky.' **1942** N. MARSH *Death & Dancing Footman* vii. It was a glancing blow.... It might have been my head.... One of them's saying to himself: 'Third time lucky.' **1993** 'C. AIRD' 'Slight of Hand' in *Injury Time* (1995) 62 'And after the second time,' mur-

mured the Commander into his drink, 'he said he hoped it would be a case of third time lucky.'
2015 *www.thenorthemecho.co.uk* 11 Jan. (*heading*) Will it be third time lucky for Cockerton developers? ■ **luck** 幸運・運 ; **superstition** 迷信

The THIRD time pays for all.
3 度目がすべての埋め合わせをする（3 度目に運が開ける）。

成功は 3 度の試みを伴うことが多い。† THIRD time lucky.「3 度目の幸運」。1954 年の用例では、3 度目の試みで仕事が完成するという意味を越えた意味で使われている。

□**1574** J. HIGGINS *Mirror for Magistrates* (1946) 93 The third payes home, this prouerbe is to true. **1599** *Wamingfor Fair Women* E3 The third time payes for all. **1855** GASKELL North & South I. xvii. 'This is th' third strike I've seen,' said she ... 'Well, third time pays for all.' **1922** *Punch* 20 Dec. 594 Mrs. Ellison has already been twice married. The third time pays for all, so they say. **1954** J. R. R. TOLKIEN *Lord of Rings* II. iv. iv. (1966) 'Gollum!' he called softly. 'Third time pays for all. I want some herbs.' **1978** S. KING *Stand* III. liv. If I could have brought myself to jump once ... I might not be here. Well, last time pays for all. ■ **perseverance** 我慢強さ ; **superstition** 迷信

third ⇒ While TWO dogs are fighting for a bone, a third runs away with it.

Thomas ⇒ On SAINT Thomas the Divine kill all turkeys, geese, and swine.

thorn ⇒ Beware of an OAK, it draws the stroke; He who PLANTS thorns should not expect to gather roses; No ROSE without a thorn; Do not grieve that ROSE-TREES have thorns....

THOUGHT is free.
思想は自由である。

□*c***1390** GOWER *Confessio Amantis* v. 4485 I have herd seid that thought is fre. **1601** SHAKESPEARE *Twelfth Night* I. iii. 64 Fair lady, do you think you have fools in hand?—Now, sir, thought is free. **1874** G. MACDONAID *Malcolm* II. Xvii. 'How do you come to think of such things?' 'Thought's free, my lord.'**1994** W. G. LYCAN *Modality and Meaning* 8 [W]e genuinely commit ourselves to ... only the Objects that we claim to find in this world, and not those which are merely objects of thought—thought is free, after all, and talk is cheap. ■ **opinions** 意見

thought ⇒ FIRST thoughts are best; SECOND thoughts are best; The WISH is father to the thought.

thousand ⇒ A journey of a thousand miles begins with a single step; One PICTURE is worth ten thousand words.

THREATENED men live long.
死に脅かされている人は長生きする。
（訳注：「一病息災」）

† 14 世紀初頭のフランス語 *Le[s] menaciez encore vivent*.「死に脅かされている人は長生きする」

☐**1534** LADY E. WHEATHELL in M. St. C. Byrne *Lisle Letters* II. ii. Tuer es a nolde sayeng thretend men lyue long. **1607** T. HEYWOOD *Fair Maid of Exchange* II. 68 Threatened men live long. **1655** T. FULLER *Church Hist. Britain* VIII. iii. Gardiner ... vowed ... to stop the sending of all supplies unto them.... But threatned folke live long. **1865** G. W. THORNBURY *Haunted London* ii. Temple Bar was doomed to destruction by the City as early as 1790.... 'Threatened men live long.' ... Temple Bar still stands. **1980** L. EGAN *Hunters & Hunted* i. The threat was an old one; and, the proverb ran, threatened men live long. ■ **mortality** 死すべき運命 ; **peril** 危険

THREE may keep a secret, if two of them are dead.
３人いてもそのうち２人死ねば秘密は守れる。

秘密を守る唯一の確実な方法はそれを知る人がただ１人しか残っていないことである。

☐**1546** J. HEYWOOD *Dialogue of Proverbs* II. V. G4ᵛ We twayne are one to many (quoth I) for men saie, Three maie keepe a counsel, if two be awaie. *c* **1595** SHAKESPEARE *Romeo & Juliet* II. iv. 190 Is your man secret? Did you ne'er hear say Two may keep counsel, putting one away? **1735** B. FRANKLIN *Poor Richard's Almanack* (July) Three may keep a secret, if two of them are dead. **1979** D. CLARK *Heberden's Seat* ii. Two of everything ... two bodies, two causes of death.... What was it? 'Three may keep a secret, if two of them are dead.' **2007** *Times* 14 Aug. 9 With their motto of 'Three can keep a secret if two are dead', initiation into the group [Hell's Angels] ensures an intense loyalty. ■ **concealment** 隠すこと・隠蔽 ; **discretion** 思慮分別

THREE removals are as bad as a fire.
引っ越し３回は火事にあうほどの災難。
（訳注：「引っ越し貧乏」）

今日よりもはるかに引っ越しが稀であった時代に生まれたことわざ。引っ越しの際の疲弊と損失は、火事にあうほどの災難である。

☐**1758** B. FRANKLIN *Poor Richard's Almanack* (Preface) I never saw an oft removed Tree, Nor yet an oft removed Family, That throve so well, as those that settled be. And again, Three Removes are as bad as a Fire. **1839** DICKENS *Letter* 14 Nov. (1965) I. 602 Did you ever 'move'? ... There is an old proverb that three removes are as bad as a fire. **1931** E. PEARSON in *Liberty* 5 Sept 28 Mr. Small's historians have traced at least six removals from place to place after he left his native Portland, and by reckoning 'three moves as bad as a fire' ... you may estimate the extent of his misfortune. **1999** *Washington Post* 17 Sept E12 In terms of general disruption, it's been said that two moves equal one fire. But unlike fires, moves can be planned and budgeted. ■ **change** 変化

THREE things are not to be trusted: a cow's horn, a dog's tooth, and a horse's hoof.
この世には信用できないものが３つ。雌牛の角、犬の歯、馬の蹄。

このことわざにおいて、dog's tooth「犬の歯」と horse's hoof「馬の蹄」はいつも登場するが、３番目の要素は様々である。†13世紀のフランス語 *Dent de chael, pé de cheval, cul d'enfant ne sunt pas a crere.*「犬の歯、馬の蹄、赤ん坊のお尻の３つは信用できない」

☐*c***1383** JOHN OF FORDON *Scotichronicon* (1759) II. xw. xxxii. Till horsis fote thou never traist, Till hondis tooth, no womans faith. **1585** S. ROBSON *Choice of Change* K2 Trust not 3 things. Dogs teeth. Horses feete. Womens Protestations. **1910** P. W. JOYCE *English as We speak it in Ireland* 110 Three things are not to be trusted—a cow's horn, a dog's tooth and a horse's hoof. **1948** T. H. WHITE *Elephant & Kangaroo* xiii. He was ... beginning to worry about being employed by a

446 three

venomous Englishman. 'Four things not to trust,' said the Cashelmor proverb: 'a dog's tooth, a horse's hoof, a cow's horn, and an Englishman's laugh.' ■ **caution** 用心; **trust and scepticism** 信用と懐疑

three ⇒ BAD things come in threes; Two BOYS are half a boy, and three boys are no boy at all; From CLOGS to clogs is only three generations; Feed a DOG for three days and he will remember your kindness for three years … ; One ENGLISHMAN can beat three Frenchmen; FISH and guests smell after three days;. It takes three GENERATIONS to make a gentleman; From SHIRTSLEEVES to shirtsleeves in three generations; TWO is company, but three is none

THRIFT is a great revenue.
倹約は大きな収入である。

†キケロ『ストア派のパラドックス』49 *Non intellegunt ominess quam magnum vectigal sit parsimonia*.「人は倹約がどれほどの収入になるか理解していない」。現在では Thrift is of great revenue. という形式で使われることが多い（慈善店についての記事における2008年の用例参照）。意味が類似したものに A PENNY saved is a penny earned.「1ペニーの節約は1ペニーの儲け」がある。

☐ 1659 J. HOWELL *Proverbs* (French) 15 Parsimony is the best revenue. 1855 H. G. BOHN *Hand-Book of Proverbs* 530 Thrift is a good revenue. 1930 *Times* 10 Oct. 13 Thrift … is not only a great virtue but also 'a great revenue'. 2008 *napavalleyregister.com* 3 July (*heading*) Thrift is of great revenue. ■ **thrift** 質素倹約

He that will THRIVE must first ask his wife.
繁栄したいと望むならまず妻に相談しなければならない。

（訳注:he =「〈関係節を伴って〉…する者は誰でも〈性別は問わない〉」。*He that* is not with me is against me.〈私に味方しない者は私に敵対する〉〈『マタイによる福音書』12章30節〉。）

妻が計画と行動に協力してはじめて夫の仕事は成功する。

☐ *a*1500 in R. L. Greene *Early English Carols* (1935) 276 Hym that cast hym for to thryve, he must ask leve of his wyff. *c*1549 J. HEYWOOD *Dialogue of Proverbs* I. xi. B8ᵛ He that will thryue, must aske leaue of his wyfe. *a*1790 E. FRANKLIN *Autobiography* (1905) I. 324 He that would thrive, must ask his wife. It was lucky for me that I had one as much dispos'd to industry and frugality as myself. 1875 S. SMILES *Thrift* viii. There is an old English proverb which says, 'He that would thrive must first ask his wife.' 2003 P. SPARKES *New Land Law* 688 The old adage was that 'He that will thrive must first ask his wife.' Surely, as this ancient saw suggests, a marriage is a joint venture in which the financial fortunes of the couple are bound up together? ■ **wives and husbands** 夫婦

thrive ⇒ ILL gotten goods never thrive; If you want to LIVE and thrive, let the spider run alive.

Don't THROW out your dirty water until you get in fresh.
きれいな水が手に入るまで汚い水を捨ててはならない。

より満足できる代替品が確実に手に入るまではそれを焦って捨ててはならない。

tiger　447

□*c*1475 in *Modern Philology* (1940) XXXVIII. 121 Heys a fole that castith a-way his olde water or he have new. **1623** W. PAINTER *Palace of Pleasure* C4ᵛ The wise prouerbe wish all men to saue Their foule water vntill they fayrer haue. **1710** S. PALMER *Proverbs* 89 Don't throw away Dirty Water till you have got Clean.... The Man being possess'd with Avarice, throws away a Certain Benefit upon uncertain … Expectations. **1842** S. LOVER *Handy Andy* xxix. 'I'll change my clothes.' … 'You had better wait.... You know the old saying, "Don't throw out your dirtywather until you get in fresh."' **1911** G. B. SHAW *Fanny's First Play* III. 208 Don't you throw out dirty water til you get in fresh. Don't get too big for your boots. **1986** M. SLUNG *More Momilies* 67 Don't throw out dirty water until you have clean. ■ **innovation** 革新

Don't THROW the baby out with the bathwater.
風呂の残り湯と一緒に赤ん坊を捨ててはならない。

不要な物の処分を急ぐあまり大切な物を捨てないように気をつけよという忠告。特に慣用句 to throw (or empty) out the baby with the bathwater「無用の物と一緒に大事な物を捨てる」の形式で比喩的に使われることが多い。少なくとも16世紀初頭に遡るドイツのことわざに由来する。† **1610** J. ケプラー『第三法則』(sub-heading) *Das ist Warnung … das sie … nicht das Kindt mit dem Badt ausschütten.*「次のことに要注意…赤ん坊を風呂の残り湯と一緒に捨てないこと」

□**1853** CARLYLE *Nigger Question* (ed. 2) 29 The Germans say, 'You must empty out the bathing-tub, but not the baby along with it.' … How to abolish the abuses of slavery, and save the precious thing in it: also, I do not pretend that this is easy. **1911** G. B. SHAW *Getting Married* (Preface) 186 We shall in a very literal sense empty the baby out with the bath by abolishing an institution [marriage] which needs nothing more than a little … rationalizing to make it … useful. **1979** J. P. YOUNG *Art of Le μ ming to Manage* 91 Do be careful that you don't throw the baby out with the bath water, and find yourself with too many people who lack experience. **2002** *Times* 9 Apr. 22 So let reform and trimming continue; but don't throw the baby out with the bathwater. ■ **prudence** 思慮・分別

throw ⇒ Throw DIRT enough, and some will stick; Those who live in GLASS houses shouldn't throw stones; Do not throw PEARLS to swine.

Thursday ⇒ Monday's CHILD is fair of face.

thyself ⇒ KNOW thyself; PHYSICIAN, heal thyself.

thysen (yourself) : ⇒ HEAR all, see all, say nowt.

tide ⇒ A RISING tide lifts all the boats; TIME and tide wait for no man.

tie ⇒ When SPIDER webs unite, they can tie up a lion; TRUST in God but tie your camel.

tiger ⇒ BETTER to live one day as a tiger … ; The BLEATING of the kid excites the tiger; He who RIDES a tiger is afraid to dismount.

448 TIME

There is a TIME and place for everything.
何事にもふさわしい時と場所がある。

There is a TIME for everything. 「何事にも潮時がある」の拡張版である。

□ **1509** A. BARCLAY *Ship of Fools* 94 Remember: there is tyme and place for euery thynge. **1862** G. BORROW *Wild Wales* II. X. There is a time and place for everything, and sometimes the warmest admirer of ale would prefer the lymph of the hill-side fountain to the choicest ale. **1986** 'C. Aird' *Dead Liberty* iv. A memory from A Midsummer Night's Dream to do with Snout serving the office of a wall welled up in Sloan's mind, but he suppressed it instantly. There was a time and a place for everything. ■ **opportunity** 機会・好機 ; **orderliness** 整然としていること ; **time** 時間

TIME and tide wait for no man.
時間と潮時は人を待たない。

(訳注 : tide =「好機、潮時」。at that *tide*〈あの時〉。「歳月人を待たず」)

好機を逃すことなく敏速に行動せよという忠告。

□ *c***1390** CHAUCER *Clerk's Tale* 1. 118 For thogh we slepe or wake, or rome, or ryde, Ay fleeth the tyme; it nil no [will no] man abyde. *a***1520** *Everyman* (1961) 1. 143 The Tyde abydeth no man. **1592** R. GREENE *Disputation between He Cony-catcher & She Cony-catcher* X. 241 Tyde nor time tarrieth no man. **1639** J. CLARKE *Parœmiologia Anglo-Latina* 233 Time and tide tary on no man. **1767** 'A. BARTON' *Disappointment* II. i. Let's step into the state-room, and tum in: Time and tide waits for no one. **1822** SCOTT *Nigel* III. ii. Come, come, master, let us get afloat.... Time and tide wait for no man. **2002** *Washington Post* 10 Mar. SC11 (*Family Circus comic strip*) Time and tide wait for no man. 'And a school bus waits for no boy.' ■ **opportunity** 機会・好機 ; **time** 時間

TIME flies.
時間は飛ぶように過ぎ去る。

(訳注 :「光陰矢のごとし」)

† ラテン語 *Tempus fugit*.「時は飛んで行く」

□ *c***1390** CHAUCER *Clerk's Tale* 1. 118 For though we slepe or wake, or rome, or ryde, Ay fleeth the tyme. **1639** J. CLARKE *Parœmiologia Anglo-Latina* 308 Time flyeth away without delay. **1776** J. W. FLETCHER *Letter* 21 Mar. in *Works* (1803) IX. 197 Time flies! Years of plenty ... disappear before the eternity to which we are all hastening. **2002** *Washington Post* 29 Mar. C9 (*Classic Peanuts comic strip*) 'Quick, Marcie, I need the answer to the third question!' 'There is no third question, sir ... we did that test last week.... ' 'Time flies when you're having fun.' ■ **time** 時間

There is a TIME for everything.
何事にも潮時がある。

『コヘレトの言葉』3 章 1 節（欽定訳聖書）To every thing there is a season.「何事にもふさわしい時期がある」を想起させる。

□ *c***1390** CHAUCER *Clerk's Prologue* 1. 6 But Salomon seith 'every thyng hath tyme'. **1540** CRANMER *Bible* (Prologue) + 3 Ther is tyme for euery thynge. **1590** SHAKESPEARE *Comedy of Errors* II. ii. 63 Well, sir, learn to jest in good time; there's time for all things. **1818** J. AUSTEN *Northanger Abbey* xxx. Your head runs too much upon Bath; but there is a time for every thing — a time for balls ... and a time for work. **1980** 'M. INNES' *Going It Alone* I. X. There is a time for everything, and he hoped that, in the present exigency, Tim wasn't going to be ... frivolous. ■ **opportunity** 機会・好機 ; **time** 時間

TIME is a great healer.
時は偉大な治療師である。

時間が傷を癒すという古来の概念から多くの表現が生まれている。以下にそのいくつか
を挙げておく。物理的な傷というより、精神的な傷を癒すという場面で使われる場合が
多い。†メナンドロス『断章』dclxxvii. (Kock) πάντων ἰατρὸς τῶν ἀναγκαίων κακῶν χρόνος ἐστίν.「時間があらゆる必要悪を癒す」

□c1385 CHAUCER *Troilus & Criseyde* v. 350 As tyme hem [them] hurt, a tyme doth hem cure.
1591 J. HARINGTON tr. *Ariosto's Orlando Furioso* VI. ii. He hurt the wound which time perhaps
had healed, weening [thinking] with greater sinne the lesse to mend. **1622** H. PEACHAM *Complete Gentleman* iv. Time, the Phisition of all. **1837** DISRAELI *Henrietta Temple* III. VI ix. Time is
the great physician. **1926** G. B. SHAW *Translations & Tomfooleries* 60 Time is the great healer.
1942 A. CHRISTIE *Body in Library* viii. He had a terrible shock and loss.... But Time, as my dear
mother used to say, is a great healer. **2001** *Washington Times* 23 Sept. C17 Time is the greatest of
healers, and during the next few weeks, sports again will provide us with a much-needed respite
from our everyday worries. ■ **time** 時間

TIME is money.
時は金なり。

τὸ πολυτελέστατον...ἀνάλωμα, τὸν χρόνον.「最も高価な出費は時間である」(アンティフ
ォンに由来する)。

□**1572** T. WILSON *Discourse upon Usury* 33 They saye tyme is precious. **1748** B. FRANKLIN *Papers* (1961) III. 306 Remember that Time is Money. He that can earn Ten Shillings a Day ... and
... sits idle one half of that Day ... has really ... thrown away Five Shillings. **1840** BULWER-
LYTTON *Money* III. vi. 'You don't come often to the club, Stout?' ... 'No, time is money.' **1980** H.
R. F. KEATING *Murder of Maharajah* xv. I can't wait here day after day.... Time's money, you
know. **2002** *Washington Times* 2 Feb. A11 When a quarterback is chosen as the Most Valuable
Player in the National Football League for the second time in three years, time is money. He can
rake in big bucks for appearing in ads, and he can also do his bit for charity by appearing in a
United Way commercial. ■ **efficiency and inefficiency** 能率と非能率 ; **time** 時間

Man fears TIME, but time fears the pyramids.
人は時を恐れるが、時はピラミッドを恐れる。

アラビアのことわざ。learned Arab of the twelfth century「12世紀の学識あるアラブ
人」(1923年の用例参照) とは誰のことなのかについてはいまだ不明である。

□**1876** E. RECLUS et al. *Earth and Its Inhabitants* 401 'All things fear time,' says the Arab proverb, 'but time fears the pyramids.' **1923** G. CAROTII *History of Art* 9 It was a learned Arab of the
twelfth century who said: 'The whole world fears time, but time fears the Pyramids.' **1926** A. F.
TOULBA *Ceylon, Land of Eternal Charm* 228 Here also, as in my own country, can we aptly apply the familiar saying 'Man fears Time, but Time fears the Pyramids. **1983** *Times* 19 Feb. (online) Khufu, first Pharaoh of the Fourth Dynasty ... built a tomb that should remain for all time.
It is written that 'Man fears Time, but Time fears the Pyramids.' **2006** *Register* (*www.theregister.
co.uk*) 26 Dec. The Great Pyramid of Giza is the sole survivor of the Seven Wonders of the
World. An Arab proverb says that: 'Man fears time, yet time fears the Pyramids', a reference to
the fact that the pyramid has survived for about 4,500 years. ■ **time** 時間

No TIME like the present.
今ほどよいときはない。
（訳注：「好機逸すべからず」）

自分が仕事を引き受けたり、他人にただちに行動するように促す際に使われる。

□ *a*1562 G. LEGH *Accidence of Armoury* 225ᵛ Mary [to be sure] sir no time better then euen now. **1696** M. MANLEY *Lost Lover* IV. i. No time like the present. **1888** M. OLIPHANT *Second Son* I. iv. 'If you were a-passing this way, sir, some time in the morning—.' 'There's no time like the present,' answered Roger. **2000** 'G. WILLIAMS' *Dr. Mortimer and Aldgate Mystery* (2001) i. 7 ' ... I was thinking in terms of an immediate start ... ' 'Oh, capital!' the doctor exclaimed.... 'No time like the present, hey?' ■ **opportunity** 機会・好機 ; **time** 時間

TIME will tell.
時間がたてばわかる。

† メナンドロス『一行格言』11 ἄγει δὲ πρὸς φῶς τὴν ἀλήθειαν χρόνος.「時間が真実を明らかにする」

□ **1539** R. TAVERNER tr. *Erasmus' Adages* 37 Tempus omnia reuelat. Tyme discloseth all thynges. **1616** T. DRAXE *Adages* 205 Time reuealeth all things. **1771** C. STUART Letter 15 Apr. in Publications of Mississippi Hist. Society (1925) V. 50 Time only will shew how far those Informations have been well founded. **1863** C. READE *Hard Cash* I. vi. I will answer ... that she will speak as distinctly to music as you do in conversation —Time will show, madam. **1913** E. H. PORTER *Pollyanna* xxiii. The doctor had looked very grave ... and had said that time alone could tell. **1929** 'J. J. CONNINGTON' *Eye in Museum* xiv. 'I'm not ... bringing any charge.' ... 'Oh ... a bright idea, perhaps. Or perhaps not so bright' 'Time will tell,' the Superintendent retorted. **2002** *New Scientist* 30 Mar. 7 'But if you look at the general principles, it's a wonderful system,' says Richard Mulligan ... 'Time will tell.' ■ **future** 未来 ; **time** 時間

TIME works wonders.
時は奇跡を生む。

時がたつと、驚くべき変化が生じることもある。

□ *a*1588 A. MARTEN *Exhortation to defend Country* F2 You ... thinke that time will worke wonders, though you your selves follow your owne pleasures. **1815** BYRON *Letter* 7 Jan. (1975) IV. 252 Time does wonders. **1845** D. W. JERROLD (*title*) *Time works wonders*. **1872** G. J. WHYTE-MELVILLE *Satanella* II. xxiv. 'I want you to like me.' ... 'They say time works wonders ... and I feel I shall.' **1982** R. DAVIES *Rebel Angels* 4 But there was time, and I was to be in his outer room, constantly under his eye. Time works wonders. ■ **time** 時間

time ⇒ There is always a FIRST time; NEVER is a long time; OTHER times, other manners; PARSLEY seed goes nine times to the Devil; PROCRASTINATION is the thief of time; One STEP at a time; A STITCH in time saves nine; THIRD time lucky; The THIRD time pays for all; WORK expands so as to fill the time available.

TIMES change and we with time.
時代は変わり、我々も時代とともに変わる。
（訳注：times〈複数形〉＝「時代、時勢」。ancient *times*〈古代〉）

† ラテン語 *Omnia* (also *tempora*) *mutantur nos et mutamur in illis*.「（時代も同様

TOMORROW 451

に）万物はつねに動いており、我々も時代とともに動いている」。西ローマ皇帝、ロタール
1世（840-55）の言葉に由来する。

□**1578** LYLY *Euphues* I. 276 The tymes are changed as Ouid sayeth, and wee are changed In the times. **1666** G. TORRIANO *Italian Proverbs* 281 Times change, and we with them.... The Latin says the same, Tempora mutantur, et nos mutamur in illis. **1943** C. MILBURN *Diary* 21 Feb. (1979) 168 1n English cities the Red Flag has been flown.... Times change indeed, and we with time. **1981** J. BINGHAM *Brock* 31 Times were changing and Melford with them. ■ **circumstances** 状況 ; **innovation** 革新

times ⇒ FALL down seven times, get up eight; MEASURE seven times, cut once; OTHER times, other manners; PARSLEY seed goes nine times to the Devil.

tinker ⇒ If IFS and ands were pots and pans, there'd be no work for tinkers' hands.

TODAY you; tomorrow me
今日はあなた、明日は私。
（訳注：「明日は我が身」）

†ラテン語*Hodie mihi, eras tibi*.「今日は私の番であり、明日はあなたの番である」。このラテン語はかつて埋葬用記念碑の碑文として使われ、参列者に誰もいつか必ず死ぬことを教えている。

□*a***1250** *Ancrene Wisse* (1962) 143 *Ille hodie, ego eras*. He to dei, and ich to marhen [he today, and I tomorrow]. **1620** T. SHELTON tr. *Cervantes' Don Quixote* II. lxv. To day for thee, and tomorrow for me. **1855** C. KINGSLEY *Westward Ho!* II. i. To-day to thee, to-morrow to me. **1906** A. CONAN DOYLE *Sir Nigel* xv. 'It is the custom of the Narrow Seas,' said they: 'Today for them; tomorrow for us.' **1929** A. W. WHEBN tr. *E. M. Remarque's All Quiet on Western Front* ix. 'Comrade,' I say to the dead man, but I say it calmly, 'To-day you, to-morrow me.' ■ **future** 未来

today ⇒ JAM tomorrow and jam yesterday, but never jam today; What MANCHESTER says today, the rest of England says tomorrow; Never PUT off till tomorrow what you can do today.

told ⇒ One STORY is good till another is told.

Tom ⇒ MORE people know Tom Fool than Tom Fool knows.

TOMORROW is another day.
明日はまた別の日である（明日は明日の風が吹く）。

問題はうまくいくという楽観的想定の下に解決を先送りしようとする際に使われる。これに対する真逆のことわざとして、下のTOMORROW never comes.「明日は決して来ない」がある。

□*c***1527** J. RASTELL *Calisto & Melebea* Cl^v Well mother to morrow is a new day. **1603** J. FLORIO tr. *Montaigne's Essays* II. iv. A letter ... beeing delivered him ... at supper, he deferred the opening of it, pronouncing this by-word. To morrow is a new day. **1824** SCOTT *St. Ronan's Well* III. We will say no more of it at present.... To-morrow is a new day. **1927** F. GREEN *Field God* I. 148

Go to it, you Mag and Lonie! To-morrow's another day, and you'll need all you can hold. **2001** K. HALL PAGE *Body in Moonlight* vii. 127 'Maybe tomorrow,' Faith said, trying to turn the corners of her mouth up. 'Tomorrow's another day.' ■ **future 未来**

TOMORROW never comes.
明日は決して来ない。

明日まで解決を先送りしてはいけないという警告。 † TOMORROW *is another day*.
「明日はまた別の日である」

□**1523** W. BERNERS *Froissart* (1901) II. 309 It was sayde every day among them, we shall fight tomorowe, the whiche day came never. **1602** J. CHAMBERLAIN *Letter* 8 May (1939) I. 142 Tomorrow comes not yet. **1678** J. RAY *English Proverbs* (ed. 2) 343 Tomorrow come never. **1756** B. FRANKLIN *Poor Richard's Almanack* (July) To-morrow, every Fault is to be amended; but that To-morrow never comes. **1889** GISSING *Nether World* III. ix. 'It's probably as well for you that tomorrow never comes.' 'Now just see how things turn out!' went on the other. **2001** *Washington Post* 27 Mar. C11 (*Jeff MacNelly's Shoe comic strip*) 'They say tomorrow never comes.' 'I sure hope so. That's when I have a math test' ■ **future 未来**; **procrastination 先延ばし**

tomorrow ⇒ BAT, drink, and be merry, for tomorrow we die; JAM tomorrow and jam yesterday, but never jam today; What MANCHESTER says today, the rest of England says tomorrow; Never PUT off till tomorrow what you can do today; TODAY you, tomorrow me.

The TONGUE always returns to the sore tooth.
舌は常に痛む歯に戻ってくる。

人は絶えず心配事に引き戻される。

□**1586** G. PETIIE tr. *S. Guazzo's Civil Conversation* (1925) II. 201 The tongue rolles there where the tooth aketh. **1659** J. HOWELL *Proverbs* (Spanish) 27 There the tongue goes where the tooth akes. **1746** B. FRANKLIN *Poor Richard's Almanack* (July) The Tongue is ever turning to the aching tooth. **1949** W. KRASNER *Walk Dark Streets* ii. He would stop ... to find the flaws in his case were standing over him, implacable, like the certainty of guilt. The tongue always returned to the sore tooth. **1985** K. S. ROBINSON in G. Dozois *Isaac Asimov's Mars* (1991) 155 In the same way that a tongue will go to a sore tooth over and over, Roger finds himself following Hans and Arthus to hear the areologist's explanation. ■ **persistence ねばり強さ**

tongue ⇒ The DEVIL makes his Christmas pies of lawyers' tongues and clerks' fingers; A STILL tongue makes a wise head; With a SWEET tongue and kindness, you can drag an elephant by a hair.

TOO many cooks spoil the broth.
料理人が多すぎるとスープをだめにしてしまう。

（訳注：「船頭多くして船山に登る」）

１つの事業に多くの人が関与しすぎると、成功の可能性が低くなる。その理由については、2014年の用例参照（少数グループの方がより良い決定ができる）。

□**1575**? J. HOOKER *Life of Carew* (1857) 33 There is the proverb, the more cooks the worse potage. **1662** B. GERBIER *Principles of Building* 24 When ... an undertaking hath been committed to many, it caused but confusion, and therefore it is a saying ... Too many Cooks spoils the

Broth. *c*1805 J. AUSTEN *Watsons* (1972) VI. 318 She professes to keep her own counse ... 'Too many Cooks spoil the Broth.' **1855** C. KINGSLEY *Westward Ho!* II. vii. As Amyas sagely re-marked, 'Too many cooks spoil the broth, and half-a-dozen gentlemen aboard one ship are as bad as two kings of Brentford.' **1979** *Guardian* 7 Nov. 6 It was a great mistake to think that ad-ministration was improved by taking on more administrators.... 'Too many cooks spoil the broth.' **2014** *Daily Mail* 25 Apr. (online) Too many cooks really do spoil the broth it seems, after new research found smaller groups make better decisions. ■ **assistance** 援助 ; **busybodies** おせっかい屋 ; **work** 仕事

You can have TOO much of a good thing.
どんなに良いものでも有り過ぎると困ることもある。

(訳注：can ＝「…のこともある」。you は総称的な用法。*You* never *can* tell what's going to happen. 〈何が起きるかは誰にもわからない〉。「薬も過ぎれば毒となる」。「過ぎたるはなお及ばざるがごとし」)

どれほど素晴らしいものでも多すぎるとかえってよくない。ただし 1985 年の用例参照。

□**1483** B. BURGH *Cato in Archiv* (1905) CXV. 313 To much is nouht of any maner thing [too much of anything is nothing]. **1611** R. COTGRAVE *Dict. French & English* s.v. Manger, A man may take too much of a good thing. **1738** SWIFT *Polite Conversation* I. 77 Fie, Miss! You said that once before; and, you know, Too much of one Thing is good for nothing. **1906** CHESTERTON *Charles Dickens* iv. We believe that you can have too much of a good thing —a blasphemous be-lief, which at one blow wrecks all the heavens that men have hoped for. **1985** *Washington Post* 2 Mar. A18 Mae West once said it was possible to have too much of a good thing and it was won-derful. **2014** *www.economist.com* 16 Aug. (*heading*) Too much of a good thing A note of warning about the way human desires are met so easily online. ■ **excess** 過剰・過度 ; **good things** よいもの

tool ⇒ A BAD workman blames his tools.

tooth ⇒ The TONGUE always returns to the sore tooth.

top ⇒ There is always ROOM at the top.

touch ⇒ If you gently touch a NBTILB it'll sting you for your pains.

He that TOUCHES pitch shall be defiled.
コールタールに触る者は手が汚れる。

(訳注：he ＝「〈関係節を伴って〉…する者は誰でも〈性別は問わない〉」。*He that* is not with me is against me. 〈私に味方しない者は私に敵対する〉〈『マタイによる福音書』12 章 30 節〉。「朱に交われば赤くなる」)

コールタールに触ると手が汚れるように、悪い人と付き合うと悪の道に引きずり込まれてしまう。†「聖書外典」『コヘレトの言葉』13 章 1 節（欽定訳聖書）He that toucheth pitch, shall be defiled therewith.「瀝青(れきせい)に触れるものは汚れる」

□**1303** R. BRUNNE *Handlyng Synne* (EETS) I. 6578 Who-so handlyth pycche wellyng hote, He shal haue fylthe therof sumdeyl [in some degree]. **1578** LYLY *Euphues* I. 250 He that toucheth pitche shall be defiled. **1710** S. PALMER *Proverbs* 249 Touch Pitch and you'll be Defil'd.... There is Danger every Way in Ill Company. **1886** H. CONWAY *Living or Dead* II. Ix. The next two months of my life ... made me take a lower and more debased view of the world.... I was touch-ing pitch, yet striving to keep myself from being defiled. **1979** *Listener* 13 Sept 345 The makers of

454 tough

the series believe that those who meddle with pitch may be defiled. **2014** *www.independent. co.uk* 26 Oct. [I]f he is intelligent enough to know that you cannot touch pitch without being defiled by it, then he is also intelligent enough to realise that exposure in the modem age depends upon your having something ripe for defilement. ■ associates 仲間；example, good and bad 好例と悪例

tough ⇒ When the GOING gets tough, the tough get going.

What goes on TOUR stays on tour.
旅先で起こることは旅先だけの話。

グループ、特にスポーツ団の遠征先での不祥事は口外すべきではない。ラグビー選手のあいだで生まれた表現であるとされる。これに相当することわざとして、What happens on the ROAD stays on the road.「道中で起こることは道中だけの話」と What happens in VEGAS stays in Vegas.「ラス・ベガスで起こることはラス・ベガスだけの話」がある。

□**2004** M. BROWN et al. *Rugby for Dummies* (2007) 303. Of course one maxim that always has to be followed is What goes on tour stays on tour—meaning that particularly funny, embarrassing or debauched moments are for consumption only by the tourists themselves and not casual listeners back home. **2012** *Mirrors* Feb. (online) What goes on tour stays on tour ... but not for a group of former public schoolboys whose private list of 'rules' for a boys' holiday went viral. ■ discretion 思慮分別；speech and silence 発言と沈黙

town ⇒ GOD made the country, and man made the town.

TRADE follows the flag.
貿易は国旗の後を行く。

貿易と植民地拡大の密接な関係は大英帝国全盛の頃に生まれた。現在でも争いの種になることが多い（1945年と1979年の用例参照）。なお、貿易と国旗が逆の順序で使われることもある（2011年の用例参照）。

□**1870** J. A. FROUDE in *Fraser's Magazine* Jan. 4 The removal of a million poor creatures to Canada and the establishment of them there ... would probably have turned out ... a profitable investment Trade follows the flag. **1945** R. HARGREAVES *Enemy at Gate* 152 There is a glib saying ... that 'trade follows the flag'; an apophthegm that succeeds in putting the cart before the horse with greater aplomb than almost any other cant phrase in common use. **1979** in C. Allen *Tales from Dark Continent* i. There is a famous old quotation that 'Trade follows the Flag' but ... in West Africa ... the reverse was true. **2011** *Times of India* 3 May (online) Business is taking India's international relations in new directions, and the flag must follow trade. Yet is the nation's traditional foreign policy community up to the task? ■ business ビジネス・商売

trade ⇒ EVERY man to his trade; JACK of all trades and master of none; There are TRICKS in every trade; TWO of a trade never agree.

transplant ⇒ You cannot SHIFT an old tree without it dying.

TREE 455

TRAVEL broadens the mind.
旅は心を広げてくれる。

旅は旅行者に何物にもかえがたい新鮮な視点を与えてくれる。マーク・トウェインがこのことわざの生みの親にされることが多いのは、彼が旅の効用に関して次のような言葉を残しているからであろう。Travel is fatal to prejudice, bigotry, and narrow-mindedness ... Broad, wholesome, charitable views of men and things cannot be acquired by vegetating in one little corner of the earth all one's lifetime. 「旅は偏見、偏屈、狭い心を消し去るのに欠かせない…人と物に対する広大で、健全で、寛大な見解は、生涯地球の片隅で暮らしていたのでは決して獲得できないものである」(『地中海遊覧記』「結論」)

☐ **1911** 'SAKI' 'Way to Dairy' in *Chronicles of Clovis* (*Short Stories of Saki*, 1958) 195 'Travel enlarges the mind, my dear Christine,' said her aunt. 'Yes, dear aunt, travel undertaken in the right spirit,' agreed Christine; 'but travel pursued merely as a means towards gambling and extravagant living is more likely to contract the purse than to enlarge the mind.' **1929** G. K. CHESTERTON *Poet & Lunatics* iii. He may be a trifle cracked, ... but that's only because his travels have been too much for his intellect. They say travel broadens the mind; but you must have the mind. **1997** *Times* 24 Dec. 14 The past may be a foreign country through which we travel as strangers. But travel still broadens the mind. **2011** S. HERRY *Barefoot Disciple* 109 Travel does not necessarily broaden the mind ... You can send a turnip around the world but it comes back a turnip.'
■ **experience** 経験 ; **travel** 旅行

travel（動詞）⇒ BAD news travels fast; It is BETTER to travel hopefully than to arrive.

He TRAVELS fastest who travels alone.
1人で旅をする者が最も早く旅をする。

(訳注：解説にある H. D. ソローは、アメリカの作家。『ウォールデン 森の生活』〈1854年〉はウォールデン池畔の森の中で自給自足の生活を送った記録をまとめたもので、その思想は後の時代の詩人や作家に大きな影響を与えたとされる)

† 1854 H. D. ソロー『ウォールデン 森の生活』78 The man who goes alone can start today; but he who travels with another must wait till that other is ready. 「1人で行く者は今日すぐにでも出発することができるが、連れがいる者は連れが準備できるまで待たねばならない」

☐ **1888** R. KIPLING *Story of Gadsby* (1889) 94 Down to Gehenna, or up to the Throne, He travels fastest who travels alone. **1921** E. WAUGH *Journal* 19 June in *Diaries* (1979) 129 Hale's gone already. I suppose he will have to. 'He travels fastest who travels alone' anyway. **1989** F. KING *Reflections in Jaundiced Eye* iv. The reason I can 'do what I do' is because I've never married. He travels fastest who travels alone, and that goes double for she. ■ **efficiency and inefficiency** 能率と非能率 ; **independence** 独立・自立 ; **travel** 旅行

tread ⇒ FOOLS rush in where angels fear to tread.

As a TREE falls, so shall it lie.
木が倒れると、その木はその場に横たわる。

死を間近にしたからと言って、長い間持ち続けてきた信念を曲げてはならない。『コヘレ

456　TREE

ト の言葉』11章3節（欽定訳聖書）If the tree fall toward the South, or toward the North, in the place where the tree falleth, there it shall be.「もし木が南か北に倒れるならば、その木は倒れたところに横たわる」を想起させる。

□ **1549** H. LATIMER *Seven Sermons* IV. M3v Wheresoeuer the tre falleth ... there it shall reste. **1578** LYLY *Euphues* I. 308 Where the tree falleth there it lyeth ... and every ones deaths daye is his domes day. **1678** J. RAY *English Proverbs* (ed. 2) 296 As a man lives so shall he die, As a tree falls so shall it lie. **1836** M. SCOTT *Cruise of Midge* II. ii. It is of no use.... As the tree falls, so must it lie—it is a part of my creed. **1937** 'F. HEDLEY *Cavalier of Crime* x. 130 'No use trying to account for the vagaries of fate, is it, Inspector? Where the tree falleth, there shall it lie.'
■ **death 死 ; fate and fatalism 運命と運命論**

The TREE is known by its fruit.
木はその実によってわかる。

『マタイによる福音書』12章33節（欽定訳聖書）The tree is known by his fruit.「木はその実によって知られる」を想起させる。

□ **1528** W. TYNDALE *Obedience of Christian Man* 88ᵛ Judge the tre by his frute, and not by his leves. **1597-8** SHAKESPEARE *Henry IV, Pt. 1* II. iv. 414 If then the tree may be known by the fruit ... there is virtue in that Falstaff. **1670** J. RAY *English Proverbs* 11 A tree is known by the fruit, and not by the leaves. **1896** J. A. FROUDE *Council of Trent* iv. Lutherans said the tree is known by its fruit. Teach a pure faith, and abuses will disappear. **1955** S. N. GROSE *Flame of Forest* I. 15 'I never judge a man by his mask.' 'A tree should be judged by its fruits,' Myna responded. ■ **appearance 外見 ; human nature 人間性**

tree ⇒ The APPLE never falls far from the tree; He that would EAT the fruit must climb the tree; When the LAST tree is cut down, ... you will realize that you cannot eat money; You cannot SHIFT an old tree without it dying; As the TWIG is bent, so is the tree inclined; WALNUTS and pears you plant for your heirs.

trick ⇒ You can't TEACH an old dog new tricks.

There are TRICKS in every trade.
あらゆる商売にはコツがある。

（訳注：trick＝「…のコツ」、trade「商売」。learn the *tricks* of the *trade*〈商売のコツを学ぶ〉）

当初の用例では、あらゆる商売人は自分の業界内で認められている手順にしたがって人を騙す独自の手口を持っているという意味で使われていた。しかし、ここ最近では、特定の業界における創業者だけが持っている商売のコツを指している。

□ **1632** M. PARKER (*title*)*Knavery in all Trades*. **1654** *Mercurius Fumigosus* 12-19 July 49 If there be not Knavery in All Trades, I shrewdly am mistaken. **1692** R. L'ESTRANGE *Fables of Aesop* clxxxiii. Jupiter appointed Mercury to make him a Composition of Fraud and Hypocrisie, and to give Every Artificer his Dose on't.... Mercury ... gave the Taylors the Whole Quantity that was Left; and from hence comes the Old Saying, There's Knavery in All Trades, but Most in Taylors. **1857** E. BENNETT *Border Rover* vi. 'I would be willing to swear you had bewitched this rifle.' ... 'Thar's tricks to all trades'cept ourn.'**1978** L. BLOCK *Burglar in Closet* xvii. You age them [bills, paper money] ... by cooking them with a little coffee-well, there are tricks in every trade—and I don't ... know some of the ones the counterfeiters have come up with. **1987** S. STEWART *Lifting the Latch* 87 'Theer's a trick in every trade,' he was fond of saying, 'bar besom[broom]-making, and the biggest stick goes in the middle theer.' ■ **business** ビジネス・商売 ; **trades and skills** 職業と技術

A TROUBLE shared is a trouble halved.
分かち合えば苦労も半分となる。

他人に自分の抱えている問題や苦しみを話すと、肩の荷が軽くなる。

□**1931** D. L. SAYERS *Five Red Herrings* ix. 'Unbosom yourself,' said Wimsey. 'Trouble shared is trouble halved.' **1966** A. CARTER *Shadow Dance* viii. He found he wanted to share the experience of the previous night with Edna (a trouble shared is a trouble halved). **1987** C. GRAHAM *Killings at Badger's Drift* 7 She had never felt more keenly the truth of the saying 'a trouble shared is a trouble halved'. But she had lived in a small village long enough to know that what she had discovered could safely be discussed with no one. **2002** *Times* 18 Mar. 12 Thorpe's estranged wife, ... acting under the principle of a problem shared is a problem halved, wanted 'the truth to come out'. ■ **trouble** やっかい・苦労

Never TROUBLE trouble till trouble troubles you.
悩み事が汝を悩ませるまでは悩み事で悩むな。

取り越し苦労をしても何にもならない。† SUFFICIENT unto the day is the evil thereof. 「その日の苦労はその日 1 日だけで十分である」

□**1884** *Folk-Lore Journal* II. 280 Never trouble trouble, till trouble troubles you. **1945** 'D. B. OLSEN' *Cats don't Smile* i. Never trouble trouble until trouble troubles you. I always wondered: what then? **1983** *Good Housekeeping* Oct 75 Talking of proverbs, there is an old Yorkshire saying: never trouble trouble, till trouble troubles thee. To which I would add the rider: and when it does trouble thee, keep it to thyself. **2002** *Spectator* 20 July 31 He was a master of procrastination or of misunderstanding what he had been told to do. 'Never trouble trouble until trouble troubles you': that was Junor's maxim where Beaverbrook was concerned. ■ **trouble** やっかい・苦労

trouble（名詞）⇒ Do not MEET troubles halfway; NEEDLES and pins, ... when a man marries, his trouble begins.

Many a TRUE word is spoken in jest.
冗談で言ったことが当たっていたということも少なくない。

（訳注：many a/an ＝「多くの」。*many a* time〈幾度も〉。「嘘から出たまこと」）

軽率に言ったこと、あるいは冗談として言ったことが本当になることもある。

□*c***1391** CHAUCER *Monk's Prologue* I. 1964 Be nat wrooth, my lord, though that I pleye. Ful ofte in game a sooth [truth] I have herd seye! *a***1628** J. CARMICHAELL *Proverbs in Scots* no. 1099 Manie suith [true] word said in bourding [jesting]. *c***1665** in *Roxburghe Ballads* (1890) VII. 366 Many a true word hath been spoke in jest. **1738** SWIFT *Polite Conversation* I. iii. 'I did a very foolish thing yesterday.' ... 'They say, many a true Word's spoken in jest.' **1979** O. LESSING *Shikasta* 356 By the time we have finished I expect we shall have a dozen or more [children].... Many a true word is spoken in jest. **2015** *www.derryjournal.com* 20 Jan. 'It's a different world up there,' a radio reporter in Belfast said with a giggle last Wednesday ... The saying, 'Many a true word was spoken in jest' came to mind. ■ **truth** 真実・真理

458　true

true ⇒ The COURSE of true love never did run smooth; What EVERYBODY says must be true; MORNING dreams come true; What is NEW cannot be true; If it SOUNDS too good to be true, it probably is.

TRUST in God but tie your camel.
神を信じよ、ただしラクダは繋いでおくように。

　アラブのことわざでイスラム教の教祖ムハンマドに関する逸話に由来する。「ムハンマドの信奉者の1人がやって来て言った。「教祖様、私は今夜ラクダの綱を緩めます。そして神の摂理に託します」。しかし、ムハンマドは賢明にも次のように答えた。「ラクダの綱はできるだけしっかり結んでおきなさい。その後で神を信じなさい」(C. H. スポルジョン『スポルジョンのクリスマスとイースターにおける説教集』〈1995〉77)。同じ趣旨に沿った、より世俗的なことわざが Trust in God but lock your car と Trust in God but lock your door.「神を信じよ、ただし車の鍵はかけておくように。神を信じよ、ただしドアの鍵はかけておくように」である。

□**1920** M. PICKTHALL *Islam and Progress* 28 Trust in God but tie your camel. **1953** *Religions: Journal of Transactions of Society for Promoting Study of Religions* 28 According to the homely Arab proverb, 'Trust in God but tie your camel.' **2000** B. MCCORMACK *Tokyo Notes and Anecdotes* 14 Even in Japan, I've learned to adhere to the wise Islamic adage: 'trust in Allah but tie your camel.' **2004** W. HUTTON & J. EAGLE *Earth's Catastrophic Past and Future* 18 The ... eruption of Krakatau was heard as a low rumble thousands of miles away. If we hear such a rumble, should we not drive as quickly as possible to grocery and drug stores to load up on necessities? As the saying goes, 'Trust in God, but tie your camel first.' ■ providence（神の）摂理 ; self-help 自助

Put your TRUST in God, and keep your powder dry.
神を信用し、火薬は濡らさぬようにせよ。

　この忠告は、英国の将軍・政治家 O. クロムウェルが言ったとされる（1834年と1856年の用例参照）。神への祈りの奨励と、火薬はつねに使用可能である状態にしておくようにという実用的な指示とを組み合わせている。後半部分（keep your powder dry）が独立して使われることも多い。

□**1834** COLONEL BLACKER *Oliver's Advice* in E. Hayes *Ballads of Ireland* (1856) I. 192 Put your trust in God, my boys, and keep your powder dry. **1856** E. HAYES *Ballads of Ireland* (ed. 2) I. 191 Cromwell ... when his troops were about crossing a river ... concluded an address ... with these words— 'put your trust in God; but mind to keep your powder dry.' **1908** *Times Literary Supplement* 6 Nov. 383 In thus keeping his powder dry the bishop acted most wisely, though he himself ascribes the happy result entirely to the observance of the other half of Cromwell's maxim. **1979** V. CANNING *Satan Sampler* iv. God ... created us for a better end.... We must put our trust in Him and keep our powder dry. **2014** *www.breitbart.com* 13 Dec. 'Keep your powder dry,' [Jeb] Bush wrote in a recent email to potential donors, hinting they should refrain from giving money to other potential candidates. ■ prudence 思慮・分別 ; self-help 自助

There is TRUTH in wine.
酒には真実がある。

　人は酔うとうっかり本心を口に出すものである。†ギリシア語 ἐν οἴνῳ ἀλήθεια.「酒に真

実がある」(紀元前 6 世紀の抒情詩人アルカイオスの言葉とされる) やラテン語版の *In vino veritas.*「酒には真実がある」もよく使われる。この言葉はエラスムスの『格言集』で使われた。

□ **1545** R. TAVERNER tr. *Erasmus' Adages* (ed. 2) H5ᵛ In wyne is trouthe. **1659** T. PECKE *Parnassi Puerpertum* 5 Grant but the Adage true, that Truth's in wine. **1869** TROLLOPE *He knew He was Right* II. li. There is no saying truer than that ... there is truth in wine. Wine ... has the merit of forcing a man to show his true colours. **1934** R. GRAVES *Claudius the God* ix. The man who made the proverb 'There's truth in wine' must have been pretty well soaked when he made it. **2002** P. LOVESEY *Diamond Dust* xi. 87 He was trying to decide if the man was capable of coherent answers. *In vino veritas* is a maxim reliable only up to a certain intake of the vino. ■ **drunkenness** 酩酊 ; **truth** 真実・真理

TRUTH is the first casualty of war.
戦争の最初の犠牲者は真実である。

ハイラム・ジョンソン議員が1918年の米国上院で演説をした際の言葉であると伝えられるが、確証はない。

□ **2015** Mrs P. SNOWDEN 'Women and War' in *Journal of Proceedings and Addresses of National Education Association* LIII. 55 Someone has finely said that 'truth is the first casualty in war'; and never was a greater untruth spoken than that war is waged for the protection of women and homes. **1928** A. PONSONEY *Falsehood in Wartime*(*epigraph*) When war is declared, Truth is the first casualty. **1975** P. KNIGHTLEY (*title*) The First Casualty: the war correspondent as hero, propagandist, and myth maker from the Crimea to Vietnam. **1998** *Independent* 12 June I. 29/1 If truth is the first casualty of war then words are the first to be crocked in the World Cup. **2002** *Consumer Reports* Feb. 62 We've all heard that truth is the first casualty of war. Still, it was surprising how fast the victim expired after the terrorist attacks of Sept. 11. ■ **truth** 真実・真理 ; **warfare** 戦争

TRUTH is stranger than fiction.
真実は小説よりも奇なり。

よく似たものに FACT is stranger than fiction.「事実は小説よりも奇なり」がある。

□ **1823** BYRON *Don Juan* XIV. ci. Truth is always strange, Stranger than Fiction. **1863** C. READE *Hard Cash* II. xv. Sampson was greatly struck with the revelation: he ... said truth was stranger than fiction. **1905** G. K. CHESTERTON *Club of Queer Trades* 133 'Do you believe that truth is stranger than fiction?' 'Truth must of necessity be stranger than fiction,' said Basil placidly. 'For fiction is the creation of the human mind, and therefore congenial to it.' **2014** *New Scientist* 4 Oct. 27 But the truth is often stranger than fiction. ■ **reality and illusion** 現実と幻想

TRUTH lies at the bottom of a well.
真理は井戸の底にある。

† ギリシア語 ἐτεῇ δὲ οὐδὲν ἴσμεν, ἐν βυθῷ γάρ ἡ. ἀλήθεια.「我々は明らかに何も知らない。なぜなら真理はとても深いところに隠れているからである」(デモクリトスに由来する)。また、ラクタンティウス『神聖教理』III. xxviii. *In puteo ... veritatem iacere demersam*.「真理は井戸の底に沈んでいる」にも挙がっている。

□ **1562** J. WIGAND *De Neutralibus* G6ᵛ The truth lyeth yet still drowned in the depe. **1578** H. WOTTON tr. *J. Iver's Courtly Controversy* 90 I shall conduct you ... vnto the Mansion where the truth so long hidden dothe inhabite, the which sage Democritus searched in the bottom of a well.

460 TRUTH

*a*1721 M. PRIOR *Dialogues of Dead* (1907) 225 You know the Antient Philosophers said Truth lay at the bottom of a Well. **1887** J. R. LOWELL *Democracy* 30 Truth … is said to lie at the bottom of a well. *c*1943 J. CORBETT *Murder minus Motive* xii. Truth … is reputed to reside at the bottom of a well. I've often conned that old saw over to myself, and … its originators must have meant that truth is often damned hard to discern. **2001** *Times* 2 31 Oct. 12 Truth may be found at the bottom of the well, but there was no well in London deep enough for that commodity. ■ con-cealment 隠すこと・隠蔽 ; truth 真実・真理

TRUTH makes the Devil blush.
真実は悪魔を恥じ入らせる。

よく似た概念は TELL the truth and shame the Devil.「真実を言うと悪魔は恥じ入る」にも含まれている。

□**1944** 'A. Gilbert' *Death at Door* (1945) viii. 81 Crook caught back a quick exclamation. Truth may make the devil blush but that doesn't mean the devil doesn't frequently get the best of it. **1955** H. KEMP *Death of Dwarf* ix. 82 'So I shall not break my rule: never to say a thing about anybody until I'm sure it's true, and not always then. Truth makes the devil blush. That's true enough; but if it turns out not to be the truth after all, it only sets him giggling.' ■ truth 真実・真理

TRUTH will out.
真実は明らかになるものだ。

(訳注：will ＝「…するものだ」〈習性・傾向〉。out は動詞。Accidents *will* happen.〈事故は避けることができないもの〉。1596年の用例〈『ヴェニスの商人』から〉では、out だけでなく、come to light も使われている)

意味と形式が類似したものに MURDER will out.「殺人は明らかになるものだ」がある。

□**1439** LYDGATE *Life of St. Alban* (1974) 203 Trouthe wil out.… Ryghtwysnesse may nat hen hid. **1596** SHAKESPEARE *Merchant of Venice* II. ii. 73 Truth will come to light; murder cannot be hid long; a man's son may, but in the end truth will out. **1822** M. EDGEWORTH *Letter* l7 Jan. (1971) 324 Whether about a novel or a murder the truth will out. **2001** *Spectator* 17 Nov. 35 It has just been announced that the EU is to hold its own public inquiry into the [foot-and-mouth] epidemic, in Strasbourg next year. At last, perhaps, truth will out. ■ concealment 隠すこと・隠蔽 ; truth 真実・真理

truth ⇒ CHIIDREN and fools tell the truth; The GREATER the truth, the greater the libel; HALF the truth is often a whole lie; A LIE is halfway round the world; TELL the truth and shame the Devil.

try ⇒ You never KNOW what you can do till you try; If at first you don't SUCCEED, try, try, try again.

tsar ⇒ GOD is high above, and the tsar is far away.

Every TUB must stand on its own bottom.
桶は皆各自独力で立たねばならない。

私たちは各自が独力で生きてゆかなくてはならない。

TURN 461

□**1564** W. BULLEIN *Dialogue against Fever* 48ᵛ Let euery Fatte [vat] stande vpon his owne bottome. **1639** J. CLARKE *Parremiologia Anglo-Latina* 66 Every tub must stand on his owne bottome. **1721** C. CIBBER *Refusal* v. 721 I have nothing to do with that.... Let every Tub stand on its own Bottom. **1948** F. THOMPSON *Still glides Stream* iv. 'Every tub must stand on its own bottom,' was one of his homely ways of expressing the individual independence desirable in children. **1994** H. N. THOMAS *Spirits in Dark* xviii. 214 I know the Old Testament tell us that the sins o' the fathers get visited on the children, but yo' mustn' have a hand in that. Let 'every tub must sit 'pon its own bottom.' ■ **independence** 独立・自立

Tuesday ⇒ Monday's CHILD is fair of face.

tug ⇒ When GREEK meets Greek, then comes the tug of war.

tune ⇒ Why should the DEVIL have all the best tunes? ; A DRIPPING June sets all in tune; When the FURZE is in bloom, my love's in tune; There's many a GOOD tune played on an old fiddle; He that LIVES in hope dances to an ill tune; He who PAYS the piper calls the tune.

TURKEY, heresy, hops, and beer came into England all in one year.
七面鳥、異教、ホップ、そしてビールはすべて 1 年でイングランドにやってきた。

1643 年の用例は食料品の構成リストだけを挙げ、該当する年が1524年であることを示しているが、heresy「異教・異端」に関しても同じことが言える。なぜなら、ルターの教義がイングランドで広まりはじめたのが1520 年代であり、一方、イングランドの東南地方でbeer「ビール」に（エールに対抗して）風味を付けるためにhops「ホップ」を栽培しはじめたのも1524 年に遡るからである。turkey「七面鳥」は米国原産の鳥で、ウィリアム・ストリックランド（1598 年没）によって16世紀前半にイングランドに持ち込まれた。

□**1599** H. BUTTES *Diet's Dry Dinner* G4 I know not how it happened (as he merrily saith) that herisie and beere came hopping into England both in a yeere. **1643** R. BAKER *Chronicle Henry VIII* 66 About [1524] ... it happened that divers things were newly brought into England, whereupon this Rime was made: 'Turke[y]s, Carps, Hoppes, Piccarell [young pike], and Beere, Came into England all in one yeere.' **1906** R. KIPLING *Puck of Pook's Hill* 235 We say—'Turkey, Heresy, Hops, and Beer Came into England all in one year.' **1979** *Observer* 16 Dec. 56 'Turkeys, heresies, hops and beer All came to England in the one year' says the rhyme, but the Romans gave us hops. ■ **innovation** 革新

turkey ⇒ On SAINT Thomas the Divine kill all turkeys, geese, and swine.

TURN about is fair play.
かわりばんこが公平である。

1755 年の用例はこのことわざがゲームに由来することを示している。ゲームでは順番を交代することがフェアプレイである。しかし、2002 年の用例では、不正を働いた相手に復讐することは容認されるという意味で使われている。

□**1755** *Life of Captain Dudley Bradstreet* 338 Hitherto honest Men were kept from shuffling the Cards, because they would cast knaves out from the Company of Kings, but we would make them know, Turn about was fair Play. **1854** SURTEES *Handley Cross* xviii. 'Turn about is fair play,' as the devil said to the smoke-jack [an apparatus for turning a roasting spit]. **1986** J. SMITH *Tourist*

462 turn

Trap xi. 'And if you hear anything about Les, you'll let me know, won't you?' 'I'll be glad to. But turn-about's fair play—if you hear something, will you let me know?' **2002** *Washington Times* 10 Apr. A16 And let's not forget: Turnabout is fair play. If we let the IRS impose U.S. tax laws on foreign banks, what's to stop foreign tax collectors from seeking to impose their laws on U.S. banks? ■ **fair dealing** 公正な取引

turn ⇒（名詞）One GOOD turn deserves another;（動詞）A BAD penny always turns up; CLERGYMEN's sons always turn out badly; There is always one who KISSES, and one who turns the cheek; Even a WORM will turn.

turneth ⇒ A SOFT answer turneth away wrath.

turning ⇒ It is a LONG lane that has no turning.

twelve ⇒ It is not SPRING until you can plant your foot upon twelve daisies.

twenty ⇒ HINDSIGHT is always twenty/twenty.

twice ⇒ FOOL me once, shame on you; Fool me twice, shame on me; He GIVES twice who gives quickly; LIGHTNING never strikes the same place twice; MEASURE twice, cut once; An OLD man is twice a child; ONCE bitten, twice shy; OPPORTUNITY never knocks twice at any man's door; THINK twice, cut once.

As the TWIG is bent. So is the tree inclined.
小枝が曲げられるように木全体も曲がるものだ。
（訳注：「三つ子の魂百まで」）

人の将来は幼少期によって大きな影響を受けるものだ。† **1530** J. PALSGRAVE *L'eclaircissement de la Langue Franr;aise.*161「細い枝（新芽）は緑色の（曲げやすい）時期なら曲げられる。そして矯正することもできる。ただしそれほど曲がっていない場合に限られる」

□**1732** POPE *Epistles to Several Persons* I. 102 'Tis Education forms the common mind, Just as the Twig is bent, the Tree's inclined. **1818** T. G. FESSENDEN *Ladies Monitor* 75 "Tis education forms the tender mind, Just as the twig is bent the tree's inclined.' This hacknied adage, not more trite than true. **1940** P. MCGINLEY Primary Education in Pocketful of Wry 16 As bends the twig, thus grows the el-em ... So, twice a month, we're bound to sell'em The doctrine of Impartial Minds. **1979** 'C. AIRD' *Some die Eloquent* viii. 'Nature, not nurture?' murmured the biologist.... 'As the twig is bent,' Sloan came back. **1996** *National Review* 9 Dec. 63 Older, bigger children defend their privileges, while younger kids try to subvert the status quo. As the twig is bent, so grows the tree. ■ **children** 子供；**human nature** 人間性；**nature and nurture** 生まれと育ち

TWO blacks don't make a white.
黒と黒を足しても白にはならぬ。

類似したものにTWO wrongs don't make a right.「悪と悪を足しても善にはならぬ」がある。

TWO　463

□**1721** J. KELLY *Scottish Proverbs* 321 Two Blacks make no White. An Answer to them who, being blam'd, say others have done as ill or worse. **1822** SCOTT *Letter* 14 Mar (1934) VII. 96 To try whether I cannot contradict the old proverb of 'Two blackies [Lockhart Life: blacks] not making a white'. **1882** A. AINGER *Charles Lamb* vii. As two blacks do not make a white, it was beside the mark to make laborious fun over Southey's youthful ballads. **1932** G. B. SHAW *Adventures of Black Girl* 28 Never forget that two blacks do not make a white. **1966** A. E. LINDOP *I start Counting* viii. 'What's the modern murderer got to fear? ... They'll only go to prison.' ... 'Two blacks don't make a white.' ■ **good and evil** 正邪

While TWO dogs are fighting for a bone, a third runs away with it.
2 匹の犬が 1 本の骨を取り合っているあいだに、第 3 の犬がそれをくわえて走り去ってしまう。
（訳注：「漁夫の利」）

同じ標的を狙っている 2 人のライバルが熾烈な争いに熱を入れ過ぎると、第 3 者が 2 人に気づかれずにやって来て獲物を奪い去るという事態も起こり得る。この道徳観は中世以降の『イソップ物語』に登場するライオン、クマ、キツネの物語に含まれている。その物語とは、ライオンとクマが小鹿を捕まえ、くたくたになるまでその獲物を巡って争っていると、キツネが忍び寄り、小鹿を奪い取ってしまうというものである。

□*c***1386** CHAUCER *Knight's Tale* I. 1177 We stryve as dide the houndes for the boon.... Ther cam a kyte, whil that they were so wrothe, And baar awey the boon betwixe hem bothe. **1534** MORE *Dialogue of Comfort* (1553) I Aiiiv Now strive there twain for vs, our lord send the grace, that the thyrde dog cary not awaie the bone from them both. **1639** J. CLARKE *Parœmiologia Anglo-Latina* 94 Two dogs strive for a bone, and the third runs away with it. **1784** *Gazette of State of S. Carolina* 17 July 2 Verifying the coarse proverb, while two dogs are fighting for a bone, a third comes and runs away with it. **1983** *Practical Computing* 5 June While the major companies continue to argue among themselves they are in a poor position to police the rest of the industry. When two alsatians are fighting over a large bone, a passing poodle can easily walk off with it. ■ **opportunity, taken** 得られた機会

TWO heads are better than one.
2 つの頭は 1 つの頭にまさる。
（訳注：「三人寄れば文殊の知恵」）

問題解決や計画立案の際にはもう 1 人の協力を仰ぐ方が賢明である。類似したものに FOUR eyes see more than two.「4 つの目は 2 つの目より多くのものを見る」がある。2001 年の用例では、head が俗語で「トイレ」を意味している。

□*c***1390** GOWER *Confessio Amantis* I. 1021 Tuo han more wit then on. **1530** J. PALSGRAVE *L'éclaircissement de la Langue Française* 269 Two wyttes be farre better than one. **1546** J. HEYWOOD *Dialogue of Proverbs* I. ix. C2v But of these two thynges he wolde determyne none Without ayde. For two hedds are better than one. **1778** S. FOOTE *Nabob* I. 5 Here comes brother Thomas; two heads are better than one; let us take his opinion. **1979** J. RATHBONE *Eurokillers* xviii. Two heads are better than one.... I'd value your advice. **2001** *Washington Post* 14 July C12 (*Jeff MacNelly's Shoe comic strip*) 'Roz is having another restroom installed here.' 'Then it's true. Two heads are better than one.' ■ **assistance** 援助

TWO is company, but three is none.
2 人だとよい連れだが、3 人だと仲間割れする。

第三者に対して、恋がたきがいることを示すためによく使われる。現代では後半部分に
three's a crowd.「3 人だと多すぎる」が使われることもある。

☐**1706** J. STEVENS *Spanish & English Dict.* s. v. Compañia, A Company consisting of three is
worth nothing. It is the Spanish Opinion, who say that to keep a Secret three are too many, and
to be Merry they are too few. **1869** W. C. HAZLITI *English Proverbs* 442 Two is company, but
three is none. **1944** *Modern Language Notes* LIX. 517 Two's company, three's a crowd. **1979** J.
LEASOR *Love & Land Beyond* viii. Two's company and three's none, so one of the three has been
taken out of the game. **2002** *Washington Post* 10 Mar. SC11 (*Family Circus comic strip*) Two's
company, three's a crowd ''specially on a tandem bike.' ■ **friends 友**

TWO of a trade never agree.
同業者の 2 人は折り合わぬ。
（訳注：agree ＝「折り合う」。「職がたき」）

同じ職業についている人たちは、つねにライバルよりも自分の方が腕前が上だと思って
いる。

☐**1630** DEKKER *Second Part of Honest Whore* II. 154 It is a common rule, and 'tis most true,
Two of one trade never loue. **1673** E. RAVENSCROFT *Careless Lovers* A2ᵛ Two of a Trade can
seldome agree. **1727** GAY *Fables* I. xxi. In every age and clime we see, Two of a trade can ne'er
agree. **1887** G. MEREDITH *Poems* (1978) I. 148 Two of a trade, lass, never agree! Parson and
Doctor!—don't they love rarely, Fighting the devil in other men's fields! **1914** 'SAKI' *Beasts & Super-Beasts* 96 The snorts and snarls ... went far to support the truth of the old saying that two of
a trade never agree. **1981** E. LONGFORD *Queen Mother* vii. There is an old adage, 'Two of a kind
never agree.' ■ **quarrelsomeness 口論になりやすさ**；**similarity and dissimilarity 類似性と相違性**；
trades and skills 職業と技術

If TWO ride on a horse, one must ride behind.
1 頭の馬に 2 人乗れば、1 人は後ろに乗らなければならない。
（訳注：「両雄並び立たず」）

1 つの組織にリーダーが 2 人いることはできない。

☐**1598-9** SHAKESPEARE *Much Ado about Nothing* III. v. 34 An two men ride of a horse, one
must ride behind. *c***1628** J. SMYTH *Berkeley* MSS (1885) III. 32 If two ride upon an horse one
must sit behinde; meaninge, That in each contention one must take the [defeat]. **1874** G. J.
WHYTE-MELVILLE *Uncle John* i. x. There is an old adage ... 'When two ride on a horse, one
must ride behind.' **1942** V. RATH *Posted for Murder* VI. iii. There comes a point hen you are very
exasperating.... 'When two ride on one horse, one must ride behind.' But I'm getting off for a
while. **1986** A. CLARKE *Mystery Lady* (1988) iv. Collaboration on a book is an awkward business.
If two people ride one horse, one of them must ride behind. ■ **cooperation 協力**

There are TWO sides to every question.
すべての問題には 2 つの立場がある。

討論や論争においては両方の主張を考慮しなければならない。†プロタゴラス『格言集』
（ディオゲネス・ラエルティオス『プロタゴラス』IX. Ii.）καὶ πρῶτος ἔφη [Protagoras]
δύο λόγους εἶναι περὶ παντὸς πράγματος ἀντικειμένους ἀλλήλοις.「すべての問題に互いに
相反する側面があると最初に言ったのはプロタゴラスであった」。プロタゴラス（紀元前

5 世紀）は古代ギリシアの修辞学・哲学・倫理学の教師であった。

□**1802** J. ADAMS *Autobiography* (1966) III. 269 There were two Sides to a question. **1817** T. JEP-PERSON *Letter* 5 May in L. J. Cappon *Adams-Jefferson Letters* (1959) II. 513 Men of energy of character must have enemies: because there are two sides to every question, and ... those who take the other will of course be hostile. **1863** C. KINGSLEY *Water Babies* vi. Let them recollect this, that there are two sides to every question, and a downhill as well as an uphill road. **1971** C. FITZGIBBON *Red Hand* iii. From the English point of view which inevitably they have applied to ... Ireland, the art of politics consists in realizing that there are two sides to every question. **2014** *news.nationalpost.com* 28 Jan. So here we were in law school, imbibing ancient sophistic tradi-tions: 'There are two sides to every question,' our professors taught us. That didn't make sense to me. ■ **fair dealing** 公正な取引

It takes TWO to make a bargain.
売買契約には 2 人要る（1 人でけんかはできない）。

売買契約に際しては両者が同意し、かつそれを守らなければならない。

□**1597** BACON *Colours of Good & Euill* x. 68 The seconde worde makes the bargaine. **1598** *Mucedorus* B2 Nay; soft, sir, tow words to a bargaine, *a*1637 MIDDLETON et al. *Widow* v. i. There's two words to a bargain ever ... and if love be one, I'm sure money's the other. **1766** GOLDSMITH *Vicar of Wakefield* II. xii. 'Hold, hold, Sir,' cried Jenkinson, 'there are two words to that bargain.' **1943** M. FLAVIN *Journey in Dark* iv. Takes two to make a bargain, and you both done mighty wrong. **1973** E. MCGIRR *Bardel's Murder* iv. My father was in skins and he had to carry a life-preserver, they got so nasty. Caveat emptor, he used to say, it taking two to make a bargain. ■ **buying and selling** 売買

It takes TWO to make a quarrel.
口論するには 2 人要る（1 人でけんかはできない）。

相手がいて、その人物が自己主張しない限り、口論にはならない。

□**1706** J. STEVENS *Spanish & English Dict*. s. v. Barajar, When one will not, two do not Quarrel. **1732** T. PULLER *Gnomologia* no. 4942 There must be two at least to a Quarrel. **1859** H. KINGS-LEY *Geoffrey Hamlyn* II. xiii. It takes two to make a quarrel, Cecil, and I will not be one. **1979** *Times* 3 Dec. 13 If it were not for the truism that it takes at least two to make a quarrel, the French and the Germans ... could fairly claim that the fault lay wholly with the United Kingdom. ■ **anger** 怒り ; **quarrelsomeness** 口論になりやすさ

It takes TWO to tango.
タンゴを踊るには 2 人必要である（責任は双方にある）。
（訳注：「けんか両成敗」）

共同活動、特に悪事や違法行為において協力関係にある両者は共に責任がある（1999 年の用例参照）。おそらく It takes two to ...（例えば「取引する」や「口論する」）「…するには 2 人必要である」という当初のことわざを基にしている。また、パール・ベイリーによって歌われたホフマンとマニングが作詞作曲した歌（1952 年の用例）は世界的にヒットし、その歌のタイトルとなったこのことわざは一躍国際的に使われるようになった。

□**1952** HOFFMAN & MANNING *Takes Two to Tango* (song title) 2 There are lots of things you can do alone! But, takes two to tango. **1965** *Listener* 24 June 923 As for negotiation ... the Presi-dent has a firm, and melancholy, conviction: it takes two to tango. **1991** *Times* 22 May 14 Re-member. It only takes two to tango, and neither of them has to be you. **1999** *Bella* 25 May 16/2 Deep down, I know it takes two to tango and the blame should lie with them equally. ■ **coopera-**

466　TWO

tion 協力

TWO wrongs don't make a right.
悪と悪を足しても善にはならぬ。

よく似たものにTWO blacks don't make a white.「黒と黒を足しても白にはならぬ」が
ある。

□**1783** B. RUSH *Letter* 2 Aug. (1951) I. 308 Three wrongs will not make one right. **1814** J. KERR *Several Trials of David Barclay* 249 Two wrongs don't make one right. **1905** S. WEYMAN *Starve-crow Farm* xxiv. He ought to see this! ... After all, two wrongs don't make a right. **1991** *Washington Post* 26 Apr. Even in law school, two wrongs don't make a right. **2014** *www. theguardian.com* 17 Dec. Two wrongs never make a right. I truly hope that we can all get beyond these mutually belligerent policies. ■ **good and evil 正邪**

two ⇒ BETTER one house spoiled than two; BETWEEN two stools one falls to the ground; A BIRD in the hand is worth two in the bush; Two BOYS are half a boy, and three boys are no boy at all; Of two EVILS choose the less; FOUR eyes ⇒ More than two; One HOUR's sleep before midnight is worth two after; NO man can serve two masters; ONE for sorrow, two for mirth; If you can't RIDE two horses at once, you shouldn't be in the circus; If you RUN after two hares you will catch neither; THREE may keep a secret, if two of them are dead; One VOLUNTEER is worth two pressed men.

tyranny ⇒ BETTER a century of tyranny than one day of chaos.

U

undone ⇒ What's DONE cannot be undone.

The UNEXPECTED always happens.
予想外の事はいつ何時でも起こるものだ。

(訳注：the unexpected ＝「予想外の事」。the は形容詞・過去分詞につけて、抽象概念を指し、単数扱いとなる。an eye for *the* beautiful〈審美眼〉。「一寸先は闇」)

NOTHING is certain but the unforeseen.「予想外の事を別にすれば、（人生において）確実なものは何もない」と類似した逆説である。†プラウトゥス『幽霊屋敷』I. iii. 197 *Insperata accidunt magi' saepe quam quae speres.*「予期せぬことは望んでいることよりもよく起こる」

□**1885** B. J. HARDY *How to be Happy though Married* xxv. A woman may have much theoretical knowledge, but this will not prevent unlooked-for obstacles from arising.... It is the unexpected that constantly happens. **1909** *Times Weekly* 12 Nov. 732 No place in the world is more familiar than the House of Commons with 'the unforeseen that always happens'. **1938** B. WAUGH *Scoop* I. iii. Have nothing which in a case of emergency you cannot carry in your own hands. But remember that the unexpected always happens. **1977** L. J. PETER *Peter's Quotations* 296 Peter's Law—The unexpected always happens. ■ **certainty and uncertainty 確かさと不確かさ；foresight and hindsight 先見の明と後知恵**

unforeseen ⇒ NOTHING is certain but the unforeseen.

UNION is strength.
団結は力なり。

特に労働組合のスローガンとしては union の代わりに unity が一般的に使われる。†ホロメス『イーリアス』XIII. 237 συμφερτὴ δ' ἀρετὴ πέλει ἀνδρῶν καὶ μάλα λυγρῶν.「弱者でさえ団結すると力を持つ」。ラテン語 *Vis unita fortior.*「団結された力は強くなる」。*c***1527** T. バセレット訳『エラスムスの賢者の言葉』A 4ᵛ Concorde maketh those thynges that are weake, mighty and stronge.「団結は弱い者を強くする」

□**1654** R. WILLIAMS *Complete Writings* (1963) VI. 280 Union strengthens. **1837** in D. Porter *Early Negro Writing* (1971) 228 In Union is strength. 1848 S. ROBINSON *Letter* 29 Dec. in *Indiana Hist. Collections* (1936) XXII. 178 'Union is strength,' and that is the only kind that can control the floods of such a 'great father of rivers [the Mississippi]'. **1877** B. WALFORD *Tales of Great Families* I. 264 The prosperity of the House of Rothschild [is due to] the unity which has attended the co-partnership of its members,... a fresh example of the saying that 'union is strength'.

468 unite

1933 H. ADAMS *Strange Murder of Hatton* xxix. Union is strength. We, by pooling our resources, ... are able ... to secure a steady income. **1981** B. AGRY *Assault Force* ix. This unfortunate mis- understanding; we must clear it up.... After all, unity is strength. ■ **strength and weakness 強弱；** **unity and division 統一と分断**

unite ⇒ When SPIDER webs unite, they can tie up a lion.

UNITED we stand, divided we fall.
団結すれば立つことができるが、分裂すれば倒れる。

団結は強固な国、組織を生み出すが、分断はそれらを破壊する。

□**1768** J. DICKINSON *Liberty Song in Boston Gazette* 18 July Then join Hand in Hand brave Americans all, By uniting we stand, by dividing we fall. **1849** G. P. MORRIS *Flag of our Union in Poems* (1853) 41 'United we stand—divided we fall!'—It made and preserves a nation! **1894** J. JACOBS *Fables of Aesop* 122 Then Lion attacked them one by one and soon made an end of all four [oxen]. United we stand, divided we fall. **2002** *Times* 2 13 June 7 Threatened ... , mocked ... , hounded ..., the churches—or at least, their more enlightened leaders—are belatedly moving towards the view that 'united we might just stand, but divided we most certainly fall'. ■ **unity and** **division 統一と分断**

unity ⇒ UNION is strength.

unlucky ⇒ LUCKY at cards, unlucky in love.

unpunished ⇒ No GOOD deed goes unpunished.

What goes UP must come down.
上がるものは必ず下がる。

（訳注：must ＝「必ず…する」〈自然法則〉。Bad seed *must* produce bad corn.〈悪い種子からは必ず実 ができる〉。「驕る平家は久しからず」）

文字通りの意味は戦争時の対空榴散弾とロケットを指すが、現在では株の変動も指す。

□**1929** F. A. POTTLE *Stretchers* vii. The antiaircraft guns always took a shot for luck. What goes up must come down, and one can be killed quite as neatly by a fragment of his own shrapnel as by the enemy's. **1949** N. MAILER *Naked & Dead* III. vi. Gravity would occupy the place of mor- tality (what goes up must come down). **1967** F. J. SINGER *Epigrams at Large* 57 'What goes up, must come down' is really a time-worn statement which wore out after the Venus and Mars probes. **2001** *Washington Post* 7 Sept B1 What goes up must come down, even 26 years later. And the aged Russian rocket that came down just before dawn yesterday did so with a glowing, pro- tracted brilliance that startled the early birds who saw it. **2014** *metronews.ca* 27 Apr. (*heading*) Summertime stock market What goes up must eventually come down. ■ **fate and fatalism 運命と** **運命論**

up ⇒ FIRST up, best dressed; PUT up or shut up; Up like a ROCKET, down like a stick.

upright ⇒ EMPTY sacks will never stand upright.

USE it or lose it.
使わないと失う。

(訳注：or ＝「〈命令文などの後で〉さもないと」。Take a vacation, *or* you'll get sick.〈休暇を取りなさい。さもないと病気になるよ〉。「宝の持ち腐れ」)

能力、性能、尽力が失われるといけないから、たえず使いこなさなければならないという警告。元になった表現は20世紀米国生まれの Abuse it and lose it.「乱用すると失う」で、それからの推論である。

□ **1893** *Homestead* [Des Moines] 16 June USE OR LOSE (*heading*) It seems to be a law of nature that use is the condition of possession. **1948** *Journal of American Judicature Society* June (*article title*) The grand jury—use it or lose it. **1985** *Times* 18 Apr. 17 The conventional answer to this loss of facilities is that it is a problem for the local community which should be solved through 'Use it or lose it' campaigns and self-help solutions. **2007** *New Scientist* 28 Apr. 48 The pendulum swung back the other way in the 20th century, when a consumeroriented culture lauded arousal and fulfilment: the injunction now was 'use it or lose it'. **2012** *ScienceDaily.com* 25 Apr. (*heading*) Protecting your brain: 'Use it or lose it'. ■ **action and inaction** 行為と非行為

use（名詞）⇒ KEEP a thing seven years and you'll always find a use for it.

V

vacuum ⇒ NATURE abhors a vacuum.

vain ⇒ In vain the NET is spread in the sight of the bird.

valet ⇒ NO man is a hero to his valet.

valour ⇒ DISCRETION is the better part of valour.

VARIETY is the spice of life.
変化は人生の薬味である。

（訳注：初例として挙がっている1785年の用例は、英国のロマン派詩人・賛美歌作者 W. クーパーの長詩『課題』〈*The Task*〉からのものである。この例の中で、作者は「変化は人生の薬味であり、それは人生にあらゆる風味を与えてくれる」と述べている）

†エウリピデス『オレステース』234 μεταβολὴ πάντων γλυκύ.「変化はつねに素晴らしい」

□**1785** COWPER *Task* II. 76 Variety's the very spice of life, That gives it all its flavour. **1854** 'M. LANGDON' *Ida May* vi. Take all de wives you can get,—bariety am de spite of life. **1954** 'M. COST' *Invitation from Minerva* 174 'Your signal is different from ours?' ... 'Variety is the spice of life,' he retorted. **2002** *Washington Post* 7 Aug. Cl5 (*Broom Hilda comic strip*) 'I have prepared our annual financial statement.' ... 'Last year you chewed it up and swallowed it.' 'Variety, lads. Spice of life and all that!' ■ **novelty** 目新しさ；**variety** 多様性

varlet ⇒ An APE's an ape, a varlet's a varlet, though they be clad in silk or scarlet.

What happens in VEGAS stays in Vegas.
ラス・ベガスで起こることはラス・ベガスだけの話。

旅行中の行きずりの性体験や粗野な振る舞いは無かったことにするという暗黙の了解を意味し、What goes on TOUR stays on tour.「旅先で起こることは旅先だけの話」と類似している。米国ネヴァダ州ラス・ベガス市は、What happens here stays here「ここで起こることは口外しない」というスローガンを掲げて、2000年初頭に観光客誘致キャンペーンを行ない、洗練された大人の客をカジノやナイトクラブに招き寄せることを意図した。地名を変えることでユーモア溢れる異形が次々と登場した。

□**2005** *usatoday.com* 4 Nov. When Jay Leno asked Laura Bush on The Tonight Show whether she had gambled or had seen a Chippendales show while visiting the Las Vegas Strip, the First

VIRTUE 471

Lady got a big hand by replying, 'Jay, what happened in Vegas, stays in Vegas.' **2014** *Times2* 17 Nov. 2 [W]hen the menfolk announced ... that they were going to 'roam and forage' for a while ... they were really heading off for the Namibian tribal equivalent of a tenday bender in Magaluf ... 'What happens on the Great Escarpment stays on the Great Escarpment!' ■ **discretion** 思慮分別; **speech and silence** 発言と沈黙

vengeance ⇒ REVENGE is a dish that can be eaten cold.

venture ⇒ NOTHING venture, nothing gain; NOTHING venture, nothing have.

vessel ⇒ EMPTY vessels make the most sound.

victor ⇒ HISTORY is written by the victors.

view ⇒ DISTANCE lends enchantment to the view; If you are not the LEAD dog, the view never changes.

It takes a whole VILLAGE to bring up a child.
子供 1 人を育てるには村全体が必要である。

ナイジェリア（イボ族とヨルバ族）のことわざで、子供の養育には村全体が役割を担うという意味である。他のアフリカ諸言語にも同様のことわざが見られる。

☐**1989** *Miami Herald* 21 May (online) We are rallying around the African proverb that it takes a whole village to raise a child. **1992** *New York Times* 18 Oct. (online) Our job as educators is to teach parents to help their kids to identify different solutions to a problem and to choose the right one ... We in the schools have to work more closely with parents on a continuous basis. There's an old saying that it takes a whole village to raise a kid. **1996** H. CLINTON (*book title*) *It Takes a Village*. **2002** 'Talking Point' posting on *www.news.bbc.co.uk* 23 Sept. Children there do not get sick, or suffer from obesity as they eat fresh food, and due to the culture of 'it takes a whole village to bring up a child', the children are cared for by every one. **2006** *British Dental Journal* vol. 200 597 There is, I understand, a proverb to the effect that 'It takes a whole village to bring up a child.' It has a folksy sort of feel about it [but] .. [m]ore importantly it suggests that it is possible for group action to create a positive outcome. ■ **children** 子供; **society** 社会

vinegar ⇒ HONEY catches more flies than vinegar; From the SWEETEST wine, the tartest vinegar.

VIRTUE is its own reward.
徳はそれ自体が報酬である。

†オウィディウス『黒海からの手紙』II. iii. *Virtutem pretium ... esse sui.*「徳はそれ自体が報酬である」

☐**1509** A. BARCLAY *Ship of Fools* 10ᵛ Vertue hath no rewarde. **1596** SPENSER *Faerie Queene* III. xii. Your vertue selfe her owne reward shall breed, Euen irrnrnortall praise, and glory wyde. **1642** BROWNE *Religio Medici* I. 87 That vertue is her owne reward, is but a cold principle. **1673** DRYDEN *Assignation* III. i. Virtue ... is its own reward: I expect none from you. **1844** DICKENS *Martin Chuzzlewit* xv. It is creditable to keep up one's spirits here. Virtue's its own reward. **2002**

472　virtue

Spectator 12 Jan. 18 Humble people lack self-esteem, and chastity is just another sexual dysfunction. Virtue is not somuch its own reward as a condition requiring therapeutic intervention.
■ **just deserts** 当然の報い ; **virtue** 長所・徳

virtue ⇒ PATIENCE is a virtue.

visitor ⇒ FISH and guests smell after three days.

The VOICE of the people is the voice of God.
民の声は神の声。

このことわざは、完全に否定されたり（1710年の用例）、皮肉としても使われる（1989年の用例）場合が多い。† *a* 804 アルクイン『書簡集』clxiv.『作品集』(1863) I. 438 *Solent dicere: vox populi, vox Dei.*「よく言われるように、民の声は神の声である」

□*c*1412 T. HOCCLEVE *Regimen of Princes* (EETS) 104 Peples vois is goddes voys, men seyne. **1450** in T. Wright *Political Poems* (1861) II. 227 The voice of the people is the voice of God. **1646** BROWNE *Pseudodoxia Epidemica* I. iii. Though sometimes they are flattered with that Aphorisme, [they] will hardly believe the voice of the people to bee the voice of God. **1710** P. A[TTERBURY] (*book title*) The Voice of the People, No Voice of God. **1822** C. C. COLTON *Lacon* II. 266 The voice of the People is the voice of God; this axiom has manifold exceptions. **1914** G. B. SHAW *Misalliance* p. lxxii. An experienced demagogue comes along and says, 'Sir: you are the dictator: the voice of the people is the voice of God.' **1989** *Washington Post* 24 Mar. C2 I imagine they are fine citizens. After all, we elected them and the voice of the people is the voice of God, remember that ■ **politics** 政治 ; **power** 力・権力 ; **rulers and ruled** 支配者と被支配者

One VOLUNTEER is worth two pressed men.
1 人の志願兵は 2 人の強制徴募兵に匹敵する。

自分の意志で仕事を引き受ける人は 1 人で強制的にやらされる人の 2 人前以上の仕事をしてくれる。pressed men とは強制的に軍隊に徴兵された兵士を指す。

□**1705** T. HEARNE *Journal* 31 Oct. in *Remarks & Collections* (1885) I. 62 'Tis S^d my Ld Seymour presently after Mr. Smith was pronounc'd Speaker, rose up, and told them, Gentlemen; you have got a Low Church man; but pray remember that 100 Voluntiers are better than 200 press'd men. **1834** MARRYAT *Jacob Faithful* I. xiii. 'Shall I give you a song?' 'That's right, Tom; a volunteer's worth two pressed men.' **1837** F. CHAMIER *Arethusa* I. iii. Don't fancy you will be detained against your will; one volunteer is worth two pressed men. **1979** M. M. KAYE *Shadow of Moon* (rev. ed.) iv. The Earl could not be persuaded to send her away.... In any case, said the Earl, Winter would need a personal maid, and in his opinion one volunteer was worth three pressed men. **2008** *www.westbriton.co.uk* 25 June (*heading*) One volunteer better than 10 pressed men.
■ **cooperation** 協力 ; **free will and compulsion** 自由意志と強制

vomit ⇒ The DOG returns to its vomit.

wag ⇒ It is MERRY in hall when beards wag all.

wait ⇒ ALL things come to those who wait; TIME and tide wait for no man.

waiting ⇒ It's ILL waiting for dead men's shoes.

If you can WALK you can dance, if you can talk you can sing.
歩けるなら踊れるし、話せるなら歌える。

　ミュージカルへの参加を勧める言葉として使われる。1998年の用例では南アフリカのジンバブエ共和国のことわざとされている。

　☐ **1947** D. E. MARSH in *Clearing House* XV. 243 (*title*) 'If You Can Walk—You Can Dance: A Social Dance Plan for Pupils'. **1998** J. C. SHUMAN & D. ROTTENBERG *Rhythm of Business* 11. I started this chapter with a saying from Zimbabwe: If you can walk/You can dance/If you can talk/You can sing. **1999** *New York Times* 17 Aug. (online) 'The only thing I am interested to know is that they will be consistent,' Mr. Leitao said. 'I do believe if you can walk you can dance. If you can talk you can sing. When you learn to shift your weight then you learn about structure and form and then you put the. melody in your body.' **2005** 'Drums that Talk' posting on *www.bowdoin.edu* 28 Mar. In West Africa, music is learned without notation and allows access to everyone, regardless of ability. Adzenyah embraces the inclusive nature of this music: 'If you can walk, you can dance. If you can talk, you can sing.' ■ **optimism** 楽観主義; **possibility and impossibility** 可能性と不可能性

We must learn to WALK before we can run.
走れるようになる前にまず歩けるようにならなければならない。

　（訳注：learn to＝「…できるようになる」。*learn* to drive.〈運転できるようになる〉）

　新しいことを覚える際は、より高度な技術に挑む前に基礎をしっかり習得しておかなければならない。慣用句 to run before one can walk「歩きもしないのに走ろうとする（＝基礎もできないのに難しいことをやろうとする）」も広く使われている。

　☐ *c***1350** *Douce MS 52* no. 116 Fyrst the cbylde crepyth and after gooth [walks]. *c***1450** *Towneley Play of First Shepherds* (EETS) 1. 100 Ffyrst must vs crepe and sythen [afterwards] go. **1670** J. RAY *English Proverbs* 75 You must learn to creep before you go. **1794** G. WASHINGTON *Letter* 20 July in *Writings* (1940) XXXIII. 438 We must walk as other countries have done before we can run. **1851** G. BORROW *Lavengro* II. ii. Ambition is a very pretty thing; but sir, we must walk before we run. **1876** J. PLATT *Business* 124 More fail from doing too much than too little. We must learn and be strong enough to walk before we can run. **1947** M. PENN *Manchester Fourteen Miles* xv. Mrs. Winstanley reproved her for being impatient. She pointed out … that everybody must learn to walk before they could run. **1980** K. AMIS *Russian Hide & Seek* iv. At the moment we can't leave it to the English to do anything. We must learn to walk before we can run. ■ **patience and impatience** 忍耐と性急

walk ⇒ AFTER dinner rest a while, after supper walk a mile.

wall ⇒ The WEAKEST go to the wall.

WALLS have ears.
壁に耳あり。
（訳注：「壁に耳あり、障子に目あり」）

よく似たものに FIELDS have eyes, and woods have ears. 「野に目あり、森に耳あり」がある。

□**1575** G. GASCOIGNE *Supposes* I. i. The table …, the portals, yes and the cupbords themselves have eares. **1592** G. DELAMOTHE *French Alphabet* II. 29 The walles may have some eares.… *Les murailles ont des aureilles.* **1620** T. SHELTON tr. *Ceruantes' Don Quixote* II. xlviii. They say Walls haue eares. **1766** D. GARRICK *Neck or Nothing* II. i. Not so fast and so loud, good master of mine—walls have ears. **1822** SCOTT *Nigel* I. vi. It is not good to speak of such things.… Stone walls have ears. **1958** L. DURRELL *Mountolive* XII. 232 She lay in the silence of a room which had housed (if walls have ears) their most secret deliberations. **2000** J. ALTMAN *Gathering of Spies* v. 91 He realized that Himmler was waiting to gain distance from the house before speaking. Walls had ears, and Nazi walls had more ears than most. ■ **eavesdroppers** 盗み聞きする人

WALNUTS and pears you plant for your heirs.
子孫のためにクルミの木と梨の木を植える。

将来の世代のために木を植えるという考えはクルミと梨に限定されず、もっと古くからある。†キケロ『大カトー』vii. 24 *'Serit arbores, quae olteri saeclo prosint,' ut ait Statius noster in Synephebis.* 「次世代の役に立つようにと木を植える者あり。（カエキリウス・）スタティウスは『老年論』の中でかく語れり」。クルミの木と梨の木はともに実が成るまでに相当長い年月がかかると考えられていたことに由来する。

□**1640** G. HERBERT *Outlandish Proverbs* no. 198 The tree that growes slowly, keepes it selfe for another. **1732** T. FULLER *Gnomologia* no. 2401 He who plants a Walnut-Tree, expects not to eat of the Fruit. **1863** A. SMITH *Dreamthorp* xi. My oaks are but saplings; but what undreamed-of English kings will they not outlive? … A man does not plant a tree for himself; he plants it for posterity. **1907** W. C. HAZUTT *English Proverbs* 361 Plant pears for your heirs. A proverb which no longer holds true, since pears are now made to yield well after a few years. **1941** C. MACICENZIE *Red Tapeworm* xv. 'Better to plant them promptly,' said Miss Quekett. 'It's only walnuts and pears you plant for your heirs.' ■ **children and parents** 親子

If you WANT a thing done well, do it yourself.
仕事を首尾よくやってもらいたければ、自らそれをやれ。
（訳注：you は総称的な用法。*You* never can tell what's going to happen.〈何が起きるかは誰にもわからない〉）

WANT 475

よく似たものに If you would be well SERVED, serve yourself.「十分に仕えてもらいたければ、自らが自らに仕えよ」がある。ナポレオンの言葉（2014年の用例）という説が一般的だが、根拠はない。

□ **1541** M. COVERDALE tr. *H. Bullinger's Christian State of Matrimony* xix. If thou wilt prospere, then loke to euery thynge thyne owne sell. **1616** T. DRAXE *Adages* 163 If a man will haue his business well done, he must doe it himselfe. **1858** LONGFELLOW *Poems* (1960) 160 That's what I always say; if you want a thing to be well done, You must do it yourself. **1975** 'B. LATHEN' *By Hook or by Crook* xxi. Do you know how I got it done in the end? I went down to Annapolis myself. I always say, if you want a thing done well, do it yourself! **1998** *Times* 20 Jan. 7 After everything that's happened, pregnancy was the last thing on my mind.... there's a lot to be said for the old adage that if you want a job doing properly, do it yourself. **2014** *www.wallstreetandtech. com* 23 Sept. Napoleon Bonaparte famously contributed the phrase, 'If you want a thing done well, do it yourself.' But even Napoleon, a well-documented micro-manager, eventually met his limits in Russia and at Waterloo. ■ **efficiency and inefficiency** 能率と非能率; **self-help** 自助

For WANT of a nail the shoe was lost; for want of a shoe the horse was lost; and for want of a horse the man was lost.
釘１本がないために蹄鉄がなくなり、蹄鉄１つがないために馬がいなくなり、馬１頭がないために兵士がいなくなる。

それ自体は取るに足らないように見えても、軽視すると厄難を招きかねないものがある。そのような事態を避けるために些細なことにも注意を払うよう奨励する言葉。多くの異形があり、1979年の用例が示すように、全文を書かずに一部だけが使われることもある。

† *c*1390 ガウワー『恋する男の告解』v. 4785 For sparinge of a litel cost Fulofte time a man hath lost The large cote for the hod [hood].「人はわずかな費用を出し渋ったためにしばしば損をし、頭巾を惜しんで大きな上衣を失うのである」

□ **1629** T. ADAMS *Works* 714 The French-men haue a military prouerbe, The losse of a nayle, the losse of an army. The want of a nayle looseth the shooe, the losse of shooe troubles the horse, the horse indangereth the rider, the rider breaking his ranke molests the company, so farre as to hazard the whole Army. **1640** G. HERBERT *Outlandish Proverbs* no. 499 For want of a naile the shoe is lost, for want of a shoe the horse is lost, and for want of a horse the rider is lost. **1880** S. SMILES *Duty* x. 'Don't care' was the man who was to blame for the well-known catastrophe: —'For want of a nail the shoe was lost, for want of a shoe the horse was lost, and for want of a horse the man was lost.' **1979** M. MCCARTHY *Missionaries & Cannibals* viii. No detail ... was too small to be passed over.... 'For want of a nail,' as the proverb said. **1995** *National Review* 12 June 10 For want of nail the battle was lost. Well, Republicans may have found just the right nail to win the entitlement battle. ■ **action and consequence** 行為と結果; **great and small** 大小

If you WANT something done, ask a busy person.
何かをしてもらいたい時は、忙しい人に頼め。

一見すると逆説的であるが、この合理的理由（忙しい人は時間の使い方がうまい）が1977年の用例に示されている。ベンジャミン・フランクリン、エルバード・ハバード、ルシル・ボールなど様々な人々の言葉とされる。

□ **1984** *Christian Science Monitor* 26 Oct. 38 It means. specifically, that you must banish all idleness; and it also means, in a general way, that if you want something done, you should ask a busy perso—like me—to do it. **1997** *Life Association News* Aug. 60 It's the old story: If you want

476 want

something done, ask a busy person. They know how to manage their time. **1998** *Times* 9 Jan. 33 They do say that if you want something done you should ask a busy person, but there must be limits. ■ **efficiency and inefficiency** 能率と非能率

want ⇒（名詞）WILFUL waste makes woeful want;（動詞）The MORE you get, the more you want; If you want PEACE, you must prepare for war; WASTE not, want not.

WANTON kittens make sober cats.
いたずら子猫も真面目な親猫になる。

若い頃は無責任で不真面目な人も分別ある大人になるものだ。

□**1732** T. FULLER *Gnomologia* no. 5415 Wanton [frolicsome] Killins may make sober old Cats. **1832** A. HENDERSON *Scottish Proverbs* 97 Wanton kittens make douce [sedate] cats. **1855** H. G. BOHN *Hand-Book of Proverbs* 551 Wanton kittens may make sober cats. **1975** J. O'FAOLAIN *Women in Wall* I. I was fleshy ... in my youth. Carnal. But wanton kittens make sober cats. ■ **youth** 若さ・若者

war ⇒ BUSINESS is war; COUNCILS of war never fight; All's FAIR in love and war; when GREEK meets Greek, then comes the tug of war; If you want PEACE, you must prepare for war; TRUTH is the first casualty of war.

warling (one who is despised or disliked): ⇒ BETTER be an old man's darling, than a young man's slave.

warm ⇒ COLD hands, warm heart.

One does not WASH one's dirty linen in public.
人前で自分の汚れた下着を洗う人はいない。

人前でプライベートな問題やスキャンダルを話しつづけるのは賢明でない。このことわざは慣用句 to wash one's dirty linen in public「内輪の恥を外へ出す」の形で使われることが多い。†フランス語 *C'est en famille, ce n'est pas en publique, qu'on lave son linge sale*.「家族の前では汚れた下着を洗うが、人前ではしない」

□**1809** T. G. FESSENDEN *Pills* 45 The man has always had a great itch for scribbling, and has mostly been so fortunate as to procure somebody who pitied his ignorance, to 'wash his dirty linen'. **1867** TROLLOPE *Last Chronicle of Barset* II. xliv. I do not like to trouble you with my private affairs; —there is nothing ... so bad as washing one's —dirty linen in public. **1942** 'P. WENTWORTH' *Danger Point* xlviii. The case ... will be dropped.... There's nothing to be gained by washing a lot of dirty linen in public. **1980** T. HOLME *Neapolitan Steak* 199 Her look raked him from head to toe. 'One does not wash one's Dirty Linen in Public, commissario.' **2014** *conginst. org* 1 Oct. (*heading*) Reforming Republican Rules—Or Why You Shouldn't Wash Your Dirty Linen in Public. ■ **discretion** 思慮分別

wash ⇒ One HAND washes the other.

water 477

WASTE not, want not.
浪費しなければ窮乏もない。

資源（食糧、金銭など）は浪費しなければ、不足して困ることもない。want は「不足」と「望み」の両方の意味で使われる。waste と want の（頭韻を含めた）関係から構成される別のことわざに WILFUL waste makes woeful want.「気ままな浪費は悲惨な欠乏を招く」がある。

□ **1772** WESLEY *Letter* 10 Aug. (1931) V. 334 he will waste nothing; but he must want nothing. **1872** T. HARDY *Under Greenwood Tree* I. I. viii. Helping her to vegetable she didn't want, and when it had nearly alighted on her plate, taking it across for his own use, on the plea of waste not, want not. **1941** C. MACKENZIE *Red Tapeworm* xxii. 'The lorry's full of children as well as rubbish.' ... 'And what is printed on the banner?' ... 'Waste Not Want Not.' **2007** 'C. AIRD' *Losing Ground* i 'There is some suggestion that the name relates to the re-use by the Anglo-Saxons of Roman stone ...' 'Waste not, want not,' observed Detective Constable Crosby to no one In particular. ■ **thrift** 質素倹約 ; **waste** 浪費

waste（名詞）⇒ HASTE makes waste; WILFUL waste makes woeful want.

A WATCHED pot never boils.
じっと見つめていると鍋はなかなか煮え立たない。

（訳注：watch には「…するのを待ち受ける」の意味がある。*watch* for the signal to change〈信号が変わるのを待つ〉。「待つ身は長い」）

何かが起こることをいらいらしながら見ていると、なかなか起こらないように感じられる。

□ **1848** GASKELL *Mary Barton* II. xiv. What's the use of watching? A watched pot never boils. **1880** M. E. BRADDON *Cloven Foot* III. viii. Don't you know that vulgar old proverb that says that 'a watched pot never boils'? **1940** C. BOOTHE *Europe in Spring* x. 'He [Mussolini] is waiting to see how the next battle turns out,' they said.... 'A watched pot never boils,' they said—only this one finally did. **2002** *Washington Post* 26 Apr. C10 (*Born Loser comic strip*) 'Whoever said, "A watched pot never boils" obviously didn't own a microwave.' ■ **patience and impatience** 忍耐と性急

Don't go near the WATER until you learn how to swim.
泳げるようになるまでは水辺に近づくな。

（訳注：「羽のはえぬ間は飛ぶな」。「急いては事をし損じる」）

必要な技術を身につけるまで何かをしようとしてはならない。

□ **1855** H. G. BOHN *Hand-Book of Proverbs* 459 Never venture out of your depth till you can swim. **1975** N. BAGLEY *Snow Tiger* xv. 'There I was.... Over-protected and regarded as a teacher's pet into the bargain.' '"Don't go near the water until you learn how to swim,"' quoted McGill. **2011** J. TURNER *Pain Through Child's Eyes* 62 Grandma Smith didn't like us being at the river. She said, 'Don't go near the water until you learn how to swim!' ■ **prudence** 思慮・分別

water ⇒ BLOOD is thicker than water; DIRTY water will quench fire; you can take a HORSE to the water, but you can't make him drink; No matter how long a LOG stays in the water ... ; The MILL cannot grind with the water that is past; You never MISS the water till the well runs dry; STILL waters run deep; STOLEN waters are sweet; Don't THROW out your dirty water

478 WAY

until you get in fresh.

The WAY to a man's heart is through his stomach.
男心をつかむには胃袋から始めよ。

料理上手の女性は男性に愛される。

☐1814 J. ADAMS *Letter* 15 Apr. In Works (1851) VI. 505 The shortest road to men's hearts is down their throats. **1845** R. FORD *Hand-Book for Travellers in Spain* I. i. The way to many an honest heart lies through the belly. **1857** N. M. MULOCK *John Halifax, Gentleman* xxx. 'Christmas dinners will be much in request.' 'There's a saying that the way to an Englishman's heart is through his stomach.'**1975** A. PRICE *Our Man in Camelot* v. The way to a man's heart wasn't through his stomach, it was through an appreciation of what interested him. **1986** J. W. RIDER *Jersey Tomatoes* xv. What she meant was in a home she could bake things and make meals for him.... The way to man's heart is through his stomach. **2001** *Washington Post* 6 Jan. C11 (*Piranha Club comicstrip*) 'And remember ladies—the way to a man's heart is through his stomach.' Unfortunately, you have to get it past his gag reflex first.' ■ **food and drink 飲食物**

There is more than one WAY to skin a cat.
猫の皮を剥ぐ方法は１つだけではない。

何かをするにはいろんな方法があるという意味のことわざの中の１つである。† There are more WAYS of killing a cat than choking it with cream.「猫を殺すにはクリームで窒息死させる以外にもいろいろ方法がある」といった、次の空想上のものもある。

☐1854 S. SMITH *Way down East* viii. 166 This is a money digging world of ours and, as it is said, 'there are more ways than one to skin a cat,' so there are more ways than one of digging for money. **1918** W. FAULKNER *Letter* 17 Oct. in J. G. Watson Thinking of Home (1992) So you see, there is more than one way to skin a cat. **2001** K. TOPPING *Slayer* (rev. ed.) 232 The Mayor [in a 1999 episode of Buffy the Vampire Slayer] knows that the statement 'There's more than one way to skin a cat' is factually accurate. ■ **ways and means 方法と手段**

way ⇒ The LONGEST way round is the shortest way home; LOVE will find a way; OTHER times, other manners; STRAWS tell which way the wind blows; A WILFUL man must have his way; Where there's a WILL, there's a way.

There are more WAYS of killing a cat than choking it with cream.
猫を殺すにはクリームで窒息死させる以外にもいろいろな方法がある。

There is more than one WAY to skin a cat.「猫の皮を剥ぐ方法は１つだけではない」という上のことわざも参照。

☐1839 S. SMITH *John Smith's Letters* 91 There's more ways to kill a cat than one. **1855** C. KINGSLEY *Westward Ho!* II. Xii. Hold on yet awhile. More ways of killing a cat than choking her with cream. **1941** 'R. WEST' *Black Lamb* I. 506 Now I see the truth of the old saying that there are more ways of killing a cat than choking it with cream. In Bosnia the Slavs did choke the Turk with cream, they glutted him with their wholesale conversions.... But here cream just &d not come into the question. **1974** T. SHARPE *Porterhouse Blue* ii. I have yet to meet a liberal who can withstand the attrition of prolonged discussion of the inessentials.... There are more ways of killing a cat than stuffing it with ... ■ **ways and means 方法と手段**

WEAKEST 479

There are more WAYS of killing a dog than choking it with butter
犬を殺すにはバターで窒息死させる以外にもいろいろな方法がある。

There are more WAYS of killing a cat than choking it with cream.「猫を殺すには
クリームで窒息死させる以外にもいろいろな方法がある」という上のことわざも参照。

□ **1845** W. T. THOMPSON *Chronicles of Pineville* 35 There's more ways to kill a dog besides
choking him with butter. **1945** F. THOMPSON *Lark Rise* xvi. A proverb always had to be capped.
No one could say, 'There's more ways of killing a dog than hanging it' without being reminded,
'nor of choking it with a pound of fresh butter.' **1955** W. C. MACDONALD *Destination, Danger* x.
It [liquor] was a lifesaver and I'm much obliged. But you can kill a dog without choking him with
butter. ■ **ways and means 方法と手段**

There are more WAYS of killing a dog than hanging it.
犬を殺すには首を絞める以外にもいろいろな方法がある。

There are more WAYS of killing a dog than choking it with butter.「犬を殺すには
バターで窒息死させる以外にもいろいろな方法がある」という上のことわざも参照。

□ **1678** J. RAY *English Proverbs* (ed. 2) 127 There are more ways to kill a dog then hanging. **1721**
J. KELLY *Scottish Proverbs* 253 Many ways to kill a Dog, and not to hang him. There be many
ways to bring about one and the same Thing, or Business. **1725** SWIFT *Drapier's Letters* X. 165 I
know that very homely Proverb, more ways of killing a Dog than hanging him. **1945** F. THOMP-
SON *Lark Rise* xvi. A proverb always had to be capped. No one could say, 'There's more ways of
killing a dog than hanging it' without being reminded, 'nor of choking it with a pound of fresh
butter.' ■ **ways and means 方法と手段**

weak ⇒ YORKSHIRE born and Yorkshire bred, strong in the arm and weak in the head.

The WEAKEST go to the wall.
一番弱い者が壁際に追いやられる。

（訳注：the weakest の the は「…な人々」の意。そのような人々を包括的に表現する。*The strong* must
help *the weak*.〈強者は弱者を助けなければならない〉）

由来に諸説ある。1つの説は、集会が教会堂の真廊（しんろう）で日常的に立って行なわれていた中
世後期、教会には年老いて体力が弱った者のために壁際の座席が取り付けられていたこ
とから生まれたというものである（1955年の用例参照）。他の説は、喧嘩で負けた者や、肉
体的な弱さゆえに通りの中央の混雑から押しのけられた者が狭い本通りに沿って並ぶ建
物の壁側に強制的に追いやられたことから生まれたというものである。本通りの中央は
歩くのに最も適した場所であったと考えられており、弱者はそこから排除されたのであ
る。慣用句 to go to the wall は「紛争や闘争で負ける」を意味する。

□ *a***1500** *Coventry Plays* (EETS) 47 The weykist gothe eyuer to the walle. *c***1595** SHAKESPEARE
Romeo & Juliet I. i. 14 That shows thee a weak slave; for the weakest goes to the wall. **1714** DE-
FOE (*title*) The weakest go to the wall, or the Dissenters sacrific'd by all parties. **1834** MARRYAT
Peter Simple I. v. You will be thrashed all day long.... The weakest always goes to the wall there.
1888 M. DOUGHTY *Travels in Arabia Deserta* I. x. There perished many among them;... it is the
weak which go to the wall. **1955** T. WARRINER *Doors of Sleep* i.'As in the early church, the weakest go to the wall,' the Archdeacon said, seating himself on the low parapet. **2014** R. DAWKINS
quoted on *www.rawstory.com* 8. Dec. What we need is a truly anti-Darwinian society. Anti-Darwinian in the sense that we don't wish to live in a society where the weakest go to the wall,

where the strongest suppress the weak … ■ **strength and weakness** 強弱；**winners and losers** 勝者と敗者

weakest ⇒ A CHAIN is no stronger than its weakest link.

wealth ⇒ The CITY for wealth, the country for health.

wealthy ⇒ EARLY to bed and early to rise, makes a man healthy, wealthy, and wise.

wear ⇒ BETTER to wear out than to rust out; If the CAP fits, wear it; CONSTANT dropping wears away a stone; GIVE a thing, and take a thing, to wear the Devil's gold ring; If the SHOE fits, wear it.

weary ⇒ Be the DAY weary or be the day long, at last it ringeth to evensong.

weather ⇒ There is no such thing as BAD weather, only the wrong clothes; ROBIN Hood could brave all weathers but a thaw wind.

web ⇒ When SPIDER webs unite, they can tie up a lion.

wed ⇒ BETTER wed over the mixen than over the moor.

One WEDDING brings another.
婚礼は婚礼を生む。

類似したものに One FUNERAL makes many.「葬式は 1 度あると何度もある」がある。表題の発想は新郎新婦の家族と友人の社交上の集まりが新たな恋をもたらすこともあるというものである。† **1818** オースティン『ノーサンガー・アビー』I. xv. Did you ever hear the old song, 'Going to one wedding brings on another?'「『結婚式に出ると恋が芽ばえる』という昔の歌を聞いたことがありますか」

□ **1634** M. PARKER in *Roxburghe Ballads* (1880) III. 54 'tis said that one wedding produceth another. **1713** GAY *Wife of Bath* I. i. One Wedding, the Proverb says, begets another. **1885** C. H. SPURGEON *Salt-Cellars* I. 88 Bridesmaids may soon be made brides. One wedding … brings on another. **1929** S. T. WARNER *True Heart* I. 54 Cheer up, Suke! I dare say you'll get a boy in time —they do say one wedding brings another. **1957** A. THIRKELL *Double Affair* i. But when he said 'One marriage always brings on another, Mrs. Hubback,' I slapped his face with a nice bit of cod's tail. ■ **weddings** 結婚式

WEDLOCK is a padlock.
結婚は南京錠。

結婚した夫婦はそこから出ることはできない。

□ **1678** J. RAY *English Proverbs* (ed. 2) 56 Wedlock is apadlock. **1821** BYRON *Don Juan* (1857) v. clviii. Thus in the East they are extremely strict, And wedlock and a padlock mean the same. **1950** C. E. VULLIAMY *Henry Plumdew* 211 Wedlock is a padlock, says our proverb. **1972** L. LEE

WELL 481

(song title) 'Wedlock is a padlock'. ■ **marriage 結婚**

Wednesday ⇒ Monday's CHILD is fair of face.

weed ⇒ ILL weeds grow apace.

weeding ⇒ ONE year's seeding makes seven years' weeding.

week ⇒ If you would be HAPPY for a week take a wife.

weep ⇒ LAUGH and the world laughs with you.

weeper ⇒ FINDERS keepers (losers weepers).

weigh ⇒ You do not FATTEN a pig by weighing it.

welcome ⇒ When all FRUIT fails, welcome haws.

WELL begun is half done.
初めうまくいけば半分できたも同然。
(訳注：「最初が肝心」)

† プラトン『法律』753^e ἀρχὴ γὰρ λέγεται μὲν ἥμιον παντὸς ἐν ταῖς παροιμίαις ἔργου. 「ことわざで言われているように、最初の部分があらゆる仕事の半分である」。ホラティウス『使徒書簡』I. ii. 40 *Dimidium facti qui coepit habet.*「最初をうまくできた者は半分できたようなものである」

□ *c*1415 *Middle English Sermons* (EETS) 148 The wise man seth that halfe he hath don that wel begynneth is werke. **1542** N. UDALL *Erasmus' Apophthegms* I. 16 Laertius ascrybeth to hym [Socrates] this saiyng also: tci haue well begoone is a thyng halfe dooen. **1616** J. WITHALS *Dict.* (rev. ed.) 555 Well begun, is halfe done. **1883** C. S. BURNE *Shropshire Folklore* 273 They also account it very unlucky to give trust [credit] for the first article sold. 'Well begun is half done,' is evidently their principle. **1981** P. O'DONNELL *Xanadu Talisman* iv. The nannie-like proverbs … Well begun is half done, The early bird catches the worm. **2014** *www.philanthropyohio.org* 3 Mar. My southern grandmother often said, 'Well begun is half done.' … But I've discovered 'well begun' isn't something that happens alone. ■ **beginnings and endings 最初と最後**

All's WELL that ends well.
終わりよければすべてよし。
(訳注：1602年の用例にあるように、シェイクスピアの喜劇のタイトルとなっている)

幸せな結末はそれまでのすべて（苦労）の埋め合わせをする。† *c*1250『アングリアことわざ集』(1881) IV. 182 Wel is him that wel ende mai.「終わりの良い人は幸せである」

□ **1381** in J. R. Lumby *Chronicon Henrici Knighton* (1895) II. 139 If the ende be wele, than is alle wele. *c*1530 R. HILL *Commonplace Book* (EETS) 110 'All ys well that endyth well,' said the gud wyff. **1602** SHAKESPEARE *All's Well that Ends Well* IV. iv. 35 All's Well That Ends Well. Still the fine's [end's] the crown. **1836** MARRYAT *Midshipman Easy* i. vi. I had got rid of the farmer, …

482 well

bull, and the bees—all's well that ends well. **1979** G. HAMMOND *Dead Game* xviii. My rank's been confirmed. So all's well that ends well. **2002** *Washington Post* 25 June Cl2 Thanks for telling us the rest of the story. All's well that ends well. ■ beginnings and endings 最初と最後 ; good fortune 幸運

well ⇒（名詞）The FROG in the well knows nothing of the sea; You never MISS the water till the well runs dry; The PITCHER will go to the well once too often; TRUTH lies at the bottom of a well.

well ⇒（名詞）LET well alone;（形容詞）The DEVIL was sick, the Devil a saint would be … ;（副詞）He LIVES long who lives well; PAY beforehand was never well served; If you would be well SERVED, serve yourself; SPARE well and have to spend; Everyone SPEAKS well of the bridge which carries him over; If a THING's worth doing, it's worth doing well; If you WANT a thing done well, do it yourself.

west ⇒ EAST is east, and west is west; EAST, west, home's best.

wet ⇒（副詞）Sow dry and set wet;（動詞）The CAT would eat fish, but would not wet her feet.

It's not WHAT you know, it's who you know.
重要なのは何を知っているかではなく、誰を知っているかである。

出世するためには、個人の技術を磨くよりも影響力を持つ人との強いネットワークを構築するほうが役に立つ。

□**1992** *Economist* 26 Dec. 20/1 'It's not what you know, it's who you know,' is the cry of the disappointed and excluded around the world. How true: intelligence and application help in life, but contacts are what count. **1998** *Housing Agenda* Apr. 12/1 Take getting a job. The old adage that 'it's not what you know but who you know' has more than a kernel of truth in it. **2014** *Telegraph* 13 Dec. (online; *article title*) It's still 'who you know not what you know that matters', say two thirds of Britons. ■ bribery and corruption 賄賂と腐敗

what ⇒ What you don't KNOW can't hurt you; What MATTERS is what works; What MUST be, must be; What you ⇒ Is what you get; What goes UP must come down.

wheel ⇒ The SQUEAKY wheel gets the grease.

while ⇒ While there's LIFE there's hope.

whirlwind ⇒ They that sow the wind shall reap the whirlwind.

whistle ⇒ Don't HALLOO till you are out of the wood; A sow may whistle, though it has an ill mouth for it.

wife   483

A WHISTLING woman and a crowing hen are neither fit for God nor men.
口笛を吹く女と時を告げるめんどりは神にも男にも好かれない。
(訳注：「めんどり歌えば家滅ぶ」)

口笛を吹くことと時を告げることはそれぞれ男性とおんどりの特権であると考えられていたので、女性や雌鶏によってなされると不自然・不吉とされた。脚韻には 3 種類が見られる (hen と men、den、end)。

☐**1721** J. KELLY *Scottish Proverbs* 33 A crooning cow, a crowing Hen and a whistling Maid boded never luck to a House. The two first are reckoned ominous, but the Reflection is on the third. **1850** *Notes & Queries* 1st Ser. II. 164 A whistling woman and a crowing hen, Is neither fit for God nor men. **1891** J. L. KIPLING *Beast & Man* ii. 'A whistling woman and a crowing hen are neither fit for God nor men,' is a mild English saying. **1917** J. C. BRIDGE *Cheshire Proverbs* 28 A whistling woman and a crowing hen will fear the old lad [the Devil] out of his den. **1933** L. I. WILDER *Farmer Boy* xi. Royal teased her, Whistling girls and crowing hens Always come to some bad ends. **1979** G. DUFF *Country Wisdom* (1983) 55 A whistling woman and a crowing hen, Will bring Old Harry out of his den. **1995** B. HOLLAND *Endangered Pleasures* 116 I was the wrong sex. Boys whistled.... As grandmothers used to say, A whistling girl and a crowing hen Both will come to a bad end. ■ **women** 女性

whistling ⇒ It is a POOR dog that's not worth whistling for.

One WHITE foot, buy him; two white feet, try him; three white feet, look well about him; four white feet, go without him.
白い足の馬で、1 本だけ白い馬は買え、2 本だけ白いのは試してみよ、3 本白いのはよく調べよ、4 本すべて白いのは買わずにおけ。

馬の売買に関する注意。馬の毛の配色において容認される白い足の数は様々で、その数に関して多くの異形がある。白い蹄のある足は黒い蹄のある足よりも丈夫でないと考えられていた。また、馬の鼻についた切り目は白いぶちである (2002 年の用例参照)。

☐**1882** *Notes & Queries* 6th Ser. V. 427 One white foot—buy him. Two white feet—try him. Three white feet—look well about him. Four white feet—go without him. **2002** E. CUTTING in *Voices: Journal of New York Folklore* XXVIII (online) One white foot, buy him. Two white feet, try him. Three white feet, deny him. Four white feet and snip on his nose, take off his hide and feed him to the crows ... Theoretically a white foot would have a softer hoof, so that it could be more easily damaged. ■ **buying and selling** 売買; **horse lore** 馬にまつわる伝承

white ⇒ It doesn't matter if a CAT is black or white ... ; FEBRUARY fill dyke, be it black or be it white; TWO blacks don't make a white.

whole ⇒ The HALF is better than the whole; HALF the truth is often a whole lie.

whore ⇒ ONCE a whore, always a whore.

wife ⇒ A BLIND man's wife needs no paint; CABSAR's wife must be above suspicion; A DEAF husband and a blind wife are always a happy couple; It's a GOOD horse that never stumbles and a good wife that never grumbles; If you would be HAPPY for a week take a wife; The HUSBAND is always the last to know; My SON is my son till he gets him a wife, but my daughter's my daughter all the days of her life; He that will THRIVE must first ask his wife.

A WILFUL man must have his way.
わがまま者は自分の流儀を通さずにはおれない。
（訳注：must ＝「…せずにはいられない」〈固執〉。She *must* have everything her own way.〈彼女は何で自分の思い通りにしないと気がすまない〉）

頑なな人は何が何でも我を通そうとする。

□**1816** SCOTT *Antiquary* I. vi. A willful man must have his way. **1907** W. DE MORGAN *Alice-for-Short* xxxvii. 'A wilful man will have his way,' says Peggy, laughing.... Alice replies: 'Never mind!' **1931** J. BUCHAN *Blanket of Dark* xii. 'Take one of my men with you.' ... He shook his head.... 'A wilful man must have his way,' she said. ■ **obstinacy 頑固さ**

WILFUL waste makes woeful want.
贅沢三昧は悲惨な貧乏暮らしを生みだす。
（訳注：「苦あれば楽あり。楽あれば苦あり」）

waste「浪費」と want「困窮」の因果関係はこのことわざが登場する以前から見られる。例えば、**1576** R. エドワーズ『上品な工夫の楽園』88 For want is nexte to waste, and shame doeth synne ensue.「困窮が浪費の隣にあるように、不名誉は罪の後に生じる」。† WASTE not, want not.「浪費しなければ不足もしない」

□**1721** J. KELLY *Scottish Proverbs* 353 Wilful waste makes woeful want. **1866** GASKELL *Wives & Daughters* II. xxix. Now young folks go off to Paris, and think nothing of the cost: and it's well if wilful waste don't make woeful want before they die. **1946** 'R. FINNEGAN' *Lying Ladies* vi. 'Well, do you want the drink or not?' ... Regan ... emptied his glass and shoved forward. 'Willful waste makes woeful want,' he declared. ■ **action and consequence 行為と結果；waste 浪費**

He that WILL not when he may, when he will he shall have nay.
やれる時にやろうとしない者はいざやろうという時にやれない。
（訳注：「鉄は熱いうちに打て」）

目の前のチャンスを逃すな。一度断ってから気が変わってもすでに手遅れである。

□*a***1000** in *Anglia* (1889) XI. 388 Nu sceal relc man efsten, thret he to gode gecerre tha hwile the he muge, thelreste, gyf he nu nelle tha hwile the he muge, eft thone he wyle, he ne mrelg [Now shall each man hasten to turn to God while he may, lest if he will not now while he may, later when he will, he may not]. **1303** R. BRUNNE *Handlyng Synne* (EETS) I. 4795 He that wyl nat when he may, He shal nat, when he wyl. *c***1450** in Brown & Robbins Index of Middle English Verse (1943) 186 He that will not when he may, When he will he shall have nay [denial]. **1624** BURTON *Anatomy of Melancholy* (ed. 2) III. ii. They omit oportunities.... He that will not when he may, When he will he shall haue nay. **1935** N. MITCHISON *We have been Warned* III. 297 'She that will not when she may, When she will she shall have nay.' Aren't you feeling a bit like that? **1958** B. PYM *Glass of Blessings* xi. 'It was a rather pretty little box, just the kind of thing you like....' 'I know,' I said. '"If you will not when you may, when you will you shall have nay."' ■ **opportunity, missed 逃した機会**

WIN 485

Where there's a WILL, there's a way.
意志 (遺志) あるところに道あり。

(訳注:「念ずれば花開く」。「精神一到何事か成らざん」)

確固たる決意があれば、どんな障害があっても道が切り開かれる。ここでwillは通常「強い意志」を意味するが、死後の財産に関する「遺言」を意味するwillという洒落もある。実は、このことわざは法律の専門家によって遺書の勧めとして使われてきた。

□ **1640** G. HERBERT *Outlandish Proverbs* no. 730 To him that will, wais are not wanting. **1822** W. HAZLITT in *New Monthly Mag.* Feb. 102 Where there's a will, there's a way.— I said so to myself, as I walked down Chancery-lane ... to inquire ... where the fight the next day was to be. **1979** E. KOCH *Good Night Little Spy* xi. I've no idea how it can be done. But where there's a will, there's a way. **2002** *Washington Times* 26 Mar. Al7 Where there's a will, there's a way. And the one thing campaign-finance reform does not do, because it cannot, is diminish the will to influence elections and politicians. ■ **persistence ねばり強さ ; ways and means 方法と手段**

will ⇒ (名詞) He that COMPUES against his will is of his own opinion still; (動詞) If ANYTHING can go wrong, it will; There's none so BLIND as those who will not see; There's none so DEAF as those who will not hear; What MUST be, must be.

He who WILLS the end, wills the means.
目的を達成しようとする者はそのための手段をも求める。

(訳注:he =「〈関係節を伴って〉…する者は誰でも〈性別は問わない〉」。*He who* has all the gold makes all the rules.〈金をすべて持つ者が法をすべて支配する〉)

希望の目的を達成したいなら、そのための手段も欠かせない。

□ **1692** R. SOUTH *Twelve Sermons* 497 That most true aphorism, that he who wills the end, wills also the means. **1910** *Spectator* 29 Oct. 677 We won a Trafalgar ... because we not only meant to win, but knew how to win—because we understood ... the maxim, 'He who wills the end wills the means.' **1980** *Listener* 13 Mar. 332 I could offer a text ... from Aneurin Bevan : 'It's no good willing the end unless you're also ready to will the means.' ■ **action and consequences 行為と結果 ; ways and means 方法と手段**

You WIN a few, you lose a few.
たまには勝てるし、たまには負ける。

(訳注:「人生、山あり谷あり」。解説にあるキップリングは英国の小説家詩人。イギリス統治下のインドを舞台にした作品、児童文学で知られる。代表作に『ジャングル・ブック』『少年キム』などがある。1907年にノーベル文学賞受賞)

米国のスポーツに由来し、慰めやあきらめの表現として使われる。また、You win some, you lose some. という形式でもよく見られる。よく似たものとして下のことわざ You can't WIN them all.「すべてに勝てるわけではない」がある。† **1897** R. キップリング『勇ましい船長』x. 'Thirty million dollars' worth of mistake, wasn't it? I'd risk it for that.' 'I lost some; and I gained some'「3千万ドルの値打ちのある失敗だったな。それくらいのリスクは覚悟だ。」「損もしたし、得もした」。**1912**『オークランド・トリビューン』21 July (*heading*) Sometimes You Win, Sometimes You Lose.「勝つときもあれば負けるときもある」

□ **1958** *New York Times* 11 Mar. Basketball and politics are somewhat similar in that you win a few, you lose a few. **1966** P. O. DONNELL *Sabre-Tooth* xrv. You win a few, you lose a few, and it's no good getting sore. **1976** *Times* 23 Nov. 14 You look like being saddled with the uninspiring Willy.... On the other hand, you seem to have got your way over Mrs. Thatcher's nominee.... You win some, you lose some. **1998** *Oldie* Jan. 32/3 Ah well, as they say in the Silver Ring, win a few, lose a few. **2001** *National Review* 19 Nov. 6 At a big Madison Square Garden event, Hillary was booed, Bill was cheered. Win some, lose some. ■ **winners and losers 勝者と敗者**

You can't WIN them all.
すべてに勝てるわけではない。

You WIN a few, you lose a few.「たまには勝てるし、たまには負ける」と同じような状況で使われる。

□**1953** R. CHANDLER *Long Good-bye* xxiv. Wade took him by the shoulder and spun him round, 'Take it easy, Doc. You can't win them all.' **1984** 'C. AIRD' *Harm's Way* xviii. 'The finger being found on the footpath was just bad luck on the murderer's part.' 'You can't win them all,' said Crosby ambiguously. **2002** *Washington Post* 18 Mar. CII (*Born Loser comic strip*) 'They say you can't win them all ... however, as evidenced by Brutus Thomapple, evidently you can lose them all!' ■ **winners and losers 勝者と敗者**

When the WIND is in the east, 'tis neither good for man nor beast.
（大陸から吹いてくる冷たい）東風は人にも獣にもよくない。

1670 年と 2002 年の用例が英国の気候に関する意味を説明している。

□**1600** R. CAWDREY *Treasury of Similies* 750 The East wind is accounted neither good for man or beast. **1659** J. HOWELL *Proverbs* (English) 19 When the wind is in the east it is good for neither man nor beast. **1670** J. RAY *English Proverbs* 41 When the wind's in the East, It's neither good for man nor beast.... The East-wind with us is commonly very sharp, because it comes off the Continent **1929** A. WYNNE *Room with Iron Shutters* xx. 'When the wind is in the East ... 'tis neither good for man nor beast' Has it ever occurred to you ... to relate the incidence of crime to meteorological conditions? **2002** *Times* 13 Mar. 24 'When the wind is from the east, 'tis neither good for man nor beast,' the old saying goes, meaning that a cold, raw, easterly wind blowing off the Continent will make life miserable. ■ **weather lore 天気にまつわる伝承**

wind ⇒ APRIL showers bring forth May flowers; GOD tempers the wind to the shorn lamb; It's an ILL wind that blows nobody any good; NORTH wind doth blow, we shall have snow; ONE for the mouse, one for the crow; A REED before the wind lives on, while mighty oaks do fall; ROBIN Hood could brave all weathers but a thaw wind; They that sow the wind shall reap the whirlwind; STRAWS tell which way the wind blows.

window ⇒ The BYES are the window of the soul; When POVERTY comes in at the door, love flies out of the window.

When the WINE is in, the wit is out.
酒が入ると理性が出ていく。

酒を飲み過ぎた人は分別と意識の両方を失うことが多い。ここでの wit は「機知に富んだ会話」ではなく「理性」を意味する。

□*c*1390 GOWER *Confessio A mantis* VI. 555 For wher that wyn doth wit aweie [does away with

WISE 487

wit], Wisdom hath lost the rihte weie [path]. **1529** MORE *Dialogue of Images* III. Xvi. Whan the wyne were in and the wyt out, wolde they take vppon them ... to handle holy cripture. **1560** T. BECON *Works* I. 536ᵛ When the wine is in, the wit is out. **1710** S. PALMER *Proverbs* 18 When the Wine's In, the Wit's Out. **1854** J. W. WARTER *Last of Old Squires* vi. None is a Fool always, every one sometimes. When the Drink goes in, then the Wit goes out. **1937** V. WII. KINS *And so—Victoria* iii. Remember what I told you last night—that with wine in, wits go out. **2011** N. J. STANZIONE *www.widenerlawreview.org* Mar. (*article title*) Granholm v. Heald: Wine In, Wit Out. ■ **drunkenness** 酩酊

wine ⇒ GOOD wine needs no bush; You can't put NEW wine in old bottles; From the SWEETEST wine, the tartest vinegar; There is TRUTH in wine.

wing ⇒ A BIRD never flew on one wing; The MOTHER of mischief is no bigger than a midge's wing.

wink ⇒ A NOD's as good as a wink to a blind horse.

wins ⇒ SLOW and steady wins the race.

WINTER never rots in the sky.
冬は決して空で腐らない。

(訳注：罪を記せば必ず天罰が下されるのである)

冬は空で消え去ったりせずに必ず地上に正確にやって来る。

□**1621** J. HALL *Contemplations* XIII in *Recollections* 32 God ... chooses out a fit season for the execution; As we vse to say of winter, the iudgements of God doe neuer rot in the side, but shall fall (if late, yet) surely. **1670** J. RAY *English Proverbs* 42 Winter never rots in the sky. **1817** W. BENTLEY *Diary* 24 Jan. (1914) N. 434 'Winter does not rot in the sky.' We have a deep snow and for the first time this season the Earth is completely covered. **1959** *Boston Herald* 13 Mar. 42 Winter never rots in the sky, says the old proverb. ■ **retribution** 天罰・報復

winter ⇒ If CANDLBMAS day be sunny and bright, winter will have another flight; A GREEN Yule makes a fat churchyard; The RICH man has his ice in the summer and the poor man gets his in the winter.

wisdom ⇒ EXPERIENCE is the father of wisdom.

It is easy to be WISE after the event.
事後に悟るのは容易である。

類似した意味のものに HINDSIGHT is always 20/20.「後智恵は常に視力が20/20である」がある。† *c*1490 P. ド・コミーヌ『回想録』(1924) I. I. xvi. *Les deux ducz ... estoient saiges après le coup* (*comme l'on dit des Bretons*)。**1596** T. ダネット訳『コミーヌの回想録』 I. xvi. These two Dukes were wise after the hurt received (as the common prouerbe saith) of the Brittons.「これら 2 人の公爵は英国人から受けた苦痛のあと賢明になった」

488 WISE

□**1616** JONSON *Epicæme* II. iv. Away, thou strange iustifier of thy selfe, to bee wiser then thou wert, by the euent. **1717** R. WODROW *Letter* 28 Sept. (1843) II. 319 Had we not verified the proverb of being wise behind the time, we might for ever [have] been rid of them. **1900** CONAN DOYLE *Great Boer War* xix. It is easy to be wise after the event, but it does certainly appear that … the action at Paardeberg was as unnecessary as it was expensive. **1977** J. PORTER *Who the Heck is Sylvia?* ii. 'It's easy enough to be wise after the event,' Babette pointed out sullenly. **2010** *www.theguardian.com* 2 June (*heading*) Warren Buffett tells US inquiry: it's easy to be wise after the event. ■ **foresight and hindsight** 先見の明と後知恵

It is a WISE child that knows its own father.
自分の父親を知っているのは賢い子供である。

（母親と違って）父親について確信を持てる者は誰もいない。「あの子は自分の父親を父親だと思っているけれど、本当はあの子の父親ではないのよね」といった陰口としてよく使われる（1823年の用例参照）。

□**1584** J. WITHALS *Dict.* (rev. ed.) IA Wise sonnes they be in very deede, That knowe their Parents who did them breede. **1589** R. GREENE *Menaphon* VI. 92 Wise are the Children in these dayes that know their owne fathers, especially if they be begotten in Dogge dales [the heat of summer], when their mothers are frantick with love. **1596** SHAKESPEARE *Merchant of Venice* II. ii. 69 It is a wise father that knows his own child. **1762** GOWSMITH *Mystery Revealed* 21 She called her father John instead of Thomas … but perhaps she was willing to verify the old proverb, that It is a wise child that knows its own father. **1823** SCOTT *Peveril* III. x. I only laughed because you said you were Sir Geoffrey's son. But no matter—'tis a wise child that knows his own father. **1983** R. DAVJES *High Spirits* 119 It's a wise child that knows its own father. How wise does a child have to be to know its own great-great-grandfather? ■ **children and parents** 親子

wise ⇒ EARLY to bed and early to rise, makes a man healthy, wealthy, and wise; A FOOL may give a wise man counsel; FOOLS ask questions that wise men cannot answer; FOOLS build houses and wise men live in them; Where IGNORANCE is bliss, 'tis folly to be wise; One cannot LOVE and be wise; PENNY wise and pound foolish; A STILL tongue makes a wise head; A WORD to the wise is enough.

The WISH is father to the thought.
そのような考えはたんなる願望によって生み出されたものにすぎない。

希望的観測（すなわち、勝手な思い込み）は、そうあって欲しいと願う人を欺いてしまう。

□**1597-8** SHAKESPEARE *Henry IV, Pt. 2* IV. V. 93 I never thought to hear you speak again. — Thy wish was father, Harry, to that thought. **1783** P. VAN SCHAACK *Letter* 5 Jan. in H. C. Van Schaack *Life* (1842) 321 My 'wish is father to the thought'. **1860** TROLLOPE *Framley Parsonage* III. xiv. The wish might be father to the thought … but the thought was truly there. **1940** E. F. BENSON *Final Edition* iii. She spied a smallish man … walking away from us. The wish was father to the thought. 'Ah, there is Lord Ripon,' she said…. He turned round. It wasn't Lord Ripon at all. **1980** A. T. ELLIS *Birds of Air* (1983) 40 Somewhere in that area of the human mind where the wish is father to the thought activity was taking place. **1988** *Washington Times* 13 Jan. A 13 The wish is father to the thought, and that timeless truism fits federal judges like a glove. ■
wanting and having 不足と所持

WOMAN   489

If WISHES were horses, beggars would ride.
もし願望が馬だったら、乞食だって馬に乗れることになろう。

身勝手な願望には意味がないという警告。

☐*a*1628 J. CARMICHAELL *Proverbs in Scots* no. 140 And [if] wishes were horses pure [poor] men wald ryde. **1721** J. KELLY *Scottish Proverbs* 178 If Wishes were Horses, Beggars would ride. **1844** J. O. HALLIWELL *Nursery Rhymes of England* (ed. 4) 501 If wishes were horses, Beggars would ride; If turnips were watches, I would wear one by my side. **1912** *British Weekly* 18 Jan. 480 If wishes were horses Unionists would ride rapidly into office. **1992** A. LAMBERT *Rather English Marriage* (1993) ix. 153 'If wishes were horses then beggars should ride,' he told her. 'Don't be too sure.' **2002** *Washington Times* 14 Aug. B5 Not only do wit 350 I remember my mother quoting the same phrase to me, she had another one: 'If wishes were horses, beggars would ride.' Both are from a bygone generation that held no truck with the 'if only' and 'I wish' mentality. ■ wanting and having 不足と所持

wit ⇒ BREVITY is the soul of wit; When the WINE is in, the wit is out.

wiving ⇒ HANGING and wiving go by destiny.

woeful ⇒ WILFUL waste makes woeful want.

Do not call a WOLF to help you against the dogs.
犬に襲われたとき、狼に助けを求めてはならない。

ロシアのことわざ。制御できないようなものに助けを求めてはならないという警告。助けを頼んだ者が敵として襲ってくることも起こり得るからである。

☐**1975** A. SOLZHENITSYN 'Words of Warning to America' in *Imprimis* Sept. We have a Russian proverb: 'Do not call a wolf to help you against the dogs.' If dogs are attacking and tearing at you, fight against the dogs, but do not call a wolf for help. Because when the wolves come, they will destroy the dogs, but they will also tear you apart. **2001** on *www.peace.ca* Which presents PBI with the classic dilemma of the unarmed civilian: Should PB! call the 'official' Colombian army for help? Or should PB! heed the Russian proverb 'If the dogs attack you don't call the wolf for help.' ■ assistance 援助 ; strength and weakness 強弱

wolf ⇒ The CARIBOU feeds the wolf, but it is the wolf who keeps the caribou strong; HUNGER drives the wolf out of the wood.

A WOMAN and a ship ever want mending.
女と船は常に修理が必要だ。

†プラウトゥス『カルタゴ人』11. 210-15 *Negoti sibi qui volet vim parare, navem et mulierem, haec duo comparato.... Neque umquam satis hae duae res omantur, neque is ulla omandi satis satietas est.*「厄介なことをたくさん抱えたい男なら船と女を持つべきだ。どちらも今だかつて十分満足したことがなく、また満足させる十分な手段もないからである」。米国では A ship and a woman are ever repairing.「船と女はつねに修理されている」が使われる。

☐**1578** J. FLORIO *First Fruits* 30 Who wil trouble hym selfe all dayes of his life, Let hym mary a woman, or buy hym a shyp. **1598** *Mirror of Policy* (1599) X2 Is it not an old Prouebe. That Women and Shippes are neuer so perfect, but still there is somewhat to bee amended. **1640** G. HERBERT *Outlandish Proverbs* no. 780 A shippe and a woman are ever repairing. **1840** R. H. DANA *Two Years before Mast* iii. As has often been said, a ship is like a lady's watch, always out of repair. **1928** A. T. SHEPPARD *Here comes Old Sailor* II. vi. There are special proverbs for us shipmen: ... 'A woman and a ship ever want mending.' ■ women 女性

A WOMAN without a man is like a fish without a bicycle.
魚に自転車が無用なように、女に男は無用だ。

一般には、米国のフェミニスト、グロリア・スタイネム (1934-) の言葉であると考えられ
ているが、匿名の落書きに由来するようである (1979年の用例参照)。

□**1979** N. REES *Graffiti Lives OK* 80 'A woman without a man is like a fish without a bicycle.' Penned as a Woman's Lib slogan, this was met by the male response: 'Yes, but who needs a stationary haddock?' **2001** *Times Literary Supplement* 28 Dec. 8 Women may have decided they need men like a fish needs a bicycle, but the pram in the hall is with us still, ruthlessly demanding attention. ■ women 女性

A WOMAN's place is in the home.
女の居場所は家庭である。

性別による役割分担があるという伝統的な考え方を表わしている。現在では A woman's
place is any place she wants to be.「女性の居場所は望むところすべてである」(『現代
ことわざ辞典より』) のような反スローガンを使ってフェミニストにより否定されている。

□**1844** 'J. Slick' *High Life* IT. 121 A woman's place is her own house, a taking care of the children. **1936** R. A. J. WALLING *Corpse with Dirty Face* iv. Mrs. Franks, being a dutiful wife, was always on the premises. 'Ah, yes—woman's place is in the home,' said Pierce. **1943** A. CHRISTIE *Moving Finger* vi. I go up in arms against the silly old-fashioned prejudice that women's place is always the home. **1979** G. WAGNER *Barnardo* v. Barnardo ... firmly believed that a woman's place was in the home. **2008** *www.independent.co.uk* 6 Aug. The gender equality fight in Britain has already peaked, with greater numbers of people convinced that a woman's place is in the home, according to new research. ■ women 女性

A WOMAN's work is never done.
女の仕事には決して終わりはない。

料理、掃除など、毎日の家事には終わりがない。

□**1570** T. TOSSER *Husbandry* (rev. ed.) 26 Some respite to husbands the weather doth send, but huswiues affaires haue neuer none ende. **1629** in *Roxburghe Ballads* (1880) III . 302 (*title*) A woman's work is never done. **1722** B. FRANKLIN *Papers* (1960) I. 19 If you go among the Women, you will learn ... that a Woman's work is never done. **1920** *Times Weekly* 12 Mar. 209 'Women's work is never done.' ... We shall never hear the whole of woman's work during the war. **1981** 'G. Gaunt' *Incomer* xiv. My grannie used to say, A woman's work is never done when it never gets started! **2009** *www.telegraph.co.uk* 6 Aug. (*heading*) Woman's work is never done—as profitably as man's. ■ women 女性 ; work 仕事

woman ⇒ HELL hath no fury like a woman scorned; A MAN is as old as he feels, and a woman as old as she looks; SILENCE isa woman's best garment; SIX hours' sleep for a man, seven for a woman, and eight for a fool; A WHISTLING woman and a crowing hen are nei-

WOOL 491

ther fit for God nor men.

women ⇒ Never CHOOSE your women or your linen by candlelight; ENGLAND is the paradise of women.

won ⇒ FAINT heart never won fair lady.

wonder ⇒ TIME works wonders.

WONDERS will never cease.
不思議なことは決して絶えることがない。

（訳注：will＝「…ものだ」〈習性：傾向〉。Truth *will* out.〈真実は明らかになるものだ〉）

予想外の事が起こったり、ある人がとうていその人らしからぬことをしでかした際に、皮肉を込めた驚きの言葉として使われる。

□ **1776** H. BATES in T. Boaden *Private Correspondence of D. Garrick* (1823) II. 174 You have heard, no doubt, of his giving me the reversion of a good living in Worcestershire.... Wonders will never cease. **1843** C. J. LEVER *Jack Hinton* I. xx. The by-standers ... looked from one to the other, with expressions of mingled surprise and dread.... 'Blessed hour.... Wonders will never cease.' **1974** A. PRICE *Other Paths to Glory* I. vii. Wonders will never cease.... Early Tudor—practically untouched. **2014** *Mail Online* 8 June Small wonders will never cease. Mini has produced its first five-door hatchback to take on the Volkswagen Golf. ■ **marvels** 不思議

wood ⇒ FIELDS have eyes, and woods have ears; Don't HALLOO till you are out of the wood; HUNGER drives the wolf out of the wood.

Happy's the WOOING that is not long a-doing.
長くかからぬ求婚は幸せである。

婚約期間は短いほうがよいという伝統的な勧め。

□ **1576** R. BDWARDS *Paradise of Dainty Devices* 71 Thrise happie is that woying That is not long a doing. **1624** BURTON *Anatomy of Melancholy* (ed. 2) III. ii Blessed is the wooing, That is not long a doing. **1754** RICHARDSON *Grandison* I. ix. What signifies shilly-shally? What says the old proverb? 'Happy's the wooing, That is not long a doing.' **1842** R. H. BARHAM *Ingoldsby Legends* 2nd Ser. ii. 40 'Thrice happy's the wooing that's not long a-doing!' So much time is saved in the billing and cooing. **1930** A. CHRISTIE *Mysterious Mr. Quin* III. The old saying ... Happy the wooing that's not long doing.' ■ **weddings** 結婚式

Many go out for WOOL and come home shorn.
羊毛を刈りに出かけ、毛を刈られて帰る者が多い。

（訳注：「ミイラ取りがミイラになる」）

出世・大儲けをしてやろうと試みる者は多いが、たいてい、身ぐるみ剝がされてしまうことになる。

□ **1599** J. MINSHEU *Dialogues in Spanish* 61 You will goe for wooll, and return home shorne. **1612** T. SHELTON tr. *Ceruantes' Don Quixote* I. vii. To wander through the world ... without once considering how many there goe to seeke for wooll, that retume againe shorne themselues.

1678 J. RAY *English Proverbs* (ed. 2) 220 Many go out for wooll and come home shorn. **1858** S. A. HAMMETT *Piney Woods Tavern* xxiii. There's a proverb about going out after wool, and coming home shorn. **1981** N. FREELING *One Damn Thing after Another* iii. One always comes back tired from holidays. 'Go for wool and come back—?' 'Shaved—no, cropped.' 'Sheared. Yes.' ∎ **ambition** 野心・野望；**misfortune** 不運；**poverty** 貧困

wool ⇒ MUCH cry and little wool.

A WORD to the wise is enough.
賢者には一言で足りる。
（訳注：「一を聞いて十を知る」）

賢明な人は短いヒントからその意味を理解する。現在では A word to the wise. と省略されることが多く、忠告や警告の導入として使われる。†ラテン語 *Verbum sat sapienti*.「賢者には一言で事足りる」と省略されることもある。

□*a*1513 DUNBAR *Poems* (1979) 206 Few wordis may serve the wyis. **1546** J. HEYWOOD *Dialogue of Proverbs* II. vii. 14ᵛ Fewe woords to the wise suffice to be spoken. *a*1605 W. HAUGHTON *Englishmen for my Money* (1616) D3 They say, a word to the Wise is enough: so by this little French that he speakes, I see he is the very man I seeke for. **1768** STERNE *Sentimental Journey* III. 164 A word, Mons. Yorick, to the wise ... is enough. **1841** DICKENS *Old Curiosity Shop* ii. 'Fred!' cried Mr. Swiveller, tapping his nose, 'a word to the wise is sufficient for them—we may be good and happy without riches, Fred.' **2002** *Washington Times* 25 Apr. ClO (*heading*) The Man With the Proverbial Word to the Wise. ∎ **hints** ヒント・暗示

word ⇒ ACTIONS speak louder than words; An ENGLISHMAN's word is his bond; FINE words butter no parsnips; HARD words break no bones; One PICTURE is worth ten thousand words; STICKS and stones may break my bones, but words will never hurt me; Many a TRUE word is spoken in jest.

All WORK and no play makes Jack a dull boy.
勉強ばかりして遊ぶことをしないとジャックは馬鹿な男の子になってしまう。
（訳注：「よく学びよく遊べ」）

仕事に人生のすべてを懸け、気晴らしと娯楽のために時間を割かずにいると、退屈極まる人間になってしまうという警告。All work and no play. と省略されることが多い。

□**1659** J. HOWELL *Proverbs* (English) 12 All work and no play, makes Jack a dull boy. **1825** M. EDGEWORTH *Harry & Lucy Concluded* II. 155 All work and no play makes Jack a dull boy. All play and no work makes Jack a mere toy. **1859** S. SMILES *Self-Help* xi. 'All work and no play makes Jack a dull boy'; but all play and no work makes him something greatly worse. **1898** C. G. ROBERTSON *Voces Academicae* I. i. 'Is that why you give garden parties yourself, eh? ... all work and no play makes Jill a very—' ... 'Plain girl. She is that already.' **1979** R. MUTCH *Gemstone* xi. 'All work and no play makes Jack a dull boy,' he observed, pouring the champagne into a glass. **2001** *Washington Post* 4 Oct. Cl3 (*Jeff MacNelly's Shoe comic strip*) 'What about your homework?' 'Later. All work and no Playstation makes Jack a dull boy.' ∎ **recreation** 気晴らし；**work** 仕事

workman 493

WORK expands so as to fill the time available.
仕事は割り当てられた時間いっぱいまで伸びる。

この言葉の生みの親である C. N. パーキンソン教授 (1909-93) にちなんで、一般に「パーキンソンの法則」として呼ばれている。

☐ **1955** C. N. PARKINSON in *Economist* 19 Nov. 635 It is a commonplace observation that work expands so as to fill the time available for its completion. **1972** M. ARGYLE *Social Psychology of Work* viii. 'Parkinson's Law' is that 'work expands so as to fill the time available'. **1976** *Scotsman* 25 Nov.14 Though there are fewer Bills than usual, MPs, being well known as exemplars of Parkinson's law, can be relied on to stretch their work to fill all the time available and more. ■ **efficiency and inefficiency** 能率と非能率 ; **work** 仕事

It is not WORK that kills, but worry.
身を滅ぼすのは勤労ではなく心労である。
(訳注：「心配は身の毒」)

ストレスに注意せよという警告。物事にくよくよ悩むことは過労死よりも死ぬ確率が高くなる。

☐ **1879** D. M. MULOCK *Young Mrs. Jardine* III. ix. Working ... all day, writing ... at night ... Roderick had yet ... never spent a happier three months ... for it is not work that kills, but 'worry'. **1909** *British Weekly* 8 July 333 It is worry that kills, they say, and not work.... The canker of care seems to eat the life away. **1930**[?] S. K. HOCKING *Mystery Man* vi. 42 'Please don't talk about bother,' she said gently and sincerely. 'Naturally we've been worried and anxious.' 'Oh, but you shouldn't worry,' and he grinned again. 'It's worry that kills, so I've been told.' ■ **stress** ストレス ; **work** 仕事

If you won't WORK you shan't eat.
働く意志がないのなら、食べさせないぞ。
(訳注：shall ＝「…させてやる」。2・3 人称主語で、目下の者や子供に用いる。「働かざる者食うべからず」)

『テサロニケの信徒への手紙二』3 章10節 (欽定訳聖書) If any would not work, neither should he eat. 「働きたくない者は、誰も食べてはならない」

☐ *c***1535** D. LINDSAY *Satire of Three Estates* (EETS) 475 *Qui non laborat, non manducet....* *Quha labouris nocht he sall not elt.* **1624** CAPT. J. SMITH *General Hist. Virginia* III. x. He that will not worke shall not eate. **1891** R. KIPLING *Life's Handicap* 362 If you won't work you shan't eat.... You're a wild elephant, and no educated animal at all. Go back to your Jungle. **1981** J. STUBBS *Ironmaster* xx. I say them as don't work shan't eat. **2009** E. VAN DE VLIERT *Climate, Affluence, Culture* 84 For paid and unpaid production activities alike the bottom line is, 'If you won't work, you shan't eat.' ■ **idleness** 怠惰 ; **work** 仕事

work ⇒ （名詞）The DEVIL finds work for idle hands to do; The END crowns the work; The EYE of a master does more work than both his hands; FOOLS and bairns should never see half-done work; If IFS and ands were pots and pans, there'd be no work for tinkers' hands; MANY hands make light work; A WOMAN's work is never done; （動詞）What MATTERS is what works; TIME works wonders.

workman ⇒ A BAD workman blames his tools.

workshop ⇒ An IDLE brain is the Devil's workshop.

world ⇒ It takes ALL sorts to make a world; All's for the BEST in the best of all possible worlds; BETTER be out of the world than out of the fashion; GOD'S in his heaven, all's right with the world; One HALF of the world does not know how the other half lives; The HAND that rocks the cradle rules the world; LAUGH and the world laughs with you; A LIE is half-way round the world; LOVE makes the world go round.

Even a WORM will turn.
（ミミズなどの）虫でさえ立ち向かうものだ。
（訳注：will ＝「…するものだ」〈習性・傾向〉。「窮鼠猫を噛む」。「一寸の虫にも五分の魂」）

最も身分の低い者でさえ度を過ぎた嫌がらせを受けたり、多すぎる仕事を押しつけられたりすると死にもの狂いで反撃する。

□**1546** J. HEYWOOD *Dialogue of Proverbs* II. iv. G4ᵛ Treade a worme on the tayle, and it must turne agayne. **1592** A. GREENE *Groatsworth of Wit* XII. 143 Stop shallow water still running. it will rage. Tread on a worme and it will turne. **1854** 'M. LANGDON' Ida May xi. Even the worm turns when he is trodden upon. **1889** W. JAMES in *Mind* XIV. 107 Since even the worm will 'turn', the space-theorist can hardly be expected to remain motionless when his Editor stirs him up. **1962** A. CHRISTIE *Mirror Crack'd* xii. He's a very meelc type. Still, the worm will turn, or so they say. **1975** 'M. INNES' *Appleby File* 98 Signs were not wanting that she was putting stuffing into Charles Vandervell, of late so inclined to unwholesome meditation of headlong dying. It was almost as if a worm were going to turn. **2011** *disgruntledradical.blogspot.com* 4 Mar. 'Even a worm will turn, just as a sausage will if you keep it long enough.' Great quote by Peter Wrigley, Keynesian Liberal, commenting on Jeremy Hunt's decision on Murdoch: ■ **retribution 天罰・報復**

worm ⇒ The EARLY bird catches the worm.

worry ⇒ It is not WORK that kills, but worry.

worse ⇒ GO further and fare worse; NOTHING so bad but it might have been worse; The more you STIR it the worse it stinks.

worst ⇒ HOPE for the best and prepare for the worst; When THINGS are at the worst they begin to mend.

The WORTH of a thing is what it will bring.
物の価値は（売れた場合に）それがもたらすもの（儲け）で決まる。
（訳注：will ＝単純未来。この場合は、言外の条件〈売れた場合〉と呼応している）

売ろうとしている商品の価値はそれを買ってくれる人がいくら払ってくれるのか、その値段でしか決められないという意味で、これから商売をしようとする者に対する警告として使われる。†ラテン語*Valet quantum vendi potest.*「物は売れる額と同じ価値がある。」15世紀のフランス語*Tant vault la chose comme elle peut estre uendue.*「物は売れる額と同じだけの価値がある」

wrong 495

□1569 J. SANFORDE tr. *H. C. Agrippa's Vanity of Arts & Sciences* xci. The thinge is so muche worthy as it maye be solde for. **1664** S. BUTLER *Hudibras* II. i. For what is Worth in any thing, But so much Money as 'twill bring? **1813** SOUTHEY *Life of Nelson* I. ii. Vouchers, he found in that country were no check whatever; the principle was, that 'a thing was always worth what it would bring'. **1847** J. O. HALLIWELL *Dict.* II. 864 The worth of a thing is what it will bring. **1908** *Spectator* 4 Apr. 535 'The real worth of anything Is just as much as it will bring'. You cannot get beyond that piece of ancient wisdom as to the determination of value. **1979** F. E. CASE in *Real Estate Economics* VII. ii. 265 (*article title*) The Value of a Thing is the Price It will Bring. ■ **buying and selling 売買 ; value 価値**

worth ⇒ A BIRD in the hand is worth two in the bush; A KING's chaff is worth more than other men's corn; An OUNCE of practice is worth a pound of precept; A PECK of March dust is worth a king's ransom; One PICTURE is worth ten thousand words; It is a POOR dog that's not worth whistling for; A SWARM in May is worth a load of hay; If a THING' s worth doing, it's worth doing well; One VOLUNTEER is worth two pressed men.

worthy ⇒ The LABOURER is worthy of his hire.

wrath ⇒ A SOFT answer turneth away wrath.

wren ⇒ The ROBIN and the wren are God's cock and hen.

write ⇒ HISTORY is written by the victors.

wrong ⇒ （名詞）He who is ABSENT is always in the wrong; The KING can do no wrong; TWO wrongs don't make a right; （副詞）If ANYTHING can go wrong, it will; （形容詞）There is no such thing as BAD weather, only the wrong clothes.

Y

year ⇒ There are no BIRDS in last year's nest; A CHERRY year a merry year; KEEP a thing seven years and you'll always find a use for it; You should KNOW a man seven years before you stir his fire; ONE year's seeding makes seven years' weeding; TURKEY, heresy, hops, and beer came into England all in one year.

yesterday ⇒ JAM tomorrow and jam yesterday, but never jam today.

YORKSHIRE born and Yorkshire bred, strong in the arm and weak in the head.
生まれも育ちもヨークシャーの者は力は強いが頭は弱い。

> ヨークシャーの代わりにイングランド（主に北部）の州と町の他の名前が使われることもある。
>
> □**1852** *Notes & Queries* 1st Ser. V. 573 Derbyshire born and Derbyshire bred, Strong i' th' arm, and weak i' th' head. **1869** W. C. HAZLIFT *English Proverbs* 273 Manchester bred: Long in the arms, and short in the head. **1920** C. H. DOUGLAS *Credit-Power & Democracy* vi. Organised labour at this time shows considerable susceptibility to the Border gibe of being 'strong i' th' arm and weak i' th' head'. **1966** J. BINGHAM *Double Agent* ii. He thought, Yorkshire born and Yorkshire bred, strong in th' arm and weak in't head; but it wasn't true, most of them were as quick as weasels and sharp as Sheffield steel. ■ **human nature** 人間性

YOUNG folks think old folks to be fools, but old folks know young folks to be fools.
若者は老人を馬鹿だと思うが、老人は若者が馬鹿であることを知っている。

> （訳注：thinkの場合は「思っている」にすぎないが、knowの場合は「事実を知っている」のである）
>
> □**1577** J. GRANGE Golden Aphroditis O2ᵛ Young men thinks old men fooles, but old men knoweth well, Yong menare fooles. **1790** R. TYLER *Contrast* v. ii. Young folks think old folks to be fools; but old folks know young folks to be fools. **1850** F. E. SMEDLEY *Frank Fairlegh* xxx. 'Young folks always think old ones fools, they say.' 'Finish the adage, Sir, that old folks know young ones to be so, and then agree with me that it is a saying founded on prejudice.' **1930** A. CHRISTIE *Murder at Vicarage* xxxi. I remember a saying of my Great Aunt Fanny's. I was sixteen at the time and thought it particularly foolish.... She used to say, 'The young people think the old people are fools—but the old people know the young people are fools!' ■ **fools** 愚か者; **old age** 老年; **youth** 若さ・若者

young 497

A YOUNG man married is a young man marred.
若くして結婚する男は若くして人生を棒に振ることになる。

まだ自立していない男性があまりに若くして結婚することに対する警告。

□**1589** G. PUITENHAM *Art of English Poesy* III. xix. 173 The maide that soone married is, soone marred is. **1602** SHAKESPEARE *All's Well that ends Well* II. iii. 291 A young man married is a man that's marr'd. **1961** R. KIRK *Old House of Fear* i. Don't forget this, though, Duncan— 'You can grave it on his tombstone, you can cut it on his card: A young man married is a young man marred.' ■ **marriage** 結婚；**youth** 若さ・若者

YOUNG men may die, but old men must die.
若者は死ぬこともあるかもしれないが、老人は必ず死ぬものだ。

(訳注：may と must の対立に注意。must ＝「必ず…する」。Bad seed *must* produce bad corn.〈悪い種子からは必ず悪い実ができる〉)

†あるローマの高貴な女性の言葉である。彼女は若い夫の死後、求婚してきた年配の男性の申し出を断るとき次のように言った。*Juvenis quidem potest cito mori; sed senex diu vivere non potest.* 「若者は実際早く死ぬかもしれないが、老人は長生きはできない」。(聖ヒエロニムス『手紙』cxxvii. 2 の中で引用されている)。

□**1534** MORE *Dialogue of Comfort* (1553) II. ii. As the younge man maye happe some time to die soone, so the olde man can never liue long. **1623** W. CAMDEN *Remains concerning Britain* (ed. 3) 276 Young men may die, but old men must die. **1758** LADY M. W. MONTAGU *Letter* 5 Sept (1967) 111. 174 According to the good English Proverb, young people may die, but old must die. **1863** B. 1. WILEY *Life of Billy Yank* (1952) xii. That is the Way of the World. The old must die and the young may die. **1970** 'D. CRAIG' (title) *Young men may die.* **1993** 'C. AIRD' *Going Concern* (1994) i. 9 Mary-Louise was the holiday party's language specialist and immediately said: '"The young die sometimes, but the old always die." That's an old Breton proverb.' ■ **death** 死；**necessity** 必要性・必然性；**old age** 老年

YOUNG saint, old devil.
若い聖人は老いると悪魔になる。

行儀が良すぎる若者はのちに正体を現わし、陰険な人物になることがある。WANTON kittens make sober cats.「いたずら子猫も真面目な親猫になる」で述べられているプロセスと逆のケースを表わしている。

□*c***1400** *Middle English Sermons from MS Royal* 18 B xxiii (EETS) 159 Itt is a comond prouerbe bothe of clerkes and of laye men, 'younge seynt, old dewell'. **1552** H. LATIMER *Seventh Sermon, Lord's Prayer in Sermons* (1844-5) 431 The old proverb, 'Young saints, old devils' … is … the devil's own invention; which would have parents negligent in bringing up their children in goodness. **1636** S. WARD *Collection of Sermons & Treatises* 269 Young Saints, will prove but old Devils … But … such as proove falling starres, never were ought but meteors. **1936** V. MCHUGH *Caleb Catlum's America* xxvii. Young saint, old devil … looks to me like you been leadin' too virtuus a life. ■ **good and evil** 正邪；**human nature** 人間性；**youth**；若さ・若者

young ⇒ BETTER be an old man's darling, than a young man's slave; whom the GODS love die young; The GOOD die young; HANG a thief when he's young, and he'll no' steal when he's old; You cannot put an OLD head on young shoulders.

498 YOUTH

YOUTH must be served.
若さは役立てられなければならない。

若者は与えられた機会を取り上げられるべきでない。

□**1829** P. EGAN. *Boxiana* 2nd Ser. II. 60 Tom Cannon made his appearance in the Prize Ring rather too late in life, under the idea that 'Youth must be served'. **1900** A. CONAN DOYLE *Green Flag* 125 There were ... points in his favour.... There was age—twenty-three against forty. There was an old ring proverb that 'Youth will be served'. **1941** G. HEYER *Envious Casca* iv. You're just an old curmudgeon, and you're upset because you didn't like young Roydon's play.... But, my dear chap, youth must be served! **2001** *Washington Times* 19 Aug. Bl And why wouldn't your clone, poor thing. have just as much claim to your constituent organs, if not more? (Youth will be served.) ■ **opportunity** 機会・好機；**youth** 若さ・若者

If YOUTH knew, if age could.
もし若者に知識があり、老人に力があったら。

†アンリ・エティエンヌ *Les Premices* (1594) 173 *O si la ievnesse scavoit, O si la vieillesse povvoit*「もし若者に知識があり、老人に力があったら」。現代フランス語の *si jeunesse savait; si vieillesse pouvait*.「もし若者に知識があり、老人に力があったら」がそのまま使われることが多い。

□**1611** R. COTGRAVE *Dict. French & English* s.v. jeunesse If youth knew what to doe, and age could doe what it knowes, no man would ever be poore. **1922** J. JOYCE *Ulysses* 30 I know, I know. If youth but knew. But what does Shakespeare say? **2002** *Times* 9 July 19 The old adage, 'If youth knew, if age but could', has been replaced by a scenario in which youth doesn't know, but age still can. ■ **old age** 老年；**youth** 若さ・若者

Yule ⇒ A GREEN Yule makes a fat churchyard.

監訳者のことば

澤田治美

　本書『オックスフォード英語ことわざ・名言辞典』は、*Oxford Dictionary of Proverbs*（2015）の日本語版です。本書には、約1200のことわざ・名言が収録されており、聖書、シェイクスピア、言語コーパスなどから用例が多数挙げられて、英語のことわざの豊穣な世界が浮き彫りにされています。テーマも、人生、仕事、暮らし、愛、結婚、友情、感情（喜び・悲しみ・怒りなど）、生き方、学問・芸術、さらには、（農事暦としての）天気にまつわる伝承・迷信など、驚くほど多岐にわたっています。ギリシア語、ラテン語から英語に入ってきたものも少なくありません。こうしたことわざにはヨーロッパの長い伝統が息づいています。英語圏で暮らす人々は子供のころからマザーグース、聖書、ことわざを身近に感じ、そのことばを日常的に使いながら暮らしているようです。ある英語の母語話者によると、"**Better late than never.**"（遅くても何もしないよりはまし）は、生徒が遅れてレポートを提出した時などに、先生が笑いながら言うそうですし、"**No pain, no gain.**"（苦労しなければ、得るものはない）は、ジムに通って体重を減らそうとする場合などに、こう言いながらジムに行くといいます。こうしたことばは日常生活に溶け込んでいるのです。

　無論、ことわざや名言は（「いろはかるた」などを通して）日本人の心の中にも深く根付いています。例えば、「論より証拠」、「ちりも積もれば山となる」、「鬼に金棒」、「急がば回れ」、「知らぬが仏」などは、日常会話でしょっちゅう使われています。また、次のことばは心に残る人生訓です。

　　ある人、弓射る事を習ふに、双矢をたばさみて的に向ふ。師の伝はく、「初心の人、二つの矢を持つ事なかれ。後の矢を頼みて、始めの矢に等閑の心あり。毎度ただ得失なく、この一矢に定むべしと思へ」と伝ふ。わづかに二つの矢、師の前にて一つをおろそかにせんと思はんや。懈怠の心、みづから知らずといへども、師これを知る。このいましめ、万事にわたるべし。

　　（ある人が弓を射ることを習うのに、二本の矢を手にして的に向かった。すると、その師が「初心者は、二本の矢を持ってはならない。後の矢をあてにして、初めの矢を射る時に油断が生じるからだ。毎回、失敗せずに、この矢一本でかならず当てようと思え」と言った。わずか二本の矢しか持たず、しかも師匠の前で彼が一本の矢をおろそかにするつもりはあるまい。しかし、二本の矢に現われた心のゆるみは、本人は気付かなくても、師匠がそれと洞察したのである。この教訓は万事に通ずるものであろう。）

　　　　　　　（『徒然草』92段『徒然草・全訳注』三木紀人著、1982、講談社学術文庫）

本書には多くのことわざ・名言が挙がっています。読者の方々にその中の幾つかを選び、咀嚼し、味わっていただければ嬉しく思います。私は次のものを選んでみました。

　　① Art is long and life is short.（技芸は長く、人生は短い）
　　② A friend in need is a friend indeed.（まさかの時の友こそ真の友）
　　③ Great oaks from little acorns grow.（樫の大木も小さなどんぐりから）
　　④ Love makes the world go round.（愛がこの世を回らせている）
　　⑤ A nation without a language is a nation without a heart.（国語を持たない国は心を持たない国である）
　　⑥ There's no place like home.（我が家に勝る所はない）
　　⑦ Truth lies at the bottom of a well.（真理は井戸の底にある）

　ことばは私たちを支え、勇気づけてくれます。私自身、島根大学 4 年の時、進路に迷いながらドイツ語を学んでいた時、Es irrt der Mensch, so lang er strebt.（人は、努力する限り迷うものだ）というゲーテのことばを見つけました。『ファウスト』の「天上の序曲」にあるこのことばは、今日までずっと心の糧となってきました。本書の中の次のことばも私の背中を押してくれました。Make haste slowly.（ゆっくり急げ）（ラテン語 festina lente.）、To err is human (to forgive divine).（過ちは人の常〈許すは神の業〉）、Be not therefore anxious for the morrow: for the morrow will be anxious for itself. Sufficient unto the day is the evil thereof.（だから、あすのことを思いわずらうな。あすのことは、あす自身が思いわずらうであろう。一日の苦労は、その日一日だけで十分である）（『マタイによる福音書』6 章34節）。

　最初のことばは島根大学時代に出会ったもの（作家の故開高健は「悠々として急げ」と名訳しました）、2 番目のことばは1986年、ハーバード在外研究員として一家でボストンに滞在していた時、クリスチャンの老夫婦の家に招かれた時に教わったもの、3 番目のことばは、結婚式で恩師から贈られたものです。安来高校時代に、授業で、Life is full of partings. を「『サヨナラ』ダケガ人生ダ（人生足別離）」（井伏鱒二『厄除け詩集』から）と、Love laughs at distance. を「惚れて通えば千里も一里」と訳したらどうかと教わった時、雷に打たれたような感動を受けました。

　英語のことわざには、古代ギリシア・ローマをはじめとするヨーロッパの長い歴史・文化・宗教・伝承の伝統が投影されています。While there's life, there's hope.（生きている限り希望がある）は古代ギリシアのことわざですし、Love laughs at locksmiths.（恋は錠前屋など物ともしない）はシェイクスピアのことばですが、考え方や感じ方は現代とちっとも変わりません。

　ことわざは英語学習にとって最高の教材となります。本書から 4 つ挙げてみましょう。第 1 に、次のことわざから、

A drowning man will clutch at a straw.（溺れる者は藁をもつかもうとする）

(i) will は「…するものだ」という「習性」を表している、(ii) clutch at は「…をつかもうとして何度も手を伸ばす（at があるため、おそらくつかめない）」ことを意味している、(iii) drowning は「溺れている」ではなく、「溺死しつつある」を表している、といったことがわかります。

第 2 に、次のことわざから、

NOTHING so bad but it might have been worse.（災難はすべて、それよりもっとひどかった可能性もある）

文頭に There is を補うと、There is nothing so bad but it might have been worse. となります。文字通りには、「もっと悪かったかもしれないということがないような悪い事というのはない」の意味です。(i) so は、否定を含意する but 節（＝…ということがない）を指している、(ii) but 節の内容である it might have been worse.（もっと悪かったかもしれない）という文は仮定法過去完了構文の帰結節だけが表されたものであり、「運が悪ければ」、「下手をすると」といった趣旨の条件節を補うことができる、といったことがわかります。どんな災難であれ、災難はすべて下手をするとそれよりもっとひどかった可能性もあるわけです。

第 3 に、次のことわざから、

You cannot have your cake and eat it.（ケーキを食べて、なおかつそれを持っているというわけにはいかない）（二ついいことはない）

"have your cake and eat it"（ケーキを食べて、なおかつそれを持っている）ということが一つのまとまった概念を成しており、それが助動詞の cannot の対象となっていることがわかります。"have your cake"（ケーキを食べる）という部分だけを cannot の対象とすることはできません。そうしてしまうと、「ケーキを食べることはできず、そしてそれを持っている」という、誤った解釈になってしまいます。

　次のことわざも、構造の上からは上のことわざと並行しています。

One cannot love and be wise.（恋と分別は両立し得ない）

You cannot run with the hare and hunt with the hounds.（野兎と一緒に逃げながら猟犬と一緒に狩をすることはできない）

というのは、"love and be wise"（恋して、なおかつ分別を持っている）、"run with the hare and hunt with the hounds"（野兎と一緒に逃げながら猟犬と一緒に狩をする）ということが一つのまとまった概念を成しており、それがcannotの対象となっているからです。

第4に、次のことわざは、「同等比較」を表す "x as ... as y" 構文の意味を解釈するのに有益です。

> **There are as good fish in the sea as ever came out of it.**（海にはこれまでに捕らえられたことのないほどのよい魚がまだまだいる）

"x as ... as y" 構文の意味は次のように解釈できます。

> "x as ... as y" は「xの…の程度はyの…の程度と同じ（くらい）」ではなく、「（少なくとも）xの…の程度はyの…程度ほどはある」という高い捉え方を表している。

こうした捉え方の下では、上のことわざにおいて、as y に当たる従属節は、（否定を含意する ever〈＝「いまだかって」〉があることからもわかるように）「これまでに捕らえられたことのないほどの」という程度が表されており、x as に当たる主節は、「（少なくとも）それと同じかそれ以上の」という高い程度が表されていることになります。このように考えると、このことわざが失恋した人に対する慰めのことばであることもうなづけます。

ことわざを通してことばを学ぶことは、ことばを通して人生を学ぶことにつながると言えましょう。ことばは私たちを励まし、救い、そして成長させてくれます。本書は英語のことわざ・名言の宝庫です。本書を紐解いて、ぜひ珠玉のことばに出会ってほしいと切に願っています。

本書の原稿を準備する中で、ことわざの解釈や訳注に関して多くの辞書・著書から恩恵を受けることができました。なかでも、『英語諺辞典』（三省堂）、『常識としての英語の諺800』（北星堂）、『三省堂英語イディオム・句動詞大辞典』（三省堂）の編者、著者、訳者の学恩に深く感謝いたします。

なお、本書に挙げられている英語のことわざの中には、現代から見ると差別的だと思われるものが含まれていますが、歴史的背景を考慮し、原典どおりといたしました。

末筆ながら、英語ことわざ・名言を日本人読者に紹介することの価値を認めて、本書の刊行に尽力された柊風舎の伊藤甫律社長と、困難な編集作業を辛抱強く丁寧に進めていただいた同社編集部の飯浜利之氏に心から感謝申しあげます。

参考文献

503

Bibliography of Major Proverb Collections and Works cited from Modern Editions

Quotations are taken from the first edition of the work in question unless otherwise stated. Standard modern editions of several major authors, particularly from the medieval and Renaissance periods, have been used for ease of reference.

Major Proverb Collections

Apperson, G. L., *Englih Proverbs and Proverbial Phrases* (London, 1929).

Bohn, H. G., *Hand-Book of Proverbs* (London, 1855).

Carmichaell, J., *James Carmichaell Collection of Proverbs in Scots*, ed. M. L. Anderson (Edinburgh, 1957).

[Clarke, J.,] *Parœmiologia Anglo-Latina ... or Proverbs English, and Latine, methodically disposed according to the Common-place heads, in Erasmus his Adages* (London, 1639).

Denham, M. A., *Collection of Proverbs and Popular Sayings relating to the seasons, the weather, and agricultural pursuits* (London, 1846).

Doyle, C. C., Mieder, W., and Shapiro, F. R., *The Dictionary of Modern Proverbs* (New Haven and London, 2012).

Draxe, T., *Bibliotheca Scholastica Instructissima, or, a Treasurie of ancient Adagies, and sententious Prouerbes, selected out of the English, Greeke, Latine, French, Italian, and Spanish* (London, 1616).

Dykes, O., *English Proverbs, with Moral Reflexions* (London, 1709).

Fergusson, D., *Fergusson's Scottish Proverbs from the Original Print of 1641 together with a larger Manuscript Collection of about the same period hitherto unpublished*, ed. E. Beveridge (Edinburgh, 1924).

Franklin, B., *Poor Richard's Almanack: Sayings of Poor Richard*, ed. P. L. Ford (Brooklyn, 1890).

Fuller, T., *Gnomologia: Adagies and Proverbs; Wise Sentences and Witty Sayings, Ancient and Modern, Foreign and British* (London, 1732).

Hart, Henry H., *700 Chinese Proverbs* (Stanford, Calif., 1937).

Hassell, J. W., Jun., *Middle French Proverbs, Sentences, and Proverbial Phrases* (Toronto, 1982).

Hazlitt, W. C., *English Proverbs and Proverbial Phrases* (London, 1869). Later editions are also cited.

Henderson, A., *Scottish Proverbs* (Edinburgh , 1832).

H[erbert]., G., *Outlandish Proverbs* (1640), and Jacula Prudentum (1651), in *Works*, ed. F. E. Hutchinson (Oxford, 1941).

Heywood, J., *Dialogue conteinyng the number in effect of all the prouerbes in the englishe tongue* (London, 1546). Later editions are also cited.

Hislop, A., *Proverbs of Scotland* (Glasgow, 1862).

H[owell]., J., *Paroimiographia. Proverbs, or Old sayed sawes & adages in English, ... Italian, French and Spanish, whereunto the British ... are added* (London, 1659).

Kelly, J., *Complete Collection of Scottish Proverbs Explained and made Intelligible to the English Reader* (London, 1721).

Kirschen, L., *American Proverbs about Women* (Westport, CT, 1998).

Lean, V. S., *Collectanea* (5 vols., Bristol, 1902- 4).

[Mapletoft, J.,] *Select Proverbs, Italian, Spanish, French, English, Scotish, British &c. Chiefly Moral* (London, 1707).

Mieder, W., Kingsbury, S. A., and Harder, K. B., *A Dictionary of American Proverbs* (New York and Oxford, 1992).

Oxford Dictionary of English Proverbs, ed. F. P. Wilson (ed. 3, Oxford, 1970).

Palmer, S., *Moral Essays on some of the most Curious and Significant English, Scotch, and Foreign Proverbs* (London, 1710).

R[ay]., J., *Collection of English Proverbs* (Cambridge, 1670). Later editions are also cited.

Stevenson, B., *Home Book of Proverbs, Maxims, and Familiar Phrases* (rev. ed., New York, 1961).

Taverner, R., *Prouebs or adagies with newe addicions gathered out of the Chiliades of Erasmus* (London, 1539).

Taylor, A., and Whiting, B. J., *Dictionary of American Proverbs and Proverbial Phrases 1820-1880* (Cambridge, Mass., 1958).

Tilley, M. P., *Dictionary of the Proverbs in England in the Sixteenth and Seventeenth Centuries* (Ann Arbor,

1950).

Torriano, G., *Dictionary English & Italian, with severall Proverbs*, first published with J. Florio's *Vocabolario Italiano & Inglese, a Dictionary Italian & English* (rev. ed., London, 1659).

Torriano, G. *Piazza universale di proverbi Italiani; or, a common place of Italian proverbs and proverbial phrases* (London, 1666).

Torriano, G. *Second alphabet consisting of proverbial phrases* (London, 1662).

Torriano, G. *Select Italian Proverbs* (Cambridge, 1642).

Tusser, T., *Husbandry: Hundreth good pointes of husbandrie* (London, 1557), *Five hundreth points of good husbandry united to as many of good huswiferie* (1573, various revised and augmented editions).

Whiting, B. J., *Early American Proverbs and Proverbial Phrases* (Cambridge, Mass., 1977).

Whiting, B. J. *Modern Proverbs and Proverbial Sayings* (Cambridge, Mass., 1989).

Whiting, B. J. *Proverbs, Sentences, and Proverbial Phrases from English Writings mainly before 1500* (Cambridge, Mass., 1968).

Works Cited from Modern Editions

Beaumont, F., and Fletcher, J., *Works*, ed. A. Glover and A. R. Waller (10 vols., Cambridge, 1905-12). *Bible: Authorised Version of the English Bible 1611* ed. W. A. Wright (5 vols., Cambridge, 1909).

Chaucer, G., *Works*, ed. F. N. Robinson (ed. 2, London, 1966).

Dekker, T., *Dramatic Works*, ed. F. T. Bowers (4 vols., Cambridge, 1953-61). Non-dramatic works are cited from the first edition.

Douce MS 52: Forster, M., 'Die Mittelenglische Sprichwortersammlung in Douce 52', *Festschrift zum XII. Allgemeinen Deutschen Neuphilologentage in Munchen, Pfingsten 1906* (Erlangen, 1906), 40-60.

Ford, J., *Dramatic Works*, ed. W. Bang and H. de Vocht (2 vols., Louvain, 1908, 1927). Gascoigne, G., *Complete Works*, ed. J. W. Cunliffe (2 vols., Cambridge, 1907-10).

Gower, J., *English Works*, ed. G. C. Macaulay (2 vols., London, 1900- 1).

Greene, R., *Life and Complete Works in prose and verse*, ed. A. B. Grosart (15 vols., London, 1881- 6).

Heywood, T., *Dramatic Works*, ed. R. H. Shepherd (6 vols., London, 1874). *Captives* is cited from the first publication of 1885.

Jonson, B., *Works*, ed. C. H. Herford, P. and E. M. Simpson (11 vols., Oxford, 1925-52). *Cynthia's Revels* is cited from the first edition.

Langland,W., *Vision of William concerning Piers Plowman*, ed. W. W. Skeat (5 vols., London, 1867-85).

Lyly, J., *Complete Works*, ed. R. W. Bond (3 vols., Oxford, 1902). Principal works cited are *Euphues: the anatomy of wit* (1578) and *Euphues and his England* (1580).

Marlowe, C., *Works and Life*, ed. R. H. Case et al. (6 vols., London, 1930- 3).

Marston, J., *Works*, ed. A. H. Bullen (3 vols., London, 1887).

Massinger, P., *Plays and Poems*, ed. P. Edwards and C. Gibson (Oxford, 1976).

Middleton, T., *Works*, ed. A. H. Bullen (8 vols., London, 1885- 6).

Milton, J., *Complete Prose Works*, ed. D. M. Wolfe et al. (8 vols., New Haven, 1953-).

Milton, J. *Works*, ed. F. A. Patterson (18 vols., New York, 1931- 8). Cited for poetical works.

Nashe, T., *Works*, ed. R. B. McKerrow (5 vols., London, 1904-10; corrected reprint 1958, 1966).

Pope, A., *Twickenham Edition of the Poems*, ed. J. Butt et al. (10 vols., London, 1939-67). The *Dunciad* and the translation of the *Odyssey* are cited from the first edition; *Letters* are cited as marked in the text.

Porter, H., *Pleasant Historie of the two angrie women of Abington*, ed. W. W. Greg (Oxford, for the Malone Society, 1912).

Romaunt of the Rose: in Chaucer, G., *Works,* supra.

Shakespeare, W., *Complete Works*, ed. P. Alexander (London, 1951).

Skelton, J., *Poems*, ed. R. S. Kinsman (Oxford, 1969). Items not found here are cited from *Poetical Works*, ed. A. Dyce (2 vols., London, 1843).

Spenser, E., *Works: a variorum edition*, ed. E. Greenlaw et al. (10 vols., Baltimore, 1932-57).

Swift, J., *Poems*, ed. H. Williams (3 vols., ed. 2, Oxford, 1958).

Swift, J. *Prose Works*, ed. H. Davis (14 vols., Oxford, 1939-68). The Polite Conversation ('S.W[agstaff].', *Complete collection of genteel and ingenious conversation, according to the most polite mode and method now used at court, and in the best companies of England* (London, 1738) is cited from the first edition.

Thompson, F., *Lark Rise to Candleford*: cited from the first collected edition of 1945. Webster, J., *Complete Works*, ed. F. L Lucas (4 vols., London, 1927).

Websites

There are a great number of websites on proverbs but few comprise more than lists of sayings culled from other dictionaries or lists and arranged either alphabetically or thematically, sometimes with a brief explanation of their meaning. A few of more ambitious, offering some kind of historical or other information, though not necessarily entirely devoted to proverbs, are listed below.

http://www.afriprov.org

www.barrypopik.com

quoteinvestigator.com

www.worldwidewords.org

参考文献

安藤邦男『テーマ別英語ことわざ辞典』東京堂出版（2008）

安藤貞雄（編）『三省堂　英語イディオム・句動詞大辞典』三省堂（2011）

金子晴勇（編訳）『エラスムス「格言選集」』知泉書館（2015）

北村孝一／武田勝昭（編）『英語常用ことわざ辞典』東京堂出版（1997）

奥津文夫『ことわざの英語』講談社（1989）

奥津文夫『ことわざで英語を学ぶ』三修社（2008）

奥津文夫『日英ことわざの比較文化』大修館書店（2008）

大塚高信／高瀬省三（編）『英語諺辞典』三省堂（1986）

大塚高信／高瀬省三（編）『英語ことわざ辞典』三省堂（1995）

Wilson,F.P. (Ed.) *Oxford Dictionary of English Proverbs*. Oxford: Oxford University Press. (1970)

R・ライダット／C・ウィティング（中西英男訳）『常識としての英語の諺800』（第8版）北星堂書店（1986）

曽根田憲三／ケネス・アンダーソン『英語ことわざ用法辞典』大学書林（1987）

武田勝昭『ことわざのレトリック』海鳴社（1992）

戸田豊『現代英語ことわざ辞典』リーベル出版（2003）

外山滋比古『現代ことわざ辞典』ライオン社（2002）

柳沼重剛（編）『ギリシア・ローマ名言集』岩波書店（2003）

山本忠尚（監修）創元社編集部（編）『新版 日英比較ことわざ事典』創元社（2007）

辞書

『小学館ランダムハウス英和大辞典』（第2版）小学館

『小学館プログレッシブ英和中辞典』（第4版）小学館

『ユースプログレッシブ英和辞典』小学館

『ウィズダム英和辞典』（第3版）三省堂

『ジーニアス英和辞典』（第5版）大修館書店

『リーダーズ英和中辞典』（第2版）研究社

『LEXICON LATINO＝JAPONICUM』（改訂版）研究社

『アクセス独和辞典』（第3版）三修社

『クラウン仏和辞典』（第6版）三省堂

シェイクスピアからの用例の和訳に際しては、基本的に『シェイクスピア全集』（小田島雄志訳、白水社）の名訳を参考にさせていただいた。また、訳注に挙げた英文ならびにその和訳に関しては、基本的に上記の英和辞典のものを借用させていただいた。記して心から感謝の意を表したい。

主題索引

absence：不在
ABSENCE makes the heart grow fonder 15
He who is ABSENT is always in the wrong 15
The BEST of friends must part 39
BLUE are the hills that are far away 57
DISTANCE lends enchantment to the view 119
OUT of sight, out of mind 344

abuse, verbal ⇒ malice：悪意・恨み；slander：誹謗中傷

accidents ⇒ misfortune：不運

action and consequence：行為と結果
AFTER the feast comes the reckoning 19
ANOTHER day, another dollar 22
ASK a silly question and you get a silly answer 26
As you BAKE, so shall you brew 32
As you BREW, so shall you bake 63
CATCHING's before hanging 78
CRIME doesn't pay 99
They that DANCE must pay the fiddler 105
DO right and fear no man 120
He who DRINKS beer, thinks beer 128
The END justifies the means 137
GARBAGE in, garbage out 180
ILL gotten goods never thrive 234
IN for a penny ... 236
As you MAKE your bed, so you must lie upon it 284
The NAIL that sticks up gets hammered down 313
NO harm, no foul 324
ONE year's seeding makes seven years' weeding 340
He who PAYS the piper calls the tune 348
He who PLANTS thorns should not expect to gather roses 356
If you PLAY with fire you get burnt 356
Who won't be RULED by the rudder must be ruled by the rock 386
Who SAYS A must say B 391
SOW an act, and you reap a habit 414
As you SOW, so you reap 414
They that SOW the wind shall reap the whirlwind 415
The more you STIR it ... 423
For WANT of a nail the shoe was lost ... 471
WILFUL waste makes woeful want 480
He who WILLS the end, wills the means 481

action and inaction：行為と非行為 ⇒ words and deeds：言動 も見よ
As good be an ADDLED egg as an idle bird 17
The BETTER the day, the better the deed 44
BETTER to light one candle ... 46
BETTER to live one day as a tiger ... 46
BETTER to wear out than to rust out 47
COUNCILS of war never fight 95
DELAYS are dangerous 110
When in DOUBT, do nowt 126
The ROAD to hell is paved with good intentions 379
If you SIT by the river for long enough ... 405
Let SLEEPING dogs lie 407
USE it or lose it 469

adversity：逆境・苦難 ⇒ good fortune：幸運 も見よ
ADVERSITY makes strange bedfellows 18

The BLOOD of the martyrs is the seed of the Church 56
The DEVIL was sick, the Devil a saint would be ... 114
A FRIEND in need is a friend indeed 177
What doesn't KILL you makes you stronger 245
If LIFE hands you lemons, make lemonade 263

advice：忠告・助言
A FOOL may give a wise man counsel 171
NIGHT brings counsel 322
Don't TEACH your grandmother to suck eggs 439

age ⇒ middle age：中年；old age：老年；youth：若さ・若者

agreement ⇒ harmony and disharmony：調和と不調和

ambition：野心・野望
Hasty CLIMBERS have sudden falls 87
The HIGHER the monkey climbs ... 217
If you are not the LEAD dog, the view never changes 257
Up like a ROCKET ... 381
There is always ROOM at the top 383
Many go out for WOOL and come home shorn 487

anger：怒り
A LITTLE pot is soon hot 268
A SOFT answer tumeth away wrath 410
Never let the SUN go down on your anger 431
It takes TWO to make a quarrel 465

animals：動物
Feed a DOG for three days ... 121
DOGS look up to you ... 125

anticipation ⇒ expectation：期待

appearance：外見
BE what you would seem to be 34
A BLIND man's wife needs no paint 55
A CARPENTER is known by his chips 74
HANDSOME is as handsome does 209
PRETTY is as pretty does 362
The PROOF of the pudding is in the eating 365
The TREE is known by its fruit 456

appearance, deceptive：偽りの外見
An APE's an ape, a varlet's a varlet ... 23
APPEARANCES are deceptive 23
BEAUTY is only skin-deep 35
You can't tell a BOOK by its cover 58
Never CHOOSE your women or your linen by candlelight 84
The COWL does not make the monk 98
All that GLITTERS is not gold 184
There's many a GOOD cock come out of a tattered bag 193
There's many a GOOD tune played on an old fiddle 195
No matter how long a LOG stays in the water ... 273
STILL waters run deep 423

appearance, significant：重要な外見
CLOTHES make the man 88
The EYES are the windows of the soul 152
FINE feathers make fine birds 163
FIRST impressions are the most lasting 166

A GOOD horse cannot be of a bad colour 194
What you SEE is what you get 394

army ⇒ soldiers：兵士

assistance：援助
EVERY little helps 142
FOUR eyes see more than two 175
MANY hands make light work 290
A MOUSE may help a lion 309
If you're not part of the SOLUTION ... 411
Everyone SPEAKS well of the bridge ... 417
TOO many cooks spoil the broth 452
TWO heads are better than one 463
Do not call a WOLF to help you against the dogs 489

associates：仲間 ⇒ example, good and bad：好例と悪例；
    friends：友 も見よ
Where BEES are, there is honey 36
BIG fleas have little fleas ... 49
BIRDS of a feather flock together 52
CAESAR's wife must be above suspicion 70
Where the CARCASE is ... 72
A man is known by the COMPANY he keeps 91
The DEVIL looks after his own 113
If you LIE down with dogs ... 262
LOVE me, love my dog 280
MORE people know Tom Fool ... 306
POLITICS makes strange bedfellows 358
If there were no RECEIVERS, there would be no thieves
    374
The ROTTEN apple injuries its neighbours 385
There is SAFETY in numbers 388
The SUN loses nothing by shining into a puddle 431
He who SUPS with the Devil should have a long spoon
    432
He that TOUCHES pitch shall be defiled 453

badness ⇒ good and evil：正邪；wrong-doers：悪事をな
    す者

beauty：美・美貌
BEAUTY draws with a single hair 35
BEAUTY is in the eye of the beholder 35
BEAUTY is only skin-deep 35

beginnings and endings：最初と最後 ⇒ finality：終末・終
    局 も見よ
It is the FIRST step that is difficult 166
There is always a FIRST time 167
A GOOD beginning makes a good ending 192
GREAT oaks from little acorns grow 199
A JOURNEY of a thousand miles begins with a single step
    240
The MOTHER of mischief is no bigger than a midge's
    wing 308
All ROADS lead to Rome 380
Good SEED makes a good crop 394
The SOONER begun, the sooner done 412
As you SOW, so you reap 414
A STREAM cannot rise above its source 426
WELL begun is half done 481
All's WELL that ends well 481

behaviour ⇒ conduct 行ない・品行；human nature：人間性

bigness ⇒ great and small 大小

bird lore：鳥にまつわる逸話
ONE for sorrow, two for mirth ... 339
The ROBIN and the wren are God's cock and hen ... 380

blessings：恵み・（神の）恩恵
BLESSED is he who expects nothing ... 53
BLESSINGS brighten as they take their flight 54
Happy is the BRIDE ... 64
Happy is the COUNTRY which has no history 96
Blessed are the DEAD ... 108
You never MISS the water till the well runs dry 300

boasting：自慢
BRAG is a good dog ... 60
EMPTY vessels make the most sound 136
One ENGLISHMAN can beat three Frenchmen 139
The KUMARA does not speak of its own sweetness 250
MUCH cry and little wool 310
SELF-PRAISE is no recommendation 395
TALK is cheap 437

boldness：大胆さ ⇒ courage：勇気 も見よ
ADVENTURES are to the adventurous 18
ATTACK is the best form of defence 27
BETTER to live one day as a tiger ... 46
The best DEFENSE Is a good offense 110
FAINT heart never won fair lady 154
You never KNOW what you can do till you try 249
If you gently touch a NETTLE ... 318
NOTHING so bold as a blind mare 330
NOTHING venture, nothing gain 330
NOTHING venture, nothing have 331
Put a STOUT heart to a stey brae 426

borrowing and lending：貸し借り
Neither a BORROWER nor a lender be 59
The EARLY man never borrows from the late man 131
He that GOES a-borrowing, goes a-sorrowing 192
LEND your money and lose your friend 259

bravery ⇒ courage：勇気

brevity and long-windedness：簡潔と冗漫
BREVITY Is the soul of wit 63
A GREAT book is a great evil 198

bribery and corruption：賄賂と腐敗
EVERY man has his price 143
There's no such thing as a FREE lunch 176
A GOLDEN key can open any door 191
KISSING goes by favour 247
It's not WHAT you know, it's who you know 482

business：ビジネス・商売
BUSINESS before pleasure 67
BUSINESS is war 67
CORPORATIONS have neither bodies to be punished ...
    95
EVERY man to his trade 144
MONEY has no smell 302
Where there's MUCK there's brass 311
If you're not PAYING, you're the product 348
PUNCTUALITY is the soul of business 367
SELL in May and go away 396

SHORT reckonings make long friends   401
TRADE follows the flag   454
There are TRICKS in every trade   456
TWO of a trade never agree   464

busybodies：おせっかい屋 ⇒ eavesdroppers 盗み聞きする
　人 も見よ
If it ain't BROKE, don't fix it   65
Let the COBBLER stick to his last   89
EVERYBODY's business is nobody's business   145
LAY-OVERS for meddlers   257
LET well alone   261
Let SLEEPING dogs lie   407
The more you STIR it ...   423
TOO many cooks spoil the broth   452

buying and selling 売買 ⇒ business：ビジネス・商売 も見よ
You BUY land, you buy stones ...   68
Let the BUYER beware   68
The BUYER has need of a hundred eyes ...   68
The CUSTOMER is always right   103
A MONEYLESS man goes fast through the market   305
SELL in May and go away   396
It takes TWO to make a bargain   465
One WHITE foot, buy him ...   483
The WORTH of a thing is what it will bring   494

calendar lore：暦にまつわる伝承 ⇒ weather lore：天気に
　まつわる伝承 も見よ
BARNABY bright, Barnaby bright ...   33
CANDLEMAS day, put beans in the clay ...   71
Ne'er CAST a clout till May be out   74
FEBRUARY fill dyke ...   159
On the FIRST of March, the crows begin to search   166
MARRY in May, rue for aye   292
MAY chickens come cheeping   293
On SAINT Thomas the Divine kill all turkeys, geese, and
　swine   390
It is not SPRING until you can plant your foot upon
　twelve daisies   419
A SWARM in May is worth a load of hay ...   433
SWEEP the house with broom in May ...   434

caution：用心 ⇒ discretion：思慮分別；risk：危険 も見よ
Let the BUYER beware   69
The BUYER has need of a hundred eyes ...   69
Be CAREFUL what you pray for, you might get it   73
If you can't be GOOD, be careful   191
LOOK before you leap   275
MEASURE seven times, cut once   294
MEASURE twice, cut once   294
Those who PLAY at bowls must look out for rubbers   356
One STEP at a time   421
He who SUPS with the Devil should have a long spoon
　432
THINK twice, cut once   443
THREE things are not to be trusted ...   445

certainty and uncertainty：確かさと不確かさ
NOTHING is certain but death and taxes   328
NOTHING is certain but the unforeseen   328
The UNEXPECTED always happens   467

change：変化 ⇒ constancy and inconstancy：安定と不安
　定；innovation：革新 も見よ
There are no BIRDS in last year's nest   51

A CHANGE is as good as a rest   79
NEW lords, new laws   320
NOTHING is for ever   328
ONE nail drives out another   339
OTHER times, other manners   342
THREE removals are as bad as a fire   445

character ⇒ human nature：人間性

charity：慈善
CHARITY begins at home   80
CHARITY covers a multitude of sins   80
He GIVES twice who gives quickly   183
KEEP your own fish-guts for your own sea-maws   244

children：子供
Monday's CHILD is fair of face ...   82
The CHILD is the father of the man   82
CHILDREN and fools tell the truth   83
CHILDREN should be seen and not heard   83
Out of the MOUTHS of babes −   310
SPARE the rod and spoil the child   415
As the TWIG is bent, so is the tree inclined   462
It takes a whole VILLAGE to bring up a child   471

children and parents：親子 ⇒ family：家族・家系 も見よ
CHILDREN are certain cares   83
CLERGYMEN's sons always turn out badly   87
Like FATHER, like son   157
Like MOTHER, like daughter   308
PRAISE the child, and you make love to the mother   362
My SON is my son till he gets him a wife ...   412
WALNUTS and pears you plant for your heirs   474
It is a WISE child that knows its own father   487

choices：選択 ⇒ decision and indecision：決断と優柔不断
　も見よ
A DOOR must either be shut or open   126
Of two EVILS choose the less   147
MANY are called but few are chosen   290
You PAYS your money and you takes your choice   348
You cannot RUN with the hare ...   387
SMALL choice in rotten apples   408

Christianity：キリスト教
The BLOOD of the martyrs is the seed of the Church   56
The CHURCH is an anvil ...   84
The NEARER the church, the farther from God   315

circumstances：状況
There is no such thing as BAD weather ...   31
There are no BIRDS in last year's nest   51
CIRCUMSTANCES alter cases   85
CUT your coat according to your cloth   104
My HOUSE, my rules   225
No matter how long a LOG stays in the water ...   273
It is a LONG lane that has no turning   274
NEW lords, new laws   320
OTHER times, other manners   342
When in ROME, do as the Romans do   382
TIMES change and we with time   450

civility ⇒ manners：礼儀・作法；politeness：礼儀正しさ

cleanliness：清潔さ
CLEANLINESS is next to godliness   86

If every man would SWEEP his own doorstep ... 433

clothing ⇒ dress：衣服

coercion ⇒ free will and compulsion：自由意志と強制

coincidence：偶然の一致
GREAT minds think alike 198
TALK of the Devil, and he is bound to appear 438

common sense ⇒ discretion：思慮分別；prudence：思慮・
分別

company ⇒ associates：仲間；friends：友

compassion ⇒ pity：哀れみ・同情

compulsion ⇒ free will and compulsion：自由意志と強制

concealment：隠すこと・隠蔽
Those who HIDE can find 216
LOVE and a cough cannot be hid 278
MURDER will out 311
THREE may keep a secret ... 445
TRUTH lies at the bottom of a well 459
TRUTH will out 460

conduct：行ない・品行 ⇒ politeness：礼儀正しさ も見よ
CAESAR's wife must be above suspicion 70
If the CAP fits, wear it 72
EVIL communications corrupt good manners 146
What can you EXPECT from a pig but a grunt? 149
HANDSOME is as handsome does 206
One might as well be HANGED for a sheep as a lamb
207
HONESTY is the best policy 220
You can't PLEASE everyone 357
PRETTY is as pretty does 362
When in ROME, do as the Romans do 382
If the SHOE fits, wear it 400
It is ill SITTING at Rome and striving with the Pope 406

confession：告白・懺悔
CONFESS and be hanged 93
CONFESSION is good for the soul 93
A FAULT confessed is half redressed 158

conscience：良心
CONSCIENCE makes cowards of us all 94
A clean CONSCIENCE is a good pillow 93
CORPORATIONS have neither bodies to be punished ...
95
DO right and fear no man 120
He who EXCUSES, accuses himself 149
A GUILTY conscience needs no accuser 202

consequences ⇒ action and consequence：行為と結果

constancy and inconstancy：安定と不安定 ⇒ change：変
化 も見よ
A DOG is for life ... 123
The LEOPARD does not change his spots 260
LOVE me little, love me long 279
It is best to be OFF with the old love ... 334
ONCE a — , always a — 337

ONCE a priest, always a priest 337
ONCE a whore, always a whore 338
A ROLLING stone gathers no moss 381

content and discontent：満足と不満足
All's for the BEST ... 38
BETTER a dinner of herbs ... 41
BETTER are small fish ... 41
BLUE are the hills that are far away 57
If it ain't BROKE, don't fix it 65
ENOUGH is as good as a feast 140
ENOUGH is enough 140
GO further and fare worse 185
GOD's in his heaven ... 188
The GRASS is always greener ... 198
What you've never HAD you never miss 203
HALF a loaf is better than no bread 203
The HALF is better than the whole 204
If you would be HAPPY for a week take a wife ... 208
HOME is home though it's never so homely 219
HOME is where the heart is 220
LET well alone 261
There's no PLACE like home 355
Do not grieve that ROSE-TREES have thorns ... 384
SOMETHING is better than nothing 411

cooperation：協力 ⇒ assistance：援助；reciprocity：相互
扶助 も見よ
If TWO ride on a horse ... 464
It takes TWO to tango 465
One VOLUNTEER is worth two pressed men 472

corruption ⇒ bribery and corruption：賄賂と腐敗

courage：勇気 ⇒ boldness：大胆さ も見よ
BETTER to die on your feet ... 45
None but the BRAVE deserve the fair 61
BRAVE men lived before Agamemnon 61
FORTUNE favours the brave 175

cowardice：臆病
A BULLY is always a coward 66
CONSCIENCE makes cowards of us all 94
COWARDS die many times before their death 98
Don't CRY before you're hurt 101

credulity ⇒ trust and scepticism：信用と懐疑

cunning ⇒ guile：狡猾・策略

curiosity：詮索好き・好奇心
ASK no questions and hear no lies 27
CURIOSITY killed the cat 102
LAY-OVERS for meddlers 257

danger ⇒ peril：危険

death：死
Good AMERICANS when they die go to Paris 21
Every BULLET has its billet 66
Let the DEAD bury the dead 107
Blessed are the DEAD that the rain rains on 108
DEATH is the great leveller 109
DEATH pays all debts 109
You can only DIE once 116
Every ELM has its man 135

One FUNERAL makes many 179
Whom the GODS love die young 189
The GOOD die young 193
A GREEN Yule makes a fat churchyard 200
There is a REMEDY for everything except death 375
SHROUDS have no pockets 402
STONE-dead hath no fellow 425
As the TREE falls, so shall it lie 455
YOUNG men may die, but old men must die 497

deception：ごまかし ⇒ guile：狡猾・策略 も見よ
APPEARANCES are deceptive 23
FEAR the Greeks bearing gifts 158
FOOL me once, shame on you 172
The HUSBAND is always the last to know 227
In vain the NET is spread in the sight of the bird 317
PROMISES, like pie-crust, are made to be broken 364

decision and indecision：決断と優柔不断 ⇒ choices：選択
  も見よ
BETWEEN two stools one falls ... 48
The CAT would eat fish ... 77
Don't CHANGE horses in mid-stream 79
COUNCILS of war never fight 95
When in DOUBT, do nowt 126
FIRST thoughts are best 167
He who HESITATES is lost 216
If you RUN after two hares you will catch neither 386

deeds ⇒ action and inaction：行為と非行為；words and
  deeds：言動

democracy ⇒ equality：平等；rulers and ruled：支配者と
  被支配者

deserts ⇒ just deserts：当然の報い

desire ⇒ wanting and having：不足と所持

despair ⇒ hope and despair：希望と絶望

desperation ⇒ necessity：必要性・必然性

destiny ⇒ fate and fatalism：運命と運命論

destruction：破壊
It is easier to PULL down than to build up 367
Don't THROW the baby out with the bathwater 447

diet ⇒ food and drink：飲食物；health：健康

difficulties ⇒ misfortune：不運；trouble：やっかい・苦労

diligence：勤勉
Where BEES are, there is honey 36
The BUSIEST men have the most leisure 67
DILIGENCE is the mother of good luck 117
The EARLY bird catches the worm 130
EARLY to bed and early to rise ... 131
GENIUS is an infinite capacity for taking pains 181
PRACTICE makes perfect 361
There is no ROYAL road to learning 385
SEEK and ye shall find 395

disappointment：失望
BLESSED is he who expects nothing ... 53

HOPE is a good breakfast but a bad supper 222
JAM tomorrow and jam yesterday ... 239
He that LIVES in hope dances to an ill tune 272
There's MANY a slip between cup and lip 289

discipline：規律
When the CAT's away, the mice will play 76
Who won't be RULED by the rudder must be ruled by the
  rock 386
SPARE the rod and spoil the child 415

discretion：思慮分別 ⇒ caution：用心 も見よ
DISCRETION is the better part of valour 118
He who FIGHTS and runs away ... 162
LEAST said, soonest mended 258
What happens on the ROAD stays on the road 379
SEE no evil, hear no evil, speak no evil 394
A SHUT mouth catches no flies 402
THINK first and speak afterwards 442
THREE may keep a secret, if two of them are dead 445
What goes on TOUR stays on tour 454
What happens in VEGAS stays in Vegas 470
One does not WASH one's dirty linen in public 476

dishonesty ⇒ honesty and dishonesty：正直と不正直

dissimilarity ⇒ similarity and dissimilardty：類似性と相違性

division ⇒ unity and division：統一と分断

doctors：医者
An APPLE a day keeps the doctor away 24
The best DOCTORS are Dr Diet ... 121
LAUGHTER is the best medicine 255
PHYSICIAN, heal thyself 352

dreams：夢
DREAM of a funeral ... 127
DREAMS go by contraries 127
MORNING dreams come true 307

dress：衣服
There is no such thing as BAD weather ... 31
Ne'er CAST a clout till May be out 74
CLOTHES make the man 88
FINE feathers make fine birds 163
NINE tailors make a man 322

drink ⇒ food and drink：飲食物

drunkenness：酩酊
He who DRINKS beer, thinks beer 128
There is TRUTH in wine 458
When the WINE is in, the wit is out 486

eavesdroppers：盗み聞きする人
FIELDS have eyes ... 161
LISTENERS never hear any good of themselves 266
LITTLE pitchers have large ears 268
WALLS have ears 474

economy, false ⇒ meanness：けち・意地悪

education see learning 学問・学び；nature and nurture：
  生まれと育ち

efficiency and inefficiency：能率と非能率
A BAD workman blames his tools　31
Never send a BOY to do a man's Job　59
Two BOYS are half a boy ...　60
The BUSIEST men have the most leisure　67
He who CAN does ...　71
It doesn't matter if a CAT is black or white ...　75
A CAT in gloves catches no mice　75
The EARLY bird catches the worm　130
HORSES for courses　224
IDLE people have the least leisure　229
KEEP no more cats than will catch mice　243
KEEP your shop and your shop will keep you　244
What MATTERS is what works　293
Never PUT off till tomorrow what you can do today　368
If you can't RIDE two horses at once ...　378
If you would be well SERVED, serve yourself　397
A SHORT horse is soon curried　401
The SOONER begun, the sooner done　412
SPEAK softly and carry a big stick　417
TIME is money　449
He TRAVELS fastest who travels alone　455
If you WANT a thing done well, do it yourself　474
If you WANT something done, ask a busy person　475
WORK expands so as to fill the time available　493

employers and employees：雇用者と被雇用者
The EYE of a master does more work ...　151
JACK is as good as his master　238
Why KEEP a dog and bark yourself?　243
A KING's chaff is worth more than other men's corn　246
The LABOURER is worthy of his hire　252
LAST in, first out　253
Like MASTER, like man　293
NO man can serve two masters　324
NO man is a hero to his valet　324
PAY beforehand was never well served　347
If you PAY peanuts, you get monkeys　347

ends ⇒ beginnings and endings：最初と最後；finality：結末・終局

enemies：敵
If you can't BEAT them, join them　34
It is good to make a BRIDGE of gold ...　64
DIAMOND cuts diamond　115
The ENEMY of my enemy is my friend　137
When GREEK meets Greek, then comes the tug of war　200
There is no LITTLE enemy　266

Englishness ⇒ national characteristics：国民性

entertaining ⇒ hospitality：もてなし

environment：環境
When the LAST tree is cut down ...　254
THINK global, act local　443

envy ⇒ content and discontent：満足と不満足；malice：悪意・恨み

equality：平等
When ADAM delved and Eve span ...　17
A CAT may look at a king　76
DOGS look up to you ...　125

JACK is as good as his master　238
The RICH man has his ice in the summer ...　377

error：間違い・過ち
He who is ABSENT is always in the wrong　15
If ANYTHING can go wrong, it will　22
A FAULT confessed is half redressed　158
GARBAGE in, garbage out　180
It's a GOOD horse that never stumbles and a good wife that never grumbles　194
HOMER sometimes nods　220
There's MANY a slip between cup and lip　289
A MISS is as good as a mile　300
If you don't make MISTAKES you don't make anything　301

evil ⇒ good and evil：正邪

example, good and bad：好例と悪例
EVIL communications corrupt good manners　146
EXAMPLE is better than precept　147
An OUNCE of practice is worth a pound of precept　343
One PICTURE is worth ten thousand words　353
Every PICTURE tells a story　353
The ROTTEN apple injures its neighbours　385
He that TOUCHES pitch shall be defiled　453

exception ⇒ 規則

excess：過剰・過度
The LAST drop makes the cup run over　253
The LAST straw breaks the camel's back　253
You can have TOO much of a good thing　453

excuses：言い訳
A BAD excuse is better than none　29
He who EXCUSES, accuses himself　149
FINGERS were made before forks　163
IGNORANCE of the law is no excuse　234
It is easy to find a STICK to beat a dog　422

exercise ⇒ health：健康

expectation：予期・期待 ⇒ disappointment：失望；hope and despair：希望と絶望 も見よ
It is BETTER to travel hopefully ...　47
Don't CRY before you're hurt　101
While the GRASS grows, the steed starves　198
It's ILL waiting for dead men's shoes　235

expense ⇒ getting and spending：取得と消費

experience：経験
The man who has once been BITTEN by the snake ...　52
A BURNT child dreads the fire　66
You cannot CATCH old birds with chaff　77
EXPERIENCE is the best teacher　150
EXPERIENCE is the father of wisdom　150
EXPERIENCE keeps a dear school　150
The same FIRE that melts the butter hardens the egg　164
The FROG in the well knows nothing of the sea　177
LIVE and learn　269
They that LIVE longest, see most　271
ONCE bitten, twice shy　338
TRAVEL broadens the mind　455

extravagance ⇒ getting and spending：取得と消費

fair dealing：公正な取引
Give CREDIT where credit is due　99
A fair EXCHANGE is no robbery　148
All's FAIR in love and war　155
FAIR play's a jewel　154
GIVE and take is fair play　182
GIVE the Devil his due　183
Be JUST before you're generous　241
Never give a SUCKER an even break　429
TURN about is fair play　461
There are TWO sides to every question　464

faith：信念
FAITH will move mountains　155
Put your TRUST in God ...　458

faithfulness ⇒ constancy and inconstancy：安定と不安定

fame and obscurity：有名と無名
BRAVE men lived before Agamemnon　61
Until the LIONS produce their own historian ...　266
MORE people know Tom Fool ...　306

familiarity：慣れ親しみ
BETTER the devil you know ...　44
BETTER wed over the mixen ...　48
EAST is east, and west is west　131
FAMILIARITY breeds contempt　156
You should KNOW a man seven years before you stir his
　fire　248
Come LIVE with me and you'll know me　271
NO man is a hero to his valet　324
There is NOTHING new under the sun　329
A PROPHET is not without honour ...　365

family：家族・家系 ⇒ children and parents：親子 も見よ
The APPLE never falls far from the tree　24
BLOOD is thicker than water　56
BLOOD will tell　57
What's BRED in the bone ...　62
From CLOGS to clogs is only three generations　88
The FAMILY that prays together stays together　156
It takes three GENERATIONS to make a gentleman　181
KEEP your own fish-guts for your own sea-maws　244
From SHIRTSLEEVES to shirtsleeves in three generations
　400
The SHOEMAKER's son always goes barefoot　400

fashion ⇒ innovation：革新；novelty：目新しさ

fate and fatalism：運命と運命論
If you're BORN to be hanged ...　58
Every BULLET has its billet　66
One DAY honey, one day onion　106
You can only DIE once　116
Every ELM has its man　135
Whom the GODS would destroy, they first make mad　189
What GOES around comes around　190
HANGING and wiving go by destiny　208
MAN proposes, God disposes　286
MANY are called but few are chosen　290
What MUST be, must be　312
As a TREE falls, so shall it lie　455
What goes UP must come down　468

Fickleness ⇒ constancy and inconstancy：安定と不安定

fiction ⇒ reality and illusion：現実と幻想

fighting ⇒ warfare：戦争

finality：結末・終局
ALL good things must come to an end　19
The END crowns the work　136
EVERYTHING has an end　145
The OPERA isn't over till the fat lady sings　341
There is a REMEDY for everything except death　375
STONE-dead hath no fellow　425

finds ⇒ gains and losses：利益と損失

folly ⇒ fools：愚か者；stupidity：愚かさ

food and drink ⇒ health：健康；hunger：飢え・空腹
An APPLE-PIE without some cheese ...　25
An ARMY marches on its stomach　25
BETTER a dinner of herbs ...　41
A BIRD never flew on one wing　51
He who DRINKS beer, thinks beer　128
You are what you EAT　132
EAT to live, not live to eat　134
ENOUGH is as good as a feast　140
GOD sends meat, but the Devil sends cooks　187
HUNGER is the best sauce　226
MAN cannot live by bread alone　285
The WAY to a man's heart is through his stomach　478

fools：愚か者 ⇒ stupidity：愚かさ も見よ
CHILDREN and fools tell the truth　83
A FOOL may give a wise man counsel　171
FOOLS and bairns should never see half-done work　172
FOOLS ask questions that wise men cannot answer　172
FOOLS build houses and wise men live in them　173
FOOLS for luck　173
FOOLS rush in where angels fear to tread　173
FORTUNE favours fools　174
Whom the GODS would destroy, they first make mad　189
Never give a SUCKER an even break　429
YOUNG folks think old folks to be fools ...　496

foresight and hindsight：先見の明と後知恵
FOREWARNED is forearmed　174
HINDSIGHT is always twenty/twenty　217
HOPE for the best and prepare for the worst　222
NOTHING is certain but the unforeseen　328
Those who PLAY at bowls must look out for rubbers　356
PREVENTION is better than cure　363
It is too late to shut the STABLB-door after the horse has
　bolted　420
A STUMBLE may prevent a fall　428
A STICH in time saves nine　424
The UNEXPECTED always happens　467
It is easy to be WISE after the event　487

forgetfulness：物忘れ
A BELLOWING cow soon forgets her calf　37
OUT of sight, out of mind　344

forgiveness：許し・寛容
Let BYGONES be bygones　69

CHARITY covers a multitude of sins 80
To ERR is human ... 141
To KNOW all is to forgive all 248
OFFENDERS never pardon 335
Never let the SUN go down on your anger 431

fortune ⇒ good fortune：幸運；misfortune：不運

free will and compulsion：自由意志と強制
He that COMPLIES against his will ... 92
FREEDOM is not free 176
You can take a HORSE to the water ... 223
One VOLUNTEER is worth two pressed men freedom 472

friends：友 ⇒ associates：仲間 も見よ
The BEST of friends must part 39
The COMPANY makes the feast 92
The ENEMY of my enemy is my friend 137
A FRIEND in need is a friend indeed 177
You should KNOW a man seven years before you stir his fire 248
LEND your money and lose your friend 259
SAVE us from our friends 391
TWO is company, but three is none 464

futility：無益 ⇒ possibility and impossibility：可能性と不可能性 も見よ
In vain the NET is spread in the sight of the bird 317
It is too late to shut the STABLE-door after the horse has bolted 420
A STERN chase is a long chase 422
SUE a beggar and catch a louse 430

future：未来
COMING events cast their shadows before 91
He that FOLLOWS freits, freits will follow him 170
LONG foretold, long last ... 274
NEVER is a long time 318
NEVER say never 319
TIME will tell 450
TODAY you; tomorrow me 451
TOMORROW is another day 451
TOMORROW never comes 452

gains and losses：利益と損失 ⇒ winners and losers：勝者と敗者 も見よ
BLESSINGS brighten as they take their flight 54
FINDERS keepers ... 162
FINDINGS keepings 161
All is FISH that comes to the net 169
All is GRIST that comes to the mill 201
What you've never HAD you never miss 203
One man's LOSS is another man's gain 277
There's no great LOSS without some gain 277
SAFE bind, safe find 388
A SLICE off a cut loaf isn't missed 407
If you don't SPECULATE, you can't accumulate 418

garden lore：庭にまつわる伝承 ⇒ weather lore：天気にまつわる伝承 も見よ
CANDLEMAS day, put beans in the clay ... 71
A CHERRY year, a merry year ... 82
If you would be HAPPY for a week take a wife ... 208
ONE for the mouse, one for the crow ... 339
ONE year's seeding makes seven years' weeding 340

PARSLEY seed goes nine times to the Devil 346
SOW dry and set wet 413

gentleness：優しさ
EASY does it 132
FAIR and softly goes far in a day 154
With a SWEET tongue and kindness ... 413

gentry：紳士階級
When ADAM delved ... 17
It takes three GENERATIONS to make a gentleman 181

getting and spending：取得と消費 ⇒ money：金・金銭；thrift：質素倹約 も見よ
EASY come, easy go 132
What is GOT over the Devil's back is spent under his belly 197
LIGHT come, light go 264
QUICKLY come, quickly go 371
SPARE at the spigot ... 415
A WOMAN and a ship ever want mending 489

giving and receiving：授受
It is BETTER to give than to receive 45
FEAR the Greeks bearing gifts 158
Never look a GIFT horse in the mouth 182
GIVE a thing, and take a thing ... 183
He GIVES twice who gives quickly 183

good and evil：正邪
Never BID the Devil good morrow ... 48
The DEVIL can quote Scripture for his own ends 111
Why should the DEVIL have all the best tunes? 112
The DEVIL is not so black ... 113
EVIL communications corrupt good manners 146
Never do EVIL that good may come of it 148
EVIL to him who evil thinks 147
Where GOD builds a church, the Devil will build a chapel 186
The GOOD die young 193
GOOD men are scarce 195
The GREATER the sinner, the greater the saint 199
IDLENESS is the root of all evil 230
ILL weeds grow apace 235
MONEY is the root of all evil 303
NOTHING so bad but it might have been worse 329
It is easier to RAISE the Devil than to lay him 373
No ROSE without a thorn 384
SEE no evil, hear no evil, speak no evil 394
SUFFICIENT unto the day is the evil thereof 430
TWO blacks don't make a white 462
TWO wrongs don't make a right 466
YOUNG saint, old devil 497

good fortune：幸運 ⇒ blessings：恵み・(神の)恩恵
Set a BEGGAR on horseback ... 36
The DEVIL looks after his own 113
FULL cup, steady hand 178
Call no man HAPPY till he dies 209
A RISING tide lifts all boats 379
TAKE the goods the gods provide 436
All's WELL that ends well 481

good things：よいもの
ALL good things must come to an end 19
The BEST is the enemy of the good 38

The BEST things in life are free　40
The GOOD is the enemy of the best　195
One STORY is good till another is told　425
You can have TOO much of a good thing　453

government ⇒ politics：政治；rulers and ruled：支配者と
　被支配者

gratitude and ingratitude：感謝と忘恩
Feed a DOG for three days …　121
Never look a GIFT horse in the mouth　182
You never MISS the water till the well runs dry　300
Do not throw PEARLS to swine　349

great and small：大小
The BEST things come in small packages　39
BIG fish eat little fish　49
BIG fleas have little fleas …　49
The BIGGER they are …　50
The DEVIL is in the details　112
DOGS bark, but the caravan goes on　124
EAGLES don't catch flies　130
EVERY little helps　142
GREAT oaks from little acorns grow　199
LITTLE fish are sweet　267
LITTLE leaks sink the ship　267
A LITTLE pot is soon hot　268
LITTLE strokes fell great oaks　268
LITTLE thieves are hanged …　269
LITTLE things please little minds　269
A LIVE dog is better than a dead lion　271
MANY a little makes a mickle　288
MANY a mickle makes a muckle　289
The MOTHER of mischief is no bigger than a midge's
　wing　308
A MOUSE may help a lion　309
PROVIDENCE is always on the side of the big battalions
　366
You cannot get a QUART into a pint pot　370
A REED before the wind lives on …　375
SMALL is beautiful　409
When SPIDER webs unite, they can tie up a lion　419
From the SUBLIME to the ridiculous is only a step　428
The SUN loses nothing by shining into a puddle　431
THINK global, act local　443
For WANT of a nail the shoe was lost …　475

greed：貪欲
The MORE you get, the more you want　307
MUCH would have more　310
The SEA refuses no river　393

guile：狡猾・策略 ⇒ deception：ごまかし も見よ
A CLEVER hawk hides its claws　87
An old POACHER makes the best gamekeeper　357
SOFTLY, softly, catchee monkey　410
Set a THIEF to catch a thief　440

guilt ⇒ conscience：良心

gullibility ⇒ trust and scepticism：信用と懐疑

habit：習慣
What's BRED in the bone …　62
The DOG returns to its vomit　123
OLD habits die hard　335

You cannot SHIFT an old tree without it dying　398
SOW an act, and you reap a habit　414
You can't TEACH an old dog new tricks　439

happiness：幸福
If you would be HAPPY for a week take a wife …　208
Call no man HAPPY till he dies　209
MONEY can't buy happiness　302
It is a POOR heart that never rejoices　358

harmony and disharmony：調和と不調和
BIRDS in their little nests agree　51
A DEAF husband and a blind wife …　109
EAST is east, and west is west　129
GOOD fences make good neighbours　193
GREAT minds think alike　198

haste：性急
HASTE is from the Devil　210
More HASTE, less speed　210
HASTE makes waste　211
Make HASTE slowly　211
MARRY in haste and repent at leisure　292
NOTHING should be done in haste but gripping a flea
　329
It is the PACE that kills　345
ROME was not built in a day　382

hatred ⇒ malice：悪意・恨み

health：健康
AFTER dinner rest a while …　19
An APPLE a day keeps the doctor away　24
The CITY for wealth …　85
The best DOCTORS are Dr Diet …　121
EARLY to bed and early to rise …　131
We must EAT a peck of dirt before we die　134
FEED a cold and starve a fever　160
One HOUR's sleep before midnight is worth two after
　225
LAUGHTER is the best medicine　255
There is NOTHING so good for the inside of a man …
　330
SIX hours' sleep for a man …　406

help ⇒ assistance：援助；reciprocity：相互扶助

heredity ⇒ family：家族・家系

hindsight ⇒ foresight and hindsight：先見の明と後知恵

hints：ヒント・暗示
A NOD's as good as a wink …　326
STRAWS tell which way the wind blows　426
A WORD to the wise is enough　492

history：歴史 ⇒ past：過去・過ぎ去った も見よ
Happy is the COUNTRY which has no history　96
HISTORY repeats itself　218
HISTORY is written by the victors　218
Until the LIONS produce their own historian …　266

holidays ⇒ recreation：気晴らし

home：家庭・母国
CHARITY begins at home　80

Every COCK will crow upon his own dunghill   90
EAST, west, home's best   132
An ENGLISHMAN's house is his castle   139
FOOLS build houses and wise men live in them   174
GO abroad and you'll hear news of home   185
HOME is home though it's never so homely   219
HOME is where the heart is   220
There's no PLACE like home   355
A WOMAN's place is in the home   490

honesty and dishonesty：正直と不正直
The DEVIL makes his Christmas pies of lawyers' tongues
   ...   113
HONESTY is the best policy   220
The more LAWS, the more thieves and bandits   256
OPPORTUNITY makes a thief   341
It's a SIN to steal a pin   404
When THIEVES fall out, honest men come by their own
   441

honour：尊敬・名誉
An ENGLISHMAN's word is his bond   140
There is HONOUR among thieves   221
The post of HONOUR is the post of danger   221
Where MACGREGOR sits is the head of the table   283
A PROPHET is not without honour ...   365

hope and despair：希望と絶望 ⇒ disappointment：失望；
   optimism：楽観主義 も見よ
Be CAREFUL what you pray for, you might get it   73
The DARKEST hour is just before the dawn   105
Whosoever DRAWS his sword against the prince ...   127
A DROWNING man will clutch at a straw   129
HOPE deferred makes the heart sick   222
HOPE is a good breakfast but a bad supper   222
HOPE springs eternal   223
If it were not for HOPE, the heart would break   223
He that LIVES in hope dances to an ill tune   272

horse lore：馬にまつわる伝承
A GOOD horse cannot be of a bad colour   194
NO foot, no horse   323
One WHITE foot, buy him ...   483

hospitality：もてなし
The COMPANY makes the feast   92
FISH and guests smell after three days   168
It is MERRY in hall when beards wag all   297
The MORE the merrier   306

houses ⇒ home：家庭・母国

human nature：人間性 ⇒ nature and nurture：生まれと
   育ち も見よ
An APE's an ape, a varlet's a varlet ...   23
BEAUTY is only skin-deep   35
The BEST of men are but men at best   39
BIRDS of a feather flock together   52
BOYS will be boys   60
What's BRED in the bone ...   62
A CARPENTER is known by his chips   74
The CHILD is the father to the man   82
The DOG returns to its vomit   123
What can you EXPECT from a pig but a grunt?   149
EXTREMES meet   151
The HIGHER the monkey climbs ...   217

KNOW thyself   249
The LEOPARD does not change his spots   260
MAN is the measure of all things   286
Because a MAN is born in a stable ...   287
ONCE a － , always a －   337
A ROLLING stone gathers no moss   381
SCRATCH a Russian and you find a Tartar   392
The STYLE is the man   428
The TREE is known by its fruit   456
As the TWIG is bent, so is the tree inclined   462
YORKSHIRE born and Yorkshire bred ...   496
YOUNG saint, old devil   497

hunger：飢え・空腹 ⇒ food and drink：飲食物
APPETITE comes with eating   24
EMPTY sacks will never stand upright   136
It's ill speaking between a FULL man and a fasting   178
GOD never sends mouths but He sends meat   187
HUNGER drives the wolf out of the wood   226
HUNGER is the best sauce   226
A HUNGRY man is an angry man   230

husbands ⇒ wives and husbands：夫婦

hypocrisy：偽善
The DEVIL can quote Scripture for his own ends   111
The DEVIL was sick, the Devil a saint would be ...   114
DO as I say, not as I do   120
FINE words butter no parsnips   163
Those who live in GLASS houses ...   184

idiosyncrasy：特異性・性癖
There is no ACCOUNTING for tastes   16
It takes ALL sorts to make a world   20
EVERY man to his taste   142
Every LAND has its own law   252
One man's MEAT is another man's poison   295
So many MEN, so many opinions   296
There's NOWT so queer as folk   331
There is REASON in the roasting of eggs
He that would go to SEA for pleasure ...   393
The STYLE is the man   428
TASTES differ   438

idleness：怠惰
As good be an ADDLED egg as an idle bird   17
It is as CHEAP sitting as standing   81
The DEVIL finds work for idle hands ...   112
An IDLE brain is the Devil's workshop   229
IDLE people have the least leisure   229
IDLENESS is the root of all evil   230
If you won't WORK you shan't eat   493

ignorance：無知・無学
There's none so BLIND ...   54
When the BLIND lead the blind ...   55
In the COUNTRY of the blind ...   96
What the EYE doesn't see ...   151
The FAT man knoweth not what the lean thinketh   157
FOOLS rush in where angels fear to tread   173
The FROG in the well knows nothing of the sea   177
One HALF of the world does not know how the other half
   lives   198
Where IGNORANCE is bliss ...   233
IGNORANCE of the law is no excuse   234
What you don't KNOW can't hurt you   249

A LITTLE knowledge is a dangerous thing 267
NOTHING so bold as a blind mare 330
A SLICE off a cut loaf isn't missed 407

illusion ⇒ reality and illusion：現実と幻想

illustration：例示
One PICTURE is worth ten thousand words 353
Every PICTURE tells a story 353

imitation：模倣
IMITATION is the sincerest form of flattery 236
What MANCHESTER says today ... 287
MONKEY see, monkey do 305

impatience ⇒ patience and impatience：忍耐と性急

impossibility ⇒ possibility and impossibility：可能性と不
可能性

improvement：改善
It is NEVER too late to mend 319
NEW brooms sweep clean 320
You can't put NEW wine in old bottles 321
When THINGS are at the worst they begin to mend 442

inconstancy ⇒ constancy and inconstancy：安定と不安定

indecision ⇒ decision and indecision：決断と優柔不断

independence：独立・自立
GOD is high above, and the tsar is far away 186
Every HERRING must hang by its own gill 216
The MOUNTAINS are high, and the emperor is far away
  309
He TRAVELS fastest who travels alone 455
Every TUB must stand on its own bottom 460

industriousness ⇒ diligence：勤勉

ingratitude ⇒ gratitude and ingratitude：感謝と忘恩

injustice ⇒ justice and injustice：正義と不正義

innovation：革新 ⇒ change：変化；novelty：目新しさ も見
よ
NEW brooms sweep clean 320
What is NEW cannot be true 320
You can't put NEW wine in old bottles 321
You can't TEACH an old dog new tricks 439
Don't THROW out your dirty water ... 446
TIMES change and we with time 450
TURKEY, heresy, hops, and beer came into England all in
  one year 461

intentions：意図
The BEST-laid schemes ... gang aft agley 39
The ROAD to hell is paved with good intentions 379

interference ⇒ busybodies：おせっかい屋

intimacy ⇒ familiarity：慣れ親しみ

just deserts：当然の報い ⇒ retribution：天罰・報復；re-
venge：復讐
Good AMERICANS when they die go to Paris 21

None but the BRAVE deserve the fair 61
Give CREDIT where credit is due 99
No GOOD deed goes unpunished 193
NO cure, no pay 323
NO penny, no paternoster 326
VIRTUE is its own reward 471

justice and injustice：正義と不正義 ⇒ fair dealing：公正な
  取引；law and lawyers：法と法律家 も見よ
JUSTICE delayed is justice denied 242
KINGS have long arms 247
One LAW for the rich and another for the poor 256
LITTLE thieves are hanged ... 269
MIGHT is right 298
The MILLS of God grind slowly ... 299

justification ⇒ excuses：言い訳

knowledge ⇒ learning：学問・学び

lateness：遅れ
BETTER late than never 43
It is NEVER too late to learn 319
It is NEVER too late to mend 319
It is too late to shut the STABLE-door after the horse has
  bolted 420

laughter ⇒ merriment：談笑・陽気な賑わい

law and lawyers：法と法律家
The DEVIL makes his Christmas pies of lawyers' tongues
  ... 113
HARD cases make bad law 209
HOME is home, as the Devil said ... 219
IGNORANCE of the law is no excuse 234
No one should be JUDGE in his own cause 241
One LAW for the rich and another for the poor 256
The more LAWS, the more thieves and bandits 256
A man who is his own LAWYER has a fool for a client
  257
SUE a beggar and catch a louse 430

laziness ⇒ idleness：怠惰

learning：学問・学び
LEARNING is better than house and land 258
A LITTLE knowledge is a dangerous thing 267
It is NEVER too late to learn 319
NEVER too old to learn 319
There is no ROYAL road to learning 385

lending ⇒ borrowing and lending：貸し借り

lies ⇒ lying：嘘をつくこと

life：人生
ART is long and life is short 26
EAT, drink, and be merry ... 133
LIFE begins at forty 262
LIFE isn't all beer and skittles 263
While there's LIFE there's hope 263
A LIVE dog is better than a dead lion 271
He LIVES long who lives well 272
MAN cannot live by bread alone 285

loans ⇒ borrowing and lending：貸し借り

long-windedness ⇒ brevity and long-windedness：簡潔
と冗漫

losers ⇒ winners and losers：勝者と敗者

loss ⇒ gains and losses：利益と損失

love：愛・恋愛 ⇒ marriage：結婚 も見よ
ABSENCE makes the heart grow fonder　15
BEAUTY is in the eye of the beholder　35
BETTER be an old man's darling ...　41
COLD hands, warm heart　90
FAINT heart never won fair lady　154
All's FAIR in love and war　154
JOVE but laughs at lovers' perjury　240
LOVE and a cough cannot be hid　278
One cannot LOVE and be wise　278
LOVE is blind　278
LOVE laughs at locksmiths　279
LOVE makes the world go round　279
LOVE me little, love me long　279
LOVE me, love my dog　280
LOVE will find a way　280
LUCKY at cards, unlucky in love　281
It is best to be OFF with the old love ...　334
PITY is akin to love　355
The QUARREL of lovers is the renewing of love　370

love, blighted：くじかれた愛
BETTER to have loved and lost ...　46
The COURSE of true love never did run smooth　97
There are as good FISH in the sea as ever came out of it
　168
HELL hath no fury like a woman scorned　215
There is always one who KISSES ...　247
When POVERTY comes in at the door ...　360

love, prosperous：順調な (恋) 愛
When the FURZE is in bloom, my love's in tune　179
When the GORSE is out of bloom, kissing' s out of fashion
　197

luck：幸運・運
It is BETTER to be born lucky than rich　45
If you're BORN to be hanged ...　58
The BREAD never falls ...　61
The DEVIL' s children have the Devil's luck　114
DILIGENCE is the mother of good luck　117
FOOLS for luck　173
FORTUNE favours fools　174
FORTUNE favours the brave　175
If you can't be GOOD, be lucky　192
There is LUCK in odd numbers　281
LUCKY at cards, unlucky in love　281
MARRIAGE is a lottery　291
See a PIN and pick It up ...　353
THIRD time lucky　443

lying：嘘をつくこと
ASK no questions and hear no lies　27
HALF the truth is often a whole lie　204
A LIAR ought to have a good memory　261

malice：悪意・恨み
BETTER a dinner of herbs ...　41
CURSES, like chickens, come home to roost　102

Don't CUT off your nose to spite your face　103
Throw DIRT enough, and some will stick　117
DOGS bark, but the caravan goes on　124
HARD words break no bones　209
HELL hath no fury like a woman scorned　215
There is no LITTLE enemy　266
MISERY loves company　299
STICKS and stones may break my bones ...　422
Never let the SUN go down on your anger　431
Never tell TALES out of school　437

manners：礼儀・作法
CHILDREN should be seen and not heard　83
CIVILITY costs nothing　86
EVIL communications corrupt good manners　146
FINGERS were made before forks　163
MANNERS maketh man　288

marriage：結婚 ⇒ love：愛・恋愛；weddings：結婚式；wives
　and husbands も見よ
BETTER one house spoiled than two　43
BETTER to marry than to burn　46
BETTER wed over the mixen ...　48
CHANGE the name and not the letter ...　79
Why buy a COW when milk is so cheap?　97
A DEAF husband and a blind wife ...　109
The GREY mare is the better horse　201
HANGING and wiving go by destiny　208
MARRIAGE is a lottery　291
There goes more to MARRIAGE than four bare legs in a
　bed　291
MARRIAGES are made in heaven　291
Never MARRY for money, but marry where money is　291
MARRY in haste and repent at leisure　292
MARRY in May, rue for aye　292
NEEDLES and pins, ... when a man marries, his trouble
　begins　316
WEDLOCK is a padlock　480
Happy's the WOOING that is not long a-doing　491
A YOUNG man married is a young man marred　497

marvels：不思議
The age of MIRACLES is past　299
WONDERS will never cease　491

masters and servants ⇒ employers and employees：雇
　用者と被雇用者

meanness：けち・意地悪
PENNY wise and pound foolish　351
Do not spoil the SHIP for a ha'porth of tar　399

means ⇒ ways and means：方法と手段

men and women：男女 ⇒ marriage：結婚；wives and
　husbands も見よ
Every JACK has his Jill　238
A MAN is as old as he feels ...　285
What's SAUCE for the goose is sauce for the gander　390

merriment：談笑・陽気な賑わい
LAUGH and the world laughs with you ...　254
LAUGHTER is the best medicine　255
It is MERRY in hall when beards wag all　297
The MORE the merrier　306
SING before breakfast, cry before night　405

methods ⇒ ways and means：方法と手段

middle age：中年
A FOOL at forty is a fool indeed　171
LIFE begins at forty　262

mischief ⇒ good and evil：正邪；wrong-doers：悪事をなす者

misfortune：不運 ⇒ trouble：やっかい・苦労 も見よ
ACCIDENTS will happen ...　16
ADVERSITY makes strange bedfellows　18
If ANYTHING can go wrong, it will　22
BAD news travels fast　30
BAD things come in threes　31
The BIGGER they are ...　50
The BLEATING of the kid excites the tiger　53
The BREAD never falls ...　61
CROSSES are ladders that lead to heaven　100
It is no use CRYING over spilt milk　101
It's an ILL wind that blows nobody any good　235
LIGHTNING never strikes the same place twice　264
MAY chickens come cheeping　293
Do not MEET troubles halfway　296
MISERY loves company　299
MISFORTUNES never come singly　300
NO cross, no crown　323
The PITCHER will go to the well once too often　354
It never RAINS but it pours　373
Help you to SALT, help you to sorrow　390
The SHARPER the storm, the sooner it's over　398
Many go out for WOOL and come home shorn　491

mistakes ⇒ error：間違い・過ち

moderation：節度・中庸
ENOUGH is enough　140
The HALF is better than the whole　204
LESS is more　260
There is MEASURE in all things　295
MODERATION in all things　301

money：金・金銭 ⇒ getting and spending：取得と消費；just deserts：当然の報い も見よ
BAD money drives out good　29
The BEST things in life are free　40
A FOOL and his money are soon parted　170
You cannot serve GOD and Mammon　185
GOLD may be bought too dear　191
A GOLDEN key can open any door　191
KEEP your shop and your shop will keep you　244
The LABOURER is worthy of his hire　252
When the LAST tree is cut down, ... you will realize that you cannot eat money　254
Never MARRY for money, but marry where money is　291
MONEY can't buy happiness　302
MONEY has no smell　302
MONEY isn't everything　302
MONEY is power　303
MONEY is the root of all evil　303
MONEY, like manure, does no good till it is spread　303
MONEY makes a man　304
MONEY makes money　304
MONEY makes the mare to go　304
MONEY talks　305

Where there's MUCK there's brass　311
He that cannot PAY, let him pray　347
If you PAY peanuts, you get monkeys　347
He who PAYS the piper calls the tune　348
You PAYS your money and you takes your choice　348
Take care of the PENCE ...　350
SHROUDS have no pockets　402
SPEAK not of my debts unless you mean to pay them　417

mortality：死すべき運命
ART is long and life is short　26
A CREAKING door hangs longest　98
We must EAT a peck of dirt before we die　133
THREATENED men live long　444

murder ⇒ violence：暴力

national characteristics：国民性
ENGLAND is the paradise of women ...　138
The ENGLISH are a nation of shopkeepers　139
One ENGLISHMAN can beat three Frenchmen　139
An ENGLISHMAN's house is his castle　139
An ENGLISHMAN's word is his bond　140
The only GOOD Indian is a dead Indian　194
When GREEK meets Greek ...　200
Every LAND has its own law　252
A NATION without a language is a nation without a heart　313
SCRATCH a Russian and you find a Tartar　392

Nature：自然・造物主
You can DRIVE out Nature with a pitchfork ...　128
GOD made the country, and man made the town　187
NATURE abhors a vacuum　314
SELF-preservation is the first law of nature　396

nature and nurture：生まれと育ち ⇒ human nature：人間性 も見よ
An APE's an ape, a varlet's a varlet ...　23
The APPLE never falls far from the tree　24
You can take the BOY out of the country ...　59
As the TWIG is bent, so is the tree inclined　462

necessity：必要性・必然性 ⇒ pragmatism：実用主義 も見よ
ANY port in a storm　20
BEGGARS can't be choosers　36
DESPERATE diseases must have desperate remedies　111
DIRTY water will quench fire　118
When all FRUIT fails, welcome haws　178
When all you have is a HAMMER ...　205
HUNGER drives the wolf out of the wood　226
MAN's extremity is God's opportunity　286
If the MOUNTAIN will not come to Mahomet ...　308
NECESSITY is the mother of invention　316
NECESSITY knows no law　316
NEEDS must when the Devil drives　317
Beware of an OAK, it draws the stroke ...　333
Who SAYS A must say B　391
SMALL choice in rotten apples　408
YOUNG men may die, but old men must die　497

neighbours：隣人
GOOD fences make good neighbours　193
What a NEIGHBOUR gets is not lost　317

news：知らせ
BAD news travels fast　30
GO abroad and you'll hear news of home　185
NO news is good news　325

novelty：目新しさ
BETTER be out of the world ...　43
There is always something NEW out of Africa　321
There is NOTHING new under the sun　329
One STORY is good till another is told　425
VARIETY is the spice of life　470

obedience：従順・服従
The FIRST duty of a soldier is obedience　165
He that cannot OBEY cannot command　334
OBEY orders if you break owners　334

obscurity ⇒ fame and obscurity：有名と無名

observation：観察
FOUR eyes see more than two　175
LOOKERS-ON see most of the game　275

obstinacy：頑固さ
Little BIRDS that can sing and won't sing ...　52
There's none so BLIND ...　54
He that will to CUPAR maun to Cupar　101
There's none so DEAF ...　109
If the MOUNTAIN will not come to Mahomet ...　308
SUSSEX won't be druv　432
A WILFUL man must have his way　484

old age：老年
BETTER to wear out than to rust out　47
A CREAKING door hangs longest　98
There's no FOOL like an old fool　171
When all FRUIT fails, welcome haws　178
The GODS send nuts to those who have no teeth　189
There's many a GOOD tune played on an old fiddle　195
They that LIVE longest, see most　271
A MAN is as old as he feels ...　285
NEVER too old to learn　319
An OLD man is twice a child　335
OLD soldiers never die　336
You cannot SHIFT an old tree without it dying　398
You can't TEACH an old dog new tricks　439
YOUNG folks think old folks to be fools ...　496
YOUNG men may die, but old men must die　497
If YOUTH knew, if age could　498

omens：前兆 ⇒ superstition：迷信 も見よ
He that FOLLOWS freits, freits will follow him　170
ONE for sorrow, two for mirth ...　342
STRAWS tell which way the wind blows　426
One SWALLOW does not make a summer　432

opinions：意見
What MANCHESTER says today ...　287
So many MEN, so many opinions　296
THOUGHT is free　444

opportunity：機会・好機
EAT, drink, and be merry ...　133
ENGLAND's difficulty is Ireland's opportunity　138
All is FISH that comes to the net　169
All is GRIST that comes to the mill　201

MAN's extremity is God's opportunity　286
When ONE door shuts, another opens　338
OPPORTUNITY never knocks twice ...　342
STRIKE while the iron is hot　427
TAKE the goods the gods provide　436
There is a TIME and place for everything　448
TIME and tide wait for no man　448
There Is a TIME for everything　448
No TIME like the present　450
YOUTH must be served　498

opportunity, missed：逃した機会
A BLEATING sheep loses a bite　53
The GODS send nuts to those who have no teeth　189
The MILL cannot grind with the water that is past　298
He that WILL not when he may, when he will he shall
　have nay　484

opportunity, taken：得られた機会
ADVENTURES are to the adventurous　18
When the CAT'S away, the mice will play　76
Every DOG has his day　122
When the GOING gets tough, the tough get going　190
MAKE hay while the sun shines　284
NATURE abhors a vacuum　314
OPPORTUNITY makes a thief　341
A POSTERN door makes a thief　359
While TWO dogs are fighting for a bone ...　463

opposites：両極
EAST is east, and west is west　131
EXTREMES meet　151
From the SWEETEST wine, the tartest vinegar　434

optimism：楽観主義
All's for the BEST ...　38
It is BETTER to travel hopefully ...　47
Every CLOUD has a silver lining　89
Don't COUNT your chickens ...　95
While there's LIFE there's hope　263
NOTHING so bad but it might have been worse　329
Don't SELL the skin till you have caught the bear　396
When THINGS are at the worst they begin to mend　442
If you can WALK you can dance ...　473

orderliness：整然としていること
FIRST come, first served　165
FIRST things first　167
A PLACE for everything, and everything in its place　355
There is a TIME and place for everything　448

origins：起源・生まれ
The APPLE never falls far from the tree　24
You can take the BOY out of the country ...　59
Because a MAN is born in a stable ...　287

past：過去・過ぎ去った ⇒ history：歴史 も見よ
Let BYGONES be bygones　69
It is no use CRYING over spilt milk　101
What's DONE cannot be undone　125
The MILL cannot grind with the water that is past　298
OLD sins cast long shadows　336
OTHER times, other manners　342
Things PAST cannot be recalled　346

patience and impatience：忍耐と性急

ALL things come to those who wait 20
BEAR and forbear 34
What can't be CURED must be endured 102
HASTE is from the Devil 210
More HASTE, less speed 210
HASTE makes waste 209
Make HASTE slowly 211
HURRY no man's cattle 227
The LONGEST way round is the shortest way home 274
There is LUCK in leisure 281
NOTHING should be done in haste but gripping a flea 329
PATIENCE is a virtue 346
Don't PUT the cart before the horse 368
REVENGE is a dish that can be eaten cold 415
ROME was not built in a day 382
If you SIT by the river for long enough ... 405
SLOW and steady wins the race 408
SLOW but sure 408
SOFTLY, softly, catchee monkey 410
One STEP at a time 421
We must learn to WALK before we can run 473
A WATCHED pot never boils 477

peace：平和
AFTER a storm comes a calm 18
If you want PEACE, you must prepare for war 349

peril：危険
Don't HALLOO till you are out of the wood 205
The post of HONOUR is the post of danger 221
If you PLAY with fire you get burnt 356
He who RIDES a tiger is afraid to dismount 378
He who SUPS with the Devil should have a long spoon 432
THREATENED men live long 444

perseverance：我慢強さ ⇒ persistence：ねばり強さ も見よ
Be the DAY weary or be the day long ... 106
It's DOGGED as does it 124
FALL down seven times ... 155
IN for a penny, in for a pound 236
It is a LONG lane that has no turning 274
Put a STOUT heart to a stey brae 426
If at first you don't SUCCEED ... 429
It is idle to SWALLOW the cow ... 433
The THIRD time pays for all 444

persistence：ねばり強さ ⇒ perseverance：我慢強さ も見よ
CONSTANT dropping wears away a stone 94
You can DRIVE out Nature with a pitchfork ... 128
ONCE a － . always a － 337
The PITCHER will go to the well once too often 354
A STERN chase is a long chase 422
The TONGUE always returns to the sore tooth 452
Where there's a WILL, there's a way 485

persuasion：説得 ⇒ tact：機転；words and deeds：言動 も見よ
EXAMPLE is better than precept 147
An OUNCE of practice is worth a pound of precept 343
The PEN is mightier than the sword 350

pity：哀れみ・同情
BETTER be envied than pitied 42
PITY is akin to love 355

politeness：礼儀正しさ
A CIVIL question deserves a civil answer 86
CIVILITY costs nothing 86
HONEY catches more flies than vinegar 221
There is NOTHING lost by civility 328
PUNCTUALITY is the politeness of princes 367

politics：政治
ENGLAND's difficulty is Ireland's opportunity 138
When the GOING gets tough, the tough get going 190
If you don't like the HEAT, get out of the kitchen 214
POLITICS makes strange bedfellows 358
REVOLUTIONS are not made with rose-water 377
The VOICE of the people is the voice of God 472

possessions ⇒ property：財産

possibility and impossibility：可能性と不可能性
ALL things are possible with God 20
You cannot get BLOOD from a stone 55
You cannot make BRICKS without straw 63
The DIFFICULT is done at once ... 116
You cannot HAVE your cake and eat it 212
Whatever MAN has done, man may do 285
You cannot get a QUART into a pint pot 370
You can't make a SILK purse out of a saw's ear 404
If the SKY falls we shall catch larks 407
A SOW may whistle, though it has an ill mouth for it 414
If you can WALK you can dance ... 473

poverty：貧困
ADVERSITY makes strange bedfellows 18
BEGGARS can't be choosers 36
From CLOGS to clogs is only three generations 88
CUT your coat according to your cloth 104
EMPTY sacks will never stand upright 136
A MONEYLESS man goes fast through the market 305
He that cannot PAY, let him pray 347
When POVERTY comes in at the door ... 360
POVERTY is no disgrace ... 360
POVERTY is not a crime 360
The RICH man has his ice in the summer ... 377
From SHIRTSLEEVES to shirtsleeves in three generations 400
Many go out for WOOL and come home shorn 491

power：力・権力
DIVIDE and rule 119
GOD is high above, and the tsar is far away 186
KINGS have long arms 247
KNOWLEDGE is power 250
MIGHT is right 298
MONEY is power 303
MONEY talks 305
The MOUNTAINS are high, and the emperor is faraway 309
POWER corrupts 361
SPEAK softly and carry a big stick 417
The VOICE of the people is the voice of God 472

pragmatism：実用主義 ⇒ necessity：必要性・必然性
The BEST of men are but men at best 39
It doesn't matter if a CAT is black or white ... 75
If you have to LIVE in the river, it is best to be friends with the crocodile 270

You cannot make an OMELETTE without breaking eggs
337

pride：誇り・うぬぼれ
Set a BEGGAR on horseback ... 36
Where MACGREGOR sits is the head of the table 283
The NAIL that sticks up gets hammered down 313
PRIDE feels no pain 363
PRIDE goes before a fall 364
Up like a ROKCET ... 381

procrastination：先延ばし
DELAYS are dangerous 110
There is LUCK in leisure 281
PROCRASTINATION is the thief of time 364
Never PUT off till tomorrow what you can do today 368
TOMORROW never comes 452

professions ⇒ trades and skills：職業と技術

property：財産
You BUY land, you buy stones ... 68
What you HAVE, hold 212
LEARNING is better than house and land 258
POSSESSION is nine points of the law 359

prosperity ⇒ good fortune：幸運

providence：(神の) 摂理
GOD helps them that help themselves 186
GOD makes the back to the burden 187
GOD never sends mouths but He sends meat 187
GOD tempers the wind to the shorn lamb 188
HEAVEN protects children, sailors, and drunken men
214
MAN proposes, God disposes 286
PROVIDENCE is always on the side of the big battalions
366
TRUST in God but tie your camel 458

prudence：思慮・分別 ⇒ caution：用心；thrift：質素倹約
It is BEST to be on the safe side 40
BETTER be safe than sorry 43
A BIRD in the hand ... 50
DISCRETION is the better part of valour 118
Don't put all your EGGS in one basket 135
FOREWARNED is forearmed 174
FULL cup, steady hand 178
One HAND for yourself and one for the ship 205
When you are in a HOLE, stop digging 219
JOUK and let the jaw go by 239
If you want PEACE, you must prepare for war 349
PREVENTION is better than cure 363
It is easier to RAISE the Devil ... 373
SECOND thoughts are best 393
It is ill SITTING at Rome and striving with the Pope 406
A STICH in time saves nine 424
A STUMBLE may prevent a fall 428
Don't THROW out your dirty water ... 446
Don't THROW the baby out with the bathwater 447
Put your TRUST in God, and keep your powder dry 458
Don't go near the WATER until you learn how to swim
477

public opinion：世論 ⇒ reputation：評判
COMMON fame is seldom to blame 91

What EVERYBODY says must be true 145
What MANCHESTER says today ... 287
No SMOKE without fire 409
Everyone SPEAKS well of the bridge which carries him
over 417

public relations：広報・宣伝活動
GOOD wine needs no bush 196
You can't PLEASE everyone 357
Any PUBLICITY is good publicity 366

punctuality：時間厳守
FIRST up, best dressed 167
PUNCTUAUTY is the politeness of princes 367
PUNCTUAUTY is the soul of business 367
SHORT reckonings make long friends 401

quarrelsomeness：口論になりやすさ
It's ill speaking between a FULL man and a fasting 178
A HOUSE divided cannot stand 225
TWO of a trade never agree 464
It takes TWO to make a quarrel 465

rain ⇒ weather lore：天気にまつわる伝承

reality and illusion：現実と幻想
FACT is stranger than fiction 153
FACTS are stubborn things 153
You do not FATTEN a pig by weighing it 157
The PROOF of the pudding is in the eating 365
If it SOUNDS too good to be true ... 413
TRUTH is stranger than fiction 459

reciprocity：相互依存
DO as you would be done by 120
DO unto others as you would they should do unto you
120
DOG does not eat dog 122
There's no such thing as a FREE lunch 176
One GOOD turn deserves another 196
One HAND washes the other 206
HAWKS will not pick out hawks' eyes 212
JUDGE not, that ye be not judged 241
LOVE begets love 278
NOTHING comes of nothing 327
NOTHING for nothing 327
You SCRATCH my back, I'll scratch yours 392
You don't get SOMETHING for nothing 411

recreation：気晴らし
A CHANGE is as good as a rest 79
He that would go to SEA for pleasure ... 393
All WORK and no play makes Jack a dull boy 492

regrets：後悔
MARRY in haste, repent at leisure 292
MARRY in May, rue for aye 292
Things PAST cannot be recalled 346
It is too late to shut the STABLE-door after the horse has
bolted 420

reputation：評判
If the CAP fits, wear it 72
The DEVIL is not so black ... 113
Give a DOG a bad name and hang him 122
Every DOG is allowed one bite 123

The only GOOD Indian is a dead Indian 194
GOOD wine needs no bush 196
If the SHOE fits, wear it 400
SPEAK as you find 416
Never SPEAK ill of the dead 416
One man may STEAL a horse, while another may not
  look over a hedge 421

retribution：天罰・報復
CURSES, like chickens, come home to roost 102
What GOES around comes around 190
ILL gotten goods never thrive 234
He who LIVES by the sword dies by the sword 272
The MILLS of God grind slowly ... 299
PRIDE goes before a fall 364
WINTER never rots in the sky 487
Even a WORM will turn 494

revenge：復讐
BLOOD will have blood 56
Don't CUT off your nose to spite your face 103
DEAD men don't bite 107
DEAD men tell no tales 108
He LAUGHS best who laughs last 255
He who LAUGHS last, laughs longest 255
Don't get MAD, get even 283
REVENGE is a dish that can be eaten cold 376
REVENGE is sweet 377
If you SIT by the river for long enough ... 405

rewards ⇒ just deserts：当然の報い；money：金・金銭

riches：富 ⇒ money：金・金銭 も見よ
It is BETTER to be born lucky than rich 45
The CITY for wealth ... 85
EARLY to bed and early to rise ... 131
The MORE you get, the more you want 307
MUCH would have more 310
The RICH man has his ice in the summer ... 377
If you don't SPECULATE, you can't accumulate 418

risk：危険 ⇒ caution：用心 も見よ
ADVENTURES are to the adventurous 18
A BIRD in the hand ... 50
One might as well be HANGED for a sheep as a lamb
  207
IN for a penny, in for a pound 236
If you don't make MISTAKES you don't make anything
  301
NOTHING venture, nothing gain 330
NOTHING venture, nothing have 331
If you don't SPECULATE, you can't accumulate 418

rules：規則
The EXCEPTION proves the rule 148
There is an EXCEPTION to every rule 148
HARD cases make bad laws 209
My HOUSE, my rules 225
RULES are made to be broken 386

rulers and ruled：支配者と被支配者
BETTER a century of tyranny than one day of chaos 40
When the BLIND lead the blind ... 55
The CAT, the rat, and Lovell the dog ... 76
In the COUNTRY of the blind ... 96
DIVIDE and rule 119

Whosoever DRAWS his sword against the prince ... 127
The FISH always stinks from the head downwards 168
GOD is high above, and the tsar is far away 186
The KING can do no wrong 246
The MOUNTAINS are high, and the emperor is far away
  309
He that cannot OBEY cannot command 334
REVOLUTIONS are not made with rose-water 377
The VOICE of the people is the voice of God 472

rumour：噂
BELIEVE nothing of what you hear ... 37
A LIE is halfway round the world ... 261
No SMOKE without fire 409
What the SOLDIER said isn't evidence 410
A TALE never loses in the telling 437

safety ⇒ security：安全

seasons ⇒ calendar lore：暦にまつわる伝承；weather
  lore：天気にまつわる伝承

secrecy ⇒ concealment：隠すこと・隠蔽

security：安全
It is BEST to be on the safe side 40
BETTER be safe than sorry 43
One HAND for yourself and one for the ship 205
Beware of an OAK ... 333
OUT of debt, out of danger 343
SAFE bind, safe find 388
There is SAFETY in numbers 388

self-help：自助
EVERY man is the architect of his own fortune
GOD helps them that help themselves 186
PHYSICIAN, heal thyself 352
If you would be well SERVED, serve yourself 397
TRUST in God but tie your camel 458
Put your TRUST in God ... 458
If you WANT a thing done well ... 475

self-interest ⇒ self-help：自助；self-preservation：自己防衛

self-preservation：自己防衛
If you can't BEAT them, join them 34
It is BEST to be on the safe side 40
BETTER be safe than sorry 43
DEVIL take the hindmost 114
EVERY man for himself 142
EVERY man for himself, and devil take the hindmost 142
EVERY man for himself, and God for us all 143
Those who live in GLASS houses ... 184
HEAR all, see all, say nowt ... 213
JOUK and let the jaw go by 239
NEAR is my kirtle, but nearer is my smock 314
NEAR is my shirt, but nearer is my skin 314
SELF-preservation is the first law of nature 396

separation ⇒ absence：不在

servants ⇒ employers and employees：雇用者と被雇用者

silence ⇒ speech and silence：発言と沈黙

similarity and dissimilarity：類似性と相違性

BIRDS of a feather flock together   52
All CATS are grey in the dark   78
COMPARISONS are odious   92
DIAMOND cuts diamond   115
Like FATHER, like son   157
FIGHT fire with fire   161
When GREEK meets Greek, then comes the tug of war   200
LIKE breeds like   264
LIKE will to like   265
Like MOTHER, like daughter   308
Like PEOPLE, like priest   352
It TAKES one to know one   436
TWO of a trade never agree   464

slander：誹謗中傷 ⇒ malice：悪意・恨み；rumour：噂 も見よ
Throw DIRT enough, and some will stick   117
Give a DOG a bad name and hang him   122
A DOG that will fetch a bone ...   124
Those who live in GLASS houses ...   184
The GREATER the truth, the greater the libel   200
Never SPEAK ill of the dead   416

sleep ⇒ health：健康

smallness ⇒ great and small：大小

society：社会
A CAT may look at a king   76
DO as you would be done by   120
DO unto others as you would they should do unto you   120
EVERYBODY loves a lord   145
One HALF of the world does not know how the other half lives   204
If every man would SWEEP his own doorstep ...   433
It takes a whole VILLAGE to bring up a child   471

soldiers：兵士
An ARMY marches on its stomach   25
The FIRST duty of a soldier is obedience   165
OLD soldiers never die   336
What the SOLDIER said isn't evidence   410

speech and silence：発言と沈黙
BETTER out than in   42
Little BIRDS that can sing and won't sing ...   52
A BLEATING sheep loses a bite   53
Out of the FULLNESS of the heart ...   178
Who KNOWS most, speaks least   250
LEAST said, soonest mended   258
NO names, no pack-drill   325
NO news is good news   325
What happens on the ROAD stays on the road   379
You can't SHOUT 'Fire' in a crowded theatre   402
A SHUT mouth catches no flies   402
SILENCE is a woman's best garment   403
SILENCE is golden   403
SILENCE means consent   403
SPEECH is silver, but silence is golden   418
A STILL tongue makes a wise head   423
STILL waters run deep   423
What goes on TOUR stays on tour   454
What happens in VEGAS stays in Vegas   470

spending ⇒ getting and spending：取得と消費

staying power ⇒ perseverance：我慢強さ；persistence：ねばり強さ

strength and weakness：強弱
The CARIBOU feeds the wolf ...   74
A CHAIN is no stronger ...   79
When ELEPHANTS fight, it is the grass that suffers   135
What doesn't KILL you makes you stronger   245
There is nothing like LEATHER   259
A REED before the wind lives on ...   375
When SPIDER webs unite, they can tie up a lion   419
UNION is strength   467
The WEAKEST go to the wall   479

stress：ストレス
CARE killed the cat   73
When the GOING gets tough, the tough get going   190
If you don't like the HEAT, get out of the kitchen   214
It is the PACE that kills   345
If you can't RIDE two horses at once ...   378
Do not call a WOLF to help you against the dogs   489
It is not WORK that kills, but worry   493

stupidity：愚かさ
ASK a silly question and you get a silly answer   26
A FOOL and his money are soon parted   172
A FOOL at forty is a fool indeed   172
There's no FOOL like an old fool   171
PENNY wise and pound foolish   351

success：成功
Every DOG has his day   122
If you can't be GOOD, be lucky   192
NOTHING succeeds like success   330
The RACE is not to the swift ...   372
If at first you don't SUCCEED ...   429
SUCCESS has many fathers, but failure is an orphan   429

superstition：迷信 ⇒ dreams：夢；omens ⇒前兆 も見よ
BAD things come in threes   31
CHANGE the name and not the letter ...   79
If you want to LIVE and thrive, let the spider run alive   270
There is LUCK in odd numbers   281
PARSLEY seed goes nine times to the Devil   346
Help you to SALT, help you to sorrow   390
SWEEP the house with broom in May ...   434
THIRD time lucky   443
The THIRD time pays for all   444

tact：機転
DIFFERENT strokes for different folks   116
EASY does it   132
FAIR and softly goes far in a day   155
LEAST said, soonest mended   258
A NOD's as good as a wink ...   326
Never mention ROPE in the house of a man who has been hanged   383
A SOFT answer turneth away wrath   410
SPEAK not of my debts unless you mean to pay them   417
With a SWEET tongue and kindness ...   434
THINK first and speak afterwards   442

talkativeness ⇒ speech and silence：発言と沈黙；words and deeds：言動

taste：趣味・味
There is no ACCOUNTING for tastes　16
BEAUTY is in the eye of the beholder　35
EVERY man to his taste　144
One man's MEAT is another man's poison　295
TASTES differ　438

teamwork ⇒ cooperation：協力

theft：窃盗
It's a SIN to steal a pin　404
STOLEN fruit is sweetest　424
STOLEN waters are sweet　424

thrift：質素倹約
CUT your coat according to your cloth　104
KEEP a thing seven years ...　243
OUT of debt, out of danger　343
Take care of the PENCE ...　350
A PENNY saved is a penny earned　351
PENNY wise and pound foolish　351
See a PIN and pick it up ...　353
SPARE well and have to spend　416
THRIFT is a great revenue　446
WASTE not, want not　477

tidiness ⇒ orderliness：整然としていること

time：時間
There is a TIME and place for everything　448
TIME and tide wait for no man　448
TIME flies　448
There is a TIME for everything　448
TIME is a great healer　449
TIME is money　449
Man fears TIME, but time fears the pyramids　449
No TIME like the present　450
TIME will tell　450
TIME works wonders　450
TIMES change and we with time　450

tolerance：寛容・忍耐
It takes ALL sorts to make a world　20
BEAR and forbear　34
GIVE and take is fair play　182
JUDGE not, that ye be not judged　241
To KNOW all is to forgive all　248
LIVE and let live　270

trades and skills：職業と技術
Let the COBBLER stick to his last　89
The COBBLER to his last ...　89
EVERY man to his trade　144
JACK of all trades and master of none　238
There are TRICKS in every trade　456
TWO of a trade never agree　464

travel：旅行
It is BETTER to travel hopefully　47
GO abroad and you'll hear news of home　185
TRAVEL broadens the mind　455
He TRAVELS fastest who travels alone　455

trouble：やっかい・苦労 ⇒ misfortune：不運 も見よ
AFTER a storm comes a calm　18
ANY port in a storm　22
Don't CARE was made to care　73
Don't CROSS the bridge ...　100
What the EYE doesn't see ...　151
GOD makes the back to the burden　187
GOD tempers the wind to the shorn lamb　188
Don't HALLOO till you are out of the wood　205
When you are in a HOLE, stop digging　219
The MOTHER of mischief is no bigger than a midge's wing　308
Those who PLAY at bowls must look out for rubbers　356
If you're not part of the SOLUTION, you're part of the problem　411
The SQUEAKY wheel gets the grease　420
A TROUBLE shared is a trouble halved　457
Never TROUBLE trouble till trouble troubles you　457

trust and scepticism：信用と懐疑
BELIEVE nothing of what you hear ...　37
SEEING is believing　395
THREE things are not to be trusted ...　445

truth：真実・真理 ⇒ reality and illusion：現実と幻想 も見よ
CHILDREN and fools tell the truth　83
What EVERYBODY says must be true　145
The GREATER the truth, the greater the libel　200
A LIE is halfway round the world ...　261
What is NEW cannot be true　320
What the SOLDIER said isn't evidence　410
TELL the truth and shame the Devil　440
Many a TRUE word is spoken in jest　457
There is TRUTH in wine　458
TRUTH is the first casualty of war　459
TRUTH lies at the bottom of a well　459
TRUTH makes the Devil blush　460
TRUTH will out　460

uncertainty ⇒ certainty and uncertainty：確かさと不確かさ

unity and division：統一と分断
A HOUSE divided cannot stand　225
When SPIDER webs unite, they can tie up a lion　419
UNION is strength　467
UNITED we stand, divided we fall　468

value：価値
GOLD may be bought too dear　191
A KING' s chaff is worth more than other men's corn　246
The NEARER the bone, the sweeter the meat　315
It is a POOR dog that's not worth whistling for　358
The WORTH of a thing is what it will bring　494

variety：多様性
It takes ALL sorts to make a world　20
VARIETY is the spice of life　470

villainy ⇒ wrong-doers：悪事をなす者

violence：暴力
BLOOD will have blood　56
When ELEPHANTS fight, it is the grass that suffers　135
KILLING no murder　245
MURDER will out　311

virtue：長所・徳
The BEST of men are but men at best 39
To the PURE all things are pure 367
VIRTUE is its own reward 471

wanting and having：不足と所持 ⇒ greed：貪欲 も見よ
APPETITE comes with eating 24
The BEST-laid schemes ... gang aft agley 39
The CAT would eat fish ... 77
He that would EAT the fruit must climb the tree 134
If IFS and ands were pots and pans ... 233
NO pain, no gain 325
NOTHING venture, nothing gain 330
NOTHING venture, nothing have 331
If you RUN after two hares you will catch neither 386
SEEK and ye shall find 395
The WISH is father to the thought 488
If WISHES were horses, beggars would ride 489

warfare：戦争
ATTACK is the best form of defence 27
COUNCILS of war never fight 95
The best DEFENSE is a good offense 110
All's FAIR in love and war 154
TRUTH is the first casualty of war 459

waste：浪費
HASTE makes waste 211
Do not throw PEARLS to swine 349
SPARE at the spigot, and let out at the bunghole 415
WASTE not, want not 477
WILFUL waste makes woeful want 484

ways and means：方法と手段
DIFFERENT strokes for different folks 116
DIRTY water will quench fire 118
EASY does it 132
Never do EVIL that good may come of it 147
FIGHT fire with fire 161
He who FIGHTS and runs away ... 162
FIRE is a good servant but a bad master 164
FIRST catch your hare 164
When all you have is a HAMMER ... 205
The LONGEST way round is the shortest way home 274
You cannot make an OMELETTE without breaking eggs 337
ONE size does not fit all 340
Don't PUT the cart before the horse 368
REVOLUTIONS are not made with rose-water 377
All ROADS lead to Rome 380
Give a man ROPE enough and he will hang himself 383
There is no ROYAL road to learning 385
SLOW and steady wins the race 408
SLOW but sure 408
SOFTLY, softly, catchee monkey 410
There is more than one WAY to skin a cat 478
There are more WAYS of killing a cat than choking it with cream 478
There are more WAYS of killing a dog than choking it with butter 479
There are more WAYS of killing a dog than hanging it 479
Where there's a WILL, there's a way 485
He who WILLS the end, wills the means 485

weakness ⇒ strength and weakness：強弱

wealth ⇒ riches：富

weather lore：天気にまつわる伝承 ⇒ calendar lore：暦にまつわる伝承
APRIL showers bring forth May flowers 25
There is no such thing as BAD weather ... 31
If CANDLEMAS day be sunny and bright ... 71
As the DAY lengthens, so the cold strengthens 106
A DRIPPING June sets all in tune 128
If in FEBRUARY there be no rain ... 159
A GREEN Yule makes a fat churchyard 200
LONG foretold, long last ... 274
MARCH comes in like a lion ... 290
So many MISTS in March, so many frosts in May 301
NORTH wind doth blow ... 327
When the OAK is before the ash ... 333
A PECK of March dust is worth a king's ransom 350
RAIN before seven, fine before eleven 372
RED sky at night, shepherd's delight ... 374
ROBIN Hood could brave all weathers but a thaw wind 381
If SAINT Paul's day be fair and clear ... 389
SAINT Swithun's day, if thou be fair, for forty days it will remain 389
SEPTEMBER blow soft, till the fruit's in the loft 397
The SHARPER the storm, the sooner it's over 398
When the WIND is in the east, 'tis neither good for man nor beast 486

weddings：結婚式
Happy is the BRIDE ... 64
Always a BRIDESMAID, never a bride 64
DREAM of a funeral ... 127
MARRY in May, rue for aye 292
One WEDDING brings another 480
Happy's the WOOING that is not long a-doing 491

wilfulness see obstinacy：頑固さ

winners and losers：勝者と敗者 ⇒ gains and losses：利益と損失
He LAUGHS best who laughs last 255
He who LAUGHS last, laughs longest 255
What you LOSE on the swings ... 276
You cannot LOSE what you never had 276
What a NEIGHBOUR gets is not lost 317
The WEAKEST go to the wall 479
You WIN a few, you lose a few 485
You can't WIN them all 486

wisdom：賢明・知恵
You cannot CATCH old birds with chaff 77
EXPERIENCE is the father of wisdom 150
FOOLS ask questions that wise men cannot answer 172
HINDSIGHT is always twenty/twenty 217
KNOW thyself 249
KNOWLEDGE is power 250
One cannot LOVE and be wise 278
Out of the MOUTHS of babes − 310
You cannot put an OLD head on young shoulders 335
A STILL tongue makes a wise head 423

wishes ⇒ wanting and having：不足と所持

wives and husbands：夫婦 ⇒ marriage：結婚 も見よ

BETTER be an old man's darling ... 45
A BLIND man's wife needs no paint 55
The GREY mare is the better horse 201
The HUSBAND is always the last to know 227
He that will THRIVE must first ask his wife 446

women：女性
Never CHOOSE your women or your linen by candlelight
　84
The FEMALE of the species is more deadly than the male
　160
The HAND that rocks the cradle rules the world 206
HELL bath no fury like a woman scorned 215
LONG and lazy, little and loud ... 273
SILENCE is a woman's best garment 403
A WHISTLING woman and a crowing hen ... 483
A WOMAN and a ship ever want mending 489
A WOMAN without a man ... 489
A WOMAN's place is in the home 490
A WOMAN's work is never done 490

words and deeds：言動
ACTIONS speak louder than words 17
A BARKING dog never bites 33
A BELLOWING cow soon forgets her calf 37
BRAG is a good dog ... 60
DO as I say, not as I do 120
EMPTY vessels make the most sound 136
EXAMPLE is better than precept 147
FINE words butter no parsnips 163
It's a GOOD horse that never stumbles and a good wife
　that never grumbles 194
MUCH cry and little wool 310
An OUNCE of practice is worth a pound of precept 343
The PEN is mightier than the sword 350
PRACTISE what you preach 361
PUT up or shut up 369
PUT your money where your mouth is 368
STICKS and stones may break my bones ... 422
TALK is cheap 437

work ⇒ diligence：勤勉 ; trades and skills：職業と技術 も
　見よ
ANOTHER day, another dollar 22
A BAD workman blames his tools 31
Never send a BOY to do a man's job 59
Two BOYS are half a boy ... 60
You cannot make BRICKS without straw 63
BUSINESS before pleasure 67
He who CAN, does ... 71

Let the COBBLER stick to his last 89
The COBBLER to his last ... 90
EVERY man to his trade 144
FOOLS and bairns should never see half-done work 172
Why KEEP a dog and bark yourself? 243
KEEP no more cats than will catch mice 243
The LABOURER is worthy of his hire 252
MANY hands make light work 290
PAY beforehand was never well served 347
A SHORT horse is soon curried 401
If a THING's worth doing, it's worth doing well 441
TOO many cooks spoil the broth 452
A WOMAN's work is never done 490
All WORK and no play makes Jack a dull boy 492
WORK expands so as to fill the time available 493
If you won't WORK you shan't eat 493

worry ⇒ stress：ストレス

wrong-doers：悪事をなす者 ⇒ error：間違い・過ち
A BAD penny always turns up 30
CHEATS never prosper 81
To ERR is human ... 141
The GREATER the sinner, the greater the saint 199
A GUILTY conscience needs no accuser 202
HANG a thief when he's young ... 207
There is HONOUR among thieves 221
An IDLE brain is the Devil's workshop 229
ILL weeds grow apace 235
LITTLE thieves are hanged ... 269
OFFENDERS never pardon 335
OLD sins cast long shadows 336
ONCE a whore, always a whore 338
An old POACHER makes the best gamekeeper 357
If there were no RECEIVERS ... 374
Give a man ROPE enough ... 383
Set a THIEF to catch a thief 440
When THIEVES fall out ... 441

youth：若さ・若者
Whom the GODS love die young 189
The GOOD die young 193
You cannot put an OLD head on young shoulders 335
SOON ripe, soon rotten 412
WANTON kittens make sober cats 476
YOUNG folks think old folks to be fools ... 496
A YOUNG man married is a young man marred 497
YOUNG saint, old devil 497
YOUTH must be served 498
If YOUTH knew, if age could 498

【編者】
ジェニファー・スピーク (Jennifer Speake)
辞典編集者。The Oxford Dictionary of Foreign Words and Phrases (1997) と The Oxford Dictionary of Idioms (1999) の初版時の編集担当。

【監訳者】
澤田治美 (さわだ・はるみ)
関西外国語大学教授。博士(英語学)。著書：『視点と主観性』(ひつじ書房)、『モダリティ』、『現代意味解釈講義』、『続・現代意味解釈講義』(以上、開拓社)、編書：『ひつじ意味論講座 1 ～ 7』(ひつじ書房)、監修書：『ビジュアル版 世界言語百科』、『ビジュアル版 世界の文字の歴史文化図鑑』(以上、柊風舎)、監訳書：『オックスフォード 英単語由来大辞典』(柊風舎)。

【訳者】
赤羽美鳥 (あかはね・みどり)
岡山理科大学非常勤講師。博士(文学)。著書：『シェイクスピアの喜劇における両義性』(翰林書房)。共訳書：『オックスフォード 英単語由来大辞典』(柊風舎)。

杉山正二 (すぎやま・しょうじ)
岡山理科大学教授。博士(文学)。共訳書：『ビジュアル版 世界の文字の歴史文化図鑑』、『オックスフォード 英単語由来大辞典』(以上、柊風舎)。

オックスフォード
英語ことわざ・名言辞典

2017年12月25日　第1刷
2019年 4月20日　第2刷

編　　者　ジェニファー・スピーク
監 訳 者　澤田治美
訳　　者　赤羽美鳥／杉山正二
装　　丁　古村奈々
発 行 者　伊藤甫律
発 行 所　株式会社　柊風舎
〒161-0034 東京都新宿区上落合1-29-7 ムサシヤビル5F
TEL 03-5337-3299 ／ FAX 03-5337-3290

印刷／文唱堂印刷株式会社
製本／小髙製本工業株式会社
ISBN978-4-86498-052-4

Japanese Text © Harumi Sawada